FIFTEENTH EDITION

THE
KOVELS'
ANTIQUES & COLLECTIBLES
PRICE LIST

A guide to the 1982-1983 market
for professionals, dealers, and collectors

by Ralph and Terry Kovel

Illustrated

D0450967

CROWN PUBLISHERS, INC.
New York

Books by Ralph and Terry Kovel

Dictionary of Marks—Pottery and Porcelain
A Directory of American Silver, Pewter and Silver Plate
American Country Furniture, 1780–1875
The Kovels' Antiques & Collectibles Price List
The Kovels' Bottle Price List
The Kovels' Collector's Guide to American Art Pottery
Kovels' Organizer for Collectors
The Kovels' Price Guide for Collector Plates, Figurines,
    Paperweights, and Other Limited Editions
The Kovels' Illustrated Price Guide to Royal Doulton
The Kovels' Illustrated Price Guide to Depression Glass
    and American Dinnerware
Kovels' Know Your Antiques
Kovels' Know Your Collectibles
The Kovels' Book of Antique Labels

Inquiries should be addressed to Crown Publishers, Inc., One Park
Avenue, New York, New York 10016

Printed in the United States of America

Published simultaneously in Canada by General Publishing Company
Limited

Library of Congress Catalog Card Number: 72-84290

ISBN: 0-517-54761-9

10 9 8 7 6 5 4 3 2 1

Introduction

The antiques market, like the rest of the economy, has had a difficult year. Prices for some pieces—Oriental rugs, top quality Tiffany lamps, Fulper pottery, silver, and art glass—have dropped. Several major auction galleries have closed or reorganized into smaller quarters. But we are concerned with the middle market in antiques, the small shops and shows and flea markets, and here the prices have not been lower. Advertising art, collectibles and memorabilia, oak furniture, dolls and toys, twentieth-century glass and art pottery, and English furniture have all continued to sell at higher prices. Some antiques shows have had poor sales, but that may be because there are so many more shows than there were five years ago. The major shows in the Midwest, South, and West have been successful for the dealers; only the Eastern shows seem to have less dollar volume.

Record auction prices are of interest because they show that the best still sells well. Most have little effect on the middle market, although they bring headlines in the daily papers.

Furniture records for the year include two English pieces: a pair of Regency girandoles, or mirrors, over 9 feet high for $180,000 and a Queen Anne black japanned bureau bookcase for $860,000. A Victorian settee by Belter, a piece of American furniture, sold in London for $38,385 and later resold to a British museum for $60,000. A Shaker tiger maple chest with 5 drawers sold for $24,000; a Queen Anne mahogany bonnet-top highboy for $105,000. A porcelain sweetmeat dish by Bonnin and Morris of Philadelphia brought $60,000 for the owner who had purchased it for $2 at a tag sale. A Tiffany glass floriform vase of lavender and green sold for $53,900 and a paperweight by an unknown maker, c. 1850, of clear glass encasing a spray of lily of the valley, sold for the record $47,300. A Remington bronze brought $205,000 and a Sebastian miniature figurine sold for $1,500. Folk art prices continue to be strong. A carved St. Bernard dog carousel figure sold for $26,000; a sheet iron angel Gabriel weather vane for $30,000, only to have the record topped by $75,000 for a molded and gilded copper Statue of Liberty weather vane. A duck drake decoy by A. Elmer Crowell sold for $15,500; a lesser yellow legs by William Bowman for $23,000; a swimming goose by Nathan Cobb for $14,000. Clothing set record prices: a Fortuny coat of green velvet sold for $7,800, a black double delphos tea gown by the same maker was $7,000. A Boston school fishing lady needlework was auctioned for $45,000; a pieced, appliquéd, and embroidered quilt brought $10,500.

Dolls brought high prices but the record was a tie with an old one: $16,500 for a French bisque AT doll. A googly faced doll sold for $8,400, a set of Dionne quintuplets for $4,200. A Britain's Boer War supply display set of lead soldiers, 27 pieces, sold for the record $7,000. One Britain's Camel Corps figure was $560; a scale model of an auto gyro was $820.

But it was the memorabilia that captured the headlines and the dollars. An original Yellow Kid comic strip sold for $6,100; a watercolor drawing from *Snow White* sold for $4,250; Judy Garland's ruby slippers brought $12,000. Bing Crosby's golf club went to a pop singer for $7,500 and the movie prop sled "Rosebud" from *Citizen Kane* was purchased by a movie director-producer for $60,500.

The prices listed in the remainder of this book are reports of the more general antiques market. All the record prices we have mentioned were set at auction. The other pieces that are listed in this book are retail prices asked when the items were offered in shops, sales, antiques shows, flea markets, or mail-order listings. They represent the actual asking price of the item, although it is possible that the buyer negotiated the final price to a slightly lower figure. *None of these prices is an estimate.* If a range of price is given, it is because we have found at least two of the identical items offered for sale at different places. The computer records the various prices and prints the high and low figures. It does not estimate. The range may represent two sales or as many as eight sales. Note that price ranges are only found in categories like pressed glass where the identical item can be accurately identified.

If you are selling your antiques and collectibles do not expect to get the retail value unless you are a dealer. Wholesale prices for antiques can be from 20 to 50 percent less than retail. Remember that the antiques dealer, like any store owner, must make a profit or go out of business.

The Margaret Woodbury Strong Museum

The Margaret Woodbury Strong Museum, the newest museum in America, opened October 12, 1982, in Rochester, New York. It is based on the collections of the founder, a serious, dedicated collector who acquired more than 300,000 objects that represent American life in the past century.

Both the collections and the method of display will interest everyone, adults and children alike, visiting the museum. The first floor is filled with exhibits that represent life in America. One exhibit shows the change in living from the farms of the 1820s to the industrialized society of the early 1900s. Another exhibit is about household furnishings, one about middle-class American women and their role, and one about the playthings of the past.

Other floors display over 4,000 toys, 350 dollhouses, the world's largest collection of dolls, plus folk art, needlework, quilts, coverlets, Oriental furniture, ceramics, metalwork, and textiles, and impressive corridors of nineteenth-century American furniture, and wall and floor coverings. Over 19,000 items are on display.

The museum library and computerized accession system permit collectors to learn about any item on display.

This is a wonderful museum for children and for all collectors as well as the serious student. Most of the furniture is in original condition with old upholstery and finish. The dolls and toys are also in original condition with the old clothing or paint. Many of the objects on view are those used by the average family. It is not a museum of great art but rather a historical society devoted to life in America.

The museum is in downtown Rochester, New York, and is surrounded by free parking. It is open Tuesday through Saturday from 10 A.M. to 5 P.M., Sunday from 1 P.M. to 5 P.M. Admission is $1.50 for adults, free for children under 8 with adults, 50¢ for students and children 8 to 16, and $1 for senior citizens. There is no lunchroom at the museum.

The physical display of items at the Strong Museum is unique and permits a special understanding of the everyday items of the past 150 years. We saw the museum while it was being assembled and noticed many details of the American furniture pieces that would not have been obvious in less extensive collections. In most museums, the extra pieces are stored in bins open only to staff. This museum has deliberately made information and artifacts available to every collector who cares to visit. Plan a short visit to just the main floor or a long, leisurely visit to study the other displays.

How to Use This Book

There are just a few simple rules to follow in using this book. Each listing is arranged in the following manner: CATEGORY (such as pressed glass, silver, or furniture); OBJECT (such as vase, spoon, table); DESCRIPTION (which includes as much information as possible about size, age, color, and pattern). Pressed glass is the only exception to this rule, and it is listed CATEGORY, PATTERN, OBJECT, DESCRIPTION. All items are presumed to be in good condition, undamaged, unless otherwise noted.

Several special categories were formed to make a more sensible listing of items possible. "Kitchen" and "tool" include special equipment. Since it would be unreasonable to expect the casual collector to know the proper name for each variety of tool, such as an "adze" or a "trephine," we have lumped them together in the special categories. Other special categories are "commemorative," "store," "nautical," "weapon," and "railroad." The index can help you locate items in these sections.

This book has several idiosyncrasies of style that must be noted before it can be used properly. The final prices are compiled by a computer, and the machine has dictated several strange rules. Everything in the book is listed alphabetically according to the IBM alphabetic system. This means that words such as "mt." are alphabetized as "M-T," not as "M-O-U-N-T." Another peculiarity of the machine alphabetizing is that all numerals come after all letters, thus 2 comes after z. A quick glance at a listing will make this clear, as the alphabetizing is consistent throughout the book. We have not listed any pieces priced over $9,999.

We have made several editorial decisions that affect the use of the book. A bowl is a bowl and not a dish unless it is a special type of dish, such as a pickle dish. A butter dish is a "butter" and a celery dish is a "celery." A salt dish is called a "salt" to differentiate it from a saltshaker. A toothpick holder is called a "toothpick." It is always a "sugar and creamer," never a "creamer and sugar." Where one dimension is given, it is the height of the piece, or if the object is round, the dimension is the diameter. Height of a picture is listed before width. Glass is clear unless a color is indicated.

This book does not include price listings of fine art paintings, books, comic books, stamps, coins, and a few other categories that are covered in specialized books. Prices for collectors' editions, bottles, Royal Doulton, depression glass, and American dinnerware are included although they are more completely reported in *The Kovels' Price Guide for Collector Plates, Figurines, Paperweights, and Other Limited Editions; The Kovels' Bottle Price List; The Kovels' Illustrated Price Guide to Royal Doulton;* and *The Kovels' Illustrated Price Guide to Depression Glass and American Dinnerware.*

Several categories such as "milk glass" and "bottles" include special reference numbers. These numbers refer the reader to the most widely known books about the category. When these numbers appear, the name of the special book is given in the paragraph heading. All these numbers take the form "B-22," "McK-G-11," and so forth. The letter is the author's initial; the number refers to a picture in the author's book.

All black-and-white pictures in *The Kovels' Antiques & Collectibles Price List* are of antiques sold during the past year. The prices are as reported by the seller. Each piece pictured is listed with the word "Illus" as part of the description. Pictures are placed as close to the price listing as is possible. Color pictures are all from the collection of The Strong Museum and no prices are given for these antiques.

There have been many misinformed comments about how this book is written. We *do* use the computer. It alphabetizes, ranges prices, sets the type, and does many other time-consuming jobs. Because of the computer, the book can be produced faster than a price book printed by conventional methods. The last entries in the book are added in June; the book is available in October at bookstores. This is about six months faster than would be possible any other way. But it is human help that finds the prices and checks the accuracy. We read everything in each book at least twice, sometimes more. We edit from 100,000 entries (prices recorded in all parts of the country) to the 45,000 entries found in this book. We remove incorrect data, correct the spelling, write the category headings, and decide on the new categories to be included. We sometimes make errors. Collector-specialists often make suggestions for changes in the way various categories are listed to make them more useful to the collector. This type of suggestion is always welcome. For example, this year for the first time both Depression glass and Carnival glass are listed by pattern name. We *do not* ask dealers or collectors to price items for the book.

We have tried to make the entries in this book as easy to find as possible. Every entry is listed alphabetically and there is also a full index. One problem we cannot solve is that of language. Several antiques terms have two meanings such as "Sheffield," "Salopian," and "snow baby." Be sure to read the paragraph headings to know the meaning we used. All the category headings are based on the language of the average person at an average show, and we use terms like "mud figures" even if that is not technically correct.

All prices included in this book are reports, not estimates. This means that somewhere in the United States, between June 1981 and June 1982, the antiques described were offered for sale at the prices we have listed. A few prices are from auctions, but most are from shops and shows. The prices have been taken from sales in all parts of the country, and variations may be caused by geographic differences in pricing. Every price has been checked for accuracy, but we cannot be responsible for any errors that may have occurred. We welcome any suggestions for future editions of this book but cannot answer letters asking for advice or appraisals.

Ralph M. Kovel,
American Society of Appraisers, Senior Member

Terry H. Kovel,
American Society of Appraisers, Senior Member

Update for Prices Available

Each year *The Kovels' Antiques & Collectibles Price List* is completely rewritten. Every entry is new because of the rapidly changing antiques market. The only way so complete a revision can be accomplished is by using a computer, making it possible to publish the bound book two months after the last price is received.

Yet many price changes occur between editions of *The Kovels' Antiques & Collectibles Price List.* Important sales produce new record prices each day. Inflation, the changing price of silver and gold, and the international demand for some types of antiques influence sales in the United States.

You can keep up with developments from month to month. *Kovels on Antiques and Collectibles* is a nationally distributed illustrated newsletter, published monthly. It covers prices, how to buy or sell, special interest antiques, refinishing and first aid for your possessions, marks, book reviews, and other pertinent antiques news.

Information about the newsletter is available from the authors at P.O. Box 22200, Beachwood, Ohio 44122.

Picture Acknowledgments

David and Linda Arman; Steve Bennett; Richard Bourne; Christie's; Don Culbertson; DuMouchelle Art Galleries; Robert C. Eldred; Gene Harris Antiques Center; Julia's Auction Barn; Maritime Auctions; Mid Hudson Galleries; Milwaukee Auction Gallery; Montgomery Auction Exchange; Morton's Auction Exchange; Richard Oliver Auction and Art Gallery; Richard Opfer; Phillip's; Lloyd Ralston; Roan Auctions; Robert W. Skinner, Inc.; Sotheby's; Auctions by Theriault; Weiss Auctions; Wolf's Shaker Galleries; Woody Auction Co.

Almaric Walter made pate-de-verre glass under contract at the Daum glassworks from 1908 to 1914. He started his own firm in Nancy, France, in 1919. Pieces made before 1914 are signed "Daum, Nancy" with a cross. After 1919 the signature is "A. Walter Nancy."

A.WALTER, Figurine, Baby Bird, Orange Feet, Blue, Aqua Pedestal, 3 1/4 In. 1200.00
   Pendant, Winged Insect, Marked, Translucent Yellow, 1 3/4 In. 260.00
   Plaque, Nude In Pool Of Water, Pate-De-Verre, 6 X 10 In. 1375.00
   Vase, Landscape, Lazy River Scene, Green, Yellow Ground, 6 In. 85.00

ABC plates, or children's alphabet plates, were popular from 1780 to 1860. The letters on the plate were meant as teaching aids for children learning to read. The plates were made of pottery, porcelain, metal, or glass.

ABC, Bowl, Child's, Baby, Teddie Bear, & Elephant, 2-Handled, 6 In. 20.00
   Bowl, Feeding, Child's, Girl, Clown Doll, Boy, Dog, 7 1/2 In. 35.00
   Bowl, Feeding, Girl In Field Of Poppies, Gold Letters Around, 7 1/2 In. 68.00
   Bowl, 4 Children Washing Clothes, German 65.00
   Creamer, Rooster, Hen, & Chicks, Germany 30.00
   Cup, Little Bopeep, Staffordshire 75.00
   Plate & Cup, Farm & Zoo Animals, Plate 6 1/4 In. 85.00
   Plate, Alphabet Outer Edge, Sign Language Inside Border 70.00
   Plate, Animals & ABC Rim, Boy & Girl In Red Car, Signed, German 55.00
   Plate, Archery, Earthenware With Raised Letters 45.00
   Plate, Blue Transfer, A Fishing Elephant, 2 Children, 1890s, 6 3/4 In. 60.00
   Plate, Bulfinch, Staffordshire 37.50
   Plate, Bulldog, My Face Is My Fortune, Blue & White, England, 7 3/8 In. 35.00
   Plate, Canary, Staffordshire 37.50
   Plate, Children & Dog, Catch It Carlos When I Throw, 6 In. 55.00
   Plate, Children & Puppies In Center, 8 1/2 In. 38.00
   Plate, Children, Parrot, Dog, Germany 40.00
   Plate, Clock Center, Clear Letters, Frosted Edge, 7 1/4 In. 30.00
   Plate, Cock Robin, Tin 45.00
   Plate, Elephant, Jumbo In Center, Embossed, Tin, 6 In. 48.00
   Plate, Embossed Alphabet On Rim, Lamb, Blue Green Ground, 8 1/2 In. 40.00
   Plate, Fork, & Spoon, Who Killed Cock Robin, Tin, 8 In. 60.00
   Plate, Franklin Farmers Scene & Proverb 75.00
   Plate, Girl On Swing, Polychrome, Tin, 3 1/2 In. 50.00
   Plate, Harry Baiting His Line, Staffordshire, 5 1/2 In. 192.00
   Plate, Hey Diddle Diddle, Metal 10.00
   Plate, Hi-Diddle, Letters & Design, Tin 45.00
   Plate, Kittens With Yarn 25.00
   Plate, Kittens, Ohio Art, Tin, 4 1/2 In. 30.00
   Plate, New Pony, Staffordshire 35.00
   Plate, Old Mother Hubbard, 7 In. 85.00

(See Page 2)

ABC, Plate, Transfer-Printed, Young Man Fishing, 19th Century

Plate, Orange Carnival, Stork In Center 35.00
Plate, Painted Farm Scene, Gold Letters, Beaded Edge, Milk Glass, 7 In. 37.00
Plate, Rooster & Chicken In Center, Porcelain, 6 1/2 In. 32.00
Plate, Rooster & Hen, Gold Trim, Gray Border, Embossed Letters, 6 In. 50.00
Plate, Stippled Letters, Scalloped, Center Medallion, 6 1/4 In. 28.00
Plate, The Baker, 5 1/4 In. 35.00
Plate, The Blind Girl, 6 1/4 In. 42.00
Plate, Tired Of Play, Staffordshire 35.00
Plate, Transfer-Printed, Young Man Fishing, 19th Century .... *Illus* 192.00
Plate, Victorian Child Center, C.1840, Soft Paste, 7 In. 85.00
Plate, 2 Cows & Chickens, Verse, Pink Border, Staffordshire, 7 1/2 In. 34.00
Tray, Oval, Glass, Miniature 70.00

> *Abingdon Pottery was established in 1934 by Raymond E. Bidwell as*
> *the Abingdon Sanitary Manufacturing Company. The company made art*
> *pottery. The factory ceased production in 1950.*

ABINGDON, Basket, Star Shape, Signed 15.00
Bowl, Ribbon, Pink 4.75
Bowl, Scroll, 14 1/2 In. 6.50
Bowl, Seashell Pattern On Outside, Pink, 9 X 4 1/4 In. 18.00
Candlestick, Pink 15.00
Console Set, Pink 20.00
Console Set, Vase, No. 507, Candleholder, No. 505 .... 26.00
Cookie Jar, Moneybag 40.00
Cornucopia, Blue 5.75
Cornucopia, Double, No. 482, Green 10.00
Cornucopia, Double, Peach 12.00
Cornucopia, Rose Horizontal, 10 In. 10.00
Cornucopia, White 5.00
Planter, Bowknot, No. 462 .... 14.00
Planter, Shell, Signed 8.00
Urn, Wreath, Yellow Crazed 10.00
Vase, Clam Shell, No. 507 .... 14.00
Vase, Classic, Rose, 10 In. .... 9.00 To 17.50
Vase, Marked, Blue Gray, 10 1/2 In. 12.00
Vase, Swirl Pattern, Marked, Gray Blue, 11 In. 15.00
Wall Pocket, Lily, Marked, Gray Green, 8 1/2 In. 8.00
Wall Pocket, Lily, Rose 22.00
Wall Pocket, Lily, Yellow 22.00

ADAMS
ENGLAND

> *Adams china was made by William Adams and Sons of Staffordshire,*
> *England. The firm was founded in 1769 and is still working.*

ADAMS, see also Flow Blue
ADAMS, Cup & Saucer, Seasons, Handleless, Pink 65.00
Dish, Vegetable, Red Rose, 1840-60, Cover, Pinwheel Mark, 12 5/8 In. 500.00
Hatpin Holder, Jasperware, Figures, Blue & White, Marked, 4 1/4 In. 55.00
Jug, Milk, Red Rose Pattern, C.1840, Foliate Border, 4 7/8 In. 75.00
Plate, Boy & Horses, Blue Transfer, 7 In. 35.00
Plate, Villa In Regents Park, Blue, 8 3/4 In. 40.00
Platter, Denton Park, Yorkshire 250.00
ADVERTISING, see Store

> *Agata glass was made by Joseph Locke of the New England Glass*
> *Company of Cambridge, Massachusetts, after 1885. A metallic stain was*
> *applied to New England Peachblow and the mottled design characteristic of*
> *agata appeared.*

AGATA, Bowl, Flared & Ruffled Top, Mottled, 5 1/2 In. 1450.00

Finger Bowl, Allover Gold Mottling, Raspberry To Pink, 5 1/4 In.Diam. 995.00
Toothpick, New England Glass Co., Green Opaque 500.00
Vase, Rosey-Red Pontil To Deep Red Top, 10 In. 1585.00

AGATE, Coffeepot, Hand-Painted Design, Porcelain Handle, Pewter Trimmed 169.00
Figurine, Cat, On Hamper, Red 400.00
Teapot, Pewter Trimmed, Blue & White 175.00
Vase, Lily, 19th Century, Glossy Finish, 9 1/4 In. 350.00

Akro agate glass was made in Clarksburg, West Virginia, from 1932 to 1951. Before that time the firm made children's glass marbles. Most of the glass is marked with a crow flying through the letter A.

AKRO AGATE, Ashtray, Match Holder, Pumpkin, Hotel Edison 28.00
Ashtray, Tab, Pink, Red, Cobalt, 4 X 2 In. 6.50
Ashtray, Tire Goodrich, White & Gray 15.00
Bowl, Green, 6 In. 10.00
Box, Powder, Colonial Lady, Blue 40.00
Box, Powder, Colonial Lady, White 30.00
Box, 2 Nude Females, Covered, Round, Green 115.00
Child's Set, Marbleized, 3 Cups & Saucers, 12 Piece 75.00
Cornucopia, White, Green, Aqua 6.00
Creamer, Concentric Ring, Blue, 1 1/4 In. 6.50
Creamer, Concentric Ring, Green, 1 1/4 In. 4.50
Creamer, Octagon, Opaque 10.00
Cup & Saucer, Marbleized, Set Of 6 .... 50.00
Cup, Green, Chicuita, 1 1/4 In. 6.00
Cup, Open Handled, Green, Octagonal, 1 1/4 In. 6.50
Cup, Pumpkin, Concentric Ring 8.00
Dish, Powder, Scotty, Blue 85.00
Flower Pot, White, 1 1/4 In. 6.00
Jar, Cigarette, Mexicali, Hat Ashtray Lid, Orange & White 40.00
Jar, Powder, Scotty Dog, Pink Opaque 45.00
Match Holder & Ashtrays, White, Oxblood, Set Of 4 .... 25.00
Mortar & Pestle, White With Original Markings 12.00
Planter, White & Orange, Rectangular 6.00
Plate, Blue, Octagonal, 3 3/4 In. 5.00
Plate, Green, Octagonal, 4 1/2 In. 3.00
Pot, Cream, Blue, Green, 2 1/2 In. 3.50
Pot, Graduated Darts, Green, 7 Darts, 5 1/4 In. 12.00
Pot, Green, 1 3/4 In. 3.00
Pot, Pumpkin, 2 1/2 In. 4.50
Sugar, Blue, Concentric Ring, 1 1/4 In. 6.50
Sugar, Concentric Ring, Green, 1 1/4 In. 4.50
Tea Set, Green & White, Boxed 55.00
Tea Set, Multicolor, Little American Maid, 17 Piece 68.00
Teapot, Child's, Raised Daisy, Blue 18.00
Tumbler, White, Stacked Disc, 2 In. 4.00
Vase, Orange & White 10.00
Vase, White & Orange, 6-Sided Foot 6.00
Water Set, Stippled Band, Jade Transoptic, 3 Tumblers 36.50

ALABASTER, Dish, Candy, Metal 6 In.Woman On Top, 5 In.Diam. 95.00
Figurine, Tiger, Carved & Stained, 21 In.Long 500.00
ALBUM, PHOTOGRAPH, see Photography, Album

Alexandrite glass was first made by Thomas Webb & Sons at the beginning of the twentieth century. It is a transparent glass shading from pale yellow to rose to blue. Stevens & Williams later produced Alexandrite glassware by plating a transparent yellow body with rose and blue glass.

ALEXANDRITE, Rose Bowl, Honeycomb, 2 1/2 In. .... 675.00 To 725.00
   Taza, Honeycomb, Fluted Edge, Citron Foot, 4 5/8 In. 695.00
   Tazza, Honeycomb, Fluted, Blue Edge Shaded To Rose, 4 5/8 In. 695.00
   Vase, Petal Top, 6 In. 750.00
   Wine, Honeycomb, 4 1/2 In. 950.00

Al hambra

Alhambra is a pattern of tableware made in Vienna, Austria, in the twentieth century. The geometric designs are applied in gold, red, and dark green.

ALHAMBRA, Butter, Rectangular, Covered, 5 1/2 X 8 In. 95.00
   Creamer 15.00
   Dish, Soup 45.00
   Plate, 8 In. 45.00
   Plate, 9 In. 85.00
   Plate, 10 In. 45.00

ALUMINUM, Ashtray, Figural Dog 2.00
   Basket, Raspberry Pattern, Farberware, 13 In. 10.00
   Cocktail Shaker, Chrysanthemum, Continental 18.00
   Crumb Tray & Scraper, Art Deco, C.1925 .... 15.00
   Ice Bucket, Chrysanthemum, Continental, Lucite Handles, Cover 30.00
   Tray, Glass Serving Dish, Farber 15.00
   Tray, Hammered, Wendell August Forge, 8 In.Long 25.00
   Tray, Pinecone Decorations, 9 X 11 In. 12.00

Amber glass is the name of any glassware with the proper yellow-brown shade. It was a popular color after the Civil War.

AMBER GLASS, Ball, Seine, Net Roping, Marked, 5 In.Diam. 30.00
   Bottle, Cologne, Enameled Flowers, Blown Stopper, 9 In. 53.00
   Bottle, Cologne, Long Stopper, 6 In. 16.00
   Bottle, Wine, White Enameled Flowers, Bubble Stopper, 1i In. 78.00
   Creamer, Bird & Floral Design, Pink & White Flowers, 5 1/2 In. 88.00
   Cruet, Enameled Foliage, Amber Bubble Stopper, 8 In. 100.00
   Cruet, French Pewter Encased, 8 1/4 In. 145.00
   Cruet, Pewter Encased, Pewter Cherub Stopper, French, 15 In. 225.00
   Cruet, Stars & Bars, Amber Stopper 75.00
   Cruet, Swirl, Amber Applied Foot, Pewter Top, Stopper, 8 1/4 In. 95.00
   Cruet, Swirl, Amber Stopper, 3 3/4 In. 25.00
   Cruet, Wine, Enameled 145.00
   Dish, Powder, Covered, Bambi, Iridescent 9.50
   Hatpin, Victorian, 10 1/2 In.Tall 18.50
   Jar, Canning, Milk Glass Scaler, Patent April 7, 1896 .... 40.00
   Match Holder, Boot Shape 60.00
   Mug, Bluebird & Berry 30.00
   Pitcher, Daisy & Button, Threaded Handle, 5 In. 67.50
   Pitcher, Enameled Flowers & Butterfly, 4 In. 58.00
   Pitcher, Thumbprint Square Mouth, Blown 75.00
   Pitcher, Water, Hobnail With Thumbprint 35.00
   Pitcher, Water, Hobnail, Reeded Handle, 7 3/4 In. 45.00
   Salt, Valencia Waffle, Master 28.00
   Smoke Bell, Daisy & Button 65.00
   Spooner, Daisy & Button, Amber Panels 55.00
   Syrup, Pilgrim Bottle 60.00
   Syrup, Rope & Thumbprint 30.00
   Table Set, Rope & Thumbprint, 4 Piece 175.00
   Toothpick, Daisy & Button, Metal Rim 35.00
   Toothpick, Inverted Thumbprint, Straight Sides, Ring Base 35.00
   Tumbler, Mitered Diamond 28.00
   Tumbler, Rose, 4 1/2 In. 75.00

Tumbler, Wildflower	30.00
Vase, Applique, Applied Edging, Pink Calla Lily, 12 1/4 In.	235.00
Vase, Blue Neck, Polished Pontil, Column Of Blue, 5 In.	45.00
Vase, Daisy & Button, Hand Shape	22.00
Vase, Paneled, Roses, Butterfly, & Flowers, Blue Foot, 13 In.	178.00

AMBERETTE, see Pressed Glass, Klondike

Amberina is a two-toned glassware made from 1883 to about 1900. It was patented by Joseph Locke of the New England Glass Company. The glass shades from red to amber.

AMBERINA, see also Baccarat; Bluerina; Plated Amberina

AMBERINA, Bell, Smoke, Hobnail, 3 5/8 In.	200.00
Bottle, Perfume, Original Stopper, Signed, Libbey, 7 In.	650.00
Bowl, Diamond Optic, 4 In.	50.00
Bowl, Diamond-Quilted, Red To Amber, 7 7/8 X 2 1/2 In.	295.00
Bowl, Finger, New England, Fluted, Fuchsia, 2 1/2 X 5 In.	250.00
Bowl, Fuchsia, 9 1/2 In.	150.00
Bowl, Gold Fan, Foliage & Bird, Ruffled, Amber Feet, 6 5/8 In.	325.00
Bowl, Hobnail, 4 3/4 In.Diam.	250.00
Bowl, Honeycomb, 10 In.	97.50
Bowl, Ruffled & Turned Down Edge, 8 In.Diam.	245.00
Bowl, Ruffled, Swirl Footed, Gold Flowers & Birds, 6 1/2 X 8 In.	325.00
Box, Powder, Covered	495.00
Butter, New England, Diamond-Quilted, Covered	850.00
Castor Set, Baby Thumbprint Pattern, 3 Piece	375.00
Celery, Diamond-Quilted, 6 1/2 In.	275.00
Celery, Square, Crimped Top.5 In.	165.00
Champagne, Hollow Stem, Amber Base & Stem, Red Bowl, 4 In.	275.00
Creamer, Inverted Thumbprint, Amber Handle, Bulbous, 5 1/2 In.	150.00
Creamer, Inverted Thumbprint, Amber Handle, Squatty, 2 3/4 In.	375.00
Creamer, Inverted Thumbprint, Ruffled Top, 6 In.	185.00
Cruet, Clear Twist Applied Handle, Clear Stopper, 6 In.	235.00
Cruet, Inverted Thumbprint, Clear Handle, Faceted Stopper, 6 In.	155.00
Cruet, Inverted Thumbprint, Mushroom Stopper, Amber Handle	225.00
Cruet, Inverted Thumbprint, Original Amber Stopper, Flint	265.00
Cruet, Swirl, Melon Stopper, 6 In.	225.00
Cup, Punch, Diamond-Quilted, Fuchsia, Amber Reeded Handle, 2 In.	130.00
Cup, Punch, Diamond-Quilted, Fuchsia, Laurel Leaves Etched, 2 In.	175.00
Cup, Punch, Ribbed, Amber Handle, 19th Century, Plated	1300.00
Cup, Punch, Thumbprint Design, Engraved Fernery, Handle	150.00
Finger Bowl, Pleated Top, 5 In.	110.00
Hall Lamp, Paneled Swirl, Brass Fittings, Cranberry To Amber	395.00
Mug, Diamond-Quilted, Amber Ribbed Handle, Child's	175.00
Pitcher, Applied Handle & Spout, Blown, 8 In.	175.00
Pitcher, Applied Handle & Spout, 8 In.	150.00
Pitcher, Clear Twisted Handle	105.00
Pitcher, Diamond-Quilted, 6 3/4 In.	450.00
Pitcher, Gold & Pink Flowers, Enameled, 11 1/2 In.	275.00
Pitcher, Hobnail, Square Mouth, 5 5/8 In.	625.00
Pitcher, Honeycomb Pattern	260.00
Pitcher, Inverted Thumbprint, Square Mouth, 4 3/4 In.	135.00
Pitcher, Melon Ribbed, Amber Handle, Ruby To Amber	150.00
Pitcher, Milk, Bulbous, Square Mouth, 6 1/2 In.	400.00
Pitcher, Milk, New England, Diamond-Quilted, Fuchsia, 6 1/2 In.	400.00
Pitcher, Paneled	195.00
Pitcher, Rattail Glass Around Collar, Braided Handle, 8 1/2 In.	400.00
Pitcher, Swirl Pattern, 6 1/2 In.	165.00
Pitcher, Water, Herringbone Pattern, 8 In.	325.00
Pitcher, Water, Hobnail, Bulbous, Square Mouth, 5 5/8 In.	650.00
Plate, Ice Cream, Daisy & Button, Ruby To Amber	170.00
Plate, Ice Cream, Daisy & Button, Scalloped Corners, 5 3/4 In.	110.00
Punch Cup, Reed Handle, Diamond-Quilted	125.00
Rose Bowl, Frosted, 6 In.	270.0

Shade, Angle Lamp, Ribbed Swirled Texture, C.1900, 8 1/4 In., Pair 100.00
Shoe Bow, Daisy & Button 20.00
Spooner 145.00
Toothpick, Baby Thumbprint .... 45.00 To 125.00
Toothpick, Daisy & Button Design, Footed, 3 In. 195.00
Toothpick, Diamond-Quilted, Square Top 195.00
Toothpick, Fine Diamond 185.00
Toothpick, Fuchsia 245.00
Toothpick, Fuchsia, Square Top 195.00
Toothpick, Inverted Baby Thumbprint 140.00
Toothpick, Pedestal 169.00
Toothpick, Venetian Diamond Pattern, 2 1/2 In. 95.00
Tray, Ice Cream, Daisy & Button Pattern, 14 X 9 In. 125.00
Tumbler, Diamond-Quilted, New England Glass Co. 125.00
Tumbler, Diamond-Quilted, 3 5/8 In. 90.00
Tumbler, Optical Ribbing, Light Fuchsia 80.00
Tumbler, Silver Plated 1900.00
Tumbler, Swirl & Thumbprint 75.00
Vase, Applied Edge Ruffle, Pear-Shaped Body, 10 1/2 In. 55.00
Vase, Bud, Amber To Dark Fuchsia, 6 3/4 In. 350.00
Vase, Crackle Glass, Applique Leaves, Flower Prunt, 6 1/8 In. 395.00
Vase, Diamond-Quilt Reverse, 8 In. 295.00
Vase, Enameled Florals, Rigaree Around Neck, Amber, 11 1/2 In. 295.00
Vase, Footed, Gold Flowers, Ruffled Edge, Cranberry To Amber, 5 In. 235.00
Vase, Footed, Swirl, Serpentine Trim, Gold Flowers, 14 1/4 In. 265.00
Vase, Inverted Thumbprint, Amber, Cranberry, 5 3/4 In. 245.00
Vase, Inverted Thumbprint, Applied Rigaree, Footed, 5 3/4 In. 245.00
Vase, Inverted Thumbprint, Jack-In-The-Pulpit 275.00
Vase, Inverted Thumbprint, 14 In. 195.00
Vase, New England, Fuchsia Over Girth Of Body, Amber Cut 330.00
Vase, Petal Feet, Ruffled, 11 1/4 In. 225.00
Vase, Roman Gold Flowers, Leaves, & Foliage, Ruffled, 11 3/8 In. 225.00
Vase, Ruffled & Crimped, Pink Overlay, Amber Rigaree, 10 3/4 In. 100.00
Vase, Ruffled Top, Roman Gold Lilies, 12 3/4 In., Pair 475.00
Vase, Swirl Glass, Cranberry To Amber, Amber Feet, 6 1/4 In. 195.00
Vase, Swirl, Amber Rigaree Top Rim, Footed, 10 5/8 In. 195.00
Vase, Swirl, Blue Floral, Amber Feet, Cranberry To Amber, 11 1/2 In. 295.00
Vase, Swirl, Gold Chrysanthemums, Cranberry To Amber, 14 1/2 In. 295.00
Vase, 6 Petal Top, Enameled Flowers, Gold Leaves, 11 3/4 In. 235.00
Water Set, Diamond-Quilted Pattern, 3 Tumblers, 8 3/4 In. 375.00
Water Set, Diamond-Quilted, 6 Tumblers, Pitcher, 8 1/2 In. 1100.00
Water Set, Inverted Diamond-Quilted, 6 Glasses, 8 1/4 In. 325.00

*American Encaustic Tiling Co. of Zanesville, Ohio, worked from 1879
to 1935. Decorative glazed, embossed, and faience tiles were made.*

AMERICAN ENCAUSTIC TILING CO., Paperweight, Ram, 3 3/4 X 5 1/2 In. 45.00
Presidential, McKinley, Signed, 3 X 3 In. 95.00
Tile, Raised Flowers 45.00

*Amethyst glass is any of the many glasswares made in the proper dark purple
shade. It was a color popular after the Civil War.*

AMETHYST GLASS, Bottle, Perfume, Daisy & Button, Clear Stopper, 4 In. 35.00
Bottle, Perfume, Floral 18.00
Bowl, Cream Soup, Moondrops, Handled 12.00
Bowl, Embossed Design, Black, Handled & Footed, 8 1/2 In. 26.00
Box, Hinged, Footed, Grapes & Leaves, 5 1/4 X 6 In.Diam. 195.00
Compote, Jelly 18.00
Cruet, S-Repeat, Original Stopper 50.00

Decanter, Silver Decoration 60.00
Dish, Candy, Covered 14.00
Lamp, Finger, Reflector 310.00
Liqueur Set, Brass Collar Opens To 6 Glasses, 8 1/4 In. 60.00
Mug, Child's 25.00
Pitcher, Water, Ruffled, Gold Flowers & Leaves 90.00
Reamer 15.00
Rose Bowl, Enameled Man At Table, Drinking, 4 1/2 X 4 In. 110.00
Rose Bowl, Overall Gold Design, 3 3/4 In. 75.00
Toothpick, Boot Shape, Embossed Star 12.00
Toothpick, Swag & Bracket, Gold Trim 40.00
Tumbler, Quilted-Diamond 40.00
Tumbler, Swag Bracket 30.00
Vase, Bud, Enameled Flowers, 10 In., Pair 95.00
Vase, Hand-Painted Deer In White, Flared, 8 3/4 In. 150.00
Vase, Imperial Jewels, Pear-Shaped, Green, Signed, 6 In. 95.00
Vase, Tulip, Scalloped, Octagonal Sides, C.1845, 10 In., Pair 725.00
Water Set, Enameled, 6 Piece 90.00

AMOS & ANDY, Ashtray, With Match Holder, Bronzed Ceramic 85.00
Card Party, Score Pads, 8 Tallies, Boxed 35.00
Doll, Jointed, Wooden, 5 1/2 In. 395.00
Jigsaw Puzzle, 1932 .... 25.00
Map, Treasure, Pepsodent 30.00
Photograph, Autographed, Black & White, Mailing Envelope 16.00
Sheet Music, The Pepsodent Hour 20.00
Toy, Fresh Air Taxi 425.00
     AMPHORA, see Teplitz
     ANDIRON and related Fireplace items, see Fireplace
     APOTHECARY JAR, see Bottle, Apothecary
     APPLE PEELER, see Kitchen, Peeler, Apple

ARCHITECTURAL, Backbar, Center Mirror, Stained Glass Doors, Oak, 12 X 9 Ft. 6000.00
Backbar, Drugstore, Stained Glass, Marble, Oak, 20 In. X 9 Ft. 1825.00
Backbar, Fretwork, Spindles Over Crown, Victorian Oak, 16 In. 2500.00
Backbar, Ice Cream Parlor, Marble Doors, Hanging Lamps, 10 Ft. 6500.00
Backbar, Ice Cream, Marble Top, Leaded Cabinets, Oak, 16 In. 1700.00
Backbar, Oval Mirror Each End, 4 Pilaster Oak Bars, 18 In. 2750.00
Backbar, Single Arch, Brunswick Oak, 24 In. 2600.00
Backbar, Soda Fountain Top, Lead Glass, Mission Oak, 14 In. 1750.00
Backbar, Stained Glass Columns, Marble Top, Dated 1910, 16 Ft. 9000.00
Backbar, Stained Glass, English Pub 3550.00
Backbar, Triple Arch, Mahogany, 20 In. 1600.00
Bar, Saloon, Leaded Glass, Bell Flower Design, Canopy 26 In. 2950.00
Bar, Saloon, Leaded Glass, Pink Roses, Canopy 50 In. 4900.00
Booth, Phone, Shelf, Light, Sliding Door, Wooden 575.00
Bracket, Tumbler & Toothbrush Holder, C.1890, Brass, 6 1/2 In. 45.00
Cab, Elevator, Paneled, Leaded Glass, Brass Accordion Door 3000.00
Cab, Elevator, Paneling Inside & Out, Leaded Glass Side 3000.00
Cabinet, Hardware Store, 32 Glass Front Oak Drawers 300.00
Cabinet, Medicine, Beveled Glass, Towel Rack, Oak, 28 X 18 In. 155.00
Cabinet, Medicine, Beveled Mirror, Walnut, 14 1/2 In.Square 95.00
Cabinet, Medicine, Green Glass Towel Bar, Pine 75.00
Cabinet, Medicine, Oak, 28 X 18 X 8 In. 150.00
Column, Fluted, Oak, C.1890, 8 1/2 Ft. X 9 In.Diam., Set Of 4 .... 2000.00
Column, Ornate Top, Cast Iron, 11 Ft., Set Of 4 .... 800.00
Cornice, Straight, 4 Column Oak Back, 16 In. 2000.00
Cornice, Wooden, Applied Carvings, Brown Paint, 44 In. 700.00
Counter, General Store, Victorian Style Designs, Pine 550.00
Counter, Sherer Seed, Windows, Drawers, Pulls, Oak, 16 Ft.Long 1600.00
Counter, 30 Glass Front Boxes, 30 Back Drawers, Oak, 12 Ft. 1500.00
Desk, Storekeeper's, Primitive 750.00

Divider, Teller Cage, Hand-Carved, 1890, 36 X 84 1/2 In., Set 700.00
Fireplace, C.1880, Victorian, White Marble, 72 X 50 In. 500.00
Fixture, Gas, Wall, Glass Shade, Brass 135.00
Flag, American, 48 Star, Electrical, 3 X 3 Ft. 5000.00
Front Bar, Brunswick, Oak, 24 In. 500.00
Gate, Elevator, Lacy Cast Iron, 4 X 7 Ft., Pair 450.00
Hinge, 1880, Brass, Fancy, Set Of 3 .... 85.00
Lavatory, Raised Back, Faucets, Vitreous China 165.00
Ornament, Eagle, Full Figure, Copper, 24 1/2 In. 425.00
Post Office, General Store, 1900s, 40 Brass Boxes, Oak 2500.00
Post Office, Money Order & General Delivery Window, Oak 2700.00
Safe, Stamp, 11 Drawers, U.S.Post Office, Metal 125.00
Seat, Toilet, 1907, Oak 45.00
Soap Dish, Shell Shape, Corner Mount, Brass, 3 3/4 X 4 1/2 In. 25.00
Soda Fountain, Adjustable, A.Eliaers, Walnut, C.1853, 42 In. 2500.00
Soda Fountain, Renaissance, Ebonized, C.1865, 6 Ft. 550.00
Thumb Latch, Hand-Forged, Colonial, Wrought Iron, 8 In. 30.00
Toilet, Flush, Scrolled Bowl, Oak Seat & Tank, Itasca 450.00
Weight, Gate, Hand & Grapes, C.1860, Cast Iron, 6 1/2 In. 130.00
Window, Beveled Glass, Brass Frame, Oval, Pair 50.00
Window, Palladian, Original Interior Trim, Black Walnut 300.00
Window, Stained Glass, Drugstore, 2 Section, 19 X 3 1/2 In. 2450.00
Window, Victorian, Beveled, Original Frame, 24 X 86 In. 995.00

Arequipa Pottery was produced from 1911 to 1918 by the patients of the Arequipa Sanitorium in Marin County Hills, California.

AREQUIPA, Vase, Crystalline, Blue Over Gray, 5 1/2 X 6 In.Diam. .... 295.00 To 325.00
Vase, Incised Butterflies, Signed, Matte Gray Blue, 6 X 5 In. 550.00
ARGY-ROUSSEAU, see G. Argy-Rousseau

ARITA, Bowl, Fruit Medallion, Petal Edges, C.1700, Blue & White, 9 5/8 In. 375.00
Bowl, Swimming Fish & Chrysanthemum, C.1860, Blue & Gray, 10 In.Diam. 700.00

Art Deco, or Art Moderne, is a style started at the Paris Exposition of 1925, characterized by linear, geometric designs. All types of furniture and decorative arts, jewelry, bookbindings, and even games were designed in this style.

ART DECO, Ashtray Holder, Hand-Painted Jiggs Cartoon, Wooden, 33 In. 65.00
Ashtray, Held By Kneeling Nude Girl 95.00
Ashtray, Metal Female Clown, Ivory Head, Marble & Alabaster, 8 In. 300.00
Basket, Hand-Painted Design, German, Signed Fireside, Pottery 50.00
Bookends, Fish, Adjustable, Brass & Enamel, 5 In. 68.00
Bookends, Girl Kneeling, Bronze Over Copper 125.00
Bookends, Nude Lady, Cast Iron 35.00
Bookends, Penguin, Silver Plated, Pair 25.00
Bookends, Stylized Antelope, White Metal, 7 1/2 In. 50.00
Bottle, Green Floral, Stippled Frosted, White Ground, 7 In. 165.00
Bottle, Perfume, Cut Crystal, Signed Marcel Franck, 3 X 3 In. 75.00
Burner, Incense, Woman On Tummy Holding Burner, Bird's Head, 13 In. 110.00
Candlestick, Brass Scones, 2 Arms In Each Anchor, 4 Sockets, 9 In. 195.00
Figurine, Head Of Jester, French, Bronze & Marble, 10 1/4 In. 1900.00
Figurine, Woman & Running Deer, Matte Green Glaze, French 400.00
Holder, Flower, Dancing Nudes, Pottery, 8 In. 35.00
Lamp, Figural, Labrador, Chasing, White Frosted Globe 65.00
Lamp, Figurine, Base, Flower & Glass Petals 20.00
Lamp, Onyx, Bronze Dancing Girl, 12 In. 350.00
Lamp, Wall, Custard Shades, Blue, Pair 300.00
Lighter, Cigarette, Turning Copper Globe, On Stand, 5 1/4 In. 32.00

Plate, 20s Scene Of Drinkers, Boaters 75.00
Tray, Geometric Reverse On Glass, Chrome Frame 125.00
Vase, Backgammon Pattern, Czechoslovakia, 7 1/4 In. 110.00
Vase, Charder, Blue Over White-Blue Frost, Signed, 10 In. 435.00
Vase, Hand-Painted, Signed Gabzlini, Gray Ground, 6 1/2 In. 175.00

> *Art glass means any of the many forms of glassware made during the late
> nineteenth century or early twentieth century. These wares were expensive and
> made in limited production. Art glass is not the typical commercial glass
> that was made in large quantities, and most of the art glass was produced by
> hand methods.*

**ART GLASS, see also separate headings such as Burmese; Nash;
Schneider; etc.**
ART GLASS, Ashtray, Silver Inlays, Gustavberg Argenta, 2 3/4 X 3 1/2 In., Pr. 48.00
Basket, Deep Cranberry, Twisted Handle, 6 In. 135.00
Basket, Ruffled, Amber Twisted Handle, Opalescent 175.00
Basket, Square Thorn Handle, Pink & White Speckled, 6 In. 110.00
Basket, White Applied Amber Handle, Leaf, 6 1/4 In. 159.00
Bell Light, Nailsea Loops, Vaseline With Opalescent 395.00
Bowl, Apple Green Top, Cobalt Blue Base, 8 In. 30.00
Bowl, Blue, Red & Clear, Pukenburg, 5 X 1 1/2 In. 60.00
Bowl, Coquille, Black, White, & Clear, Flygfors, 9 X 10 1/2 In. 75.00
Bowl, Creamy White To Robin's Egg Blue, 1885, 5 1/2 In. 45.00
Cracker Jar, Enameled Design, Pink To Clear, Meriden B-Co., 6 In. 110.00
Cracker Jar, Silver Plated Handle, Milk Glass, 8 1/4 In. 35.00
Creamer, Powder Blue, Dark Blue Handle, 4 1/4 In. 52.00
Inkwell, Geometric Design, Brass Collar, Clear Inset, 3 1/2 In. 250.00
Obelisk, Frosted, Clear Casing, Ivenini, Blue, 1o 1/2 In. 125.00
Pitcher, Pale Green, Tree Branch Design, 1880, 5 In. 75.00
Purple Iridescent, Enameled Yellow Flowers, 10 1/2 In. 100.00
Rose Bowl, Purple Overshot Ribs, 5 X 5 In. 95.00
Shade, Banquet, Opalescent Hobs, Ripple Rim 150.00
Shade, Luster Art, Feather Design, Gold Threading 120.00
Shade, Orange & Blue 30.00
Shade, 1/2 Green & Gold Loops, Signed, Set Of 5 .... 750.00
Vase, Art Deco Roosters, French, Black Glass, 7 1/4 In. 225.00
Vase, Austrian, C.1900, Pale Green & Blue, 8 1/2 In. ....*Illus* 1550.00
Vase, Cased Black, Red, & Clear, Pulled Spiral, Kosta, 12 1/2 In. 150.00
Vase, Cased White, Red & Yellow Stripes, 10 1/2 X 5 1/2 In. 28.00
Vase, Darcy, Blue & White, 14 In. 350.00
Vase, Green Stretch, Copier Leerdam, 8 1/2 In. 225.00
Vase, Hand-Painted Flower, Signed Kolek, 3 1/2 In. 47.50
Vase, Purple Stretch, Copier Leerdam, 16 In. 300.00
Vase, Reverse Painted Leaves & Pods, Signed Ambero, C.1900, 18 In. 400.00
Vase, White To Orange, Tree Design, 1885, 4 1/2 In. 65.00
Vase, White, Pink, Yellow Trim, Flowers, C.1900, 6 In., Pair 150.00
Wager Cup, Upper Portion Of Lady Is Gilded, Enameled, 7 1/4 In. 90.00

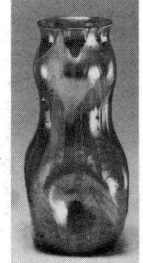

Art Glass, Vase, Austrian, C.1900,
Pale Green & Blue, 8 1/2 In.

Art Nouveau, a style characterized by free-flowing organic design, reached its zenith between 1895 and 1905. The style encompassed all decorative and functional arts from architecture to furniture and posters.

ART NOUVEAU, see also Furniture; various glass categories; etc.

ART NOUVEAU, Ashtray & Match Holder, Bronze	90.00
Candlestick, Demure Maiden, Pewter & Brass, 3 Sockets, 11 In.	395.00
Card Holder, Gold Over Pewter, Smiling Girl, 13 X 5 1/2 In.	385.00
Chamberstick, Lily Lotus Pad, Copper, Copper Match Holder	79.00
Lamp, Nude Lady On Each Side, Threaded Glass Light, Bronze	125.00
Wine, Enameled, Iridescent Orange Flower, Ruffled Foot	165.00

ART POTTERY, see under factory name

ART POTTERY, Vase, Ivory & Green, Tuskegee Institute, 9 1/2 In.	155.00
Vase, Pinched Sides, Green, Hellosine Ware, Austria, 5 In.	85.00
Vase, 1923, Gustavsburg, 5 In.	85.00
ARTHUR OSBORNE, see Ivorex	

AURENE

Aurene glass was made by Frederick Carder of New York about 1904. It is an iridescent gold glass, usually marked Aurene or Steuben.

AURENE, see also Steuben

AURENE, Atomizer, Blue, Signed, 8 1/2 In.	280.00
Atomizer, Perfume, Blue, 7 1/2 In.	350.00
Basket, Blue Handle, Calcite, Gold, 11 X 11 1/2 In.	675.00
Bottle, Perfume, Acorn Stopper, 4 1/4 In.	375.00
Bottle, Perfume, Pedestal Shape, Mirror Finish, Blue, Signed, 8 In.	850.00
Bottle, Perfume, Pedestal Shape, Signed, 8 In.	850.00
Bowl, Blue, Signed, Carder, 3 1/4 X 8 In.	600.00
Bowl, Blue, 3 X 10 In.Diam.	375.00
Bowl, Calcite, Gold, 7 In.Diam.	475.00
Bowl, Calcite, Gold, 8 In.Diam.	295.00
Bowl, Calcite, 10 1/2 In.	150.00
Bowl, Finger, Calcite, Gold, Underplate	200.00 To 265.00
Bowl, Teakwood Base, Purple, Signed, 6 In.	150.00
Candlestick, Calcite, Gold, 6 In., Pair	400.00
Candlestick, Signed, 8 In.	185.00
Candlestick, Twisted Stem, Blue, Signed, 8 In., Pair	355.00
Candlestick, Twisted Stem, Blue, Signed, 13 In., Pair	1250.00
Chalice, Trumpet Shape, Gold, Purple Highlights, 6 1/2 In.	285.00
Compote, Blue, 4 Applied Buttons, Signed, 5 3/4 In.	450.00
Compote, Calcite, Blue, 6 1/2 X 7 In.	550.00
Compote, Calcite, Gold, 8 In.Diam.	245.00
Cup, Gold, Pedestal, Signed, 3 1/2 In.	200.00
Darner, Stocking, Gold	430.00
Finger Bowl, Gold, Signed	260.00
Flower Frog, Gold, 2 X 3 In.	90.00
Orange Bowl, Signed, 14 X 7 1/2 In.	175.00
Plate, Stretched Edge, Signed, 7 1/2 In.	130.00
Salt, Gold Iridescent, Signed	95.00
Shade, Calcite	80.00
Shade, Diamond-Quilted, Gold, Pulled Green Feathers	300.00
Shade, Gold, Bell Shape, Signed, Set Of 4	350.00
Shade, Gold, Fishnet Design Over Calcite	195.00
Shade, Gold, Ribbed, 5 1/2 In.	75.00
Shade, Gold, 2 1/4 In., Pair	250.00
Shade, Ribbed, Scalloped Rim, Gold, 6 1/2 In., Pair	100.00
Sherbet & Liner, Gold, Signed	210.00
Sherbet & Underplate, Gold, Calcite	225.00
Toothpick, Dimpled, Gold Iridescence, Signed, 2 1/4 In.	165.00

Vase, Blue, 6 In. 600.00
Vase, Blue, Signed, 8 In. 675.00
Vase, Blue Iridescent, Signed, 8 In. 325.00
Vase, Cylindrical, White, Red Arches, Signed, 6 In. 1600.00
Vase, Gold Ruby Swirl, Ruffled, Blue 350.00
Vase, Gold, Double Gourd, 6 In. 425.00
Vase, Gold, 4 In. 350.00
Vase, Gold, 6 In. 300.00
Vase, Inverted Bell Form, Ribbed, C.1904, Signed, 6 3/4 In. 350.00
Vase, Ivorene Body, Gold Random Threads, Signed, 5 In. 675.00
Vase, M Handles, Gold, Signed F.Carder, 7 In. 650.00
Vase, Paper Label, Signed, 10 In. 575.00
Vase, Pond Lily, Signed, 7 3/4 In. 650.00
Vase, Stretched 3-Cornered Ruffled Top, Gold, Signed, 4 In. 175.00
Vase, Trumpet Form, Signed, 8 In. 200.00
Vase, Waisted, Flared Top, Signed, 4 1/4 In. 185.00

Auto parts and accessories are collectors' items today.

AUTO, Gas Pump Globe, Bang That Food Gas, Gilmore Refining Co.Red, 30 In. 80.00
Gas Pump Globe, Cavalier Diesel 110.00
Gas Pump Globe, Champlin 77.50
Gas Pump Globe, Clarks 65.00
Gas Pump Globe, Clock Face 550.00
Gas Pump Globe, Crown Oil 110.00
Gas Pump Globe, Crown, Red 150.00
Gas Pump Globe, Derby 110.00
Gas Pump Globe, Dino Sinclair Supreme 55.00
Gas Pump Globe, Esso Extra, Metal Frame 150.00
Gas Pump Globe, Esso, Metal Frame 125.00
Gas Pump Globe, Flame Shaped, Painted Red, Milk Glass 225.00
Gas Pump Globe, Marathon Mile Maker, Red, White, & Blue Lettering 65.00
Gas Pump Globe, Mobile Regular 77.50
Gas Pump Globe, Mobile Supreme 77.50
Gas Pump Globe, Phillips 66 .... 125.00
Gas Pump Globe, Red Crown Gasoline, Porcelain, 30 In.Diam. 125.00
Gas Pump Globe, Red Crown, Porcelain, 24 In.Diam. 145.00
Gas Pump Globe, Red Head 125.00
Gas Pump Globe, Regular McMurray Gasoline 145.00
Gas Pump Globe, Richfield Gas, Picture Of Eagle, 15 In.Diam. 175.00
Gas Pump Globe, Shell 125.00
Gas Pump Globe, Simpson's Premium Ethyl 135.00
Gas Pump Globe, Sinclair Dino Gasoline 70.00
Gas Pump Globe, Skelly Keotane 60.00
Gas Pump Globe, Skelly Regular 55.00
Gas Pump Globe, Sohio 90.00
Gas Pump Globe, Standard Oil, Crown, Milk Glass, Never Painted 225.00
Gas Pump Globe, Texaco, Leaded Stained Glass 1450.00
Gas Pump Globe, U.S.Motor McMurray 145.00
Gas Pump Globe, Wadham's Antiknock, Metal Globe, Exterior Lights 350.00
Gas Pump Globe, White Eagle .... 600.00 To 750.00
Gauge, Radiator, Boyce Moto-Meter, 1930s Ford 32.00
Gauge, Tire, Packard, Pouch 85.00
Gauge, Tire, Schrader, 1909 .... 5.00
Gearshift Knob, Finger Grooves, Dog Under Glass Center 35.00
Gearshift Knob, Swirl, Glass, Green & White 20.00
Headlight Lens, Ford, 1936 .... 5.00
Headlight, Bar & Ooga Horn, 1929 Cadillac 250.00
Holder, License Plate, 1933 Century Of Progress, Emblem, Brass 22.00
      AUTO, HOOD ORNAMENT, see also Lalique
Hood Ornament, Bulldog, Mack 12.00
Hood Ornament, Flying Bird, Metal 22.00
Hood Ornament, Nude, Ford, Chrome 52.00
Hood Ornament, Pontiac Indian Head 7.75

Horn, Ford, 1936	8.00
Jar, Battery, Electrodes, Cobalt Blue, Round	45.00
Knob, Gearshift, Marbleized	15.00
Knob, Gearshift, Marbleized Orange, Brown, & White Agate	15.00
Lamp, Franklin, 1910, Brass, Pair	150.00
Lamp, Oil, Ford, 1917, Bull's-Eye Lens, Brass Top & Rim	90.00
Lamp, 1910, Knickerbocker, Electrified, Brass	85.00
License Plate, Dealer, Mississippi, 1932	30.00
License Plate, Iowa, 1942	4.00
License Plate, Mississippi, 1932	5.00
License Plate, Missouri, 1932	7.00
License Plate, New York, 1933	8.50
Light, Cowling Side, Hudson, Pair	10.00
Light, Driving, Red Side Lens, Gray & Davis, Amesbury, Bracket Mount	100.00
Light, Oil, Side, Ford, Signed	18.00
Liscense Plate, Ohio, 1922	20.00
Ornament, Hood, Mercedes	20.00
Ornament, Nude Woman	24.00
Padlock, Standard Oil Co., Brass	10.00
Rack, Luggage, Fits Running Board	35.00
Rack, Luggage, Large	12.00
Rack, Luggage, Model T	40.00
Rack, Luggage, Small	18.00
Side Light, Bracket, 1914 Cadillace, Brass	95.00
Tester, Delco, Tube & Magneto	10.00
Vase, U.S.Glass, Paper Label, Blue	22.50
Wrench, Model A Ford, Marked	5.50

Autumn Leaf pattern china was made for the Jewel Tea Company from 1933. Hall China Company of East Liverpool, Ohio, Crooksville China Company of Crooksville, Ohio, Harker Potteries of Chester, West Virginia, and Paden City Pottery, Paden City, West Virginia, made dishes with this design. Autumn Leaf dishes have been made in the 1970s.

AUTUMN LEAF, Base, Candle Warmer, Jewel Tea, Round	75.00
Bowl, Mixing, Jewel Tea, Set Of 3	27.50
Bowl, Vegetable, Covered	28.50
Butter, Covered, Jewel Tea	125.00
Butter, Hall, 1/4 Pound	90.00
Butter, Jewel Tea, Cover, Sealed Factory Box	125.00
Butter, Jewel Tea, Covered, Box	125.00
Can, Fruitcake, Jewel Tea, 7 In.	5.00
Candle Warmer, Jewel Tea	75.00
Canister, Bittersweet, Jewel Tea	35.00
Canister, Jewel Tea, Plastic Lid, White	10.00
Casserole, Covered	22.50
Casserole, Covered, Pink	26.00
Coaster, Jewel Tea, Set Of 8	30.00
Coffee Server, 10 Cup Size	30.00
Coffeepot, Jewel Tea, Cover	40.00
Cookie Jar, Pink	65.00
Cup & Saucer	4.50 To 6.50
Cup, St.Dennis	14.00
Custard Cup, Jewel Tea	10.50
Dish, Pickle, Jewel Tea, Oval	18.00
Dish, Vegetable, Covered, Oval	25.00
Goblet, Jewel Tea, 9 Ounce	16.50
Gravy Boat, Jewel Tea	10.00
Hot Pad, Round	10.00

Marmalade Set, 3 Piece	50.00
Mustard, 3 Piece	45.00
Percolator, Electric, Hall	160.00
Pitcher, Iced Tea	24.00 To 25.00
Pitcher, Jewel Tea, Small	12.00
Pitcher, Milk, Jewel Tea	18.00
Pitcher, Milk, Jewel Tea, Meakin, Copper	115.00
Pitcher, Milk, Jewel Tea, 6 In.	12.00
Pitcher, Tilt	35.00
Pitcher, Utility	17.50
Plate, Jewel Tea, 6 In.	2.50 To 3.75
Plate, Jewel Tea, 7 In.	3.90 To 4.25
Plate, Jewel Tea, 8 In.	4.75 To 5.00
Plate, Jewel Tea, 9 In.	5.50
Platter, Jewel Tea, 11 In.	10.00
Platter, 13 1/2 In.	10.00
Range Set, Jewel Tea, 4 Piece	26.50
Range Set, 3 Piece	30.00
Salt & Pepper, Jewel Tea, Small	8.00
Server, Coffee, Jewel Tea	37.50
Souffle, Jewel Tea	10.50
Sugar & Creamer, Jewel Tea	18.00 To 30.00
Sugar, Covered, Jewel Tea	12.50
Teapot, Aladdin	25.00
Teapot, Jewel Tea, Aladdin, Strainer	28.00
Teapot, Jewel Tea, Gold	95.00
Teapot, Jewel Tea, Gooseneck Spout	15.00
Teapot, Long Spout	45.00 To 60.00
Teapot, Pink	62.00
Tray, Tidbit, 3 Tier	60.00
Tumbler, Jewel Tea, 14 Ounce	13.50
Vase, Jewel Tea, Gold Trim	95.00
Warmer, Base, Candle, Jewel Tea	75.00

AVON POTTERY, Pitcher, Olive Green Stripes, Signed, 4 In.	60.00

Baccarat glass was made in France by La Compagnie des Cristalleries de Baccarat, located 150 miles from Paris. The factory was started in 1765. The firm went bankrupt and began operating again about 1822. Cane and millefiori paperweights were made during the 1860 to 1880 period. The firm is still working near Paris making paperweights and glasswares.

BACCARAT, Bobeche, Amberina Swirled, Marked, 4 In.Diam.	15.00
Bottle, Perfume, Art Deco, Stylized Lines, 4 In.	50.00
Bottle, Perfume, Mannequin, Bust, 4 1/2 In.	50.00
Bottle, Perfume, Swirl, Original Stopper, 5 3/4 In.	37.50
Bottle, Ribbed, Bell Shape, Stopper, Signed	40.00
Bowl, Freeform, 8 Starfish Points, 11 1/2 X 7 In.	200.00
Bowl, Rose Teinte, Ormolu Mounting, Oval, 7 1/2 X 12 In.	225.00
Box, Crystal, Angular Designs, Covered, Signed, 4 X 4 In.	125.00
Cake Plate, Swirled Floral Pattern, Marked, 8 In.Diam.	68.00
Compote, Swirl, Depose, Signed, Green, 6 3/8 In., Pair	160.00
Decanter Set, Gilt-Bronze & Glass, Late 19th Century	*Illus* 1900.00
Dresser Set, Diamond-Cut Pattern, Signed, 4 Piece	375.00
Holder, Card, Holder Is Fan, Butterflies Base, Signed	160.00
Holder, Toothbrush, Amberina, Signed	65.00
Jar, Covered, 6 Panels, Cut Crystal, Original Ladle, 5 1/2 In.	95.00
Lamp, Fairy, Pinwheel Pattern, Matching Plate, Marked, 5 3/4 In.	265.00
Lamp, Fairy, Sunburst Pattern, Amberina, 3 3/4 X 5 5/8 In.	195.00
Lamp, Fairy, Swirl Pattern, Amberina, Signed	345.00
Lamp, Peg, Swirl, Amber, Pair	325.00
Paperweight, Buttercup, Ringed By Millefiori Canes, Star Cut Base	5200.00

(See Page 13)

Baccarat, Decanter Set, Gilt-Bronze & Glass,
Late 19th Century

Paperweight, Canes, Crown, Millefiori, 7 In.	350.00
Paperweight, Concentric Circle, Dated 1969, Signed	150.00
Paperweight, Concentric Millefiori, Canes, 2 3/8 In.	390.00
Paperweight, Coronation, Fan Cut Ground, 1953	250.00
Paperweight, Eisenhower, Overlay	450.00
Paperweight, Filigree Twists, Bull's-Eye Cane, 2 5/8 In.	300.00
Paperweight, Flower, Center Cane, Aqua Ground, 1971, 3 1/4 In.	275.00
Paperweight, Flower, Center Cane, Blue Ground, 1974, 3 In.	400.00
Paperweight, Flowers, 3 Buds, Swirling Latticinio, 3 1/8 In.	310.00
Paperweight, Garland, 10 Stippled Petals, Honeycomb Center, 6 In.	1000.00
Paperweight, Hunter, Dog, Woodland, Red Ground, 3 1/4 In.	2100.00
Paperweight, Kennedy, John & Jackie, Overlay Gold Design	100.00
Paperweight, Liberty Bell, Faceted Blue Ground	175.00
Paperweight, Luther, Martin, Blue Base	180.00
Paperweight, Magnum Pattern, Green, White, Blue, Claret, Yellow	4800.00
Paperweight, Millefiori With Animals, Canes, Dated 1848, 2 3/4 In.	1450.00
Paperweight, Mount Rushmore, Overlay	400.00
Paperweight, Paine, Thomas, 1976	75.00
Paperweight, Pansy, Flowers, Purple, Yellow, Pink, White, 2 1/4 In.	450.00
Paperweight, Pansy, Purple, Pink & White Star, Green Stalk, 6 In.	260.00
Paperweight, Pansy, 2 Buds, Opalescent Ground, Signed, 1972	150.00
Paperweight, Pope John, Yellow Overlay Base	110.00
Paperweight, Pope Pius XII, Overlay	120.00
Paperweight, Rayburn, Sam, Overlay	450.00
Paperweight, Seahorse, Coiled Tail, 3 1/4 In.	310.00
Paperweight, Silhouettes, Dog, Goat, Cockerel, 1 3/4 In.	200.00
Paperweight, Silhouettes, Horses, Dog, Devil, Dated 1847, 2 In.	700.00
Paperweight, Sulfide, Zodiac, Cancer	80.00
Paperweight, Truman, Harry, Double Overlay, Blue & White	225.00
Paperweight, Truman, Harry, Gold Star Cut Base	100.00
Salt, Pedestal, Signed	60.00
Tumbler, Paneled, Windows, Topaz & Crystal, 4 1/2 In., Set Of 6	330.00
Vase, Amberina Swirl, 9 In.	105.00
Vase, Bud, Teardrop Shape, Signed, 7 In.	45.00
Vase, Swirled Rib, Flared Top, Signed, 5 In.	55.00
Wine, Footed, Etched, C.1900, Signed	22.00
BADGE, American Legion Grand Promenade, Austin, Texas, 1938	7.50
American Secret Service, Lieutenant Protective League	95.00
Cap, The Grayline, Sightseeing Everywhere, Porcelain	45.00
Chicago Real Estate Board, 1915	7.50

Chief, Fire Engine, Steam, German, Silver 85.00
Constable, Colfax County, Cimarron, New Mexico, Eagle Top 60.00
Deputy Sheriff, Cook County, Illinois 50.00
Deputy Sheriff, Lampasas Co., Texas Star Center, Ballpoint 60.00
Detective, Star, Philadelphia Street Railway 40.00
Dress Hat, G.A.R., Brass Laurel Wreath 15.00
Fireman's, C.1930, Conemaugh, Pennsylvania 19.00
Fireman's, Enameled Lettering, Weymouth, Mass., State Seal 20.00
Fireman's, 1903, Candor, New York, Silver Eagle 22.00
Game Warden, Texas, State Seal 35.00
Guard, Security, Butler Bros., Enameled Seal Of North Carolina 15.00
Las Vegas Canine Patrol 45.00
Massachusetts Reformatory, Massachusetts Seal 47.50
New York City Detective 12.50
New York City Police 12.50
Orlando Police, Shield Shape, Eagle Top, Hallmarked 50.00
Patrol Man, Police, Lake Ozard, Missouri 40.00
Plant, Willy's Overland 18.00
Police, Investigator, Hawaii Five-O, State Logo, Blue Enamel 25.00
Police, Oiltown, Oklahoma 70.00
Police, Sergeant, Enameled State Seal, New Hampshire, Gold Plated 20.00
Post Adjutant, Beaumont, Texas, 1936 .... 7.50
Post Office, New York 15.00
Postal Transportation Service 37.50
Railroad Express Agency Employee, Gold Plated 40.00
Regimental, Russian, C.1870, Imperial Eagle & Banner On Wreath 80.00
Ringling Bros.Circus 20.00
School Safety Patrolman 15.00
Sheriff, Deputy, Cole County, Missouri, Porcelain 35.00
Shield, Publix Cab & Telephone Number 35.00
Southern California Telephone Co. 35.00
Telephone, Blue Porcelain 16.00
Texas Ranger, 6 Point 95.00
Traffic, Police, Coat Of Arms 7.00
U.S.Census, 1910 .... 40.00
V.F.W., Houston, Texas, 1850 .... 7.50
Woman's Relief Corps, Dated 1883, Red, White, & Blue 6.00
    BAG, BEADED, see Beaded Bag

*Metal banks have been made since 1868. There are still banks, mechanical
banks, and registering banks (those which total money deposited on the face of
the bank). Many old banks have been reproduced since the 1950s in iron
or plastic.*

BANK, Acorn Stove, Pottery, Green 35.00
Airdale, Cast Iron 55.00
American Can Co., Declaration Of Independence 10.00
Andy Gump, Thrift 225.00
Antlered Deer, Cast Iron 30.00
Apple, Red, Pottery 18.00
Arabian Safe, Cast Iron .... 37.00 To 75.00
Aunt Jemima, Cast Iron .... 40.00 To 68.00
Babe Ruth 45.00
Baby In Papoose, C.D.Kenny, German 25.00
Bank Building, Cast Iron, Silver, Square 45.00
Bank Building, Chimney, Tin 50.00
Bank Building, Dome Roof, Cast Iron 20.00
Bank Building, Red Paint, Yellow & Green Trim, Cast Iron, 5 1/2 In. 85.00
Bank Building, With Cupola, Cast Iron 35.00
Barrel, Cast Iron 75.00
Barrel, Happy Days 20.00
Baseball Player, Cast Iron 110.00
Bear, Standing, Cast Iron, 5 3/4 In. 85.00

Beehive Shape, Pointed Finial, Redware, Black Slip, 4 X 6 In. 175.00
Beehive, Iron, 1920s 27.50
Beehive, Savings Bank, Commercial Bank Of Eau Claire, Wisc., Cast Iron 135.00
Bell, Buckled Harness Strap 295.00
Big Bertha Bomb, Iron Cross, 1914 Date, Metal 165.00
Billiken, Good Luck, Cast Iron .... 46.00 To 80.00
Billiken, Steel 35.00
Black Beauty, Cast Iron 60.00
Black Man, 2 Face, Cast Iron, 3 1/4 In. 85.00
Black Sharecropper, Cast Iron 90.00
Bokar Coffee 12.00
Bonzo, Nodder, Papier-Mache, 8 1/2 In. 175.00
Boston Bull, Seated, Cast Iron 90.00
Boston Bulldog, Cast Iron, 9 In. 22.50
Bottle, Lincoln 15.00
Boy Scout, Cast Iron 75.00
Boy Scout, With Staff, Doughboy Uniform, 5 3/4 In. 50.00
Bozo The Clown, Chalkware, 20 In. 18.00
Buffalo, Amherst, Cast Iron 200.00
Buffalo, Cast Iron .... 55.00 To 110.00
Buffalo, Gold Paint, 3 In. 70.00
Bugs Bunny, 1972 .... 15.00
Building, Cast Iron, 4 1/2 X 2 In.Diam. 35.00
Building, Handmade, Wooden, Steeple, 9 X 5 X 5 1/2 In. 45.00
Building, 13 Story, 6 Roof Tower, Iron, 3 1/2 X 4 1/2 X6 1/2 In. 55.00
Bulldog, Cast Iron 65.00
Bulldog, Seated, Cast Iron 35.00
Bulldog, Seated, Cast Iron, 4 1/4 In. 55.00
Bulldog, Seated, Husky, Studded Collar, 4 1/2 In. 50.00
Bulldog, Sitting, Cast Iron, Gold Color 50.00
Bullet, World War I, Cast Iron 50.00
Buster Brown & Tige, Cast Iron 100.00
Camel, Cast Iron .... 50.00 To 70.00
Camel, Cast Iron, Small 40.00
Camel, Cast Iron, 4 1/4 In. 65.00
Cannon Shell, Cast Iron 25.00
Cannon, Cast Iron, 10 1/2 In.Long 45.00
Car, Antique, Lowell 5 Cent Savings 20.00
Cat In Tub, Cast Iron 80.00
Cat With Tie, Cast Iron 49.00
Cat, C.1840, Chalkware, Blue & White Paint, 9 3/4 In. 300.00
Cat, Seated, Black & Gold Paint, Cast Iron, 5 X 4 X 4 In. 45.00
Champion, Combination, Cast Iron 50.00
Charlie Chaplin, Glass, Partial Color 90.00
Christ Child With Lamb, Original Yellow Paint, Cast Iron, 8 1/2 In. 45.00
Church, Chein, Tin 14.00
Church, Day By Day, A Penny A Meal, Tin 55.00
Circus Elephant, Stand On 2 Hind Legs, Trunk To Side, Cast Iron 75.00
Circus Pony, Prancing, Cast Iron 60.00
Clock With Pendulum, Cast Iron 325.00
Clock, Money Saved, Cast Iron 35.00
Clown, Cast Iron .... 75.00 To 110.00
Clown, Grapette, Closure, 7 In. 10.00
Clown, Redhead, Riding Pig, Chalkware, Dated 1949, 11 1/2 In. 27.50
Clown, 6 1/2 In. 15.00
Combination Safe Bank, Safe Deposit, Pat. '87 .... 45.00
Cow, Cast Iron 100.00
Deer, Cast Iron .... 50.00 To 70.00
Deer, Light In Nose, White Metal 15.00
Deer, Original Gold Paint, Cast Iron 65.00
Deer, With Antlers, Cast Iron .... 35.00 To 52.00
Derby Hat, Cast Iron 150.00

Dime, Superman, 1940s, Original Paint 45.00
Dog With Pack, Cast Iron, 3 3/4 In. 65.00
Dog, Bee On Hip, Cast Iron 60.00
Dog, Cocked Ear, Cast Iron 45.00
Dog, Pack On Back, Black Paint, 5 1/2 In. 65.00
Dog, Scotty, White 40.00
Dog's Head, Roseville 175.00
Donald Duck, Long Bill, Papier-Mache 35.00
Donkey With Saddle, Cast Iron, Silver Color 60.00
Donkey, Army Mule, Saddled & Bridled, Red Trim, 4 1/2 In. 60.00
Donkey, Cast Iron, Gray Paint, 4 1/4 In. 125.00
Donkey, Standing, Cast Iron .... 45.00 To 85.00
Donkey, With Saddle, Cast Iron 40.00
Doughboy Hat, World War I 115.00
Dresser Shape, Rockingham Glaze, Pottery, 8 1/2 X 6 In. 135.00
Duck On Tub, Cast Iron .... 55.00 To 85.00
Duck, Standing, Cast Iron 85.00
Dutch Cleanser, Tin, Advertising 18.00
Dutch Girl, Cast Iron 85.00
Dutch Shoe, Century Of Progress, Chicago, 1933, Carved, Scenic 20.00
Eagle, McCoy Pottery 12.00
Electrolux, Cast Iron 35.00
Elephant On Bench Sitting On Tub, Iron, 4 In. .... 95.00 To 125.00
Elephant With Howdah, Cast Iron, Gold Color, 3 In. 50.00
Elephant, Cast Iron .... 25.00 To 45.00
Elephant, Hand-Painted, Occupied Japan, 3 X 2 1/2 In. 12.00
Elephant, Sitting, Grapette, Glass 25.00
Elephant, Trunk Down, Gilt Paint, Iron, 3 In. 75.00
Elk, With Antlers, Arcade Co., Gilt Paint, 6 1/2 X 4 In. 50.00
Excelsior, Semimechanical 65.00
Fido, Cast Iron .... 45.00 To 55.00
Fireman 190.00
Flatiron Building, Cast Iron 75.00
Foxy Grandpa, Cast Iron 285.00
GE Refrigerator, Iron .... 50.00 To 150.00
General Pershing, Cast Iron 75.00
German Shepherd, Iron, Original Paint, 9 In. 75.00
Get Rich Quick 45.00
Globe, Chein, 1930s 10.00
Globe, With Eagle, Cast Iron 150.00
Hippo, 1948, Tin 15.00
Home Budget, Tin, 6 Slots 7.00
Home Savings Bank, Cast Iron, Olive Green, Red Trim, 2 1/4 X 2 1/2 X 3 ...... 35.00
Home, Tin, Red House On Blue Base 7.00
Honeybee House, Yellow Paint Worn, Milk Glass 45.00
Horse & Wagon, Removable Wagon Seats, 12 1/2 In. 80.00
Horse Beauty, Iron 50.00
Horse, Prancing, Cast Iron .... 40.00 To 45.00
Horse, Prancing, Cast Iron, 4 1/4 In. .... 25.00 To 59.00
Horse, Prancing, Iron, Gilt Paint, 4 1/2 In. 85.00
Horse, Rearing, Pebbled Base, Flowing Tail, 7 1/2 In. 120.00
Horse, Saddle & Bridle, Cast Iron, Small 265.00
Horse, Standing, Cast Iron .... 25.00 To 45.00
Horse, Wheels, Cast Iron 235.00
Horseshoe, Horseheads On Sides, 3 1/4 X 3 1/2 In. 75.00
House, Coin Drop In Roof, Black & Orange, Metal, 4 In.Square 15.00
House, Porch Left Side, Cast Iron, Small 45.00
House, Porch Right Side, Cast Iron, Large 65.00
House, Porch, Slot In Roof, Cast Iron 75.00
House, Roll-Top, Bear Finial, Cast Iron 78.00
House, Victorian, Copper Gilt, 3 X 2 1/4 In. 50.00
House, White, Green, Red, Iron, 3 1/8 In. 35.00

House, With Porch, Cast Iron 95.00
House, 2 Chimneys, Dated July 25, 1908, Cast Iron, 3 In. 60.00
Indian Head, Cast Iron 28.00
Israeli Independence, 1940s, Blue, Map Of Israel 30.00
Junior Safe Deposit, Leafy Design, Copper Colored Lock, 4 1/2 In. 50.00
Kewpie, Black, Chalkware 45.00
Kewpie, Standing 22.00
Kitten, Cast Iron 30.00
Liberty Bell, Arcade, Cast Iron 20.00
Liberty Bell, Cast Iron, Small 55.00
Liberty Bell, Cast Iron, 4 1/2 In. 60.00
Liberty Bell, Embossed Glass, 1776, 4 1/2 In. 35.00
Lighthouse, Removable Top, C.1870, Treen, 3 3/4 In. 75.00
Lincoln High Hat, Cast Iron 70.00
Lincoln, Figural, Metal 15.00
Lindy 120.00
Lion Head, Iron 39.00
Lion On Circus Tub, Begging, Red Sash, Iron, 5 In. 110.00
Lion On Tub, Circus, Gold Paint, 4 1/4 In. 70.00
Lion, Maned, Standing, Iron, Original Paint, 4 1/4 In. 75.00
Lion, Standing, Cast Iron .... 15.00 To 75.00
Lion, Standing, Open Mouth, Silver Paint, 3 3/4 In. 20.00
Little Red Riding Hood, Hull 200.00
Log Cabin, Glass 15.00
Log Cabin, Original Label, Westmoreland Mustard, Milk Glass 95.00
Log Cabin, Van Dyke Tea, Brown Glaze, Pottery 38.00
Lucky Jog, Glass 12.00
Mailbox, Cast Iron, Green, Red Design, 2 1/2 X 5 In. 52.00
Mailbox, Cast Iron, Large 45.00
Mailbox, Cast Iron, Medium 40.00
Mailbox, Cast Iron, Small 35.00
Mailbox, Eagle, W123, Iron 45.00
Mailbox, Hanging, Cast Iron .... 45.00 To 50.00
Mammy, With Spoon, Cast Iron, 8 In. 95.00
Mammy, With Spoon, Plaster 40.00

> Mechanical banks were first made about 1870. Any bank with moving parts is
> considered mechanical, although those most collected are the metal banks made
> before World War I. Reproductions are being made.

Mechanical, Alway Did Spise A Mule .... 295.00 To 465.00
Mechanical, Baseball Player, Cast Iron 85.00
Mechanical, Box Next To Glass Candy Container Bank, Marx 295.00
Mechanical, Boys Stealing Watermelon, Cast Iron ....Illus 4000.00
Mechanical, Cabin, Cast Iron ....Illus 225.00
Mechanical, Calumet Baking Powder, Tin 150.00
Mechanical, Chest Of Drawers 25.00
Mechanical, Chest Of Drawers, Celluloid 65.00
Mechanical, Clown On Globe, Original Wooden Box 700.00
Mechanical, Columbian Exposition Building, 1892 .... 225.00
Mechanical, Creedmoor 250.00
Mechanical, Dog On Turntable, Iron 225.00
Mechanical, Dog, Speaking, Iron 425.00
Mechanical, Eagle & Eaglets .... 425.00 To 650.00
Mechanical, Elephant, Chein, Tin 38.00
Mechanical, Elephant, Howdah, Man Pops Out, Iron .... 200.00 To 225.00
Mechanical, Elephant, Trunk Wiggles, Cast Iron, 3 1/2 In. .... 45.00 To 65.00
Mechanical, Hal's Lilliput, Cast Iron ....Illus 125.00
Mechanical, Jolly Nigger, Cast Iron 65.00
Mechanical, Jolly Nigger, Dated 1893, Shepard's Hardware 190.00
Mechanical, Jolly Nigger, March 14, 1882 .... 300.00
Mechanical, Jonah & The Whale 50.00
Mechanical, Lion & 2 Monkeys, Iron 375.00

Mechanical, Magic, Cast Iron ....*Illus* 850.00
Mechanical, Magician 550.00
Mechanical, Milk Pail Shape, Registers Penny Put In, Cast Iron 85.00
Mechanical, Monkey, Tips Hat, Chein, Tin 30.00
Mechanical, Nashua, N.H., Trust Co., Round 12.50
Mechanical, Nodding Scotsman, 50 Percent Paint 185.00
Mechanical, Organ Boy & Girl, Cast Iron, No Trap 550.00
Mechanical, Organ, Book Of Knowledge Series 65.00
Mechanical, Organ, Boy & Girl, Iron 225.00
Mechanical, Organ, Dog, Cat Revolves, Monkey Tips Hat, Pat.June 18, 1822 .... 225.00
Mechanical, Organ, Monkey, Iron 225.00
Mechanical, Owl, Glass Eyes, Turns Head 325.00
Mechanical, Owl, Turns Head .... 225.00 To 265.00
Mechanical, Paddy & His Pig, Dated Oct.8, 1882 .... 650.00

Banks, Mechanical, top row: Hal's Lilliput, Cast Iron ; Boys Stealing Watermelon,
Cast Iron; Popeye Knockout, Lithographed, Tin ; bottom row, Cabin, Cast Iron;
Stump Speaker, Cast Iron ; Magic, Cast Iron

Mechanical, Paddy & The Pig, Iron 475.00
Mechanical, Penny Pineapple, Hand Feeds Coin To Mouth, Yellow 350.00
Mechanical, Popeye Knockout, Lithographed, Tin ....*Illus* 450.00

Mechanical, Punch & Judy 265.00
Mechanical, Punch & Judy, Tin, 1930s 150.00
Mechanical, Rocket Ship, Tin 15.00
Mechanical, Signal Cabin, Iron 475.00
Mechanical, Southern Comfort 125.00
Mechanical, Spaceship, Plane Shoots Coins, Metal, C.1935 .... 25.00
Mechanical, Speaking Dog, Dated July 14, 1885, Cast Iron .... 265.00 To 350.00
Mechanical, Stump Speaker, Cast Iron ....*Illus* 1000.00
Mechanical, Tammany 185.00
Mechanical, Teddy & The Bear .... 475.00 To 580.00
Mechanical, Tut Tut, Lehman 650.00
Mechanical, Watchdog Safe, Iron 235.00
Mechanical, Wild West, Boxed 65.00
Mechanical, William Tell 350.00
Mechanical, Woodpecker, Tin, Germany 18.75
Mexican On Mule, Pot Metal 15.00
Middy, Cast Iron 145.00
Monkey, Thank You, Tin 35.00
Monkey, Tips Hat, Chein 45.00
Moon, Papier-Mache 26.50
Mr.Peanut Golden Anniversary 45.00
Mule, Cast Iron 60.00
Nash's Mustard, Lucky Joe, Glass 5.00
Nipper Dog, R.C.A., White Fuzz On Metal, 6 In. 125.00
Nipper, Ceramic, 12 In. 40.00
Old Decker's Pig, Iron 75.00
Onion Shape, Mushroom Button Finial, Redware, 4 X 4 1/2 In. 65.00
Organ Grinder, Cast Iron 110.00
Oscar The Goat, C.1910, Original Paint, Cast Iron, 8 In.Long 250.00
Owl On Stump, Cast Iron 100.00
Owl, Pawtucket Institution For Savings, Bronzed Metal 22.00
Pabst Blue Ribbon Beer, Small Can 11.00
Pail, Germany, Tin, 3 In. 9.00
Panda Bear, Cast Iron 35.00
Panther, On Tub, Cast Iron 60.00
Parking Meter, Cast Iron 55.00
Peanut Vendor, Original Box 100.00
Pershing, Bust, Cast Iron 100.00
Pershing, 7 3/4 In. .... 115.00 To 250.00
Pig, Cast Iron .... 20.00 To 40.00
Pig, Dress Suit & Tie, Old Paint, Cast Iron, 7 1/2 In. 130.00
Pig, Marbled Glaze, Pottery, 5 1/2 In. .... 65.00 To 75.00
Pig, Red Strawberries, C.1910 .... 25.00
Pig, Seated, Cast Iron 65.00
Pig, Thrifty, Smiling, Ivory, Gray, Pink Ears, Hobley, 1936, 6 In. 50.00
Pittsburgh Paint, 1940s, Glass 20.00
Popeye Dime Register, 1929 .... 28.00
Porky Pig, Bisque 45.00
Puppy, Cast Iron .... 40.00 To 55.00
Puppy, With Bee, Iron 45.00
Rabbit, Amber Glass 15.00
Rabbit, Oyster Shell, 6 In. 13.00
Radio, Cast Iron .... 45.00 To 55.00
Radio, 3 Dials, Cast Iron 45.00
Red Goose Shoes, Cast Iron 115.00
Register, Art Nouveau, C.1918, American Can, 5 In. 95.00
Register, Ben Franklin, Tin 35.00
Register, Burdick Corbin, Dime, 1902, Copper 45.00
Register, Chein, Dime, Tin 8.00
Register, Jackie Robinson, Dime 100.00
Register, Kopey, Dime 100.00
Register, Master Lock Shape, Dime, Tin 15.00

Register, Penny, Milk Pail, Cast Iron 85.00
Register, Snow White & 7 Dwarfs 25.00
Register, Treasury, Day & Amount, Chrome 16.00
Register, Uncle Sam, Tin 35.00
Register, 3 Coin, Marx 30.00
Register, 3 Coin, Uncle Sam, Black Metal 25.00
Rig, Tuxedo 45.00
Roller Safe, Roller Skating Scenes, Cast Iron 60.00
Rooster, Cast Iron 70.00
Rooster, Mean Looking, Red Comb, Gold Paint, 4 3/4 In. 60.00
Roy Rogers & Trigger, Tin 25.00
Safe Deposit, Brass Lock, Iron, 1888, 4 3/4 In. 55.00
Safe, Center Post, Gothic Arch, Floral Design, Key, Cast Iron 20.00
Safe, Combination, Cast Iron 35.00
Safe, Daisy, Cast Iron 50.00
Safe, Double Door, Combination, Cast Iron 100.00
Safe, J. & E.Stevens Co., Cast Iron 55.00
Safe, Key, Silver, Cast Iron 50.00
Safe, Roller, Cast Iron 55.00
San Diego Padres Cap 8.00
Santa Claus, Save Your Pennies, Tin 90.00
Second National Duck, Tin 75.00
Sheep, Iron, Original Paint, 5 1/2 In. 95.00
Shell, 1 1/2 In. 50.00
Slot Machine, Dime Makes Reel Spin, Tin 50.00
Sparkle Plenty, Savings, Boy With Arms Extended 12.00
St.Bernard, With Pack, Cast Iron, Silver 45.00
State Bank Building, Cast Iron, Silver Color, 2 1/2 X 5 1/2 In. 53.00
State Bank Building, Cast Iron, 3 X 2 1/2 X 4 In. 48.00
State Bank, Brown & Yellow Finish, Iron, 6 1/2 In. 75.00
State Bank, Cast Iron, 5 1/2 In. 130.00
Statue Of Liberty, Cast Iron 60.00
Steamboat, Cast Iron 150.00
Stove, Cast Iron, Green 50.00
Stove, Kenton, 1875, Cast Iron 25.00
Strongbox, Tin 15.00
Superman 28.00
Tabby 325.00
Tally Ho, Cast Iron 65.00
Tammany, Cast Iron .... 210.00 To 350.00
Tank, Cast Iron 75.00
Tank, World War I, Tin 45.00
Treasure Chest, Mickey Mouse 175.00
Truck, Armored, Tin, 9 1/2 X 4 In. 24.00
Trunk, Prudential Insurance Co., Tin 24.00
U.S.Mailbox, Cast Iron, 1 1/2 X 1 3/4 X 3 3/4 In. 18.00
U.S.Mailbox, Eagles, Key, Dark Blue, Metal, 9 In. 45.00
U.S.Mailbox, Tin .... 10.00 To 18.00
Uncle Sam Register, Cast Iron 20.00
Uncle Sam, Cast Iron 80.00
Union Bank, Filigree Work, Kenton Brand, Iron, 3 1/2 X 2 1/2 In. 30.00
Vault, On Wheels, Mosler, Jr., Cast Iron, 7 X 9 In. 18.00
Woolworth Building, Cast Iron .... 20.00 To 110.00
Woolworth Building, Cast Iron, Small 40.00
World War I Cannon Shell, Cast Iron 25.00
World's Fair, 1893, Cast Iron 98.00
Young America Rapid Fire Gun, Dated 2-19-07, 6 1/2 X 6 1/2 In. 340.00
Zeppelin, Cast Iron 130.00

Banko is a Japanese pottery first produced at Kuwana, Ise Province,
in the seventeenth century. Many potters produced this ware and marked it
with the Banko seal. It is still being produced.

BANKO, Pitcher, 2 Oriental Figures, Wine Keg, Black Matte Ground, 12 1/2 In. 395.00
    Teapot, Elephant 115.00
    Teapot, Stem Handle, Yellow 125.00
    Teapot, Translucent Enameled, Birds On Branch 119.00
    Teapot, 5 Molded Masks, Marbleized 425.00
    Tumbler, 2 Raised Action Figures, 3 1/2 In. 85.00
    Vase, Enameled Scene Of House, Pagoda, & Man In Boat, 5 In. 60.00
    Vase, Monkeys In Several Groups, Red Matte Ground, 12 X 6 In. 295.00
    Vase, Tapestry Effect, Raised Gold Flowers, 3 1/4 In. 75.00

BARBER, Chair, Child's, Old Car Shape, Paidar 1100.00
    Chair, Child's, Wooden Horsehead 1450.00
    Chair, Paidar, Porcelain 250.00
    Chair, Red Brocade Velvet, C.1900 .... 1200.00
    Pole, Acorn Finials, Wooden 325.00
    Pole, Floor Model, Porcelain, 8 Ft. X 16 In.Diam. 395.00
    Pole, Hanging, 19th Century, 32 In. 200.00
    Pole, Revolving Glass, Red, White, & Blue Cylinder, 26 In. 165.00
    Pole, 19 X 66 In. 375.00
    Pole, 19th Century, Old Red, White, & Blue Paint, Wooden, 8 X 32 In. 235.00

BAROMETER, A.S. & J.A.West, Rochester, New York, Walnut 550.00
    B.Pike & Sons, New York, Mid-19th Century, Rosewood 650.00
    Bro's.Kendall, New Lebanon, New York, 19th Century, Walnut 700.00
    C.A.Wheeler, Peterboro, New Hampshire, Walnut 250.00
    C.Wilder, Peterborough, N.H., Stick, 19th Century, Walnut, 38 In. 800.00
    C.Wilder, Peterborough, New Hampshire, Gimbal Style, Cherry 425.00
    Conrad Michael Brenner, Columbiana, Ohio, Walnut 350.00
    Deacon Fecit, C.1790, 36 In. 500.00
    Double Column, H.A.Clum, New York, C.1860, 37 1/2 In. 800.00
    Double Dolphin Crest, 19th Century, Carved Maple, 40 In. 500.00
    E.Kendall, New Lebanon, Walnut, Veneer 600.00
    H.A.Clum, Rochester, N.Y., C.1860, Double Column, Mahogany 800.00
    Hayden & Gibbard, Auburn, N.Y., 19th Century, Walnut, 39 In. 575.00
    Humboldt Barometer Co., Fredonia, New York, Cherry 300.00
    Humboldt Barometer Co., Fredonia, New York, Oak 100.00
    Humboldt Co., N.Y., 19th Century, Stick, Cherry, 43 1/2 In. 300.00
    J.Davis, London, Wheel, Victorian, Mirror, Mahogany, 4 Feet 1540.00
    J.Westcott & Co., Montreal, Stick, C.1864, Walnut, 38 In. 550.00
    Kendall Bros., N.Y., 19th Century, Stick, Walnut, 35 1/2 In. 700.00
    Meroid, Sewill, Liverpool, 19th Century, Brass Case, 6 In. 90.00
    Negretti & Zambra, 8 Day French Movement, Drawer, 17 In.Wide 635.00
    P.L.Teeple, Mansfield, Ohio, Walnut 350.00
    Queen & Co., Phila., 19th Century, Stick, Oak, 37 In. 250.00
    Shell Inlaid, Hygrometer Dial, English, 38 1/2 In. 412.00
    Stick, Ohio 385.00
    Timby's Patent, 1857, J.M.Merrick & Co., Worcester, Mass., Rosewood 400.00
    Wall, Double Dolphin Form Crest, Maple, 40 In. 550.00
    Watkins & Hill, London, Wheel, Inlaid, 19th Century, 4 Feet 1650.00
    Woodruff's Patent, 1860, C.Wilder, Peterborough, N.H., Walnut 800.00

BASKET, Amana Colony, Oak Handle, Willow, Oval, 16 X 19 X 12 In. 65.00
    Apple, New England, Notched Handles, Nailed Rim, Bentwood, 19 X 12 In. 100.00
    Apple, New England, Plank Bottom, Wide Splint, 1/2 Bushel 60.00
    Apple, New Hampshire, Swing Bail Handle, C.1880, 14 1/4 X 9 3/4 In. 75.00
    Berry, Natural & Purple Dyed Splint, 1/2 Pint 14.50
    Berry, 4 Baskets Joined By Single Handle 525.00
    Bicycle, Willow, 10 X 14 X 9 In. 15.00
    Braided Handles, Natural, Willow Wicker, C.1890, 10 X 5 1/2 In. 25.00
    Buttocks, Bentwood Handle, Melon Ribbed, Splint, 13 X 13 1/2 In. 175.00
    Buttocks, Double Rim, Rectangular, 14 In.Long 100.00
    Carrier Pigeon, Wicker 67.50

Cheese, 4 In.Wide Handles, 19th Century	175.00
Cheese, 19th Century, 17 X 6 In.	495.00
Creel, Bombe Sides, C.1890, Hinged Cover, Splint, 12 1/2 X 7 1/2 In.	40.00
Double-Wrapped Rim, Carved Swing Handle, 5 3/4 X 10 In.Diam.	225.00
Dough, Rye Straw	49.00
Egg, Bulbous, Footed, Handled, Wire, 13 1/2 In.	65.00
Egg, Carved & Notched Handle, C.1870, Splint, 5 X 8 X 11 In.	130.00
Egg, Collapsible	22.00
Egg, Notched Bentwood Handle, Splint, Round, 10 X 14 In.	65.00
Egg, Splint, Wooden Handle, 5 X 8 1/2 In.Diam.	60.00
Egg, Virginia, Splint	78.00
Egg, Wood Handle, Splint, 5 X 8 1/2 In.Diam.	65.00
Egg, Wrapped Handle, Wicker Body, Ribs, & Splint, 11 1/2 X 13 1/2 In.	50.00
Farm, Dark Green	75.00
Feather, Bentwood Handle, Cover Slides Up & Down, Splint, 11 X 9 In.	135.00
Feather, Bombe-Sided, Cover Slides Up & Down, Handle, 9 X 12 In.	65.00
Field, Oak Splint, Carved Bow Handles, 14 X 18 X 9 In.	85.00
Gathering, Bentwood Handle, Splint, 6 1/2 X 9 X 5 3/4 In.	30.00
Gathering, Splint, Boat Shaped, 14 In.Long	95.00
Handle, Cover, Painted Red, 9 X 9 In.	22.50
Handleless, Old Green Paint, 16 X 11 3/4 In.	115.00
Loom Room, Handles Built Into Framework, 19 1/2 X 12 X 12 In.	90.00
Lunch, Woven Plaits, Double Drop Handle, Wire Latch, C.1910	25.00
Market, Gizzard Weave, 13 1/2 X 9 In.	95.00
Melon, Handle, 9 X 5 In.	35.00
Mending, Wrapped Rim, Round Top, Square Base, Splint, 11 X 4 In.	35.00
Mose, Bentwood Rim, Hand-Notched Handles, Splint, 13 3/4 X 15 In.	185.00
Nantucket, Fred S.Chadwick, 19th Century, Splint Ash & Willow, 9 In.	500.00
Nantucket, Marked Sylvaro, Splint Ash & Willow, 10 1/2 In.	450.00
Nantucket, Swing Handle, Sylvaro, Mass., Splint Ash, 14 3/4 In.	600.00
Nantucket, W.D.Appleton, 19th Century, Splint Ash & Willow, 6 1/2 In.	450.00
Notched Handle, Splint, 8 1/2 X 5 X 11 In.	65.00
Pennsylvania, Rye Straw, Nesting Set Of 3	55.00
Pennsylvania, Rye, 5 X 16 In.Diam.	89.00
Picnic, C.1930, Redman Indian Seal, 11 X 20 In.	48.00
Picnic, Suitcase Type, Straw	15.00
Picnic, Wicker, Tin Lined	25.00
Picnic, Wide Splint, Brass Hasp, Hinged Cover, 12 1/4 X 7 1/4 In.	18.50
Pine Needle, 14 In.Diam.	24.00
Potato, Maine, Bentwood Handle, Woven Black Ash, 17 3/4 X 13 In.	95.00
Potato, 2 Handles, Maine, 12 1/2 X 18 In.Diam.	55.00
Pull Finule, Covered, Sweet Grass, 6 1/2 X 2 5/8 In.	18.50
Red Berry Stain, Covered, 8 1/4 In.	95.00
Reed Woven, Handle, 18 X 7 In.	75.00
Rye Straw, Ovoid, 12 In.	65.00
Sewing, Braided Handle, Cover, Grass & Raffia, C.1910, 8 1/2 In.Diam.	35.00
Sewing, Curved Handle, Latch, Willow & Raffia, Square, 7 X 7 X 4 In.	35.00
Sewing, Hinged Cover, Bombe Sides, Splint & Sweet Grass, 9 In.Diam.	35.00
Shopping, Victorian, Braided Rim, Wicker, 15 X 21 3/4 X 18 In.	125.00
Solid Bottom, Ash Splint, Painted Green, 16 In.Diam.	120.00
Splint, Woven Handle, 10 In.Long	80.00
Splint, 8 7/8 X 6 1/4 X 8 1/2 In.	70.00
Split Oak, Flared Sides	75.00
Storage, Blue Bands, Splint, Oval, 10 X 1o X 6 In.	65.00
Storage, New Hampshire, Red Dye & Natural, 14 1/2 X 9 3/4 In.	60.00
Storage, Stovepipe, Squared Bottom, C.1860, Rim 10 In.	225.00
Storage, Wrapped Rim, Wide Splint, Barn Red, 5 1/2 X 9 X 4 1/4 In.	16.50
Sweet Grass, Cover, 1 1/2 X 2 In.Diam.	15.00
Swing Handle, Oak	260.00
Transport, Carrier Pigeon, Wicker, Large	65.50
Utility, North Carolina Mountain, Honeysuckle Vines	65.00
Waste, Blackberry Dye & Natural Bands, Splint, 8 1/4 X 12 In.	18.50
Winnowing, Laced Around Bottom, 19th Century, 17 3/8 In.	135.00

Woven Reed, Willow Base, Handle, Original Paint, 2 1/2 X 7 In.	35.00
Woven Splint, 2 1/4 X 4 In.Diam.	18.00
BATMAN, Cup	10.00

Battersea enamels are enamels painted on copper and made in the Battersea district of London from about 1750 to 1756. Many similar enamels are mistakenly called Battersea.

BATTERSEA, Box, May You Be Happy, Enameled	130.00
Box, Nelson's Victory, Enameled	210.00
Box, Patch, Dog's Head	325.00
Box, Pump Room Bath, Enameled	150.00
Snuffbox, Lady & Child In Garden, 1 1/2 X 2 X 1 In.	300.00

Bavaria was a district where many types of pottery and porcelain were made for centuries. The words "Bavaria, Germany," appeared after 1871.

BAVARIA, see also Rosenthal

BAVARIA, Bowl, Floral, 8 In.Diam.	25.00
Cake Plate, Fruit Decor, Pierced Rim, Gold, 11 In.	35.00
Chocolate Set, 7 Piece	165.00
Hatpin Holder, Violets, Hand-Painted	18.50
Plaque, Hand-Painted, Baker's Chocolate Lady, 4 X 5 In.	150.00
Plate, Grapes, A.Koch, 7 In.	18.00
Plate, Roses, Hand-Painted, 9 In.	25.00
Plate, Water Lily, Hand-Painted, Gold Leaf Border, Signed, 13 In.	75.00
Sugar & Creamer, Hand-Painted, Gold Trim, Artist Signed & Dated	95.00
Teapot, Forget-Me-Nots, Gold, 6 Cup Size, Schumann	25.00

BAYONET, see Sword, Bayonet

BEACH BABIES, see also Sand Babies

BEACH BABIES, Planter, Blue Mark	112.00

BEADED BAG, Bakelite Handle, Mirror, Fringe, Black, 4 X 9 In.	23.00
Blue, Black, & Violet	50.00
Loops Around Top & Bottom, 5 X 8 In.	45.00

BEATLES, Head Scarf, Triangular	17.00
Holder, Record	45.00
Lunch Box	24.50
Lunch Box, Thermos	35.00
Stationery, Yellow Submarine	15.00
Tie Tack, On Original Card	15.00

BECK, see also Buffalo Pottery

BECK, Plate, Deer & Doe In Forest, Autumnal Foliage, 12 3/8 In.	65.00
Plate, Spaniel With Pheasant In Mouth, Signed, 9 1/4 In.	65.00
Platter, Grazing Deer, Signed, 18 In.	95.00

BED WARMER, 19th Century, Turned Wood Handle, American	200.00

Beehive, Austria, or Beehive, Vienna, china includes all the many types of decorated porcelain marked with the famous beehive mark. The mark has been used since the eighteenth century.

BEEHIVE, see also Royal Vienna

BEEHIVE, Bowl, Signed A.Kauffmann, Oval, 11 X 8 1/2 In.	189.00
Charger, Signed Constance, Marked, 14 1/4 In.Diam.	290.00
Dish, Pickle, Artist Signed, Open Handles, 8 X 4 In.	75.00
Plate, Ruth Holding Wheat, Gold Trim, 9 In.	250.00
Sauce, Classic Portraits, Dark Green, Maroon, & Gold	125.00
Tray, Dresser, Marked, 13 X 10 In.	39.00

Vase, Green, Magenta, & Gilt, Grecian Maidens & Cupid, 6 In. 150.00

Beer cans have been made since the 1930s. Collectors search for old or new cans.

BEER CAN, A-I, Flat Top	6.00
Banner, Flat	12.00
Bay State Ale, Green	650.00
Billy	.25 To 3.00
Black Forest, Cleveland Home Brewing, Red, Black, & White	300.00
Blatz, Flat Top	6.00
Blatz, 1936, Cone Top	40.00
Brauhaus, By General	8.00
Brockert Porter, Brockert Brewing, Massachusetts, Green & Yellow	2750.00
Buccaneer Beer, Gulf Brewing, Texas, Gold, Brown, & White	625.00
Buffalo Beer, Buffalo Brewing, California, Gold & Brown, C.1936	325.00
Bulldog Malt Liquor, Gold & Blue	12.00
Dawson's Master Ale, Dawson Brewing, New Medford	325.00
El Rancho, Yellow Can, Cactus	20.00
Esslinger's Premium Beer, Esslinger's, Pennsylvania, Yellow & Red	225.00
Falstaff, Flat Top	4.00
Fox Deluxe Bock	225.00
Golden Crown Draft	15.00
Harvard Ale	50.00
Herrenhaufer, Flat	25.00
Imperial	60.00
Iron City, Three River Stadium	7.00
Jax Beer, Flat Top	20.00
Krueger Ale	190.00
McEwan's Pale Ale, 15 1/2 Oz.	12.00
Narragansett Ale	100.00
Neuweiler's Cream Ale, Cone, 32 Ounce	38.00
Ohio State Flag	1.50
Old Georgetown, Flat	100.00
Old Topper, Cone Top	70.00
Rainier	50.00
Red Lion Sparkling Ale, Burger Brewing, Ohio, Red, Black, & White	2000.00
Regal Select Draft	15.00
Ruppert Beer	100.00
Schmidt's Tiger Brand, Cone, 32 Ounce	28.00
Storz All-Grain Beer, Storz Brewing, Nebraska, Blue Sky, Red Roof	2600.00
Tiger Ale, Cone Top, 32 Ounce	28.00
Wunderbar	10.00

Bells have been made of china, glass, or metal. All types are collected.

BELL, Animals, Heads, & People, Bronze, Marked, 9 1/2 X 8 1/2 In.	125.00
Colonial, Cross Clapper, 1908, Brass	25.00
Cow, Brass Plated, 5 In.	8.00
Cow, Cast Iron	10.00
Cow, Leather Strap & Buckle, Iron Clapper, Sheet Iron, 5 1/4 In.	15.00
Cow, Leather Strap, Brass, 5 1/2 In.	30.00
Desk, Hotel, Spinner, Large	15.00
Embossed Assyrian Figures, Brass, 5 1/8 X 6 1/2 In.	110.00
Engraved, Mutton Fat Jade Handle, Chinese, Small	75.00
Figural, Belgian Country Woman, Brass	65.00
Figural, Clara Barton	58.00
Figural, Napoleon, Wrapped In Cloak, Scenes Of Waterloo, Brass	175.00
Figural, Woman In Elizabethan Dress, Bronze, 4 3/8 In.	90.00
Figural, Woman, Clapper Feet, Brass, 3 1/2 In.	14.50
For Shafts, Brass, Iron Clapper, 2 3/4 In.	12.00
Gold, White Handle	2.00
Hand, Heraldic Eagle Forms Handle, Bronze, 5 In.	20.00

Locomotive, Brass, Large	350.00
Neck, Animal, Acorn, Brass, Leather Strap & Buckle, 2 3/4 In.	25.00
Plantation, Rocker Arm, Cast Iron, 13 X 10 In.	375.00
School, Brass, 6 In.	15.00
School, Heavy Copper, Black Wooden Handle	35.00
School, Wood Turned Handle, Brass, 8 1/2 In.	45.00
Schoolmaster's, Walnut Handle, Iron Clapper, Brass, 8 1/4 In.	60.00
Servant, Figural, Man Holding Bell On Head, Brass, 7 In.	165.00
Sheep, Cast Iron Clapper, Sheet Iron, 2 X 2 1/2 X 3 In.	14.50
Sheep, Leather Strap	15.00
Shop, Wire Coil Spring, Pull To Ring, Brass	75.00
Sleigh, Graduated, On Leather, Set Of 26	210.00
Sleigh, Leather Strap, Loop Type, Brass, 6 Bells, 15 3/4 In.	40.00
Sleigh, Leather, Strap, Brass, 42 Bells	130.00
Sleigh, Loop, Leather Strap, Set Of 6	40.00
Sleigh, Original Strap, 12 Graduated Sizes	125.00
Street Car, Brass, Fare, 11 1/2 In.	150.00
Tap, Teacher's	15.00
Trolley, Brass	65.00

Belle Ware was made in 1903 by Carl V. Helmschmied. In 1904 he started a corporation known as the Helmschmied Manufacturing Company. His factory closed in 1908 and he worked on his own until his death in 1934.

BELLE WARE, Box, Lid, Pink Rose, Buds, Pebbled Finish, Marked, 2 3/4 In.Diam.	375.00

Belleek china is made in Ireland, other European countries, and the United States. The glaze is creamy yellow and appears wet. The first Belleek was made in 1857. All pieces listed are Irish Belleek. The mark changed through the years: First mark, black, dates 1863 to 1890. Second mark, black, dates 1891 to 1926 and includes the words "Co. Fermanagh, Ireland." Third mark, black, dates 1926 to 1946 and has the words "Deanta in Eirinn." Fourth mark, same as third mark but green, dates 1946 to 1955. Fifth mark, green, dates 1955 to 1965 and has the R in a circle added in the upper right. Sixth mark, green, dates after 1965 and the words "Co. Fermanagh" have been omitted.

BELLEEK, see also Ceramic Art Co.; Haviland; Lenox; Matt Morgan; Ott & Brewer; Willets

BELLEEK, Basket, Envelope, Pearl, 2nd Black Mark, 4 1/4 In.	265.00
Basket, Lily, Three Strand, 10 1/2 In.Diam.	1190.00
Basket, Multicolored Flowers, 4 Strand, 6 In.Diam.	300.00
Basket, Open-Work, 4 Strand Bottom, Handle, 11 In.Long	550.00
Basket, Shamrock, 3 Strand, 5 In.	420.00
Basket, Trefoil Shape, Budding Roses, Marked, 5 1/4 In.	300.00
Bowl, Powder, Mask Ware, Covered, Black Mark	175.00
Bowl, Shamrock & Basket Weave, 3rd Black Mark, 3 1/2 In.Diam.	50.00
Bowl, Tea, Shell, 2nd Black Mark	75.00
Box, Acorn Finial, 3rd Black Mark, 2 1/2 X 3 1/2 X 3 1/2 In.	85.00
Box, Powder, Mask, Covered, 3rd Black Mark	225.00
Box, Trinket, 3rd Black Mark, 3 1/4 In.	200.00
Bread Plate, Tridacna	190.00
Cabaret Set, Thistle, Pearl Luster, 2nd Black Mark	150.00
Candleholder, Boy On Dolphin, 1st Black Mark, 7 1/2 In.	1150.00
Candlestick, 2nd Black Mark, 7 In., Pair	590.00
Chamberstick, Figural, Green & Gilded, 1st Impressed Mark, 7 In.	2900.00
Coffee Set, White, Gold Trim, Marked, 3 Piece, Monogram B	225.00
Coffeepot, Bowl & Underplate, Harp Shamrock, 6th Mark, 3 Piece	195.00
Compote, Prince Of Wales, Pearl, 1st Black Mark, 9 1/2 In.	1400.00
Compote, Yellow, Lavender, Florals, Gold Handles, Marked, 9 In.	75.00
Condiment Set, Orange, Leaves, Gold Top, Marked	75.00
Creamer, Bow & Ribbon, Green Mark	22.00
Creamer, Celery Top, 2nd Black Mark	60.00

Creamer, Green Ribbon, Porcelain, 2nd Black Mark, 3 1/4 In.	75.00
Creamer, Green, Hexagon, 2nd Black Mark	55.00
Creamer, Green, Tridacna, 2nd Black Mark	55.00
Creamer, Irish Pot, 2nd Black Mark	60.00
Creamer, Ivy Pattern, Black Mark	55.00
Creamer, Lily, 3rd Black Mark	50.00
Creamer, Lotus, 3rd Black Mark	35.00
Creamer, Pink, Neptune, 2nd Black Mark	55.00
Creamer, Pink, Tridacna, 2nd Black Mark	55.00
Creamer, Plain, Cone, 2nd Black Mark	55.00
Creamer, Shamrock, 2nd Black Mark	55.00
Creamer, Shamrock, 3rd Black Mark	40.00
Crucifix, Applied Flowers, 1st Black Mark, 3 In.	275.00
Cup & Saucer, Clover Shape, Green 3-Leaf Clovers, 1st Green Mark	50.00
Cup & Saucer, Clover, 3rd Black Mark	47.50
Cup & Saucer, Cream, Green 3 Leaf Clover, 1st Green Mark	42.00
Cup & Saucer, Echinus, 1st Black Mark	120.00
Cup & Saucer, Green, Neptune, 2nd Black Mark	55.00
Cup & Saucer, Horseshoe & Fan, Pearlized, 1st Black Mark	125.00
Cup & Saucer, Pink Rim, 1st Black Mark	75.00
Cup & Saucer, Shamrock & Basket Weave, 3rd Black Mark	40.00 To 45.00
Cup & Saucer, Shamrock, 2nd Black Mark	55.00
Cup & Saucer, Shamrock, 3rd Black Mark	45.00 To 52.00
Cup & Saucer, Shaped Of 3 Leaf Clover, 1st Green Mark	50.00
Cup & Saucer, Tridacna, Neptune, 2nd Black Mark, Green	55.00
Cup & Saucer, Tridacna, Pink Trim, Gilt Rims, 2nd Black Mark	200.00
Cup, Demitasse, Serpent Mark, Roses, Dragon Handle	40.00
Cup, Tridacna, 3rd Black Mark	25.00
Dish, Heart-Shaped, Bud Border, 4 Strand	295.00
Dish, Mint, Shamrock, Handled, 3rd Black Mark	30.00
Dish, Nut, Wheel On Coral, 2nd Black Mark, 2 1/2 In.	200.00
Dish, Shell, Marked	28.00
Dish, Twig Handle, Shamrock, Basket Weave, 2nd Black Mark, 5 1/2 In.	38.00
Eggcup, Shamrock, 2nd Black Mark, 2 1/2 In.	125.00
Epergne, Coral, Shells, 4 Trumpet Vases, Black Mark, 11 In.	350.00
Ewer, Dark Red Roses, Gold Handle, Ruffled Spout, Signed, 8 In.	155.00
Ewer, Red Currants Design, Palette Mark, 6 X 6 In.	175.00
Figurine, Boxer On A Pillow, 1st Black Mark, 3 X 4 1/4 In.	1250.00
Figurine, Bust Of Joy & Sorrow, Green Mark	275.00
Figurine, Cherub On Dolphin, Pink Trim, 1st Black Mark, 7 1/2 In.	1350.00
Figurine, Cherub On Dolphin, White, 1st Black Mark, 7 1/2 In.	1100.00
Figurine, Erin Unveiling, 1st Black Mark	5800.00
Figurine, Girl With Basket, Pearl, 1st Black Mark, 9 In.	950.00
Figurine, Greyhound, Female, 1st Black Mark, 6 1/2 In.	720.00
Figurine, Greyhound, 1st Black Mark, 6 1/2 In.	720.00
Figurine, Greyhound, 3rd Black Mark	615.00
Figurine, Leprechaun, Porcelain, 2nd Black Mark, 5 1/2 In.	550.00
Figurine, Swan, 2nd Black Mark, 4 1/2 In.	130.00
Figurine, Swan, 3rd Black Mark, 4 1/2 In.	100.00
Flower Holder, Bas-Relief, Prince Of Wales, 1st Black Mark, 8 In.	2900.00
Harp, Shamrock, 3rd Black Mark, 8 1/2 In.	190.00
Holder, Flower, Sea Horse, 2nd Black Mark	165.00
Holder, Menu, Pearl Glaze, 2nd Mark, 3 In.	220.00
Humidor, Full Face Of Indian Chief, Brown To Cinnamon, Marked	245.00
Jar, Shamrock, 3rd Black Mark	88.00
Jug, Aberdeen, Pearl Luster, 3rd Black Mark, 6 In.	220.00
Jug, Cream, Neptune Mask, 1st Black Mark, 3 1/2 In.	150.00
Jug, Harp Handle, Pearl, 1st Black Mark, 5 1/2 In.	290.00
Jug, Milk, Harp Handle, 1st Black Mark	265.00
Jug, Nautilus, Coral Colored Handle, 1st Black Mark, 5 In.Long	290.00
Jug, Snail, Pearl, 1st Black Mark, Large	310.00
Kettle, Hot Water, Neptune Pattern, Pink Trim, 2nd Black Mark	425.00
Kettle, Water, Grasses Pattern, 1st Black Mark, Large	695.00

Mirror, Applied Florals, Convex Frame, Beaded, C.1880, Oval, 16 In. 225.00
Mug, Gold Dragon Handle & Trim, Vassar College Seal 50.00
Mug, Gooseberries 100.00
Mug, Head Of Deer, Gold Dragon Handle, Hand-Painted 110.00
Mug, Shamrock, Green Mark 24.00
Mug, Shamrock, 2nd Black Mark 65.00
Night-Light, Figural, Lighthouse, 1st Black Mark, 7 3/4 In. 400.00
Pitcher, Cider, Corn Design, Gold Trim, Red Brown Ground 165.00
Pitcher, Cider, Pink Roses, Gold Handles, Marked, 9 In. 110.00
Plate, Bacchus Pattern, Masks, Strawberry, Ivy, Yellow, Marked, 8 In. . 95.00
Plate, Bread, Hexagon Design, Green Trim, Gold Edge, 2nd Black Mark .. 35.00
Plate, Christmas, 1975 .... 40.00
Plate, Dessert, Green, 2nd Black Mark, 9 In. 50.00
Plate, Green Shamrocks, 3rd Black Mark, 7 In. 35.00
Plate, Limpet, 3rd Black Mark, 8 1/4 In. , Set Of 5 .... 210.00
Plate, New Shell Pattern, Gold Rim, Pink Shells, 1st Green Mark 54.00
Plate, Sandwich, 1st Black Mark, 8 1/2 In. 160.00
Plate, Shamrock, 2nd Black Mark, 6 In., Set Of 6 .... 140.00
Plate, Tridacna, Pink Border, 2nd Black Mark, 8 3/4 In. 85.00
Plate, Tridacna, 3rd Black Mark, 8 In. 40.00
Plate, White, Green Leaf & Berry Design, 2nd Black Mark, 10 In. 35.00
Pot, Flower, Applied Flowers, All White, Green Mark 85.00
Pot, Shamrock, 3 Footed, 2nd Black Mark, 3 1/2 X 5 In. 60.00
Rose Bowl, Flowers, Tassels, 2nd Black Mark, 1891, 3 In. 140.00
Rose Bowl, Quilted Diamond Design, Dots In Center, Gold Lines 75.00
Salt, Shamrock 12.00
Server, Cake, Four Strand, Large 275.00
Server, Egg, Pink Trim, 5 Cups, 1st Black Mark, 7 In.Diam. 1350.00
Shaving Mug, Sterling Silver Overlay 65.00
Spill, Double Root, Pink Blossoms, Root Base, 1st Black Mark 425.00
Spill, Rock, 3rd Black Mark, 5 1/2 In. 105.00
Sugar & Creamer, Artichoke, Green Mark 37.00
Sugar & Creamer, Lotus, Pink Handle, Yellow Interior, Marked 90.00
Sugar & Creamer, Mask Pattern, 3rd Black Mark 85.00
Sugar & Creamer, Ribbon, 3rd Black Mark .... 60.00 To 70.00
Sugar & Creamer, Shamrock, 2nd Black Mark 95.00
Tankard, Green Ground, Purple Grape Clusters, Marked, Signed 260.00
Tankard, Multicolored Roses, Jeweled, Marked, 14 1/4 In. 329.00
Tankard, Purple Grapes, Green Ground, Signed & Dated, Marked 240.00
Tazza, Dolphin Base, 1st Black Mark, 10 1/2 In. 425.00
Tea Set, Basket Weave & Shamrocks, 3rd Black Mark 250.00
Tea Set, Erne, 2nd Mark, Set Of 5 Pieces 850.00
Tea Set, Fan Pattern, Pearl Luster, 7 Piece 690.00
Tea Set, Flying Geese, Pine Trees, Ivory, Yellow, Green, 3 Piece 275.00
Tea Set, Limpet, Yellow Trim, 8 Cups & Saucers, Black Mark, 20 Piece . 695.00
Tea Set, Tridacna, Pink Trim, Gilt Rims, 2nd Black Mark, 3 Piece 425.00
Tea Set, White & Green Ground, Red Roses, Gold Handles, Marked 150.00
Tea Set, 2nd Black Mark, Tray, 16 In., 7 Piece 950.00
Tea Strainer, Floral Design, 2 Pieces 125.00
Teakettle, Grass Pattern, 1st Black Mark 450.00
Teakettle, Shamrock, Basket Weave Pattern, 3rd Black Mark 185.00
Teakettle, Tridacna, Pink Trim, 1st Black Mark, 6 1/4 In. 295.00
Teapot, Bamboo Design, Pearl Glaze, 1st Black Mark, 5 In. 535.00
Teapot, Blarney Pattern, Pink & Gilded, 2nd Black Mark, 7 In.Long 475.00
Teapot, Neptune Design, 2nd Black Mark 245.00
Teapot, Neptune, 3rd Black Mark, Green, Large 225.00
Teapot, Shamrock, Large, 3rd Black Mark 140.00
Teapot, Shamrock, 2nd Black Mark 150.00
Teapot, Shamrock, 3rd Black Mark, Small 155.00
Teapot, Tridacna, 2nd Black Mark, Green 155.00
Toothpick, Seahorse, 1st Black Mark 195.00
Tray, Echinus Pink, 1st Black Mark, 18 In. 790.00

Tray, Hawthorne Design, Spider Web, Rust Color, 1st Black Mark 1200.00
Tray, Limpet, 3rd Black Mark, 7 3/4 X 5 In. 75.00
Tray, Pink, Echinus, 1st Mark, 18 In. 790.00
Tray, Tridacna, Pink Trim, 1st Black Mark 460.00
Tub, Butter, Lidded, Shell, Black Mark 140.00
Vase, Aberdeen, Flowers, 3rd Black Mark, 6 In. 135.00
Vase, Aberdeen, Glazed, 2nd Black Mark, 6 In. 225.00
Vase, Basket Weave, Flowers, Handled, 2nd Black Mark, 4 1/2 In. 485.00
Vase, Corn, Pearl, 1st Black Mark, 6 1/2 In. 345.00
Vase, Cornucopia, Pink Trim, 2nd Black Mark, 3 1/2 In. 115.00
Vase, Creamy White, Gold Handles, 12 In. 75.00
Vase, Daisy Spill, 3rd Black Mark 95.00
Vase, Flowers, 2nd Black Mark, 4 In. 250.00
Vase, Hoof Tripod, Porcelain, 1st Black Mark, 13 In. 750.00
Vase, Horse & Snake, Parian Glazed, 1st Green Mark, 16 1/2 In. 4200.00
Vase, Nile, Pearl Luster, Yellow Leaves, 3rd Black Mark, 13 In. 350.00
Vase, Pearl, 3rd Black Mark, 6 1/2 In. 125.00
Vase, Portrait, Ivory, Japanese Maidens, Cherry Trees, Marked, 10 In. 265.00
Vase, Prince Arthur, Applied Flowers, 5th Mark, 10 1/2 In, Pair 300.00
Vase, Prince Arthur, Pearl, 3rd Black Mark, 11 In. 790.00
Vase, Prince Arthur, 3rd Black Mark, 11 In. 790.00
Vase, Prince Of Wales, 1869, 8 1/2 In. 1490.00
Vase, Rathmore Pattern, 3rd Black Mark, 7 1/2 In. 160.00
Vase, Ribbon, 3rd Black Mark, Pair 475.00
Vase, Rock Spill, Cornucopia Form, Rocky Ledge, 5 1/2 In., Pair 150.00
Vase, Roses, Mauve Ground, 13 1/2 In. 225.00
Vase, Scalloped Rim, Harp Hound, & Castle, Harp Handles 80.00
Vase, Shamrock Trunk Stump, 2nd Black Mark 145.00
Vase, Thistle, Pearl Glaze, 2nd Black Mark, 8 1/2 In. 590.00
Vase, Wind-Blown Flowers, Autumn Colors, 15 In. 155.00
Wall Pocket, Swan, Gilded, 1st Black Mark, 9 In. 1790.00

Bennington ware was the product of two factories working in Bennington, Vermont. Both firms were out of business by 1896. The wares include brown and yellow mottled pottery, Parian, scroddled ware, stoneware, graniteware, yellowware, and Staffordshire-like vases.

BENNINGTON, see also Rockingham
BENNINGTON TYPE, Marble, Blue & White, Small 55.00
Marble, Brown & White, Large 55.00
Teapot, Souvenir, Tea Company, Hartford, Connecticut 15.00

BENNINGTON, Bedpan 40.00
Bedpan, Figural, Bird 125.00
Bottle, Coachmen, Holding Mug, Marked, 10 1/2 In. 170.00
Bottle, Shoe Form 40.00
Bowl, Fluted Pattern, Covered, 4x 6 In.Diam. 65.00
Bowl, Wash, Signed, 1849 .... 375.00
Canteen Flask, Rockingham Glaze, Leather Strap, Figural, 7 In. 170.00
Coffeepot, Flint Enamel, 1849 Mark 900.00
Cream Pot, Speckled Breasted Bird, Blue On Gray, 2 Gallon 150.00
Crock, Brown, Tan, & Red Slip, L.Norton & Son, 7 In. 60.00
Crock, Butter, No Handles, E.Norton & Co., 5 In. 50.00
Crock, Floral 425.00
Cuspidor, Diamonds On Bottom Half, Italian Blue, Tan & Cream 95.00
Cuspidor, Rockingham, Scalloped, Marked, 5 1/2 In. 40.00
Cuspidor, Scalloped Ribbed Pattern, 5 1/2 In. 50.00
Figurine, Dove, Parian, Ornament, Bird In Flight, 7 In. 500.00
Figurine, Woman, Parian 95.00
Flask, Book, Mottled, 4 1/2 X 6 1/4 In. 350.00

Jar, Snuff, L.Norton & Son, Brown Shiny Slip, 8 3/4 In. 60.00
Jug, 2 Leaves, Trailing Squiggle, Blue, L.Norton & Son, 1 Gallon 245.00
Pan, 8 1/2 In. 75.00
Pitcher & Bowl, 1849 Mark, Flint 900.00
Pitcher, Brown & White, Parian, Palm Trees, Marked, 7 In. 90.00
Pitcher, Cow, 6 3/4 In. 85.00
Pitcher, Hound Handle, Beige, Miniature 30.00
Pitcher, Hound Handle, 11 In. 600.00
Pitcher, Hunters Chasing Deer 150.00
Pitcher, Hunting Scene, Brown, Hound Handle, Marked 175.00
Pitcher, Hunting Scene, Horses, 7 In. 95.00
Pitcher, Hunting Scene, 10 In. 325.00
Pitcher, Parian, Brown & White, Palm Trees, Exotic Flowers, 7 In. 90.00
Pitcher, Parian, Corn 550.00
Pitcher, Parian, Spinning Wheel, Blue Ground, 4 1/2 In. 45.00
Pot, Blue Lead, Handled, Semiovoid, Salt Glaze, 1 Gallon 95.00
Syrup, Hinged Pewter Lid 38.00
Vase, Parian Ware, Right & Left Hand, Pair 95.00
Vase, White, Salt Glaze 85.00
Vegetable Dish, Oval, 9 In. 65.00

*Berlin, a German porcelain factory, was started in 1751 by Wilhelm Kaspar
Wegely. In 1763 the factory was taken over by Frederick the Great and
became the Royal Berlin Porcelain Manufactory. It is still in operation today.*

BERLIN, Charger, Temple Of Jupiter, Blue Ground, Marked, 16 In. 500.00
Chocolate Pot, Ovoid Body, Puce Flowers, Covered, Marked, 8 In. 175.00
Plaque, Maiden, Renaissance Dress, Marked, 12 In. 950.00
Plaque, Ruth, Gray Robe, Wheat Field, Marked, 10 In. 2500.00
Plaque, Seated Gentleman, Writing With Quill, Scepter Mark, 9 3/4 In. 500.00
Vase, Family Training Falcons, Green Ground, Marked, 16 In. 375.00
Vase, Lovers, Flowers, Marked, 16 In., Pair 1000.00
Vase, Scenes, Gold Leafed Griffin Handles, C.1880, 18 In. 850.00

BESWICK, Figurine, Dog, Old Mark, 11 1/2 In. 55.00
Figurine, Mr.Benjamin Bunny & Peter Rabbit, 1975 .... 30.00
Figurine, Mrs.Tiggy Winkle, 1948 .... 55.00
Figurine, Pheasant, No.1226 .... 75.00
Figurine, Ribby, 1951 .... 50.00
Figurine, Tabitha Twitchett, 1961 .... 35.00
Teapot, Dolly Varden, No.1203 .... 49.00

BETTY BOOP, Playing Instruments, Bisque, Set Of 3 .... 275.00
Sugar, Creamer, & Teapot, Child's 75.00

BICYCLE, Lenox, Syndicate Trading Co., Model L, N.Y., 73 X 44 In. 385.00
Shaft Driven, Made In Chicago 100.00
Tricycle, Coventry Rotary Type, Single Drive .... *Illus* 4500.00

Bicycle, Tricycle, Coventry Rotary
Type, Single Drive

Bing & Grondahl is a famous Danish factory making fine porcelains from 1853 to the present. Their Christmas plates are especially well known.

BING & GRONDAHL, Figurine, Bird, No.1242	46.00
Figurine, Dog, No. 1998, Signed, 5 1/2 In.	75.00
Figurine, Eskimo, No.2253, Cast Mark, 13 1/2 X 13 X 9 In.	650.00
Figurine, Girl, Pigtails, Holding Puppy, Porcelain, 7 In.	100.00
Figurine, Madonna, Holding Infant In Arms, White, 9 In.	45.00
Figurine, Monkey, Seated, Looking At Turtle In Palm, 8 In.	165.00
Figurine, Polar Bear, Head Raised, 5 1/2 X 7 1/2 In.	175.00
Figurine, Snow Owl, Sitting, Signed Jensen, 17 1/2 In.	685.00
Figurine, Standing Boxer, Tan, 6 X 6 In.	50.00
Figurine, The Kissers, No.2162	225.00
Figurine, Waltzing Couple, 8 In.	225.00
Madonna, Holding Infant, 9 In.	40.00
Plate, Christmas, 1961	65.00 To 195.00
Plate, Christmas, 1963	200.00
Vase, Birds, Blue, 5 In.	38.00
Vase, Lily-Of-The-Valley, 7 In.	45.00
BINOCULARS, Lady's, Racetrack, Pearl-Handled	90.00
U.S.Civil War, Brass	40.00
BIRDCAGE, Cathedral Style, Brass, Complete	60.00
De Wayside Inn, Dome-Shaped, Milk Glass & Amber Feeder	250.00
Dome Shape, 2 Celluloid Parrots, C.1930	50.00
Form Of Church, Parquet Floor, Painted Clock, Steeple, Wooden	6400.00
Hendryx, Dome, Brass, 14 In.	195.00
Hendryx, Glass Feeders, Complete, Brass	55.00
Inlaid Mahogany, Federal, 1790-1810, 18 In.	750.00
Porcelain Bird, Famille Rose Design, French, 18 X 10 In.Diam.	450.00

Bisque is an unglazed baked porcelain. Finished bisque has a slightly sandy texture with a dull finish. Some of it may be decorated with various colors. Bisque gained favor during the late Victorian era when thousands of bisque figurines were made.

BISQUE, see also named porcelain factories

BISQUE, Bottle, Figural, Boot, Leather Strap, Gold Spur, Black, Cork Top, 6 In.	110.00
Creamer, Heron In Bulrushes, Shepherd's Crook Handle, 3 1/4 In.	45.00
Figurine, Boy Holding Racket, Blue & White, Gold Trim, 14 1/2 In.	275.00
Figurine, Gentleman & Lady, Bal Masque Costume, C.1900, 21 1/2 In.	450.00
Figurine, Googlie Girl, Crow, Pastels, Star & Crown Mark, 4 1/4 In.	88.00
Figurine, Lady Holding Bird, 19th Century, French, 19 1/4 In.	210.00
Group, Kneeling Boy With 2 Infants, 10 In.Long	70.00
Night-Light, Figural, Bull, Glass Eyes, German	1950.00
Night-Light, Figural, Cat, Glass Eyes, German	175.00
Night-Light, Figural, Dog, Glass Eyes, German	175.00

Black amethyst glass appears black until it is held to the light, then a dark purple can be seen. It was made in many factories from 1860 to the present.

BLACK AMETHYST, Ashtray, Coal Hood, Bail Handle	7.00
Ashtray, 4 1/2 In.	3.50
Basket, Applied Crystal Handle, 7 1/2 In.	45.00
Bottle, Cologne, Hobnail, Bulbous, 6 In.	75.00
Bowl, Centerpiece, Attached Candleholders, Oval	35.00
Bowl, Handled & Footed, Embossed Design On Side, 8 In.	28.00
Bowl, Holed Rim, 11 In.Diam.	14.00
Bowl, Silver Designs, Signed, Oval, 12 1/2 In.Long	175.00
Bowl, 4 Medallions Of Fruit, Leaves, Scrollwork, 12 In.	65.00
Box, Cigarette, Allover Flowers, Silver Overlay, Covered	45.00
Box, Cigarette, Elephant Cover	27.00
Box, Heron & Flowers, Pedestal, Hinged, 4 7/8 X 5 1/4 In.	110.00
Candleholder, Classical Design, Gold Foot, 6 1/2 In.	40.00

Candlestick, Blown, 9 3/4 In., Pair 45.00
Candlestick, Gold Trim, Cambridge, 7 1/2 In., Pair 40.00
Candlestick, Silver Overlay, 9 In., Pair 45.00
Candlestick, 3 In., Pair 8.00
Candlestick, 3 1/2 In., Pair 22.00
Console Set, Zaricor, Candlesticks, 9 In., Bowl, 10 In.Diam. 45.00
Figurine, Scottish Terrier, Seated, Red Collar, 4 In. 60.00
Figurine, Swan, Silver Trim, 8 In. 45.00
Figurine, Swan, Traces Of Gold, 8 1/2 In. 95.00
Flowerpot, 3 In. 7.00
Plate, S Border, Square, 3 1/4 In. 15.00
Plate, Sandwich, Center Handle, Pointed Outer Edge, 12 In. 29.00
Server, Silver Flower Pattern, Handled, Octagon 16.50
Vase, Applied Flowers, Marked, 14 In. 30.00
Vase, Basket Weave Pattern, Triangular Top, 6 In. 22.00
Vase, Bud, 7 3/4 In. 16.00
Vase, Deco, Applied Flowers, Marked Czech, 14 In. 30.00
Vase, Etched, 9 3/4 In. 145.00
Vase, Loving Cup, Lady Design, 8 In., Pair 35.00
Vase, Pan & Wood Nymphs At Base, 9 In. 25.00
Vase, Prayer Rug Pattern, 6 In. 40.00
Vase, Silver Painted Florals, Ruffled Top, 5 1/2 In. 8.00
Vase, Urn, Dancing Girls, 7 In. 50.00

BLACK, Amos & Andy, Ashtray, Chalk 35.00
Ashtray, Amos & Andy .... 75.00 To 95.00
Ashtray, Black Boy On Bedpan, China 20.00
Ashtray, Black Boy, Porcelain, Germany, 2 In. 35.00
Ashtray, Black Boy, The Early Bird Catches The Worm 75.00
Ashtray, Child On Potty, Metal 35.00
Bell, Black Figure, Porcelain 35.00
Box, Aunt Jemima, Pancake Flour 65.00
Box, Jelly Bean, Pickaninnies, Black & Orange, 10 Lbs., 12 X 5 In. 85.00
Box, Recipe, Aunt Jemima, Yellow 20.00
Brush, Shaving, Mammy, Figural Handle, Wooden 12.50
Button, Negro Eating Watermelon, Porcelain 225.00
Cookie Jar, Aunt Jemima .... 45.00 To 65.00
Cookie Jar, Lady, Ceramic 45.00
Cookie Jar, Mammy, Celluloid 65.00
Cookie Jar, Mammy, Porcelain 35.00
Creamer, Uncle Moe 28.00
Cup & Saucer, Coon Chicken Inn, With Stand 65.00
Dinner Bell, Aunt Jemima 40.00
Doll, Lady, Jamaica, 16 In. 35.00
Doll, Mammy, Cloth, Pearl Eyes, Earrings, Kerchief, Apron, 9 In. 20.00
Doll, Mammy, Made From A Pecan Nut, 8 In. 15.00
Doll, Mammy, Walking, 1940s, Wooden 15.00
Doll, Man, Wood, Walnut, Carrying Bag Of Cotton, 12 In. 35.00
Figurine, Girl, Wearing Yellow Dress, White Hat, German, 3 In. 135.00
Figurine, Stork Carrying Black Baby 110.00
Figurine, 3 Boys Sitting On Log, Eating Corn On Cob, Bisque, 5 In. ... 135.00
Firecracker Pack, Boy Sitting On River, Fishing, Eating Melon 10.00
Game, Child's, Shooting Target, Sambo 50.00
Game, Poor Jenny, Contents & Boxed 75.00
Holder, Match, Boy Eating Watermelon 38.00
Holder, String, Aunt Jemima, Wall, Porcelain, 6 3/4 X 3 3/4 In. 12.50
Holder, String, Mammy 30.00
Jewelry Box, Black Boy Shaking Dice, Wood, 6 X 3 In. 40.00
Lamp, Black Man, 12 1/2 In. 65.00
Mammy Kitchen Hang-Up, Memo, 1920s, 10 1/2 In.Tall 45.00
Mammy Memo, Figural, Pad & Pencil Holder, Wood 15.00
Mammy, Sweeping, Lindstrom, Boxed 125.00

Match Holder & Pot, Aunt Jemima, Wall	35.00
Matchbook, Dinah's Shack	12.00
Menu, Coon Chicken Inn, 12 In.	75.00
Note Pad, Aunt Jemima, Celluloid	35.00
Pad, Memo, Mammy, Celluloid	37.00
Pencil Sharpener, Black Minstrel, Iron	45.00
Pencil Sharpener, Black Minstrel, Japan	50.00
Piebird	20.00
Pinball Machine, Black Minstrel, Bells, Lights, Gottlieb & Co.	1200.00
Placemat, Coon Chicken Inn	25.00
Planter, Black Boy Eating Watermelon, Ceramic, 5 In.	35.00
Plaque, Cook & Chef	40.00
Plate, Dinner, Coon Chicken Inn, 9 3/4 In.	95.00
Playing Cards, Lady, Basket Of Cotton, Boxed	6.00
Porter, Lead, From Train Garden	15.00
Potholder, Figural, Girl	12.00
Rack, Potholder, Aunt Jemima, Carved, Wooden	15.00
Salt & Pepper, Aunt Jemima	12.00 To 20.00
Salt & Pepper, Aunt Jemima & Uncle Mose, Celluloid	10.00
Salt & Pepper, Aunt Jemima & Uncle Mose, 5 In.	22.00
Salt & Pepper, Aunt Jemima, Green Glaze, Boston, Massachusetts	18.00
Salt & Pepper, Chefs, Ceramic, 5 In.	10.00
Salt & Pepper, Man & Woman, Ceramic	21.00
Spice Set, Aunt Jemima	65.00
Statue, Watermelon Scene, Chalk, 15 In.	135.00
Stickpin, Black Rolling Eyes	95.00
String Holder, Black Lady, Red, Orange, Green, & Blue	30.00
Sugar & Creamer, Aunt Jemima	30.00
Sugar & Creamer, Aunt Jemima & Uncle Mose	38.00
Syrup, Aunt Jemima	15.00
Syrup, Aunt Jemima & Mose	20.00
Syrup, Aunt Jemima, Plastic	11.00
Syrup, Mammy, Plastic	19.00
Thermometer, Diaper Dan, Boxed, 1949, 5 In.	85.00
Tin, Aunt Dinah, 4 1/2 In.	20.00
Towel, Aunt Jemima	20.00
Toy, Pull, Eyes Roll, Tin, Germany, 1915	25.00
Toy, Shuffling Sam, Wood, Primitive	95.00
Water Faucet Handle, Negro's Head, Figural	75.00
Whiskbroom, Aunt Jemima	24.00
BLANC DE CHINE, Cup, Libation	295.00

Blown glass was formed by forcing air through a rod into molten glass. Early glass and some forms of art glass were hand blown. Other types of glass were molded or pressed.

BLOWN GLASS, Bank, Deep Amber, Lily Pad Foot, Pontil Mark, 4 In.	190.00
Bottle, Bulbous, Olive Green, Diamond Sunburst Pattern, 7 In.	290.00
Bowl, Deep Amethyst, Ruffled Edge, Pontil Mark, 4 1/2 In.	70.00
Bowl, Pale Green, Rolled Lip, Pontil Mark, 9 In.	140.00
Bowl, Sapphire Blue, Pontil Mark, 4 1/2 In.	140.00
Bowl, Sapphire Blue, Rolled Edge, C.1720, Pontil Mark, 5 In.	70.00
Candlestick, Amethyst, C.1840, 7 1/2 In., Pair	250.00
Canister, Sapphire Blue Rings, Covered, C.1820, 11 1/2 In.	550.00
Cruet, Expanded 24 Ribs, Crimped Blown Handle, 9 1/4 In.	185.00
Decanter, Original Stopper, 10 In.	170.00
Decanter, Petticoat Design, 19th Century, 10 In., Pair	85.00
Dome, Flint & Rings, Oval, 8 X 4 In.	25.00
Flytrap, Original Pressed Drop Strap, Footed, 6 In.	115.00
Holder, Twine, Blue Wheel Floral Engraving, 5 X 5 In.	265.00
Jar, Candy, Circular Foot, Covered, 15 1/2 In.	70.00
Jar, Candy, Electric Blue, C.1850, Pear Shape, Covered, 19 In.	400.00

Pitcher, Applied Handle, 2 Icicles, 7 In. 135.00
Pitcher, Deep Amethyst, Rolled Lip, Strap Handle, 5 1/4 In. 200.00
Pitcher, Enameled Cherries, Green 90.00
Pitcher, Sapphire Blue, 15 Panels, Strap Handle, 12 In. 200.00
Pitcher, 4 Raised Rings, Applied Strap Handle, 8 1/2 In. 80.00
Pitcher, 2 Applied Rings On Body, Boston Glass, C.1815 .... 350.00
Pitkin, Double Pattern Vertical Ribbing, Olive Green, 6 1/4 In. 350.00
Plate, Opalescent Swirl, 7 In. 40.00
Rolling Pin, Green, White Flecked, Saratoga Glass, 15 1/2 In. 225.00
Salt, Master, Fish Handles 60.00
Salt, Ribbed, Ogee Shape, 18th Century, American, 3 3/4 In. 75.00
Sugar, Cobalt Blue, Diamond Quilted Design, 6 1/2 In. 275.00
Vase, Amethyst, Hyacinth Type, Witch Ball Cover, 13 In. 200.00
Vase, Apothecary, Ruby Red, C.1840, 18 In. 110.00
Vase, Green, Hyacinth Type, Witch Ball Cover, 13 In. 220.00
Vase, Red Amethyst, Hyacinth Type, Witch Ball Cover, 11 In. 110.00
Vase, Trumpet, Sapphire Blue, Witch Ball Cover, Pedestal, 8 In. 1500.00
Wall Pocket, Sea Green, Folded Edge, Triangular Hanger, 5 In. 160.00
Wine, Conical Bowl, Bubble Stem, C.1830, 8 In. 70.00
Witch Ball & Stand, Red & White Looping, Footed, Clear, 6 In. 1150.00
Witch Ball, Clear, Pink & White Looping, 6 1/2 In.Diam., Pr. 525.00
Witch Ball, Red & Gray Looping, Black Stand, 5 1/2 In.Diam. 360.00
Witch Ball, Red Splotches, White Ground, 5 In.Diam. 375.00
      BLUE AMBERINA, see Bluerina
      BLUE GLASS, see Cobalt Blue
      BLUE ONION, see Onion

*Blue Willow pattern has been made in England since 1780. The pattern
has been copied by factories in many countries, including Germany, Japan, and
the United States. It is still being made. Willow was named for a pattern that
pictures a bridge, birds, willow trees, and a Chinese landscape.*

BLUE WILLOW, Boat, Gravy, Buffalo 75.00
Bowl, Adams, 9 1/2 In.Diam. 50.00
Bowl, Cereal, Adams, 6 1/4 In. 13.50
Bowl, Flow Blue, Royal Doulton, 7 In. 65.00
Bowl, Flow Blue, Royal Doulton, 8 In. 75.00
Bowl, Royal, 10 In.Diam. 16.50
Bowl, Vegetable, Adams, Oval 45.00
Bowl, Vegetable, Allerton, 9 In.Diam. 25.00
Bowl, Venton Ware, 4 3/4 In.Diam. 5.00
Bowl, Venton Ware, 8 1/2 In.Diam. 15.00
Bowl, Venton Ware, 9 In. 35.00
Bowl, 5 1/2 In. 3.00
Bowl, 9 In. 8.00
Bowl, 10 In. 12.00
Butter Pat, Allerton 15.00
Butter, Patterned Insert, Adams 65.00
Butter, Scalloped, Allerton 149.50
Compote, Dark Blue, Birds, Pedestal, 2 1/4 In. 65.00
Creamer 8.50
Creamer, Adams, 4 In. 35.00
Creamer, Soho, England, 3 1/2 In. 15.00
Cup & Saucer, Allerton 25.00
Cup & Saucer, Children's 5.00
Cup & Saucer, Gold Trim, Burleighware 7.50
Cup & Saucer, Homer Laughlin .... 5.00 To 6.00
Cup & Saucer, Royal 6.00
Cup & Saucer, Tea, Adams 12.50
Cup & Saucer, Wood & Sons 10.00
Cup, Myott & Son 7.50
Cup, Restaurant, Buffalo 3.00
Dipper, Wood Handle 10.00

Dish, Pickle, Victorian Leaf Shaped, 6 In.	32.00
Dish, Soap, Decal, 4 X 8 X 3 In.	5.00
Dish, Vegetable, Baker, England, Covered, 12 X 9 In.	75.00
Dish, Vegetable, Lion Finial, Allerton, Square, Covered	65.00
Dish, Vegetable, Scalloped, Allerton, 9 In.	45.00
Dish, Vegetable, Soho, England, 8 1/2 X 6 1/2 In.	15.00
Eggcup, Booths, Set Of 4	10.00
Gravy Boat	12.00
Gray, Scalloped, Allerton	59.50
Pitcher & Bowl, Decals, Pitcher, 11 In.	32.50
Plate, A.B.Jones Grafton, 9 In.	5.00
Plate, Adams, 6 In.	7.50
Plate, Adams, 7 In.	8.50
Plate, Adams, 9 In.	12.50
Plate, Adams, 10 In.	12.50
Plate, Allerton, 7 In.	20.00
Plate, Allerton, 9 In.	18.00
Plate, Allerton, 10 In.	18.00
Plate, Bradley's, Light Blue	2.50
Plate, Children's	3.50
Plate, Cookie, Yorktown Relish, 3 In.	24.00
Plate, Fishtail Birds, Gold Trim, 6 In.	3.00
Plate, Royal, 12 In.	15.00
Plate, Scalloped, Allerton, 10 In.Diam.	18.00
Plate, Soup, Adams, 8 In.	15.50
Plate, Soup, Allerton, Large	28.00
Plate, Soup, Scalloped Rim, Marked, 7 In., Pair	50.00
Plate, Venton Ware, 9 In.	9.00
Platter, Adams, 13 In.	65.00
Platter, Adams, 15 In.	50.00
Platter, Baker, 9 X 12 In.	35.00
Platter, Homer Laughlin, Oblong, 11 1/4 In.	22.00
Platter, Homer Laughlin, 11 1/4 In.	10.00
Platter, Homer Laughlin, 13 1/4 In.	12.50
Platter, Impressed Mark, 15 3/4 X 12 1/2 In.	75.00
Platter, Incised Name, 12 X 9 1/2 In.	20.00
Platter, James O'Neill, England, 9 X 11 In.	32.50
Platter, Laughlin, 14 In.	15.00
Platter, Oval, Marked, 14 In.	83.00
Platter, Ridgway, 16 In.	20.00
Platter, Soho, England, 10 X 12 In.	35.00
Platter, 11 1/2 X 9 1/2 In.	22.00
Saucer, Homer Laughlin	3.00
Saucer, Japan	1.75
Shaker, Handled	12.00
Soup, Allerton, 8 In.	35.00
Soup, Ridgway, 7 In.	35.00
Teapot, Children's	6.50
Tray, Change, Advertising, Staffordshire, C.1850	30.00
Tray, 2 People On Arched Bridge, Gilded Rim, 6 X 7 1/4 In.	30.00
Tureen, Covered, Adams, Square, 9 1/2 In.	85.00

Bluerina is a type of art glass which shades from light blue to ruby. It is often called blue amberina.

BLUERINA, Sugar Shaker, Original Top	125.00

Boch Freres factory was founded in 1841 in La Louviere in eastern Belgium. The wares resemble the work of Villeroy & Boch. The factory is still in business.

BOCH FRERES, Vase, Art Deco, 8 In.	250.00

BOEHM, Figurine, African Elephant, Horse & Crown Mark, 8 In. 450.00
Figurine, Angels, Brother & Sister, Pair 250.00
Figurine, Chipmunk, No.1513 .... 375.00
Figurine, Common Tern, Horse & Crown Mark, 4 1/2 In. 200.00
Figurine, God Anubis, 9 3/4 X 13 1/2 In. 315.00
Figurine, Madonna, White, Marked, 4 1/2 In. 75.00
Figurine, Mallard, 10 1/2 In., Pair 1900.00
Figurine, Mouse, Trenton, N.J., 3 1/2 In. 195.00
Figurine, Poodle, Trenton, N.J., 3 X 5 In. 195.00

*Bohemian glass is an ornate, overlay, or flashed glass made during the
Victorian era. It has been reproduced in Bohemia, which is now a part of
Czechoslovakia. Glass made from 1875 to 1900 is preferred by collectors.*

BOHEMIAN GLASS, Biscuit Jar, Deer & Castle, Covered 85.00
Bottle, Cologne, Frosted Deer & Castle, Ruby Red 45.00
Bottle, Wine, Deer, Castle, Birds, Stopper, 16 In. 85.00
Compote, Deer & Castle Scene, Amber, 4 X 8 1/2 In. 45.00
Compote, Deer In Landscape, , 19th Century, 12 In., Pair 800.00
Compote, Scrolling Lip, Bull's-Eyes & Stars, 8 1/2 In., Pair 300.00
Compote, Vines, Leafage, Trefoil Base, 2 Part, 10 1/2 In., Pair 650.00
Decanter Set, Deer & Castle Design, Set Of 6 Glasses 285.00
Decanter, Etched Animals, 3 Glasses, Blue Edges, 9 In. 95.00
Decanter, Etched Stag Pattern, 8 In. 40.00
Decanter, 3 Stemmed Glasses, Red 145.00
Ewer & Goblet, Ruby Flash & White 425.00
Goblet, Stag & Doe, Covered 100.00
Jar, Leaf & Bead, Covered, 6 In. 55.00
Punch Bowl, Underplate, White To Clear, 12 1/2 In. 400.00
Stein-Etched Landscape, Pewter Fittings, C.1900, 6 In. 275.00
Stein, Red Design On Clear Glass, 3 1/2 In. 75.00
Tankard, Engraved Virgin, Swags, Flowers, 8 1/2 In. 1100.00
Tumbler, Amber Flash, Dated 1848, Thistle Sprays, 12 In. 250.00
Tumbler, Green & Amber, C.1850, Engraved Trophies, 11 In. 240.00
Vase, Bear's Hunt, Diamond Cut Design, C.1815, 8 1/4 In. 880.00
Vase, Deer Castle, Amber, 18 1/2 In. 110.00
Vase, Etched Wolf, Deer, & Birds, Pedestal, Amber, 7 In. 97.00
Vase, Flowers, Animals & Man, Ruby Flashed, 10 1/4 In. 120.00
Vase, Overlay Luster, Blue, 8 In. 250.00
Vase, Turn-Out Lip, Frosted Panels, Ruby Birds, 8 3/4 In. 50.00
Water Set, Deer & Castle, 5 Piece 150.00
Wine Set, Deer & Castle, 6 Stemmed Glasses, Ruby 175.00
Wine, Hunting Party, Knopped Stem, Enameled, 7 1/4 In. 440.00

BONN, Plate, Portrait, Marie Louise, 8 1/2 In. 35.00
BOOK, see Paper, Book; and others
BOSTON & SANDWICH CO., see Sandwich Glass; Fireglow; Lutz

BOTTLE OPENER, Baseball Cap, Iron 13.00
Black Egyptian Woman, Iron 15.00
Black Face 65.00
Brass Fish, With Corkscrew 15.00
Bulldog 45.00
Bulldog, Cast Iron 15.00
Dead Man In Coffin Box, 1932, Cast Iron 45.00
Dog, Figural 25.00
Donkey .... 15.00 To 20.00
Donkey, Smiling 20.00
Drunk At Lamppost 6.00
Drunk At Sign Post 6.00
Drunk Leaning On Palm Tree, Cast Iron 14.00
Drunk, Wall Mount, Cast Iron 28.00
Duck, Figural 25.00

False Teeth, Pink & White, Iron, 3 1/2 In.	70.00
Forest Park Butter	6.00
Gold Ball	8.50
Golf Club	6.00
Goose, White Body, Black Head & Neck	40.00
Haberle Congress Beer	3.00
Irish Setter, Cast Iron	17.00
Lobster, Iron	17.50
Man With Palm Tree, Figural	25.00
Man With 4 Eyes, Cast Iron	20.00
Man's Head, Wearing Top Hat, Wall Mounted, Brass, 5 In.	28.00
Miller's Forge	3.00
Mouth With Teeth, Wall Mount	25.00
Negro Head, Figural, Cast Iron, 3 3/4 X 4 1/4 In.	65.00
Nude, Brass, Art Deco	15.00
Nymph On Rock, White Rock, Cast Iron	20.00
Old Snifter	35.00
Orange Crush	6.00
Parrot On Perch, Polychrome Paint, 5 In.	55.00
Parrot On Stand, Figural	25.00
Parrot, Cast Iron	35.00
Parrot, Iron, Green, Red	20.00
Parrot, Standing	25.00
Pelican, Figural	25.00
Scotty Dog, Figural, Iron	10.00
Sea Gull, Cast Iron	14.00
Woman With 4 Eyes, Cast Iron	19.50 To 22.00

Bottle collecting has become a major American hobby. There are several general categories of bottles such as historic flasks, bitters, household, figural, and others. For modern bottle prices and more old bottle prices see the book "The Kovels' Bottle Price List" by Ralph and Terry Kovel.

BOTTLE, Apothecary, Blown & Cut Stopper, Enameled Label, Amber, 5 7/8 In.	20.00
Apothecary, Clear, Blown, Stopper, Label, 7 3/4 In.	12.50
Apothecary, Cobalt Blue, Blown, Paper Label, Stopper, 9 1/4 In.	40.00
Apothecary, Glass Label, Ground Stopper, Amber, Square, 9 3/4 In.	30.00
Apothecary, Pressed Stopper, Eglomise Label, 4 1/2 In.	15.00

Avon started in 1886 as the California Perfume Company. It was not until 1929 the name Avon was used. In 1939 it became Avon Products, Inc. Each year Avon sells figural bottles filled with cosmetic products. Ceramic, plastic, and glass bottles are made in limited editions.

Avon, Automobile, Electric Charger	3.00
Avon, Automobile, Rolls-Royce	6.00
Avon, Automobile, Stanley Steamer	4.00
Avon, Bell, Currier & Ives	8.00
Avon, Candle Shape, Chipmunk	4.00
Avon, Candle Shape, Fostoria	5.00
Avon, Candle, Nesting Dove	3.00
Avon, Chess Set, Complete	300.00
Avon, Cologne, White Moire	49.50
Avon, Cruet Set, Colored	15.00
Avon, Defender Cannon	15.00
Avon, Dueling Pistol	5.00
Avon, Figural, Good Fairy	8.00
Avon, Flask, Alpine, Boxed	60.00
Avon, Pipe Shape, Brown, Full	3.00
Avon, Pipe Shape, Calabash	6.00
Avon, Pitcher, Mount Vernon	12.00
Avon, Stanley Steamer	2.00
Barber, Amethyst, White Enamel Design	110.00

Barber, Black Amethyst, Enameled White Daisies	85.00
Barber, Deep Amethyst, White Enamel Design	75.00
Barber, Enameled Design, Cobalt Blue, White Milk Glass Stopper	60.00
Barber, Enameled, Stopper, Amethyst, Pair	275.00
Barber, Hobbs, Blue	80.00
Barber, Spatter, Blue, White, & Clear, 8 In.	30.00
Barber, Talc, Clambroth, Glass, Metal Cap	20.00
Barber, White Enamel Beading, Amethyst	62.00
Barber, Witch Hazel, Clambroth	15.00

Beam bottles are made to hold Kentucky Straight Bourbon made by the James B.Beam Distilling Company. The Beam series of ceramic bottles began in 1953.

Beam, Blue Fox	130.00
Beam, Carmen	300.00
Beam, Figaro	290.00
Beam, Locomotive	42.00
Beam, Madama Butterfly	575.00
Beer, Moehn Brewery, Amber	5.00
Bitters, Augauer Bitters Co., Chicago	52.50
Bitters, Big Bill's Best	25.00
Bitters, Brown's Celebrated Indian Herb, Patented 1868, Green	1000.00
Bitters, Dr. Geo. Pierce's Indian Restorative, Aqua, 7 In.	30.00
Bitters, Dr. Soule Hop Bitters	22.50
Bitters, National, Patented 1867, Light Brown	700.00
Bitters, Richardson's Jamaica Root, Wheaton Glass Co., Blue	5.00
BOTTLE, COCA-COLA, see Coca-Cola, Bottle	
Cod Liver Oil, Fish Shape, 9 In. ....*Illus*	22.50
Cologne, Basket Weave, Blown, Pontil, Aqua	42.00
Cologne, Cut Stars, Thumbprints, Ruby Cut Crystal, Stopper, 8 3/4 In.	145.00
Cologne, Gold Decorated, Green Cut To Crystal, Stopper, 9 1/2 In.	135.00
Drugstore, Cobalt Blue, C.1875, 18 In.	45.00
Extract, Shoe Shaped	40.00
Ezra Brooks, Casey Jones Train	45.00
Ezra Brooks, Lincoln Continental	30.00
Ezra Brooks, Snow Leopard	46.00
Figural, Boy, Holding Up Shirt Exposing Himself, German, 3 In.	95.00
Figural, Buster Brown, Comic Strip Character, Tolet Water	30.00
Figural, Eagle Claw Holding Egg, 14 1/2 In.	65.00
Figural, Kaiser Wilhelm II, Kaiserin Augusta Victoria, 12 In., Pair	150.00
Figural, Lady, Victorian Laced High Shoe, Ribbed Stocking, 12 In.	65.00
Figural, Man Strolling, Hands On Umbrella, Tans, German, 10 In.	90.00
Figural, Monk, Head Stopper, Black Body, Zanesville, 9 1/2 In.	70.00
Flask, Double Eagle, Historical, Olive Green, Open Pontil, 6 In.	180.00
Flask, Pikes Peak, Aqua	125.00
Fruit Jar, Atlas E-Z Seal, Amber, Quart	30.00
Fruit Jar, Atlas E-Z Seal, Aqua	2.00
Fruit Jar, Flaccus Bros., Steerhead, Lid, Clear	29.00
Fruit Jar, Hartells	45.00

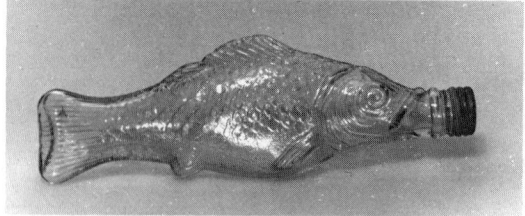

Bottle, Cod Liver Oil, Fish Shape, 9 In.

Bottle, Fruit Jar, Quick Seal, Aqua, Pint

Bottle, Fruit Jar, Mason's Patent No.30, Aqua, Pint

Fruit Jar, Mason's Patent No.30, Aqua, Pint .... *Illus*	4.00
Fruit Jar, Midget Mason, Original Lid, Aqua	10.00
Fruit Jar, Millville, Ct.	25.00
Fruit Jar, Quick Seal, Aqua, Pint .... *Illus*	5.00
Fruit Jar, Woodbury, No.2, 9 In.	30.00
Ginger Ale, Belfast, Aqua, Blob Top, Round Bottom	12.00
Hair Tonic, Lucky Tiger, Embossed, Girl & Tiger, 1930s	20.00
Ink, Cart, Ma & Pa, Pair	80.00
Lady's Shape, Dear, Signed, 6 1/2 In. .... *Illus*	35.00
Lionstone, Fire Hydrant	50.00
Lionstone, Hockey Player	22.00
Medicine, Allens Anti-Fat, Buffalo, Cobalt Blue	30.00
Medicine, Dr.Kilmer's Swamp Root Remedy, Embossed, 4 In.	8.00
Medicine, Dr.W.B.Caldwell's, Full, Boxed, Clear .... *Illus*	15.00
Medicine, H.H.H., Reverse D.O.J., 1868, Aqua, 5 In. .... *Illus*	12.00

Bottle, Lady's Shape, Dear, Signed, 6 1/2 In.

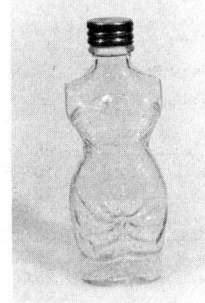

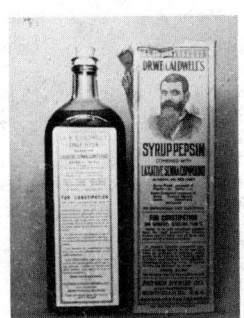

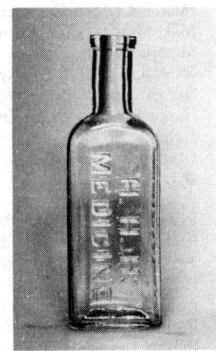

Bottle, Medicine, Dr.W.B.Caldwell's,
Full, Boxed, Clear

Bottle, Medicine, H.H.H., Reverse D.O.J., 1868, Aqua, 5 In.

Bottle, Milk, Meadow Gold,
Amber, Quart

Bottle, Miniature, Scotch Whisky,
Pottery, 7 In.

Bottle, Perfume, Florida Water, Murray
& Lanman, New York, 9 In.

Bottle, Soda, Ginger Beer, Titus
Greenwood, Pottery, 8 In.

Medicine, Warner's Safe Diabetes Cure, Embossed, Amber, 9 In. 55.00
Milk, Baby Face One Side, Brookfield Dairy, Hellertown, Pa., 1/2 Pint 10.00
Milk, Baby Face Top 12.00
Milk, Meadow Gold, Amber, Quart ....*Illus* 4.50
Mineral Water, Farmville Lithis, Embossed, Lady, Aqua, 9 In. 35.00
Miniature, Scotch Whisky, Pottery, 7 In. ....*Illus* 75.00
Numol Tonic Nervine, Pottery Container 25.00
Nursing, Baby's Friend, Embossed Eagle, 1880s, Boxed 65.00
Nursing, Figural, Black Baby, Germany, Miniature 20.00
Orange Crush, 1920s 45.00
Owl Family, Screech, Gallon 425.00
Perfume, Floral Stopper, Sterling Silver Overlay, C.1906, 4 3/4 In. 220.00
Perfume, Florida Water, Murray & Lanman, New York, 9 In. ....*Illus* 10.00
Perfume, Lucky Lindy, C.1927 .... 12.00
Perfume, Negro, Germany, 2 In. 40.00
Perfume, Romona, C.1930 .... 50.00
Perfume, Swirl, Cranberry Opalescent, Clear Stopper, 6 1/4 In. 125.00
Perfume, Transparent Green, Silver Overlay, 3 1/4 In. 110.00
Poison, Not To Be Taken, 6 Sided, Cobalt Blue 7.00

Powder Horn, Flat, Metal Screw Lid, Clear 16.00
Quaker, Embossed Picture, With Lid 10.00
Scent, 15K Gold & Agate, C.1840 .... 2250.00
Ski Country, Birth Of Freedom, Gallon 2500.00
Ski Country, Owl, Great Horned, Gallon 1100.00
Snuff, Ivory, Oriental Nobleman, Wife With Book, 4 1/2 In., Pair 235.00
Snuff, Lapis Lazuli, White Jade Stopper, 3 In. 65.00
Soda, Ginger Beer, Titus Greenwood, Pottery, 8 In. .... *Illus* 8.00
Soda, John Graf Milwaukee, Amber, Embossed, Blob Top 20.00
Sunburst, Blown-In-Mold, New England, C.1825, Green, 6 1/4 In. 900.00
Syrup, Flask, Ben Franklin, Green 4.00
Violin, Blue, 8 In. 9.00
Whiskey, Adolph Harris & Co., Light Amber, 12 In. 115.00
Whiskey, Blumauer & Hoch, Amber, 11 1/2 In. 20.00
Whiskey, Boot Shape, Imperial Green 10.00
Whiskey, Cartan, McCarthy & Co., Amber, 11 3/4 In. 35.00
Whiskey, Cerruti Mercantile Co., Inc., Amber, 11 3/8 In. 20.00
Whiskey, Cranberry Swirl 295.00
Whiskey, Dave D.Gibbons & Co., Amber, 11 In. 40.00
Whiskey, E.A.Fargo Co., Dark Amber, 11 1/2 In. 20.00
Whiskey, F.Chevalier & Co., Green, 11 7/8 In. 10.00
Whiskey, F.Zimmerman & Co., Light Amber, 12 In. 15.00
Whiskey, Geo.Wissemann, Amber, 11 1/8 In. 20.00
Whiskey, Hall, Luhrs & Co., Light Amber, 11 3/4 In. 20.00
Whiskey, Hawkins, Aqua, Rye In Circle On Front, 10 5/8 In. 15.00
Whiskey, Hildebrandt, Posner & Co., Dark Amber, 11 3/4 In. 30.00
Whiskey, J.Aronson, Amber, 12 In. 12.00
Whiskey, J.H.Cutter, Amber, Blob Top, 12 In. 4500.00
Whiskey, J.H.Cutter, Greenish Amber, 12 In. 30.00
Whiskey, Jesse Moore & Co., Light Amber, 11 5/8 In. 15.00
Whiskey, Jos.Herscher Co., Amber, Rectangle, 13 3/4 In. 20.00
Whiskey, Kellogg's, Amber, 11 3/4 In. 20.00
Whiskey, Levaggi Co., Amber, 11 In. 20.00
Whiskey, Louis Taussig & Co., Dark Amethyst, 11 1/2 In. 15.00
Whiskey, Louis Taussig & Co., Medium Amber, 12 In. 45.00
Whiskey, M.Cronan & Co., Light Amber, 11 3/4 In. 15.00
Whiskey, Miniature, Fiddle Shape, Label 8.00
Whiskey, Phoenix, Medium Amber, 11 3/4 In. 75.00
Whiskey, The Rothenberg Co., Light Amber, 11 1/2 In. 35.00
Whiskey, Wheaton, Log Cabin, Amber, 8 In. 50.00
Whiskey, Wilmerding-Loewe Co., Amber, 11 1/2 In. 15.00

*Boxes of all kinds are collected. They were made of thin strips of inlaid
wood, metal, tortoiseshell, embroidery, or other material.*

BOX, see also Ivory, Box; Porcelain, Box; Shaker, Box; Store,
Box; Tin, Box; and various porcelain categories

BOX, Anheuser-Busch Brewery, Paducah & St.Louis, 24 X 14 In. 85.00
Art Deco, Hand-Wrought Metal, Laird Argental, Enameled Top, 3 X 5 In. 35.00
Ballot, Fenton Metallic Mfg., Jamestown, N.Y., Metal, 14 X 16 X 18 In. 60.00
Ballot, George III, English, C.1800 .... *Illus* 1200.00
Ballot, Inside Divider, C.1850, Black Walnut, 9 1/2 X 5 3/4 In. 50.00
BOX, BATTERSEA, see Battersea, Box
Beveled Sliding Top, Original Red Paint, 12 X 3 1/4 X 3 3/4 In. 65.00
Bible, Brown Graining 120.00
Bible, Chester County, Pennsylvania 4500.00
Bride's, Birch Laced, Norwegian, Pine 135.00
Bride's, Hand-Forged Nails, Dome Topped, C.1850, Grained, 23 3/4 X 12 In. ... 110.00
Butter, Swing Handle, Wood Grip, Black Paint, Bentwood, 11 1/4 In. 150.00
Cake, Schlepp's, Tin, 2 Shelves 65.00
Candle, Dovetailed, Salmon Paint 200.00
Candle, Hanging, Dark Gray Paint, Pine, 14 1/2 In. 160.00
Candle, Incised & Designs, Pennsylvania 495.00

Box, Ballot, George III, English, C.1800

(See Page 41)

Candle, Slide Top, Mitered Keyed Corners	15.00
Candle, Sliding Lid, Dovetailed, Oak, 8 X 3 X 12 In.	90.00
Candle, Square Nails, Slide Cover, C.1840, Pine, Blue, 18 X 7 3/4 In.	295.00
Candle, Wall, Hand-Forged Square Nails, C.1820, 3 X 4 X 12 In.	95.00
Candle, Wooden, Compartment, Sliding Cover, Chamfered Base, Signed D.Fail	90.00
Candle, 2-Drawer, Hand-Forged Nails, Buttermilk Red, Pine, 5 1/2 X 17 In.	385.00
Chippendale Carved, Painted Pine, C.1740	1400.00
Cigar, Admiral Dewey	50.00
Cigar, Dated 1861-1961, Souvenir	10.00
Cigar, La Palina, Wooden	9.00
Cigarette, Scovill Mfg.Co. 125th Anniversary, 1927, Silver Plated	60.00
Collar, Portrait Bust Of General Chester A.Arthur, Gutta-Percha Top	40.00
Cylinder, Red Circle Display Case Co., Top Red Patina, Crank Handle	87.50
Deed, Hand-Carved, Wooden	85.00
Deed, Lock, Mahogany, 4 X 7 X 2 In.	18.00
Document, New England, 19th Century, Ivory & Shell, Mahogany, 10 1/2 In.	475.00
Dovetailed, Dome Top, Old Red, Wooden, 3 X 16 1/2 X 13 1/2 In.	115.00
Dressing, Inset Mirror, C.1840, Mahogany & Maple, 10 1/2 X 4 In.	80.00
Elastic Starch, Old Sadiron, 14 X 22 In.	22.00
Fan, Underglaze, Germany, Green	10.00
Foliage & Flowers, French, 1787, 2-Color Gold & Enamel, 2 3/8 In.Diam.	2000.00
Genre Design, Spirit Lock, Pigskin	500.00
Grand Republic Cigarros, Eagle Inside Lid, Wooden, 5 X 12 In.	20.00
Handle, Walrus Ivory, Russian Trade Bead, Engraved Eskimo Scene, 10 In.	450.00
Herb, Slide Top, C.1860, Black Paint, 3 1/2 X 4 In.	60.00
Iron Lock, Key, Leather Handle, Red Paint, Signed, C.1860, 8 3/4 X 18 In.	135.00
Jewel, Coach, Top Removes, Wheels Turn, Enameled, 5 X 3 1/2 In.	800.00
Jewel, Leather & Brass Buttoned, Domed Hinged Lid, 9 In.	115.00
Jewelry, Rosewood, Fitted With A Tray, 9 1/2 In.	45.00
Knife, George III, English, C.1790, Pair	*Illus* 2300.00
Knife, Hand-Carved, Arched Divider, Pine, C.1880, 9 3/8 X 12 In.	65.00
Knife, Signed Wallace Nutting	110.00
Knife, 3 Sections, Handle Grip, 9 3/4 X 14 1/2 In.	25.00
Knife, 19th Century, Painted Pine & Rosewood, 12 3/4 X 8 3/4 In.	80.00
Music, Enameled & Gilt Metal, Austrian, Chest Form, 5 1/2 In.	425.00

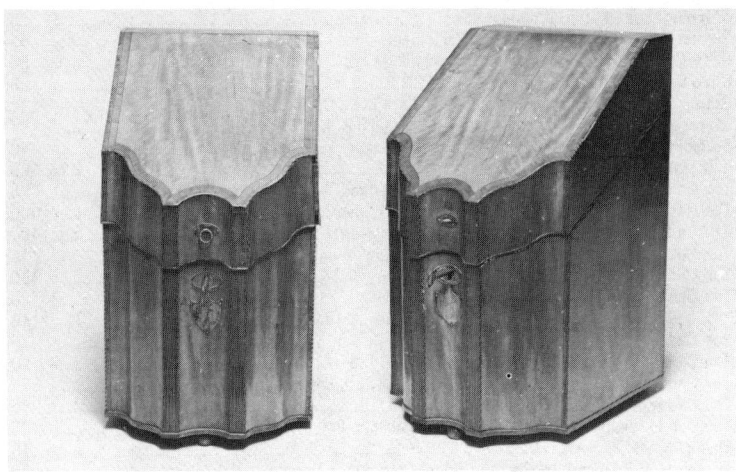

Box, Knife, George III, English, C.1790, Pair

Needle, Victor, Tin	3.25
Oriental Scene, Mother-Of-Pearl & Lacquer	17.50
Pantry, Blue, 9 X 17 In.Diam.	195.00
Pantry, Colonial, Stitched Laps, Oval, Black-Blue Paint, 10 In.	125.00
Pantry, Gray Tan Patina, 6 1/4 In.Diam.	30.00
Pantry, Original Crackled Yellow Paint, Wooden, 8 In.Diam.	75.00
Pantry, Painted, Stack Of 5	525.00
Pantry, Shellac Finish, 6 1/2 In.	38.00
Pantry, Signed J.Burr, Salmon Red, Bentwood, 3 X 6 1/2 In.Diam.	65.00
Pantry, Uneven Headed Nails, Nut Brown, 11 In.	58.00
Pantry, V Lap Top & Bottom, Early Nails, 4 In.	50.00
Pantry, Wire Bail, Wood Grip Handle, Cover, 9 In.Diam.	32.00
Pantry, Wooden Pegged, Copper Nails, Bentwood, 6 1/2 In.Diam.	35.00
Pantry, 5 Laps, Copper Rivets, Green Paint, 6 X 4 1/4 X 3 In.	150.00
Paper Covered, C.1830, Oval, 7 3/4 X 5 1/2 In.	85.00
Paper Covered, Wood, C.1830, Signed Nancy Barnum	8000.00
Pencil, Jackie Coogan, Tin, Green	10.00
Pencil, Little Jack Horner, Dovetailed, 2 1/2 X 7 3/4 In.	40.00
Pencil, Mother Goose, Wooden	12.50
Pencil, Universal Dairy, 1920s, Wooden	100.00
Pigskin, Chinese, Polychrome Floral & Birds, 12 1/2 X 28 X 18 In.	375.00
Queen Of Virginia Tobacco, Square Corners	60.00
Rosewood, Tea Caddy, 10 3/4 In.	65.00
Saffron, Made By Joseph Lehn, August 7, 1889, Covered, 5 1/2 In.	450.00
Salt, Hand-Carved Nitch, Ink Marked B.W.Pressy, 5 X 9 X 4 1/4 In.	45.00
Salt, Table, Freeman & Sears, Boston, Label, Bentwood, 6 In.Diam.	55.00
Salt, Yellow Sponging On Red Ground	165.00
Satinwood & Cut Steel, C.1810	635.00
Seashell	18.00
Seed, Briggs Bros., Label, Oak, 10 1/2 X 7 In.	40.00
Seed, Ferry's, Oak, 11 1/2 X 7 In.	25.00
Seed, Hart's, Display, Dovetailed, Paper Labels	85.00
Seed, Hiram Sibley Co., Dovetailed, Pine, 12 X 29 In.	35.00
Seed, Manderville & King Co., Superior Flowers	36.00
Seed, Ross, Label, Vegetables & Flowers, Wooden	65.00

Shipping, Keen Kutter, Wooden 28.00
Signed J.Webb, On Cover, Forged Nails, Bentwood, 17 1/4 X 7 In. 85.00
Slide Cover, Cut-Nail Construction, Brown, 6 1/2 X 2 1/4 In. 28.00
Slide Cover, Uneven Headed Nails, 6 1/2 X 2 3/8 In. 28.00
Stamp, Doghouse Shape, Bulldog Head, Glass Eyes, Cover, 3 1/2 X 2 1/8 In. ... 28.00
Storage, Square Nails, Original Red, 11 1/2 X 28 X 13 In. 195.00
Sunshine Biscuit, Blue Boy Paper Inset, Tin 40.00
T.M.Myers, House & Carriage Painter, 1876 .... 395.00
Tea Caddy, Chippendale, Mahogany, Beaded Edges, 6 1/4 X 10 In. 275.00
Tea Caddy, Fruitwood, Form Of Melon, Hinged Cover, 5 In. 1000.00
Tea Caddy, Fruitwood, Form Of Pear, Hinged Cover, 7 In. 1400.00
Tea Caddy, George III, C.1790, Inlaid, Mahogany, 6 In. 715.00
Tea Caddy, Mahogany, Pear Form, 19th Century, 6 1/2 In. 990.00
Tea Caddy, Mahogany, William II, Rectangular, 4 1/2 In. 60.00
Tea Caddy, Rosewood, Coffret Form, 2 Sections, C.1810, 5 In. 140.00
Tea Caddy, Rosewood, Inlay, Bracket Feet, 13 X 7 In. 70.00
Tea Caddy, Rosewood, Victorian, Octagonal, 4 X 6 1/2 In. 60.00
Tea Caddy, Spiral Pedestal, Blossom Finial, C.1850, English 575.00
Tea Caddy, Tortoiseshell 385.00
Tea Caddy, Victorian, Domed Hinged Top, Walnut, 8 1/4 X 6 1/4 In. 125.00
Thread, Coats & Clark, Plaid Scenic 18.00
Thread, J. & P.Coats Best Six Cord Spool Cotton, 4 In.Diam. 20.00
Thread, J. & P.Coats, 3-Shelf, Metal 29.00
Tobacco, Seal Of North Carolina, 7 In. 65.00
Tool, Machinist's, 7 Drawers, Top Compartments, Golden Oak 245.00
Tulipwood, French Porcelain, Mounted, 6 1/2 In. 325.00
Union Biscuit, Blue & Gold, Tin 38.00
Utensil, Arched Handle, Gray Blue Paint 95.00
Viennese, Draped Nude On Lid, Blue Enamel, C.1925, 1 5/8 In.Square 1000.00
Wallpapered, Newspaper Lined, 6 1/2 In.Diam. 110.00
William Hershey, Hingham, Mass., Original Label, Oval 162.50
Winchester, Ammo.Wooden 15.00
Writing, Fitted Interior, Maple, 5 3/4 X 12 X 18 In. 85.00
BOY SCOUT, Ax, Trademark 32.50
Book, Adventuring For Senior Scouts, C.1942 .... 10.00
Book, In Coal Caverns, 1913, By Major Fletcher, 1913 .... 12.50
Book, With Byrd, 1931, 33 Photographs, Siple 10.00
Bugle, Rexcraft, Brass 40.00
Camera, Boxed 12.00
Compass & Sundial, Metal Case, 1921 .... 15.00
Cub, Jackknife, Boker Barlow, 1953 .... 10.00
Drum, Tin 50.00
Game, Scout Trail, 1920, Henricksen Mfg. Co. 25.00
Hand Book, Rockwell Cover, 1938 .... 12.50
Hand Book, Rockwell Cover, 1940 .... 12.50
Handkerchief & Clasp 6.50
Hat, Scoutmaster 15.00
Kit, First Aid, Tin, Contents, 1932 .... 25.00
Kit, First Aid, 1932 .... 15.00
Knife, Marbles 25.00
Knife, Marked Kent 15.00
Match Safe, Emblem, Hanging Ring, Nickeled Brass, 3/4 X 3 In. 32.00
Membership Booklet, 1919 .... 18.00
Pin, 10th World Jamboree 45.00
Pin, 11th World Jamboree 25.00
Plaque, Bronze, Lady Liberty, Scout With Sword, 3 1/2 X 2 In. 25.00
Plate, Commemorative, Baden-Powel Picture, Royal Gouda, 1937 .... 30.00
Signal Set, Battery Operated, Boxed 12.00
Signal Set, Triple, Original Box, 1930s 30.00
Tablet, Writing, 1820 .... 5.00
Watch Fob 50.00
Yearbook, 1915 .... 9.00

Bradley & Hubbard Manufacturing Company made lamps and other metal work in Meriden, Connecticut, around the turn of the century.

BRADLEY & HUBBARD, Bookends, Lincoln Memorial, Silver Color	20.00
Bookends, Spanish Galleons, Brass	45.00
Candlestick, Brass, 8 In., Pair	125.00
Candlestick, Square Base, 11 In., Pair	75.00
Humidor	26.00
Lamp Base, Bronze	95.00
Lamp.Oil, Green, Floral, Ball Shade, Signed, 16 In.	195.00
Lamp, Banquet, Floral Milk Glass Globe, C.1890, 47 In.	425.00
Lamp, Clambroth Embossed Shade, Electrified, 25 In.	150.00
Lamp, Crown Half Shade, Polychrome Floral, 20 In.	180.00
Lamp, Hanging, Brass, 8 Socket, Gas, Electric, Signed, 32 In.	225.00
Lamp, Hanging, Country Store, Nickel Plated Brass, Large	245.00
Lamp, Kerosene, Fierce Creature, Brass, 12 3/4 In.	375.00
Lamp, Reverse Painted Shade, Bronze, Shade 17 In.Diam.	395.00
Lamp, Student, Double, Electrified	600.00
Lamp, Student, Duplex Burner, Acorn Finials, Shade 10 In.	695.00
Lamp, Table, Art Glass Allover, Lily Pad Base, 24 In.	1850.00
Lamp, Table, Overlay Shade, Signed, Brass, 24 In.	375.00
Lamp, Table, Reverse Painted, 4-Paneled, Shade, 14 In.	695.00
Lamp, 6 Chocolate Glass Panels, 24 In.	375.00

Brass has been used for decorative pieces and useful tablewares since ancient times. It is an alloy of copper, zinc, and other metals.

BRASS, see also Bell; Tool; Trivet; etc.

BRASS, Ashtray, Elsie, Figural	38.00
Ashtray, Squirrel	5.00
Barrel, Biscuit, Victorian, Porcelain Lining, 6 1/2 In.	60.00
Basin, Spun, Detailed Side Handles, 19 In.	60.00
Bed, Double Size, Tubular Design, Side Rails	160.00
Bedwarmer, English, Etched, Turned Oak Handle, 44 1/2 In.	200.00
Bedwarmer, Etched, English, Turned Oak Handle, 42 In.	325.00
Bookends, Civil War Drum & Fife Team, American Flag	25.00
Bookends, Horsehead, Horse & Sulky Below	28.00
Bookends, Indian, Full Headdress, 8 X 5 In.	110.00
Bookends, Nude Ladys, Pair	40.00
Bookends, Scotty	35.00
Box, Embossed Leaves On Lid, Applied Copper Leaves, 4 3/4 In.Diam.	20.00
Box, Tobacco, Oval, Hunting Scene, Copper, 6 1/2 In.	400.00
Bucket, Bail, 3 Gallon	55.00
Bucket, Candy, 10 In.	85.00
Bucket, Dovetailed, Lion Handles, 9 X 10 In.	110.00
Bucket, English Regency, Spherical Body, 2 Lions Heads Mount, 15 In.	375.00
Bucket, Marked H.W.Haydens, Pat.1873, Mfd.By E.Miller & Co., 2 Gallon	110.00
Bucket, Spun, Patent Label, 11 3/4 In.	60.00
Bucket, Swinging Handle, Dated 1866, 10 X 14 1/2 In.Diam.	100.00
Candelabra, Cutout Work, Burnished, 7-Light, 16 3/4 In.	155.00
Candelabra, Floral, 19th Century French, 35 In., Pair	225.00
Candelabra, 3-Branch, 13 1/2 In., Pair	79.00
Candelabra, 5-Branch, 21 In.Tall	325.00
Candle Sconce, Double, 2 Hinged Arms, Vining Flowers, 8 In.	85.00
Candleholder, Held By Soldier, Pair	110.00
Candlestick Holder, 3 Lions At Base, Goats' Heads & Grapes At Top	75.00
Candlestick, Beehive, English, 9 In., Pair	95.00
Candlestick, C.1790, 10 In., Pair	160.00
Candlestick, C.1810, English, 11 In., Pair	95.00
Candlestick, Chinese Dragon, 7-Socket, 17 In.	180.00
Candlestick, Chinese, Fancy Scrolls, 13 In., Pair	198.00
Candlestick, Chinese, 2 Storks & 2 Fish, C.1906, 19 In., Pair	230.00

Candlestick, Early 19th Century, Pair 225.00
Candlestick, Elongated Socket, Baluster Stem, Domed Base, 8 1/2 In. 125.00
Candlestick, English, 18th Century, Octagonal Base, 6 1/2 In., Pair 300.00
Candlestick, English, 18th Century, Petal-Form Cup, 8 1/4 In., Pair 650.00
Candlestick, Georgian, Push-Ups, 6 1/4 In., Pair 85.00
Candlestick, Octagonal Base, Threaded Baluster Stem, 5 In. 325.00
Candlestick, Persian Style Design, 16 In., Pair 100.00
Candlestick, Petal Form, Baluster Stem, Marked Ed. Durnall, 7 In. 550.00
Candlestick, Queen Anne, 18th Century, 8 In. 195.00
Candlestick, Russian, 3-Socket Candelabra, 2 Animal Figures, 14 In. 75.00
Candlestick, Square Base, Four Rectangular Feet, Ring Column, 12 In. 80.00
Candlestick, Square Base, Screw-In Baluster Stem, 5 In. 400.00
Candlestick, Student Lamp, English, C.1740 .... 375.00
Candlestick, Victorian, Push-Ups, 10 3/4 In., Pair 60.00
Case, Pince-Nez, Papier-Mache, Hinged, Black, 2 1/4 X 3 1/4 X 1 In. 13.00
Chamberstick, Push-Up, 4 1/2 In., Pair 110.00
Chandelier, French, 4-Light, Glass Shades 135.00
Coat Rack, Splendor, Coil Design, 72 In. 95.00
Coffeepot, Hinged Cover, Double Eagle Mark, Russian, 15 In. 90.00
Collar, Dog, Bands Joined By Brass Chain, Philadelphia, 1840 .... 150.00
Condiment Server, Regency 765.00
Cow Bell, Leather Strap, Identification Number, 5 X 5 X 3 In. 70.00
Cuspidor, Removable Cover, 3 3/4 X 10 In.Diam. 85.00
Cutter, Cigar, Monkey, Ashtray, Tail Cuts, Brass, 5 In. 225.00
Dipper, Forged Iron Handle, Rattail Hook-End, 15 In. 230.00
Dipper, Iron Handle, 17 1/4 In. 85.00
Dish, Alms, Adam & Eve, Germany, 15th Century, 10 In. 1850.00
Dish, Alms, Repousse Medallion, Floral Forms, Germany, 15th Century 1650.00
Dish, Soap, Over Tub 22.50
Door Knocker, Lady's Hand, Lace & Beaded Cuff, Ringed Finger, 5 In. 180.00
Doorknob, Egg Shape, Pair 10.00
Doorknob, Inscribed Public School City Of New York 10.00
Doorstop, Cavalrymen, Mounted 95.00
Easel, 8 X 5 1/2 In. 28.00
Ewer, Dragon Spout, Snake Handle, C.1870, 20 In. 125.00
Ewer, 2-Handled, 14 In. 90.00
Figurine, Racehorse, On Base, Jockey Has Red Coat, 8 In. 75.00
Flask, Powder, Black, Embossed, Ribbed Melon, 8 In. 72.50
Gauge, Steam 15.00
Gong, Held By Spaniel, White Metal, Glass Eyes, Striker, 10 X 6 1/4 In. 195.00
Harpoon, Attached Tag, Patented 1844, 4 1/2 In. 125.00
Headband, Oxen, Heart Design, Leather Strap, 9 1/2 X 14 In. 45.00
Holder, Spool, 4 Tiers Over Seated Mythical Figure, Brass, 17 In. 700.00
Hook, Hinged Arm & Star Bracket, 9 1/2 In. 55.00
Hook, Wall, Horsehead, Set Of 8 .... 70.00
Humidor, Hammered Surface, Art Deco Design, Ball Feet, 3 X 9 In. 65.00
Humidor, La Palinas Senators, Cork Lined 20.00
Inkwell, Glass, Onyx, 7 X 3 In. 50.00
Inkwell, Pyramid, Covered, Clear Insert 35.00
Inkwell, Top Hinged, Small Flowers On Top 20.00
Jardiniere, 19th Century, Imperial Mark, 10 X 8 In. 165.00
Kettle, Bulbous, 3 Chippendale Bail, Ball Feet, 13 1/4 In. 225.00
Lamp, Oil, Mesh Cargo, 15 In. 45.00
Lamp, Piano, Ribbed Font, Swirled Leaf Molding, Paw Feet, 63 In. 275.00
Lamp, Student, Bulbous Font, Scrolled Arm, Milk Glass Shade, 8 In. 150.00
Lamp, Student, Single, Green Shade, Adjustable 325.00
Lantern, Farm, Dietz, 11 In. 175.00
Lock, Canoe Oar, Pair 43.00
Lock, Horseshoe, Good Luck 45.00
Lock, Keen Kutter 80.00
Mold, Chocolate, 4-Row, Each Line A Letter To Spell Baker, 6 X 19 In. 110.00
Mold, Thimble, Used By Silversmith, Size 5 .... 35.00

Mortar & Pestle, C.1825, Marked	125.00
Nozzle, Gas Pump	55.00
Padlock, Eagle	12.00
Padlock, U.S.Navy, 2 Keys	25.00
Pail, Spun, Marked E.Miller & Co., Patented 1870, 13 X 9 In.	75.00
Pan, Warming, Floral Design, Chestnut Handle, 13 1/4 In.	250.00
Pan, Warming, Pierced Cover, Floral Design, Wooden Handle, 43 In.	225.00
Pedestal, Onyx Top, Ornate, 31 In.	50.00
Penholder, Victorian, Holds 4 Pens, 4 In.	30.00
Planter, Claw Feet, Russian, 5 1/2 In.	25.00
Pot, Flared Top, 3 Peg Legs, 5 X 8 In.Diam.	45.00
Pump, Boat, Wooden Plunger, Rubber Bailing Hose, C.1884, 30 In.	40.00
Sadiron, Gate Lifts For Coals	45.00
Samovar, Complete With Kettle, 16 In.	135.00
Samovar, Repousse, 29 In.	100.00
Scale, Balance, Hanging, 18 In.Pan	150.00
Sconce, Cherub Climbing Vine, 2-Arm, 19 In.	55.00
Sconce, Settle, Punched Brass, European	150.00
Sconce, 2-Light, Prisms, Floral Arms, Pierced Back, 15 In., Pair	125.00
Scoop, Candy, Tubular Handle, Fruit Design, 11 In.Long	35.00
Shoehorn, Lion Head On Top	18.00
Sign, Funeral Home	22.00
Smoking Set, Chinese, Tray, Ashtray, Cigarette Box, Matchbox Holder	52.50
Snuffer, Candle, Deer Head, Wooden Handle, Brass	10.00
Spit Dogs, Cresset, Circular Cup, Scroll Hook, Arched Foot, 28 In., Pr.	200.00
Spittoon, Gray Graniteware Drain Pan	55.00
Spurs, Lady Leg With Garter, Marked Sims, Pair	50.00
Spurs, U.S. G.A.R.Marked, Pair	40.00
Stamp, Initial M, Rosewood Handle	18.00
Stand, Book, Adjustable, Pierced Rack, 8 In.	50.00
Stand, Dish, Georgian, Adjustable	25.00
Stand, Shoeshine, Pair	70.00
Stand, Umbrella, Hand-Tooled Design, 38 In.	90.00
Stencil, Apple, Extra Selected Kings, Dome-Topped, 13 3/4 X 12 In.	60.00
Stencil, Barrel Head, Fruits & Vegetables, 14 In.Diam.	45.00
Stencil, Love U S A , Hang-Up Hole, 5 X 3/4 In.	25.00
Tamper, Tobacco, Figural, Man, 18th Century, 3 In.	130.00
Teakettle, Alcohol Burner & Stand, Manning & Bowman	85.00
Teakettle, Stand, Ovoid, Scrolling Spout, Hoof Feet, 11 3/4 In.	500.00
Teapot, 4 1/2 X 5 1/4 In.Diam.	35.00
Tool, Pipe Cleaning, Hand Shape, 2 1/8 In.	14.00
Tray, Floral Design, 1900s, Chinese, 3 In.Diam.	8.00
Umbrella Stand, Embossed Tavern Scene, Rose Border	75.00
Urn, Hammered Bird, Animal, Fern, Flower, 10 1/4 In.	40.00
Washboard, Advertising Logo On Top	15.00
Wax Jack, English, 6 1/2 In.	880.00
Whistle, Steam, 12 In.	25.00
Whistle, Steamship, 36 X 6 In.	500.00
BREAD PLATE, see various Pressed Glass patterns	
BRETBY, Vase, High Gloss, Blue, 5 1/2 In.	35.00

Brides' baskets of glass were usually one-of-a-kind novelties made in American and European glass factories. They were especially popular about 1880 when the decorated basket was often given as a wedding gift. Cut glass baskets were popular after 1890. All brides' baskets lost favor about 1905.

BRIDE'S BASKET, Apricot To White, Deep Ruffling	85.00
Blue Opalescent, Hobnail, Clear Handles, 8 1/2 X 10 In.	95.00
Bowl, Cranberry Ribbon, Fluted	165.00
Clear Inside, Blue To White Outside, Clear Edge, 11 In.	185.00

Cranberry Bowl, Signed Pairpoint Holder	495.00
Cranberry Glass Bowl, White Rim, Silver Plated Holder	125.00
Crimped, Pink Inside, White Outside, Silver Plated Holder	375.00
Insert, Mint Green To White Crimped Edge, 6 1/2 In.	60.00
Orange Enameling, Silver Plated Holder, 12 1/4 X 10 In.	180.00
Pears & Cherries, Silver Plated Holder	165.00
Ruby Enameled, Gold Design, 12 In.	450.00
Triple Overlay, Opaque White, Spangle, Clear, 11 In.	125.00
Waffle Pattern, Ornate Foot, Sand	65.00
White Cased With Blue, Meriden Holder	160.00
BRIDE'S BOWL, Pink Ruffled Edge, Cased, 10 In.	75.00
Ruffled, Enameled Design, Blue, 2 1/2 X 6 3/4 In.Diam.	65.00

*Bristol glass was made in Bristol, England, after the 1700s. The
Bristol glass most often seen today is a Victorian, lightweight opaque glass
that is often blue. Some of the glass was decorated with enamels.*

BRISTOL, Biscuit Jar, Enameled Herons, Flowers, Strawberry Finial, Blue	135.00
Biscuit Jar, Floral Design, Silver Plate Lid, Green Ground	145.00
Buscuit Jar, Pink Flowers, Silver Plated Top Rim & Handle, Green	95.00
Jar, Powder, Floral Pattern, Semiopaque Frosted, 6 In.	50.00
Jar, Tobacco, Off-White, Autumn Color Decoration	75.00
Vase, Art Nouveau, Tulip Design, Frosted, 7 X 9 In.	48.00
Vase, Barrel Shape, Design, 5 1/4 X 12 1/2 In.	75.00
Vase, Blue, Gold, & Copper Design, Beads On Flowers, 11 1/4 In., Pair	135.00
Vase, Bud, Enameled Hummingbird & Flowers, 7 1/2 In.	85.00
Vase, Butterflies & Flowers, Frosted, 11 In.	75.00
Vase, Cream, Enameled Water Flowers, 4 In.	35.00
Vase, Florals & Leaves, Gold Trim, Frosted, 9 In.	25.00
Vase, Green, Hand-Painted, C.1890, 11 1/2 In., Pair	345.00
Vase, Pale Yellow Ground, Cameo Reserve, 13 In.	70.00
Vase, Rose, Red Neck, Gold Beading, 10 1/2 In.	24.00
Vase, Stick, Painted Sienna Floral Design, 9 1/2 In.	35.00
Vase, Turkeys, Trees, White Beading, Pink Top, 18 In., Pair	500.00
Vase, White & Orange Flowers, Leaves, C.1880, 9 In., Pair	80.00
Vase, White, Orange & Gold, Pedestal, Ruffled Edge, 7 In.Pair	100.00
BRITANNIA, see Pewter	
BRONZE, Ashtray, Dog With Duck In Mouth	45.00
Base, Lamp, Ram's Head	150.00
Bell, Cow, Tassel, Cast Clapper, 5 In.	13.00
Bell, Locomotive, Clapper & Stationery Mount, 13 In.Diam.	300.00
Bell, On Yoke, Pearson's Son	850.00
Bell, Rampant Lion, Iron Stand, 57 In.	175.00
Bit, Horse, 1800-800 B.C., Persia, Twisted Pattern, 8 In.	135.00
Bookends, Angelus	60.00
Bookends, Austrian, Girl Seated On Draped Persian Carpet, 4 1/8 In.	170.00
Bookends, Bengal Tiger, Rearing, China, 8 X 6 1/2 In.	425.00
Bookends, Bonjeur, Horses	50.00
Bookends, Bust Of Washington	45.00
Bookends, The Aviator, Lindbergh, Dated 1929	50.00
Bookends, The Hunters	50.00
Bowl, Raised Figure Of Woman Warrior, Signed, Dated 1867, 10 In.	375.00
Box, Lidded, Shape Of Standing Rig, 3 X 4 In.	100.00
Burner, Incense, Allover Turtle Design, Foo Dog Finial, 4 1/4 In.	135.00
Burner, Incense, Form Of Eagle, 19th Century, Oriental, 24 In.	600.00
Burner, Incense, Japanese, 5 In.	110.00
Bust, Chariclea, French Woman, Signed, 15 3/4 In.	275.00
Bust, Charles Dickens, 18 In.	1050.00
Bust, Houdon, Madame Recamier, Green Patina, 24 1/2 In.	1200.00
Bust, Kauba, Portrait, Mozart, 8 In.	325.00
Bust, Napoleon Bonaparte, Marked, C.1808, 17 3/4 In.	450.00
Bust, R.Colombo, Napoleon Bonaparte, Dated 1885, 22 In.	2500.00

Candelabra, Austria, Woman, Bird, 2 Deer, Signed L.Hagenauer, 16 In. 595.00
Candelabra, Circular, Dish In Center, 6-Candle, 22 In. 115.00
Candlestick, Cobra, Striking Position, 8 1/2 In., Pair 250.00
Candlestick, Danish, Nude Male Figures, C.1920, 12 In., Pair 250.00
Candlestick, Flying Dragon, 7 X 7 In. 150.00
Candlestick, Japanese Phoenix, Cloisonne Socket, 2-Candle, 11 1/2 In. 750.00
Cup, French, C.1870, Leaves & Berries, Basalt Base, Handled, Pair 950.00
Desk Set, Seated Military Figure, Marble Base, French, 16 X 11 In. 1075.00
Door Knocker, Hand Holding Pearl Of Bronze, Ruffled Cuff 85.00
Ewer, French, 19th Century, Verde Antico Marble, 14 In., Pair 950.00
Ewer, Ovoid, Double Handle, Water Nymph, Sitting By Pond, 16 In. 2000.00
Figurine, A Le Veel, Drummer, 19th Century, 19 In. 700.00
Figurine, Adnet, Couple Dancing The Tango, 13 3/8 In. 8000.00
Figurine, Arabian Thoroughbred, Marble Plinth, 13 In. 1300.00
Figurine, Ariadne, French, C.1900, 32 In. 900.00
Figurine, Augustus Caesar, Ebonized Wood Pedestal, 86 In. 4100.00
Figurine, Austria, Bull, Ivory Horns, 10 1/4 X 6 1/4 In. 375.00
Figurine, Austria, Children Riding Goats, C.1900, 3 In. 175.00
Figurine, Austria, Mare & Foal, Marble Base, 7 X 5 7/8 In. 140.00
Figurine, Bacchante, Young, Sitting On Grapes, 8 1/2 In. 500.00
Figurine, Barye, Hunting Dog, Signed, 4 5/8 X 9 1/2 In. 1500.00
Figurine, Barye, Panther Seizing Stag, Marked, 21 In. 1400.00
Figurine, Barye, Spaniel, Golden Brown Patina, Marked, 6 1/2 In. 275.00
Figurine, Barye, Walking Tiger, Marked, 15 1/4 In. 800.00
Figurine, Boar, Being Attacked By 3 Dogs, Circular Base, 5 In. 375.00
Figurine, Bonheur, Fox, Peers Into Ledge For Food, 21 X 10 In. 2950.00
Figurine, Boy On Elephant, American Coin Foundry Mark 340.00
Figurine, Boy, Nude, With Arrows, Marble Base 350.00
Figurine, Brenda Putnam, Nude Child, 1923, Kunst Foundry, N.Y. 2250.00
Figurine, Buddha, Ceylon, 5 In. 150.00
Figurine, Bull, Ivory Horns, Head Lowered, 7 In. 250.00
Figurine, Bulldog, Standing, 2 3/4 In. 16.00
Figurine, Bulldog, 6 In. 125.00
Figurine, C.Corschann, Shepherdess & Flock, Founder's Mark, 15 In. 1500.00
Figurine, Child, Enfant A La Mouche, C.1900, 22 1/2 In. 1400.00
Figurine, Chinese Scholar, On Horseback, Reading Book, 13 In. 750.00
Figurine, Chotka, Eagle On Rock, 9 In.Wingspread, Austria, 6 In. 325.00
Figurine, Cornworth, Girl & Boy Looking At Nest Of Birds, 15 In. 3000.00
Figurine, Cougar, On Rocks, Cold Cast, 6 In. 65.00
Figurine, Cow, Standing, Raised Head, Oval Base, 9 1/2 In. 425.00
Figurine, Dalous, A Worker, Spade In Hand, Marked, 8 In. 850.00
Figurine, Dante, Basalt Base, Marked, 20 In. 700.00
Figurine, Discobolus, Discus Thrower, 19 1/4 In. 1950.00
Figurine, E.Fremiet, Dog, Stretching Pose, 7 1/2 X 3 1/2 In. 750.00
Figurine, E.Gruet, Nude, Head In Hands, Foundry Mark, 7 In. 750.00
Figurine, E.T.C., Madonna & Child, Gorham Founders, 1931, 11 5/8 In. 160.00
Figurine, Elephant, Ivory Tusk, 5 1/2 In. 100.00
Figurine, Exotic Dancer, Ivory Face & Arms, Marble Base, 21 In. 7000.00
Figurine, F.Iffland, Child With Wheat, Dated 1886 .... 600.00
Figurine, F.Ouillon Carrere, Nude On Toes, 1919, 21 1/2 In. 625.00
Figurine, F.Pautrot, Bird, Wings Lifted, Head Down, C.1870, 4 7/8 In. 200.00
Figurine, F.Pautrot, Partridge Hen & Chick, C.1870, Signed, 5 1/8 In. 100.00
Figurine, F.Pautrot, Rabbit, Crouching, Signed, 3 3/8 X 5 3/8 In. 600.00
Figurine, Falkin, Girl Holding Cloche Against Wind, 4 In. 225.00
Figurine, Farmer, Brown Patina, Marked, 24 In. 1000.00
Figurine, Female Golfer, C.1925, Beret & Pantaloons, 12 3/4 In. 800.00
Figurine, Flute Player, Brown Patina, Inscribed, 28 In. 1700.00
Figurine, Foo Lion, Sits On Haunches, Oriental Table Base, 9 In. 125.00
Figurine, French, Sans Famille, Orphaned Itinerant Musician, 19 In. 1300.00
Figurine, Girl On Basket, French, Cherie 30, Signed, Dated 295.00
Figurine, Girl, Holding Cloche Against Wind, Signed, 4 In. 225.00
Figurine, Greguire, Woman, Classical, Brown Patina, 27 In. 1700.00
Figurine, Greugante, Boxer, 23 In. 1950.00

Figurine, H.Muller, Whippet, Ears Perked, Signed, 8 1/4 X 7 1/2 In. 300.00
Figurine, Harriet W.Frishmuth, Star, Nude Woman, 1918, 20 In. 2600.00
Figurine, Hirobi, Samurai, Gilded Hat, Meiji Period, Signed, 8 1/2 In. 2800.00
Figurine, Hoko, Samurai, Gilded Kimono, Signed, 10 3/4 In. 1300.00
Figurine, Horse, C.1880, Oriental, 6 In. 135.00
Figurine, Hunter & Huntress, Basalt Base, 26 1/2 In. 2000.00
Figurine, I.Bonheur, Les Animalier, Racehorse & Jockey, Signed, 46 In. 7500.00
Figurine, J. De Roncourt, Man In Chains, C.1820, Signed, 28 X 17 In. 375.00
Figurine, J.Moigniez, Bird, 19th Century, Marked, 13 1/2 In. 900.00
Figurine, J.Pollet, Star Of Evening, Allegorical Figure, 48 5/8 In. 4200.00
Figurine, Jacques Bousseau, Soldier Bending A Bow, 18 1/2 In. 750.00
Figurine, Jas.L.Clark, Water Buffalo, C.1913, Marked, 17 1/4 In. 1500.00
Figurine, Jean-Leon Gerome, Bather, Foundry Seal, 12 1/4 In. 3000.00
Figurine, Jester & Puppet, Brown Patina, Marked, 22 In. 1100.00
Figurine, Jo Davidson, Reginal C.Vanderbilt, Signed 600.00
Figurine, Kauba, Crouching Indian With Bow & Arrow 350.00
Figurine, Kauba, Indian, Little Soldier, 7 1/2 In. 450.00
Figurine, Kauba, Kneeling Indian Holding Rifle, Signed 500.00
Figurine, Kauba, Lohengrin, C.1900, 28 In. 1700.00
Figurine, Keck, Dancer, Flowing Frock, Raised Leg, Signed, 5 In. 170.00
Figurine, Knight, Credo, Red Marble Base, Tan Stand, Marked, 15 In. 550.00
Figurine, Kossowski, Laborer, Allegorical, C.1900, Marked, 12 1/2 In. 500.00
Figurine, Kubart, Stag, Marble Base, Dark Patina, 10 In. 395.00
Figurine, Lecon De Danse, 26 1/2 In. 3500.00
Figurine, Leda & The Swan, Green Onyx Base, Signed, 9 3/4 In. 525.00
Figurine, Lobster, Spiny, Life Size, Joints Move, 9 1/2 In. 250.00
Figurine, Lorenzal, Pierette, C.1920, Art Deco, 5 1/2 In. 575.00
Figurine, Luxor, Tutankhamen, The Harpooner, 1922, 9 1/2 X 11 In. 395.00
Figurine, M.Montagne, Mercury, Brown Patina, 1867, Marked, 32 In. 1400.00
Figurine, Maris, Equestrian, Signed, 34 X 34 In. 3500.00
Figurine, Max Kruse, Nenikhkamen, Nude Male Runner, 23 X 19 In. 1200.00
Figurine, Mercury, Stepped Basalt Base, 25 In. 400.00
Figurine, Moigniez, Setter, Long Haired, Pointing Stance, 9 X 13 In. 575.00
Figurine, Monkey, Basket Strapped To Back, Brown Patina, 8 In. 350.00
Figurine, Moreau, Girl, Signed, 18 In. 375.00
Figurine, N.Greb, Dancing Maiden, C.1900, Movable, Marked, 5 7/8 In. 650.00
Figurine, Oriental Dancing Girl, C.1900, 5 1/2 In. 100.00
Figurine, Otter, Fish On Rock, Signed, 6 X 5 In. 225.00
Figurine, P.Dubois, Boy Street Vendor, With Jug, Signed, 16 1/8 In. 375.00
Figurine, P.J.Mene, Arab Stallion, C.1850 .... 2400.00
Figurine, P.J.Mene, Cavalier King Charles Spaniel, C.1840 .... 300.00
Figurine, P.J.Mene, Greyhound & King Charles Spaniel, C.1848 .... 600.00
Figurine, P.J.Mene, Pointer, Standing Pose, Signed, 7 5/8 In. 150.00
Figurine, P.J.Mene, Setter, Signed, 5 X 5 1/2 In. 215.00
Figurine, P.J.Mene, Stallion & Dog, Saddled, Rock Base, 27 In. 4250.00
Figurine, Pan & Grappilleuse, Green Patina, Marked, 1900, 29 In. 1400.00
Figurine, Panther, Reclining, Wolf Caught In Trap, 6 1/2 In. 250.00
Figurine, Peasants, Two, Inscribed Picault, 22 In. 1600.00
Figurine, Peiffer, Child & Setter, Signed, 11 3/4 X 10 In. 425.00
Figurine, Pelicans, Silvered, Ivory, 9 5/8 In., Pair 600.00
Figurine, Piat, Blackamoors, Male & Female, Marked, 27 1/2 In., Pair 4250.00
Figurine, Podany, Dewdrops, 2 Women, C.1900, Marked, 24 3/4 In. 1600.00
Figurine, Pointer, Leafy Ground, Brown Patina, 12 1/2 In. 300.00
Figurine, Putti, French, Mounted On Gray Marble, 9 In., Pair 900.00
Figurine, R.Bagatti, Lioness, Nubian, 26 1/2 In. 8000.00
Figurine, Richard The Lionhearted In Battle Dress, 15 In. 375.00
Figurine, Roman Charioteer, Marble Base, Inscribed, 16 In. 1300.00
Figurine, Rosa Bonheur, Cow, 4 3/4 X 3 1/4 In. 400.00
Figurine, Ruffled Grouse, On Tree Trunk, Geshutz, 4 3/4 In. 290.00
Figurine, Russian, Men On Horses, 12 In. .... *Illus* 700.00
Figurine, Samurai On Horse, Exposition Paris 1900, 13 1/4 In. 3300.00
Figurine, Spaniel, Bird In Mouth, Rabbit On Side, 6 In. 350.00

Bronze, Figurine, Russian, Men On Horses, 12 In.

Figurine, Stag, Listening, Standing, Raised Head, 7 In. 300.00
Figurine, Stags, Two, Fighting, Greenish Brown Patina, 21 In. 1100.00
Figurine, T.Cartier, Panther, Preparing To Pounce, Marked, 15 1/2 In. 400.00
Figurine, Temple Dancer, 5 In. 250.00
Figurine, Thai Dancers, Headdress, Costumes, Wood Base, 44 In., Pr. 3500.00
Figurine, Trodoux, Partridge On Rock, Signed, C.1875, 7 3/8 In. 250.00
Figurine, Two Wolves, Silver Finish, Signed, French, 15 1/2 In. 850.00
Figurine, V.Chemin, Boar, Green Marble Plinth, 7 1/4 X 7 1/4 In. 185.00
Figurine, Vienna, Antlered Deer, 2 1/4 In. 95.00
Figurine, Vienna, Black Boy Lying Prone, Looking At Kettle, 5 1/2 In. 175.00
Figurine, Vienna, Black Couple, He Pleads For Forgiveness 275.00
Figurine, Vienna, Brown Bulldog, Seated Inside Lady's Glove, 3 In. 150.00
Figurine, Vienna, Cat Playing With Ball 60.00
Figurine, Vienna, Dachshund Lying On Back On Pillow 85.00
Figurine, Vienna, Dachshund Sitting, Singing Over Sheet Music 85.00
Figurine, Vienna, Dancing Harem Girl With Mask, Onyx Base, 9 1/2 In. 160.00
Figurine, Vienna, Fox, Seated, Red-Brown, White Chest, 2 In. 85.00
Figurine, Vienna, Red-Tufted Woodpecker, 3 X 4 In. 115.00
Figurine, Vienna, Stallion, Brown With Black Mane, 6 X 5 In. 225.00
Figurine, Vienna, Terrier, 5 In.Long 250.00
Figurine, Vienna, Woman On Gray Mule, Foundry Mark, 5 1/2 In. 495.00
Figurine, Waagan, Whippet, Signed, 20 1/2 X 16 In. 3500.00
Figurine, Waagen, Terrier, Playing With Ball, Signed, C.1869, 4 1/4 In. 100.00
Figurine, Woman, Farm, Bag Over Shoulder, Marked, 4 1/2 In. 225.00
Figurine, Woman, Seated, Breton, Holding Umbrella, 5 5/8 In. 200.00
Figurine, Zach, Three Nymphs, Dancing With Flower Garland, 14 In. 1200.00
Flowerpot, Incised Iris, Austrian, Miniature 25.00
Frame, Easel, Grotesque Fat At Top & Corners, 5 X 7 In. 75.00
Group, Caresse De L'amour, Brown Patina, Marked, 36 In. 3250.00
Group, Claude Michel Clodion, Three Satyrs & A Nymph, Signed, 30 In. 2500.00
Group, Reveil De Genie, Allegorical, Foundry Mark, 4 Ft. 4 In. 4000.00
Group, Two Bacchantes, Brown Patina, Marble Base, 27 In. 3000.00
Hibachi, 4-Panel Relief, Elephant Handles, 1840-1850, 10 In. 450.00
Incense Burner, Foo Dog Lid, Monster Head Handles, 4 1/2 X 4 1/2 In. 235.00
Inkwell, Conch Form, Pen Tray, 2 Tritons On Rim, French, 10 3/8 In. 3600.00
Iron, Charcoal, Oriental, Dragons & Floral Design, Set Of 3 .... 70.00
Lamp, C.Perron, Illuminated, C.1900, Lavender Shade, 26 1/2 In. 875.00

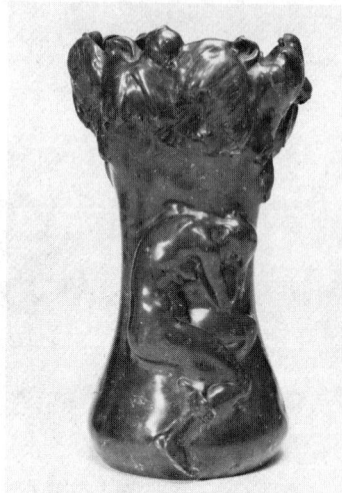

Bronze, Vase, 19th Century, French, Vital Cornu

Bronze, Urn, Japanese, Revolves, 30 In.

Lamp, Champleve, 26 In. 200.00
Lamp, Gold-Painted, Austrian, Signed Bergman, 30 In. 3950.00
Lamp, Th.Ullman, Cowboy On Rearing Horse, 15 In. 850.00
Lamp, 19th Century Chinese, Glass Dome Shade, 29 In. 800.00
Lighter, Cigarette, Ivory Boar Head, 6 In. 250.00
Mirror & Brush, Painting On Ivory, French, Signed 325.00
Mirror, Circular, Stylized Art Deco Foot, 19 1/4 In. 1300.00
Mirror, Pierced Scroll, Leaf Crest, Signed Oscar B.Bach, 28 1/2 In. 70.00
Mortar & Pestle, Bust Of French Monarch, 4 3/4 In. 180.00
Mortar, Earlike Side Ornaments, 5 1/2 In. 155.00
Mortar, Flower Design, Small Handles, 4 5/8 In. 125.00
Mortar, 4 Faces Crowned Monarch, 4 1/4 In. 75.00
Plaque, Young Boy, Edgar, Jr., Nantucket, 1911, Framed, 18 X 18 In. 350.00
Plate, Kneeling Nymph, A.Ledru, Polychrome, 1o 1/4 In., Pair 750.00
Seal, Figural, Foo Dog, Pair 100.00
Seal, Figural, Owl, Garnet Eyes 145.00
Tamper, Tobacco, Standing Nude Woman, 18th Century 130.00
Tazza, Oval, Heads & Torso Of Nymphs, Signed England, 8 In. 1500.00
Tray, Art Nouveau, Woman's Portrait, C.1900, 5 In. 120.00
Urn, Japanese, Revolves, 30 In. .... Illus 1000.00
Vase, Applied Dragon, Dragon Stand, 19th Century, Japanese, 35 1/2 In. 2600.00
Vase, Double Gourd Form, 3 Carp Swimming, Hanging Wisteria, 21 In. 700.00
Vase, Dragon, Clouds, Elephant Head Handles, 8 3/4 In. 110.00
Vase, Draped Nymph Rising From Pansies, Signed Lorschann, 17 In. 2400.00
Vase, Gu-Form, Abstract Design, Scalloped Ridges, 10 1/4 In. 50.00
Vase, Oriental, Ibis, Hibiscus, Leaves, Geometric Border, 14 In. 200.00
Vase, Putto Above Birds, Fluted Lip, Signed H.F.Moreau, 22 In. 700.00
Vase, Silver Thistle Design, C.1912, Signed, 8 In. 225.00
Vase, Sterling Silver Overlay, Marked & Dated 1912, 5 In. 90.00
Vase, 19th Century, French, Vital Cornu .... Illus 1000.00
Weight, Desk, Reclining Nymph, On Elbows, French, 12 1/2 X 4 3/8 In. 1100.00

*Brownies were first drawn in 1883 by Palmer Cox. They are
characterized by large round eyes, down-turned mouths, and skinny legs.*

BROWNIES, Book, Brownies & Their Book, Illustrated, Century, 1915	15.00
Book, The Brownies, Their Book, Signed Palmer Cox, 1915	49.50
Cup, Child's, Palmer Cox On Sides	40.00
Dish, Feeding.Black & White	28.00
Figurine, Lithographed, Wooden, Palmer Cox, 10 In., Set Of 10	275.00
Game, Palmer Cox	30.00
Lithograph, Palmer Cox, C.1900, Wooden, 10 In.	280.00
Mug, Brownies On Seesaw, Palmer Cox, Sterling Silver	115.00
Paper Toy, Dude On Donkey, Palmer Cox, 3 X 4 3/4 In.	12.50
Paperweight, Palmer Cox	30.00 To 55.00
Plate, Palmer Cox, 7 In.	45.00
Plate, Ripple Edge, Palmer Cox, 7 In.Diam.	30.00
Stamping Blocks, 1 Black, 11 Brown	45.00
Stickpin, Palmer Cox	18.00
Tea Set, Palmer Cox, Playing Musical Instruments, 12 Piece	150.00
Tray, Palmer Cox	40.00
BUCK ROGERS, Atomic Pistol	95.00
Battle Cruiser, Tootsietoy	35.00 To 50.00
Bomb Sight	60.00
Book, Big Little Book, Moons Of Saturn	19.50
Book, Kelloggs	100.00
Book, Pop-Up	185.00
Game, Dart Gun	35.00
Gun, Daisy, 25th Century	65.00
Gun, Smoke Ring Ray, Ammo	37.00
Gun, Sonic Ray	45.00
Laboratory, Chemical, 1937, Gropper Toys	750.00
Pencil Box, No.3609, 1936	45.00
Pistol, Atomic, Book, Boxed	100.00
Pistol, Liquid Helium, Tin, Lithograph	150.00 To 300.00
Pistol, Pop, Daisy, C.1934	75.00
Pistol, Pop, 25th Century, Daisy	47.50
Pistol, Water, Metal, Repeater	13.00
Ray Gun, Metal	75.00
Roller Skates	1800.00
Space Kit	85.00
Spaceship, Boxed	585.00
Stamp, Rubber, On Wooden Block	25.00
Tumbler, Supersonic, Plastic, 1953	12.50
Watch, Pocket	55.00 To 185.00

*Buffalo pottery was made in Buffalo, New York, after 1902. The company
was established by the Larkin Company, famous manufacturers of soap. The
wares are marked with a picture of a buffalo and the date of manufacture.
Deldare ware is the most famous pottery made at the factory. It is a
khaki-colored transfer-decorated ware.*

BUFFALO POTTERY DELDARE, Bowl, Village Scenes, 9 In.	450.00
Bowl, Ye Village Tavern, C.1909, Signed, 9 1/8 In.	330.00
Bowl, Ye Village Tavern, Signed K.Stewart, 9 In.	295.00
Bowl, Ye Village Tavern, 9 3/4 In.	340.00
Bowl, Yellow Roses, Green Ground, Gold Trim, Marked	85.00
Candlestick, Signed, 9 In., Pair	595.00
Charger, An Evening At Ye Lion Inn, Signed	425.00
Charger, The Fallowfield Hunt, Signed, 14 In.	615.00
Cider Set, Fallowfield Hunt, C.1909, 6 Piece	1700.00
Cream & Sugar, Artist Signed	325.00
Cup & Saucer, Ye Olden Days	160.00

Cup, Ye Olden Days 65.00
Hair Receiver 249.00
Humidor, Ye Lion Inn, Artist Signed, 7 In. 575.00
Mug, Fallowfield Hunt, At Three Pigeons 240.00
Mug, Hunt Scene, 4 1/2 In. 265.00
Pitcher, Fallowfield Hunt, Breaking Cover 350.00
Pitcher, Go Collect Rent, 8 1/2 In. .... 395.00 To 440.00
Pitcher, Manner Of Telling Stories, Signed, 6 In. 365.00
Pitcher, Village Scenes, 7 In. 85.00
Pitcher, Ye Lion Inn, C.1908, Signed, 10 1/8 In. 385.00
Pitcher, 1908, Artist P.Wall Altman, 6 1/2 In. 350.00
Plate, An Evening At Ye Lion Inn, Signed 425.00
Plate, At Ye Lion Inn, 6 1/4 In. .... 100.00 To 110.00
Plate, Card, Fallowfield Hunt, 7 In. 185.00
Plate, Chop, An Evening At Ye Lion Inn, 13 3/4 In. 375.00
Plate, Chop, The Start, Signed, 14 In. 300.00
Plate, Dr.Syntax Disputing Bill, Blue, 9 In. 95.00
Plate, Fallowfield Hunt, Breaking Cover 135.00
Plate, Fallowfield Hunt, The Death, 8 1/4 In. 155.00
Plate, Fallowfield Hunt, The Start .... 150.00 To 180.00
Plate, Fallowfield Hunt, The Start, 7 1/2 In. 125.00
Plate, Olden Times, Signed Wade 225.00
Plate, Ye Olden Times, 9 1/2 In. 150.00
Plate, Ye Town Crier, Signed A.Wade, 8 1/2 In. 165.00
Plate, Ye Village Street, 1908, 7 In. 100.00
Platter, Game, Deer At Stream, Oval, Signed, 15 In. 75.00
Sugar, Covered, Scene Of Village Life, 1925, Signed 100.00
Teapot, Breaking Cover, Signed 170.00
Tile, Dr.Syntax 500.00
Tile, Ye Olden Days, 6 1/4 In.Square 125.00
Tray, Calling Card, Fallowfield Hunt 270.00
Tray, Dancing Ye Minuet, Signed, 9 X 12 In. 495.00
Tray, Dr.Syntax, Rural Sports, 12 1/4 X 9 1/4 In. 850.00
Tray, Fallowfield Hunt, 1909, Signed, 7 In. 125.00
Wash Set, Cairo Pattern 350.00

BUFFALO POTTERY EMERALD, Cup & Saucer, Dr.Syntax & Bookseller 110.00
Plate, Introduction To Courtship 300.00
Plate, Misfortune At Tulip Hall, 8 1/2 In. 425.00
Sugar & Creamer, Scenes Of Village Life, 1924 .... 385.00
Tile, Traveling In Ye Olden Times 275.00

BUFFALO POTTERY, Bowl, Blue Willow, 1909, Square, 4 X 9 In. 45.00
Bowl, Vegetable, Vienna Pattern, Oval 22.00
Cup & Saucer, Roosevelt Bears, 2 1/2 In. 75.00
Gravy Boat, Underplate, Flowers On White 30.00
Hot Toddy Set, Silver Plate Holder 75.00
Pitcher, Bluebirds, 7 In. .... 45.00 To 110.00
Pitcher, Gaudy Willow, 1907, 5 In. 185.00
Pitcher, George Washington, 7 1/2 In. .... 350.00 To 375.00
Pitcher, Geranium 145.00
Pitcher, Marine Jug, 1903, Marked, 9 1/4 In. ....*Illus* 140.00
Pitcher, Pilgrim, Dated 1907, 9 In. 475.00
Pitcher, Pilgrim, Dated 1908 .... 475.00
Pitcher, Robin Hood 295.00
Pitcher, Roosevelt Bears, Dated 1907, 8 In. 395.00
Pitcher, Teddy Roosevelt Bears, Signed 595.00
Plate, Blue Willow, 1910, 9 In. 15.00
Plate, Canton, Green & White, 10 In. 40.00
Plate, Dusky Grouse, Green, 9 In. 40.00
Plate, Faneuil Hall, Boston, Blue & White, 10 In. 43.00
Plate, Faneuil Hall, Boston, 4 In. 40.00

Buffalo Pottery, Pitcher, Marine Jug,
1903, Marked, 9 1/4 In.

Plate, Flying Ducks, 9 In.	40.00
Plate, Geometric Design, 1923, Roycroft Mark, 9 1/4 In., Pair	150.00
Plate, Independence Hall, Philadelphia, Blue & White, 10 In.	43.00
Plate, McKinley Monument, Blue & White, 7 1/2 In.	20.00
Plate, Mt.Vernon, Green, 7 1/2 In.Diam.	35.00
Plate, Niagara Falls, 10 In.	38.00
Plate, Pavilion At Columbia Gardens, Butte, Mont., 7 In.	85.00
Plate, Washington's Home, Blue Green, 10 In.	35.00
Plate, White House, Green & White, 10 In.	40.00
Plate, Wild Ducks, 1907, 9 1/4 In.	50.00
Platter, Blue Willow, 16 X 12 3/4 In.	65.00
Platter, Blue Willow, 1909, 14 X 11 In.	45.00
Platter, Flowers On White, Olive Green, 11 X 15 In.	30.00
BUGGY, Baby, Wicker	250.00

*Burmese glass was developed by Frederick Shirley at the Mt.Washington
Glass Works in New Bedford, Massachusetts, in 1885. It is a two-toned
glass, shading from peach to yellow. Some have a pattern mold design. A few
Burmese pieces were decorated with pictures or applied glass flowers of
colored Burmese glass.*

BURMESE, see also Gunderson

BURMESE, Bowl, Phantom Diamond-Quilted, Leaf Feet, Mt.Washington, 5 1/2 In.	485.00
Candlestick, Twisted Stem, Pair	800.00
Condiment Set, 3 Ribbed Bottles, Pairpoint Holder, Mt.Washington	725.00
Creamer, Yellow Handle, Acid Finish	295.00
Cruet, Melon Ribbed, Pointed Stopper, Mt.Washington	695.00
Cup & Saucer, Mt.Washington	485.00
Hat, Bryden, Upside Down Top Hat, 2 3/4 X 3 1/2 In.	65.00
Lamp, Fairy, Creamy Yellow To Deep Rose, 4 In.	175.00
Lamp, Fairy, Drape Pattern, Inverted Lip Under Dish, 6 In.	150.00
Lamp, Fairy, Gold Pinecones, Marked Clarke Base, 5 1/4 In.	395.00
Mug, Lemonade, Lemon Yellow	290.00
Mug, Lemonade, Lemon, Blush Of Salmon	385.00
Mug, Lemonade, Yellow, Salmon	385.00
Pitcher, Enameled Yellow Rose, Verses, Mt.Washington, 6 In.	1450.00
Pitcher, Hobnail, Mt.Washington, 5 1/2 In.	475.00
Pitcher, Hobnail, 5 1/2 In.	350.00 To 450.00
Pitcher, Satin Finish, Mt.Washington, 3 1/2 In.	435.00
Pitcher, Squat, 19th Century, 6 3/4 In.	325.00
Pitcher, Water, Applied Reed Handle, 10 In.	250.00
Plate, Lemon Yellow, Gold Design, Ruffled, 6 In.	450.00
Plate, Lemon Yellow, Gold Design, Ruffled, 8 In.	650.00

Plate, Salmon To Yellow, Mt.Washington, 9 1/4 In.Diam. 325.00
Rose Jar, Raised Enameled Blossoms, Gold Trim, Mt.Washington, 4 In. 475.00
Salt & Pepper, Ribbed, Tufts Silver Plated Holder, Mt.Washington 285.00
Sugar, Glossy, Pedestal Foot, Open, Mt.Washington, 2 X 3 1/4 In. 195.00
Toothpick, Diamond-Quilted 275.00
Toothpick, Diamond-Quilted, Acid Finish, Square 300.00
Top Hat, Upside Down, Basket Weave Design, 2 3/4 X 3 1/2 In. 45.00
Tumbler, Diamond-Quilted, Miniature 250.00
Urn, 2-Handled, Acid Finish, 20th Century, Mt.Washington, 13 1/2 In. 675.00
Vase, Bud, Sprig Of Forget-Me-Nots, Enameled, C.1890, 9 3/4 In. 375.00
Vase, Gourd Shape, Blue Machine Stitch 400.00
Vase, Lily, Acid Finish, New Bedford, Mass., 13 In. 250.00
Vase, Lily, Acid Finish, 9 In. 495.00
Vase, Lily, Yellow Edge, Mt.Washington, 6 In. 375.00
Vase, Long Neck, 4 Legs, Yellow To Salmon Pink, Mt.Washington, 8 In. 1100.00
Vase, Ovoid Shape, Low Neck, C.1886, 4 1/2 In. 70.00
Vase, Pulpit, 11 In. 595.00
Vase, Ruffled, Bulbous, Flare Neck, C.1886, 4 1/2 In. 275.00
    BURMESE, WEBB, see Webb Burmese

BUSTER BROWN, Bank, Iron Horseshoe, With Tige 150.00
Blocks, Alphabet, Puzzle & Pictures 105.00
Book, And The Donkey, Muslin Cloth, 1905, Signed Outcault 45.00
Book, No.4, 1910, Blue Ribbon Shoes 35.00
Button, With Tige, Buster Brown Blue Ribbon Shoes 10.00
Camera, With Tige, Original Box, 1910 .... 275.00 To 350.00
Child's Set, Knife, Fork, & Spoon, Silver Plate 45.00
Cup & Saucer, Buster Pouring Water 25.00
Game, Pin The Tie On, Cloth 95.00
Knife & Fork, Salad 35.00
Knife, Coin Silver 18.50
Mannequin, 1930s, 36 In. 150.00
Mirror, Pocket With Tige, Dated 1946 .... 5.00
Mug 85.00
Pencil, Mechanical 12.00
Pillow, With Tige 45.00
Pin, Bread 20.00
Plate, Buster Pouring Tea For Tige 45.00
Postcard, 1909 .... 8.00
Poster, Buster's Mix-Up, Laid On Linen, C.1919 .... 165.00
Roly Poly, 4 3/8 In. 138.00
Stationery, Color, Lithograph Picture With Tige, 6 X 9 In. 2.00
Tin, Mustard 23.00
Tobacco Jar, Tam Lifts Off As Lid 150.00
Toy, Dog Tige 45.00
Tray, Pin 35.00
Whistle 18.00
    BUTTER MOLD, see Kitchen, Mold, Butter
    BUTTERMILK GLASS, see Custard Glass

Buttons have been known throughout the centuries, and there are millions of styles. Only a few are listed for comparison.

BUTTON, Advertising, Red Comb Poultry, Celluloid 6.00
Art Nouveau, Lady With Flowing Hair, 4/5 In. 8.00
Child In Dance Position, Signed Chi, Nickel Size 3.00
Cloisonne, 1 1/4 In., Pair 15.00
Cupid, Sterling Silver, English 10.00
Eagle & Wreath, Civil War, Brass 5.00
Fireman's, Beaded Rim, Fire Horn In Relief, 1 In.Diam., Set Of 6 .... 12.00
German Shepherd Dog Encased In Glass 3.00
Gibson Girl, 1 1/2 In. 20.00
Glass, Opalescent Pink, Set Of 4 .... 8.00

Heart, Sterling Silver, English 12.00
Paperweight, Pairpoint, Set Of 5 .... 15.00
Persian Nobleman, Ivory Encased In Sterling Silver & Glass 45.00
Raised Sphinx & Word Egypt 8.00
Rope Edge, Bead Center, Sterling Silver, 1 1/8 In.Diam., Set Of 8 .... 125.00

BUTTONHOOK, Advertising, F.L.George, Dery, N.H. 12.00
Buy W.J.Youngs, One Side, Rochester Shoe, Other Side 5.00
Doll, Wire, 2 1/2 In. 5.00
Embossed Floral Handle, Unger Brothers Mark 30.00
Figural, Lady's Leg With High Button Top Shoe 45.00
Folding, Walk-Over Shoes 7.50
Glove, Brass Handle, Engraved 22.50
Shoe, Pearl Handle, Large 10.00

BYBEE, Candleholder, Twisted Column, Domed Base, Turquoise, 3 X 6 In. 6.00
    CALCITE, see Steuben

CALENDAR PAPER, 1873, Scovill's Farmers & Mechanics 6.50
1877, Liverpool Almanac, Advertising, Blue, White, 7 3/4 In. 195.00
1879, Pocket, Home Insurance Co., Children 3.50
1880, Scottish Insurance Company 22.00
1888, Carnrich Food, Picture Of Baby 38.00
1889, Clarks Thread, Framed 22.00
1889, Hood's Sarsaparilla 14.00
1891, Walter A.Wood Co., Farm Equipment, Cord Tied, 6 X 7 In. 19.00
1892, Hood's Sarsaparilla 38.00
1894, Hood's Sarsaparilla 35.00
1895, Sanford Ginger Ale 39.00
1897, Sweet Message, Tuck 40.00
1898, Prudential Insurance 35.00
1899, Hoods 40.00
1899, Lord's Fish 10.00
1900, Fairy Soap, Patriotic Girl, 10 X 12 1/2 In. 45.00
1900, Haines General Mds., Penna., 13 X 15 1/2 In. 31.50
1901, Grand Union Tea Company 50.00
1901, 3 Month, Phoenix Insurance, Framed 18.00
1902, Hood's Sarsaparilla, Columbia's Daughters 15.00
1904, Edgerton, Minnesota, Bouquet Of Roses, 20 In. 15.00
1904, National Life Ins.Co., 8 In.Diam. 35.00
1904, Ohio Farmers Insurance 30.00
1904, Val Blatz 300.00
1905, Bell-Cap-Sic Plaster 10.00
1905, Continental Fire Insurance 18.00
1905, Flower Lifts To Reveal Months, Trinidad, Colorado 85.00
1905, National Life Ins.Co., 8 In.Diam. 35.00
1906, Autumn, Philip Boileau, 10 X 19 In. 50.00
1906, Glavanic Soap, Die Cut 32.00
1906, Grandma, Child Wearing Specs, Reading, Framed 35.00
1906, National Life Ins.Co., 8 In.Diam. 35.00
1908, Dr.Daniel's Tonic Pills, Sepia, 8 3/4 X 12 In. 22.50
1908, Metropolitan Life Insurance Co., Boileau 125.00
1909, DeLaval, Mailing Tube 37.50
1909, Gibson Type Girl, 8 In. 18.00
1909, Grafton, West Virginia 35.00
1909, Holly Wreath, Wisconsin Advertising 28.00
1909, Peaches & Blackberries, Illinois Advertising 28.00
1909, Roses & Lilac, Oregon Advertising 33.00
1909, Water Lilies, Nebraska Advertising 33.00
1910, A Passing Glance, Philip Boileau, 5 X 10 In. 30.00
1910, Betsy Ross, Flag, & Washington 25.00
1910, Chrysanthemum, Illinois Advertising 15.00

1910, Gibson Girl, Rose Border, Signed A.Gumn	25.00
1911, Biplane	50.00
1911, Delft, Windmill Scene	48.00
1911, Double Poppies, West Virginia Advertising	30.00
1911, Scenic, Flowers, Advertising	26.00
1912, Brewery Poster Girl, Springfield Breweries	195.00
1912, Fidelity Phoenix Insurance	18.00
1912, Woman, Beer Wagons	11.00
1912, Zetts Beer	200.00
1913, Flowers, Advertising Muskegon, Mich, , 9 1/4 In.	20.00
1913, Hold To Light Art, Lady With Basket, 9 3/8 In.	65.00
1913, Selby Ammunition, 21 X 27 In.	195.00
1914, Singer Sewing Machine	19.00
1916, Atlantic Refining Co., Card	3.00
1917, Chero Cola, Brunette Holding Bottle, 36 X 20 In.	350.00
1918, Metropolitan Life Ins. Co., Infant, Mother, 9 X 14 In.	12.50
1920, Winchester, Hunter & Son Unloading Ducks, 20 X 39 In.	575.00
1922, Savage Stevens, Deer On Mountain, 14 X 28 In.	295.00
1923, Each Month Has Movie Actor & Actress	30.00
1924, Advertising, Ranger, Texas	25.00
1924, Mountain & Lake Scene	17.00
1926, Fisk Tire, Desk	22.50
1926, Littletown Bakery, Pa., Pretty Girl	12.00
1927, Florida East Coast Fertilizer Co.	8.00
1927, Savage & Stevens	125.00
1927, Wrigley Double Mint Gum	25.00
1928, Vulcan Tool Mfg. Co., Artist Signed, 7 1/4 X 9 1/4 In.	7.50
1930, Boston, Maine R.R.	95.00
1930, DeLaval Separator, Norman Price Illustrations	25.00
1930, Edison Mazda, M.Parrish, 8 X 18 In.	225.00 To 250.00
1931, Wyeth McCormick Reaper	50.00
1932, Robinson Paint Supplies, Dogs, 2 1/2 X 11 In.	6.50
1933, G.E.Mazda Lamps, Sunrise, Signed Maxfield Parrish	125.00
1936, Dionne Quints	7.50
1936, Hercules Powder Co.	135.00
1936, In Golden Hunting Grounds, 20 X 15 In.	15.00
1936, Phillips 66, Truck Shape, Desk	15.00
1937, Hercules Powder Co.	135.00
1937, Kinter Milling Co., Hunter Petting Dog, 36 X 18 In.	125.00
1937, Traveler's Insurance Co., Lithograph, 10 X 13 1/2 In.	6.50
1939, Picture, 4 X 11 In.	3.00
1939, Rock Island	26.50
1939, Utica Beer, Franklin Roosevelt	75.00
1940, John Morrell Co., Wyeth Illustrations, 12 Prints	25.00
1941, Dionne Quintuplets	15.00
1945, Boy Scout, Rockwell Illustration	18.00
1945, Esquire, Varga, Envelope	32.00
1948, Dr.Pepper	43.00
1948, Dr.Pepper, Cover Sheet	35.00
1949, Dr.Pepper	40.00
1949, Ruppert Beer & Ale	12.00
1949, Squirt	18.00 To 35.00
1950, Ruppert, Envelope	20.00
1952, Nude Marilyn Monroe	9.00
1952, Red & White Grocery, Elves	10.00
1952, Tydol & Veedol	8.00
1953, Marilyn Monroe, Nude	12.00
1953, Orange Crush	40.00
1960, Ward's Drugs, Athol, Mass.	12.00
1970, Remington, 12 Full-Color Game Pictures	45.00
1977, Ken Dallison, 12 Vintage Autos, Full Color, 21 X 23 In.	250.00

Calendar plates were very popular in the United States from 1906 to 1929. Since then plates have been made every year. A calendar, the name of a store, a picture of flowers, a girl, or a scene was featured on the plate.

CALENDAR PLATE, 1908, New Year's Greeting, 7 1/2 In.	30.00
1909, Fruit, Illinois Advertising, 7 1/2 In.	27.50
1909, Livermore Falls, Maine	24.00
1909, Multicolored Poppies, 9 1/2 In.	15.00
1910, Betsy Ross	30.00
1910, Poppies, Missouri Advertising, 8 1/2 In.	25.00
1910, Portrait, Signed	35.00
1910, Washington House At Mt.Vernon, 10 In.	30.00
1910, 2 Angels Ringing Liberty Bell	25.00
1911, Carnations With Advertising	25.00
1911, Double Poppies, California Advertising, 8 1/2 In.	30.00
1911, 2nd Anniversary, Jarl Bros., Woodburn, Iowa	15.00
1912, Martha Washington, 9 In.	25.00
1912, Owl On Book, Ruff & Son, Bremen, Ohio	35.00
1915, Panama Canal, New York Advertising, 7 In.	25.00
1919, Pheasants	45.00
1920, World War, Advertising, 7 In.	27.50
1921, Bluebirds Around Border	25.00

CAMARK, Planter, Cornucopia	9.00
Planter, Doe, Sticker, Green, 5 In.	4.00
Vase, Bulbous, Loop Top Handles, Matte Green Over Brown, 4 1/2 In.	8.00
Vase, Drip Green, Yellow, 8 In.	22.50
Vase, Pink, 5 3/4 In.	20.00
Vase, Tulip, Green, 6 In.	12.50
Vase, Volcanic Shape, Marked, Drizzled Gray & Yellow, 5 X 6 In.	6.00

CAMBRIDGE COCKTAIL, Nude Stem, Green	65.00

Cambridge art pottery was made in Cambridge, Ohio, from about 1895 until World War I. The factory made brown glazed decorated wares marked with a variety of marks including an acorn, the name Cambridge, the name Oakwood, or the name Terrhea.

CAMBRIDGE POTTERY, Vase, Brown Glaze, Oakwood, 8 In.	125.00

Cambridge Glass Company was founded in 1901 in Cambridge, Ohio. The company closed in 1954, reopened briefly, and closed again in 1958. The firm made all types of glass. Their early wares included heavy pressed glass with the mark "Near Cut." Later wares included etched stemware, crystal, colored, and Crown Tuscan. The firm used a C in a triangle mark after 1920.

CAMBRIDGE, Ashtray & Cigarette Holder, Cobalt Blue	23.00
Ashtray Set, Shell Pattern, Box & Labels, 8 Piece	75.00
Ashtray, Caprice, Yellow, 3 In.	5.00
Ashtray, Crown Tuscan, 7 In.	26.00
Ashtray, Red, 7 In.	22.00
Ashtray, Shell, 8 Piece	50.00
Ball, Ivy, Amethyst, 8 In.	35.00
Basket, Novelty, Pistachio Green, Handled, 5 In.	20.00
Basket, Rose Point, 2-Handled, 5 In.	30.00
Bell, Acid Etched	12.00
Berry Set, Marjorie, 7 Piece	60.00
Bonbon, Caprice, Handle, Blue, 6 In.Square	15.00
Bonbon, Elaine, Gadroon Rim, 5 In.	18.00

Bonbon, Rose Point, Etched, Handled 22.50
Bookends, Eagle, Pair 135.00
Bookends, Roaring Lion, Pair 750.00
Bookends, Scotty Dog, Clear, 5 X 3 X 6 1/4 In., Pair 70.00
Bottle, Water, Figural, Dog With Glass Cap, Pink 65.00
Bowl & Underplate, Etched Lace Border, Pink, 12 In. 75.00
Bowl, Adonis, Footed, 12 In. 35.00
Bowl, Alpine, Nappy, Square, Blue, Handles, 7 In. 22.50
Bowl, Amber, 10 In. 15.00
Bowl, Azurite, 9 1/2 In.Diam. 30.00
Bowl, Caprice, Blue, 12 1/2 In.Diam. 42.00
Bowl, Caprice, 4-Footed, Blue, 10 1/2 In. 22.50
Bowl, Cleo, Etched, Gold Trim, Pink, 12 In. 35.00
Bowl, Console, Diane, 10 In. 35.00
Bowl, Console, Honeycomb, Amberina 95.00
Bowl, Diane, 4-Footed, 12 In. 40.00
Bowl, Elaine, Etching, 10 In.Diam. 16.00
Bowl, Etched Floral, Flared, Pink, 12 1/2 In.Diam. 45.00
Bowl, Etched Pattern, Ruffled, 13 X 5 In. 32.00
Bowl, Everglades, Dolphin Footed, Amber, 11 In. 40.00
Bowl, Everglades, Dolphin Footed, Amber, 12 In. 40.00
Bowl, Everglades, Footed, 10 3/4 In. 55.00
Bowl, Everglades, Green Swans, 14 In.Diam. 100.00
Bowl, Everglades, Indians & Buffalo, Pink, 16 In.Diam. 95.00
Bowl, Everglades, Tulip Shape, Amber 40.00
Bowl, Flying Nude, Crown Tuscan 275.00
Bowl, Gold Trim, Footed, Crown Tuscan, 12 In. 150.00
Bowl, Helio, Gold Laurel Band, 8 3/4 In. 55.00
Bowl, Heliotrope, Gold Band, 11 3/4 In.Diam. 65.00
Bowl, Metal Handle, Cleo, Pink, 4 1/2 In. 18.00
Bowl, Nautilus, Flower Center, Footed, Crown Tuscan, 6 In. 85.00
Bowl, Nautilus, Shell Feet, Crown Tuscan, 8 In. 35.00
Bowl, Poppy, Etched, 13 In. 23.00
Bowl, Primrose, 12 In.Diam. 52.00
Bowl, Punch, Wild Rose, Carmen, Bowl, Base & 4 Cups 650.00
Bowl, Ram's Head, Clear 75.00
Bowl, Ram's Head, Jade 90.00
Bowl, Rose Point, Bold Trim, Oval, 12 In. 55.00
Bowl, Rose Point, Footed, 9 3/4 In. 45.00
Box, Candy, 3-Handled, Cover, Crown Tuscan 37.50
Box, Cigarette, Caprice, Blue, Covered 20.00
Box, Cigarette, Caprice, Cover 20.00
Box, Cigarette, Dolphin Footed, Pink, Green, & Rose, Crown Tuscan 55.00
Box, Cigarette, Paneled Lid, Crown Tuscan, 6 In.Square 30.00
Box, Heart Shape, Crown Tuscan 30.00
Box, Scroll Handle, Paneled Lid, Crown Tuscan, 4 X 6 In. 35.00
Brandy, Nude, Light Pink, 1 Ounce 75.00
Butter & Sugar, Colonial, Child's, Covered 55.00
Butter, Colonial, Child's, Covered, Green 40.00
Butter, Gloria, Covered 65.00
Butter, Rose Point, Covered, Round, 5 1/2 In. 145.00
Cake Plate, Gold Encrusted Handle, Footed, Crown Tuscan 110.00
Cake Plate, Rose Point, Handled, 13 1/2 In.Diam. 30.00
Cake Server, Dragon, Light Blue 14.00
Candleholder, Adonis, Double Branch, Pair 45.00
Candleholder, Caprice, Blue, 2 1/2 In.Diam., Pair 35.00
Candleholder, Dolphin, Mt. Vernon Base, Light Green, Pair 140.00
Candlestick, Caprice, Blue, Low, Pair 25.00
Candlestick, Caprice, Blue, With Prisms, 7 In. 50.00
Candlestick, Caprice, Double, Gold, Pair 45.00
Candlestick, Caprice, Low, Crystal 10.00
Candlestick, Caprice, 3-Light, Blue 35.00
Candlestick, Daffodil, 2-Light, Etched, Pair 50.00

Candlestick, Dolphin, Green, Pair	145.00
Candlestick, Dolphin, Mt.Vernon, Custard Glass, 9 1/2 In.	150.00
Candlestick, Doric Column, Pair	125.00
Candlestick, Double Keyhole, Crown Tuscan, Pair	50.00
Candlestick, Double Keyhole, Diane, Pair	50.00
Candlestick, Everglades, 2-Light, Blue	50.00
Candlestick, Green Satin Finish, Pair	65.00
Candlestick, Heliotrope Column, Pair	160.00
Candlestick, Hexagon Jade, Gold Trim, Pair	55.00
Candlestick, Jade Twist, 8 In., Pair	30.00
Candlestick, Rose Point, Bobeches & Long Prisms, Pair	65.00
Candlestick, Rose Point, Key, 5 1/2 In., Pair	130.00
Candlestick, Star Shape, Ice Flute, 5 In., Pair	50.00
Candlestick, Twist, Jade, 8 1/2 In.	35.00
Candlestick, Windsor Blue, Pair	175.00
Candlestick, 2-Light, Crown Tuscan, Pair	64.00
Candlestick, 2-Light, Moonlight Blue, 6 In, Pair	55.00
Candy, Caprice, Covered, 3 Footed	26.00
Champagne, Diane	12.00
Champagne, Rose Point	21.00
Cheese & Cracker Set, Heliotrope, Platter, 13 1/2 In.	95.00
Claret, Rose Point	45.00
Cocktail Set, Shaker, 6 Nude Stems, Farber Ware Holder	125.00
Cocktail Set, 6 Farber Ware Tulip Holders, Purple Inserts	75.00
Cocktail Shaker, King Edward, Cut	45.00
Cocktail, Amber, Nude, 3 Ounce	80.00
Cocktail, Caprice	8.00
Cocktail, Diane	14.00
Cocktail, Laurel Wreath, 3 Ounce	12.00
Cocktail, Nude, Amethyst, 3 Ounce	65.00
Cocktail, Nude, Dark Green, 3 Ounce	65.00
Cocktail, Nude, Mandarin Gold, 3 Ounce	65.00
Cocktail, Nude, Moonlight Blue, 3 Ounce	105.00
Cocktail, Nude, Royal Blue, 3 Ounce	85.00
Cocktail, Rose Point	30.00
Compote, Amethyst, Farber Ware, 7 In.Diam.	18.00
Compote, Azurite, 8 In.	58.00
Compote, Candy, Chantilly, Sterling Silver Pedestal	35.00
Compote, Candy, Nude Stem, Crown Tuscan	135.00
Compote, Clear Keyhole Stem, Green	17.50
Compote, Enameled Florals, Gold Trim, Crown Tuscan, 7 In.	60.00
Compote, Flying Nude, Crown Tuscan, 15 In.	200.00
Compote, Jade, 7 1/2 In.	40.00
Compote, Nude Stem, Amethyst, Farber Ware	26.00
Compote, Nude Stem, Blue Cup	90.00
Compote, Nude Stem, Shell Shape, Crown Tuscan, Pair	250.00
Compote, Nude Stem, Shell Top, Crown Tuscan	125.00
Compote, Nude, Emerald	125.00
Compote, Primrose, Gold Engraved Trim, 6 X 6 3/4 In.	45.00
Compote, Primrose, 7 X 3 1/2 In.	15.00
Compote, Rosette & Palms, Open, 8 In.	13.50
Compote, Seashell Pattern, Sailboat, Pier, Crown Tuscan, 8 In.	100.00
Compote, Silver Berries & Leaves, Footed Marked	35.00
Compote, Wildflower Design, Gold Encrusted	45.00
Condiment Set, Caprice, 5 Cruets, Salt & Pepper, Tray	45.00
Console Set, Azurite, Ram's Head	385.00
Console Set, Calla Lily Candlesticks, Bowl	75.00
Console Set, Jade, 2 Twisted Stem, 9 1/2 In.Bowl, Holders, 8 In.	120.00
Cordial, Achilles, 1 Ounce	30.00
Cordial, Amber, 1 Ounce	3.00
Cordial, Caprice, Crystal, 1 Ounce	28.00
Cordial, Flat, 1 Ounce	3.00
Cordial, Rose Point, 1 Ounce	40.00

Cordial, Wildflower, 1 Ounce	20.00
Cornucopia, Seashell Pattern, 9 1/2 In.	35.00
Cornucopia, Shell Base, Crown Tuscan, 5 In.	20.00
Creamer, Colonial, Child's	10.00 To 35.00
Creamer, Colonial, Child's, Green	35.00
Creamer, Wheat Sheaf, Child's	18.00
Cruet, Buzz Saw Pattern, 3 In.	35.00
Cruet, Etched Elaine	35.00
Cruet, Rose Point	50.00
Cruet, Snowflake	45.00
Cup & Saucer, Caprice, Blue	25.00 To 32.00
Cup & Saucer, Cascade	10.00
Cup & Saucer, Decagon, Pink	7.50
Cup & Saucer, Elaine, Etched	30.00
Cup & Saucer, Mt.Vernon	7.00
Cup & Saucer, Optic, Amber	6.00
Cup & Saucer, Rose Point	30.00
Cup, Caprice, Amber	15.00
Cup, Nut, Caprice, Crystal	7.50
Cup, Nut, Shell, Footed, Pink	9.00
Cup, Punch, Colonial, Clear	4.50
Decanter, Caprice, Clear	24.00
Decanter, Clear Stopper, Red	60.00
Decanter, Cordial, Amethyst, 12 Ounce	20.00
Decanter, Cordial, Crystal Stopper, 4 Glasses, Amethyst, 12 Ounce	32.00
Decanter, Nautilus, Amber, 12 Ounce	25.00
Decanter, Rose Point, Stopper, Amethyst, 32 Ounce	32.00
Dish, Alpine, Blue, Oval, Handled, 10 In.	22.50
Dish, Candy, Elaine, Etched Ram's Head, Covered	75.00
Dish, Candy, Rose Point, Scalloped Edge, Handle	30.00
Dish, Candy, Turkey, Lid	18.00
Dish, Candy, Wildflower, 3 Section, Covered	25.00
Dish, Candy, 3-Section, Covered, Crown Tuscan, 8 In.	50.00
Dish, Cheese, Majestic, Cover	75.00
Dish, Cheese, Wildflower Design, Domed, Covered	125.00
Dish, Mint, Chantilly, Footed, Divided Relish, 3 1/4 In.	40.00
Dish, Nut, Shell	6.00
Dish, Shell, Pedestal, Crown Tuscan, 6 In.	55.00
Figurine, Bashful Charlotte, 8 In.	75.00
Figurine, Sea Gull	65.00
Figurine, Swan, Crown Tuscan, 3 1/2 In.	20.00
Figurine, Swan, Crystal, 3 In.	17.00
Figurine, Swan, Emerald, Green, Turned Neck, 3 1/2 In.	62.00
Figurine, Swan, Marked, Apple Green, 3 1/2 In.	25.00
Figurine, Swan, Milk Glass, 4 1/2 In.	60.00
Figurine, Swan, Peach Blow, Signed, 3 In.	27.50
Figurine, Swan, Yellow, Signed, 3 In.	32.00
Flower Frog, Bashful Charlotte, Clear, 8 In.	60.00
Flower Frog, Bashful Charlotte, Pink, 12 1/2 In.	195.00
Flower Frog, Dated April 11, 1915, 6 Holes, Crystal	7.00
Flower Frog, Draped Lady, Clear, 8 1/2 In.	55.00
Flower Frog, Footed, Crown Tuscan, 6 In.	85.00
Flower Frog, Gull	45.00
Flower Frog, Lady, Satin Finish, 13 1/2 In.	285.00
Flower Frog, Rose Lady, Green, 9 In.	165.00
Flower Frog, Rose Point, 8 In.	34.00
Flower Frog, Sea Gull	20.00 To 65.00
Flower Frog, Seashell Pattern, Crown Tuscan, 7 1/2 In.	75.00
Flower Frog, Seashell, Crown Tuscan, 8 In.	120.00
Flower Frog, September Morn, Ribbed Base, 6 1/2 In.	57.50
Flower Frog, September Morn, Scalloped Base, Pink, 13 In.	225.00
Flower Frog, 2 Kids, Frosted Green	85.00
Flower Holder, Rose Point, 8 In.	32.00

Flower Holder, Sea Gull, Crystal	65.00
Flower Holder, Windsor, Blue Shell	145.00
Goblet, Adonis	18.00
Goblet, Caprice, Blue, 10 Ounce	28.00
Goblet, Caprice, Clear, 5 3/4 In.	10.00
Goblet, Laurel Wreath, 9 Ounce	12.00
Goblet, Martha Washington, Ritz Blue	35.00
Goblet, Martha Washington, 9 Ounce	15.00
Goblet, Mt.Vernon, 5 3/4 In.	7.00
Goblet, Rose Point, Gold Trim	35.00
Goblet, Rose Point, 10 Ounce	20.00 To 28.00
Ice Bucket, Caprice, Tongs, Clear	33.00
Ice Bucket, Martha	23.00
Ice Bucket, Poppy Etched, Clear	30.00
Ice Bucket, Royal Ruby, Tongs	23.50
Ice Bucket, Vintage, Etched, Pink	25.00
Ice Tub, Rose Point	55.00
Iced Tea, Rose Point, Footed, 12 Ounce	25.00
Ivy Ball, Black, 7 1/2 In.	35.00
Ivy Ball, Crown Tuscan, Ring Stem, 8 In.	40.00
Ivy Ball, Rose Point	45.00
Jar, Candy, Mt.Vernon, Covered, Carmen, 1 Pound	95.00
Jar, Desiccator, Cover, Original Box & Label, 11 1/2 X 10 1/2 In.	120.00
Jug, Ball, Nautilus, Amber	30.00
Jug, Ball, Nautilus, Forest Green	30.00
Jug, Chantilly, Sterling Silver Base	130.00
Jug, Rose Point, Ball Shape, 80 Ounce	225.00
Jug, Rose Point, Tilt, Amber, 80 Ounce	44.00
Jug, Rose Point, Tilt, Amethyst, 80 Ounce	44.00
Juice, Caprice, Blue, 5 Ounce	24.00
Marmalade, Rose Point, Lid	65.00
Mayonnaise Set, Azurite, 1920s, 2 Piece	30.00
Mayonnaise Set, Chantilly, Gold Encrusted, 3 Piece	45.00
Mayonnaise Set, Rose Point, 3 Piece	30.00
Mug, Argus, Master, Flint	15.00
Mug, Carmen Red, Handled, 12 Ounce	24.00
Mug, Mt.Vernon, Crystal Handle, Ruby	38.00
Nut Cup & Card Holder, Blue, Caprice	10.00
Nut Cup, Rose Point, Master	35.00
Oil & Vinegar, Nautilus, Tray, Amethyst	40.00
Pitcher, Amethyst, Applied Handle, 6 1/2 In.	20.00
Pitcher, Ball, Cobalt Blue, 80 Ounce	45.00
Pitcher, Feather, Signed, 5 3/4 In.	43.00
Pitcher, Nautilus, Amber	50.00
Pitcher, Rose Point, Ball Tilt, 80 Ounce	135.00
Pitcher, Rose Point, 76 Ounce	150.00
Pitcher, Water, Chantilly Etched, Sterling Silver Base, 9 In.	165.00
Pitcher, Water, Colonial, Child's	10.00
Plate, Alpine, Blue, Handles, 7 1/2 In.	22.50
Plate, Alpine, Blue, Round, Handles, 7 In.	30.00
Plate, Apple Green, 8 In.	5.00
Plate, Caprice, Blue, 8 1/2 In.	20.00
Plate, Caprice, Blue, 9 In.	16.00
Plate, Caprice, Footed, 14 In.	42.50
Plate, Caprice, 7 1/2 In.	6.00
Plate, Caprice, 8 1/2 In.	8.00
Plate, Chantilly, 8 1/2 In.	6.50
Plate, Elaine, Etched, Amber, 7 In.	8.00
Plate, Elaine, Etched, 10 In.	34.00
Plate, Etched Flowers, 9 In.	45.00
Plate, Etched, Signed, Green, 6 In.	24.00
Plate, Everglades, Blue, 17 In.	115.00
Plate, Gloria, Square, 10 In.	27.00

Plate, Handled, Amethyst, 12 In.	18.00
Plate, Martha Washington, Dark Green, 9 In.	7.00
Plate, Open Handles, Black, 6 In.Square	6.00
Plate, Rose Point, Etched, 8 1/4 In.	18.00
Plate, Rose Point, Handled, 12 1/2 In.	45.00
Plate, Rose Point, Rimmed, Footed, 12 1/2 In.	45.00
Plate, Rose Point, 6 In.	12.00
Plate, Rose Point, 7 1/2 In.	12.00
Plate, Rose Point, 8 1/2 In.	10.00 To 12.00
Plate, Sandwich, Fleur-De-Lis, Center Handle, Blue	20.00
Plate, Sandwich, Keyhole, Yellow	20.00
Pot, Jam, Farber Ware Holder, Chrome Lid, 4 1/4 In.	10.00
Relish, Apple Blossom, Yellow Divided Handle	20.00
Relish, Candlelight, 5-Part, 12 In.	75.00
Relish, Caprice, 3-Compartment, Footed	28.50
Relish, Eagle	25.00
Relish, Portia Etch, 3 Compartments	32.00
Relish, Rose Point, Etched, 3-Sectioned, 15 1/2 In.	60.00
Relish, Rose Point, 2-Compartment, 7 1/4 In.	32.50
Relish, Rose Point, 3-Part	25.00
Relish, Rose Point, 5-Part, 12 In.	85.00
Relish, Rose Point, 9 1/2 In.	30.00
Salt & Pepper, Rose Point	40.00
Salt, Swan Shape, Crown Tuscan, 3 1/2 In.	30.00
Saltshaker, Rose Point, Footed	18.00
Saltshaker, Squat, Crystal Base & Top	12.00
Sandwich Plate, Fleur-De-Lis, Center Handle, Blue	20.00
Sandwich Plate, Heliotrope, Center Loop Handle, 10 1/2 In.	75.00
Sandwich Plate, Heliotrope, Handled, 10 1/2 In.	30.00
Server, Sandwich, Heliotrope, Center Loop Handle, 10 In.	75.00
Sherbet, Caprice, 5 3/4 In.	7.00
Sherbet, Laurel Wreath	12.00
Sherbet, Mt.Vernon, 4 1/4 In.	6.00
Sherbet, Rose Point, Tall	18.50
Sherbet, Rose Point, 6 Ounce	22.00
Sign, Triangle, Ritz Blue	80.00
Spooner, Colonial, Child's, Emerald Green	20.00
Spooner, Colonial, Child's, Green	28.00
Spooner, Colonial, Cobalt Blue	30.00
Sugar & Creamer, Alpine, Blue	30.00
Sugar & Creamer, Caprice	9.00
Sugar & Creamer, Carmen	45.00
Sugar & Creamer, Elaine, Etched Gadroon	45.00
Sugar & Creamer, Gloria	45.00
Sugar & Creamer, Mt.Vernon, Carmen	67.00
Sugar Shaker, Leaning Panel, Amber, Aluminum Top	50.00
Sugar, Colonial, Child's	15.00
Sugar, Mt.Vernon, Cover, Clear	25.00
Sugar, Wildflower, Blue, Covered	24.00
Swan, Crystal, 8 1/2 In.	40.00
Swan, Mandarin, Gold, Signed, 3 In.	32.00
Table Set, Child's, Colonial	65.00
Table Set, Child's, Colonial, Green, 3 Piece	80.00
Table Set, Child's, Whirligig Pattern, 4 Piece	65.00
Table Set, Colonial, Child's, Green, 4 Piece	100.00
Table Set, Fernland, 4 Piece	125.00
Toothpick, Thistle, Shades To Ebony	35.00
Tray, Cream & Sugar, Caprice, Blue, Small	40.00
Tumbler, Colonial, Child's	5.00
Tumbler, Georgian, Red, 3 1/4 In.	7.50
Tumbler, Georgian, 5 Ounce	10.00
Tumbler, Georgian, 9 Ounce	10.00

Tumbler, Mt.Vernon, Footed, 3 Ounce	6.50
Tumbler, Mt.Vernon, 10 Ounce	6.50
Tumbler, Nearcut, Child's	8.00
Tumbler, Rose Point, Cobalt Blue Bowl, 12 Ounce	60.00
Tumbler, Rose Point, Flat Bottom	45.00
Tumbler, Rose Point, Footed, 5 Ounce	23.00 To 28.00
Tumbler, Rose Point, 10 Ounce	20.00
Vase, Caprice Blue, 4 1/2 In.	20.00
Vase, Caprice, Amber, 8 1/2 In.	125.00
Vase, Caprice, Green, 6 1/2 In.	55.00
Vase, Chantilly, 11 In.	59.90
Vase, Colonial, Marked, 15 In., Pair	28.00
Vase, Conch Shell, Amethyst, 7 X 8 In.	48.00
Vase, Cornucopia, Crown Tuscan, Seashell Base, 10 In., Pair	85.00
Vase, Cornucopia, Ebony, 10 In.	70.00
Vase, Everglades, Fan Shape, Frosted, Crystal Dragonflies, 8 In.	45.00
Vase, Floral & Anemones, Rose & Magenta, Signed Peynaud, 10 In.	275.00
Vase, Floral Design, 12 In.	70.00
Vase, Gloria, Crystal, Footed, Dark Green Top, 10 In.	95.00
Vase, Gold Chintz, Signed, Crown Tuscan, 12 In.	175.00
Vase, Gold Chintz, Signed, Crown Tuscan, 13 In.	210.00
Vase, Keyhole, Apple Green, 10 In.	35.00
Vase, Keyhole, Crystal Base, Cobalt Blue, 10 In.	50.00 To 58.00
Vase, Nautilus, Crown Tuscan, 8 In.	90.00
Vase, Pinched Neck, Gold Etching, Crown Tuscan, 7 In.	55.00
Vase, Portia, Gold Etched, Ring Stem, Crown Tuscan, 12 In.	125.00
Vase, Rose Point, Crystal & Gold	45.00
Vase, Rose Point, Gold, Crown Tuscan, Etch, 10 In.	43.00
Vase, Rose Point, 10 1/2 In.	74.00
Vase, Rose Point, 12 In.	70.00
Vase, Sculptured Flowers, Green, 12 In.	40.00
Vase, Sea Horse Design, Sterling Silver Trim, Crown Tuscan	175.00
Water Glass, Rose Point, 5 Ounce	27.50
Water Set, Nearcut, Child's, 4 Piece	48.00
Water Set, Peacock, Clear, 6 Tumblers	600.00
Water Set, Peacock, 7 Piece	600.00
Wine, Amber, Farber Holder	5.00
Wine, Imp Hunt Etch, Pink With Green Base, Footed, Set Of 4	110.00
Wine, Mt.Vernon, 3 Ounce	7.00
Wine, Nude, Ebony Stem, 6 1/2 In.	45.00
Wine, Rose Point, 3 Ounce	38.00

Cameo glass was made in much the same manner as a cameo in jewelry. Parts of the top layer of glass was cut away to reveal a different colored glass beneath. The most famous cameo glass was made during the nineteenth century.

CAMEO GLASS, see also under factory names

CAMEO, Bottle, Perfume, Lay-Down, White Carving, Green, English, 9 1/2 In.	1500.00
Bottle, Shell Design, Sterling Silver Cap, Olive Ground, English	750.00
Carafe, English, Rosebuds, Foliage, Silver Plated Lid, Green, 9 In.	1050.00
Vase, Boat & Lighthouse, Navy Blue To Peach, Signed, French, 10 1/8 In.	1100.00
Vase, Flowers, Citron, English, 15 In.	1500.00
Vase, Flowers, Raspberry To Pink Body, Signed, Cameo, 4 3/4 In.	375.00
Vase, Green Grapes, Arsall, 14 In.	800.00
Vase, Mottled, Frosted Ground, Gondola With Man, French, 8 1/2 In.	1200.00
Vase, Passion Flowers, Red Ground, Dragonfly, English, 5 In.	1950.00
Vase, Sailboat Scene, Brown To Yellow, French, 8 1/2 In.	875.00
Vase, White Flowers & Leaves On Frosted Blue Ground, English, 3 In.	1450.00
Vase, White Flowers & Leaves, Yellow Ground, English, 4 3/4 In.	895.00
Vase, White On Cranberry Satin Glass, English, 10 1/4 In.	2500.00

CAMPAIGN, see Political

Candelabra, Floral, French, 19th Century,
Cast Brass, 35 In., Pair

CAMPBELL KIDS, Puzzle, Teddy Bear 15.00
   Spoon & Fork 16.00
   Teaspoon, Figural 15.00

*Camphor glass is a cloudy white glass that has been blown or pressed. It
was made by many factories in the Midwest during the mid-nineteenth century.*

CAMPHOR GLASS, Box, Powder, Figural, Owl, Cover, 6 X 4 In. 40.00
   Ewer, Clear Handles, Gold Design 60.00
   Figurine, Bulldog, Jewel Eyes 5.00
   Holder, Place Card 16.00
   Shoe, 6 In. 15.00
   Vase, Enameled Birds & Flowers, Smoky, Pair 85.00
      CANARY GLASS, see Vaseline Glass
CANDELABRA, Floral, French, 19th Century, Cast Brass, 35 In., Pair .... *Illus* 225.00
   5-Light, Classical Figures, C.1870, Bronze & Marble, 22 In., Pair 550.00

      CANDLEHOLDER, see also Brass; and various porcelain categories
CANDLEHOLDER, Costumed Lady & Man, 18th Century, Bisque, 15 In., Pair 170.00
   Hand-Wrought, Ox Shoe Base 155.00
   Pricket, Brass, C.1800 .... 180.00

      **CANDLESTICK, see also Brass, Candlestick; Pewter, Candlestick;
      Sandwich Glass, Candlestick; Silver-Sterling, Candlestick;
      and various porcelain categories**
CANDLESTICK, Blue Spiral Glass, C.1920, Pair 95.00
   Brass & Ruby Glass, American, C.1850, 9 1/2 In., Pair 150.00
   Column Form, C.1790, Brass Mounted, Mahogany, 15 1/2 In., Pair 1045.00
   Diamond Design, 9 In., Pair 95.00
   Dolphin, Amber, 1890-1900, 10 1/2 In. 75.00
   Edwardian, Silver Inlaid Tortoiseshell Stems, 5 1/2 In., Pair 2420.00
   Elkington, Italian Renaissance, Electrotype, 13 7/8 In., Pair 300.00
   Flint Enamel 675.00
   French Porcelain, Blue & White, Flowers, 10 In., Pair 125.00
   French, Metal Soldiers, Holding Lances, 14 In., Pair 250.00
   Hand Wrought Iron, 1820-40, 16 In., Pair 225.00
   Hog Scraper 60.00
   Hog Scraper, Signed Shaw, Cast Iron, 7 In. 75.00

Iridescent Glass, Blue, 10 In., Pair	69.00
Knopped Stem, Bell Based, 17th Century, Germany	875.00
Octagonal Ruffled Base, French, 1810-20, Brass, 9 1/2 In.	350.00
Oriental Pewter, 1850s, Pricket Style, 8 3/4 In., Pair	150.00
Threaded Shaft, Adjustable Socket, Cast Iron, Patent 1848	85.00
Triple Wedding Ring, Hog Scraper	395.00
Victorian, Bell Brass, Open Twist, 1835-45, 17 In., Pair	400.00
4-Section, Triangular Base, Brass, 11 In.	225.00

Candy containers, especially those made of glass, have been popular since the late Victorian era. The S-XX numbers refer to the book "A Century of Glass Toys" by Mary Louise Stanley.

CANDY CONTAINER, Airplane	39.00 To 40.00
Airplane With Pilot, Spirit Of Goodwill	55.00 To 75.00
Airplane, Spirit Of Goodwill, S-18	125.00
Airplane, Spirit Of St.Louis	125.00 To 275.00
Angeline Trolley	20.00
Auto Lamp, S-637	75.00
Auto, Paint, Closure, Candy, Beveled Glass Window, 4 In.	95.00
Auto, Streamlined	20.00
Auto, Streamlined, Yellow	25.00
Barney Google, S-294	100.00 To 150.00
Baseball	28.00
Battleship	15.00
Battleship, Paper Closure	20.00
Battleship, S-220	85.00
Bean Kettle, Handle, Paper Lid	7.00
Bear, Performing, Clear, S-168	135.00
Boat	15.00
Boot	3.50
Bottle, Baby, Glass, Rubber Nipple	10.00
Bottle, Goldfish, Figural, Scale Embossed, 8 In.	28.00
Bulldog	26.00 To 27.00
Camera On Tripod, S-590	205.00 To 225.00
Candlestick Telephone, Metal Mouthpiece, Wooden Receiver	37.50
Cane, 18 In.	22.00
Car, Rumble Seat, Original Paint	40.00
Car, Victory Glass Co., Green Paint	20.00
Cat, Black, 1920s	22.00
Charlie Chaplin, Borgfeldt, 3 7/8 In.	65.00 To 95.00
Charlie McCarthy	26.00
Chick By Cracked Egg, Papier-Mache	15.00
Chick On Nest	25.00
Chick, Standing, Original Closure	110.00
Chick, Standing, 3 3/8 In.	32.00
Chicken & Nest, Original Paint, 5 In.	42.00
Chicken On A Basket	10.00 To 40.00
Chicken On Nest, Paper Closure	22.00
Chicken On Solid Nest	30.00
Chicken, Papier-Mache, Large	15.00
Chicken, Sagging Basket	140.00
Chicken, Solid Nest	29.00
Clock, Bank	125.00
Clown On Rocking Horse	55.00
Clown, Rocking Horse, S-502	125.00
Coal Scuttle, Blue, Wire Bale, Victorian Design	35.00
Dime Bank, Kiddie Clock, Time Zone, Glassine Window	18.00
Dog, Cobalt Blue	16.00
Dog, Hound, Clear, With Candy	4.00
Dog, Papier-Mache	25.00
Dog, Scotty	10.00
Doll Nurser, Embossed Dog	12.50

Donkey Cart	23.00
Donkey Pulling Cart, 4 In.	7.00 To 12.00
Drum Mug	22.00
Duck, Standing	25.00
Dutch Maid, Bell Shape	30.00
Dutch Windmill	26.00 To 30.00
Easter Bunny	25.00
Electric Iron	20.00
Elephant, Genteel, S-372	100.00
Engine	16.00
Fat Boy On Drum, S-301	135.00
Fire Engine	10.00 To 30.00
Fire Engine, Original Enclosure & Candy	25.00
Fire Engine, Paper Insert	13.00 To 20.00
Fire Truck	11.00
Fire Truck, Antique	19.00
Flat Iron, S-519	250.00
Football, Germany	15.00
Frosty The Snowman, 12 In.	18.00
Gay Head Lighthouse	25.00
Girl With 2 Geese	25.00
Gun	15.00 To 20.00
Half-Doll, Easter	75.00
Halloween, Lady With Monkey Face, Papier-Mache, Germany	110.00
Hen, Sagging Basket	50.00
Hen, 3 1/2 In.	20.00
Horn, Plastic Top & Base	10.00
Hound Dog, Cobalt Blue	15.00
Hound Pup, Original Metal Bell Around Neck	5.00
Hurricane Lamp, Small	45.00
Independence Hall	225.00
Jack-O-Lantern, Embossed Face, Red, White, Black, 4 In.	110.00
Jack-O-Lantern, Slanted Eyes, Lid & Bail, Clear	50.00
Jack-O-Lantern, Yellow Eyes, Black Mouth, Tin Rim & Handle	35.00
Jackie Robinson, 5 In.	45.00
Jeep, Millstein	16.00
Jeep, Scout Car, Willy's, Paper Closure	20.00
Kettle	10.00
Kettle, Ruby Stained, Bail	30.00
Kewpie	55.00
Kewpie By Barrel	40.00
Kewpie By Barrel, Original Closure	90.00
Lamp, Hurricane, Miniature	25.00
Lantern, Bail Wire Handle	25.00
Lantern, Metal Screw Cap & Handle	16.00
Lantern, Original Candy	20.00
Lantern, 1882, S-1292	45.00
Liberty Bell, Amber	75.00
Light Bulb, Amber	45.00
Lighthouse	22.00
Limousine, S-42	80.00
Limousine, Westmoreland	45.00
Little Boiler	33.00
Locomotive	15.00
Locomotive, Jeanette, Clear, 4 In.	40.00
Locomotive, Marked USA, 1 1/2 Ounce	35.00
Locomotive, Tin Closure	17.50
Locomotive, Tin Lithograph, Closure	35.00
Log Cabin	25.00
Madonna & Child	38.00
Man In Fire Truck	18.50
Man In Jeep	22.00

Melon Head	20.00
Midget Washer	30.00
Military Cap	16.00
Military Hat	20.00
Moon Mullins	23.00 To 35.00
Motorcycle, S-1269	300.00
Nude Boy	15.00
Nurser, Nipple Type, Jeanette Label, 2 1/4 In.	10.00
Oaken Bucket	10.00 To 11.00
Opera Glass	55.00
Phonograph, Home Sweet Home	25.00
Pierce Arrow, 1920, Tin Top	25.00
Pistol	8.00 To 18.50
Pistol, C.1900	15.00
Pistol, Cap, 8 In.	18.00
Pistol, Metal Cap	10.50
Planters Printed, Peanut Shape, Plastic	6.50
Puppy, Sitting, 3 In.	10.00
Rabbit In Shell	45.00
Rabbit Wheelbarrow, S-843	125.00
Rabbit, Crouching, S-864	75.00
Rabbit, Ears Laid Back	22.00
Rabbit, Eating Carrot	30.00
Rabbit, Emerging From Egg	45.00
Rabbit, Papier-Mache, 3 In.	22.00
Rabbit, Paws Next To Body	30.00
Rabbit, S-854	60.00
Rabbit, Sitting, Jeanette, Pa., 6 1/2 In.	28.00
Rabbit, Sitting, 5 In.	30.00
Rabbit, Standing, 3, Nodders, Glass Eyes	30.00
Rabbit, Wearing Pants, S-840	500.00
Racer No.12, S-88	60.00
Radio, Horn Speaker	38.00
Radio, S-778	75.00
Radio, Speakers	75.00
Railroad Engine, Lithographed	75.00
Revolver	17.50
Revolver, Screw Cap	27.00
Revolver, 8 In.	20.00
Sailboat, Metal Sail	10.00
Santa Claus	40.00 To 75.00
Santa Claus Boot, Papier-Mache, 7 3/4 X 4 In.	10.00
Santa Claus Boot, 3 In.	10.00
Santa Claus Climbing Down Chimney, Original Paint	95.00
Santa Claus Climbing Down Chimney, Victory Glass Co.	75.00
Santa Claus In A Stocking, Papier-Mache & Cloth, 6 In.	40.00
Santa Claus In A Stocking, Papier-Mache, 6 In.	40.00
Santa Claus, Papier-Mache, 7 In.	30.00
Santa Claus, Plastic Head, Clear	36.00 To 45.00
Santa Claus, Plastic Head, 5 7/8 In.	39.00
Santa Claus, S-882	90.00
Santa Claus, S-886	130.00
Santa Claus, S-890	100.00
Santa Claus, S-891	110.00
Santa Claus, 5 3/4 In.	55.00
Scotty	5.00 To 15.00
Sedan	15.00
Sedan, Chrysler, S-49	50.00
Skater's Lantern, Bail Handle, Screw Lid	65.00
Snowman, Musical	15.00
Snowman, Papier-Mache, 13 In.	35.00
Spark Plug, Metal Bottom, No Paint	70.00
Spark Plug, Metal Closure	10.00 To 27.50

Spark Plug, S-110 .... 110.00
Spinning Top, Original Top 30.00
Straw Hat, Milk Glass 35.00
Suitcase .... 22.00 To 28.00
Suitcase, Handle, Metal Closure .... 25.00 To 45.00
Swimming Duck 55.00
Tank .... 22.00 To 24.50
Tank, Man 10.00
Tanker, Bank 6.00
Telephone .... 15.00 To 38.50
Telephone, Candlestick, Wooden Receiver, Victory Paper End 35.00
Telephone, French, Clear, With Candy 12.00
Telephone, Label 30.00
Telephone, Metal Mouthpiece 30.00
Telephone, Metal Mouthpiece, Wooden Receiver 40.00
Telephone, Musical 18.00
Telephone, Redlichs, S-908 .... 150.00
Telephone, Whistle, Wood Receiver, Candy 25.00
Telephone, Wooden Receiver 20.00
Terrior, Marked 24.00
Top 20.00
Tot Telephone 20.00
Train .... 15.00 To 16.00
Train Engine, 4 1/2 In. 8.50
Trunk 25.00
Tune In Radio 80.00
Turkey 25.00
Turkey, Papier-Mache, 7 X 5 X 5 In. 20.00
Turkey, S-206 .... 65.00
U.S.Army Tank, Bottle Neck, 3 In. 25.00
Washer 30.00
Wheelbarrow 35.00
Wheelbarrow, S-1175 .... 65.00
Willy's Jeep 15.00
Willy's Jeep, Glass, Embossed, 4 1/4 In. 25.00
Witch, Papier-Mache, 4 In. 110.00
Witch, Pumpkinhead, S-469 .... 300.00
15-P-7 Army Bomber 15.00

CANE, Alligator Carved In-The-Round Handle, C.1890, 35 1/2 In. 68.00
Carved Bone Bulldog, Sterling Silver Band 190.00
Ebony, Whalebone Top, Ebony Bands, Tapering Ebony Stick, 33 1/2 In. 50.00
Gold Head, Ebony 40.00
Hand-Carved, Bearded Man With Skullcap & Ivory Inset Eyes 165.00
Head, Carved Wolf's Head 65.00
Ivory Handled 75.00
Natural Animal Horn, Sterling Silver Band 90.00
Scrimshaw Whalebone & Ivory, Carved Bone Shaft, Ivory Knob, 1840s 375.00
Scrimshaw, Turned Knob Finial, Diamond Crosshatch, 32 3/4 In. 170.00
Snakeskin, Man's 50.00
Stag Handle 25.00
Top, Gold Filled, Small 11.50
Twisted Handle & Base, Glass, Green, 39 In. 58.00
Walking Stick, Animals's Head Forms Handle, Black Paint, 35 In. 30.00
Walking Stick, Carved Oak Leaves, Acorns, Lizard At Top, 32 In. 120.00
Walking Stick, Carved Snake, 36 In. 65.00
Walking Stick, Carved Wire-Haired Terrier Handle, Painted 150.00
Walking Stick, Man's Head Forms Knob, 33 1/2 In. 55.00
Walking Stick, Water Buffalo Horn 25.00
Walking Stick, 6 Snakes Spiraled Between Dividers, Knob Handle, 36 In. 205.00
Wooden, Knob Handle, Lizard, Beaver, Turtle, Snake, 33 In. 175.00

Canton china is a blue-and-white ware made near Canton, China, from about 1785 to 1895. It is hand-decorated with Chinese scenes.

CANTON, Bottle, Water, Bulbous Body	250.00
Bowl, Pavilion, Island, Square, 9 1/2 In.	600.00
Bowl, Rice, C.1860, Marked, 5 1/4 In.	55.00
Bowl, Shallow, Flat Rim, 13 In.	750.00
Bowl, Shaped Rim, 9 1/2 In.	425.00
Bowl, 6 In.	50.00
Box, Cylindrical Form, Landscape, Mountains, Covered, 7 1/2 In.	600.00
Box, Rectangular, Covered, 3 X 7 In.	1050.00
Candlestick, Inverted Trumpet Shape, 8 In.	550.00
Creamer, Helmet	230.00
Cup, Syllabub, Covered, Fruit Design, 3 In., Set Of 5	550.00
Dish, C.1840, 6 In.Diam.	40.00
Dish, Curry, Butterfly Form Handle, 10 In.	475.00
Dish, Hot Water, 10 1/2 In.	270.00
Dish, Hot Water, 11 In.	260.00
Dish, Serving, Ju-1 Form, 10 3/4 In.	300.00
Dish, Serving, Oval, 8 In.	240.00
Dish, Vegetable, Covered, 10 In.	350.00
Dish, Vegetable, Covered, 8 X 9 1/4 In.	390.00
Dish, Vegetable, Lozenge Shape, 11 1/2 In.	330.00
Dish, Vegetable, Open, 8 X 9 In.	210.00
Dish, Vegetable, Oval, 9 In.	150.00
Ginger Jar, 7 In.	130.00
Jar, Cylindrical, Saucer Form Cover	525.00
Jar, 6 In.	165.00
Plate, Serving, Hot Water, 9 In.	150.00
Platter, Octagonal, 9 1/2 X 12 In.	220.00
Platter, Octagonal, 10 1/2 In.	210.00
Platter, Octagonal, 12 X 16 In.	230.00
Platter, Octagonal, 13 1/2 X 10 1/2 In.	225.00
Platter, Octagonal, 15 In.	150.00 To 300.00
Platter, Octagonal, 17 1/2 In.	300.00
Platter, Pierced Liner, 17 In.	1300.00
Platter, Well Insert, Oval, 10 X 13 1/4 In.	170.00
Platter, 6 X 7 1/2 In.	130.00
Sugar	125.00
Sugar, Twisted Handles	125.00
Teapot	140.00
Teapot, Covered, Entwined Handle, 7 In.	260.00 To 375.00
Teapot, Ovoid Body, Domed Cover, 10 In.	350.00
Tureen, Soup, Flower Bud Design, Boar's Head Handles, Covered, 12 In.	725.00

Capo-Di-Monte porcelain was first made in Naples, Italy, from 1743 to 1759. The factory moved near Madrid, Spain, and reopened in 1771 and worked to 1834. Since that time the Doccia factory of Italy acquired the molds and is using the N and crown mark.

CAPO-DI-MONTE, Bowl, Cherubs, Scroll, Gold Rim, Floral Center, Marked, 10 In.	325.00
Box, Covered, Oval, Dancing Putti, 5 1/2 In.	100.00
Box, Tavern Scenes, Cavaliers On Horseback, Crown Mark	495.00
Coffee Set, C.1840, 4 Cups & Saucers, 11 Piece	650.00
Compote, Cherub Design, Cherub Finial & Handles, Marked, 9 In.	225.00
Figurine, African Crowned Crane, Natural Coloring, 14 In.	160.00
Figurine, Lady Dancing, Blue Crown N Mark, 10 In.	100.00
Figurine, Romantic Couple, Signed Pucci, 9 1/2 In.	250.00
Figurine, Sandpiper, 8 X 6 1/2 In.	95.00
Figurine, 3 Classically Draped Women, Cherub, Flowers, 12 In.	100.00

Jug, Bacchanalian Mask, Crown Mark, 3 1/2 In. 100.00
Ladies In Garden, Gold Trim, Crown Mark, 18 1/2 X 12 1/2 In. 185.00
Lamp, Cherub & Flower Base, Flower & Leaf Shade, 19 In. 320.00
Mustard, Raised Cupids, Crown Finial, Nude Man On Spoon 75.00
Plaque, Children In Garden, Brass Frame, 3 X 4 1/4 In. 110.00
Tea Set, Dragon Spout, Portrait Fronts, Scenic Backs, 11 Piece 375.00
Tea Set, Dragon Spout, Red & Gold, Figures, 4 Cups 425.00
Tea Set, Floral Detail In Relief, 11 Piece 450.00
Urn, Scenic, 7 1/2 In. 275.00

CAPTAIN MARVEL, Bank, Dime Register, Flat 125.00
Toy, Lightning Racing Cars 225.00
Wristwatch, Leather Strap 95.00

CAPTAIN MIDNIGHT, Badge, Flight Patrol 10.00
Cup & Mug 35.00
Decoder .... 15.00 To 32.00
Decoder, Keyomatic 30.00
Decoder, Secret Squadron Mystery Dial 27.50
Decoder, 1941-48, Set 275.00
Decoder, 1945 .... 22.00
Decoder, 1948 .... 35.00
Figurine, Plaster 12.00
Flight Patrol Wings 20.00
Medal, Membership, Brass 9.00
Mug, Ovaltine 12.50
Mug, Shake-Up, Papers Inside 65.00
Photograph, 1939 .... 12.00
Photomatic Code-O-Graph 27.50
Pin, Flight Patrol Wings 10.00
Ring, Printing 35.00
Token, Brass Spinner, Membership 10.00
Token, Flight Patrol, Brass, 1940 .... 14.00
    CARAMEL SLAG, see Chocolate Glass

    CARD, see also Postcard
CARD, Arcade, Scantily Clad Ladies, 1927, Sepia, 3 1/4 X 5 1/4 In., Set Of 20 .... 40.00
Baseball, Honus Wagner, Lithograph Star Label, C.1910, 4 X 4 In. 3000.00
Baseball, Joe DiMaggio, 1939 .... 100.00
Baseball, Joe DiMaggio, 1948 .... 95.00
Baseball, Pee Wee Reese, 1957 .... 15.00
Christmas, Double-Sided, Children & Floral, Fringed, Set Of 5 .... 20.00
Christmas, Parrish 7.00
Christmas, Toonerville Trolley, Fountaine Fox, Signed 25.00
Consolidated Coffee Co., 4 Bulldogs Wearing Glasses, 4 X 5 In. 7.00
Germania House Hotel, Cincinnati, C.1870, Street Scene 3.00
J. & P.Coats Thread, Girl Offering Food To Dogs, 3 X 4 In. 3.75
Lobby, Laurel & Hardy, 1940s, 12 X 16 In. 12.00
New Year, Prang, Silk Fringed, Signed, 1882, 3 3/4 X 4 1/4 In. 6.50
Playing, Dr.Pepper, 1940s, Sweater Girl 65.00
Playing, Jack Daniels, Double Deck, Tin Box 35.00
Playing, Los Angeles Scenes, Flower & Liberty Bell On Back, M.Rieder 45.00
Playing, Maxfield Parrish, Unopened 15.00
Playing, Old English Pipe Tobacco 12.50
Playing, 52 American Beauties, Elvgren, Pinups In Color 7.50
Soapine Soap, Kendall Mfg.Co., Fan Shaped, Girl, 3 X 4 In. 3.50
Trade, Kate Greenaway, Series 501, Signed, 3 1/4 X 4 1/2 In., Set Of 4 .... 325.00
Trade, Kis-Me-Pepsin Gum, Little Boy Cook, 3 7/8 X 5 In. 7.50
Trading, Baseball, Quaker Puffed Rice, 1930s, Set Of 26 .... 5.00
Trading, Belding Bros., 1876 Centennial Exposition, 3 X 5 In. 5.00
Trading, D.M.Moore, Tailor, Easel Shape, 3 X 5 1/2 In. 2.50
Trading, Ed.Kakas Of Boston, Furs, Prang, Dated 1877, Fox & Squirrel 4.50
Trading, Edison Phonograph, Signed Picture Of T.Edison, 3 1/2 X 5 In. 6.00

Trading, Eureka Silk, Novelty, To See Man Swallow Ball, 3 X 4 1/2 In. 3.50
Trading, J. & P.Coats Thread, Cow & Frog 2.50
Trading, J. & P.Coats Thread, Lion & Mouse 2.50
Trading, J.P.Bush, Bovine Elixir, Hold To Light, Woman With Product 7.50
Trading, Kate Greenaway, Series 501, Signed, 3 1/4 X 4 1/2 In., Set Of 4 .... 325.00
Trading, Mason & Hamlin Organ & Piano Co., 4 Models, 3 1/4 X 5 In. 3.50
Trading, Soapine Soap, Kendall Mfg.Co., Fan Shaped, Girl, 3 X 4 In. 3.50
Trading, Sterling Piano & Organ Co., Child Playing With Cat, 3 X 5 In. 3.50
Valentine, Boy & Girl With Umbrella, Fold-Out, 1920, 6 X 9 In. 14.00
Valentine, Boy & Girl With Wheelbarrow, Fold-Out, C.1920, 3 X 4 In. 7.00
Valentine, Boy Running, Germany 7.50
Valentine, Cherubs, Color, Set Of 3 .... 4.50
Valentine, Child Riding Dragonflies, 2-Fold 25.00
Valentine, Fold-Out, Around Merry-Go-Round, Cupid Center, 8 1/2 In. 8.00
Valentine, Howland Type, Whitney, C.1880, Set Of 6 .... 35.00
Valentine, Jiggs, 1930s 10.00
Valentine, Mechanical, Perry At North Pole, Nister 50.00
Valentine, Mechanical, Youth Plays Piano, 1920s, Germany, 5 1/2 X 9 In. 11.00
Valentine, Mickey Mouse, 1939 .... 25.00
Valentine, Mr.Peanut, Foil Label, Logo 5.50
Valentine, Opens To Children At Chalkboard, Tuck 25.00
Valentine, Sailor, Think Of Me, 9 In. 48.00
Valentine, Sailor's, Hearts & Stars, 13 3/4 In. 400.00
Valentine, Satin & Lace 5.00
Valentine, Teddy Bear, Squeaker, Movable Head, 8 1/2 In. 52.50
Valentine, Victorian Fold-Up 5.00
Valentine, Young Girl, Fringed, 1908, 4 X 5 1/2 In. 10.00
Valentine, 1900, Cat & Mouse, Germany 15.00
     CARDER, see Aurene; Steuben
CARLETON, Bowl, Rouge Royale, Gold Feet & Rim 50.00

*Carlsbad, Germany, is a mark found on china made by several factories in
Germany. Most of the pieces available today were made after 1891.*

CARLSBAD, Bowl, Scenic, Signed, 10 In. 35.00
  Box, Dresser, Portrait, Gold Scrollwork Trim, Beehive Mark, 17 In. 125.00
  Fish Set, Yellow Florals, 12 Plates, Platter, 8 1/2 X 20 In. 350.00
  Ice Cream Set, Purple Flowers, Scalloped, Set Of 6 Dishes 75.00
  Mug, Portrait, Friar With Violin, 4 In. 65.00
  Oyster Plate 50.00
  Pitcher, Dragon Handle, Victoria, Carlsbad Mark, 8 In. ....*Illus* 85.00
  Pitcher, Pink & Purple, Blue Leaves, Signed, 5 1/4 In. 45.00
  Rose Jar, Gilt Raspberry Finial, Piercing Over Cover, 6 3/4 In. 75.00
  Sugar Shaker, Egg Shape, Flowers, Bird Perched On Stem, Marked 55.00
  Urn, Blue Ground, Ormolu Mount, Covered, 17 1/2 In., Pair 225.00

Carlsbad, Pitcher, Dragon Handle, Victoria, Carlsbad Mark, 8 In.

Vase, Gold & Yellow Flowers, Cobalt Blue, Handled, 8 In. 50.00
Vase, Ivory Ground, Floral Design, 8 In. 55.00
Vase, Peacock Feather, Iridescent, 4 Gold Ribbon Handle, 6 In. 135.00
Vase, Poppies, Cream Ground, Red Mark, 8 In. 60.00
Vase, Stick, Flowers On Crackled Coralene Ground, Gold Trim, 10 In. 150.00

*Carlton ware was made at the Carlton Works of Stoke-on-Trent,
England, about 1890. The firm traded as Wiltshaw & Robinson until
1957. It was renamed Carlton Ware Ltd. in 1958.*

CARLTON WARE, Lamp, Birds, Brown & Gilt, 8 In. 65.00
Pitcher, C.1898, Floral, Gilt, Pewter Lid, 6 1/2 In. 85.00
Pitcher, Classical Women, Pewter Lid, Signed, Salmon, 9 In. 85.00
Pitcher, Multicolored Floral, Pewter Lid, Beige Ground, 6 In. 85.00
Plate, Baby, Jack & Jill, Hand-Tinted 26.00

*Carnival, or taffeta, glass was an inexpensive, pressed, iridescent glass made
from about 1907 to about 1925. Over 1,000 different patterns are known.
Carnival glass is currently being reproduced. If the letter N for
Northwood is included in the description, it appears on the piece of glass.*

      CARNIVAL GLASS, see also Northwood
CARNIVAL GLASS, Acanthus, Plate, Clambroth, 10 1/2 In. 200.00
  Acanthus, Plate, Smokey 110.00
      ACORN BURRS & BARK, see Acorn Burrs
Acorn Burrs, Berry Bowl, Purple 18.00
Acorn Burrs, Berry Set, Purple, 7 Pieces 445.00
Acorn Burrs, Bowl, Master Berry, Purple 145.00
Acorn Burrs, Bowl, Punch, White 950.00
Acorn Burrs, Cup, Punch, Cobalt Blue 75.00
Acorn Burrs, Cup, Punch, Green 30.00
Acorn Burrs, Cup, Punch, Marigold, Northwood 35.00
Acorn Burrs, Cup, Punch, Purple .... 25.00 To 32.00
Acorn Burrs, Cup, Punch, Purple, Northwood 34.00
Acorn Burrs, Pitcher, Water, Marigold 300.00
Acorn Burrs, Pitcher, Water, Purple, Northwood 350.00
Acorn Burrs, Punch, Base, Amethyst 100.00
Acorn Burrs, Tumbler, Amethyst, Northwood 52.00
Acorn Burrs, Tumbler, Purple 49.00
Acorn Burrs, Water Set, Marigold, Northwood, 7 Piece 495.00
Acorn Burrs, Water Set, Purple, 7 Piece 800.00
Acorn, Bowl, Cobalt Blue, 7 1/2 In. 42.00
      AMARYLLIS, see Tiger Lily
      AMERICAN BEAUTY ROSES, see Wreath of Roses
Apple Blossom Twigs, Bowl, Dark Purple, 9 3/4 In. 75.00
Apple Blossoms, Bowl, Marigold, Northwood, 9 In. 35.00
Apple Blossoms, Bowl, Marigold, 5 3/4 In. 15.00
Apple Blossoms, Bowl, Marigold, 6 1/2 In. 20.00
Apple Blossoms, Bowl, White, Fluted, 9 In. 110.00
Apple Blossoms, Lamp, Marigold, 3 In. 325.00
Apple Blossoms, Pitcher, Water, Marigold, Northwood 155.00
Apple Tree, Pitcher, White, Ruffled Top 450.00
Apple Tree, Water Set, Marigold, 5 Piece 340.00
Apple Tree, Water Set, Marigold, 7 Piece .... 295.00 To 375.00
      ARCHED HOBSTAR, see Hobstar Band
      ARGONAUT SHELL, see Nautilus
Asters, Compote, Green, Millersburg 1300.00
      ASTRAL STAR, see Curved Star
      AUTUMN, see Wild Berry
Autumn Acorns, Bowl, Cobalt Blue, 8 1/2 In. 40.00
Banded Drape, Mug, Marigold 26.00

BASKETWEAVE & CABLE BAND, see Basketweave & Cable
Basketweave & Cable, Sugar & Creamer, Marigold 45.00
   BATTENBURG LACE NO.1, see Hearts & Flowers
   BATTENBURG LACE NO.2, see Captive Rose
   BATTENBURG LACE NO.3, see Fanciful
Beaded Cable, Rose Bowl, Aqua .... 175.00 To 200.00
Beaded Cable, Rose Bowl, Marigold 100.00
Beaded Cable, Rose Bowl, Purple 65.00
Beaded Shell, Mug, Purple 70.00
Beaded Shell, Tumbler, Amethyst 45.00
Beaded Swirl, Table Set, Green With Gold 265.00
Beads, Bowl, Green, Hat Shaped, Northwood, 8 X 3 1/4 In. 40.00
Beauty, Vase, Bud, Purple, 8 3/4 In. 58.00
Birds & Cherries, Bowl, Cobalt Blue, 10 1/2 In. 275.00
Birds & Cherries, Nappy, Cobalt Blue, 2-Handled 78.00
   BIRDS ON BOUGH, see Birds & Cherries
   BLACKBERRY A., see Blackberry
Blackberry Wreath, Bowl, Amethyst, Millersburg, 7 1/2 In. 42.00
Blackberry Wreath, Bowl, Green, Millersburg, 10 In. 87.00
Blackberry, Bowl, Marigold, Footed, 8 1/2 In. 45.00
Blossoms & Spears, Plate, Marigold, 8 In. 35.00
Bo Peep, Mug, Marigold, Handled 75.00
Bottle, Cologne, Grape & Cable, Northwood, Purple 135.00
Bouquet & Lattice, Plate, Grill, Marigold 5.00
Bouquet, Tumbler, Marigold .... 25.00 To 30.00
Bouquet, Water Set, Marigold, 7 Piece 300.00
Broken Arches, Cup, Punch, Amethyst 20.00
Broken Arches, Punch Set, Marigold, Bowl, Base, 12 Cups 350.00
Brooklyn Bridge, Bowl, Marigold, 8 1/2 In. .... 325.00 To 350.00
   BUSY CHICKENS, see Farmyard
Butterfly & Berry, Berry Bowl, Marigold, Footed .... 18.50 To 40.00
Butterfly & Berry, Berry Set, Marigold, 7 Piece 149.00
Butterfly & Berry, Bowl, Green, Flared, Peacock Tail Inside 110.00
Butterfly & Berry, Bowl, Marigold, Panther, 10 In. 90.00
Butterfly & Berry, Bowl, Marigold, 3-Footed, 8 1/4 In. 65.00
Butterfly & Berry, Creamer, Marigold 50.00
Butterfly & Berry, Hatpin Holder, Marigold 550.00
Butterfly & Berry, Pitcher, Water, Marigold 70.00
Butterfly & Berry, Sauce, Purple 32.00
Butterfly & Berry, Spooner, Marigold 50.00
Butterfly & Berry, Sugar, Marigold, Covered 59.00
Butterfly & Berry, Table Set, Marigold, 4 Pieces 230.00
Butterfly & Berry, Tumbler, Amethyst 245.00
Butterfly & Berry, Tumbler, Marigold .... 12.00 To 35.00
Butterfly & Berry, Vase, Marigold, 7 1/4 In. 22.00
Butterfly & Berry, Vase, Red, 8 1/2 In. 250.00
Butterfly & Berry, Water Set, Cobalt Blue, 5 Piece 450.00
Butterfly & Berry, Water Set, Cobalt Blue, 7 Piece 230.00
Butterfly & Berry, Water Set, Cobalt Blue, 8 Piece 225.00
Butterfly & Berry, Water Set, Marigold, 6 Piece 250.00
Butterfly & Berry, Water Set, Marigold, 7 Piece .... 180.00 To 450.00
   BUTTERFLY & CABLE, see Springtime
Butterfly & Fern, Tumbler, Amethyst 30.00
Butterfly & Fern, Tumbler, Marigold .... 25.00 To 36.50
Butterfly & Fern, Water Set, Marigold, 7 Piece .... 395.00 To 440.00
   BUTTERFLY & GRAPE, see Butterfly & Berry
   BUTTERFLY & PLUME, see Butterfly & Fern
Butterfly & Tulip, Bowl, Marigold, Flared, 11 In. 300.00
Butterfly & Tulip, Bowl, Marigold, Square 225.00
Butterfly & Tulip, Bowl, Purple, Footed, Square 1300.00
   CABBAGE ROSE & GRAPE, see Wine & Roses
   CACTUS LEAF RAYS, see Leaf Rays

Captive Rose, Bowl, Cobalt Blue, 8 1/2 In. 65.00
Captive Rose, Bowl, Green, Fluted 45.00
Captive Rose, Bowl, Green, 8 In. 55.00
Captive Rose, Bowl, Green, 9 In. 45.00
Captive Rose, Bowl, Marigold, 9 In. 40.00
Captive Rose, Plate, Marigold 95.00
Carolina Dogwood, Bowl, Peach, 8 1/2 In. 125.00
Carolina Dogwood, Bowl, Purple 235.00
Carolina, Bowl, Marigold With Clambroth Piecrust Edge 75.00
    CATTAILS & FISH, see Fisherman's Mug
    CATTAILS & WATER LILY, see Water Lily & Cattails
Chatelaine, Tumbler, Amethyst 225.00
Chatelaine, Tumbler, Purple 185.00
    CHERRIES & HOLLY WREATH, see Cherry Circle
    CHERRIES & MUMS, see Mikado
Cherry Chain, Bonbon, Marigold, 2-Handled 30.00
Cherry Chain, Bowl, Marigold, 10 1/2 In. 37.00
Cherry Circle, Bowl, Marigold, 2-Handled, 7 5/8 In. 30.00
Cherry Circle, Water Set, Amethyst, Pitcher, 2 Tumblers 325.00
Cherry Smash, Bowl, Pale Marigold, 7 1/2 In. 18.00
    CHERRY WREATHED, see Wreathed Cherry
Cherry, Banana Boat, Purple 165.00
Cherry, Banana Boat, 6 Sauces, Red 285.00
Cherry, Bowl, Marigold, Footed, 8 1/2 X 3 1/4 In. 65.00
Cherry, Bowl, Peach, Ruffled, 3-Footed, 7 1/2 In. 135.00
Cherry, Bowl, Purple, Jeweled Heartback, Large 75.00
Cherry, Bowl, Purple, Millersburg, 7 1/4 In. 95.00
Cherry, Compote, Amethyst, Millersburg 500.00
Cherry, Punch Bowl, Marigold, Millersburg 250.00
Christmas Compote, Compote, Purple 2750.00
    CHRISTMAS PLATE, see Poinsettia
    CHRISTMAS ROSE & POPPY, see Six-Petals
Chrysanthemum Sprig, Tumbler, Northwood, Blue, Set Of 4 .... 550.00
Chrysanthemum, Bowl, Green, 9 In. 55.00
Chrysanthemum, Bowl, Marigold, 10 1/2 In. 45.00
Chrysanthemum, Bowl, Red, 9 In. 1250.00
Chrysanthemum, Plate, Marigold, 10 1/2 In. 535.00
Circled Scroll, Tumbler, Marigold 145.00
Classic Arts, Jar, Powder, Marigold, Covered, 4 1/2 In. 250.00
Cobblestones, Bowl, Purple, 9 In. 45.00
Coin Dot, Bowl, Green, 6 In. 30.00
Coin Spot, Compote, Marigold, 4 X 6 In. 20.00
    COLONIAL, see Colonial Carnival
Colonial Carnival, Candlestick, Olive Green, 8 1/4 In., Pair 100.00
    COMET, see Ribbon Tie
Concave Diamonds, Pitcher, Pink, 9 In. 95.00
Concave Diamonds, Tumbler, Ice Blue 85.00
Concave Diamonds, Tumbler, Pink 40.00
    CONSTITUTION, see God & Home
Coral, Bowl, Green, 8 1/2 In. 175.00
Corinth, Bowl, Amethyst, 7 In. 25.00
Corn, Bottle, Marigold 300.00
Corn, Vase, Green 400.00
Corn, Vase, Ice Green, N 195.00
Cosmos & Cane, Table Set, White 675.00
Cosmos Variant, Bowl, Amethyst, 10 1/2 In. 75.00
Cosmos Variant, Bowl, Marigold, 10 In. .... 35.00 To 40.00
Cosmos Variant, Bowl, Marigold, 9 In. .... 18.00 To 30.00
Country Kitchen, Butter, Amethyst, Millersburg, Covered 40.00
Crab Claw, Tumbler, Marigold 40.00
Crab Claw, Water Set, Marigold, 7 Pieces 350.00
Crackle, Vase, Auto, Ice Green, Paneled Inside 25.00

Crackle, Vase, Auto, Marigold 20.00
Crackle, Vase, Auto, Paneled Inside, Lime Green 25.00
Crackle, Water Set, Marigold, Imperial, 6 Goblets 185.00
Curved Star, Bowl, Marigold, Flared, 12 1/2 In. 50.00
Curved Star, Bowl, Marigold, 7 3/4 In. 20.00
Curved Star, Bowl, Marigold, 9 1/4 In. 25.00
Cut Arcs, Bowl, Marigold, 9 In. 18.00
Cut Flowers, Vase, Marigold 65.00
Dahlia, Sauce, White 35.00
Daisies & Drape, Vase, Aqua 400.00
Daisies & Drape, Vase, Marigold, Ribbed, 9 In. 150.00
Daisies & Drape, Vase, White, 6 1/4 In. 200.00
        DAISY & LATTICE BAND, see Lattice & Daisy
Daisy & Plume, Compote, Marigold, Clear Stem 22.00
Daisy & Plume, Rose Bowl, Amethyst, Footed 1050.00
Daisy & Plume, Rose Bowl, Amethyst, Northwood, Stemmed 70.00
Daisy & Plume, Rose Bowl, Green, Footed 85.00
Daisy & Plume, Rose Bowl, Marigold, Northwood 85.00
Daisy & Plume, Rose Bowl, Marigold, Pedestal 60.00
Daisy & Plume, Rose Bowl, Pedestal, Marigold 60.00
        DAISY BAND & DRAPE, see Daisies & Drape
Daisy Basket, Basket, Marigold 30.00
Daisy Chain, Shade, Marigold, Set Of 5 .... 245.00
Dandelion, Mug, Amethyst .... 175.00 To 425.00
Dandelion, Mug, Green 325.00
Dandelion, Mug, Marigold, Northwood 75.00
Dandelion, Pitcher, Purple 125.00
Dandelion, Tankard, Cobalt Blue, Paneled 495.00
Dandelion, Tumbler, Amethyst, Paneled 38.00
Dandelion, Tumbler, Marigold, Northwood 42.00
Dandelion, Tumbler, Purple 45.00
Dandelion, Water Set, Green, Paneled, 7 Piece 595.00
Dandelion, Water Set, Marigold, Paneled, 5 Piece 425.00
Detroit Elk, Bowl, Green 600.00
        DIAMOND & CABLE, see Fentonia
Diamond & Rib, Vase, Green, 11 In. 24.00
Diamond & Rib, Vase, Green, 12 In. 28.00
Diamond & Sunburst, Wine, Marigold 15.00
Diamond Jewel Lily, Epergne, Peach 250.00
Diamond Lace, Pitcher, Purple 165.00
Diamond Lace, Pitcher, Water, Purple .... 65.00 To 225.00
Diamond Lace, Water Set, Purple, 3 Piece 365.00
Diamond Lace, Water Set, Purple, 5 Piece 300.00
Diamond Lace, Water Set, Purple, 7 Piece .... 320.00 To 525.00
        DIAMOND POINT & DAISY, see Cosmos & Cane
Diamond Point Columns, Vase, Amethyst, 16 1/2 In. 35.00
Diamond Point Columns, Vase, Marigold 12.00
Diamond Point Columns, Vase, Marigold, 12 In. 20.00
Diamond Point, Creamer, Marigold 12.00
Diamond Point, Vase, Purple 35.00
Diamond Ring, Bowl, Smoky, 8 In. 50.00
        DOGWOOD & MARSH LILY, see Two Flowers
Double Dutch, Bowl, 8 1/2 In. 50.00
Double Loop, Compote, Aqua, Northwood 50.00
Double Star, Tumbler, Green .... 44.00 To 55.00
Double-Stem Rose, Bowl, Purple, 8 In. 45.00
Dragon & Berry, Bowl, Green, Footed, 9 1/2 In. 500.00
Dragon & Lotus, Bowl, Amethyst, Candy Ribbon Edge, 9 In. 55.00
Dragon & Lotus, Bowl, Amethyst, 8 3/4 In. 40.00
Dragon & Lotus, Bowl, Green 45.00
Dragon & Lotus, Bowl, Green, Ribbed Rim, 9 In. 55.00
Dragon & Lotus, Bowl, Ice Green 775.00

Dragon & Lotus, Bowl, Marigold, Flat Base, 8 1/2 In. 35.00
Dragon & Lotus, Bowl, Marigold, Fluted Rim, 8 In. 50.00
Dragon & Lotus, Bowl, Marigold, Footed, 8 In. 45.00
Dragon & Lotus, Bowl, Marigold, Ruffled, 9 In. .... 30.00 To 35.00
Dragon & Lotus, Bowl, Marigold, 7 In. 38.00
Dragon & Lotus, Bowl, Marigold, 8 In. 45.00
Dragon & Lotus, Bowl, Marigold, 8 1/2 In. 28.00
Dragon & Lotus, Bowl, Red, 8 1/2 In. 675.00
Dragon & Lotus, Bowl, Red, 9 In. .... 350.00 To 500.00
Dragon & Lotus, Creamer, Purple 75.00
Drapery, Dish, Candy, Ice Blue 95.00
Drapery, Rose Bowl, Aqua 215.00
Drapery, Vase, Ice Green, Northwood, 8 In. 55.00
    EGYPTIAN BAND, see Round-Up
    EMALINE, see Zippered Loop Lamp
Embroidered Mums, Bonbon, White, Stemmed, 2-Handled 165.00
Estate, Sugar & Creamer, Peach 150.00
    FAN & ARCH, see Persian Garden
Fanciful, Plate, Purple 110.00
Fanciful, Plate, White, Ruffled, 8 3/4 In. 90.00
    FANTASY, see Question Marks
Farmyard, Bowl, Purple, Ruffled, Square 1250.00
Fashion, Punch Set, Marigold, Bowl, 12 1/4 In., 6 Cups 245.00
Fashion, Punch Set, Smoky, 8 Piece 750.00
Fashion, Tumbler, Marigold .... 22.00 To 30.00
Feather & Heart, Tumbler, Amethyst 60.00
    FEATHER & HOBSTAR, see Inverted Feather
    FEATHER & SCROLL, see Quill
Feathers, Bowl, Green, 8 In. 14.00
Fentonia, Tumbler, Marigold 32.00
Fern Panels, Hat, Marigold 15.00
Fern Panels, Hat, Red 295.00
    FIELD ROSE, see Rambler Rose
Fieldflower, Pitcher, Amber 325.00
Fieldflower, Pitcher, Amethyst 249.00
Fieldflower, Pitcher, Water, Marigold .... 75.00 To 80.00
Fieldflower, Tumbler, Marigold 25.00
Fine Cut & Roses, Bowl, Ice Blue, Northwood 225.00
Fine Cut & Roses, Rose Bowl, Amythyst 29.00
Fine Cut & Roses, Rose Bowl, Green, Footed .... 85.00 To 130.00
Fine Cut & Roses, Rose Bowl, Ice Blue 160.00
Fine Cut & Roses, Rose Bowl, Purple .... 65.00 To 75.00
Fine Cut & Roses, Rose Bowl, White 75.00
Fine Rib, Vase, Aqua, Ruffled, 9 In. 45.00
Fine Rib, Vase, Aqua, 10 1/2 In. 65.00
Fine Rib, Vase, Cobalt Blue, 14 1/2 In. 25.00
Fine Rib, Vase, Marigold, 15 1/2 In. 20.00
Fine Rib, Vase, Marigold, 9 1/2 In. 12.00
Fine Rib, Vase, Purple, 9 3/4 In. 25.00
Fine Rib, Vase, Red, 10 3/4 In. 175.00
    FINECUT & STAR, see Star & File
    FISH & FLOWERS, see Trout & Fly
Fisherman's Mug, Mug, Marigold 110.00
Fisherman's Mug, Mug, Purple .... 75.00 To 95.00
Fishscale & Beads, Plate, Marigold, 7 In. 18.00
    FLORAL & DIAMOND POINT, see Fine Cut & Roses
Floral & Grape, Bonbon, Amethyst, Fenton, Handled 20.00
Floral & Grape, Pitcher, Cobalt Blue 150.00
Floral & Grape, Pitcher, Marigold .... 70.00 To 150.00
Floral & Grape, Pitcher, Water, Purple 200.00
Floral & Grape, Pitcher, White 149.00
Floral & Grape, Tumbler, Amethyst 20.00

Floral & Grape, Tumbler, Cobalt Blue 40.00
Floral & Grape, Tumbler, Marigold .... 13.00 To 25.00
Floral & Grape, Water Set, Amethyst, 5 Piece 249.00
Floral & Grape, Water Set, Cobalt Blue, 7 Piece .... 290.00 To 335.00
Floral & Grape, Water Set, Marigold, 5 Piece .... 200.00 To 225.00
Floral & Grape, Water Set, Marigold, 6 Piece .... 200.00 To 325.00
Floral & Grape, Water Set, Marigold, 7 Piece 200.00
    FLORAL & GRAPEVINE, see Floral & Grape
    FLOWER POT, see Butterfly & Tulip
    FLOWERING ALMONDS, see Peacock Tail
Flowers & Frames, Bowl, Pedestal, Purple 57.00
Flowers, Bowl, Marigold, Footed, 7 1/2 In. 12.00
    FLUFFY BIRD, see Peacock
Flute & Cane, Pitcher, Milk, Marigold 165.00
Flute, Berry Bowl, Marigold 10.00
Flute, Breakfast Set, Purple 125.00
Flute, Sugar & Creamer, Purple 95.00
Flute, Toothpick, Green 80.00
Flute, Toothpick, Marigold .... 35.00 To 49.00
Flute, Toothpick, Purple .... 70.00 To 95.00
Four Flowers, Bowl, Marigold, 9 1/4 In. 40.00
Four-70-Four, Punch Set, Green, 7 Piece 425.00
Frosted Block, Plate, Clambroth, 9 1/2 In. 50.00
Fruit & Flowers, Bonbon, Aqua 375.00
Fruit & Flowers, Bonbon, Green 350.00
Fruit & Flowers, Bonbon, Marigold, 2-Handled 35.00
Fruit & Flowers, Bonbon, Pastel Marigold 100.00
Fruit & Flowers, Bonbon, White 150.00
Fruit & Flowers, Bowl, Ice Green, 10 In. 110.00
Fruit & Flowers, Plate, Green, 7 In. 175.00
Garland, Rose Bowl, Marigold, N .... 35.00 To 40.00
Gay Nineties, Pitcher, Amethyst, Millersburg 2400.00
God & Home, Water Set, Purple, 7 Piece 150.00
Good Luck, Bowl, Aqua, Ruffled, Northwood 450.00
Good Luck, Bowl, Cobalt Blue 100.00
Good Luck, Bowl, Green, 9 In. 140.00
Good Luck, Bowl, Marigold .... 55.00 To 69.00
Good Luck, Bowl, Marigold, Basket Weave Back, Ruffled 78.00
Good Luck, Bowl, Marigold, Basket Weave Back, 9 In. 37.50
Good Luck, Bowl, Pastel Marigold, 8 1/2 In. 125.00
Good Luck, Bowl, Purple, 8 1/2 In. .... 110.00 To 135.00
Good Luck, Plate, Purple 235.00
Grape & Cable, Banana Boat, Amethyst, 7 In. .... 180.00 To 200.00
Grape & Cable, Banana Boat, Marigold 150.00
Grape & Cable, Banana Boat, Purple, Northwood 175.00
Grape & Cable, Banana Bowl, Footed, Marigold 180.00
Grape & Cable, Banana Bowl, Marigold, Footed 180.00
Grape & Cable, Berry Bowl, Purple 28.00
Grape & Cable, Bonbon, Purple, 2-Handled 47.00
Grape & Cable, Bottle, Cologne, Amethyst, Stopper 200.00
Grape & Cable, Bottle, Cologne, Marigold .... 165.00 To 190.00
Grape & Cable, Bottle, Cologne, Purple, Northwood 135.00
Grape & Cable, Bottle, Perfume, Marigold .... 285.00 To 300.00
Grape & Cable, Bottle, Perfume, Purple 435.00
Grape & Cable, Bowl, Amethyst, Footed, 8 In. 40.00
Grape & Cable, Bowl, Amethyst, 9 In. 20.00
Grape & Cable, Bowl, Fruit, White, Footed, 10 1/2 X 5 1/4 In. 350.00
Grape & Cable, Bowl, Green, Footed, 8 In. 49.50
Grape & Cable, Bowl, Green, Northwood, 9 In. 45.00
Grape & Cable, Bowl, Ice Cream, Green, 11 In. 150.00
Grape & Cable, Bowl, Ice Cream, White 235.00
Grape & Cable, Bowl, Marigold, Basket Weave, Piecrust Edge 50.00
Grape & Cable, Bowl, Marigold, Northwood, 9 In. 35.00

Grape & Cable, Bowl, Purple, Footed, 8 In. 62.50
Grape & Cable, Bowl, Purple, Northwood 100.00
Grape & Cable, Butter, Covered, Amethyst 175.00
Grape & Cable, Butter, Green, Covered 179.00
Grape & Cable, Butter, Marigold, Northwood 165.00
Grape & Cable, Butter, Purple, Covered 185.00
Grape & Cable, Butter, Purple, Northwood 200.00
Grape & Cable, Candlestick, Green 99.00
Grape & Cable, Candlestick, Light Marigold, Northwood 70.00
Grape & Cable, Candlestick, Marigold, Northwood 35.00
Grape & Cable, Compote, Amethyst, Covered, Large 525.00
Grape & Cable, Compote, Purple, Open .... 275.00 To 495.00
Grape & Cable, Compote, Sweetmeat, Purple .... 190.00 To 350.00
Grape & Cable, Cookie Jar, Marigold 145.00
Grape & Cable, Cookie Jar, Marigold, Covered 225.00
Grape & Cable, Cookie Jar, Purple 350.00
Grape & Cable, Creamer, Amethyst 70.00
Grape & Cable, Cup, Punch, Marigold .... 15.00 To 16.00
Grape & Cable, Cup, Punch, Purple 30.00
Grape & Cable, Decanter, Amethyst, Whiskey, Northwood, 12 In. 600.00
Grape & Cable, Dish, Ice Cream, White, Basket Weave Bottom 195.00
Grape & Cable, Dish, Sweetmeat, Purple 185.00
Grape & Cable, Hatpin Holder, Amethyst 125.00
Grape & Cable, Hatpin Holder, Green .... 150.00 To 169.00
Grape & Cable, Hatpin Holder, Marigold .... 140.00 To 250.00
Grape & Cable, Hatpin Holder, Purple .... 125.00 To 180.00
Grape & Cable, Humidor, Amethyst, Northwood 75.00
Grape & Cable, Humidor, Marigold, Tobacco 215.00
Grape & Cable, Jar, Powder, Amethyst 90.00
Grape & Cable, Jar, Powder, Green, Covered 675.00
Grape & Cable, Jar, Powder, Purple, Covered .... 45.00 To 115.00
Grape & Cable, Nappy, Marigold, Handled 30.00
Grape & Cable, Pitcher, Water, Amethyst, Thumbprint, N 235.00
Grape & Cable, Plate, Amethyst, Fenton, Footed, 9 In. 95.00
Grape & Cable, Plate, Green, Fenton, Footed, 9 In. 95.00
Grape & Cable, Plate, Green, Footed, 9 In. .... 65.00 To 75.00
Grape & Cable, Plate, Marigold, Footed, 9 In. 55.00
Grape & Cable, Plate, Marigold, Meander Back, Footed, 9 In. 95.00
Grape & Cable, Plate, Purple, 7 3/4 In. 45.00
Grape & Cable, Plate, Purple, 9 In. 145.00
Grape & Cable, Punch Bowl, Base, White 50.00
Grape & Cable, Punch Set, Amethyst, 8 Piece .... 300.00 To 850.00
Grape & Cable, Punch Set, Marigold, Northwood, 8 Cups 1000.00
Grape & Cable, Punch Set, Marigold, 7 Piece 400.00
Grape & Cable, Punch Set, Purple, Northwood, 8 Piece 375.00
Grape & Cable, Punch Set, Purple, 6 Cups, Bowl 11 In. 995.00
Grape & Cable, Sherbet, Amethyst 20.00
Grape & Cable, Shot Glass, Amethyst 150.00
Grape & Cable, Shot Glass, Marigold, Northwood 125.00
Grape & Cable, Spooner, Amethyst 110.00
Grape & Cable, Spooner, Purple, Northwood 175.00
Grape & Cable, Sugar, Purple 175.00
Grape & Cable, Sugar, Purple, Northwood, Covered 210.00
Grape & Cable, Tray, Dresser, Purple, 11 In. .... 190.00 To 250.00
Grape & Cable, Tray, Pin, Green 135.00
Grape & Cable, Tray, Pin, Marigold 75.00
Grape & Cable, Tumbler, Green .... 39.00 To 45.00
Grape & Cable, Tumbler, Light Marigold 14.00
Grape & Cable, Tumbler, Marigold 25.00
Grape & Cable, Tumbler, Marigold, Stippled, Northwood, 1915 .... 100.00
Grape & Cable, Tumbler, Purple 35.00
Grape & Cable, Water Set, Amethyst, Northwood, 5 Piece 350.00

Grape & Cable, Water Set, Marigold, 6 Piece 295.00
Grape & Cable, Water Set, Marigold, 7 Piece 295.00
Grape & Cable, Water Set, Purple, 7 Piece .... 395.00 To 425.00
Grape & Gothic Arches, Berry Bowl, Marigold 35.00
Grape & Gothic Arches, Butter, Marigold, Covere .... 75.00 To 85.00
Grape & Gothic Arches, Creamer, Marigold .... 25.00 To 32.00
Grape & Gothic Arches, Saucer, Green 28.00
Grape & Gothic Arches, Sugar, Marigold, Covered 30.00
Grape & Gothic Arches, Table Set, Marigold 275.00
Grape & Gothic Arches, Table Set, Marigold, 4 Piece 275.00
Grape & Gothic Arches, Water Set, Marigold, 7 Piece 200.00
Grape & Gothic, Water Set, Green, 7 Piece 625.00
Grape Arbor, Pitcher, Water, Marigold 185.00
Grape Arbor, Tumbler, Ice Blue 115.00
Grape Arbor, Tumbler, Marigold, Northwood 35.00
Grape Arbor, Tumbler, Purple .... 45.00 To 50.00
Grape Arbor, Tumbler, Purple, Northwood 55.00
Grape Arbor, Tumbler, White .... 100.00 To 110.00
Grape Arbor, Water Set, Ice Blue, 7 Piece 1500.00
Grape Arbor, Water Set, Marigold, 5 Piece 279.00
Grape Arbor, Water Set, Marigold, 7 Piece .... 380.00 To 410.00
Grape Arbor, Water Set, Purple 900.00
  GRAPE DELIGHT, see Vintage
Grape Leaves, Bowl, Amber, 7 In. 25.00
Grape Leaves, Bowl, Clambroth, 9 In. 35.00
Grape Leaves, Bowl, Marigold, 8 In. 35.00
Grape Leaves, Bowl, Purple 75.00
Grape, Bottle, Water, Marigold, Imperial, Pair 150.00
Grape, Bottle, Water, Purple, Imperial .... 120.00 To 165.00
Grape, Bowl, Cobalt Blue, Northwood, 9 In. 95.00
Grape, Bowl, Marigold, Imperial, 8 In. 28.00
Grape, Bowl, Marigold, Northwood, 9 In. 35.00
Grape, Bowl, Purple, Northwood, 8 In. 95.00
Grape, Candlestick, Green, Northwood, Pair 250.00
Grape, Cup, Green, Imperial 60.00
Grape, Cup, Punch, Green, Northwood 25.00
Grape, Decanter, Purple, Stopper, Imperial 150.00
Grape, Dish, Candy, Purple, Northwood 185.00
Grape, Goblet, Marigold, Imperial 30.00
Grape, Marigold, Fenton, 9 In. 39.00
Grape, Pitcher, Marigold, Imperial .... 50.00 To 165.00
Grape, Pitcher, Water, Green, Imperial 100.00
Grape, Pitcher, Water, Purple, N 250.00
Grape, Plate, Green, N, 9 In. 85.00
Grape, Plate, Marigold, Imperial, 8 3/4 In. 38.00
Grape, Plate, Purple, Northwood, 9 In. 55.00
Grape, Punch Bowl, Marigold, Pedestal, Northwood, 11 In. 200.00
Grape, Punch Bowl, Purple, Northwood, 11 In. 300.00
Grape, Sugar, Green, Covered, Northwood 55.00
Grape, Tumbler, Amber, Imperial, 6 .... 75.00
Grape, Tumbler, Marigold, Imperial .... 10.00 To 22.50
Grape, Water Set, Marigold, Imperial, 7 Piece .... 165.00 To 245.00
Grape, Wine Set, Amethyst, Imperial, 7 Piece 200.00
Grape, Wine Set, Green, Imperial, 6 Piece 125.00
Grape, Wine Set, Purple, 3 Goblets, Decanter 225.00
  GRAPEVINE DIAMONDS, see Grapevine Lattice
Grapevine Lattice, Tumbler, Purple 25.00
Grapevine Lattice, Water Set, Marigold, 7 Piece 575.00
Greek Key, Bowl, Green, 8-Sided, Signed, 4 In. 48.00
Greek Key, Compote, Green 45.00
Greek Key, Pitcher, Green 750.00
Greek Key, Tumbler, Amethyst 40.00

Greek Key, Tumbler, Green 85.00
Greek Key, Tumbler, Green, Set Of 6 .... 550.00
Greek Key, Tumbler, Purple 65.00
Greek Key, Water Set, Green, Northwood, 7 Piece 1250.00
Greek Key, Water Set, Purple 1500.00
Hatpin Holder, Purple, Northwood 160.00
Hattie, Bowl, Marigold, 8 1/2 In. 35.00
Headdress, Compote, Marigold 20.00
Heart & Vine, Plate, Cobalt Blue, 10 In. 150.00
    HEART BAND & HERRINGBONE, see Feather & Heart
Hearts & Flowers, Bowl, Ice Blue, 8 3/4 In. 30.00
Hearts & Flowers, Bowl, Purple, 8 1/2 In. 55.00
Hearts & Flowers, Bowl, White, 9 In. 80.00
Hearts & Flowers, Compote, Ice Blue 200.00
Hearts & Flowers, Compote, White 83.00
Heavy Prisms, Celery, Marigold, 6 In. 50.00
    HERON & RUSHES, see Stork & Rushes
    HOBSTAR, see Hobstar, Carnival
Hobstar & Feathers, Cup, Punch, Marigold 20.00
    HOBSTAR & TORCH, see Double Star
Hobstar Band, Tumbler, Marigold 30.00
Hobstar Band, Water Set, Marigold, 7 Piece 285.00
Hobstar, Carnival, Bowl, Marigold, 4 1/4 In. 35.00
Hobstar, Carnival, Cookie Jar, Marigold, Covered 65.00
    HOLLY & BERRY, see Holly, Carnival
    HOLLY CHRISTMAS COMPOTE, see Christmas Compote
    HOLLY SPRAY, see Holly Sprig
Holly Sprig, Bowl, Amethyst, 7 In. 35.00
Holly Whirl, Bowl, Amethyst 45.00
Holly Whirl, Bowl, Purple, Hat Shaped, 7 In. 35.00
Holly, Bowl, Red, Carnival, 9 In. 450.00
Holly, Carnival, Bowl, Cobalt Blue, 8 In. 65.00
Holly, Carnival, Bowl, Marigold, 8 1/2 In. 45.00
Honeycomb & Clover, Bonbon, Purple 50.00
    HONEYCOMB & FOUR LEAF CLOVER, see Honeycomb & Clover
    HONEYCOMB COLLAR, see Fishscale & Beads
Horses' Heads, Bowl, Cobalt Blue, 7 1/2 In. 75.00
Horses' Heads, Bowl, Marigold 75.00
Horses' Heads, Dish, Candy, Purple, Footed .... 485.00 To 900.00
Horses' Heads, Plate, Marigold, 7 1/2 In. 150.00
Horses' Heads, Rose Bowl, Marigold, Footed 120.00
Horses' Heads, Rose Bowl, Smoky 195.00
Imperial Grape, Bottle, Water, Green 110.00
Inverted Coin Dot, Tumbler, Marigold .... 22.00 To 48.00
Inverted Feather, Cookie Jar, Green 180.00
Inverted Strawberry, Basket, Aqua, Crimped, Handled 27.50
Inverted Strawberry, Candlestick, Amethyst, 6 1/4 In., Pair 40.00
Inverted Strawberry, Candlestick, Marigold, Pair 150.00
Inverted Strawberry, Creamer, Green, Signed Near Cut 85.00
Inverted Strawberry, Water Set, Marigold, Millersburg 1400.00
Iris, Goblet, Amethyst 40.00
Iris, Heavy, Water Set, Amethyst, 7 Piece 375.00
Iris, Heavy, Water Set, Marigold, 7 Piece 225.00
Iris, Heavy, Water Set, Purple, 7 Piece 750.00
Iris, Herringbone, Water Set, Marigold, 9 Piece 100.00
Iris, Pitcher, Light Marigold 250.00
Iris, Tumbler, Marigold 50.00
Iris, Water Set, Marigold, 7 Piece 600.00
Iris, Water Set, Purple, 7 Piece 900.00
    IRISH LACE, see Louisa
Jefferson Glass Co., Compote, Aqua 40.00
Jeweled Heart, Tumbler, Marigold 50.00

KIMBERLY, see Concave Diamonds
Kingfisher, Bowl, Purple, Australia, 9 1/2 In. 125.00
Kittens, Bowl, Cereal, Marigold 125.00
Kittens, Bowl, Marigold, Ruffled, Child's 140.00
Kittens, Bowl, Marigold, Scalloped 90.00
Kittens, Cup & Saucer, Marigold 210.00
Kittens, Cup & Saucer, Marigold, Child's 250.00
Kittens, Cup, Marigold 90.00
Kittens, Dish, Marigold, Fluted Top, 3 1/4 In. 85.00
Kittens, Dish, Marigold, 4 Sides Turned Up 100.00
Kittens, Spooner, Marigold .... 95.00 To 150.00
Kittens, Toothpick, Marigold 110.00
Kittens, Vase, Cobalt Blue, Fluted Edge, 3 In. 175.00
Kittens, Vase, Marigold, Fluted Edge, 3 In. 140.00
    LABELLE ELAINE, see Primrose
    LABELLE POPPY, see Poppy Show
    LABELLE ROSE, see Rose Show
    LATE IRIS, see Iris, Herringbone
    LATE LATTICE, see Bouquet & Lattice
Lattice & Daisy, Tumbler, Marigold .... 12.00 To 20.00
Lattice & Grape, Water Set, Marigold, 5 Piece 200.00
Lattice & Grape, Water Set, Marigold, 7 Piece 275.00
    LATTICE & GRAPEVINE, see Lattice & Grape
Leaf & Beads, Dish, Candy, Green 35.00
Leaf & Beads, Rose Bowl, Amethyst .... 135.00 To 250.00
Leaf & Beads, Rose Bowl, Aqua 145.00
Leaf & Beads, Rose Bowl, Cobalt Blue 60.00
Leaf & Beads, Rose Bowl, Marigold .... 15.00 To 45.00
Leaf Chain, Bowl, Green, 8 1/2 In. 30.00
Leaf Chain, Bowl, Marigold, Ruffled, 6 In. 60.00
Leaf Chain, Bowl, White, 8 1/4 In. 60.00
Leaf Chain, Plate, White, 7 1/2 In. 43.00
Leaf Chain, Plate, White, 9 In. .... 95.00 To 110.00
    LEAF MEDALLION, see Leaf Chain
Leaf Rays, Nappy, Marigold 20.00
Leaf Rays, Nappy, Purple 35.00
Leaf Rays, Nappy, White 40.00
Lion, Bowl, Marigold 160.00
Lion, Dish, Marigold, Ruffled, Fenton, 7 In. 75.00
Little Fishes, Berry Bowl, Marigold, Master, Footed 90.00
Little Fishes, Bowl, Marigold, Footed, 6 In. 75.00
Little Fishes, Bowl, Marigold, Footed, 9 1/2 In. 110.00
Little Flowers, Berry Bowl, Green, Small 22.00
Little Flowers, Berry Set, Green, 6 Piece 160.00
Little Flowers, Berry Set, Purple, 6 Piece 160.00
Little Flowers, Bowl, Amethyst, Millersburg 89.00
Little Flowers, Rose Bowl, Marigold, Fenton 35.00
Loganberry, Vase, Marigold 175.00
Long Thumbprint, Vase, Amethyst, 11 1/2 In. 22.00
    LOOP & COLUMN, see Pulled Loop
Louisa, Rose Bowl, Amber, Footed 40.00
Louisa, Rose Bowl, Green 50.00
Louisa, Rose Bowl, Purple 45.00
Lustre & Clear, Sherbet Set, Clambroth, Set Of 6 .... 50.00
Lustre Flute, Sugar, Green, Northwood 24.00
Lustre Flute, Vase, Marigold, Hat Shaped, 6 In. 20.00
Lustre Rose, Bowl, Amber, 8 1/2 In. 35.00
Lustre Rose, Butter, Marigold, Covered 65.00
Lustre Rose, Spooner, Marigold 20.00
Lustre Rose, Table Set, Marigold, 4 Piece .... 125.00 To 195.00
Lustre Rose, Tumbler, Green 35.00
Lustre Rose, Tumbler, Marigold 12.00

Lustre Rose, Water Set, Marigold, 8 Tumblers 200.00
    MAGNOLIA & POINSETTIA, see Water Lily
    MAINE COAST, see Seacoast
Many Fruits, Pitcher, Green, Millersburg 2400.00
Many Fruits, Pitcher, Marigold, Millersburg 4400.00
Many Fruits, Punch Set, Marigold, 8 Piece 550.00
Maple Leaf, Bowl, Ice Cream, Amethyst, Master 75.00
Maple Leaf, Bowl, Ice Cream, Purple, Pedestal 75.00
Maple Leaf, Butter, Purple, Base 45.00
Maple Leaf, Creamer, Purple 40.00
Maple Leaf, Pitcher, Water, Marigold 140.00
Maple Leaf, Tumbler, Amethyst, Set Of 6 .... 150.00
Maple Leaf, Tumbler, Marigold 26.00
Maple Leaf, Tumbler, Purple .... 38.00 To 40.00
Maple Leaf, Water Set, Purple, 5 Piece 375.00
Maple Leaf, Water Set, Purple, 7 Piece .... 325.00 To 495.00
    MARYLAND, see Rustic
    MAYFLOWER, see Four-70-Four
    MELINDA, see Wishbone
    MELON & FAN, see Diamond & Rib
Memphis, Bowl, Fruit, Purple 110.00
Memphis, Cup, Punch, Amethyst 25.00
Memphis, Cup, Punch, Marigold 24.00
Memphis, Cup, Punch, Marigold, Northwood .... 12.00 To 24.00
Memphis, Cup, Punch, White .... 25.00 To 40.00
Memphis, Punch Set, Green, 8 Piece 265.00
Memphis, Punch Set, Purple, 8 Piece .... 265.00 To 500.00
Mikado, Compote, Cobalt Blue 190.00
Mikado, Compote, Marigold, 10 X 7 1/4 In. 175.00
Milady, Jar, Powder, Marigold 72.00
Milady, Tumbler, Cobalt Blue 15.00
Millersburg Courthouse, Bowl, Amethyst 395.00
Millersburg's Grape Leaves, Bowl, Amethyst, 5 In. 35.00
Morning Glory, Tankard, Amethyst, Millersburg 6700.00
Morning Glory, Tankard, Marigold, Millersburg 4200.00
    MULTI FRUIT & FLOWERS, see Many Fruits
    MUMS & GREEK KEY, see Embroidered Mums
My Lady's Powder Jar, Jar, Powder, Marigold 77.00
My Lady's Powder Jar, Jar, Powder, Marigold, Lid 125.00
Nautilus, Sugar, Purple 230.00
Nippon, Bowl, Green, 8 1/2 X 3 In. 40.00
Northern Star, Bonbon, Marigold 15.00
Northwood's Jack-In-The-Pulpit, Vase, Purple, 7 1/2 In. 35.00
Nu Art, Shade, Marigold 20.00
    OAK LEAF & ACORN, see Acorn
Octagon, Cruet, White, Imperial, Stopper 30.00
Octagon, Pitcher, Marigold, Small 49.00
Octagon, Tumbler, Marigold 18.00
Octagon, Water Set, Amethyst, 6 Piece 400.00
Octagon, Water Set, Marigold, 5 Piece 130.00
    OLD FASHION FLAG, see Iris
    OLE CORN, see Corn Bottle
Open Rose, Bowl, Amber, 8 1/2 In. 48.00
Open Rose, Bowl, Marigold, Footed, 10 3/4 In. 15.00
Open Rose, Bowl, Marigold, 9 In. 30.00
Open Rose, Bowl, White, 9 1/4 In. 34.00
Open Rose, Lamp, Marigold 1700.00
Open Rose, Plate, Amber 49.00
Open Rose, Plate, Marigold, 9 In. 40.00
Open Rose, Water Set, Marigold, Imperial, 7 Piece 110.00
    ORANGE TREE & CABLE, see Orange Tree Orchard
Orange Tree Orchard, Tumbler, White 75.00

Orange Tree, Bowl, Fruit, Cobalt Blue, 3-Footed 95.00
Orange Tree, Bowl, Marigold, Footed, 9 In. 35.00
Orange Tree, Bowl, Marigold, Spatulated Feet, 10 In. 70.00
Orange Tree, Butter, Cobalt Blue, Covered 85.00
Orange Tree, Compote, Jelly, Marigold, Footed 17.50
Orange Tree, Goblet, Marigold, 5 1/2 In. .... 35.00 To 39.00
Orange Tree, Hatpin Holder, Cobalt Blue 140.00
Orange Tree, Jar, Powder, Cobalt Blue 70.00
Orange Tree, Jar, Powder, Marigold 38.00
Orange Tree, Loving Cup, Cobalt Blue 30.00
Orange Tree, Loving Cup, Green 180.00
Orange Tree, Loving Cup, White 200.00
Orange Tree, Mug, Amethyst 45.00
Orange Tree, Mug, Cobalt Blue 45.00
Orange Tree, Mug, Marigold .... 25.00 To 75.00
Orange Tree, Mug, Red .... 325.00 To 350.00
Orange Tree, Plate, White, 9 In. .... 85.00 To 95.00
Orange Tree, Plate, White, 9 1/2 In. .... 85.00 To 125.00
Orange Tree, Punch Bowl & Base, Marigold, Fenton 250.00
Orange Tree, Punch Bowl, Marigold 75.00
Orange Tree, Punch Set, Marigold, 8 Piece 120.00
Orange Tree, Punch Set, White, 5 Cups 450.00
Orange Tree, Shaving Mug, Marigold 135.00
Orange Tree, Sugar & Creamer, Amethyst 135.00
Orange Tree, Sugar, Marigold 25.00
Orange Tree, Tumbler, White, Footed 70.00
Orange Tree, Water Set, Marigold, Footed, 7 Piece 400.00
Orange Tree, Water Set, Purple, Footed 400.00
Orange Tree, Wine, Marigold 40.00
Oriental Poppy, Tumbler, Amethyst 40.00
Oriental Poppy, Tumbler, Marigold 30.00
Oriental Poppy, Tumbler, Purple 39.00
Oriental Poppy, Water Set, Amethyst, 7 Piece 900.00
Oriental Poppy, Water Set, Marigold, 5 Piece 545.00
Oriental Poppy, Water Set, Marigold, 6 Piece 400.00
Oriental Poppy, Water Set, Purple, 6 Piece 750.00
Oriental Poppy, Water Set, Purple, 7 Piece .... 775.00 To 825.00
Oriental Poppy, Water Set, White, 5 Piece 1250.00
PANELED BACHELOR BUTTONS, see Milady
Pansy, Bowl, Marigold, 9 In. 35.00
Pansy, Bowl, Purple, 8 In. 75.00
Pansy, Bowl, Purple, 8 1/2 In. 45.00
Pansy, Nappy, Green 32.00
Pansy, Relish, Green 39.00
Pansy, Tray, Amber, 8 In. 100.00
Panther, Berry Bowl, Marigold, Footed, 5 1/4 In. 35.00
Panther, Berry Set, Marigold, 7 Piece .... 160.00 To 325.00
Panther, Bowl, Marigold, Footed, 5 In. 47.00
Panther, Bowl, Marigold, 5 In. 60.00
Panther, Saucer, Marigold 45.00
PARROT TULIP SWIRL, see Acanthus
Pastel Swan, Figurine, Purple 15.00
Peach & Pear, Banana Boat, Marigold 50.00
Peacock & Dahlia, Bowl, Marigold, 7 In. 35.00
Peacock & Grape, Bowl, Amethyst, 9 In. 75.00
Peacock & Grape, Bowl, Green, Footed, 8 In. 50.00
Peacock & Grape, Bowl, Green, 8 3/4 In. 38.00
Peacock & Grape, Bowl, Marigold, 9 In. 39.00
Peacock & Grape, Bowl, Red, 9 In. 325.00
Peacock & Grape, Plate, Green, 9 In. 215.00
Peacock & Urn, Berry Set, Purple, 5 Piece 230.00
Peacock & Urn, Bowl, Amethyst 60.00

Peacock & Urn, Bowl, Ice Cream, Marigold 125.00
Peacock & Urn, Bowl, Ice Cream, White .... 180.00 To 235.00
Peacock & Urn, Bowl, Ice Cream, White, N, 13 1/2 In. 250.00
Peacock & Urn, Bowl, Marigold, Beaded Berry On Reverse, 9 In. 35.00
Peacock & Urn, Bowl, Marigold, 8 3/4 In. 95.00
Peacock & Urn, Bowl, Marigold, 9 In. 72.00
Peacock & Urn, Compote, Marigold .... 30.00 To 40.00
Peacock At Fountain, Berry Bowl, Green, 9 1/4 X 5 3/4 In. 90.00
Peacock At Fountain, Berry Bowl, Ice Blue 65.00
Peacock At Fountain, Berry Bowl, Marigold 21.00
Peacock At Fountain, Berry Set, Marigold, 7 Piece 180.00
Peacock At Fountain, Bowl, Fruit, Marigold, Footed 165.00
Peacock At Fountain, Bowl, Ice Cream, Marigold 100.00
Peacock At Fountain, Bowl, Purple, Northwood 220.00
Peacock At Fountain, Butter, Marigold, Covered 30.00
Peacock At Fountain, Pitcher, Water, Marigold, 1 Tumbler 195.00
Peacock At Fountain, Pitcher, Water, Purple, Signed 200.00
Peacock At Fountain, Punch Set, Marigold, 6 Cups 435.00
Peacock At Fountain, Saucer, Marigold, Northwood 12.00
Peacock At Fountain, Sugar, White, Covered 10.00
Peacock At Fountain, Table Set, Marigold 225.00
Peacock At Fountain, Tumbler, Amethyst .... 38.00 To 45.00
Peacock At Fountain, Tumbler, Marigold 32.00
Peacock At Fountain, Tumbler, Purple 30.00
Peacock At Fountain, Tumbler, Purple, Northwood 45.00
Peacock At Fountain, Water Set, Cobalt Blue, 5 Piece 490.00
Peacock At Fountain, Water Set, Cobalt Blue, 7 Piece 540.00
Peacock At Fountain, Water Set, Marigold, Northwood, 5 Piece 345.00
Peacock At Fountain, Water Set, Marigold, 5 Piece 300.00
Peacock At Fountain, Water Set, Marigold, 7 Piece 500.00
Peacock At Fountain, Water Set, Purple, 7 Piece 500.00
Peacock At Fountain, Water Set, White, 7 Piece 875.00
PEACOCK EYE, see Scroll Embossed
PEACOCK EYE & GRAPE, see Vineyard
Peacock Tail, Berry Bowl, Marigold 20.00
Peacock Tail, Bowl, Marigold, 10 1/2 In. 45.00
Peacock Tail, Compote, Green 35.00
Peacock Tail, Nappy, Amber 30.00
Peacock, Bowl, Aqua, Northwood, 8 3/4 In. 500.00
Peacock, Bowl, Green 300.00
Peacock, Bowl, Ice Cream, White, Northwood, Large 165.00
Peacock, Bowl, Marigold, Northwood 69.00
Peacock, Bowl, Purple, Ruffled, Northwood, 8 3/4 In. 110.00
Peacock, Dish, Marigold, Ruffled, Northwood, 9 In .... 80.00 To 95.00
Peacock, Lamp, Red 400.00
Peacock, Plate, Ice Green, Northwood, 9 In. 200.00
Peacock, Plate, Pastel Green, Northwood 22.00
Peacock, Plate, Purple, Northwood 190.00
Peacock, Plate, White, Northwood, 9 In. .... 156.00 To 225.00
Peacock, Tumbler, Green 75.00
Persian Garden, Bowl, Fruit, Amethyst 60.00
Persian Garden, Bowl, Ice Cream, White .... 150.00 To 230.00
Persian Medallion, Bonbon, Aqua, 2-Handled 100.00
Persian Medallion, Bonbon, Marigold 40.00
Persian Medallion, Bowl, Purple 15.00
Persian Medallion, Dish, Candy, Marigold 50.00
Persian Medallion, Hair Receiver, Marigold 38.00
Persian Medallion, Rose Bowl, Marigold 55.00
Petals & Fan, Berry Set, Peach, 5 Piece 200.00
Petals, Compote, Amethyst 42.00
Peter Rabbit, Bowl, Green 750.00
Peter Rabbit, Bowl, Marigold, 9 In. 1300.00

PINE CONE WREATH, see Pine Cone

Pine Cone, Bowl, Marigold, 6 In.	20.00
Pine Cone, Plate, Cobalt Blue, 6 In.	45.00
Pine Cone, Plate, Green, 6 1/2 In.	45.00
Pineapple, Creamer, Marigold	18.00
Pinwheel, Plate, White, 9 1/4 In.	110.00
Poinsettia, Pitcher, Milk, Marigold	27.00 To 95.00

POLKA DOT, see Inverted Coin Dot
PONY ROSETTE, see Pony

Pony, Bowl, Marigold, 8 1/2 In.	40.00 To 70.00
Pony, Bowl, Marigold, 9 In.	65.00

POPLAR TREE, see Feathers

Poppy Show, Plate, Green	325.00
Poppy, Compote, Green, Millersburg	200.00
Primrose, Bowl, Amethyst, Ruffled, Millersburg, 9 3/4 In.	80.00
Primrose, Bowl, Green, Millersburg, 9 1/2 In.	65.00

PRINCESS LACE, see Octagon

Pulled Loop, Vase, Peach, 9 3/4 In.	50.00
Puzzle, Bonbon, White, 2-Handled	45.00

QUEENS CROWN, see Royalty

Question Marks, Compote, Marigold, Handled	20.00
Question Marks, Compote, Purple, Stemmed, 2-Handled	38.00
Question Marks, Compote, White	69.00
Quill, Pitcher, Purple	*Illus* 1700.00
Raindrops, Bowl, Peach, Pedestal	59.00
Raindrops, Bowl, Purple, Dome, Footed, 9 1/2 In.	45.00
Raindrops, Bowl, Purple, 10 In.	40.00
Rambler Rose, Tumbler, Marigold	30.00
Rambler Rose, Water Set, Marigold, 7 Piece	230.00 To 325.00
Rambler Rose, Water Set, Marigold, 9 Piece	350.00
Rambler Rose, Water Set, Purple, 7 Piece	130.00
Ranger, Tumbler, Marigold	60.00
Raspberry, Pitcher, Milk, Ice Green	895.00
Raspberry, Pitcher, Milk, Marigold	105.00
Raspberry, Pitcher, Milk, Purple, Northwood	150.00 To 158.00
Raspberry, Tumbler, Marigold	30.00
Raspberry, Tumbler, Marigold, Set Of 5	100.00
Raspberry, Tumbler, Purple	33.00
Raspberry, Tumbler, Purple, Northwood	40.00
Raspberry, Water Set, Green, 7 Piece	90.00
Raspberry, Water Set, Marigold, 7 Piece	250.00
Raspberry, Water Set, Purple, 7 Piece	495.00
Reamer, Green, 2 1/2 In.	6.50

Carnival Glass, Quill, Pitcher, Purple

Ribbon Tie, Bowl, Marigold, 8 In. 25.00
Ripple, Vase, Aqua, 14 1/4 In. 72.00
Ripple, Vase, Marigold, 8 In. 25.00
    ROBIN RED BREAST, see Robin
Robin, Mug, Marigold 40.00
    ROSE & RUFFLES, see Open Rose
Rose Show, Bowl, Amethyst, 9 In. 175.00
Rose Show, Bowl, Aqua, 8 3/4 In. 300.00
Rose Show, Bowl, Ice Blue, 8 In. 225.00
Rose Show, Bowl, Marigold, 8 1/2 In. 175.00
Rose Show, Bowl, Marigold, 9 In. 250.00
Rose Show, Bowl, Purple .... 175.00 To 195.00
Rose Spray, Goblet, Marigold 22.00
    ROSES & LOOPS, see Double-Stem Rose
Round-Up, Plate, Peach, 9 In. 450.00
Royalty, Cup, Punch, Marigold 12.00
Rustic, Vase, Cobalt Blue, 18 In. 75.00
Rustic, Vase, Marigold, 18 In. 25.00
Rustic, Vase, Purple, 15 In. 12.00
S-Repeat, Creamer, Purple 65.00
S-Repeat, Cup, Punch, Purple 32.00
    SAILBOAT & WINDMILL, see Sailboats
Sailboats, Bowl, Aqua, Ruffled, 6 1/4 In. 95.00
Sailboats, Bowl, Marigold, 6 In. .... 20.00 To 24.00
Scale Band, Pitcher, Marigold 95.00
Scroll Embossed, Plate, Marigold, 9 1/2 In. 50.00
    SCROLL-CABLE, see Estate
    SEA LANES, see Little Fishes
Seacoast, Tray, Pin, Purple 265.00
Shell & Jewel, Sugar & Creamer, Green, Covered 50.00
    SHELL & WILD ROSE, see Wild Rose
Ship & Stars, Plate, Marigold, 8 1/2 In. 30.00
Singing Birds, Butter, Marigold, Covered .... 95.00 To 110.00
Singing Birds, Butter, Marigold, Northwood, Covered 165.00
Singing Birds, Creamer, Amethyst 55.00
Singing Birds, Mug, Amethyst, Northwood 59.00
Singing Birds, Mug, Cobalt Blue 79.00
Singing Birds, Mug, Marigold, Northwood 38.00
Singing Birds, Mug, Purple, Northwood .... 57.00 To 59.00
Singing Birds, Pitcher, Amethyst 350.00
Singing Birds, Pitcher, Water, Marigold 195.00
Singing Birds, Pitcher, Water, Purple, Northwood 375.00
Singing Birds, Tumbler, Green .... 30.00 To 38.00
Singing Birds, Tumbler, Water, Purple, 4 3/8 In. 40.00
Singing Birds, Water Set, Green, 7 Piece .... 525.00 To 615.00
Single Flower, Bowl, Peach, 9 In. 45.00
Six-Petals, Bowl, White, Fluted, 7 1/2 In. 65.00
Ski-Star, Berry Bowl, Peach, Deeply Fluted, 5 In. 60.00
Ski-Star, Bowl, Peach, Ruffled, 10 In. 69.00
Ski-Star, Bowl, Peach, 11 In. .... 65.00 To 75.00
Ski-Star, Bowl, Purple, Compass Exterior, 5 1/2 In. 40.00
Ski-Star, Saucer, Purple 38.00
Smooth Panels, Epergne, Green, 14 In. 295.00
Soda Gold, Water Set, Smoky, 4 Piece 550.00
Soldier's & Sailors Home, Plate, Quincy, Ill., Marigold, 8 In. 950.00
    SPIDER WEB, see Soda Gold
Split Diamond, Creamer, Marigold 20.00
Split Diamond, Pitcher, Marigold, 3 In. 18.00
    SPRING FLOWERS, see Bouquet
Springtime, Bowl, Marigold, 5 1/2 In. 10.00
Springtime, Butter, Marigold, Covered 195.00
Springtime, Creamer, Marigold 65.00

Springtime, Pitcher, Water, Marigold .... 225.00 To 375.00
Springtime, Spooner, Marigold 80.00
Springtime, Sugar, Marigold, Covered 150.00
Stag & Holly, Bowl, Amethyst, 7 3/4 In. 100.00
Stag & Holly, Bowl, Cobalt Blue, Footed, 11 In. 160.00
Stag & Holly, Bowl, Marigold, Footed, 10 In. 89.00
Stag & Holly, Bowl, Marigold, Footed, 10 1/2 In. 85.00
Stag & Holly, Bowl, Marigold, Footed, 11 In. .... 65.00 To 165.00
Stag & Holly, Bowl, Marigold, Spatula Footed, 7 3/4 In. 60.00
Stag & Holly, Bowl, Marigold, 8 1/2 In. 95.00
Stag & Holly, Bowl, Purple, Scalloped Edge, Footed, 7 7/8 In. 75.00
Stag & Holly, Bowl, Purple, 8 1/2 In. 95.00
Stag & Holly, Rose Bowl, Marigold 210.00
Stag & Holly, Spatula, Bowl, Marigold, Footed, 7 1/4 In. 65.00
Star & File, Decanter Set, Marigold, 6 Wines 285.00
Star Medallion, Bowl, Smoky, 7 1/2 In. 25.00
Star Medallion, Goblet, Marigold 35.00
Star Medallion, Pitcher, Milk, Smoky 55.00
Star Medallion, Pitcher, Milk, 1 Tumbler, Marigold 50.00
Star Medallion, Plate, Clambroth, 9 1/2 In. 20.00
Star Medallion, Tumbler, Marigold, Set Of 6 .... 150.00
Star Of David & Bows, Bowl, Amethyst, Footed, 8 1/2 In. 50.00
Star Of David & Bows, Bowl, Amethyst, 7 In. 35.00
      STAR OF DAVID MEDALLION, see Star of David & Bows
Star Of David, Bowl, Green, Ruffled, 9 In. 39.00
Star Of David, Bowl, Green, 8 In. 40.00
Star Of David, Bowl, Purple, Fluted, 2 1/2 X 9 In. 95.00
Star Of David, Bowl, Purple, 8 In. 30.00
      STIPPLED DIAMOND & FLOWER, see Little Flowers
Stippled Flower, Bowl, Peach, 7 In. 25.00
      STIPPLED LEAF & BEADS, see Leaf & Beads
      STIPPLED POSY & PODS, see Four Flowers
Stippled Rays, Berry Bowl, White, Scale Band 85.00
Stippled Rays, Bonbon, Marigold, 2-Handled .... 15.00 To 25.00
Stippled Rays, Bonbon, Purple 15.00
Stippled Rays, Bowl, Amethyst, Ruffled, Northwood, 9 In. 60.00
Stippled Rays, Bowl, Amethyst, Ruffled, 8 1/b In. 35.00
Stippled Rays, Bowl, Marigold, 10 In. 28.00
Stippled Rays, Bowl, Purple, 6 In. 18.00
Stippled Rays, Bowl, Purple, 8 1/2 In. 35.00
Stippled Rays, Bowl, Purple, 9 In. 45.00
Stippled Rays, Bowl, Red, Northwood, 9 1/2 In. 375.00
Stippled Rays, Bowl, Red, Scalloped, 6 1/2 In. 250.00
Stippled Rays, Bowl, Red, 6 1/2 In. 70.00
Stippled Rays, Bowl, Red, 10 1/2 In. 600.00
Stippled Rays, Compote, Green 25.00
Stippled Rays, Nappy, Purple, 3-Cornered 18.00
Stippled Rays, Plate, Marigold, Scale Band, 7 In. 15.00
Stippled Rays, Sugar, Marigold 22.00
Stippled Rays, Tumbler, Purple 4.00
Stork & Rushes, Mug, Marigold 25.00
Stork & Rushes, Mug, Marigold, Lattice Band 12.00
Stork & Rushes, Tumbler, Marigold .... 16.00 To 24.00
      STRAWBERRY, see Wild Strawberry
Strawberry Intaglio, Bowl, Marigold, 9 3/4 In. 100.00
Strawberry, Bonbon, Marigold, 2-Handled 35.00
Strawberry, Bowl, Amethyst, 9 In. 65.00
Strawberry, Bowl, Peach, Northwood, 8 In. 95.00
Strawberry, Compote, Marigold, Short & Flat 85.00
Strawberry, Plate, Marigold, 8 1/2 In. 85.00
Strawberry, Plate, Northwood, Amethyst, 9 In. 70.00
Strawberry, Plate, Purple, 8 3/5 In. 85.00

Stream Of Hearts, Compote, Marigold 55.00
    SUNFLOWER, see Dandelion
    SUNFLOWER & WHEAT, see Fieldflower
Sunflower, Bowl, Green, 5 3/4 In. 9.00
Sunflower, Bowl, Marigold, 7 In. 30.00
Swan Covered Dish, Dish, White, 8 X 6 In. 200.00
Swan, Carnival, Bowl, Marigold 95.00
Swirl, Bowl, Marigold, Northwood, 8 1/2 In. 22.00
    TEARDROPS, see Raindrops
Thin Rib, Vase, Amethyst, Northwood, 11 In. 24.00
Thistle & Thorn, Bowl, Marigold, Footed, 5 In. 18.00
Thistle & Thorn, Creamer, Marigold 20.00
Thistle & Thorn, Sugar, Marigold 25.00
Thistle, Banana Boat, Marigold, Fenton, Thistle On Inside 70.00
Three Fruits, Bonbon, Purple, Stemmed 65.00
Three Fruits, Bowl, Aqua 325.00
Three Fruits, Bowl, Green, Northwood, 9 1/2 In. 48.00
Three Fruits, Bowl, Green, 9 1/2 In. .... 48.00 To 75.00
Three Fruits, Bowl, Marigold, Northwood, 8 1/4 In. 20.00
Three Fruits, Bowl, Pastel Marigold 55.00
Three Fruits, Plate, Amethyst, 9 In. .... 60.00 To 85.00
Three Fruits, Plate, Marigold, Basket Weave Outside, 9 In. 95.00
Three Fruits, Plate, Marigold, Stippled, 9 In. 75.00
Three Fruits, Plate, Marigold, 8-Sided 60.00
Three Fruits, Plate, Marigold, 12-Sided 75.00
Three-In-One, Berry Set, Marigold, 7 Piece 40.00
Tiger Lily, Tumbler, Green 25.00
Tiger Lily, Tumbler, Marigold 15.00
Tiger Lily, Water Set, Marigold, 5 Piece 220.00
Tiger Lily, Water Set, Marigold, 7 Piece 230.00
Toothpick, Flute, Green 50.00
Tree Bark, Pitcher, Marigold 29.00
Tree Bark, Water Set, Marigold, 5 Piece 65.00
Tree Of Life, Tumbler, Marigold 50.00
Tree Trunk, Vase, Purple, 6 3/4 In. 37.00
Trout & Fly, Bowl, Green .... 285.00 To 310.00
Trout & Fly, Bowl, Marigold, Satin Finish, 9 1/2 In. 185.00
    TWO BAND, see Scale Band
Two Flowers, Bowl, Cobalt Blue, 3-Footed, 11 In. 35.00
Two Flowers, Bowl, Marigold, Footed, 10 In. 25.00
Two Flowers, Bowl, Purple, Footed, 10 In. 75.00
Two Flowers, Plate, Chop, Marigold, Footed, 13 In. 400.00
Vineyard, Pitcher, Water, Marigold .... 59.00 To 90.00
Vineyard, Tumbler, Marigold .... 18.00 To 70.00
Vineyard, Water Set, Marigold, 7 Piece 250.00
Vineyard, Water Set, Purple, 7 Piece 475.00
Vintage Banded, Mug, Marigold .... 25.00 To 35.00
Vintage Banded, Tumbler, Marigold 30.00
Vintage, Bowl, Amethyst, Millersburg, Center Leaf, 6 1/2 In. 70.00
Vintage, Bowl, Green, 8 1/2 In. .... 38.00 To 48.00
Vintage, Bowl, Marigold, 7 1/2 In. 27.00
Vintage, Bowl, Nut, Marigold, 6-Footed 40.00
Vintage, Dish, Candy, Amethyst, 6-Footed 62.00
Vintage, Epergne, Marigold, Small 95.00
Vintage, Jar, Powder, Marigold, Covered 40.00
Vintage, Jar, Powder, Purple, Covered 35.00
Vintage, Plate, Sandwich, Marigold, Glass Center Handle 30.00
Vintage, Rose Bowl, Purple .... 65.00 To 85.00
    WAFFLE BAND, see Lustre Flute
Waffle Block, Punch Bowl, Marigold 125.00
Water Lily & Cattails, Bonbon, Pink, 3-Cornered, 5 1/2 In. 68.00
Water Lily & Cattails, Saucer, Marigold 20.00
Water Lily & Cattails, Spooner, Marigold, Small .... 45.00 To 65.00

Water Lily & Cattails, Tumbler, Marigold .... 20.00 To 22.00
Water Lily, Bowl, Ice Cream, Marigold, Footed, 10 In. 75.00
Water Set, Oriental Poppy, Purple, 6 Piece 750.00
Wide Panel, Bowl, Aqua, 8 In. 35.00
Wide Panel, Bowl, Green, 8 In. 35.00
    WIDE SWIRL, see Swirl
Wild Berry, Bowl, Amethyst, 9 1/4 In. 36.50
    WILD GRAPES, see Grape Leaves
Wild Rose, Bowl, Green, Northwood, Footed 35.00
Wild Rose, Bowl, Marigold, 8 In. 48.00
Wild Rose, Table Set, Marigold, Child's, 4 Piece 260.00
Wild Strawberry, Plate, Purple, N, 8 In. 85.00
Windflower, Bowl, Amethyst, 8 1/4 In. 35.00
Windflower, Bowl, Marigold, Ruffled Edge 30.00
Windflower, Bowl, Marigold, 8 1/2 In. 25.00
Windflower, Bowl, Purple, 8 1/2 In. 85.00
Windflower, Bowl, Purple, 8 3/4 In. 40.00
Windflower, Nappy, Marigold, Handled 40.00
Windflower, Plate, Marigold 45.00
Windmill & Checkerboard, Plate, Marigold, 8 In. 8.00
Windmill, Bowl, Marigold, 8 In. 250.00
Windmill, Pitcher, Milk, Green 70.00
Windmill, Pitcher, Milk, Smoky 85.00
Windmill, Plate, Marigold 10.00
Windmill, Tumbler, Amethyst 40.00
Wine & Roses, Goblet, Marigold, Clear Stem 35.00
Wine & Roses, Water Set, Marigold, 7 Piece 380.00
Wishbone & Spades, Bowl, Peach, 6 1/4 In. 80.00
Wishbone & Spades, Bowl, Purple, Ruffled, 6 In. 58.00
Wishbone & Spades, Plate, Purple, 6 1/4 In. 80.00
Wishbone, Bowl, Green, Footed 85.00
Wishbone, Bowl, Green, Scalloped Edge, Footed, 8 In. 68.00
Wishbone, Bowl, Purple, Footed, 8 1/2 In. 70.00
Wishbone, Bowl, Purple, 8 1/4 In. 55.00
Wishbone, Bowl, Purple, 10 In. 105.00
Wishbone, Plate, Marigold, 10 In. 450.00
Wishbone, Water Set, Purple, Millersburg, 4 Piece 1750.00
Woodpecker, Vase, Wall, Marigold 30.00
Wreath Of Roses, Bonbon, Green, Footed, Handled 50.00
Wreath Of Roses, Compote, Marigold 20.00
Wreath Of Roses, Cup, Punch, Marigold 14.00
Wreath Of Roses, Punch Set, Purple, 7 Piece 375.00
Wreath Of Roses, Rose Bowl, Amethyst, Small 55.00
Wreath Of Roses, Rose Bowl, Marigold .... 35.00 To 55.00
Wreathed Cherries, Banana Boat, Purple .... 140.00 To 145.00
Wreathed Cherry, Banana Boat Set, Marigold, 7 Piece 195.00
Wreathed Cherry, Banana Boat, Amethyst 110.00
Wreathed Cherry, Berry Set, Marigold 285.00
Wreathed Cherry, Tumbler, Marigold 29.00
Wreathed Cherry, Water Set, Marigold, 7 Piece 250.00
Zippered Loop Lamp, Lamp, Marigold, Oil 180.00
Zippered Loop Lamp, Lamp, Smoky, Oil 325.00
CAROUSEL, Chariot, Hand-Carved, 1912, Herschell-Spillman, Pair 1000.00
  Goat, Euclid Beach Park, C.1900, 50 X 62 In. 5600.00
  Horse, American Flag On Side, Dog Behind Saddle, Parker, Wooden 3500.00
  Horse, American, 19th Century, Carved & Painted, Wooden, 56 In. 2000.00
  Horse, Armored, Ear Of Corn Behind Saddle, Parker, Wooden 3500.00
  Horse, Brown Body, Gems On Collar, 1930s, Signed & Dated 1850.00
  Horse, C.1900, Charles Carmel, Carver, Stripped 5500.00
  Horse, Child's, Pinto Brothers, Coney Island, New York, Metal 250.00
  Horse, Dapple Gray, Wooden, Horsehair Tail 2000.00
  Horse, Glass Eyes, Hair Tail, Rocking Stand, A.Herschell 2000.00

Horse, Jeweled, Dog Head Carved Behind Saddle, Parker 3300.00
Horse, Painted White, Red Saddle, Bells At Neck, Metal, 33 X 25 In. 575.00
Horse, Parker, Armored, Ear Of Corn Behind Saddle 3500.00
Horse, Parker, Glass Eyes, American Flag On Side, Wooden 3500.00
Horse, Parker, Metal, 1950s 350.00
Horse, Prancing, American, 19th Century, Glass Eyes, 57 1/2 In. 2000.00
Horse, Red Saddle, 1930s, Allan Herschell 875.00
Horse, Rocking, Wooden, 5 Ft. 1 In. X 5 1/2 Feet 3500.00
Horse, Trojan, Herschell 1250.00
Horse, Trojan, High-Roached Man, Herschell-Spillman 2650.00
Horse, Wooden, C.1900, Armitage Herschell 2500.00
Ornament, Court Jester, Cast Metal 175.00
Seat, Pelican 165.00

CARRIAGE, Baby Buggy, Red & Black Design, Yellow 475.00
Baby, C.1915, Haywood, Wakefield, Windscreen & Headlight 5500.00
Baby, Victorian, Reel-Turned Spindles, Wire Wheels 175.00
Baby, Walker, Pennsylvania Dutch, C.1800, Pine 1100.00
Baby, Wicker, Black Bumpers, C.1929, Germany, 34 X 33 In. 500.00
Child's, Original Painted Design, C.1850, Black & Red, 50 X 37 In. 550.00
Child's, Wicker 250.00
Sleigh, Horse Drawn, C.1880 .... 2500.00
Sleigh, 2-Seater, Horse Drawn, Portland Cutter, C.1790, Red Trim 795.00
Surry, Spoke Wheels, Blue Upholstery, Canton, Ohio, 1890 .... 4200.00
Wagon, Coster, American Roller Bearing, Stenciling 175.00
Wagon, Farm, Original Painting & Striping, Spring Seat, 1/2 Size 1000.00

CASH REGISTER, Audit, Candy Store Size, Cast Iron 695.00
Candy Store, Brass, Small 600.00
Candy, National, Brass 1000.00
Michigan, Brass, Soda Fountain Size 225.00
National, Floor Model, 64 In. 2200.00
National, Model 33, Patent 1891, Brass 550.00
National, Model 310, Brass 500.00
National, Model 313, Brass .... 650.00 To 1295.00
National, Model 313, Candy Store, Brass 750.00
National, Model 332 .... 450.00 To 1095.00
National, Model 332, Brass 1095.00
National, Model 455-A, Brass 495.00
National, Model 1054X-C, Brass 1395.00
National, No.1503529, Dated June 8, 1915, Brass 750.00
National, Rings To 1 Dollar, Brass 795.00
National, Saloon Model, 1/2 Pint, Pint, & Quart Keys, 2-Drawer 1250.00
National, Time Clock & Card Stamp, 1 Drawer, Oak & Brass 950.00

*Castor sets have been known as early as 1705. Most of those found today
date from Victorian times. A castor set usually consists of a silver plated
frame that holds three to seven condiment bottles. The pickle castor is a
single glass jar about six inches high, held in a silver frame. A cover and
tongs were kept with the jar. They were popular from 1890 to 1900.*
CASTOR SET, see also various porcelain and glass categories
CASTOR SET, 4-Bottle, Daisy & Button, Silver Plated Holder, Meriden 200.00
4-Bottle, Etched Bottles, Silver Plated Holder, Wilcox 185.00
5-Bottle, Gothic Arched 75.00
5-Bottle, Revolving, Blue Bottles, Silver Plated Frame 175.00
5-Bottle, Revolving, Pressed Glass Bottles, Silver Plated Frame 250.00
6-Bottle, Engraved Flowers, Dated 1881, Silver Plated Holder 85.00
6-Bottle, Pressed Glass Bottles, Ball Feet, Bird Center Handle 175.00

CASTOR, PICKLE, see also various glass categories
CASTOR, Pickle, Amber Insert 135.00
Pickle, Beaded Plume, Melon Ribbed, Cranberry, Double, 6 X 5 In. 395.00
Pickle, Blue Glass Inserts, Tongs, Meriden, Silver Plated 175.00

Pickle, Bowtie Insert 25.00
Pickle, Cane Crystal Insert, Bird's Head Holds Tongs, Pewter 45.00
Pickle, Cut Crystal Bottle, Silver Plated Carrier, C.1879 .... 125.00
Pickle, Double, Spread Eagle On Top, Fork, Blue 175.00
Pickle, Enamel Design, Silver Plated Flower Form Frame, Cranberry 195.00
Pickle, Inverted Thumbprint, Blue 150.00
Pickle, Stork & Rushes, Quadruple Plate Frame & Tongs 135.00
Pickle, Tongs, Clear Threaded Glass, Silver Plate Holder & Cover 65.00
Pickle, Vaseline Glass Cut Insert, Sterling Silver Frame, 10 1/2 In. 135.00
Pickle, Vertical Cuttings On Clear, Meriden, Silver Plated Holder 145.00
     CATALOG, see Paper, Catalog

The firm Cauldon Limited worked in Staffordshire, Great Britain,
and went through many name changes. John Ridgway made porcelain at
Cauldon Place, Hanley, until 1855. The firm of John Ridgway, Bates
and Co. of Cauldon Place worked from 1856 to 1859. It became the
Bates, Brown-Westhead-Moore and Co. from 1859 to 1862. Brown-
Westhead, Moore and Co. worked from 1862 to 1904. About 1890 this firm
started using the word Cauldon or Cauldon ware as part of the mark.
Cauldon Ltd. worked from 1905 to 1920, Cauldon Potteries from 1920
to 1962.

     CAULDON, see also Indian Tree
CAULDON, Cup & Saucer, Demitasse, Red & Gold Trim, Cream Ground, Set Of 12 .... 190.00
Dinner Set, Service For 18 .... 1000.00
Game Plate, Center Bird, Blue Ground, J.Birbeck, 9 In., Set Of 14 .... 2000.00

Celadon is a Chinese porcelain having a velvet-textured green-gray glaze.
Japanese, Korean, and other factories also made a celadon-colored glaze.

CELADON, Bowl, Chinese, Dragons, Locust Interior 265.00
Bowl, Green, 6 In. 45.00
Charger, Do-I-Mari, Wedding Carriage, Blue, 15 X 12 In. 675.00
Creamer, Green, Individual 15.00
Jardiniere, Square, 7 X 5 1/2 In. 65.00
Mug, Floral, Bird & Butterfly Design, Ribbon Handle, 4 3/4 In. 175.00
Planter, Blooming Prunus Tree, Blue & White Enamel, 5 X 7 1/2 In. 55.00
Planter, Blue & White, Prunus Trees, Rectangular, 5 X 7 In. 65.00
Planter, Pink, Flowers, Footed, 6 In. 25.00
Pockets, Wall, Iris Flower, Set Of 3, 12 In. 38.00
Sugar & Creamer, Signed 110.00
Tea Set, Red & Pink Floral, Green Foliage, 3 Piece 175.00
Teapot, Rope Handle, Bulbous 75.00
Umbrella Stand, Swimming Carp, Bands Of Scrollwork, 25 In. 1500.00
Vase, Blue Design, Phoenix, Mums, 2 Pierced Handles, 16 In. 125.00
Vase, Figures Engaged In Contests, Crackleware, C.1880, 11 In. 125.00
Vase, Oriental Design, C.1910, 12 X 8 In. 150.00
Vase, Peony Design, Ming 750.00
Vase, Pink Flowers, Bluebird, Quilted Background, 15 In. 160.00
Vase, Polychrome Floral & Birds, 19th Century, 23 In. 300.00
Vase, Sea Bottom Design, 14 In. 225.00
Vase, Urn Shape, Ring Handles, Crackle Finish, Green, 11 In., Pair 225.00

CELLULOID, Box, Basket Weave Design On Sides, Covered, 3 X 1 1/2 X 1 1/2 In. 3.50
Bracelet, Scarab, Colored 55.00
Brush & Comb Set, Case With Mirror 25.00
Case, Cigarette, Tortoiseshell, C.1920, 3 X 3 1/2 In. 40.00
Comb & Mirror, Topaz & Amber 10.00
Comb, Teardrop Shaped Amber Tops 8.00
Compact, Mirror & Comb, Pink 5.00
Doll, Nude, Occupied Japan, 5 In. 10.00
Doll, Sailor, Blue Velvet Suit, Marked 35.00
Dresser Box & Hand Mirror 49.00
Dresser Set, Marblelike Yellow, 11 Piece 25.00

Dresser Set, Marked Patent 1868, Diatite, 3 Piece 60.00
Dresser Set, Original Case, 11 Piece 54.00
Dresser Set, Original Case, 13 Piece 100.00
Dresser Set, 3 Boxes, Tray, Beveled Mirror, 2 Oval Frames 50.00
Figurine, Goofy, Hand-Painted, Disney 150.00
Letter Opener, Indian Smoking Pipe 17.00
Mirror, Hand, Child's, Pink 6.50
Mirror, Hand, Green 10.00
Mirror, Shaving, Round 7.50
Rattle, Google Eyes 25.00
Razor, Straight, Nude Design 20.00
Rooster, Metal Legs, 4 In. 25.00

The Ceramic Art Company of Trenton, New Jersey, was established in 1889 by J. Coxon and W. Lenox, and was an early producer of American Belleek porcelain.

CERAMIC ART CO., Mug, Berries, Hand-Painted, 5 In. 45.00
Mug, Landscape, 5 In. 175.00
Mug, 3-Handled, Pink & Blue, Gold Design, Palette Mark 65.00
Pitcher, Flowers, Ivy, Gold, Hand-Painted, 7 In. 125.00
Tankard, Roses, Belleek, Hand-Painted, Palette Mark, 14 In. 329.00
Tea Set, Flowers, Gold, Hand-Painted, 3 Piece 300.00
Vase, Molded Design Edged In Gold, Green Mark, 5 1/2 In. 95.00
Vase, Prism Design, Green, Yellow, Palette Mark, 10 1/2 In. 102.00
Vase, Red & White Roses, Dated 1903, Signed, 15 In. 325.00

Chalkware is really plaster of Paris decorated with watercolors. The pieces were molded from known Staffordshire and other porcelain models and painted and sold as inexpensive decorations.
CHALKWARE, FIGURINE, see also Kewpie
CHALKWARE, Bank, Figural, Cat, American, 19th Century, Smoking Pipe, 9 3/4 In. 300.00
Bulldog, Seated, 7 In. 55.00
Bust, Lincoln, Boston Sculpture Co., Copyright 1908, 13 In. 85.00
Cat, Black & White Stripes, Red Ribbon, 5 X 2 1/2 In. 23.00
Cat, Sleeping, Brown Spots, Red & Blue Bow, Gold Bell, 10 X 4 In. 45.00
Clock, Mantel, Figural, Art Nouveau Female, 1902, 24 In. 425.00
Dog, Scratching Fleas 20.00
Frog, Seated, Old Paint, 3 X 3 1/2 X 5 In. 130.00
Girl & Boy, Oriental, Nodder 22.00
Girl Feeding Deer, Deco, White 50.00
Lady & Greyhound, Deco Nude, White 35.00
Lady Reclining With Dove, Signed Arnove 274 .... 35.00
Lady Sewing, Victorian 20.00
Lady, Art Deco, 2 Hounds, Sticker, 13 1/4 In. 80.00
Old Lady Sitting In Wing Chair, Cat At Her Feet, Large 20.00
Rabbit, Sitting, White, Pink Paws, Ears, Nose, 6 In. 110.00
Spaniel, 7 1/4 In. 150.00
Statue, Oshkosh B'Gosh, Uncle Sam & Little Boy 110.00
Terrier 18.00
Victor Dog 12.50
Victorian Lady Sewing 20.00

CHARDER, Compote, 3-Color, Pinecones In Cameo Relief, 11 In.Diam. 450.00

CHARLIE CHAPLIN, Doll, Rag, Porcelain Face, Hand, & Feet, Boxed, 24 In. 38.00
Pocket Knife, Figural 30.00
Toy, Windup, Moving Feet, Cane, & Hat, Spanish, 5 X 7 In. 45.00

CHARLIE MC CARTHY, Bank, Composition, 9 In. 15.00
Bank, Mouth Is Money Slot, Composition 125.00

Book, Coloring, The Artist, 1938	15.00
Car, Marx, Lithographed Tin	150.00
Clock, Animated	350.00 To 400.00
Doll, Composition, 32 In.	400.00
Doll, Soap	35.00
Game, Card	18.00
Game, Topper, 8 Wood Hats, Deck Of Cards, 1938	35.00
Puppet, Composition Head	75.00
Puppet, Party, Envelope, Paper	15.00
Spoon, Cereal Premium, Souvenir	15.00
Toy, Benzine Buggy	160.00
Toy, Crazy Car, Windup, Marx	325.00

Chelsea grape pattern was made before 1840. A small bunch of grapes in a raised design, colored with purple or blue luster, is on the border of the white plate. Most of the pieces are unmarked. The pattern is sometimes called Aynsley or Grandmother. Chelsea sprig is similar but has a sprig of flowers instead of the bunch of grapes.

CHELSEA GRAPE, Bowl, Waste, Luster Trim	35.00
Butter Pat, 4 In., Set Of 4	35.00
Plate, Luster, 6 1/4 In.	8.00
Tea Set, C.1825, 24 Piece	500.00
CHELSEA KERAMIC ART WORKS, see Dedham	
CHELSEA SPRIG, Dish, 4 3/4 In.	40.00
Tea Set, C.1840, Davenport, Service For 8, 30 Piece	850.00

Chelsea porcelain was made in the Chelsea area of London from about 1745 to 1784. Recent copies of this work have been made from the original molds.

CHELSEA, Bottle, Applied Flowers, Cobalt Blue & Gold, 18 1/2 In., Pair	3950.00
Coffeepot, Large	185.00
Cup & Saucer, Handleless, Raised Harps & Flowers, White	22.50
Figurine, Girl Holding Basket Of Flowers, Marked, 6 In.	95.00
Figurine, Wooly Lambs, Reclining, Gold Anchor Period, 3 1/2 In., Pair	275.00
Jug, Gray Glaze, Squatty, C, 1870, Stamped Chelsea, 6 In.	55.00
Pitcher, Handled, Blue Anchor Mark	275.00
Plate, Tropical Birds Center, Basket Weave Border, 10 In., Pair	275.00
Teapot, Red & Green Design	65.00
Vase, Gilt Scroll Design, Swan's Neck Handles, 11 In., Pair	445.00

Chinese export porcelain is all the many kinds of porcelain made in China for export to America and Europe in the eighteenth and nineteenth centuries.

CHINESE EXPORT, see also Canton; Celadon; Nanking

CHINESE EXPORT, Basin, Blue & White, Boy, Water Buffalo, Marked, 15 In.	650.00
Bowl, Butterfly & Cabbage, Chinese Character Mark, 9 In.	200.00
Bowl, Coat Of Arms Of Duke Of Melford	150.00
Bowl, Famille Rose, C.1850, Gold Rim, 13 1/2 In.Diam.	550.00
Bowl, Floral Design, Diapered Valance, 5 1/2 In.	90.00
Bowl, Floral Spandrels, C.1820, Blue & White, 9 X 4 In.	575.00
Bowl, Mandarin Palette, C.1785, Gilt Back, 10 1/4 In.	750.00
Bowl, Rose, Purple, Red, Yellow, Black, C.1780, 7 1/2 In.	200.00
Bowl, Tree Peony, Blue Ground, Famille Rose, 10 3/8 In.	280.00
Box, Octagonal, Hinged Cover, Stand, Black Lacquer, 20 In.	880.00
Creamer, Basket Of Flowers, Fish Scale, 4 In.	85.00
Creamer, Helmet Shape, Floral Design, Bough Handle, 5 In.	65.00
Creamer, Rose Mandarin, Bulbous, 3 1/2 In.	90.00
Cup & Saucer, Eagle & Shield Transfer	350.00
Cup & Saucer, Mandarin In Landscape Scene	80.00

Cup, Blue & Red Design, White Ground, Loop Handle, 6 In.	225.00
Cup, Famille Rose, Floral Design, White Ground, 6 In.	275.00
Dish, Hot Water, Blue Fitzhugh, C.1825, 11 1/8 In.	325.00
Dish, Lozenge Shape, Blue Fitzhugh, 10 1/2 In.	250.00
Dish, Sweetmeat, Enameled, Bird Medallion, Turquoise Ground	27.50
Dish, Top, Floral, Bird, Insect Design, 9 In.	80.00
Figurine, Cat, Sleeping, Salmon, Red Ribbon, Bells, 6 3/4 In.	550.00
Figurine, Star Gods, C.1850, 10 In., Set Of 3	900.00
Jar, Blue & White, Happiness Sign, Covered, 9 In.	140.00
Jar, Ginger, Crackle Glaze, C.1800, 13 In.	1200.00
Jar, Ginger, Famille Verte, 3 Chinese Ladies, 8 1/2 In.	700.00
Lamp, Glazed Garniture, Mounted As Lamp, 22 1/2 In., Set Of 3	1100.00
Plate, Arms Of New York, 7 3/4 In., Pair	275.00
Plate, Butterfly & Cabbage, Long-Life Symbol, 8 1/2 In.	45.00
Plate, Figures & Boats, C.1745, Gilt Border, 9 1/8 In.	350.00
Plate, Flower & Bough Design, Scroll, 9 In.	275.00
Plate, Rose Mandarin, 6-Sided, 6 3/4 In.	37.50
Plate, Rose, Carmine, Violet, & Green, 9 In., Pair	100.00
Platter & Strainer, Blue Fitzhugh, Oval, C.1825, 14 In.	800.00
Platter, Blue & White, C.1820, Pagodas, Boats, 11 In.	125.00
Platter, Blue & White, Fitzhugh Design, 14 X 10 1/2 In.	250.00
Platter, Blue Fitzhugh, Oval, C.1825, Pinecone, 10 In.	400.00
Platter, Tobacco Leaf Pattern, C.1775, Oval, 13 In.	2300.00
Platter, Well & Tree, Green Floral, Gold Rim, 13 X 16 In.	425.00
Pot, Brush, American Eagle, Diaper Pattern Border, 5 In.	125.00
Sauceboat & Tray, Blue & Gold, Lozenge Shape, 7 In.	150.00
Tea Bowl, Gold Flower Spray, 18th Century, 4 1/3 In.Diam.	72.00
Tea Set, Butterfly & Cabbage, Rose Border, 9 Piece	275.00
Teapot & Cover, Blue & White, Chinaman Fishing, 5 In.	150.00
Teapot, Arms Of New York State, C.1790, Shield, 5 1/2 In.	325.00
Teapot, Black Lacquer, Octagonal Form, 7 X 10 In.	225.00
Teapot, Oriental Men, Flattened Bulbous Shape, Blue & White	395.00
Teapot, Peach Form, Cadogan, Early 19th Century	175.00
Tureen, Brown, Berries, Leaves, Cover, Stand, C.1810, 7 3/8 In.	600.00
Tureen, Carp-Form, Iron Red, Black Eye, Fin Cover, 11 In.	1000.00
Tureen, Duck Form, Yellow, Green, Pink, Blue Ground, 13 In.	525.00
Tureen, Famille Rose, Mandarin Design, C.1790, Covered	2000.00
Tureen, Rooster Form, Rose Palette, 13 1/2 In.	450.00
Tureen, Turtle Form, Coral Red, Dragon, Phoenix, Covered	600.00
Vase, Bronze, Dog Head Handles, Dragon Relief, Marked, 11 In.	195.00
Vase, Famille Rose, Cylinder, 5 X 12 In.	60.00
Vase, Figural, Schoolmaster, Desk, Marked, 11 In.	110.00
Vase, Pink Flowers, Baluster Form, Signed, 17 1/4 In.	100.00

Chocolate glass, sometimes mistakenly called caramel slag, was made by the Indiana Tumbler and Goblet Company of Greentown, Indiana, from 1900 to 1903.

CHOCOLATE GLASS, Berry Bowl, Cactus Design, 7 1/4 In.	115.00
Berry Bowl, Leaf Bracket, 8 In.	75.00
Berry Set, Cactus, Greentown, 7 Piece	295.00 To 385.00
Berry Set, Leaf Bracket, Greentown, 7 Piece	395.00
Bowl, Bull's-Eye & Beaded Base, Fluted, 8 1/2 In.	79.00
Bowl, Cactus, Footed, 7 1/2 In.	90.00
Bowl, Shell & Leaf, Footed, 8 In.Diam.	45.00
Butter, Cactus, Covered	175.00 To 185.00
Butter, Leaf Bracket, Covered	100.00 To 150.00
Compote, Cactus, Scalloped Rim, 5 1/2 X 5 In.Diam.	110.00
Compote, Cactus, 5 1/2 In.	115.00
Compote, Dolphin Greentown, Cover	265.00
Compote, Jelly, Geneva Pattern, Footed	165.00
Compote, Jelly, Greentown	85.00
Cracker Jar, Cactus, Covered	115.00 To 210.00

Creamer, Greentown	75.00
Creamer, Sultan	65.00
Cruet, Cactus, Original Stopper, Greentown	140.00 To 165.00
Cruet, Leaf Bracket, Red Agate Stopper	160.00
Cruet, Leaf Bracket, Stopper, 6 3/4 In.	50.00 To 100.00
Dish, Dolphin, Covered, Footed	95.00
Dish, Dolphin, Fish Finial	200.00
Dish, Honeycomb, Rectangular	350.00
Dish, Leaf Bracket, Scalloped, Oblong, 7 1/4 X 4 3/4 In.	75.00
Figurine, Cat On Hamper, Tall	265.00
Figurine, Dolphin	50.00
Jar, Cracker, With Lid, Greentown	150.00
Lamp, Duffner Filigree, Paneled, Bronze Base	775.00
Lamp, Kerosene, Wild Rose, Greentown, 9 In.	50.00 To 100.00
Mug, Cactus	70.00
Mug, Drinking Scene, Greentown, 5 1/2 In., Pair	45.00 To 65.00
Mug, Herringbone Buttress	60.00
Nappy, Cactus, 4 In.	35.00
Nappy, Leaf Bracket, Greentown	25.00 To 35.00
Nappy, Masonic Insignia	150.00
Pitcher, Cactus	83.00
Plate, Serenade, 6 In.	200.00
Plate, Serenade, 8 1/4 In.Diam.	165.00
Saltshaker, Leaf Bracket, Greentown	55.00
Saltshaker, Leaf Bracket, Original Lid, Greentown	85.00
Sauce, Leaf Bracket	25.00
Shade, Curved Panels, Mast Metal Frames, 2 1/4 In., Pair	175.00
Shade, Lamp, Curved Panels Held By Metal Frame, Brass	150.00
Shade, 8 Curved Panels, Metal Border, 15 1/2 In.Diam.	365.00
Spooner, Cactus	75.00
Stein, Drinking Scene, Greentown	70.00 To 125.00
Sugar, Covered, Miniature	35.00
Syrup, Cactus, Dewey Lid	95.00
Syrup, Cord Drapery	150.00 To 170.00
Syrup, Shuttle, Greentown	125.00
Teapot, Castle Scene, Greentown	135.00
Toothpick, Cactus	125.00
Toothpick, Chrysanthemum Leaf	195.00
Tray, Wild Rose & Bowknot, Greentown, 8 1/2 X 10 1/2 In.	265.00
Tumbler, Cactus	45.00 To 75.00
Tumbler, Lemonade, Cactus, Greentown	75.00
Tumbler, Shuttle	85.00
Tumbler, Uneeda Milk Biscuit, Signed, 5 1/2 In., Pair	150.00

CHRISTMAS PLATE, see Collector Plate

CHRISTMAS TREE, Decoration, Snow Baby, On Skis, Cotton, C.1920, 5 In.	35.00
Light Bulb, Aviator, 3 In.	20.00
Light Bulb, Bell With Santa Claus Head	15.00
Light Bulb, Betty Boop	55.00
Light Bulb, Birdcage, Red Trimmed, 2 1/2 In.	10.00
Light Bulb, Bluebird	5.00
Light Bulb, Bubble Lights, Nova, Box	35.00
Light Bulb, Candle	10.00
Light Bulb, Cat	15.00
Light Bulb, Clown Head, 2 1/2 In.	25.00
Light Bulb, Cluster Of Grapes, 3 1/2 In.	12.00
Light Bulb, Dick Tracy, 3 1/4 In.	40.00
Light Bulb, Double Faced Santa Claus	20.00
Light Bulb, Elephant, Trunk Up, Thin Milk Glass	30.00
Light Bulb, Elephant, 3 In.	15.00
Light Bulb, Flash Gordon, 1934, Set	175.00
Light Bulb, Frog	28.00

Light Bulb, Harlequin Clown 20.00
Light Bulb, House, 6-Sided, 3 In. 10.00
Light Bulb, Jiminy Crickett 15.00
Light Bulb, Lantern, Milk Glass .... 4.50 To 14.00
Light Bulb, Lion With Tennis Racquet, 3 1/2 In. 20.00
Light Bulb, Lion, With Pipe & Smoking Jacket 32.00
Light Bulb, Mickey Mouse 20.00
Light Bulb, Mickey Mouse, Noma 110.00
Light Bulb, Mickey Mouse, Paramount 100.00
Light Bulb, Mickey Mouse, 8 Shades 125.00
Light Bulb, Minnie Mouse 20.00
Light Bulb, Moon Mullins 35.00
Light Bulb, Noma, String Of 9, Boxed 24.00
Light Bulb, Orange 15.00
Light Bulb, Orphan Annie, Milk Glass, 3 In. 40.00
Light Bulb, Parakeet .... 8.00 To 20.00
Light Bulb, Parrot, 3 In. 15.00
Light Bulb, Pear 15.00
Light Bulb, Pig With Violin 11.00
Light Bulb, Pluto 15.00
Light Bulb, Popeye, Boxed, Set 135.00
Light Bulb, Rabbit With Banjo, 3 1/4 In. 15.00
Light Bulb, Rosettes, Nippon, Pair 20.00
Light Bulb, Santa & Snowman, Milk Glass, Pair 20.00
Light Bulb, Santa Claus, Japan, 7 In. 30.00
Light Bulb, Santa Claus, Pair 10.00
Light Bulb, Santa Claus, 2-Sided, Milk Glass 15.00
Light Bulb, Santa, Celluloid 20.00
Light Bulb, Snowball, Milk Glass 7.00
Light Bulb, Snowman .... 5.00 To 6.00
Light Bulb, Snowman, Milk Glass, Large 10.00
Light Bulb, Strawberry, Clear, 2 In. 3.00
Light Bulb, String Of Lanterns, Occupied Japan, Boxed 34.00
Light Bulb, Terrier 9.00
Light Bulb, Zeppelin, Milk Glass, 3 In. 25.00
Ornament, Acorn, Dresden, Gold, 2 3/8 In. 4.00
Ornament, Anchor, Dresden, Silver, 2 3/8 In. 4.00
Ornament, Angel Face, Lithograph, Spun Glass Wings, 6 In.Wide 10.00
Ornament, Angel Head, Dresden, Affixed To Cardboard Star 28.50
Ornament, Angel, Basket Of Flowers, Heavy Paper, Tinsel, 3 In. ... 15.00
Ornament, Angel, Blonde, Toy Basket, Die Cut, Paper, 6 3/4 In. ... 18.00
Ornament, Angel, Die Cut, Cotton Batting, 18 In. 110.00
Ornament, Angel, Full Body, Scrap Litho, Spun Glass Wings 28.00
Ornament, Angel, Litho, Ring Of Tinsel, 4 In. 12.50
Ornament, Angel, Standing, Silver, Glass, 1920s, 6 In. 85.00
Ornament, Angel, Treetop, Wax, Holder, Early 1900s, 6 In. 115.00
Ornament, Angel, Wax, Fiberglass, Wings 65.00
Ornament, Automobile, Red, Silver Trim, C.1930, Glass, 3 In. 75.00
Ornament, Baby Carriage, Blue & Gray, Cardboard, 2 1/2 In. 12.00
Ornament, Baby In Manger On Red Heart, Glass, 1900-10, 2 In. ... 75.00
Ornament, Baby, Silver Basket, Dresden, 3 3/4 X 3 1/2 In. 55.00
Ornament, Beaded Tassel, Dresden 8.50
Ornament, Bell, Red Silk, Berries, Candy Container, 3 1/2 In. 15.00
Ornament, Bird, Clip-On 10.00
Ornament, Boot, Papier-Mache, Red, 3 1/2 In. 3.00
Ornament, Bulb, Shoe, Glass, Gold 25.00
Ornament, Butterfly, Dresden, Gold, Flat, 2 In. 8.50
Ornament, Butterfly, Dresden, Silver, Flat, 2 In. 8.50
Ornament, Camel, Dresden, Cardboard, 2 In. .... 8.50 To 18.50
Ornament, Candy Container, Walnut, Dresden 35.00
Ornament, Carrot, 4 1/2 In. 65.00
Ornament, Cello, Brown Glass 22.00

Ornament, Cello, Gold	16.50
Ornament, Celluloid Ring, Green, Yellow Parrot, 4 In.	15.00
Ornament, Chandelier, 6 Branches For Candles, 4 1/2 In.	75.00
Ornament, Chimney Candy Container	22.50
Ornament, Clown	35.00
Ornament, Clown Head, Scrap Litho, Spun Glass Robe	10.00
Ornament, Clown On Ball	35.00
Ornament, Cornucopia, Composition Santa Head, Silver	27.50
Ornament, Cottage, 1900s, German, 4 1/2 In.	15.00
Ornament, Crescent, Dresden, Silver, Deep Embossing, 2-Sided	7.50
Ornament, Cross, Dresden, Gold, 2-Sided, Flat	6.00
Ornament, Dirigible, Tinsel-Wrapped	45.00
Ornament, Dog, Seated, Pink, Blue Ears, Glass, C.1920, 2 3/4 In.	65.00
Ornament, Doll Head, Red Mouth, Hood, Glass, C.1910, 2 1/2 In.	75.00
Ornament, Drum, Sticks, Gold Paper, Dresden, 3 In.Diam.	45.00
Ornament, Ear Of Corn, 4 In.	65.00
Ornament, Elephant, Pearly White, Glass, C.1910, 3 1/4 In.	125.00
Ornament, Father Christmas, Blown, 80 Percent Paint	25.00
Ornament, Father Christmas, Die Cuts, Cotton Batting, 18 In.	125.00
Ornament, Father Christmas, Ring Of Tinsel, 4 In.	15.00
Ornament, Fish, Glass, 6 1/2 In.	50.00
Ornament, Fish, Red Gills, Spun Glass Tail, 5 1/2 In.	60.00
Ornament, Fish, Tinsel Outline, Cotton, Tinsel Eye, 7 In.	18.50
Ornament, Fish, 4 In.	25.00
Ornament, Football, Tan, Dresden, Candy Container, 2 1/2 In.	75.00
Ornament, Frosted Lemons, Fabric Leaf, Glass, C.1890, 2 In.	95.00
Ornament, Fruit Basket	8.00
Ornament, Girl, Die Cut, Cotton Batting, Brown, Hair, 18 In.	95.00
Ornament, Gondola, Tinsel	85.00
Ornament, Heart	8.00
Ornament, Heart, Dresden, Gold, Embossed Border, 2-Sided, Flat	6.50
Ornament, Horn, Blown Glass, White & Silver	6.00
Ornament, Horn, Glass, Painted	5.00
Ornament, House	14.00
Ornament, Indian Head, Orange-Gold, Glass, C.1910, 2 In.	85.00
Ornament, Lyre, Dresden, Silver, Red Gel Insert, Flat	9.50
Ornament, Lyre, Tinsel Outline, Blue Cotton, 4 X 5 In.	30.00
Ornament, Mandolin, Wire-Wrapped, Green, Glass, C.1900, 5 In.	35.00
Ornament, Moth, Silver, Candy Container, Dresden, 3 In.	195.00
Ornament, Mushroom	20.00
Ornament, Owl, Frosted Purple & White, 3 1/2 In.	25.00
Ornament, Owl, 1930s, 3 1/2 In.	20.00
Ornament, Parrot, Clip-On	15.00
Ornament, Peach, Frosted Glass	11.00
Ornament, Peach, Glass Particles Attached, 1920s, 3 In.	30.00
Ornament, Peacock, 1930s, 5 1/2 In.	10.00
Ornament, Peanut, Candy Container, Dresden, 1 1/2 X 3 In.	40.00
Ornament, Pelican, Blown	25.00
Ornament, Pickle, 5 In.	60.00
Ornament, Pinecone, Blown Glass, Blue, 3 In.	6.00
Ornament, Reindeer, Celluloid, White	5.00
Ornament, Robin, Holly Lithograph Center, Cotton	35.00
Ornament, Rocking Horse, Red & Green, Cardboard, 2 3/4 In.	10.00
Ornament, Rooster, Gold, Grass, Flowers, Dresden, 2 1/2 In.	20.00
Ornament, Rose Vase, Sugared, Clip	60.00
Ornament, Rose, Patented January, 1927, 4 In.	35.00
Ornament, Rose, Unsilvered, White, Glass, C.1900, 3 In.	45.00
Ornament, Sailboat, Paper Anchor & Sail, 1920s, 5 1/2 In.	40.00
Ornament, Sailboat, 2 Cloth Sails, Pennant, Dresden, 3 In.	165.00
Ornament, Santa Carrying Tree, Scrap Litho, Spun Glass, 8 In.	75.00
Ornament, Santa Claus On Sleigh, 2 Reindeer, Celluloid	18.00
Ornament, Santa Claus, Push & Whiskers Move, Wooden	90.00

Ornament, Santa Claus, 1930s, Czechoslovakia, 3 In. 10.00
Ornament, Santa Head, Dresden, Affixed To Cardboard Star 37.50
Ornament, Santa Head, Papier-Mache 32.00
Ornament, Santa Head, Ring Of Tinsel, 3 In. 7.00
Ornament, Santa Head, Scrap Litho, Spun Glass Robe, 3 1/2 In. 12.50
Ornament, Santa Head, Set-In Eyes, Glass, 1920-30, 3 In. 75.00
Ornament, Santa Holding Tree, Glass 6.00
Ornament, Santa, Celluloid Face, Papier-Mache Feet 55.00
Ornament, Santa, Red Sack, On Sleigh Box, Red 29.50
Ornament, Santa, Tinsel Rope Outline, Yellow Cotton, Flat 42.50
Ornament, Santa, White Paper-Cotton, Lithograph Face, White 45.00
Ornament, School Boy, Bobsled, Spun Glass Knickers, 7 1/2 In. 48.50
Ornament, Slipper, White, Paper Baby Face, Glass, 3 In. 30.00
Ornament, Snow White, Seven Dwarfs, Glass 450.00
Ornament, Snowman 35.00
Ornament, Snowman With Broom, Green Trim 35.00
Ornament, Songbird, Pastel Tinting, C.1910, 6 1/2 In. 12.00
Ornament, Songbird, Trimmed With Feathers, 1900s, 6 In. 20.00
Ornament, Spaniel, Walking, Dresden, Gold-Pressed, 4 In. 30.00
Ornament, Spider Web, With Spider, Gold Wire 10.00
Ornament, Spun Glass Circle, 2 Angel Heads, 5 1/2 In. 25.00
Ornament, Star, Dresden, Tinsel Comet, Gold, Double-Sided 12.50
Ornament, Star, Litho Santa Head In Center, White Cotton 25.00
Ornament, Strawberries 3.00
Ornament, Swan Gondola, Seated Santa Claus 70.00
Ornament, Tassel, Beaded, Dresden, 4 3/4 In., Flat 8.50
Ornament, Teapot, Red Glass 27.50
Ornament, Turnip, Spun Cotton 22.00
Ornament, Two Children, Sled, Paper Die Cut, Tinsel, 8 In. 12.00
Ornament, Umbrella, Tinsel Wrapped 22.00
Ornament, Wax Angel, Spun Glass Wings, Candy Container, 4 In. 40.00
Ornament, Zulu Warrior, Shield & Spear, Cotton Doll 68.50
Ornament, 3 Angel Heads, Tinsel Outline, Gold Paper, 7 In. 22.00
Ornaments, Santa, Clip On 45.00
Stand, Angels & Stars 137.50
Stand, Lighted, Disney 15.00
Stand, Musical, Eckardt, German, Key Wind, 2 Tunes, 14 In.Base 425.00
Stand, Musical, German, Spring Wound, Marked DRGM 1901 .... 395.00
Stand, Noma, Electric 30.00

Art Deco chrome items became popular in the 1930s. Collectors are most interested in pieces made by the Chase Brass and Copper Company of Waterbury, Connecticut.

CHROME, Andirons, Chrome & Lucite Blocks, 8 In. 300.00
  Cigarette Case, Brown Plastic Trim, 1930s 25.00
  Cigarette Lighter, Enameled, Black Bartender, Ronson, 7 In. 500.00
  Cocktail Shaker, Red Lucite Handle, Line Design 35.00
  Compact, Chain, Lipstick In Box, Richard Hudnut, Blue Enamel 65.00
  Server, Snack, Electric, Chase, 13 In.Diam. 110.00

CIGAR STORE FIGURE, Indian, Polychrome Colors, Counter Top, 27 In. 1500.00
  Punch, 1870-90, Carved & Painted ....*Illus* 6000.00

Cinnabar is a vermilion or red lacquer. Some pieces are made with hundreds of thicknesses of the lacquer that is later carved.

CINNABAR, Ashtray, Temple Design, 3 1/8 In. 25.00
  Box, Carved Soapstone Center, 3 X 1 In. 30.00
  Box, Floral & Leaves, Removable Lid, C.1900, 9 1/2 X 9 1/2 X 3 In. 70.00
  Box, Inlaid Ivory On Cover, 5 X 3 1/2 In. 25.00
  Box, Overall Flower & Figure Carving, Cover, 7 X 4 In. 110.00
  Inro, 5 Cases, Scene Of 5 Sages, Iron Red Lacquer 425.00

Cigar Store Figure, Punch, 1870-90,
Carved & Painted

Tray, Dragons Carved On Inside, Incised Mark, 2 X 7 X 11 1/2 In.	120.00
Vase, Baluster Shape, Mountains, Pagodas, Pine Trees, Red, 7 In., Pair	125.00

Civil War mementos are important collectors' items. Most of the pieces are military items used from 1861 to 1865.

CIVIL WAR, Bayonette Scabbard, U.S., Brass	35.00
Bayonette, 45-70 Trowel	120.00
Belt Plate, Cartridge, Hook, Oval U.S.Type	40.00
Bond, Confederate, Pictures Alexander Stephens, Framed, 17 X 21 In	50.00
Book, History, 1912, Brady Photographs, Set Of 16	150.00
Brush, Curry, Leather, Marked U.S. & Herbert Brush Mfg.Co., Pair	35.00
Buckle & Belt, Leather, 45 In.	35.00
Case, Cartridge	105.00
Chest, Horstmann Bros. & Co., Dated 1915, 18 X 10 1/2	125.00
Cup, Drinking, Collapsible, Hard Rubber, 2 1/2 In.Diam.	79.50
Drum, Haverhill, Mass.	800.00
Flag, 34 Star	150.00
Flask, Powder, Brass	95.00
Lantern, Signal, Kerosene, Tin	35.00
Mess Gear, Clasp Knife Shape, Horn Handles, Silver Spoon	84.50
Mirror, Hand, Soldier's, Marked U.S., 2 X 7 In.	75.00
Mold, Bullet, Pistol, Brass	30.00
Saber & Scabbard, Cavalry, Marked U.S.	175.00
Sword, Dress	150.00
Sword, Infantry, Scabbard, Marked U.S., 1863, Brass Handle, Belt	225.00
Telescope, 3-Draw, French, Extended 30 1/2 In.	135.00
CKAW, see Dedham	

Clambroth glass, popular in the Victorian era, is a grayish color and is semiopaque like clambroth.

CLAMBROTH, Basket, Souvenir, Havana, N.D.	26.00
Bottle, Barber, Stopper	30.00
Box, Trinket, Winged Scroll, Heisey, Souvenir	35.00
Compote, Captive Rose, Blue	75.00
Shaker, Talcum	15.00
Shaving Mug, Bird & Wheat	35.00

Spooner	200.00
Spooner, Sandwich Glass	400.00
Toothpick, Oregon	20.00
Vase, 4 3/4 X 9 In.	25.00

CLARICE CLIFF, Coffee Set, Gayday, Multicolored, 6 Piece	175.00
Coffee Set, Multicolored, 16 Piece	375.00
Jar, Cylindrical, Geometric, Covered, 3 1/2 In.	120.00
Plate, Coronation, 1953, 6 1/2 In.	25.00
Sugar & Creamer, Tray, Blue & White	25.00

Clewell ware was made in limited quantities by Charles Walter Clewell
of Canton, Ohio, from 1902 to 1955. Pottery was covered with a thin coating of bronze, then treated to make the bronze turn different colors. Pieces
covered with copper, brass, or silver were also made. Mr. Clewell's
secret formula for blue patina bronze was burned when he died in 1965.

CLEWELL, Mug, Nail Handle	90.00
Mug, Nailhead Copper	95.00
Vase, Green Patina, 8 1/2 In.	130.00 To 165.00
Vase, Green, 10 In.	175.00
Vase, Patina, 6 1/2 In.	145.00

Clews pottery was made by George Clews & Co. of Brownhill Pottery,
Tunstall, England, from 1806 to 1861.

CLEWS, see also Flow Blue

CLEWS, Bowl, Soup, Oriental Scenery	85.00
Cup & Saucer, Jessamine, Handleless	65.00
Plate, St.Catherine Hill Near Guildford, 1818-34 Mark, 9 In.	165.00

The Clifton Pottery was founded by William Long in Clifton,
New Jersey, in 1905. He worked there until 1908 making a line
called Crystal Patina. The Clifton pottery made art pottery. Another
firm, the Chesapeake Pottery, sold majolica marked Clifton ware.

CLIFTON, Bowl, Indian, Mile Run Inscription, 8 In.Diam.	65.00
Pitcher, Crystal, Lid, 5 1/2 In.	85.00
Pitcher, Lid, Crystal Patina, 5 1/2 In.	150.00
Vase, Arizona Indian, Squatty, 8 In.	80.00

CLOCK, Acorn, Double Columns, Cartouche Face, Thermometer, Barometer, French	525.00
Acorn, Wall, Time, Strike, Thermometer, Barometer, French, C.1880	795.00
Adkins, 8-Day, Rosewood	175.00
Advertising, Ac Spark Plugs	75.00
Advertising, Budweiser, Revolving, Picture Of Duck On Back	27.50
Advertising, Canada Dry	20.00
Advertising, Dr.Pepper, Electric, Square	25.00
Advertising, Drink Coca-Cola In Bottles, Electric, Wood Frame, 16 In.	185.00
Advertising, Edward P.Baird & Co., Tobacco, Seth Thomas	875.00
Advertising, Ever-Ready, Pendulum	*Illus* 1700.00
Advertising, Father Knickerbocker Drinking Beer, Square	45.00
Advertising, Figure Eight, Baird & Co., Seth Thomas, 31 In.	450.00
Advertising, Gallery, Nestles Milk, C.1890, Tin	600.00
Advertising, Gas Globes & Lenses, White Eagle	750.00
Advertising, General Electric Refrigerator, Electric, 8 1/2 In.	160.00
Advertising, Hudson Motor Car Co., Wall	75.00
Advertising, Humble Oil & Gasoline	15.00
Advertising, K.M.Y.R. 710 Sunday, Seven Ten P.M., Black	185.00
Advertising, Lucky Strike Cigarettes	750.00
Advertising, Lux, Beer Drinkers, Animated	125.00
Advertising, Marlboro Cigarettes, Rectangular, Large	40.00

Clock, Advertising, Ever-Ready, Pendulum

Advertising, Milkmaid Milk, Now's The Time To Buy It	600.00
Advertising, Miller High Life, Jumping Lights	50.00
Advertising, Mr.Peanut, Alarm, Original, Boxed	55.00
Advertising, Mr.Peanut, Lux Time Maker, Alarm Bell On Top	75.00
Advertising, Nash's Happy Time Mustard, Original Label	18.00
Advertising, New Haven, School, Lewis Red Jacket Bitters, 21 1/2 In.	500.00
Advertising, Nu Grape, Electric, 14 1/2 In.Diam.	50.00
Advertising, Oil Zum Motor Oil, Pictures Masked Man	75.00
Advertising, Old Mr, Boston, Bottle Shape	135.00
Advertising, Orange Crush	20.00
Advertising, Pabst	45.00
Advertising, Pepsi-Cola, Talking	175.00
Advertising, Piel's Beer, Figural, Bert & Harry, 1959	25.00
Advertising, Postal Telegraph	70.00
Advertising, Procter & Gamble	40.00
Advertising, Red Goose, 3-D, Papier-Mache	125.00
Advertising, Reed's Tonic, Grandfather, Miniature	800.00
Advertising, Royal Crown Cola, Electric, 15 In.Diam.	27.50
Advertising, Sauer's Extracts, Gilbert Works, C.1907, Wall	1150.00
Advertising, Skelly Premium, 12 1/2 In.Diam, Pair	175.00
Advertising, Smith Jewelers	25.00
Advertising, St.Joseph Aspirin	45.00
Advertising, Sunoco Dynafuel, 15 In.Diam.Pair	175.00
Advertising, Vantaga Cigarettes	20.00
Advertising, Wall Street Journal Sold Here, 10 Cents, Electric	20.00
Alarm, Charlie The Tuna	35.00
Alarm, New Haven, Oak	140.00
Alarm, Popeye, Initial, C.1929, New Haven	675.00
Alarm, Seth Thomas, Empire Cornice & Column	450.00
Alarm, Waterbury, 1920s, Boxed With Guarantee	50.00
Amimated, F.D.R.At The Wheel For A New Deal, Electric	65.00
Animated, Betty Boop	400.00
Animated, Big Bad Wolf	155.00 To 250.00
Animated, F.D.R., Bartender, Prohibition, White Metal	115.00
Animated, Mickey Mouse, Eyes Move, Alarm, Germany	30.00
Animated, Mickey Mouse, Ingersoll	175.00
Animated, Mickey Mouse, Ingersoll, Alarm, C.1934	190.00 To 300.00
Animated, Organ Grinder With Monkey	150.00
Animated, Pluto	110.00
Animated, Roy Rogers	115.00
Animated, Woody Woodpecker	155.00
Ansonia, Blue With White China, 6 1/2 In.	150.00
Ansonia, Cherub At Top, China, Green, 11 In.	400.00
Ansonia, Crystal Regulator, Time & Strike	595.00
Ansonia, Grandfather, C.1900, Solid Mahogany	3995.00
Ansonia, King Model, 8-Day, Time & Strike, Spool Pendulum, 24 In.	300.00
Ansonia, King, Shelf, Spool Pendulum, 24 In.	275.00

Clock, Ansonia, Royal Bonn Case,
Open Escapement

Ansonia, Kitchen, 8-Day, Beehive Bears, Walnut 225.00
Ansonia, LaGrace, Royal Bonn 395.00
Ansonia, LaVergna, Royal Bonn 525.00
Ansonia, Mantel, Greek Temple, Open Escapement, Time & Strike 215.00
Ansonia, Mantel, 1/4 Hour, Westminster Chimes, Mahogany 135.00
Ansonia, Mission, Kitchen, 8-Day, Time & Strike, Oak 95.00
Ansonia, Onyx, Gilded Visible Escapement, Fancy Dial 250.00
Ansonia, Queen Mary 650.00
Ansonia, Regulator, Mercury Pendulum, Beveled Glass, 9 In. 375.00
Ansonia, Regulator, Mirror Side 500.00
Ansonia, Royal Bonn Case, Open Escapement ....*Illus* 1500.00
Ansonia, School, Time & Strike, Oak, Large 350.00
Ansonia, Solid Brass, 6 In. 100.00
Ansonia, Teardrop, Time & Strike 325.00
Ansonia, Wall, Major Model, C.1875, Walnut, 29 1/2 In. 1200.00
Ansonia, Wall, Queen Elizabeth, Time & Strike 750.00
Atkins, School, Rosewood 275.00
Auguste Courvoisier, Carriage, C.1830, Calendar Dial, Agate Sides 8500.00
Austrian, Grandfather, Bombe, C.1860, Burl Walnut, 8 Ft. 10 In. 8500.00
Banjo, Chelsea, Brass Eagle On Top, Reverse Painting, 40 In. 1750.00
Banjo, Gilbert, Bim Bam, 40 In. 325.00
Banjo, Howard, Davis & Dennison, Roxbury, No.5 .... 2500.00
Banjo, Ingraham, Nyanza 325.00
Banjo, Ingraham, Treasure Isle, 8-Day, Time & Strike, 39 In. 500.00
Banjo, Job Wilbour, Providence, R.I. 4250.00
Banjo, New Haven, Bim Bam, 33 In. 200.00
Banjo, New Haven, 8-Day, Pendulum Pictures Ship, 33 In. .... 195.00 To 225.00
Banjo, Weight Driven, Rosewood Case, Nickel Plated Brass Face 850.00
Boston, Crystal Regulator, Delphus Model, Gold Plated Case 750.00
Brewster & Sons, Steeple, 8-Day 295.00
Bruney, Louis XV, Bronze Dore, 19th Century, 22 In. 250.00
Bundy, Regulator, Oak, 50 In. 450.00
Calendar, Gilbert, Walnut, Gingerbread, 21 1/2 In. 300.00
Calendar, Ithaca, Double Dial, 26 In. 1100.00
Calendar, Ithaca, Farmer's Model, C.1880, 25 In. 975.00
Calendar, Meriden, Lovell Mfg.Co., Grain Painted Pine Case 450.00
Calendar, Seth Thomas, Parlour 875.00
Calendar, Wignall, Ormskirk, Dial & Moon Phase, 1760-85, England 2800.00
Carriage, Ansonia Movement, Porcelain Double Face, Strike, 9 3/4 In. 560.00
Carriage, Bigelow-Kinnard Co., 4-Sided, Beveled Glass 395.00
Carriage, Brass, Arabic Numerals, White Enamel Dial, 4 3/4 In. 375.00
Carriage, Chelsea, Raised Numerals, Bronze Resonator, 11 In. 1500.00
Carriage, Dienzle, Music Box, Alarm, 1890s, 6 In. 145.00

Carriage, French Striker, Chimes, Brass Finish, 5 X 3 In. 565.00
Carriage, Musical, White Metal & Brass, German 250.00
Carriage, Seth Thomas, Roman Numerals, Chrome, Brass, 5 X 6 In. 145.00
Carriage, Striking, Alarm, C.1890, Curved Sides, Gilt Metal 1500.00
Carriage, Waterbury, Brass, Miniature, Leather Case, 3 X 2 In. 415.00
Carriage, 8-Day, Time & Strike, French 350.00
Cartel, C.1900, Arabic Numerals, Strike, Enamel Dial, Bronze, 34 In. 1100.00
Chelsea, Navy, Time Only, Black, 6 In. 150.00
Chelsea, Ship, Silvered Dial, U.S.Marine Corps, Nickel, 7 In.Diam. 225.00
Chelsea, Table, 2-Tone Metal Face & Frame, English, 8 In. 55.00
Chelsea, 1 Weight, Quarter-Sawed Oak 3250.00
Crystal Regulator, Green Onyx, Visible Escapement, Porcelain Dial 600.00
Cuckoo, German, Wood, 2 Weights, 19th Century 170.00
Desk, Calendar, C.1900, 8-Day, Gilt Metal 450.00
Detex, Night Watchman's, Leather Case, Keys 35.00
Drum Movement, Outside Countwheel, C.1850, Meissen, 21 In. 2200.00
E.Howard & Co., No.75, Oak 2800.00
E.Ingraham & Co., Mantel, 20 In. 145.00
E.N.Welch, Walnut Gingerbread, Sandwich Glass Pendulum 195.00
Ebensee, Wall, Porcelain Dial, Brass Weights & Pendulum, C.1890 .... 1400.00
Edward Stanton, William & Mary, Brass, 15 1/2 In. 330.00
Electric, Roosevelt, Man Of The Hour 75.00
Eli Bentley, Grandfather, C.1770, Rocking Ship Movement, Walnut, 8 Feet 3500.00
Eli Terry, Wooden Works, 8-Day, Carved Mahogany Case 1400.00
F.C.Andrews, Triple Decker, 8-Day, Weight Driven, Reverse Paintings 575.00
F.Kroeber, Mantel, Brass, Owl & Fox Motifs, 1874 .... 500.00
Forestville Mfg.Co., Biston, Conn., Triple-Shelf, Mahogany On Pine 300.00
French, Barometer, 19th Century .... *Illus* 3500.00
French, Beveled Glass, C.1910, Walnut Burl & Marquetry, Ormolu Trim 795.00
French, Crystal Regulator, Mercury Pendulum, Frederick Japi, 12 In. 800.00
French, Garniture, Dial Signed Deniere, 26 1/4 In., 3 Piece 3000.00
French, Porcelain, Fish Form, Basket Flowers, Time & Strike, 16 In. 275.00
French, Regulator, Mercury Pendulum, Porcelain Dial, Beveled Glass 395.00
French, Travel, C.1900 .... 300.00
French, Wag-On-Wall, Tin Face Housing & Pendulum, Morbier, 43 In. 1200.00
G.B.Owens, Shelf, Drawer In Base, Time & Strike 425.00
Gallery, Fussee, Walnut Case, English, Brass Bezel 750.00
German, Box Regulator, Time & Strike, 11 X 30 In. 125.00
German, Bracket, Westminster Chimes, Brass Works, Wurttemberg 285.00
German, 3-Weight, Quarter-Hour Chime, Carved Case & Inlay 1100.00
Gilbert, Gingerbread, Oak 115.00
Gilbert, Regulator, 8-Day, 38 In. 450.00

Clock, French, Barometer, 19th Century

Gilbert, Rounded Top, 3-Hour, Time & Strike, Rosewood Case 75.00
Gilbert, Shelf, Alarm, Original Glass, Walnut 295.00
Gilbert, Teardrop, Time & Strike 295.00
Gilbert, Time & Strike, Blue China 375.00
Grandfather, Ansonia, Mahogany, No.5, C.1900 .... 4000.00
Grandfather, David Goebrecth, Calendar Movement, Pine, 93 In. 1200.00
Grandfather, Eastlake, Walnut, C.1885, 8 Ft. 1 In. 200.00
Grandfather, G.Parker, Cherry, Signed Dial 7500.00
Grandfather, George III, Moon Dial, Tubular, C.1880, 3 Weights, 96 In. 1900.00
Grandfather, Herschede, Cincinnati 5100.00
Grandfather, John Wood, George III, Japanned, 7 Ft. 2 In. 3750.00
Grandfather, Levi & Abel Hutchins, Painted Moon-Phase Dial 6250.00
Grandfather, Mudge, Calendar, English, Mahogany, 7 Ft. 10 In. 1870.00
Grandfather, Painted Face, Calendar Dial, English, C.1700, 87 1/2 In. 3500.00
Grandfather, Sheraton, Broken Arch Bonnet, 8-Day, C.1810, Cherry 2550.00
Grandfather, Thomas Norton, C.1800, Carved, Cherry, 7 Ft. 11 In. 4250.00
Grandfather, Wallace Nutting, 2-Weight, Mahogany, 7 Ft. 10 In. 4000.00
Grandfather, Willard, C.1800, Moon Register, Mahogany, 7 Ft. 7 In. 9000.00
Hall, Colonial Westminster, Mahogany Case, 5-Tube, C.1919 .... 3900.00
Hall, German, 9-Tube Chimes, Mahogany, 7 1/2 Feet 1400.00
Hamilton, Chronometer, Ship's, Model 21 .... 1600.00
Hamilton, Navy, Time Only, 3-Part Mahogany Box 1600.00
Henry Brown, Carriage, Brass Frame, Classical Scene On Dial, 5 In. 200.00
Henry Capt.Geneve, Carriage, Enamel Face, Beveled Glass, Repeater 350.00
Illinois, Sangamo Special, 23-Jewel 375.00
Ingraham, King, Time & Strike 325.00
Ingraham, Niagara 250.00
Ingraham, School, Time & Strike, Walnut 275.00
International Wagon Wheel 1200.00
International, Self-Winding, Mercury Pendulum, 5 1/4 Feet 500.00
Iron, Colonial Rotund Man Form, Clock In Stomach, 19 In. 475.00
Ithaca, Double Dial, Farmers Model, Marked, 1866, 26 In. 875.00
Ithaca, Regulator, No.2, Bank 2400.00
Ives, Black Dancer, Brass & Mahogany, Tap Dances, 1873, 7 In. 1200.00
J.J.Bertand A Gembloux, Long Case, Painted & Parcel Gilt, 7 Ft. 8 In. 1500.00
J.Windmills, Bracket, Musical, English, Silver & Gilt Metal, 18 1/2 In. 1100.00
Jerome & Co., Cottage, C.1850, Time & Strike, 30-Hour 115.00
Jerome & Co., Shelf, Gothic Revival, Mahogany & Rosewood, 14 1/2 In. .. 105.00
Jerome & Darrow, Mirror, Wooden Works, C.1855 .... 350.00
Jerome & Darrow, Ogee, 30-Hour, Original Paper, Stenciling 200.00
Jerome, Weight Driven, Reverse Painting, Exchange Building 595.00
Jewelers, Regulator, Floor Standing, Oak 3500.00
Jughans, Carriage, 2 Tunes, Triple Dial, Glass Sides, 6 In. 210.00
Kroeber, Shelf, 8-Day, Time & Strike, Plymouth, Glass Pendulum 295.00
Le Coultre, Desk, Swings On Stand, Bronze 125.00
Long Case, William Lambert, Calendar, Inlaid, Burr Walnut, 7 Ft. 5 In. 7150.00
Lux, Beer Drinkers 150.00
Lux, Organ Grinder 195.00
Lux, Spinning Wheel, Double Animation 110.00
Mantel, Ansonia, Black Lacquer, Lion's Head, 8 1/2 In. 75.00
Mantel, Astrological, Calendar Dial, French, C.1870, Marble, 19 3/4 In. 750.00
Mantel, Black, Empire Style Design, Gilbert Clock Co. 65.00
Mantel, Boston Clock Co., Inlaid Marble, Tandem Wind 250.00
Mantel, Brass Figure On Top, Marble, French, C.1877 .... 250.00
Mantel, Bronze & Marble Statue, Time & Strike, C.1820 .... 895.00
Mantel, C.1900, Gilt Bronze & Champleve Enamel, French, 18 3/4 In. 2500.00
Mantel, C.1900, Gilt Bronze & Enamel, French, 16 1/2 In. 2000.00
Mantel, C.1900, Gilt Bronze, French, 26 In. 550.00
Mantel, Chelsea, Tambour Shape, C.1900, Bronze 595.00
Mantel, Classic Figure In Armor, Time & Strike, Bronze, French 850.00
Mantel, Connecticut Clock Co., Beehive, Paper & Painting 200.00
Mantel, Floral Design, C.1890, Stand, Porcelain, German, 14 In. 350.00
Mantel, Georgian, Brown Lacquered, Chinoiserie, 5 Chimes, 16 In. 350.00

Mantel, Iron, Blue, White, Pendulum, C.1900, 21 In. 1875.00
Mantel, Louis XV/XVI, Transitional, Ormolu Case, 26 X 14 In. 1300.00
Mantel, Marble, Brass Columns, Top Ornament, French, 17 X 16 1/4 In. 250.00
Mantel, Marble, French, Porcelain Dial, Visible Escapement 150.00
Mantel, Pewter, English, C.1900, Flaring Sides, 13 In. 885.00
Mantel, Porcelain Panels, Gilt, French, 14 1/2 In. 475.00
Mantel, Swollen Sides, Beveled Glass, 8-Day, French, 12 1/8 In. 450.00
Mantel, Waterbury, Iron Case, 10 1/2 X 9 1/2 In. 110.00
Mantel, 3-Piece Dore Bronze & Onyx Set, French, C.1880 .... 1895.00
New Haven, Banjo, Porcelain Dial, Miniature 125.00
New Haven, Banjo, Reverse Paint, Congressional Library, 40 In. 325.00
New Haven, Cathedral, Westminster Chime 125.00
New Haven, Cottage, 8-Day 150.00
New Haven, Folding Travel, Brass, Red Leatherette 32.00
New Haven, Iron Case, Open Escapement, Silver Design, 11 In. 125.00
New Haven, Miniature, China, 7 In.Tall 125.00
New Haven, Ogee, Original Mirror On Door, Weight Driven 200.00
New Haven, Round Top, Time & Strike, 8-Day, 10 In. 45.00
New Haven, Shelf, Christmas Tree, Time & Strike 250.00
New Haven, Standing Flower Girl, Open Escapement 325.00
O.S.Sperry, Ogee, Original Frosted Tablet, Flower Design 200.00
Oliver Weldon, Wooden Cased, Wooden Works, Weight Driven, 25 1/2 In. 395.00
Pewter & Enamel, Shield Form, Blue, Green Design, C.1900, 9 In. 725.00
R.Johns, Figural, Castle Shape, Dated 1885, Iron, 13 In. 140.00
Regulator, Vienna, Spring Driven, Junhans, 36 In. 350.00
Rodney Brace, Torrington Movement, Carved 1/4 Column 1250.00
Rosenahling, Wag-On-Wall, Red Roses, Blue Anemones 425.00
Samuel Terry, Pillar & Scroll 1200.00
Schoolhouse, New Haven, Marquetry On Bezel, 8-Day, Time & Strike 550.00
Schoolhouse, New Haven, Satinwood Inlaid With Oak, 27 In.Long 490.00
Schoolhouse, Waterbury, Burled Walnut, Calendar, 12 In. 350.00
Schoolhouse, Waterbury, Oak, 10 In.Dial 250.00
Sessions, Banjo, 38 In. 275.00
Sessions, Gingerbread, Time & Alarm, Oak 200.00
Sessions, Railroad Station, Walnut 300.00
Sessions, Shop Regulator, Time Only, C.1890, Oak 495.00
Sessions, Tambour, 8-Day, Westminster Chimes 125.00
Seth Thomas, Alarm, Mahogany Case 15.00
Seth Thomas, Banjo, Reverse-Painted Glasses, 29 In. 265.00
Seth Thomas, Beehive, 1/4 Hour Strike, 18 In. 500.00
Seth Thomas, Calendar, Double Dial, Parlor No.5 .... 675.00
Seth Thomas, Calendar, No.13, Office 1950.00
Seth Thomas, Cottage, C.1885, Time & Strike, 30-Hour 95.00
Seth Thomas, Crystal Regulator, Bow Front 425.00
Seth Thomas, Crystal Regulator, Porcelain Dial 325.00
Seth Thomas, Crystal Regulator, Time & Strike, Columns 750.00
Seth Thomas, Double Dial Calendar, 20 In. 750.00
Seth Thomas, Double Dial Fashion, Walnut, 16 X 31 In. .... *Illus* 1325.00
Seth Thomas, Gingerbread, Original Level & Thermometer, Walnut 350.00
Seth Thomas, Locomotive, Brass 150.00
Seth Thomas, Mercury Pendulum, Convex Beveled Glass Sides, 11 In. 650.00
Seth Thomas, Mercury Pendulum, Crystal Regulator, 12 1/2 In. 590.00
Seth Thomas, No.2, Second Hand, Oak Case, 37 In. 1500.00
Seth Thomas, No.3, Parlour, Calendar 175.00
Seth Thomas, Oak Gallery, Pendulum, 12 In.Dial 200.00
Seth Thomas, Pillar & Scroll, Label 1950.00
Seth Thomas, Railroad, No. 2, 1880s 700.00
Seth Thomas, Regulator No.2, Oak, 80-Beat 875.00
Seth Thomas, Regulator, No.2, Etched Lion's International Logo, Cherry 975.00
Seth Thomas, Regulator, Office, Reverse Painted Glass, C.1900, Oak 495.00
Seth Thomas, Regulator, 1880-83, Burl Walnut, 8 Ft. 4 In. 4000.00
Seth Thomas, Schoolhouse, Time & Strike, Rosewood 300.00
Seth Thomas, Schoolhouse, 30-Day, Long Drop 600.00

Clock, Seth Thomas, Double Dial Fashion,
Walnut, 16 X 31 In.

(See Page 107)

Clock, Waterbury, Mirror-Sided, Walnut

Seth Thomas, Ship's Bell, Exposed Bell, Brass Case	450.00
Seth Thomas, Sonora, Chime 5 Bells, Oak Case	385.00
Seth Thomas, Store, Painted Metal Dial, 8-Day, Poplar, 15 1/2 X 36 In.	350.00
Seth Thomas, Tambour, Westminster Chime, Double Works	350.00
Seth Thomas, 4 Bell Sonora Chimes	500.00
Shelf, Daniel Pratt, Rosewood	145.00
Shelf, Gothic Design, Rosewood Case, 16 In.	90.00
Shelf, Rosewood, Connecticut, Mirrored Panel Door, Flat Top, 17 In.	200.00
Sheraton, Tall Case, Broken Arch Bonnet, Pennsylvania, C.1810, Cherry	2550.00
Ship, Fusee, Brass Case, C.1840	400.00
Ship, Wall Mount, 30-Hour, C.1850, 9 In.Diam.	150.00
Shreve, Crump, Regulator, Mercury, C.1900, Brass Case, 12 1/2 In.	450.00
Statue, Mercury, Marble Base	350.00
Street, 3 Faces, Corner Mounted, Bronze & Copper, 10 Ft. X 46 In.	2500.00
Stromberg, Master, Pendulum, Light Oak, 5 Feet	500.00
Stromberg, Master, Second Beat, Pendulum, C.1938, 5 1/2 Feet	600.00
Switzerland, C.1925, Enamel & Sterling Silver, 2 In.	350.00
Tall, Brass-Mounted, French, C.1900, 5 Feet 4 In.	2200.00
Tall, R, Whiting, Winchester, Silas Hoadley Cabinet, C.1815	2234.00
Thwaites & Reed, Rolling Drum, London, Mahogany, 28 In.Long	1000.00
CLOCK, TIFFANY, see Tiffany, Clock	
Travel, French, Time & Strike	350.00
Vienna, Regulator, Spring Wind, Time & Strike, Porcelain Dial, 29 In.	175.00
Vienna, Regulator, 3 Weight	1275.00
Vienna, Walnut, Case, Wall, 39 In.	650.00
Vienna, 1 Wt., 3 In.Dial, Pulley, Pendulum, Beat Scale, 8-Day	2795.00
Vincenti, Figural, C.1840, Dore Bronze	425.00
Wag-On-Wall, Provincial, Arched Top, Red, Green Floral, 17 In.	125.00
Wag-On-Wall, Time & Strike, C.1910, Wood & Metal Works	290.00
Wall, Beveled Glass, C.1935, Walnut, German, 30 In.	100.00
Wall, Gilbert, Light Oak, 25 In.	155.00
Wall, Gilbert, Regulator, No.2, Walnut	895.00
Wall, Gustav Becker, Porcelain Dial, Brass Weight & Pendulum, C.1890	1595.00
Wall, Moillet, Flarcie, Gilt Bronze, C.1900, 32 In.	2400.00
Wall, Vienna Regulator, 16 X 48 In.	695.00
Walnut, Victorian Case, Double Dial, Fashion, Seth Thomas, 16 In.	1325.00
Waterbury, Beehive Case, Dated 1915, Key Wind, 16 1/4 In.	335.00
Waterbury, Beehive, Oak Case, 14 In.	150.00
Waterbury, Carriage, 8-Day Repeater	375.00
Waterbury, Gingerbread, Time, Strike, & Alarm, Walnut, 19 In.	250.00
Waterbury, Jeweler's Regulator, Pinion Movement, Walnut, 6 1/2 Feet	2800.00
Waterbury, Mirror-Sided, Walnut	*Illus* 750.00

Waterbury, Octagon Drop, Golden Oak, Dial 10 In. 250.00
Waterbury, Pinwheel Regulator, Golden Oak, 75 In. 4200.00
Waterbury, Pinwheel Regulator, Wall, Lyre Pendulum, 6 1/4 Feet 3500.00
Waterbury, Regulator, Oak, 34 In. 375.00
Welch, Carving, Inlaid, 8-Day, Time & Strike, Bell Chimes, Mirror, 36 In. 500.00
Welch, Mantel, Brass Face, Black 110.00
Welch, Mantel, Gold Decal Door Glass, 8-Day, Time & Strike, 24 In. 90.00
Welch, Spring & Co., Regulator, 8-Day, C.1880, Rosewood 2800.00
Willard, Banjo, Signed 1750.00
William Marshall, Tall Case, 8-Day, Late 18th Century, Edinburgh 2500.00
Williams, Orton, & Preston, Shelf, Farmington, Conn., Paper 550.00

Cloisonne enamel was developed during the tenth century. A glass enamel was applied between small ribbonlike pieces of metal on a metal base. Most Cloisonne is Chinese or Japanese.

CLOISONNE, Ashbowl, Cigar, Square, 4 In. 35.00
Base, Lamp, Double Socket, Brass 95.00
Bottle, Snuff, Double Gourd 600.00
Bottle, Snuff, Turquoise, White, Black & Gold, Flying Cranes 189.00
Bowl, Birds & Flowers, On White, 5 In. 100.00
Bowl, Candy, Red & Pink Peonies, Green Border Design, Marked China 180.00
Bowl, Happy Dragon, 8 In. 285.00
Bowl, Multicolored Flowers, Green, Marked China, 4 In. 37.50
Bowl, Plique-A-Jour, Multicolor Flowers, Green Ground, 4 3/4 In. 1200.00
Bowl, 5 Claw Dragons, Seal On Bottom, 8 In. 250.00
Box, Allover Butterflies, 4 Compartments, Black 225.00
Box, Black, Brass Scrolls, Deco Floral Design, 6 X 3 1/4 In. 225.00
Box, Cigarette, Blue & White, Ashtray 80.00
Box, Cigarette, Flowers, Black Ground, 2 Compartments, 6 X 5 In. 175.00
Box, Cigarette, Footed, Green & Turquoise 145.00
Box, Covered, 3 1/2 In.Diam. 165.00
Box, Floral Design, 2 1/2 X 4 X 5 In. 150.00
Box, Florals & Butterflies, Covered, 4 3/4 In.Diam. 495.00
Box, Flowers, Black Ground, Covered, Round 110.00
Box, Jigsaw Design, Flowers, 7-Color, Signed, 3 In.Diam. 145.00
Box, Rocks, Flowers, Blue Ground, Silver Scroll, 6 In. 275.00
Box, Scroll Cloisons, Foil Butterflies, Covered, 6 X 1 3/4 In. 155.50
Box, 3 Compartment, White Flower, Covered, 3 X 7 In. 125.00
Cachepot, Floral Designs, 19th Century, 9 X 7 In. 350.00
Charger, Bluebird On Bamboo Arch, Flowers, Copper Edge, 14 1/2 In. 400.00
Charger, Fans, Flowers, & 3 Birds, 19th Century, 15 1/2 In.Diam. 675.00
Charger, Flowers & Birds, 12 In. 395.00
Cocoa Pot, Diaper Pattern, Foil Goldfish, 3 1/2 In. 295.00
Containers, Swan, Chinese, C.1900, 5 X 5 In., Pair 2000.00
Cup, Rust, Flowers, Fishscale, Marked, 1 1/2 In. 20.00
Dish, Dragon On White, 7 In. 150.00
Figurine, Crane, Feather & Scrollwork, Brown, 7 1/2 In. 655.00
Figurine, Crane, Standing, Brown Ground, Blue, Green, Yellow, 7 In. 675.00
Figurine, Daibutsu, Seated, Wearing Robe, C.1900 .... 600.00
Figurine, Horse, Prancing, Scrolls Of Enamel, Blue Ground, Pair 1150.00
Figurine, Prancing Horse, Blue Ground, Gilded, 5 X 6 In., Pair 990.00
Figurine, Standing Cranes, Feather & Scroll, Enameled, 7 1/2 In. 655.00
Frame, Easel Back, Oval Center, 5 In. 36.00
Ginger Jar, Blue, 4 1/2 In. 135.00
Ginger Jar, Flowers, Dark Ground, 5 In., Pair 125.00
Ginger Jar, Turquoise Ground, Multicolored Lotus, 3 In., Pair 450.00
Holder, Cigarette, Goldstone, Ivory Stem 95.00
Jar, Birds & Plants, Japanese, Blue Ground, 9 3/4 In. 800.00
Jar, Covered, Multicolored Flowers, Black, 5 1/2 In. 135.00
Jar, Elephant Form, Ring Handles, Japanese, 13 1/2 In., Pair 800.00
Jar, Flowers & Birds, Black Ground, 13 In. 400.00
Jar, Ginger, Black Ground, Pink & Red Flowers, 4 1/2 In., Pair 165.00
Jar, Ginger, Flowers, Rust Ground, Covered, 4 In., Pair 125.00

Cloisonne, Platter, One Thousand Wire,
Stand, Cobalt Blue

Jar, Prunus Design, White Ground, Covered, 5 1/2 In.	50.00
Jar, Rose Petal, White Ground, Covered, 5 1/2 In.	115.00
Jar, Rose, Enameled, Patchwork, Floral, Insect, 5 3/8 In.	90.00
Lamp, Chinese, 37 In.	1250.00
Lamp, Green, Marked China, 10 1/2 In.	125.00
Open Salt & Pepper Shaker, Green	95.00
Pitcher, Urn Shape, Gold Flecks, Black Ground, 4 In.	140.00
Plate, Fans, Cloud Scrolls, Flowers, Black Ground, 14 1/8 In.	500.00
Plate, Floral Center, 6 Medallions On Rim, 11 3/4 In.	395.00
Plate, Rust, Green And Red Center, 10 In.	240.00
Plate, Turquoise, 12 In.	550.00
Platter, One Thousand Wire, Stand, Cobalt Blue _Illus_	6500.00
Purse, Blue, Red, Pink & White, 3 In.Wide	275.00
Salt & Pepper, Open Salt, Green	95.00
Smoke Set, Covered Box, Ashtray, Matchbox Holder, Tray 9 In.	250.00
Smoking Set, Chinese, Floral Design, 8 X 16 In.	600.00
Teapot, Blue, Butterflies, Porcelain, Creamer, Sugar	600.00
Teapot, Butterflies, Birds, Flowers, Miniature	210.00
Teapot, Diaper Pattern, Foil Goldfish	215.00
Teapot, Phoenix Birds, Diaper Pattern, Goldstone Ground, 5 In.	485.00
Toothpick, Allover Color, 2 1/4 In.	80.00
Tray, Birds, Flowers, & Butterflies, 8 1/4 X 9 3/4 In.	245.00
Tray, Multicolored Flowers, Fans, Blue, 7 1/2 In.	100.00
Urn, Dragon Head Handles, Blossoms, Teakwood Stand, 14 1/2 In.	695.00
Vase, Art Deco, Stylized Egrets, Light Blue & White, 8 In.	200.00
Vase, Artist Signed, China Mark, 1i 1/2 In.	225.00
Vase, Bird & Flowers, Pink Ground, 5 1/2 X 12 In.	1000.00
Vase, Bird Of Paradise Design, 7 1/2 In.	30.00
Vase, Blue, Luster Trim, Birds On Blossom Branch, 8 In.	70.00
Vase, Butterflies, Dark Blue, 3 3/4 In., Pair	165.00
Vase, Cased Fish Scale, 5 3/4 In.	103.00
Vase, Copper, Chrysanthemum, Polychrome Design, 6 3/4 In.	150.00
Vase, Dragon Design, 10 1/2 In.	75.00
Vase, Dragon Head Handles, Teakwood Base, 14 1/2 In.	485.00
Vase, Fish Scale, Foiled, Bird On Flowers, Signed, 7 In.	295.00
Vase, Fish Scale, Green To White, Lavender & Red Flowers, 7 In.	165.00
Vase, Fish Scale, Light Green To White, Red Flowers, 7 In.	175.00
Vase, Fish Scale, Sunset Lit Sky, Trees, 8 In., Pair	595.00
Vase, Fleur-De-Lis, Colored Foil, Fishnet Ground, 6 1/2 In., Pair	145.00
Vase, Floral Design, Blue & Green, Marked, 5 1/2 In., Pair	110.00
Vase, Florals, Red & Green, 8 In., Pair	495.00
Vase, Flower Design, 9 1/2 In.	70.00
Vase, Flowering Plants, Flared Foot, Japanese, Blue, 9 1/2 In.	375.00
Vase, Flowers, Brown & Turquoise, 9 In., Pair	220.00
Vase, Gold On Black, Dragon Design, 9 In.Pair	130.00
Vase, Herons, Green Dragons At Top, Gray Ground, 12 1/8 In.	650.00
Vase, Japanese, Swallow Flying, Plum Tree, Green, Brown, 7 In.	180.00

Vase, Multicolored Flowers, Geometric Ground, Marked China, 5 In. 75.00
Vase, Multicolored Flowers, 7 In. 50.00
Vase, Multicolored, Signed, 18 Pounds, 18 X 14 In.Diam. 1790.00
Vase, Oxblood, 9 1/2 In. 175.00
Vase, Peony Blossoms, Red, Purple, Silver Foil, 7 In. 125.00
Vase, Plants & Feathers, Beige Ground, Baluster Hasp, 15 In., Pr. 1250.00
Vase, Plique-A-Jour, Multicolor Florals, Green Ground, 5 In. 800.00
Vase, Prunus Blossoms, Clouds, Flying Bird, Blue Ground, 9 1/2 In. 225.00
Vase, Red Ground, Silver Mount, 3 Butterflies, 7 In. 390.00
Vase, Royal Blue, Red Flowers, Green Leaves, 5 1/2 In. 150.00
Vase, White & Red Roses, Emerald Green Fish Scale, 7 1/2 In., Pair 290.00
Vase, White Lotus Scrolls, Russet, 6 1/2 In. 135.00
Vase, White, Yellow, Red, Blue Florals, Impressed China, 4 In. 45.00
Vase, Woven Wire Pattern, Flower Petals, 10-Color, C.1885, 6 In. 285.00
Whistle, Bobby, Bright Coloring 180.00
    CLOTHING, see Textile

> *Cluthra glass is a two-layered glass with small air pockets that form white spots. The Steuben Glass Works of Corning, New York, made it after 1903. Kimball Glass Company of Vineland, New Jersey, made Cluthra from about 1925.*

    CLUTHRA, see also Steuben
CLUTHRA, Vase, Blue With Yellow, Signed, 18 In. 450.00
Vase, Bottle Shape, Royal Blue & Clear, Pontil 60.00
Vase, Yellow, White, Orange, Green, Bulbous, Kimball, Signed, 6 1/2 In. 795.00
Vase, 3-Color, Flared Rim, Bulbous, 6 1/2 In. 495.00
Vase, 4-Color, Bulbous, Flared Rim, Signed, 7 In. 595.00

Coalport ware has been made by the Coalport Porcelain Works of England from 1795 to the present time.

    COALPORT, see also Indian Tree
COALPORT, Boat & Underplate, Cupids, Revelry Design, 5 In. 35.00
Cup & Saucer, Demitasse, Blue & Green Jeweled 150.00
Cup & Saucer, Demitasse, Pink, Gold Tracery, Enamel Dots, C.1900 .... 185.00
Cup & Saucer, Tea, Tree Of Life 20.00
Cup & Saucer, Tree Of Life .... 25.00 To 35.00
Cup, Bouillon, Floral Trim, Green & Gold, Set Of 6 .... 150.00
Demitasse Set, Porcelain, 8 Pieces 50.00
Dish, Teniers Design, C.1820, Oval .... Illus 125.00
Figurine, Penelope, 6 1/4 In. 45.00
Figurine, Rosalinda, 6 1/4 In. 45.00
Flower Pot, 2 X 2 In. 15.00
Mastiff, C.1825 .... 750.00
Plate, Cookie, Tree Of Life 35.00
Plate, Hand-Painted Center Bird, Signed J.H.Plant, 9 1/2 In. 275.00

Coalport, Dish, Teniers Design, C.1820, Oval

Plate, Strawberries, Flowers, Polychrome, C.1820, 9 1/2 In.	130.00
Vase, Baluster, Floral, Covered, C.1830, 16 1/2 In.	250.00

Cobalt blue glass was made using oxide of cobalt. The characteristic bright dark blue identifies it for the collector. Most cobalt glass found today was made after the Civil War.

COBALT BLUE, see also Shirley Temple

COBALT BLUE, Basket, Flared, Rope Handle, 12 In.	80.00
Bottle, Perfume, Gold Scrolls & Trim, 2 1/8 In.	75.00
Bowl, Royal Lace, 3-Leg, Straight Edge, 10 In.Diam.	37.50
Cake Set, Charades, 4 Plates, 4 Cups & Saucers	50.00
Candleholder, Double, Silver Deposit Around Rim, Pair	36.00
Condiment Set, White Panels, Violets, 6 Bottles, 6 1/2 In.	40.00
Decanter, Enameled, Stopper	50.00
Dresser Set, Florals, Tray, 8 1/4 X 12 1/2 In., 4 Piece	245.00
Ewer, Enameled Lily-Of-The-Valley Design, 11 1/2 In., Pair	98.00
Figurine, Swan, 8 In.	45.00
Hat, Blue, 2 1/4 X 2 1/2 X 3 In.	24.00
Lamp, Diamond Band & Shield, Flat Finger, C.1865	295.00
Tomahawk, Indian Chief On Head, No Inscription	45.00
Toothpick, Elephant Pedestal	45.00
Toothpick, Hat Shape	12.00
Toothpick, Wheelbarrow	40.00
Vase, Etched Leaves Allover, 10 3/4 In.	65.00
Vase, White Design, 10 1/4 In., Pair	100.00

Coca-Cola advertising items have become a special field for collectors.

COCA-COLA, Bank, Dispensing, Battery Operated, Linemar	285.00
Barrel, Lithograph Label, 6 Iron Bands, Bung, Old Red, 10 Gallon	185.00
Billfold, Leather	45.00
Board, Chinese Checkers, 1940s	50.00
Book, Safe Driving, Copyright 1940	18.00
Booklet, The Truth, 1907	50.00
Bottle Opener & Ice Pick, 1940s	5.00
Bottle Opener, Have A Coke	2.00
Bottle Opener, Wall Mount, Cast Iron	8.50
Bottle, Advertising, Free Standing, Rubber, 43 In.	495.00
Bottle, Christmas, Dec.25, 1923, Thermopolis, Wyo.	50.00
Bottle, Columbus, Ohio, Amber	40.00
Bottle, Display, Christmas Coke, December 25, 1923, 20 In.	150.00
Bottle, Display, 1933	125.00
Bottle, Oshkosh, Stars, Aqua	9.50
Bottle, Pittsburgh, Amber	30.00
Buckle, Belt, Art Nouveau, Brass	3.00
Calendar, 1855	20.00
Calendar, 1922, Full Pad	325.00
Calendar, 1923, Full Pad	350.00
Calendar, 1955	30.00
Cards, Playing, 1915	35.00
Clock, Advertising, Baird	3200.00
Clock, Art Deco, 1950s	100.00
Clock, Wall, Curved Glass, Slanted Sides, Logo, Electric, 15 1/4 In.	55.00
Cooler, Picnic, Red Metal	30.00
Cooler, Salesman Sample, 1939, 10 X 12 In.	695.00
Cooler, 1950s, 2 X 3 1/2 Feet	150.00
Cribbage Board	45.00
Darts	35.00
Door Pull, Bottle Shape	60.00
Door Push, Porcelain	65.00
Fan, Hand With Coke Bottle, 1942	15.00
Game Kit, Serviceman's, World War II, Red Box	225.00
Glass, With Measure, Marked	10.00

Hat, Vendor's, Paper, Dated 1929	18.00
Ice Pick	3.00 To 8.00
Jar, Gum	350.00
Knife, At All Fountains, 5 Cents	20.00
Knife, Pocket, 1933, World's Fair, Chicago	25.00 To 32.00
Light, Red Button Type, Drink Coca-Cola, 1948	125.00
Mirror, Advertising, 1904	120.00
Mirror, 1917, Elaine	110.00
Ornament, Santa Claus, Box, 1960	5.00
Paddles, Ping-Pong	40.00
Pencil, Mechanical, Bottle Clip, Red	24.00
Penlight, 1950s, 3 1/2 In.	3.50
Pitcher, Tumbler Shape, Logo In White, 10 In.	85.00
Plate, Advertising On Back, Vienna Art, Wooden Frame, 1911	275.00
Poster, 3 Girls With Umbrellas, Garland Of Flowers	675.00
Raft, 2-Man, Oars & Cushion, Inflatable	40.00
Rule, Wooden	4.00
Sharpener, Pencil, Red Metal, 1933	10.00
Sign, Bottle, Embossed Tin, 1923, 27 X 20 In.	125.00
Sign, Double-Sided, Porcelain, 1932, 36 X 60 In.	350.00
Sign, Drink Coca-Cola, Pictured Bottle, Metal, 54 X 18 In.	25.00
Sign, Drug Store, Porcelain, 28 X 16 In.	95.00
Sign, Fountain Service, Porcelain	60.00
Sign, Fountain, Drink Coca-Cola, Porcelain, 12 X 28 In.	32.00
Sign, Mother & Girl In Garden, Litho, 25 X 11 In.	40.00
Thermometer	55.00
Thermometer, Bottle Shape	14.00
Thermometer, C.1941, 15 In.	65.00
Thermometer, Thirst Knows No Season	45.00
Thermometer, Wooden, 1900	275.00
Toothpick, Red Enamel & Gold Fluted Edge	20.00
Train Set, Lionel, Track & Transformer, 1974	125.00
Train, Engine, 1974	35.00
Tray, T.V., 1961, Thanksgiving Scene	25.00
Tray, Tip, 1905, Juanita	250.00
Tray, Tip, 1909, Coca-Cola Girl	145.00 To 150.00
Tray, Tip, 1912	*Illus* 85.00
Tray, Tip, 1914, Betty	*Illus* 110.00
Tray, Tip, 1917, Elaine	*Illus* 115.00
Tray, Tip, 1920, Garden Girl	85.00
Tray, 1909, Hamilton King's Coca-Cola Girl	250.00
Tray, 1909, Rectangular	85.00
Tray, 1917, Elaine	65.00 To 165.00

Coca-Cola, Tray, Tip, 1914, Betty

Coca-Cola, Tray, Tip, 1912

Coca-Cola, Tray, Tip, 1917, Elaine

Tray, 1920, Oval 375.00
Tray, 1921, Summer Girl 200.00
Tray, 1922, Autumn Girl 275.00
Tray, 1923, Flapper Girl .... 75.00 To 115.00
Tray, 1925, Girl At Party 200.00
Tray, 1926, Sports Couple .... 185.00 To 300.00
Tray, 1927, Curb Service .... 125.00 To 400.00
Tray, 1929 .... 225.00
Tray, 1930, Bathing Beauty .... 60.00 To 135.00
Tray, 1930, Girl With Telephone .... 75.00 To 90.00
Tray, 1931, Farm Boy With Dog .... 375.00 To 450.00
Tray, 1932 .... 250.00
Tray, 1934, Johnny Weismuller, Maureen O'Sullivan .... 125.00 To 400.00
Tray, 1935, Madge Evans 200.00
Tray, 1936, Hostess 65.00
Tray, 1937, Running Girl .... 45.00 To 50.00
Tray, 1939, Springboard Girl .... 42.00 To 65.00
Tray, 1940, Sailor Girl Fishing 40.00
Tray, 1941, Girl Ice Skater .... 45.00 To 55.00
Tray, 1942, Two Girls At Car .... 35.00 To 52.00
Tray, 1943, Girl With Wind In Her Hair 35.00
Tray, 1950, Girl With Fence .... 16.00 To 25.00
Tray, 1950, Girl With Menu 25.00
Tray, 1953 .... 25.00
Tray, 75th Anniversary, Euclid Beach, Cleveland, Ohio 14.00
Truck, Delivery, 1950, 12 In. 95.00
Truck, 6 Cases & Bottles, Smith-Miller, Boxed 450.00
Watch Fob, Girl & Glass 125.00
Watch Fob, 1917, Elaine 95.00
Wrapper, Gum, Spearmint 260.00

*Coffee grinders, home size, were first made about 1894. They lost favor by
the 1930s.*

COFFEE GRINDER, Arcade Imperial, Cast-Iron Top, Oak 70.00
    Arcade, Crystal No. 4 .... 65.00
    Arcade, Miniature 65.00
    Challenge Fast Grinder, Table Model, Wooden 75.00
    Clamps On Table, Tin 45.00
    Crystal, Wall Mount, Original 75.00
    Daisy, 1-Drawer, Iron Cup, 2 1/2 X 2 Feet 52.00
    Dated 1888 .... 69.50
    Delmew Coffee Mills, Simons Hardware, Wooden 60.00
    Dovetailed Drawer, Tin Top & Handle, Wooden, 5 1/2 In.Square 38.00
    Elma, Tin, Lap .... 30.00 To 44.00
    Enterprise Co., Eagle Finial, Wheels 17 In.Diam. 300.00
    Enterprise, Hand Crank, Iron Drawer, 12 In. 95.00
    Enterprise, Iron Drawer, 2-Wheel, 8 1/2 In. 280.00
    Enterprise, Original Paint, Wheels, 9 In. 385.00
    Enterprise, Two 18 In.Wheels 350.00
    Enterprise, 23 In.Wheels 375.00
    Hoffman's Old Time 275.00
    Iron Top & Handle, Square, Wooden, 5 X 5 X 4 In. 40.00
    Kenrick, Porcelain-Lined Cup, Iron Drawer, 6 X 4 1/2 In. 69.00
    Parker, No.50, Embossed Eagle, Cast Iron & Tin, Black 40.00
    Regal, Wall Mount 15.00
    Root-Heath Mfg.Co., Iron, 17 1/2 In. 32.50
    Swift, Hill, Lane Bros., Poughkeepsie, N.Y., No.15, Cast Iron 395.00
    Table Mounted, Dated 1905, Iron & Tin 30.00
    Telephone Mill, Wall Mount 245.00
    Universal No.3314 .... 32.50
    Wall, A. & P.Co., Advertising 85.00
    3 Grinds, Coffeepot Shape, 30 In. 700.00

COIN SPOT, Creamer, Blue, 4 In. 35.00
  Creamer, Clear Handle, Cranberry, 4 In. 38.00
  Creamer, Reeded Handle, Blue, 4 In. 38.00
  Cruet, Blue, 7 3/4 In. 70.00
  Dish, Pleated Rim, Vaseline Opalescent, 10 In.Diam. 65.00
  Hat, Cranberry Glass 22.00
  Lamp, Cranberry Font, Clear Pedestal 196.00
  Lamp, Raised Leaves & Strawberries On Base, Dated 1872, Handled ... 185.00
  Pitcher, Bulbous, Clear Handle, Cranberry Glass 75.00
  Pitcher, Fluted Top, Bulbous, Opalescent 125.00
  Pitcher, Opalescent, White, 9 1/2 In. 70.00
  Pitcher, Ruffled Top, Blue Opalescent, 8 1/2 In. 125.00
  Pitcher, Spherical, Ruffled Lip, White Opalescent On Clear, 1 Qt. ... 115.00
  Pitcher, Tri-Cornered Top, Opalescent 100.00
  Pitcher, Water, Bulbous, Fluted, Blue Handle, Blue, 10 In. 125.00
  Pitcher, Water, Fluted, Blue Opalescent 115.00
  Pitcher, 4 Matching Tumblers, Ruffled Top, Blue, 10 In. 70.00
  Rose Bowl, Opalescent Cranberry, 6 1/2 X 6 In. 75.00
  Sugar Shaker, Original Top 95.00
  Sugar Shaker, 9-Panel, Blue Opalescent 60.00
  Syrup, Blue 85.00
  Syrup, Blue Opalescent 75.00
  Syrup, Opalescent Overlay, Cranberry 95.00
  Syrup, Ring Neck, Blue 100.00
  Syrup, Ring Neck, Blue Opalescent 75.00
  Syrup, Ring Neck, Rubena 120.00
  Syrup, Syrup, With Swirl, Blue 50.00
  Syrup, White, Tall 65.00
  Syrup, 9-Panel 140.00
  Toothpick, White Opalescent 55.00
  Tumbler, Cranberry Opalescent, 3 3/4 In. 22.00
  Tumbler, Opalescent Cranberry 35.00
  Tumbler, White Opalescent 20.00
  Vase, Cranberry, Crimped Ruffled Top, 8 In. 50.00
  Vase, Sandwich, Pink & White, 7 In. 95.00
  Vase, White Ruffled Rim, 4 1/4 In. 22.00
  Water Set, 6 Tumblers, Green Opalescent 240.00

COIN-OPERATED MACHINE, Candy, Hershey Bar, 1 Cent, 2 Feet ... 55.00
  Checkerboard, Rol-A-Top, 5 Cent 2800.00
  Claw, Exhibit Supply Digger 1150.00
  Crane, Arcade, 25 Cent 1550.00
  Dice, Mills, 25 Cent 2995.00
  Discount Bicycle Wheel, Trade Stimulator, C.1900 .... 1500.00
  Dispenser, Diamond Book Match, Cast Iron 250.00
  Gem, Champion, L-Shape, Oak, 4 Column, 1890 .... 450.00
  Grip Tester, Exhibit Supply Hercules 1395.00
  Gum, Pulver Chocolate Cocoa, Patent 1889 .... 675.00
  Gum, Pulver, Yellow Kid 380.00
  Gum, Spin-A-Pack, Penny 275.00
  Gum, The Baker Boy, 1 Cent 1095.00
  Gum, Watling, 1 Cent, Stand 1650.00
  Gumball, Blackjack, Daval's 200.00
  Gumball, E-Z Chew Gambling, Original Tin Marque 600.00
  Gumball, E-Z, Cast Iron 900.00
  Gumball, Jennings Dutchess, 1 Cent 1695.00
  Gumball, Master, 1 Cent, Red 185.00
  Gumball, Puritan Bell 225.00
  Gumball, Scoppy 750.00
  Gumball, Superior Confection, Brass Body & Top 245.00
  Gumball, Watling, 1 Cent 2395.00
  Horsehead Bonus, Mills, 5 Cent 1950.00
  Little Duke, Single Jackpot, 1 Cent 1350.00

Love Tester, Hercules 1250.00
Match Vendor, Pat.1904, Kelley Mfg.Co., Cast Iron 650.00
Movies, 8 For 10 Cents, Oak, 3 X 7 Feet 995.00
Mutoscope, Girlie Reel, Tin 350.00
Peanut, Advance, 1923 .... 95.00
Peanut, Northwestern, 1 To 5 Cent 200.00
Peep Show, 15 Stereoviews, 5 Cent, Nudes 325.00
Penny Drop, Game Of Chance, Wooden 200.00
Pinball, Big Broadcast, Tabletop, Manual, 5 Cent 2250.00
Pinball, Gottlieb, Baffle Ball, C.1931 .... *Illus* 550.00
Racehorse, Bally 4000.00
Skill Roll, Bally 225.00
Skittles Game, Slate Top, Felt, Oak, 37 X 72 In. 975.00
Slot, Buckley, Criss-Cross, 5 Cent 1895.00
Slot, Buckley, Electronic, 10-Cent Pointmaker 500.00
Slot, Caille, Cadet, 5 Cent 800.00
Slot, Caille, Silver Cup, Chicago Electric Keyboard 2900.00
Slot, Caille, Superior, Nude Front 3000.00

Coin-Operated Machine, Pinball, Gottlieb, Baffle Ball, C.1931

Slot, Caille, Superior, 4 Reel, 5 Cent 1975.00
Slot, Caille, Superior, 5 Cent 1250.00
Slot, Caille, Victoria, Center Pull 6800.00
Slot, Caille, 1 Wheel, 4 For 1.25 Cent, Counter Top 5900.00
Slot, Evans, Big 6 Dice Wheel, 60 In. 1950.00
Slot, Jennings, Chief Model, 10 Cent 1000.00
Slot, Jennings, Gooseneck, Skill Buttons, 10 Cent 2200.00
Slot, Jennings, Indian Chief, 25 Cent 1995.00
Slot, Jennings, Lightup, 5 Cent 1375.00
Slot, Jennings, Operator's Bell, Cast Iron & Wood 1600.00
Slot, Jennings, Rockaway, 1 Cent, Five Jacks 1050.00
Slot, Jennings, Silver Chief Sportsmen, 10 Cent 1150.00
Slot, Jennings, Standard Chief, 5 Cent 1150.00
Slot, Jennings, Victory Chief, 5 Cent 1150.00
Slot, Little Duke, 1 Cent 2895.00
Slot, Mills, Baseball O.K.Vender, 5 Cent 3250.00
Slot, Mills, Black Cherry, 5 Cent .... 1100.00 To 1450.00
Slot, Mills, Bursting Cherry, 10 Cent .... 1150.00 To 1250.00
Slot, Mills, Bursting Cherry, 25 Cent .... 1200.00 To 1400.00
Slot, Mills, Bursting Cherry, 5 Cent .... 1150.00 To 1600.00
Slot, Mills, Castle Front, Gold Award, 25 Cent 1550.00

Slot, Mills, Castle Front, 5 Cent .... 1100.00 To 1650.00
Slot, Mills, COK Gooseneck, 25 Cent 1350.00
Slot, Mills, Dewey, 5 Cent 7800.00
Slot, Mills, Diamond Front, 25 Cent 1450.00
Slot, Mills, Double Jackpot, 10 Cent 1650.00
Slot, Mills, Extraordinary, 5 Cent 1250.00
Slot, Mills, Four Column FOK Vender, 5 Cent 1650.00
Slot, Mills, Futurity, 5 Cent 2500.00
Slot, Mills, Liberty Bell, Cast Iron 8500.00
Slot, Mills, Lion Front, Single Jackpot, 5 Cent 1650.00
Slot, Mills, Poinsettia, 5 Cent, Freeplay 1st Lemon 1500.00
Slot, Mills, Punching Bag, 1 Cent 1000.00
Slot, Mills, Quartoscope 2195.00
Slot, Mills, Rock-Ola, 10 Cent 975.00
Slot, Mills, Roman Head, 25 Cent 2850.00
Slot, Mills, Skyscraper, 5 Cent 1375.00
Slot, Mills, Vest Pocket, 5 Cent .... 275.00 To 525.00
Slot, Mills, War Eagle, 5 Cent .... 1750.00 To 1800.00
Slot, Mills, 5 Cent Hi-Top, Guaranteed Jackpot 1100.00
Slot, Pace, Comet, 10 Cent 1500.00
Slot, Pace, Eight Star, 10 Cent 875.00
Slot, Pace, Fancy Front, 1935, 1 Cent 1850.00
Slot, Pace, Four Star, 25 Cent 1375.00
Slot, Service Novelty Co., Operator's Bell, 50 Cent 2950.00
Slot, Skyscraper, 1 Cent, Tokens & Side Vendor 1850.00
Slot, Steeplechase 400.00
Slot, Vest Pocket, 5 Cent 500.00
Slot, Watling, Blue Seal, Gooseneck, 25 Cent 1995.00
Slot, Watling, Blue Seal, 5 Cent 1750.00
Slot, Watling, Full Deck, 5 Arrow Stimulator 5000.00
Slot, Watling, Rol-A-Top, 5 Cent, Fortune .... 2500.00 To 3850.00
Slot, Watling, Rol-A-Top, 25 Cent 3500.00
Slot, Watling, Treasury, 5 Cent .... 4500.00 To 4600.00
Slot, Watling, Wonder, 2 Column, 5 Cent 2000.00
Smilin' Sam From Alabam, The Peanut Man, C.1925 .... 995.00
Standard Chief, 10 Cent 1200.00
Steeplechase Marble Horse Race 300.00
Talking Scale, 5 Cent, 1902 .... 4500.00
Target Practice, Mills, Penny Drop 385.00
Trade Stimulator, Griswold 375.00
Uncle Sam Personality Tester 1495.00
Wood Gun, Gum Mechanism, Bull's Eye, Rings Bell 450.00

Collector plates are modern plates produced in limited editions. Some will
be found listed under the company. Pictures and more price information can
be found in "The Kovels' Price Guide for Collector Plates, Figurines,
Paperweights, and Other Limited Editions."

COLLECTOR PLATE, Belleek, Christmas, 1974 .... 120.00
    COLLECTOR PLATE, BING & GRONDAHL, see Bing & Grondahl
DeGrazia, Flower Girl, 1978 .... 190.00
DeGrazia, White Dove, 1977 .... 150.00
Disney, Christmas, 1973 .... 135.00 To 165.00
Ferrandiz, Christmas, 1973, Wooden 195.00
Goebel, Annual, 1976 .... 32.00
Goebel, Annual, 1977 .... 43.00
Granget, Annual, 1977, Bears 50.00
Haviland, Christmas, 1970 .... 70.00
Haviland, Christmas, 1974 .... 15.00
Hibel, Colette & Child 500.00
Hummel, Anniversary, 1971 .... 800.00
Hummel, Annual, 1971 .... 795.00
Hummel, Annual, 1972 .... 85.00

Hummel, Annual, 1973	195.00
Ispanky, Ten Commandments, 1979	89.50
Jansen, Becky & Baby, 1977	59.50
Jansen, Jeanette & Julie, 1978	50.00
Lenox, Wildlife, 1973	85.00
Lenox, Wildlife, 1974	27.50
Lenox, Wildlife, 1975	79.50
Rockwell, Four Seasons, 1973	145.00
Rockwell, Four Seasons, 1977	100.00
Rockwell, Scotty Gets Tree	145.00
Rosenthal, Christmas, 1913	175.00
Rosenthal, Christmas, 1915	149.50
Rosenthal, Christmas, 1916	175.00
Royal Bayreuth, Mother's Day, 1974	50.00
COLLECTOR PLATE, ROYAL COPENHAGEN, see Royal Copenhagen	
Szabo, The Whaler, 1979	50.00
Wedgwood, Christmas, 1978, 10th Anniversary, 2-Color	60.00
COMIC ART, Amos & Andy, 1935, Sunday, 1/2 Page	12.00
Buck Rogers, Sunday, Full Color Page, June 16, 1935	50.00
Celluloid, Mickey Mouse, The Sorcerer's Apprentice, 5 In.	2600.00
Chicago Sunday Sun, May 23, 1923, The Spirit, Mr.Mystic, Lady Luck	7.00
Nancy & Sluggo, Ernie Bushmiller, Original Art	300.00
Popeye, Watercolor & Ink, Dated 1947, Signed Bud Sagendurf, Framed	200.00
4 Sections Of Aurora Beacon News, Illinois, June 14, 1936	4.00

Commemoration items have been made to honor members of royalty and those of great national fame. World's fairs and important historical events are also remembered with commemorative pieces.

COMMEMORATIVE, see also Coronation; World's Fair	
COMMEMORATIVE, Bell, Prince Charles, Lady Diana, 5 1/4 In.	28.00
Bowl, King Edward VIII, Portrait, Coat of Arms, 7 3/4 In.	55.00
Bowl, King George VI, Visit To Canada & U.S.A., 1939, 3 In.	30.00
Box, Queen Elizabeth II Silver Jubilee, Lid, 4 In.Square	29.00
Calendar, King George VI, Queen Elizabeth, Souvenir	40.00
Cup, King Edward VII, Queen Alexandra Portraits, 3 In.	80.00
Dish, Candy, Princess Ann, Wedgwood, White On Blue, 4 1/4 In.	15.00
Dish, Candy, Queen Elizabeth, Portrait & Flags, 1953, Covered	45.00
Dish, Sir Winston Churchill, Blue & White, Jasperware, 4 In.	20.00
Mug, Queen Elizabeth II, Prince Philip, 25th Anniversary	75.00
Mug, Queen Victoria Diamond Jubilee	65.00
Paperweight, Prince Charles & Lady Diana	32.00
Plate, George VI & Elizabeth, Profiles, 1937, 9 In.	40.00
Plate, God Bless The Prince Of Wales, 3 In., Pair	20.00
Plate, Hartford Scenic, 8 In.	17.50
Plate, Marblehead, W.Adams & Son, 8 In.	17.50
Plate, New Haven Scenic, Marked England, 8 In.	17.50
Plate, Panama Canal	19.00
Plate, Queen Elizabeth II, Silver Jubilee, Wedgwood, 8 In.	35.00
Plate, Queen Mother Elizabeth, 80th Birthday, 10 1/4 In.	69.00
Plate, Queen Victoria, 1887, Sepia Picture, Jubilee, 9 In.	40.00
Slipper, Queen Victoria, 1837-97, 6 In.Long	85.00
Tankard, Prince Charles, Lady Diana, Bells, 5 3/4 In.	25.00
Tin, King George V, Queen Mary, Silver Jubilee, 1910-35	55.00
Tin, Queen Elizabeth & Prince Philip Silver Jubilee, 6 In.	14.00
Tin, Queen Elizabeth II, Prince Philip, St.Lawrence Seaway	18.00
Toothpick, Silver Jubilee Of George V & Queen Mary, 1935	45.00
Tray, Pin, Queen Elizabeth II, Princess Ann, Prince Charles	52.00
Vase, Queen Victoria, Dominion Of Canada, Handled, 5 In.	85.00
Vase, Queen Victoria, Portrait, Canada Provinces, 5 1/2 In.	85.00

Coors ware was made by a pottery in Golden, Colorado, owned by the Coors Beverage Company. It was produced from the turn of the century until the pottery was destroyed by fire in the 1930s. The name Coors is marked on the back.

COORS, Ashtray, Signed	10.50
Creamer, Cover, Paper Label, Green	15.00
Holder, Fountain Straw, Metal Lid	45.00
Plate, Rosebud, Maroon, 10 In.	9.00
Pot, Melting, Pharmacist's	5.00
Stein, 1 1/2 In.	25.00
Vase, Art Deco, Blue Matte, 6 In.	15.00
Vase, Blue & White, 6 In.	27.00
Vase, Blue & White, 11 In.	55.00
Vase, Bulbous, Flaring Mouth, Triangular Stamp, 8 1/2 In.	18.00
Vase, Orange, White, Handled, 6 In.	38.00
Vase, Small Handles, Matte Green, 7 In.	12.00
Vase, Yellow, 8 In.	15.00

COPELAND

W.T.Copeland & Sons, Ltd., ran the Spode Works in Staffordshire, England, from 1847 to 1976. Copeland & Garrett was the firm name from 1833 to 1847.

COPELAND SPODE, see also Flow Blue; Spode

COPELAND SPODE, Bowl, Blue & White, Footed, Registry Number, 8 In.	70.00
Bowl, Blue & White, 7 1/2 In.	35.00
Bowl, Underplate, Fluted Sides & Edges, 9 In.Diam.	150.00
Coffeepot, Green, Beige, White Classical Figures, 8 In.	95.00
Cup & Saucer, Blue & White, Large	45.00
Cup & Saucer, Gainsborough, Demitasse	25.00
Dish, Cheese, Tower Scene, Blue & White	95.00
Pitcher, Blue Cameo, C.1900, 8 In.	75.00
Pitcher, Blue & White, 9 X 9 In.	60.00
Plate, Bird, Blue & White, Woodcock, Duck, 10 In.	40.00
Plate, Fruit Center, Signed, Flower Border, Set Of 12	165.00
Plate, Leaves & Bird, Hand-Painted Flowers, 7 In.	20.00
Plate, Souvenir, Shakespeare, Black & White, Country Scene	25.00
Plate, University Of New Hampshire Buildings, Set Of 5	125.00
Plate, Willoware, Signed, 12 1/2 In.	60.00
Teapot, Blue & White, Italian, Dog Design, Inscribed	135.00

COPELAND, see also Copeland Spode; Spode

COPELAND, Mug, Going To The Derby, Handled, Signed, 7 In.	165.00
Pitcher, Milk, Figures, Dark Blue	75.00
Planter, Scrolls & Masks, White, Blue Ground, 8 In.	375.00
Plate, Mandarin II, 1882-83, 10 In.	17.50
Platter, Greek Pattern, Blue	47.50
Platter, Mandarin II, Oval, 7 X 9 In.	37.50
Vase, Jeweled Porcelain, 19th Century, Gilt Mark, 10 3/4 In.	1100.00

COPPER LUSTER, see Luster, Copper

COPPER, Bedwarmer, English, Oak Handle, 19th Century	100.00
Bookend, Figural, Parrot, 5 1/2 X 6 1/4 In.	55.00
Bookends, Green Design, Craftsman	45.00
Bowl, Crimped, Marked Craftsman, C.1915, 15 In.Diam.	165.00
Box, Document, Hinged Lid, 4 Feet, Top Handle, 9 1/2 In.	65.00
Box, Snuff, Heart Form, C.1840, 3 In.	165.00
Candlestick, Removable Salamanders, 4 Claw Feet, 11 In., Pair	120.00
Canteen, 1863, German	55.00
Coal Scuttle, Embossed Woman, Man, In Front Of Fireplace, 25 1/2 In.	25.00
Coffeepot, Brass Finial, 8 3/4 In.	15.00

Copper, Planter, Dirk Van Erp, 11 X 17 In.Diam.; 8 1/4 X 12 In.Diam.

Desk Set, C.1910, G.Stickley, Stamped Mark, Inkwell 5 1/2 In., 5 Piece	360.00
Figurine, Buddha, Seated, Tablet, 4 In.	450.00
Funnel, Brewery, Lap Seaming, C.1850, Burnished, 12 In.Diam.	60.00
Hot Dog Steamer, Queen Anne Brass Legs, Double Top, 11 X 17 In.	300.00
Inkwell, Riveted Edge, C.1910, G.Stickley, Copper, 5 1/2 In.Diam.	110.00
Kettle, Apple Butter	375.00
Kettle, Dovetailed, Gooseneck Spout, Acorn Finial, 13 3/4 In.	295.00
Kettle, Handle, Marked Thomas Bishop	80.00
Kettle, Iron Handles, C.1865, 12 In.	125.00
Kettle, Rome, Swing Handle, Black Grip, 1 Gallon	45.00
Kettle, Victorian, 19th Century, Brass & Porcelain Swing Handle	50.00
Mug, Drinking, Lead Lining, 2-Handled, 1800s	145.00
Mug, Lap Seaming, Lapped Copper Handle, C.1860, 3 3/4 In.	60.00
Pan, Jam, English, Swing Handle	75.00
Pan, Sauce, Dovetailed, Solid Brass Finial Iron Handle, Marked N.Y.	260.00
Pitcher, Beer, Vertical Glass Window On Side, 1848, 8 1/2 In.	95.00
Pitcher, Middle Eastern, 11 3/4 In.	20.00
Pitcher, Milk, With Lid	210.00
Planter, Dirk Van Erp, 8 1/4 X 12 In.Diam. ....*Illus*	2000.00
Planter, Dirk Van Erp, 11 X 17 In.Diam. ....*Illus*	4000.00
Samovar, Stand, Burner, 12 In.	45.00
Scuttle, Coal, English, Circular Form, Concave Center, Handles	50.00
Sifter, Flour, C.1800	60.00
Sink, C.A.Blessing, Phila., Copper Covered Tin, 20 X 14 1/2 X 7 In.	155.00
Skillet, Wrought Copper Handle, 8 1/2 In.	30.00
Spittoon, Arts & Crafts, 9 In.	375.00
Spittoon, Bulldog & Cut Plug Emblem	30.00
Still, Dome-Topped, Folding Handle, 3 Gallon	210.00
Still, Moonshine, With Stove, Complete	400.00
Tank, Beer, Marked Portsmouth Brewing Co., Tinned Inside, 15 3/4 In.	475.00
Teakettle, Dovetailed, Norwegian	75.00
Teakettle, Gooseneck Spout, Oval, 8 1/2 In.	40.00
Teakettle, Marked Hummerman, Boston	1425.00
Teakettle, Regency Style, Gooseneck Spout, Paw Feet, 10 In.	150.00
Teakettle, Stand & Burner	75.00
Teapot, Marked Majestic, Brass Handle	185.00
Tray, Art Nouveau, 2-Figure, Marked 58, 9 1/2 In.	250.00
Tray, Arts & Crafts, Gorham, 5 1/2 In.	60.00
Tray, Crumb, Scenes Of Yellowstone Park	10.00
Tub, Dovetailed Construction, Hand-Forged Handles	195.00
Urn, Handmade, 7 1/2 In.	20.00
Urn, 3 Brass Ball Feet, Chased Flowers, Leaves, Bulbous, 3 1/2 In.	18.00
Washing Machine Cover, Embossed ABC, 24 X 23 In.	24.00

Tiffany, Lamp, Table, Favrile, 1896, 33½ In.

Flow Blue, Plate And Teapot, Kremlin, Samuel Alcock & Co., C. 1845

Dedham, Cup And Saucer And Plate, Rabbit, 1900

Adams, Platter, Caledonia, C. 1850

Mt. Washington, Bride's Bowl, Pink, 1880, 13 In.

Copeland, Vase, Acropolis, Jeweled, Samuel Alcock, C. 1893, 19 In.

Lamps, Kerosene, Windmill Decoration, 1900, 28 In.; Wild & Wessel, Germany, C. 1895, 22 In.

Niloak, Vase, 9¾ In.

Doll, Japanese, Samurai Warrior, Composition, C. 1900, 17 In.

Fulper, Compote, C. 1910, 7¾ In.

Silver Plate, Coffee Urn, Floral, U.S., 16 In.

Silver Plate, Tilting Water Pitcher, Two Goblets, Victorian, Reed & Barton

Silver Plate, Bonbon, Parker Casper & Co., 1867–69, 8 In. Diam.; Figural, Napkin Ring, Cupid, Floral, C. 1900, 3¼ In.; Coffee Maker, Locomotive, English, 1875–90

Coffee Grinders, Enterprise, Pat. Oct. 21, 1873, 15 In.; Wall Model, C. 1900, 14 In.; Landers, Frary & Clark, Pat. Feb. 14, 1905, 7¼ In.

Food Can Labels, C. 1900

Store, Poster, Mellin's Food,
Chromolithograph,
28½ X 12½ In.

Silver-American, Teapot, Gorham, Floral Repousse, 1881–86

Souvenir, Spoons, Sterling Silver, Atlanta, Enamel
Watercolor; New York, Enamel Flag

Skeletonized Leaf In Dome, C. 1875

Potichomania, Glass Globe,
Decorated With Cigar Bands

Carnival Glass, Pitcher, Windmill,
6½ In.

Pressed Glass, Wildflower,
Compote, Amber, Covered,
1874–1900, 9½ In.

Cranberry Glass, Syrup Jug,
Enameled Flowers, Silver Plated
Top

Satin Glass, Vases, Blue, C. 1890, 5½ In.; Pink, C. 1890; Pink, Footed,
C. 1880, 7¼ In.

Washing Machine, Voss, 1915 .... 150.00

CORAL, Figurine, Buddha, 1 1/2 In. 45.00
  Figurine, Chinese Lady, 2 1/2 In. 50.00
  Figurine, Maiden, Holding Basket Of Fruit, 9 7/8 In. .... *Illus* 1000.00
  Figurine, Maiden, Holding Vase, Pinkish White, 6 In. 275.00
  Figurine, Maiden, Robe, Basket Of Flowers, Orange Tone, 9 1/2 In. 1800.00
  Figurine, Sampan, Man At Tiller, Waves, Fish, 3 3/4 In. .... *Illus* 1900.00

*Coralene glass was made by firing many small colored beads on the outside
of glassware. It was made in many patterns in the United States and
Europe in the 1880s. Reproductions are made today.*

CORALENE, JAPANESE, see Japanese Coralene
CORALENE, Basket, Signed, Cobalt Blue & Gold Trim, Japanese, 4 3/4 In. 50.00
  Box, Powder, Dated 1909 .... 55.00
  Communion Set, Blown, Cobalt Blue, 7 Piece 60.00
  Ewer, Pink, Gold, Coral, Cream Base, Thorn Handle, 11 In. 875.00
  Pitcher, Tan Ground, Patent February 9, 1909, 12 In. 275.00
  Sugar & Creamer, Gold & White Over Pastels, Handled 135.00
  Vase, Bird Design, Ruffled Top, 6 In. 250.00
  Vase, Blue, Yellow, & Red, 1908, 9 In. 335.00
  Vase, Green, Yellow, & Orange Beading, 1909 Mark, 5 In. 190.00
  Vase, Inverted Thumbprint, Floral, Cranberry, 5 1/4 In. 390.00
  Vase, Japanese, Iris Design, Loop Handles, Marked, 8 1/2 In. 135.00
  Vase, Lady's Slipper In Lilac, Pink, & Yellow, Shell Feet, 10 In. 900.00
  Vase, Poppy Design, Dated 1902, 16 1/2 In. 335.00
  Vase, Rose, Diamond-Quilted, Mother-Of-Pearl, Pink, Yellow, 4 In. 495.00
  Vase, Seaweed Design, Lavender To Yellow, 6 In. 385.00
  Vase, Shaded Green Ground, Purple Flowers, C.1909, Marked, 12 In. 295.00
  Vase, Yellow Flowers, Blue Handles, Purple 1909 Mark, 4 7/8 In. 200.00

*Cordey China Company was founded in 1942 by Boleslaw Cybis in
Trenton, New Jersey. The firm produced gift shop items. Production
stopped in 1950 and Cybis Porcelains was founded.*

CORDEY, Bottle, Perfume, Male Bust 45.00
  Bowl, Rose Bouquets On Top Of Handles, 9 1/2 In.Diam. 78.00
  Box, Jewelry, Roses & Petals, Gold Trim, 3 5/8 X 2 1/4 In. 38.00
  Box, Pink Roses On Lid, Square, 4-Footed, Signed, 5 X 4 In. 75.00
  Bust, Junior Miss, No.5026, Draped Scarf Over Head, Marked, 7 In. 90.00
  Bust, Lady, Rose Leaves, Hat, Gold Trim, 6 1/4 In. 79.00
  Bust, Lady, Roses, Man, Washington Hairdo, Marked & Numbered 125.00

Coral, Figurine, Maiden, Holding
Basket Of Fruit, 9 7/8 In.

Coral, Figurine, Sampan, Man At Tiller,
Waves, Fish, 3 3/4 In.

Bust, Male, Colonial 3-Cornered Hat, No.4013 .... 55.00
Cup & Saucer, Free-Form, Rococo, Floral & Leaves, Signed 37.00
Dish, Clusters Of Flowers Each End, Scalloped, 12 In. 48.00
Figurine, Blonde Girl With Bonnet, No.5028/161, 6 1/2 In. 135.00
Figurine, Colonial Gentleman, Signed, 16 1/4 In. 75.00
Figurine, Girl With Basket, Gathering Fruit, No.304, 16 In. 225.00
Figurine, Grape Worker, Burgundy Hat & Coat, No.305, 16 In. 85.00
Figurine, Lady, No.5084, 12 In. 95.00
Figurine, Man & Lady, No.302, 303, 16 In., Pair 190.00
Figurine, Oriental, 12 In. 100.00
Figurine, Young Girl, Blonde, Curled, Bonnet, Roses, Gray Color, 6 In. 80.00
Lamp, Colonial Gentleman 300.00
Lamp, Marie Antoinette 300.00
Lamp, Oriental, Signed 250.00
Vase, Blownout Figure Of Geisha, Applied Florals, 8 3/4 In. 70.00
Vase, Stylized Leaves Around Middle, Gray Iridescent Glaze, 8 In. 20.00
Wall Pocket, Swirled Cone Shape, Nude Draped Lady, 8 1/2 In. 115.00

CORKSCREW, Advertising, Diehl & Lord Beer, Large 15.00
Anheuser Busch Malt-Nutrine, Brass 30.00
Bottle-Shaped, Kelly's Private Stock Whiskey, Brass 20.00
Brubaker Pudding 10.00
Figural, Nude Outer Space Type Man, Jeweled Eyes 12.50
Figural, Pig's Hindquarters, Metal 24.00
Figural, The Christian Brothers, Wooden 6.50
File Design On Iron, Ebony Handle, 5 In. 22.00
Green River Whiskey, Folding, Metal 16.00
Horn Handle, 19th Century, Handmade 12.00
Marked Listerine, Folding 5.00
Remnants Of Brush, Turned Handle, 18th Century 23.00

*Coronation cups have been made since the 1800s. Pottery or glass with a
picture of the monarch and date have been souvenirs for many coronations.*
CORONATION, see also Commemorative
CORONATION, Ashtray, Queen Elizabeth II, Glass .... 12.00 To 120.00
Beaker, King Edward VIII, Portrait, 4 1/4 In. 45.00
Cup & Saucer, Queen Elizabeth II, Portrait 45.00
Cup, Queen Elizabeth, Alfred Meakin 10.00
Dish, Queen Elizabeth II, Wade, 4 1/2 In.Diam. 16.00
Jar, Queen Elizabeth II, June 2, 1953, Lid 40.00
Mug, King Edward, 8, May, 1937, Burleigh, England 25.00
Mug, Queen Elizabeth II, Portrait, Flags, 3 In. 30.00
Pitcher, King Edward VIII, Crown, 5 1/4 In. 60.00
Plate, King Edward VIII, 6 1/4 In. 20.00
Plate, Queen Elizabeth II, Portrait, 6 3/4 In. 20.00
Saucer, Elizabeth II, June 2, 1953, Taylor & Kent 4.50
Teaspoon, George VI, 1937 .... 15.00
Tray, Pin, Queen Elizabeth II, Ellr, 3 In. 22.00
Tray, Pin, Queen Elizabeth II, Royal Minton 18.00

Cosmos pattern glass is a pressed milk glass pattern with colored flowers.

COSMOS, Butter, Covered 135.00
Butter, Enameled Flowers, Pink Band, Covered 165.00
Condiment Set, Cosmos Handled Frame, Pink Band, 3 Piece .... 195.00 To 265.00
Creamer 110.00
Lamp, Pink Band, Original Chimney & Burner, Miniature .... 70.00 To 172.00
Lamp, Table, Pink Band Shade, Yellow Band Base, Eagle Burner, 16 In. 300.00
Pitcher, Water 215.00
Salt & Pepper, Pink, Cased 85.00
Spooner 50.00
Sugar & Creamer, Pink Band 295.00
Sugar, Covered 20.00
    COUNTRY STORE, see Store

Cowan pottery was made in Cleveland, Ohio, from 1913 to 1931. Most pieces of the art pottery were marked with the name of the firm in various ways.

COWAN, Bowl, Allover Craquelure, C.1930, V.Schrechengost, Marked, 16 3/4 In.	825.00
Candleholder, 3-Light, Centerpiece, Ivory Lattice	32.00
Candlestick, Blue Luster, 8 In., Pair	68.00
Candlestick, Handled, Ivory, Pair	24.00
Candlestick, Seahorse, Ivory, Pair	22.00
Match Holder, Seahorse	25.00
Vase, Blue, 8 1/2 In., Pair	70.00
Vase, Green Crystalline, 8 X 5 In.	80.00

CRACKER JACK, Badge, Police, Tin	9.00
Bookmark, Bulldog, Tin	8.00 To 13.00
Bookmark, Dog Head	8.00
Jumping Frog, Cardboard	10.00
Pullcart, Tin	15.00
Sulky, Tin	15.00
Tablet, School, 1936	18.00
Toonerville Trolley	350.00 To 425.00
Top, Metal	6.00
Toy, Cart, Wooden Tongue, Metal	15.00
Toy, Horse & Wagon, Tin	15.00
Trick, Paper Foldout, Eat Cracker Jack & Grow Big, Metal	10.00
Truck, Tin, Lithograph	30.00
Wagon, Horse-Drawn, Tin	25.00
Watch, Pocket	15.00
Whistle, Tin	5.00 To 12.00

Crackle glass was originally made by the Venetians, but most of the ware found today dates from the 1800s. The glass was heated, cooled, and refired so that many small lines appeared inside the glass. It was made in many factories in the United States and Europe.

CRACKLE GLASS, see also Fry

CRACKLE GLASS, Bride's Basket, Bird Finial, Silver Plated	200.00
Dish, Cheese, Applied Knob Finial	150.00
Pitcher, Lemonade, Blue Handle, Covered, Green	45.00
Vase, Auto, Marigold, Pair	14.00
Vase, Enameled White & Gold Flowers, Sapphire Blue, 5 1/4 In.	125.00
Vase, Garniture, Rose & Water Lillies, 11 In., Pair	100.00
Vase, Medallions, Iron Red Lattice Ground, Chinese, 3 5/8 In.	110.00

Cranberry glass is an almost transparent yellow-red glass. It resembles the color of cranberry juice.

CRANBERRY GLASS, see also Northwood; Rubena Verde; etc.

CRANBERRY GLASS, Basket, Clear Handle, 7 In.	35.00
Basket, Handled, 5 In.	50.00
Basket, Hobnail, Silver Plated Holder	75.00
Bell, Smoke, 8 3/4 In.	60.00
Bell, White Cut To Cranberry, Gold Tracery, 7 In.	375.00
Bottle, Barber, Swirl, Opalescent	85.00
Bottle, Perfume, Cased, Sterling Silver Hinged Top	30.00
Bottle, Perfume, Enameled Flowers, Gold Trim, 2 7/8 In.	95.00
Bottle, Perfume, Gold Flowers, Pink & White Leaves, 5 In.	110.00
Bottle, Perfume, Gold Foliage, Coral Flowers, 4 3/4 In.	110.00
Bottle, Perfume, Gold Intaglio Design, Pink Rose, 5 5/8 In.	110.00
Bottle, Perfume, Gold Thistles & Leaves, Aqua, 4 3/4 In.	115.00
Bottle, Perfume, Sterling Silver Overlay, 3 3/4 In.	65.00
Bottle, Smelling Salts, Sterling Silver Hinged Top	28.00
Bottle, Wine, Rib Optic	85.00
Bowl, Finger, Underplate, Ground Bottom	40.00
Bowl, Opalescent Threading, Clear Feet, 6 In.	85.00

Bowl, Pierced Sheffield Silver Holder, 7 1/4 In.Diam. 155.00
Bowl, Ruffled, Quilted Pattern, 10 In.Top Diam. 85.00
Bowl, Ruffled, 4 X 10 In.Diam. 75.00
Bowl, Thumbprint, 2 7/8 X 4 In.Diam. 37.50
Box, Design, Hinged, Signed, 3 In.Diam. 125.00
Box, Knobbed Lid, Gold & White Enamel, 2 3/4 In.Diam. 150.00
Box, Overall Enamel Design, Ormolu Feet, Hinged Lid, 4 In. 165.00
Box, Powder, Hinged, Gold & Blue Enamel, 2 3/4 In. 110.00
Butter, Crystal Applique Ruffle, Thorn Finial, Covered 135.00
Candleholder, Finger Ring 45.00
Carafe, Water, Seaweed Pattern, Clear Stopper 85.00
Castor, Pickle, Cone Pattern 250.00
Castor, Pickle, Inverted Thumbprint, Silver Plated Frame 235.00
Castor, Pickle, Inverted Thumbprint, 4 1/4 In. 85.00
Cookie Jar, Lettered, For Ma, Etched, 8 1/4 In. 199.00
Creamer, Clear Applied Foot, Reeded Handle, 2 3/4 In. 60.00
Creamer, Embossed Wheat, Clear Handle, 4 In. 125.00
Creamer, Inverted Thumbprint Pattern, Clear Handle, 5 In. 130.00
Cruet, Clear Handle, Gold Scrolls, White Dots, 11 3/4 In. 145.00
Cruet, Enameled Scrolls & Flowers, Gold Trim, 7 1/2 In. 145.00
Cruet, Hobnail, Crystal Reeded Handle 48.00
Cruet, Inverted Thumbprint, Floral Pontil, 5 In. 60.00
Cruet, Lacy Gold Enamel Scrolls, 7 3/8 In. 118.00
Cruet, Optic Mold, Clear Handle & Stopper, 3-Cornered Spout 165.00
Cruet, Polished Pontil, Clear Ball Stopper, 6 3/4 In. 65.00
Cup & Saucer, Multicolor Enameled Flowers, Saucer 5 In. 125.00
Decanter, Bulbous, 6 Stemmed Wines, Clear Stems, 9 In. 225.00
Decanter, Clear Bubble Stopper, Enameled Dots, 9 1/8 In. 150.00
Decanter, Figural, Bird, Brass Feet, Legs & Head, Beak Opens 175.00
Decanter, Optic Swirl, Clear Pedestal, Faceted Stopper 65.00
Decanter, Square, Bulbous, Clear Handle, Stopper, 8 3/4 In. 110.00
Dish, Candy, Clear Knob 40.00
Dish, Sweetmeat, Silver Plated Holder, 6 1/2 In.Diam. 100.00
Dresser Set, Gold Enamel, Scrolls, Flowers, 6 Piece 395.00
Epergne, Single Lily, 19 In. 135.00
Epergne, 2 Hanging Baskets On Crystal Arms, 2 Lilies 375.00
Epergne, 3-Trumpet Vases, Gold-Flecked Filigree 185.00
Epergne, 4 Lilies, Crimped, 19 In. 345.00
Finger Bowl, Plate, Threaded, Scalloped Rims, Opalescent 85.00
Finger Bowl, Underplate, Allover Gold, Berry Feet 110.00
Goblet, Clear Base & Stem, Set Of 6 .... 40.00
Goblet, Sunburst, Paneled Sawtooth Stem, 8 3/4 In. 25.00
Goblet, Wedding, Clear Stem & Foot, Dated 1896, 6 1/4 In. 65.00
Hat, Optic Dot, Small 35.00
Hat, Polished Pontil, 3 1/2 X 2 In. .... 40.00 To 55.00
Jam Pot, Sterling Silver Holder, Signed, 4 1/4 In. 165.00
Jar, Pickle, Inverted Thumbprint, Silver Holder 140.00
Lamp, Bull's-Eye, Miniature, Base, 6 1/2 In. 70.00
Lamp, Dated 1888, Pewter Collar 75.00
Lamp, Fairy, Clear, 4 3/4 In. 190.00
Lamp, Fairy, Pyramid Shape, Clarke Base, 3 1/4 In. 110.00
Lamp, Fairy, Verre Moire, White Loopings, 5 1/4 In. 150.00
Lamp, Hanging, Wall 160.00
Light, Hall, Victorian, Swirl Design, 14 In. 180.00
Muffineer, Inverted Thumbprint 60.00
Muffineer, 12 Panels, Silver Plated Domed Top 72.00
Nappy, Combed Open Handle, Hand Blown, 4 3/4 In. 55.00
Pitcher, Clear Applied Handle, Gold & Enameling, 9 In. 115.00
Pitcher, Clear Handle, 7 1/2 In. 95.00
Pitcher, Clear Reeded Handle, Enameled Florals, 7 1/2 In. 165.00
Pitcher, Cut Dragonfly & Leaves In Gold, 6 1/2 In. 160.00
Pitcher, Enamel Design, Ruffled, Clear Handle, Blown Ribbing 135.00
Pitcher, Fluted, Enameled Dot Design, Gold Trim, 6 1/2 In. 115.00

Pitcher, Hobnail, 5 1/2 In.	48.00
Pitcher, Inverted Thumbprint, Clear Handle	190.00
Pitcher, Inverted Thumbprint, Enameled Flowers, 6 In.	120.00
Pitcher, Inverted Thumbprint, Reeded Handle, 6 3/4 In.	135.00
Pitcher, Inverted Thumbprint, 4-Sided Mouth, 7 1/2 In.	165.00
Pitcher, Overshot Back, 7 In.	98.00
Pitcher, Overshot Back, 9 In.	135.00
Pitcher, Paneled, 7 In.	75.00
Pitcher, Ribbed, Clear Applied Handle, 7 1/2 In.	125.00
Pitcher, Sanded Design, Enameled Dots, 4 1/4 In.	100.00
Pitcher, Swirl Design, Clear Reeded Handle, 5 In.	90.00
Pitcher, Turned Down Ruffled Top, Gold & Enamel, 9 In.	150.00
Pitcher, Water, Leaf Umbrella, Northwood	165.00
Pitcher, Water, Nailsea, Bulbous, Applied Handle, 7 In.	175.00
Pitcher, White Enamel Design, Running Deer	175.00
Pitcher, White Enamel Dots, Gold Trim, Fluted, 6 1/2 In.	115.00
Rose Bowl, Enameled Florals, Blue & White, 3 X 3 1/2 In.	118.00
Rose Bowl, Enameled White Lace, 3 In.	145.00
Rose Bowl, Gold Enameling, 2 1/2 In.	45.00
Salt & Pepper, Inverted Thumbprint, Tufts Holder	65.00
Salt, 5 Clear Applied Feet, Ruffled Rim	45.00
Saltshaker, Leaf Umbrella	40.00
Saltshaker, Paneled Sprig	48.00
Sherbet, Cut To Clear	29.50
Sugar & Creamer, Rigaree, Petal Feet, Reeded Handle	350.00
Sugar Shaker, Inverted Thumbprint, 9 Panel	65.00
Sugar Shaker, Leaf Mold, Shiny Spatter	145.00
Sugar Shaker, Leaf Umbrella, Blue	150.00
Sugar Shaker, Panel Cut	60.00
Sugar Shaker, Ribbed Pillar, White Spatter	110.00
Sugar Shaker, Spatter Ring Neck	45.00
Syrup, Inverted Thumbprint	80.00
Syrup, Leaf Mold, Vaseline Spatter	275.00
Syrup, Pitcher, Clear Handle, Silver Collar & Lid, 6 In.	165.00
Syrup, Spanish Lace	140.00
Syrup, 1000-Eye	89.00
Toothpick, Delaware	85.00
Toothpick, Florette, Pink	45.00
Tumbler, Commemorative, Lebanon Fair, 1916	18.00
Tumbler, Enameled Florals	20.00
Tumbler, Gold, Enamel Brazier	28.00
Tumbler, Inverted Thumbprint	25.00
Tumbler, Leaf Mold, Vaseline Spatter	65.00
Tumbler, Ribbed Pillar Pattern, White Spatter	30.00
Tumbler, White & Yellow Enameled Flowers, 3 3/4 In.	30.00
Urn, Thorny Knob Finial, Gold Scrolls, Covered, 11 1/4 In.	275.00
Vase, Applied Crystal Leaves, Thorny Nubs, 8 1/4 In.	110.00
Vase, Applied Pinecone & Crystal Handle, 7 1/8 In.	85.00
Vase, Applied Shell Trim Around Center, 7 3/4 In.	75.00
Vase, Bulbous, Gold Flecked, Marked, 4 X 4 In.	35.00
Vase, Butterflies, Dot Edge, Enamel Foliage, 4 1/4 In., Pair	175.00
Vase, Crystal Applied Flowers, Tricornered Top, 5 In.	195.00
Vase, Cut To Clear, 12 1/2 In.	90.00
Vase, Double Crimp, 5 X 4 1/2 In.	30.00
Vase, Enameled Floral Design, White & Green, 8 In.	185.00
Vase, Enameled Floral, Brass Feet & Handles, 10 1/2 In., Pr.	400.00
Vase, Enameled Gold, Yellow, White Flowers, 4 3/4 In., Pair	145.00
Vase, Enameled Leaves, White Outlined, Florals, 10 5/8 In.	150.00
Vase, Flower Prunts At Base Of Handle, 11 1/2 In.	195.00
Vase, Fluted, White Trim, 10 In.	35.00
Vase, Gold Bands, Allover Design, Scalloped, 5 3/4 In.	100.00
Vase, Gold Branches & Flowers, Pedestal, 16 In.	125.00
Vase, Gold Scrolls, Enameled Flowers, 15 In., Pair	550.00

Vase, Gold Spangles, Clear Handle & Edging, 9 3/4 In. 195.00
Vase, Lily Of The Valley, Gold Leaves, 6 3/4 In., Pair 135.00
Vase, Paisley Design, Gold Trim. 3 3/4 In. 45.00
Vase, Ribbon Wrap, Clear Feet, 6 In. 65.00
Vase, Ruffled Rim, 5 X 4 In. 35.00
Vase, Shell Feet, Solid Mass Of Shells For Base, 5 In. 375.00
Vase, Spiral Optic, Matching Pair, 12 In. 235.00
Vase, Threaded, Ormolu Mounted, 7 1/2 In. 350.00
Vase, Trumpet Shape, Ruffled, Clear Foot, C.1870, 11 1/2 In. 78.00
Vase, Vaseline Applied Spiral Trim, Heart-Shaped Top, 9 In. 95.00
Vase, Wheel-Etched, 11 In., Pair 80.00
Vase, White Enameled Stag & Foliage, 10 1/4 In. 145.00
Vase, White Enameled Tree Scene, Gold Flowers, 9 In. 165.00
Vase, White Ruffle, 4 1/4 X 3 1/2 In. 25.00
Vase, Windows, Ruffed Rim, 8 In. 60.00
Water Set, Leaf Umbrella, 7 Piece 675.00

*Creamware, or queensware, was developed by Josiah Wedgwood about
1765. It is a cream-colored earthenware that has been copied by many factories.*
CREAMWARE, see also Wedgwood
CREAMWARE, Cup & Saucer, Copper Luster, C.1850 .... 50.00

*The Creil Factory at Oise, France, made earthenware from 1794 to
1895. It joined the firm of Montereau in the early nineteenth century.*

CREIL, Cachepot, Black Side Transfers, Oval Reserves, Marked, 6 In. 650.00
Cafe Pot, Dome Top, Marked, 12 In. 1000.00
Creamer, 4 1/2 In. 220.00
Sucrier, Marked, 6 In. 550.00
CROESUS, see Pressed Glass, Croesus

*Crown Derby is the nickname given to the works of the Royal Crown
Derby factory which began working in England in 1859. An earlier and
more famous English Derby factory existed from 1750 to 1848. The two
factories were not related. Most of the porcelain found today with the
Derby mark is the work of the later Derby factory.*
CROWN DERBY, see also Royal Crown Derby
CROWN DERBY, Bowl, Butterfly Handle, Footed, Covered, 6 1/2 In. 40.00
Bowl, Butterfly Handle, Gold & Opaque, Footed, Covered, 6 In. 40.00
Creamer, Miniature, Imari Pattern, C.1875, 2 1/2 In. 65.00
Cup & Saucer, Daffodils, Flowers, Gold, Marked 55.00
Cup & Saucer, Gold & White, Sculptured 50.00
Cup & Saucer, View In Cumberland, Blue & Gilt 200.00
Dish, Japan Pattern, Lozenge, C.1815, 8 1/4 In., Pair 375.00
Jug, Milk, Japan Pattern, Pewter Lid, Marked, 6 1/2 In. 130.00
Jug, Milk, King's Pattern, C.1880, Printed Mark, 7 1/2 In. 100.00
Plate, Japan Pattern, Crossed Swords, 10 1/4 In., Set Of 12 .... 500.00
Plate, Soup, Japan Pattern, 1940 Mark, 9 1/4 In. 50.00
Sugar & Creamer, Orange, Blue Cypher Mark 98.00
Toothpick, Green Ground, Floral Reserve, 3 1/2 In. 235.00
Vase, Bud, Cream Ground, Florals, Handled, 4 1/2 In., Pair 535.00
Vase, Bud, Teardrop Form, Floral Design, Blue, Red, Marked, 7 In. 80.00
Vase, Buff Ground, Paisley Design, Jeweling, 9 In. 425.00
Vase, Cabinet, Yellow Ground, Florals, Gilding, 6 1/2 In. 365.00
Vase, Hawthorne, Japanese Design, Blue Ground, Marked, 5 In., Pr. 250.00
Vase, Melon Fern Body, Lotus Design, Ball Knop, Marked, 9 In. 550.00
Vase, Ovoid, Floral Design, Polychrome, Marked, 7 1/4 In. 200.00
Vase, Pear Form, Floral Design, Teal Green, Marked, 12 In. 180.00
Vase, Pink Ground, Blossoms, 10 In. 245.00
Vase, Plum Ground, Scrollwork Design, C.1884, Marked, 9 In. 190.00
Vase, Swelling Vessel, Jeweled, Blue Ground, Marked, 19 In. 1750.00
Vase, Trumpet-Shape, Florals, Cream Ground, 8 In., Pair 600.00

Crown Ducal is the name used on some pieces of porcelain made by A.G. Richardson and Co., Ltd., England. The name has been used since 1916.

CROWN DUCAL, Plate, Bar Scenes, 8 In. 8.00
Plate, Transfer Of Bar Scene, 8 In. 10.00

Crown Milano glass was made by Frederick Shirley about 1890. It had a plain biscuit color with a satin finish. It was decorated with flowers, and often had large gold scrolls.

CROWN MILANO, Biscuit Jar, Gold Flowers, Coral & Yellow Ground, 8 In. 1250.00
Biscuit Jar, Melon Ribbed, Mottled Blue, Gold Beading 395.00
Bowl, Flowers, Gold Design, Crown Mark, 9 In.Diam. 945.00
Box, Florals, Fluted Base, Gold & Magenta Enamels, Lid, Signed 595.00
Bride's Basket, Painted Pansies, Pairpoint Holder, 11 In.Diam. 2800.00
Cracker Jar, Albertine, Burmese Shading, Mt.Washington Lid 695.00
Cracker Jar, Floral, Gold Scrolls, Signed 395.00
Cracker Jar, Flowers, Brass Fittings, Bail, Signed, 10 In. 289.00
Cracker Jar, Queen's, Sterling Silver Fittings, 7 5/8 In. 275.00
Cracker Jar, Twig Handle, Stripes, C.1890, 4 3/4 In. 300.00
Cracker Jar, Wild Roses, Silver Plated Fittings, 6 1/2 In. 300.00
Ewer, Floral, Bulbous, Footed, 7 1/2 X 4 1/2 In. 750.00
Jar, Marmalade, Pastel Pansies, Silver Plated Lid 885.00
Jar, Mustard, Acorns, Oak Leaves, Yellow Ground, 3 3/4 In. 210.00
Jar, Sweetmeat, Diamond Pattern, Taupe & Gold, Metal Top, 4 In. 500.00
Muffineer, Opaque Green, Melon Shape, Flowers, 4 1/2 In. 575.00
Pitcher, Rope Handle, Enameled Thistles, Leaves, Tan Background 1850.00
Vase, Enameled Florals, Custard Satin, Signed & Dated, 3 In. 350.00
Vase, Floral Design, 8 1/2 In. 145.00
Vase, Gold Floral Design, Mottled Ground, Paper Label 1295.00
Vase, Pink To White Mums, Signed, 5 X 4 In. 450.00
Vase, Shadow Fern, Gold Trim, 8 In. 750.00
Vase, Shadow Leaves, Gold Roses, 8 In. 1495.00
Vase, 3 Large Nosegays, 10 Smaller Ones, Signed, 8 3/4 In. 1250.00
        CROWN TUSCAN, see Cambridge

Cruets of glass or porcelain were made to hold vinegar or oil. They were especially popular during Victorian times.
        CRUET, see also various glass sections
CRUET, Blown Molded, Clear, 7 1/2 In. 65.00
Cranberry Glass, Cut Glass Stopper, 2 1/2 In. 75.00
Cranberry Glass, Thumbprint 12.50
Cut Glass, Sterling Stopper 120.00
Inverted Thumbprint, Stopper 75.00
Plain, Applied Handle, Cut Glass Stopper, Fostoria 22.50
Spatter Glass, Red, White, Blue Spatter 45.00

CT Germany porcelain was made by C. Tielsch & Company of Altwasser, Silesia, in 1845. It is a hard-paste porcelain.

CT GERMANY, Cup & Saucer, Flowers, Altwasser 30.00
Plate, Floral Border, Violets, Dogwood, 8 In. 15.00
Plate, Game, Pheasant, Tan, Brown, Gold, 8 1/2 In. 25.00
Plate, Queen Louisa, White Scarf, 10 1/2 In. 50.00

Cup plates are small glass or china plates that held the cup, while a gentleman of the mid-nineteenth century drank his coffee or tea from the saucer. The most famous cup plates were made of glass at the Boston and Sandwich factory located in Massachusetts.

CUP PLATE, Benjamin Franklin, Sailship, B.F.On Flag, Sandwich Glass	35.00
Cadmus, Sandwich Glass	25.00
Eagle Center, Dated 1831, Sandwich Glass	27.50
Eagle, Dark Blue, Lacy	600.00
Eagle, Lacy, Ft.Pitt Glass Works, Dark Blue .... *Illus*	600.00
Harp, Lacy, Blue, Midwestern	325.00
Heart, Green, Lacy, 3 1/2 In.	300.00
Heart, Lacy, Peacock Blue Scalloped .... *Illus*	140.00
Heart, Lacy, Violet Blue .... *Illus*	260.00
Heart, Sandwich Glass, Opalescent .... *Illus*	100.00
Henry Clay, Peacock Blue	110.00 To 120.00
Log Cabin, Amber	350.00
Pansy & Rose, Sandwich Glass	20.00
Peacock Feather Border, Fort Pitt Eagle Center, Sandwich Glass	35.00
Philadelphia Area, Clear .... *Illus*	200.00
Washington, Octagonal, Clear .... *Illus*	775.00

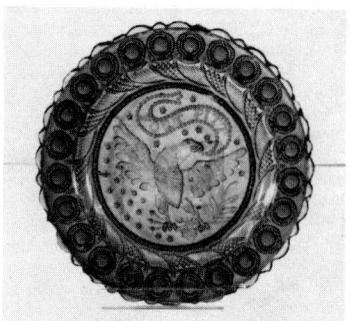

Cup Plate, Eagle, Lacy, Ft.Pitt Glass
Works, Dark Blue

Cup Plate, Heart, Lacy, Peacock Blue, Scalloped

Cup Plate, Heart, Lacy, Violet Blue

Cup Plate, Heart, Sandwich Glass, Opalescent

Cup Plate, Philadelphia Area, Clear

Cup Plate, Washington, Octagonal, Clear

Currier & Ives made the famous American lithographs marked with their name from 1857 to 1907.

CURRIER & IVES, A Home In The Wilderness, 1870, 8 X 12 1/2 In.	325.00
American Country Life, Wife, Children & Dog Greet Hunters	875.00
Autumn Fruits	160.00
Bewildered Hunter	425.00
Brook Trout Fishing, An Anxious Moment	2750.00
Brother & Sister, Framed, 16 X 12 In.	85.00
Burning Of The Steamship Austria, Ship Nears Burning Ship	245.00
Children's Picnic, Children In Woodland, Girl On Swing	65.00
Clipper Ship Great Republic	345.00
Cooling Stream, 11 1/4 X 15 3/4 In.	125.00
Cottage Life, Summer, Children With Toys	175.00
Darktown Fire Brigade, 1885	175.00
Descent From The Cross, 8 1/2 X 12 In.	30.00
Expresss Train, 1870	950.00
Fashionable Turnouts In Central Park, 18 1/8 X 28 3/4 In.	1550.00
Fearnaught Stallions, 1875, Team Pulling Sleigh	895.00
Flower Vase, Young Woman In Blue On Vase Of Flowers	145.00
General Grant & Family, Black & White	85.00
Harvest Field, Women & Children With Bales Of Wheat	295.00
Highland Fling, Dancing Figure, 1846, Oval	100.00
Idlewild, On The Hudson, Cascading River, Wooded Mountains	145.00
Inconvenience Of Single Life	110.00

Currier & Ives, Life In The Country

Indian Buffalo Hunt, Framed	150.00
Life In The Country	*Illus* 4200.00
Life Of A Fireman, Steam & Muscle, 17 1/4 X 25 3/4 In.	1300.00
Mambrino Gift, 1874, Trotter Broadside To Right	110.00
Mollie McCarthy, 1878, Race Horse In Full Stride	145.00
Moonlight, The Ruins	65.00
Moosehead Lake, Deer In Foreground	185.00
Morning Prayer, Boy, Framed	23.00
Mountain Spring, West Point 1862, Steamer & Sailing Ships	675.00
New Suspension Bridge, Niagara Falls, American & Canadian	235.00
Niagara Falls, From Goat Island, Moonlight Scene	160.00
Not Caught	185.00
Partridge Shooting	275.00
Queen Of The Turf, Lady Thorn, 13 1/2 X 17 1/2 In.	195.00
Railroad Suspension Bridge, Niagara Falls	495.00
Sinking Of The Steamship Ville Du Havre, 1873	185.00
Soldier's Memorial, 10th Battery, Massachusetts	85.00
Southern River Scenery, Couple In Rowboat, 1870	110.00
Stag At Bay, Rocky Shore	165.00
Sunnyside-On-Hudson, Home Of Washington Irving	165.00
Through To The Pacific, Train Passing Through Town, 1870	545.00
Tomb Of Washington, Mt.Vernon, Virginia	75.00
Trade Card, A Bare Chance, 1879	65.00
Tree Of Life, 8 1/2 X 12 In.	55.00
Trotters On The Snow, 12 1/2 X 17 In.	425.00
Trotting Cracks At Home, Model Stable, 19 3/4 X 29 1/2 In.	1500.00
Vase Of Flowers, 1870	65.00
Washington At Valley Forge, Cannon & Troops, 1777-78	170.00
Washington Crossing The Delaware, Standing In Boat, Troops	395.00
Wreck Of The Atlantic, 1873	140.00
CURRIER, City Hall, New York, Wide Margins	225.00
City Of New York, From Jersey City, 9 Keyed Names At Bottom	475.00
Death Of Harrison, 1841, 8 Names Of Persons At Bedside	65.00
Death Of Washington, Names Of Persons At Bedside	68.00

Dr.Friedrick Hecker, 1/2 Length 30.00
English Snipe, Bird's-Eye Maple Frame 140.00
Fox Chase, Hunters & Racing Dogs 275.00
Lucky Escape, 10 1/4 X 14 3/4 In. 175.00
Naval Bombardment Of Vera Cruz, 1847 .... 165.00
No You Don't, Boy Tries To Take Rose From Girl 95.00
Old Homestead, 1855, 9 7/8 X 14 3/4 In. 210.00
Ruth, Framed, 16 1/2 X 12 1/2 In. 45.00
Snipe Shooting, 1852, Long Island Hunting Scene 5495.00
Two Sister, Heads Of 2 Young Girls 36.00
Waiting For A Drink, Cartoon 68.00
Washington's Reception By Ladies On Passing Bridge, Trenton, 1789 .... 160.00
William Penn's Treaty With The Indians 48.00

Custard glass is an opaque glass sometimes known as buttermilk glass. It
was first made in America after 1886 at the La Belle Glass Works,
Bridgeport, Ohio.

CUSTARD GLASS, see also Maize
CUSTARD GLASS, Banana Boat, Autumn Pattern, Green 25.00
Berry Bowl, Beaded Swag, Roses, Souvenir Clayton, Wisconsin 65.00
Berry Bowl, Chrysanthemum Sprig, Footed, Oval, Marked 205.00
Berry Bowl, Chrysanthemum Sprig, Gold Trim, Master 165.00
Berry Bowl, Delaware, Boat Shape, Green Design, Small 75.00
Berry Bowl, Fluted Scrolls, Footed, Gold Design, Master 100.00
Berry Bowl, Georgia Gem, Gold Design, Master 95.00
Berry Bowl, Victoria, Master 185.00
Berry Set, Geneva, Red & Green Design, 7 Piece 295.00
Berry Set, Inverted Fan & Feather, Pink & Gold, 5 Piece 485.00
Berry Set, Louis XV, 7 Piece 575.00
Berry Set, Victor, 6 Piece 575.00
Berry Set, Winged Scroll, 7 Piece 525.00
Biscuit Jar, Brass Lid, English 200.00
Bonbon, Bluebirds, Fenton, Handled 30.00
Bonbon, Prayer Rug Pattern, Handled 50.00
Bonbon, Prayer Rug Pattern, 2 Handled 50.00
Bottle, Cologne, Grape & Cable 95.00
Bottle, Cologne, Northwood Grape, Nutmeg Stain 300.00
Bowl, Banana, Grape & Cable, Satin Blue Stain 375.00
Bowl, Pedestal, Cable & Thumbprint, Nutmeg Stain 35.00
Bowl, Pier & Wave, Footed, 8 1/2 In.Diam. 38.00
Bowl, Rose, Canary, Opalescent, Button Sent 35.00
Bowl, Sugar, Chrysanthemum Sprig, Covered 110.00
Bowl, Winged Scroll, 4 In. 40.00
Box, Candy, Heart Shape .... 22.00 To 30.00
Butter, Argonaut Shell, Covered 55.00
Butter, Chrysanthemum Sprig, Covered, Gold Trim 245.00
Butter, Geneva, Design, Covered 185.00
Butter, Georgia Gem, Gold Trim, Covered .... 145.00 To 165.00
Butter, Grape & Gothic Arches, Covered, Pearlized Finish 195.00
Butter, Intaglio, Gold & Green Trim, Covered 165.00
Butter, Louis XV, Covered 215.00
Butter, Maple Leaf, Covered 215.00
Butter, Ring Band, Covered, Gold Trim 225.00
Celery, Chrysanthemum Sprig, Gold Trim, Northwood, Blue 950.00
Compote, Greek Key & Shell Pattern, 5 In. 70.00
Compote, Intaglio, Green & Gold, 7 1/2 X 5 1/2 In. 225.00
Compote, Jelly, Argonaut Shell, Design 85.00
Compote, Jelly, Intaglio, Gold & Green Design 80.00
Creamer, Argonaut Shell, Signed Northwood 135.00
Creamer, Beaded Swirl, Green 43.00
Creamer, Chrysanthemum Sprig, Blue 350.00
Creamer, Cut Block, Rose Design, Souvenir, Stanquist, Minn. 42.50
Creamer, Geneva, Red & Green Design 75.00

Creamer, Intaglio, Green, Gold Trim	85.00
Creamer, Iris, Gold Trim	110.00
Creamer, Louis XV, Gold Trim	37.50
Creamer, Maple Leaf, Gold Trim	95.00
Creamer, Souvenir, Standish, Maine	22.00
Cruet, Blue Chrysanthemum Sprig, Gold, Original Stopper, 7 In.	675.00
Cruet, Chrysanthemum Sprig, Original Stopper	200.00
Cruet, Intaglio Green & Gold, Clear Stopper	200.00
Cruet, Louis XV, Gold Trim	150.00 To 200.00
Dish, Berry, Louis XIV, Footed, 5 1/2 X 4 In.	42.00
Dish, Ice Cream, Peacock & Urn, Nutmeg Design	195.00
Dish, Peacock & Urn, Small	65.00
Dish, Rampant Lions & Trees Inside, Grapes Out, 6 In.	135.00
Goblet, Beaded & Floral, Independence, Kansas	65.00
Goblet, Beaded Swag, Souvenir, Richfield, Wisconsin	55.00
Goblet, Grape & Gothic Arch, Nutmeg Rim	45.00
Hat, Grape Arbor, Nutmeg Stain	50.00
Holder, Toothpick, Ivorine Verde, Gold Trim, 2 1/2 X 2 In.	75.00
Jar, Mustard, Thousand Eye, Emerald Green	28.00
Jar, Sweetmeat, Birds & Flowers, Handle	125.00
Lamp, Hanging, Heart Shape	175.00
Lemonade Set, Elizabeth, Hand-Painted Violets, 4 Tumblers	40.00
Light Shade, Poppies, Paneled, Nutmeg Stain, Satin Finish	575.00
Maple Leaf, Tumbler	55.00
Mug, Balaton, Minn.	50.00
Mug, Beaded Shell, Twig Handle, 4 In.	68.00
Mug, Punty Band, Souvenir, Collins, Wisconsin	40.00
Mug, Roses, Paris 1911, Signed	50.00
Mug, Scalloped Gold Edge, Floral, Monona, Iowa	55.00
Mug, Souvenir, Sebasco, Maine, Green	25.00
Mug, Star & Punty, Locust St.Market, Dover, N.H., 3 1/4 In.	28.00
Nappy, Grape & Lotus, Handled	50.00
Pitcher, Diamond With Peg, Roses, Signed, 7 1/2 In.	135.00
Pitcher, Georgian Gem, 6 1/2 In.	205.00
Pitcher, Hobnail, Reeded Handle	250.00
Pitcher, Water, Argonaut Shell, Gold Trim	235.00
Pitcher, Water, Chrysanthemum Sprig, Footed, Gold Trim	195.00
Pitcher, Water, Thumbprint	135.00
Pitcher, Water, Victor, Green	350.00
Plate, Horse Medallions, 7 1/2 In.Diam.	90.00
Punch Set, Tom & Jerry, 6 Mugs	75.00
Salt & Pepper, Corn, 3 1/4 In.	45.00
Salt & Pepper, Diamond With Peg, Red Rose, Original Lids	90.00
Salt & Pepper, Gold & Green	115.00
Salt & Pepper, Louis XV, Gold Trim	165.00
Salt, Geneva	65.00
Saltshaker, Chrysanthemum Sprig, Original Top, Blue	100.00
Saltshaker, Dithridge Princess Swirl, Enameled Flowers	35.00
Sauce, Argonaut Shell	40.00
Sauce, Chrysanthemum Sprig, Blue	85.00
Sauce, Victoria	55.00
Shot Glass, State Historical Library, Madison, Wi., View	45.00
Spooner, Argonaut Shell	75.00 To 125.00
Spooner, Chrysanthemum Sprig	95.00
Spooner, Chrysanthemum Sprig, Blue	285.00
Spooner, Diamond With Peg, Conneaut Lake, Pennsylvania	50.00
Spooner, Everglades	135.00
Spooner, Geneva	75.00
Spooner, Geneva, Red & Green	55.00 To 80.00
Spooner, Grape & Gothic Arches, Nutmeg Stain	75.00
Spooner, Intaglio, Green & Clear	80.00
Spooner, Jackson	30.00
Spooner, Leaf Medallion, Green	65.00

Spooner, Louis XV .... 60.00 To 95.00
Spooner, Maple Leaf, Gold Trim, 3-Handled 125.00
Spooner, Sheraton, Amber 32.00
Spooner, Tiny Optic, Purple 30.00
Spooner, Victoria 80.00
Spooner, Wild Bouquet 150.00
Sugar Shaker, Diamond With Peg 35.00
Sugar, Creamer, & Spooner, Winged Scroll 395.00
Sugar, Grape & Gothic Arches, Covered, Pearlized 100.00
Sugar, Louis XV 75.00
Sugar, Louis XV, Gold Trim 65.00
Sugar, Winged Scroll, Covered, Gold Trim 120.00
Table Set, Argonaut Shell, Northwood, 4 Piece .... 500.00 To 675.00
Table Set, Chrysanthemum Sprig, 4 Piece 495.00
Table Set, Diamond Maple Leaf, Gold Trim, 4 Piece 625.00
Table Set, Fan, Gold Trim, 4 Piece 650.00
Table Set, Georgia Gem, Gold Trim, 4 Piece 395.00
Table Set, Intaglio, Green, 4 Piece 500.00
Table Set, Jefferson Ribbed Drape, Rose Design, 4 Piece 475.00
Table Set, Louis XV 480.00
Table Set, Maple Leaf 645.00
Tankard, Winged Scroll, Gold Trim, 9 In. 290.00
Toothpick, Argonaut Shell, Northwood 295.00
Toothpick, Bay City, Michigan, Gold Trim 40.00
Toothpick, Chrysanthemum Sprig, Northwood, Signed 360.00
Toothpick, Georgia Gem 65.00
Toothpick, Green Vermont Rim 45.00
Toothpick, Harvard 35.00
Toothpick, Maple Leaf 400.00
Toothpick, Public School, Parkersburg, Iowa 50.00
Toothpick, Quixote, Enfield, N.H., Green 26.00
Toothpick, Ribbed Drape, Roses Design 145.00
Toothpick, Ring Band, Souvenir, Boston 50.00
Toothpick, Souvenir, Sault Saint Marie 40.00
Toothpick, Sprig, Northwood, Blue 350.00
Toothpick, Winged Scroll 80.00
Tray, Pin, Delaware Pattern, Blue Design 48.50
Tumbler, Beaded Circle 45.00
Tumbler, Chrysanthemum Sprig, Gold Decoration 35.00
Tumbler, Clambroth, Souvenir Spencer, South Dakota 31.50
Tumbler, Fan 40.00
Tumbler, Geneva, Red & Green, Set Of 2 .... 50.00
Tumbler, Green, Rose & Purple Poppies, Leaves & Buds 45.00
Tumbler, Intaglio, Blue 55.00
Tumbler, Intaglio, Gold & Green 55.00
Tumbler, Jackson 35.00
Tumbler, Jefferson Optic, Red Rose 38.00
Tumbler, Louis XV .... 40.00 To 45.00
Tumbler, Ring Band, Souvenir 75.00
Tumbler, Souvenir Bruning, Nebraska, Green 37.50
Vase, Nutmeg On Grape & Cable, Signed Northwood 50.00
Vase, Red Rose, Gold Trim, Souvenir, Twin Mt., N.H., 5 3/4 In. 35.00
Water Set, Chrysanthemum Sprig, 7 Piece .... 550.00 To 725.00
Water Set, Jackson, 5 Piece 375.00
Water Set, Louis XV, 7 Piece 550.00
Water Set, Maple Leaf, 5 Piece 600.00

*Cut glass has been made since ancient times, but the large majority of the
pieces now for sale date from the brilliant period of glass design, 1880 to
1905. These pieces had elaborate geometric designs with a deep miter cut.*
CUT GLASS, see also listings under factory name
CUT GLASS, Banana Boat, Harvard Cut, Floral Pattern 200.00
  Banana Boat, Hobstars, Strawberry, Fan, & Diamond, 9 1/2 In. 225.00

Basket, Acorns & Oak Leaves, Intaglio, 16 1/2 X 11 1/2 In.	40.00
Basket, Chain Of Hobstars Each Side, Leaves, 17 1/2 In.	375.00
Basket, Florence Pattern, Hobstar Base, 16 In.	1650.00
Basket, Harvard & Floral, 16 X 12 In.	450.00
Basket, Pinwheel, Hobstar, & Zipper, Handled, 6 In.Diam.	175.00
Basket, Twisted Handle, Hobstars, Fan, Buzz, 6 1/2 In.	125.00
Bishop's Hat, Sunflower Pattern, 11 1/2 In.Diam.	350.00
Bonbon, Ring Handle, 6 In.	38.00
Bottle, Barber, Sterling Stopper	225.00
Bottle, Cologne, Hobstars & Strawberry, Diamonds, Pair	125.00
Bottle, Cologne, Jewel Pattern, T.B.Clark, 1896, 6 In., Pair	495.00
Bottle, Cologne, Pyramidal Star & Buttons, 5 1/2 In., Pair	220.00
Bottle, Perfume, Diamond Points, Starred Base, 7 1/4 In.	48.00
Bottle, Perfume, Harvard Cut Sides, Faceted Stopper, 4 1/2 In.	47.50
Bottle, Perfume, Orange, Square Shape, Fine Cut Design, 5 In.	110.00
Bottle, Perfume, Panel Flute Design, Sterling Silver Top	135.00
Bottle, Perfume, Sterling Silver Top, Cobalt Blue To Clear	365.00
Bottle, Perfume, Stopper, Square Bottom, 6 3/4 X 2 1/4 In., Pair	75.00
Bottle, Scent, C.1845, Gold Overlay, Faceted Cover, 4 7/8 In.	750.00
Bottle, Water, Pineapple & Fine Cut	65.00
Bottle, Wine, Diamond Pattern, 12 In.	45.00
Bottle, Wine, Hobbs, Pinwheels, 6-Sided Neck, 10 3/4 In.	145.00
Bowl, Allover Hobstars, Crossed Ovals & Diamond Point, 10 X 4 In.	525.00
Bowl, Allover Hobstars, 9 In.Diam.	95.00
Bowl, Brilliant Cut, Serrated Rim, 2 X 7 In.Diam.	55.00
Bowl, Caviar, Silver Plate Rim, Handles, & Cover	275.00
Bowl, Checkerboard Pattern, 10 In.	350.00
Bowl, Chrysanthemum, 10 In.	360.00
Bowl, Crosscut Diamond, Dorflinger, 4 1/2 X 10 In.Diam.	230.00
Bowl, Crystal, Hobstar Cut, Variegated Rim, 6 In.	300.00
Bowl, Cut In Hunt Royal, 8 In.	285.00
Bowl, Diamond Fields & Stars, Scalloped Rim, 9 In.	80.00
Bowl, Dorflinger Parisian Pattern, Fan, Hobstar, 10 In.	325.00
Bowl, Expanding Star Pattern, 9 In.Diam.	295.00
Bowl, Feathered Pinwheels, Hobstar, Scallop Sawtooth Rim, 8 In.	70.00
Bowl, Feathered Star, Bands Of Cane, 9 In.Diam.	225.00
Bowl, Finger, & Underplate, Signed Sinclaire	70.00
Bowl, Fruit, Gloria Design, 9 In.	295.00
Bowl, Fruit, Scalloped Rim, Hobnail Band Under Rim, C.1900, 9 In.	50.00
Bowl, Garland Pattern, P. & B., 9 X 4 In.	325.00
Bowl, Harvard Bottom, Scalloped Edge, 10 In.	270.00
Bowl, Harvard Pattern, Canoe Form, 11 1/2 In.	70.00
Bowl, Heart, Hobstars, Fan, 8 X 3 1/2 In.	95.00
Bowl, Hobstar & Fan, Fan Bottom, Signed Clarke, 7 X 3 In.	100.00
Bowl, Hobstar, Whipped Cream, 8 1/2 In.	225.00
Bowl, Hobstars, Silver Rim, Gorham 1904 Mark, 9 X 4 In.	295.00
Bowl, Hunt Royal Design, 8 In., Diam.	285.00
Bowl, Parisian Pattern, 4 Turned-In Edges, Dorflinger, 5 In.	595.00
Bowl, Punch, Brilliant Cut, C.1880, 11 1/2 X 12 1/4 In.	1000.00
Bowl, Punch, Crystal, Hobstar & Vessica Cut, C.1900, 9 In.	150.00
Bowl, Punch, Hobstars & Strawberry Diamond Design, 2 Pieces	70.00
Bowl, Punch, Tulip Shaped, On Stand, 18 X 14 In.	4000.00
Bowl, Russian Pattern, Cut Bottom, 8 1/4 X 2 3/4 In.	550.00
Bowl, Sawtooth Edge, Hobnail Pattern, American, C.1910, 11 1/2 In.	75.00
Bowl, Sawtooth Rim, Hobstar, Cane & Crosshatch, C.1890, 11 1/2 In.	1500.00
Bowl, Split Heart Pattern, 8 In.Diam.	245.00
Bowl, Star Design, 9 In.	295.00
Bowl, Strawberry & Diamond In X Cut, 9 1/2 In.Diam.	195.00
Bowl, Strawberry Diamond & Cross Hatch, Pedestal, 10 1/2 In.	265.00
Bowl, Strawberry Diamond, Fan Pattern, Clear, Footed, 7 1/2 In.	240.00
Box, Dresser, Allover Harvard Pattern, Rayed Base, 6 X 3 1/2 In.	160.00
Box, Dresser, Cupid & Floral Design, Sterling Lid	150.00
Box, Dresser, Sterling Silver Lid With Cupid & Flowers, 6 In.	225.00

Box, Heart Shaped, Hobstars, Hobnail, Fan, Covered, 6 In. 200.00
Box, Jewel, Allover Cut, Hinged, 5 In. 225.00
Box, Jewelry, Thumbprint Around, Flowers & Leaves Top, 6 In. 239.00
Box, Powder, C.1890, Hinged Cover, 4 1/2 In.Diam. 150.00
Butter Tub, Arcadia Pattern, Underplate 350.00
Butter Tub, Brilliant Cut, Eared, 4 1/2 X 7 1/2 In.Wide 195.00
Butter Tub, Flowers, Leaves, Fans, & Hobnail, 6 X 4 1/2 In. 125.00
Butter, Covered, Harvard Pattern 155.00
Butter, Covered, Hobstars, Crosshatching, & Fans, Signed Dorflinger 485.00
Butter, Diamond Fan, High Domed Cover 275.00
Butter, Hobstars, Cross Hatching, & Fans, Signed Dorflinger 475.00
Candlestick, Flute Cut, Teardrop Stem, Star Foot, Signed, 8 In. 390.00
Candlestick, Intaglio Cut, Teardrop Stem, 12 In., Pair 295.00
Candlestick, Intaglio Tulips, Amethyst Socket, Square Base, 10 In. 130.00
Candlestick, Starflower Pattern, Teardrop, 8 In., Pair 210.00
Candlestick, Teardrop Stem, Green To Clear, 11 In. 150.00
Canoe, Harvard Pattern, Paul Richter & Co., 4 1/2 X 12 In. 105.00
Canoe, Persian Pattern, 10 In.Long 375.00
Carafe, Broadway Pattern, Notched Edges, 7 1/2 In. 115.00
Carafe, Comet Pattern, Patent 1910, Signed J.Hoare 495.00
Carafe, Hobstar & Beading Variant, 7 In. 225.00
Carafe, Hobstars, Brilliant Cut, 8 In. 80.00
Carafe, Pinwheels, Strawberry Diamond, Clear 125.00
Carafe, Stawberry Fan, 24-Ray Star On Bottom, 9 X 6 In. 60.00
Carafe, Water, Crosscut, Pineapple, 8 1/2 In. 10.00
Celery, Greek Key & Laurel Pattern, Sinclaire, 13 X 6 1/2 In. 95.00
Celery, Joan Pattern, 12 X 4 In. 100.00
Celery, Regal Pattern, Intaglio & Geometric, 13 X 5 1/2 In. 130.00
Celery, 4 Elipses Join In Center, Flower & Leaves, 12 1/2 In. 120.00
Champagne, Hobstars, Flashed Hobs, Fans, Hollow Stemmed, 5 In. 65.00
Cheese Dish, Allover Hobstars, High Dome 375.00
Cheese Dish, Blown Black, Hobstars, Buzz, Diamond Cane & Fan 275.00
Cheese Dish, Flower & Harvard, Dome Plate, 7 3/4 In. 400.00
Clock, Boudoir, Harvard & Cosmos Base, 5 1/2 X 4 In. 240.00
Clock, Boudoir, Harvard Pattern, 5 1/2 X 4 In. 200.00
Cologne, Dorflinger, 8 In. 140.00
Compote, Allover Hobstar, Daisy, & Fan, Scalloped, 9 3/4 X 12 In. 650.00
Compote, Amethyst, 7 1/2 In.Diam., Pair 185.00
Compote, Candy, Sawtooth Rim, Buzz Star Design, 8 1/2 In. 85.00
Compote, Cobalt Cut To Clear, Willow Pattern, 9 X 5 1/2 In. 650.00
Compote, Diamond & Fan, 9 1/2 X 11 1/4 In. 275.00
Compote, Grape & Leaf Design, 7 3/4 In. 25.00
Compote, Hobstars & Crosscut, 4 1/4 X 5 In. 70.00
Compote, Hobstars, Fan, Scalloped Hobstar Base, 7 X 8 1/2 In.Diam. 250.00
Compote, Hobstars, Sterling Silver Edge, 4 3/4 In. 137.00
Compote, Hobstars, Teardrop In Stem, 7 3/4 In. 350.00
Compote, Intaglio Floral Design, Teardrop Stem, 9 In. 175.00
Compote, Paperweight Base, Pedestaled, Hobnail & Fan, 11 In. 250.00
Compote, Pedestaled, 2 Handled, Harvard, 9 X 6 1/2 In. 190.00
Compote, Rayner Pattern, Empire Cut Glass, 5 X 5 In. 115.00
Compote, Redmond Pattern, 10 X 9 In.Diam. 575.00
Compote, Tulip & Butterfly, 7 In. 170.00
Compote, Vertical Double X Strawberry Diamonds, 8 X 8 In. 375.00
Cookie Jar, Pinwheel, Beading, & Fan, Brass Rim, 8 1/2 In. 175.00
Cream & Sugar, Hobstars, Flashed Fan, Stars, Handles 115.00
Creamer, Heart Design 45.00
Creamer, Venetian, Hawkes 95.00
Crucifix, Russian Cut, Miniature 250.00
Cruet, Buzz Saw & Rayed Base, Prism Stopper, Applied Handle 48.00
Cruet, Buzz Saw, Panel Notching, Lighthouse Shape, 7 In. 55.00
Cruet, Buzz Saw, Rayed Base, Prism Cut Stopper, 3-Way Spout 48.00
Cruet, Crosshatched Diamond & Fan, Tricornered Spout, 7 In., Pair 75.00
Cruet, Cut & Blown, Signed Hoare 45.00

Cruet, Flashed Fan, Flairs, & Hobstars, Teardrop Stopper 115.00
Cruet, Hobstars, Strawberry, & Diamonds, 3-Lipped 65.00
Cruet, Intaglio Stars, Orange, Pewter Stopper, 8 In. 95.00
Cup, Loving, Priscilla Pattern, 2 Handled, Signed, 6 X 8 In. 525.00
Cup, Punch, Hobnail, Fan, Rayed Bottom, Set Of 12 .... 175.00
Decanter, Bulbous, Elongated Neck, Flared Spout, C.1910, 10 1/4 In. 60.00
Decanter, C.1820, Ring-Turned Neck, 8 In., Pair 200.00
Decanter, Captain's, Rigaree, 10 X 6 In. 125.00
Decanter, Crosshatch & Herringbone, Pedestal, 10 In. 160.00
Decanter, Cut In Hobstars, Cane, Fans, Flare Neck, 11 In. 350.00
Decanter, Cut Through Dark Blue, Whie, Clear, Stopper, 8 In. 595.00
Decanter, Diamond & Prism 85.00
Decanter, Fern & Flashed Star, Handled 145.00
Decanter, Floral & Harvard, Bowling Pin, 15 In. 300.00
Decanter, Globular Body, Mitre Cut, American, C.1900, 12 1/2 In. 50.00
Decanter, Green, Hobstar, Crosshatch, Inverted, 16 In. 200.00
Decanter, Harvard & Cosmos, Pedestal 225.00
Decanter, Hobstar & Fan, Step Cut Neck, 11 3/4 In. 350.00
Decanter, Hobstars & Canes, Mushroom Stopper 250.00
Decanter, Hobstars & Variants, Ring-Turned Neck, 12 3/4 In. 325.00
Decanter, Hobstars, Pinwheel, & Fan, 9 In. .... 150.00 To 165.00
Decanter, Intaglio Cut Band, Diamond Point, Lavender, 15 In. 95.00
Decanter, Russian Pattern, Cut Button, 12 In., Pair 1500.00
Decanter, St. Louis Handle, Stopper, Zipper & Thumbprint 125.00
Decanter, Tracks Pattern, Ball Stopper, Square, 10 In. 67.00
Decanter, Tuthill, Primrose Design, Hobstars, 9 In. 650.00
Decanter, Whiskey, Hobstar Pattern, 12 In. 285.00
Decanter, Zipper Pattern, Handled, 9 In. 125.00
Dish, Candy, Divided, Harvard Top, Hobstar & Diamonds, 10 In. 170.00
Dish, Candy, Hobstars, Diamonds, & Fan, Handled, 6 1/2 X 3 In. 60.00
Dish, Cane, Heart Shape, Handled, 6 X 5 1/2 In. 110.00
Dish, Chrysanthemum, Rectangular, 9 X 4 1/4 In. 275.00
Dish, Dessert, Allover Cutting, Serrated Rim, Set Of 6 .... 225.00
Dish, Expanding Star, 4-Section, 8 In. 380.00
Dish, Good Luck Pattern, Harvard Border, 9 In. 550.00
Dish, Heart Shaped, Hob Style Design, 10 In. 150.00
Dish, Ice Cream, Crosscut Diamond & Fan, Set Of 6 .... 115.00
Dish, Lemon, Sterling Silver Band, 5 In. 95.00
Dish, Pickle, Rosaceae Design, Signed Tuthill, 4 1/2 X 6 3/4 In. 330.00
Dish, Russian Pattern, Cut Buttons, Crescent Shape 225.00
Dish, Stick, Murillo Design 150.00
Dish, Tuthill, Hobstars, Fans, Stars, Signed, 5 In. 60.00
Dish, 4 Compartment, Expanding Star Pattern, 7 In.Diam. 135.00
Flower Center, Empress Design, 10 In. 575.00
Flower Center, Hobstars, Honeycomb Cut, Signed, Egginton, 8 In. 395.00
Flower Center, Hobstars, Honeycomb, Checkering, Signed, 5 In. 395.00
Goblet, Water, Hobstars, Notched Stem, 24-Point Star Base 50.00
Hair Receiver, Sterling Top 40.00
Holder, Tatting, Prism Pattern, Sterling Silver Top, 3 1/4 X 3 In. 250.00
Humidor, Marlboro Pattern, Single Star Bottom, 10 In. 1050.00
Humidor, Marlboro Pattern, Single Star Bottom, 11 In. 1150.00
Ice Bucket, Brilliant & Intaglio 75.00
Ice Bucket, Harvard Variant Pattern, 6 X 6 In. 270.00
Ice Bucket, Hobstars & Fans, Tab Handles 210.00
Ice Bucket, Sawtooth Border, Hobstar Base, 5 1/2 X 7 In. 70.00
Inkwell, Block Cut Base, Beveled, Hinged, 1 7/8 In. 36.00
Inkwell, Blue, Cube Shape 75.00
Inkwell, Cane Pattern, Sterling Silver Cap 275.00
Inkwell, Fluted & Notched Panels, Silver Top, 3 In. 50.00
Jar, Condiment, Covered, 2 1/2 X 3 In. 95.00
Jar, Condiment, Hobstars, Fans, Straight Sides, Stopper, 7 In. 130.00
Jar, Crystal, Russian Cut, Hobstar Design, Covered, 14 In. 275.00
Jar, Horseradish, Pinwheel & Zipper, Covered, 5 In. 90.00

Jar, Jam, Zipper, Underplate	75.00
Jar, Mayonnaise, Flowers, 2 Handles, Stopper, Signed, 6 In.	160.00
Jar, Talcum Powder, Sterling Silver Lid	68.00
Jug, Whiskey, Geometric Pattern, Strap & Button Handle	650.00
Juice Set, Pinwheel & Star, 6 Tumblers, Pitcher 9 In.	155.00
Juice, American Pattern, Hobstar Base, Set Of 6	375.00
Ladle, Pairpoint, Hobstars & Fan	300.00
Lamp Shade, Hobstars, Fans, Prisms, 14 In.	385.00
Lamp, Alternating 5 & 4 In.Prisms, 24 In.	1400.00
Lamp, Boudoir, Prisms, Buzz Diamond & Fan, 13 1/4 In.	495.00
Lamp, Floral Pattern, Prisms, 20 In.	895.00
Loving Cup, Buzz Star & Cane, 5 1/2 In.	395.00
Loving Cup, Engraved Leaves, Flowers, 8 In.	295.00
Mayonnaise, Set, Notched Prism, Hobstars, Plate 7 In.	550.00
Muffineer, Cobalt Blue To Clear, 6 In.	165.00
Muffineer, Hobstars, Fan, & Crosscut Hatch, Sterling Silver Top	85.00
Mug, Purple To Clear, Marked From Karlsbaad, 5 In., Pair	75.00
Mustard, Hobstars, 16-Point Star Base, 4 1/2 In.	45.00
Mustard, Vertical Notching, Hobstars, Fan Ray Base	35.00
Napkin Ring, Russian Cut	125.00
Nappy, Cane Vesica & Hobstar, 6 1/4 In.	145.00
Nappy, Comet Pattern, Handled, 7 In.	160.00
Nappy, Florence Pattern	145.00
Pitcher, Allover Hobstar & Fan, 8 In.	175.00
Pitcher, Allover Interlocking Serpentine, 10 3/4 In.	350.00
Pitcher, Bull's-Eye Handle, Hobstar Design, 8 In.	275.00
Pitcher, Champagne, Planeta Pattern, Step-Cut Handle, 12 1/4 In.	595.00
Pitcher, Cider, Brilliant Deep Cut, 7 X 5 In.	150.00
Pitcher, Cider, Deep Brillant Cut, Body Handle, 7 In.	160.00
Pitcher, Cider, Hobstars, Strawberries, & Fans, 6 In.	350.00
Pitcher, Feather Design, Signed, 8 In.	425.00
Pitcher, Flashed Star, Double Thumbprint, Diamond & Fan, 8 In.	225.00
Pitcher, Flower Pattern, Notched Handle & Rim, 7 1/2 In.	65.00
Pitcher, Harvard Diamonds Variants, 8 1/2 In.	110.00
Pitcher, Heavily Cut, 6 3/4 In.	250.00
Pitcher, Hobstars & Notched Prisms, Pedestal, 10 In.	995.00
Pitcher, Hobstars Top Half, Signed Hoare, 1853, 8 1/2 In.	450.00
Pitcher, Hobstars With Chains Of Smaller Hobstars, 8 1/2 In.	135.00
Pitcher, Hobstars, Pineapple, & Diamonds, Ice Lip, 6 1/2 X 9 In.	415.00
Pitcher, Iris Design, Signed Hawkes	595.00
Pitcher, Lotus Pattern, Egginton, Hobstar Base, 7 In.	425.00
Pitcher, Pinwheel, Hobnail & Cane Design, 10 In.	90.00
Pitcher, Pinwheels, Nailhead, & Diamond, 13 In.	135.00
Pitcher, Silver Overlay Grapes, Wide Border	195.00
Pitcher, Thumbprint Handle, Star Base, Hobstars & Strawberries	225.00
Pitcher, Triple Overlay, Royal Blue, White To Crystal, 10 In.	495.00
Pitcher, Water, Comet With Fern, 7 1/2 In.	225.00
Pitcher, Water, Frosted Floral, Rayed Bottom	60.00
Pitcher, Water, Pinwheel Pattern, Notched Handle, 9 In.	65.00
Plate, Chain Of Crosshatched Diamonds, Serrated Rim, 9 In.	175.00
Plate, Deep Blue Out To Clear, Willow Pattern, 9 1/2 In.	150.00
Plate, Harvard Pattern, Signed J.Hoare, 7 In.	300.00
Plate, Hobstars & Cross Hatching, Signed, 7 In.	50.00
Plate, Lemon, Diamond Crosscut Diamonds, Sterling Silver Band	95.00
Plate, Marlboro Pattern, Dorflinger, 7 In., Set Of 8	400.00
Plate, Russian Pattern, Persian Buttons, 6 In.Diam.	110.00
Plate, 6 Panels, With Cut Thistle, Signed, 11 1/2 In.	265.00
Platter, Ice Cream, Russian Ambassador Pattern, 14 X 7 1/2 In.	250.00
Pokals, Pineapple, Facet Cut Knob, Star Cut Feet, 14 In.	600.00
Punch Bowl, Flashed Hobstars, C.1900, Stand, 14 In.	700.00
Punch Bowl, Meriden Cut, C.1900, 12 In.Diam., 2 Piece	1200.00
Punch Bowl, Strawberry, Diamond, & Hobstar, Silver Plate Ladle	1400.00
Punch Set, Egginton, C.1900, 14 1/2 In., 9 Piece	1200.00

Ring Tree, Florence Pattern 110.00
Rose Bowl, Fan Cutting, Scallop Top, Footed, 6 In. 175.00
Rose Bowl, Hunt's Royal Pattern 550.00
Rose Bowl, Strawberry Diamond Pattern, 5 X 4 In.Diam. 175.00
Rose Bowl, Strawberry, Diamond, & Fan, Miniature 60.00
Rose Jar, Genda Pattern, Clarke, 6 1/2 In. 525.00
Salt & Pepper, Notched Prism & Crosshatched Diamonds 50.00
Salt & Pepper, Ribbed Cut, Pair 25.00
Spill Holder, Pink & White To Clear, Star Cut Bottom, 4 1/2 In. 275.00
Spooner, Allover Cut, Brilliant Buzzstar 110.00
Spooner, Allover Harvard, Hobstar Bottom, 4 3/4 In. 170.00
Spooner, Corset Shape, Allover Hobstars 115.00
Spooner, Harvard Cut 135.00
Spooner, Starburst, Diamond & Fan, 2 Handled, Notched 95.00
Sugar & Creamer, Allover Hobs & Prisms, Fluted Lip, 7 X 6 In. 325.00
Sugar & Creamer, Allover Hobs, Button Centers, 3 1/2 In. 95.00
Sugar & Creamer, Allover Hobstars 125.00
Sugar & Creamer, Allover Hobstars, Miniature 195.00
Sugar & Creamer, Beverly Pattern, Greek Key Border 105.00
Sugar & Creamer, Buzzes, Hobstars & Prisms 95.00
Sugar & Creamer, Corinthian Pattern 180.00
Sugar & Creamer, Cut Flowers, Harvard Design, Handles, 5 In. 210.00
Sugar & Creamer, Flashed Hobstars, Crossed Bars, Stars, Fans 95.00
Sugar & Creamer, Flower & Butterfly 130.00
Sugar & Creamer, Harvard Allover Cut 150.00
Sugar & Creamer, Hobstar, Cane, & Strawberry Diamonds, 5 In. 500.00
Sugar & Creamer, Russian Pattern, Footed 395.00
Sugar & Creamer, Thumbprint Design, Pinwheel Pattern 125.00
Sugar Shaker, Hobstars, Bull's-Eyes, Crosscut, Rayed Base 175.00
Sugar, Venice Pattern, Signed P. & B. 85.00
Syrup, Graduated Punties, Sterling Silver Lid, 7 In. 250.00
Tankard, Encore Pattern, Strauss, 12 In. 395.00
Tazza, Teardrop Center, 7 3/4 In. 245.00
Teapot, Marie Antoinette Pattern, Sinclaire, Signed 1250.00
Toothpick, Egg Shape, Pedestal 50.00
Toothpick, Harvard Pattern 40.00
Tray, Bread, Harvard & Florence Pattern, 10 1/2 X 6 1/2 X 4 In. 175.00
Tray, Bread, Hobstars, Turned-In Sides 315.00
Tray, Celery, Hobstars, Fans, Vesicas, 12 X 4 1/4 In. 85.00
Tray, Cosmos, 14 X 8 In. 195.00
Tray, Dresser, Jars, Ring Tree 125.00
Tray, Hobstars & Diamonds, Kidney Shape, Handled, 8 X 3 1/2 In. 75.00
Tray, Ice Cream, Chain Of Hobstars, 16 X 10 In. 425.00
Tray, Ice Cream, Harvard Pattern, 8 X 14 In. 350.00
Tray, Ice Cream, Hobstar, Hobnail, & Crosshatching, 14 X 7 1/2 In. 185.00
Tray, Kidney-Shape Handled, Hobstars, Diamond & Star, 8 X 4 In. 95.00
Tumbler, Hobstar & Fan, Signed Hoare, Pair 75.00
Tumbler, Hobstars & Crosshatching, 4 In. 20.00
Tumbler, Louis XIV Pattern, Signed Hawkes 65.00
Tumbler, Monarch Pattern 25.00
Tumbler, Russian Pattern, Clear Button 45.00
Tumbler, Winfield Pattern, Set Of 6 .... 150.00
Vase, Athens Pattern, Single Star Base, 4 1/2 X 10 In. 295.00
Vase, Basket Shape, Hobstar & Thistles, Step Cut Ends, 7 In. 145.00
Vase, Brunswick Design, Signed Hawkes, 16 In. 1050.00
Vase, Bull's-Eye Flowers, Corset Shape, 10 In. 85.00
Vase, Butterflies, 10 In. 50.00
Vase, Chalice, Green Cut To Clear, Colias Design, 14 In. 250.00
Vase, Cranberry Overlay, Hobstar, Cane, Fan, Clear Stem, 10 In. 200.00
Vase, Crystal, Hobstar & Fan Pattern, 15 In. 225.00
Vase, Flower, Crystal, Baluster Form, Pinwheel & Fan, 13 In. 150.00
Vase, Harvard Band, Floral & Leaves, 16-Point Star Base, 6 In. 55.00
Vase, Harvard Design, 3-Footed, 13 In. 850.00

Vase, Harvard Pattern, Intaglio Flowers, 12 In. 95.00
Vase, Hobstar, Narrow At Bottom, Flared Top, 10 In. 175.00
Vase, Hobstars, Cane, & Nailhead Diamonds, Handled, 12 In. 1100.00
Vase, Intaglio Cut, Amethyst, C.1900, 12 1/2 In. 100.00
Vase, Melon-Shaped Body, Vertical Vesicas, 5 1/2 X 13 3/4 In. 750.00
Vase, Monarch Pattern, 2-Handled, 12 In. 1375.00
Vase, Pinwheel & Buzzstar, Hobstar On Sides, Signed, 9 In. 125.00
Vase, Pinwheel Pattern, Heavy Black, 6 1/2 In. 85.00
Vase, Pinwheel, Buzzstar, Hobstars On Side, Signed Ry, 4 In. 125.00
Vase, Pinwheels, Hobstars, Fans, 3 1/4 In. 135.00
Vase, Stratford Design, Signed Sinclaire, 16 In. 275.00
Vase, Strawberry, Diamond, & Fan, Maple Leaf Signature, 14 In. 175.00
Vase, Trumpet-Shaped, 12 In. 300.00
Vase, Trumpet, Hobstar, Fan, & Crosshatching, 10 In. 150.00
Vase, Trumpet, Hobstars & Crosshatching, Rayed Base, 12 In. 165.00
Vase, Trumpet, Hobstars & Notched Prism, 15 In. 295.00
Vase, Trumpet, Hobstars, Cane, Fans, & Stars, Maple City, 12 1/4 In. 150.00
Vase, Urn-Shaped, Hobstars, Signed Sinclaire, 8 In. 140.00
Water Set, Fan & Pineapple, Pitcher, 6 Tumblers 175.00
Water Set, Pinwheels, Crosscut Diamond & Fan, 4 Tumblers, 5 Piece 300.00
Wine, Colonial Pattern, C.1893, Knobbed Stem, Dorflinger, Set Of 4 .... 200.00
Wine, Pear Shape, Etched Top 25.00
Wine, Plymouth Pattern, Hollow Stem, Meriden Co., Set Of 4 .... 350.00
Wine, Rhine, Twist Stem, Clear, Cranberry, & Chartreuse, 7 1/4 In. 250.00
Wine, Strawberry Diamond Facet Cut Knob, 21 Point Base, Set Of 6 .... 132.00

D'Argental is a mark used by the St.Louis, France, glassworks. The
firm made multilayered, acid-cut cameo glass in the late nineteenth and
twentieth centuries. D'Argental is the French name for the city of
Munzthal, home of the glassworks. Later they made enameled etched glass.
Compagnie des Cristalleries de St. Louis is still working.

D'ARGENTAL, Bowl, C.1920, Conical Contour, Siena Overlay, Signed, 8 3/4 In. 650.00
Bowl, Cameo, Brown Floral On Beige Ground, 5 1/2 In. 1050.00
Vase, Boat Scene, Frosted Purple To White, Signed, 5 3/4 In. 675.00
Vase, Boat Scenic, 3 Acid Cuttings, Signed, 5 3/4 In. 650.00
Vase, Cameo, Yellow, Brown, Scrolling Vines, Signed, 13 In. 550.00
Vase, Lily Pond, Red Amber, Yellow & Amber Ground, 4 X 4 In. 550.00
Vase, Maroon, Cream Ground, Flowers, Ivys, Cameo, 6 In. 400.00
Vase, Rooftop Scene, Storks, Salmon Sides, Signed, 12 In. 2200.00
Vase, Trumpet Blossoms, Yellow, Red, Signed, 17 In. 1500.00

D'Aurys is a mark found on French cameo glasswares of the nineteenth
century.

D'AURYS, Vase, Red, Green Flowers, 8 In. 400.00
        DAGUERREOTYPE, see Photography, Daguerreotype
        DANISH CHRISTMAS PLATE, see Bing & Grondahl; Royal Copenhagen

DAUM
NANCY

Daum Nancy is the mark used by Auguste and Antonin Daum on pieces of
French cameo glass made after 1875.

DAUM NANCY, Bottle, Perfume, Stylized Flowers, Green Ground, Signed, 7 1/2 In. 180.00
Bowl, Cameo, Orange & White, 5 In. 475.00
Bowl, Emerald Green, To Clear, Berries, Leaves, 9 1/2 In. 475.00
Bowl, Gray, Green & Pink, Blossoms, Signed, 12 In. 225.00
Bowl, Lake Scene, 4 Crimps, Mottled Ground, Signed, 8 In. 1200.00

Bowl, Molded Leaves, Irregular Form, Marked, Yellow, 6 In.Diam. 280.00
Bowl, Orange, Green Ground, 15 Sailing Ships, Signed, 5 In. 545.00
Bowl, Thistle Leaves & Stems, Gray & Gilt, Signed, 4 3/4 In.Diam. 500.00
Bowl, Transparent Yellow, Silver Flecks, Marked, 18 In. 6200.00
Bowl, Trefoil Form, Blue-Gray, Mountain Scene, Signed, 7 In. 495.00
Bowl, Verseau, 24 In.Diam. 150.00
Bowl, Winter Scene, Frosted Gold Ground, Square, Signed, 6 In. 550.00
Bowl, Yellow, Orange Ground, Leaves, Cherries, Browns, 5 1/2 In. 595.00
Bowl, Yellow, Orange, & Brown, Signed 635.00
Box, Covered, Leaves & Cones, Yellow, Signed, 4 In.Wide 475.00
Box, Covered, Winter Scene, Signed, 3 In.Wide 695.00
Box, Etched & Enameled, Signed, 2 1/2 In. 700.00
Box, Red Flowers, Gold Design, Signed, 3 X 3 In. 750.00
Box, Winter Scene, Covered, Tangerine Ground, 3 In.Wide 595.00
Cachepot, Forest Scene, Gray Ground, Signed, 5 1/2 X 4 1/2 In. 995.00
Chandelier, Blue Bells & Berries, White Ground, 14 In.Diam. 1450.00
Compote, Cameo, Black, Green & Red Ground, 11 1/2 X 12 In. 1750.00
Cordial, Clear, Bubble Top, Wafer Stem Feet, Signed, 3 In. 45.00
Ewer, Enameled Flowers, Silver Top & Handle, C.1898, Signed 250.00
Inkwell, Gold Foil Between Layers, Red Orange, Gold, 5 In. 750.00
Inkwell, Layered Gold Foil, Knob Top, 5 In.Square 850.00
Juice, Barrel Shape, Cameo & Enameled White Flowers 125.00
Lamp, C.1910, Wild Flowers, Wrought Iron, Signed, 14 1/2 In. 2000.00
Lamp, Iron, Orange, Yellow, Burgundy, Signed, 12 In. 2750.00
Lamp, Table, Translucent, Shouldered Dome Shade, Marked, 18 In. 6500.00
Rose Bowl, Winter Scenic, Mottled Gold Ground, Marked, 6 In.Diam. 1250.00
Salt, Cameo, Gold Enamel Design, Green, Oval, Signed 295.00
Salt, Turquoise To Crystal, Frosted, Thistles, Leaves, 2 In. 545.00
Salt, Windmills, Ships, 1 3/4 In. 388.00
Salt, Winter Scene 395.00
Salt, Yellow Ground, Forest Scene, Signed 525.00
Toothpick, Enameled Trees & Houses, Marked, C.1900, 1 3/4 In. 700.00
Toothpick, Winter Scene, Cameo & Enamel, Signed, 2 In. 395.00
Tumbler, Blue Summer Scenic, Barrel Shape, Mottled Ground, Signed 695.00
Tumbler, Summer Scene, Signed, 5 In. 550.00
Tumbler, Yellow To Orange, Barrel Shape, 4 In. 155.00
Vase, Allover Yellow & Orange Leaves, Berries, Signed, 14 1/2 In. 975.00
Vase, Applied Flowers, Signed, Yellow & Blue, 5 3/4 In. 620.00
Vase, Bellflowers, Double Overlay, Signed, Opalescent, 11 3/4 In. 2700.00
Vase, Black Raspberry, Black, Red, Yellow, 8 In. 575.00
Vase, Blue, Green, Purple, Poppy Blossoms, Signed, 10 In. 1350.00
Vase, Bud, Apricot-Yellow, Green Foot, Leafless Tree, Signed, 6 In. 875.00
Vase, Bud, Landscape, Blue, Gray, Orange, Salmon, Village, 5 In. 775.00
Vase, C.1930, Band Of Hexagonal Links, Signed, Brown, 13 In. 1300.00
Vase, Carved Thistle, Gold Enamel, Signed, Square, 4 1/2 In. 325.00
Vase, Cross Of Lorraine, Serpentine Handle, Mottled 420.00
Vase, Deco Floral, Lorain Acid Cutback, 6 In. 175.00
Vase, Deep Rust & Yellow Orange, Signed, 8 In. 600.00
Vase, Flowers, Yellow, Purple Ground, 3-Layer, Signed, 4 1/2 In. 455.00
Vase, Fox & Raven, Enameled On Front, Emerald Green Top, 8 In. 1275.00
Vase, Gondola & Gondolier, Enameled, C.1900, Signed, 5 In. 1425.00
Vase, Gray, Iris & Leafage, Stars, Flowers, Signed, 10 In. 880.00
Vase, Green Floral On Martele Opalescent Blue, 24 In. 2700.00
Vase, Green, Blue, & Brown, 8 In. 800.00
Vase, Honey Amber, Cut Back, Raised Round Foot, 13 1/2 In. 650.00
Vase, Iris, 9 1/2 In. 675.00
Vase, Iris, 9 3/4 In. 675.00
Vase, Lacy Layer, Sunflowers, Red, Streaked Dark Green, 16 In. 1750.00
Vase, Landscape, Salmon, Mustard, Gray, River Scene, 13 In. 1350.00
Vase, Landscape, Yellow To Orange, Sailing Junks, 4 3/4 In. 675.00
Vase, Leaves, Carved Begonias, Tear Dop Shape, Signed, 9 1/4 In. 1300.00
Vase, Marbleized, Red, Yellow Streaked, Green Trees, Marked, 16 In. 2600.00
Vase, Mottled Colors, Signed, 11 In. 465.00

Daum Nancy, Vase, Overlay Etched, 15 1/4 In.

Vase, Mottled Green & Blue, Rectangular & Oval, 7 X 4 3/4 In. 200.00
Vase, Mushrooms, C-Shaped Handles, Enameled, Signed, 7 3/4 In. 2900.00
Vase, Olive Green, Etched Columns, Geometric Design, Marked 1100.00
Vase, Orange & Dark Green Daisies, Baluster, Marked, 6 In. 800.00
Vase, Overlay Etched, 15 1/4 In. .... *Illus* 4000.00
Vase, Pedestal, Scenic, Mottled Gold Ground, Signed, 13 3/4 In. 1100.00
Vase, Purple Violets, Green Leaves, Signed, 2 1/4 X 4 1/2 In. 510.00
Vase, Purple Violets, Green Leaves, Signed, 4 1/2 In. 470.00
Vase, Purple, Green, & Red, 24 In. .... *Illus* 1800.00
Vase, Red Berries, Chartreuse Leaves, Mottled, Signed, 15 In. 875.00
Vase, Snow Laden Trees, Orange & Yellow, Signed, 4 1/4 In. 675.00
Vase, Spring Scenes, Cameo Cut & Enameled, 11 In. 1350.00
Vase, Spring Scenic, Carved Trees & Mountains, Signed, 1 1/2 In. 475.00
Vase, Summer Scene, Acid Cut & Enameled, Green, Signed, 4 3/4 In. 650.00
Vase, Swallows Flying In Sunrise, Enameled, Signed, 10 In. 1500.00
Vase, Transparent Blue, Etched Fish, Seaweed, Marked, 11 In. 150.00

Daum Nancy, Vase, Purple, Green, & Red, 24 In.

Vase, Trees, Balustered, Signed, Carnation Ground, 11 1/4 In. 2000.00
Vase, Trees, River, Gold Frosted Ground, 9 1/4 In. 1695.00
Vase, Trees, Streams, & Mountains, Enameled, Signed, 8 In. 1185.00
Vase, Winter Scene, Flattened Oval, Signed, 6 3/4 In. 875.00
Vase, Winter Scene, Orange Ground, Brown Tree, Snow, Signed, 3 In. 425.00
Vase, Yellow Ground, Orange, Leaves & Cherries, Browns, Signed 635.00
Vase, Yellow, Mauve, Burgundy, Rose, Green, Marked, 15 In. 850.00
Vase, Yellow, Orange Shading, Burgundy Base, Bellflowers, Signed 1000.00
Vase, Yellow, Plum, Burgundy & Green, Buds, Signed, 15 In. 600.00
Vase, Yellow, 16-Sided Foot, Baluster, Signed, 11 In. 400.00
Vase, 3 Shades Of Red, Yellow Ground, Signed, 8 In. 995.00
Vase, 4 Applied Handles, Etched In Green, Brown, Orange, Marked 400.00

DAVENPORT
LONGPORT
STAFFORDSHIRE

Davenport pottery and porcelain were made at the Davenport factory in Longport, Staffordshire, England, from 1793 to 1887. Earthenwares, creamwares, porcelains, ironstone wares, and other products were made. Most of the pieces are marked with a form of the word Davenport.

DAVENPORT, Compote, Hand-Painted Scenic Center, 11 X 8 1/2 In., Pair 395.00
    Cup & Saucer, Shades Of Rose, Allover Gold Scrolling, 1830-37 .... 50.00
    Pitcher, Winchester Cathedral, Purple Luster, Marked, 8 In. 295.00
    Plate, Clematis Pattern, Scalloped Edge, C.1848, 6 In.Diam. 55.00
    Plate, Hand-Painted Castle & Mountain Scene, 9 In. 55.00
    Tea Service, Fluted, Berry Vines, C.1800, Anchor Mark, 32 Piece 770.00

DAVY CROCKETT, Bowl & Mug 10.00
    Bowl, Cereal 12.00
    Coat, Shirt, Bag, Tie, & Flashlight 49.00
    Figurine, Crockett On Horse 10.00
    Gun, Pirate 22.00
    Hat With Badge, Boxed 30.00
    Knife, Pocket 5.00
    Lamp, Figural, Metal, 10 1/2 In. 30.00
    Lunch Box 12.00
    Ring 10.00
    Ring, Metal 12.00
    Spoon, Souvenir 3.50
    Toy, Wagon 65.00
    Tumbler, Davy & Indians In Canoe 15.00
    Watch 10.00

William De Morgan made art pottery in England from the 1860s to 1907. He is best known for his luster glazed Moorish inspired pieces.

DE MORGAN, Vase, Lion Design, Ruby Luster, 18 3/8 In. .... *Illus* 5900.00

DE PANTIN, Vase, Carved, Oranges, White Ground, Cameo, Signed, 10 In. 450.00

DE VEAU, Vase, Peacock, Frosted Gold Ground, Signed, Cameo, 10 In. 1150.00

De Vez is a name found on special pieces of French cameo glass made by the Cristallerie de Pantin about 1890. Monsieur de Varreux was the art director of the glassworks and he signed pieces "de Vez."

DE VEZ, Bowl, Tricorn Shape, Gold Ground, Landscape, Signed, 4 7/8 In.Diam. 850.00
    Vase, Boat & Village Scene, Scene In Navy, Pink Ground, 16 1/8 In. 2250.00
    Vase, Boat Scene, Blue Cut To Yellow, Signed, 8 1/4 In. 795.00
    Vase, Cameo, Frosted Gold Ground, Man In Gondola, Signed, 6 1/8 In. 775.00
    Vase, Fisherman & Boats, Pink & White Lining, Signed, 7 1/2 In. 2000.00
    Vase, Frosted Gold Ground, Perched Bird, Gold Plated Base, 18 3/4 In. 2250.00

De Morgan, Vase, Lion Design,
Ruby Luster, 18 3/8 In.

Vase, Man In Gondola, Green To Rose, Gold Ground, Signed, 6 1/8 In.	795.00
Vase, Mosque & Palm Trees, Blue To Rose, Signed, 11 3/4 In.	1175.00
Vase, Roman Temple, Scenic, 3 Acid Cuttings, Signed, 8 In.	1100.00
Vase, Sailing Ships On Pink, Yellow, & Orange Ground, 3 X 7 In.	995.00
Vase, Scalloped Top, Island & Houses, Yellow & Blue, Signed, 8 In.	375.00

Decoys are carved or turned wooden copies of birds. The decoy was placed in the water to lure flying birds to the pond for hunters.

DECOY, American Merganser, H.Conklin, Manahawkin, N.H., Hollow, Pair	250.00
American Merganser, H.Shourds III, N.Y., Signed, Hollow Cedar	150.00
American Merganser, Morse, Miniature	290.00
Bird, Tack Eyes, Old Alligatored Paint, Wooden, 11 In.	40.00
Bird, Tin, Pat.1874	45.00
Black Duck, Barnegat Boy, C.1920, Hollow Cedar	70.00
Black Duck, J.Pierce, Havre De Grace, Maryland, Original Paint, 15 In.	65.00
Black Duck, Joe King, N.J., C.1900, Leather Thong, Hollow Cedar	125.00
Black-Bellied Plover, Jamaica Bay, N.Y.	1400.00
Black-Bellied Plover, Shourds	2700.00
Black-Breasted Plover, Beetle Head, Tack Eyes, Split Tail	825.00
Blue Wing Teal, Drake, Capt. Harry Jobes	60.00
Bluebill, Carved & Signed Ernest Ouimet, Pair	150.00
Bluebill, Drake, Chunky, Oshkosh, C.1920, Glass Eyes, Old Paint, 12 In.	45.00
Bluebill, Duck, Carved Layers Of Feathers On Back, 13 1/2 In.	95.00
Bluebill, Duck, Glass Eyes, Carved Feathers, New York, Pine	160.00
Bluebill, Miniature, 19th Century, 3 1/4 In.	325.00
Bluebill, Repainted	400.00
Bluewing Teal, Drake, Turned Head, Tack Eyes, 11 In.	80.00
Brant, Duck, Harry Shourds, New Jersey	1000.00
Brant, Hand-Carved By M.Schult	145.00
Broadbill Drake, C.1936	1400.00
Bufflehead, Drake, Glass Eyes, Original Paint, Wooden, 9 3/4 In.	60.00
Bufflehead, Preening, Glass Eyes, Original Paint, 9 In.	50.00
Bufflehead, Working, New Hampshire, C.1900	50.00
Canada Goose, Brown, Glass Eyes, 2-Piece Head, 24 In.	325.00
Canada Goose, Canvas On Slat, C.1902, By Captain Clarence Bailey	1600.00
Canada Goose, Captain Harry Jobes, Maryland, Original Paint, Cedar	225.00
Canada Goose, Cork Body, Wooden Head, Glass Eyes, 18 In.	65.00
Canada Goose, Crowell, Miniature	425.00
Canada Goose, Hollow-Carved, Stick Up, By Charles Hart	5250.00

Canada Goose, Hollow, Swimmer, Tack Eyes, Original Paint, 21 In.	135.00
Canada Goose, Morse, Miniature	300.00
Canada Goose, Served As Duck Blind Weight	395.00
Canada Goose, Silhouette, Finger Lakes Region	25.00
Canada Goose, Stick Up, Tack Eyes, 23 In.	50.00
Canada Goose, Swimmer, Jim Love, Aberdeen, Maryland, 29 In.	325.00
Canada Goose, Tack Eyes, Doweled Head, Original Paint	600.00
Canada Goose, Tack Eyes, One Piece	250.00
Canada Goose, Turned Head, Used On Ice, 27 1/2 X 16 1/2 In.	175.00
Canvasback, Bald Head & Bill, Glass Eyes, Black & White	50.00
Canvasback, Drake, Capt. Harry Jobes	100.00
Canvasback, Duck, Male & Female, Glass Eyes, 17 1/2 In., Pair	190.00
Canvasback, Duck, Old Paint	55.00
Canvasback, Feeding, Crowell, Miniature	325.00
Canvasback, Glass Eyes	130.00
Canvasback, Hen, Charles Joiner, Maryland, Original Paint	100.00
Canvasback, Hen, Crowell, Miniature	250.00
Canvasback, Hen, Mason Standard Grade, Glass Eyes, Original Paint	190.00
Canvasback, Hen, Ward Bros.	3500.00
Canvasback, Mason, Glass Eyes, Original Paint	120.00
Coot, Fat, Tack Eyes, Old Paint, C.1900, 11 In.	75.00
Coot, Glass Eyes, Handmade	17.50
Coot, Ken Anger, Dunville, Ontario, Original Paint	550.00
Coot, Michigan, 1920	85.00
Country Goose, Wide Breast, Black & White Paint, 2-Piece Head, 22 In.	135.00
Crow, Wooden	70.00
Crown, Hinged Wings	40.00
Curlew, By Nathan Cobb	3900.00
Curlew, Harry Shourds III, N.J., Original Paint, Solid Cedar	150.00
Curlew, Long Island, C.1860, Solid Construction	1760.00
Curlew, Tullytown, Penna., Original Paint, Mounted, Solid Cedar	250.00
Dowitcher, H.V.Shourds	65.00
Duck, Black, Inlet Head, Open Bill, Original Paint, By Gus Wilson	3000.00
Duck, Black, New Hampshire	60.00
Duck, Black, Rose-Folding, Original Paint, Chicago	25.00
Duck, Black, Turned Head, Glass Eyes, Original Paint, 14 In.	105.00
Duck, Bluebill, Hollow Body, C.1820	70.00
Duck, Hollow Black, Tack Eyes, Original Paint, 16 1/2 In.	80.00
Duck, Paper, Calendar, 1917, Gems Of Thought	20.00
Duck, Teal Hen, Feathers & Tail, C.1920, 10 In.	160.00
Eider, Working, Glass Eyes	45.00
Fish, Handmade, Tin Fins & Tail, Glass Eyes, White Body, 9 1/2 In.	30.00
Fish, Metal Fins, Ocher, Brown, & Black Paint	350.00
Fish, Sturgeon	210.00
Golden Plover, John Dilley, Long Island	9000.00
Goldeneye, Crowell, Miniature	225.00
Goldeneye, Drake, Oversized, Glass Eyes, 17 In.	50.00
Goose, Barnegat Bay	190.00
Goose, Blue, Field Stick Up, Tack Eyes, Original Paint, 27 In.	90.00
Goose, Canvas On Wire	95.00
Goose, Head In Dozing Retracted Neck, Hand-Carved, Cedar, 20 1/2 In.	125.00
Goose, Madison Mitchell	185.00
Goose, North Carolina, C.1900	2100.00
Goose, Sleeper, Head & Neck Turned 180 Degrees, Painted, 18 1/2 In.	175.00
Greater Yellowlegs, Cape Cod, C.1870, Tack Eyes, Split Tail	605.00
High-Neck Canvasback, McLaughlin, Pair	2100.00
Hooded Merganser, Morse, Miniature	290.00
Kingfisher, Crowell	1000.00
Loon, Nova Scotia, Tail Cut Out, C.1900, 18 1/4 In.	65.00
Mallard, Crowell, Miniature, Pair	575.00
Mallard, Drake, Glass Eyes, Original Paint, 15 3/4 In.	60.00
Mallard, Drake, Glass Eyes, Original Paint, 17 In.	65.00
Mallard, Drake, Hollow Body, Perry Wilcox, Liverpool, Il., 1920s	175.00

Mallard, Hen, Glass Eyes, Original Paint, 18 In.	55.00
Mallard, Mason, Pair	325.00
Mallard, Morse, Miniature	225.00
Merganser, American, Glass, Eyes, Original Paint, 19 1/4 In.	55.00
Merganser, Amine	175.00
Merganser, Hand-Carved, Bobwhite	160.00
Merganser, Hen, Hollow-Carved, Mason	6800.00
Merganser, Huey	975.00
Merganser, Red Breasted, Fat Bodied, Glass Eyes, 16 In.	75.00
Owl, Glass Eyes, Large	46.50
Pheasant, Crowell, Miniature	400.00
Pigeon, Hand-Carved, Original Paint	145.00
Pintail, Challenge, Hollow Carved, Original Paint, Pair	5250.00
Pintail, Drake, Eastern Shore Virginia, Glass Eyes, Cedar	150.00
Pintail, Drake, Flying, Tin Wings, Original Paint	275.00
Pintail, Drake, High Head, Elongated Tail, Original Paint, 17 In.	85.00
Pintail, Drake, Turned Head, Original Paint, 19 In.	80.00
Pintail, Duck, Glass Eyes, C.1930, Signed Arnes	115.00
Pintail, Duck, Handmade, Glass Eyes, Wooden	17.50
Pintail, Duck, Mason Decoy Factory, Detroit, 1800s, Pair	5250.00
Quail, Crowell, Miniature	525.00
Redbreasted Merganser, Hen, Tack Eyes, Original Paint, 15 1/4 In.	85.00
Redbreasted Merganser, Morse, Miniature	310.00
Redbreasted Merganser, 17 1/2 In.	170.00
Redhead, Drake, Fat Cheeks, Turned Head, Wood, 13 1/4 In.	60.00
Redhead, Drake, Glass Eyes, Al Ragg, Ontario, 14 3/4 In.	80.00
Redhead, Drake, Henry Keyes Chadwick	800.00
Redhead, Duck, Hand-Carved, Wooden	68.00
Redhead, Hen, Tack Eyes, Original Paint	325.00
Ring Billed, Drake, Button Eyes, C.1890, Maine	110.00
Ruddy Duck, Elvirah Wright	1700.00
Ruddy Duck, John Williams	2500.00
Ruffed Grouse, Crowell, Miniature	425.00
Scoter, Hollow Carved, Dated, Lem Steve Wards, Pair	4100.00
Shadow Goose, Original Paint	250.00
Slat Goose, Crowell	375.00
Snipe, Late 19th Century, Original Paint, Tin, 11 X 6 X 3 1/2 In.	135.00
Swan, Life Size, By Capt, Harry Jobes, 32 In.	175.00
Teal Duck, Hen, Carved Feathers & Tail, C.1920, 10 In.	160.00
Tern, Crowell	900.00
Tern, Crowell, Miniature	300.00
Western Grebe, Haertel	1400.00
Widgeon, Oversize, Glass Eyes, Original Paint	225.00
Winter Gull, Eastern Shore, Glass Eyes, Turned Head, Original Paint	125.00
Wooduck, Drake, Relief Carving, Glass Eyes, Branded Clare, 14 1/2 In.	105.00
Yellowlegs Bird, H.V.Shourds	60.00
Yellowlegs Bird, In Feeding Position	45.00
Yellowlegs, Boyd	2600.00
Yellowlegs, Crowell, Miniature	475.00

Chelsea Keramic Art Works was established in 1872 in Chelsea, Massachusetts, by members of the Robertson family. The factory closed in 1889, and was reorganized as the Chelsea Pottery U.S. in 1891. It became the Dedham Pottery of Dedham, Massachusetts, in 1895. The factory closed in 1943. It was famous for its crackleware dishes, which picture blue outlines of animals, flowers, and other natural motifs.

DEDHAM, Ashtray, Rabbit	165.00
Bowl, Azalea, 5 In.	125.00
Bowl, Rabbit, 4 3/8 In.	160.00
Bowl, Rabbit, 5 1/2 In.Diam.	50.00
Charger, Rabbit	395.00

Creamer, Rabbit, 4 1/2 X 2 In. 200.00
Cup & Saucer, Horse Chestnut 150.00
Cup & Saucer, Rabbit 90.00
Cup Plate, Rabbit 38.00
Cup, Rabbit 45.00
Mug, Rabbit Pattern, Marked, Crazed Off-White Ground, 5 1/2 In., Pair 440.00
Paperweight, Rabbit 300.00
Pitcher, Morning-Evening 400.00
Plate, Azalea, 6 In. 125.00
Plate, Azalea, 7 1/2 In. 90.00
Plate, Butterfly, 6 In. 150.00
Plate, Crab, 6 In. 260.00
Plate, Grape, 8 1/2 In. 95.00
Plate, Horse Chestnut, 6 In. 85.00
Plate, Horse Chestnut, 8 1/2 In. 100.00
Plate, Iris, Maude Davenport, 8 In. .... 115.00 To 135.00
Plate, Iris, 6 In. .... 125.00 To 140.00
Plate, Lotus, 10 In. 120.00
Plate, Magnolia, 8 In. 75.00
Plate, Polar Bear, 7 1/2 In. 295.00
Plate, Rabbit, 7 1/2 In. 75.00
Plate, Rabbit, 8 In. 85.00
Plate, Rabbit, 8 1/2 In. .... 75.00 To 130.00
Plate, Rabbit, 9 3/4 In. 95.00
Plate, Rabbit, 10 In. 140.00
Plate, Rabbit, 12 In. 295.00
Plate, Snowtree, 6 In. 75.00
Plate, Snowtree, 10 In. 160.00
Plate, Turkey, 8 1/2 In. 165.00
Plate, 3 Rabbit, 6 In. 125.00
Saucer, Elephant, 6 In. 125.00
Tea Tile, Rabbit, 5 1/2 In. 250.00
Vase, Caramel Drip Glaze, 8 In. 250.00
Vase, Green & Blue Glaze, Signed, 5 1/2 In. 450.00

Delatte glass is a French cameo glass made by Andre Delatte. It was first made in Nancy, France, in 1921. Lighting fixtures and opaque glassware in imitation of Bohemian opaline were made.

DELATTE, Bottle, Art Deco, Enameled, White Floral, Blue Ground, Stopper 525.00
Vase, Bud, Morning Glories, Purple, 6 1/2 In. 190.00
Vase, Cut Leaves & Berries, Bulbous Shape, 6 In. 450.00
Vase, Scenic, Windmill & Trees, 2 Cuttings, Green & Brown, 5 In. 525.00
   DELAWARE, see Custard Glass; Pressed Glass
   DELDARE, see Buffalo Pottery Deldare

Delft is a tin-glazed pottery that has been made since the seventeenth century. It is decorated with blue on white or with colored decorations. Most of the pieces sold today were made after 1891, and the name Holland appears with the Delft factory marks.

DELFT, Bottle, Blue & White, C.1750, Floral Spray, English, 6 7/8 In. 275.00
Bowl, Barber's, White, Pierced For Hanging, English, 10 In. 385.00
Bowl, Blue & White Lotus Pattern, C.1755, Irish, 7 1/8 In. 990.00
Bowl, Exotic Birds On Shrubbery, Polychrome, 9 5/8 In.Diam. 500.00
Bowl, Polychrome, Iron, Iron Red, Green, Blue, Birds, Floral, 9 In. 500.00
Bowl, Punch, Blue & White, Peony Plate, C.1770, London, 12 In. 165.00
Canister Set, People, Sailboat, & Windmills, Blue & White, 10 Piece 165.00
Charger, Blue & White, Yellow Band, Marked, 13 1/2 In. 50.00
Charger, Blue, Green, Rust, & Yellow, Cornflowers, 13 In. 325.00
Charger, Holland Scene, 12 In. 145.00
Clock, Wall, Blue & White 95.00

Coffee Grinder, Wall	195.00
Creamer, Cow, Blue, Hand-Painted, Signed	65.00
Creamer, Windmill Scene	22.00
Dish, Hot Water, White, Strap Handles, English, 7 In.	605.00
Figurine Horse, White, Grassy Mound, 6 3/4 In., Pair	900.00
Figurine, Boar, Standing, Green Base, Polychrome, Marked, Dutch, 5 In.	2000.00
Figurine, Duck, Brown Head, Ocher Beak, Swimming, Marked, 4 5/8 In.	800.00
Figurine, Duck, C.1750, Brown Head, Wings, & Tail, Polychrome, 4 5/8 In.	800.00
Flask, House Shaped, 3 1/4 In.	55.00
Jar, Floral, Embossed Scrolls, Sailing Scene, Covered, 16 In., Pair	325.00
Jug, Wine, Ovoid Body, Floral Sprigs, Blue & White, Marked, 8 1/4 In.	325.00
Picture, 12-Tile, Butterflies & Insects, Framed, 20 1/2 X 15 3/8 In.	1400.00
Plate, Birds, Stylized Rockwork Center, Paneled Rim, 1700, 13 1/8 In.	325.00
Plate, Blue & White, Chinamen, River, Fishing, C.1760, English, 8 In.	2750.00
Plate, Blue & White, Oriental Figure, C.1750, London, 10 In.	600.00
Plate, Blue & White, Oriental Lady, C. 1760, London, 9 In.	110.00
Plate, Blue & White, Peony Branches, C.1760, London, 13 1/4 In.	220.00
Plate, Blue, Green, Red, Oriental Lady, Garden, Marked, 13 1/4 In.	800.00
Plate, Green, Blue, Yellow, Brown, Peacock Design, 8 In.	100.00
Plate, Hand-Painted Canal Scene, Trees & Birds, Marked, 12 In.	95.00
Plate, Polychrome, Blue, Green, Red, C.1760, English, 10 In.	192.00
Plate, Polychrome, English, C.1730, 9 In.	325.00
Plate, Tea Plant Pattern, De Witte Starre, 1723-41, 13 7/8 In.	300.00
Pot, Bulb, Form Of Louis XV Commode, Blue, Yellow, Green, 5 In.	375.00
Slipper, Floral Sprigs, Polychrome, Dutch, 5 1/4 In.	950.00
Tile, Stork Above Word Gravenhage, 4 1/2 In.Square	35.00
Tile, Windmill & Water Scene, 4 1/2 In.Square	35.00
Tobacco Jar, Blue & White, Pipe Smoking Indian, Marked, 8 In., Pair	1400.00
Tobacco Jar, Pipe-Smoking Indians, Brass & Copper Lid, 8 3/4 In., Pair	1400.00
Toothpick, 1 3/4 X 2 1/2 In.	20.00
Vase, Blue & White, Baluster, Figure Strolling, Garden, 9 In., Pair	300.00
Vase, Blue & White, Covered, Birds, Blossoms, Domed Cover, 13 In.	275.00
Vase, Dark Blue, Picture Panel, Octagon Shape, 13 1/2 In.	165.00
Vase, Flaring Cylindrical Body, Floral Medallions, 7 1/2 In.	125.00
Vase, Garden In Panel, De Twee Scheepjes, 1850-75, 9 3/8 In., Pair	300.00
Vase, Hand-Painted Birds, Stylized Foliage, Cover, Marked, 13 7/8 In.	275.00

DENTAL, Cabinet, Beveled Glass, Metal	145.00
Cabinet, Marble Top, Sandwich Glass Knobs, Black Walnut	975.00
DENTIST, see Medical	

> Depression glass was an inexpensive glass manufactured in large quantities
> during the 1920s and early 1930s. It was made in many colors and patterns by
> dozens of factories in the United States. The name "Depression glass"
> is a modern one.

DEPRESSION GLASS
ACCORDION PLEATS, see Round Robin

Adam & Sierra, Butter, Pink, Covered	575.00
Adam, Ashtray, Crystal	12.00
Adam, Ashtray, Green, 4 1/2 In.	15.00
Adam, Ashtray, Pink	15.00
Adam, Bowl, Cereal, Pink	15.00 To 22.50
Adam, Bowl, Green, 4 1/2 In.	9.00
Adam, Bowl, Pink, 4 3/4 In.	8.50
Adam, Bowl, Vegetable, Pink, Covered, 9 In.	30.00
Adam, Bowl, Vegetable, Pink, Oval	14.50
Adam, Butter, Green, Covered	195.00
Adam, Butter, Pink, Covered	65.00 To 67.50
Adam, Cake Plate, Green	15.00
Adam, Cake Plate, Pink	10.00 To 13.00
Adam, Candleholder, Green, Pair	59.50
Adam, Candlestick, Pink, Pair	45.00

Depression Glass, Adam & Sierra

Depression Glass, Adam

Depression Glass, American Sweetheart

Adam, Coaster, Green, 3 1/2 In.	10.00
Adam, Coaster, Pink	18.50
Adam, Creamer, Green	10.00
Adam, Cup & Saucer, Green	15.00 To 17.50
Adam, Cup & Saucer, Pink	12.00 To 19.50
Adam, Dish, Candy, Pink, Covered	35.00 To 55.00
Adam, Pitcher, Green	24.00
Adam, Pitcher, Pink, Round Base, 32 Ounce	34.00
Adam, Plate, Green, 6 In.	8.50
Adam, Plate, Green, 8 3/4 In.	9.00
Adam, Plate, Green, 10 1/2 In.	12.00
Adam, Plate, Grill, Green	12.00
Adam, Plate, Pink, 6 In.	3.00
Adam, Plate, Pink, 9 In.	7.00 To 11.00
Adam, Plate, Pink, 9 1/2 In.	14.00
Adam, Plate, Pink, 10 In.	14.50
Adam, Platter, Pink	12.50
Adam, Salt & Pepper, Pink, Footed, 4 In.	38.00
Adam, Saltshaker, Pink	18.00
Adam, Sherbet, Pink	12.00
Adam, Sugar & Creamer, Pink	25.00
Adam, Tumbler, Green	16.00
Adam, Tumbler, Green, Footed, 5 1/2 In.	20.00
Adam, Tumbler, Pink	16.00
AMERICAN BEAUTY, see English Hobnail	
American Pioneer, Cup & Saucer, Crystal	4.75
American Pioneer, Sugar, Crystal	5.00
American Sweetheart, Berry Bowl, Pink	20.00 To 25.00
American Sweetheart, Berry Bowl, Pink, 3/4 In.	25.00

American Sweetheart, Berry Bowl, Pink, 9 In. 15.00
American Sweetheart, Bowl, Cereal, Monax 8.50
American Sweetheart, Bowl, Cereal, Pink .... 7.00 To 8.00
American Sweetheart, Bowl, Console, Red, 18 In. 700.00
American Sweetheart, Bowl, Monax, 5 3/4 In. 9.50
American Sweetheart, Bowl, Pink, 9 In. .... 14.00 To 15.00
American Sweetheart, Bowl, Vegetable, Monax, Oval 35.00
American Sweetheart, Butter, Red, Covered 25.00
American Sweetheart, Creamer, Pink 7.00
American Sweetheart, Cup & Saucer, Monax 10.50
American Sweetheart, Cup & Saucer, Pink .... 10.00 To 15.00
American Sweetheart, Cup & Saucer, Red 95.00
American Sweetheart, Cup, Pink .... 2.50 To 7.00
American Sweetheart, Cup, Red 80.00
American Sweetheart, Plate, Green, 6 In. 3.50
American Sweetheart, Plate, Monax, 6 1/2 In. 3.25
American Sweetheart, Plate, Monax, 8 In. 7.00
American Sweetheart, Plate, Monax, 9 1/4 In. 8.00
American Sweetheart, Plate, Monax, 9 3/4 In. 14.50
American Sweetheart, Plate, Monax, 10 In. 10.00
American Sweetheart, Plate, Monax, 12 1/2 In. 10.00
American Sweetheart, Plate, Monax, 15 3/4 In. 110.00
American Sweetheart, Plate, Pink, 6 In. .... 2.25 To 2.50
American Sweetheart, Plate, Pink, 6 1/2 In. 3.00
American Sweetheart, Plate, Pink, 8 In. .... 6.00 To 7.00
American Sweetheart, Plate, Pink, 10 In. .... 12.00 To 13.50
American Sweetheart, Plate, Pink, 10 1/2 In. 12.00
American Sweetheart, Plate, Pink, 11 1/2 In. 10.00
American Sweetheart, Plate, Pink, 12 In. 10.00
American Sweetheart, Plate, Red, 8 In. .... 70.00 To 75.00

Depression Glass, American Sweetheart, Plate

Depression Glass, Bubble, Plate

Depression Glass, Cameo, Plate

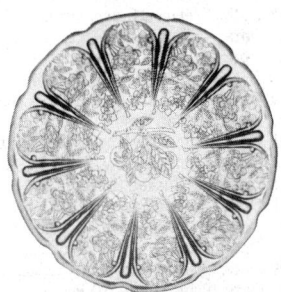

Depression Glass, Cherry Blossom, Plate

American Sweetheart, Plate, Red, 15 1/2 In. 270.00
American Sweetheart, Platter, Pink, Oval 15.00
American Sweetheart, Salt & Pepper, Monax 195.00
American Sweetheart, Salver, Red, 12 In. 125.00
American Sweetheart, Saucer, Monax .... 2.00 To 2.50
American Sweetheart, Saucer, Red .... 35.00 To 40.00
American Sweetheart, Sherbet, Green 8.00
American Sweetheart, Sherbet, Monax 13.50
American Sweetheart, Sherbet, Monax, Footed 13.00
American Sweetheart, Sherbet, Pink .... 7.50 To 10.00
American Sweetheart, Sherbet, Pink, Footed, 4 In. 11.00
American Sweetheart, Soup, Cream, Pink 15.00
American Sweetheart, Soup, Dish, Green, 9 1/2 In. 20.00
American Sweetheart, Soup, Dish, Pink, 10 In. 20.00
American Sweetheart, Sugar & Creamer, Red 190.00
American Sweetheart, Sugar, Monax, Open 6.00
American Sweetheart, Sugar, Pink, Open 6.00
American Sweetheart, Tumbler, Pink, 9 Ounce 30.00
Anniversary, Cup, Pink 3.50
Anniversary, Dish, Candy, Pink, Covered 24.00
Anniversary, Vase, Wall, Pink 25.00
    APPLE BLOSSOM, see Dogwood
Aunt Polly, Plate, Blue, 8 In. 7.00
    AURORA, see Petalware
Avocado, Sugar, Green 15.00
    BALLERINA, see Cameo
    BANDED CHERRY, see Cherry Blossom
    BANDED FINE RIB, see Coronation
    BANDED PETALWARE, see Petalware
    BANDED RAINBOW, see Ring
    BANDED RIBBON, see New Century
    BANDED RINGS, see Ring
    BASKET, see No. 615
Beaded Block, Bowl, Orange, 8 1/2 In. 13.00
Beaded Block, Celery, Orange Iridescent, 8 In. 13.00
Beaded Block, Parfait, Crystal 3.00
Beaded Block, Soup, Dish, Opal Blue 18.50
Beaded Block, Sugar, Crystal 5.00
Beaded Block, Sugar, Green 12.50
Beaded Block, Vase, Opal, Dark Blue 45.00
    BELMONT, see Rose Cameo
    BLOCK, see Block Optic
Block Optic, Bowl, Cereal, Green 5.50
Block Optic, Bowl, Green, 4 1/4 In. 2.75
Block Optic, Bowl, Green, 5 1/4 In. 6.00
Block Optic, Bowl, Green, 8 1/2 In. 10.00
Block Optic, Butter, Green, Covered 20.00
Block Optic, Creamer, Green, Cone Shape 5.50
Block Optic, Creamer, Green, Flat 5.50
Block Optic, Cup, Green 4.00
Block Optic, Cup, Green, Flat 4.00
Block Optic, Cup, Green, Flat Bottom 4.00
Block Optic, Cup, Pink .... 2.50 To 3.00
Block Optic, Gobler, Pink, 5 3/4 In. 9.00
Block Optic, Goblet, Pink, Iced Tea, Footed 12.00
Block Optic, Goblet, Yellow, 7 1/4 In. 17.50
Block Optic, Ice Bucket, Green 12.00
Block Optic, Pitcher, Green, 8 1/2 In. 30.00
Block Optic, Plate, Green, 6 In. 2.00
Block Optic, Plate, Green, 8 In. 2.50
Block Optic, Plate, Green, 9 In. 10.50
Block Optic, Plate, Green, 10 In. 9.00
Block Optic, Plate, Pink, 8 In. 3.25

Block Optic, Plate, Yellow, 6 In. 2.50
Block Optic, Plate, Yellow, 8 In., Set Of 6 .... 18.00
Block Optic, Plate, Yellow, 8 1/2 In. 4.50
Block Optic, Salt & Pepper, Green, Footed 52.50
Block Optic, Saltshaker, Green, Flat, Single 13.00
Block Optic, Saucer, Green, Small Ring 4.00
Block Optic, Sherbet, Green, Cone Shape 3.00
Block Optic, Sherbet, Yellow, Low 4.50
Block Optic, Sugar & Creamer, Pink, Cone Shape 10.00
Block Optic, Sugar, Crystal, Footed 3.00
Block Optic, Sugar, Green, Flat 4.00
Block Optic, Tumbler, Green, Flat .... 7.00 To 8.75
Block Optic, Tumbler, Pink, Flat, 5 In. 6.00
Boopie, Tumbler, Forest Green, Footed 2.50
        BOUQUET & LATTICE, see Normandie
Bowknot, Plate, Green, 7 In. 5.50
        BRIDAL BOUQUET, see No. 615
Bubble, Berry Bowl, Blue, Large 6.50
Bubble, Berry Bowl, Crystal, Large 4.00
Bubble, Berry Bowl, Crystal, 4 In. 2.00
Bubble, Bowl, Cereal, Blue 5.50
Bubble, Bowl, Fruit, Blue, 4 1/2 In. 5.75
Bubble, Bowl, Fruit, Crystal, 4 1/2 In. 2.00
Bubble, Creamer, Blue 13.00
Bubble, Cup & Saucer, Blue .... 3.00 To 4.00
Bubble, Cup, Blue 3.25
Bubble, Cup, Forest Green 2.50
Bubble, Goblet, Green, Water 5.00
Bubble, Pitcher, Ruby 20.00
Bubble, Plate, Blue, 6 1/2 In. .... 1.00 To 1.50
Bubble, Plate, Blue, 9 1/2 In. 10.00
Bubble, Plate, Blue, 10 In. 4.00
Bubble, Plate, Grill, Blue 5.75
Bubble, Platter, Blue .... 5.98 To 6.00
Bubble, Platter, Crystal 4.00
Bubble, Soup, Dish, Blue 5.50
Bubble, Sugar & Creamer, Blue 25.00
Bubble, Sugar & Creamer, Crystal 6.50
Bubble, Sugar & Creamer, Green 11.50
Bubble, Sugar, Green 6.00
Bubble, Tumbler, Red, Juice 6.00
Bubble, Tumbler, Red, Water 5.00
        BULLSEYE, see Bubble
        BUTTONS & BOWS, see Holiday
        CABBAGE ROSE, see Sharon
        CABBAGE ROSE WITH SINGLE ARCH, see Rosemary
        CABBAGE ROSE WITH TRIPLE ARCH, see Mayfair Federal
Cameo, Bottle, Green, Vinegar .... 18.00 To 20.00
Cameo, Bowl, Cereal, Green 13.50
Cameo, Bowl, Green, 7 1/2 In. .... 24.00 To 28.00
Cameo, Bowl, Green, 8 1/2 In. 22.00
Cameo, Bowl, Salad, Green .... 20.00 To 24.00
Cameo, Bowl, Vegetable, Green, Oval 13.50
Cameo, Bowl, Yellow, 5 1/2 In. 15.00
Cameo, Butter, Green, Covered 80.00
Cameo, Cake Plate, Green, Footed 12.00
Cameo, Cake Plate, Yellow, 2-Legged 22.00
Cameo, Cookie Jar, Green, Covered .... 27.00 To 35.00
Cameo, Creamer, Green .... 13.00 To 15.00
Cameo, Cup & Saucer, Topaz 10.50
Cameo, Cup & Saucer, Yellow 7.00
Cameo, Cup, Green 9.00
Cameo, Cup, Yellow 4.50

Cameo, Decanter, Green 48.00
Cameo, Dish, Candy, Green, Tall 115.00
Cameo, Dish, Candy, Green, 4 In. .... 30.00 To 38.00
Cameo, Goblet, Green .... 28.00 To 32.00
Cameo, Ice Bowl, Green .... 65.00 To 100.00
Cameo, Mayonnaise Set, Green 35.00
Cameo, Pitcher, Green, Juice, 6 In. 40.00
Cameo, Pitcher, Green, Water 32.00
Cameo, Plate, Green, Square, 8 1/2 In. 24.00
Cameo, Plate, Green, 6 In. .... 2.50 To 4.00
Cameo, Plate, Green, 8 In. 6.00
Cameo, Plate, Green, 10 In. .... 10.00 To 12.00
Cameo, Plate, Grill, Amber 9.00
Cameo, Plate, Grill, Green .... 6.00 To 7.00
Cameo, Plate, Grill, Yellow .... 5.00 To 7.00
Cameo, Plate, Grill, Yellow, Close Handled 6.50
Cameo, Plate, Yellow, Close Handled, 10 1/2 In. 7.00
Cameo, Plate, Yellow, 6 In. .... 2.25 To 2.50
Cameo, Plate, Yellow, 10 1/2 In. .... 6.25 To 7.00
Cameo, Platter, Green, Oval 14.00
Cameo, Platter, Yellow, 10 1/2 In. 18.00
Cameo, Relish, Green .... 8.00 To 12.50
Cameo, Salt & Pepper, Green 50.00
Cameo, Sherbet, Green, Tall 20.00
Cameo, Soup, Dish, Green, Flat 27.50
Cameo, Sugar & Creamer, Topaz 20.00
Cameo, Sugar & Creamer, Yellow 40.00
Cameo, Sugar, Green 8.00
Cameo, Tumbler, Green, Flat, 4 In. 16.50
Cameo, Tumbler, Green, Flat, 5 In. 18.00
Cameo, Tumbler, Green, Footed, 5 In. 18.50
Cameo, Tumbler, Yellow, Footed, 5 In. 11.00
Cameo, Vase, Green, 5 3/4 In. .... 80.00 To 100.00
Cameo, Vase, Green, 8 In. .... 15.00 To 18.50
Cameo, Wine 15.00
Cape Cod, Cocktail, Crystal, Footed 3.50
Cape Cod, Goblet, Crystal, Footed, 5 1/2 In. 6.00
Cape Cod, Sugar, Crystal 3.50
CHAIN DAISY, see Adam
CHERRY, see Cherry Blossom
Cherry Blossom, Berry Bowl, Green, 4 3/4 In. 9.00
Cherry Blossom, Berry Bowl, Green, 8 1/2 In. 14.50
Cherry Blossom, Berry Bowl, Pink, 4 3/4 In. 8.75
Cherry Blossom, Berry Bowl, Pink, 8 1/2 In. 15.00
Cherry Blossom, Bowl, Cereal, Green 18.00
Cherry Blossom, Bowl, Delphite, Handled, 9 In. 18.00
Cherry Blossom, Bowl, Delphite, 4 3/4 In. 10.00
Cherry Blossom, Bowl, Green, Footed, 10 In. 37.50
Cherry Blossom, Bowl, Pink, 4 3/4 In. .... 6.50 To 9.00
Cherry Blossom, Bowl, Vegetable, Pink, Oval, 9 In. 19.00
Cherry Blossom, Butter, Green, Covered .... 70.00 To 75.00
Cherry Blossom, Butter, Pink, Covered 65.00
Cherry Blossom, Cake Plate, Green .... 20.00 To 27.00
Cherry Blossom, Cake Plate, Pink .... 12.50 To 17.00
Cherry Blossom, Coaster, Green .... 8.50 To 9.00
Cherry Blossom, Coaster, Pink .... 10.00 To 12.50
Cherry Blossom, Creamer, Green .... 8.50 To 13.00
Cherry Blossom, Creamer, Pink .... 8.50 To 15.00
Cherry Blossom, Cup & Saucer, Delphite, Child's 36.00
Cherry Blossom, Cup & Saucer, Green 17.00
Cherry Blossom, Cup & Saucer, Pink .... 13.75 To 17.50
Cherry Blossom, Cup, Pink 12.50
Cherry Blossom, Dinner Set, Delphite, Child's, 14 Piece 195.00

Cherry Blossom, Goblet, Pink, Scalloped Bottom	20.00
Cherry Blossom, Pitcher, Delphite, 6 1/2 In.	85.00
Cherry Blossom, Pitcher, Green, Cone Shape	30.00
Cherry Blossom, Pitcher, Pink, Scalloped Base	30.00
Cherry Blossom, Plate, Delphite, 9 In.	13.00
Cherry Blossom, Plate, Green, Handled, 10 In.	12.00
Cherry Blossom, Plate, Green, 7 In.	14.00
Cherry Blossom, Plate, Grill, Green	16.00 To 16.50
Cherry Blossom, Plate, Pink, Handled, 10 1/4 In.	14.00
Cherry Blossom, Plate, Pink, 6 In.	4.50 To 5.50
Cherry Blossom, Plate, Pink, 7 In.	10.00 To 14.00
Cherry Blossom, Plate, Pink, 9 In.	11.00 To 13.50
Cherry Blossom, Plate, Pink, 10 In.	10.00 To 12.00
Cherry Blossom, Platter, Pink, Divided, Large	35.00
Cherry Blossom, Platter, Pink, Handled, 10 1/2 In.	15.00
Cherry Blossom, Saucer, Green	4.50
Cherry Blossom, Saucer, Pink	4.00 To 5.00
Cherry Blossom, Sherbet, Green	10.00 To 11.00
Cherry Blossom, Sherbet, Pink	9.00 To 11.00
Cherry Blossom, Sherbet, Pink, Footed	9.00
Cherry Blossom, Soup, Dish, Pink, Flat	32.00
Cherry Blossom, Sugar & Creamer, Green, Covered	34.00
Cherry Blossom, Sugar & Creamer, Pink	25.00 To 27.00
Cherry Blossom, Sugar, Delphite	12.50
Cherry Blossom, Sugar, Green	10.00
Cherry Blossom, Sugar, Green, Covered	8.00 To 30.00
Cherry Blossom, Sugar, Pink, Covered	15.00 To 22.50
Cherry Blossom, Tray, Delphite, 10 1/2 In.	18.00
Cherry Blossom, Tray, Pink, 2-Handled	15.00
Cherry Blossom, Tumbler, Green, Footed, 4 1/2 In.	28.00
Cherry Blossom, Tumbler, Green, Juice, Flat, 3 In.	12.00
Cherry Blossom, Tumbler, Green, Juice, Footed, 3 In.	12.00
Cherry Blossom, Tumbler, Green, 4 1/4 In.	16.50
Cherry Blossom, Tumbler, Pink, Footed, 4 1/2 In.	20.00
Cherry Blossom, Tumbler, Pink, Juice, Footed, Set Of 6	12.00
Cherry Blossom, Tumbler, Pink, 3 1/2 In.	12.50
Cherry Blossom, Tumbler, Pink, 4 1/4 In.	20.00
Chinex Classic, Butter, Ivory	15.00
Chinex Classic, Plate, Ivory, 6 1/4 In.	2.00
Circle, Bowl, Green, 4 1/2 In.	5.50
Circle, Sherbet, Green, Short	3.50
Circle, Sherbet, Green, Tall	5.50
Circle, Tumbler, Green, 5 In.	6.50
CIRCULAR RIBS, see Circle	
Cloverleaf, Ashtray, Black	50.00
Cloverleaf, Bowl, Cereal, Green	15.00
Cloverleaf, Bowl, Green, 4 In.	12.00
Cloverleaf, Cup & Saucer, Black	9.00 To 12.50
Cloverleaf, Cup & Saucer, Green	5.75
Cloverleaf, Cup & Saucer, Pink	6.00 To 6.50
Cloverleaf, Cup, Black	8.00
Cloverleaf, Plate, Black, 8 In.	9.00 To 10.00
Cloverleaf, Plate, Green, 6 In.	3.50 To 5.50
Cloverleaf, Salt & Pepper, Green	25.00
Cloverleaf, Saucer, Green	1.75
Cloverleaf, Sherbet, Black	12.00
Cloverleaf, Sherbet, Black, Footed, 3 In.	15.00
Cloverleaf, Sherbet, Pink	4.50
Cloverleaf, Sherbet, Yellow	7.00
Cloverleaf, Sugar & Creamer, Black	16.50 To 20.00
Cloverleaf, Sugar & Creamer, Yellow	16.50
Cloverleaf, Sugar, Black	8.00
Cloverleaf, Sugar, Green	5.50

Cloverleaf, Tumbler, Yellow, Footed, 5 3/4 In. 20.00
Colonial, Bowl, Green, 4 1/2 In. .... 5.50 To 7.00
Colonial, Bowl, Green, 9 In. 11.50
Colonial, Bowl, Vegetable, Green, Oval, 10 In. 12.00
Colonial, Butter, Crystal 25.00
Colonial, Butter, Crystal, Covered .... 12.00 To 14.00
Colonial, Butter, Pink, Covered 225.00
Colonial, Cocktail, Crystal, 4 In. 6.50
Colonial, Goblet, Green, 6 In. .... 16.00 To 20.00
Colonial, Pitcher, Pink, 7 3/4 In. 40.00
Colonial, Plate, Crystal, 10 In. 14.50
Colonial, Plate, Green, 6 In. 3.00
Colonial, Plate, Grill, Green .... 9.00 To 14.00
Colonial, Platter, Green, Oval, 12 In. 10.00
Colonial, Salt & Pepper, Crystal 60.00
Colonial, Salt & Pepper, Green 75.00
Colonial, Saltshaker, Green 75.00
Colonial, Sherbet, Green 7.50
Colonial, Sherbet, Green, Footed 8.00
Colonial, Soup, Cream, Green .... 17.50 To 30.00
Colonial, Sugar & Creamer, Green 23.00
Colonial, Sugar, Green, Open 9.00
Colonial, Sugar, Pink, Covered 20.00
Colonial, Tumbler, Crystal, Footed, 4 In. 5.00
Colonial, Tumbler, Green, Lemonade 27.00
Colonial, Tumbler, Green, 3 In. 9.50
Colonial, Whiskey, Green 8.00
Colonial, Wine, Crystal, 4 1/2 In. 6.75
Columbia, Plate, Crystal, 9 In. 4.50
Coronation, Berry Bowl, Pink, 8 In. 7.00
Coronation, Berry Bowl, Ruby Red, 8 In. 10.50
Coronation, Berry Set, Red, Master, 5 Bowls 28.00
Coronation, Plate, Pink, 6 In. 3.50
Coronation, Tumbler, Pink, Footed .... 5.00 To 6.00
   CRISS CROSS, see X Design
Cubist, Butter, Green, Covered 42.00
Cubist, Coaster, Green 3.50
Cubist, Creamer, Pink, 3 In. 4.00
Cubist, Cup & Saucer, Green 8.50
Cubist, Cup & Saucer, Pink 7.50
Cubist, Dish, Candy, Green, Covered .... 17.00 To 19.00
Cubist, Jar, Powder, Green .... 13.50 To 15.00
Cubist, Jar, Powder, Pink 13.50
Cubist, Pitcher, Pink, 8 3/4 In. .... 75.00 To 90.00
Cubist, Plate, Green, 6 In. 2.00
Cubist, Plate, Green, 8 In. 5.50
Cubist, Salt & Pepper, Green 17.00
Cubist, Salt & Pepper, Pink 22.00
Cubist, Sherbet, Green .... 5.50 To 6.00
Cubist, Sugar & Creamer, Amber 12.00
Cubist, Sugar & Creamer, Green 10.50
Cubist, Sugar & Creamer, Pink .... 4.00 To 6.00
Cubist, Sugar, Crystal 2.50
Cubist, Sugar, Green, Covered, Large 19.00
Cubist, Sugar, Pink, Covered, Large 10.00
Cubist, Tumbler, Green 27.00
   DAISY, see No. 620
   DAISY PETALS, see Petalware
   DANCING GIRL, see Cameo
   DANISH CRYSTAL, see Raindrops
   DIAMOND, see Windsor
   DIAMOND PATTERN, see Miss America
   DIAMOND POINT, see Petalware

Depression Glass, Cubist, Plate

Depression Glass, Dogwood, Plate

Depression Glass, Floral

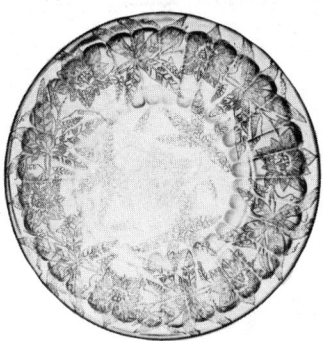

Depression Glass, Floral, Plate

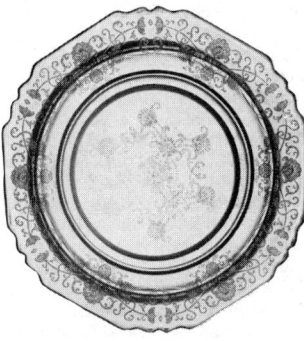

Depression Glass, Florentine No. 1, Plate

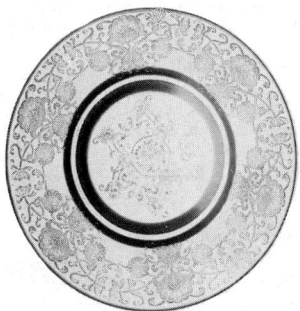

Depression Glass, Florentine No. 2, Plate

Diamond Quilted, Creamer, Green 6.50
Diamond Quilted, Cup, Black 5.50
Diamond Quilted, Dish, Candy, Pink 6.00
Diamond Quilted, Sugar & Creamer, Green 15.00
Diana, Bowl, Pink, 5 In. 4.25
Diana, Cup, Pink 4.75
Dish, Candy, Green, Covered 36.00
Dogwood, Bowl, Cereal, Pink 12.00
Dogwood, Cup & Saucer, Pink .... 10.00 To 11.50
Dogwood, Plate, Crystal, 8 In. 4.00
Dogwood, Plate, Grill, Pink 10.00
Dogwood, Plate, Pink, 6 In. .... 3.00 To 22.50
Dogwood, Plate, Pink, 8 In. .... 3.50 To 4.00
Dogwood, Plate, Pink, 9 1/4 In. .... 14.00 To 17.00
Dogwood, Saucer, Pink 3.00
Dogwood, Sugar & Creamer, Pink, 3 1/4 In. 21.00
Dogwood, Tumbler, Pink, Juice 5.00
Dogwood, Water Set, Pink, 5 Tumblers 250.00
Dolphin, Candlestick, Amber, 6-Sided Base, Pair 20.00
Doric & Pansy, Cup, Pink 22.00
Doric & Pansy, Tumbler, Teal, 4 1/2 In. 20.00
Doric, Bowl, Pink, 8 1/4 In. 9.00
Doric, Creamer, Green 5.00
Doric, Creamer, Pink .... 5.00 To 6.50
Doric, Dish, Candy, Delphite, 3-Section, Metal Holder 30.00
Doric, Dish, Candy, Pink 35.00
Doric, Dish, Candy, Pink, Covered 20.00
Doric, Pitcher, Pink, Flat, 6 In. 22.00
Doric, Plate, Green, 10 In. 7.50
Doric, Plate, Pink, 6 In. 3.50
Doric, Salt & Pepper, Green .... 12.50 To 35.00
Doric, Saltshaker, Pink 12.50
Doric, Sherbet, Pink 6.00
Doric, Sugar & Creamer, Green 35.00
Doric, Sugar, Pink, Covered 20.00
Doric, Tray, Green, 4 X 4 In. 7.50
Doric, Tray, Pink, Square 10.00
Doric, Tumbler, Green, 4 1/2 In. 45.00
    DOUBLE SHIELD, see Mt. Pleasant
    DOUBLE SWIRL, see Swirl
    DRAPE & TASSEL, see Princess
    DUTCH ROSE, see Rosemary
English Hobnail, Salt & Pepper, Green .... 50.00 To 95.00
Fairfax, Bowl, Black, Open Handled 11.50
Fairfax, Cup & Saucer, Topaz 7.00
Fairfax, Plate, Topaz, 8 3/4 In. 6.00
    FAN & FEATHER, see Adam
    FINE RIB, see also Homespun
Fine Rib, Pitcher, Blue, Juice 25.00
Fine Rib, Salt & Pepper, Blue 12.00
Fine Rib, Tumbler, Blue, 4 In. 5.75
    FLAT DIAMOND, see Diamond Quilted
Floragold, Ashtray, Iridescent 5.50
Floragold, Bowl, Iridescent, Square, 8 1/4 In. 10.00
Floragold, Bowl, Pink, Square 2.50
Floragold, Plate, Cheese & Cracker, Iridescent 45.00
Floragold, Plate, Green, 8 1/2 In. 1.50
Floragold, Plate, Iridescent, 10 In. 15.00
Floragold, Sherbet, Iridescent 7.50
Floral & Diamond Band, Sherbet, Green 4.50
Floral & Diamond Band, Tumbler, Green, 4 In. 7.50
Floral, Bowl, Green, Oval, 9 In. 10.00
Floral, Bowl, Pink, 4 In. 12.00

Floral, Butter, Pink, Covered .... 65.00 To 85.00
Floral, Candlestick, Green, Pair 57.00
Floral, Candlestick, Pink, Pair 40.00
Floral, Coaster, Green 7.50
Floral, Coaster, Pink 6.50
Floral, Creamer, Green 9.50
Floral, Creamer, Pink 9.00
Floral, Cup & Saucer, Green 15.00
Floral, Cup & Saucer, Pink 12.50
Floral, Dish, Candy, Green, Covered .... 29.00 To 33.50
Floral, Dish, Candy, Pink 25.00
Floral, Dish, Candy, Pink, Covered 20.00
Floral, Ice Tub, Pink, 8 1/4 In.Long 250.00
Floral, Lamp Base, Green 65.00
Floral, Pitcher, Green, Lemonade, 10 1/4 In. 225.00
Floral, Pitcher, Green, 8 In. 22.00
Floral, Pitcher, Pink, Lemonade, 10 1/4 In. 140.00
Floral, Pitcher, Pink, 8 In. .... 15.00 To 26.00
Floral, Plate, Green, 6 In. 4.50
Floral, Plate, Green, 8 In. 9.50
Floral, Plate, Green, 9 In. 14.50
Floral, Plate, Pink, 6 In. 3.50
Floral, Plate, Pink, 8 In. 7.50
Floral, Plate, Pink, 9 In. 10.50
Floral, Platter, Pink, 10 3/4 In. 10.00
Floral, Salt & Pepper, Green, Footed 32.00
Floral, Salt & Pepper, Pink, Flat 27.50
Floral, Salt & Pepper, Pink, Footed .... 25.00 To 30.00
Floral, Saltshaker, Pink, Footed, Single 15.00
Floral, Sherbet, Pink 9.50
Floral, Sugar & Creamer, Green 17.50
Floral, Sugar & Creamer, Green, Covered 30.00
Floral, Sugar & Creamer, Pink 20.00
Floral, Sugar, Green, Covered 15.75
Floral, Sugar, Pink, Covered 25.00
Floral, Tumbler, Green, 4 In. 12.00
Floral, Tumbler, Pink, Footed, 4 3/4 In. .... 8.00 To 11.50
Floral, Tumbler, Pink, 4 3/4 In. 12.00
Florentine No.1, Butter, Pink, Covered 150.00
Florentine No.1, Creamer, Clear 5.00
Florentine No.1, Creamer, Clear, Ruffled 15.00
Florentine No.1, Creamer, Green 6.75
Florentine No.1, Creamer, Pink 9.00
Florentine No.1, Cup & Saucer, Clear 5.00
Florentine No.1, Cup & Saucer, Green 12.00
Florentine No.1, Cup & Saucer, Pink 10.00
Florentine No.1, Cup & Saucer, Yellow 10.00
Florentine No.1, Pitcher, Clear, Footed, 6 1/2 In. 25.00
Florentine No.1, Pitcher, Green, 6 1/2 In. 28.50
Florentine No.1, Pitcher, Pink, 6 1/2 In. 40.00
Florentine No.1, Plate, Green, 9 In. 5.00
Florentine No.1, Plate, Pink, 6 In. 4.50
Florentine No.1, Plate, Yellow, 10 In. 11.50
Florentine No.1, Salt & Pepper, Pink 45.00
Florentine No.1, Saltshaker, Crystal 10.00
Florentine No.1, Sherbet, Green 8.50
Florentine No.1, Sherbet, Pink 7.00
Florentine No.1, Sugar & Creamer, Green, Covered 27.50
Florentine No.1, Tumbler, Green, Footed, Juice 8.75
Florentine No.1, Tumbler, Green, Footed, 4 3/4 In. 15.00
Florentine No.1, Tumbler, Pink, Footed, 5 In. 15.00
Florentine No.1, Tumbler, Yellow, Juice, Footed, 3 1/4 In. 12.00
Florentine No.2, Berry Bowl, Green, Small 8.50

Florentine No.2, Berry Bowl, Yellow, Large, 8 1/2 In. 22.00
Florentine No.2, Butter, Yellow, Covered 85.00
Florentine No.2, Coaster, Green 8.00
Florentine No.2, Creamer, Yellow .... 7.50 To 10.00
Florentine No.2, Cup & Saucer, Green 10.00
Florentine No.2, Cup & Saucer, Yellow 10.00
Florentine No.2, Cup, Yellow 6.00
Florentine No.2, Gravy Boat, Yellow 37.50
Florentine No.2, Gravy Boat, Yellow, Underplate 55.00
Florentine No.2, Pitcher, Yellow, Flat, 8 In. 125.00
Florentine No.2, Pitcher, Yellow, Footed, 7 1/2 In. 17.50
Florentine No.2, Plate, Green, 6 In. 1.50
Florentine No.2, Plate, Yellow, 6 In. 4.00
Florentine No.2, Salt & Pepper, Green .... 25.00 To 30.00
Florentine No.2, Salt & Pepper, Yellow 37.50
Florentine No.2, Saltshaker, Yellow 16.50
Florentine No.2, Sherbet, Green 7.50
Florentine No.2, Sherbet, Yellow .... 7.00 To 8.50
Florentine No.2, Soup, Cream, Green .... 7.00 To 7.50
Florentine No.2, Sugar & Creamer, Yellow 30.00
Florentine No.2, Sugar, Yellow, Covered 25.00
Florentine No.2, Tumbler, Green, Flat, 4 In. .... 8.50 To 11.00
Florentine No.2, Tumbler, Pink, Juice, 3 1/2 In. 12.50
Florentine No.2, Tumbler, Pink, 4 In. 9.50
Florentine No.2, Tumbler, Yellow, Footed, 3 1/4 In. 10.00
    FLOWER BASKET, see No. 615
Forest Green, Tumbler, 5 Ounce 1.50
Forest Green, Tumbler, 10 Ounce 2.50
Fortune, Dish, Candy, Pink, Covered 4.50
    FROSTED BLOCK, see Beaded Block
Fruits, Sherbet, Green 4.75
Fruits, Sherbet, Pink 3.75
Georgian, Bowl, Green, 4 1/2 In. 4.25
Georgian, Bowl, Green, 5 3/4 In. .... 9.00 To 10.00
Georgian, Bowl, Green, 6 1/2 In. 35.00
Georgian, Bowl, Green, 7 1/2 In. .... 32.00 To 35.00
Georgian, Butter, Green, Covered .... 55.00 To 60.00
Georgian, Creamer, Green 6.50
Georgian, Cup & Saucer, Green .... 8.50 To 9.50
Georgian, Hot Plate, Crystal, 5 In. 5.00
Georgian, Plate, Sherbet, Green, 6 In. 2.00
Georgian, Saucer, Green .... 1.75 To 2.25
Georgian, Sherbet, Green .... 6.50 To 7.50
Georgian, Sugar & Creamer, Green, Covered .... 30.00 To 35.00
Georgian, Tumbler, Green, 4 In. .... 25.00 To 27.00
Georgian, Tumbler, Green, 5 1/4 In. 40.00
    GLADIOLI, see Royal Lace
Grape, Vase, Pink, Crystal Foot, 8 In. 5.00
    HAIRPIN, see Newport
    HANGING BASKET, see No. 615
Heritage, Bowl, Crystal, 10 1/2 In. 6.50
Heritage, Creamer, Crystal 10.00
Heritage, Cup & Saucer, Crystal 4.75
Heritage, Cup, Crystal 2.50
Heritage, Plate, Crystal, 8 In. 4.00
Heritage, Plate, Crystal, 10 In. 5.50
Heritage, Plate, Crystal, 12 In. 5.00
    HINGE, see Patrician
Hobnail, Cup & Saucer, Pink 4.50
Hobnail, Plate, Pink, 8 1/2 In. 2.50
Holiday, Berry Bowl, Pink, 8 In. 6.00
Holiday, Berry Bowl, Pink, 8 1/2 In. 12.50
Holiday, Butter, Pink, Covered .... 27.50 To 30.00

Holiday, Creamer, Pink	6.00
Holiday, Cup & Saucer, Pink	6.00
Holiday, Cup, Pink	4.50
Holiday, Pitcher, Iridescent, Milk, 4 3/4 In.	12.00
Holiday, Pitcher, Pink, Milk, 4 3/4 In.	45.00
Holiday, Pitcher, Pink, 6 3/4 In.	25.00
Holiday, Plate	1.75
Holiday, Plate, Pink, 6 1/2 In.	2.50
Holiday, Plate, Pink, 8 1/2 In.	2.50
Holiday, Plate, Pink, 9 In.	7.50
Holiday, Plate, Pink, 10 1/2 In.	8.00
Holiday, Platter, Iridescent, Oval, 11 3/8 In.	10.50
Holiday, Platter, Pink, Oval, 11 3/8 In.	8.50
Holiday, Saucer, Pink	2.00 To 2.50
Holiday, Saucer, Pink, Rayed	2.50
Holiday, Sherbet, Pink, Footed	5.00
Holiday, Tray, Iridescent, Handled, 10 1/2 In.	6.00
Holiday, Tumbler, Iridescent, Juice, Footed	5.00
Holiday, Tumbler, Pink, Flat, 4 In.	11.00
HOMESPUN, see also Fine Rib	
Homespun, Cup, Pink	5.75
Homespun, Tumbler, Pink, Flat, 4 In.	5.00
Homespun, Tumbler, Pink, Footed, 5 1/4 In.	15.00
Homespun, Wine, Pink, Footed	5.00
Honeycomb, Creamer, Green	3.50
Honeycomb, Mixing Bowl, Delphite, 1 1/2 Gallon	22.50
Honeycomb, Saltshaker, Green	6.00
HORIZONTAL RIBBED, see Manhattan	
HORIZONTAL ROUNDED BIG RIB, see Manhattan	
HORIZONTAL SHARP BIG RIB, see Manhattan	
HORSESHOE, see No. 612	
Indiana Custard, Bowl, White, 8 3/4 In.	17.50
IRIS & HERRINGBONE, see Iris	
Iris, Bowl, Crystal, Ruffled, 9 1/2 In.	9.00
Iris, Bowl, Crystal, Ruffled, 11 In.	11.00
Iris, Bowl, Iridescent, 4 1/2 In.	5.50
Iris, Butter, Iridescent, Covered	28.00
Iris, Cake Plate, Amber	12.00
Iris, Coaster, Crystal	35.00
Iris, Creamer, Crystal	4.00 To 5.00
Iris, Creamer, Iridescent	5.50
Iris, Cup & Saucer, Crystal	10.00
Iris, Cup & Saucer, Iridescent	10.50 To 11.00
Iris, Cup, Iridescent	8.00
Iris, Goblet, Crystal, 4 Ounce	10.00 To 12.75
Iris, Plate, Crystal, 9 In.	18.00 To 25.00
Iris, Sherbet, Crystal, 4 In.	10.00
Iris, Sugar, Crystal, Covered	10.00
Iris, Sugar, Marigold, Covered	7.00
Iris, Tumbler, Iridescent, Footed, 6 In.	8.50
KNIFE & FORK, see Colonial	
Lace Edge, Bowl, Cereal, Pink	8.50
Lace Edge, Bowl, Pink, Ribbed, 9 1/2 In.	10.00 To 20.00
Lace Edge, Bowl, Pink, 3-Footed, 10 1/2 In.	100.00
Lace Edge, Bowl, Pink, 7 1/2 In.	7.50 To 18.50
Lace Edge, Bowl, Pink, 7 3/4 In.	7.50
Lace Edge, Bowl, Pink, 9 1/2 In.	9.00 To 12.00
Lace Edge, Butter, Pink	30.00
Lace Edge, Butter, Pink, Covered	20.00 To 40.00
Lace Edge, Cookie Jar, Pink	38.50
Lace Edge, Creamer, Pink	12.00
Lace Edge, Cup & Saucer, Pink	20.00
Lace Edge, Cup, Pink	12.50

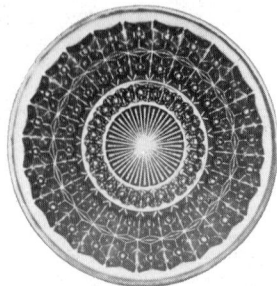

Depression Glass, Holiday

Depression Glass, Iris, Beaded Edge

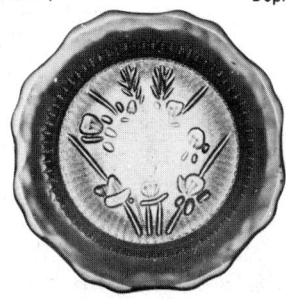

Depression Glass, Iris, Ruffled Edge

Depression Glass, **Laurel**

Depression Glass, Madrid

Depression Glass, Open Rose

Lace Edge, Flower Bowl & Frog, Pink 15.00
Lace Edge, Plate, Grill, Pink .... 10.00 To 15.00
Lace Edge, Plate, Grill, Yellow 11.00
Lace Edge, Plate, Pink, 7 1/4 In. 11.00
Lace Edge, Plate, Pink, 8 3/4 In. .... 7.00 To 8.50
Lace Edge, Platter, Pink, 4-Part .... 15.00 To 20.00
Lace Edge, Platter, Pink, 5-Part, 12 3/4 In. 15.00
Lace Edge, Relish, Pink, 10 1/2 In. .... 12.00 To 15.00
Lace Edge, Relish, Yellow, 10 1/2 In. 12.50
Lace Edge, Saucer, Pink 5.50
Lace Edge, Sherbet, Pink, Footed .... 28.50 To 50.00
Lace Edge, Sugar & Creamer, Pink 20.00
Lace Edge, Sugar, Pink 12.00
Lace Edge, Tumbler, Pink, Flat 9.00
Lace Edge, Tumbler, Pink, Footed 32.00
    LACEY DAISY, see No. 618
Laurel, Bowl, Green, 11 In. 12.50
Laurel, Bowl, Ivory, 6 In. 6.50
Laurel, Bowl, Ivory, 9 In. 11.00
Laurel, Plate, Green, 9 1/4 In. .... 4.50 To 7.00
Laurel, Plate, Grill, Ivory 7.00
Laurel, Tea Set, Child's, Red Band, 14 Piece 220.00
    LIBERTY WORKS, see American Pioneer
    LILY MEDALLION, see American Sweetheart
    LINCOLN DRAPE, see Princess
Lincoln Inn, Goblet, Jade 10.00
    LOOP, see Lace Edge
    LORAIN, see No. 615
    LOUISA, see Floragold
    LOVEBIRDS, see Georgian
    LYDIA RAY, see New Century
Madrid, Bowl, Amber, Square, 9 1/2 In. 18.00
Madrid, Bowl, Amber, 9 1/2 In. .... 18.00 To 22.50
Madrid, Bowl, Amber, 10 In. 8.00
Madrid, Bowl, Console, Pink 7.50
Madrid, Bowl, Pink, 5 In. 4.00
Madrid, Bowl, Vegetable, Green, Oval 10.00
Madrid, Cake Plate, Amber 10.50
Madrid, Candlestick, Amber, Pair 15.00
Madrid, Candlestick, Crystal, Single 4.50
Madrid, Candlestick, Iridescent, Pair 10.00
Madrid, Candlestick, Pink, Pair 18.00
Madrid, Cookie Jar, Amber, Covered 28.00
Madrid, Cup & Saucer, Amber 6.50
Madrid, Jar, Jam, Amber 14.00
Madrid, Jell-O Mold, Amber .... 5.00 To 8.00
Madrid, Pitcher, Amber, Water, 8 1/2 In. 45.00
Madrid, Pitcher, Amber, 5 1/2 In. 20.00
Madrid, Pitcher, Amber, 8 In. .... 26.00 To 32.00
Madrid, Plate, Amber, Square, 7 1/2 In. 7.00
Madrid, Plate, Grill, Amber 8.50
Madrid, Platter, Amber .... 8.50 To 11.00
Madrid, Platter, Blue 22.00
Madrid, Relish, Pink 7.50
Madrid, Salt & Pepper, Amber 30.00
Madrid, Salt & Pepper, Amber, Flat .... 35.00 To 48.00
Madrid, Saltshaker, Green 25.00
Madrid, Saucer, Pink 3.50
Madrid, Sherbet, Amber, Cone Shaped .... 5.00 To 5.50
Madrid, Sherbet, Amber, Footed .... 4.50 To 5.00
Madrid, Soup, Dish, Amber 7.00
Madrid, Sugar & Creamer, Amber 25.00
Madrid, Sugar & Creamer, Amber, Open 12.50

Madrid, Sugar, Amber 5.00
Madrid, Sugar, Amber, Covered 25.00
Madrid, Sugar, Blue, Covered 100.00
Madrid, Tumbler, Amber, Juice, Flat 12.50
Madrid, Tumbler, Amber, 5 1/2 In. 14.00
Madrid, Tumbler, Green, Footed, 10 Ounce 24.00
Madrid, Tumbler, Pink, 4 1/4 In. 9.00
   MAGNOLIA, see Dogwood
Manhattan, Ashtray, Crystal 5.25
Manhattan, Ashtray, Crystal, Square 12.00
Manhattan, Pitcher, Crystal, 42 Ounce 11.50
Manhattan, Plate, Crystal, 10 In. 10.00
Manhattan, Relish, Ruby, Inserts 4.00
Manhattan, Salt & Pepper, Pink .... 15.00 To 18.00
Manhattan, Sugar & Creamer, Pink 14.00
Manhattan, Sugar & Creamer, Pink, Scalloped 22.50
Manhattan, Tumbler, Crystal, Footed 5.00
Manhattan, Tumbler, Pink 8.50
   MANY WINDOWS, see Roulette
Mayfair Federal, Bowl, Vegetable, Amber, Oval, 10 In. 12.00
Mayfair Federal, Creamer, Crystal 6.50
Mayfair Federal, Saucer, Amber 2.00
Mayfair Federal, Saucer, Crystal 1.50
Mayfair Federal, Soup, Cream, Crystal 8.50
Mayfair Federal, Soup, Cream, Green 5.00
Mayfair Federal, Sugar, Footed, Amber 10.00
Mayfair Federal, Tumbler, Green, 4 1/2 In. 15.00
   MAYFAIR OPEN ROSE, see also Rosemary
Mayfair Open Rose, Bowl, Cereal, Pink 11.50
Mayfair Open Rose, Bowl, Green, Flat, 11 3/4 In. 16.50
Mayfair Open Rose, Bowl, Green, 12 In. 14.00
Mayfair Open Rose, Bowl, Pink, Covered, 10 In. 50.00
Mayfair Open Rose, Bowl, Pink, Handled, 7 In. 15.00
Mayfair Open Rose, Butter, Blue, Covered 225.00
Mayfair Open Rose, Cake Plate, Footed, Blue 35.00
Mayfair Open Rose, Cake Plate, Green, Center Handle 20.00
Mayfair Open Rose, Cake Plate, Pink, Handled, 12 In. 27.00
Mayfair Open Rose, Cocktail, Pink, 3 1/2 Ounce 40.00
Mayfair Open Rose, Creamer, Pink, Footed 11.00
Mayfair Open Rose, Cup & Saucer, Pink 15.00
Mayfair Open Rose, Cup, Blue 28.00
Mayfair Open Rose, Cup, Pink 10.50
Mayfair Open Rose, Decanter, 6 Shot Glasses, Pink 350.00
Mayfair Open Rose, Dish, Candy, Pink 38.00
Mayfair Open Rose, Dish, Candy, Pink, Covered .... 36.00 To 37.50
Mayfair Open Rose, Goblet, Pink, Set Of 5, Water, 5 3/4 In. 175.00
Mayfair Open Rose, Goblet, Pink, Water, 5 3/4 In. 20.00
Mayfair Open Rose, Goblet, Pink, Wine, 4 1/2 In. 45.00
Mayfair Open Rose, Pitcher, Pink, 6 In. .... 19.00 To 37.50
Mayfair Open Rose, Pitcher, Pink, 8 In. .... 22.00 To 30.00
Mayfair Open Rose, Plate, Blue, 10 In. 30.00
Mayfair Open Rose, Plate, Pink, 8 1/2 In. .... 9.00 To 14.00
Mayfair Open Rose, Plate, Pink, 10 In. 28.00
Mayfair Open Rose, Platter, Blue, 12 In. 18.50
Mayfair Open Rose, Relish, Blue, 10 In. 19.50
Mayfair Open Rose, Sandwich Plate, Blue .... 28.50 To 40.00
Mayfair Open Rose, Sandwich Plate, Green 18.50
Mayfair Open Rose, Sandwich Plate, Pink, Large Handle 27.50
Mayfair Open Rose, Sherbet, Blue 45.00
Mayfair Open Rose, Soup, Cream, Pink 28.00
Mayfair Open Rose, Sugar & Creamer, Blue 70.00
Mayfair Open Rose, Sugar, Pink, Frosted 10.00
Mayfair Open Rose, Tumbler, Blue, Flat, 4 1/4 In. 55.00

Mayfair Open Rose, Tumbler, Pink, Footed, 5 1/2 In.	18.00
Mayfair Open Rose, Tumbler, Pink, 6 1/2 In.	25.00
Mayfair Open Rose, Vase, Sweet Pea	62.50
Mayfair Open Rose, Vegetable, Bowl, Blue, Covered	65.00
Mayfair, Plate, Pink, 6 In.	7.50
MEADOW FLOWER, see No. 618	
MEANDERING VINE, see Madrid	
Miss America, Berry Bowl, Pink, 6 1/4 In.	9.00
Miss America, Bowl, Green, Oval, 10 In.	14.00
Miss America, Bowl, Pink, Oval, 10 In.	12.50 To 18.50
Miss America, Butter, Crystal, Metal Top	25.00
Miss America, Butter, Pink, Paneled	150.00 To 350.00
Miss America, Cake Plate, Pink, Footed, 12 In.	30.00
Miss America, Candy Jar, Pink	75.00
Miss America, Coaster, Pink	18.50
Miss America, Creamer, Pink	9.50 To 11.00
Miss America, Cup & Saucer, Pink	15.50 To 16.50
Miss America, Cup, Green	6.00 To 10.00
Miss America, Dish, Candy, Crystal	60.00
Miss America, Dish, Relish, Crystal	6.00
Miss America, Goblet, Pink, 5 1/2 In.	20.00
Miss America, Goblet, Wine, Pink, Footed	42.50
Miss America, Pitcher, Crystal, Ice Lip, 8 In.	48.00
Miss America, Pitcher, Pink, 8 In.	80.00
Miss America, Plate, Crystal, 10 1/4 In.	8.00
Miss America, Plate, Grill, Crystal	6.00
Miss America, Plate, Grill, Pink	10.00
Miss America, Plate, Pink, 8 1/2 In.	8.50
Miss America, Platter, Pink, 12 1/4 In.	10.00 To 16.50
Miss America, Salt & Pepper, Pink	30.00 To 45.00
Miss America, Sherbet, Crystal	6.00
Miss America, Sherbet, Pink	10.00
Miss America, Sugar & Creamer, Crystal	15.00
Miss America, Sugar & Creamer, Pink	25.00 To 38.50
Miss America, Sugar, Crystal	7.00
Miss America, Tumbler, Pink, Flat, 4 1/2 In.	20.00
Miss America, Tumbler, Pink, 6 3/4 In.	42.00
MODERNE ART, see Tea Room	
Moderntone, Bowl, Cobalt Blue, 5 In.	9.00
Moderntone, Creamer, Cobalt Blue	4.00
Moderntone, Cup & Saucer, Cobalt Blue	8.00 To 10.00
Moderntone, Cup, Pink	1.50
Moderntone, Custard, Cobalt Blue	6.00
Moderntone, Dish, Candy, Cobalt Blue, Ruffled	18.75
Moderntone, Plate, Cobalt Blue, 7 3/4 In.	1.00 To 3.50
Moderntone, Plate, Cobalt Blue, 8 7/8 In.	6.50
Moderntone, Plate, Cobalt Blue, 10 1/2 In.	6.00 To 16.50
Moderntone, Plate, Pink, 8 7/8 In.	1.25
Moderntone, Salt & Pepper, Cobalt Blue	16.00 To 20.00
Moderntone, Salt & Pepper, Pink	4.00
Moderntone, Saucer, Cobalt Blue	1.00
Moderntone, Sherbet, Yellow	1.75
Moderntone, Soup, Cream, Cobalt Blue, Pair	15.00
Moderntone, Sugar & Creamer, Cobalt Blue	6.00 To 18.00
Moderntone, Sugar, Cobalt Blue	4.00 To 5.00
Moderntone, Sugar, Pale Green	2.00
Moderntone, Tumbler, Cobalt Blue, 4 1/4 In.	10.00
Moondrops, Butter, Amber, Covered	190.00
Moondrops, Cup & Saucer, Amber	5.00
Moondrops, Goblet, Wine, Amber, 4 In.	7.50
Moondrops, Goblet, Wine, Ruby, Chrome Stem, 5 1/4 In.	9.50
Moondrops, Pitcher, Red, Ice, Lip	200.00
Moondrops, Plate, Amber, 9 3/8 In.	5.00

Moondrops, Sugar, Amber	4.00
Moondrops, Tumbler, Red, 4 7/8 In.	16.00
Moonstone, Bottle, Cologne, Stopper	9.50 To 15.00
Moonstone, Bowl, Cloverleaf	8.00 To 9.00
Moonstone, Bowl, Crimped, 5 1/2 In.	4.00
Moonstone, Bowl, Crimped, 7 3/4 In.	7.50
Moonstone, Candleholder, Pair	9.00 To 13.50
Moonstone, Cup & Saucer	7.00
Moonstone, Jar, Powder, Covered	9.20 To 15.00
Moonstone, Plate, 6 In.	4.75
Moonstone, Relish	5.00 To 6.50
Moonstone, Relish, Divided	6.00 To 6.50
Moonstone, Sherbet	4.00 To 6.00
Moonstone, Sugar & Creamer	8.20 To 15.00
Moonstone, Tumbler, Footed	14.00
Mt. Pleasant, Bowl, Cobalt Blue, Square, 4 In.	10.00
Mt. Pleasant, Bowl, 3-Legged, Cobalt Blue, 5 1/2 In.	15.00
Mt. Pleasant, Cup & Saucer, Cobalt Blue	9.50
Mt. Pleasant, Plate, Black, Open Handled, 8 In.	8.50
Mt. Pleasant, Salt & Pepper, Cobalt Blue	35.00
Mt. Pleasant, Saltshaker, Cobalt Blue	17.50
Mt. Pleasant, Tumbler, Cobalt Blue	10.00 To 11.00
New Century, Butter, Green, Covered	40.00
New Century, Cup, Green	5.00
New Century, Pitcher, Cobalt Blue, 8 1/2 In.	30.00
New Century, Tumbler, Amethyst, Flat, 4 1/8 In.	7.50
New Century, Tumbler, Cobalt Blue, 3 1/2 In.	7.00
New Century, Tumbler, Cobalt Blue, 5 1/4 In.	5.50
Newport, Bowl, Cereal, Amethyst	8.50
Newport, Bowl, Cobalt Blue, 4 1/4 In.	8.00
Newport, Creamer, Amethyst	5.50
Newport, Cup & Saucer, Amethyst	6.50
Newport, Cup & Saucer, Cobalt Blue	5.50 To 8.50
Newport, Cup, Cobalt Blue	4.50 To 5.75
Newport, Plate, Amethyst, 6 In.	4.50
Newport, Plate, Amethyst, 8 1/2 In.	4.50 To 5.00
Newport, Plate, Cobalt Blue, 8 1/2 In.	6.00
Newport, Platter, Cobalt Blue	10.50
Newport, Salt & Pepper, Cobalt Blue	27.50
Newport, Saucer, Amethyst	2.00
Newport, Sherbet, Amethyst	6.00 To 7.50
Newport, Sherbet, Cobalt Blue	8.00

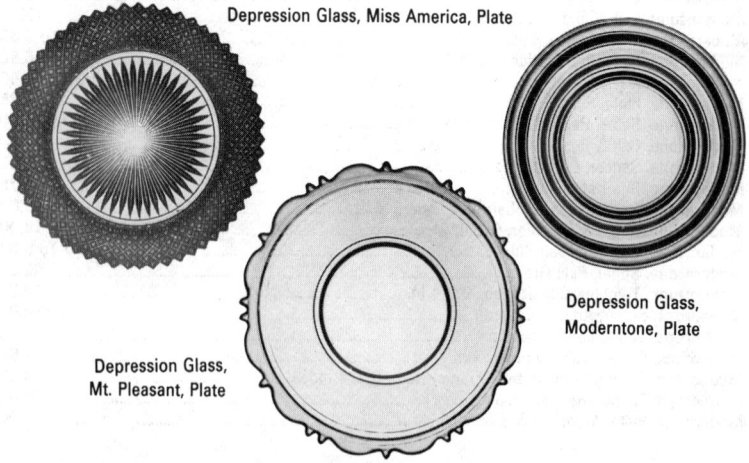

Depression Glass, Miss America, Plate

Depression Glass,
Moderntone, Plate

Depression Glass,
Mt. Pleasant, Plate

Depression Glass, No. 612

Newport, Sherbet, White	3.00
Newport, Sugar & Creamer, Cobalt Blue	13.50
Newport, Sugar, Amethyst	5.00
No.610, Berry Bowl, Yellow, 4 3/4 In.	20.00
No.610, Bowl, Vegetable, Pink, Oval	35.00
No.610, Creamer, Yellow	25.00
No.610, Water Set, Yellow, Footed Tumblers, 9 Piece	760.00
No.612, Bowl, Iridescent, 8 In.	10.00
No.612, Butter, Green, Covered	400.00
No.612, Creamer, Yellow	15.00
No.612, Cup & Saucer, Green	9.00 To 12.50
No.612, Pitcher, Green, Footed, 8 3/4 In.	125.00
No.612, Plate	3.75
No.612, Plate, Green, 8 3/8 In.	6.50
No.612, Plate, Yellow, 6 In.	3.50
No.612, Platter, Yellow	10.00 To 12.50
No.612, Saucer, Green	3.00
No.612, Sherbet, Green	9.00
No.612, Sugar & Creamer, Yellow	15.00
No.612, Sugar, Green	9.50
No.612, Tumbler, Green, Footed, 9 Ounce	12.50
No.615, Bowl, Yellow, 7 1/2 In.	32.50 To 45.00
No.615, Cup, Yellow	12.00
No.615, Dish, Candy, Crystal, 8 3/4 In.	12.00
No.615, Plate, Yellow, 5 1/2 In.	5.00
No.615, Plate, Yellow, 7 3/4 In.	8.00 To 8.50
No.615, Plate, Yellow, 10 1/2 In.	32.00
No.615, Relish, Crystal	10.00
No.615, Relish, Yellow	18.00
No.615, Relish, Yellow, 8 In.	12.50
No.615, Saucer, Yellow	3.50
No.615, Sherbet, Yellow	20.00 To 25.00
No.616, Coaster, Yellow	15.00
No.616, Cup & Saucer, Crystal	7.50
No.616, Cup & Saucer, Yellow	16.00
No.616, Cup, Yellow	9.00
No.616, Pitcher, Yellow, 60 Ounce	30.00
No.616, Sherbet, Yellow	12.50
No.616, Sugar, Yellow, Covered	25.00
No.616, Tumbler, Yellow, Footed, 5 In.	20.00
No.618, Bowl, Crystal, 6 In.	16.00
No.618, Creamer, Amber	10.00
No.618, Platter, Crystal	9.00
No.618, Sugar, Crystal	5.50
No.620, Berry Bowl, Amber, Large	16.50
No.620, Berry Bowl, Amber, Small	5.50
No.620, Cake Plate, Amber, 11 1/2 In.	8.00
No.620, Plate, Amber, 8 3/8 In.	5.00

No.620, Plate, Green, 8 In. 7.50
No.620, Relish, Amber 14.50
No.620, Sherbet, Green 4.50
No.620, Soup, Cream, Amber .... 5.00 To 5.50
Normandie, Bowl, Cereal, Iridescent 5.50
Normandie, Bowl, Vegetable, Iridescent, Oval 8.50
Normandie, Cup & Saucer, Iridescent 5.50
Normandie, Cup, Iridescent 4.00
Normandie, Pitcher, Amber 45.00
Normandie, Plate, Grill, Iridescent 5.00
Normandie, Platter, Iridescent 7.50
Normandie, Sherbet, Amber 4.00
Normandie, Sherbet, Iridescent 2.75
Normandie, Tumbler, Amber, 6 In. 105.00
Normandie, Water Set, 6 Tumblers, Amber 105.00
Old Cafe, Dish, Candy, Pink .... 5.00 To 7.00
Old Cafe, Dish, Candy, Ruby, Covered 7.50
Old Cafe, Saucer, Crystal 3.50
Old Cafe, Tumbler, Pink, Flat, 4 In. 12.50
          OLD FLORENTINE, see Florentine No. 1
          OPEN LACE, see Lace Edge
          OPEN ROSE, see Mayfair Open Rose
          OPEN SCALLOP, see Lace Edge
          OPTIC DESIGN, see Raindrops
          ORIENTAL POPPY, see Florentine No. 2
          OREGON GRAPE, see Woolworth
          OVIDE, see also New Century
Oyster & Pearl, Relish, Pink, Oblong, 10 1/2 In. 5.00
          PANELED ASTER, see Madrid
          PANELED CHERRY BLOSSOM, see Cherry Blossom
          PARROT, see Sylvan
Patrician, Berry Bowl, Amber, 8 1/2 In. 25.00
Patrician, Berry Bowl, Pink, 5 In. 9.50
Patrician, Bowl, Amber, 5 In. 6.50
Patrician, Bowl, Green, 8 1/2 In. 15.00
Patrician, Butter, Amber, Covered .... 47.50 To 65.00
Patrician, Butter, Green, Covered .... 65.00 To 70.00
Patrician, Butter, Pink, Covered 180.00
Patrician, Cookie Jar, Amber .... 25.00 To 45.00
Patrician, Creamer, Amber 5.00
Patrician, Creamer, Pink 7.00
Patrician, Cup & Saucer, Amber 10.50
Patrician, Cup & Saucer, Green 8.50
Patrician, Cup, Green 5.00
Patrician, Pitcher, Amber, 8 1/2 In. 60.00
Patrician, Pitcher, Green, 8 1/2 In. 80.00
Patrician, Plate, Amber, 6 In. 6.00
Patrician, Plate, Amber, 7 1/2 In. 5.75
Patrician, Plate, Amber, 10 1/2 In. .... 4.00 To 6.00
Patrician, Plate, Green, 9 In. 6.50
Patrician, Salt & Pepper, Amber .... 24.00 To 35.00
Patrician, Salt & Pepper, Green 45.00
Patrician, Sherbet, Amber .... 4.25 To 8.00
Patrician, Soup, Cream, Amber .... 5.50 To 8.00
Patrician, Sugar & Creamer, Amber, Covered 32.00
Patrician, Sugar & Creamer, Green 15.00
Patrician, Sugar, Amber, Covered 28.50
Patrician, Tumbler, Amber, Flat, 4 1/2 In. 12.00
Patrician, Tumbler, Amber, Footed .... 22.00 To 25.00
Patrician, Tumbler, Amber, 4 In. .... 15.00 To 18.50
Patrician, Tumbler, Green, Footed, 5 1/2 In. 30.00
Patrician, Tumbler, Green, 4 In. 25.00
Patrician, Tumbler, Pink, 5 1/2 In. 30.00

Peacock & Wild Rose, Bowl, Console, Footed, Pink, 13 In. 35.00
    PETAL, see Petalware
Petalware, Cereal Bowl, Monax 3.50
Petalware, Cup, Cremax 2.50
Petalware, Cup, Monax 3.00
Petalware, Jar, Mustard, Cobalt Blue, Covered 7.50
Petalware, Plate, Cremax, 9 In. 3.50
Petalware, Saucer, Monax 1.50
Petalware, Sherbet, Pink 7.00
Petalware, Sugar & Creamer, Red & Yellow Flowers 12.50
    PINEAPPLE & FLORAL, see No. 618
    PINWHEEL, see Sierra
    POINSETTIA, see Floral
    POPPY NO. 1, see Florentine No. 1
    POPPY NO. 2, see Florentine No. 2
Primo, Cup & Saucer, Yellow 5.50
    PRIMUS, see Madrid
Princess, Berry Bowl, Green, Large 24.00
Princess, Berry Bowl, Green, 4 1/2 In. 14.00
Princess, Berry Bowl, Pink 11.00
Princess, Bowl, Cereal, Green, 5 1/4 In. 14.00
Princess, Bowl, Cereal, Pink 15.00
Princess, Bowl, Cereal, Yellow 20.00
Princess, Bowl, Green, Hat Shape, 9 1/2 In. .... 18.00 To 22.00
Princess, Bowl, Green, Octagonal 22.50
Princess, Bowl, Pink, Hat Shaped 15.00
Princess, Bowl, Yellow, Octagonal, 9 In. 79.50
Princess, Butter, Green, Covered .... 52.00 To 65.00
Princess, Butter, Pink, Covered 65.00
Princess, Coaster, Green .... 16.00 To 18.50
Princess, Cookie Jar, Green, Covered 31.50
Princess, Cookie Jar, Pink 18.00
Princess, Creamer, Yellow 9.00
Princess, Cup & Saucer, Green 8.00
Princess, Cup & Saucer, Pink .... 5.00 To 7.50
Princess, Cup & Saucer, Yellow .... 6.50 To 8.00
Princess, Cup, Pink 5.00
Princess, Pitcher, Green, 8 In. 30.00
Princess, Plate, Green, 8 In. 6.00
Princess, Plate, Green, 9 1/2 In. 13.50
Princess, Plate, Grill, Green, Closed Handle .... 8.50 To 10.00
Princess, Plate, Grill, Pink, Closed Handle, 11 1/2 In. 7.00
Princess, Plate, Grill, Yellow, 9 1/2 In. 6.50
Princess, Plate, Luncheon, Yellow 5.50
Princess, Plate, Pink, 5 1/2 In. 3.50
Princess, Plate, Pink, 8 In. 6.00
Princess, Plate, Pink, 9 1/2 In. 9.00
Princess, Plate, Sandwich, Pink, Handled, 11 1/2 In. 8.00
Princess, Plate, Topaz, 8 In. 4.50
Princess, Plate, Yellow, 6 In. 3.00
Princess, Plate, Yellow, 8 In. 6.00
Princess, Plate, Yellow, 9 1/2 In. 9.00
Princess, Platter, Green, 12 In. 12.50
Princess, Relish, Green, Divided .... 13.00 To 19.50
Princess, Relish, Pink 18.75
Princess, Salt & Pepper, Green 25.00
Princess, Sherbet, Green, Footed .... 8.00 To 12.00
Princess, Sherbet, Pink .... 9.00 To 10.00
Princess, Sherbet, Yellow .... 3.50 To 21.00
Princess, Spice Shaker, Green 12.50
Princess, Sugar & Creamer, Green, Covered 25.00
Princess, Sugar & Creamer, Pink 15.00
Princess, Sugar & Creamer, Yellow 37.50

Princess, Sugar, Green, Covered 12.50
Princess, Sugar, Open, Yellow 12.00
Princess, Sugar, Pink 9.00
Princess, Sugar, Yellow, Open 12.00
Princess, Tumbler, Footed, Yellow, 5 1/4 In. 18.50
Princess, Tumbler, Pink, Flat, 4 In. 10.00
Princess, Tumbler, Pink, Footed, 5 1/4 In. .... 12.50 To 15.00
Princess, Tumbler, Pink, Iced Tea, Flat, 5 1/4 In. 15.00
Princess, Tumbler, Yellow, Iced Tea, 5 1/4 In. .... 15.00 To 22.50
Princess, Tumbler, Yellow, 4 In. 17.50
    PROVINCIAL, see Bubble
    PYRAMID, see No. 610
Queen Mary, Berry Set, Pink, 8 In., 7 Piece 22.50
Queen Mary, Bowl, Cereal, Pink, 6 In. 5.00
Queen Mary, Bowl, Pink, 2-Handled, 5 1/2 In. 4.50
Queen Mary, Butter, Pink, Covered 75.00
Queen Mary, Candlestick, Red, Double, Pair 22.00
Queen Mary, Cup, Pink 4.00
Queen Mary, Plate, Pink, 6 In. 2.50
Queen Mary, Plate, Pink, 9 3/4 In. 15.00
Queen Mary, Plate, Sandwich, Crystal, 12 In. 4.50
Queen Mary, Saucer, Crystal, Ringed 3.00
Queen Mary, Saucer, Pink, Ringed 6.50
Queen Mary, Sherbet, Pink 4.50
Queen Mary, Tumbler, Crystal, Footed 8.50
Queen Mary, Tumbler, Pink, Footed 14.50
Queen Mary, Tumbler, Pink, Juice, 3 1/2 In. 5.00
Radiance, Bowl, Amber, 6 In. 8.00
Radiance, Cordial, Ruby, Stemmed, Set Of 6 .... 110.00
Radiance, Cup & Saucer, Amber 9.00
Radiance, Cup, Punch, Amber 5.20
Radiance, Punch, Ladle, Crystal 25.00
Radiance, Saltshaker, Amber 14.50
Radiance, Sugar & Creamer, Red 28.00
Radiance, Tumbler, Red 13.50
Radiance, Vase, Red, 10 In. 55.00
Raindrops, Cup & Saucer, Green 5.00
Raindrops, Nappy, Green 3.25
Raindrops, Sherbet, Green 1.75
    RASPBERRY BAND, see Laurel
    REX, see No. 610
    RIBBED, see Manhattan
Ribbon, Cup & Saucer, Green 9.50
Ribbon, Plate, Green, 6 1/4 In. .... 2.00 To 2.50
Ribbon, Sherbet, Green 4.50
Ring, Decanter, Blue 12.50
Rose Cameo, Sherbet, Green 5.00
    ROSE LACE, see Royal Lace
    ROSEMARY, see also Mayfair Open Rose
Rosemary, Berry Bowl, Amber, 5 In. 4.50
Rosemary, Plate, Amber, 6 3/4 In. 2.25
Rosemary, Plate, Pink, 10 In. 11.50
Rosemary, Sugar & Creamer, Pink 16.00
Roulette, Bowl, Fruit, Green, 9 In. 8.00
Roulette, Cup & Saucer, Green 9.50
Roulette, Plate, Green, 6 In. 1.50
Roulette, Plate, Green, 8 1/2 In. 4.00
Roulette, Tumbler, Footed, Green, 5 1/2 In. 11.00
Round Robin, Saucer, Green 1.50
Round Robin, Saucer, Iridescent 1.50
Round Robin, Sherbet, Iridescent, Footed 4.00
Roxana, Sherbet, Yellow, Footed 3.50
Royal Lace, Berry Bowl, Blue, 10 In. .... 27.50 To 35.00

Royal Lace, Berry Bowl, Pink, 10 In. 15.00
Royal Lace, Bowl, Blue, Rolled Edge, 10 1/2 In. 37.50
Royal Lace, Bowl, Green, Ruffled, 3-Legged, 10 In. 25.00
Royal Lace, Butter, Blue 320.00
Royal Lace, Butter, Green, Covered .... 190.00 To 200.00
Royal Lace, Butter, Pink, Covered .... 90.00 To 110.00
Royal Lace, Candlestick, Blue, Rolled Edge, Single 40.00
Royal Lace, Console Set, Blue, 3 Piece 190.00
Royal Lace, Cookie Jar, Blue 175.00
Royal Lace, Cookie Jar, Blue, Covered 200.00
Royal Lace, Cookie Jar, Crystal .... 25.00 To 27.00
Royal Lace, Cookie Jar, Green 48.50
Royal Lace, Cookie Jar, Pink 38.50
Royal Lace, Cracker Jar, Blue, 7 1/4 In. 170.00
Royal Lace, Creamer, Blue .... 20.00 To 25.00
Royal Lace, Creamer, Pink 11.00
Royal Lace, Cup & Saucer, Blue 24.00
Royal Lace, Dish, Candy, Crystal, Ruffled Edge 42.00
Royal Lace, Hot Toddy Set, Blue 125.00
Royal Lace, Pitcher, Blue, Straight Sided 75.00
Royal Lace, Pitcher, Blue, Water, 86 Ounce, 8 In. 95.00
Royal Lace, Pitcher, Green, 8 1/2 In. 97.00
Royal Lace, Plate, Blue, 6 In. 7.50
Royal Lace, Plate, Blue, 8 In. 20.00
Royal Lace, Plate, Blue, 10 In. 25.00
Royal Lace, Plate, Green, 10 In. 14.00
Royal Lace, Plate, Grill, Pink .... 8.50 To 15.00
Royal Lace, Platter, Green, 13 In. 25.00
Royal Lace, Salt & Pepper, Green 110.00
Royal Lace, Salt & Pepper, Pink 50.00
Royal Lace, Saltshaker, Green 65.00
Royal Lace, Saltshaker, Pink 20.00
Royal Lace, Saucer, Green 4.50
Royal Lace, Sherbet, Crystal 7.50
Royal Lace, Sherbet, Green 15.00
Royal Lace, Sherbet, Pink 9.50
Royal Lace, Soup, Cream, Pink 10.00
Royal Lace, Sugar & Creamer, Blue, Covered 85.00
Royal Lace, Sugar & Creamer, Crystal 14.50
Royal Lace, Sugar, Crystal 5.00
Royal Lace, Sugar, Pink 9.00
Royal Lace, Toddy Set, Amethyst, 6 Roly-Poly Tumblers 120.00
Royal Lace, Tumbler, Blue, Juice, 3 1/2 In. 24.00
Royal Lace, Tumbler, Blue, 4 7/8 In. 25.00
Royal Lace, Tumbler, Crystal, 4 1/8 In. .... 8.00 To 9.00
Royal Lace, Tumbler, Green, Juice, 3 1/2 In. 16.00
Royal Lace, Tumbler, Green, 4 1/8 In. 15.00
Royal Lace, Tumbler, Pink, Juice, 3 1/2 In. .... 10.00 To 13.50
Royal Lace, Tumbler, Pink, 4 1/4 In., Set Of 6 .... 40.00
Royal Lace, Tumbler, Pink, 4 1/8 In. .... 12.00 To 12.50
Royal Ruby, Berry Bowl, 4 1/4 In. 3.50
Royal Ruby, Berry Set, 6 Bowls, Master Bowl 8 1/2 In. 25.00
Royal Ruby, Bowl, Salad 15.00
Royal Ruby, Cup & Saucer .... 4.00 To 4.50
Royal Ruby, Goblet, Ball Stem .... 6.00 To 8.00
Royal Ruby, Goblet, Footed, 3 1/2 In. 8.50
Royal Ruby, Plate, 7 In. 4.00
Royal Ruby, Plate, 9 In. 5.00
Royal Ruby, Punch Set, Bowl, 11 Cups 60.00
Royal Ruby, Sherbet 8.50
Royal Ruby, Sugar & Creamer 8.00
Royal Ruby, Tumbler, Footed, 5 In. .... 5.50 To 6.00

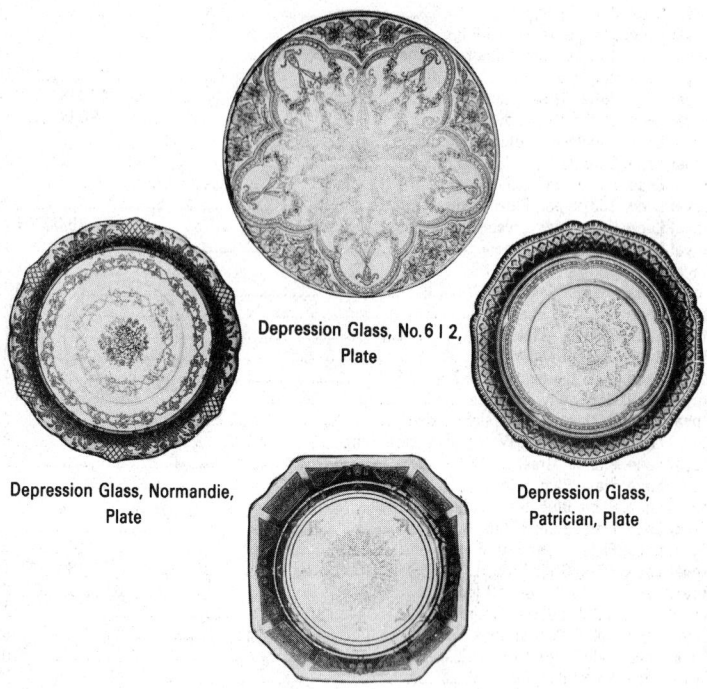

Depression Glass, No.6 l 2,
Plate

Depression Glass, Normandie,
Plate

Depression Glass,
Patrician, Plate

Depression Glass, Princess, Plate

Royal Ruby, Tumbler, 4 1/2 In.	6.00
RUSSIAN, see Holiday	
S Pattern, Cup & Saucer, Amber	4.50
S Pattern, Plate, Amber, 6 In.	5.00
S Pattern, Sherbet, Amber, Footed	4.75
Salt & Pepper, American Sweetheart, Monax	195.00
Sandwich Hocking, Berry Bowl, Crystal	3.50
Sandwich Hocking, Berry Bowl, Green	2.25
Sandwich Hocking, Bowl, Green, 6 1/2 In.	18.50
Sandwich Hocking, Butter, Crystal	20.00
Sandwich Hocking, Creamer, Crystal	5.50
Sandwich Hocking, Crystal, 6 1/2 In.	4.50
Sandwich Hocking, Pitcher, Green, Juice, 6 In.	100.00
Sandwich Hocking, Sugar & Creamer, Green	25.00
SAWTOOTH, see English Hobnail	
SAXON, see Coronation	
SHAMROCK, see Cloverleaf	
Sharon, Berry Bowl, Amber, 5 In.	5.00
Sharon, Berry Bowl, Amber, 8 1/2 In.	4.00 To 4.50
Sharon, Berry Bowl, Green, 8 1/2 In.	15.00
Sharon, Berry Bowl, Pink, 5 In.	6.00
Sharon, Berry Bowl, Pink, 8 1/2 In.	12.50
Sharon, Bowl, Cereal, Amber, 6 In.	9.00
Sharon, Bowl, Cereal, Pink, 6 In.	9.00
Sharon, Bowl, Fruit, Amber, 10 1/2 In.	12.00 To 12.50
Sharon, Bowl, Fruit, Green, 10 1/2 In.	20.00
Sharon, Bowl, Fruit, Pink, 10 1/2 In.	17.00 To 18.00

Depression Glass, Royal Lace

Sharon, Bowl, Vegetable, Amber, Oval, 9 1/2 In.	8.50
Sharon, Bowl, Vegetable, Pink, Oval, 9 1/2 In.	10.00 To 12.00
Sharon, Butter, Amber, Covered	20.00 To 35.00
Sharon, Butter, Green	65.00 To 70.00
Sharon, Butter, Pink, Covered	28.00 To 45.00
Sharon, Cake Plate, Amber, Footed, 11 1/2 In.	14.50
Sharon, Cake Plate, Crystal, Footed	7.50
Sharon, Cake Plate, Crystal, 11 1/2 In.	4.50
Sharon, Cake Plate, Pink	15.00 To 22.50
Sharon, Creamer, Pink	7.50 To 9.50
Sharon, Cup & Saucer, Amber	7.50
Sharon, Cup & Saucer, Pink	12.00 To 14.00
Sharon, Cup, Amber	6.50 To 7.50
Sharon, Cup, Green	9.00
Sharon, Cup, Pink	5.00
Sharon, Dish, Candy, Amber	20.00 To 35.00
Sharon, Dish, Candy, Green	90.00
Sharon, Dish, Candy, Pink	22.00 To 35.00
Sharon, Dish, Cheese, Amber	70.00
Sharon, Pitcher, Amber, Ice Lip	87.50 To 90.00
Sharon, Pitcher, Pink, Ice Lip	80.00 To 85.00
Sharon, Plate, Amber, 6 In.	3.00 To 3.50
Sharon, Plate, Amber, 7 1/2 In.	8.00 To 11.00
Sharon, Plate, Amber, 9 1/2 In.	7.00 To 9.50
Sharon, Plate, Green, 6 In.	4.50 To 6.00
Sharon, Plate, Green, 9 1/2 In.	9.50 To 10.00
Sharon, Plate, Green, 9 1/2 In., Set Of 5	40.00
Sharon, Plate, Pink, 6 In.	4.50
Sharon, Platter, Amber, Oval, 12 1/2 In.	8.50
Sharon, Platter, Green, 12 1/2 In.	13.00 To 15.00

Depression Glass, Royal Lace

Sharon, Platter, Pink 10.00
Sharon, Salt & Pepper, Amber .... 27.50 To 32.00
Sharon, Salt & Pepper, Green 65.00
Sharon, Salt & Pepper, Pink .... 40.00 To 45.00
Sharon, Saltshaker, Green 28.00
Sharon, Saucer, Amber 3.00
Sharon, Sherbet, Amber, Footed .... 7.00 To 8.50
Sharon, Sherbet, Pink, Footed .... 6.50 To 9.50
Sharon, Soup, Cream, Amber, 5 In. .... 12.00 To 12.50
Sharon, Soup, Cream, Green 22.00
Sharon, Soup, Cream, Pink 20.00
Sharon, Sugar & Creamer, Amber, Covered 40.00
Sharon, Sugar & Creamer, Pink, Covered .... 22.50 To 35.00
Sharon, Sugar & Creamer, Pink, Open 20.00
Sharon, Sugar, Pink, Open 8.50
Sharon, Tumbler, Amber, Flat, 4 1/8 In. 16.50
Sharon, Tumbler, Pink, Footed, Set Of 5 .... 28.00
Sharon, Tumbler, Pink, Footed, 15 Ounce .... 32.50 To 37.50
Sharon, Tumbler, Pink, 4 1/8 In. 18.50
      SHELL, see Petalware
Sierra, Bowl, Cereal, Green, 5 1/2 In. 5.75
Sierra, Bowl, Vegetable, Pink, Oval 25.00
Sierra, Butter, Green, Covered 42.00
Sierra, Cup & Saucer, Green 10.00
Sierra, Pitcher, Pink, 6 1/2 In. .... 32.00 To 42.50
Sierra, Plate, Pink, 9 In. .... 8.00 To 9.50
Sierra, Salt & Pepper, Pink 20.00
Sierra, Sugar, Pink, Covered .... 17.50 To 18.00
Sierra, Tray, Green, Handled 6.00
Sierra, Tray, Pink, Handled 8.00
      SMOCKING, see Windsor
      SNOWFLAKE, see Doric
      SPIRAL OPTIC, see Spiral
Spiral, Ice Tub, Green 16.50
Spiral, Plate, Green, 6 In. 1.50
Spiral, Plate, Green, 8 In. 2.00
Spiral, Sugar & Creamer, Green, Footed 10.50
      SPOKE, see Patrician
      STIPPLED ROSE BAND, see S Pattern
Strawberry, Sherbet, Pink .... 7.00 To 8.75
Sunflower, Cup & Saucer, Pink 8.00
Sunflower, Sugar & Creamer, Green 25.00
Swirl, Bowl, Cereal, Pink, 5 1/4 In. 4.00
Swirl, Butter, Ultramarine 180.00
Swirl, Candleholder, Ultramarine, Double 14.00
Swirl, Coaster, Pink 4.50
Swirl, Creamer, Ultramarine 5.00
Swirl, Plate, Pink, 12 1/2 In. 6.00
Swirl, Plate, Ultramarine, 7 1/2 In. 7.50
Swirl, Sherbet, Pink 5.00
Swirl, Sugar & Creamer, Ultramarine 10.00
Swirl, Tumbler, Pink, 4 1/4 In. 6.00
      SWIRLED BIG RIB, see Spiral
      SWIRLED SHARP RIB, see Diana
Sylvan, Butter, Green, Covered, 6 3/4 In. 275.00
Sylvan, Cup & Saucer, Amber 20.00
Sylvan, Cup & Saucer, Green 26.00
Sylvan, Plate, Green, 10 1/2 In. 27.00
Sylvan, Plate, Grill, Amber 10.00
Sylvan, Plate, Grill, Green 19.00
Sylvan, Salt & Pepper, Green .... 145.00 To 187.50
Sylvan, Sherbet, Amber, Set Of 8 .... 48.00
Sylvan, Sherbet, Green .... 9.00 To 16.00

Sylvan, Sherbet, Green, Pair 30.00
Sylvan, Sugar, Green, Covered 75.00
    TASSELL, see Princess
Tea Room, Creamer, Green, Large 15.00
Tea Room, Creamer, Green, Small 12.50
Tea Room, Creamer, Pink, Large 15.00
Tea Room, Creamer, Pink, Small 12.50
Tea Room, Sugar & Creamer, Green, Small 25.00
Tea Room, Sugar & Creamer, Pink, Footed 25.00
Tea Room, Sugar, Creamer, & Tray, Pink 45.00
Tea Room, Sugar, Green, Footed 8.50
Tea Room, Vase, Green, Ruffled Edge, 9 1/2 In. 35.00
Tea Room, Water Set, Green, 6 Tumblers 225.00
Thistle, Plate, Pink, 8 In. .... 8.00 To 8.50
    THREE PARROT, see Sylvan
    VERNON, see No. 616
    VERTICLE RIB, see Queen Mary
Victory, Bowl, Amber, 6 1/2 In. 4.50
    VIVID BANDS, see Petalware
    WAFFLE, see Waterford
Waterford, Berry Bowl, Crystal 9.50
Waterford, Cake Plate, Crystal, Metal Handled 6.00
Waterford, Pitcher, Crystal, Juice 10.00
Waterford, Pitcher, Pink, Water .... 95.00 To 125.00
Waterford, Salt & Pepper, Crystal, Pair 5.00
Waterford, Tumbler, Pink, 3 1/2 In. 9.50
    WEDDING BAND, see Moderntone
    WILD ROSE, see Dogwood
    WILDFLOWER, see No. 618
    WINDSOR DIAMOND, see Windsor

Depression Glass, Royal Lace

Depression Glass, Sharon

Depression Glass, Swirl

Depression Glass, Sylvan

Depression Glass, Windsor

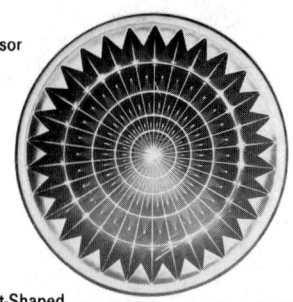

Windsor, Bowl, Green, Boat-Shaped 17.00
Windsor, Bowl, Green, 4 1/2 In. 4.50
Windsor, Bowl, Pink, Boat Shape 15.00
Windsor, Bowl, Pink, 12 1/2 In. .... 25.00 To 29.00
Windsor, Butter, Crystal, Covered 20.00
Windsor, Butter, Pink, Covered 25.00
Windsor, Cake Plate, Pink, 10 In. 17.00
Windsor, Candlestick, Pink, Pair 48.50
Windsor, Coaster, Pink 4.00
Windsor, Cup & Saucer, Green 8.50
Windsor, Cup & Saucer, Pink 6.50
Windsor, Cup, Pink .... 3.50 To 4.00
Windsor, Jar, Jam, Pink 25.00
Windsor, Pitcher, Pink, 6 3/4 In. 20.00
Windsor, Plate, Pink, Open Handled, 10 In. 18.00
Windsor, Plate, Pink, 9 In. 7.00
Windsor, Platter, Green, Oval 12.50
Windsor, Salt & Pepper, Green, Pair 32.00
Windsor, Salt & Pepper, Pink, Pair 20.00
Windsor, Sherbet, Green 6.50
Windsor, Sugar & Creamer, Pink 12.50
Windsor, Sugar, Pink, Covered .... 5.00 To 9.00
Windsor, Tumbler, Pink, 4 In. 8.50
   WINGED MEDALLION, see Madrid
X Design, Reamer, Green 18.00

*Derby porcelain was made in Derby, England, from 1756 to the present.
The factory changed names and marks several times. Chelsea Derby (1770-
1784), Crown Derby (1784-1811), and the modern Royal Crown Derby are
some of the most famous periods of the factory.*
   DERBY, see also Chelsea; Crown Derby; Royal Crown Derby
DERBY, Candelabra, The Skater, Polychromed In Blue & Gold, C.1790, 13 In. 675.00
   Cup & Saucer, C.1889, Impressed S 45.00
   Figurine, Autumn, C.1830, Young Girl, Crossed Swords Mark, 7 1/2 In. 400.00
   Figurine, Dog, C.1810 .... 475.00
   Tureen, Sauce, King's Pattern, C.1825, Covered, 9 1/2 X 8 1/2 In. 300.00
   Vase, Hand-Painted Flowers, C.1800, Marked, 12 1/2 In., Pair 2100.00

DE VILBISS, Atomizer, Green Art Glass, Cut Leaf Design, Signed 59.00
   Atomizer, Throat 10.00
   Bottle, Perfume, Clear Pressed Flower Stopper, Marked 15.00
   Bottle, Perfume, Encrusted Gold, Stopper Gold & Black, 4 In. 35.00
   Bottle, Perfume, Green Satin Glass 55.00
   Bottle, Perfume, Raised Feathers, Gold Plated 15.00
   Bottle, Perfume, 3 Etched Panels & Foot, Gold Trim, Signed, 5 In. 75.00

DICK TRACY, Badge, Detective Club, Brass 7.00
   Book, Big Little Book, Encounters 4.50

Book, Pop-Up	85.00
Camera, Hard Plastic	30.00
Car, Magic Garage, Marx	75.00
Flashlight, Boxed	25.00
Game, Electronic Target	55.00
Gun	12.50 To 20.00
Gun, Click, Jr., Boxed	50.00
Hat, Felt, War Planes On Brim	65.00
Pinback, Detective	18.00
Pistol, Pop, Boxed	50.00
Pistol, Siren, Decal, Red	45.00
Pistol, Water, 1951	10.00 To 12.50
Poster, Radio Premium, Dated 1939, 20 X 12 In.	50.00
Puzzle, 1952	19.00
Radio, Wrist, Battery Operated, Remco, C.1951	45.00
Ring, Embossed Straight Arrow	40.00
Ring, Profile	35.00
Ring, Secret Compartment	55.00
Suspenders, Detective Set, Boxed	28.00
Target, Tin, 1941, Boxed	26.00
Toy, Car, Tin	75.00

DICKENS WARE, see Royal Doulton; Weller

DIONNE QUINTUPLETS, Book, Story Of DQ, Soon We'll Be Three	17.00
Calendar, 1937, Wholesum	22.50
Calendar, 1942, Colors Flowing Gowns	35.00
Doll, In High Chair, 7 1/2 In.	125.00
Fan	10.00
Paper Dolls, All Aboard Shut Eye Town, Uncut	85.00
Postcard, 10 X 16 In., Pair	350.00
Spoons, Set Of 5	85.00

DISNEYANA, Alarm Clock, Ingersoll, Mickey Mouse	320.00
Ball, Sun Rubber Co., Mickey Mouse, 5 In.	16.00
Bank, Bugs Bunny, On Barrel	65.00
Bank, Donald Duck, Carnival	30.00
Bank, Donald Duck, Glass, Tin Top, 1940	100.00
Bank, Donald Duck, Tongue Retracts, Drop Coin, Tin	75.00
Bank, Pinocchio, World's Fair, 1934, Hand-Painted, Metal	125.00
Bank, Post Office, Mickey & Minnie Mailing Letters, Red, Tin	45.00
Bank, Snow White, Dime, 1938	43.00
Bell, Bicycle, Mickey Mouse, 1933	25.00 To 30.00
Book, Mickey Sees The U.S.A., Hard Cover, 138 Pages	95.00
Book, No.2, Mickey Mouse	50.00
Book, Pop-Up Circus, Mickey Mouse, 1933	165.00
Book, Seven Dwarfs, Linen	55.00
Book, The Adventures Of Mickey Mouse, 1931	55.00
Book, Walt Disney Circus, 1944	30.00
Bookend, Mickey Mouse, Cast Iron, Pair	125.00
Bottle, Donald Duck, Pop, 1940s	25.00
Bowl, Mickey Mouse Beetleware	15.00
Box, Paint, Donald Duck, 1945	16.00
Bracelet, Three Little Pigs, Enameled	170.00
Camera, Donald Duck	25.00 To 50.00
Car, Donald Duck, Friction, Tin, Linemar	110.00
Car, Donald Duck, Rubber	25.00 To 50.00
Car, Mickey Mouse, Circus Dining, Tin, 1930	115.00
Car, Roadster, Parade, Boxed	200.00
Card, Birthday, Mickey Mouse, 1932	15.00
Card, Birthday, Mickey, 1936, 19 X 23 In.	25.00
Cards, Snow White & Dwarfs, Boxed	95.00
Choo-Choo, Mickey Mouse, Red	250.00
Christmas Light, Mickey Mouse, Noma, Boxed	235.00

Clothes Brush, Mickey Mouse, Silver & Black Metal 65.00
Coffee Set, Minnie Mouse, Signed Walter E.Disney, 7 Piece 155.00
Comb, Fold-Up, Mickey Mouse Club 12.00
Cookie Jar, Birthday, Mickey, Ceramic 55.00
Cookie Jar, Donald Duck, 1940s .... 40.00 To 70.00
Cookie Jar, Dumbo, 1940s .... 60.00 To 90.00
Cookie Jar, Mickey Mouse, Turnable, 1940s 70.00
Cookie Jar, Thumper, Original Paint 48.00
Corn Popper, Mickey, 1936 .... 275.00
Costume, Halloween, Minnie Mouse, 1930s 215.00
Cuff Links, Mickey Mouse 20.00
Cup, Mickey Mouse, Lid, Handle, Cap Ears 6.00
Dish, Feeding, Mickey Mouse, Patriot 65.00
Dish, Soap, Donald Duck, Rubber 15.00
Display, Mickey Mouse, Revolving Light Makes Eyes Change 350.00
    DISNEYANA, DOLL, see Doll
Embroidery Set, Snow White & Dwarfs, 1960s, Boxed 15.00
Figurine, Doc, Frosted Glass, 5 3/8 In. 65.00
Figurine, Donald Duck, Chalkware, 1940s .... 20.00 To 50.00
Figurine, Donald Duck, Hard Rubber 6.00
Figurine, Dopey, Bisque, 5 1/2 In. 40.00
Figurine, Dwarfs, Rubber, Set Of 7 .... 45.00
Figurine, Mickey & Minnie, Celluloid, Hand-Painted, 1928-30, Pair 175.00
Figurine, Mickey Mouse, Pie-Eyed, Holding Umbrella, Marked 40.00
Figurine, Mickey Mouse, Wooden, 1930s, 12 In. 60.00
Figurine, Mickey, Minnie, & Pluto, Christmas, Grolier 195.00
Figurine, Snow White & Seven Dwarfs, 8 Pieces 265.00
Fire Truck, Mickey Mouse & Donald Duck, Hard Rubber 22.00
Fire Truck, Mickey Mouse, Rubber 50.00
Fountain Pen, Mickey Mouse, Deluxe Model, With Pictures 100.00
Game, Donald Duck, 1938 .... 45.00
Game, Mickey Mouse Club 18.00
Game, Old Maid, Mickey Mouse, Boxed, 1937 .... 50.00
Game, Pin Tail On Mickey, 1930s .... 55.00 To 75.00
Game, Uncle Remus-Br'er Rabbit, Boxed 35.00
Globe, Mickey Mouse, Tin 125.00
Hairbrush, Mickey Mouse, 1930s 15.00
Kaleidoscope, Makes Mickey Mouse Design .... 25.00 To 35.00
Kartooner Drawing Board, Mickey Mouse Club 20.00
Machine, Gumball, Mickey Mouse, Plastic, 9 In. 12.50
Mask, Sneezy, Cloth & Felt 40.00
Mirror, Pocket, Rectangular 3.00
Moviejector, Mickey Mouse, 2 Films 200.00
Mug, Bowl & Plate, Mickey Mouse 75.00
Mug, Ludwig Von Drake 12.00
Music Box, Mickey Mouse 10.00
Night-Light & Music Box, Mickey Mouse, Boxed 30.00
Nodder, Donald Duck, Celluloid 400.00
Noisemaker, Mickey Mouse, Cardboard, 1930s 65.00
Nurse Kit, Minnie Mouse 25.00
Pail, Sand, Mickey Mouse & Minnie Mouse 45.00
Pail, Sand, Treasure Island, Mickey Mouse, Shovel 37.50
Party Horn, Mickey & Minnie, 1930 .... 55.00
Pencil Holder, Mickey Mouse, Dixon, Composition, 1930s, 6 In. 235.00
Pencil Sharpener, Donald Duck 25.00
Pencil Sharpener, Donald Duck Figure, Celluloid 145.00
Pencil, Mechanical, Mickey Mouse Head On Top 60.00
Pistol, Water, Mickey Mouse Club, Embossed Mickey 45.00
Pitcher, Donald Duck .... 22.00 To 25.00
Pitcher, Dumbo, Ceramic .... 25.00 To 45.00
Planter, Bambi .... 15.00 To 16.00
Planter, Pluto, Ceramic 16.00
Planter, Thumper 15.00

Plate, Donald Duck, Christmas, 1976	15.00
Plate, Little Pigs, China, 7 In.	55.00
Projector, Mickey Mouse Club	25.00
Puppet, Hand, Minnie Mouse, 11 In.	20.00
Puppet, Hand, Pluto, 11 In.	15.00
Puzzle, Mickey Mouse, 1930s, 10 X 7 3/4 In.	50.00 To 75.00
Rug, Mickey Mouse, 21 X 13 In.	25.00
Salt & Pepper, Donald Duck	18.00 To 35.00
Saucer, Big Bad Wolf, Green, Tin, 4 In.	40.00
Scissors, Donald Duck, Linemar	75.00
Shaker, Minnie	9.00
Sheet Music, Uncle Remus	20.00
Sheet Music, Who's Afaid Of The Big Bad Wolf, 1932	15.00
Soap, Ferdinand The Bull, Boxed	12.00
Soap, Figural, Mickey Mouse	40.00
Soap, Snow White & Seven Dwarfs, Boxed, 1938	85.00
Spoon, Mary Poppins	12.00
Spoon, Mickey Mouse, Silver Plate	10.00
Stationery, Alice In Wonderland, Boxed	8.00
Stationery, Mickey Mouse, Boxed	11.00
Stencil Set, Oswald Lucky Rabbit	46.00
Tambourine, Mickey Mouse	150.00
Target Set, Mickey Mouse, 1930s	90.00
Tea Set, Alice, Boxed	45.00
Tea Set, Child's, Mickey & Minnie	40.00 To 95.00
Tea Set, Donald Duck, China, Luster, 13 Piece	55.00
Tea Set, Mickey Mouse, Boxed, 1930s, 23 Piece	350.00
Teaspoon, Pinocchio	7.00
Thermometer, Mickey Standing On Pluto's House Pointing, Metal	185.00
Toothbrush Holder, Donald Duck	250.00
Toothbrush Holder, Mickey & Minnie	60.00
Toothbrush Holder, 3 Pigs	35.00
Top, Mickey Mouse & Gang, Tin, 8 In.	40.00
Top, Spinning, Disney Enterprises	100.00
Toy, Donald Duck & Nephews, Windup, Marx, Plastic, Boxed	125.00
Toy, Donald Duck On Skis, Linemar, Windup, Tin	285.00
Toy, Donald Duck, Playing Drums, Linemar	105.00
Toy, Donald Duck, Pull, Fisher Price	15.00
Toy, Donald Duck, Push, Fisher Price, 1939	20.00
Toy, Drum Major, Mickey Mouse, Pull, Wooden, 1940s	75.00
Toy, Drum, Mickey Mouse, Ohio Art	165.00
Toy, Express, Disneyland, Windup, Engine & 2 Cars	25.00
Toy, Ferdinand, Windup, Tin	75.00
Toy, Ferris Wheel, Hercules, Tin, Windup, 1950	110.00
Toy, Ferris Wheel, Mickey Mouse, Chein	175.00
Toy, Fire Truck, Mickey Mouse, Hard Rubber, Brown & Red, 6 In.	25.00
Toy, Hand Car, Mickey & Minnie Mouse, Lionel	575.00
Toy, Majorette, Mickey Mouse, Plastic, Battery Operated, 9 In.	75.00
Toy, Mickey Mouse Drives Race Car, 1930	95.00
Toy, Mickey Mouse, Drummer, Battery Operated, Linemar	250.00
Toy, Mickey Mouse, Drummer, Fisher Price	55.00
Toy, Mickey Mouse, Marching, Boxed	50.00
Toy, Minnie Mouse, With Shopping Cart, Battery Operated, Boxed	25.00
Toy, Pinocchio The Acrobat	275.00
Toy, Pluto, Blows Horn, Linemar	125.00
Toy, Pluto, Drum Major, Boxed	175.00
Toy, Pluto, Pulling A Wagon, Friction, Tin, Linemar	75.00
Toy, Porky Pig, Windup, Dated 1939	385.00
Toy, Refrigerator, Snow White, Tin, 15 In.	30.00
Toy, Rhythm Maker, Mickey Mouse, Emenee, Boxed, 1950s	125.00
Toy, Rocking Chair, Minnie Mouse, Linemar, Windup, Tin	195.00
Toy, T.V., Mouseketeer, Electric, Tin, 13 1/2 In.	150.00

Toy, X-Press, Pinocchio, Pull, Wooden 55.00
Tractor, Mickey Mouse, Sun Rubber Co. 50.00
Train, Donald Duck, Wooden, 1940s 50.00
Train, Mickey Mouse, Wooden, Pull 50.00
Typewriter, Mickey Mouse, Boxed 65.00
Umbrella, Donald Duck, Handled 50.00
Umbrella, Mickey Mouse, Figural Handle 50.00
Umbrella, Mickey, Pluto, Goofy, Orange Rayon 60.00
Wagon, Donald Duck, Wooden, Pull, Twirling Baton, 1940s 50.00
Washing Machine, Mickey & Minnie, Plastic, 1950 .... 65.00
Watch Fob, Mickey Mouse, Zinc 35.00
Watch, Mickey Mouse, Pocket, Ingersoll 95.00
Wood Blocks, Mickey Mouse, With Suitcase 18.00
Wristwatch, Mickey Mouse, Black Leather Band, 1930s 185.00
Wristwatch, Mickey Mouse, Metal Band 250.00
Wristwatch, Snow White 25.00
Xylophone, Mickey Mouse, Metal, Boxed, 1950 .... 85.00
Xylophone, Mickey Mouse, Pull Toy, Fisher Price, 1939 .... 45.00
Yo-Yo, Mickey Mouse 22.00
     DOCTOR, see Medical

Doll entries are listed by marks printed or incised on doll, if possible.
If there are no marks, the doll is listed by name of subject or country.

DOLL, A.B.G., 30 In. 600.00
A.M. 100, Dream Baby, 12 In. 285.00
A.M. 323, Googly, Original Clothes, 7 In. 595.00
A.M. 323, Googly, 6 1/2 In. 500.00
A.M. 329, Baby, Open Mouth, Blue Eyes, Dressed, Marked, 18 In. 325.00
A.M. 341, Dream Baby, Brown Eyes, 15 In. 675.00
A.M. 351/3k, Character, Composition Body, Bent Limbs 385.00
A.M. 351/8k, Rock-A-Bye Dream Baby, Bisque, Bent Limbs, 22 In. 550.00
A.M. 370, Bisque Head, Ball-Jointed, Kid Body, 15 In. 175.00
A.M. 370, Bisque Head, Blue Glass Eyes, 24 In. 250.00
A.M. 370, Kid Body, Sleep Eyes, Ball-Jointed Arms, 22 In. 350.00
A.M. 390, Bisque, Ball-Jointed Body, Royal Blue Outfit, 20 1/2 In. 200.00
A.M. 390, Boy, Scotch, Bisque, Matching Scotch Plaid Box, 12 In. 165.00
A.M. 390, Brown Sleep Eyes, Ball-Jointed, 28 In. 450.00
A.M. 390, Sleep Eyes, Blonde Wig, Ball-Jointed, Dressed, 38 In. 1695.00
A.M. 390, Sleep Eyes, Composition Ball-Jointed Body, Dressed, 24 In. 425.00
A.M. 390, Sleep Eyes, Lashes, Ball-Jointed, Ecru Dress, 22 In. 425.00
A.M. 390n, Child, 33 1/2 In. 750.00
A.M. 560, Bisque, Glass Eyes, Composition Body, White Dress, 9 In. 325.00
A.M. 560a, Blue Sleep Eyes, Open Mouth, Ball-Jointed, 16 1/2 In. 795.00
A.M. 590, Baby, Closed Mouth, Brown Sleep Eyes, 8 In. 550.00
A.M. 600, Character Boy, Bisque Shoulder & Head, Kid Body, 15 In. 550.00
A.M. 971, Character Baby, Blue Eyes, Open Mouth, Bent Limbs, 13 In. 265.00
A.M. 975, Baby, Sleep Brown Eyes 300.00
A.M. 985, Character, Dimpled, Blue Eyes, 16 In. 450.00
A.M. 985, Sleep Blue Eyes, 16 In. 400.00
A.M., Baby Gloria, Molded Blonde Hair, Dimples, 14 In. 550.00
A.M., Baby, Open Mouth, Sleep Eyes, Velvet Dress, Incised Mark, 18 In. 325.00
A.M., Bisque, Socket Head, Composition Body, Blue Eyes, 13 In. 130.00
A.M., Brown Sleep Eyes, Bisque Handle, 22 In. 250.00
A.M., Dream Baby, Blue Sleep Eyes, Cloth Body, Composition Hands, 8 In. 250.00
A.M., Dream Baby, Blue Sleep Eyes, 5-Piece Composition Body, 8 1/2 In. 350.00
A.M., Duchess, Sleep Brown Eyes, Open Mouth, Silk Dress, Germany, 28 In. .. 495.00
A.M., Floradora, Bisque Head & Arms, Kid Body, 24 In. 475.00
A.M., Just Me, Painted Bisque, Riding Habit, 10 In. 225.00
A.M., Mabel, Dressed, 16 In. 165.00
A.M., Scotsman, Bisque Head, Paperweight Eyes, 8 In. 125.00
Advertising, Purina Scarecrow, 20 In. 20.00
Alabama Baby, Blue Boots, 22 In. 495.00
     DOLL, ALEXANDER, see Doll, Madame Alexander

Alice In Wonderland, Brown Eyes, Parian, 11 In. 375.00
Alice In Wonderland, 1965 .... 65.00
Alice In Wonderland, 8 In. 300.00
Amberg 1361, Baby, Cry Box, 13 In. 300.00
American Character, Debutante, Walking, Composition, 18 In. 125.00
Arlesford, Baby Celia, Blown Glass Eyes, Pink Dress, Soft Body, 16 In. 78.00
    DOLL, ARMAND MARSEILLE, see Doll, A, M.
B.P.585 Character, Glass Eyes, Closed Mouth, Molded Tongue, 20 In. 1350.00
Babe Ruth, Hallmark, Boxed 15.00
Baby Bud, Jointed Arms, Bisque, 5 1/2 In. 100.00
Baby Yawnie, Black, Boxed, 14 In. 20.00
Baby, Boy, Bisque, Jointed Arms & Hips, Incised Japan, 5 In. 15.00
Baby, Brass Head, Rubber Hands, Cloth Body 150.00
Baby, Jointed Body, Molded Hair, Painted Eyes, 1930s, 10 In. 15.00
Baby, Mechanical, Crawler 150.00
Baby, Molded & Painted Features, Open-Close Mouth, 19 In. 20.00
Bartenstein, Signed 550.00
Beadwork, 7 In. 13.00
Bebe, Body Signed, Eiffel Tower Mark, 17 In. 3175.00
Belton, Bisque Head, Paperweight Eyes, Pierced Ears, 1 1/2 In. 1450.00
Belton, Glass Eyes, Human Hair Wig, Composition 5-Piece Body, 8 In. 485.00
Belton, Jumeau, Original Wig & Clothes, Pierced Ears, 14 In. 2850.00
Belton, Paperweight Eyes, Blonde Human Hair Wig, 14 In. 1250.00
Belton, Sleep Eyes, 6 In. 395.00
Belton, Twins, Original, 8 In. 800.00
Ben Casey, Doctor's Outfit, Hard Plastic & Vinyl, Boxed, 29 In. 125.00
    DOLL, BERGMANN, see also Doll, S & H; Doll, Simon & Halbig
Bergmann, Bisque, Swivel Head, Brown Sleep Eyes, 1916, 24 In. 250.00
Bergmann, Blue Sleep Eyes, Long Brown Hair, Ball-Jointed, 24 In. 525.00
Bergmann, Girl, Mohair Wig, Taffeta Dress, 29 In. 700.00
Bergmann, Simon & Halbig, Sleep Eyes, Lashes, Bisque, Dressed, 24 In. 450.00
Bergmann, Sleep Eyes, Human Hair Wig, Ball-Jointed, Dressed, 25 In. 585.00
Bernard Ravca, Stocking Face, Paris 1924, Cloth Body, 15 In. 100.00
Betsy McCall, 26 In. 125.00
Betty Boop, Bisque, 7 In. 50.00
Betty Boop, Painted Hair & Eyes, Segmented Limbs, 12 In. 45.00
Biedermeier, Ball Head, Original Blonde Wig, 17 1/2 In. 425.00
Biskoline Baby, Painted Eyes, Molded Hair, 1912, 11 In. 125.00
Bisque Head, Cloth Body, Marked Morimura, Japan, 15 In. 85.00
Bisque, Baby Phyllis, Sleep Eyes, Original Cloth Body, 12 In. 595.00
Bisque, Dutch Boy & Girl, German, 1 5/8 In. 55.00
Bisque, Glass Eyes, Cloth Body, Bisque Arms & Legs, Dressed, 6 1/2 In. 465.00
Bisque, Googly Toddler, Intaglio Eyes, Molded Hair, Black, 6 1/2 In. 675.00
Bisque, Molded Teeth & Long Black Stockings, Swivel Head, 7 In. 750.00
Bisque, Original Red Cross Uniform, C.1900 .... *Illus* 9800.00
Black Baby, Talks, Cloth Body, Glass Sleep Eyes, 18 In. 100.00
Bonnie, Plaid Lassie Doll, 20 In. 28.00
Bottle, Black, Gray Dress, Checked Apron, Bandana, Earrings, 13 In. 32.00
Bru 9, Walker, Dressed In French Clothes, 21 In. 4500.00
Bru, Bisque Head, Paperweight Eyes, Pierced Ears, Marked, 10 In. 3995.00
Bru, Closed Mouth, Brown Eyes, 15 In. 8500.00
Bru, French Bisque, Mannikin, C.1880, 46 In. .... *Illus* 5750.00
Bru, Lady Head, Life-Size, Paperweight Eyes, Closed Mouth, Head, 19 In. 2500.00
Bru, Nursing, Bisque, 19 In. 5975.00
Bru, Paperweight Eyes, Open Mouth, Blue Velvet Dress, 31 In. 7500.00
Bru, Violet Paperweight Eyes, Ball-Jointed, Marked, Bisque, 17 In. 3000.00
Bruckner, Topsy Turvy, All Original, Label, Signed 350.00
Bruno Schmidt, Oriental, All Original, 18 In. 2200.00
Bye-Lo, All Original, Label On Dress, Head Circumference 10 In. 450.00
Bye-Lo, Baby, Bisque Dome Head, Celluloid Hands, Cloth Body, 12 In. 500.00
Bye-Lo, Baby, Bisque Head, Cloth Body, Artist Joyce Hogarth, 9 In. 225.00
Bye-Lo, Baby, Blue Sleep Eyes, Original Body & Clothes, 12 1/2 In.Head 595.00
Bye-Lo, Baby, Composition, 13 In. 250.00

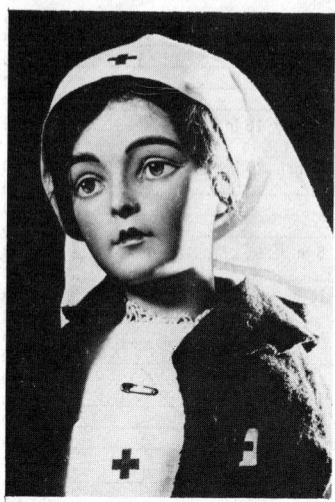

Doll, Bisque, Original Red Cross
Uniform, C.1900

(See Page 179)

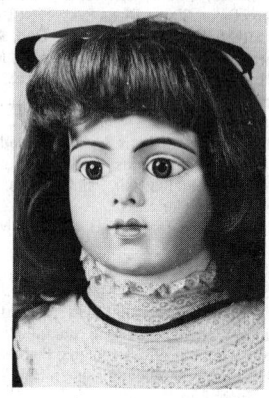

Doll, Bru, French Bisque, Mannikin,
C.1880, 46 In.

Bye-Lo, Baby, Glass Eyes, Jointed Arms & Legs, Dress & Bonnet, 4 1/4 In.	550.00
Bye-Lo, Baby, Stamped Body, Head, 14 In.	725.00
Bye-Lo, Blue Sleep Eyes, Marked Head & Body, Head Circumference 13 In.	525.00
Bye-Lo, Brown Eyes, Signed Head & Body, 10 1/2 In.	395.00
Bye-Lo, Brown Eyes, Swivel Neck, Original Dress, Bisque, 6 In.	600.00
Bye-Lo, Cloth Body, Celluloid Hands, Dressed, 10 1/2 In.	150.00
Bye-Lo, Composition Body, Sleep Brown Eyes, Original Clothes, 13 In.	1200.00
Bye-Lo, Fully Jointed, Hard, Painted Eyes, Japan, 4 In.	45.00
Bye-Lo, Glass Eyes, Swivel Neck, Trunk, Layette, Marked, 8 In.	1200.00
Bye-Lo, Movable Arms & Legs, Bisque, Romper Suit, 4 In.	550.00
Bye-Lo, Open-Close Gray Eyes, Blonde Wig, Bisque, 7 In.	550.00
Bye-Lo, Painted Eyes, Cloth Body, Wax, 21 In.	2000.00
Bye-Lo, Painted Eyes, Jointed Hips & Shoulders, Bisque, 5 In.	350.00
Bye-Lo, Sleep Eyes, Cloth Head & Body, Celluloid Hands, 12 1/2 In.	550.00
Campbell Kid, Centennial, Vinyl, 10 In.	25.00
Campbell Kid, Cloth Body, Marked	150.00
Celluloid, Boy, Buckskin Suit & Hat, Turtlemark, 16 In.	90.00
Celluloid, Boy, German Turtlemark, Blue Glass Eyes, 22 In.	175.00
Ceresota Flour Boy, Stuffed	90.00
Chad Valley, Girl, Glass Eyes, Plaid Skirt & Tam	120.00
Chad Valley, Little Red Riding Hood, 24 In.	450.00
Chad Valley, Margaret Rose, Redhead, 15 In.	395.00
Charlie McCarthy	35.00
Chase, Baby, Original Clothes, 14 In.	145.00
Chase, Boy, 26 In.	325.00
Chatty Baby, Black, Original	75.00
Chatty Cathy, 1960, Boxed	75.00
Cloth, Art Fabric Mills Cutout, 8 1/2 In.	50.00
Cloth, C.1850, Checkered Dress	325.00
Cloth, Dolly Dimples, Original Envelope	145.00
Cloth, Embroidered Face, Yarn Hair, Leather Shoes, Movable Arms, 23 In.	50.00
Cloth, Raggedy Ann, I Love Your Heart	100.00
Clown, Schoenhut	125.00
Countess Dagmar, Parian, 14 In.	450.00
Cream Of Wheat Man, Stuffed	45.00
Creche, Original Dress, 11 In.	350.00

Creche, Polychromed Terra-Cotta, Italian, 12 In. 190.00
Cuno & Otto Dressel, Bisque, Socket Head, Wing Mark, 20 In. 240.00
Cuno & Otto Dressel, Sleep Eyes, Ball-Jointed Body, Dressed, 18 In. 485.00
D.D.K.260, Blue Sleep Eyes, 33 In. 1575.00
Deanna Durbin, Gypsy Princess Costume, 14 In. 235.00
Dimples, Composition 95.00
Dionne Quintuplets, Toddler, Original Outfit, 11 In. 350.00
Dionne Quintuplets, 12 In., Set 1150.00
Doll, Mr.Peanut, Character, Wood-Jointed 115.00
Dollhouse, Mother, Grandmother, & Butler, Molded Hair, Bisque, 6 In. 210.00
Dollikins Baby, Jointed, Rooted Hair, Uneeda, 21 In. 55.00
Dolly Dimples, Cloth, Uncut, Packaged 150.00
Donald Duck, Jointed, Celluloid, 3 1/2 In. 175.00
Dondi, Comic Character, Vinyl, All Original 45.00
Dr.Doolittle, Original Clothes, 22 In. 25.00
Dream Baby 341, Closed Mouth, Cloth Body, 12 In. 275.00
Dream Baby, Dressed, 8 1/2 In. 325.00
Dressel, Bisque, Socket Head, Jointed Composition Body, 22 In. 675.00
E.G.Goldberger, Composite Head, Arms, Legs, Cloth Body, Navy Dress 35.00
Eden Bebe, Bisque Head, Paperweight Eyes, Pierced Ears, Marked, 17 In. 1700.00
Eden Bebe, Closed Mouth, Paperweight Eyes, 25 In. 2550.00
Eden Bebe, Dressed As Bride, Open Mouth, All Original, 27 In. 2900.00
Effanbee, Ann Shirley, Bride, White Satin Gown, Human Hair Wig, 21 In. 180.00
Effanbee, Ann Shirley, 15 In. 68.00
Effanbee, Antique Bride, Ecru Lace Gown, 18 In. 65.00
Effanbee, Baby Dainty, Composition, With Pin 95.00
Effanbee, Baby, Dy-Dee, Caracul Wig 75.00
Effanbee, Barbara Lou, Smiling, Metal Heart Bracelet, 21 In. 850.00
Effanbee, Boy, 1967 .... 22.00
Effanbee, Dewees Cochran, American Child, Open Mouth, 21 In. 495.00
Effanbee, Dewees Cochran, Cindy 395.00
Effanbee, Dewees Cochran, Ice Queen, Sleep Eyes, Marked, 14 In. 425.00
Effanbee, Dewees Cochran, Self-Portrait, 1977 .... 165.00
Effanbee, Dewess Cochran, Boy, Blue Suit, American Child, Tags, 1930s 1000.00
Effanbee, Dy-Dee Gro, Jointed, Sleep Eyes, Vinyline, Wets, 20 In. 40.00
Effanbee, Dy-Dee Jane, 17 In. 75.00
Effanbee, Girl Scout, Black, 1966, Boxed 25.00
Effanbee, Girl, Composition, Original Clothes, 27 In. 225.00
Effanbee, Grandes Dames, Daphne, 18 In. 44.00
Effanbee, Grandes Dames, Opal, 18 In. 44.00
Effanbee, Grandes Dames, Topaz, 18 In. 44.00
Effanbee, Honey, Ball Gown, 15 In. 90.00
Effanbee, Little Lady, Composition, Cloth, Yarn Hair, 1942, 20 In. 95.00
Effanbee, Lovums, Composition Body, 21 In. 125.00
Effanbee, Lovums, Gold Bracelet, Original, 30 In. 225.00
Effanbee, Lovums, Sleep Eyes, Movable Teeth, Cloth Body, 16 In. 25.00
Effanbee, Maid Marian & Robin Hood, Pair 70.00
Effanbee, Mary Ann, Long Curls, 19 In. 175.00
Effanbee, Mary Ann, Plaid Dress, Red Hair, Heart Bracelet, 1928 .... 200.00
Effanbee, Mickey Sailor Boy, Rubber 20.00
Effanbee, Patricia, Green Sleep Eyes, Lashes, Blonde Wig, 16 In. 135.00
Effanbee, Patsy Joan, 16 In. 130.00
Effanbee, Patsy, Original Dress & Bracelets 225.00
Effanbee, Patsy, Redressed, 14 In. 85.00
Effanbee, Patsy, 19 In. 190.00
Effanbee, Patsyette, Original Dress & Bonnet, 9 In. 90.00
Effanbee, Rosemary, Walk, Talk, Sleep, Open Mouth, 24 In. 125.00
Effanbee, Skippy, Boxed 185.00
Effanbee, Sugar Baby, Dressed, 23 In. 100.00
Effanbee, Sugar Baby, Open & Close Green Eyes, Molded Hair, 1936 .... 95.00
Effanbee, Sweetie Pie, Blue Flirty Eyes, Red Wig, Composition 90.00
Effanbee, Tinkerbell 35.00
Effanbee, Tommy Tucker, Brown Flirty Eyes 55.00

Effanbee, W.C.Fields .... 50.00 To 60.00
Einco, Googly, Blue Eyes, Metal Lever Mechanism, Ball-Jointed, 13 In. 6000.00
Elizabeth Taylor, 3 Changes Of Clothes, Horsman, Boxed, 12 In. 45.00
Ella Cinders, Original Clothes, 16 1/2 In. 325.00
Emma Clear, Danny Boy, 17 In. 310.00
Emmett Kelly 75.00
English, Hillary, Blonde, Blue Coat Over Pink Dress, Porcelain, 24 In. 112.50
English, Sharon, Auburn Brown Jumper, Porcelain, 24 In. 112.50
F.G., Bisque Head, Paperweight Eyes, Composition Jointed Body, 20 In. 2650.00
F.G., Child, Closed Mouth, Paperweight Eyes, French Body, 20 In. 2400.00
F.G., Child, Original Clothes, Bisque, 12 In. 2875.00
F.G., Closed Mouth, Paperweight Eyes, Pull-String Voice, 24 In. 2900.00
F.G., Fashion, Original Wig, Shoes, Trunk & Accessories, 23 In. 2850.00
F.G., French, Child, Blue Eyes, Closed Mouth, 20 In. 2000.00
F.G., French, Closed Mouth, Blue Glass Eyes, Swivel Head, Marked, 17 In. 850.00
F.G., French, Closed Mouth, Human Hair Wig, 8 1/2 In. 675.00
F.G., Kid Fashion Body, Blue Paperweight Eyes, Closed Mouth, 15 In. 1200.00
F.G., Leather Body, Blue Paperweight Eyes, Closed Mouth, 12 In. 1200.00
F.G., Original Clothes, 15 In. 1400.00
F.G., Original Clothes, 17 In. 1800.00
F.S. & Co., Breather Baby, Blue Sleep Eyes, Wobble Tongue, 27 In. 1250.00
Fanny Brice, Ideal, 12 1/2 In. 225.00
Fashion, Mulatto, Kid Body, Paperweight Eyes, Marked, 13 In. 2000.00
Flapper, Bisque, 3 In. 45.00
Floradora, Bisque Head, Kid Body, Glass Eyes, Velvet Dress, 19 In. 140.00
Floradora, Bisque, Leather Body, Dressed, 23 In. 265.00
Floradora, Kid Body, Bisque Forearms, Dressed 12 In. 225.00
French, Black, Original Wig, Ball-Jointed Body, 11 1/2 In. 2200.00
French, Closed Mouth, Dancing Automaton On Inlaid Music Box 1150.00
French, Fashion, Extra Hats, Dresses, & Gloves, Basket, 10 1/2 In. 1350.00
French, Fashion, Kid Body, Wood Upper Arms, Bisque Hands, 15 In. 2250.00
French, Jointed, French, Eagle Mark 40.00
French, Lady, Musical Automaton, 20th Century *Illus*1800.00
French, Le Conte, Brown Eyes, Blonde Hair, Silk Plaid Outfit, 18 In. 900.00
French, Marie Antoinette, Cobalt Blue Eyes, Original Wig, 20 1/2 In. 3000.00
French, Open Mouth, Blue Paperweight Eyes, Marked, 15 In. 595.00
French, Open Mouth, Brown Paperweight Eyes, Long Hair, 24 In. 1500.00
French, Sleep Eyes, Human Hair Wig, Original Clothes, Bonnet, 24 In. 1575.00
French, 5-Piece Body, Glass Eyes, 5 In. 300.00
Frozen Charlie, Molded Eyelids, Pink, C.1850, 16 In. 265.00
Frozen Charlotte, Blonde, 16 1/2 In. 500.00
Frozen Charlotte, Brown Eyes, Pink Luster Face, 15 1/4 In. 350.00
Frozen Charlotte, German, 2 In. 25.00
Frozen Charlotte, Mohair Wig, Braids, Painted Features, 3 1/4 In. 75.00
Frozen Charlotte, Pink Luster Face, 16 In. 475.00
    DOLL, FULPER, see also Doll, Horsman
Fulper, Girl, Linen Dress, 19 In. 500.00
Furniture, Closet, 2 Glass Doors, Stenciling, Mirror, White, 20 X 10 In. 65.00
Furniture, Kitchen, Refrigerator, Green, Opens, Tootsietoy 12.00
Furniture, Kitchen, Server, Green, Opens, Tootsietoy 10.00
G.S.& Co., Blue Sleep Eyes, Ball-Jointed, 23 In. 395.00
Gebruder Krauss, Pouty Boy, Painted Eyes, Ball-Jointed Body, 16 In. 695.00
Gebruder Kuhnlenz, Boy, Bisque, Composition Limbs, Native Dress, 9 In. 75.00
General MacArthur, Molded Hat, Composition, Pin Button, 18 In. 225.00
Georgene Averill, Baby, Cloth Body, Head 14 In. 625.00
Gerber Baby, Christening Gown & Basket, Flirty Eyes, 12 In. 45.00
German, Baby Boy, Bisque Head, Sleep Eyes, Marked 1992/0, 11 1/2 In. 125.00
German, Baby, Bisque, Clover Mark, 5 In. 60.00
German, Bisque-Headed, Poured Wax Shoulders, 19th Century ....*Illus* 225.00
German, Bisque, Brown Hair, Open Eyes, Kid Body, 15 In. 200.00
German, Bisque, Flapper Girls, Different Dresses, 2 1/2 In., Box Of 6 .... 250.00
German, Black, Closed Mouth, 5-Piece Body, 13 In. 650.00
German, Clown, White Bisque 850.00

Doll, French, Lady, Musical Automaton,
20th Century

Doll, German, Bisque-Headed, Poured
Wax Shoulders, 19th Century

Doll, German, Fashion, Bisque
Swivel Neck, 19th Century

German, Fashion, Bisque Swivel Neck, 19th Century ....*Illus*	725.00
German, Fashion, Closed Mouth, Cloth Body, 11 In.	675.00
German, Fashion, Kid Body, Paperweight Eyes, 10 In.	300.00
German, Girl, Bisque, Head, Blonde, Dressed, Composition Body, 21 1/2 In.	250.00
German, Girl, Blue Eyes, Composition Body, Bisque Head, Marked 21, 14 In.	145.00
German, Girl, Closed Mouth, Blue Eyes, Bisque, 9 1/2 In.	225.00
German, Girl, Composition Body, Blonde Wig, Marked Germany 1916, 24 In.	275.00
German, Girl, Pink Tinted Complexion, Molded Lids, Cloth Body, 20 In.	350.00
German, K.H.Walkure, No.253, Sleep Eyes, Brown Wig, 16 In.	175.00
German, Little Sweetheart, Bisque, Original Box, 23 In.	600.00
German, No.182, Stationary Blue Eyes, 35 In.	950.00
German, Open-Close Mouth, Sleep Eyes, Kid Body, Bisque Arms, 14 In.	425.00
German, Paperweight Eyes, Ball-Jointed, Bisque Head, Marked, 18 In.	1500.00
German, Parian-Type Bisque Turned Head, Kid Body, 15 In.	850.00
German, Stationary Eyes, Open Mouth, Ball-Jointed, 22 In.	495.00
German, Toddler, Wobble Tongue, Bent Limbs, Marked, 26 1/2 In.	950.00
Ginger Rogers, Composition, Clothes Tagged, Wendy Face, 21 In.	450.00
Girl, Art Fabric, Printed Undies, Signed, 18 In.	100.00
Goebel, Coquette, Lacy Dress, Painted Shoes, 2 Straps	395.00
Goebel, Coquette, Painted Eyes To Side, Open-Close Mouth, 6 3/4 In.	195.00
Goodyear, Rubber, C.1850, Original Clothes	650.00
Googly 165, Bisque Head, Composition Toddler Body, 13 In.	2600.00
Greiner, Black Haired	350.00
Greiner, Leather Arms, Painted Eyes, 23 In.	350.00

H & C, Viola, Original Clothing & Wig, Germany, 32 In.	750.00
Handwerck 283, Girl, 28 In.	495.00
Handwerck 79, Stationary Brown Eyes, Bisque, 18 In.	275.00
Handwerck 99, Girl, Long Blonde Wig, Blue Eyes, Pierced Ears, 32 In.	725.00
Handwerck, Blue Paperweight Eyes, Open Mouth, Ball-Jointed Body, 38 In.	1650.00
Handwerck, Blue Sleep Eyes, Lashes, Ball-Jointed, 33 1/4 In.	1495.00
Handwerck, Child, Brown Sleep Eyes, Pierced Ears, Bisque, 29 In.	850.00
Handwerck, Flirty Eyes, Mohair Ringlets, Silk Dress, Cape, 22 In.	675.00
Handwerck, Girl, Brown Hair, Composition, Bisque Head & Arms, 17 In.	395.00
Handwerck, Girl, Paperweight Eyes, Ball-Jointed Body, 33 1/2 In.	1495.00
Handwerck, Lady, Composition Body, Sleep Blue Eyes, 14 1/2 In.	950.00
Handwerck, Open Mouth, Bulging Eyes, Kid Body, 17 In.	225.00
Handwerck, Sleep Blue Eyes, Jointed, 25 In.	400.00
Handwerck, Sleep Blue Eyes, Original Body, 29 In.	900.00
Handwerck, Sleep Brown Eyes, All Original, 18 In.	395.00
Handwerck, Sleep Eyes, Ball-Jointed Body, Original Clothes, 29 In.	795.00
Happifats, Boy & Girl, Marked, 4 In.	600.00
Harriet Hubbard Ayers, Ideal	85.00
Heeby Sheeby, Blue Boots, Bisque, 4 In.	600.00
Heidi Ott, Hand-Painted Vinyl Head, Lucie, Holding Own Baby, 19 In.	265.00
Helen Jenson, Gladdie, Boy, Composition, Biskaloid Legs, Arms, & Head	800.00
Herm Steiner, Baby, Sleep Eyes, Celluloid Hands, Baby Dress, 10 In.	395.00
Heubach Koppelsdorf 267, Baby, Sleep Eyes, Bisque, 5-Piece Body, 20 In.	325.00
Heubach Koppelsdorf 267, Toddler, Sleep Eyes, Composition Body, 18 In.	425.00
Heubach Koppelsdorf 300, Baby, Blonde Hair, Brown Eyes, 12 In.	350.00
Heubach Koppelsdorf 399, Toddler, Closed Mouth, Sleep Eyes, 15 In.	585.00
Heubach Koppelsdorf 520 7/0, Character Baby, Boy, Bisque, 12 In.	250.00
Heubach Koppelsdorf, Shoulder Head, Leather Arms, Glass Eyes, 20 In.	125.00
Heubach 8191, Closed Mouth, Molded Teeth, Bent Limbs, 15 In.	500.00
Heubach 8192, Girl, 9 1/2 In.	400.00
Heubach, American Schoolboy, 15 In.	450.00
Heubach, Baby, Flirty, Blue Dress	455.00
Heubach, Boy, Flocked Hair, With Hobby Horse, Square Mark, 5 1/2 In.	475.00
Heubach, Boy, Watermelon Mouth, Jointed Arms, 4 1/4 In.	150.00
Heubach, Character, Mechanical, Toddler Taking First Step, 11 In.	1425.00
Heubach, Dream Baby, Closed Mouth, 15 In.	600.00
Heubach, Easter Bunny Children With Eggs For Candies, 5 1/2 In.	475.00
Heubach, Googly Baby, Sleep Eyes, 5-Piece Body, 7 In.	395.00
Heubach, Googly Girl, 7 In.	575.00
Heubach, Laughing Boy, 7 In.	250.00
Heubach, Pouty Baby, 17 In.	445.00
Heubach, Pouty Boy, Intaglio Eyes, 16 In.	880.00
Heubach, Pouty, Girl, Flocked Hair, 11 1/2 In.	700.00
Highland Mary, Parian, 27 In.	495.00
Highland Mary, Pink Luster, White Leather Arms, 20 1/2 In.	225.00
Hilda, Blue Sleep Eyes, Bisque, Head, 10 In.	1920.00
Hina, Emperor & Empress, C.1920, 10 In., Pair	145.00
Horsman, Baby Magic Skin, Original Box	35.00
Horsman, Blonde, Sleep Eyes, Rooted Hair, Rubber Stuffed, 14 In.	10.00
Horsman, Little Bo Peep Outfit, Pouty Mouth, Mohair Pigtails, 22 In.	150.00
Horsman, Poor Pitiful Pearl, Original Clothes & Tags, 17 In.	35.00
Howdy Doody, Mouth Moves, Boxed, 12 In.	35.00
Howdy Doody, Wood, Jointed, Pristine	175.00
Hummel, Vinyl, Goebel Incised Bee Mark, 10 In.	20.00
Ideal, Baby Dreams, 16 In.	40.00
Ideal, Baby Sparkle Plenty, Sleep Eyes, Hard Plastic Head, 14 In.	68.00
Ideal, Bam Bam, 16 In.	20.00
Ideal, Betsy Wetsy, 17 In.	20.00
Ideal, Bonnie Braids, Holding Toothbrush, Tagged Dress	50.00
Ideal, Cameo, Baby Mine	125.00
Ideal, Campbell Kids, Boy, Cloth Body, Rubber Appendages, 12 In.	25.00
Ideal, Deanna Durbin, All Original, 21 In.	375.00
Ideal, Fanny Brice's Baby Snooks, Flexible Body	170.00

Ideal, Kiss Me Baby, 1951	65.00
Ideal, Little Miss Revlon, Lingerie & Pearls, 1957, 10 1/2 In.	25.00
Ideal, Miss Peep, Cameo	35.00
Ideal, Peter Playpal, Original, 38 In.	250.00
Ideal, Play'n Jane, Battery Operated, Plays Tic-Tac-Toe	24.00
Ideal, Saucy Walker, 22 In.	25.00
Ideal, Shirley Temple, Blue Dress, New Wig, 22 In.	150.00
Ideal, Shirley Temple, Flirty Eyes, 1950s	200.00
Ideal, Shirley, 1972	45.00
Ideal, Tiffany Taylor, Boxed, 18 In.	12.00
Ideal, Tiny Tears	15.00
Ideal, Toni, Brunette, Hand-Painted, Tagged, 20 In.	125.00
Ideal, Toni, 1948, 14 In.	45.00
Ideal, Triple Head, Lever Behind Neck Activates, Plastic, 22 In.	65.00
DOLL, INDIAN, see Indian, Doll	
Indian Maiden, Velvet Body, Felt Clothes, Painted Face, Quebec	35.00
Italian, Creche, 8 1/2 In.	140.00
DOLL, J.D.K., see also Doll, Kestner	
J.D.K.151, Baby, 13 In.	210.00
J.D.K.164, Brown Sleep Eyes, Ball-Jointed, Signed, 18 In.	495.00
J.D.K.171, Sleep Brown Eyes, Original Wig, 24 In.	125.00
J.D.K.211, Baby Sammy, Blue Eyes, 17 In.	675.00
J.D.K.211, Jointed Toddler Body, 11 1/2 In.	425.00
J.D.K.211, Sammy Baby, Blue Eyes, 17 In.	675.00
J.D.K.221, Googly, All Original, 12 In.	2600.00
J.D.K.257, Baby, Blonde With Black Eyelashes	500.00
J.D.K.257, Baby, Blue Sleep Eyes, 14 In.	495.00
J.D.K.257, Baby, Open Mouth, Blue Sleep Eyes, Blonde Wig, Marked, 15 In.	325.00
J.D.K.257, Baby, Sleep Eyes, 16 In.	475.00
J.D.K.260, Character, Stationary Brown Eyes, Original Wig, 27 In.	1000.00
J.D.K.260, Toddler, Fully Jointed, 33 In.	1575.00
Jane Withers, Closed Mouth, Tagged, 13 In.	850.00
Japan, Wedding Veil, Celluloid, 10 In.	20.00
Japanese Kyugetsu	150.00
Japanese, Porcelain Head, Dressed, 8 1/2 In.	100.00
Jensen, Gladdie, 16 In.	850.00
Judy Garland, Sitting On Stool, Dressed In Tuxedo, 30 In.	380.00
Jumeau, Bisque Head, Paperweight Eyes, Composition Body, Dressed, 26 In.	3000.00
Jumeau, Blue Paperweight Eyes, Bisque, 30 In.	2550.00
Jumeau, Blue Paperweight Eyes, Closed Mouth, Signed, 24 In.	3600.00
Jumeau, Blue Paperweight Eyes, Closed Mouth, 11 In.	2500.00
Jumeau, Blue Paperweight Eyes, Marked, 1907, 31 In.	2850.00
Jumeau, Blue Paperweight Eyes, Pale Bisque, Signed Head, 27 In.	3675.00
Jumeau, Brown Paperweight Eyes, Original Marked Body, 27 In.	3400.00
Jumeau, Closed Mouth, Blue Paperweight Eyes, Marked, 15 In.	2900.00
Jumeau, Closed Mouth, Paperweight Eyes, Marked Head & Body, 17 In.	2450.00
Jumeau, Closed Mouth, Paperweight Eyes, 26 In.	3000.00
Jumeau, Closed Mouth, 20 In.	3400.00
Jumeau, Fashion, C.1875, Bisque	*Illus* 2300.00
Jumeau, French Fashion, Brown Eyes, Stamped Body, 14 In.	1450.00
Jumeau, Long Face, Original Pink Satin Dress & Hat, 21 In.	9975.00
Jumeau, Long Face, 28 In.	4500.00
Jumeau, Mechanical, Walker, Voice Box, Throws Kisses, 21 In.	2000.00
Jumeau, Open Mouth, Blue Open & Close Eyes, Bisque, Marked, 28 In.	950.00
Jumeau, Open Mouth, Brown Open & Close Eyes, Marked, 18 In.	950.00
Jumeau, Open Mouth, Glass Eyes, Velvet Dress, Curls, 30 In.	3000.00
Jumeau, Open Mouth, Open & Close Eyes, Brown Hair Wig, Marked, 23 In.	950.00
Jumeau, Open Mouth, Original Body, Wig, & Clothes, 25 In.	1995.00
Jumeau, Open Mouth, Paperweight Eyes, Pierced Ears, Dressed, 24 In.	2400.00
Jumeau, Open Mouth, Paperweight Eyes, 22 In.	2300.00
Jumeau, Original Clothes, Signed Head & Body, 30 In.	4900.00
Jumeau, Paperweight Eyes, Ball-Jointed, Velvet Dress, 20 In.	2000.00
Jumeau, Paperweight Eyes, Bisque, Straight Wrists, Signed, 29 In.	5500.00

Doll, Jumeau, Fashion, C.1875, Bisque

(See Page 185)

Jumeau, Paperweight Eyes, Closed Mouth, Head Marked, 15 In.	2850.00
Jumeau, Paperweight Eyes, Dressed In Cranberry Velvet, 32 In.	2950.00
Jumeau, Paperweight Eyes, Original Body, Marked, 22 In.	1850.00
Jumeau, Paperweight Eyes, Walking Body, 24 In.	3100.00
Jumeau, Voice Box With Pull Strings, Paperweight Eyes, 19 In.	6500.00
Juno, Tin Head	30.00
Just Me, Bisque Head, 9 In.	1100.00
Just Me, Original Clothes & Wig, Biskaloid, 9 1/2 In.	400.00
Jutta, No.1349, Clown, Sleep Eyes, Blonde Human Hair, 28 In.	750.00
K & K 39, Open Mouth, Blue Eyes, Germany, Kahl & Kohle, 21 In.	250.00
K * R 26, Open Mouth, Brown Eyes, Original Clothes, 9 1/2 In.	400.00
K * R 100, Baby, 11 In.	550.00
K * R 101, Gray Painted Eyes, Brown Mohair Wig, 12 In.	1400.00
K * R 101, Marie, Intaglio Eyes, 5-Piece Body, White Dress, 11 In.	2000.00
K * R 114, Hans, Sailor Suit, Ear Missing, 18 In.	1495.00
K * R 116a, Baby, Open-Close Mouth, 17 In.	2100.00
K * R 117, Flirty Sleep Eyes, Ball-Jointed, 30 In.	2650.00
K * R 117, Flirty, Dressed, 25 In.	1200.00
K * R 117, Mein Liebling, Sleep Eyes, Girl Body, 31 In.	5200.00
K * R 117, Simon & Halbig, Flirty Eyes, Antique Clothes, 20 In.	900.00
K * R 117n, Flirty Eyes, Antique Clothes, 20 In.	900.00
K * R 117n, Toddler, Print Costume, Sleep Eyes, 21 In.	1500.00
K * R 121, Baby, Dimples, Christening Clothes, 26 In.	900.00
K * R 122, Baby, Mechanical, Closes Eyes, Moves Tongue, 22 In.	2200.00
K * R 126, Baby, Blue Eyes, Brown Wig, Original Clothes, 10 1/2 In.	350.00
K * R 126, Baby, Flirty Brown Eyes, 16 In.	595.00
K * R 126, Baby, Pre-1900, 29 In.	1200.00
K * R 126, Toddler, Flirty Eyes, 23 In.	495.00
K * R 126, Toddler, Sleep Eyes, Open Mouth, 2 Teeth, Sundress, 6 In.	250.00
K * R 128, Baby, 16 In.	550.00
K * R 403, Blue Sleep Eyes, Blonde, Ball-Jointed, 20 1/2 In.	450.00
K * R 717/70, Flirty Eyes, Celluloid Head, Jointed Above Knees, 27 In.	475.00
K * R 1228, Toddler, Open Mouth, 2 Upper Teeth, Movable Tongue, 17 In.	995.00
K * R, Blue Flirty Eyes, Ball-Jointed, Pierced Ears, 25 In.	795.00
K * R, Blue Sleep Eyes, Brown Human Hair Wig, Antique Dress, 27 In.	750.00
K * R, Child, Bisque Head, Sleep Eyes, Open Mouth, 6 In.	285.00

K * R, Flirty Brown Eyes, Pierced Ears, Dressed, 19 In. 825.00
K * R, Flirty Eyes, Ball-Jointed Body, Human Hair, 28 In. 950.00
K * R, Flirty Eyes, 29 In. 2150.00
K * R, Girl, Sleep Brown Eyes, 26 In. 500.00
K * R, Open Mouth, Cloth-Stuffed Body, German, Incised Mark, 16 In. 375.00
Kaiser, Baby, Brown Eyes, 14 1/2 In. 575.00
Kallas, Pete, Jointed, Wooden, 12 In. 175.00
Kampkins, 18 In. 400.00
Kathy Kruse, Boy, Original Attire, 17 In. 750.00
Kenner, Darci, Boxed, 12 1/2 In. 10.00
      DOLL, KESTNER, see also Doll, J.D.K.
Kestner 12, Sleep Eyes, Open Mouth, 2 Teeth, Ball-Jointed, 19 In. 795.00
Kestner 64/14, German Girl, Kid Body, Bisque Head, 17 In. 225.00
Kestner 118, Kid Body, Dressed, 19 In. 350.00
Kestner 136, Girl, Brown Eyes, All Original, 24 In. .... 495.00 To 520.00
Kestner 143, Sleep Brown Eyes, Original Wig & Underwear, 8 In. 350.00
Kestner 143, Sleep Eyes, Ball-Jointed, 20 In. 775.00
Kestner 143, Sleep Eyes, Open Mouth, 2 Upper Teeth, 22 In. 1275.00
Kestner 146, Brown Sleep Eyes, Ball-Jointed, 24 In. 395.00
Kestner 149, Sleep Eyes, Human Hair Wig, Original Dress, 19 1/2 In. 795.00
Kestner 150, Sleep Eyes, All Bisque, 9 1/2 In. 795.00
Kestner 152, Baby, Gray Eyes, 14 In. 315.00
Kestner 152, Character Baby, Blue Sleep Eyes, 21 In. 550.00
Kestner 154, Blonde Braids, Original Clothes, 27 In. 285.00
Kestner 154, Kid Body, Composition Arms, Original Wig, 29 In. 750.00
Kestner 154, Schoolgirl, Human Hair Wig, Leather Body, 24 In. 495.00
Kestner 154, Sleep Brown Eyes, Kid Body, 28 In. 395.00
Kestner 154, Sleep Eyes, Kid Pin-Jointed Body, Bisque Arms, 23 In. 475.00
Kestner 156, Child, Lashed Blue Eyes, Blonde Wig, 24 In. 550.00
Kestner 163, Bisque Head, Glass Sleep Eyes, Composition Body, 13 In. 2500.00
Kestner 164, Boy, Sailor Suit, Open Mouth, Eyelashes, 34 In. 1500.00
Kestner 164, Girl, 29 In. 595.00
Kestner 164, Human Hair Wig, Ball-Jointed Body, 30 1/2 In. 595.00
Kestner 164, Sleep Eyes, Human Hair Wig, Original Dress, 19 In. 495.00
Kestner 165-9, Googly, Closed Watermelon Mouth, Blonde Wig, 19 1/2 In. 4500.00
Kestner 166, Sleep Eyes, Old Clothes, 22 In. 425.00
Kestner 167, Girl, Sleep Eyes, Curly Wig, Dressed, 18 1/2 In. 375.00
Kestner 168, Sleep Blue Eyes, All Original, 20 In. 395.00
Kestner 171, Blue Sleep Eyes, 19 In. 295.00
Kestner 171, Character, Sleep Eyes, Human Hair Wig, Bisque Head, 28 In. 925.00
Kestner 171, Daisy, Sleep Eyes, Ball-Jointed, Marked, 30 In. 850.00
Kestner 171, Paperweight Blue Eyes, Bisque Arms, 17 In. 495.00
Kestner 179, Closed Mouth, Painted Amber Eyes, Human Hair Wig, 15 In. 1650.00
Kestner 192, Bisque Head, 28 In. 475.00
Kestner 196, Sleep Eyes, Fur Eyebrows, Ball-Jointed, White Dress, 30 In. 1200.00
Kestner 208, Bisque, Sleep Eyes, 9 In. 690.00
Kestner 215, Fur Eyebrows, Spring Strung, 24 In. 425.00
Kestner 221, Googly, 12 In. 3500.00
Kestner 226, Sleep Eyes, Bent Limbs, Double Chin, 24 In. 500.00
Kestner 240, Googly, 12 In. 2200.00
Kestner 257, Baby, Bisque Head, Glass Eyes, Dressed, 8 In. 250.00
Kestner 257, Baby, Character, Human Wig, Sleep Eyes, Bisque, 17 In. 375.00
Kestner, Baby, Intaglio Eyes, 10 In. 275.00
Kestner, Baby, Kid Body, Lower Arms Bisque, Christening Dress, Blanket 425.00
Kestner, Baby, Open Mouth, Blue Sleep Eyes, Incised Mark, 12 In. 295.00
Kestner, Baby, Solid Dome, Open-Close Mouth, 12 In. 375.00
Kestner, Bisque, Shoulder Head, Kid Body, Brown Sleep Eyes, 14 In. 130.00
Kestner, Boy, Closed Mouth, 19 In. 1800.00
Kestner, Character, Closed Mouth, Ball-Jointed, 16 In. 985.00
Kestner, Closed Mouth, Turned Head, French Cut 1150.00
Kestner, Gibson Girl, Closed Mouth, Original Wig, 18 In. 2650.00
Kestner, Girl, Kid Body, Brown Set Eyes, Closed Mouth 550.00
Kestner, Hilda Baby, Marked, 12 In. 800.00

Kestner, Long Face On Kid Body, 23 In. 425.00
Kestner, Sleep Eyes, Ball-Jointed Body, Blue Crepe Dress, 30 In. 995.00
Kestner, Sleep Eyes, Ball-Jointed Body, Pink Eyelet Dress, 21 1/2 In. 495.00
Kestner, Turned Head, Bisque Arms, Original Clothing, 23 In. 425.00
    DOLL, Kewpie, see Kewpie
Kid Body, Sleep Eyes, Teeth, Coat Trimmed With Mink, Marked, 20 1/2 In. 250.00
Kley & Hahn 526, 19 1/2 In. 3150.00
Kley & Hahn, Baby, Bald Head, Open-Close Eyes, Sweater & Cap, 16 In. 625.00
Kley & Hahn, Baby, Character Face, 5-Piece Bent-Limb Body, 12 In. 595.00
Kley & Hahn, Bisque Head, Wooden, Jointed, 10 In. 425.00
Kley & Hahn, Character Boy, Intaglio Eyes, Open-Close Mouth 595.00
Kley & Hahn, Walkure, Dressed, 26 In. 450.00
Knickerbocker, Pinocchio, 14 In. 350.00
Knickerbocker, Snow White 60.00
Knickerbocker, Snow White & Seven Dwarfs, Hard Rubber, Set 395.00
L.A.S., Baby, C.1914, Head 9 In. 375.00
L.A.S., Baby, C.1914, Head 16 In. 650.00
Lady, Jointed, Original Paint & Dress, 15 In. 98.00
Lady, Wax Over Papier-Mache, Original Dress, C.1880, 20 In. 325.00
Lenci 300, Boy, Original Clothes, Marked, 21 In. 600.00
Lenci, Bernise, Original Clothing, Tagged, 15 In. 395.00
Lenci, Boy, 1933, 33 In. 1495.00
Lenci, Child, Brown Eyes, Original Costume, 17 In. 545.00
Lenci, Child, Hollow Torso, 18 In. 895.00
Lenci, Girl, Original Blue Felt Dress, Ball, 14 In. 275.00
Lenci, Girl, Original Dress & Hat, 18 In. 250.00
Lenci, Girl, Scotch, Boxed 175.00
Lenci, Goose Girl, Labeled, 8 In. 195.00
Lenci, Holding Duck, Original Box, 11 In. 295.00
Lenci, Lady, Cloth Face, Braids & Bun, Tagged, 14 In. 350.00
Lenci, My Dearie, Bisque Head, Glass Eyes, Ball-Jointed, 24 In. 550.00
Lenci, Pouty Girl, Pink Organdy Dress, 18 In. 650.00
Lenci, Schoolgirl Costume, Felt, Jump Rope, 17 In. 365.00
Lenci, Suzanna, Boxed 250.00
Limoges, Character, Blue Paperweight Eyes 1100.00
Limoges, Lady, Lorraine, Bisque, Molded Teeth, 17 In. 1200.00
Madame Alexander, Agatha, 1975 .... 375.00
Madame Alexander, Agatha, 1979, 21 In. .... 225.00 To 275.00
Madame Alexander, Alice In Wonderland, Blue Sleep Eyes, 19 In. 275.00
Madame Alexander, Alice In Wonderland, Composition, 14 In .... 75.00 To 110.00
Madame Alexander, Alice In Wonderland, Plastic, 18 In. .... 225.00 To 395.00
Madame Alexander, Amish Boy, 8 In. 475.00
Madame Alexander, Amy, 1963 .... 140.00
Madame Alexander, Annabelle, 15 In. .... 175.00 To 275.00
Madame Alexander, Baby Brother & Sister, 14 In., Pair 90.00
Madame Alexander, Baby Brother & Sister, 20 In., Set 200.00
Madame Alexander, Baby Brother, 20 In. 80.00
Madame Alexander, Baby Huggims 25.00
Madame Alexander, Baby Lynn 165.00
Madame Alexander, Baby McGuffey, 18 In. 225.00
Madame Alexander, Baby Precious, 14 In. 150.00
Madame Alexander, Baby Snooks, Blue Print Outfit, Tags 150.00
Madame Alexander, Baby Victoria, 14 In. .... 20.00 To 55.00
Madame Alexander, Betsy McCall, 8 In. 60.00
Madame Alexander, Billy, 1959, 8 In. 320.00
Madame Alexander, Binnie Walker, Long Ball Gown 125.00
Madame Alexander, Binnie Walker, Tagged Dress, Yellow Pinafore, 19 In. 175.00
Madame Alexander, Bitsey 125.00
Madame Alexander, Black Baby Ellen, 14 In. 100.00
Madame Alexander, Blue Ballerina, 8 In. 145.00
Madame Alexander, Bopeep, 8 In. 32.00
Madame Alexander, Bride, Lace, 14 In. 195.00
Madame Alexander, Brigitta, Sound Of Music 250.00

Madame Alexander, Butch, Composition, Cloth, 1940, Mohair Wig, 11 In. 200.00
Madame Alexander, Caroline, Original Clothes, Tagged, 14 In. 225.00
Madame Alexander, Cinderella, Ball Gown 60.00
Madame Alexander, Cinderella, Ball Gown, 14 In. .... 60.00 To 85.00
Madame Alexander, Cinderella, Boxed 55.00
Madame Alexander, Cissette, Ballerina 165.00
Madame Alexander, Cissette, Queen 300.00
Madame Alexander, Cissette, 10 In. 70.00
Madame Alexander, Cissy, Binnie Walker, Tagged 95.00
Madame Alexander, Cissy, Bride, 1957 .... 350.00
Madame Alexander, Cissy, Queen .... 350.00 To 450.00
Madame Alexander, Cleopatra, 12 In. 65.00
Madame Alexander, Cornelia, 1972 .... 475.00
Madame Alexander, Cornelia, 1976, Boxed, 21 In. 325.00
Madame Alexander, Creche, Man, Terra-Cotta, 12 In. 190.00
Madame Alexander, Deanna Durbin, Redressed 225.00
Madame Alexander, Deanna Durbin, 21 In. 400.00
Madame Alexander, Dionne Quintuplet, Sleep Eyes, Tagged Dress, 11 In. 275.00
Madame Alexander, Dionne Toddler, Sleep Eyes, Composition, 19 In. 275.00
Madame Alexander, Easter Girl, 8 In. 395.00
Madame Alexander, Ecuador, 8 In. 350.00
Madame Alexander, Elise Ballerina, Dressed In Blue 140.00
Madame Alexander, Elise Ballerina, Silver, Crown 75.00
Madame Alexander, Elise Ballerina, 17 In. .... 70.00 To 150.00
Madame Alexander, Elise Bride, 1966, 17 In. 95.00
Madame Alexander, Elise Bride, 1976, 17 In. 175.00
Madame Alexander, Elizabeth Montgomery, First Set 165.00
Madame Alexander, Enchanted Doll, 8 In. .... 375.00 To 425.00
Madame Alexander, Fairy Princess, Wrist Tag, Necklace, Tiara, 14 1/2 In. 325.00
Madame Alexander, Gainsborough, 1978 .... 375.00
Madame Alexander, Ginny, Trunk, Original Wardrobe 210.00
Madame Alexander, Godey Boy, 14 In. 525.00
Madame Alexander, Godey, Yellow Gown, 14 In. 200.00
Madame Alexander, Grandma Jane, 14 In. 225.00
Madame Alexander, Groom, Marked 350.00
Madame Alexander, Happy 125.00
Madame Alexander, Heidi, 14 In. 75.00
Madame Alexander, Hiawatha, Bent Knees, Boxed, 8 In. 400.00
Madame Alexander, Huggums, Dressed In Silk 125.00
Madame Alexander, Indonesia, Hard Plastic, Bent Knees, 8 In. 105.00
Madame Alexander, Jacqueline, Inaugural Gown 795.00
Madame Alexander, Janie Baby 125.00
Madame Alexander, Japan, Bent Knee Walker, Maggie Face, Boxed 300.00
Madame Alexander, Jeannie Walker, Composition, Pink Dress, Tagged, 18 In 250.00
Madame Alexander, Jenny Lind, Lace On Dress, 14 In. 475.00
Madame Alexander, Jenny Lind, Original Clothes, 11 In. 550.00
Madame Alexander, Jo, Little Women, Tagged Clothes, 14 1/2 In. 165.00
Madame Alexander, Kathy Nurser, 1954, 16 In. 38.00
Madame Alexander, Kathy Tears, Original Clothes, Tagged, 1961 .... 55.00
Madame Alexander, Kelly 150.00
Madame Alexander, Korea, Maggie Face 425.00
Madame Alexander, Leslie Ballerina, Black 250.00
Madame Alexander, Leslie Ballerina, 18 In. 250.00
Madame Alexander, Lissy, Ball Gown, Fur Scarf, 12 In. 225.00
Madame Alexander, Little Colonel, Original, 24 In. 500.00
Madame Alexander, Little Genius, Christening Gown, 8 In. 115.00
Madame Alexander, Little Women & Laurie, Box, 12 In. 300.00
Madame Alexander, Little Women, Boxed, 12 In. 45.00
Madame Alexander, Littlest Angel, Vinyl, Cloth, Wrist Tag, 9 In. 200.00
Madame Alexander, Lord Fauntleroy, 12 In. 95.00
Madame Alexander, Madelaine, Original Clothes, Tagged 135.00
Madame Alexander, Maggie Mix-Up, 1960, Original Box 65.00

Madame Alexander, Magnolia, 1977	475.00
Madame Alexander, Majorette, Bent Knees	750.00
Madame Alexander, Marc Anthony & Cleopatra, Boxed, Pair	100.00
Madame Alexander, Margaret O'Brien, Girl Scout Outfit, 21 In.	595.00
Madame Alexander, Margaret O'Brien, Original Clothes, Tagged, 14 In.	400.00
Madame Alexander, Margot, Bikini, Boxed, 10 In.	225.00
Madame Alexander, Maria, Sound Of Music	250.00
Madame Alexander, Marme, 1966	110.00
Madame Alexander, Marta, 8 In	125.00
Madame Alexander, Mary Martin, Gown, 18 In.	495.00
Madame Alexander, Mary Poppins	40.00
Madame Alexander, McGuffey Ana, Auburn Mohair Wig, 14 In.	145.00
Madame Alexander, McGuffey Ana, Original Clothes, Tagged, 9 In.	150.00
Madame Alexander, McGuffey Ana, 1937, 21 In.	250.00
Madame Alexander, Meg, 12 In.	50.00
Madame Alexander, Meg, 14 In.	315.00
Madame Alexander, Melanie, 1979, 21 In.	225.00
Madame Alexander, Mimi, 1971	650.00 To 1000.00
Madame Alexander, Nancy Drew, Blue & White Suit, All Original, 12 In.	275.00
Madame Alexander, Napoleon & Josephine, Pair	115.00 To 130.00
Madame Alexander, Napoleon, 1i In.	60.00
Madame Alexander, Newborn, Victoria, 14 In.	45.00
Madame Alexander, Nina Ballerina, 1947, 14 In.	200.00
Madame Alexander, Peruvian Boy, Bent Knees, Boxed, 8 In.	375.00 To 475.00
Madame Alexander, Peter Pan	250.00
Madame Alexander, Polly Pigtails, Yellow Tagged Dress, 14 In.	315.00
Madame Alexander, Polly, Red Hair, Sequins, Pink Dress, 17 In.	200.00
Madame Alexander, Poor Cinderella	55.00
Madame Alexander, Presidents' Ladies, First Set	1100.00 To 1200.00
Madame Alexander, Presidents' Ladies, Second Set	550.00 To 650.00
Madame Alexander, Princess Elizabeth, Composition, Sleep Eyes, 23 In.	350.00
Madame Alexander, Princess Elizabeth, Original Tagged Outfit, 17 In.	175.00
Madame Alexander, Princess Elizabeth, Red Mohair Wig, Composition Body	100.00
Madame Alexander, Princess Elizabeth, Short Party Dress, 17 In.	300.00
Madame Alexander, Puddin', 14 In.	50.00
Madame Alexander, Pussycat, Black, 14 In.	75.00 To 97.00
Madame Alexander, Pussycat, Boxed, 24 In.	85.00
Madame Alexander, Pussycat, 20 In.	65.00
Madame Alexander, Quizkin	350.00
Madame Alexander, Rag, Funny, 18 In.	50.00
Madame Alexander, Red Cross Nurse, Boxed, 7 In.	150.00
Madame Alexander, Red Riding Hood, Bent Knees, 7 1/2 In.	125.00
Madame Alexander, Renoir Girl, Cotton Dress, Straw Hat, 1978	275.00
Madame Alexander, Renoir Girl, 1967	150.00
Madame Alexander, Romeo & Juliet, Pair	105.00
Madame Alexander, Romeo, Boxed, 12 In.	65.00
Madame Alexander, Rosamund, Bridesmaid, 15 In.	200.00
Madame Alexander, Rosey Posey, Large	175.00
Madame Alexander, Scarlett, Green Velvet Dress, 21 In.	275.00
Madame Alexander, Scarlett, White Dress, 14 In.	75.00
Madame Alexander, Scootles, Black, Composition	600.00
Madame Alexander, Shari Lewis, 14 In.	225.00
Madame Alexander, Shirley Temple, 13 In.	225.00
Madame Alexander, Sleeping Beauty, 17 In.	350.00 To 400.00
Madame Alexander, Smarty, Original Clothes, Tagged, 1962, 12 In.	125.00
Madame Alexander, Snow White, Gold Skirt, Velvet Top, 17 In.	275.00
Madame Alexander, So Big	125.00
Madame Alexander, Sonja Henie, Smiling Mouth, Composition, 21 In.	350.00
Madame Alexander, Sonja Henie, 18 In.	185.00
Madame Alexander, Southern Belle, Green Ribbon, Boxed	375.00
Madame Alexander, Spanish Boy & Girl	450.00
Madame Alexander, Sweet Tears, With Layette	76.00

Madame Alexander, Sweet Tears, 1965, 13 In.	30.00
Madame Alexander, Sweet Violet, 18 In.	125.00
Madame Alexander, Swiss Walker, Bent Knees, 8 In.	110.00
Madame Alexander, Tinkerbell, 10 In.	325.00
Madame Alexander, Toddler, Vinyl & Cloth, Sleep Eyes, 21 In.	55.00
Madame Alexander, Tommy Bangs, 14 In.	525.00
Madame Alexander, Vietnam, Bent Knees, Maggie Face, Boxed, 8 In.	450.00
Madame Alexander, Walker, Blonde, Tagged, 15 In.	85.00
Madame Alexander, Wendy, Bridesmaid, Composition, 15 In.	175.00
Madame Alexander, Wendy, Maid Of Honor, Composition, 15 In.	195.00
Mammy Doll, Handmade, Patterned Dress, Painted Face, 1930s, 10 In.	48.00
Mascotte, Brown Paperweight Eyes, Closed Mouth, Marked, 11 1/2 In.	2250.00
Mascotte, Original Wig, Antique Clothes & Shoes, 21 In.	3550.00
Mascotte, Paperweight Eyes, Closed Mouth, Marked, 24 In.	2250.00
Mason & Taylor, Child, Striped Dress, Original Paint, 12 In.	750.00
Mason & Taylor, Jointed, Pewter Hands & Feet, Wooden	550.00
Mattel, Baby Come Back, 1976	20.00
Mattel, Barbie, No.3	100.00
Mattel, Barbie, No.850, Titian Ponytail, Boxed	85.00
Mattel, Ken, In Tuxedo, 1967	12.00
Mattel, Mrs.Beasley	20.00
Mechanical, Baby Rising Out Of A Cabbage	2300.00
Mechanical, Baby, Wax, 1860, Plays Music	1600.00
Mechanical, Mama Katzenjammer, Mouth Opens, 1920s, 10 In.	225.00
Mechanical, Pussy Cat	65.00
Melitta, Baby, Open Mouth, 5-Piece Compositon Body, 16 In.	1500.00
Mickey Mouse, Boxing Gloves, 1930s, 11 In.	215.00
Mickey Mouse, Homemade Rag, 1930s, 18 In.	69.00
Mickey Mouse, Pull String To Talk, 13 In.	45.00
Mickey Mouse, Rubber, Sun Rubber Co., 10 In.	40.00
Morimura Bros., Bisque Head, Blue Eyes, Ball-Jointed, Marked, 24 In.	285.00
Mortimer Snerd, Composition Head & Hands, Wood Feet, 12 1/2 In.	175.00
Mr.Peanut, Cloth	12.00
Nancy Ann Storybook, Bisque, Boxed, 8 In.	50.00
Nancy Ann Storybook, Plastic, Mink Stole, 10 1/2 In.	125.00
Nippon, Baby, Blue Sleep Eyes	225.00
Nippon, Bisque, Human Hair, 6 1/2 In.	75.00
Nippon, Boy, Sleep Eyes, Ball-Jointed Body, Human Hair Wig, 20 1/2 In.	250.00
Nippon, Girl, Composition Body, Waxed Eyes, 18 In.	215.00
Nippon, Open Mouth, Gray Sleep Eyes, Composition Body, Marked, 20 In.	275.00
Norah Wellings, Indian, 9 In.	75.00
Norah Wellings, Mexican, 13 1/2 In.	75.00
Norah Wellings, Sailor, 10 In.	45.00
Nun, Flying Nun White Headdress, Rosary Beads	45.00
P.M.914, Googly, Sleep Eyes, Papier-Mache Body, 8 In.	725.00
P.M.914, Toddler, Molded Teeth & Tongue, Pink & White Dress, 22 In.	675.00
Pansey 1, Germany, Brown Sleep Eyes, Lashes, Dressed, 23 In.	425.00
Pansey, Sleep Eyes, Human Hair Wig, Ball-Jointed Body, 22 In.	395.00
DOLL, PAPER, see Paper Doll	
Papier-Mache, Blonde Hair, 36 In.	350.00
Papier-Mache, Boy & Girl, Amish Costume, 10 1/2 In., Pair	55.00
Papier-Mache, French, Fashion Pink Kid Body, Dressed, 23 1/2 In.	950.00
Papier-Mache, Goldsmith Body, 28 In.	385.00
Papier-Mache, Indian, German, 11 In.	75.00
Papier-Mache, Santa Claus, Red Suit, 9 In.	25.00
Parian, Alice In Wonderland, Satin & Lace, Shoes, 24 In.	892.00
Parian, Black Band, Cloth Corset, Body, Wired Leather Hands, 16 In.	495.00
Parian, Fancy Dress, 16 In.	200.00
Parian, Lady, Molded Hair, Bisque Arms, Cloth Body	475.00
Parsons Jackson, Baby, Celluloid, Double Chin, Jointed At Neck, 11 In.	75.00
Parsons Jackson, Character, Boy, Bisque, Stork Mark, 15 In.	220.00
Patsy Lou, Original	250.00
Patty Play Pal, 36 In.	50.00

Peter Pan, HP, 1953 .... 335.00
Peter Play Pal, 38 In. 50.00
Phoenix Bebe, Paperweight Eyes, Bisque & Tinting, Ball-Jointed, 15 In. 1250.00
DOLL, PINCUSHION, see Pincushion Doll
Pinocchio, Walt Disney, Wood 140.00
Poor Pitiful Pearl, Boxed, 12 In. 40.00
Pouty, Intaglio Eyes, Composition Body, Closed Mouth, 8 In. 450.00
President Harry Truman, Cloth & Wood, 11 In. 90.00
Princess Elizabeth, 1937, Boxed, 13 In. 275.00
Princess, Japanese, Nishi, Porcelain Face & Feet, Wig & Fan, 15 In. 100.00
Pudgy Girl, Sleep Eyes, 6 1/2 In. 135.00
Queen Anne, Wood Head & Torso, Wire Limbs, C.1780, 9 1/4 In. 1595.00
Queen Louise, 13 In. 225.00
Quiz Kid, Hard Plastic, Mohair Braids, 10 1/4 In. 35.00
R & B, Composition & Cloth Body, 19 In. 95.00
R.D., Bisque Head, Paperweight Eyes, Jointed, Marked R.2D, 20 In. 3600.00
R.D., Closed Mouth, Blue Paperweight Eyes, Incised Mark R2D, 22 In. 2850.00
R.D., Paperweight Eyes, Bisque, Wood & Papier-Mache Sockets, 17 In. 3500.00
Recknagel, Bisque, Blue Stationary Eyes, Wooden Torso, 9 In. 70.00
Revalo, Blue Sleep Eyes, Original Wig, 25 In. 500.00
Revalo, Set Eyes, Cotton Shift & Underwear, Bisque, 18 In. 295.00
Revalo, Stationary Glass Eyes, Ball-Jointed, Print Dress, 19 In. 450.00
Rohmer, Fashion, Blue Eyes, Dark Eyeliner, Signed, 18 In. 4500.00
Rohmer, French, Glass Eyes, Kid Body, China Arms & Head, 21 In. 3795.00
S & H III, Blue Sleep Eyes, Lashes, Ball-Jointed Body, 24 1/2 In. 550.00
S & H 126, Bent Limb Body, Blue Velvet Boy's Suit, 18 In. 535.00
S & H 905, Swivel Head On Bisque Shoulder, Cloth Body, 11 In. 995.00
S & H 949, Blue Eyes, Closed Mouth, Ball-Jointed Body, 27 In. 2250.00
S & H 949, Closed Mouth, Swivel Head On Bisque Shoulder Plate, 19 In. 1600.00
S & H 950, Kid Body & Feet, Bisque Arms, Taffeta Dress, 19 In. 1025.00
S & H 1009, Brown Sleep Eyes, Ball-Jointed, 22 1/2 In. 475.00
S & H 1010, Kid Body, 23 In. 250.00
S & H 1079, Blonde Hair, Blue Eyes, 15 1/2 In. 395.00
S & H 1079, Brown Eyes, 31 1/2 In. 750.00
S & H 1079, Brown Sleep Eyes, Ball-Jointed, 27 In. 495.00
S & H 1079, French Body, Brown Eyes & Hair, 16 1/2 In. 395.00
S & H 1079, Girl, Brown Wig, White Cotton Dress, 29 In. 750.00
S & H 1159, Lady, Sleep Eyes, Molded Brows, Ball-Jounted Body, 27 In. 2500.00
S & H 1079, Sleep Brown Eyes, Blonde Wig, Ball-Jointed Body, 12 In. 265.00
S & H 1109, Velvet Outfit, 16 In. 495.00
S & H 1249, Santa Claus, Open-Close Blue Eyes, Bisque, 24 1/2 In. 765.00
S & H 1299, Brown Sleep Eyes, Ball-Jointed, 18 In. 800.00
S & H 1428, Character Baby, 12 1/2 In. 1475.00
S & H, Baby Blanche, 24 In. 500.00
S & H, Bisque Head, Ball-Jointed Composition Body, Marked, 32 In. 1175.00
S & H, Bisque, Socket Head, Sleep Eyes, Long Hair, 1909, Marked, 18 In. 225.00
S & H, Blue Sleep Eyes, Ball-Jointed, Star Mark, 22 In. 395.00
S & H, Girl, Dollhouse, Molded Hair, 5 In. .... 195.00 To 200.00
S & H, Girl, Flirty Eyes, Blue & White Organdy Dress, 18 In. 595.00
S & H, Lady, All Original, Price Tag, 17 In. 1050.00
S & H, Stationary Eyes, Black Wig, Fruit Basket On Head, Marked, 14 In. 675.00
S.F.B.J., Blue Paperweight Eyes, Ball-Jointed Body, Jumeau Face, 33 In. 2250.00
S.F.B.J., Flirty Eyes, Pierced Ears, Ball-Jointed, Satin Dress, 23 In. 2200.00
S.F.B.J., Googly, 8 In. 2595.00
S.F.B.J., Open Mouth, Bisque Head, Paperweight Eyes, Jointed, 20 In. 1100.00
S.F.B.J., Sleep Eyes, Kid Body, Original Clothes, & Wig, 19 In. 295.00
S.F.B.J.60, Open Mouth, Jointed, 14 In. 425.00
S.F.B.J.226, Baby, Paperweight Eyes, 5-Piece Body, Dressed, 13 1/2 In. 650.00
S.F.B.J.226, French Boy, Closed Mouth, Blue Paperweight Eyes, 17 In. 975.00
S.F.B.J.227, Character, Smiling, Paperweight Eyes, Bisque, 14 In. 2600.00
S.F.B.J.235, Boy, Molded Hair, Blue Eyes, 13 In. 1050.00
S.F.B.J.236, French Character, Open-Close Mouth, Incised Mark, 18 In. 1200.00
S.F.B.J.236, French Toddler, Sleep Blue Eyes, 27 In. 2100.00

S.F.B.J.236, Laughing Child Jumeau, Sleep Eyes, Incised Mark, 26 In. 1950.00
S.F.B.J.236, Laughing Jumeau, Blue Sleep Eyes, Incised Mark, 23 1/2 In. 1750.00
S.F.B.J.236, Laughing Jumeau, Brown Sleep Eyes, Red Wig, 19 In. 995.00
S.F.B.J.236, Laughing Jumeau, Open-Close Mouth, Bent Limb Body, 14 In. 1395.00
S.F.B.J.236, Laughing Jumeau, Toddler Body, 13 1/2 In. 1495.00
S.F.B.J.236, Paris Laughing Baby, 12 In. 1400.00
S.F.B.J.247, Bisque Head, Sleep Eyes, 2 Upper Teeth, Dressed, 16 In. 1900.00
S.F.B.J.247, Twirp, Sleep Blue Eyes, Toddler Body, Bisque, 18 In. 2600.00
S.F.B.J.247, Twirp, 29 In. 1650.00
S.F.B.J.251, Baby, 26 In. 600.00
S.F.B.J.251, Bisque Head, Blue Sleep Eyes, Open Mouth, 2 Teeth, 19 In. 1250.00
S.F.B.J.251, Sleep Eyes, Movable Tongue, Ball-Jointed, 13 In. 1800.00
S.F.B.J.251, Toddler, Sleep Eyes, Ball-Jointed, Checked Dress, 18 In. 2300.00
S.F.B.J.301, Brown Sleep Eyes, Lashes, Ball-Jointed Body, 22 1/2 In. 1250.00
S.F.B.J.301, French, Blue Sleep Eyes, Original Clothes & Box, 15 In. 985.00
S.F.B.J.301, Paperweight Eyes, Ball-Jointed, Taffeta Costume, 30 In. 2000.00
S.P.B.H., Hanna, Lashes, Ball-Jointed Toddler Body, 24 In. 1200.00

DOLL, S & H, see also Doll, Bergmann; Doll, Simon & Halbig

Sandy McCall, 26 In. 175.00
Santa Claus, German, Cotton Body, Wax Face, Wood Sled, 6 X 3 1/2 X 2 In. 43.00
Santa Claus, German, Cotton, Painted Composition Face, 6 In. 46.00
Santa Claus, Stuffed Cloth Body, Painted Face, 20 In. 95.00
Santa, Papier-Mache 55.00
Sasha, Baby, Jointed, Black Series, England, 12 In. 30.00
Scarlett O'Hara, Flowered Gown, Original Straw Hat, 8 In. 300.00
Schmidt, Boy, Blue Eyes, Dark Red Velvet Suit, 19 In. 495.00
Schmidt, Brown Paperweight Eyes, Closed Mouth, Incised Mark, 16 In. 4350.00
Schoenhut, Baby Face, Original Clothes & Paint, 11 In. 550.00
Schoenhut, Bareback Rider, Bisque Head 295.00
Schoenhut, Blue Intaglio Eyes, Molded Hair Band, Marked, 15 In. 895.00
Schoenhut, Boy, Mohair Wig, Sailor Suit, Label, 14 In. 275.00
Schoenhut, Boy, Original Clothes, Brown Eyes, 19 In. 750.00
Schoenhut, Boy, Undressed, C Mark In Circle, 13 In. 400.00
Schoenhut, Girl, Blue Eyes, Original Shoes & Stockings, 19 In. 750.00
Schoenhut, Girl, Decal Eyes, Open-Close Mouth, 20 In. 395.00
Schoenhut, Girl, Decal Eyes, 20 In. 400.00
Schoenhut, Girl, Original Dress, 22 In. 435.00
Schoenhut, Girl, Playwear, New Wig, Old Dress, 22 In. 365.00
Schoenhut, Milkman, 7 1/2 In. 350.00
Schoenhut, Painted Eyes, 3 Molded Teeth, Knit Costume, 16 In. 485.00
Schoenhut, Pouty Girl, Original, Marked, 20 In. 395.00
Schoenhut, Pouty Toddler, Marked, 11 In. 275.00
Schoenhut, Santa Rolly, 9 In. 750.00
Schoenhut, Santa Rolly, 10 3/4 In. 950.00
Schoenhut, Spring-Jointed Wood Body, Painted Eyes, Brown Wig, 19 In. 375.00
Schoenhut, Toddler, 16 In. 375.00
Schoenhut, Wooden, Girl, Tin Eyes, Jointed, 1911 .... 495.00

DOLL, SHIRLEY TEMPLE, see Shirley Temple
DOLL, SIMON & HALBIG, see also Doll, Bergmann; Doll, S & H

Simon & Halbig 117a, Bisque Face, Signed K R, 24 In. 3950.00
Simon & Halbig 550, Original, 21 In. 395.00
Simon & Halbig 1039, Blue Flirty Eyes, Blonde Eyelashes, 23 In. 1050.00
Simon & Halbig 1039, Strung To Throw Kisses, Bisque, 23 In. 995.00
Simon & Halbig 1078, Open Mouth, Blue Eyes, Ball-Jointed, 38 In. 1800.00
Simon & Halbig 1079, Brown Sleep Eyes, Ball-Jointed, 26 In. 595.00
Simon & Halbig 1079, Brown Sleep Eyes, 30 In. 650.00
Simon & Halbig 1079, Sleep Eyes, Molded Brows, Ball-Jointed, 26 In. 550.00
Simon & Halbig 1160, Closed Mouth, 8 In. 225.00
Simon & Halbig 1160, 8 In. 250.00
Simon & Halbig 1249, Santa, Head Circumference 17 In., 36 In.Long 1850.00

Doll, Standing Arab, Automaton, Cook
Co., Philadelphia, 1930s

Simon & Halbig 1349, Sleep Eyes, Ball-Jointed Body, 16 In. 350.00
Simon & Halbig, Child, Blue Sleep Eyes, Ball-Jointed, Dressed, 23 In. 850.00
Simon & Halbig, Little Women, 9 In. 265.00
Simon & Halbig, Max Handwerck, Original, 22 In. 395.00
Simon & Halbig, No.939 .... 750.00
Simon & Halbig, Turned Head, Paperweight Eyes, Original Clothes, 17 In. 465.00
Sipple Coe, Blonde Wig, Blue Eyes, Old Clothes, Germany, 14 In. 400.00
Skookum Chief, Boxed 35.00
Smokey The Bear, Vinyl 6.00
Snookums, Papier-Mache, C.1930 .... 30.00
Snuffy Smith, Original Clothes 14.00
Sonja Henie, Composition, Red Skating Suit, Marked, 21 In. 250.00
Sonja Henie, 14 In. 160.00
Southern Belle, Mollye, 21 In. 375.00
Standing Arab, Automaton, Cook Co., Philadelphia, 1930s ....*Illus* 5000.00
Steiff, Mickey Mouse 395.00
Steiner, A Series, Closed Mouth, Paperweight Eyes, 16 In. 2675.00
Steiner, Bisque Head, Blue Glass Eyes, Pierced Ears, Human Hair, 23 In. 3200.00
Steiner, Bisque Head, Composition Jointed Body, Incised *86, 15 In. 1650.00
Steiner, Bourgoin, Wire-Eyed, Straight Wrists, 22 1/2 In. 4775.00
Steiner, Brown Wire-Eyed, Human Hair Wig, 17 In. 2200.00
Steiner, Closed Mouth, Blue Paperweight Eyes, 13 In. 2100.00
Steiner, Closed Mouth, 8 1/2 In. 1800.00
Steiner, Girl, Closed Mouth, 32 In. 4995.00
Steiner, Girl, Completely Original Condition, 8 1/2 In. 1850.00
Steiner, Mechanical, Head Turns, Throws Kisses, Marked, 31 In. 1950.00
Steiner, Mechanical, Turns Head, Lifts Arms, & Kicks, 18 In. 1800.00
Steiner, Open Mouth, Double Row Of Fish Teeth, 18 1/2 In. 2800.00
Steiner, Paperweight Blue Eyes, Closed Mouth, Braided Wig, 15 In. 2200.00
Steiner, Paperweight Eyes, Closed Mouth, Incised Mark, 16 In. 2750.00
Stockinette Grandpa, Original Chair 425.00
Superman, Wood, Jointed, Boxed 450.00
Sweet Sue, 25 In. 55.00
Tete Jumeau, Blue Paperweight Eyes, Auburn Human Wig, 36 In. 3800.00
Tete Jumeau, Blue Paperweight Eyes, Open Mouth, Marked, 27 In. 2375.00
Tete Jumeau, Blue Paperweight Eyes, Open Mouth, Marked, 30 In. 1650.00

Tete Jumeau, Blue Sleep Eyes, Open Mouth, Pierced Ears, Marked, 35 In. 2850.00
Tete Jumeau, Brown Paperweight Eyes, Closed Mouth, Marked .... 2775.00 To 2900.00
Tete Jumeau, Closed Mouth, Paperweight Blue Eyes, Stamped, 21 In. 2500.00
Tete Jumeau, Closed Mouth, Straight Wrists, 19 In. 2895.00
Tete Jumeau, Closed Mouth, 20 In. 2495.00
Tete Jumeau, Open Mouth, 31 In. 2295.00
Tete Jumeau, Paperweight Eyes, Closed Mouth, Marked Head & Body, 27 In. 3000.00
Tete Juneau, Paperweight Eyes, Human Hair, White Dress, Marked, 26 In. 4000.00
Three-Face, Bisque Head, 12 In. 1500.00
Tina, No.7, Grandpa's Little Ballerina 140.00
Tiny Tears, Rubber Body, Composition Head, Dress & Bonnet, 13 In. 35.00
Toddler, Sleep Eyes, Ball-Jointed Body, Hobby Horse Toy, 1o 1/2 In. 350.00
Topsy, 16 In. 125.00
Uncle Sam, Bisque Head, Original Clothes, 14 In. 1250.00
Unis, France, Open Mouth, Blue Sleep Eyes, Incised Mark, 22 In. 495.00
Unis, No.301, Open Mouth, France, 27 In. 1200.00
Unis, No.301, Open Mouth, 29 In. 1500.00
Unis, 5-Piece Slender Body, Dark Blonde Hair, 18 In. 550.00
Vogue, Ginny, Bride, Tagged, 15 In. 45.00
Vogue, Ginny, Ice Skates, 8 In. 35.00
Vogue, Ginny, Vinyl, 8 In. 15.00
Vogue, Girl, Blonde Wig, Sleep Eyes, Straw Hat, Black Snap Shoes 85.00
Vogue, Sailor Boy, Cracker Jack, Cloth Body, 12 In. 12.50
Wax Over Composition, China Legs, Wooden Arms, 1893, 10 In. 70.00
William Goebel 120, Blue Eyes, Ball-Jointed, Marked, 25 In. 650.00
Wooden Shoulder Head, Cloth Body & Arms 2800.00
Wooden, Closed Mouth, Blue Painted Eyes, Carved Hair & Body, 17 In. 1490.00
Wooden, Hand-Carved, Jointed, Yellow Dress, Pre-1850 .... 110.00
Wooden, Jointed, Painted Hair & Features, Lavender Outfit 50.00
Wooden, Painted Eyes, Shaped Kid Body, Hand, & Feet, 15 In. 950.00
Wooden, Queen Anne, Original Paint, Carved Fingers, Wooden Arms, 14 In. 2500.00
Wooden, Queen Anne, Original Paint, Carved Fingers, 12 In. 2200.00
      DONALD DUCK, see Disneyana
      DOORSTOP, see Iron, Doorstop
DORFLINGER, Bowl, Kalana Lily, Frosted Decoration, Underplate 95.00

       Doulton pottery and porcelain were made by Doulton and Co. of Burslem,
       England, after 1882. The name Royal Doulton appeared on their wares
       after 1902.
      DOULTON, see also Royal Doulton
DOULTON, Biscuit Jar, Burslem, Cream Ground, Silver Lid, Marked, 7 3/4 In. 195.00
Biscuit Jar, Pink Roses, Beige Ground, Silver Lid, Marked, 7 1/4 In. 125.00
Creamer, Lambeth, Hunt Scene 75.00
Decanter, Lambeth, Art Nouveau, Green Ground, Artist Signed 55.00
Ewer, Hand-Painted, Floral Gilding, C.1890, Blue, Pair 390.00
Jug, Lambeth, Beading, Signed Eliza Simmance, Dated 1876, 6 In. 195.00
Jug, Lambeth, Busts Of Young & Old Queen Victoria, 7 1/2 In. 175.00
Jug, Lambeth, Saltglaze, Applied Figures, Tan & Brown, 5 1/2 In. 85.00
Pitcher, Allover Florals, Flow Blue, Marked, 5 1/4 In. 85.00
Pitcher, Burslem, Blue Willow, 8 1/2 In. .... *Illus* 125.00
Pitcher, Burslem, Jacobean Design, Luster, 9 In. .... *Illus* 80.00
Pitcher, Burslem, Tapestry Band, Incised Lilies, Gold Flower, Signed 160.00
Pitcher, Flow Blue, Hunting Scene, 7 In. 105.00
Pitcher, Lambeth, Brown Fruit Decoration, Beige, Signed, 4 In. 75.00
Pitcher, Lambeth, Camel, Leaves, & Berries, 1891, Signed, 6 In. 125.00
Pitcher, Lambeth, Dated 1874, Artist Initials 175.00
Pitcher, Syrup, Lambeth, Hunt Scene, Brown, Oatmeal, C.1898, 6 1/2 In. 125.00
Pitcher, Whiskey, King Edward VII, Incised Mark, Tan & Brown 175.00
Plate, Burslem, Overlaid Gold Flower & Vine Design, Signed, 9 In. 395.00
Plate, Sunflower, Dated 29 May, 1879, 10 In. 30.00
Platter, Burslem, Windmill & Castle, Blue & White, 16 In. 100.00
Platter, Yale, C.1892, Gold Trim, Blue Transfer, 16 X 11 1/2 In. 75.00

Doulton, Pitcher, Burslem, Blue Willow, 8 1/2 In.

Doulton, Pitcher, Burslem, Jacobean
Design, Luster, 9 In.

(See Page 195)

Punch Bowl, Burslem, Iris Design, 17 In.	450.00
Teapot, Lambeth, Incised Flowers, Green, White, & Tan Ground, Signed	145.00
Teapot, Lambeth, Tapestry Design, Tan Ground, Artist Signed	150.00
Toby Jug, Seated Man, Black Face & Hat Lid, C.1860	875.00
Vase, Burslem, Dancing Ladies & Children, Flow Blue, Marked, 4 In.	98.00
Vase, Burslem, Morrisian Ware, Ladies In Black, Marked, 7 1/4 In.	125.00
Vase, Etched Horses, Green Bands, Gold Inside, Dated 1886, 11 In.	795.00
Vase, Flambe Woodcut, Hunting Scene, 9 In.Tall, 24 1/2 In.Diam.	225.00
Vase, Lambeth, C.1890, Central Cattle Frieze, Marked, 16 7/8 In.	700.00
Vase, Stoneware, Blue, Brown, White Dots, Animals, 10 1/2 In.	375.00
Vase, Stoneware, Green Top, Fuchsia, Gray Ground, Marked, 6 1/4 In.	85.00
Vase, Stoneware, 8 Incised Sheep, Signed Barlow, 15 1/2 In., Pair	1450.00

       DR.SYNTAX, see Adams; Staffordshire

*Dresden china is any china made in the town of Dresden, Germany. The
most famous factory in Dresden is the Meissen factory.*

       DRESDEN, see also Meissen

DRESDEN, Basket & Candleholders, Crossed Swords	225.00
Box, Magenta Scene, Twig Handle On Lid, C.1875, 3 1/2 X 4 In.	115.00
Box, Trinket, Polychrome Florals, Gilded Scrolls, C.1900, 3 In.	70.00
Bust, Colonial Man & Woman, Green, Pink, 9 1/2 In., Pair	150.00
Candlestick, Applied Rose Each Side, Gold Trim, Double, 7 In., Pair	260.00
Candlestick, Entwined Vine, C.1900, Gilt Mounted, 16 1/4 In., Pair	500.00
Candlestick, Figural, Young Boy, Girl, Studying, 8 In., Pair	90.00
Candlestick, Foliage Of Blooming Flowers, 6 1/2 In., Pair	240.00
Candlestick, Pink, Yellow Roses, Gold Trim, F Crown N, Pair	260.00
Centerpiece, Angels, Floral Bouquets, 12 X 6 In.	450.00
Compote, Figural, White, 12 In.	165.00
Cruet, Thorn Handle, Floral Design, White Ground, 6 In., Pair	95.00
Cup & Saucer, Demitasse, Yellow Portrait, Gold Rose Mark	225.00
Cup & Underplate, Dated 1914, Gilded, Landscape, Pair	130.00
Demitasse, Pirkenhammer, C.1920, White & Floral, Set Of 6	50.00
Figurine, Ballerina, Signed, 4 In.	65.00 To 85.00
Figurine, Black Boy, Serving His Lady, 6 1/2 In.	50.00
Figurine, Blue Boy, 11 1/2 In.	300.00
Figurine, Boy Holding Basket, Girl Holds Lamb, 4 In., Pair	80.00
Figurine, Boy, Seated Playing Flute, Goat, Sheep, 4 X 6 In.	225.00
Figurine, Colonial Couple On Settee, 9 1/2 X 10 1/2 In.	585.00
Figurine, Colonial Woman & Gentleman, Seated On Settee, 10 X 10 In.	485.00

Figurine, Girl Wearing Bonnet, Blooming Flowers, 3 1/4 In. 90.00
Figurine, Girl Wearing Bonnet, Sprigs Of Flowers & Feather, 5 In. 185.00
Figurine, Girl, Bonnet Of Flowers & Feather, 5 In. 185.00
Figurine, God On Wine On Goat, Crossed Swords, 8 1/2 In. 395.00
Figurine, Lady, Seated, Mandolin, Man Standing, Holds Music 65.00
Figurine, Nude, Flesh-Colored Boy, Porcelain Plinth, Signed, 11 In. 125.00
Figurine, Parrots, Perched On Tree Stumps, Foliage, 6 1/2 In. 345.00
Figurine, Summer, Golden-Haired Putto Rests, Wheelbarrow 125.00
Figurine, The Musical Vagabond, Signed, 7 In. 145.00
Figurine, Young Colonial Gentleman & Woman, 9 1/2 X 10 1/2 In. 585.00
Lamp, Lithophane Shade, Flowered Finial, 20th Century, 15 1/2 In. 450.00
Mirror, Vanity, Cupids Around Frame, Roses & Scrolls, 13 X 18 In. 525.00
Pitcher, Yellow Flowers, Gold Edging, 5 1/2 In. 30.00
Plaque, Baby Moses, Ark, Bulrushes, Pharaoh's Daughter, 8 X 5 In. 1100.00
Plaque, Fruit Garland, Nudes, Fruit On Back, Numbered, 7 X 9 3/4 In. 1100.00
Plaque, German Bride, Pious Maiden, 7 1/8 X 5 In., Pair 1300.00
Plaque, Good Night, Maiden, Candlelight, White Dress, 8 X 5 In. 1100.00
Plaque, Gypsy Girl, White Blouse, Rose Scarf, Tambourine, 8 X 4 In. 175.00
Plaque, Lady Godiva, Carved Wood Frame, 6 In. 300.00
Plaque, Lovers, Initialing Tree, C.1910, Framed, 7 X 4 7/8 In. 650.00
Plaque, Portrait Of Beatrice Cenci, Marked, 11 3/4 X 8 7/8 In. 1900.00
Plaque, Queen Of Roses, Maiden, Lace Bonnet, Pink Gown, 7 X 5 In. 1300.00
Plaque, The Fruit Garland, C.1900, Marked, 6 7/8 X 9 3/4 In. 3000.00
Plaque, The Grape Harvesters, Peasants, Gazing At Coin, 7 In. 600.00
Plate, Cat, 7 1/2 In. 24.00
Plate, U.S.Indian School, Grand Junction, Colorado, 7 1/2 In. 21.00
Plate, Young Ladies With Sheep, Decal 15.00
Salt & Pepper, On Tray, Laurel & Hardy, Marked 45.00
Sconces, Wall, Putto Holding Garland, Floral Border, 9 In., Pair 400.00
Shoe, Floral Rosettes, Design Inside & Out, Marked ....Illus 50.00
Tureen, Convex Top, Scalloped Tray, Applied Roses, 9 1/2 In. 200.00
Vase, Bird Form Finials, Hydrangeas, Floral Ground, 22 In., Pair 2200.00
Vase, Floral, Shepherdess, Minstrel, Cherubs, Covered, 19 In. 400.00

*Duncan & Miller glass was made at the George A. Duncan and Sons
Company in Washington, Pennsylvania. The company was started in 1894,
with James E. Duncan, president, and Edwin C. Miller, secretary.*

DUNCAN & MILLER, Ashtray, Dogwood 12.50
Ashtray, Duck, 5 In. .... 9.00 To 20.00
Ashtray, Terrace, Ruby, 4 In. 16.00
Basket, Crystal, 5 1/2 In. 12.00
Basket, Hobnail, Handled, 5 In. 25.00
Bottle, Cologne, Hobnail, Pink, 7 In. 55.00
Bowl, Canterbury, Chartreuse 25.00
Bowl, Canterbury, Crimped, 13 In. 12.50
Bowl, First Love, 14 In. 45.00
Bowl, Murand, Chartreuse, 8 X 4 In. 35.00
Bowl, Rose, Hobnail, Clear, Footed, Crimped Top 20.00
Bowl, Salad, Crimped, Amber, 13 In.Diam. 15.00
Box, Cigarette, Covered, Duck 40.00
Butter, Double Snail, Covered 125.00
Candleholder, American Way, Pink Opalescent, Pair 55.00
Candleholder, Etched Indian Tree 45.00
Candleholder, Figural, Swan, Ruby 40.00

Dresden, Shoe, Floral Rosettes, Design Inside & Out, Marked

Candleholder, Granda, 3-Light, Pair 55.00
Candleholder, Magnolia, 2-Light, Pair 60.00
Candleholder, Murano, Frosted, Pair 45.00
Candleholder, Red Swan, Clear Neck & Head, Pair 65.00
Candlestick, Ebony, Silver Design, 6 In. 30.00
Candlestick, Hobnail, Pink Opalescent, Pair 45.00
Candlestick, Hobnail, 4 In. 55.00
Candlestick, Jack-In-Pulpit Design, C.1940, 6 In., Pair 45.00
Cocktail Shaker, Chanticleer, Ruby .... 95.00 To 125.00
Cocktail Shaker, Etched Mallard 42.00
Cocktail, Hobnail 8.50
Compote, Blue Opalescent, Hobnail, 6 1/2 In. 35.00
Compote, Canterbury, Crystal 8.00
Compote, Flower Scrolls, 5 In. 35.00
Compote, Green, 7 X 5 In. 25.00
Compote, Puritan, Green, Shallow, Footed 6.00
Compote, Tree Of Life, Hand On Stem, Scalloped, 6 3/4 In. 60.00
Console Set, Caribbean, Cape Cod Blue, 3 Piece 145.00
Cornucopia, First Love, 8 1/4 In. 45.00
Creamer, Amberette, 5 In. 65.00
Creamer, Child's, Wooden Pail 30.00
Creamer, Jeweled Shell, 4 1/2 In. 12.00
Creamer, Nailhead 15.00
Creamer, Teardrop 8.00
Cup, Hobnail 5.00
Dish, Candy, Blue Opalescent, Lid, 3-Part 59.00
Dish, Candy, First Love, Covered 35.00
Dish, Candy, Hobnail, Footed, Green Opalescent, 6 In. 48.00
Dish, Candy, Hobnail, 2-Handled, Blue Opalescent 15.00
Dish, Leaf Shaped, 5 3/4 In. 7.00
Dish, Nut, Teardrop 5.00
Dish, Sanibel, 3-Section 45.00
Dish, 3-Section, First Love, 3 Feather, Sterling Silver Base 35.00
Goblet, Canterbury .... 8.00 To 9.00
Goblet, Dover, Red 15.00
Goblet, Hobnail, 9 Ounce 8.50
Goblet, Teardrop 8.00
Hat, Blue Opalescent .... 17.50 To 20.00
Heron, 7 In. .... 60.00 To 75.00
Ice Bucket, 2 Side Handles, Amber 25.00
Juice, Hobnail, Set Of 6 .... 38.00
Lamp, Gothic, Green, 10 In. 70.00
Lamp, Oil, Larkin, Brass-Colored Metal, Paneled Shade 225.00
Mayonnaise Set, Blue Opalescent, 3 Piece 60.00
Mayonnaise Set, Teardrop, 3 Piece 25.00
Pall Mall Swan, 10 1/2 In. 20.00
Pall Mall Swan, 7 In. 8.00
Plate, Cambria, 6 In. 12.50
Plate, Canterbury, 8 1/2 In. 4.50
Plate, First Love, 6 In., Set Of 5 .... 38.00
Plate, Priscilla, 10 In.Diam. 25.00
Plate, Teardrop, 10 1/2 In. 17.00
Plate, Torte, 12 In. 24.00
Relish, 3-Compartment, Pink Opalescent 38.50
Relish, 4-Compartment, Cape Cod Blue 27.50
Sherbet, Canterbury 8.00
Sherbet, Charmain Rose 16.00
Sherbet, Cretan 16.00
Sherbet, Indian Tree 16.00
Spooner, Child's, Mardi Gras 35.00
Spooner, Diamond 20.00
Spooner, Mardi Gras .... 25.00 To 35.00
Sugar & Creamer, Canterbury 12.00

Sugar & Creamer, Pink, Hobnail	38.00
Sugar & Creamer, Teardrop	16.00
Sugar, Teardrop	6.00
Swan, Chartreuse, 8 In.	38.00
Swan, Clear Neck, Ruby, 12 1/2 In.	55.00
Swan, Clear, 7 In.	15.00
Swan, Clear, 8 In.	18.00 To 24.00
Swan, Clear, 9 In.	10.00
Swan, Crystal Neck, Blue Opalescent, 5 1/2 In.	52.00
Swan, Green, Clear Neck, 10 In.	50.00
Swan, Green, 3 In.	80.00
Swan, Green, 8 In.	25.00
Swan, Green, 12 In.	30.00
Swan, Ruby & Crystal Neck, 10 1/2 In.	39.00
Swan, Ruby, Clear Neck, 7 1/2 In.	28.00
Swan, Ruby, 7 In.	25.00
Swan, Solid, 3 In.	18.00
Swan, Solid, 4 1/2 In.	20.00
Swan, Spread Wing, Clear, 12 In.	40.00
Swan, Trimmed In Gold, Crystal, 8 In.	42.50
Syrup, Eyewinker	55.00
Syrup, Henrietta	35.00
Toothpick, Ladder & Diamond	25.00
Tray, Cream & Sugar, Teardrop	18.00
Tray, Handled, 14 In.	25.00
Tumbler, Arliss, Ruby	25.00
Tumbler, Teardrop, 8 Ounce	5.00
Vase, Canterbury, Pink Opalescent, 3 In.	12.00
Vase, Canterbury, Pink Opalescent, 5 X 5 In.	30.00
Vase, Chanticleer, 3 In.	25.00
Vase, Fluted, 5 1/2 In., Pair	45.00
Vase, Hobnail, Pink Opalescent, Flared, Fluted Top, 5 1/2 In.	29.00
Vase, Pink Opalescent, 3 In.	25.00
Vase, Pink Opalescent, 4 In.	27.50
Vase, Violet, Pink Opalescent, Hobnail, Footed, 5 In.	45.00
Water Set, Scroll, Swans, Amber Over Crystal, 5 Piece	225.00
Wine, Teardrop	4.00
Wine, Tepee	13.00

Durand glass was made by Victor Durand from 1879 to 1935 at several factories. Most of the iridescent Durand glass was made by Victor Durand, Jr., from 1912 to 1924 at the Durand Art Glass Works in Vineland, New Jersey.

DURAND, Bowl, Centerpiece, White Pulled Feather, Ruby Flashed, Pink Bands	445.00
Bowl, White Pulled Feathers, Ruby Flashed, 15 Pink Bands, 12 In.Diam.	445.00
Box, Green Luster Glass, Gold Luster King Tut Design, 3 1/2 In.	950.00
Candlestick, Feather Pattern, Blue & Oil Luster, 3 In.	65.00
Compote, Feather Pattern, Signed, Blue & Oil Luster, 13 In.Diam.	160.00
Compote, Peacock, Starburst Pattern, Yellow Foot, 8 In.	300.00
Compote, 1921, Turquoise, Small, 3 X 6 In.	215.00
Goblet, White & Red Feathers, Pedestaled, 6 1/2 In.	175.00
Lamp Base, Figural, Two Children Back To Back, Tooting Horns	125.00
Lamp Base, King Tut, Gold Luster, Blue, 24 In.	275.00
Lamp Base, Pulled Feather, Engraved Floral, Fluted, 9 In.	225.00
Lamp, Gold Iridescent, Threading, 13 In., Pair	1400.00
Lamp, King Tut Design	315.00
Lamp, Moorish Crackle, Platinum, 14 In.	425.00
Parfait, Feather Pattern, 5 1/2 In.	70.00
Plate, Lustered Glass, Red Peacock Feather Design, 8 In.	115.00
Plate, Peacock, Pulled Feather On Ruby, C.Link Engraver, 8 In.	295.00
Plate, Pulled Feather, Red, 8 In.Diam.	175.00
Rose Bowl, Clear Bubbles, Signed, 4 In.	225.00
Shade, Bell Shape, Gold Leaves, Ivory Outside, Gold Inside, 5 In.	110.00

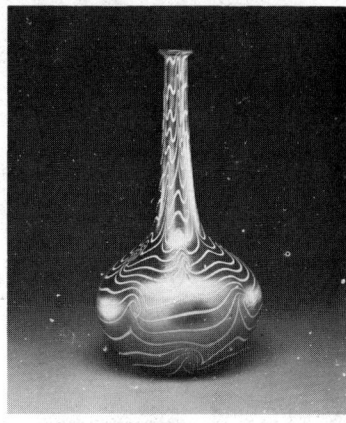

Durand, Vase, Amber Iridescence, Opalescent,
C.1915, 15 1/2 In.

Sherbet Set, Cranberry	75.00
Sherbet, Oil Luster, Green Thread Rim	30.00
Vase, Amber Iridescence, Opalescent, C.1915, 15 1/2 In. .....*Illus*	885.00
Vase, Beehive, Iridescent Blue, Gold Highlights, Signed, 6 In.	685.00
Vase, Blue & Clear Egyptian Crackle Glass, 12 In.	550.00
Vase, Blue Luster, Iridescent, Signed & Numbered, 8 1/2 In.	485.00
Vase, Blue Luster, White & Silver King Tut Pattern, 9 1/2 In.	675.00
Vase, Blue Luster, White King Tut Design, 9 1/2 In.	785.00
Vase, Blue, Gold Aurene Lining, Crackle Glass, 9 1/2 In.	600.00
Vase, Brown, Red Exterior, 8 In.	350.00
Vase, Bulbous, Flared Rim, Orange Iridescent, Signed, 6 1/2 In.	275.00
Vase, Cased Green Striped Leaves, Beige Pink Ground, 8 1/2 In.	300.00
Vase, Cream, Gold, Blue Feathers, Gold Iridescent, Signed, 9 In.	675.00
Vase, Deep Blue Iridescence, Light Blue Pattern, Signed, 7 1/4 In.	425.00
Vase, Deep Blue, Purple, Green, Gold Trim, Signed, 5 3/4 In.	685.00
Vase, Egyptian Crackle, Blue & Clear, 12 In.	550.00
Vase, Egyptian Crackle, Blue, Luster Crystal, 13 In.	345.00
Vase, Gold Iridescent, Blue Green Design, 10 1/2 In.	575.00
Vase, Gold Threading, Cream, Gold, & Blue, Signed, 17 In.	675.00
Vase, Green Cut To Clear, Signed, 8 In.	350.00
Vase, Green Hearts & Vines, Orange Iridescent Ground, Signed, 12 In.	650.00
Vase, Green King Tut Design, Gold Luster, 6 1/2 In.	595.00
Vase, Green Peacock Feather Full Design, Signed & Numbered, 13 In.	590.00
Vase, Iridescent Blue, Applied Blue Stringing, Signed, 8 In.	350.00
Vase, Iridescent Gold, 9 1/2 In.	525.00
Vase, Iridescent Green, Red, & Blue, 5 1/2 In.	200.00
Vase, Iridescent, Amber, Scrolling Waves, Signed, 15 In.	885.00
Vase, King Tut Design, Silver, Blue, Gold, & Green, Signed, 7 In.	585.00
Vase, King Tut Pattern, Orange Iridescent, Blue, Signed, 8 1/2 In.	475.00
Vase, King Tut Pattern, Ruffled, Gold & Green, Signed, 6 3/4 In.	875.00
Vase, King Tut, Gold Iridescence Over White, 8 1/2 In.	650.00
Vase, King Tut, Green Opalescent, 9 In.	550.00
Vase, King Tut, Purple & Green, 10 In.	750.00
Vase, Lily Pads In Green, Gold, Signed & Numbered, 11 1/8 In.	750.00
Vase, Modern Shape, Blue Iridescent, Signed, 7 In.	325.00
Vase, Moorish Crackle, Blue Luster, White Ground, 13 In.	300.00
Vase, Moorish Crackle, Blue On Lustered Crystal, 13 In.	365.00
Vase, Orange Iridescent, Signed, 10 In.	325.00
Vase, Orange, Gold, 8 1/2 In.	150.00

Vase, Oviform, White, Green, King Tut Design, 11 In.	1400.00
Vase, Pearl, 9 1/2 In.	475.00
Vase, Pink & Gold Iridescent, Signed, 7 1/2 In.	650.00
Vase, Pink, Gold, Signed, 7 1/2 In.	495.00
Vase, Ribbed Lavender, Signed	140.00
Vase, Ribbed, Squat Body, Signed, Purple, 5 1/2 In.	150.00
Vase, Ruby Red, Purple Ribbon Design, Signed, 8 In.	570.00
Vase, Spherical, Applied Gold Threading, Inscribed, 8 In.	360.00
Vase, Triple Overlay, Blue, White, & Green Case Glass, Signed, 8 In.	465.00
Vase, Trumpet, Red, Stretched Brown Interior, Footed, 8 In.	350.00
Wine, Ruby Bowl, Spanish Yellow Stem, 7 In.	225.00
Wine, Spanish Yellow Stem & Foot, Ruby, 7 1/4 In.	225.00
ELVIS PRESLEY, Belt, Picture Of Elvis, Dated 1956	25.00
Cards, Playing, Full-Color Photographs	7.50
Cover, Pillow	15.00
Mirror, Pocket, Signed & Dated 1956	1.00
ENAMEL WARE, see Graniteware	
ENAMEL, Clock Garniture, C.1900, Onyx Mounted, 21 1/2 In., 3 Piece	3000.00
ENAMEL, RUSSIAN, see also Faberge	
Russian, Charm, Teapot, Blue Enamel On Silver Gilt	190.00
Russian, Niello, Enameled Farm Scene, Cigar Box, 1856, 4 In.	490.00
Russian, Salt Dip & Spoon, 3 Ball Feet, Marked 84	375.00
Russian, Salt Spoon	150.00
Russian, Salt, 6 Colors	325.00
Russian, Spoon, Marked 84, 4 1/2 In.	125.00
Russian, Spoon, Tea Caddy, Green Ground, Hallmarked, 4 1/2 In.	650.00
Vase, Pearl-Set, Fluted Panels, Bell Shape, Swiss, Gold, 3 In.	1600.00
END OF DAY GLASS, see Spatter Glass	

ES Germany porcelain was made at the factory of Erdmann Schlegelmich from 1861 to 1925 in Suhl, Germany. The porcelain was sold decorated or undecorated.

ES GERMANY, Dish, 3 Portraits, 3-Compartment, Handled, 10 In.Diam.	200.00
Ewer, Girl, Birds, Pearlized, Gold Handles, 8 In.	65.00
Holder & Hair Receiver, Yellow White & Fuchsia Flowers	70.00
Holder, Hatpin, & Hair Receiver, Yellow, White, Fuchsia	70.00
Plaque, Pheasant, Chickens, 12 1/2 In.	195.00
Plaque, Portrait, Pink & Gold Border, 10 In.	65.00
Plate, Portrait, Medallions, 10 In.	95.00
Plate, Two Half-Nude Ladies, Water, Red & Gold Border, 8 In.	55.00
Tankard, Portrait, 11 In.	275.00
Tray, Portrait, Open Handled, 10 1/4 X 6 1/2 In.	135.00
Tray, Portrait, Three Ladies & Cherubs, Green Border & Handle	75.00
Vase, Bud, Portrait Of Ladies, Cupid, Handled, 6 In.	75.00
Vase, Florals, Signed, 10 In.	59.00
Vase, Lady Holding Roses, Pink & Yellow, Petals Form Neck	65.00
Vase, Maroon Ground, Turquoise Neck, Handles, 7 1/4 In.	275.00
Vase, Portrait, Red Luster Ground, Gold Trim, Blue, 7 1/2 In.	159.00
Vase, Portrait, Woman, 11 1/2 In.	275.00
Vase, Portrait, 12 1/2 In.	195.00
ES PRUSSIA, Chocolate Pot	125.00
Dish, Hand-Painted Classical Scene, Gold Banded, 10 1/2 In.	95.00
Hair Receiver, Yellow Roses, Cream Ground, C.1911	45.00
Hair Receiver, Yellow Roses, 1811	40.00
Tray, Dresser, Yellow Roses	125.00
Vase, Pink, White, Blue, Gold, Double, Wall, Bird Mark, 10 3/4 In.	90.00
ES SUHL, Relish, Rose Buds, Gold Tracery, Beaded Rim, Red Mark, 7 In.	85.00

ESKIMO, Bone, Polar Bear, 3 In.Long 350.00
   Container, Harpoon Blades, Walrus Ivory, Fluke Effigy, 4 1/4 In. 200.00
   Doll, Original Fur-Lined Clothes, 12 In. 125.00
   Doll, Walrus Ivory, Prehistoric, Rudimentary, 7 1/2 In. 1600.00
   Doll, Walrus Ivory, St. Lawrence Island, Prehistoric, 7 1/2 In. 1600.00
   Figurine, Bear, Bone, In Relief, 2 1/8 In. 65.00
   Figurine, Bone, Dogsled, 6 In.Long 150.00
   Mask, Nunivak Island, C.1890 .... 3000.00
   Sculpture, Man With Spear, Signed 215.00
   Snow Knife, Walrus Tusk, Scrimshawed Eagle, Whale, & Scenes, 18 In. 975.00
   Stone Carving, Seal, Writing On Base, Black, 4 1/2 In. 90.00
      ETRUSCAN MAJOLICA, see Majolica

КФ   *Faberge was a firm of jewelers and goldsmiths founded in St.
Petersburg, Russia, in 1842, by Gustav Faberge. Peter Carl
Faberge, his son, was jeweler to the Russian Imperial Court from
about 1870 to 1914.*

FABERGE, Barometer, Desk, Silver, C.1900, Circular Form, Marked, 3 1/4 In. 2420.00
   Coffee Set, Tray, Silver, Hoof Feet, Greek Key Design, 3 Pieces 6050.00
   Dish, Silver & Translucent Enamel, C.1900, Triangular, 4 1/2 In. 4400.00
   Lighter, Cigarette, Gold, C.1900, Reeded, Sapphire Thumbpiece, 2 In. 715.00
   Punch Set, Silver & Jeweled, Cranberry Glass, Moscow, 1894 .... 5500.00
   Ring, Scarf, Sapphire & Diamond, Gold, 2 Rope Strands, 1 1/4 In. 2860.00
   Spoon, Demitasse, Silver Gilt, Translucent Enamel, Set Of 12 .... 3300.00

FAIENCE, Charger, Coat Of Arms Of Francois I 80.00
   Flask, Book Form, Harbor Scene, Flower Spine, Dutch, 4 5/8 In. 250.00
   Jug, Blue Persian, Floral Sprays, White Bands, Nevers, 7 3/4 In. 950.00
   Jug, C.1800, Polychrome, Pewter-Mounted, Schrezheim, 9 3/8 In. 600.00
   Jug, Masonic, Dated 1791, Heart-Shaped Wreath, Schrezheim, 8 1/4 In. 750.00
   Jug, Persian, Blue Ground, Ocher, White, Floral Sprays, 7 3/4 In. 950.00
   Jug, Polychrome, Blue, Green, Masonic Design, 8 In. 750.00
   Plate, Blue & White, Nurnberg, Flowering Plant, Scrolls, 8 In. 200.00
   Plate, C.1730, Central Plant, Splotchy Blues, Nurnberg, 8 3/4 In. 200.00
   Spoon, Sifter, Molded As Branch, Veined, French, 7 3/4 In. 350.00
   Tankard, Pear Shape, Pewter Rim & Handle, Dated 1692, 10 1/4 In. 425.00
   Tankard, Pewter Mounted, Pear Shaped, Sponge All Over, 10 1/4 In. 425.00

      *Fairings are small souvenir china boxes sold at country fairs during the
      nineteenth century.*

FAIRING, Box, Trinket, Baby Sitting On Dresser Looking In Mirror 85.00
   Box, Trinket, Drawers, Open Mirror Frame 45.00
   Box, Trinket, Little Girl On Lid 48.00
   Box, Trinket, Man, Lady, Walking, 19th Century, Marked 52.00
   Figurine, Boy, Girl, In Cart 80.00
   Figurine, Husband, Wife, Man Under Bed 120.00
   Figurine, Married Blessedness, Man Holding Twins 125.00
   Figurine, Orphans, Three Dogs On A Chair 120.00
   Figurine, Reception At 3 O'clock, Woman Spanking Man 75.00
   Figurine, Twelve Months Of Marriage 75.00
   Figurine, Welsh Spinning Party, Two Women & Spinning Wheel 75.00
   Figurine, Welsh Tea Party, Three Women At Tea 75.00

FAN, Advertising, Hintermeister, Child Feeding Doll, Collie 33.00
   Advertising, Liquid Medicine, C.1935, Wicket Handle 3.50
   Advertising, Shelburne Grill, Atlantic City 10.00
   Black Lacquered, Gold Figures Both Sides 125.00
   Black Ostrich Feathers, Tortoiseshell Sticks .... 35.00 To 75.00
   Black Satin, Blue Embroidery, Framed, 15 X 24 In. 125.00
   Black Silk With Sequins, Carved Ebony Sticks, Opens To 18 In. 30.00
   Calendar, 1914, Lacy Fold-Out 22.50

Celluloid	8.00
Cockade, Red Cloth, Man's	15.00
Creamy Black Ostrich, Tortoise Sticks, 1850	110.00
Dayton, Brass Blade	50.00
Depicting Harlequin, Pierrot & Figures, Pearl Stick, 12 In.	130.00
Drink Moxie On Each Celluloid Segment, 10 3/4 In.	85.00
Elks, 1909, Advertising	14.00
Feather, 1920s, Blue	20.00
French, Black Luscious Ostrich Plumes, Mother-Of-Pearl Sticks, 1860	185.00
Ivory & Embroidered Mythological Chinese Dragon, 1830	75.00
Ivory, Chinese, Pagodas, Pavilions, Mandarins, Lace, Carved	375.00
Ivory, Hand-Painted Silk, Gold Leaf Case	450.00
Lace & Sequins, Gold Trim, Black Lacquer, Lacquer Box	125.00
Maribou, Fuchsia	45.00
Mother-Of-Pearl & Lace, Painted Inserts, French	95.00
Moxie, 2-Sided	12.00
Organdy, Silver Sequins, Carved Sticks, Black, 8 1/2 In.	35.00
Ostrich Feather, Pink, Plastic Handle, Boxed, 11 In.	35.00
Palmetto, Braided Design Along Edge, 12 X 10 In.	15.00
Peacock Feather, 13 X 10 In.Diam.	20.00
Peacock Feathers, Two Birds, Carved Teakwood Braces, Tassel, Open 21 In.	85.00
Pennsylvania Dutch, Satin, Carved Tulips, Ebony Sticks, 1870	115.00
Pierced Celluloid, Bride's, 1915	12.00
Pink Ostrich Feathers, Amber Sticks	30.00
Poole Stores, Wooden Handle	9.00
Putnam Dyes	9.00
Scenic, Gothic Lovers, Ivory Lucite, 9 In.	22.00
Silk & Ivory	24.00
Silk, French, Peep Fan Horn, Ivory Sticks, 1820	145.00
Silk, Hand-Painted, Silver Studded Ivory Sticks, 1850	110.00
Silk, Lace, Peach Mother-Of-Pearl Sticks, Hand-Painted, 1850	135.00
Sprays Of Flowers, 19th Century, Watercolor On Velvet, 16 In., Pair	200.00
The English Girl, 1906, Paper	20.00
Valentine, Cardboard	5.00
Valentine, Prang, Late 1800s	24.00
Victorian, Lace & Silk, Portraits	89.00
White Lace On Silk, Sequins, Black Silk With Sequins, Pair	45.00
White Lace On White Silk With Sequins, Ivory Sticks, Opens To 18 In.	40.00

*Fenton Art Glass Company, founded in Martins Ferry, Ohio, by
Frank L.Fenton, is now located in Williamstown, West Virginia. It
is noted for early carnival glass produced between 1907 and 1920.
Many other types of glass were also made.*

FENTON, Basket, Beaded Melon, White Outside, Green Inside, 7 In.	50.00
Basket, Beaded Melon, White Over Green	55.00
Basket, Clear Handle, Blue, 7 In.	50.00
Basket, Hanging, Heart, Turquoise	50.00
Basket, Overlay Outside, Green Inside, Beaded Melon, 7 In.	50.00
Basket, Peachcrest, Beaded Melon, White Handle, 10 In.	125.00
Basket, Purple, Silvery Iridescent, 2 Open Rows	25.00
Basket, Ruby, Nappy, Crimped	18.00
Basket, Silver Crest, Marked, 5 1/2 In.	12.00
Basket, Silver Crest, 11 In.	40.00
Basket, Spiral, Blue Opalescent	27.50
Basket, 2 Row Open Edge, Ice Green, 7 In.	70.00
Bell, Hobnail, Cameo Opalescent	12.50
Bell, Sydenham, Topaz Opalescent	10.00 To 19.50
Bonbon, Daisy & Button, Tricornered, Handled, Rose	12.50
Bottle, Cologne, Green	45.00
Bottle, Perfume, Hobnail, Apple Green, 7 In.	25.00
Bowl, Black Rose, 9 In.	40.00
Bowl, Coin Dot, Honeysuckle, 6 In.	32.00

Bowl, Console, Black, 9 In. 45.00
Bowl, Cranberry, 9 In.Diam. 45.00
Bowl, Crest Shell, Peach 65.00
Bowl, Diamond Lace, Blue, 10 1/2 In. 40.00
Bowl, Dot Optic, Blue, 7 In. 35.00
Bowl, Ebony, Dolphin, Silver Design, Handled, C.1934 ..... 99.00
Bowl, Emerald Crest, 7 1/2 In. 22.50
Bowl, Floral & Leaf Cutting, Dolphin Handle, Pink, 9 In.Diam. 25.00
Bowl, Honeysuckle, Coin Dot, Ruffled Rim, 3 1/2 X 7 In. 55.00
Bowl, Maple Leaf, 8 In. 55.00
Bowl, Pink, September Morn Nymph, Hobnail 95.00
Bowl, Rose, Rose Satin 25.00
Bowl, Rose, Ruffled Top, Rose Mist, Speckled Rose & White 30.00
Bowl, Silver Crest, Heart-Shaped Handle, 6 3/4 In. 22.00
Bowl, Spiral Fluted, French Opalescent, 9 In. 22.00
Bowl, Spiral Fluted, 9 In.French Opal 22.00
Bowl, Wild Flower, 3-Footed, Rosalene 19.00
Box, Candy, Melon Rib, Blue Overlay, Covered, 5 1/2 In. 28.00
Box, Candy, Spiral Optic, Covered, Blue Opalescent 25.00
Box, Candy, Water Lily Pattern, Covered 32.00
Butter, Child's, Beaded Swirl, Covered 35.00
Butter, Child's, Sawtooth, Clear 75.00
Cake Plate, Silver Turquoise, Footed, 13 In. 38.50
Candle, Gold Crest, 5 1/2 In., Pair 38.50
Candle, Silver Crest, 3 1/2 In., Pair 18.50
Candleholder, Child's, Angle, Pair 35.00
Candleholder, Cornucopia, Ming Pattern, Pair 35.00
Candleholder, Cranberry, Pair 45.00
Candlestick, Black, Pair 20.00
Candlestick, Blue Opalescent, Pair 28.00
Candlestick, Cornucopia, Gold Crest, 6 In., Pair 38.50
Candlestick, Double, Jade, Pair 70.00
Candlestick, Logo, Low, Blue Opalescent, Pair 28.00
Compote, Bicentennial, Patriot Red ..... 70.00 To 150.00
Compote, Dogwood, 5-Petal, Blue 45.00
Compote, Persian Medallion, Satin, Lime 10.00
Compote, Silver Crest, 8 In. 18.50
Console Set, Block & Star, Turquoise, Bowl 10 In.Diam. 50.00
Cornucopia, Hobnail, Opalescent White 12.00
Creamer, Cobalt Handle, Blue Opalescent 25.00
Creamer, Coin Dot, 4 In. 38.00
Creamer, Sawtooth, Child's 25.00
Cruet, Burmese, Rose 45.00
Cruet, Cranberry, Hobnail, Opalescent 50.00
Cruet, White Opalescent, 4 1/2 In. 18.00
Cup, Punch, Hobnail, Milk Glass, Opalescent 5.00
Decanter, Polka Dot Optic, Cone-Shaped Indentions, Stopper, Aqua 55.00
Decanter, Ribbed, 6 Wines, Cranberry 300.00
Decanter, Wine, 5 Wineglasses 125.00
Dish, Candy, Covered, Hobnail, Footed, French Opalescent 30.00
Dish, Candy, Dolphin, Velva Rose 75th Anniversary, Covered 35.00
Dish, Candy, Hobnail, Footed, French Opalescent 30.00
Dish, Nut, Cameo, Opalescent 12.50
Dish, Relish, Apple Blossom, Heart-Shaped 45.00
Egg, Glass Flowers, Pedestal, Custard Glass 18.50
Epergne, 1 Lily, Peachblow, 12 X 7 In. 150.00
Fan, Crystal, C.1937 ..... 10.00
Figurine, Cat, Peking Blue, Small 19.00
Flower Frog, Standing Nude, Opaline Base, Jade Green, 7 In. 75.00
Goblet, Hobnail, Blue Opalescent, 5 1/4 In. 18.00
Goblet, Lincoln Inn, 6 In. 12.00
Guest Set, Pitcher, Tumbler Fits As Cover, Green, Cobalt Blue Handle 65.00
Hat, Blue, 3 1/4 In. 25.00

Hat, Hobnail, 2 1/2 In.	12.50
Hobnail, Epergne, Green Pastel, 3 Lily, Miniature	90.00
Ivy Ball, Thumbprint, Footed, Green	38.00
Jar, Candy, Celeste Blue	35.00
Jug, Dot Optic, Cramberry, Handled, 8 1/2 In.	35.00
Jug, Peach Crest, Handled, 8 1/2 In.	55.00
Jug, Peach Crest, 5 1/2 In.	35.00
Lamp, Candle, Chou Ting, Rosalene	38.00
Lamp, Candle, Dogwood, Hurricane, Blue, Pewter Finish, 5 Petal	48.00
Lamp, Candle, Log Cabin	30.00
Lamp, Fairy, Rosalene, Owl	25.00
Lamp, Hanging Heart, Custard	175.00
Lamp, Hurricane, Cranberry, Snow Crest, Wrought-Iron Base	55.00
Lamp, Student, Rose Burmese, 20 In.	170.00
Lemonade Set, Dot Optic, Ice Lip Pitcher, 4 Tumblers, Set	150.00
Lemonade Set, Dot Optic, Ice Lip, Black Handle, Blue, 5 Piece	150.00
Macaroon Jar, Cookies Pattern, Handled, Ebony	125.00
Mug, Bicentennial, White Satin	25.00
Mustard & Spreader, Hobnail, Blue Opalescent	15.00
Nappy, Aqua Crest, 6 In.	15.00
Nappy, Heart-Shaped, Crimped Snow Crest Rim, Red	25.00
Nappy, Rose Crest, 6 In.	12.00
Paperweight, Eagle, White Satin	22.50
Perfume, Blue, Coin Dot	65.00
Pitcher, Water, Green Opalescent	165.00
Pitcher, Water, Hobnail, Blue	75.00
Planter, Rosalene, Floral	45.00
Plate, Bicentennial Eagle, Red	23.00
Plate, Cake, Footed, Rose Pastel	45.00
Plate, Emerald Crest, 8 1/4 In.	18.50
Plate, Lincoln Inn, Red, 8 In.	10.00
Plate, Rosalene, 25th Anniversary	125.00
Plate, Rose Pastel, 9 In.	45.00
Plate, Stretch, Topaz, 6 In.	15.00
Punch Set, Hobnail, French Opalescent, 15 Piece	150.00
Relish, Petticoat, Heart-Shaped, Handled, White With Red	25.00
Rose Bowl, Hanging Hearts, Blue	25.00
Rose Bowl, Persian Medallion, Stemmed, Topaz	17.50
Rose Bowl, Rose Burmese, Labels	16.50
Rose Bowl, Rose Mist, Ruffled	30.00
Shade, Hurricane, Dot Optic, Milk Glass Candleholder Base, Turquoise	75.00
Shade, Hurricane, Silver Turquoise, 8 In.	25.00
Shaker, Red, Diamond-Quilted	40.00
Sherbet, Aqua Crest	18.50
Slipper, Cat, Hobnail, Green Opalescent	15.00
Spooner, Water Lily & Cattails, Blue Opalescent	65.00
Sugar & Creamer, Colonial, Green	22.50
Sugar & Creamer, Hobnail, Blue, Large	20.00
Sugar & Creamer, Hobnail, Frosted, 3 In.	25.00
Sugar & Creamer, Jade, Footed	35.00
Sugar, Child's, Beaded Swirl, Cover	30.00
Top Hat, Coin Dot, 3 1/2 In.	38.00
Tumbler, Lincoln Inn, Crystal, 5 In.	12.00
Vanity Set, Melon Ribbed, Crystal Tops, 3 Piece	42.00
Vase, Basket Weave, 5-Petal, Blue	40.00
Vase, Beaded Melon, Peach Crest, 5 In.	35.00
Vase, Bud, Cactus Pattern, Silver & Rose Label, Milk Glass	8.50
Vase, Bud, Colonial, Amber	10.00
Vase, Bulb, Honeysuckle, Coin Dot, Ruffled Top, 5 In.	65.00
Vase, Cased Ruffled Top, Lilac, 6 1/2 In.	38.00
Vase, Coin Dot, Blue, 10 In.	65.00
Vase, Coin Dot, White, Bottle Shape, 6 In.	22.00
Vase, Crest, Triangle, Peach, 5 In.	35.00

Vase, Diamond Optic Fan, Dolphin Handles, Orchid, 5 In.	28.00
Vase, Dogwood, 5-Petal, Basket Weave, Blue	40.00
Vase, Dot Optic, Yellow, Bottle, 7 In.	30.00
Vase, Double Crimp, Cranberry, 5 In.	25.00
Vase, Double Crimp, 5 1/2 In.	17.00
Vase, Empress & Mandarin, Peking Blue, Logo, Pair	60.00
Vase, Fan, Black, 5 1/4 In.	35.00
Vase, Fan, Diamond Optic, Dolphin Handles, Orchid	28.00
Vase, Fan, Mandarin Red, 8 In.	35.00
Vase, Flared, Mandarin Red, 6 1/2 In.	50.00
Vase, Flared, Mongolian Green, 8 In.	45.00
Vase, Gold Crest Triangle, 4 In.	14.00
Vase, Green Overlay, White Lining, 6 In.	18.00
Vase, Handkerchief, Colonial, Green	15.00
Vase, Hobnail, Blue Opalescent, 4 1/2 In.	25.00
Vase, Hobnail, Blue Opalescent, 5 X 6 3/4 In.Diam.	30.00
Vase, Hobnail, Cranberry, 4 In.	10.00
Vase, Hobnail, Ruffled & Crimped Rim, 5 In.	32.00
Vase, Mulberry, 8 In.	75.00
Vase, Peachblow Hobnail, Ruffled, 6 In.	45.00
Vase, Pulled Feather, Blue, 9 1/2 In.	110.00
Vase, Rose Crest, 11 1/2 In.	48.50
Vase, Snow Crest, Amber, 8 3/4 In.	55.00
Vase, Spiral Optic, White, 6 X 4 1/2 In.	35.00
Vase, Tulip, Aqua Crest, Ribbed Bottom, 4 In.	28.00
Vase, Tulip, White Swirl, 6 X 4 1/2 In.	30.00
Water Set, Dark Blue, Cherries & Blossoms	100.00
Water Set, Hanging Heart Pattern, Blue, 5 Piece	265.00

Fiesta dinnerware was introduced in 1936 by the Homer Laughlin China Co., redesigned in 1969, and withdrawn in 1973. The simple design was characterized by a band of concentric circles, beginning at the rim. Cups had full-circle handles until 1969, when partial-circle handles were made. Harlequin and Riviera were related wares.

FIESTA WARE, Ashtray, Aqua, Marked	28.50
Ashtray, Red	35.00
Ashtray, Turquoise	12.00
Ashtray, Yellow	14.00 To 20.00
Bowl, Forest Green, 5 1/2 In.	9.00
Bowl, Forest Green, 6 In.	18.00
Bowl, Fruit, Chartreuse	7.00
Bowl, Fruit, Gray, 4 3/4 In.	8.00
Bowl, Fruit, Rose, 4 3/4 In.	6.50
Bowl, Fruit, Yellow, 5 1/2 In.	6.50
Bowl, Gray, 4 3/4 In.	8.50
Bowl, Gray, 5 1/2 In.	9.00
Bowl, Green, 8 In.	8.00
Bowl, Medium Green, 5 1/2 In.	9.00
Bowl, Orange Tree Pattern, 6 Quart	12.00
Bowl, Red, 4 3/4 In.	8.50
Bowl, Red, 5 1/2 In.	9.00
Bowl, Red, 7 5/8 In.	10.00
Bowl, Red, 8 1/2 In.	14.00
Bowl, Rose, 6 In.	18.00
Bowl, Salad, Medium Green	20.00
Bowl, Salad, Yellow, 10 In.	40.00
Bowl, Soup, Gray, 8 1/2 In.	15.00
Candleholder, Bulb Type, Red	22.50
Candleholder, Tripod, Red	50.00
Carafe, Old Ivory	25.00
Carafe, Turquoise	25.00
Carafe, Yellow	25.00

Casserole, Covered, Rose	15.00 To 22.50
Casserole, Green	35.00
Casserole, Green, Covered	40.00
Casserole, Old Ivory	35.00
Casserole, Red, Covered	60.00
Casserole, Red, Individual	85.00
Casserole, Turquoise, Covered	40.00
Coffeepot, Demi, Yellow	69.50
Coffeepot, Old Ivory, 2 Piece	26.00
Coffeepot, Red	25.00
Coffeepot, Yellow	40.00
Compote, Old Ivory, 12 In.	827.00
Compote, Red, 12 In.	40.00 To 45.00
Compote, Turquoise, 12 In.	32.00
Creamer, Chartreuse	10.00
Creamer, Forest Green	6.00
Creamer, Gray	6.00
Creamer, Old Ivory	4.00
Creamer, Orange	12.00
Creamer, Red	7.00 To 10.00
Creamer, Yellow	15.00
Cup & Saucer, Forest Green	14.00 To 17.00
Cup & Saucer, Gray	20.00
Cup & Saucer, Medium Green	17.00
Cup & Saucer, Old Ivory	20.00
Cup & Saucer, Red	20.00 To 35.00
Cup & Saucer, Turquoise	12.00
Cup & Saucer, Yellow	85.00
Cup & Saucer, Yellow, Demitasse	20.00
Cup, Chartreuse	16.00 To 20.00
Cup, Gray	16.00 To 20.00
Cup, Medium Green	16.00
Cup, Old Ivory	2.00
Cup, Red	2.50 To 14.00
Cup, Turquoise	10.00
Eggcup, Red	25.00
Eggcup, Turquoise	10.00
Eggcup, Yellow	10.00
Gravy Boat, Gray	16.50
Gravy Boat, Red	16.00 To 39.50
Gravy Boat, Rose	25.00
Gravy Boat, Turquoise	20.00
Gravy Boat, Yellow	20.00
Jar, Marmalade, Covered, Green	65.00
Jar, Marmalade, Covered, Yellow	55.00
Jar, Yellow, Covered	56.00
Jug, Yellow, 1 Pint	20.00
Mug, Coffee, Red	22.00 To 30.00
Mug, Tom & Jerry, Decal	28.00
Mug, Turquoise	23.00
Mug, Yellow	20.00
Mustard, Covered, Blue	45.00
Nappy, Ivory, 8 1/2 In.	16.00
Nappy, Red, 8 1/2 In.	15.00 To 20.00
Nappy, Rose, 8 1/2 In.	20.00 To 25.00
Nappy, Turquoise, 8 1/2 In.	12.00
Nappy, Yellow, 8 1/2 In.	12.00
Pepper Shaker, Red	6.00
Pepper Shaker, Rose	3.00
Pitcher, Ice Lip, Blue, 2 Pt.	35.00
Pitcher, Juice, Yellow, 30 Ounce	17.50
Pitcher, Water, Dish, Turquoise	25.00
Pitcher, Water, Green, 2 Quart	22.00

Pitcher, Water, Red	30.00
Pitcher, Water, Yellow	16.00 To 20.00
Plate, Blue, 6 In.	2.00 To 2.50
Plate, Blue, 10 In.	6.00 To 10.00
Plate, Calendar, Good Luck, Old Ivory	25.00
Plate, Chartreuse, 7 In.	5.00
Plate, Chop, Green, 13 In.	12.00
Plate, Chop, Red, 13 In.	25.00
Plate, Chop, Turquoise, 13 In.	12.00
Plate, Chop, Yellow, 13 In.	12.00
Plate, Dessert, Green	8.00
Plate, Dinner, Yellow, 10 In.	6.00
Plate, Forest Green, 6 In.	3.50
Plate, Forest Green, 9 In.	9.00
Plate, Gray, 6 In.	3.00
Plate, Gray, 7 In.	3.75
Plate, Gray, 9 In.	6.25
Plate, Green, 10 In.	8.00
Plate, Medium Green, 6 In.	3.50
Plate, Medium Green, 9 In.	6.00
Plate, Old Ivory, 6 In.	2.00
Plate, Old Ivory, 9 In.	5.00
Plate, Old Ivory, 10 In.	9.00
Plate, Red, 6 In.	3.00 To 3.50
Plate, Red, 7 In.	4.00
Plate, Red, 9 In.	7.00
Plate, Red, 10 In.	8.00 To 10.00
Plate, Turquoise, 7 In.	3.75
Plate, Turquoise, 9 In.	2.00 To 6.25
Plate, Turquoise, 10 In.	4.00 To 8.00
Plate, Yellow, 6 In.	1.50 To 2.50
Plate, Yellow, 9 In.	5.00
Plate, Yellow, 10 In.	4.00 To 14.00
Platter, Blue, 12 In.	12.00
Platter, Old Ivory, 12 In.	9.00 To 12.00
Platter, Oval, Medium Green, 12 In.	12.00
Platter, Oval, Turquoise, 13 In.	14.50
Platter, Yellow, 12 In.	7.00 To 12.00
Refrigerator Stacking Set, Yellow, 4 Piece	95.00
Relish, Old Ivory, 6 Parts	45.00
Salt & Pepper, Handled	16.50
Salt & Pepper, Medium Green	15.00
Salt & Pepper, Turquoise	5.00
Saltshaker, Red	6.00
Saltshaker, Rose	3.00
Saltshaker, Turquoise	3.00
Saucer, Fruit, Red, 5 1/2 In., Set Of 4	50.00
Saucer, Gray	2.50
Saucer, Medium Green	2.50
Saucer, Old Ivory	1.50
Saucer, Red, 5 1/2 In.	9.00
Saucer, Rose	2.50
Saucer, Turquoise, 5 1/2 In.	2.50 To 7.00
Saucer, Yellow, 5 1/2 In.	1.50 To 7.00
Serving Set, Kitchen Kraft, Spoon, Fork, & Server, Red	175.00
Soup, Blue	12.00
Soup, Gray, 8 1/2 In.	15.00
Soup, Rose	18.00
Sugar & Creamer, Gray, Chartreuse, & Green, Cover	20.00
Sugar & Creamer, Old Ivory, Covered	13.00
Sugar, Covered, Dark Green	11.00
Sugar, Covered, Gray	14.00
Sugar, Open, Medium Green	7.00

Sugar, Red	8.00
Syrup, Cover, Purple	75.00
Syrup, Original Top, Red	100.00 To 125.00
Syrup, Original Top, Turquoise	70.00 To 125.00
Syrup, Yellow	85.00
Teapot, Light Green, 6 Cups	30.00
Teapot, Turquoise	24.00
Tray, For Sugar & Creamer, Royal Blue	25.00
Tray, Sugar & Creamer, Blue	15.00
Tray, Turquoise	9.00
Tray, Utility, Blue	16.00
Tray, Utility, Green	10.00
Tray, Utility, Yellow	10.00
Tumbler, Blue	20.00
Tumbler, Green	12.00 To 20.00
Tumbler, Juice, Blue	14.00
Tumbler, Juice, Old Ivory, 5 Ounce	7.50
Tumbler, Juice, Turquoise	10.00
Tumbler, Juice, Yellow	10.00
Tumbler, Red	25.00
Tumbler, Yellow	14.00 To 20.00
Utility Tray, Turquoise	20.00
Vase, Bud, Navy	25.00
Vase, Bud, Old Ivory	25.00
Vase, Bud, Yellow	20.00
Vase, Yellow, 6 In.	30.00
Vase, Yellow, 8 In.	135.00

Findlay, or onyx, glass was made using three layers of glass. It was manufactured by the Dalzell Gilmore Leighton Company about 1889 in Findlay, Ohio. The silver, ruby, or black pattern was molded into the glass. The glass came in several colors, but was usually white or ruby.

FINDLAY ONYX, Bowl, 2 3/4 X 8 In.Diam.	900.00
Muffineer, Platinum	250.00
Salt, Cream	245.00
Spooner, Raspberry	395.00
Sugar, Ivory With Platinum, Covered	650.00
Syrup, Silver Design, Cream Ground	775.00

FIREFIGHTING, Alarm Box, Gamewell, C.1905, Window Front, Bell, 12 X 45 In.	595.00
Alarm Box, Gamewell, Cast Iron, 17 In.	95.00
Alarm Box, Hand Holding Electricity, 17 X 12 1/2 X 6 In.	37.50
Ax, Hooked Handle	130.00
Ax, Nickel Plated, Red Handle	50.00
Belt, Parade, Dress, New York	40.00
Brazier, Wooden Handle, 18th Century, Copper, 10 In.	495.00
Bucket, Italian Design, Leather, 1700s	350.00
Bucket, Leather, 1700s	195.00
Bucket, Leather, 1875	195.00
Bucket, S.Murdock, Leather	150.00
Crane Plate, Wrought-Iron Bail, Swivel Ring, 18th Century	75.00
Extinguisher, Auto, Pyrene, Brass	39.50
Extinguisher, Bulldog	10.00
Extinguisher, Dashout, Glass	15.00
Extinguisher, Hanging, Glass	25.00
Extinguisher, Kent, Brass, Gauge, 21 In.	22.50
Extinguisher, Phoenix, 22 In.	24.00
Extinguisher, Pioneer, Lithograph Of Pioneer, Tin, 22 In.	15.00
Extinguisher, Polished Copper, Tall	32.50
Extinguisher, Pump, Copper & Brass	50.00
Extinguisher, Pyrene, Copper & Brass	30.00
Extinguisher, Red Comet, Clear Grenade, Wall Bracket	12.50

Extinguisher, Shur-Stop, Red Liquid, Hangar, Bulb Shape	20.00
Gauge, Steam Boiler, Fire Engine, American LaFrance	150.00
Grenade, C. & N.W.Ry., Glass, 17 1/2 In.Long	100.00
Grenade, Hazelton, Keg	135.00
Grenade, Wall Mount, Kill-Fyr	15.00
Hat, Eagle Crest, Ohio Valley, 19th Century	65.00
Hat, High Profile Front, Brass Eagle On Top, Leather	245.00
Helmet, Austrian	195.00
Helmet, Brass Eagle, Leather, Marked Cairns, N.Y.C.	80.00
Helmet, Dress, French, Brass	270.00
Helmet, Dyersburg	25.00
Helmet, Eagle On Top, Leather	85.00
Helmet, English, Brass	175.00
Helmet, French, Brass	125.00
Helmet, German, Black	175.00
Nozzle, A.J.Morse & Son, Boston, Brass, 15 1/4 In.	45.00
Nozzle, Esso, Brass	20.00
Nozzle, Hose, Powhatan, Brass, 12 In.	22.00
Nozzle, 2-Hand Grip, Brass, 30 In.	60.00
Pump, Hand, Ship's	117.00
Red Shield, Fearless Imprinted, Leather, 41 In.	40.00
Spotlight, Engine, Handle, Brass, 9 1/2 In.Diam.	75.00
Sprinkler Head, Dated 1911	6.00

*Fireglow glass resembles English Bristol glass, but a reddish-brown
color can be seen when the piece is held to the light. It is a form of art
glass made by the Boston and Sandwich Glass Co.of Massachusetts, and
other companies.*

FIREGLOW, Vase, Enameled Bird, Branch, Berries, 3-Legged, 6 1/2 In.	90.00

FIREPLACE, Andirons, American Federal, C.1790, Brass, 14 In.	330.00
Andirons, Arched Spurred Supports, Ball Feet, Brass, 21 In.	200.00
Andirons, Black Man & Woman, Comic, 16 In.	425.00
Andirons, Brass & Iron, Arch Foot, Ring Top, 18th Century	150.00
Andirons, Brass, Bell Foot, Faceted Shafts, 23 In., Pair	100.00
Andirons, Brass, Federal, C.1820, Ball Finials, 12 1/2 In.	200.00
Andirons, Brass, French, 11 X 13 In., Pair	60.00
Andirons, C.1800, American, Brass, 22 5/8 In.	625.00
Andirons, Chippendale, Brass	350.00
Andirons, Christmas Tree Shape, Brass Knobs	75.00
Andirons, Cupids, Screen, French, Bronze, 29 In.	900.00
Andirons, Eastlake, Cast Iron, 15 X 8 In.	95.00
Andirons, Federal, American, 19th Century, Ball Finial, 17 1/2 In.	200.00
Andirons, Federal, Hunneman, Boston, 19th Century, 11 1/2 In.	600.00
Andirons, Figural, Boy, Feet Set Apart, C.1825, Cast Iron, 13 In.	325.00
Andirons, Figural, George Washington, Cast Iron, 20 In.	195.00
Andirons, Gooseneck, Penny Feet, Iron, 18 In.Pair	150.00
Andirons, Kindling, Arched Penny Footed Gooseneck, 13 1/2 In.	300.00
Andirons, Lemon Top, Firedogs, Gold Paint, Brass, 20 In.	375.00
Andirons, Ring Top, Hearts, Iron, 15 1/2 In., Pair	85.00
Andirons, Straight Blades Curl Forward, Trestle Feet, 13 3/4 In.	195.00
Ball Top, Snake Feet, Late 18th Century, Brass, 17 In.	295.00
Bellows, Brass, Victorian, 2-Wheel Mechanism, Iron, Stand, 20 In.	200.00
Bellows, Bull's-Eye Medallion Center, Leather, Tin End, 18 1/2 In.	40.00
Bellows, Cast Brass Nozzle, French	24.00
Bellows, Handmade, Leather & Wood	65.00
Bellows, Original Design, Leather, Maine	200.00
Bellows, Red Leather, Hand-Carved Mahogany	40.00
Bellows, Turtleback, Gilt Stenciled Basket Of Fruit, 17 In.	85.00
Broom, Hearth, Hand-Tied, Wooden Handle, 40 In.	12.50
Carrier, Ember, Wrought-Iron Handle Into Wooden Handle, 32 In.	115.00
Chenets, Brass, Double Urn, Brass Boot, Angel Bust Detail, 11 In.	150.00

Chenets, French, Gilt, 19th Century, 21 In. 800.00
Chenets, French, Lion Surmount, Gilt, 16 1/2 In. 1200.00
Crane, Curled End, 36 In. 55.00
Crane, 28 In. 35.00
Crane, 38 In. 42.00
Fender, Brass, Curved Front, Pierced Fretwork, 4 Paw Feet 225.00
Fender, Brass, English, Pierced Foliate Design, 3 Oval Feet 100.00
Fender, Brass, Pierced, Spiral-Twist Design, Paw Feet, 40 In. 100.00
Fender, Footed, Brass, Openwork, 34 X 8 In. 80.00
Fender, Paw Feet, Brass, 42 1/2 X 12 In. 145.00
Fender, Putti, Lion's Heads, & Leafage, Bronze Dore, 60 In. 550.00
Fireback, Basket Of Flowers, Scrollwork, Iron, 18 X 28 In. 115.00
Frypan, Long Handled, Footed, 16 1/4 In. 145.00
Frypan, Wrought-Iron, Handled, 42 In. 125.00
Hook, Trammel, Swivel, Wrought Iron 30.00
Ladle, Double Pouring Lip, Wrought Iron, 22 1/2 In. 50.00
Mantel, Pine, Blue Paint, Shelf, 64 1/2 X 61 In. 65.00
Peel, Bread, Hand-Forged Iron, Mushroom Knob, C.1860, 50 In. 50.00
Plate, Crane, Footed, Bail, Swivel Ring, 18th Century, Wrought Iron 75.00
Poker, Ram's Horn Top, Wrought Iron, 54 In. 95.00
Pot, Wrought-Iron Bail, 3-Footed, Cast Iron, 8 1/4 X 10 In.Diam. 75.00
Roasting Jack, Meat, Clockwork, Brass 85.00
Screen, African, Bone & Mother-Of-Pearl Inlaid, Fruitwood, 48 In. 400.00
Screen, Copper, 31 In. 100.00
Screen, Petitpoint Dutch Scene, Open Handled, Walnut Frame 195.00
Screen, Stained Glass Insets, Marquetry, Mahogany, 30 1/2 In. 385.00
Shovel, Oak Handle, Brass, 13 In. 45.00
Skimmer, Brass Ferrule, Iron Ladle, Drain Holes, C.1880, 32 In. 50.00
Teakettle, Hanging, Wrought-Iron Stand, Copper & Brass 145.00
Tile, Hunting Dogs, Doe With Fawn, Buck Deer, 6 X 18 In., 3 Piece 750.00
Tile, Two Colonial Girls, One Man, Framed, 6 X 18 In., 3 Piece 675.00
Toaster, Rotating, Center Dividers, Handle, 6 1/2 X 16 1/4 In.Long 235.00
Toaster, Rotating, 3 Sets Twisted Wrought-Iron Bars, 13 In.Wide 220.00
Toaster, Serpentine Curves Of Wire, Footed Plate, 30 In. 65.00
Toaster, Whirling, 18th Century, Wrought Iron, 19 In. 450.00
Tongs, Ember, Brass Handle 12.00
Tongs, Penny End, Wrought Iron 18.00
Tool Set, Chased Stand & 4 Tools 90.00

*Fischer porcelain was made in Herend, Hungary. The factory was founded
in 1839, and has continued working into the twentieth century. The wares are
sometimes referred to as Herend porcelain.*

FISCHER, Dish, Leaf-Shaped, Handled, Emerald Green 36.00
Figurine, Music Lesson, 7 In. 125.00
Jug, Blue Butterflies, Deer, Flowers 380.00
Vase, Battle Frieze, C.1900, Covered, Marked, 9 1/2 In. 600.00
Vase, Filigree, 2-Handled, 6 1/2 X 6 1/2 In. 145.00
Vase, Flowers, Wedding Rings, Cobalt Handles, Signed, 12 In. 229.00
Vase, Pastel Flowers, 4 Wedding Rings, Cobalt Handles, Signed, 12 In. 229.00
Vase, Reticulated Allover, Multicolored, 4 Handles, Marked, 15 In. 550.00

FISHING, Box, Bait, Worn On Belt, Iron Hinges, Copper, 3 X 5 3/4 X 2 3/4 In. 35.00
Box, Tackle, 13 Lures, Cedar 100.00
Creel, Applied Bronze Shellfish On Cover, Woven Bronze 250.00
Lure, Al Foss, Lithographed Box, C.1930, Brass 15.00
Lure, C.1940, Wooden, Original Boxes, Set Of 50 .... 250.00
Lure, Fishmaster, Minnow, 1940s 5.00
Lure, Orcher Spinner, Milward's, Redditch, England, Original Card 10.00
Lure, Skinner's No.5 Spoon, Feathered Treble, Fluted Spoon 7.00

Pflueger Skilkast, 1953 .... 8.00
Reel, Bait Casting, South Bend, No.350a 8.00
Reel, Edwards No.30, Aluminum Fly Reel 4.50
Reel, Fly, Rainbow 7.50
Reel, Hendryx, Nonlevel 8.00
Reel, Ocean City, No.1591 .... 5.50
Reel, Pflueger Summit, 1993L 10.00
Reel, Shakespeare 1837 Tru-Art Automatic Trout, Box 18.00
Reel, Tripart, 580, 1909 .... 17.50
Reel, Winchester 70.00
Reel, Wonderreel Deluxe Model GE 16.00
Rod & Reel, Winchester 150.00
Rod, Fly, South Bend, Split Bamboo, 2 Extra Sections, Guides 50.00
Rod, Split Bamboo, Montague, No.4 SC, Extra Tip, Tube Container 150.00
Rod, Sport King, No. 8 1/2 .... 17.50
    FLAG, see Textile, Flag

FLASH GORDON, Arresting Ray Gun, Boxed 100.00
Cap Pistol, Atomic Disintegrator 69.00
Christmas Tree Lights, 1934, Boxed 175.00
Gun, Disintegrator, Original Wrapper, Tin, Red 85.00
Kite, Paper, 1930s 35.00
Kite, Pictorial, 1942 .... 11.00
Map, World Battle Front, Macy's World War II Giveaway 90.00
Radio Repeater, Boxed 100.00
Ring, Post Toasties 10.00
Rocketship .... 185.00 To 250.00
Space Compass, Boxed 8.00
Telephone, 2-Way, Original Cord 35.00

> *Flow blue, or flo blue, was made in England about 1830 to 1900. The plates
> were printed with designs using a cobalt blue coloring. The color flowed from
> the design to the white plate so the finished plate had a smeared blue design.
> The plates were usually made of ironstone china.*

FLOW BLUE, Ashtray, Boat Shaped, Floral Design, 2 1/2 X 5 1/4 In. 25.00
Berry, Kyber, Adams, 5 In. 45.00
Bone Dish, Dorothy, Set Of 4 .... 120.00
Bone Dish, Holland, Meakin 25.00
Bone Dish, La Belle, Signed 35.00
Bone Dish, Oxford 25.00
Bone Dish, Portman, Grindley, Set Of 4 .... 179.50
Bowl, Albany, Round Handled 58.00
Bowl, Centerpiece, Italian Scenery, Adams, 10 In. 295.00
Bowl, Cereal, Melbourne, 7 1/2 In. 30.00
Bowl, Clayton, Johnson Bros., 10 In. 18.00
Bowl, Delph, Bourne & Leigh, 10 1/2 In. 55.00
Bowl, Delph, E.Bourne & J.Leech, 10 1/2 In. 48.00
Bowl, Dorothy 15.00
Bowl, Kyber, Rectangular, 7 1/2 In. 89.50
Bowl, La Belle, Embossed Flower Ends, Oval, 12 1/4 X 9 3/4 In. 125.00
Bowl, La Belle, Footed, Large 325.00
Bowl, Nonpareil, 7 3/4 In. 40.00
Bowl, Oriental, 6 X 8 In. 40.00
Bowl, Rhone, 10 In. 58.00
Bowl, Scinde, 10 3/4 X 8 1/4 In. 130.00
Bowl, Shortcake, Touraine, 6 1/4 In. 35.00
Bowl, Soup, Ashburton, Grindley 14.00
Bowl, Soup, Florida, Johnson Bros. 46.00
Bowl, Soup, Togo, Grindley, Rimmed 25.00
Bowl, Vegetable, Adams, Oval Sided, 13 In. 95.00
Bowl, Vegetable, Baltic, Covered, 12 X 7 1/4 In. 110.00
Bowl, Vegetable, Canton, Edwards, Open, 10 1/4 In.Diam. 145.00
Bowl, Vegetable, Daisy, Scalloped, Open, 9 X 11 In. 42.50

Bowl, Vegetable, Hong Kong, C.Meigh, Open, C.1845, 12 In.Diam. 150.00
Bowl, Vegetable, Individual, Rose, Grindley 22.50
Bowl, Vegetable, Melbourne, Grindley, 10 In.Diam. 20.00
Bowl, Vegetable, Scinde, Square Finial, Covered, 10 X 13 In. 425.00
Bowl, Waldorf, New Wharf Pottery, 9 In. .... 40.00 To 69.00
Bowl, Waste, Marie, Grindley 55.00
Bowl, Waste, Scinde, Alcock 130.00
Butter Pat, Argyle, Grindley 26.50
Butter Pat, Clarence 28.00
Butter Pat, Clifton, Grindley 22.50
Butter Pat, Colonial 20.00
Butter Pat, Gainsborough, Ridgway 19.50
Butter Pat, La Francais 12.00
Butter Pat, Linda 12.00
Butter Pat, Nonpareil 15.00
Butter Pat, Oxford, J.B. 15.00
Butter Pat, Portman, Grindley 22.50
Butter Pat, Savoy, Johnson Bros. 14.50
Butter Pat, Touraine .... 14.00 To 20.00
Butter Pat, Waverly 9.00
Butter Pat, Wentworth, Hanley 12.00
Butter, Neapolitan, Covered, Drainer 95.00
Butter, Rose, Grindley, Covered 45.00
Butter, Shanghai, Drainer, Covered 100.00
Cake Plate, Coburg, Closed Handles, Octagonal, 9 In. 65.00
Celery, La Belle, Strawberry Design 100.00
Charger, Fairy Villas, 15 In. 128.00
Charger, La Belle 99.50
Chocolate Pot, Warwick 175.00
Coffeepot, Manilla, Podmore Walker 450.00
Coffeepot, Washington, T.Walker, 1850 .... 180.00
Creamer, Canton, Edwards 195.00
Creamer, Ebor, Ridgway 127.50
Creamer, Linda, J.Maddock 65.00
Creamer, Lobelia 78.00
Creamer, Marechal Neil, Grindley 75.00
Creamer, Marie, Grindley, 5 In. 55.00
Creamer, Oregon 225.00
Creamer, Saxon, Blue Border 45.00
Creamer, Sydney, Wood & Son 59.50
Creamer, Touraine 125.00
Creamer, Watteau, Doulton 34.50
Cup & Saucer, Brunswick Evangeline, Libertus 20.00
Cup & Saucer, Canton, Handleless, C.1845 .... 65.00
Cup & Saucer, Cashmere, Handleless 110.00
Cup & Saucer, Chapoo, Demitasse 99.50
Cup & Saucer, Conway, New Wharf Pottery 45.00
Cup & Saucer, Dahlia 65.00
Cup & Saucer, Ebor, Ridgway 64.50
Cup & Saucer, Gem, Maddock, Set Of 6 .... 270.00
Cup & Saucer, Haddon, Grindley 55.00
Cup & Saucer, Heath's Flower, 2 Handles 95.00
Cup & Saucer, Indian Jar, Handleless 75.00
Cup & Saucer, Italia, Floral & Lattice On Inner Rims 79.00
Cup & Saucer, Kendal, Ridgway 40.00
Cup & Saucer, Kyber, Adams 35.00
Cup & Saucer, Lancaster, New Wharf Pottery 40.00
Cup & Saucer, Manhattan, Alcock 37.50
Cup & Saucer, Nonpareil .... 40.00 To 55.00
Cup & Saucer, Oregon 45.00
Cup & Saucer, Osborne, Grindley, Set Of 4 .... 198.50
Cup & Saucer, Peking, Handleless, C.1845 .... 75.00
Cup & Saucer, Pelew, Challinor, Handleless .... 75.00 To 95.00
Cup & Saucer, Pelew, Handleless 70.00

Cup & Saucer, Rhine, Handleless, Dated	50.00
Cup & Saucer, Savoy	67.50
Cup & Saucer, Scinde, Alcock	95.00
Cup & Saucer, Shanghai	55.00 To 70.00
Cup & Saucer, Sobraon, Handleless, Set Of 4	300.00
Cup & Saucer, Splendid, Maastricht	55.00
Cup & Saucer, Temple, Walker	95.00
Cup & Saucer, Touraine	45.00 To 69.50
Cup & Saucer, Waldorf, New Wharf Pottery	55.00
Cup & Saucer, Windsor, Edwards & Sons	55.50
Cup Plate, Amoy	39.00
Cup, Touraine	24.00 To 55.00
Dish, Candy, La Belle, Cloverleaf Shape, Blue, 9 X 7 1/2 In.	85.00
Dish, Honey, Hong Kong	38.00
Dish, Osborne, Cloverleaf Shape, Ridgway, Cover	65.00
Eggcup, Madras, Royal Doulton	53.50
Eggcup, Montana, Johnson	95.00
Eggcup, Osborne, Ridgway	95.00
Eggcup, Touraine, Maastricht	165.00
Gravy Boat & Underplate, Paisley, Mercer	50.00
Gravy Boat & Undertray, Marguerite, Grindley	55.00
Gravy Boat, Irene	45.00
Gravy Boat, Marie, Grindley	55.00
Gravy Boat, Minton, C.1874	40.00
Gravy Boat, Oriental, Alcock	125.00
Gravy Boat, Tivoli	100.00
Gravy Boat, Touraine	77.50
Gravy, Paris	22.00
Gravy, Waldorf	45.00
Jardiniere, Sebring	297.00
Ladle, Sauce, Small Florals On White, Gold Trim, 7 In.	25.00
Ladle, Soup, Lotus, Grindley, 12 In.	100.00
Pitcher, California, C.1849, 8 In.	95.00
Pitcher, Crawford Cooking Ranges, C.1885, 6 In.	75.00
Pitcher, Hot Water, Clifton	279.50
Pitcher, Melton, 7 1/2 In.	45.00
Pitcher, Melton, 8 1/4 In.	55.00
Pitcher, Milk, Clarence, Grindley	145.00
Pitcher, Milk, Kyber	100.00
Pitcher, Milk, Madras	150.00
Pitcher, Water, Indian, Pratt, Bulbous, 6 1/2 In.	335.00
Pitcher, Water, Touraine	175.00 To 229.50
Plate, Acantha, 8 In.	14.00
Plate, Acantha, 9 In.	18.00
Plate, Acantha, 10 In.	22.00
Plate, Alaska, Grindley, 10 In.	24.00
Plate, Albany, Grindley, 7 In.	17.00
Plate, Albany, Johnson Brothers, Cobalt Blue, 10 In.	32.00
Plate, Amoy, Davenport, 10 In.	94.50
Plate, Amoy, 7 1/4 In.	48.00
Plate, Amoy, 10 In.	127.50
Plate, Arabesque, Mayer, 10 In.	85.00
Plate, Argyle, 8 In.	35.00
Plate, Argyle, 9 In.	23.00 To 42.00
Plate, Atalanta, Wedgwood & Co., 10 In.	49.50
Plate, Beauties Of China, 8 1/2 In.	40.00
Plate, Canton, Ashworth, Slate Gray, 8 In.	20.00
Plate, Canton, Edwards, 10 1/4 In.	70.00
Plate, Canton, 10 3/4 In.	80.00
Plate, Cashmere, 9 In.	75.00
Plate, Chapoo, Wedgwood, 8 1/4 In.	57.00
Plate, Chapoo, Wedgwood, 9 1/4 In.	90.00
Plate, Chapoo, 7 1/2 In.	60.00

Plate, Chapoo, 8 1/2 In.	55.00 To 75.00
Plate, Chapoo, 9 1/2 In.	80.00
Plate, Chusan, Clementson, 6 In.	45.00
Plate, Chusan, Clementson, 9 In.	65.00
Plate, Chusan, 10 1/2 In.	75.00
Plate, Claremont, Johnson Bros., 7 3/4 In.	24.50
Plate, Claremont, Johnson Bros., 9 1/2 In.	50.00
Plate, Colonial, Hanley, 10 In.	25.00
Plate, Commemorative, Death Of Captain Lawrence	30.00
Plate, Conway, New Wharf Pottery, 10 In.	35.00
Plate, Conway, 6 In.	15.00
Plate, Corean, Mulberry, 9 In.	30.00
Plate, Cuba, 9 In.	39.50
Plate, Cuba, 10 In.	43.50
Plate, Cyprus, 9 1/2 In.	20.00
Plate, Delph, 10 In.	25.00
Plate, Devon, 7 In.	18.00
Plate, Fairy Villas, 8 1/2 In.	22.00
Plate, Formosa, Mayer, 9 1/2 In.	65.00
Plate, Geneva, Adams, 10 In.	75.00
Plate, Geneva, Royal Doulton, 8 1/2 In.	75.00
Plate, Grecian Statue, 9 3/4 In.	40.00
Plate, Holland, Meakin, 10 In.	45.00
Plate, Hong Kong, Meigh, 8 In.	40.00
Plate, Hong Kong, 10 1/2 In.	55.00
Plate, Idris, Grindley, 8 In.	12.00
Plate, Indian Jar, Furnival, 9 In.	65.00
Plate, Indian, Pratt, 6 In.	45.00
Plate, Indian, Pratt, 8 1/4 In.	65.00
Plate, Indian, Pratt, 9 In.	75.00
Plate, Keele, Grindley, 9 In.	35.00
Plate, Kyber, Adams, 10 In.	85.00
Plate, Kyber, W.Adams & Sons, 10 In.	45.00
Plate, La Belle, Cup Ring, 6 1/2 In.	92.50
Plate, La Belle, 9 In.	24.00 To 44.50
Plate, Leicester, Sampson Hancock, 9 In.	28.00
Plate, Madras, Doulton, 9 1/2 In.	32.00 To 58.50
Plate, Marie, 10 In.	32.00
Plate, Martha Washington, 9 In.	85.00
Plate, Melbourne, 10 In.	48.00
Plate, Moorish Palace, 9 1/2 In.	35.00
Plate, Muriel, 10 In.	30.00
Plate, Nonpareil, 8 1/2 In.	30.00
Plate, Oregon, 10 In.	60.00
Plate, Oriental, 7 In.	30.00
Plate, Osborne, Grindley, 9 1/2 In.	35.00
Plate, Osborne, T.R. & Co., 10 3/4 In.	37.00 To 47.00
Plate, Oxford, Johnson Bros., 8 In.	28.00
Plate, Pekin, Wedgwood, Bentley, 10 1/4 In.	75.00
Plate, Pekin, 12 In.	50.00
Plate, Pelew, Challinor, 8 1/2 In.	40.00
Plate, Persian, 9 In.	25.00
Plate, Poppy, 9 In.	35.00
Plate, Rhine, T.Dimmock, 10 1/2 In.	50.00
Plate, Richmond, Meakin, 10 In.	50.00
Plate, Rock, 10 1/2 In.	60.00
Plate, Romeo, Wedgwood, 10 In.	22.00
Plate, Rose, Grindley, 7 1/2 In.	27.50
Plate, Rose, Grindley, 9 In.	20.00
Plate, Rose, Grindley, 10 In.	25.00
Plate, Rose, Grindley, 12 In.	27.50
Plate, Scinde, Alcock, 8 1/4 In.	65.00
Plate, Scinde, Alcock, 9 1/2 In.	60.00

Plate, Scinde, Alcock, 10 In.	50.00
Plate, Scinde, Scalloped Curved Rim, 10 3/4 In.	65.00
Plate, Scinde, Staffordshire, 9 1/2 In.	52.00
Plate, Scinde, T.Walker, 9 1/2 In.	58.00
Plate, Seville, New Wharf, 7 In.	13.00
Plate, Shanghai, J.F. & Co., 8 In.	42.50
Plate, Temple, P.Walker, 7 1/2 In.	48.00
Plate, Temple, Pearlstone Ware, Podmore & Walker	60.00 To 75.00
Plate, Temple, Pearlstone Ware, Podmore & Walker, 9 1/2 In.	95.00
Plate, Togo, 7 In.	25.00
Plate, Togo, 9 In.	37.00
Plate, Togo, 10 In.	45.00
Plate, Tokio, Johnson Bros., 10 In.	47.00
Plate, Tokio, 10 In.	42.00
Plate, Touraine, Meakin, 10 In.	55.00
Plate, Touraine, 6 1/2 In.	20.00
Plate, Touraine, 8 In.	28.00
Plate, Touraine, 8 3/4 In.	40.00
Plate, Touraine, 9 In.	30.00
Plate, Troy, 9 1/4 In.	35.00
Plate, U.S.Capitol, 10 1/4 In.	135.00
Plate, Waldorf, Fan Edge, New Wharf Pottery, 10 In.	28.00
Plate, Waldorf, New Wharf Pottery, 9 In.	35.00 To 42.00
Plate, Waldorf, New Wharf Pottery, 10 In.	55.00
Plate, Waldorf, 9 In.	28.00 To 55.00
Plate, Whampoa, 7 1/4 In.	40.00
Platter, Alaska, Grindley, 13 In.	110.00
Platter, Arabesque, Mayer, 13 1/2 X 10 1/2 In.	125.00
Platter, Argyle, 10 In.	42.50
Platter, Argyle, 12 In.	80.00
Platter, Argyle, 15 X 10 1/2 In.	127.00
Platter, Astoria, 14 In.	65.00
Platter, Belmont, 15 1/2 In.	65.00
Platter, Burleigh, 10 In.	40.00
Platter, Carlton, 13 X 10 In.	85.00
Platter, Chapoo, Wedgwood, 16 In.	150.00
Platter, Chusan, Clementson, 8 X 10 1/4 In.	225.00
Platter, Claremont, Johnson, 1i 1/2 In.	135.00
Platter, Claremont, Johnson, 14 1/2 In.	165.00
Platter, Clayton, Johnson Bros., 12 1/2 In.	15.00
Platter, Conway, New Wharf Pottery, 11 X 8 In.	60.00
Platter, Crown & Banner, Lancaster, England, Blue, 9 X 12 In.	60.00
Platter, Del Monte Pattern	82.00
Platter, Formosa, 12 1/2 X 9 1/2 In.	250.00
Platter, Geisha, Meakin, 9 X 12 In.	40.00
Platter, Gothic, J.F. & Co., 12 1/2 X 16 In.	265.00
Platter, Hong Kong, 13 1/2 X 10 In.	275.00
Platter, Indian Plant, T.Dimmock, C.1844, 18 X 15 In.	200.00
Platter, Indian, 17 In.	135.00
Platter, Janette, 15 In.	85.00
Platter, Kyber, Adams, 16 3/4 In.	195.00
Platter, Kyber, Small	87.50
Platter, La Belle, Floral	20.00
Platter, Lasas, Ridgway, 9 X 12 In.	45.00
Platter, Melbourne, 14 X 10 In.	75.00
Platter, Nelson, 16 X 12 In.	75.00
Platter, Nonpareil, B & L, 18 In.	195.00
Platter, Normandy	89.50
Platter, Olympia, Grindley, 14 X 10 In.	62.50
Platter, Onion, Oval, Marked, 12 1/2 In.	125.00
Platter, Oregon, 15 1/2 X 12 In.	350.00
Platter, Paisley, Mercer, 15 1/2 In.	75.00
Platter, Pekin, Vase On Table, 12 In.	85.00

Platter, Pekin, 15 In. 35.00
Platter, Pelew, 15 1/2 X 12 In. 350.00
Platter, Poppy, Oval, 12 X 9 1/4 In. 117.00
Platter, Rhine, 15 X 12 In. 130.00
Platter, Scinde, Alcock, 7 1/4 In. 175.00
Platter, Scinde, Alcock, 13 1/2 In. 265.00
Platter, Scinde, Alcock, 16 In. 345.00
Platter, Scinde, 14 X 16 In. 325.00
Platter, Sobraon, 12 X 16 In. .... 100.00 To 140.00
Platter, Stanley, 14 X 10 In. 50.00
Platter, Temple, J.Wedgwood, 13 1/4 In. 175.00
Platter, Temple, Podmore & Walker, Pearlstone Ware, 13 1/4 In. 150.00
Platter, Tivoli, Notched Corner, 16 In. 95.00
Platter, Touraine, Stanley, 12 1/2 X 8 1/2 In. 55.00
Platter, Touraine, Stanley, 15 In. 85.00
Platter, Turkey, 19 X 16 1/2 In. 225.00
Platter, Waldorf, New Wharf Pottery, 16 In. 235.00
Platter, Waldorf, 9 X 11 In. 25.00
Platter, Waldorf, 10 1/2 In. 45.00
Platter, Waverly, Grindley, 12 X 8 1/4 In. 59.50
Relish, Madras, Paneled 65.00
Sauce, Arabesque 35.00
Sauce, Arcadia, Wilkinson, Set Of 8 .... 100.00
Sauce, Berry, Chapoo, Wedgwood, 5 1/2 In. 55.00
Sauce, Florida 17.00
Sauce, Rose, Grindley 49.50
Sauce, Savoy, Johnson Bros, ... 67.50
Sauce, Scinde, Alcock 55.00
Sauce, Touraine 20.00
Saucer, Kyber, Coffee 12.50
Saucer, La Belle 20.00
Saucer, Maniela, P.W. & Co. 20.00
Shaving Mug, Campion, Grindley 79.50
Shaving Mug, Wagon Wheel 127.50
Soup, Ancient Ruins 28.00
Soup, Dish, Chapoo 75.00
Soup, Dish, Claremont, Johnson Bros., Flange, 8 3/4 In. 40.00
Soup, Dish, Clayton, Johnson Bros. 7.50
Soup, Dish, Lancaster, New Wharf Pottery, Flange 37.50
Soup, Dish, Roseville 40.00
Soup, Dish, Touraine 33.50
Soup, Dish, Waldorf, New Wharf Pottery, 9 In. 40.00
Soup, Formosa, 10 1/2 In. 80.00
Soup, Lugano 45.00
Soup, Roseville 28.00
Soup, Waldorf, 9 In. 30.00
Soup, Willow, 10 In. 80.00
Spittoon, Willow, Dark Blue 265.00
Sugar & Creamer, Plymouth 185.00
Sugar, Hong Kong, Covered 280.00
Sugar, Lobelia 165.00
Sugar, Mongolia, Johnson Bros., Covered 75.00
Sugar, Montana, Johnson Bros., Covered 87.50
Sugar, Paisley, Mercer, Covered 60.00
Sugar, Peruvian, Wedgwood, 16 Panels 85.00
Sugar, Rose, Grindley, Covered 25.00
Sugar, The Bolingbroke, Ridgway, Covered 85.00
Sugar, Touraine, Cover, Large 115.00
Tea Set, Gothic, Furnival 500.00
Teapot, Fern, Bunch Of Grapes Finial 450.00
Teapot, Neapolitan 100.00
Teapot, Sugar, & Creamer, Kaolinware, Thos.Dimmock 500.00
Toilette Set, Stoke On Trent, Flower Garlands, 4 Piece 350.00

Tray, Dresser, La Belle, Wheeling 70.00
Tureen, Argyle, Covered, Grindley, Oval, 9 1/2 In. 200.00
Tureen, Claremont, Covered, Johnson, Oval, 9 1/2 In. 185.00
Tureen, Gothic, Footed, Covered, 12 1/2 In. 225.00
Tureen, Kyber, 8-Sided, Covered, Adams 235.00
Tureen, Lonsdale, Covered, 11 1/2 In. 135.00
Tureen, Soup, Chusan, Morley, Pedestal Base 460.00
Tureen, Soup, Duchess, Grindley & Co., Platter & Ladle 375.00
Tureen, Soup, Togo, F.Winkle 125.00
Tureen, Watteau, Doulton, Pedestal, Covered 275.00
Vase, Double Handled, Scenic, 8 Panels, 12 In. 260.00
Vase, Iris, Square, C.1865 .... 129.50
Vase, Little Girl With Doll, 4 3/4 In. 125.00
Vegetable, Ancient Ruins, Covered 275.00
Vegetable, Astoria, Covered, 10 In. 85.00
Vegetable, Conway, Open, Round, 9 In. 45.00
Waste Bowl, Chapoo, Wedgwood 135.00
Waste Bowl, Claremont, Johnson 85.00
Waste Bowl, Ning Po 100.00

FLYING PHOENIX, see Phoenix Bird

Folk Art is listed in many sections of the book under the actual name of
the object. See categories such as Box; Cigar Store Indian; Weather
Vane; Wooden; etc.

FOLK ART, Board, Black & White Pig, 7 1/2 X 12 In. 45.00
Certificate, Baptismal Wish, Dated April 12, 1825, European 85.00
Certificate, Birth & Baptismal, For George Saltzmann, Dated 1793 .... 600.00
Certificate, Birth & Baptismal, For Johannes Saltzmann, Dated 1791 .... 625.00
Certificate, Birth & Baptismal, Men With Rooster, Virginia 5300.00
Certificate, Birth & Baptismal, Printed By Eagle Book Store 15.00
Certificate, Birth & Baptismal, Printed By Peters, Harrisburg 17.50
Duck, Black, Original Paint, Glass Eyes, 7 In., Pair 250.00
Family Record, Calligraphic, Gardner & Cornelia Garey 300.00
Figure, Dancing, Young Man, Cap, Wire, Spring Board, 20 In. 400.00
Figure, Man, Bald Head, Jointed, Wood & Papier-Mache, 27 In. 265.00
Figure, Seated Sad-Eyed Spaniel Dog, 3 X 2 X 2 In. 20.00
Figurine, Black Native, Polychrome Paint, 21 1/4 In. 400.00
Figurine, German Man With Hat, Signed L.S., 12 In. 125.00
Figurine, Turtle, Concrete, Wooden Base, 12 In. 13.00
Horse, Rope Forelock & Tail, Small 32.00
Horse, Wood, Black Paint, C.1900, 5 X 4 X 1 In. 25.00
Log Cabin, Church, 30 X 23 X 42 In. 140.00
Model, Boat, Square-Rigged, 9 In. 70.00
Ornament, Lawn, Duck, C.1900, 13 In. 18.00
Roly-Poly Clown, Papier-Mache, Original Paint, 6 X 2 In. 40.00
Sculpture, Dog, Reclining, Carved Sandstone, 1870, 14 X 9 1/2 In. 225.00
Stagecoach & 4 Horse Team, 10 Windows, 2 People, Harness, 19 In. ... 550.00
Wagon, Pulled By Pair Oxen, Wood, Cloth Top, 20 In. 85.00
Whale, Wooden, Metal Button Eye, Upturned Tail, 28 In. 90.00
Whirligig, Arms Old Red Paddles That Turn, Wooden, 7 1/2 In. 22.00
Whirligig, Confederate Soldiers, 11 In. 295.00
Whirligig, Dove, C.1880 .... 1250.00
Whirligig, Jigs Sawing Wood, Original Paint, 1930s 125.00
Whirligig, Lady In Rocker 100.00
Whirligig, Lady In Rocker, Under Tree, C.1930, Tin & Wood 100.00
Whirligig, Man Sawing Wood, 1930s 68.00
Whirligig, Paddle-Arm Sailor 28.00
Whirligig, Pecking Bird, Copper & Wood 160.00
Whirligig, Pigeon, Original Paint, 19th Century 850.00
Whirligig, Policeman, Brass Button, C.1920, Wooden, 18 X 7 In. 300.00
Whirligig, Rooster, Tin Wings, Wooden, Large 300.00
Whirligig, Sailor, Original Paint 1400.00
Whirligig, Stylized Soldier, Polychrome Paint, 15 In. 200.00

Whirligig, Windmill, Black Mammy Scrubbing Clothes, 10 3/4 In.	350.00
Whirligig, Woodpecker, Red Head, Pecks Branch, 17 X 12 X 12 In.	160.00
Whirligig, 4 Motorboats On Wheel, Movable, 62 In.	375.00

Foo dogs are mythical Chinese figures, part dog and part lion. They were made of pottery, porcelain, carved stone, and wood.

FOO DOG, Figurine, Soapstone, 3 1/2 In.	12.50
Green, Marked China, 8 In.	95.00
Jade, 3 1/4 X 3 In.	265.00
Marked China, Blue, 5 3/4 In.	65.00
Seated On Plinth, Soapstone, Tan, Marble, 4 X 6 X 9 1/2 In.	120.00
Turquoise Glaze, Late 19th Century, Chinese, Pair, 10 In.	200.00

FOOT WARMER, Blue Onion Pattern, Grimwade Mark, 11 In.Diam.	85.00
Brass Portholes, Tin Lid & Interior Base, 7 1/4 X 9 1/4 In.	300.00
Carpet Covered, Charcoal Drawer, Clark Heater Co.	45.00
Colonial, Walnut, Tin Top, Vents, Wire Bail, 8 X 6 In.	350.00
Halstead, Oval Sheet Iron, Footed, Handle, Drawer, Carpet Cover	40.00
Interior Pan, Punched Tin, Wooden Frame, 10 3/4 X 7 1/2 In.	85.00
Patent 1912, Henderson Pottery	65.00
Pierced Diamond Design, Tin & Wood, 9 X 7 1/2 In.	95.00
Pierced Diamonds & Circle Pattern, Old Red Finish On Wood, Tin	130.00
Pierced Tin, Maple	125.00
Pierced Tin, Soapstone Insert On Top, Whale Oil Burner	120.00
Punched Tin Top, Charcoal Pan, Walnut, 8 In.Square	350.00
Stamped OK Foot Warmer, Blue Letters	175.00
Velvet & Brass	25.00
Wire Bail Handle Heat & Flannel Wrap, Soapstone, 6 X 9 In.	20.00
Wire Bail Handle, Soapstone, 6 X 9 In.	22.50
Wooden Case, Wire Handle, Square Nails, Soapstone, 10 X 7 In.	48.00
5-Pointed Stars On Sides, Bail Handle, Wood Frame, 8 X 9 In.	165.00

FOSTORIA

Fostoria glass was made in Fostoria, Ohio, from 1887 to 1891. The factory was moved to Moundsville, West Virginia, and most of the glass seen in shops today is a twentieth-century product.

FOSTORIA, see also Milk Glass

FOSTORIA, Bookends, Horsehead	32.50
Bookends, Rearing Horse	45.00 To 55.00
Bowl, American, Salad, 10 In.Diam.	16.00
Bowl, American, 4 1/2 In.	4.25
Bowl, Console, June, Mushroom, Blue, 12 In.	65.00
Bowl, Fagot Pattern, Clear & Frosted, 9 1/2 In.	35.00
Bowl, Fairfax, Divided, Green, 9 In.	10.00
Bowl, June, Mushroom, Oval, Blue, 14 1/2 In.	85.00
Bowl, Royal Pattern, Oval, 10 In.	35.00
Bowl, Royal Pattern, 9 In.	30.00
Butter, American, Dome, Covered	45.00
Butter, Georgian Lovebird, Covered	65.00
Butter, Priscilla, Covered, Gold Trim, Green	100.00
Butter, Priscilla, Emerald Green, Gold, Covered	100.00
Cake Stand, American, Round, Pedestal	45.00
Candleholder, Baroque, 3-Light, Pair	35.00
Candlestick, Bell, Pair	125.00
Candlestick, Double, Plume	30.00
Candlestick, Fairfax, Mushroom, Green, Pair	27.50
Candlestick, June, Pink, 3 In., Pair	15.00
Candlestick, June, Scroll, Yellow, 5 In., Pair	65.00
Candlestick, Meadow Rose, Double, Flame, Pair	35.00
Candlestick, Versailles, Scroll, Yellow, Pair	65.00
Celery, Willomere	9.00
Champagne, June, Pink	14.00

Champagne, Meadow Rose	12.00 To 22.50
Champagne, Navarre	13.50
Champagne, New Vintage, Etched	7.00
Champagne, Romance	6.00
Coaster, Fostoria, Pink	3.50
Cocktail, June, Blue	20.00
Cocktail, Oyster, Fruits, 5 Ounce	14.00
Compote, American, Covered, 5 In.Diam.	37.50
Compote, Candy, 3 Diverters, Open Loop Handle, Ice Blue	135.00
Compote, Jelly, American, Covered	9.50
Compote, Jelly, Footed, Covered	20.00
Compote, Puritan, Green	6.00
Compote, Versailles, Blue, 6 1/2 In., Pair	45.00
Console Set, Baroque	45.00
Creamer, Georgian Lovebird, Tall	10.00
Creamer, Priscilla, Gold Trim, Green	40.00
Creamer, Sunray, Clear	5.00
Creamer, Sylvan, 1902, Individual	9.00
Cruet, American, Stopper	18.00
Cruet, Sidney	35.00
Cup & Saucer, Fairfax, Amber	4.50
Cup & Saucer, Fairfax, Azure Blue	8.00
Cup & Saucer, Fairfax, Green	7.50
Cup & Saucer, Fairfax, Pink	5.75
Cup & Saucer, Georgian Lovebird	15.00
Cup & Saucer, June, Blue	40.00
Cup & Saucer, Pioneer, Green	11.00
Cup & Saucer, Royal Pattern, Footed	20.00
Cup & Saucer, Seville, Green	18.00
Cup & Saucer, Versailles, Blue	30.00
Cup & Saucer, Versailles, Topaz, Demitasse	32.50
Cup, Fairfax, Blue	4.00
Cup, Vesper, Green	15.00
Dish, Candy, American, Covered	22.50
Dish, Candy, American, Handled, Small	6.00
Dish, Candy, Blue Baroque, Scalloped Edge, 3 Feet	15.00
Dish, Figural, Standing Rooster, Frosted, Covered, 6 1/2 X 8 3/4 In.	38.00
Dish, Pickle, Baroque, Yellow, 8 In.	25.00
Dish, Relish, American, Divided, Boat Shape	8.75
Glass, Deer, Figural	28.00
Goblet, American	9.00
Goblet, American, 7 In.	9.00
Goblet, Colony, 5 1/2 In.	6.00
Goblet, June, Blue	22.00
Goblet, June, Topaz	12.00
Goblet, Mayflower, 5 1/2 In.	14.50
Goblet, Mystic, 9 Ounce	14.00
Goblet, Purple, Knop Stem, Signed, Set Of 12, 7 1/2 In.	225.00
Goblet, Romance	8.00
Goblet, Royal Pattern	25.00
Goblet, Shirley	10.00
Goblet, Topaz Bowl, Crystal Stem	12.00
Goblet, Versailles, Etched, Azure Blue	37.50
Goblet, Willowmere, Etched, 10 Ounce	14.00
Goblet, Woodland Design, 9 Ounce	6.00
Ice Bucket, Chintz, Tongs	45.00
Ice Bucket, June, Yellow	60.00
Ice Bucket, Versailles, Metal Handle, Pink	35.00
Jug, American, 1/2 Gallon	30.00
Jug, Cutting Allover, Footed, Crystal	70.00
Jug, Woodland Pattern, 10 1/2 In.	30.00
Ladle, Punch, Clear	42.00
Mustard Set, American, Spoon	25.00

Parfait, Baronet, Amber, 6 In.	10.00
Plate, Colony, 7 In.	2.00
Plate, Dewdrop & Star, 6 In.	10.00
Plate, Dewdrop & Star, 7 In.	18.00
Plate, Fairfax, Azure Blue, 7 1/2 In.	4.75 To 4.85
Plate, Fairfax, Green, 6 1/4 In.	3.00
Plate, Fairfax, Green, 7 1/2 In.	4.50
Plate, Fairfax, Green, 8 1/2 In.	7.50
Plate, Grill, Fairfax, Green	7.50
Plate, Grill, Trojan, Pink	12.50
Plate, June, Blue, 7 1/2 In.	8.50
Plate, June, Blue, 8 1/2 In.	13.00
Plate, June, Blue, 10 1/2 In.	28.00
Plate, June, Pink, 7 1/4 In.	5.50
Plate, Sandwich, Romance	28.00
Plate, Torte, 13 In.	18.00
Plate, Trojan, 9 In.	15.00
Plate, Vernon Green, 10 In.	10.00
Plate, Versailles, Topaz, 7 1/2 In.	8.00
Plate, Vesper, Green, 8 3/4 In.	8.50
Plate, Vesper, Green, 10 3/4 In.	17.50
Platter, June, Pink, 12 In.	30.00
Platter, Royal Pattern, 12 In.	35.00
Relish, Pickle, Royal Pattern	18.00
Rose Bowl, Sylvan, 3 1/2 In.	20.00
Salt & Pepper, American Pattern	10.00
Salver, Diana, 9 In.	22.50
Saucer, Fairfax, Azure Blue	3.25
Saucer, Versailles, Blue	4.00
Shade, Green Feather, Gold Outline On Opalescent	125.00
Shaker, Colony, Clear	5.00
Shaker, Topaz, Versailles	38.00
Sherbet, Colony	3.00
Sherbet, Mayflower, Clear, Footed	8.00
Sherbet, Pioneer, Green	8.50
Sherbet, Priscilla, Green	15.00
Sherbet, Versailles, Etched, Azure Blue	25.00
Sherbet, Versailles, Topaz, High	16.00
Sherbet, Yellow, Set Of 6	40.00
Spooner, Priscilla, Gold Trim, Green	40.00
Sugar & Creamer, American, Small	12.00
Sugar Bucket, Plain Panels, Green, 14 In.	30.00
Sugar, American, Clear	5.50
Sugar, Georgian Lovebird, Covered, Large	30.00
Sugar, Pioneer, Amber, Frosted, Etched	6.00
Sugar, Priscilla, Covered, Gold Trim, Green	60.00
Sugar, Priscilla, Green	3.50
Sugar, Sunray, Clear	3.00 To 5.00
Tankard, Peacocks, Etched, Set Of 4 Tumblers	65.00
Toothpick, Rosby	18.00
Tray, June, Handled, Blue, 9 1/2 In.	17.50
Tray, Romance, Handled, 11 In.	18.50
Tumbler, American, Flat, 4 1/4 In.	7.50 To 8.00
Tumbler, Edgewood, Set Of 6	38.00
Tumbler, Fairfax, Green, 5 In.	5.50
Tumbler, Fashmir, Topaz, Footed, Flared, 5 1/4 In.	10.00
Tumbler, June, Footed, Pink	12.00
Tumbler, Royal Pattern, Footed	20.00
Tumbler, Sunray, Clear, Footed, 5 1/2 In.	6.00
Tumbler, Vernon Green, Footed, 9 Ounce	10.00
Tumbler, Versailles, Footed, Yellow, 5 1/2 In.	13.00 To 18.00
Tumbler, Vesper, Green, 6 In.	15.50
Tumbler, Whiskey, American, 2 Ounce	8.00

Tumbler, Woodland Pattern, Footed, Cone-Shaped	5.00
Vase, American, Footed, 9 1/2 In.	22.00
Vase, Azure, Spool, 6 In.	22.00
Vase, Bud, American, Flared, 5 1/2 In.	7.00
Vase, Bud, American, Flared, 7 1/2 In.	12.00
Vase, Bud, American, Flared, 10 In.	15.00
Vase, Morning Glory Cream, 7 1/2 In.	32.00
Vase, Spool, Azure, 6 In.	24.00
Vase, Tut, Black Ebony, 8 1/2 In.	14.50
Wine, Amber, White Striping & White Rim, Signed, 3 In.	45.00
Wine, Carmen	16.00
Wine, Romance	8.00

FOVAL, see Fry Foval

Francisware is an amber hobnail glassware made by Hobbs Brockunier and Company, Wheeling, West Virginia, in the 1880s.

FRANCISWARE, Berry Set, Frosted Hobnail, Amber, 7 Piece	175.00
Bowl, Amber Knob & Trim, Covered, 5 1/2 In.Diam.	95.00
Bowl, Frosted Hobnail, Amber Rim, Square	40.00
Bowl, Frosted Hobnail, Amber Trim, 8 In.Diam.	135.00
Dish, Candy, Hobnail, Frosted Amber, 5 1/4 X 5 1/2 In.	95.00
Dish, Frosted, Square, 4 In.	37.50
Dish, Ice Cream, Frosted, Yellow Amber, 5 3/4 In.	35.00
Dresser Set, Forget-Me-Not, 10 Piece	45.00
Lemonade Set, Cloverleaf Tray, Pitcher, 2 Tumblers, Finger Bowl	385.00
Lemonade Set, Hobnail, Amber Frost, 7 Piece	345.00
Pitcher, Frosted, 7 In.	285.00
Pitcher, Lemonade, Frosted Hobnail	195.00
Sauce, Square, Frosted	35.00
Spooner, 5 X 4 In.	40.00
Table Set, Hobnail, 4 Piece	295.00
Toothpick, Frosted, Amber Rim	67.50
Toothpick, Hobnail, Frosted	40.00
Tray, Celery, Frosted Amber	55.00
Tray, Swirl, Frosted, Amber Rim, Oval, 12 1/4 X 6 3/4 In.	35.00

Frankart, Inc., New York, New York, mass-produced nude "dancing-lady" lamps, ashtrays, and other decorative Art Deco items in the 1920s and 1930s. They were made of white lead composition and spray painted. Frankart Inc. and the patent number and year were stamped on the base.

FRANKART, Ashstand, Nude Woman On Ball, Green	350.00
Ashtray, Kneeling Lady, Green Insert, Dated December 25, 1932	240.00
Ashtray, Seagull	29.50
Bookends, Sailor Boy, C.1930, 7 1/4 In.	140.00
Bust, Woman, Art Deco	69.00
Figurine, Elk, Gold Bronze Patina	115.00
Figurine, Lady, Upside Down, 10 In.	175.00
Figurine, Nude, Large	500.00
Holder, Ashtray, Two Nudes Back To Back, Cigarette Holder	350.00
Holder, Card, Woman On Pillow, Dated '27, Metal	165.00
Lamp, Greenie	175.00
Planter, Nude Lady, Steuben Glass Insert, Wrought Iron	300.00
Plaque, Woman's Portrait In Gold-Tone, Signed, 1930s	125.00

FRANKENTHAL, Plate, Flowering Tree, 1759-62, Iron Red, 10 3/4 In.	990.00

Frankoma Pottery was originally known as The Frank Potteries when John F. Frank opened shop in 1933. The factory is now working in Sapulpa, Oklahoma.

FRANKOMA, Ashtray, Large	10.00
Ashtray, Road Runner	3.00

Ashtray, Shamrock	4.50
Bowl, Pink Over Red, 6 X 11 1/2 X 3 In.	18.00
Bowl, Swirled Molded Sides, Matte Green, Bronze Shadows, 11 1/2 In.	15.00
Christmas Plate, 1967	60.00
Cup, Road Runner, Large	7.00
Cup, Soup, Lazybones, 11 Ounce	3.00
Dish, Flower Shape, Flat	6.50
Figurine, Cat, Black, 1971	15.00
Figurine, Elephant, Red	35.00
Holder, Candle, Double, Brown & Sand, Pair	8.00
Mug, Donkey, Yellow	17.50
Mug, Elephant, 1968	70.00
Mug, Elephant, 1973, Nixon & Agnew, Gold	27.00
Mug, Elephant, 1976	5.00
Mug, Elephant, 1977	5.00
Mug, Elephant, 1978	5.00
Mug, GOP Elephant 1979	5.00
Mug, Nixon, Agnew, 1969	70.00
Pitcher, Green & Bronze, Signed, 9 In.	10.00
Pitcher, Lavender, Small	8.00
Planter, Duck, Signed, 10 1/2 In.	22.00
Plate, Christmas, 1965	220.00
Plate, Christmas, 1966	80.00
Plate, Christmas, 1967	70.00
Plate, Christmas, 1969	15.00
Plate, Easter, 1972, White	10.00
Plate, Plainsman, 6 1/2 In.	2.50
Plate, Wagon Wheel, Green, 10 In.	6.00
Salt & Pepper, Wagon Wheels, Green Bronze	17.00
Sign, Dealer	45.00
Syrup, Green Over Brown, 3 X 6 In.	7.00
Teapot, Desert Gold, 6 Cup	10.00
Tile, Good Luck, Brown & Green	8.00
Tile, Rooster, Brown	8.00
Toothpick, Brown & Green	4.00
Vase, Bud, Snail, Brown	4.00
Vase, Cactus & Oklahoma, Cream, Brown, 7 In.	35.00
Vase, Dark Blue, Panther Mark, 4 In.	26.00
Vase, No.835, Brown, 1 Handle, 8 1/2 In.	15.00
Vase, Trumpet Shape, 8-Sided, Marked, 6 1/2 In.	7.00
Vase, Urn Shape, Ram's Head Handles, Marked, 6 In.	12.50
Wall Pocket, Acorn Shape, Green	35.00
FRUIT JAR, see Bottle, Fruit Jar	

Fry glass was made by the H.C.Fry Glass Company of Rochester, Pennsylvania. It includes cut glass, but the famous Fry glass today is the foval, or pearl, art glass. This is an opal ware decorated with colored trim. It was made from 1922 to 1933.

FRY FOVAL, Candlestick, Blue Spiral Thread, Wafer Foot, 10 3/4 In., Pair	200.00
Candlestick, Twisted Stem, Delft Blue Trim, 11 In., Pair	275.00
Cup & Saucer, Delft Blue Handle	95.00
Lemonade Set, Opalescent, Green, Glasses, 10 1/4 In., 5 Piece	150.00
Pitcher, Pedestal Base, Ball-Shaped Lower Body, Signed, 8 In.	300.00
Sugar & Creamer, Green Jade Handles, Covered, 4 3/4 In.	160.00
Syrup, Light House Shape, 6 In.	75.00
Teapot, Delft Blue Handle & Spout	125.00
Tumbler, Lemonade, Jade Pedestal & Handle	65.00
Vase, Blue Base & Trim, 6 In.	100.00
Wine, Jade Foot	75.00

FRY, see also Cut Glass

FRY, Coffeepot, Applied Handle, Complete Insert, Covered	147.00

Mug, Radio Ware, Jade Handles & Base 125.00
Pitcher, Crackle Glass, Applied Blue Thorn Handle, 19 In. 145.00
Pitcher, Lemonade, Crackle Glass, Applied Green Handle, 8 I .... 90.00 To 110.00
Shade, Tulip Shape, Blue Opalescent 45.00
Vase, Orange Cased, Cut & Threaded Design, 8 In. 95.00

Fulper is the mark used by the American Pottery Company of
Flemington, New Jersey. The art pottery was made from 1910 to 1929.
The firm had been making bottles, jugs, and housewares from 1805. Doll
heads were made about 1928. The firm became Stangl Pottery in 1929.

FULPER, see also Doll, Fulper

FULPER, Bookend, Figural, Stacked Books, Blue & Gray, Marked, Pair 140.00
Bookend, Grotesque Face, Triangular, Olive & Beige, 5 1/2 In., Pair 280.00
Bowl, Art Deco Handle, Tan Over Brown, Mirror Green, 9 In.Diam. 75.00
Bowl, Blue Flambe Over Rose, 11 In. 85.00
Bowl, Brown Flambe, Cream Interior, 10 1/2 In. 65.00
Bowl, Bulb, Tiger's Eye, Brown, 8 1/2 In. 85.00
Bowl, Centerpiece, Flared, Green & Brown, 16 In.Diam. 70.00
Bowl, Chinese Relief, Cream To Blue Mirror, Marked, 6 1/2 In. 55.00
Bowl, Console, Matte Rose, 13 In. 85.00
Bowl, Crystalline, Green, 16 In.Diam. 130.00
Bowl, Green & Brown Flambe, 9 In.Diam. 60.00
Bowl, Melon Ribbed, Green Crystalline, 15 In. 75.00
Bowl, Running Glaze, Green & Yellow, 10 1/2 In. 85.00
Bowl, Scalloped, Signed, Blue Crystalline, 11 X 4 In. 100.00
Box, Powder, Figural, Girl, Porcelain, 6 1/2 In. 145.00
Box, Powder, Lady 125.00
Box, Puff, Figural, Lady With Fan, 6 1/2 In. 185.00
Candleholder, Black With White Blossom & Butterfly, 4 1/2 In. 40.00
Candlestick, Crystalline, Art Deco Handles, Green, Pair 90.00
Candlestick, Cylindrical, Brown To Rose Glaze, C.1910, 16 3/4 In., Pr. 250.00
Candlestick, Green & Rose, 4 In., Pair 65.00
Centerpiece, Folded Back, Holes For Flowers, Yellow, Blue, 11 In. 300.00
Chocolate Pot, Flambe, Copper & Cream 115.00
Console Set, Marked, Candlesticks 10 1/2 In. 150.00
Dish, Bulb, Dark Green, 2 X 8 In. 25.00
Jug, Whiskey, Sterling Silver Overlay, Brown & Caramel Glaze 330.00
Lamp, Perfume, Ballerina, 6 1/4 In. 175.00
Lamp, Perfume, Dutch Girl Holding Out Skirt, 8 In. 225.00
Lamp, Stained Glass & Pottery, Crystalline, C.1915, Marked, 17 In. 5000.00
Mug, Black, Brown, Crystalline, 4 In. 55.00
Sugar & Creamer, Green, Black, Brown, Flambe Glaze, 2 1/2 In. 150.00
Vase, Art Deco, Copper Crystalline Glaze, 10 In. 200.00
Vase, Ball Shape, Flared Rim, Pale Green Lava Semi Gloss, 6 In. 80.00
Vase, Beige & Light Green Flambe, Drip Glaze, 6 In X 3 1/2 In. 65.00
Vase, Beige Top, Brown, 7 In. 50.00
Vase, Black Glaze, 2-Handled, Marked, C.1925, 12 In. 140.00
Vase, Blue Wisteria, Chinese Blue Ground, Paper Label, 11 In. 200.00
Vase, Blue, Brown, 7 In. .... 26.00 To 65.00
Vase, Brown, Crystalline, 2-Handled, Signed, 11 In. 200.00
Vase, Bud, Matte Green, 8 In. 35.00
Vase, Bud, White Drip Over Brown, 8 1/4 In. 110.00
Vase, Crystalline Leopard Skin, Green, 9 In. 165.00
Vase, Cucumber Green, Wide Rim, Bulbous, C.1914, 12 In. 100.00
Vase, Cylindrical, Marked, Black Streaked Crystalline, 17 1/4 In. 300.00
Vase, Elongated Ovoid Form, C.1915, Blue Glaze, Marked, 13 In. 195.00
Vase, Famille Rose, 8 1/2 In. 80.00
Vase, Fan Shape, Green & Rose, Handles, 8 In. 60.00
Vase, Fan Shape, Green & Rose, 125th Anniversary Sticker, 9 In. 65.00

Vase, Gourd, Swan & Flowers Frog, 6 In. 125.00
Vase, Green, Rose, Ivy, Arches, 8 3/4 In. 70.00
Vase, Green, Squatty, Rectangular Handles, Ink Mark, 4 In. 55.00
Vase, Metallic Sheen, Green & Black, 8 In. 90.00
Vase, Mission Form, Light To Dark Green, Signed, 5 In. 55.00
Vase, Olive, Turquoise, Scattered Crystals, 8 1/2 In. 85.00
Vase, Oviform, Paper Label, Pink, Navy, Olive, & Black Glaze, 8 In. 180.00
Vase, Ovoid Form, Crystals Over Tan Ground, C.1910, 13 In. 1100.00
Vase, Primrose, Ball-Shaped, Handled, Blue, 6 1/2 In. 50.00
Vase, Rectangular Handles, Marked, Flambe Glaze, 14 1/2 In. 280.00
Vase, Scattered Large Crystals, Gold Trim, 5 In. 120.00
Vase, Signed, Blue Green, 8 In. 50.00
Vase, Spherical, Looped Handles, Marked, Black & Olive, 10 1/2 In. 380.00
Vase, Volcanic Blue, 6 1/2 In. 75.00
Vase, 7-Sided, Marked & Paper Label, Glazed, 10 In. 260.00

FURNITURE, Armchair, American Gothic, C.1845, Rosewood 400.00
Armchair, American Gothic, C.1845, Walnut 500.00
Armchair, American Renaissance, C.1865, Ebonized Walnut, Pair 800.00
Armchair, American Renaissance, Peter Timmes Sons, C.1895, Pair 1100.00
Armchair, American Rococo, C.1855, Belter, Laminated Rosewood, Pair 2250.00
Armchair, American, Masonic, C.1870, Walnut & Rosewood, Pair 800.00
Armchair, Art Moderne, C.1937, Peterson Studios, Fruitwood, 4 Piece 400.00
Armchair, Black Painted, Cane Seat, Gild Design, C.1810 .... 250.00
Armchair, Brace Back, Windsor, C.1770 .... 475.00
Armchair, Brass Capped Feet, Caned Seat, Wicker 350.00
Armchair, C.1760, Dipped Top Rail, Carved Walnut, Pair 5500.00
Armchair, C.1910, 6 Back Slats, Mission Oak 2100.00
Armchair, Carved Frieze, Upholstered, C.1860, English, Mahogany 650.00
Armchair, Carved Mahogany, Empire Period 120.00
Armchair, Carved Oriental Dragon, 19th Century, 33 1/2 In., Pair 700.00
Armchair, Carved Scrolls & Leaves, C-Scroll Arms, Walnut 325.00
Armchair, Carved Splat, Teak, C.1930, 35 1/2 In. 275.00
Armchair, Child's, Needlepoint Upholstered, C.1680, Walnut 2200.00
Armchair, Child's, Windsor, Branded Lapham, Pair 3500.00
Armchair, Chinese, Mother-Of-Pearl, Deer Medallion, Pair 1500.00
Armchair, Chippendale, Carved Crest, American, C.1930, Pair 350.00
Armchair, Corner, Acanthus Carved Front Legs, C.1740, Walnut 2500.00
Armchair, Corner, English, C.1750, Mahogany 880.00
Armchair, Corner, George III, Carved, Oak, Pair 1550.00
Armchair, Eastlake, C.1875, Walnut 250.00
Armchair, Embossed & Painted Leather Upholstery, Italian, Walnut 2300.00
Armchair, Empire, Bronze-Mounted, Mahogany 1900.00
Armchair, English, C.1750, Carved, Mahogany 4675.00
Armchair, English, C.1750, Leaf & C-Scroll Top Rail, Mahogany 4200.00
Armchair, English, Gothic Arched Top Rail, C.1765, Mahogany 2000.00
Armchair, Fanback, Wicker, Marked 175.00
Armchair, Fanback, Windsor, New England, C.1800, Painted Black 3750.00
Armchair, Gentleman's & Lady's, C.1865, Incised Walnut, Pair 550.00
Armchair, Gentleman's, C.1855, Laminated Rosewood 7500.00
Armchair, George III, Gold Brocade, Claw & Ball Feet, 46 In. 1650.00
Armchair, Gondola Back, Lyre Splat, Scrolled Arms, Mahogany, Pair 225.00
Armchair, Iron, Garden, C.1800, Reeded Frame, Slatted Seat 1870.00
Armchair, Library, C.1760, Upholstered, Carved Mahogany 5200.00
Armchair, Library, Walnut, George II, Shell Carved Legs 300.00
Armchair, Limbert, Oak 55.00
Armchair, Louis XVI, C.1780, Beechwood, Pair 1000.00
Armchair, Mahogany Rosewood, Gothic Revival 225.00
Armchair, Mahogany, C.1780, Chamfered Legs 325.00
Armchair, Mahogany, Drop-In Seat, Tapered Legs, C.1790 .... 400.00
Armchair, Mahogany, Foliage Inlay 55.00
Armchair, Mahogany, Pierced & Carved Splat 350.00

Armchair, Masonic, C.1879, Walnut & Rosewood, Pair	800.00
Armchair, Masonic, Walnut, Chippendale, C.1760, 51 In.	3400.00
Armchair, Medallion Back, Carved, C.1870, Mahogany, 40 1/2 In.	100.00
Armchair, Mid-Victorian, Upholstered, C.1860, Walnut	250.00
Armchair, Oak, Queen Anne, Slip Seat, Cabriole Legs	275.00
Armchair, On Rockers, C.1865, Carved Frame, Upholstered, Walnut	325.00
Armchair, Open Wing, 14 Slats, 10 Shape Cushion, J.Hoggmann, 28 In.	1700.00
Armchair, Papier-Mache, Victorian, Mother-Of-Pearl, C.1860	1400.00
Armchair, Queen Anne, Delaware Valley, 1740-60, Trifid Feet, Walnut	3750.00
Armchair, Reclining, Austrian Art Deco, C.1930, Footstool, 2 Piece	1100.00
Armchair, Regency, C.1820, Morgan & Samuels, Mahogany	2200.00
Armchair, Rocking, Mahogany Arms, Painted Yellow, American	500.00
Armchair, Rococo Revival, Carved Crest Rail, American, Walnut	200.00
Armchair, Rosewood, Victorian, 19th Century	275.00
Armchair, Shield Back, C.1790, Prince Of Wales Plume, Painted, Pair	6600.00
Armchair, Slat Back, New England, First Finish, Maple & Ash	1800.00
Armchair, Swivel, M.W.King & Son.N.Y., 19th Century, 31 In.	110.00
Armchair, Teak, Barrel Back, Bird Carving, 33 In.	400.00
Armchair, Teak, Carved, Oriental, Dragons, Carved Back & Arms	375.00
Armchair, Victorian, Walnut & Burl, Swivel, Office, C.1870	90.00
Armchair, Voluted Arms, Upholstered Back & Seat, C.1855, Walnut	375.00
Armchair, Walnut, Geometric Back, Fretwork Design, 25 In.	1000.00
Armchair, Walnut, Italian Rococo, C.1750, Scrolled Toes	1200.00
Armchair, Walnut, Rococo Revival, Tufted Back, C.1850	375.00
Armchair, Windsor Gothic, C.1770, Yew & Elmwood, Pair	8800.00
Armchair, Windsor, Bow Back, American, 11 Spindle	1900.00
Armchair, Windsor, Bow Back, Chestnut & Ash, 35 In.	1900.00
Armchair, Windsor, Bow Back, 7 Spindles, 35 In.	500.00
Armchair, Windsor, Comb Back, 9 Spindle	2000.00
Armchair, Windsor, Fanback, Crest, Saddle Seat, 44 In.	700.00
Armchair, Windsor, Fanback, 7 Spindles, Saddle Seat, 44 In.	700.00
Armchair, Windsor, Step-Down, Bamboo Legs, C.1810, 31 In.	450.00
Armchair, Wing, Cabriole Legs, Claw & Ball Feet, C.1930, Mahogany	425.00
Armchair, Wing, Chippendale, Red Leather, Brass Tacks	300.00
Armchair, Wing, Mahogany, Chippendale, Loose Cushion, C.1780	5000.00
Armchair, Wing, Queen Anne, Kittinger, Buffalo, 46 In.	450.00
Armchair, Wing, Queen Anne, Walnut, Cabriole Legs, Pad Feet	1250.00
Armchair, Wing, Queen Anne, Walnut, Canted Back, Crest, Trifid Feet	3250.00
Armchair, Wingback, Chippendale, Mahogany Base	1100.00
Armchair, Writing, Windsor, Bamboo, 18 In.	300.00
Armchair, 5 Vertical Slats, G.Stickley, C.1910, Decal	400.00
Armchair, 5-Slat, Delaware Valley, Pair	4750.00
Armoire, Austrian, Paneled Door, 19th Century, Walnut, 5 Ft. 5 In.	600.00
Armoire, Carved Rosewood, 2 Gothic Paneled Doors, 93 In.	900.00
Armoire, Chippendale, Raised Doors, Mahogany, 77 X 23 X 50 In.	1475.00
Armoire, Chippendale, Raised Panel Doors, English, 50 X 77 In.	1475.00
Armoire, Empire, Paneled Doors, C.1835, Mahogany, 68 X 97 In.	800.00
Armoire, Mahogany, Double Door, Arched, 113 X 58 1/2 In.	1050.00
Armoire, Oak, Louis XV, Cornice, 8 Ft. X 4 Ft. X 11 In.	2500.00
Armoire, Pegged Pine	500.00
Armoire, Victorian, Single Door, C.1850, Rosewood, 44 X 25 X 89 In.	475.00
Armoire, Virginia, Pine & Poplar	950.00
Armoire, Walnut, Empire, 2 Paneled Doors, 95 X 58 In.	700.00
Basin Stand, Corner, Bow Front, Mahogany, Federal, C.1800, 39 In.	1200.00
Basin Stand, Mahogany, Bow Front, George III, 33 In.	1200.00
Basin Stand, Tripod, Mahogany, C.1780, 29 1/2 In.	950.00
Bed, Acorn Post, Rope, Maple, 7 Feet	1175.00
Bed, American Empire, Sleigh, Walnut, 1840s, Double	500.00
Bed, Base & Ring Turned, C.1820, Cherry, Full Size	2200.00
Bed, Brass, Double Size	600.00
Bed, C.1890, Italian, Walnut, 6 Ft. 4 In. X 4 Ft. 10 In.	1400.00
Bed, Cannonball, Grain Painted, Gold Balls & Rings, Original Paint	275.00
Bed, Cannonball, Rope, Rock Maple	450.00

Bed, Canopy, Reverse Paintings, Carved Sides, Chinese, 80 X 91 In. 5500.00
Bed, Canopy, Tall Post, Birch, Federal, Original Red, 76 X 72 In. 1500.00
Bed, Carved, New Orleans, C.1850, 73 X 54 X 101 In. 3200.00
Bed, Country, Bird's-Eye Maple, Yellow & Ocher, C.1820, 53 In. 350.00
Bed, Day, Louis XVI, Fluted Uprights, 18th Century, 41 In. 1650.00
Bed, Day, Mahogany, Empire X, Molded Feet, 42 X 50 In. 1320.00
Bed, Double, Carved Snowflakes Design, 74 In. 275.00
Bed, Eastlake, Rope Twist Design, 3/4 Size 400.00
Bed, Ecole De Nancy, C.1900, Walnut, 4 Ft. 11 In.High ....*Illus* 1870.00
Bed, Four-Poster, American, Pineapple, Mahogany, 4 Ft. 10 In. 650.00
Bed, Four-Poster, C.1765, Urn Finials, Mahognay, 7 Ft. 6 1/2 In. 4250.00
Bed, Four-Poster, Mahogany, Federal, 77 X 57 In. 1100.00
Bed, Four-Poster, Walnut, Round Post, Arched, 96 X 73 In. 800.00
Bed, G.Stickley, 5 Vertical Slats Head & Foot, C.1910 .... 1000.00
Bed, Half-Canopy, Baluster & Ball Forms, Brass, Double 450.00
Bed, Half-Tester, Paneled Headboard, Rosewood Grained, 89 1/2 In. 1700.00
Bed, Jenny Lind, Single 160.00
Bed, Lion Head Highback, Silver & Pearl Inlay, Walnut 1000.00
Bed, Low-Post, Pine, Shaped Headboard, Turned Legs, Red, 48 In. 200.00
Bed, Mahogany, Federal, Four-Poster, C.1810, 4 Ft. 6 In. 9000.00
Bed, Murphy, Victorian, Poplar, Canted Front, 56 X 43 In. 150.00
Bed, Pencil Post, Federal, Tiger Maple 6000.00
Bed, Pencil Post, New England, 18th Century, Birch, 4 Ft. 4 In. 275.00
Bed, Pine & Maple, Stenciled, Oak Leaves, 6 Ft. 4 In. 3410.00
Bed, Post, Empire, Mahogany, Pineapple Carved Design, 62 In. 725.00
Bed, Post, Federal Maple, 2 Ring Turned Posts, Pine, 52 In. 300.00
Bed, Post, Maple, Federal, C.1800, Urn Turned Posts, 52 In. 1300.00
Bed, Poster, Mahogany, Empire, 64 X 58 X 76 In. 750.00
Bed, Rope, Four-Poster, 1700s, Maple, 7 Feet High 5000.00
Bed, Rope, Original Red Paint, Pine 375.00
Bed, Rope, Trundle, Built-In Wooden Wheels, 69 X 20 In. 225.00
Bed, Rosewood, Portuguese, Shell & Scroll, 5 Ft. 9 In. 375.00
Bed, Rosewood, Victorian, New Orleans, C.1850, 95 X 54 In. 2250.00
Bed, Scrolled Cornice, Thonet, C.1895, Bentwood, Double, 80 In. 2200.00
Bed, Sheraton, Four-Poster, Carved, Mahogany, 55 X 74 X 88 In. 1500.00
Bed, Sleigh, Mahogany, Empire, Carved, 37 X 73 In. 550.00

Furniture, Bed, Ecole De Nancy, C.1900, Walnut, 4 Ft. 11 In.High

Bed, Stamped C.Lee, No.3, C.1845, Walnut, 4 Ft. 7 1/4 In. X 8 Feet 4000.00
Bed, Tall Post, Old Blue Paint, 3/4 Size 2000.00
Bed, Tester, Coat Of Arms, Parcel Gilt Mahogany, 8 1/4 Feet 935.00
Bed, Tester, Four-Post, Turned Walnut & Pine, Federal, C.1805 .... 2300.00
Bed, Tester, Maple, Federal, C.1820, 6 Ft. X 6 Ft. 4 In. 550.00
Bed, Tubular Structure, Medallion Form, Brass, American, Single 350.00
Bed, Two-Tester, Pencil Post, C.1800, Maple, 3/4 Size 1900.00
Bed, Urn-Form Finials, Four-Poster, Birch, C.1810, 4 1/2 Feet 2800.00
Bed, Vertical Slats At Head & Foot, C.1910, G.Stickley, 45 1/2 In. 900.00
Bed, Victorian, Arched Headboard, Walnut, 78 1/2 X 72 In. 300.00
Bed, Victorian, Panel Headboard, Carved Crest, C.1850, Walnut 1100.00
Bed, Walnut, Paneled Headboard, Carved Shell, 93 X 75 In. 950.00
Bed, Walnut, Pewter Scrolls, Ivory Heads, Flowers, Side Rails 10,000.00
Bed, Wrought Iron, Late 19th Century 165.00
Bed, Youth, Spool-Turned 285.00
Bedroom Set, Armoire, 3 Chairs, Claw Foot, Oak, 8 Piece 2750.00
Bedroom Set, Bamboo, C.1880, Maple & Bird's-Eye Maple, 3 Piece 2500.00
Bedroom Set, C.1890, Victorian, Walnut, 3 Piece 5000.00
Bedroom Set, Marble Tops, C.1880, Half-Tester Bed, Walnut, 4 Piece 4000.00
Bedroom Set, Rocker, Dressing Table, Double Bed, Bird's-Eye Maple 500.00
Bedroom Set, Step-Down Dresser, Bed, Walnut 675.00
Bedroom Set, Victorian, Marble-Top Dresser, Walnut, 2 Piece 2350.00
Bench Table, Pennsylvania, 7 Feet 4400.00
Bench, Adams, C.1810, Cane Seat 1300.00
Bench, American Renaissance, C.1870, John McLean, 43 1/2 In. 225.00
Bench, Amish Pine, Crest On Square Stiles, 59 In. 350.00
Bench, Bucket, Nailed Walnut & Poplar 135.00
Bench, Bucket, Pine 200.00
Bench, Bucket, Walnut 235.00
Bench, Cherrywood, Scrolling Arms, Tapered Legs, 6 Ft. 3 In. 350.00
Bench, Deacon's, Carved Back Inserts, Golden Oak 850.00
Bench, Deacon's, Pine 295.00
Bench, Deacon's, Windsor, Pine & Ash, C.1820, 152 In. 375.00
Bench, Double Seat, Triple Slat Back, Caned Seat, 35 In. 375.00
Bench, Fruitwood, Regency, Scrolled Arms, Curule Base, 24 In. 70.00
Bench, Garden, American, C.1865, Cast Iron .... Illus 375.00

Furniture, Bench, Garden, American, C.1865, Cast Iron

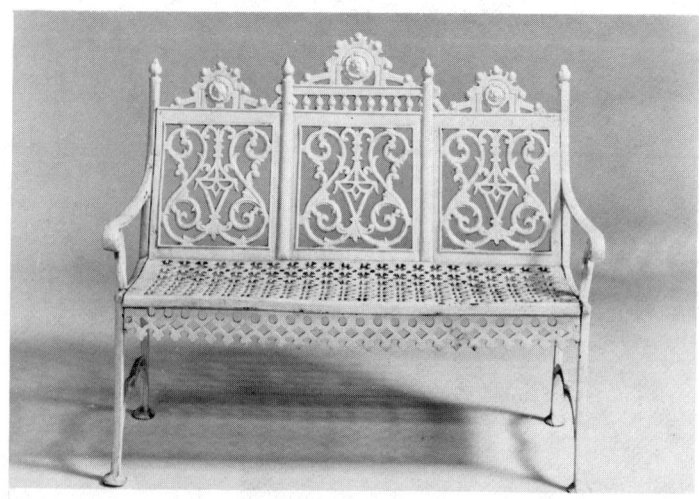

Furniture, Bench, Garden, American, C.1880, Cast Iron

Furniture, Bench, Garden, C.1855, Painted Rococo Cast Iron, Pair

Bench, Garden, American, C.1880, Cast Iron .... *Illus*	400.00
Bench, Garden, C.1855, Painted Rococo Cast Iron, Pair .... *Illus*	3250.00
Bench, Garden, Eastlake, American, C.1870, Cast Iron .... *Illus*	250.00
Bench, Garden, Rococo, Iron, American, C.1870, 44 1/2 In.	750.00
Bench, Hall, Jacobean Style, 41 X 35 In.	75.00
Bench, Italian Baroque Style, Silver Gilt, 4 Ft. 10 In.	1650.00
Bench, Italian Rococo, Scrolled Toes, Painted, 5 Ft. 10 In.	4000.00
Bench, Kneeling, Church, Pine, 5 3/4 X 41 X 7 In.	90.00
Bench, Kneeling, Walnut, 6 1/2 In.	40.00
Bench, Louis XV, Painted White, Gilt Highlights, 17 In.	140.00
Bench, Louis XVI, Parcel Gilt, 15 X 20 In.	500.00

Furniture, Bench, Garden, Eastlake, American, C.1870, Cast Iron

(See Page 229)

Bench, Mammy's, Shoe Feet, Half Of Seat Lifts Up, Blue Paint	950.00
Bench, Mammy's, Windsor, 1820-30, Yellow, Red, & Black Paint	900.00
Bench, Pennsylvania Dutch, Pine, 33 In.	450.00
Bench, Photographer's, Wicker	700.00
Bench, Pine, Provincial, Flat Panel Inserts, 40 In.	60.00
Bench, Pine, Tombstone Ends, Old Red Paint, 31 X 24 In.	80.00
Bench, Plank Seat, Spindle Back, Stained Brown, 95 In., Pair	1200.00
Bench, Prayer, Gilt Wood, Needlepoint Seat, 48 In.	200.00
Bench, Renaissance, Caned Oak, Grape & Vine Design	950.00
Bench, Rosewood, Empire, Serpentine Form, Bracket Feet, 41 In.	300.00
Bench, Turkish, Wicker	500.00
Bench, Wash, Red Paint, 30 X 18 X 16 In.	50.00
Bench, Wash, Trace Of Red & Green Paint, Pine, 17 1/2 X 27 In.	150.00
Bench, Water, Bootjack Ends, Ash & Hickory, Green, 26 X 28 In.	175.00
Bin, Slant Top, Slide Tray Inside, Pine	165.00
Bookcase, American, Grain Painted, 4 Doors, 19th Century, 81 In.	250.00
Bookcase, American, Mahogany, 3 Section, C.1820, 36 X 51 In.	325.00
Bookcase, Bureau, Double Domed, Walnut, George I, 6 Ft. 5 In.	8000.00
Bookcase, Bureau, George III, Mahogany, C.1790, 91 X 44 In.	2900.00
Bookcase, Cabinet, George III, Glazed Doors, Mahogany, 7 1/2 Ft.	2850.00
Bookcase, Carved, 2 Door, 2 Drawer, Walnut, C.1870, 57 X 94 In.	1100.00
Bookcase, Cherry, 2 Glazed Doors, 7 Drawers, C.1930, 81 1/2 In.	350.00
Bookcase, Chest, Carved, Mahogany, C.1770, 6 Ft. 6 1/2 In.	5775.00
Bookcase, Desk, L. & J.G.Stickley, Marked, C.1910, 40 In.Wide	165.00
Bookcase, Eastlake Style, 3 Door, Walnut, C.1880, Pair	1500.00
Bookcase, Eastlake, English, Oak, C.1880, 8 Ft. 2 In.	800.00
Bookcase, Federal, Mahogany, Glass Doors, Gothic Arches, 93 In.	550.00
Bookcase, French Books, Painted & Grained, C.1835, 10 In.	75.00
Bookcase, G.Stickley, Decal, Mahogany, C.1905, 4 Ft. 10 In.	2750.00
Bookcase, G.Stickley, 2 Door, 8 Panes Of Glass, C.1910	1300.00
Bookcase, Leaded Glass Doors, Stickley	950.00
Bookcase, Louis XV, Glazed Doors, Bronze-Mounted, 30 X 61 In.	1600.00
Bookcase, Mahogany, Empire, Glass Doors, C.1840, 59 X 37 In.	575.00
Bookcase, Mission Style, 1 Drawer, 3 Shelves, 17 X 12 X 45 In.	55.00
Bookcase, Oak, Arched Cornice, Glass Doors, 90 X 53 In.	1050.00
Bookcase, Oak, Glass Front, Mission Style, 69 X 39 In.	125.00
Bookcase, Oak, Stickley, C.1912, Signed, 44 X 39 In.	1550.00
Bookcase, Open, 2 Shelves, Cherry	185.00
Bookcase, Regency, Mahogany, Bureau, C.1810, 82 X 40 In.	4000.00
Bookcase, S-Top & Bottom, 4-Section Stack, Oak	240.00

Bookcase, Satinwood & Tulipwood, C.1900, 5 Ft. 3 1/2 In. 1200.00
Bookcase, Secretary Desk, Drop Front, Beveled Mirror 895.00
Bookcase, Secretary, Astragal Glazed Doors, Mahogany, 50 X 85 In. 900.00
Bookcase, Secretary, Barrel Front, Walnut 795.00
Bookcase, Secretary, Empire, Mahogany, 43 1/2 X 90 In. 605.00
Bookcase, Secretary, Mahogany, Empire, C.1840, 93 X 42 In. 1500.00
Bookcase, Secretary, Mahogany, Empire, Glass Doors, 3 Drawers 425.00
Bookcase, Secretary, Mahogany, Federal, C.1815 .... 6500.00
Bookcase, Secretary, Oak & Mahogany, 3 Drawers, 40 X 19 In. 550.00
Bookcase, Secretary, Victorian, Rocco Style, Fall Front, 70 In. 250.00
Bookcase, Secretary, Walnut, C.1860, 43 1/4 X 113 1/2 In. 1550.00
Bookcase, Stack, Globe Wernicke, Mahogany, 3 Sections, 48 In. 175.00
Bookcase, Stickley, 4 Shelf, 2 Door, Oak, 53 1/2 X 55 In. 2500.00
Bookcase, Triple Door, 12 Panel Glass Each Door, Oak 975.00
Bookcase, Two Female Figures, Oak, 68 1/2 X 18 X 63 1/2 In. 2750.00
Bookcase, Victorian, Walnut, Plinth Base, 3 Sections 750.00
Bookcase, Walnut, Open, C.1880, 66 X 48 X 10 1/2 In. 260.00
Bookcase, Walnut, Sectional, 34 X 49 In. 150.00
Bookstand, L. & J.G.Stickley, Label, 4 Shelves, C.1905, 41 3/4 In. 715.00
Bookstand, William IV, C.1830, Mahogany, 4 Ft. 4 1/2 In. 850.00
Box, Blanket, Breadboard Edge, Mustard Grained, 18 1/2 X 38 In. 750.00
Box, Blanket, C.C.Whitehouse, N.H., 19th Century, Pine, 43 1/4 In. 125.00
Box, Blanket, Snipe Hinges, Green Paint, Sabbathday Lake, Shaker 800.00
Box, Calendar, Day-Date, Wood Inlay 295.00
Box, Dough, Sliding Cover, Pennsylvania, Hand Pegged, Splay Legs 375.00
Box, Knife, George III, Serpentine Front, C.1790, Mahogany 385.00
Box, Salt, Hanging, Pine, 10 3/4 X 6 In. 50.00
Box, Spice, Red & Blue Paint, 6 Drawer, 11 1/2 X 7 3/4 X 10 In. 295.00
Box, Stationery, Victorian, Calamander Wood, 13 In. 450.00
Bracket, Victorian, Shaped Marble Top, Gilt Wood, 18 In., Pair 800.00
Breakfast, George III, C.1790, 4 Doors, Mahogany, 7 Ft. 8 In. 5750.00
Breakfront Bookcase, Bronze-Mounted, Mahogany, C.1880, 7 Ft. 8 In. 9000.00
Breakfront Bookcase, 4 Doors, C.1770, Mahogany, 4 Ft. 2 In. 5775.00
Buffet, Animal Theme Carvings, Oak 3400.00
Buffet, Oak, Provincial, Regency, Molded Doors, 41 In. X 5 Feet 1870.00
Buffet, Paneled Cupboards, Shelves, Oak, 6 Ft. 10 In. 1500.00
Buffet, Victorian, Mirrored, Marble Top, Side Shelves, Burl Walnut 3900.00
Buffet, Walnut, Louis XV/XVI, Provincial, 3 Drawers, 5 Feet 2200.00
Bureau, Bookcase, George III, Mahogany, 7 Ft. 6 1/2 In. 1430.00
Bureau, Bookcase, Silk Interior, Mahogany, C.1770, 7 Ft. 8 In. 6600.00
Bureau, Bookcase, Slant Front, Mahogany, C.1770, 39 1/2 In. X 8 Ft. 5225.00
Bureau, Bow Front, Federal, Cherry, 4 Drawers, 38 X 21 In. 1400.00
Bureau, Cabinet, Dutch Neoclassical, Mahogany, Burr Walnut, 7 Ft. 4500.00
Bureau, Crest, Mirror, Candle Brackets, C.1870, Walnut, 103 1/2 In. 950.00
Bureau, Cylinder, Louis XVI, Inlaid Mahogany & Rosewood, 44 In. 800.00
Bureau, Cylinder, Writing Surface, Mahogany, C.1800, 38 In. 300.00
Bureau, Dressing, Mahogany, Victorian, C.1845, 8 Ft. X 2 Ft. 6 In. 2250.00
Bureau, Empire, 2 Drawers, Brass Knobs, Marked 1848, 9 In. 275.00
Bureau, Fruitwood, Louis XV, 31 X 29 X 48 In. 1000.00
Bureau, George III, Mahogany, Fall Front, C.1790, 42 1/2 In. 950.00
Bureau, Lady's, Writing Surface, Brass Gallery, 33 1/2 X 34 In. 400.00
Bureau, Leather Top, Mahogany, 5-Drawer, C.1900, 54 1/2 X 30 In. 3750.00
Bureau, Leather Top, 2-Drawer, Bronze-Mounted Kingwood, 30 1/2 In. 6000.00
Bureau, Mahogany, Tambour-Fronted, Cylinder, C.1790, 37 In. 2500.00
Bureau, Plat, Mahogany & Tulipwood, Louis XVI, 29 X 57 In. 1500.00
Bureau, Princess, Corner, C.1870, Mahogany, 66 X 82 In. 550.00
Bureau, Slant Front, C.1770, English, Mahogany .... *Illus* 2900.00
Bureau, Slant Front, C.1790, Inlaid Mahogany, 39 X 44 1/2 In. 2200.00
Bureau, Slant Front, Fitted Interior, C.1740, Walnut, 41 1/2 In. 4125.00
Bureau, Slant Front, Inlaid, Walnut, C.1740, 36 X 42 In. 3653.00
Bureau, Slant Front, Inlaid, Walnut, C.1740, 36 1/2 X 42 In. 4400.00
Bureau, Stand, Slant Front, Inlaid, Walnut, C.1710, 38 In. 5500.00

Furniture, Bureau, Slant Front, C.1770,
English, Mahogany *(See Page 231)*

Bureau, Tulipwood, Gilt-Bronze, Louis Xv, 2 Drawers, 4 Feet 1400.00
Bureau, 2-Door, Wooden Knobs, Shaker, 19th Century, Pine, 45 In. 2100.00
Butler, Pantry, Mahogany, Baker, Fold-Out, 28 In. 425.00
Cabin-On-Chest, Polychrome Design, C.1680, Black Lacquer, 6 Feet 9500.00
Cabinet, Apothecary, Pine, 30 Drawer, 43 X 60 In. 500.00
Cabinet, Arched Opening, Carved, Stained Pine, 7 Ft. 11 In. 3750.00
Cabinet, Baroque, Pietra Dura & Ebony, Stand, 4 Ft. 4 1/2 In. 5500.00
Cabinet, Bookcase, Mission Oak, Black Trim, 4 Feet 8 In. 700.00
Cabinet, Bowed Sides & Door, Mirrored, C.1940, Mahogany, 47 In. 325.00
Cabinet, Bronze-Mounted, Ebonized, C.1865, 3 Ft. 11 1/2 In. 2000.00
Cabinet, China, Glass Sides, Glass Door, Mirror-Backed Top, Oak 450.00
Cabinet, China, Inlaid Frieze, Mahogany, 81 3/4 X 68 3/4 In. 700.00
Cabinet, China, Mahogany, Double Door, Glass, 56 X 60 In. 150.00
Cabinet, China, Oak, Bowed Glass, 3 Shelves, 3 X 5 In. 250.00
Cabinet, China, 2-Drawer, English, Mahogany, 43 3/4 X 48 1/2 In. 300.00
Cabinet, Continental Baroque, Ivory-Mounted Ebony, 5 1/2 Feet 2500.00
Cabinet, Corner, Biedermeier, Fruitwood, 7 1/4 Feet 1400.00
Cabinet, Corner, Bow Front, C.1790, Mahogany, 7 Ft. 4 1/2 In. 3850.00
Cabinet, Corner, Curio, 2-Door, English, Mahogany, 34 X 51 In. 225.00
Cabinet, Corner, Hanging, C.1800, Italian Green, Japanned, 38 In. 880.00
Cabinet, Curio, Bronze-Mounted, Louis XVI, 7 X 40 X 9 In., Pair 4250.00
Cabinet, Curio, Bronze-Mounted, 40 X 84 In., Pair .... *Illus* 4250.00
Cabinet, Curio, French, Gold Leaf Curved Glass, 38 X 18 1/2 In. 2000.00
Cabinet, Curio, Mahogany, Brass Floral Mounts, 68 1/2 X 34 In. 550.00
Cabinet, Display, Japanese, Black Lacquer, Sliding Doors, 5 Ft. 600.00
Cabinet, Display, Mahogany, Victorian, Domed Top, 64 X 26 In. 425.00
Cabinet, Display, Sliding Glass Doors, Oak, 73 X 20 In. X 7 Feet 1500.00
Cabinet, European, C.1900, Carved, 56 X 90 In. .... *Illus* 2000.00
Cabinet, Federal, Paneled Doors, Cherry, 48 1/2 X 83 1/2 In. 525.00
Cabinet, Hoosier 150.00
Cabinet, Hoosier, Kitchen, Sugar & Flour Bins 550.00
Cabinet, Japanned, Red Lacquered, Hanging, 48 1/2 X 30 1/2 In. 175.00
Cabinet, Lift Top, Gilt Flowers & Butterflies, Lacquer, 14 In. 220.00
Cabinet, Louis XV, Curved Glass, Mirrored, 26 X 70 In. 2200.00
Cabinet, Louis XVI, Marble Top, Mahogany, 4 Ft 3 In. 4500.00
Cabinet, Miniature, Carved Walnut, German, C.1860, 23 X 19 X 8 In. 80.00
Cabinet, Mother-Of-Pearl & Teakwood, 13 X 6 X 15 In. 130.00
Cabinet, Music, Sheet, Mirrored, Felt Lined, 20 X 47 In. 90.00
Cabinet, Music, Walnut, Glass Door, 33 X 20 In. 70.00
Cabinet, Over Chest Of Drawers, Hancock, Massachusetts Colony 9500.00
Cabinet, Pedestal, Mahogany, Empire, Removable Top, 20 In. 192.00
Cabinet, Phonograph, Austrian Art Deco, C.1930, 35 In. 300.00

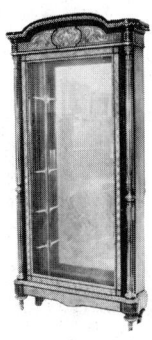

Furniture, Cabinet, Curio, Bronze-
Mounted, 40 X 84 In., Pair

Furniture, Cabinet, European, C.1900,
Carved, 56 X 90 In.

Cabinet, Side, Bow Front, Incised & Ebonized, 6 Ft. X 44 In. 650.00
Cabinet, Side, Carved Pine, George III, C.1790, 7 Ft. 6 In. 5000.00
Cabinet, Side, Fruitwood, Biedermeier, Glazed Doors, Block Feet 2200.00
Cabinet, Side, Victorian, C.1840, 3 Drawers, Rosewood, 4 Ft. 3 In. 550.00
Cabinet, Side, Walnut, Victorian, Floral Marquetry, 44 X 30 In. 200.00
Cabinet, Spool, Cylinder, Merrick's Cotton, Oak, 20 X 18 In.Diam. 375.00
Cabinet, Spool, 4-Drawer, Slant Lift Top, Inkwell, Oak 145.00
Cabinet, Storage, Record, Victor V 200.00
Cabinet, Wall, New England, 19th Century, Sponge Graining, 27 In. 475.00
Cabinet, Wall, Victorian, Bird's-Eye Maple, C.1875, 26 In. 3800.00
Cabinet, Watercolor On Paper, 18th Century, Walnut, 13 1/4 In. 1100.00
Caddy, Tea, Carved Rosewood, Mother-Of-Pearl Inlaid, 13 In. 450.00
Caddy, Tea, Octagonal, Ivory Edged, Tortoiseshell, 4 In. 880.00
Canape, Louis XV, Fruitwood, Scroll Feet, Velvet, 33 X 56 In. 350.00
Canape, Louis XV, Walnut Scroll Legs, Pale Green, 29 1/2 In. 250.00
Candlestand, American, 18th Century, Tin Cups, Cherry, 17 1/2 In. 600.00
Candlestand, Birdcage, Tripod, C.1780, Tilting Top, Cherry, 27 In. 625.00
Candlestand, Chamfered Top, Connecticut, C.1780, Cherry 595.00
Candlestand, Cherry, Chippendale, Tripod Base, Snake Feet, 27 In. 600.00
Candlestand, Cherry, Turned Pedestal, Sawn Legs, 25 1/2 In. 325.00
Candlestand, Cherrywood, Federal, Tripod Base, Snake Feet, 24 In. 900.00
Candlestand, Chippendale, Cherry, 3 Legs, 17 X 16 In. 350.00
Candlestand, Cross-Based, Pilgrim, 2o 1/2 In. 685.00
Candlestand, Curly Maple, Baluster Form, Shaker, 25 In. 1320.00
Candlestand, Hepplewhite, Shaped Top, Red Paint 425.00
Candlestand, Maine, 18th Century, Walnut 545.00
Candlestand, New England, 1810-30, Painted & Grained Maple, 27 In. 4500.00
Candlestand, Pennsylvania, C.1760, Snake Feet, Cherry, 28 1/2 In. 2200.00
Candlestand, Smoke Design, Gray Black Outline, 26 In. 900.00
Candlestand, Tilt Top, Carved Base, C.1840, Mahogany, 28 In. 125.00
Candlestand, Tilt Top, Cherry, Federal, Spider Leg Base, 27 In. 850.00
Candlestand, Tilt Top, Chippendale, Walnut, C.1750, 28 1/2 In. 6000.00
Candlestand, Tilt Top, Mahogany, Turned Post, Spider Legs, 25 In. 300.00
Candlestand, Turned Maple, Shaker, South Family, 26 3/4 In. 3300.00
Candlestand, Windsor, Checkerboard Top, First Black 850.00
Cane Stand, Sailor Figure Holds Tray, Iron & Wood, 27 1/4 In. 1300.00
Cane Stand, Victorian, C.1840, Brass & Mahogany, 29 1/2 In. 600.00
Canterbury, Federal, Mahogany, C.1810, X-Form Uprights, 20 In. 3300.00
Canterbury, Mahogany, Federal, Cock-Beaded Drawers, 7 3/4 In. 550.00
Canterbury, Mahogany, Regency, C.1815, 4 Bays, 1 Drawer, 22 In. 500.00
Canterbury, Victorian, C.1840, Rosewood, 19 3/4 X 24 1/2 In. 750.00
Canterbury, Victorian, C.1855, Mahogany & Burl Walnut, 23 3/4 In. 600.00

Canterbury, Walnut, Victorian, Fretwork Gallery, Drawer 800.00
Canterbury, William IV, 3 Divisions, C.1830, Rosewood, 22 In. 2310.00
Case, Display, Mirrored Sliding Doors, Oak, 8 Feet Long 300.00
Case, 38 Drawers, Old Red On Drawer Fronts, Grain Painting, Pine 2300.00
Cellaret, Lead Lined, C.1790, Satinwood, 17 1/2 X 15 1/2 In. 1870.00
Cellaret, Mahogany, Regency, Arched Panel, Handles, 21 X 17 In. 400.00
Cellaret, Stand, C.1790, Hexagonal, Brass-Bound Mahogany, 23 In. 1100.00
Cellaret, Stand, C.1790, Marquetry Inlaid Satinwood, 17 X 29 In. 1450.00
Chair Table, American, 18th Century, Painted Pine, 5 1/2 Feet 1600.00
Chair Table, Boot Jack Ends, 19th Century, Pine, 60 X 30 In. 650.00
Chair Table, C.1800, Old Red Paint, Pine & Maple 1800.00
Chair Table, Red Paint With Black Graining, Poplar 750.00
Chair, American Gothic, Walnut, C.1835, Set Of 4 .... 1700.00
Chair, American Rococo, Cast Iron, C.1850, Pair .... *Illus* 300.00
Chair, American Rococo, Laminated Rosewood, C.1855 .... 3500.00
Chair, American Rococo, Mahogany, C.1855, Pair 175.00
Chair, American Rococo, Rosewood, C.1855, Pair 350.00
Chair, American Rococo, Rosewood, C.1855, 36 In., Pair 250.00
Chair, Balloon Back, Needlepoint Seat, Rosewood, Set Of 5 .... 375.00
Chair, Balloon Back, Plank Bottom, Decorated, Set Of 6 .... 1050.00
Chair, Ballroom, Rosewood, Victorian, Upholstered Seat 75.00
Chair, Baluster Splat, Walnut, C.1740 .... 550.00
Chair, Bamboo-Turned Legs 350.00
Chair, Banister Back, Japanned 4600.00
Chair, Baroque, Dutch, Inlaid Ebonized Oak, C.1900, Set Of 4 .... 2500.00
Chair, Belter, Pierce-Carved Laminated Rosewood, C.1850 .... 2500.00
Chair, Boudoir, Louis XV, Concave Back, Turned Legs 50.00
Chair, Captain, 1-Board Seat, Red Brown Paint, Set Of 6 .... 850.00
Chair, Carved Oak, Animal Arms, Pawed Feet 90.00
Chair, Carved, Shell Top Rail, Mahogany, C.1760, Pair 1430.00
Chair, Centennial, Prince Of Wales Feathers, Pair 1300.00
Chair, Chamber Pot, Hinged Seat & Cover, Walnut, 17 X 19 X 18 In. 175.00
Chair, Child's, C.1850, Upholstered Splat, Rosewood, Pair 1300.00
Chair, Child's, C.1910, G.Stickley, Decal, Oak 275.00
Chair, Child's, Cane Seat, New England, 19th Century, 18 1/2 In. 210.00

Furniture, Chair, American Rococo, Cast Iron, C.1850, Pair

Furniture, Chair, Child's, Turned &
Painted, Maple, American

Chair, Child's, Signed Thonet, Bentwood Oak, Caned Seat 125.00
Chair, Child's, Slat Back 48.00
Chair, Child's, Turned & Painted, Maple, American .... *Illus* 550.00
Chair, Child's, Windsor, C.1800 .... 475.00
Chair, Chinese Export, Ebony, C.1845, Pair 800.00
Chair, Chinese, Chippendale Style, Bamboo Design, Set Of 4 .... 550.00
Chair, Chinese, Floral, Bird, Dragon Form Legs, 19 In. 125.00
Chair, Chippendale Style, Wing, Mahogany 300.00
Chair, Chippendale, Crest Rail, Cherry, C.1780 .... 625.00
Chair, Chippendale, Mahogany, C.1780, Pair 1300.00
Chair, Chippendale, New York, Mahogany, 1760-80, Pair 4500.00
Chair, Chippendale, Pierced Splat, Mahogany, Set Of 6 .... 2750.00
Chair, Chippendale, Rush Seat, Maple, C.1750, 42 In. 5500.00
Chair, Club, Empire, Inlaid Marquetry, C.1920 .... 225.00
Chair, Club, Parquetry Veneer, French, C.1925, Low 415.00
Chair, Continental Ash, C.1880, Carved Dolphins 300.00
Chair, Continuous Spindle Arm, Shaker 525.00
Chair, Corner, Cherry, Straight-Legged, Chippendale Style Splats 600.00
Chair, Corner, Chippendale, 1930, Mahogany, 30 In. 150.00
Chair, Corner, Mahogany & Oak, Rolled Crest, George III 350.00
Chair, Corner, New England, Rush Seat, Painted Maple, C.1860 .... 1200.00
Chair, Corner, Queen Anne, Maple, C.1750, Spanish Foot, 31 In. 450.00
Chair, Corner, William & Mary, Rush Seat, Spanish Foot, 29 In. 1900.00
Chair, Corner, 18th Century .... *Illus* 600.00
Chair, Curly Maple, Cane Seat, Pair 3800.00

Furniture, Chair, Corner, 18th Century

Chair, Dining, Flower Head, Tassel Rail, Mahogany, C.1780, Set Of 8 .... 3190.00
Chair, Dining, Jacobean Style, Crest-Carved, 19th Century, Set Of 8 .... 1400.00
Chair, Dining, L. & J.G.Stickley, Oak, 4 Side & 1 Arm, C.1910 .... 195.00
Chair, Dining, Queen Anne, Yoke Crest, American, C.1930, Set Of 6 .... 800.00
Chair, Dining, Regency, C.1815, Gilt & Grained, Set Of 8 .... 4400.00
Chair, Dining, Solid Back, Mission Oak, C.1910, Set Of 6 .... 300.00
Chair, Dining, V-Back, G.Stickley, C.1910, Set Of 6 .... 1500.00
Chair, Dining, Vase-Shaped Splat, Carved, Mahogany, Set Of 6 .... 8525.00
Chair, Eastlake, Brass-Mounted, Ebonized, C.1885 .... 250.00
Chair, Eastlake, C.1875, Incised & Ebonized Walnut 150.00
Chair, Eastlake, Needlepoint Seat, Stained Cherry, C.1880 .... 325.00
Chair, Eastlake, Velvet Covered, Dated 1871 .... 195.00
Chair, Empire, Caned Seat, Whimsical Scenes, Pair 1500.00
Chair, Empire, Fruitwood, Bowed Crest, Carved Apron 150.00
Chair, Federal, Shieldback, Mahogany, Spade Feet, C.1790 .... 1300.00
Chair, Folding, Piedmont Cigarettes, Porcelain Front & Back, 1900s 190.00
Chair, French Empire, Mahogany & Parcel Gilt, C.1810 .... 1000.00
Chair, French Empire, Mahogany, Ram's Head, C.1810 .... 1300.00
Chair, G.Hunzinger, Ebonized Walnut, C.1870 .... 400.00
Chair, G.Hunzinger, Painted Walnut, C.1870, Pair 200.00
Chair, G.Stickley, Oak, C.1910, Set Of 4 .... 880.00
Chair, G.Stickley, Paper Label, Oak, C.1910, Pair 110.00
Chair, G.Viardot, Stained Maple, Upholstered, C.1880, Pair 900.00
Chair, Gentleman's, Finger-Carved Crest, American, C.1860, Walnut 175.00
Chair, Gentleman's, Victorian, Walnut, Serpentine Seat, 44 In. 175.00
Chair, George I, Needlepoint Seat, Walnut, C.1700 .... 880.00
Chair, George II, Shell Rail, Walnut, C.1740, Pair 3080.00
Chair, George III, C.1810, Gilt & White Painted, Set Of 4 .... 3750.00
Chair, Gilt Wood, Medallion Back, C.1900, 38 1/2, Set Of 4 .... 650.00
Chair, Gilt-Stenciled, Needlepoint Seat, French, Gilt Wood 50.00
Chair, Gilt-Stenciled, Rush Seat, C.1815, 16 In. 120.00
Chair, Gondola Back, Mahogany, 33 1/2 In., Set Of 8 .... 600.00
Chair, Hall, Mahogany, Victorian, Leaf-Carved Back, C.1840 .... 80.00
Chair, Hall, Regency, C.1810, Solid Seat, Mahogany, Pair 990.00
Chair, Hall, Walnut, Carved & Upholstered, Red Fabric 90.00
Chair, Hitchcock, Rush Seats, C.1950, 33 In., Set Of 5 .... 300.00
Chair, Hitchcock, Signed L.Stuart, Set Of 6 .... 750.00
Chair, Horn, Moose Antlers, 19th Century 475.00
Chair, Ice Cream, Child's, Original Green Paint, 20 In. 95.00
Chair, Italian Neoclassical, Ball Feet, 18th Century 330.00
Chair, Italian, Louis XVI, Blue & Gold Paint, Pair 1800.00
Chair, J. & J.Kohn, Bentwood, C.1904, Pair .... *Illus* 900.00
Chair, Jacobean Revival, Carved, Oak, 2 Arm & 6 Side 1600.00
Chair, L. & J.G.Stickley, Decal, Oak, C.1910, Set Of 4 .... 275.00
Chair, Ladder Back, Child's, Flowers On Slats, Mustard, 17 3/4 In. 25.00
Chair, Ladder Back, Green Paint, 3 Curved Slats 700.00
Chair, Ladder Back, Hepplewhite, Pine, Rush Seat 550.00
Chair, Ladder Back, Rush Seat, C.1750 .... 550.00
Chair, Ladder Back, Turned Design, Rush Seat, Set Of 4 .... 200.00
Chair, Lady's, Leon Marcotte, C.1860, Ebonized Walnut 350.00
Chair, Lawyer's Swivel, Upholstered Seat, Back, & Arms, Oak 325.00
Chair, Leaf-Carved Top Rail, Carved Mahogany 495.00
Chair, Leather Upholstered, X-Legs, Jean M.Frank, 32 In. 1000.00
Chair, Leaves & Peacocks, C.1850, Ohio, Hand Stenciled, Set Of 6 .... 695.00
Chair, Lolling, Federal, Mahogany, Bow Front, C.1800 .... 1300.00
Chair, Louis XV, Carved C-Scroll, Walnut, Pair 190.00
Chair, Louis XVI, Aubusson Tapestry Seat, Gilded 70.00
Chair, Lucite, 1940s 250.00
Chair, Lyre Splat, Mahogany, C.1840, Set Of 4 .... 400.00
Chair, Majorelle, Fruitwood, C.1900, Pair 1100.00
Chair, Maple, Chippendale, Crest Rail, Rush Seat, 41 In. 150.00
Chair, Maple, Tilters, Shaker .... *Illus* 3600.00
Chair, Matching Lady's & Gentleman's, Rose Velvet 1200.00

Furniture, Chair, J. & J.Kohn, Bentwood, C.1904, Pair

Chair, Meeks, Carving Outlining Backs 3500.00
Chair, Midnight Blue Mohair, Branded Legs, 19 In., Pair 2000.00
Chair, Morris, C.1905, G.Stickley, Decal, Oak 1000.00
Chair, New England, C.1780, Rush Seat, Painted Maple, Pair 1600.00
Chair, New England, C.1800, Bamboo-Turned & Painted Black 450.00
Chair, North Italian, Marquetry, Walnut, C.1800 .... 125.00
Chair, Nursing, Papier-Mache, Victorian, C.1845, Drop-In Seat 1200.00
Chair, Office, Thonet, N.Y., Walnut, Signed, 34 X 16 In. 245.00
Chair, Parlor, Carved Rosewood, Original Beaded Upholstery 200.00
Chair, Parlor, Victorian, Gilt Incised & Ebonized, C.1865, Pair 650.00
Chair, Pennsylvania, C.1800, Strapwork Slat Back, Mahogany 500.00
Chair, Philadelphia, C.1760, J.M.Whitall, Mahogany 7250.00
Chair, Piano, Rosewood, Charles X, Leather Seat, C.1820 .... 1045.00
Chair, Potty, Child's, Arched Back, Bootjack Feet, Hinged 770.00
Chair, Potty, Child's, Red & Black Graining, Gold Crest 45.00
Chair, Potty, Windsor, Plank Seat 50.00
Chair, Pressed-Back, Child's, Set Of 6 .... 450.00
Chair, Pressed-Back, Northwind Design, Oak 155.00
Chair, Queen Anne, Baluster Splat, Japanned, Pad Feet 100.00
Chair, Queen Anne, Carved Rail, Rush Seat, Spanish Feet 600.00
Chair, Queen Anne, Maple & Cherrywood, Rush Seat, C.1750 .... 850.00
Chair, Queen Anne, Walnut, Claw Feet, Splat Back 375.00
Chair, Queen Anne, Walnut, Shoe Pad Feet, Slip Seat, C.1750 .... 6500.00
Chair, Reclining, Victorian, Walnut, Leaf Design, Curved Legs 50.00
Chair, Regency, Brass Rosettes, Rail Banding, C.1810, Set Of 6 .... 2400.00
Chair, Renaissance Revival, Ebonized Rosewood Inlaid, C.1870 .... 150.00
Chair, Renaissance, C.1860, Walnut & Burl Walnut 325.00
Chair, Rococo Style, 19th Century, Portuguese, Mahogany 250.00
Chair, Rococo, C.1850, Belter, Laminated Rosewood, Pair 1800.00
Chair, Rolled Arm, Spider Back, Wicker 1300.00
Chair, Rush Seat, Crest, Green, Yellow, & Red, Rosewood Ground 302.00
Chair, Scallop Crest, Slat Back, Oak, 37 1/2 In. 225.00
Chair, School, 1840s, Maple 60.00
Chair, Scrolled Open Back, Upholstered, C.1860, Walnut, Pair 400.00
Chair, Shell-Carved Crest, Balloon Seat, C.1930, Mahogany, Pair 275.00
Chair, Sheraton, Amberican, Turtleback, Rush Seat, Pair 180.00
Chair, Sheraton, American, Maple, Set Of 6 .... 2100.00
Chair, Sheraton, Cane Seat, Original House & Tree Design, Set Of 4 .... 400.00
Chair, Sheraton, Old Black Paint, Set Of 8 .... 1500.00
Chair, Side, C.1880, Eastlake, Walnut Marquetry, Pair 500.00
Chair, Side, Rocking, No.3, Shaker, New York, Acorn Design, Tape Seat 500.00
Chair, Slipper, Candy-Striped Upholstery 15.00

Furniture, Chair, Maple, Tilters, Shaker
(See Page 236)

Chair, Slipper, Ebonized Frame, Carved, Upholstered, C.1850	175.00
Chair, Slipper, Renaissance Revival, C.1860, Rosewood	175.00
Chair, Southern, Slat Back, Caned Seat, Maple & Hickory, Set Of 4	850.00
Chair, Spindle Back, Rabbit Ear, High, Original Red Paint, 35 In.	135.00
Chair, Spindle Back, Stenciled, Brown Ground, Set Of 6	375.00
Chair, Spool, Victorian, Original Paint & Cane, Set Of 4	365.00
Chair, Steerhorn & Hide	2500.00
Chair, Tall Back, L. & J.G.Stickley, C.1910, Decal Mark, Oak	1750.00
Chair, Tapestry Upholstered, C.1760, Mahogany, Set Of 4	7150.00
Chair, Thumb Back, 3 Splats, Rush Seat, Fruit Design, 33 In.	300.00
Chair, Tub, Child's, Mahogany, George III, C.1790, Bow Front	600.00
Chair, Tub, Leaf-Carved Frame, Bow Front, C.1780, Mahogany	3575.00
Chair, Turned Feet, Rush Seat, 4 Vertical Slats, Pair	200.00
Chair, Upholstered, Wicker	200.00
Chair, V-Back, G.Stickley, C.1910, Oak, Pair	300.00
Chair, Victorian, Balloon Back, C.1840, Brocade Covered, Pair	225.00
Chair, Victorian, Oval Frame, Upholstered, Walnut, 38 3/4 In.	150.00
Chair, Victorian, Pierce-Carved, Mahogany *Illus*	400.00
Chair, Walnut, Baroque, Bow-Arched Top, 42 In.	250.00
Chair, Walnut, Elizabethan, Needlepoint Seat	150.00
Chair, Walnut, Hepplewhite, Shield-Back, Marlborough Feet	50.00
Chair, Wicker, Star Design	175.00
Chair, Wicker, Upholstered Seat, C.1900, 33 In.	200.00
Chair, William IV, Carved, C.1830, Mahogany, Pair	450.00
Chair, Windsor, Bamboo, Pair	250.00
Chair, Windsor, Bamboo, Step-Down Crest, 17 3/4 In., Pair	450.00
Chair, Windsor, Birdcage, Arched Crest, Brown	300.00

Furniture, Chair, Victorian, Pierce-Carved, Mahogany

Furniture, Chaise Longue, M.Breuer, C.1960, Laminated Plywood

Chair, Windsor, Birdcage, C.1820, Set Of 5 .... 650.00
Chair, Windsor, Birdcage, Pennsylvania, C.1810, Set Of 6 .... 1250.00
Chair, Windsor, Black Over Red 645.00
Chair, Windsor, Bow Back, Ash & Maple, Bamboo-Turned Legs, 36 In. 325.00
Chair, Windsor, Bow Back, Ash & Maple, 36 3/4 In. 325.00
Chair, Windsor, Bow Back, Brace Back, C.1770 .... 450.00
Chair, Windsor, Bow Back, Brace Back, 9 Spindles, 38 In. 850.00
Chair, Windsor, Bow Back, C.1780 .... 850.00
Chair, Windsor, Bow Back, Green Paint, 18 In. 335.00
Chair, Windsor, Bow Back, New England, Original Red Finish 395.00
Chair, Windsor, Bow Back, Old Black Paint, Pair 2850.00
Chair, Windsor, Bow Back, Richmond, Virginia, C.1780, Pair 2400.00
Chair, Windsor, Bow Back, 7 Spindle 950.00
Chair, Windsor, Bow Back, 7 Spindle Back, C.1765 .... 400.00
Chair, Windsor, Cincinnati Manufacturer 550.00
Chair, Windsor, Comb Back, 16 In. 150.00
Chair, Windsor, Comb Back, 9 Spindle, Red & Gold Design 800.00
Chair, Windsor, Continuous Arm, Brace Back, C.1770 .... 475.00
Chair, Windsor, Fanback, C.1780 ....1150.00
Chair, Windsor, Fanback, Chestnut, Maple, Ash, 36 In. 600.00
Chair, Windsor, Fanback, Crest Rail, 9 Spindles, 17 In. 650.00
Chair, Windsor, Fanback, Saddle Seat, Black, 17 In. 400.00
Chair, Windsor, G.Gammon Warranted, Grained, Set Of 6 ....2800.00
Chair, Windsor, Loop Back, Bamboo Turnings 150.00
Chair, Windsor, Low Back, New England, C.1800 .... 450.00
Chair, Windsor, New England, Set Of 4 .... 900.00
Chair, Windsor, Rhode Island Turning, Set Of 6 ....1600.00
Chair, Windsor, Shaped & Carved Seats, C.1800, Set Of 4 ....1650.00
Chair, Windsor, Signed I.C.Tuttle, Painted 265.00
Chair, Windsor, Step-Down 225.00
Chair, Windsor, Thumb Back, Yellow, Set Of 4 .... 995.00
Chair, Windsor, Waters & Barrett, 1873 .... 300.00
Chair, Youth, Signed & Dated 1817, Original Green Paint & Stencil 215.00
Chaise Longue, M.Breuer, C.1960, Laminated Plywood .... *Illus* 715.00
Chaise, Victorian, Brass-Capped Feet, C.1890, Wicker, 39 1/2 In. 500.00
Chest-On-Cabinet, Molded Drawers, Mass., 79 1/2 In. .... *Illus* 9500.00
Chest-On-Chest, C.1790, Inlaid, Mahogany, 6 Ft. 4 1/2 In. 2900.00
Chest-On-Chest, C.1790, 5-Drawer Top, Mahogany, 4 X 6 Ft. 7 In. 3300.00
Chest-On-Chest, Chippendale, C.1780, Mahogany, 6 Ft. 8 In. 3500.00
Chest-On-Chest, George III, Mahogany, C.1780, 72 X 43 1/4 In. 2700.00
Chest-On-Chest, Georgian, Chamfered Corners 2100.00
Chest-On-Chest, Queen Anne, C.1750, Trifid Feet, Walnut, 5 1/2 Ft. 1500.00

Furniture, Chest-On-Cabinet, Molded
Drawers, Mass., 79 1/2 In.

(See Page 239)

Chest-On-Chest, 5 Drawer, C.1790, Inlaid Mahogany, 6 Ft. 3 In. 2000.00
Chest-On-Chest, 5 Drawer, Inlaid, Burr Walnut, 41 X 6 Feet 3575.00
Chest-On-Frame, New England, C.1740, Curly Maple, 5 Feet 2750.00
Chest, American, 19th Century, 4 Drawer, Basswood, 24 X 7 In. 250.00
Chest, Apothecary, Beveled Front, 17 Drawer, 36 X 44 In. 550.00
Chest, Apothecary, C.1795, Basswood 1500.00
Chest, Apothecary, Zinc Lined, Brass Binders, Mahogany, 18 X 7 In. 140.00
Chest, Apothecary, 35 Drawer, Pine, 54 X 70 In. 1100.00
Chest, Austrian, Painted, Floral Sprays, Carrying Handles, 26 In. 220.00
Chest, Bachelor's, George III, Mahogany, C.1790, 30 X 31 In. 1600.00
Chest, Backboard Scallop, Yellow Pine 525.00
Chest, Blanket, American, C.1825, Painted Design, Pine, 43 1/2 In. 1000.00
Chest, Blanket, Brown, Vermont, Knobs, 36 X 40 In. 1650.00
Chest, Blanket, By H.Brenneman, Penna., Dated March 4, 1888 ....4250.00
Chest, Blanket, C.1860, Green Paint, 11 3/4 X 23 1/4 X 10 1/4 In. 165.00
Chest, Blanket, Chippendale, 3 Drawer, C.1780, Grain Painted Pine 1150.00
Chest, Blanket, Dated 1887, Grained Red Over Yellow, Miniature 185.00
Chest, Blanket, Design By Angela Britin, Ohio 725.00
Chest, Blanket, Double-X Design, C.1910, Mission Oak, 4 Ft.3/4 In. 350.00
Chest, Blanket, Dovetailed Bracket Base, Yellow & Red Designs 595.00
Chest, Blanket, Dovetailed Construction 235.00
Chest, Blanket, Drawer, Dark Green Over Light Green Paint 1100.00
Chest, Blanket, Flower, Leaf Design, Yellow, Red, White, Green, 43 In. 1430.00
Chest, Blanket, Grain Painted, C.1850 .... 255.00 To 425.00
Chest, Blanket, New England, Green Sponge Over Red, 39 X 36 In. 1250.00
Chest, Blanket, Old Red, Footed 195.00
Chest, Blanket, Pennsylvania, Grained Design, C.1800 .... 350.00
Chest, Blanket, Pine, Bracket Feet, Brown, Shaker, 25 X 23 In. 1320.00
Chest, Blanket, Pine, Federal, Applied Molded Edge, Green, 43 In. 275.00
Chest, Blanket, Pine, Grained Single Drawer 320.00
Chest, Blanket, Pine, Lift Top, 2 Drawer, 33 X 39 In. 575.00
Chest, Blanket, Pine, 2 Drawer, Turned Feet, 29 In. 500.00
Chest, Blanket, Queen Anne, C.1750, 2 Drawer, Red 875.00
Chest, Blanket, Queen Anne, C.1750, 5-Drawer Facade, 36 X 40 In. 1525.00
Chest, Blanket, Queen Anne, 2 Drawer, C.1750, Old Red Paint 875.00

Chest, Blanket, Rose, Yellow Tulips, Trees, Green, 3 X 6 In. 1650.00
Chest, Blanket, Ship's Portrait Design, Blue Painted 1000.00
Chest, Blanket, Smoke Design, Red 130.00
Chest, Blanket, Sponge Painting, Red Stippling, Poplar, 47 3/4 In. 600.00
Chest, Blanket, Vinegar Graining, Tan, 2 Drawer, 43 X 39 In. 650.00
Chest, Blanket, Walnut, Federal, Inlaid Leaf, Inlaid Hearts, 11 In. 800.00
Chest, Blanket, Yellow Smoke Design 470.00
Chest, Blanket, 2 Drawer, Iron Hinges, Bear Trap Lock, Walnut 525.00
Chest, Blanket, 2 Drawer, Script 1847 Date, Tiger Maple 1200.00
Chest, Bonnet, Federal, C.1800, Georgia Piedmont, Walnut 3250.00
Chest, Bow Front, C.1800, 6 Drawer, Inlaid Mahogany, 36 In. 850.00
Chest, Bow Front, Federal, Inlaid & Veneered, C.1790, 41 In. 2500.00
Chest, Bow Front, George III, Mahogany, 35 1/2 In. 750.00
Chest, Bow Front, Hepplewhite, Cherry, C.1790 .... 1650.00
Chest, Bow Front, Hepplewhite, French Feet, C.1790, Cherry 1550.00
Chest, Bow Front, Mahogany, Federal, 4 Drawer, 38 X 40 In. 850.00
Chest, Bow Front, Mahogany, George III, C.1790, 35 In. 500.00
Chest, Bow Front, Mahogany, Regency, 5 Drawer, 39 In. 325.00
Chest, Bow Front, Mahogany, String Inlay, 4 Drawer 2200.00
Chest, Bow Front, New England, C.1800, Mahogany & Birch, 39 In. 1200.00
Chest, Bow Front, Slover & Taylor, C.1802, Mahogany, 38 In. 6000.00
Chest, Butler, Hepplewhite, Mahogany Inlaid, Ivory, Elm 600.00
Chest, Campaign, Brass Bound, Camphorwood 625.00
Chest, Campaign, 2-Part, 2 Drawer, Bracket Feet, 40 X 36 In. 700.00
Chest, Cherry & Tiger Maple, 4 Full Drawers, 2 Small Drawers 1450.00
Chest, Cherry, Chippendale, 4 Drawer, Bracket Base 1800.00
Chest, Cherry, Chippendale, 4 Drawer, Bracket Feet, 36 In. 3100.00
Chest, Cherry, Federal, 3 Drawer, New England, C.1800, 44 In. 800.00
Chest, Cherry, 6 Drawer, Tall 2950.00
Chest, Chippendale, Bracket Feet, Cherry, Connecticut, C.1780 .... 2150.00
Chest, Chippendale, Ogee Feet, Walnut 2850.00
Chest, Chippendale, Tiger Maple, 5 Drawer, 37 X 18 In. 3000.00
Chest, Chippendale, 3 Over 2 Over 5 Graduated, 1750-1800, Walnut 2000.00
Chest, Chippendale, 4 Drawer, C.1770, Mahogany, 37 X 19 X 33 In. 2100.00
Chest, Chippendale, 4 Graduated Drawers, Bracket Base 850.00
Chest, Chippendale, 5 Drawer, C.1780, Pennsylvania, Cherry 5400.00
Chest, Chippendale, 6 Drawer, Vermont, C.1780, Original Finish 4950.00
Chest, Country Federal, C.1800, Grain Painted, 40 1/2 X 38 In. 650.00
Chest, Country Federal, C.1800, Grain Painted, 41 X 37 1/2 In. 450.00
Chest, Country Hepplewhite, Cherry 850.00
Chest, Country Sheraton, 4 Drawer, Half Spindles, Cherry, 44 In. 575.00
Chest, Double, North Family, Shaker, Pine, 32 3/4 In. ....*Illus* 4750.00

Furniture, Chest, Double, North Family, Shaker, Pine, 32 3/4 In.

Chest, Double, Pine, Shaker, North Family, 32 3/4 X 68 In. 4750.00
Chest, Dovetailed Drawers, Gilded Brasses, Birch, 49 1/2 In. 2250.00
Chest, Dower, New York, Blue-Green Base, Red & Yellow Design 8000.00
Chest, Dowry, High Arch Lid, 1821, Oak, 50 X 25 X 30 In. 1500.00
Chest, Empire, Caulk Beading, Inlaid Keyholes, Cherry Top 375.00
Chest, Empire, Mahogany, 4 Drawer, C.1830, 39 3/4 X 43 1/4 In. 175.00
Chest, Empire, Mahogany, 4 Drawer, C.1850, 50 1/2 X 39 In. 225.00
Chest, Empire, Mahogany, 6 Drawer, C.1840, 26 X 23 1/2 In. 275.00
Chest, Empire, Mirror, C.1840, Rosewood Veneer 350.00
Chest, Empire, Mirror, Walnut Over Pine 350.00
Chest, Empire, Rope Columns, Ivory Pulls, 6 Drawer, 8 1/2 In. 195.00
Chest, Empire, Tile Like Design, C.1820, American 795.00
Chest, Empire, 4 Drawer, C.1830, Mahogany, 39 3/4 X 43 1/4 In. 175.00
Chest, Federal, American, 19th Century, Inlaid Walnut, 39 In. 900.00
Chest, Federal, Ball Feet, Cherry, 43 1/4 X 46 1/2 In. 525.00
Chest, Federal, Cherry, C.1790, 4 Drawer, 39 In. 1400.00
Chest, Federal, Cherry, 4 Drawer, C.1800, 40 X 42 In. 600.00
Chest, Federal, Mahogany & Birch, C.1790, Bowed Drawers, 40 In. 2600.00
Chest, Federal, Mahogany, Back Splash, 2 Drawer, C.1835, 50 In. 500.00
Chest, George I, 4 Drawer, Inlaid Burr Walnut, 42 X 32 1/2 In. 2530.00
Chest, German Rococo, Serpentine Fronted, Walnut Veneered, 31 In. 1000.00
Chest, German Rococo, 19th Century, Brass-Mounted, Walnut, 29 In. 1200.00
Chest, Hepplewhite, Bow Front, Inlaid Skirt, C.1790, Cherry 1650.00
Chest, Hepplewhite, French Feet, Walnut, 4 Drawer, C.1795 .... 1450.00
Chest, Hepplewhite, Original Brasses, 4 Drawer, Cherry, 38 In. 800.00
Chest, Hepplewhite, Skirt, Tiger Maple 2250.00
Chest, Hepplewhite, Walnut, French Feet, 40 1/2 X 37 In. 2300.00
Chest, Hepplewhite, 1785-1810, Curly Maple 2300.00
Chest, Hepplewhite, 4 Drawer, Chambersburg, Penn., C.1790, Cherry 1650.00
Chest, Hepplewhite, 4 Drawer, Maple With Tiger Maple 3700.00
Chest, Hepplewhite, 4 Inlaid Drawers, Cherry, 35 1/2 In.Wide 1500.00
Chest, Hepplewhite, 6 Drawer, Pennsylvania, Original Brasses 1200.00
Chest, Italian Renaissance Style, Walnut, 36 X 48 In. 200.00
Chest, Korean, Elmwood, 4 Drawer, Brass Mounts, 40 X 35 In. 300.00
Chest, Korean, Inlaid, Brass Mounts, 55 X 15 In. 250.00
Chest, Lacquer & Mahogany, 4 Drawer, Disc Knobs, 45 In. 1700.00
Chest, Leather Covered, Chinese, 19th Century 650.00
Chest, Lift Top, False Drawer, Turned Legs, 19 1/2 In. 180.00
Chest, Lift Top, Pine, Yellow Design, Fish, Red Ground, 24 In. 1045.00
Chest, Mahogany, Chippendale, 4 Cock-Beaded Drawers, 39 In. 900.00
Chest, Mahogany, English, 4 Drawer, Brasses, C.1770, 37 X 33 In. 2100.00
Chest, Mahogany, George III, C.1780, 4 Drawer, 29 In. 1500.00
Chest, Mahogany, George III, C.1780, 4 Drawer, 35 1/2 X 32 In. 1870.00
Chest, Mahogany, George III, 4 Drawer, Bracket Feet, 36 In. 475.00
Chest, Mahogany, Victorian, 4 Drawer, C.1880, 40 X 44 In. 200.00
Chest, Mahogany, 4 Drawer, Bracket Feet, C.1780 .... 800.00
Chest, Mahogany, 4 Drawer, C.1780, 31 X 30 1/2 In. 2750.00
Chest, Mahogany, 6 Drawer, Rope Columns, Ivory Pulls, 8 1/2 In. 195.00
Chest, Maple & Cherry, 6 Drawer, C.1810 .... 1450.00
Chest, New England, Carved & Painted Maple & Pine, C.1780, 36 In. 1800.00
Chest, New England, Cherry & Birch, 4 Graduated Drawers 875.00
Chest, New England, 2 Drawer, 19th Century 1250.00
Chest, New England, 4 Drawer, Cock-Beaded, Cherry, C.1780 .... 1700.00
Chest, New Hampshire, Yellow & Brown Grain 450.00
Chest, New York, Cabriole Legs, Mahogany, C.1760, 36 In. 400.00
Chest, Oak, Continental, 2 Drawer, Straight Legs, 26 In. 302.00
Chest, Original Sandwich Glass Pulls, Tiger Maple & Cherry 875.00
Chest, Outthrust Upper Drawer, Mahogany & Cherry, 40 3/4 In. 655.00
Chest, Pennsylvania, Red & Black Design 450.00
Chest, Pillow & Blanket, Lift Top, Red Paint, 48 X 39 In. 650.00
Chest, Pine, Pennsylvania, Dated 1781, Tulips, Flowers, 28 In. 6500.00
Chest, Pine, Shaker, South Family, Rope Handles, 14 X 35 In. 1300.00
Chest, Pine, 4 Drawer, Higgins Bros., N.H., 39 X 35 In. 125.00

Chest, Pine, 5 Drawer, Nailed Construction, 15 X 19 In. 105.00
Chest, Rattail Hinges, C.1760, Dark Green, 32 X 19 X 19 1/2 In. 420.00
Chest, Regency, Mahogany, Bow Front, C.1810, 3 Drawer, 41 In. 750.00
Chest, Reverse Serpentine Front, Dated 1797, Cherry, 33 In. 4000.00
Chest, Reverse Serpentine, Mahogany, Chippendale, C.1760, 31 In. 6500.00
Chest, Sea, Pine, Carved, Lion, Gentleman, Horse, 17 X 43 In. 5225.00
Chest, Serpentine Front, Frieze, Mahogany, C.1780, 31 1/2 In. 4500.00
Chest, Serpentine Front, Inlaid Satinwood, 37 X 35 1/2 In. 8800.00
Chest, Serpentine Front, Mahogany, C.1790, 36 X 36 In. 3850.00
Chest, Serpentine Front, Massachusetts, Mahogany, C.1770, 35 In. 4500.00
Chest, Sheraton, Bow Front, Biscuit Top, Walnut 4200.00
Chest, Sheraton, Dovetailed Case 795.00
Chest, Sheraton, Grain Painted, All Original, C.1820 .... 1500.00
Chest, Sheraton, New Hampshire, C.1820 .... 350.00
Chest, Sheraton, Original Brasses, Mahogany 695.00
Chest, Sheraton, Tall, Tiger Maple & Cherry 1450.00
Chest, Sheraton, 4 Drawer, Half Spindle, Cherry, 40 X 20 X 44 In. 575.00
Chest, Storage, Butternut & Chestnut, Flush Iron Handles, 18 In. 412.00
Chest, Storage, Pine, Iron Strap, 2 Sections, Shaker, 22 X 6 Ft. 1320.00
Chest, Strap Hinges, Dated 1774, Walnut, Miniature 1500.00
Chest, Tiger Maple Dovetailed Drawers, Old Finish, 17 1/2 In. 600.00
Chest, Tiger Maple Front, 6 Drawer 450.00
Chest, Victorian, Miniature, 3 Drawer, 10 X 11 X 8 In. 60.00
Chest, Victorian, Walnut, 3 Drawer, Domed Mirror & Candle Shelves 475.00
Chest, Victorian, Walnut, 4 Drawer, Fruit Pulls 325.00
Chest, Victorian, 3 Drawer, Drop Pulls, Glass Top, 28 X 37 In. 175.00
Chest, Walnut & Fruitwood, George I, C.1720, 37 1/2 In. 880.00
Chest, Walnut, Federal, 4 Drawer, C.1800, 37 1/2 In. 3500.00
Chest, Walnut, George I, Graduated Drawers, Stand, 4 Ft. 52 In. 1100.00
Chest, Walnut, George I, 5 Drawer, Inlaid, 41 X 39 In. 1400.00
Chest, Walnut, George I, 5 Drawer, Oak Sides, 37 X 38 In. 1300.00
Chest, William & Mary, Oak & Pine, On Frame, 26 X 30 In. 6500.00
Chest, William & Mary, Oyster Veneered, Burr Walnut, 34 In. 5500.00
Chest, William & Mary, Walnut, 5 Drawer, Ball Feet 950.00
Chest, 3 Drawer, Double Arched Bootjack Ends, 6 1/2 In. 90.00
Chest, 3 Drawer, Mahogany, 32 1/2 X 32 In. 2100.00
Chest, 3 Drawer, 2 Candlestands, Teardrop Pulls, Oak 245.00
Chest, 3 Full & 4 Half Drawers, Grain Painted, 15 X 16 In. 325.00
Chiffonier, Fruitwood, Louis XVI, Salmon & Gray, 4 Ft. X 26 In. 2090.00
Chiffonier, Grained, Regency, Brass Inlay, Lion's Head Pull, 53 In. 450.00
China Cabinet, Butternut & Walnut 425.00
China Cabinet, G.Stickley, Label, Oak, C.1910, 41 1/2 In. X 5 Ft. 1750.00
China Closet, 2 Doors, Glass Sides, Stickley, 67 In. 900.00
Coal Box, Victorian Mahogany, White Marble Top 125.00
Coatrack, Hanging, 6 Hooks.8 X 37 In.Long 65.00
Coatrack, Thonet Bros., C.1900, Bentwood, 6 Ft. 8 In. .... *Illus* 660.00
Coatrack, Umbrella Stand, Bentwood, C.1900, 6 Ft. 660.00
Commode, Bedside, Bow Front, Mahogany, George III, 33 X 23 In. 900.00
Commode, Bedside, Walnut, C.1850, 29 1/4 X 23 X 16 In. 275.00
Commode, Bombe, Marble Top, Inlaid Parquetry, Kingwood, 45 X 34 In. 1300.00
Commode, Burl Fruitwood, Biedermeier, 4 Drawer, C.1820, 30 In. 1200.00
Commode, Edwardian, Inlaid, Mahogany, 13 1/2 X 13 1/2 X 30 1/2 In. 125.00
Commode, English Victorian Mahogany, Leather Potty, 32 In. 90.00
Commode, George III, Lift Top, C.1790, Mahogany, 25 X 30 In. 850.00
Commode, Louis XV, Marble Top, Bronze-Mounted, Rosewood, 34 In. 3250.00
Commode, Louis XV, Metal-Mounted, Black Lacquer .... *Illus* 6500.00
Commode, Louis XV, Vernis Martin & Lacquer .... *Illus* 4750.00
Commode, Louis XVI, Rosewood & Tulipwood Parquetry, 35 1/2 In. 2250.00
Commode, Marble Top & Splash, Burl Drawer & Doors, C.1865, 43 In. 450.00
Commode, Marble Top, Satinwood & Kingwood, C.1900, 35 1/2 In. 1600.00
Commode, Oak, 3 Drawer, Geometric Panels, 33 X 24 In. 625.00
Commode, Petite, Louis XV, 3 Drawer, Mahogany, France, 17 In. 650.00
Commode, Pink Marble Top, 3 Drawer, 1 Door, Walnut 575.00

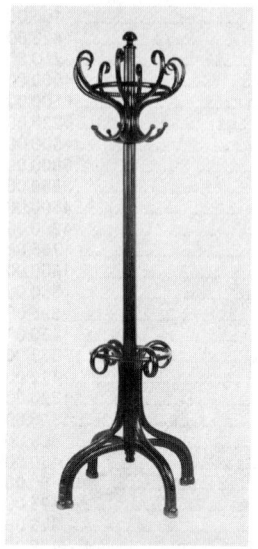

Furniture, Coatrack, Thonet Bros., C.1900,
Bentwood, 6 Ft. 8 In.   *(See Page 243)*

(See Page 243)

Furniture, Commode, Louis XV, Metal-Mounted, Black Lacquer

Furniture, Commode, Louis XV, Vernis Martin & Lacquer

(See Page 243)

Furniture, Cradle, French Empire, 19th Century, Bronze-Mounted

Commode, Step, Hinged Top, Mahogany, C.1860, 17 1/2 X 16 1/2 In.	75.00
Commode, Walnut, Demilune, Biedermeier, Marble Slab, C.1830, 33 In.	1500.00
Cooler, Wine, Lead Lined, Brass Bound, Mahogany, 7 1/2 In., Pair	6000.00
Couch, Edwardian, Carved, Leather Upholstery, Griffins, 82 In.	2800.00
Couch, Tufted, Victorian, Rounded Back & Arms, 68 In.	600.00
Cradle-On-Frame, Sheraton, C.1795, Santo Domingo Mahogany	1350.00
Cradle, Baby, French Empire, Bronze Mounting	1900.00
Cradle, Cherry, Chippendale, Arched Hood, C.1750, 42 In.	260.00
Cradle, Cherry, Shaker, Pierced Handholds, C.1800, 41 1/4 In.	770.00
Cradle, French Empire, 19th Century, Bronze-Mounted	*Illus* 1900.00
Cradle, Hooded, Original False Grained Paint	850.00
Cradle, Lattice Ribs, Suspended From Bentwood Frame, 46 In.	325.00
Cradle, Pine, Unfinished, Square Nails, 1800s, 33 5/8 In.	200.00
Cradle, Swings From Frame, Boat Shape, Wooden, 4 Feet	450.00
Credenza, Walnut, 2 Drawers, 2 Doors, 43 X 59 In.	3000.00
Crib, Hand-Turned, Wooden, C.1830	175.00
Cupboard & Dry Sink, Shaker, Pine	4900.00
Cupboard, Bedside, George III, Inlaid Mahogany, 32 In.	150.00
Cupboard, Bedside, Tambour-Fronted, Mahogany, C.1790, 31 In.	1600.00
Cupboard, Broken Arch, Dovetailed Case, Cherry, 2 Piece	6900.00
Cupboard, Chimney, Molded Base	165.00
Cupboard, Chippendale, Flat Wall, Dovetailed Feet, Cherry	5800.00
Cupboard, Corner, American, C.1780, Carved Pine, 5 Ft. 4 In.	2100.00
Cupboard, Corner, American, 19th Century, Blue, Cherry, 7 Ft. 4 In.	2900.00
Cupboard, Corner, Chamfered Doors, Cherry, 35 1/2 X 81 1/2 In.	2700.00
Cupboard, Corner, Cherry, Handmade Glass, Pegged, C.1800, 7 X 4 Ft.	2895.00
Cupboard, Corner, H-Hinges, Wood Pegged, Handmade Nails, C.1930	3200.00
Cupboard, Corner, Hanging, C.1770, Glazed Door, Drawer, Oak, 4 Feet	350.00
Cupboard, Corner, Hepplewhite, Broken Pediment, 8 1/2 Feet	2600.00
Cupboard, Corner, Molded & Carved Frieze, C.1780, Pennsylvania	3950.00
Cupboard, Corner, Mustard & Orange Paint, 1820s, 2 Piece	4500.00
Cupboard, Corner, Paneled Door, Turnip Feet, 7 3/4 Ft.High	1650.00
Cupboard, Corner, Pine, Painted, 1 Door, Red, 74 1/2 In.	1000.00
Cupboard, Corner, Reeding & Fluting, Chester County, Pa., Cherry	3975.00
Cupboard, Corner, Walnut & Butternut	1350.00
Cupboard, Corner, Walnut, 7 Feet	1050.00
Cupboard, Corner, 2-Part, 9-Light Boor, Rupp, Softwood, 84 1/2 In.	2500.00
Cupboard, Corner, 4 Pane Door, Pine, 33 1/2 X 89 In., 2 Piece	2600.00
Cupboard, Corner, 12 Pane Single Door, Pennyslvania, Walnut	1750.00
Cupboard, Corner, 12 Pane Windows, Pine	1990.00
Cupboard, Corner, 15 Glazed Panels, 18th Century, 2 Piece	3800.00
Cupboard, Dish, Spice Drawers, Oak	1025.00

Cupboard, Double Doors, 18 Glass Panes, Pennsylvania, 1810, Walnut 6800.00
Cupboard, Dry Sink, Grain Painted 875.00
Cupboard, Dutch, Painted, C.1625 .... 3500.00
Cupboard, Dutch, Rattail Hinges, Walnut 6800.00
Cupboard, Dutch, Yellow Graining 3900.00
Cupboard, Filing, Trays & Pigeonholes, Schoharie County, Grained 265.00
Cupboard, Flatwall, Harvard, Mass., Narrow 1200.00
Cupboard, Flatwall, Pennsylvania, C.1820, Cherry, 2 Piece 6850.00
Cupboard, Jelly, Bracket Feet, Scalloped Gallery, Pine, Old Red 750.00
Cupboard, Jelly, Completely Original, C.1860 .... 1050.00
Cupboard, Jelly, Gray Paint, Dovetailed Gallery 685.00
Cupboard, Jelly, 2 Small Upper Drawers, Grained 325.00
Cupboard, Jelly, 3 Recessed Drawer Top 450.00
Cupboard, Kitchen, Seller Oak 225.00
Cupboard, Old Red, Mustard Trim, Child's, 30 In. 195.00
Cupboard, Panel Front, Ohio Shaker, Brown Stain 1195.00
Cupboard, Pennsylvania, C.1800, 2-Part, Painted Pine, 7 Ft. 1 In. 6500.00
Cupboard, Pewter, French, Cherry 1750.00
Cupboard, Pewter, Open Top, Pine 1395.00
Cupboard, Pewter, Step-Back, Dentil Molding, Canadian 2750.00
Cupboard, Pewter, 3 Molded Shelves, 2 Panel Doors, 18th Century 1200.00
Cupboard, Pewter, 3 Open Shelves, 2 Doors, C.1775, Pine, 2 Piece 1650.00
Cupboard, Pine, Cutout Feet, 2 Drawers, 25 X 48 In. 525.00
Cupboard, Raised Panel Door, Sabbathday Lake, Green 3700.00
Cupboard, Step Gallery, 3 Drawers, 2 Doors, C.1830, 63 X 84 In. 5500.00
Cupboard, Stepback, Old Red Paint 1750.00
Cupboard, Stepback, Pine, 8 Feet 575.00
Cupboard, Wall, Panel Doors, C.1830, Grain Painted, 8 X 37 In. 300.00
Cupboard, 2 Drawer, Thumbnail Molding, Green Paint, Pine, 3. In. 325.00
Cupboard, 9-Light Door, Virginia, Pine & Poplar 775.00
Cupboard, 18th Century, Pennsylvania, Softwood 3600.00
Daybed, Jenny Lind, Spool-Turned, Casters, Walnut, 76 3/4 X 30 In. 200.00
Daybed, Mahogany, C-Scroll Feet, Seat Rail, 92 In. 550.00
Daybed, Regency, C.1815, Brass Inlaid, Rosewood, 6 Ft. 8 1/2 In. 1870.00
Daybed, 11 Vertical Slat Back, C.1910, Mission Oak, 6 Ft. 11 In. 345.00
Decanter Stand, Mahogany, Shell Inlaid, George III, 29 In. 700.00
Desk & Game Table, Lady's, Carved Scrolls, Rosewood, 41 1/4 In. 650.00
Desk, Bookkeeper's, Removable Top, Pink, 72 X 31 X 79 In. 2100.00
Desk, Butler's, Mahogany, Empire, C.1840, 48 X 42 In. 475.00
Desk, Butler's, New York, C.1790, Mahogany, 45 3/4 X 45 1/2 In. 1000.00
Desk, Butler's, Victorian, Walnut, 6 Drawers, 55 X 40 In. 1000.00
Desk, C.1910, G.Stickley, Decal, Oak 2200.00
Desk, Carlton House, Satinwood, 37 X 45 In. 2200.00
Desk, Carved Gallery, Brass Pulls, Walnut, Davenport, 24 X 35 In. 990.00
Desk, Child's, Lift Top, Victorian, Double Slate, 1860s 375.00
Desk, Chippendale, Mahogany & Walnut, Slant Top, 3 Drawers 525.00
Desk, Chippendale, Slant Front, C.1780, Cherry, 37 In.Wide 3450.00
Desk, Chippendale, Slant Front, Maple 6200.00
Desk, Cylinder, C.1860, English, Mahogany, 51 X 28 X 44 In. 1500.00
Desk, Cylinder, Pierced Gallery Top, Oak 495.00
Desk, Cylinder, Walnut & Burl, Renaissance Revival, C.1865 .... 1950.00
Desk, Davenport, Burled Walnut, C.1860, 22 1/2 X 22 X 33 In. 2750.00
Desk, Davenport, Lift Dome Top, C.1870, Bird's-Eye Maple, 35 In. 750.00
Desk, Davenport, Walnut, Brass Trim 990.00
Desk, Drop Front, Brass-Mounted, Gallery, French Style 280.00
Desk, Drop Front, C.1905, G.Stickley, Decal, Oak, 27 X 47 1/2 In. 9100.00
Desk, Drop Front, Carved Lid & Legs, Oak 325.00
Desk, Empire, 2 Beaded Doors, C.1840, Mahogany, 52 1/4 X 52 In. 750.00
Desk, Fall Front, Burr Veneer, Biedermeier 1100.00
Desk, Fall Front, G.Stickley, Oak, Red Decal .... *Illus* 2200.00
Desk, Fall Front, Shaker, 19th Century, Cherry, 43 1/2 X 43 In. 3000.00
Desk, Federal, Line Inlaid, Tambour, C.1800, Mahogany, 38 X 47 In. 7200.00
Desk, Flat Red Leather Top, Oak, Cabinets & Drawers, 29 In. 600.00

Furniture, Desk, Fall Front, G.Stickley, Oak, Red Decal

Desk, French Restoration, 19th Century, Rosewood, 51 X 40 In. 425.00
Desk, Hanging, Scalloped Backboard, Divided Interior, Walnut 950.00
Desk, Innkeeper's, C.1880, Secret Drawer, Pine, 2 Piece 600.00
Desk, Italian Rococo, Slant Front, Carved, Walnut, 39 In. 900.00
Desk, Kneehole, Mahogany, George III, 7 Drawers 300.00
Desk, Lacquered & Metal, Semicircular, 3 Drawers, 50 In. 3800.00
Desk, Lady's, Eastlake, Brass Galleried, C.1870, 45 1/2 X 30 In. 350.00
Desk, Lady's, Eastlake, Mirrored Top, C Roll, Walnut, 31 X 59 In. 625.00
Desk, Lady's, Marble Top, Mirrored Doors, C.1870, Mahogany, 44 In. 600.00
Desk, Lady's, Ogee Slant Lid, Bombe Case, Oak, C.1920, 40 In. 300.00
Desk, Lady's, Ormolu Mounts, Hand-Painted, French, C.1885 .... 2200.00
Desk, Lamp, Pine, Hinged Lid, 2 Drawers, 6 3/4 X 11 1/2 In. 225.00
Desk, Lap, Art Nouveau Silver Scroll Applied 175.00
Desk, Lap, Brass Hinges, Oak, 13 1/2 X 11 1/2 X 3 1/2 In. 22.00
Desk, Lap, C.1860, Side Drawer, Mahogany, 12 X 5 1/2 In. 150.00
Desk, Lap, George III, Mahogany, Brass-Mounted, C.1800, 6 X 20 In. 200.00
Desk, Lap, Inlays, C.1870, Rosewood, 14 1/2 X 11 X 4 1/2 In. 350.00
Desk, Lap, Mahogany, Brass Inlay, Covered Box, 20 X 10 In. 200.00
Desk, Lap, N.Starkey, Philadelphia, 1845, , Walnut, 18 X 6 1/2 In. 425.00
Desk, Lap, Original Ink Bottles, Velvet Lined, Oak 160.00
Desk, Lap, Papier-Mache, Victorian, Mother-Of-Pearl Inlay, 23 In. 200.00
Desk, Lap, Regency, C.1825, Velvet Lined, Brass Inlaid, 10 X 20 In. 520.00
Desk, Lap, Rosewood, Mother-Of-Pearl Inlaid, Inkwell, 13 In. 275.00
Desk, Lap, Tambour, C.1790, Carved, Mahogany, 13 X 6 In. 350.00
Desk, Lap, Walnut Campaign, Brass Bound, C.1840, 18 In. 225.00
Desk, Lap, Walnut, Brass Inlaid, Victorian, 10 X 19 In. 175.00
Desk, Louis XV, Bronze Mounted Woman At Corners, 53 X 29 In. 1300.00
Desk, Old Red Paint, Cherry 6500.00
Desk, Original Brass, New England, C.1780, Birch, 18 1/2 X 45 In. 4500.00
Desk, Partner's, C.1800, Gilt Leather Inset, Mahogany, 31 In. 5500.00
Desk, Partner's, C.1825, Mahogany, 49 1/2 X 30 In. 650.00
Desk, Partner's, Railway Express Co. Office, Oak 895.00
Desk, Partner's, Raised Panels, Oak 200.00
Desk, Partner's, 2-Man, Oak, Hillsdale, Mich., R.R. Depot 225.00
Desk, Pen Tray & Inkwell, Charles P. Limbert, Oak, 41 3/4 In. 500.00
Desk, Plantation, 2 Piece, 3 Burled Walnut Doors, C.1810, Walnut 2150.00
Desk, Plantation, 2 Piece, 3 Door Panels, Walnut, C.1810 .... 2150.00
Desk, Queen Anne, Slant Top, Maple, Writing Height 30 5/8 In. 9500.00
Desk, Roll Top, Beveled Panels On Drawers, Dated 1884, Oak, 50 In. 2895.00
Desk, Roll Top, C Curve, Oak 1100.00
Desk, Roll Top, Matching Chair, Oak, 48 X 29 In. 1500.00
Desk, Roll Top, Oak, Typewriter Compartment, 5 Ft. X 43 In. 475.00
Desk, Roll Top, Oak, 60 In. 1400.00
Desk, Roll Top, 5 Drawer, Filing Section, C.1890, 48 X 45 In. 975.00
Desk, Rosewood, Spinet, American, 53 X 34 In. 450.00

Furniture, Desk, Slant Front, English,
Mahogany, 42 X 42 In.

Desk, Rosewood, Victorian, Traveling 100.00
Desk, S Roll Top, Hinged & Removable Wings, Oak 2275.00
Desk, S Roll Top, S.Schwarzwaelder & Co., Mahogany, 60 In. 1950.00
Desk, Schoolmaster's, Federal, Inkwell, 2 Drawer, 36 X 36 In. 600.00
Desk, Schoolmaster's, Hepplewhite, Walnut, 3 Drawer, 32 X 32 In. 375.00
Desk, Schoolmaster's, Lift Top, Black Feather Design Over Red 500.00
Desk, Schoolmaster's, Poplar, Turned Legs, Pigeonholes, 33 In. 150.00
Desk, Secretary's, English, Mahogany, 1830 .... 6500.00
Desk, Ship's, Ivory Escutcheons, Owned By Captain Hancock, 1819 .... 2500.00
Desk, Slant Front, C.1840, Bamboo, Bird's-Eye Maple, 4 Ft. 7 In. 1900.00
Desk, Slant Front, Chippendale, C.1770, Carved, Walnut, 43 In. 8500.00
Desk, Slant Front, English, Mahogany, 42 X 42 In. .... *Illus* 1500.00
Desk, Slant Front, English, 38 X 42 1/2 X 19 In. .... *Illus* 1600.00
Desk, Slant Front, Fan Inlaid Lid, Mahogany, 33 X 40 In. 300.00
Desk, Slant Front, Federal, Carved, Cherry, 23 1/4 X 27 1/2 In. 275.00
Desk, Slant Front, Hepplewhite, 18th Century, American, Walnut 1800.00
Desk, Slant Front, Mahogany, English, Flat Front, 38 X 42 In. 1600.00
Desk, Slant Front, Mahogany, Serpentine Front, 36 In. 325.00
Desk, Slant Front, New England, C.1750, Carved, Maple, 40 In. 4500.00
Desk, Slant Front, Pigeonholes, 3 Drawers, Carved Pulls, Walnut 1250.00
Desk, Slant Front, Victorian, American Oak 900.00
Desk, Slant Front, Walnut, 4 Drawers, Eagle Brasses, 28 In. 4800.00
Desk, Slant Front, 1750-80, Tiger Maple 3400.00
Desk, Slant Front, 19th Century, Carved, Cherry, 18 X 25 1/2 In. 750.00
Desk, Stand-Up, C.1870, Norwegian, Locks, Original Salmon Paint 875.00
Desk, State-O'-Maine, Birch 2500.00
Desk, Student, Double, Slant Top, 19th Century, Shaker, 24 In. 190.00
Desk, Tabletop, Slant Top, Inside Shelf, Gray, 24 X 18 3/4 In. 185.00

Furniture, Desk, Slant Front, English,
38 X 42 1/2 X 19 In.

Desk, Teacher's, 5 Side Drawers, 1 Large Drawer, Oak	235.00
Desk, Traveling, Rosewood, Brass Bound, Side Drawer, 20 X 11 In.	375.00
Desk, Wells Fargo, Walnut, C.1885, 43 1/2 X 32 1/2 In.	950.00
Desk, Wooton, Glass Window In Back, Elephant Feet, Black Walnut	9000.00
Desk, Wooton, Wells Fargo, Walnut, Renaissance	8500.00
Desk, Writing, Lady's, Federal Style, 32 X 16 X 35 In.	45.00
Desk, Writing, Walnut, Queen Anne, 3 Small Drawers, 32 X 40 In.	125.00
Desk, 19th Century, Unpainted Wicker	600.00
Dictionary Stand, C.1760, Brass-Mounted, Mahogany, 30 In.	1700.00
Dining Set, Marble Top Buffet, 6 Chairs, Carved Animals, 51 In.	2850.00
Dining Set, Oxbow Sideboard, 6 Fan & String Inlay Chairs, C.1940	550.00
Dining Set, Sheraton, Drop Leaf Table, Mahogany, 40 X 74 In.	850.00
Dining Table, Drop Leaf, Signed Wallace Nutting, Walnut	800.00
Dough Box, Sliding Lid, Pennsylvania, Hand-Pegged, Splay Legs, Pine	375.00
Dresser, Beveled Mirror, Claw Feet, 4 Drawer, Oak	295.00
Dresser, Burled Detail, Walnut	425.00
Dresser, Curly Maple, Serpentine, Brass Posts, C.1900	360.00
Dresser, Double, English, Mahogany, C.1860, 87 X 60 In.	1600.00
Dresser, Eastlake, Glove Box, Marble Top, Walnut	495.00
Dresser, George III, Bow Front, Mahogany, C.1810, 45 X 41 In.	800.00
Dresser, Lady's, Louis XV, Floral Marquetry, 26 X 33 In.	1000.00
Dresser, Mahogany, Mirror, Marble Top, Scrolled Feet, 75 X 41 In.	425.00
Dresser, Mahogany, Mirror, Marble Top, 3 Drawers, 85 X 43 In.	750.00
Dresser, Mahogany, New Orleans, Wig Cupboards, C.1840, 92 In.	1500.00
Dresser, Marble Top, C.1860, Carved Fruit, 45 1/4 X 89 1/2 In.	475.00
Dresser, Oak, Victorian, Beveled Tilt Mirror, 41 X 78 In.	150.00
Dresser, Oak, 4 Open Shelves, 5 Drawer, C.1740, 6 1/2 Feet	4500.00
Dresser, Princess, Eastlake, Marble Top	500.00
Dresser, Renaissance, Marble Top, Walnut, C.1860, 46 X 100 In.	800.00
Dresser, Victorian, Arched Mirror, Carved, Walnut, 45 1/2 X 96 In.	950.00
Dresser, Victorian, Marble Top, Rosewood, C.1860, 44 X 86 3/4 In.	650.00
Dresser, 2 Section, Cupboard & Drawers, Oak, C.1780, 6 Ft. 8 In.	4000.00
Dressing Glass, Mahogany, 2 Drawer, C.1825, 24 In.	175.00
Drop Leaf Table, C.1860, Pine, 72 In.	500.00
Dry Sink, Pine, Drawer, Doors, Bracket Feet, Red, Yellow, 31 In.	7700.00
Dry Sink, Pine, Pierced For Basin, Shaker, 25 X 17 1/2 In.	3210.00
Dry Sink, Pine, Shaker, New York, 2 Doors, 25 X 44 X 17 In.	2100.00
Dry Sink, Vermont, Dusty Gray Green Paint	435.00
Dry Sink, 1 Drawer, Pine, 54 X 26 1/2 X 34 In.	750.00
Dry Sink, 2 Door, Shaker, Pine, 25 1/2 X 44 1/2 In.	*Illus* 2100.00

Furniture, Dry Sink, 2 Door, Shaker, Pine, 25 1/2 X 44 1/2 In.

Drying Rack, 4-Legged, Ten Arms, Shaker 450.00
Dumbwaiter, Mahogany, George III, 2 Tiers, 19 In. 200.00
Dumbwaiter, Mahogany, 2 Hinged Platforms, C.1780, 3 Feet 1500.00
Easel, Carved Arched Top, 19th Century, Mahogany, 4 Ft. 11 In. 4180.00
Easel, Eastlake, Pierced, Gold Highlights, Back Brace, C.1875 .... 375.00
Easel, Folding, Brass-Mounted, Mahogany, 19th Century, 6 Feet 880.00
Etagere, Chinese Chippendale, Mahogany, C.1880, 4 1/2 Feet 550.00
Etagere, Mahogany, 5 Tiers, Bamboo Supports, 36 X 53 In. 150.00
Etagere, Regency, Mahogany, 3-Tier, C.1820, 4 Ft. 5 1/2 In. 825.00
Etagere, Rosewood, Rococo, American, C.1860, 8 Ft. X 5 Ft. 6000.00
Etagere, Victorian, Beveled Glass Mirrors, Walnut 395.00
Etagere, Walnut, Shell Carvings, Oak Drawers, Separate Mirror 960.00
Fern Stand, Chinese, Hardwood, Marble Top, 36 In. 260.00
Fern Stand, Mahogany, Octagonal, Louis XVI, 40 In. 400.00
Fern Stand, Rouge Marble Top, Carved, Oriental, 23 3/4 In. 175.00
Fern Stand, Victorian, Shelves, Beaded Molding, C.1890 .... 60.00
Fernery, Scrolls, Grapes, Iron, American, C.1880, 33 1/4 X 30 In. 275.00
Folio Rack, C.1865, Gilt Incised & Ebonized Walnut, 48 1/2 In. 2000.00
Footstool, Empire, C.1840, Mahogany, 21 1/2 X 13 In., Pair 320.00
Footstool, English, Head Beaded Center 50.00
Footstool, Label, Shaker's, Mt.Lebanon, N.Y., Pine, 7 In. 180.00
Footstool, Leather Cushion, Mission Oak, C.1910, 15 In. 45.00
Footstool, Mahogany, Needlepoint Seat 110.00
Footstool, Needlepoint Cover, Walnut, C.1840, 13 X 16 X 6 In. 90.00
Footstool, Needlepoint Top, Pink Roses, Walnut 28.00
Footstool, Oak, Turned Legs, Floral Top, 10 X 14 X 7 In. 30.00
Footstool, Painted Red, 12 X 5 1/2 X 6 3/4 In. 30.00
Footstool, Pine, Applied Scrolled Leg, 8 X 10 In. 15.00
Footstool, Serpentine Form, Needlepoint Seat, Walnut, 18 In. 80.00
Footstool, Upholstered Top, Cabriole Legs, 19th C., Pair 825.00
Footstool, Victorian Lacy Iron, Original Cover 50.00
Footstool, Victorian, Ebonized, Leaf Frame, Paw Feet, 30 In. 400.00
Footstool, Walnut, Queen Anne, Slip Seat, Cabriole Legs 1800.00
Girandole, Regency, C.1820, Eagle Crest, Gilt Wood, 39 1/2 In. 1430.00
Globe, Terrestrial, Calculated To 1848, Mahogany Stand, 46 1/2 In. 4950.00
Hall Seat, C.1905, G.Stickley, Decal, Oak, 4 Ft. 8 In. 9400.00
Hall Seat, Oak, Beveled Mirror, Clothes Hooks, Lift Top 375.00
Hall Seat, Renaissance, C.1885, Italian, Walnut 750.00
Hall Stand, Bentwood, C.1900, 75 In. 200.00
Hall Stand, Beveled Mirror, Seat Opens, Hooks, Oak 600.00
Hall Stand, C.1880, Mahogany, 68 1/2 In. 275.00
Hall Stand, Carved Scrolls, Iron Pan, Mahogany, 35 1/2 X 75 In. 200.00
Hall Stand, Oak, 2 Beveled Mirrors, Ornate Brass Hooks 800.00
Hall Stand, Victorian, Carved, 19th Century, 89 1/2 In. 470.00
Hall Stand, Walnut, Victorian, Beveled Mirror, 48 X 93 In. 550.00
Hall Tree, Oak, Victorian, C.1900, Mirror, Brass Racks, 39 In. 300.00
Hall Tree, Victorian, C.1880, Cast Iron & Brass, 7 1/2 Feet 1200.00
Hall Tree, Victorian, Marble Shelf, Walnut .... Illus 1650.00
Hamper, Baby Clothes, Wicker 48.00
Hamper, Laundry, Wicker, Wide Weave 30.00
Hat Rack, 6-Arms, Center Carving Of Benjamin Franklin, Walnut 120.00
High Chair, Back, Wicker 85.00
High Chair, Cane Seat, Carved Back, Folds Into Rocker, Oak 650.00
High Chair, Cane Seated 150.00
High Chair, Child's, Windsor, Yellow, Bamboo Legs, 32 1/2 In. 400.00
High Chair, Lithograph, Red Trim, Tray, 1800s 75.00
High Chair, New England, Old Blue Paint 165.00
High Chair, Stroller, Cherry, Turned Spindle Back, Cane Seat 175.00
Highboy Top, Painted Grain, Mid-19th Century, Pine 1400.00
Highboy, American, William & Mary, C.1740 .... 1500.00
Highboy, Bonnet Top, C.1760, Tiger Maple 3800.00
Highboy, Bonnet Top, Shell Carving, Mahogany, C.1930, 80 In. 800.00
Highboy, C.1740, Burled Veneer Drawers .... Illus 1500.00

Furniture, Hall Tree, Victorian,
Marble Shelf, Walnut

Highboy, New England, C.1750, Maple & Walnut, 6 Ft. 5 In. 9500.00
Highboy, Queen Anne, Philadelphia, Walnut, 6 Ft. 8 In. 1300.00
Highboy, Queen Anne, Tiger Maple, Two Sections, 72 X 38 In. 4100.00
Highboy, Queen Anne, Walnut, Mahogany & Cherry, 77 X 38 In. 1500.00
Highboy, Vermont, C.1760, 2-Part, Painted Maple, 5 Ft. 2 In. 4000.00
Highboy, William & Mary, C.1710, 12 Drawers, Tiger Maple Fronts 2500.00
Highboy, William & Mary, C.1730, Old Red Paint, 39 X 66 In. 5800.00
Highboy, William & Mary, 12 Drawer, C.1710, Maple Fronts, 7 Feet 2500.00
Huntboard, Federal, 3 Drawer, C.1790, Walnut, 42 X 16 X 41 1/2 In. 5250.00
Huntboard, Oak, 3 Drawer, Teardrop Pulls, Block Legs, 31 In. 550.00
Hutch, Water, Painted, Country Pine 1500.00
Ice Cream Parlor, Child's, 4 Chairs, Oak Top & Seats, Bent Iron 265.00
Ice Cream Parlor, Oak Top Table, 1890, Copper Legs, 5 Piece 550.00
Jardiniere, 3 Legs, Liner, Bronze-Mounted, Mahogany, 33 In. 1500.00
Kas, 18th Century, Lancaster County, Decorated By D.Y.Ellinger 4200.00
Kettle Stand, Queen Anne, 3 Cabriole Legs, C.1750, 27 X 14 In. 375.00
Knife Box, George III, Mahogany, Hinged Lid, Set Of 3 .... 1550.00
Ladder, Folding, 8 Rungs, Shaker, 19th Century, Pine, 8 Feet 250.00
Ladder, Library, Mahogany, George III, Folding, 100 In. 1000.00
Lamp Stand, C.1790, Inlay Around Keyholes, Chestnuts 125.00
Lamp, Hall, Cased, Enameled Art Glass 300.00
Library Ladder, C.1800, Mahogany, 5 Ft. 11 In. 950.00
Library Steps, Folding, C.1800, Mahogany, 28 1/2 In. 950.00
Library Steps, Mahogany, Folds Into Bench, Needlepoint Seat 100.00
Linen Press, 2-Part, Grain-Painted, 48 X 74 3/4 In. 400.00
Living Room Set, Mohair, Burgundy & Gold, 3 Piece 1200.00
Love Seat & Armchair, Sheraton, Matching, Inlay & Reeded Legs 595.00
Love Seat, Carved Trim, Green Velvet, Matching Lady's Chair 950.00

Furniture, Highboy, C.1740,
Burled Veneer Drawers

Love Seat, Dragon & Phoenix Carvings, Oriental, 72 X 56 X 24 In. 3950.00
Love Seat, Finger Carved Crest Rail, American, C.1875, Walnut 250.00
Love Seat, Finger Roll, Victorian 800.00
Love Seat, Mahogany, George III, Wing Arms, Claw Feet, 53 In. 600.00
Love Seat, Upholstered, Wicker 275.00
Love Seat, Walnut, Queen Anne, Cabriole Legs, 35 In. 1000.00
Love Seat, Wicker 375.00
Lowboy, George III, Mahogany, 3 Drawer, Ball Feet, 32 In. 650.00
Lowboy, Maple, Queen Anne, 1740-60, Pad Feet, 30 X 30 In. 3750.00
Lowboy, Trumpet Turnings, C.1690, Original Hardware, Walnut 1700.00
Lowboy, Walnut, Queen Anne, Delaware Valley, C.1740, 26 In. 7000.00
Magazine Rack, Hanging, Wicker 450.00
Marquise, Walnut, Louis XVI, Bow Front, 37 In. 3575.00
Mirror, Acanthus Design, C.1880, Gold Leaf, 19 X 32 In. 80.00
Mirror, American Southwest, Horn & Wood, 40 X 48 In. 200.00
Mirror, Beveled, C.1795, Oval, 32 X 26 In. 150.00
Mirror, Bull's-Eye, Pink Opalescent Basket, English, 12 X 8 In. 350.00
Mirror, Cape Cod, Polychrome & Gesso, Roses, 20 In. 400.00
Mirror, Carved & Gilded, Plate, 25 X 22 In. 80.00
Mirror, Carved Egg & Dart Border, Gilt Wood, 5 1/2 Feet 4125.00
Mirror, Carved Rosette Corners, Gilded, 48 1/2 X 51 1/2 In. 225.00
Mirror, Carved, Oak, C.1880, 16 X 50 In. 50.00
Mirror, Cherry Frame, Matching Top & Bottom Crest, 8 X 18 In. 285.00
Mirror, Cheval, Feather Carved Supports & Florals 3200.00
Mirror, Cheval, Mahogany, 19 1/2 X 23 In. 40.00
Mirror, Chippendale, Mahogany, C.1815, 38 1/2 X 20 In. 900.00
Mirror, Chippendale, Mahogany, Scrolled Crest, 20 In. 150.00
Mirror, Chippendale, Scrolled Cutouts, 8 X 9 1/2 In. 185.00
Mirror, Chippendale, 13 X 18 In. 265.00
Mirror, Chippendale, 18th Century, Mahogany, Gilt Wood, 26 1/4 In. 600.00
Mirror, Comb Pocket, Towel Bar, Carvings Of Birds & Stars 220.00
Mirror, Convex, Eagle Crest, Gilt Wood, C.1820, 4 Ft. 11 In. 2640.00
Mirror, Convex, Empire, 2 Candle Arms, Gilt Wood, C.1825, 40 In. 1500.00
Mirror, Courting, Eglomise Panels, Floral Design, Undertray, 14 In. 750.00
Mirror, Dressing, Drawer, Papier-Mache, C.1850, 24 X 29 1/2 In. 650.00
Mirror, Dressing, Pineapple Uprights, Mahogany, C.1815, 30 1/2 In. 400.00
Mirror, Empire Frame, Columns, Reverse Painted Fruit, 21 X 11 In. 85.00
Mirror, Empire Gilt, Convex, C.1820 ....1200.00
Mirror, Empire, Divided Plate, Gilt Frame, Mahogany, 54 In., Pair 400.00
Mirror, Federal, American, 19th Century, Gilt Wood, 39 In. 250.00
Mirror, Federal, C.1815, 3 Plates, Gilt Wood, Gesso, 4 Ft. 5 In. 950.00
Mirror, Federal, Eglomise Panel, 15 1/2 X 43 1/4 In., Pair 325.00
Mirror, Federal, Gilt Wood & Eglomise, C.1820, 30 In. 500.00
Mirror, Federal, T.Biggs, Phila., 19th Century, Mahogany, 18 In. 325.00
Mirror, Folding, 3-Part, Beveled Glass, Oak 65.00
Mirror, George III, Beaded & Gadrooned, Gilt Wood, 42 1/2 In. 935.00
Mirror, George III, C.1770, Gadrooned, Gilt Wood, 4 Ft. 4 In. 2750.00
Mirror, Gesso, Persia, Floral Crest, Polychrome Border, 24 In. 125.00
Mirror, Girandole, Federal, Gilt, C.1800, 37 X 18 In. 750.00
Mirror, Hall, Carved Frame, Walnut 175.00
Mirror, Hall, Eastlake, Walnut, 6 Brass Hooks, 44 In. 140.00
Mirror, Hand, Pine, C.1791, 8 In. 375.00
Mirror, Hanging, Walnut, Victorian, Renaissance Period, 51 In. 130.00
Mirror, Italian Neoclassical, Parcel Gilt, Arched, 5 Ft. 225.00
Mirror, Italian Rococo, Foliate Cresting, 5 Feet 4 In. X 26 In. 880.00
Mirror, Italian Rococo, Parcel Gilt, 5 Ft. 4 In. X 26 In. 880.00
Mirror, Leaves & Rosettes, Shepherd Cartouche, 36 X 52 In. 175.00
Mirror, Leaves & 11 Flowers, Venetian, Oval, 23 X 14 1/2 In. 385.00
Mirror, Louis XVI, Gesso & Gilt, Grape Leaf Design, 42 In. 250.00
Mirror, Louis XVI, Gilt Wood, Floral Cresting, 38 In. 250.00
Mirror, Mahogany, Chippendale, Eagle Crest, 37 In. 325.00
Mirror, Mahogany, Chippendale, Eagle Pediment, 31 X 16 In. 300.00
Mirror, Mantel, Baluster Frame, Broken Cornice, Gilt, 56 X 32 In. 325.00

Mirror, Napoleon III, C.1855, Gilt Wood, 6 Ft. 10 In. X 47 In. 2800.00
Mirror, Napoleon III, Gilt Wood, C.1860, 34 X 29 In. 325.00
Mirror, Oak, Beveled, Oblong, 6 Feet 125.00
Mirror, Ogee, Mahogany, Empire, Molded Edge, Gilt Trim, 46 In. 300.00
Mirror, Overmantel, Cherry, 60 X 30 X 10 In. 195.00
Mirror, Overmantel, Walnut, Eastlake Style, C.1880, 56 X 63 In. 300.00
Mirror, Ovolo & Beaded Edges, C.1850, Gilded, 51 3/4 X 65 In. 325.00
Mirror, Pier, Queen Anne, Black Japanned, 19 In. X 4 Ft. 3 In. 800.00
Mirror, Pier, Victorian, Mahogany, C.1900, 74 1/2 X 31 1/2 In. 200.00
Mirror, Plateau, Beveled, Chain Of Sunbursts, Floral Feet, 12 In. 65.00
Mirror, Plateau, Double Bevel, Silver Plate Border, 12 In. 155.00
Mirror, Plateau, Embossed Flower Form Feet, 8 1/2 X 3 In. 75.00
Mirror, Plateau, Filigree, Bronze Tone, 12 1/2 In. 95.00
Mirror, Plateau, Lion Head & Claw Feet, Scroll & Floral, 12 In. 120.00
Mirror, Plateau, Petal Forms, Beading, Beveled, 5-Footed 67.00
Mirror, Plateau, Rococo Embossed, Florals, Scrolls, 15 1/4 In. 105.00
Mirror, Plateau, Scrolled Floral Feet, Bull's-Eye Chain, 19 In. 90.00
Mirror, Prince Of Wales Feather Ornament, Boston, C.1808, 23 In. 230.00
Mirror, Queen Anne, Mahogany Veneer, Scrolled, 24 In. 650.00
Mirror, Queen Anne, Mahogany, Crest, Pendant, Frame, 21 In. 525.00
Mirror, Queen Anne, Walnut & Gilt Wood, 34 1/2 X 13 3/4 In. 500.00
Mirror, Regency, Ebonized & Gilt Wood, Oval, C.1820, 29 In. 1210.00
Mirror, Regency, Gilt Frame, Convex, C.1820, 45 1/2 X 29 In. 1100.00
Mirror, Reverse Painting Of House, 11 X 20 1/4 In. 55.00
Mirror, Rococo, Gilt Wood, Carved Foliage, 51 X 28 In., Pair 400.00
Mirror, Rococo, Tole, Cartouche Shape, Flowers, 44 In. 550.00
Mirror, Scandinavian, Molded Frame, Painted Pine, 8 X 5 1/2 In. 80.00
Mirror, Shaped Within C-Scroll, Gilt Wood, 7 Ft. 4 In. 500.00
Mirror, Shaving, Bamboo, Free Standing, Brass Trim 57.50
Mirror, Shaving, Eastlake Frame 125.00
Mirror, Shaving, Federal, String Inlay 185.00
Mirror, Shaving, Mahogany, Hepplewhite, 1 Drawer 140.00
Mirror, Shaving, Rosewood, Rococo, C.1845, 5 Ft. X 17 In. 400.00
Mirror, Shaving, Scrolled Medallions, Walnut, C.1880, 25 In. 35.00
Mirror, Shaving, Signed Edwards & Roberts, Walnut, 16 X 23 In. 1050.00
Mirror, Shaving, Simple Cherry, Adjustable Frame, 13 X 12 In. 45.00
Mirror, Sheraton, Reverse Painting On Glass, Farm Building, 33 In. 650.00
Mirror, Table, French, C.1900, Gilt Bronze & Malachite, 22 1/2 In. 1200.00
Mirror, Triple, Dresser Top, Oak Frame, Beveled Glass 100.00
Mirror, Walnut, Queen Anne, Crest Center, Beveled, 4 Ft. 6500.00
Music Stand, Fruitwood, Biedermeier, Tripod Base, 47 In. 715.00
Music Stand, Italian, Iron, Pair, 60 In. 550.00
Parlor Set, American, Cherry & Rattan, C.1885, 4 Piece 300.00
Parlor Set, Empire, Bronze-Mounted, Mahogany, 5 Piece 1800.00
Parlor Set, Ice Cream, 1890 .... 600.00
Parlor Set, Louis XV, Carved Rosettes, Damask Covered, 5 Piece 1700.00
Parlor Set, Rococo Revival, Scrolls, Rosewood, C.1850, 6 Piece 4400.00
Pedestal, American, Marble Top, Ebonized, C.1865, 42 1/4 In., Pair 850.00
Pedestal, Louis XVI, Bronze-Mounted, Mahogany, 43 1/2 In., Pair 2000.00
Pedestal, Marble Top, Inlaid Brass, Mahogany, C.1900, 48 1/4 In. 225.00
Pedestal, Marble, Fluted Column, Molded Top, Green, 42 3/4 In., Pair 400.00
Pedestal, 2-Tier Form, Ormolu-Mounted Marble Top, Walnut, 34 In. 275.00
Pew, Carved Ends, Golden Oak, 16 Ft. 175.00
Pew, Church, Oak, Small 190.00
Pie Safe, Gallery, Turned Legs 300.00
Pie Safe, Poplar, Screen Panels, Brown Paint, 49 X 53 In. 95.00
Pie Safe, Tins Dated 1883, Sevier County, Tennessee, Cherry 650.00
Pie Safe, 12 Tins Of Stars & Hearts, Pine 645.00
Plant Stand, Heart Design, C.1870 .... 385.00
Plant Stand, Wicker 250.00
Planter, Baskets On Scrolling Feet, Cast Iron, C.1850, 37 In. 400.00
Plate Stand, Mahogany, 3 Folding Tiers, C.1890, 36 In. 110.00
Pool Table, B.Collander, Bird's-Eye Maple & Walnut, C.1885, 9 Ft. 4500.00

Furniture, Pool Table, Brunswick, Inlaid Rosewood, C.1885

Pool Table, Brunswick, Inlaid Mahogany, C.1885, 9 Ft. 5000.00
Pool Table, Brunswick, Inlaid Rosewood, C.1885 .... *Illus* 4500.00
Pool Table, Brunswick, Pearl & Holly Inlay, Mahogany, C.1920 .... 5000.00
Pool Table, Brunswick, Quartered Oak, C.1890, 4 X 8 Ft. 6000.00
Potty Chair, American, Early 19th Century .... *Illus* 770.00
Rack, Boot, Mahogany, English, 24 X 38 In. 95.00
Rack, Drying, Tripod Base, 5 Slats, Shaker, 19th Century, 57 In. 275.00
Rack, Drying, Wall, 11 Bars Retract Under Shelf, Pine, 27 1/2 In. 60.00
Rack, Drying, 5 Frames, Shaker, Cherry & Walnut, Closed, 78 In. 150.00
Rack, Game, Scalloped Base, 7 Wrought-Iron Hooks 90.00
Rack, Hat, Portraits Of Women On 3 Brass Hooks, Walnut 50.00
Rack, Magazine, Hanging, Wicker, 1800s 65.00
Rack, Magazine, Walnut, Carved Bear 135.00
Rack, Music, Victorian, Walnut, Lyre Style 275.00
Rack, Quilt, 3 Section, Folding, Wooden Hinges, 29 X 60 In. 175.00
Recamier, C.1855, J.H.Belter, Laminated Rosewood, 39 In., Pair 9000.00
Recamier, Pierced Carved Grapevine, 19th Century .... *Illus* 1100.00
Rocker, Arrow Back, Bamboo Turnings, 3-Slat Back 90.00
Rocker, Arrow Back, Comb Back 750.00
Rocker, Back & Seat Cushions, Bluebird Print, Child's, Wicker 125.00
Rocker, Bentwood, Cane Backrest & Seat, C.1900 .... 550.00
Rocker, Boston, Black Paint, C.1830 .... 125.00
Rocker, Boston, Original Paint & Stenciling 195.00
Rocker, Boston, Turned Legs, Scrolled Seat & Arms, Blue Green 50.00
Rocker, Bow Back, Saddle Seat 700.00

Furniture, Potty Chair, American, Early 19th Century

Furniture, Recamier, Pierced Carved Grapevine, 19th Century

Rocker, Brother Gregory, Arms, Shaker	475.00
Rocker, Brother Gregory, Shaker	375.00
Rocker, Carved Mahogany ....*Illus*	350.00
Rocker, Child's, Bentwood, Adirondack Style, 20 X 18 X 14 In.	50.00
Rocker, Child's, Boston, Original Red, Signed A.N.Britan	95.00
Rocker, Child's, Hitchcock, Original Condition	295.00
Rocker, Child's, Oak, Spindles, Turned Legs & Arms	135.00
Rocker, Child's, Pressed Back, Spindles, Turned Arms & Legs, Oak	135.00
Rocker, Child's, Slatted Back & Seat, Shaker Style, Dated 1878	150.00
Rocker, Child's, Victorian, Wicker Back, Reel Spindles	30.00
Rocker, Child's, Windsor, Red, Green, & Yellow Paint, C.1830	500.00
Rocker, Chrome Yellow Paint, Shaker	8000.00
Rocker, Church Design, Birds, Yellow, Rosewood Ground	1540.00
Rocker, Horizontal Slats, G.Stickley, C.1910, Oak, 32 In.	250.00
Rocker, Inset Green Velvet Seat, Curly Maple	895.00
Rocker, Ladder Back, Groveland, Shaker	375.00
Rocker, Ladder Back, Pennsylvania, Old Black Paint Over Red	325.00
Rocker, Ladder Back, Shaker Decal, Mt.Lebanon, 34 3/4 In.	225.00
Rocker, Ladder Back, Shawl Bar, Shaker, 19th Century, 33 1/2 In.	375.00
Rocker, Ladder Back, Tape Seat, Shaker, 19th Century, 40 In.	650.00
Rocker, Lady's, Flat Back, Rush Seat, G.Stickley, 1910	225.00
Rocker, Leather Seat & Back Rest, Steer Horn ....*Illus*	1200.00
Rocker, Mission, Oak	65.00
Rocker, No.3, Shaker, Brown Finish, Red & Black Tape Seat, Label	400.00
Rocker, Oak, Spindles, Pressed Back, C.1910	185.00

Furniture, Rocker, Carved Mahogany

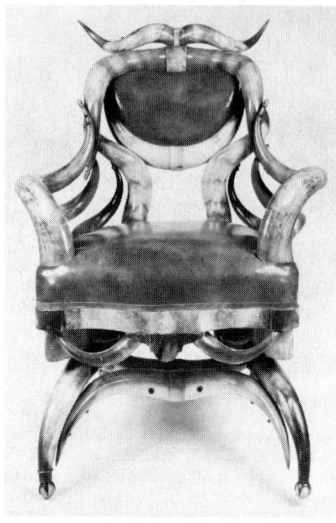

(See Page 255)

Furniture, Rocker, Leather Seat
& Back Rest, Steer Horn

Rocker, Oak, Tooled Leather Back 35.00
Rocker, Original Brown Paint, Green Decoration 1200.00
Rocker, Platform, Carved Rail, Padded Headrest, Hunzinger, C.1883 .... 275.00
Rocker, Platform, Walnut, Turned, Renaissance, C.1885 .... 400.00
Rocker, Pressed-Back, Spindles, Leather Seat, Oak 195.00
Rocker, Red & Black Graining, Yellow Floral Design 285.00
Rocker, Rolled Arm, Platform, Wicker 400.00
Rocker, Salem, Crest, 7 Spindles, Bamboo Legs, Yellow 375.00
Rocker, Salem, Crest, 7 Spindles, Curved Seat, 41 In. 100.00
Rocker, Salem, Decorated & Grained, 41 In. 100.00
Rocker, Shaker, No.4, Shawl Bar, 33 In. 150.00
Rocker, Shaker, Taped Back & Seat, Turned Finials, 34 In. 175.00
Rocker, Shaker, 7 Spindle Back, Taped Seat, 34 1/2 In. 150.00
Rocker, Side, Shaker, No.3, Acorn Finial, Arched Slats 550.00
Rocker, Spindled Sides, Stickley, Oak, Armless, C.1906, 36 1/4 In. 1200.00
Rocker, Steer Horn, Upholstered In Green Hide, C.1860 .... 1200.00
Rocker, Tape Back, Finials, Arms, Shaker 525.00
Rocker, Tape Seat, Shakers Trademark, Carved, Painted ....*Illus* 500.00
Rocker, Tape Seat, 3 Slat Back, Shaker, Red Stain, C.1860, 36 In. 300.00
Rocker, Tape Seat, 4 Slat Back, Shaker, 18th Century, 45 In. 1000.00
Rocker, Thonet Bros., C.1900, Bentwood ....*Illus* 550.00
Rocker, Vertical Post Back, Rush Seat, Shaker, Cherry, 37 1/2 In. 325.00
Rocker, Victorian, C.1890, Wicker 225.00
Rocker, Victorian, Hunzinger, Upholstered, Walnut, C.1880 .... 165.00
Rocker, Victorian, Wicker 595.00
Rocker, Wicker, White With Bluebird Print On Seat & Back 125.00
Rocker, Windsor, Comb Back 800.00
Rocker, Windsor, Rod Back, Whale-Shaped Arms, Red Paint 225.00
Rocker, Windsor, Rod Back, Whale-Shaped Arms, Red Paint 225.00
Rocker, 5 Slat, John Ware, South Jersey 750.00
Salon Set, Josef Hoffmann, C.1904, Bentwood, 6 Piece ....*Illus* 5000.00
Schrank, Carved Clothes Pegs, Original Red Brown Paint, Poplar 695.00
Screen, Coromandel, 4-Panel, 19th Century, 1 Ft. 3 3/4 In. 1600.00
Screen, Folding, Leather 300.00
Screen, Japanese, 3-Panel, Landscape, Red Lacquer Border, 48 In. 400.00
Screen, Monkeys, 6-Fold, Japanese, Panel 1 Ft. 11 1/2 In., Pair 5000.00
Screen, Pole, Needlepoint, Adjustable, C.1850, Mahogany, 54 In. 200.00

Furniture, Rocker, Tape Seat, Shakers
Trademark, Carved, Painted

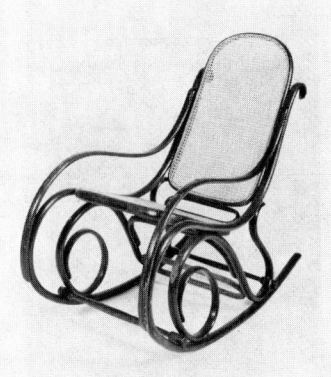

Furniture, Rocker, Thonet Bros.,
C.1900, Bentwood

Furniture, Salon Set, Josef Hoffmann, C.1904, Bentwood

Screen, 2-Fold, Red Lacquer Ground, Teakwood & Ivory, 58 In.	550.00
Screen, 3-Fold, Art Nouveau, Glass & Bentwood	Illus 3000.00
Screen, 4-Panel, Lacquer	350.00
Screen, 12-Panel, Palace, Birds & Flowers, On Reverse	Illus 8000.00
Secretary Bookcase, Top Glazed Doors, Mahogany, 7 Ft. 7 In.	4200.00
Secretary Bookcase, 3 Drawer, Mahogany, C.1790, 7 Ft. 8 In.	3630.00
Secretary Breakfront, Inlaid Drawers, Mahogany, C.1790	8500.00
Secretary Breakfront, 4 Glazed Doors, Mahogany, 60 X 90 In.	4250.00
Secretary Cabinet, Mirrored Doors, Satinwood, 2 Part, 5 Ft. 5 In.	8250.00
Secretary, Austrian, C.1810, Bronze Mounts, Walnut, 42 In. X 6 Ft.	4000.00
Secretary, Austrian, Fall-Front, 19th Century, Walnut, 4 3/4 Ft.	1800.00
Secretary, Block-Front, Chippendale Style, Mahogany, 86 In.	1100.00
Secretary, Butler's, Boston, Mahogany, C.1930, 38 X 75 1/2 In.	535.00
Secretary, Butler's, Pull-Down Drawer Front, Walnut, C.1865, 91 In.	1150.00
Secretary, Chinese Export, Black Lacquer, 4 Ft. 5 In.	1600.00
Secretary, Chippendale, Pennsylvania	4850.00
Secretary, Empire Mahogany, Figured Maple, C.1825, 6 Ft.	2100.00
Secretary, Fall-Front, Mahogany, C.1810, 4 Ft.8 1/2 In.	1400.00
Secretary, Federal American, Mahogany	Illus 4000.00

Furniture, Screen, 3-Fold, Art Nouveau,
Glass & Bentwood *(See Page 257)*

Furniture, Screen, 12-Panel, Palace, Birds & Flowers, On Reverse *(See Page 257)*

Furniture, Secretary, Federal
American, Mahogany

(See Page 257)

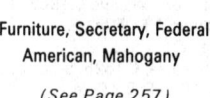

Secretary, German Neoclassical, Fall-Front, Mahogany, 5 Ft. 1 In. 1000.00
Secretary, Glass Door In Upper Section, Walnut & Ash, 2 Piece 750.00
Secretary, Hepplewhite, Blind Doors, Inlaid Medallions, Walnut 1000.00
Secretary, Hepplewhite, Inlaid, Cherry, 18th Century 7500.00
Secretary, Leather Inset, Mahogany, C.1800, 31 1/2 X 45 1/2 In. 7700.00
Secretary, Mahogany & Bird's-Eye Maple, C.1815, 40 X 64 1/2 In. 1805.00
Secretary, Marble Top, Fall-Front, 40 1/2 X 45 1/2 In. 4250.00
Secretary, New England, 19th Century, 2-Part, Mahogany, 46 In. 1300.00
Secretary, Wedgwood Plaques, Mahogany, C.1880, 4 Ft.1 In. 2000.00
Server, Empire, Splashboard, 2 Shelves, Mahogany, 56 X 47 1/2 In. 275.00
Server, 3 Drawer, Plate Rail, Mission Oak, C.1910, 44 In. 550.00
Settee, American, Carved Mahogany, 19th Century, 6 Ft.3 In. 1000.00
Settee, American, Shaped Arms, 19th Century, 6 Ft.5 In. 3000.00
Settee, Aubusson Tapestry Cover, Painted, 19th Century, 5 1/3 Ft. 4000.00
Settee, Beechwood, George I, Three Cushions, Pad Feet, 76 In. 2600.00
Settee, Bentwood, Trefoil Back, Paned Panels, C.1900, 5 Ft. 725.00
Settee, Caned Back, Ebony, 3 Cushion, Vase Legs, 25 In. 100.00
Settee, Crest Rail, Plank Seat, Scrolled Arms, 33 X 72 In. 200.00
Settee, Curved Crest, Walnut Arms, Serpentine Seat, 67 In. 350.00
Settee, Eastlake, Carved, Pierced Back, 63 In. 175.00
Settee, Eastlake, Walnut, Carved, Red Upholstery 130.00
Settee, Fruitwood, Ecole De Nancy, Cane Seat, C.1900, 46 In. 335.00
Settee, Garden, C.1800, Reeded Frame, Open Backrest & Arms, 40 In. 2650.00
Settee, Georgian Style, Mahogany, C.1900 .... 700.00
Settee, Hepplewhite Style, Mahogany, Camelback, C.1900, 70 In. 400.00
Settee, Italian Empire, C.1820, Inlaid Walnut, 5 1/2 Ft. 1500.00
Settee, Italian, Neoclassical, Painted, Parcel Gilt, 5 Ft. 605.00
Settee, Mahogany, George III, Arched Back, Square Legs, 72 In. 3520.00
Settee, Oak & Walnut, Paneled Back, Shallow Hood 400.00
Settee, Pickled Rosewood, Rococo, Arched Back, C.1855, 84 In. 9000.00
Settee, Rolled Arm, Wicker 500.00
Settee, Serpentine Crest, Padded Arms, American, Walnut, 60 In. 325.00
Settee, Serpentine, Upholstered, Mahogany, C.1780, Ft. 6 1/2 In. 3300.00
Settee, U-Shaped Back, Horseshoe Stretched, J.Hoffmann, 47 In. 1100.00
Settee, Upholstered Seat, Back, Biedermeier, Fruitwood, 5 1/2 Ft. 1100.00
Settee, 3-Chairback, Windsor, C.1770, Yew & Elmwood, 5 Ft. 7 In. 9900.00
Settle, Gustav Stickley, C.1910, Upholstered Seat .... *Illus* 2200.00
Settle, L. & J.G.Stickley, Marked, Oak, C.1910, 6 Ft. 1050.00
Settle, Paneled Backrest, C.1740, Oak, 5 1/2 Ft. 950.00
Settle, Pine & Walnut 800.00
Settle, V-Back, C.1910, Leather Seat, G.Stickley, Mark, 47 3/4 In. 2200.00
Settle, Windsor, Bent Arrow Back, C.1810, Red Brown Finish, 6 Ft. 1075.00
Settle, 1 Horizontal Slat Back, C.1910, Mission Oak, 6 1/2 Ft. - 2400.00

Furniture, Settle, Gustav Stickley, C.1910, Upholstered Seat

Sewing Stand, Mahogany & Veneered, Federal, 2 Drawer, 17 In. 250.00
Sewing Stand, 2 Drawer, Tiger Maple 275.00
Sewing Stand, 2-Tier, Shaker, Walnut, Wooden Pull, 1880, 7 In.Wide 135.00
Shaving Stand, Art Deco, Beveled Mirror 350.00
Shaving Stand, Dresser Top, Drawer 180.00
Shaving Stand, Triple Folding Mirror, Bamboo 450.00
Shaving Stand, Victorian, Adjustable Height, Oak 475.00
Shelf, Gallery Top, Carved Medallions, C.1880, Walnut, 60 X 29 In. 250.00
Shelf, Hanging, Canted, Dark Brown, 24 X 26 In. 350.00
Shelf, Hanging, Pine, Rectangular, 3 Shelves, Shaker, 21 X 15 In. 550.00
Shelf, Pine, Shaker, 3 Shelves, Rectangular Feet, 30 In. 220.00
Sideboard Secretary, Alexander Danner, 1833, Signed, Cherry, 6 Ft. 7000.00
Sideboard, American, Curly Maple, 19th Century, 4 Ft. 1 1/2 In. 400.00
Sideboard, Bow Front, C.1790, Inlaid Mahogany, 6 Ft. X 38 In. 3650.00
Sideboard, Bow Front, Mahogany, George III, 6 Ft. 4 In. 950.00
Sideboard, Carved Crest, Center Lion Head, C.1900, Oak, 99 In. 115.00
Sideboard, Cellaret Drawer, Marquetry Mahogany, 6 Ft. X 36 In. 3575.00
Sideboard, Chippendale, Hand-Cut Dovetailing, Oak 495.00
Sideboard, Country, 7 Dovetailed Drawers, Ball Feet, C.1820, Pine 950.00
Sideboard, Eastlake, Cherry, Basket Weave Panels, C.1875, 75 In. 650.00
Sideboard, Etched Beveled Mirror, Original Brass, Walnut 1265.00
Sideboard, Federal, Inlaid Mahogany, 4 Drawer, C.1790, 41 In. 5500.00
Sideboard, Federal, Mahogany, Kidney Shaped, C.1790, 38 In. 2000.00
Sideboard, French Victorian, 1860, Signed 2000.00
Sideboard, Hepplewhite, Flower Inlays, C.1800 .... 2700.00
Sideboard, Hepplewhite, Serpentine Inlays 4500.00
Sideboard, J. & J.W.Meeks, Marble Top, Oak, C.1855, 5 Ft. X 36 In. 850.00
Sideboard, Mahogany, Chippendale, 39 3/4 X 55 X 19 In. 180.00
Sideboard, Mahogany, Concave Front, 2 Sliding Doors, 44 In. 500.00
Sideboard, Mahogany, Empire, C.1835, 54 X 66 In. 400.00
Sideboard, Mahogany, Federal Style, Inlaid, Bow Front, 37 In. 675.00
Sideboard, Mahogany, Federal, Backsplash, Cupboard, Paw Feet 650.00
Sideboard, Oak, Hunter, Ornate Animal Covering Allover 4000.00
Sideboard, Oak, On Legs, Original Mirror, 54 X 42 X 18 In. 150.00
Sideboard, Oval Beveled Mirror, English, Burl Walnut 480.00
Sideboard, Regency, Mahogany, Lion Handles, C.1800, 45 In. 2700.00
Sideboard, Renaissance Revival, Carved Lion's Heads, 1880s 1895.00
Sideboard, Serpentine-Fronted, Mahogany, 4 Ft. X 34 1/2 In. 1750.00
Sideboard, Server, Tiger Oak, Carved Fruit, Flowers, Beveled Mirror 1800.00
Sideboard, Sheraton, American Cherry, C.1810 .... 4800.00
Sideboard, Sheraton, Mahogany, Fluted Legs, Bow Front, 66 1/2 In. 350.00
Sideboard, Variegated Marble Shelf, Austrian, Walnut, 40 X 94 In. 2900.00
Sideboard, Victorian, Brown Marble Top, Walnut With Burl Veneer 1250.00
Sideboard, Victorian, Walnut, Marble Top, 48 X 36 In. 225.00
Sideboard, Walnut, Renaissance, C.1865, 7 Ft. 9 In. X 6 Ft. 2000.00
Sideboard, Walnut, 2 Shelves, Marble Top, C.1880, 90 X 48 In. 400.00
Sideboard, 4 Drawer, Mission Oak, C.1910, 4 1/2 Ft. X 37 In. 475.00
Sofa, American Rococo, Rosewood, C.1855, 6 Ft. 10 In. 2250.00
Sofa, Beaded Frame, Upholstered, Gilt Wood, C.1780, 6 Ft. 2 In. 1870.00
Sofa, Birch, Country, Crest Rail, C.1830, 40 In. 300.00
Sofa, Carved Basket Of Fruit Crest, Walnut, C.1860, 80 In. 200.00
Sofa, Carved Mahogany, Federal, Salem, C.1800, 75 1/2 In. 3000.00
Sofa, Carved Rosewood, France, 19th Century, 75 In. 650.00
Sofa, Child's, 18th Century, Red Upholstery 1200.00
Sofa, Country, Birch, Canada, Crest Rail, C.1830, 40 X 71 In. 200.00
Sofa, Eastlake, Herter Bros., Inlaid Rosewood, C.1880, 6 Ft. 2 In. 4000.00
Sofa, Eastlake, Tufted Back, Center Leg, Inlay Design 4000.00
Sofa, Empire, Carved, Winged Paw Carved Feet, Mahogany, 60 In. 525.00
Sofa, Empire, Ogee Feet, Mahogany, C.1840, 85 In. 625.00
Sofa, Federal, Mahogany, Crest Rail, Turned Feet, C.1825, 72 In. 550.00
Sofa, Federal, Square Back, Mahogany, C.1790, 32 1/2 In. Wide 550.00
Sofa, Finger Carved, Walnut, Yellow Velvet 350.00
Sofa, Fruitwood, Hand-Carved, Italian Provincial, Louis XVI 1400.00

Sofa, Gold Leaf, Queen Anne, Louis XIV 1300.00
Sofa, Louis XV, Petit Point, 19th Century, Walnut, 78 In. 1400.00
Sofa, Mahogany, Empire, Carved, C.1840, 88 In. 475.00
Sofa, Mahogany, Empire, Leaf Carved Panels, Paw Casters, 7 Ft. 600.00
Sofa, Mahogany, Sheraton, Bow Front, Reeded Arm, 56 In. 500.00
Sofa, New York, Padded Armrests, Mahogany, C.1815, 7 1/2 Ft. 1300.00
Sofa, Renaissance Revival, Finger Carved, Walnut, 68 In. 300.00
Sofa, Rose & Grape Carved Crest, Medallion Back, Walnut, 70 In. 550.00
Sofa, Sheraton, Arched Crest Rail, Mahogany, 84 In. 1400.00
Sofa, Tete-A-Tete, Upholstered, Carved, Mahogany, 1890, 54 X 26 In. 385.00
Sofa, Upholstered, Wicker 400.00
Sofa, Victorian, Hand-Carved Roses 1500.00
Sofa, Victorian, Mahogany, C.1840, 78 In. 550.00
Sofa, Victorian, Mahogany, Yellow Upholstery, C.1840 .... 120.00
Sofa, Wicker, Upholstered 400.00
Spinning Wheel, Flax, By Samuel Ring 275.00
Stand, Abalone Shell Top, China, Teak & Marble, 20 1/4 In. 250.00
Stand, Acanthus & Rope Carved Turned Legs, 2 Drawer, Brass Pulls 600.00
Stand, American Rococo, 3-Tier, Rosewood, C.1850, 35 3/4 In. 1000.00
Stand, Beaded Edge, Pierced Skirt, Teak, Marble, C.1890, 33 1/2 In. 200.00
Stand, Birch, Turned Legs, Drawer, Board Top, 28 In. 75.00
Stand, Burl Veneer & Walnut, 3-Tier, C.1870, 39 1/2 In. 375.00
Stand, Cherry, 2 Drawer, Drop Leaf 170.00
Stand, Dovetailed Drawer, Pine 375.00
Stand, Economite, Original Rose-Carved Pulls 1600.00
Stand, French Renaissance, Bronze, C.1885, 36 1/2 In. 1300.00
Stand, Gadrooned Border, China, Teak & Marble, C.1880, 35 In. 200.00
Stand, Gadrooned Edge, Marble Top, China, C.1880, 23 1/2 In., Pair 400.00
Stand, Inlaid Mahogany, 3-Tier, Carved Oak Leaves, 39 In. 3000.00
Stand, Marble Top, Cabriole Legs, China, Teak, C.1880, 33 In. 375.00
Stand, Marble Top, Demon Face Legs, China, Teak, C.1900, 36 In. 225.00
Stand, Marble Top, Pierced Apron, China, Teak, C.1910, 31 3/4 In. 100.00
Stand, Old Red Paint, Softwood 295.00
Stand, Renaissance Revival, Oval Top, Walnut, C.1870, 21 1/2 In. 225.00
Stand, Round, Ornate, Wicker 350.00
Stand, Scrolled Legs, Marble Top, C.1870, Walnut, 28 1/2 In. 100.00
Stand, Taper Leg, 1 Drawer, 2 Piece Top, Maple & Cherry, 24 In. 950.00
Stand, Tiger Maple, Federal, 1795, Serpentine Top, 29 In. 1300.00
Stand, Turned Legs, Drawer, Board Top, Red Paint, 28 In. 225.00
Stool, Carved & Painted Pine, Shaker, Red, 19th Century 225.00
Stool, Chair, Desk, Northern Italian Rococo, Painted & Caned 2300.00
Stool, Mahogany, Victorian, Needlepoint Seat, C.1870, 18 In. 85.00
Stool, Mortised, Pine 65.00
Stool, Needlepoint Cover, French, Gilt Wood, 9 1/2 In. 70.00
Stool, Organ, High Back 279.00
Stool, Organ, Walnut, Renaissance Revival, C.1870, 20 In. 50.00
Stool, Organ, Wood, Swivel, Square Upholstered Seat 25.00
Stool, Piano, Adjustable, Black Walnut 112.00
Stool, Piano, Adjustable, Brass Claw With Ball Feet, Walnut 70.00
Stool, Piano, Claw Feet 85.00
Stool, Piano, Italian, C.1885, Revolving, Walnut 4500.00
Stool, Piano, New York, C.1830, Needlework Seat, Mahogany 550.00
Stool, Pine, Rectangular, Peg Legs, Red, Black, 7 In. 412.00
Stool, Rails, Silk Upholstered, Green-Painted & Gilt Wood, C.1790 .... 150.00
Stool, Soda Fountain, Iron Base 23.00
Stool, Walnut, Carolingian, Needlepoint Top, 17 X 21 In. 200.00
Stool, William IV, X-Form, Carved Leaf & Scroll, Rosewood, 21 In. 2420.00
Table & Chair, Plywood, Isokon, Ebonized Legs, Set Of 4 Chairs 2800.00
Table, Acanthus Carved Post, Boston, C.1910, Mahogany, 30 In. 150.00
Table, American Rococo, C.1855, Marble Top, Cherry, 29 1/4 In. 1300.00
Table, American Rococo, Marble Top, C.1845, Walnut, 32 1/2 In. 700.00
Table, American, C.1935, Aluminum & Glass .... *Illus* 1320.00
Table, Architect's, Walnut, Trestle Base, English, 28 In. 1100.00

Furniture, Table, American, C.1935, Aluminum & Glass

(See Page 261)

Table, Bamboo Turned Legs, Single Board Pine Top	975.00
Table, Banquet, Mahogany, Empire, Oval, C.1900, 29 X 62 In.	475.00
Table, Bedside, Walnut, Louis XVI, Provincial, 28 1/2 In.	522.00
Table, Berkey & Gay, C.1870, Walnut & Burl Walnut, 29 In.	500.00
Table, Billiard, Phelan & Collender, Cues, Counters, 9 Ft.	4000.00
Table, Blackjack, Claw Feet, 1890s	1800.00
Table, Bouillotte, Louis XVI, Marble Top, Mahogany, 28 1/4 In.	200.00
Table, Bow Front, Molded Frieze, C.1830, Mahogany, 36 In.	1200.00
Table, Breakfast, Drop Leaf, Mahogany, Victorian, 26 X 23 In.	325.00
Table, Breakfast, George III, Mahogany, 4 Ft. 10 In. X 29 In.	1760.00
Table, Breakfast, Tilt Top, C.1780, Mahogany, 4 1/2 Ft.	1450.00
Table, Breakfast, Tilt Top, Inlaid Mahogany, 5 Ft. 1/2 In.	3600.00
Table, Breakfast, Tilt Top, Regency, Mahogany, 46 X 59 In.	300.00
Table, Bronze-Mounted, Rosewood Marquetry, C.1865, 47 X 29 In.	900.00
Table, Butler's, Mahogany, Oval Handle, Burlap Straps, 37 In.	425.00
Table, Card, Brass Rosettes, Mahogany, C.1825, 34 1/4 X 30 1/2 In.	200.00
Table, Card, Console, Mahogany, Hepplewhite, 30 X 17 X 33 In.	675.00
Table, Card, Empire, Lyre Pedestal, Mahogany, 34 X 29 1/2 In.	140.00
Table, Card, Empire, Mahogany, C.1830, 36 X 29 3/4 In.	180.00
Table, Card, Greco-Roman Revival, Mahogany, 29 In.	500.00
Table, Card, Mahogany & Figured Birch, Federal, C.1790, 29 In.	9500.00
Table, Card, Mahogany, Federal, Beaded Edge, 29 In.	550.00
Table, Card, Mahogany, Federal, Folding Top, 29 X 17 In.	600.00
Table, Card, Mahogany, Federal, Reeded Legs, C.1790, 36 1/2 In.	1700.00
Table, Card, Mahogany, Inlaid, Federal, Hidden Drawers, 28 In.	1600.00
Table, Card, Maryland, Hinged Top, Mahogany, C.1790, 28 1/2 In.	600.00
Table, Card, Maryland, Hinged Top, Mahogany, C.1800, 29 1/2 In.	2700.00
Table, Card, Pennsylvania, Mahogany, 2 Part, C.1790	1150.00
Table, Card, Pine, D-Shaped, Square Legs, Green, Yellow, 30 In.	6600.00
Table, Card, Rosewood, William IV, C-Scroll Feet, C.1835, 30 In.	300.00
Table, Card, Serpentine Front, Lyre Base, Pennsylvania	450.00
Table, Card, Sheraton, Flip Top, Inlaid Apron, Mahogany, 36 X 30 In.	225.00
Table, Card, Sheraton, Reeded Legs, Bird's-Eye Maple Panels	950.00
Table, Card, Sheraton, Reeded Legs, Pennsylvania, C.1800, Mahogany	595.00
Table, Card, Tilt Top, Salem Area, Acanthus-Carved, Mahogany	650.00
Table, Card, 1 Drawer, Birch & Bird's-Eye Maple	960.00
Table, Carved Dragon Heads On Legs, 29 1/2 X 35 In.Diam.	400.00
Table, Carved Leaf Design, 1 Leaf, Round, Oak	650.00
Table, Carved Lotus Blossom & Lily Pad, China, C.1930, 26 In.	150.00
Table, Center Leg, Square, 5 Chairs, Eagle Claw Footed	1395.00

Table, Center, Adam Style, Oval, Spade Feet, 30 In. 225.00
Table, Center, Cloisonne & Green Onyx, Ormolu Mounted, 30 In. 1800.00
Table, Center, Dutch Marquetry, Oval Top, 30 X 36 In. 325.00
Table, Center, Fruitwood, Continental, Rococo, Stained, 28 In. 1650.00
Table, Center, Louis XV, Carved Flowers, Walnut, 29 1/2 In. 3250.00
Table, Center, Mahogany, Charles X, Tripod Base, C.1825, 30 In. 1430.00
Table, Center, Marble Top, Italian Neoclassical, 4 Ft. 3 In. 300.00
Table, Center, Marble Top, Mahogany, C.1840, 29 1/2 In. 1100.00
Table, Center, Oak, Marble Top, 20 X 29 In. 175.00
Table, Center, Oak, Provincial, Louis XV, 5 Ft. 4 In. X 29 In. 1750.00
Table, Center, Teakwood, Burmese, Round, Foo Dogs Base, 54 In. 1600.00
Table, Center, Walnut, Burl Walnut, English, 28 X 60 X 44 In. 1100.00
Table, Central Plaque, C.1910, Gilt Wood & Porcelain, 29 In. 4500.00
Table, Chess, Regency, Pen Work, River & Landscape Edge, 20 In. 1300.00
Table, Chippendale, Shaped Apron, Leaves, Cherry 950.00
Table, Coffee, Art Deco, Blue Mirror, 27 X 15 In. 60.00
Table, Coffee, Carved & Scrolled Marble Top, Turtleback 600.00
Table, Coffee, Drop Flap, Oval, Oak, 19 X 27 In. 80.00
Table, Concave Front, Bow Back, Mahogany, 1810, 36 In. 1870.00
Table, Conference, Drawers On Each Side, Blonde Oak 800.00
Table, Conference, Leather Surface, English, Mahogany, 96 X 30 In. 160.00
Table, Console, Demilune, Mahogany, 30 X 44 1/2 X 18 In. 90.00
Table, Console, Eagle Form Support, Gilt Wood, 38 X 29 1/2 In. 3850.00
Table, Console, George III, Parcel-Gilt Satinwood, C.1770, 40 In. 4250.00
Table, Console, Italian Rococo, Marble Top, Flower Heads, 35 In. 1760.00
Table, Console, Italian Rococo, Marble Top, 6 Ft. 10 In. 3500.00
Table, Console, Mahogany, Federal Style, Brass Feet 30.00
Table, Console, Marble Top, Mahogany, 48 1/2 X 33 1/2 In. 425.00
Table, Console, Marble Top, Ogee Carved Base, 39 In.Wide 550.00
Table, Console, Victorian, Iron, Serpentine Form, C.1840, 33 In. 2200.00
Table, Curio, Louis XV, Removable Top, Bronze Mounted, 40 In. 1400.00
Table, Curly Maple, Double Butterfly, William & Mary, 4 Ft. 2500.00
Table, Cushioned Frieze Drawer, Scarlet Japanned, 38 X 32 In. 8800.00
Table, Cutout Corners, Georgia Piedmont, C.1800, Walnut, 27 In. 450.00
Table, Demilune, Painted & Inlaid Satinwood, C.1790, 30 1/2 In. 990.00
Table, Desk, Pine, Drawer, Flowers, Leaves, Red, Black, 12 In. 2090.00
Table, Dining, Brass Paw Casters, Mahogany, 44 X 29 1/2 In. 4125.00
Table, Dining, Charles Rohlfs, Oak, 1901, 4 Ft.Diam. 7700.00
Table, Dining, Claw Feet, Oak, 48 In.Diam. 600.00
Table, Dining, Curved Corners, 2 Leaves, Mahogany, 59 X 28 7/8 In. 375.00
Table, Dining, Drop Leaf & Gate Leg, C.1800, Mahogany, 7 3/4 Ft. 1900.00
Table, Dining, Drop Leaf, Georgia Piedmont, Walnut, 48 X 29 In. 1200.00
Table, Dining, Drop Leaf, Grain Painted, C.1820, 43 In.Diam. 425.00
Table, Dining, Drop Leaf, Mahogany, C.1815, 61 X 30 In. 750.00
Table, Dining, Drop Leaf, Mahogany, Empire, C.1840, 29 X 38 In. 250.00
Table, Dining, Drop Leaf, Mahogany, Federal, C.1810, 28 In. 900.00
Table, Dining, Drop Leaf, Mahogany, Georgian, Pad Feet, 28 In. 500.00
Table, Dining, Duncan Phyfe, Mahogany, Overhanging, 42 X 108 In. 400.00
Table, Dining, Eastlake, 4 Leaves, Pedestal Base, 45 X 28 1/2 In. 275.00
Table, Dining, Extending, Circular, Mahogany, Regency, 48 In.Diam. 475.00
Table, Dining, G.Stickley, Label, Oak, C.1910, 4 1/2 Ft.Diam. 2200.00
Table, Dining, G.Stickley, 3 Leaves, Oak, C.1910, 4 Ft.Diam. 1200.00
Table, Dining, G.Stickley, 6 Leaves, Oak, C.1910, 4 1/2 Ft.Diam. 1775.00
Table, Dining, George III, 2 Pedestal, Mahogany, 7 1/2 Ft. Long 1320.00
Table, Dining, Mahogany, 2 Pedestal, George III, 28 In. 1300.00
Table, Dining, Sheraton, Drop Leaf, Rope Legs, 1825-40 .... 850.00
Table, Dining, Tilt Top, Regency, Mahogany, Saber Legs, 29 In. 350.00
Table, Dining, Victorian, Mahogany & Veneer, Round Top, 31 In. 275.00
Table, Dining, Victorian, 5 Leaves, Walnut 1300.00
Table, Dining, 2 Leaves, Mission Oak, C.1910, 4 1/2 Ft.Diam. 220.00
Table, Dining, 3 Pedestal, Mahogany, C.1820, Open 10 Ft. 8 In. 7500.00
Table, Dining, 5 Legs, 5 Leaves, G.Stickley, Oak, 48 In. 800.00
Table, Dining, 6 Leaves, G.Stickley, C.1910, Oak 2000.00

Furniture, Table, Dressing, Inlaid, Rosewood

Furniture, Table, Drop Leaf, G.Stickley,
Oak, Red Decal, 32 In.

Table, Dressing, Bow Front, Inlaid Mahogany, C.1800, 32 1/2 In. 1900.00
Table, Dressing, Cherry & Walnut, C.1840, 34 1/2 X 20 1/2 X 36 In. 450.00
Table, Dressing, Country, Grain Painted, C.1820 .... 225.00 To 275.00
Table, Dressing, Eastlake, Inlaid Oak, C.1870, 5 Ft. 3 1/2 In. 500.00
Table, Dressing, English, Painted Satinwood, C.1900, 5 Ft. 7 In. 2000.00
Table, Dressing, Federal, Grain Painted, Red, 34 X 29 In. 375.00
Table, Dressing, Federal, Mahogany, C.1830, 42 1/2 X 76 In. 475.00
Table, Dressing, Federal, Maple, Scrolled Backboard 700.00
Table, Dressing, Frieze Drawer, Carved, Walnut, 32 1/2 X 29 1/2 In. 1650.00
Table, Dressing, Frieze Drawer, Walnut, C.1740, 32 1/2 X 26 1/2 In. 1675.00
Table, Dressing, Gentleman's, Mahogany, George III, 31 In. 650.00
Table, Dressing, George II, 3 Drawer, Inlaid, Walnut, 28 In. 990.00
Table, Dressing, Gilt Drawer Pulls, C.1815, Yellow Paint 750.00
Table, Dressing, Inlaid Mahogany, C.1790, 32 X 31 In. 400.00
Table, Dressing, Inlaid, Rosewood .... *Illus* 650.00
Table, Dressing, Lift Top, Rosewood, C.1860, 24 1/2 X 17 1/2 In. 600.00
Table, Dressing, Long Drawer, 2 Smaller Drawers, Claw Feet 425.00
Table, Dressing, Maple, Federal, C.1800, Ring-Turned Columns 700.00
Table, Dressing, Pine & Poplar, Turned Legs, Drawer, 24 X 28 In. 135.00
Table, Dressing, Swing Mirror, Carved, Walnut, C.1880, 33 X 64 In. 300.00
Table, Dressing, 2 Drawer, Stripping, Painted Fruit Design 900.00
Table, Dressing, 3 Drawer, Inlaid Burr Walnut, 32 X 29 In. 2100.00
Table, Dressing, 3 Drawer, Red Graining, Pine Poplar, 34 1/2 In. 525.00
Table, Drop Leaf, Alfred Colony, Shaker, Curly Maple 3000.00
Table, Drop Leaf, Cherry, Drawer, Shaker, Square Legs, 29 X 39 In. 1540.00
Table, Drop Leaf, Cherry, Shaker, 1 Drawer, 36 X 29 In. 3000.00
Table, Drop Leaf, Empire, Mahogany, Clover Shape, C.1815, 29 In. 420.00
Table, Drop Leaf, Federal, Mahogany, Skirt Seat, Rope Legs, 28 In. 200.00
Table, Drop Leaf, G.Stickley, Oak, Red Decal, 32 In. .... *Illus* 1100.00
Table, Drop Leaf, George II, Mahogany, C.1750, 44 X 28 In. 550.00
Table, Drop Leaf, George II, Oval, Mahogany, C.1750, 29 In. 3100.00
Table, Drop Leaf, George III, Mahogany, Square Legs, 28 In. 225.00
Table, Drop Leaf, Hepplewhite, New England, Old Red Paint 1050.00
Table, Drop Leaf, Hinged Top, C.1750, Mahogany, 4 1/2 Ft. X 28 In. 990.00
Table, Drop Leaf, Mahogany, Chippendale Style, Swing Leg, 29 In. 400.00
Table, Drop Leaf, Mahogany, Empire, C.1840, Lyre Pillar, 27 In. 300.00
Table, Drop Leaf, Mahogany, Federal, C.1840, 28 X 36 In. 220.00
Table, Drop Leaf, Maple, 1700s, 39 X 42 In. 1500.00
Table, Drop Leaf, New England, Carved, Walnut, C.1780, 27 1/2 In. 400.00

Table, Drop Leaf, Oak, Queen Anne, Pad Feet, 27 X 58 In. 275.00
Table, Drop Leaf, Oval, Oak, C.1700, 18 1/2 X 28 In. 1200.00
Table, Drop Leaf, Pine, C.1860, 72 In. 500.00
Table, Drop Leaf, Pine, Federal, Red & Black, 4 Ft. 10 In. 1925.00
Table, Drop Leaf, Queen Anne, Maple, Duck Feet, 15 X 26 In. 2500.00
Table, Drop Leaf, Queen Anne, Walnut, Pennsylvania, 10 X 15 In. 300.00
Table, Drop Leaf, Reeded Legs, Mahogany, C.1930, 39 X 28 In. 200.00
Table, Drop Leaf, Shaker, Cherry, 36 X 29 In. 3000.00
Table, Drop Leaf, Tiger Maple, Dated 1876 .... 2500.00
Table, Drop Leaf, Turned Cherry Legs, Tiger Maple 750.00
Table, Drop Leaf, 2 Drawer, Cherry 195.00
Table, Drop Leaf, 2 Drawer, Lyre Trestle, Fruitwood, 41 X 30 In. 1500.00
Table, Drop Leaf, 2 Drawer, Walnut 200.00
Table, Drum, Mahogany, Regency, 4 Drawer, 38 3/4 In. 675.00
Table, Drum, Regency, 4 Drawer, Mahogany, C.1820, 47 1/2 In.Diam. 3080.00
Table, Drum, Revolving Top, Leather Top, Mahogany, 29 1/2 In. 3300.00
Table, Drum, Revolving Top, Mahogany, C.1820, 43 1/2 In.Diam. 1650.00
Table, Drum, 4 Frieze Drawers, Rosewood, C.1815, 4 Ft. 1/2 In. 4950.00
Table, Eastlake, Marble Top, Beveled Edge, 28 X 28 In. 125.00
Table, Eastlake, Oval Top, White Marble Top, 20 1/2 X 28 1/2 In. 225.00
Table, Empire, Black, Tan, & Gray Marble Top, Mahogany, 36 In.Diam. 425.00
Table, Empire, Faceted Frieze, Mahogany, C.1835, 36 3/4 X 30 In. 200.00
Table, Export, Oriental, Rose Design, Bamboo Legs, 19 In. 1500.00
Table, Farm Bench, Pine, 69 X 32 1/2 X 30 In. 190.00
Table, Farm, Lift-Off Top, 1 Drawer, Red Paint 145.00
Table, Farm, Queen Anne, 1 Drawer, Walnut 310.00
Table, Federal, Pembroke, Cherry, C.1790, 26 1/2 In. Wide 1400.00
Table, Flaming Birch, Swing Leg, Drop Leaf, C.1800, 52 In. 675.00
Table, Flip Top, Gate Leg, C.Baudoine, Rosewood, C.1850, 28 1/2 In. 1700.00
Table, Flip Top, Hunzinger Label, Mahogany, 30 X 26 In. 300.00
Table, Frank Lloyd Wright, Cypress & Laminated Wood, Pair .... *Illus* 880.00
Table, Frieze Drawer, C.1870, Marquetry, Rosewood, 42 X 44 1/2 In. 1400.00
Table, Game, Backgammon & Chess 1100.00
Table, Game, Baize-Lined Top, Inlaid, Mahogany, C.1790, Pair 9900.00
Table, Game, Chess Top, Sliding Backgammon Board, Painted 1200.00
Table, Game, Chessboard Surface, C.1825, Rosewood, 29 1/2 In. 1430.00
Table, Game, D-Shaped Top, C.1810, Inlaid Mahogany, 36 X 30 In. 2000.00
Table, Game, Empire, Fold-Over, Mahogany, 33 X 28 In. 140.00
Table, Game, Flip Top, Brass Casters, Satinwood, C.1790, 29 In. 5225.00
Table, Game, Flip Top, Carved Base, Walnut, C.1860, 36 X 28 In. 350.00
Table, Game, Flip Top, Mahogany, Empire, C.1840, 35 X 31 In. 350.00

Furniture, Table, Frank Lloyd Wright, Cypress & Laminated Wood, Pair

Table, Game, Flip Top, Mahogany, Empire, Serpentine Top, 29 In. 450.00
Table, Game, Flip Top, Marquetry, C.1898, 40 X 30 In. 1100.00
Table, Game, Hepplewhite Period, Mahogany, Wood Inlay, 36 In. 2800.00
Table, Game, Italian Neoclassical, Fruitwood, 31 X 37 In. 660.00
Table, Game, Leather Inset, C.1740, Mahogany, 35 1/2 X 28 1/2 In. 3000.00
Table, Game, Louis XVI, Mahogany, 2 Drawer, C.1820, 29 In. 1900.00
Table, Game, Mahogany, C.1790, 30 In. 175.00
Table, Game, Mahogany, Charles X, Concave Sides, 29 X 36 In. 385.00
Table, Game, Mahogany, Concertina Action, C.1770, 29 In. 800.00
Table, Game, Papier-Mache, Victorian, Chessboard Top, 28 In. 475.00
Table, Game, Portuguese, Walnut, Marble Top, 28 1/2 X 34 In. 3750.00
Table, Game, Semicircular, Inlaid Mahogany, C.1790, 36 X 29 In. 2450.00
Table, Game, Swivel, Mahogany, Inlaid, Edwardian, C.1900, 26 In. 600.00
Table, Game, Triple Top, Baize-Lined, Mahogany, C.1750, 34 X 29 In. 1675.00
Table, Gateleg, Drop Leaf, Country Sheraton, 46 X 29 In. 375.00
Table, Gateleg, Elizabethan Revival, Walnut, 48 X 33 1/2 X 28 In. 175.00
Table, Gateleg, Pine Top, Walnut 350.00
Table, Gateleg, William & Mary, Drop Leaves, 28 X 41 In. 500.00
Table, Gothic Revival, Rosewood, 27 X 22 1/2 In. 200.00
Table, Half-Round, New England, Pine 375.00
Table, Harvest, Federal, Painted, Drop Leaves, Red, 28 In. 2500.00
Table, Harvest, New England, Old Red Paint, 8 Ft. 3800.00
Table, Harvest, Pine, Sawbuck, Cross Legs, Red Paint, 30 In. 1800.00
Table, Harvest, Shaker, Pine & Birch, C.1820, 140 X 29 1/2 In. 900.00
Table, Hinged Top, Satinwood, 27 1/2 In., Pair 4675.00
Table, Hutch, Pine & Maple, Trestle Feet, Red, Yellow, 29 In. 1900.00
Table, Hutch, Tulip & Poplar Wood, Top 35 X 62 In. 650.00
Table, Hutch, 3-Board Top, Pine 1475.00
Table, Indian Style, Bone & Mother-Of-Pearl Inlaid, 33 In. 800.00
Table, Inlaid Daffodil Sprays, Marble Top, G.Homar, 49 X 14 In. 2000.00
Table, Italian Rococo, Lacquered, 31 X 43 In. 1045.00
Table, Kidney Shaped Top, Ball Finials, 27 X 17 In., Pair 300.00
Table, Kitchen, Drop Leaf, Pine 85.00
Table, L. & J.G.Stickley, Lower Shelf, Oak, C.1910, 24 X 29 In. 195.00
Table, Lamp, Elizabethan Revival, Mahogany, C.1850, 29 1/2 In. 175.00
Table, Lamp, Marble Top, Walnut, Renaissance Revival, C.1870 .... 200.00
Table, Lazy Susan, Country Pine, Turned Legs, 36 In. 500.00
Table, Leather Inset Top, 3 Drawer, Burr Walnut, 5 Ft. 10 In. 8000.00
Table, Leon Marcotte, Rosewood & Curly Maple, C.1870, 28 3/4 In. 1200.00
Table, Library, Eastlake, Herter Bros., Mahogany, C.1880, 5 1/2 Ft. 800.00
Table, Library, Eastlake, Reeded Legs, Floral Design, 23 X 30 In. 100.00
Table, Library, Lions, Carved Lion Legs, C.1880 .... 750.00
Table, Library, Mahogany, C.1840, 51 3/4 X 28 1/4 In. 225.00
Table, Library, Mahogany, 3 Drawer, Trestle Base, 30 In. 900.00
Table, Library, Satinwood & Rosewood, C.1865, 4 Ft. 3 In.Long 900.00
Table, Library, Walnut, Renaissance Revival, 2 Drawer, 30 In. 1050.00
Table, Library, 3 Drawer, G.Stickley, Oak, C.1910, 54 In. 1000.00
Table, Library, 4 Carved Lions, C.1880, Mahogany 780.00
Table, Loo, Columns, English, Walnut, 1860, 46 1/2 X 29 1/2 In. 300.00
Table, Louis XV, Fruitwood, Cabriole Legs, 19 In. 275.00
Table, Louis XV, Ormolu & Alabaster, 19th Century, 30 In. 900.00
Table, Louis XV, 2-Tier, Bronze-Mounted Kingwood, 36 In.Diam. 3500.00
Table, Louis XVI, Marble Top, Gilt-Metal Mounted, 30 X 22 In. 275.00
Table, Louis XVI, Tulipwood Marquetry, 26 1/4 In. 1000.00
Table, Low, Walnut, Victorian, Inlaid, 29 X 48 In. 650.00
Table, Mahogany, Bowed Sides, Ormolu Pulls, 31 In. 2500.00
Table, Mahogany, George III, Tapered Legs, C.1780, 28 In. 100.00
Table, Mahogany, 2-Tier, Butterflies, Signed Galle, 15 In. 1400.00
Table, Mandarin, Mahogany, Carved Top, Inlaid Eyes In Birds, 32 In. 2500.00
Table, Maple & Pine, Hutch, Square Legs, 30 In. 1800.00
Table, Marble Top, American Rococo, Walnut, C.1845, 32 1/2 In. 1200.00
Table, Marble Top, Carved, 4-Footed, Oval, Walnut 2200.00
Table, Marble Top, Gilt Wood Side, Regency, Baluster Legs, 44 In. 1200.00

Table, Marble Top, Mahogany, C.1740, 4 Ft. 5 1/4 In. X 35 In. 7700.00
Table, Marble Top, Marquetry Frieze Apron, 46 X 29 1/2 In. 1350.00
Table, Marble Top, Victorian, Walnut, Carved Skirt, 30 In. 200.00
Table, Marble Top, Walnut, Victorian, Molded Legs, 29 In. 275.00
Table, Marquetry, Demilune, C.1800, 30 X 24 In. 1600.00
Table, Marquetry, Fruitwood, Galle, Landscape, C.1900, Signed 1100.00
Table, Mother-Of-Pearl Inlaid, Moroccan Ebonized, 29 X 30 In. 225.00
Table, Napoleon III, Rosettes & C-Scrolls, Onyx & Brass, 31 In. 1800.00
Table, Nest Of 4, Carved Tops, Bamboo Edge & Legs, Ash, 26 1/2 In. 175.00
Table, Nest, Bamboo Supports, Mahogany, C.1815, 28 1/2 In., Set Of 3 .... 825.00
Table, Never Painted Poplar Top, Gray Blue Painted Body 545.00
Table, Night, Burl Satinwood, Ebene De Macassar, 23 In. 550.00
Table, Onyx, Gilt Metal, Victorian, 31 X 15 X 15 In. 80.00
Table, Oval Top, Maple, New Hampshire, C.1740 .... 6000.00
Table, Pastry, Drop Leaf & Gateleg, Pine, 40 1/2 X 28 1/2 In. 260.00
Table, Pedestal, Carved, Marble Top 800.00
Table, Pedestal, Claw Feet, Oak, 48 In.Diam. 600.00
Table, Pedestal, Hinged Top, 2 Drawer, Rosewood, C.1820, 30 In. 2300.00
Table, Pedestal, Oriental, Carved, Marble Insert, 34 1/2 In. 775.00
Table, Pembroke, Bow Front Drawer, Mahogany, C.1790, 28 1/2 In. 1080.00
Table, Pembroke, Cut Corners, Cherry, C.1810 .... 735.00
Table, Pembroke, Demilune Leaves, Mahogany, C.1940, 17 1/2 In. 275.00
Table, Pembroke, Ebony Inlaid, Elmwood, C.1810, 28 1/2 In. 8250.00
Table, Pembroke, Federal, Mahogany, Drop Leaf, C.1795, 29 In. 400.00
Table, Pembroke, Frieze Drawer, Mahogany, C.1780, 25 X 28 In. 605.00
Table, Pembroke, Frieze Drawer, Mahogany, C.1790, 18 X 28 1/2 In. 1540.00
Table, Pembroke, Frieze Drawer, Oval, Inlaid Satinwood, 30 In. 2100.00
Table, Pembroke, George III, Shaped Flaps, Mahogany, 28 1/2 In. 1980.00
Table, Pembroke, Inlaid, Mahogany, C.1790, 30 X 28 In. 1450.00
Table, Pembroke, Mahogany, C.1790, 28 1/2 X 28 1/2 In. 2850.00
Table, Pembroke, Mahogany, Deep End Drawers, 28 In. 350.00
Table, Pembroke, Mahogany, Federal, Drop Leaf, 29 In. 400.00
Table, Pembroke, Mahogany, George III, C.1800, 29 In. 450.00
Table, Pembroke, Pennsylvania, Mahogany, C.1775, 28 3/4 In. 2200.00
Table, Pembroke, Philadelphia, Walnut, C.1770, 28 1/4 In. 1800.00
Table, Pembroke, Turned Feet, Cherry, C.1810, 38 X 29 1/2 In. 475.00
Table, Pier, Mahogany, Chippendale, Salem, Claw Feet, C.1760, 26 In. 4500.00
Table, Pier, Marble Top, Philadelphia, Mahogany, C.1820, 41 In. 900.00
Table, Pietra Dura, Ebonized, Eastlake, Geometric Inlaid, 26 In. 350.00
Table, Pine, 1 Drawer, Shaker, New York, 19th Century, 28 X 37 In. 2300.00
Table, Pool, Brunswick, Slate Bed, 4 1/2 X 9 Ft. 2000.00
Table, Pool, Quarter Cut Oak, Victorian 3000.00
Table, Poudre, French, Inlaid 525.00
Table, Pub, Cast Iron 395.00
Table, Queen Anne, Birdcage, Snake Foot, Mahogany, 33 1/2 In.Diam. 900.00
Table, Queen Anne, Pennsylvania, Walnut 3400.00
Table, Raised Platform On Paw Feet, C.1880, 24 X 29 In. 80.00
Table, Refectory, Oak, Ribbed Edge, Trestle Top Base, 26 In. 1000.00
Table, Refectory, Oak, Shoe Feet, Rectangular Top, 33 In. 2000.00
Table, Refectory, Pine, Continental, Block Feet, 9 Ft. 2860.00
Table, Regency, Octagonal Top, C.1880, 29 In., Nest Of 4 .... 650.00
Table, Regency, Octagonal Top, Stenciled, C.1810, 18 X 28 In. 600.00
Table, Repousse Design, Indian, Silvered, 15 X 8 In., Pair 900.00
Table, Rope Legs, Cherry, 29 1/2 X 17 In.Square 90.00
Table, Rosewood & Marquetry Inlaid, C.1870, 29 X 29 1/2 In. 1000.00
Table, Rosewood & Satinwood, Napoleon III, 4 Ft. 5 In. 3250.00
Table, Rosewood, Octagonal, Victorian, C.1840, 30 In. 175.00
Table, Sawbuck, Birch & Pine, Cape Cod, 27 X 36 In. 275.00
Table, Sawbuck, Pine, Cross Legs, 24 In. 325.00
Table, Serpent Carved Legs, 19th Century, 22 X 30 1/2 In. 200.00
Table, Serving, Bow Front, 2 Drawer, C.1815, Mahogany, 60 X 42 In. 950.00
Table, Serving, Drop Leaf, Mahogany, Empire, 27 1/2 X 17 1/2 In. 110.00
Table, Sewing, American Empire, Drop Leaf, Mahogany, C.1830, 29 In. 225.00

Table, Sewing, American, Flaps, Inlaid Mahogany, C.1830, 33 1/4 In. 1700.00
Table, Sewing, Birch, Federal, Square Legs, C.1800, 27 In. 400.00
Table, Sewing, Bird's-Eye Maple Panels, Mahogany 450.00
Table, Sewing, Bow Front, Regency, Mahogany, Medial Drawers 900.00
Table, Sewing, Drop Leaf, Empire, Mahogany, C.1840, 37 X 29 1/2 In. 300.00
Table, Sewing, Drop Leaf, Walnut, 2 Drawer, Spool Turned Legs 135.00
Table, Sewing, Drop Leaf, 2 Drawer, C.1840, 36 1/2 X 28 1/2 In. 275.00
Table, Sewing, Empire, American, 19th Century, Mahogany, 28 1/4 In. 225.00
Table, Sewing, Empire, Drop Leaf, Mahogany, C.1835, 20 X 29 In. 200.00
Table, Sewing, Federal, Mahogany, Salem, 1 Drawer, C.1800, 28 In. 2200.00
Table, Sewing, Federal, 1 Drawer, Birch, C.1840, 17 1/2 X 27 1/2 In. 150.00
Table, Sewing, Federal, 1 Drawer, Cherry, C.1840, 18 X 28 3/4 In. 175.00
Table, Sewing, Folding Legs, Oak 69.00
Table, Sewing, Folding, Maple 85.00
Table, Sewing, George III, Mahogany, C.1780, 21 X 29 In. 600.00
Table, Sewing, Hinged Top, 2 Compartments, Mahogany, C.1800, 29 In. 950.00
Table, Sewing, Lift Top, Bamboo, Wicker, & Rattan, C.1885, 29 1/2 In. 175.00
Table, Sewing, Mahogany, Federal, Carved Leaves, C.1790, 30 In. 7000.00
Table, Sewing, Mahogany, Federal, Octagonal Top, C.1805, 30 In. 5750.00
Table, Sewing, Mahogany, Satinwood, Federal, Salem, C.1800, 29 In. 5250.00
Table, Sewing, Papier-Mache, Mother-Of-Pearl Inlaid, 29 X 28 In. 450.00
Table, Sewing, R.Pierce, Drop Leaf, Mahogany, C.1830, 29 In. 1100.00
Table, Sewing, Regency, Mahogany, Work Basket, C.1830, 28 X 32 In. 300.00
Table, Sewing, Ring-Turned Legs, Mahogany, 19th Century, 28 1/4 In. 300.00
Table, Sewing, Rosewood, Victorian, Lyre Supports, C.1850, 31 In. 325.00
Table, Sewing, Shaker, Cherry & Pine, C.1800, 21 X 20 In. 225.00
Table, Sewing, Shaker, Pine Top, Maple Base, 2 Drawer, 91 In.Long 3600.00
Table, Sewing, Shenandoah Valley, Fluted Legs 695.00
Table, Sewing, Walnut & Ebonized, Renaissance Revival, 30 In. 225.00
Table, Sewing, Walnut, Neoclassical, Continental, 28 In. 350.00
Table, Sewing, Walnut, Rococo Revival, 1 Drawer, Curved Legs, 29 In. 200.00
Table, Sewing, 2 Drawer, North Family, Pine & Maple ....*Illus* 5000.00
Table, Single Drawer, Square Legs, Maple, 26 X 19 In. 180.00
Table, Sofa, Hinged Top, Brass Casters, Mahogany, 1820, 28 1/2 In. 3300.00
Table, Sofa, Regency, Hinged Top, Inlaid Rosewood, 36 X 28 In. 2530.00
Table, Splay-Legged, Tiger Maple 1850.00
Table, Spool Turned, 24 X 18 In. 45.00
Table, Steel, Black Lacquer & Chromed, C.1930, 30 In. 900.00
Table, Step-Down, Grain Painted, C.1830, 30 X 37 In. 550.00
Table, Tavern, Cast-Iron Pedestal Base, Oak, 42 In.Diam. 150.00
Table, Tavern, H-Stretcher, Cherry, 40 X 62 X 28 In. 650.00

Furniture, Table, Sewing, 2 Drawer, North Family, Pine & Maple

Furniture, Table, Tilt Top, English,
Mahogany, 29 1/2 In.Diam.

Table, Tavern, Maple & Pine, Queen Anne, 26 X 24 In. 950.00
Table, Tavern, Pine & Maple, William & Mary, 24 1/2 In. 900.00
Table, Tavern, Provincial Oak, Ring Legs, Beaded Top, 22 In. 125.00
Table, Tavern, Queen Anne, Maple, Square Skirt, 1 Drawer, 27 In. 800.00
Table, Tavern, Stretcher Base, C.1800, Walnut 1500.00
Table, Tavern, William & Mary, Maple & Pine, 25 X 31 In. 1450.00
Table, Tavern, 2-Board Top, Brown Paint, Hardwood 135.00
Table, Tavern, 4 Turned Legs, 42 X 29 In. 300.00
Table, Tea, Articulated, 2-Tier, Mahogany, 29 X 17 In. 1600.00
Table, Tea, Carved Birdcage Support, Connecticut, Cherry 4500.00
Table, Tea, Chippendale, Cabriole Legs, Spade Foot 2850.00
Table, Tea, Dish Top, Mahogany, George III, 27 X 23 In. 275.00
Table, Tea, F.Linke, Ormolu-Mounted Mahogany, C.1880, 37 In. 2200.00
Table, Tea, Fireside, Collapsible, Doubles As Fire Screen 75.00
Table, Tea, Folding, Kingwood, & Mahogany, Louis XV, 29 X 37 In. 1800.00
Table, Tea, Gallery, Drawer Each End, Mahogany, 30 1/2 In. 140.00
Table, Tea, Piecrust, Chippendale, Mahogany, 1760-80, 29 In. 5500.00
Table, Tea, Queen Anne, Drop Leaf Top, Oval, Cherry 1900.00
Table, Tea, Tilt Top, Chippendale, Piecrust, Pennsylvania, C.1770 .... 3400.00
Table, Tea, Tilt Top, Mahogany, Massachusetts, C.1760, 28 In. 6500.00
Table, Tea, Tilt Top, Pennsylvania, Mahogany, C.1760, 27 1/4 In. 300.00
Table, Tea, Tilt Top, Pennsylvania, Walnut, C.1770, 28 1/2 In. 2000.00
Table, Tea, Tilt Top, Snake Feet, Rhode Island, C.1740, 26 In.Diam. 795.00
Table, Tea, 2-Tier, Emile Galle, Signed, Mahogany, 30 1/2 In. 2000.00
Table, Tiered, C.1900, Brass Inlaid Rosewood, 22 3/4 In. 120.00
Table, Tilt Top, Carved, Mahogany, C.1750, 30 1/2 X 28 1/2 In. 4400.00
Table, Tilt Top, Chippendale, Mahogany, C.1930, 30 X 29 1/2 In. 350.00
Table, Tilt Top, Chippendale, Mahogany, Snake Feet, 28 X 26 In. 850.00
Table, Tilt Top, English Piecrust, Mahogany, 29 X 28 In. 575.00
Table, Tilt Top, English, Mahogany, 29 1/2 In.Diam. .... *Illus* 725.00
Table, Tilt Top, Marquetry, 19th Century 335.00
Table, Tilt Top, New Hampshire, Oval, Spider Legs 525.00
Table, Tilt Top, Piecrust, Mahogany, George III, 28 1/2 In. 300.00
Table, Tilt Top, Revolving, Pennsylvania, Walnut, C.1760, 30 In. 4750.00
Table, Tilt Top, Tripod Base, Mahogany, 31 1/2 X 30 In. 225.00
Table, Tilt Top, Tripod, Mahogany, C.1750, 42 X 29 1/2 In. 2640.00
Table, Tilt Top, Walnut, Tripod Base, Slipper Feet, 27 In. 350.00
Table, Tilt Top, 18th Century, Inlaid Mahogany, 29 1/2 In. 350.00
Table, Tilt Top, 19th Century, Inlaid Mahogany, 41 In.Diam. 350.00
Table, Trestle, Baroque, Continental, Trestle Feet, 31 In. 950.00
Table, Trestle, Wooden Top, Cast Iron, 58 X 30 1/4 In. 700.00
Table, Tripod, Leather Top, Federal Style, 3 Footed Columns 95.00
Table, Tripod, Octagonal Top, Carved, Mahogany, 26 In. 1600.00
Table, Tripod, Tilt Top, Carved Mahogany, C.1755, 29 1/2 In. 2640.00
Table, Tripod, Tilt Top, Mahogany, Pad Feet, C.1770, 28 In. 475.00

Furniture, Table, Writing, Victorian, English, Burr Walnut

Table, Turned Legs, Washboard White Top, Maple, C.1865, 6 X 4 Ft.	250.00
Table, Turned Spool Supports, Scroll Feet, Mahogany, 29 In.	150.00
Table, Victorian, Bamboo & Oak, 21 X 30 1/4 In.	250.00
Table, Victorian, Mahogany, Leaf Design, 29 In.	375.00
Table, Victorian, Marble Top, Curved	600.00
Table, Victorian, Marble Top, Walnut, C.1860, 34 X 27 1/2 In.	450.00
Table, Victorian, Marble Top, Walnut, C.1870, 31 1/2 X 27 1/2 In.	300.00
Table, Victorian, Walnut, Marble Top, 20 X 25 In.	190.00
Table, Victorian, White Marble Top, Carved Railing, Walnut	225.00
Table, Walnut & Burl, Renaissance Revival, C.1870, 31 In.	400.00
Table, Walnut, George II, Pad Feet, C.1730, 26 In.	1900.00
Table, Walnut, William & Mary, Serpentine Top, 30 In.	450.00
Table, Wine, Hinged Horseshoe-Shaped Top, C.1830, 29 In.	6000.00
Table, Writing, Art Deco, C.1930, Burled Walnut & Fruitwood, 29 In.	500.00
Table, Writing, Brass-Bound Mahogany, C.1810, 42 1/2 X 30 1/2 In.	2500.00
Table, Writing, Bronze-Mounted Thuyawood, C.1880, 41 1/2 In.	1600.00
Table, Writing, Drawer, Oval, Mahogany, C.1890, 36 X 29 In.	900.00
Table, Writing, English, Burr Walnut	8000.00
Table, Writing, Frieze Drawer, C.1800, Inlaid Mahogany, 33 In.	4400.00
Table, Writing, Leather Inset, Frieze Drawers, Mahogany, 31 1/2 In.	2750.00
Table, Writing, Leather Surface, 5-Drawer, C.1860, 47 X 30 In.	850.00
Table, Writing, Leather Top, Frieze Drawers, Mahogany, 31 1/2 In.	2750.00
Table, Writing, Napoleon III, Brass Inlaid, Ebonized, 31 In.	900.00
Table, Writing, Victorian, English, Burr Walnut	*Illus* 8000.00
Table, Writing, 3-Tier, Mahogany, C.1830, 32 1/2 X 46 In.	1100.00
Table, 1-Drawer, New York, Shaker, Pine, 28 X 37 In.	*Illus* 2300.00

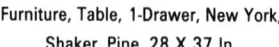

Furniture, Table, 1-Drawer, New York,
Shaker, Pine, 28 X 37 In.

Table, 2 Frieze Drawers, 17th Century, Oak, 40 X 31 1/2 In. 495.00
Table, 2-Tier, Fruitwood, Butterflies, Galle, Signed, 28 In. 2100.00
Table, 2-Tier, G.Stickley, Red Decal, Oak, C.1910, 24 X 29 In. 330.00
Table, 4 Frieze Drawers, Carved, English, Oak, 30 1/2 X 51 In.Diam. 550.00
Tables, Nesting, Marquetry, Galle, Blossoms, Signed, C.1900 .... 990.00
Tabouret, Mother-Of-Pearl, Bone Inlaid, Moorish Design, 19 In. 150.00
Tea Caddy, George III, Brass, Geometric Border, Paw Feet, 4 In. 80.00
Tea Cart, Glass Top, Walnut, Tray 250.00
Towel Stand, Turned Supports, Walnut 50.00
Tray, Butler's, Folding Stand, Mahogany, 38 3/4 X 23 In. 475.00
Tray, C.1900, Mother-Of-Pearl Inlaid Teakwood, 13 1/2 X 41 In. 70.00
Tray, Fruitwood, Marquetry, Landscape, Galle, Signed, C.1900, 19 In. 1325.00
Tray, George III, C.1790, Oval, Mahogany, 26 1/2 In. 440.00
Tray, George III, Mounted On Tripod Table, C.1870, 28 1/2 In. 600.00
Tray, Kidney-Shaped, Mahogany, Inlaid, George III, 23 In. 125.00
Tray, Mahogany, Edwardian, C.1900, Brass Handles, 26 In. 260.00
Tray, Tea, Inlaid Mahogany, Burl Maple, Rosewood, 14 In. 550.00
Tray, Victorian, Mahogany & Beadwork, C.1870, 25 X 13 In. 150.00
Trolley, 3-Tier, Fluted Finials, English, Mahogany, 47 X 40 In. 375.00
Trundle Seat, Serpentine Shape Frame, Mahogany, 46 X 29 1/2 In. 300.00
Trunk, Bone Top, Yellow & Black, Red Ground, 22 X 12 X 12 In. 375.00
Umbrella Stand, Bronze Handle, C.1870, Ebonized Walnut, 44 In. 2200.00
Umbrella Stand, C.1910, Oak, 32 In. 275.00
Umbrella Stand, Cast Iron, English 220.00
Umbrella Stand, Tapering, G.Stickley, Oak, C.1910, 33 In. 165.00
Urn Stand, French, Marble Top, Mahogany, C.1880, 4 Ft. 700.00
Urn Stand, George III, Galleried Top, Mahogany, 27 In. 2300.00
Urn Stand, Scalloped Gallery, Satinwood, C.1900, 22 In. 550.00
Urn, Knife, Regency, C.1840, English, Hardwood, 25 In., Pair 1000.00
Urn, Mahogany, Victorian, C.1840, 23 1/2 In. 1400.00
Valet Stand, Mahogany, 47 In. 25.00
Valise Stand, Mahogany, Victorian, C.1900 .... 60.00
Vitrine, Glazed Door, Bronze-Mounted Mahogany, 5 Ft. 4 In. 4000.00
Wardrobe, Brandon, Wisconsin, Germanic 1350.00
Wardrobe, Eastlake, Walnut 400.00
Wardrobe, Federal, Flared Cornice, C.1815, Mahogany, 54 X 80 In. 2000.00
Wardrobe, Knockdown, Fan Finial, Walnut, Burl Veneer, 24 X 97 In. 900.00
Wardrobe, Triple, Mahogany, Gothic Design, Maple Interior 700.00
Wardrobe, Victorian, Carved, American, Oak, 7 Ft. High 500.00
Wash Bench, Rounded Bootjack Ends, Pine 75.00
Washstand, Corner, Mahogany, 19th Century, 39 X 43 In. 200.00
Washstand, Country Empire, Black & Red Graining, Stenciled Fruit 350.00
Washstand, Country Sheraton, Original Paint 495.00
Washstand, Empire, Convex Drawer, Mahogany, C.1840, 22 X 33 In. 125.00
Washstand, Empire, Serpentine Marble, Mahogany, C.1845, 29 In. 180.00
Washstand, Federal, Mahogany, 1 Drawer, C.1810, 34 X 20 In. 150.00
Washstand, French, Walnut, Marble Top, Sink, Plumbing, 48 X 35 In. 1200.00
Washstand, Mahogany, Empire, 36 X 35 X 17 1/2 In. 240.00
Washstand, Mahogany, George III, Pewter Basin, 21 In. 750.00
Washstand, Marble Top & Backsplash, Mahogany, 31 1/2 In. 250.00
Washstand, Marble Top, Walnut 350.00
Washstand, Marble Top, Walnut, C.1870, 38 X 30 X 16 In. 300.00
Washstand, Marble Top, 1 Drawer, Mahogany, C.1840, 30 1/2 In. 200.00
Washstand, New England, 19th Century, Painted & Grained, 39 In. 100.00
Washstand, Victorian, Wood, 2 Drawers, 1 Door, 32 X 29 In. 150.00
Washstand, Walnut, Matched Pair 600.00
Washstand, 1 Drawer, Towel Rods, Pine 95.00
Whatnot, American Southwest, 4 Tier, Horn & Wood, 27 1/2 X 55 In. 200.00
Whatnot, Corner, Walnut, Victorian, 6 Shelves 130.00
Whatnot, Corner, 6 Graduated Shelves, Walnut, 72 In. 200.00
Window Seat, Mahogany, C.1770, Scrolled Ends, 4 Ft. 9 In. 800.00
Window Seat, Mahogany, George III, Stuffed Seat, Square Legs 700.00

G-ARGY-
ROUSSEAU

Gabriel Argy-Rousseau, born in 1885, was a French glass artist
who produced a variety of objects in Art Deco style. His mark,
G. Argy-Rousseau, was usually impressed.

G.ARGY-ROUSSEAU, Ashtray, Flower Form, Tiered, Pate-De-Verre, Signed 1200.00
  Beatles Pin Tray, Pate-De-Verre 950.00
  Lamp, Swirls, Band, & Triangles, Blue, Signed, 7 1/2 In. 2900.00
  Vase, Purple Streaked, Pate-De-Verre, C.1925, 8 5/8 In. 1000.00

Galle glass was made by the Galle factory founded in 1874 by Emile
Galle of France. The firm made cameo glass, furniture, and other
Art Nouveau items, including some pottery. After Galle's
death in 1904, the firm continued in production until 1935.

GALLE POTTERY, Planter, Egyptian Scenes, C.1890, Signed, 14 1/2 X 4 1/2 In. 1200.00
  Vase, Beetle & Lotus, 8 In. 675.00

GALLE, Bottle, Cologne, Dark To Light Burgundy, 4 1/4 In. 825.00
  Bottle, Perfume, Clusters Of Berries & Leaves, Signed, Amber, 4 3/4 In. 495.00
  Bottle, Scent, Aquatic Flowers, Silver Cover, Hallmarked, 5 1/4 In. 9200.00
  Bowl, Butterflies, Pale Green, Purple, & Lavender, Signed, 8 In.Diam. 525.00
  Bowl, Flower Form Top, 2 Cuttings, 4 Colors, Signed, 7 X 4 1/2 In. 1500.00
  Box, Amethyst To Frosted Ground, Dragonflies, Water Lilies, Signed 1000.00
  Box, Blue Tint, Amber Etched, Water Lilies, Dragonfly, Signed, 6 In. 1600.00
  Box, Covered, 2-Color, Lid & Base, Signed, 6 X 3 In. 775.00
  Chandelier, Bronze Mounted, Orange Tint, Chartreuse, Brown, 13 In. 1700.00
  Compote, Polished Flowers, Leaves, Pink, Green, Camphor, 8 1/2 X 4 In. 1350.00
  Decanter, Enameled Lily & Butterflies, Signed, Yellow, 10 1/2 In. 1800.00
  Dish, Landscape, Leaf Form, Lavender, Brown, River, Signed, 10 In. 825.00
  Egg, Dark Green Ferns, Light Green Background 1500.00
  Ewer, Etched Grapevines, Silver-Mounted Overlay, 11 1/2 In. 900.00
  Figurine, Cat, Blue, White, Yellow Ground, Glass Eyes, Marked, 13 In. 550.00
  Glass, Shot, Crystal & Enamel, Amber Ribbed Body, Signed, 1 3/4 In. 225.00
  Jar, Sea Creatures On Lid, Pottery, 1900, Signed, 4 X 8 In.Diam. 1500.00
  Lamp, Acid Cutback, Wheel Engravings, Yellow, Red, White, 17 In.Dome 3500.00
  Lamp, Blue & Pink, Matching Shade, Signed, 18 In. 2900.00
  Lamp, Clematis, Conical Shade, Trumpet -Shaped, Signed, 26 1/2 In. 7500.00
  Lamp, Domed Shade, Yellow, Sapphire, Purple, Brown, Signed, 15 In. 8000.00
  Lamp, Flowers & Stems, Topaz, Yellow, Peach, & Green, Signed, 4 X 14 In. 5000.00
  Lamp, Flowers, Mushroom Shade, Signed, 24 In. 9500.00
  Lamp, Leaves On Column, Bronze Mounted, Signed, 14 1/4 In. 3800.00
  Lamp, Marsh Marigolds & Dragonfly, Signed, Yellow Tinted, 21 In. 3500.00
  Lamp, Perfume, Cameo, Acorns, Leaves, 3 Cuttings, Bronze Base, 4 3/4 In. 1400.00
  Lamp, Swallows, Matching Shade, Signed, Double Overlay, 11 1/2 In. 2600.00
  Lamp, Table, Red Butterflies, Wrought Iron, Marble Base, 5 1/2 In. 1600.00
  Lamp, Topaz, Yellow, & Peach, Flowers, Signed, 14 X 7 In.Diam. 5000.00
  Nesting Tables, C.1900, Fruitwood Marquetry, 27 1/2 In. .... *Illus* 990.00
  Night-Light, Bleeding Hearts, Polished Red, Gold Ground, 5 In. 1350.00
  Tazza, Leaves & Strawberries, Swirled Stem, Signed, Yellow, 9 3/4 In. 3200.00
  Vase, Acorns & Leaves, Flask Shape, Green To Frosted, 5 1/4 In. 1050.00
  Vase, Allover Design, Carnelian, Signed, 14 1/4 In. 1875.00
  Vase, Amber Pinecones, Needles, Yellow, White, Brown Ground, 9 In. 650.00
  Vase, Amber Sides, Cornflowers, Blue, Signed, 6 3/4 In. 1775.00
  Vase, Avocado Sides, Spring Flowers, Raindrops, Signed, 4 In. 675.00
  Vase, Blown-Out Flowers, Purple & Blue, 6 1/2 In. .... *Illus* 3100.00
  Vase, Blown-Out Leaves, Stems, Pods, Yellow Ground, Signed, 9 1/2 In. 5500.00
  Vase, Blue & Gray, Oxblood, Vines, Signed, 13 In. 2500.00
  Vase, Brown Trees, Green Ground, Shaded To Pink, 9 1/2 In. 300.00
  Vase, Brown, Orange, & Rust, Signed, 5 1/4 In. 600.00
  Vase, Bud, Cameo, Flower Design, 6 In. 400.00
  Vase, Butterflies, Oviform, Signed, Martele Ground, 4 3/4 In. 2300.00
  Vase, Candlestick Shape, 3 Shades Of Brown Leaves, Signed, 4 1/2 In. 950.00

Galle, Nesting Tables, C.1900, Fruitwood Marquetry, 27 1/2 In.

Vase, Cascading Wisteria, Lavender Blossoms, Signed, 12 3/8 In. 3200.00
Vase, Cherries & Leaves, Apricot To Red Shading, Signed, 4 In. 600.00
Vase, Clematis, Oviform, Peach Ground, Violet, Blue, Signed, 6 In. 1600.00
Vase, Cut Purple Iris & Leaf Design, Signed, 16 In. 1500.00
Vase, Cylindrical, Burnt Orange Nasturtium, Signed, 23 1/4 In. 825.00
Vase, Cylindrical, Etched Algae, Seaweed, Starfish, Signed, 15 In. 1900.00
Vase, Dark Purple, Plum Base, Buttercups, Frosted Ground, 10 In. 825.00
Vase, Detailed Lakeside Landscape, 3-Color, 6 In. 1025.00
Vase, Enameled Anemones, Spherical, Signed, Green Ground, 8 In. 550.00
Vase, Etched Roses, Green Overlay, Signed, 6 1/2 In. 3200.00
Vase, Fire Polish, Cameo, Purple & Lavender, 3 Toe, 8 In. 645.00
Vase, Flask Form, Boughs Of Fuchsia, Double Overlay, Signed, 8 3/4 In. 1600.00
Vase, Flattened Ovoid, Hydrangea Blossoms, Signed, 1904-10, 8 In. 400.00
Vase, Flattened Tear Form, Teal Blue, Yellow, Signed, C.1900, 7 1/2 In. 650.00
Vase, Floral Carving, Pink & Orange, 4 In. 375.00
Vase, Floral, Frosted, Signed, Mauve To Clear, 4 In. 350.00
Vase, Flower Design, Purple, Signed, 9 1/2 In. 725.00
Vase, Flower Petals Over Surface, Double Overlay, Signed, 7 1/4 In. 2600.00
Vase, Gray Sides, Rose & Red Overlay, Signed, C.1900, 8 In. 1200.00
Vase, Gray-Blue Body, Golden Brown Pines, Signed, 11 In. 550.00
Vase, Gray, Cherry Red, Lotus Blossoms, Signed, 22 In. 3900.00
Vase, Gray, Green Neck, Brown, River Scene, Signed, 13 In. 1000.00
Vase, Gray, Purple, Iris Blossoms, Leaves, Signed, 5 1/4 In. 795.00
Vase, Gray, Rose & Olive Blossoms, Signed, 5 In. 775.00
Vase, Green & Brown Pine Stems & Blossoms, Frosted, Signed, 7 In. 675.00
Vase, Green Flowers & Leaves, Pink Frosted Ground, Signed, 17 1/4 In. 1950.00
Vase, Hibiscus, Flattened Oviform, Signed, Martele Ground, 5 In. 2200.00
Vase, Insect In Flight, Pink Overlay, Martele Ground, Signed, 5 1/4 In. 5500.00

Galle, Vase, Blown-Out Flowers, Purple & Blue, 6 1/2 In.

Vase, Iris, 2-Toned, Double-Lipped, Signed, White Ground, 8 1/4 In. 1400.00
Vase, Irises & Bee, Green & Amber Overlay, Speckled, Signed, 6 In. 3000.00
Vase, Landscape, Browns & Tones, Signed, 5 1/2 In. 750.00
Vase, Landscape, Yellow, Blue, Green, Brown, Lake Scene, Signed, 8 In. 2750.00
Vase, Landscape, Yellow, Gray, Blue, Purple, River, Signed, 14 In. 3000.00
Vase, Lavender Floral On White, Fire Polished Wet Look, 8 1/4 In. 725.00
Vase, Lavender Flowers & Leaves, Yellow Ground, 8 1/8 In. 575.00
Vase, Lavender Flowers, Yellow Ground, Signed, 4 In. 495.00
Vase, Lavender Leaves & Flowers, Yellow Ground, 8 1/2 In. 575.00
Vase, Lavender To Frosted, Peach Bottom, 13 In. 1125.00
Vase, Leaves & Gherkins, Balustered, Signed, Translucent, 7 1/4 In. 3400.00
Vase, Lemon Yellow, Primrose, Leafage, Signed, 8 3/4 In. 1650.00
Vase, Lilies, Pink & Crimson Overlay, Signed, Aquamarine Ground, 26 In. 2200.00
Vase, Magenta Cut To Clear, Fern, Grasshopper Design, Signed, 12 In. 850.00
Vase, Man Rowing Boat On Lake, Brown Foliage, 7 X 4 1/2 In. 1750.00
Vase, Marqueterie-De-Verre, Applied Blades Of Grass, Signed, 8 1/4 In. 9100.00
Vase, Mellow Casing, Cut Chinese Red Lilies, 13 1/4 In. 1900.00
Vase, Oak Leaves & Acorns, Tricolor Ground, 9 3/4 In. 1250.00
Vase, Orange Etched, Poppies, Signed, 13 1/4 In. 1700.00
Vase, Orange Ferns, 2 Acid Cuttings, Signed, 4 In. 389.00
Vase, Orange, Yellow, 5 In. 550.00
Vase, Orchids, Martele Ground, Double-Gourd Form, Signed, 6 1/2 In. 3500.00
Vase, Overlaid Seaweed, Sea Urchin, Jellyfish, Signed, 7 1/2 In. 6200.00
Vase, Overlay Colored Hydrangea Blossoms, Pink Ground, Signed, 3 In. 395.00
Vase, Oviform, Orange Ground, Brown Mums, Signed, 7 3/4 In. 1200.00
Vase, Oviform, Scarlet, Lavender, Leaves, Grasshopper, Signed, 2 In. 1450.00
Vase, Pale Rose, Flower & Leaves, Signed, 5 In. 800.00
Vase, Pedestal, Trumpet Shape, Jade Green, Paper Label, 9 1/4 In. 750.00
Vase, Pink Covered By Chartreuse, Blue Gray Ground, 9 1/2 In. 1750.00
Vase, Polished Berries & Leaves Allover, Gold & Orange, 13 In. 1150.00
Vase, Polished Flowers & Leaves, Gold Ground, 4 X 3 In. 750.00
Vase, Polished Flowers, Leaves, Blue Gray Background, Pink, 9 1/2 In. 1575.00
Vase, Purple & Yellow Leaves & Acorns, Signed, 2 1/2 In. 325.00
Vase, Purple Flowers, Signed, 4 3/4 In. 350.00
Vase, Purple Polished Hydrangeas, Leaves, Blue Background, 13 In. 1575.00
Vase, Purple, Green, White, 17 1/2 In. 1650.00
Vase, Raspberry, Rose Blossoms, Leafage, Signed, 17 In. 1775.00
Vase, Red & Yellow Flowers, 8 1/2 In. .... *Illus* 1725.00
Vase, Red & Yellow, Polished, 4 In. 650.00
Vase, Red Flowers, Yellow Ground, Rose Bowl Shape, Signed, 2 1/2 In. 375.00
Vase, Roses, Double Overlay, Signed, Yellow Ground, 14 3/4 In. 1800.00
Vase, Royal Blue, White & Blue Background, Signed, 7 In. 975.00
Vase, Rust Cut To Italian Yellow, 4 1/4 In. 350.00
Vase, Scenic, Pink & Brown, 5 1/2 In. .... *Illus* 1125.00
Vase, Scenic, 4 Color, 7 1/2 In. 1195.00
Vase, Shaded Brown Leaves, Candlestick Shape, Signed, Black, 4 1/2 In. 950.00
Vase, Spherical, Yellow Ground, Red, Crimson Etched, Signed, 4 In. 850.00
Vase, Sunflower Plants, Double-Gourd Form, Signed, 8 3/4 In. 2800.00
Vase, Sunflowers, Silver Foil Inclusions, Khaki Ground, 13 3/4 In. 4200.00
Vase, Water Lilies & Lily Pads, Green Ground, Signed, 8 1/4 In. 3200.00
Vase, Water Scene, Green Trees, Pink Ground, 19 In. 2750.00
Vase, Wild Rose, Yellow Ground, Blue & Purple Rosebuds, Signed, 9 In. 3000.00
Vase, Yellow Ground, Red, Pink & Maroon Flowers, Signed, 7 In. 1400.00
Vase, Yellow Ground, Sapphire Etched, Bellflowers, Signed, 10 In. 2200.00
Vase, Yellow Sides, Blue Overlaid, Berries, Signed, 10 In. 1100.00
Vase, Yellow Sides, Blue Sprays, Signed, 5 1/4 In. 1225.00
Vase, 3-Color Landscape, 6 In. 975.00

Game plates are any type of plate decorated with pictures of birds, animals, or fish. The game plates usually came in sets consisting of twelve dishes and a serving platter. These game plates were most popular during the 1880s.

GAME PLATE, Quail In Woods, C.1800, Gold Rim, Limoges, 12 In. 150.00
Rococo Gold, Scalloped & Embossed Border, 10 In. 50.00

Galle, Vase, Red & Yellow Flowers, 8 1/2 In.

Galle, Vase, Scenic, Pink & Brown, 5 1/2 In.

GAME, Alice, Parker Brothers	95.00
Anagrams, Dated 1934, Instructions	27.50
Annie Oakley, 1955	12.00
Authors, Milton Bradley, 1896, Boxed	18.00
Bagatelle, 1932	15.00
Barney Google & Spark Plug, King Features, 1923	48.00 To 80.00
Beatle Flip You Wig	55.00
Blondie & Dagwood, 1941, Original Box	18.00
Blondie Goes To Leisureland, Westinghouse	15.00
Board, Checkerboard & Parcheesi, Red On Natural, 17 In.Square	70.00
Brownie Auto Race Marble, Color Litho Tin, 10 1/2 In.	50.00
Camelot, 1930s, Parker Bros., Boxed	20.00
Card, Batman	8.00
Carpet Balls, Set Of 13	500.00
Checkerboard, Banner Lye	22.00
Checkerboard, Bittersweet & Slate Blue Squares, 1 Piece Wood	210.00
Checkerboard, C.1890, Gray White Ground, Round, 2 Piece	275.00
Checkerboard, Early 20th Century, Handmade, 20 X 18 In.	130.00
Checkerboard, Painted Squares, Mustard & Cream, 12 3/8 X 11 In.	125.00
Checkerboard, Reverse On Glass	65.00
Checkerboard, Yellow & Black Paint, Wooden	155.00
Checkers, Quaker Oats	10.00
Chess Set, Ivory, King 6 1/2 In., Pawn 3 1/2 In.	2500.00
Cock Robin, McLoughlin Bros., Boxed	5.00
Comic Conversation Cards, McLoughlin, Silhouettes	38.00
Cribbage Board, Original Cards & Ivory Sticks, Wooden, 3 1/2 X 5 In.	45.00
Croquet, Parlor, Bliss, Set	42.50
Crossword, Simplex Spelltray, 1924	25.00
Dick Tracy Detective, 1937, Chester Gould, Boxed	18.50
Dick Tracy Super Detective Mystery Card, Gould, 1941, Boxed	22.00
Dominoes, Elephants On Back, Set	10.00
Eddie Cantor, Tell It To The Judge	65.00
Electric Questioner, Knapp, 20 Assorted Cards	15.00
Felix, 1960	15.00
Fortune Telling, Parker Brothers	15.00
Get Smart, Time Bomb Game	15.00
Golf, Bing Crosby	35.00
Gunsmoke, 1958	10.00
Happy Hooligan, 1925	125.00
Hidden Titles, Parker Bros., Box & Directions	15.00
Howdy Doody, Card, Boxed	5.00
Howdy Doody, TV Game	35.00

I Spy, Board	12.00
I've Got A Secret, Garry Moore, 1950s	6.00
Jerome Park, Steeplechase, McLoughlin Bros.	55.00
Jigsaw Puzzle, Annie Oakley	5.00
Keno Goose	525.00
Komical Conversations	8.00
Land & Sea War, 1941, Boxed	15.00
Laws, Remington, 1910	5.00
Li'l Abner, Copyright 1946	25.00
Little Black Sambo	24.00
Lotto, Boxed, Germany, Instructions	5.00
Magic Dots For Little Tots, Milton Bradley, 1907, Boxed	15.00
Mah-Jong Set, Ivory Tiles, Wood Racks, Carrying Case	75.00
Neck & Neck, Horse Racing, Tin, Wolverine	45.00
Peggity, Parker Brown	6.00
Pit, Dated 1919, Germany, Instructions	5.00
Pit, Parker Brothers, 1919	8.00
Pitch-A-Ring, Lithograph On Lid, Milton Bradley, All Wood	20.00
Playtime, Ideal, Dated 1912	25.00
Poosh-M-Up, 5 Games In 1	25.00
Popeye Ring Toss, 1935	25.00
Puzzle Blocks, German, Lithographed Animals, 10 X 7 1/2 In.	30.00
Puzzle Book, Hood's Four-In-One, 1896, 4 3/4 X 7 In.	8.50
Puzzle, Block, C.1925, Wooden Box	32.00
Puzzle, Blondie, Dagwood, Wooden	19.00
Puzzle, Bringing Up Father, Box Of 4	20.00
Puzzle, Charlie McCarthy, Boxed	30.00
Puzzle, Chicago World's Fair Picture Jigsaw, 1933, 300 Pieces	12.00
Puzzle, Cisco Kid, 1960	8.00
Puzzle, Fire, McLoughlin	150.00
Puzzle, Hood's Sarsaparilla, Wedding In Catland	75.00
Puzzle, Hood's Sarsaparilla, 2-Sided, Dated 1891	200.00
Puzzle, Rainy Day, Hood's Sarsaparilla, Boxed	45.00
Puzzle, Uncle Wiggly, Boxed, 1939	10.00
Puzzle, United States, 1915, Parker Brothers	20.00
Radio Game, 1920s	18.00
Radio Questionaire, C.1928, Boxed	15.00
Ring Toss, Elf, Standing, Wooden, C.1920, 14 X 8 X 8 In.	25.00
Rook, Edition A, Parker Bros., Patented 1910	12.00
Round The World Fliers, Playing Board, 1922, Tin	28.00
Royal Jack Straws, Victorian Era, Wooden Straws, Colorful Lid	8.00
Scouting For Boy Scouts, Milton Bradley, 1920, Boxed	25.00
Solitaire, Marble, 19th Century	435.00
Space Target, 1950, Knickerbocker	50.00
Target, Windup, Wyandotte	65.00
The Fortune Teller, 1905, Color Litho Box, Milton Bradley	40.00
The Great American Baseball Hustler Toy Co.	25.00
Tiddly-Winks, Milton Bradley, 1932, Boxed	5.00
Tom Corbett Puzzle	68.00
Uncle Wiggly Board	26.00
Uncle Wiggly, 4 Metal Figures, 1949	15.00
Walter Johnson Baseball	135.00
Winky Dink Magic Kit	12.00
Winnie The Pooh, 1933	20.00

Gaudy Dutch pottery was made in England for America from about 1810 to 1820. It is a white earthenware with Imari style decorations of red, blue, green, yellow, and black. Only sixteen patterns of Gaudy Dutch were made: Butterfly, Carnation, Dahlia, Double Rose, Dove, Grape, Leaf, Oyster, Primrose, Single Rose, Strawflower, Sunflower, Urn, War Bonnet, Zinnia, and No Name. Other similar wares are called Soft Paste, Gaudy Ironstone, or Gaudy Welsh.

GAUDY DUTCH, Cup & Saucer, War Bonnet Pattern	500.00
Plate, Butterfly Pattern, C.1825, 7 3/8 In.	325.00
Plate, Carnation Pattern, C.1825, 7 1/2 In.	275.00
Plate, Carnation Pattern, 9 1/4 In. .....*Illus*	350.00
Saucer, Single Rose	125.00

Gaudy Dutch, Plate, Carnation Pattern,

9 1/4 In.

GAUDY IRONSTONE, Cup, Handleless, Luster Band, Cobalt Blue Trim	45.00
Dish, Vegetable, Indiana, Blue & Red Rim, 12 In.	45.00
Plate, Blackberry Pattern, 9 3/4 In.	86.00
Plate, Cup & Saucer, Cotton Plant	38.00
Plate, Indiana, Blue & Red Border, 10 In.	12.00
Plate, Urn Pattern, C.1840, 9 In.	95.00
Platter, Indiana, Blue & Red Rim, 14 1/2 In.	50.00

Gaudy Welsh is an Imari decorated earthenware with red, blue, green, and gold decorations. It was made after 1820.

GAUDY WELSH, Bowl, Oyster Pattern	48.00
Creamer, Oyster Pattern, Allerton	25.00
Creamer, Porcelain, 5 In.	45.00
Creamer, Tulip Design, 3 7/8 In.	60.00
Cup & Saucer, C.1840	75.00
Cup & Saucer, C.1850	55.00
Cup & Saucer, Columbia Pattern	55.00
Cup & Saucer, Wagon Wheel Pattern	60.00
Ginger Jar, Gold, Rust, & Cobalt Blue, Crossed Swords, 7 1/4 In.	75.00
Jug, Oyster Pattern, C.1820, Soft Paste, 5 3/4 In.	185.00
Jug, Pink Luster Rim, Encircling Fruit, Soft Paste, C.1800, 5 In.	95.00
Mug, Tulip Pattern, 2 1/2 In.	45.00
Pitcher, Milk, Wagon Wheel Pattern, 8 1/2 In.	125.00
Pitcher, Oyster Pattern, 3 1/4 In.	50.00
Pitcher, 4-Petal Blossoms, Segmented Handle, 5 1/2 In.	65.00
Plate, Decagonal, Flowers, Leaves, 9 1/2 In.	75.00
Plate, Wagon Wheel, 5 1/2 In.	32.00
Sugar & Creamer, Cake Plate, Lusterware, 6 Cups & Saucers	250.00
Tea Set, Columbine Pattern, C.1810, 17 Piece	475.00

GEISHA GIRL, Tea Set, 9 Piece	50.00

GENE AUTRY, Badge, Club	15.00
Boots, Rubber	58.00
Cap Pistol, Holster, Cast Iron	45.00

Charm, Gene, Champion, Original Card Dated 1946 .... 45.00
Cutouts, Cardboard 18.00
Galoshes, Boxed 35.00
Guitar, Boxed 50.00
Gun, Cap, Iron, 8 In. 36.00
Sign, Display, 9 X 12 In. 100.00

Black and blue decorated Gibson Girl plates were made in the early 1900s. Twenty-four different 10 1/2 inch plates were made by the Royal Doulton Pottery at Lambeth, England. These pictured scenes from the book "A Widow and Her Friends" by Charles Dana Gibson. Another set of twelve 9 inch plates featuring pictures of the heads of Gibson Girls had all blue decoration.

GIBSON GIRL, Pillow, Gold Velvet, Signed 55.00
Plate, A Message From The Outside World 65.00
Plate, Day After Arriving At Her Journey's End .... 65.00 To 80.00
Plate, Failing To Find Rest In Country 95.00
Plate, Fancy Dress Ball 65.00
Plate, Miss Babbles, The Authoress, Calls & Reads Aloud 65.00
Plate, Mr. Waddles Arrives Late, 10 1/2 In. 85.00
Plate, Mrs.Diggs Is Alarmed, 10 1/2 In. 85.00
Plate, She Contemplates The Cloister .... 65.00 To 85.00
Plate, She Decides To Die In Spite Of Dr.Bottles .... 65.00 To 85.00
Plate, She Finds Exercise Doesn't Improve Spirit .... 68.00 To 85.00
Plate, She Goes Into Colors 85.00
Plate, She Is Disturbed By A Vision .... 35.00 To 80.00
Plate, She Looks For Relief Among The Old Ones .... 50.00 To 85.00
Plate, Some Think She Has Remained In Retirement .... 65.00 To 85.00
Plate, They Go Fishing .... 65.00 To 88.00
Plate, They Take A Morning Run 85.00

GILLINDER

Gillinder pressed glass was first made by William T. Gillinder of Philadelphia in 1863. Many glass items were made for the Centennial.

GILLINDER, Bust, Lincoln, Dated 1876, Frosted 300.00
Bust, Washington, Frosted, Dated 1876 .... 300.00

GLASSES, Lorgnette, Carved Tortoiseshell, C.1880 .... 55.00
Lorgnette, Tortoiseshell & Sterling Silver 135.00

Porcelain has been made by three branches of the Goldscheider family. The family left Vienna in World War II and started factories in England and in Trenton, New Jersey.

GOLDSCHEIDER, Ashtray, Dutch Girl 30.00
Box, Head Of German Shepherd On Lid 65.00
Dish, Mermaid, Terra-Cotta, 8 In. 200.00
Figurine, Bulldog, Reclining 30.00
Figurine, Chinese Poet & Chinese Guitarist, Pair 100.00
Figurine, Duchess Of Devonshire, Signed 48.00
Figurine, Elephant, Gray, 3 In. 55.00
Figurine, Lady, Gloved, 40s Attire, Label, 12 In. 30.00
Figurine, Lady, Pink Dress & Hat, 14 In. 55.00
Figurine, Madame Pompadour, Signed 48.00
Figurine, Madonna Of The Kitchen, Italian, 7 In. 45.00
Figurine, Prince Of Wales 48.00
Lamp Base, Minstrel Clown, Serenading Lady, 25 In. 125.00

Goofus glass was made from about 1900 to 1920 by many American factories. It was originally painted gold, red, green, bronze, pink, purple, and other bright colors.

GOOFUS GLASS, Bowl, Fluted, Serrated Rim, Thistles, Red & Gold, 7 In.Diam.	8.50
Bowl, Gold & Red Roses, Crimped, 9 In.Diam.	20.00
Bread Plate, Last Supper	48.00 To 50.00
Jar, Butterflies, Small	10.00
Nappy, Turned Up Side Handle, Gold On Gold	7.00
Plate, Easter, Chick Coming Out Of Egg	48.00
Plate, Red Grapes, Gold Trim, 11 In.Diam.	18.00
Plate, Red Rose Center, Gold Trim, 8 1/4 In.Diam.	8.50

W.H.COSS

Goss china has been made since 1858. English potter William Henry Goss first made it at the Falcon Pottery in Stoke-on-Trent. In 1934 the factory name was changed to Goss China Company when it was taken over by Cauldon Potteries. Goss china resembles Irish Belleek in both body and glaze. The company also made popular souvenir china.

GOSS, Box, Trinket, Horseshoe Shape, Cheltenham	7.50
Bucket, Swiss Milk, Warmer	17.50
Bust, Sir Walter Scott, 5 1/2 In.	65.00
Cauldron, Kirkwall, Macbeth Verse, 2 1/2 In.	30.00
Cottage, Shakespearean, Signed	295.00
Cup & Saucer, Orange Luster, Demitasse	18.00
Jar, Water, Egyptian Style, Aylesbury	10.00
Plate, Cake, Transfer Design, Clachan, Empire Exhibition	50.00
Shoe, Victorian, Ramsgate, 3 In.	10.00

324
SCHOONHOVEN
HOLLAND
CORE
E

Pottery has been made in Gouda, Holland, since the seventeenth century. Two firms, The Zenith pottery, established in the eighteenth century, and the Zuid-Hollandsche pottery, made the brightly colored Art Nouveau wares marked Gouda from 1880 to about 1940.

GOUDA, Bowl, Damascus, Marked, 8 In.	80.00
Carafe, Sunflower Design, House Mark, Covered, 11 In.	105.00
Chamberstick, Handle, Drip Catch, Forum House Mark, 5 X 6 In.Diam.	45.00
Creamer, Signed Gratius, 2 1/2 In.	50.00
Humidor, Pale Yellow, Brass Lid	65.00
Humidor, Rust, Green, Blue & Yellow, Plazuid Mark, 4 1/2 In.	100.00
Jar, Tobacco, Art Deco Design, 7 In.	150.00
Jug, House Mark, 6 1/2 In.	65.00
Toothpick, Regina	38.00
Vase, Art Deco Center, Black Top & Bottom, Gold & Blue, 5 1/2 In.	65.00
Vase, Art Deco Design, House Mark, Black, Gray, & Green, 6 1/2 In.	65.00
Vase, Cubistic, 5 In.	70.00
Vase, Flowers, Black & Tan Ground, Marked, 9 1/2 In.	120.00
Vase, Lattice Top, Flowers, Ivory, 7 1/2 In.	48.00
Vase, Nouveau Flowers, 6-Colored, House Mark, 6 In.	115.00
Vase, Scenic Band, Green Ground, Marked, 2 1/2 X 3 In.	30.00
Vase, Stylized Lion's Design, Distal Mark, 11 1/2 In.	75.00
Vase, 2 Handles, Bird Each Side, House Mark, 8 1/2 X 8 1/2 In.	165.00

Graniteware is an enameled tinware that has been used in the kitchen from the late nineteenth century to the present. Earlier graniteware was green or turquoise blue, with white spatters. The later ware was gray with white spatters. Reproductions are being made in all colors.

GRANITEWARE, Basin, Marbleized Royal Blue, 6 3/4 In.	12.00
Basin, Wash, Blue & White	14.00
Basin, Wash, Gray	12.50
Bathtub, Baby's, Blue, White Dots, Oval, 13 3/4 In.	30.00 To 50.00
Bedpan, Gray	6.00 To 15.00
Bottle, Gray	58.00

Bowl, Blue & White, 3 X 8 In.	15.00
Bowl, Mixing, Gray, 3 X 6 In.	4.50
Bucket, Dinner, Bail Handle, White, Black Edge, 5 1/2 X 6 1/2 In.	15.00
Butter, Pewter Trim, Covered, Gray	210.00
Can, Milk, Gray, 2 Quart	28.00
Canister, Looking Lid, Wire Handle, Germany, Brown, 5 7/8 In.	22.00
Casserole, Covered, Gray	20.00
Chamber Pot, Gray, With Lid	10.00
Coffee Cup, White Enameled, 4 1/2 In.	3.50
Coffee Mug, Handled, Mottled Gray, 2 1/2 X 3 1/2 In.	12.50
Coffeepot, Bail Handle, Chuck Wagon, Gray, 12 In.	45.00
Coffeepot, Camp, Bail Handle, Gray, 11 1/2 In.	40.00
Coffeepot, Gooseneck Spout, Gray	28.00 To 30.00
Coffeepot, Gooseneck, Teal & White, 7 In.	32.50
Coffeepot, Gray, 9 In.	23.50
Coffeepot, Hinged Dome Cover, Green Trim, Beige, 8 1/2 In.	22.50
Coffeepot, Hinged Dome Lid, Green, White Enameled Interior	40.00
Coffeepot, Knob On Lid, Blue	10.00
Coffeepot, Lid, Dark Green	10.00
Coffeepot, Log Spout, Blue & White	30.00
Coffeepot, Nash's Coffee Decal, Gray	30.00
Coffeepot, Patent 1876, Pewter Spout, Lid, & Fittings, 11 In.	130.00
Coffeepot, Percolator, Red Poppies, Pyrex Knob, Cream	20.00
Coffeepot, Percolator, 1920s	18.00
Coffeepot, Pewter Trim, Pewter Spout & Collar, Gray, 9 1/4 In.	135.00
Coffeepot, Swirled, Brown & White, 10 In.	45.00
Coffeepot, Tin Lid, Gray	15.00
Coffeepot, Tin Top, Wire Bail, Knob, 8 In.	25.00
Coffeepot, White Swirl, Cobalt Blue	35.00
Colander, Double Handled	10.00
Colander, Gray	5.00
Colander, Red Edge, White	5.00
Colander, Speckled, Side Handles, 4 1/4 X 11 1/4 In.	35.00
Cup, Cesco Label, Gray	3.00
Cup, Measuring, Calibrating Lines, Gray, 4 1/4 X 4 1/2 In.	14.50
Dipper, Gray	2.00
Dipper, Handle Hole For Hanging, Striated Pearl Gray, 9 1/2 In.	16.50
Dipper, Hook Handle, Black Trim, White, 13 In.	6.00
Dipper, Round Bottom, Curved Handle	12.00
Dipper, White, Black Trim, Hook Handle, 13 In.	6.00
Dish Pan, Red Edge, White	10.00
Double Boiler, Tin Cover, Gray	8.00
Flask, Gray	63.00
Frypan, Handle, Hole For Hanging, 5 X 5 3/4 In.	14.50
Funnel, Fruit Jar, Gray On Gray	22.50
Funnel, Side Handle, Dark Blue Trim	8.50
Jar, Fruit, Gray	7.00
Kettle, Iron, Navy & White	73.00
Kettle, Oval Shape, Dark Blue & White Enamel	110.00
Kettle, Preserving, Bail Handle, Gray, 15 X 7 1/2 In.	32.50
Kettle, Preserving, Brown	30.00
Kettle, Preserving, Gray	10.00
Ladle, Black	7.00
Ladle, Blue, Rounded Bottom	10.00
Ladle, Cream	3.00
Ladle, Gray	20.00
Lobster Steamer Pot, Cover, Handles, Gray On Gray, 14 In.Diam.	50.00
Lunch Box, Gray	38.00
Lunch Box, Inside Tray, Bail Handle	45.00
Lunch Box, Miner's, Gray	30.00
Lunch Pail, Gray	22.50
Milk Can, Domed Tin Cover, Gray, 1/2 Gallon	35.00
Mold, Food, Fluted, Gray, 2 In.	40.00

Mold, Food, Turk's Head, Scalloped, Gray, 2 1/2 X 10 In.	25.00
Mug, Blue & White, Miniature	20.00
Mug, Brown & White Speckled	10.00
Mustard Pot, Mug Shape	20.00
Pail, Dinner, Child's, Lid & Bail Handle, Black Trim	12.50
Pail, Milk, Bail Handle, Brown & White Speckled	26.50
Pail, Tin Cover, 1 Gallon	10.00
Pail, Wire Bail Handle, Gray, 4 1/2 X 6 In.	35.00
Pan, Baking, Mottled Green Gray, 11 X 16 In.	5.00
Pan, Cake, Gray	3.00
Pan, Cake, Royal Blue & White, White Inside	6.50
Pan, Cake, Speckled 2 Shades Of Gray, 9 1/4 In.	6.50
Pan, Green Handle & Matching Lid	6.00
Pan, Meat Loaf, Slant Sided, Mottled Gray, 5 1/2 In.	6.00
Pan, Muffin, Gray-On-Gray Zebra Striped, 11 1/2 X 15 1/4 In.	30.00
Pan, Pudding, Brown	15.00
Pan, Pudding, Striations Of White, Blue, 2 1/2 X 6 1/4 In.	12.50
Pan, Pudding, Turquoise Blue & White, White Interior	13.50
Pan, Roasting, Grip Handles, Gray, 12 1/4 In.Square	12.50
Pan, Side Handled & Bail, Gray	4.00
Pan, Stew, Wire Bail Handle, Light Gray	7.50
Pan, Swirl, Cobalt Blue & White, 10 In.	22.50
Pie Pan, Bluish Gray, 8 7/8 In.	6.50
Pie Pan, Brown & White Speckled	9.50
Pie Pan, Dark Gray, 6 In.	5.50
Pie Pan, Gray, 9 In.	5.00
Pie Pan, Gray, 9 3/4 In.	.40 To 5.00
Pie Pan, White Interior, Blue & White Sponged, 9 3/4 In.	7.50
Pie Pan, 10 In.	7.00
Pitcher, Water, White Enamel, Blue Handle & Rim, 1/2 Gallon	10.00
Plate, Soup, Green Edge, Cream, 8 1/2 In.	5.00
Poacher, Egg, Black, Powder Gray Speckles, 3 3/4 In.Diam.	12.50
Poacher, Fish, Insert, Gray	55.00
Pot, Double Boiler, Cover, Blue Marbleized	27.50
Pot, Double Boiler, White	9.00
Pot, Swing Handle, Domed Cover, Lavender, Blue, & White, 8 In.	22.50
Potty, Child's, Blue & White Speckled, Original Label	16.00
Potty, Gray, 10 X 10 In.	30.00
Roaster, Mottled, Oval	10.00
Rolling Pin, Advertising, Blue & White	210.00
Rooster, Mottled Gray, Oval	10.00
Saucepan, Handled, Bluish Gray, 5 X 6 In.	7.50
Saucepan, Handled, Gray, 8 In.	9.00
Saucepan, Square, Yellow With Black Trim	9.50
Scoop, Grocery, Gray	52.00
Sifter, Four, Apple Decal, Bromwell, 3 Cup	7.00
Skimmer, Long Handled, Gray, 6 In.Diam.	15.00
Soap Dish, Removable Strainer, White, 5 X 3 1/2 In.	22.50
Spittoon, Blue & White	35.00
Spittoon, Gray, 2 Piece	32.00
Spittoon, Green	20.00
Spittoon, Lady's, Gray	25.00
Strainer Ladle, Hooked End, Signed, Iron Clad, 12 In.	22.50
Strainer, Tea, Ring Handle, White	15.00
Strainer, 2 Handled, Gray	20.00
Tablespoon, Blue	10.00
Teakettle, Gooseneck, Blue & White	13.00
Teakettle, St, Louis Iron Works, Blue & White	65.00
Teapot, Child's, Gray	24.00
Teapot, Gooseneck Spout, Ivory & Black Dots, 1 Cup	15.00 To 22.50
Teapot, Gooseneck Spout, Tin Cover	25.00
Teapot, Gray, Gooseneck	25.00 To 28.00
Teapot, Green, 1 Cup	8.00

Teapot, Pewter Top, Copper Trim 60.00
Tray, Flanged Rim, Cobalt Blue, White Speckled, 12 In.Diam. 18.50

> *Greentown glass was made by the Indiana Tumbler and Goblet Company of Greentown, Indiana, from 1894 to 1903. In 1899, the factory name was changed to National Glass Company. A variety of pressed, milk, and chocolate glass was made.*

GREENTOWN, see also Chocolate Glass; Custard Glass; Holly Amber; Milk Glass; Pressed Glass

GREENTOWN, Butter, Dewey Pattern, Covered, Yellow 60.00
Butter, Dewey, Covered, Amber .... 65.00 To 70.00
Butter, Dewey, Vaseline, Covered, 1 1/4 Pounds .... 90.00 To 165.00
Butter, Teardrop & Tassel, Covered, Blue 150.00
Compote, Clear, 6 1/2 X 6 1/2 In. 40.00
Compote, Pleat Band, Open 25.00
Creamer, Child's, Austrian, Canary 95.00
Creamer, Cruet, Dewey, Green, Original Stopper 135.00
Creamer, Honeycomb & Flower Band, Dark Blue 40.00
Creamer, Teardrop & Tassel 100.00
Cruet, Dewey, Stopper, Nile Green 750.00
Dish, Hen On Nest Cover, Blue 70.00
Dish, Hen On Nest Cover, Milk Glass Head, Amber 115.00
Figurine, Dolphin, Red Agate 295.00
Goblet, Austrian 45.00
Goblet, Beehive, Clear 75.00
Mug, Dewey, Amber 40.00
Mug, Elf, Opaque Blue .... 40.00 To 65.00
Mug, Serenade Scene, Marked 38.00
Mug, Serenade, Blue 45.00
Mug, Serenade, Custard 48.00
Nappy, Leaf Bracket, Red Agate, Triangular 65.00
Pitcher, Water, Clear, Heron 195.00
Pitcher, Water, Dewey, Amber 80.00
Pitcher, Water, Diamond, 8 1/2 In. 65.00
Pitcher, Water, Ruffled Eye, Green 45.00
Plate, Dewey, Vaseline, Footed 65.00
Plate, Pekingese, Lacy Edge, Dog's Head In Relief, 6 In. 18.00
Plate, Serenade, Milk Glass, 6 In. 35.00
Sauce, Berry, Dewey, Vaseline 30.00
Sauce, Brazen Shield 6.00
Spooner, Beaded Panel 30.00
Spooner, Dewey, Amber 17.50
Stein, Serenade, Nile Green 55.00
Sugar, Covered, White Opaque 35.00
Sugar, Diamond, Clear 55.00
Tray, Dewey, Serpentine, Amber, 10 In. 42.50
Tumbler, Austrian, Gold Trim 35.00
Tumbler, Dewey, Green 48.00
Tumbler, Teardrop & Tassel, Blue 40.00
Wine, Herringbone Buttress, Green, 4 In. 160.00
Wine, Inverted Thumbprint, Pear Stem 12.50
Wine, Shuttle 8.00

> *Grueby Faience Company of Boston, Massachusetts, was incorporated in 1897 by William H. Grueby. Garden statuary, art pottery, and architectural tiles were made until 1920.*

GRUEBY, Bowl, Raised Swirl Interior, Glazed Exterior, C.1900, Marked, 8 In. 165.00
Bowl, Vase, Matte Blue, 6 1/2 X 5 In. 325.00
Tile, Knight, 6 X 6 In. 225.00
Tile, Landscape, Green, Blue & Tan, Impressed Mark, C.1900, 4 In. 140.00

Tile, Mermaid, 6 X 6 In. 225.00
Tile, Stylized Trees, 4 X 4 In. 175.00
Tile, 1 Green Lily Pads, 1 Ivory Water Lilies, Marked, 6 In., Pair 220.00
Tile, 4-Color, Windmill, 4 X 4 In. 125.00
Vase, Bowl Shape, Clotted Matte Blue, 6 1/2 X 5 In. 310.00
Vase, Buds & Leaves, Green, 8 In. 200.00
Vase, Flat Leaves & Buds, Matte Green, Marked, C.1900, 6 1/4 In. 495.00
Vase, Flat Leaves, Ovoid, C.1900, 11 1/4 In. 600.00
Vase, Leaves & Buds, Matte Green, Marked, C.1900, 11 In. 880.00
Vase, Leaves In Matte Green, Lillian Newman, C.1907, 7 1/4 In. 440.00
Vase, No Design, Green, 8 In. 250.00
Vase, Overlapping Leaves, R.Erickson, Matte Green, C.1900, 9 3/4 In. 770.00
Vase, Pebble Grain, Blue, 6 1/2 In. 350.00
Vase, Pumpkin Shape, Ribbed, Yellow, Label, 3 X 4 In. 150.00
Vase, Spherical, 2 Bands Of Leaves, Marked, Matte Green, 12 3/4 In. 800.00
Vase, Waisted Baluster, Leaves, 7 Handles, Marked, 11 1/4 In. 4500.00
Vase, 5-Pointed Rim, Molded Leaves & Buds, Marked, Green, 7 3/4 In. 300.00

GUM BALL MACHINE, see Store, Machine

GUN, Blunderbuss, Boarding, British Naval, C.1720, Relief Carved, 25 In. 1450.00
Carbine, Burnside, 4th Model, Block Letter Name 375.00
Carbine, Burnside, 4th Model, 54 Caliber, 39 1/2 In. 230.00
Carbine, Joslyn M1864 .... 550.00
Carbine, Merrill, Civil War, Side Button For Lever Latch 425.00
Carbine, Remington, Split Breech, Civil War, US On Butt 450.00
Carbine, Spencer Saddrling 650.00
Carbine, Winchester 1876, Saddle Ring, Full Forend, Marked NWMp 850.00
Carbine, 1873 Springfield 325.00
Derringer, Kentucky Style, C.1810, Marked, 42 In. 1250.00
Flintlock, Belgian, D.B., Engraved Birds, 50 In. 495.00
Flintlock, Kentucky, Curly Maple 450.00
Flintlock, Kentucky, Octagon Barrel, Lechler & Lancaster, C.1810 .... 1750.00
Flintlock, Kentucky, Silver Mounted, Curly Maple Stock, C.1810, 39 In. 1850.00
Flintlock, Kentucky, Silver Name Plate, C.1840, 72 In. 2475.00
Musket, Brown Bess, Flintlock, English, Bayonet, 57 1/2 In. 750.00
Musket, Civil War, Steel, Brass Plate, Austrian 225.00
Musket, Confederate, Marked Richmond, CS, Va., 1863 .... 350.00
Musket, Flintlock, American, 36 In. Bore Barrel, 52 In. 175.00
Musket, French, Used In American Revolution, Charleville Markings 695.00
Musket, Harpers Ferry, 1836 .... 300.00
Musket, Palmetto Armory, Columbia, S.C., 1850, Percussion, Marked 1295.00
Musket, Percussion, U.S., Model 1842, 69 Caliber, 57 1/2 In. 375.00
Musket, Springfield, Model 1817, 54 Caliber, 57 1/2 In. 300.00
Musket, U.S.Springfield 1816, Type III Style 425.00
Musket, 1864 Springfield, 58 Caliber, Civil War 375.00
Percussion Cap, C.1870, Chance & Son, Dondon, Half Octagon Barrel 120.00
Percussion Cap, Single Shot, C.1870, English 125.00
Percussion, Single Shot, J.Bland, London, C.1870 .... 120.00
Pistol, Box Lock, C.1860, Screw-Off Barrel, Walnut Stock, English 137.50
Pistol, Cap, Belt, Percussion, French Model 1837, 11 5/8 In. 302.00
Pistol, Colt Derringer, Model No.3 .... 250.00
Pistol, Colt 1879, Double Action, Frontier, 45 Caliber 675.00
Pistol, Dueling, Percussion, Damascene Barrel, French, C.1845, Pair 3275.00
Pistol, Flintlock, French, 12 In. Barrel, Brass Fittings, 19 In. 150.00
Pistol, Flintlock, French, 18th Century, Brass Trigger, 22 In. 375.00
Pistol, Flintlock, Tapered Cannon Form Barrel, C.1660, 12 In. 1395.00
Pistol, Flintlock, 12 1/2 In. Barrel, Wood Stock, 20 In. 100.00
Pistol, French, Percussion, Engraved, Original Case, C.1845, Pair 3275.00
Pistol, H.Alson, 1851 .... 295.00
Pistol, Military, Flintlock, C.1910, Walnut Stock, European 210.00
Pistol, Naval Boarding, C.1810, Brass Barrel, British, Pair 1650.00
Pistol, Pepper Box, 4-Shot, Sharps Breech, Model 4b, 5 1/2 In. 200.00
Pistol, Pepper Box, 4-Shot, Sharps Breech, 30 Caliber, 6 1/4 In. 190.00
Pistol, Remington, Derringer 198.00

Pistol, Remington, M1871, Rolling Block 500.00
Pistol, Remington, M1871, Rolling Block, Civilian Model 500.00
Pistol, Single Shot Percussion, C.1845, Marked Moore, London 70.00
Pistol, Springfield, Stagecoach, Case 9.00
Pistol, U.S.Army, Model 1842, H.Aston 150.00
Pistol, 6-Shot Colt, Lightning, C.1890 .... 150.00
Pistol, 1875 Smith & Wesson, 32 Caliber, Spur Trigger, Pair 365.00
Pistol, 1878 Marlins, Spur Trigger, 32 Caliber, Pair 355.00
Revolver, Cap, Army, Percussion, Colt, Model 1960, 14 In. 357.00
Revolver, Colt 44, Army, 1860 .... 375.00
Revolver, Colt, 31 Caliber, 1849 .... 225.00
Revolver, Navy, Colt, Model 1861, Brass Trigger, 13 In. 660.00
Revolver, Pocket, Marlin XX, Standard 1873, 6 1/2 In. 90.00
Revolver, Police, Conversion Of Colt's 1862, 36 Caliber, Ivory Grip 425.00
Revolver, S & W Model 1, 22 Caliber, Rosewood Grip, 7 In. 80.00
Revolver, Smith & Wesson 22, Model No.1, 2nd Issue 225.00
Revolver, Smith & Wesson, Model 1, 2nd Issue, 22 Caliber 150.00
Revolver, 5-Shot, Hopkins & Allen Dectator Model, 3 Caliber 30.00
Rifle, Air, Winchester, .177 Caliber, Model 422 .... 80.00
Rifle, B-B, Daisy Red Ryder Carbine 32.00
Rifle, Brunswick, Indian Inscription, Attached Bayonet, British 275.00
Rifle, Cap, Jaeger, Percussion, German, Walnut Stock, 41 In. 110.00
Rifle, Flintlock, Kentucky, Maple Stock, 40 In.Barrel 600.00
Rifle, For Maharajah Of Hyderabab, Solid Silver Design, C.1800, 47 In. 3500.00
Rifle, German, Exposed Hammer, Breech Loading, Double Barrel 750.00
Rifle, German, Over & Under Exposed Hammer, 43 1/2 In. 800.00
Rifle, Kentucky, Marked F.Beerstecher's Patent, Union City, Pa., 36 In. 595.00
Rifle, Kentucky, Marked H.Elwell, Patch Box, Brass Trim, Walnut, 61 In. 650.00
Rifle, Kentucky, Marked M.M. Marlin, Brass Trim, 58 In. 900.00
Rifle, Kentucky, Pearl Inlay, Patch Box, J.Poe In Sterling Silver 850.00
Rifle, Kentucky, Percussion, 46 Caliber, Brass Trigger, Patch Box, 37 In. 850.00
Rifle, Kentucky, Silver Plate With Name, C.1840, 72 In. 2475.00
Rifle, Long, Pennsylvania, Maple Stock, Brass & Silver Design, 54 In. 467.00
Rifle, Mississippi Percussion, 54 Caliber, Robbins & Lawrence, 1850 .... 650.00
Rifle, Needle Fire, American, 1860s, Brass Frame Walnut Stock, 22 In. 750.00
Rifle, Parker 16 P.H.E., Original Carrying Case 3000.00
Rifle, Pepper Box, Worcester, Allen, & Wheelock, 6-Shot, 34 Caliber 280.00
Rifle, Remington, Combination, 10 Gauge 1000.00
Rifle, Swiss Vertelli, Bolt Action, 7.5 Caliber, 52 In. 30.00
Rifle, Trapdoor, Model 1873, 45-70 Caliber, 51 1/2 In. 200.00
Rifle, Winchester 1873, Black Painted, Round Barrel, 24 In. 225.00
Rifle, Winchester, 22 Caliber, Peep Sight, 1903 .... 275.00
Shotgun, Double Barrel, C.1860, English 125.00
Shotgun, Double Barrel, C.1880, Lever Below Trigger, English 100.00
Shotgun, Double Barrel, Wells Fargo 750.00

> *Gunderson glass was made at the Gunderson Pairpoint Works of New
> Bedford, Massachusetts, from 1952 to 1957. Gunderson Peachblow is
> especially famous.*

GUNDERSON, Cup & Saucer, Peachblow, Raspberry, White Reeded Handle 275.00
Decanter, Peachblow 95.00
Pitcher, Burmese, Pink Fluted, Lemon Bottom & Handle, 5 1/2 In. 250.00
Pitcher, Peachblow, Ruffled Rim, Ridged Handle, 6 In. 85.00
Toothpick, Shades From Lemon To Rose, Flared 120.00
Urn, Bubble Ball, Clear Handles, Large 225.00
Vase, Burmese, 5 In. .... 95.00 To 150.00

GUTTA-PERCHA, see also Photography, Daguerreotype Case
GUTTA-PERCHA, Buckle, Belt, Carved Female Bust 32.00
Mirror, Dresser, Deer Head Embossed On Back 38.00
Mirror, Hand, Egyptian Figures, Dated 1866 .... 35.00

HAEGER, Candlestick, Calla Lily, Green, Pink, 5 In., Pair 15.00

Planter, Boy Holding Basin, Pink, 10 In.	20.00
Vase, Swordfish, Pink, Blue, Green, 9 X 13 In.	45.00

Hall China Company started in East Liverpool, Ohio, in 1903. The firm made all types of wares, including Autumn Leaf pattern dishes. It is still working.

HALL, see also Autumn Leaf

HALL, Ashtray & Matchbox Holder, Maroon Lines	5.00
Bean Pot, Chinese Red	27.00
Bowl, Orange Poppy, 8 3/4 In.	9.00
Bowl, Salad, Clamshell, Original Paper Label	75.00
Bowl, Soup, Flat, Red Poppy	10.50
Canister, Red Poppy, Cover, Metal, 6 In.	6.00 To 10.00
Casserole, Red Poppy, Covered	21.50
Cereal, Red Poppy	5.50
Coffeepot, Drip, Aluminum Insert, Floral Pattern	28.50
Coffeepot, Maroon & Silver, Big Boy	20.00
Coffeepot, Red Poppy	18.00
Coffeepot, Step-Down Type, Gold Lines, Green & White, 10 Cup Size	7.00
Cookie Jar, Gold Polka Dots, White Ground	15.00
Cookie Jar, Tavern Scene	69.00
Cracker Jar, Cream Ground, Blue Flowers, Green Leaves, Satin Finish	150.00
Dish, Refrigerator, Orange, 4 In.Square	10.00
Dispenser, Coffee, Crocus, Wall, Metal	18.00
Jug, Ball, Autumn Leaf	18.00
Jug, Red Poppy	15.00
Mustard Set, Autumn Leaf, 3 Pieces	35.00
Pepper Shaker, Poppy	4.00
Pepper Shaker, Red Poppy	7.50
Pitcher, Hotpoint	12.00
Pitcher, Ice Lip, Yellow	15.00
Pitcher, Juice, White Initial	10.00
Pitcher, Rose Parade, Blue, 6 In.	12.50
Pitcher, Tilt, Blue	12.00
Plate, Dinner, Red Poppy, 9 In.	5.50
Pot, Bean, Orange Poppy, Handled	30.00
Roaster, Westinghouse, Covered, Yellow, Large	8.00
Spittoon, Blue	65.00
Sugar & Creamer, Signed Eva Zeisel	8.00
Teapot, Airflow, Cobalt Blue	40.00
Teapot, Airflow, Yellow	20.00 To 25.00
Teapot, Aladdin, Canary	18.00
Teapot, Aladdin, Poppy Red	40.00
Teapot, Albany, Brown	40.00
Teapot, Baltimore, Lettuce Green	45.00
Teapot, Basket, Emerald Green	85.00
Teapot, Birdcage, Maroon	130.00
Teapot, Cobalt Blue	18.00
Teapot, Doughnut, Ivory	175.00
Teapot, French, Cobalt Blue	45.00
Teapot, Hollywood, Lettuce Green	25.00
Teapot, Hollywood, Maroon	25.00
Teapot, Hook Cover, Cadet Blue	20.00
Teapot, Los Angeles, Cobalt Blue	40.00
Teapot, Manhattan, Brown	25.00
Teapot, McCormick, Turquoise	25.00
Teapot, Morning Glory	13.50
Teapot, Parade, Canary	18.00 To 20.00
Teapot, Philadelphia, Turquoise	25.00

Teapot, Streamline, Canary	20.00
Teapot, Streamline, Chinese Red	50.00
Teapot, Streamline, Tavern Scene	125.00
Teapot, Surfside, Emerald	65.00
Teapot, Tricolator, Circle Mark	18.00
Teapot, Victoria, Monterrey	25.00
Teapot, Windshield, Camellia	20.00
Tom & Jerry Set, 9 Piece	60.00
Tom & Jerry Set, 10 Mugs	60.00
Tray, Glass With Wooden Handles, Autumn Leaf	45.00

HALLOWEEN, Candleholder, Pumpkin	22.00
Candy Container, Lady With Monkey Face, Papier-Mache	110.00
Costume, Mickey Mouse	15.00
Costume, Pogo, 1968, Boxed	12.00
Counter Box, Country Store, Wooden, Black Kids, Jelly Bean Blimp	250.00
Egg With Witch On Broom, Celluloid	40.00
Jack-O'-Lantern, Cat Face, Orange, Cardboard	22.00
Mold, Ice Cream, Skeletal Head, Crossbones, Pewter	110.00
Pumpkin With Legs, Celluloid	40.00
Pumpkins, Papier-Mache, 8 In.	20.00
Toy, Sparklet, Pumpkin Head, Tin	25.00
Witch Driving Car, Celluloid	40.00
Witch Pulling Wagon, Celluloid	40.00
Witch, 8 Paper Bridge Tallyies, Pull Tab, Witch Pops In & Out	10.00

Hampshire pottery was made in Keene, New Hampshire, between 1871 and 1923. Hampshire developed a line of colored glazed wares as early as 1883, including a Royal Worcester-type pink, olive green, blue, and mahogany.

HAMPSHIRE, Bowl, Raised Flowers, 6 In.Diam.	60.00
Candle Shield, Green	60.00
Chamberstick, Turned-In Sides, 7 X 3 In.	48.00
Creamer, Clear	12.00
Mug, Hand-Painted Girl, 7 In.	85.00
Mug, Oval Portrait Of Indian, Handle, Gold Trim, 7 In.	125.00
Pitcher, Matte Green, Marked, 8 1/4 In.	58.00
Vase, Chocolate Brown Mirror Glaze, 5 1/2 In.	85.00
Vase, Grape Design, Green, 4 In.	37.00
Vase, Green, 4 X 4 1/2 In.	35.00
Vase, 12 Molded Base To Shoulder Ribs, Marked, 9 In.	65.00

Philip Handel worked in Meriden, Connecticut, about 1885 and in New York City from about 1900 to the 1930s. His firm made art glass and other types of lamps.

HANDEL, Base, Lamp, 3-Socket, Geometric Design, Signed, Bronze, 20 1/4 In.	225.00
Candlestick, Teroma, Windmill Design, Signed	725.00
Chandelier, 12-Sided, Red Band Top, Leaded, Signed, 23 In.	2200.00
Desk Set, Scarab Design, 10 Piece	1400.00
Humidor, Cigar, 2 Bears, Signed & Dated 1904, 6 In.	345.00
Humidor, No.4060, Lioness, 3 Nursing Kittens, Brown & Green Ground	585.00
Humidor, Tavern Scene, Milk Glass	195.00
Humidor, 2 Hares, Pipe On Cover, Signed, Green Ground	325.00
Inkwell, Cannonball, Vaseline, Signed, 4 In.	225.00
Lamp, Bronze & Painted, Pastoral Scene, Bronze Base, 24 In.	1900.00
Lamp, Deep Purple, Signed, 16 In.Diam.	450.00
Lamp, Desk, Bronze Base, Green Shade, Signed, 6 1/2 In.Diam.	1900.00
Lamp, Desk, Cased Glass, Brown Matte, Signed	1400.00
Lamp, Domical Reverse Painted Shade, C.1900	400.00

Handel, Lamp, Hand-Painted Bird Of
Paradise, Patinated Metal

Lamp, Floor, Gooseneck, Green & Beige Leaded Shade, Bronze, 5 Ft. 1500.00
Lamp, Floor, Harp Holder, Bronze 375.00
Lamp, Floral, 25 1/2 In. 3850.00
Lamp, Hand-Painted Bird Of Paradise, Patinated Metal .... *Illus* 1350.00
Lamp, Hexagonal Mottled Glass, Classical Base, Signed, C.1915, 24 In. 2100.00
Lamp, Hexagonal Panel Shade, Signed, 21 In. 375.00
Lamp, Landscape, Glass & Patinated Metal, Signed, C.1915, 26 In. 2300.00
Lamp, Leaded Geometric Greens, Brass Base, Signed, 20 In. 1600.00
Lamp, Reverse Painted Chipped Ice Shade, Bronze Base, Signed, 14 In. 1150.00
Lamp, Reverse Painted Shade, 2 Gold Peacocks, Signed 3000.00
Lamp, Rose Bouquet, Reverse Painted, C.1918 .... *Illus* 3500.00
Lamp, Table, Border Shade .... *Illus* 1200.00
Lamp, Table, Chipped Ice Shade, Signed & Numbered, 20 In. 1350.00
Lamp, Table, Gold Teroma Shade, Tassels, Signed & Numbered, 20 1/4 In. 1900.00
Lamp, Table, Green Leaf Design On Lower Part, Brass, Signed 425.00
Lamp, Table, Maple Leaf Border, Signed & Numbered, 20 1/4 In. 1750.00
Lamp, Table, Reverse Painted & Bronze, Grape Cluster, Signed, 18 In. 1800.00
Lamp, Table, Reverse Painted Glass, Bronze Base, 15 In. 1200.00
Lamp, Table, Sunset, Flowing Brook, Trees, Signed, Numbered, 20 1/4 In. 2100.00

Handel, Lamp, Table, Border Shade

Lamp, Tree Trunk Base, 3 Sockets	850.00
Lamp, Tree Trunk Base, 24 In.	850.00
Lamp, Wall, Frosted Glass Panels, Metal Beading, Signed, Pair	500.00
Lamp, Wall, Hanging, Pair	325.00
Lamp, 4 Lilies, 2 Buds, Green, Whtte, Bronze Base, Signed, 16 X 22 In.	1950.00
Lamp, 4 Lilies, 2 Buds, Lily Pad Bronze Base, Signed, 16 In.	2250.00

Harlequin dinnerware was produced by the Homer Laughlin Company from 1938 to 1964, and sold without trademark by the F.W. Woolworth Co. It has a concentric ring design like Fiesta, but the rings are separated from the rim by a plain margin and cup handles were angular in shape.

HARLEQUIN WARE, Ashtray, Maroon	27.50
Ashtray, Red	25.00
Bowl, Cereal, Chartreuse, 6 1/2 In.	5.00
Bowl, Cereal, Rose, 6 1/2 In.	5.00
Bowl, Cereal, Turquoise, 6 1/2 In.	5.00
Bowl, Fruit, Green	3.00
Bowl, Fruit, Rose	3.00
Bowl, Fruit, Turquoise	3.00
Cream Soup, Rose	6.00
Creamer, Mauve, Individual	6.00 To 18.00
Creamer, Novelty, Rose	6.00
Creamer, Red	6.00
Creamer, Red, Individual	25.00
Creamer, Spruce, Individual	18.00
Creamer, Turquoise, Individual	18.00
Cup & Saucer, Chartreuse	6.00
Cup & Saucer, Dark Green	6.00
Cup & Saucer, Gray	3.00
Cup & Saucer, Light Green	6.00
Cup & Saucer, Rose	6.00
Cup & Saucer, Yellow	6.00
Cup, After Dinner, Light Green	15.00
Cup, After Dinner, Mauve	15.00
Cup, After Dinner, Turquoise	15.00
Cup, After Dinner, Yellow	15.00
Cup, Rose	4.50
Cup, Spruce Green	4.50
Cup, Yellow	4.50
Dish, Nut, Red, 3 In.	5.00
Dish, Nut, Spruce, 3 In.	5.00
Dish, Nut, Turquoise, 3 In.	5.00
Eggcup, Mauve, Individual	8.50
Eggcup, Red, Double	8.00
Eggcup, Spruce, Double	8.00
Eggcup, Yellow	7.00
Figurine, Penguin, Mauve	40.00
Jug, Water, Mauve	15.00
Nappy, Red, 9 In.	8.00
Plate, Gray, 6 In.	2.00
Plate, Gray, 9 In.	3.00
Plate, Green, 6 1/2 In.	.75
Plate, Red, 6 In.	2.00
Plate, Red, 7 In.	2.00
Plate, Red, 9 In.	3.00
Plate, Rose, 6 In.	2.00
Plate, Rose, 9 In.	3.00
Plate, Turquoise, 6 In.	2.00
Plate, Turquoise, 7 In.	2.00
Plate, Turquoise, 9 In.	2.00 To 3.00
Plate, Yellow, 6 In.	2.00
Platter, Light Green, 11 In.	6.00
Platter, Rose, 11 In.	6.00

Sauceboat, Rose	8.00
Saucer, After Dinner, Mauve	5.00
Saucer, After Dinner, Red	5.00
Saucer, Blue	2.00
Saucer, Rose	2.00
Saucer, Spruce Green	2.00
Saucer, Turquoise	1.00 To 2.00
Sugar & Creamer, Floral, Pink	17.00
Sugar & Creamer, Mauve	12.00
Tumbler, Red	10.00
Tumbler, Turquoise	10.00

HATPIN HOLDER, see Porcelain and various porcelain categories

HAVILAND & CO.

Haviland china has been made in Limoges, France, since 1842. The factory was started by the Haviland Brothers of New York City. Other factories worked in the town of Limoges making a similar chinaware.

HAVILAND, Blotter, Hand-Painted Violets	30.00
Bowl, The Countess, 5 3/4 X 2 1/2 In.	12.50
Bowl, Vegetable, Ranson Pattern, White With Green, Marked, 11 In.	50.00
Bowl, White, Ivy, Gold On Edge, Footed, 9 In.	40.00
Butter Pat, Gold Rim	5.50
Butter Pat, Princess	9.00
Butter, Covered, Allover Floral Sprays	48.00
Chocolate Pot, Floral, Marked	140.00
Chocolate Pot, Hand-Painted Roses Yellow Ground, Gold Trim	150.00
Chocolate Pot, Ribbon Handle & Finial, 10 In.	169.00
Coffeepot, Bird Design	20.00
Coffeepot, Floral, Double Marked	40.00
Cup & Saucer, Bretagne	22.50
Cup & Saucer, Gotham Pattern	20.00
Cup & Saucer, Lavender Flowers Inside Cup	29.00
Cup & Saucer, Montabello	28.00
Cup & Saucer, Pasadena	22.50
Dish, Vegetable, Drop Rose, Gold Pressed Edge, Handled, 11 In.	175.00
Fish Plate, Hand-Painted, C.1905, Signed, 9 In.Diam.	45.00
Gravy Boat, Attached Underplate, Gotham Pattern	45.00
Invalid Feeder	14.00
Oyster Plate, Gold Flowers, 4 Wells, Flower Shape Sauce Well	37.50
Oyster Plate, Green Seaweed, 5 Impressions, Pink Ground, 8 1/2 In.	55.00
Oyster Plate, Hand-Painted Flowers, Gold Border, Blue, 8 1/2 In.	70.00
Oyster Plate, Starfish Center, 6 Wells, Hand-Painted, 8 1/2 In.	95.00
Pitcher, Milk, Drop Rose, Red, 8 In.	185.00
Pitcher, Milk, Flying Cranes, Gold Rope Handle, 6 1/2 In.	50.00
Pitcher, Milk, Norma Pattern, 7 In.	85.00
Plate, Gotham Pattern, 6 1/2 In.	12.00
Plate, Gotham Pattern, 9 In.	15.00
Plate, Gotham Pattern, 10 1/2 In.	18.00
Plate, Hand-Painted Red Poppies, 12 In.	85.00
Plate, Pink & Blue Garlands On Rim, Scalloped, Gold Edge, 9 1/2 In.	16.00
Plate, Pink Flowers, Leaves, 10 In., Set Of 8	200.00
Platter, Gotham Pattern, 14 In.	65.00
Platter, Pink Carnations, 18 X 12 1/2 In.	65.00
Sign, Dealer, French, Porcelain	75.00
Snack Set, Yellow Flowers, Gold Trim, Curved Mark	25.00
Sugar & Creamer, Violet, Hand-Painted	45.00
Tea Set, Flowers, Blue, Pink, Gold Trim, Skirted Base	249.00
Tea Set, Gold Scalloped Base, 3 Piece	230.00
Tea Set, Hand-Painted Gold Flowers, Scalloped Base, 3 Piece	229.00

Tea Set, Ranson Pattern, 3 Piece	95.00
Teapot, Frontenac	88.00
Tray, Dresser, Island Scene, Sun Bird, Sky Blue Edge, 8 3/4 In.	20.00
Tray, Sandwich, Daisies, Purple Clover, 11 X 6 1/2 In.	38.50
Tumbler, Ale, Mephistopheles	35.00
Vase, Hatted Ladies & Flowers, Paneled, Limoges, 5 1/4 In.	350.00

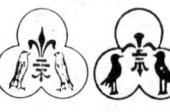

T.G.Hawkes & Company of Corning, New York, was founded in 1880. The firm cut glass made at other firms until 1962. Many pieces are marked with the trademark, a trefoil ring enclosing a fleur-de-lis and two hawks.

HAWKES, see also Cut Glass

HAWKES, Ashtray, Gilt Sterling Silver Overlay, Yellow, Signed, 3 1/2 In.	125.00
Beverage Set, Thistle Pattern, 1 Quart Jug, 4 Glasses, Silver Rim, Set	250.00
Bottle, Bitters, Thumbprint, Square Cut Base, Silver Plated Top, 5 In.	50.00
Bottle, Oil & Vinegar, Sterling Silver Stopper, Signed, 7 1/2 In.	125.00
Bottle, Water, Brunswick Pattern, Signed	225.00
Bowl, Candy, Crossed Bars, Stars, Signed, 5 1/2 In.	95.00
Bowl, Cosmos Pattern, Gravic, C.1900, 2 3/4 In.	36.00
Bowl, Delft Diamond, 8 1/4 In.	165.00
Bowl, Flowers, Leaves, Geometric Design, Signed, 5 X 6 In.	110.00
Bowl, Flowers, 8-Point Hobstars, Signed, 8 In.Diam.	185.00
Bowl, Gravic, Strawberry Pattern, Signed, 8 1/2 In.	365.00
Bowl, Hobstars Alternating With Flowers & Leaves, 8 In.	145.00
Bowl, Kohinoor & Honeycomb, Signed, 5 X 10 In.Diam.	295.00
Bowl, New Princess Pattern, Signed, 8 In.Diam.	135.00
Bowl, Stylized Flowers, 8 In.	155.00
Box, Barrel Shaped, Fans & Hobstars In Diamonds, Signed, 6 1/2 In.	495.00
Candlestick, Round Bottom & Top, Blown, Signed, 4 In., Pair	340.00
Carafe, Water, Brazilian Pattern, Single Star Base, Signed, 7 1/2 In.	525.00
Carafe, Water, Chrysanthemum Pattern, Hobstar Base, 7 1/2 In.	595.00
Carafe, Water, Venetian Pattern	285.00
Celery, Classic Pattern, Signed, 10 1/4 X 4 1/2 In.	210.00
Compote, Copper-Wheel Floral, Green Stem & Foot, 7 X 7 In.	135.00
Compote, Green Floral Etched Rim, C.1925, 2 In.	120.00
Compote, Queen's Pattern, Pedestal, Faceted Knob, Signed, 12 In.	825.00
Console Set, Rose Of Sharon Pattern, C.1910, Bowl, 4 1/4 In.	90.00
Cordial, Chelsea Rose, 4 3/4 In.	22.00
Cordial, Delft Diamond, 3 3/4 In.	40.00
Cordial, Floral & Leaf Cutting, Signed	18.00
Cordial, St.Regis Pattern, 4 3/8 In.	40.00
Cruet, Cut Glass, Hobstars, Notched Handle, 7 In.	99.50
Decanter, Cut & Rye Pattern, 12 In.	125.00
Decanter, Paneled, Starburst Base, Stopper, Marked, 7 1/4 In., Pair	160.00
Decanter, Sierra Pattern, Set Of 6 Goblets	375.00
Dish, Leaf, Hobstars, Signed	125.00
Frame, Picture, Oval, Etched Floral Design, C.1900, 7 In.	150.00
Goblet, Aragon Pattern, Green Stem & Foot	30.00
Goblet, Ramsey Pattern, 6 3/8 In.	25.00
Goblet, Sierra Pattern, 7 5/8 In.	75.00
Goblet, Water, Flowers, Flutes, Swags, & Miters, Signed, 8 1/2 In.	125.00
Goblet, Wild Rose, 6 1/2 In.	45.00
Goblet, Wine, Floral & Leaf Cutting, Signed, 2 Oz.	18.00
Ice Tea, Cornwall Pattern, 5 3/4 In.	30.00
Ice Tub, Queen's Pattern, Hobstar Base, 4 1/2 X 6 In.Diam.	575.00
Jar, Candy, Floral Cutting, Footed, Signed, 9 In.	70.00
Jar, Jam, Copper Wheel, Engraved, Crystal, Sterling Knob	48.00
Jug, Rye, Gravis Cut, Intaglio Work, Signed	725.00
Knife Rest, Signed	22.50
Nappy, Classic Pattern, Handle, Signed	175.00
Perfume, Teutonic Pattern, Sterling Top, 7 In.	150.00
Pitcher, Etched Game Bird, Applied Handle, 16 In.	48.00

Pitcher, Intaglio Cosmos & Hobstars, 4 Tumblers, Signed 425.00
Pitcher, Iris Pattern, Signed, 8 In. 595.00
Pitcher, Martini, Floral Cut 185.00
Pitcher, Water, Iris Pattern, Gravic, C.1900, 8 1/2 In. 200.00
Plate, Enameled, Pink, Blue Flowers, Gold Rim & Lattice, 7 In. 25.00
Plate, Fleur-De-Lis In Trefoil, Stamped Twice, 8 In. 10.00
Plate, Green, Crystal, Signed, 7 1/2 In. 15.00
Plate, Henley Pattern, 8 1/2 In. 20.00
Plate, Three Fruits, 8 1/4 In. 87.00
Rose Bowl, Etched Flowers, Gold Rim, Green, Signed 65.00
Rose Bowl, Queen's Pattern, Signed 250.00
Salt, Trefoil, Signed, 1 7/8 In. 12.00
Sherbet, Colonial Pattern, 2 1/2 In. 45.00
Sherbet, Foley Pattern, 4 1/2 In. 30.00
Sherbet, Henley Pattern, 4 7/8 In. 20.00
Sherbet, Laurel Pattern, 4 7/8 In. 20.00
Sherbet, Marquis Of Waterford, 4 1/4 In. 30.00
Sherbet, Wild Rose, 5 In. 45.00
Sherry, Henley Pattern, 5 1/4 In. 20.00
Sugar & Creamer, Flutes & Greek Border, 3 X 3 1/2 In. 285.00
Sugar & Creamer, Footed, 4 Feet, Rock Crystal, Victorian Shape, Signed 750.00
Sugar & Creamer, Glass Base, Sterling Silver Band, 4 In. 155.00
Sugar & Creamer, Sterling Silver Base, Marked 125.00
Tray, Centauri Pattern, Signed, 12 In. 955.00
Tray, Panel, Type Cutting, Signed, 10 In.Diam. 875.00
Tray, Serving, Jar In Center, Chain Of Hobstars, Signed, 11 In.Diam. 425.00
Tumbler, Centauri Pattern, Signed, Set Of 5 .... 450.00
Tumbler, Conquest Pattern, 3 7/8 In. 35.00
Tumbler, Doris Pattern, 3 5/8 In. 40.00
Tumbler, Juice, Marquis Of Waterford, 3 5/8 In. 20.00
Tumbler, Molded Crest On Side, 5 In. 18.00
Tumbler, Oxford Pattern, 3 3/4 In. 40.00
Tumbler, Queen's Pattern 155.00
Tumbler, York Pattern, Signed, Set Of 9 .... 405.00
Vase, Copper Wheel Engraved, Signed, Green, 8 1/2 In. 55.00
Vase, Dark Cranberry, Cut To Clear, Silver Deposit Trim, 9 In. 125.00
Vase, Dragon, Enameled Crystal, Engraved, Signed, 8 In. 85.00
Vase, Flowers, Gravic Style, 14 In. 144.00
Vase, Gravic, Chrysanthemum Pattern, Signed, 10 1/2 In. 550.00
Vase, Iris Pattern, Flared, Silver Base, Marked, 12 In. 325.00
Vase, Isis Pattern, Blue, 7 3/4 In. 225.00
Vase, Isis Pattern, Clear, 3 7/8 In. 40.00
Vase, Mum Pattern, Gravic Cut, Signed, 10 1/2 In. 575.00
Vase, Scalloped Hobstars Top, Bull's-Eye Cutting, Signed, 11 7/8 In. 350.00
Vase, Scalloped Rim, Wheel Cut Floral Design, C.1910, 9 3/4 In. 80.00
Vase, Stars, Engraved Flowers, Signed, 5 In. 175.00
Vase, Trumpet, Signed, 14 1/2 In. 230.00
Vase, Trumpet, Venetian Pattern, 8 In. 265.00
Vase, Urn Shape, Wheel Engraved, Cobalt Trim, 4 In. 75.00
Wine, Brazilian Pattern, Knobbed Teardrop Stem, Signed, Set Of 4 .... 525.00
Wine, Floral & Leaf Cutting, 2 Ounce, Set Of 6 .... 60.00
Wine, Marquis Of Waterford, 7 In. 30.00
Wine, Parfait Shape, Grapevine Pattern, 5 5/8 In. 40.00
Wine, Wheat Pattern, 5 3/8 In. 30.00

Heintz Art Metal shop made jewelry, copper, silver, and brass in Buffalo, New York, from 1915 to about 1935. It became Heintz Brothers Manufacturers about 1935.

HEINTZ ART, Vase, Iris, Silver Overlay, 6 In. 75.00
Vase, Roses, Sterling Silver Overlay, Bronze, 8 In. 125.00

H

Heisey glass was made from 1895 to 1958 in Newark, Ohio, by A.H. Heisey and Co., Inc.

HEISEY, see also Custard Glass

HEISEY, Ashtray, Empress, Sahara	130.00
Basket, Fruit, Butterfly Cut	150.00
Bell, Victorian Belle	125.00
Berry Set, Beaded Swag, Signed, 7 Piece	250.00
Berry Set, Ridgeleigh, 4 Piece	35.00
Berry, Beaded Swag, Custard Glass	37.50
Bonbon, Crystolite	23.00
Bonbon, Silver Plated Basket, Oval, Marigold, Recessed Panel, 9 In.	85.00
Bookends, Fighting Rooster	145.00
Bookends, Fish	85.00 To 210.00
Bookends, Smiling Fish, Crystal	70.00
Bottle, Bitters, Tally Ho	110.00
Bottle, Cologne, Etched, Crystal	60.00
Bottle, Ridgeleigh, Oil & Vinegar	25.00
Bottle, Water, Fancy Loop	60.00
Bottle, Water, Punty & Diamond Point	60.00
Bowl & Candleholders, Wampum	100.00
Bowl, Base, Punch, Sunburst, Signed	50.00
Bowl, Berry, Peerless	25.00
Bowl, Colonial, Signed, 7 1/2 In.	20.00
Bowl, Cornucopia, Warwick, Cobalt Blue, 11 In.	275.00
Bowl, Crystolite, Oval, 13 In.	30.00
Bowl, Dolphin, Empress, Footed, Signed, 11 In.	249.00
Bowl, Fandango, 8 In.	25.00
Bowl, Flared Flute, Signed & Dated, 1 1/2 X 5 In.	16.00
Bowl, Fruit, Queen Ann, Marked, 8 In.	35.00
Bowl, Gardenia, Waverly, Enchantress Cutting, 13 In.	65.00
Bowl, Greek Key, 8 In.	24.00 To 55.00
Bowl, Narrow Flute, Signed, Dated, 8 In.	26.00
Bowl, Octagon, Pink, 10 1/2 In.	75.00
Bowl, Orchid Etch, 7 In.	25.00
Bowl, Oval, Flamingo & Crystal, 10 In.	38.50
Bowl, Pillows, Signed, 8 1/2 In.	50.00
Bowl, Pinwheel & Fan, 8 In.	55.00
Bowl, Punch, Greek Key, Pedestal, 15 In.	185.00
Bowl, Punch, Prison Stripe, Pedestal, Silver Overlay, 8 Cups	395.00
Bowl, Queen Ann, Floral, 11 In.	45.00
Bowl, Ridgeleigh, Dawn Color, 8 In.	30.00
Bowl, Rose, Ring Band, 8 In.	150.00
Bowl, Twist, Green, 8 In.	30.00
Bowl, Victorian Pattern, 8 In.	40.00
Bowl, Waverly, Flowers, 11 In.	25.00
Bowl, Waverly, Seahorse Footed, 11 In.	50.00
Box, Candy, Waverly, Footed	85.00
Box, Cigar, Horsehead	75.00
Box, Cigarette, Crystolite	30.00
Box, Cigarette, Ridgeleigh, Covered, Signed, 4 In.	18.00 To 23.00
Box, Cigarette, Waverly, Seahorse Handle, Marked, 5 1/2 In.	82.50
Box, Dresser, Lady With Flowing Hair	150.00
Box, Powder, Colonial, Sterling Silver Top, 4 In.Diam.	35.00
Butter, Custard Ring Band, Red Roses, Gold, Marked	175.00 To 195.00
Butter, Plantation, Covered	50.00
Cake Set, Empress, Sahara, Old Colony Etched	90.00
Candelabra, Ipswich, Insets, Prisms, Pair	150.00
Candelabra, Sahara, 2-Light, Low	350.00
Candleholder, Crystolite, 3-Light	40.00
Candleholder, Moongleam, 3 In., Pair	30.00

Candleholder, Stanhope, 2-Branch	45.00
Candleholder, Trident, 2-Light, Pair	48.00
Candleholder, Wampum, Crystal, 3 1/2 In., Pair	30.00
Candlestick, Acorn, Lead Crystal, 3 Branch, 5 In., Pair	145.00
Candlestick, Cascade, 3-Light, Pair	88.00
Candlestick, Chintz Etch, Sahara, Pair	90.00
Candlestick, Cornucopia, Pair	35.00
Candlestick, Crystolite, 1-Light, Pair	25.00
Candlestick, Empress, Sahara, Dolphin Footed, Pair	175.00
Candlestick, Flamingo, Cherub, Frosted	300.00
Candlestick, Lariat, Pair	200.00
Candlestick, Liberty, Amber, 3 In., Pair	35.00
Candlestick, New Era, 2-Light, Amber, Pair	68.00
Candlestick, Orchid Etch, 1-Light, 3 In., Pair	65.00
Candlestick, Orchid, 1-Light	45.00
Candlestick, Regency, Double, Pair	25.00
Candlestick, Sparky, Amber, 6 In., Pair	65.00
Candlestick, Swan, Pair	275.00
Candlestick, Toy, Signed, Pair	40.00
Candlestick, Trident, Flamingo.Pair	105.00
Candy Jar, Colonial, Hand-Painted, Gold Trim, Covered, Footed	45.00
Celery, Amber Flashed, Oval, 12 In.	35.00
Celery, Empress, Flamingo, 12 In.	25.00
Celery, Flamingo	22.00
Celery, Flamingo, Twisted End, 12 In.	15.00
Celery, Moongleam	22.00
Celery, Sahara	24.50
Champagne, Ipswich, Sahara, Footed, Signed	35.00
Champagne, Minuet, Etch, Symphone Stem	10.00
Champagne, Moonglo	18.00
Champagne, Oxford, Signed	15.00
Champagne, Peerless	8.00
Champagne, Priscilla, Signed, 4 Ounce	12.50
Champagne, Tyrolean, 6 Ounce	25.00
Cigarette Holder, Ridgeleigh	16.00
Cigarette Holder, Winged Scroll, Emerald Green	135.00
Claret, Oxford, Etched	25.00
Claret, Priscilla, Signed, 4 Ounce	22.00
Claret, Rose Etch, 4 1/2 Ounce	60.00
Coaster, Crystolite, 4 In.Diam.	3.25
Cocktail Set, Country Club, 6 Clarets	200.00
Cocktail Shaker, Chintz	200.00
Cocktail Shaker, Cutting Of Pheasants In Forest Scene, 3 Piece	275.00
Cocktail Shaker, Intaglio Etch Of Hunter & Dog, Strainer	75.00
Cocktail Shaker, Orchid, 1 Quart, 3 Piece	130.00
Cocktail Shaker, Rooster	68.00 To 87.50
Cocktail Shaker, Tally Ho, 1 Quart, 3 Piece	140.00
Cocktail Shaker, Tally Ho, 3 Piece, 2 Quart	165.00
Cocktail Shaker, 4 Roly Poly, Cobalt Blue, Signed	200.00
Cocktail, Albermarle, 3 Ounce	10.00
Cocktail, Caliente, Skier Etch, Aqua	65.00
Cocktail, Colonial, Signed, 3 Ounce	14.00
Cocktail, Crystolite, 3 1/2 Ounce	22.00
Cocktail, Goose Stem, Frosted Goose	145.00
Cocktail, Ipswich	10.00
Cocktail, Midcentury	12.00
Cocktail, Rooster Head	60.00
Cocktail, Skier, Footed, 4 Ounce	90.00
Cocktail, Tyrolean, 4 Ounce	37.50
Cocktail, Zodiac, Marked	18.00
Cologne, Lariat	45.00
Compote, Fandango, 10 In.	85.00
Compote, Fluted, 5 1/2 In.	35.00

Compote, Jelly, Coarse Rib, Marked 25.00
Compote, Jelly, Paneled Cane, Marked 30.00
Compote, Jelly, Peerless, Flared, Footed, 4 1/2 In. 25.00
Compote, Kalonyal Pattern 38.00
Compote, Lariat With Moonglow Etch, Covered, Marked, Crystolite 35.00
Compote, Pedestal, Copper Wheel Design, Covered 38.00
Compote, Queen Ann, Flared Edges, Stem Design, Marked, 6 1/4 In. 40.00
Compote, Queen Ann, Oval, 6 In. 25.00
Compote, Sahara, Pedestal, 6 In. 30.00
Compote, Waverly, Oval 60.00
Console Set, Center Fishbowl, Candlesticks, Marked, Bowl, 8 1/2 In. 675.00
Console Set, Sunflower, Signed, 3 Piece 45.00
Console Set, Wampum, Bowl & Candlesticks 55.00
Cordial, Beaded Swag, Souvenir 35.00
Cordial, Narrow Flute, Marked, 2 Ounce 15.00
Cordial, Narrow Flute, 1 Ounce 20.00
Cornucopia, Cobalt Blue, Footed, Marked 225.00
Cream & Sugar, Crystolite, Oval, Signed 30.00
Creamer, Beaded Swag 20.00
Creamer, Custard Punty Band, Souvenir, Lebanon, N.H., Individual 45.00
Creamer, Fancy Loop, Emerald, Individual 50.00
Creamer, Orchid, Crystal, Footed 35.00
Creamer, Pineapple & Fan, Green & Gold 29.00
Creamer, Punty Band, Souvenir, Ft.Wayne, Indiana 45.00
Creamer, Rose Design, Ring Band 75.00
Creamer, Sawtooth 25.00
Creme De Menthe, Colonial, Signed, 2 1/2 In. 12.50
Cruet, Banded Flute, 4 Ounce 22.50
Cruet, Colonial, Stopper .... 25.00 To 30.00
Cruet, Crystolite 48.00
Cruet, Flared Panel, Stopper 35.00
Cruet, Lariat, Original Stopper 28.50
Cruet, Medium Flat Panel 30.00
Cruet, Pineapple & Fan, Green, Gold Trim 195.00
Cruet, Pineapple & Fan, Stopper 65.00
Cruet, Pineapple, Marked, 6 1/4 In. 40.00
Cruet, Plantation 60.00
Cruet, Pleat & Panel, Flamingo .... 57.50 To 65.00
Cruet, Puritan .... 14.00 To 30.00
Cruet, Queen Ann, Sahara, Original Stopper 40.00
Cruet, Saturn .... 35.00 To 45.00
Cruet, Sunken Panels, Tapered 20.00
Cruet, Waverly, Pair 35.00
Cruet, Yeoman, Stopper 18.00
Cup & Saucer, Demitasse, Sahara 25.00
Cup & Saucer, Orchid 35.00
Cup & Saucer, Queen Ann 30.00
Cup & Saucer, Revere, Sahara, Gold Bands, Signed 16.00
Cup & Saucer, Swirl, Green 25.00
Cup & Saucer, Yeoman, Flamingo Etch 15.00
Cup, Bouillon, Moongleam, Underplate, Handled, Set Of 4 .... 140.00
Cup, Lariat 8.00
Cup, Nut, Flamingo, Dolphin, Footed 15.00
Cup, Punch, Beaded Panel & Sunburst, Silver Overlay 12.00
Cup, Punch, Colonial, Rayed Base 7.00
Cup, Punch, Plantation 20.00
Cup, Punch, Rib & Panel, Signed 8.00
Cup, Punch, Victorian 8.00
Custard, Priscilla, 5 Ounce 6.00
Decanter, Bell Shape, Marked 85.00
Decanter, Carcassone Alexandrite 350.00
Decanter, Panel & Sunburst 85.00
Decanter, Penguin, Stopper 175.00
Decanter, Rooster Head, Stopper, 3 Pieces, 16 In. 75.00

Decanter, Sandwich, Crystal	135.00
Decanter, Tally Ho, Etched, 32 Ounce	150.00
Decanter, Whiskey, Stopper	75.00
Dish, Butter, Bottom, Pineapple & Fan	35.00
Dish, Butter, Custard, Ring Band, Signed	220.00
Dish, Candy, Bowtie, Covered, Marked	95.00
Dish, Candy, Etched Panel, Footed, Silver Plate Overlay	46.50
Dish, Candy, Greek Key, Open, 3 X 6 In.	45.00
Dish, Candy, Lariat, Orchid Shape, Handle Etched, 6 3/4 In.	40.00
Dish, Candy, Waverly, Covered	60.00
Dish, Colonial Design, Set Of 12, 4 1/2 In.	50.00
Dish, Honey, Orchid, Footed, 6 In.	32.50
Dish, Leaf, Crystolite	7.00
Dish, Octagon, Marigold, 2-Handled	25.00
Dish, Sauce, Custard Glass, Beaded Swag	40.00
Duck, Flower Frog, Flamingo	285.00
Figurine, Asiatic Pheasant, Marked	375.00
Figurine, Asiatic Pheasant, 10 1/2 In.	100.00
Figurine, Cygnet, Marked	185.00
Figurine, Donkey, Imperial Slag	42.00
Figurine, Donkey, Meadowbrook Green, Iridized, Numbered	150.00
Figurine, Elephant, Baby	175.00
Figurine, Elephant, Imperial Slag	40.00
Figurine, Elephant, Marked, Large	275.00
Figurine, Elephant, Medium	195.00 To 220.00
Figurine, Gazelle	1350.00
Figurine, Geese, Set Of 3	495.00
Figurine, Giraffe, Head Turned	140.00 To 195.00
Figurine, Goose, Wings Down	80.00 To 350.00
Figurine, Goose, Wings Halfway	65.00 To 110.00
Figurine, Goose, Wings Up	75.00 To 95.00
Figurine, Hen	425.00
Figurine, Mallard, Wings Down, Caramel Slag	300.00
Figurine, Mallard, Wings Half Up	30.00
Figurine, Piglets, Marked	95.00
Figurine, Plug Horse	75.00 To 95.00
Figurine, Ponies, Set Of 3	295.00
Figurine, Pony, Kicking, Blue, Imperial	20.00
Figurine, Pony, Rearing, 3 3/4 In.	20.00 To 190.00
Figurine, Pony, Standing	40.00 To 75.00
Figurine, Pony, Standing, Amber	280.00
Figurine, Pony, Standing, Imperial Slag	20.00
Figurine, Pony, Standing, Ultra Blue	40.00
Figurine, Pouter Pigeon	500.00
Figurine, Ringneck Pheasant	95.00 To 120.00
Figurine, Rooster	475.00
Figurine, Rooster, Fighting	90.00 To 115.00
Figurine, Scotty	75.00 To 100.00
Figurine, Sparky	95.00
Figurine, Sparky, Imperial Slag	25.00
Figurine, Sparrow	75.00 To 80.00
Figurine, Wood Duck, Imperial Slag	35.00
Finger Bowl, Underplate, Amethyst	17.50
Glass, Bar, Old Sandwich, Signed	12.00 To 15.00
Glass, Old-Fashioned, Coleport, Marked	9.00
Glass, Old-Fashioned, Equestrian	50.00
Glass, Pilsner, Signed, 10 Ounce	22.50
Goblet, Albermarle, 8 Ounce	15.00
Goblet, Bead Swag	50.00
Goblet, Bobwhite, 10 Ounce	25.00
Goblet, Carcassonne, Sahara, Old Colony Etched	16.00 To 18.00
Goblet, Charter Oak, Marked	14.00
Goblet, Chintz, Etched	25.00
Goblet, Colonial, Signed, 9 Ounce	22.00

Goblet, Crystolite	15.00 To 18.00
Goblet, Duquesne, Normandie Etch	18.00 To 25.00
Goblet, Fairacre, Moongleam Stem & Foot, Marked	20.00
Goblet, Fancy Loop, Green	55.00
Goblet, Greek Key, 7 Ounce	180.00
Goblet, Ice Tea, Midcentury	10.00 To 12.00
Goblet, Ipswich	20.00
Goblet, Lariat, 10 Ounce	30.00
Goblet, Midcentury, Marked	23.00
Goblet, Monte Cristo, Olympiad Etch	15.00
Goblet, Moonglo	20.00
Goblet, New Era	10.00
Goblet, Normandie, Etched	25.00
Goblet, Old Colony Etch, Sahara	14.00
Goblet, Old Colony, Carcassonne, Etched	20.00
Goblet, Old Dominion, 10 Ounce	30.00 To 50.00
Goblet, Old Sandwich, Low Footed, Marked	15.00
Goblet, Olympiad, Spanish Stem	28.00
Goblet, Orchid	25.00 To 35.00
Goblet, Penn Charter, Checkerboard Optic, Amber	27.00
Goblet, Plantation	18.00 To 25.00
Goblet, Plateau, Flamingo	12.00 To 15.00
Goblet, Portsmouth, Amber	15.00
Goblet, Portsmouth, Flamingo	22.00
Goblet, Rose Etched	40.00
Goblet, Sabrino, Etch	15.00
Goblet, Spanish, Cobalt Blue Bowl, 10 Ounce	75.00
Goblet, Stanhope, Swingtime Etch	33.00
Goblet, Sussex, Green Bowl, Clear Stem, Signed	37.50
Goblet, Trojan, Stemmed, Etched, Flamingo, 8 Ounce	22.00
Goblet, Tyrolean, Short, 10 Ounce	30.00
Goblet, Victorian	15.00
Goblet, Wabash Frontenac, Etched	22.50
Goblet, Wabash, Moongleam Stem & Foot, Frontenac Etch, Marked	23.00
Goblet, Wabash, Pied Piper Etch, Marked	20.00
Goblet, Water, Fancy Loop, Emerald	15.00
Goblet, Water, Narrow Flute, Marked	15.00
Goblet, Water, Victorian, Yellow	10.00
Goblet, Whirlpool, Marked	13.00
Highball, Astor	20.00
Honey, Orchid, Footed	30.00
Humidor, Greek Key, 10 In.	95.00
Ice Bucket, Dolphin Feet, Sterling Silver Overlay Grape & Leaf	65.00
Ice Bucket, Empress, Sahara, Tongs	125.00
Ice Bucket, Twist	105.00
Ice Cream Set, Sunburst, Signed, 7 Piece	95.00 To 120.00
Ice Tea, Symphony Minuet, Etched, 12 Ounce	25.00
Ice Tea, Tyrolean, 12 Ounce	30.00
Ice Tea, Wabash Frontenac, Etched, Footed	20.00
Ice Tea, Zodiac, Silver Overlay	15.00
Ice Tub, Flamingo, Handled, Cut	98.50
Ice Tub, Ridgeleigh	50.00
Jar, Candy, Colonial, Gold Trim, Covered, Footed, Blue, Pink, & Green	45.00
Jar, Candy, Imperial, Amethyst	45.00
Jar, Catsup, Colonial, Stopper	35.00
Jar, Crushed Fruit, Flat Panel Pattern, Marked & Dated 1908, 2 Quart	95.00
Jar, Fruit, Greek Key, Covered, Large	325.00
Jar, Marmalade, Plantation, Spoon, Milk Glass	50.00
Jar, Mustard, Twist, Pink	40.00
Jelly, Puritan, Signed, Handled	22.00
Jug, Cider, Old Williamsburg, Cobalt Blue	225.00
Jug, Fandango, Squat	450.00
Juice, El Rancho, Footed, Signed	15.00

Juice, Old Dominion, Footed, Set Of 8	40.00
Juice, Tally Ho	47.50
Juice, Tyrolean, 5 Ounce	37.50
Lamp, Ridgeleigh	50.00
Marmalade Set, Plantation, Tray, Spoons	300.00
Marmalade, Plantation, Covered.Signed	60.00
Mayonnaise Set, Empress, Etch, Octagon, Footed	25.00
Mayonnaise Set, Provincial Limelight, 3-Handled	85.00
Mayonnaise Set, Waverly, Orchid, Etched, 8 In.	20.00 To 55.00
Mayonnaise, Empress, Flamingo, Footed, Signed, 5 1/2 In.	35.00 To 40.00
Mayonnaise, Empress, Sahara	30.00
Mug, Beaded Swag, Souvenir, Pan Am Exposition, Buffalo, 1901	65.00
Mug, Beer, Club Drinking Scene	125.00
Mug, Beer, Moongleam, 12 Ounce	250.00
Mug, Beer, Old Sandwich, Sahara, 16 Ounce	150.00
Mug, Beer, Sportsman Etched, Marked	175.00
Mug, Custard, Devils Lake & Baraboo, Wis., Signed	50.00
Mug, Punty Band, Custard, Signed	35.00 To 40.00
Mustard, Victorian	37.50
Nappy, Colonial, Signed, 9 In.	20.00
Nappy, Empress, Flamingo, 2-Handled, 5 In.	20.00
Nappy, Flat Panel, Signed, 4 1/2 In.	10.00
Nappy, Ice Cream, Colonial, Signed, Set Of 5, 5 1/2 In.	38.00
Nappy, Locket On Chain	35.00
Nappy, Prison Stripe, Marked	18.00
Nappy, Sunburst, Scalloped, Silver Overlay	29.00
Nappy, Sunflower, Signed, 12 In.	35.00
Nappy, Twist, Green, 4 In.Diam.	5.00
Nut Cup, Moongleam, Green, Marked, Pair	22.00
Paperweight, Figural, Rabbit, Milk Glass	12.00
Pitcher, Colonial, Squatty	50.00
Pitcher, Narrow Flute, Signed, 1 Pint	50.00
Pitcher, Narrow Flute, Signed, 3 Pint	75.00
Pitcher, Plantation	175.00
Pitcher, Puritan, Signed, 1 Quart	60.00
Pitcher, Puritan, Signed, 1/2 Gallon	75.00
Pitcher, Rib & Panel, 2 Quart	35.00
Pitcher, Sunburst	140.00
Pitcher, Water, Beaded Swag, Ruby Stained Etched Band, Gold Beading	150.00
Pitcher, Water, Colonial, Gold Trim	35.00
Pitcher, Water, Flute, Marked	65.00
Pitcher, Water, Pinwheel & Fan	95.00
Pitcher, Water, Queen Ann, Red Flashing	250.00
Plate, Cake, Beaded Swag	125.00
Plate, Cake, Flamingo, Marked	15.00
Plate, Cake, Twist, 4-Footed, Pink	35.00
Plate, Cheese & Cracker, Crystal, 2 Tier	38.00
Plate, Cheese, Frog, Green	150.00
Plate, Crystolite, Crystal, Signed, 13 In.	20.00
Plate, Empress, Sahara, 8 In.Square	20.00 To 50.00
Plate, Empress, Tangerine, 7 In.	95.00
Plate, Flamingo Twist, 7 In., Set Of 6	30.00
Plate, Flat Panel, Signed, 9 1/4 In.	16.00
Plate, Groove & Slash	5.00
Plate, Ipswich, 7 In.	12.00
Plate, Ipswich, 8 In.	12.00 To 16.00
Plate, Lariat	6.00
Plate, Lariat, Sides Up, 8 In.	15.00
Plate, Mah-Jong, 12 In.	125.00
Plate, Minuet, Etch, 8 In.	10.00
Plate, Moongleam, Beehive, 8 In.	35.00
Plate, Moongleam, Signed, Square, 6 In.	10.00
Plate, Moongleam, 7 In.	5.00

Plate, Moongleam, 8 In.	10.00
Plate, Orchid Etch, 7 In.	20.00
Plate, Orchid, 8 In.	27.50
Plate, Queen Ann	10.00
Plate, Sahara, 7 3/8 In.Square	7.50
Plate, Sahara, 8 In.Diam.	7.50
Plate, Sahara, 8 In.Square	12.00
Plate, Sandwich Star	250.00
Plate, Sandwich, Waverly, Orchid Etch, 10 1/2 In.	25.00
Plate, Swirl, Green, 7 In.	20.00
Plate, Torte, Queen Ann, Orchid Etched	55.00
Plate, Torte, Waverly, Orchid Etched, 14 In.	35.00
Plate, Waverly, Flowers, 8 In.	10.00 To 17.50
Plate, Waverly, Rose, 7 In.Diam.	15.00
Plate, Yeoman, Flamingo Etch, 8 In.	4.00
Platter, Fern, Zircon Color, 15 In.	75.00
Platter, Skier, Etching Fern Design, Marked, 14 In.	185.00
Punch Bowl & Base, Sunburst	250.00
Punch Bowl, Colonial	25.00
Punch Bowl, Colonial Pattern, 8 Cups, Bowl, 11 1/2 X 11 1/2 In.	285.00
Punch Bowl, Pineapple, 12 Cups, Signed	295.00 To 395.00
Punch Cup, Beaded Swag	9.00
Punch Cup, Colonial Panel, Signed, 4 1/2 In.	10.00
Punch Cup, Puritan, 4 1/2 Ounce	8.00
Punch Cup, Victorian	8.00
Punch Set, Colonial Design Bowl, Marked, 12 Cups	275.00
Punch Set, Colonial, 8 Cups, Marked, Bowl, 11 1/2 X 11 1/2 In.	285.00
Punch Set, Plantation, Underplate, 8 Cups, Hangers, Ladle, & Bowl	650.00
Relish, Crystolite, 3 Compartment	12.00
Relish, Lariat, Etched, 3 Part	23.00
Relish, Orchid, 3-Section, Oblong	65.50
Relish, Plantation, 2 Compartment	25.00
Relish, Queen Ann, Sahara, Engraved, 12 X 4 In.	35.00
Relish, Waverly, 3 Part, Orchid Etched, 11 In.	35.00
Rose Bowl, Fandango, 4 In.	90.00
Rose Bowl, Moongleam, 9 In.	150.00
Rose Bowl, Waverly, Barcelona Cutting, Metal Base, 7 In.	75.00
Salad Set, Flamingo, 4 Plates, Bowl, 10 In.	60.00
Salt & Pepper, Crystolite	15.00
Salt & Pepper, Flamingo, Signed, 3 In.	45.00
Salt & Pepper, Plantation	39.50
Salt & Pepper, Waverly, Silver Overlay	25.00
Salt Dip, Crystolite, Leaf	12.50
Salt, Square In Diamond	18.00
Saltshaker, Punty Band, 1904 Etched	22.00
Sauce, Fancy Loop, Gold Trim	9.00
Sauce, Provincial, Limelight, Signed	30.00
Saucer, Demitasse, Sahara	10.00
Sherbet, Athena	18.00
Sherbet, Carcassonne, Lafayette Etch	10.00
Sherbet, Chintz	15.00
Sherbet, Greek Key, Marked	11.00
Sherbet, Ipswich	10.00 To 12.00
Sherbet, Orchid	25.00
Sherbet, Paneled & Stemmed	34.00
Sherbet, Peerless, Fluted, Signed, 4 1/2 Ounce	22.00
Sherbet, Peerless, Low, Footed, Signed, 5 Ounce	12.50
Sherbet, Rib & Panel	10.00
Sherbet, Spanish, Titania Etch	23.00
Sherbet, Wagon Wheel, Signed	6.00
Sherbet, Yeoman, Moongleam Etch	8.00
Shot Glass, Tally Ho, Etched	30.00
Shot Glass, Victorian	15.00 To 18.00

Soda, Donna, 12 Ounce	49.50
Soda, Fisherman, 12 Ounce	70.00
Soda, Golf Scene, Marked, 12 Ounce	150.00
Soda, Ipswich, Footed, 5 Ounce	10.00
Soda, Lancaster, 8 Ounce	55.00
Soda, Moongleam Twist	12.00
Soda, Nimrod, 12 Ounce	35.00
Soda, Normandie, Footed	18.00
Soda, Tally Ho, 8 Ounce	30.00
Soup, Cream, Yeoman, Moongleam Etch, 6 1/2 In.	12.00
Soup, Moongleam, Yeoman	12.00
Spooner, Colonial	27.00
Spooner, Fancy Loop, Gold Rim	45.00
Spooner, Sawtooth	25.00
Stopper, Horsehead, 4 In.	60.00
Sugar & Creamer, Colonial, Flamingo Etch	35.00
Sugar & Creamer, Crystolite	20.00 To 30.00
Sugar & Creamer, Dolphin, 3-Handled, Footed	40.00
Sugar & Creamer, Fandango	50.00
Sugar & Creamer, Lariat	22.00 To 25.00
Sugar & Creamer, Narrow Flute, Individual, Almond Silver Overlay	79.50
Sugar & Creamer, Orchid Etch	37.50 To 40.00
Sugar & Creamer, Peerless, Pair	30.00
Sugar & Creamer, Peerless, Tray, Individual	20.00
Sugar & Creamer, Pleat & Panel, Silver Overlay	22.50
Sugar & Creamer, Sahara, Tray, Individual	50.00
Sugar & Creamer, Stanhope	23.00
Sugar & Creamer, Whirlpool	30.00
Sugar & Creamer, Yeoman, Daisy Cutting	35.00
Sugar & Creamer, Yeoman, Moongleam	45.00
Sugar Shaker, Fandango, Original Lid	35.00
Sugar Shaker, Plantation	77.00
Sugar, Beaded Swag, Covered	25.00
Sugar, Empress, Dolphin Footed, Crystal	25.00
Sugar, Flute, Child's	45.00
Sugar, Footed, Moongleam, Signed	17.00
Sugar, Moongleam, Hotel Twist	15.00
Sugar, Pillows Design, Open, Signed	25.00
Sugar, Sawtooth, Open	25.00
Sugar, Winged Scroll, Handled	48.00
Syrup, Beaded Swag, Milk Glass	110.00
Syrup, Plantation	49.50 To 77.00
Table Set, Banded Flute, Signed	145.00
Table Set, Beaded Swag, Gold Trim, 4 Piece	250.00
Table Set, Winged Scroll, Emerald Green, 4 Piece	400.00
Tankard, Pineapple & Fan, Souvenir, 1/2 Pint	25.00
Toothpick, Colonial	30.00
Toothpick, Fancy Loop	60.00 To 70.00
Toothpick, Fandango	55.00
Toothpick, Priscilla, Silver Overlay, Marked	55.00
Toothpick, Punty Band, Custard Glass	50.00
Toothpick, Ring Band, Custard Glass	55.00 To 60.00
Toothpick, Sawtooth Bands	35.00
Toothpick, Sweet Scroll	70.00
Toothpick, Winged Scroll	150.00
Tray, Card, Crystolite, Pedestal	22.00
Tray, Celery & Olive, Lariat, 3 Sections, Signed	12.50
Tray, Crystolite, Oval, Signed, 11 X 8 In.	25.00
Tumbler, Colonial, Signed, 8 Ounce	16.00
Tumbler, Fancy Loop, Gold Rim	30.00
Tumbler, Ipswich, Footed	16.00
Tumbler, Old Sandwich, Sahara, Signed	15.00
Tumbler, Ring Band	45.00

Tumbler, Tally Ho 47.50
Tumbler, Thumbprint, 4 In. 10.00
Tumbler, Winged Scroll, Emerald Green 45.00
Vase, Empress, Grape Etching, 9 In. 85.00
Vase, Greek Key, 10 In. 38.00
Vase, Mermaid Ball, Marked, 4 In. 250.00
Vase, Plantation, 6 In. 50.00
Vase, Plantation, 14 In. 175.00
Vase, Punch Bowl, Sunburst & Panel 22.00
Vase, Ridgeleigh, Signed, 4 In. 18.00
Vase, Sahara, Dolphin Feet, 9 In. 75.00
Water Set, Prince Of Wales, 7 Piece 275.00
Water Set, Sahara Empress, Cut Daisy, 7 Piece 225.00
Wine, Athena, Reverse S 35.00
Wine, Beaded Swag, Ruby Flashed 65.00
Wine, Fancy Loop 45.00
Wine, Flute, Marked 10.00
Wine, Jamestown, Barcelona Cut 25.00
Wine, New Era 10.00
Wine, Optic Tooth, Iridescent Blue Base, Amber Stem, Set Of 12 .... 600.00
Wine, Pan American, 4 Ounce 12.00
Wine, Plantation 37.00
Wine, Spanish, Titania Etch 50.00
Wine, Victorian, 2 Ounce .... 5.00 To 24.00
Wine, Zodiac, Marked 25.00
       HEREND, see Fischer

> *Gebruder Heubach, a German firm working from 1820 to 1925, is best known for bisque dolls and doll heads, their principal products. They also manufactured bisque figurines, including piano babies, beginning in the 1880s, and glazed figurines in the 1900s.*

HEUBACH, Dutch Children, Kissing, Fighting, Red & Green, 4 1/2 In., Pair 175.00
Figurine, Bear, Gray & White, Fan Mark, 3 1/2 X 3 In. 135.00
Figurine, Boy Seated With Arms Up, Leg Out To Side, Numbered 95.00
Figurine, Children In Nighties, With Songbooks, 10 In. 395.00
Figurine, Crawling Baby, Signed, 4 X 2 1/2 In. 85.00
Figurine, Dog, Sitting, Gray & Off-White, Marked, 3 1/2 X 3 1/2 In. 95.00
Figurine, Dog, 8 X 3 1/2 In. 75.00
Figurine, Dove, Marked, White 265.00
Figurine, Dove, White, Signed 265.00
Figurine, Dutch Boy & Girl, Russet & Green Clothing, Marked, Pair 185.00
Figurine, Dutch Boy & Girl, 5 In., Pair 245.00
Figurine, Dutch Boy, Gray-Blue & White, Marked, 7 In. 88.00
Figurine, Dutch Girl, Blue & White, Marked, 4 3/8 In. 88.00
Figurine, Dutch Girl, Red Skirt, Marked, 4 1/2 In. 60.00
Figurine, Dutch Girl, Seated, Signed, 4 In. 140.00
Figurine, Female Dancer, Marked, 11 3/4 In. 140.00
Figurine, Girl Tennis Player, Bisque, Gold Trim, 12 1/8 In. 135.00
Figurine, Girl, Bonnet, Hay Fork, Pastel, Marked, 3 1/4 In. 165.00
Figurine, Girl, Dancing Pose, Trellis Base, Green & Pink, 7 In. 125.00
Figurine, Girl, Bonnet, Hay Fork, Pastel Painted, 10 In. 165.00
Figurine, Googly, 3 1/2 In. 110.00
Figurine, Great Dane, On Stomach, Head Erect, Crossed Paws, 4 X 8 In. ... 110.00
Figurine, Grumpy, 5 In. 150.00
Figurine, Mouse, Eating From Floral & Leaves, White, Marked, 3 In. 115.00
Figurine, Mouse, White, Sitting On Haunches, Eating Leaves, Marked 105.00
Figurine, Rabbit, Sitting, Pink Eyes, 3 X 5 In. 190.00
Figurine, Sea Gull, Forms Tray, Gray, White, & Pink, 9 In. 99.00
Figurine, Shaggy Dog, White, Sitting Up, 9 In. 225.00
Figurine, Spaniel, Scratching Himself, Sad Eyes, 6 X 6 In. 100.00
Figurine, Young Girl Holding Pleated Pink Skirt, 9 3/4 In. 385.00
Nude Baby, Sitting, Throwing Kisses, Wears Bathing Cap, 5 In. 220.00
Planter, Woven Rattan Trunk, 2 Children Peering, Marked, 3 X 3 In. 110.00

Tobacco Jar, Boy Head, Intaglio Eyes, Hat Is Lid, Bisque, 4 7/8 In. 135.00
Vase, Art Nouveau Lady, Handled, Gold Interior, Green Ground, 7 In. 175.00
Vase, Pink Iris, Gray Ground, 8 1/2 In. 75.00
Vase, Silver Overlay, 2 In. 95.00

H I G

Higbee glass was made by the J.B.Higbee Company of Bridgeville,
Pennsylvania, about 1900.
HIGBEE, see also Pressed Glass
HIGBEE, Cruet, Palm Leaf Fan Pattern 30.00
    HISTORIC BLUE, see Adams; Clews; Ridgway; Staffordshire

Hobnail glass is a pattern of glass with bumps in an allover pattern.
Dozens of hobnail patterns and variants have been made. Reproductions of
many types of hobnail glass can be found.
HOBNAIL, see also Francisware
HOBNAIL, Cruet Set, English, Clear 35.00
    Cruet, Blue Handle & Stopper, Amber, 8 In. 95.00
    Pitcher, Blue, Small 20.00
    Pitcher, Bulbous, Amber, 8 In. 85.00
    Pitcher, Trefoil Spout, Amber 50.00
    Punch Cup, Amber 17.50

Hochst, or Hoechst, porcelain was made in Germany from 1746 to 1796. It
was marked with a six-spoke wheel.
HOCHST, Basket, Center Spray Of Blossoms, Handled, C.1760, 9 In. 935.00

Holly amber, or golden agate, glass was made by the Indiana Tumbler and
Goblet Company from January 1, 1903 to June 13, 1903. It is a pressed
glass pattern featuring holly leaves in the amber-shaded glass.
HOLLY AMBER, Berry Bowl, 8 1/2 X 3 1/2 In. 650.00
    Butter, Covered 1250.00
    Dish, Sauce, 4 3/4 In.Diam. .... 275.00 To 285.00

HOPALONG CASSIDY, Badge, Colorful, Tin 9.00
    Bank .... 15.00 To 20.00
    Bedspread 145.00
    Binoculars, Boxed 30.00
    Book, Pop-Up 10.00
    Book, Sticker, 1951 .... 8.00
    Bottle, Milk, 1/2 Gallon 25.00
    Bowl, Hoppy In Blue 18.00
    Box, Paint, Ideal 35.00
    Camera, Flash, Boxed 30.00
    Card, Birthday, Pop-Up 15.00
    Clock, Alarm, Picture On Face, Black Metal Case 60.00
    Comic, Dated 1950 .... 8.00
    Cup .... 8.00 To 15.00
    Dart Board, Tin .... 14.00 To 18.00
    Gun & Holster Pin 20.00
    Gun, Magic Picture, Boxed 60.00
    Gun, Ranger Model 10.00
    Handkerchief, Topper 13.00
    Horseshoe, Good Luck, Bar 20 Ranch, Dated 1950, 6 In. 2.00
    Jar, Round, Glass 20.00
    Key Chain, On Card 38.00
    Knife, Pocket .... 18.00 To 22.00
    Lamp, Figural, Gun, Aladdin 145.00

Lamp, Horsehead, Alacite 115.00
Lasso Game 65.00
Mask, Latex, Boxed 55.00
Mirror, Picture, Signature, Framed, 4 X 6 In. 20.00
Mug 6.50
Pen, Black, Silver Cap, Hopalong Cassidy Written On Side 28.00
Photo Album 47.00
Plate, Glass 10.00
Radio, Arvin, Red & Silver .... 45.00 To 90.00
Record, Square Dance, Holdup, Pictures 34.00
Ring 10.00
Shooting Gallery, Automatic Toy Co. .... 85.00 To 95.00
Spoon 7.00
Toy, On Rocking Horse, Moving Arms, Tin, Lithograph 140.00
Toy, Windup 18.00
Tumbler .... 10.50 To 12.00
Wallet, Picture On Outside 12.00
Wristwatch .... 25.00 To 45.00

HOWDY DOODY, Cookie Tin, All Howdy Doody Characters On Carousel 30.00
Cup 20.00
Game, Card, Original Box 8.00
Game, Puzzle 5.00
Game, TV 15.00
Glass 5.00
Key Holder 20.00
Mirror, Clara Belle, Celluloid 30.00
Mug 15.00
Night-Light 95.00
Puppet, Steiff 25.00

Hull pottery is made in Crooksville, Ohio. The factory started in 1903
as the Acme Pottery Company. Art pottery was first made in 1917.

HULL, Ashtray, Heart-Shaped, Butterfly Center, Relief Flowers, 7 X 7 In. 16.00
Ashtray, Serenade, Enameled, Yellow, Large 14.00
Basket, Blossom Flite, 6 In. 15.00
Basket, Dogwood, 7 1/2 In. 40.00
Basket, Ebb Tide, Shrimp Color, 8 In. 16.00
Basket, Embossed Strawberries, All White, 6 1/2 In. 25.00
Basket, Flowers & Leaves, Cream Ground, 11 In. 30.00
Basket, Parchment & Pine, 8 X 5 In. 35.00
Basket, Parchment & Pine, 9 1/2 In. 65.00
Basket, Pink & Green, Scroll 20.00
Basket, Tokay, Greens & Whites, 8 In. 20.00
Basket, Tokay, 11 In. 25.00
Basket, Tulip Blue 35.00
Basket, Water Lily, Pink & Blue, 10 1/2 In. 85.00
Basket, Wild Flower, Brown & Yellow, Original Seal, 10 1/2 In. 85.00
Basket, Woodland, Pink & Green, 8 3/4 In. 40.00
Basket, Woodland, 10 1/2 In. 25.00
Bowl, Console, Atached Candleholder, Tokay, Pink 25.00
Bowl, Dogwood, Oval 28.00
Butter, Little Red Riding Hood, Covered 45.00
Candleholder, Magnolia, Pair 20.00
Candleholder, Water Lily, Brown & Cream, 4 1/2 In., Pair 35.00
Compote, Serenade, Yellow 19.50
Console Set, Pink, Gold Luster & Green, 3 Piece 25.00
Cookie Jar, Clown 28.50
Cookie Jar, Duck 20.00
Cookie Jar, Red Riding Hood .... 45.00 To 49.00
Cornucopia, Bowknot 35.00
Cornucopia, Magnolia Pattern, 8 1/2 In. 18.00

Cornucopia, Open Rose, 8 1/2 In. 35.00
Cornucopia, 7 1/2 In. 25.00
Creamer, Red Riding Hood, 5 In. .... 18.00 To 45.00
Ewer, Dogwood, Italian Blue Shading To Pink, 11 1/4 In. 40.00
Ewer, Iris, Pink & Blue, 13 1/2 In. 60.00
Ewer, Magnolia, Pink & Blue, 7 In. 30.00
Ewer, Magnolia, Pink Top, Blue Bottom, 7 1/2 In. 25.00
Ewer, Orchid, Blue, 13 In. 58.00
Ewer, Parchment & Pine, Handled, 14 1/2 X 11 In. 35.00
Ewer, Rosella, 7 In. 20.00
Ewer, Wild Flower, 5 1/2 In. 18.00
Ewer, Woodland, Glossy, 5 1/2 In. 15.00
Ewer, 2 Birds, Handled, 13 In. 45.00
Figurine, Rooster, Large 10.00
Jardiniere, Fluted, 2 Shades Of Green, 9 X 9 In. 20.00
Jardiniere, Tulip, 5 In. 15.00
Pitcher, Bowknot, Blue, 5 1/2 In. 35.00
Pitcher, Ewer Shaped, Matte Ivory, Raised Birds, 7 In. 14.00
Pitcher, Milk, Red Riding Hood .... 50.00 To 60.00
Pitcher, Narcissus, 8 In. 35.00
Pitcher, Sunglow, 5 1/4 In. 16.00
Planter, Basket Girl, 8 In. 10.00
Planter, Bucket Shape, Handle, Glossy Tan, 5 In. 8.00
Planter, Butterfly, Footed 12.00
Planter, Cat, Pink, 6 X 6 In. 20.00
Planter, Dancing Lady 14.00
Planter, Figural, Cat, 7 In. 15.00
Planter, Footed, Drip Effect On Top Edge 8.00
Planter, Hanging, Varicolored Blues, Aqua, & Red, H In Circle, 5 1/4 In. ... 20.00
Planter, Long-Necked Goose, Plumed Hat, 12 1/4 In. 25.00
Planter, Parrot 9.50
Planter, Serenade, Yellow, 12 In. 20.00
Planter, Swan, Pink, Green .... 8.00 To 22.00
Planter, Woodland, Oblong 28.00
Pocket, Wall, Woodland, Royal 9.00
Rose Bowl, Poppy, Original Seal, 4 3/4 In. 35.00
Salt & Pepper, Red Riding Hood, 3 In. .... 10.00 To 15.00
Stein, Alpine Pattern, Brown & Tan 14.00
Sugar & Creamer, Bowknot, Blue With Pink Bow, Signed 35.00
Sugar & Creamer, Red Riding Hood .... 50.00 To 65.00
Sugar & Creamer, Serenade, Pink 40.00
Sugar, Avocado Green 25.00
Sugar, Red Riding Hood, Open 45.00
Tea Set, Magnolia, Pink & Blue, 3 Piece .... 50.00 To 95.00
Tea Set, Water Lily, 3 Piece 60.00
Tea Set, Woodland 85.00
Teapot & Lid, Red Riding Hood 95.00
Teapot, Magnolia, Aladdin Lamp Shape 35.00
Teapot, Magnolia, Pink & Blue, 6 1/2 In. 45.00
Vase, Bowknot, 8 1/2 In. 45.00
Vase, Calla Lily, 6 In. 18.00
Vase, Cornucopia, Chartreuse & Dark Green, 9 In. .... 14.00 To 18.00
Vase, Cornucopia, Parchment & Pine, 12 In. 17.00
Vase, Cornucopia, Rose & Blue, Original Label, 8 In. 25.00
Vase, Cornucopia, Wild Flower, Pink & Blue, 8 1/2 In. 28.00
Vase, Dogwood Pattern, 8 1/2 In. 7.00
Vase, Dogwood, Peach, 10 1/2 In. 30.00
Vase, Dogwood, Pink & Black, 8 1/2 In. 18.00
Vase, Ebb Tide, Maroon & Green, 11 3/4 In. 35.00
Vase, Magnolia, Pink Top, Blue Base, 6 1/4 In. 15.00
Vase, Magnolia, Pink Top, Blue Base, 8 1/2 In. 18.00
Vase, Magnolia, Pink Top, Blue Base, 18 In. 65.00
Vase, Magnolia, Yellow Top, Pink Base, C.1946, 6 3/4 In. 12.50

Vase, Magnolia, 6 1/4 In.	8.00 To 16.00
Vase, Magnolia, 8 1/2 In.	20.00
Vase, Magnolia, 12 In.	55.00
Vase, Open Rose, 6 1/2 In.	25.00
Vase, Open Rose, 8 1/2 In.	20.00 To 35.00
Vase, Orchid, 6 In.	20.00
Vase, Pale Pink To Tan, Wild Flowers, 6 1/2 In.	20.00
Vase, Pink, Blue Flowers, 6 1/2 In.	12.00
Vase, Rosella, 6 1/2 In.	22.00
Vase, Serenade, Yellow, 12 In.	45.00
Vase, Thistle, Blue, 6 1/2 In.	28.00
Vase, Tulip, Pink & Blue	20.00
Vase, Tulip, Scalloped, Lavender Base, 8 1/2 In.	26.00
Vase, Water Lily, Matte, 1/ 1/2 In.	35.00
Vase, Water Lily, Tan, 10 1/2 In.	38.00
Vase, Water Lily, 6 1/2 In.	16.00
Vase, Wild Flower, Fan-Shaped, 10 1/2 In.	45.00
Vase, Wild Flower, Pink, Signed, 6 1/2 In.	12.00
Vase, Wild Flower, W-8, Matte, 7 1/2 In.	17.00
Vase, Wild Flower, 5 1/2 In.	15.00
Vase, Wild Flower, 6 1/2 In.	16.00
Vase, Wild Flower, 7 1/4 In.	25.00
Vase, Wild Flower, 12 1/2 In., Pair	110.00
Vase, Woodland, 2-Handled, 8 1/2 In.	25.00
Vase, Woodland, 6 1/2 In.	14.00
Vase, Yellow & Pink, 5 In., Pair	8.00
Vase, Yellow Rose, Blue Shading To Yellow & Pink, 18 In.	35.00
Wall Pocket, Blue Whisk Broom, Floral	25.00
Wall Pocket, Bowknot, Blue	45.00
Wall Pocket, Match Holder, Red Riding Hood	300.00
Wall Pocket, Royal Woodland	9.00
Wall Pocket, Shell, 7 1/2 In.	17.00
Wall Pocket, Sunglow, Broom	15.00
Wall Pocket, Wild Flower	17.00
Wall Pocket, Woodland, Glazed Pink & Gold, 7 1/4 In.	35.00
Wall Pocket, Woodland, 7 1/2 In.	40.00

Hummel figurines, based on the drawings of Berta Hummel, are made by the W. Goebel Porzellanfabrik of Oeslau, Germany. They were first made in 1934. The mark has changed slightly through the years. The following are approximate dates for each of the marks: "Crown" mark, 1935 to 1949; "U.S. Zone, Germany," 1946 to 1948; "West Germany," after 1949; full bee," 1950 to 1959; "stylized bee," 1960 to 1972; "three line mark," 1968 to 1979; "vee over gee," 1972 to 1979; "new mark," 1979 to present.

HUMMEL, Ashtray, Boy With Bird, No.166, Full Bee	185.00
Bookends, Playmates & Chick Girl, No.61/a & B, Full Bee	450.00
Figurine, A Fair Measure, No.345, Three Line, Eyes Open	500.00
Figurine, Accordion Boy, No.185, Full Bee	125.00 To 155.00
Figurine, Adoration, No.23/1, Full Bee, 6 1/4 In.	*Illus* 285.00
Figurine, Angel Duet, No.146, Stylized Bee	50.00
Figurine, Angel Serenade, With Lamb, No.83, Full Bee	325.00 To 350.00
Figurine, Angelic Care, No.194, Full Bee, 6 3/4 In.	*Illus* 225.00
Figurine, Apple Tree Boy, No.142, Stylized Bee	75.00 To 95.00
Figurine, Apple Tree Girl, No, 141/i, Full Bee	140.00
Figurine, Auf Wiedersehen, No, 153/0, Stylized Bee, 5 1/2 In.	105.00
Figurine, Baker, No.128, Full Bee	145.00
Figurine, Begging His Share, No.9, Stylized Bee	95.00 To 100.00
Figurine, Bird Duet, No.169, Stylized Bee	125.00
Figurine, Birthday Serenade, No.218, Full Bee	425.00
Figurine, Blessed Event, No.333, Three Line Mark	275.00
Figurine, Bookworm, No.8, Full Bee	165.00 To 170.00

Hummel, Figurine, Adoration,
No.23/1, Full Bee, 6 1/4 In.

Hummel, Figurine, Follow The
Leader, No.369, V Over G, 7 In.

Hummel, Figurine, Angelic Care,
No.194, Full Bee, 6 3/4 In.

Figurine, Boots, No.143, Full Bee	450.00
Figurine, Chick Girl, No.57/0, Stylized Bee	90.00
Figurine, Close Harmony, No.336, Three Line Mark	325.00
Figurine, Congratulations, No.17/3, Stylized Bee	110.00 To 145.00
Figurine, Culprits, No.56/a, Full Bee	160.00 To 200.00
Figurine, Doctor, No.127, Full Bee	170.00
Figurine, Doctor, No.137, Stylized Bee	90.00
Figurine, Doll Mother, No.67, Full Bee	190.00
Figurine, Farm Boy, No.66, Full Bee	150.00 To 160.00
Figurine, Feeding Time, No.199, Full Bee	300.00
Figurine, Feeding Time, No.199, Full Bee, 5 1/2 In.	400.00
Figurine, Festival Harmony, No.173, Three Line Mark	140.00
Figurine, Flower Madonna, No.10/i, Full Bee	175.00
Figurine, Follow The Leader, No.369, V Over G, 7 In.	*Illus* 250.00
Figurine, Good Hunting, No.307, Three Line Mark	145.00
Figurine, Goose Girl, No.47/0, Crown Mark, 5 1/4 In.	185.00
Figurine, Happiness, No.86, Stylized Bee	130.00
Figurine, Happy Pastime, No.69, Stylized Bee	120.00
Figurine, Hear Ye, Hear Ye, No.15/o, Full Bee	156.00
Figurine, Heavenly Protection, No.88/ii, Full Bee, 9 In.	300.00
Figurine, Heavenly Protection, No.88, Stylized Bee	*Illus* 260.00
Figurine, Joseph, No.214/b, Three Line Mark	90.00
Figurine, Kiss Me, No.311, Three Line Mark	310.00
Figurine, Latest News, No.184, Full Bee	425.00
Figurine, Letter To Santa Claus, V Over G, 7 1/4 In.	*Illus* 130.00
Figurine, Letter To Santa, No.340, Three Line Mark	325.00
Figurine, Little Fiddler, No.4, Full Bee	150.00
Figurine, Little Fiddler, No.4, Stylized Bee	175.00
Figurine, Little Gabriel, No.32, Stylized Bee	140.00
Figurine, Little Gardener, No.74, Crown Mark	170.00

Hummel, Figurine, Heavenly Protection, No.88, Stylized Bee
(See Page 305)

Hummel, Figurine, Mail Is Here, No.226, Stylized Bee, 6 In.

Figurine, Little Goat Herder, No.200/0, Stylized Bee	95.00
Figurine, Little Goat Herder, No.200, Full Bee	198.00
Figurine, Little Guardian, No.145, Crown Mark	210.00
Figurine, Little Helper, No.73, Stylized Bee	100.00
Figurine, Little Scholar, No.80, Stylized Bee	80.00
Figurine, Little Sweeper, No.171, Stylized Bee	65.00
Figurine, Mail Is Here, No.226, Stylized Bee, 6 In. ....*Illus*	310.00
Figurine, Merry Wanderer, No.7/0, Full Bee	400.00
Figurine, Merry Wanderer, No.11/2/0, Full Bee	100.00
Figurine, Mother's Darling, No.175, Stylized Bee	185.00
Figurine, Playmates, No.58/0, Crown Mark	285.00
Figurine, Prayer Before Battle, No.20, Stylized Bee	115.00
Figurine, Retreat To Safety, No.201/2/0, Stylized Bee	80.00
Figurine, Ring Around The Rosie, No.348, Stylized Bee ......*Illus*	1300.00
Figurine, Saint George, No.55, Full Bee, 6 3/4 In. ....*Illus*	310.00
Figurine, School Boy, No.82/0, Stylized Bee	75.00
Figurine, School Boys, No.170, Full Bee, 10 In.	750.00
Figurine, School Girl, No.81/0, Stylized Bee	75.00
Figurine, School Girls, No.177, Full Bee, 9 1/2 In.	750.00

Hummel, Figurine, Ring Around The Rosie, No.348, Stylized Bee

Hummel, Figurine, Saint George, No.55, Full Bee, 6 3/4 In.

Hummel, Figurine, Spring Dance, No.353, Three Line, 6 3/4 In.

Hummel, Figurine, Letter To Santa Claus,
V Over G, 7 1/4 In.

(See Page 305)

Hummel, Figurines, Umbrella Girl, No.152/B, Three Line, 4 3/4 In; Stormy Weather, No.71, Full Bee, 6 1/4 In. Umbrella Boy, No.152/A, Three Line 4 3/4 In.

Figurine, Sensitive Hunter, No.6/0, Stylized Bee	95.00
Figurine, Serenade, No.85/0, Full Bee	300.00
Figurine, Serenade, No.85/0, Stylized Bee	80.00
Figurine, She Loves Me, No.174, Eyes Open, Stylized Bee	135.00 To 150.00
Figurine, She Loves Me, She Loves Me Not, No.174, Three Line	100.00
Figurine, Shepherd Boy, No.64, Full Bee	160.00
Figurine, Sister, No.98/0, Stylized Bee	90.00
Figurine, Soloist, No.135, Full Bee	100.00
Figurine, Spring Dance, No.353, Three Line, 6 3/4 In. *Illus*	300.00
Figurine, Stormy Weather, No.71, Full Bee, 6 1/4 In. *Illus*	330.00
Figurine, Stormy Weather, No.71, Stylized Bee	230.00
Figurine, Sweet Music, No.186, Full Bee	160.00
Figurine, Telling Her Secret, No.196/0, Three Line Mark	125.00
Figurine, Telling Her Secret, No.196, Full Bee, 6 3/4 In.	400.00
Figurine, Trumpet Boy, No.97, One Line	70.00
Figurine, Umbrella Boy, No.152/A/II, Full Bee	550.00
Figurine, Umbrella Boy, No.152/A, Full Bee, 7 5/8 In.	1100.00
Figurine, Umbrella Boy, No.152/A, Three Line, 4 3/4 In. *Illus*	300.00
Figurine, Umbrella Girl, No.152/B, Three Line, 4 3/4 In. *Illus*	360.00
Figurine, Village, Boy, No.51/0, Full Bee	140.00
Figurine, Wayside Devotion, No.28, Stylized Bee *Illus*	185.00
Figurine, Whitsuntide, No.163, Full Bee	1000.00

Hummel, Figurine, Wayside Devotion,
No.28, Stylized Bee
(See Page 307)

Figurine, Worship, No.84/0, Crown Mark	265.00
Figurine, Worship, No.84/0, Full Bee	145.00
Figurine, Worship, No.84/0, Full Bee, 5 1/4 In.	175.00
Lamp, Apple Tree Boy & Girl, No.229 & 230, Three Line Mark, Pair	350.00
Lamp, To Market, No.223, Stylized Bee	265.00
Plaque, Retreat To Safety, No.126, Full Bee	250.00
Wall Vase, Boy, No.360/B, Stylized Bee	40.00
Wall Vase, Girl, No.360/C, Stylized Bee	400.00

LORENZ
HUTSCHEN REUTER

GERMANY

*Hutschenreuther Porcelain Company of Selb, Germany, was established
in 1814 and is still working.*

HUTSCHENREUTHER, Cake Plate, Floral, Green Ground, Handle, 12 In.	60.00
Candlestick, 2 Cherubs Hold Candle, White, 6 In.	75.00
Figurine, Bird, Parian, Open Mouthed, 7 In.	75.00
Figurine, Brown Dog, Standing, 3 1/4 X 4 1/2 In.	75.00
Figurine, Canary, On Branch, Insect In Beak, 5 X 4 In.	160.00
Figurine, Cardinal, Signed Granget	95.00 To 110.00
Figurine, Cockatoo, White, Gold Trim, Signed, 5 In.	75.00
Figurine, Cocks, Fighting, 6 1/2 In., Pair	250.00
Figurine, Dachshund, 4 In.	95.00
Figurine, Duck	30.00
Figurine, Elephant	45.00
Figurine, Green Bird, Flying Over Flower, 4 1/4 In.	85.00
Figurine, Maiden, Gown, Crying Cupid At Feet, 9 1/2 In.	140.00
Figurine, Monkey, White, Pair	35.00
Figurine, Porpoise, Leaping Over Waves, Signed, 4 1/2 In.	125.00
Figurine, Robins On Branch, Signed Tutter, Pair	115.00
Figurine, Spotted White-Tail Deer, Signed, 4 X 5 1/2 In.	395.00
Figurine, 2 Kittens Playing With Ball, Signed, 4 In.	50.00
Plaque, Girls Whispering, Marked, 7 1/4 X 5 1/4 In.	350.00
Plaque, Maiden In Forest, C.1910, 7 1/8 X 5 In.	1000.00
Plate, Bouquet Cent, Roses, Scalloped Gold Rim, 6 1/4 In.	9.50
Plate, Maiden, Seated, C.1910, Shield Mark, 9 1/2 In.	325.00
Plate, Portrait Of Princess Louise, C.1910, 9 1/2 In.	400.00
Plate, Portrait, Duchess Of Devonshire, C.1900, 9 1/2 In.	600.00
Plate, Seated Lady Center, C.1900, Marked, 9 5/8 In.	500.00
Sugar & Creamer, White, Papyrus Design, Embossed	15.00
Tray, Blue, White, Pink Flowers, Gold Trim, 12 X 5 1/2 In.	35.00
Vase, Evening Star, Cupids, C.1910, Shield Mark, 20 1/4 In.	2300.00
ICEBOX, see Kitchen, Icebox	
ICON, Hand-Painted, Pictorials, Brass, 10 X 12 In. & 7 X 9 In., Pair	800.00
Russian, Holy Man & Angel, On Porcelain, Ivory Frame, 3 3/4 X 2 3/4 In.	200.00

Imari patterns are named for the Japanese ware decorated with orange and blue stylized flowers. The design on the Japanese ware became so characteristic that the name Imari has come to mean any pattern of this type. It was copied by the European factories of the eighteenth and early nineteenth centuries.

IMARI, Bottle, Sake, White Ground, Red & Blue Design, 5 In., Pair	175.00
Bowl, Birds, Flowering Trees, Polychrome, 7 In.	400.00
Bowl, Central Kirin Medallion, Clouds & Birds, Formal Edge, 11 7/8 In.	225.00
Bowl, Cobalt & Red, C.1900, 10 In.	350.00
Bowl, Cover, Signed With Chop Mark, 2 1/2 X 5 In.Diam.	125.00
Bowl, Flowering Tree, Flowers, Globular Form, 11 In.	100.00
Bowl, Flowers & Pomegranate, Red & Gilt, C.1900, 9 3/4 In.	400.00
Bowl, Punch, Floral Design, Orange & Blue, Footed, 12 1/4 In.	600.00
Bowl, Rice, Covered, Set Of 6	37.50
Bowl, Scalloped Rim, 7 1/2 In.	210.00
Bowl, Tiger, Coins & Clouds, Cartouches, 18th Century, 8 3/4 In.	1700.00
Bowl, 5 In.Diam.	60.00
Bowl, 6 In.Diam.	50.00 To 60.00
Bowl, 7 In.Diam.	60.00
Bowl, 10 In.Diam.	350.00
Bowl, 19th Century, 9 In.	120.00
Charger, Blue & White, 18 In.	295.00
Charger, Blue Genre Scene, Orange & White Flowers, Red Ground, 18 In.	225.00
Charger, Blue, Red, Green, Yellow, Landscape, C.1900, 22 In.	700.00
Charger, Cobalt Blue Design, Peonies & Flowering Tree, 21 In.	125.00
Charger, Cobalt Blue Medallion, Orange Dragons, 15 1/2 In.	175.00
Charger, Cobalt Blue, Floral Design, 2 Small Birds, 13 3/4 In.	100.00
Charger, Cobalt Bluebirds, Chrysanthemums, Trees, 22 1/2 In.	45.00
Charger, Eagle Overlooking Scene, C.1790, 18 1/2 In.	495.00
Charger, Eagle With Scene, Blue & White, C.1850, 1 1/2 In.	495.00
Charger, Floral Center, Flying Herons, Blue, 13 3/8 In.	185.00
Charger, Flower-Filled Palette, Vase Center, Blue Ground, 24 In.	1600.00
Charger, Flowers & Birds, Rickshaw, Impressed Mark, 14 7/8 In.	145.00
Charger, Fluted Edge, Lined, 2 Scenes, C.1810, Blue & White, 16 In.	295.00
Charger, Houses, Boats, & People, Blue, 4 1/2 In.Diam.	145.00
Charger, Landscape, Waterfall, Tree, Blue & White, 14 1/2 In.	50.00
Charger, Medallion Center, Flowers & Birds, 12 In.	175.00
Charger, Orange, Blue, Octagon, C.1840, 14 In.	490.00
Charger, Red, Blue, Gold Design, 12 In.	130.00
Charger, Sky, Mountain, Landscape, Fish, Blue, White, Red, 13 In.	65.00
Charger, 18 In.	250.00
Cracker Jar, Stylized Flowers, Covered, 5 1/4 In.	100.00
Dish, Blue & White, Dragon, Peacock Feathers, Oval, Signed, 6 In.	30.00
Dish, Fluted Rim, 7 In., Pair	100.00
Dish, Scalloped Edge, 9 In.	130.00
Dish, Serving, Blue & Orange Floral Design, Elongated, 10 In.	225.00
Ginger Jar, Ribbed Body, Covered, 12 In.	280.00
Jar, Blue, Orange, Fan Design, Domed Cover, 12 In.	250.00
Jar, Cracker, Cylindrical, Stylized Flowers, 5 1/4 In.	100.00
Jar, Temple, 18 In.	1950.00
Plate, Blue, Iron Red & Green, Scalloped Border, 8 1/2 In.	95.00
Plate, Crane, Extended Wings Around Sides, 18th Century, 8 1/2 In., Pr.	650.00
Plate, Fan Design, Oval, 10 In.	150.00
Plate, Fish, Blue & Iron Red, Gold Trim, 14 In.	425.00
Plate, Iron Red Ground, Panels Of Sake Bottles, Flowers, 10 In.	150.00
Plate, Orange & Cobalt Blue, Scalloped Edge, 8 1/2 In.	75.00
Plate, Orange & Cobalt, Flowers In Center, C.1900, 8 In.	85.00
Tray, Oval, 13 X 10 In.	110.00
Urn, Rust, Blue, & Gold, C.1852, Signed, 12 X 18 In.	1950.00
Vase, Animal Heads At Neck, Blue, Orange, Birds, Flowers, 18 In.	775.00
Vase, Birds & Flowers, Geometric Design, 12 3/4 In.	475.00
Vase, Cobalt Blue & Orange, Bird & Floral Design, 10 In.	150.00
Vase, Cobalt Blue Design, Peonies, Baluster Form, 18 In.	175.00

Vase, Cobalt Blue Outlined, Flowers, 16 In., Pair		650.00
Vase, Cobalt Blue, Red, Paw Feet, Pedestal Base, 8 X 6 In.		95.00
Vase, Fan Shaped, Brocade Ground, C.1840, 16 1/2 In.		500.00
Vase, Figures, Various Pursuits, Flowers, 9 3/4 In., Pair		175.00
Vase, Floral Ground, Orange & Blue, Bulbous, 10 In.		250.00
Vase, Ribbed, Animal Heads, Underglaze Blue, Orange, & Ocher, 18 In.		775.00
Vase, Temple, Deep Blue, Black Ground, Flowers, Butterflies, 30 In.		175.00
Vase, Temple, Red, Orange Ground, Floral Design, Birds, Trees, 24 In.		650.00

IM PE
RI AL

Imperial Glass Corporation was founded in Bellaire, Ohio, in 1902.
Stretch glass and art glass are two of the many kinds of glass made.

IMPERIAL, Bowl, Blue, Green, & Purple Iridescence, 3 1/4 X 5 1/2 In.		60.00
Bowl, Rose, Green, Amethyst, Flaring Lip		65.00
Candlewick, Divided Dish, 6 In.		8.00
Compote, Blue Gray, Signed, 8 1/2 In.		49.00
Dish, Candlewick, Divided, 6 1/4 In.		3.50
Pitcher, Rubigold, 3 Pint		30.00
Rose Bowl, Signed, Pearl Green Luster, Amethyst		125.00
Swan, Milk, Blue, 4 1/2 In.		15.00
Vase, Candlewick, Fan Shape, 8 1/2 In.		8.50
Vase, Clear, 5 1/2 X 4 3/4 In.		52.00
Vase, Freehand, Green Leaves, Pearl Luster Ground, 11 In.		335.00
Vase, Freehand, Jack-In-The-Pulpit, Orange Rim, Label, 10 1/2 In.		275.00
Vase, Freehand, Leaf & Vine, Orange Lining, Luster Ground, 9 In.		295.00
Vase, Green Iridescent, White Hearts & Vines, 10 In.		175.00
Vase, Iridescent Amethyst, Old Block Mark		150.00
Vase, White Looping On Gold, Freehand, 10 In.		162.00
Vase, White Loops, Yellow, Orange Luster Interior, 11 In.		185.00
Vase, White Lotus Flower To Blue Field, 10 In.		110.00

Indian Tree is a china pattern that was popular during the last half of
the nineteenth century. It was copied from earlier patterns of English
china that were very similar. The pattern includes the crooked branch of a
tree and a partial landscape with exotic flowers and leaves. It is colored
green, blue, pink, and orange.

INDIAN TREE, Cup & Saucer, Coalport, Set Of 6		30.00
Cup & Saucer, Demitasse, Marked Minton		35.00
Cup & Saucer, Stoke On Trent		12.00 To 15.00
Eggcup, Ironstone, Johnson Bros.		20.00
Plate, Blue, Pink, & Green, Gold Trim, Spode, 10 In.Diam.		22.50
Plate, Myott, Set Of 8		75.00
Vegetable, Oval, 9 3/4 In.		30.00

Indian art from North America has attracted the collector for many years.
Each tribe has its own distinctive designs and techniques. Baskets, jewelry,
and leatherwork are of greatest collector interest.

INDIAN, Apron, Dance, Apache, Buckskin, C.1875, 16 X 26 In.		450.00
Ax, Head, Ohio		37.50
Bag, Bandoleer, Chippewa, Child's		650.00
Bag, Bandoleer, Chippewa, Loom Beaded, Black Velvet, 5 Tabs		350.00
Bag, Nez Perce, Cornhusk, Tree Design		275.00
Bag, Pipe, Woodland, Beaded, Buckskin, Fringe, C.1840, 27 In.		375.00
Bag, Plains, Beaded, Canvas, Red, Green, Orange, 9 In.		150.00
Basket, Apache, Burden, Red, Brown, Squares, 15 In.		600.00
Basket, Apache, Olla, Figures Of Dogs & Men, C.1900		1850.00
Basket, Buttocks, Slat Handle, White Oak, Signed, 11 1/2 X 6 3/4 In.		95.00
Basket, California, Diamond Design, 5 1/4 In.Diam.		70.00
Basket, Cherokee, Melon Shape, 19th Century, 24 X 14 1/2 In.		200.00
Basket, Chippewa, Curlicue, Green & Natural, Cover, 5 In.		25.00
Basket, Chippewa, Strawberry Curlicue Lid, Red & Natural		20.00

Basket, Choctaw, Cane Splint, Diamond Design, Brown, Orange, 14 In. 300.00
Basket, Choctaw, Cane Splint, Orange, Brown, Splint Design, 7 In. 175.00
Basket, Coil, Rabbits & Butterflies 600.00
Basket, Curlicue Sides, Sweet Grass Cover, Pink & Green 12.00
Basket, Curly Rim, Red & Tan Splint, Sweet Grass, 3 3/4 X 2 1/4 In. 12.50
Basket, Drop Handle, Split Ash, 8 X 6 In. 45.00
Basket, Eastern Woodland, Splint, Red, Yellow, Blue, 10 In. 175.00
Basket, Grain, Pima, 10 3/4 In. 125.00
Basket, Hopi, Coiled, 10 1/2 X 5 1/2 In. 55.00
Basket, Lines Of Blue & Beige Splint, Braided Handle, 7 X 14 In. 60.00
Basket, Makah, Covered, Blue Banded Design, 2 1/4 In. 175.00
Basket, Makah, Covered, Orange & Blue, 2 1/4 In. 150.00
Basket, Makah, Covered, Oval, C.1893 .... 110.00
Basket, Makah, Green, Purple, Blue, Geometric Design, Covered, 3 In. 50.00
Basket, Needle, Sweet Grass 4.00
Basket, North American, Beige & Brown, Round, 16 In.Diam. 65.00
Basket, Northeast, Covered, Sweet Grass, Green Dyed, Splint, 9 1/2 In. 65.00
Basket, Northeast, Curlicue Waistline, Splint, 9 1/2 X 4 1/2 In. 35.00
Basket, Northwest, Loops & Curlicues, Purple & Orange, Handle, 12 In. 65.00
Basket, Papago, 1930s, 8 In. 45.00
Basket, Passamoquoddy, Covered, Sweet Grass, C.1940, 9 X 4 3/4 In. 45.00
Basket, Pima, Diamond Design, Cover, Miniature, 1 7/8 In. 175.00
Basket, Pima, Round, C.1900, 5 In. 75.00
Basket, Pima, 4 Ladies, Oval Shape, 2 1/4 In. 150.00
Basket, Pomo, Boat Shape, Brown Design, 5 3/4 In. 350.00
Basket, Pomo, Canoe Shape, Bead & Feather Work, 18 In. 800.00
Basket, Pomo, Canoe Shape, Geometric Design, Black, 3 1/4 In. 125.00
Basket, Pomo, Round, Zig Zag Design, 1 1/4 In. 175.00
Basket, Salish, Brown, Black, White, Natural Ground, 12 In. 300.00
Basket, Sewing, Pink & Green, 7 In.Diam. 12.00
Basket, Sides Woven To Make Dome Shape, Cover, 19 3/4 X 11 1/2 In. 145.00
Basket, Southwest, Black & Red Design 110.00
Basket, Storage, Northeast, Curlicue Splinting, C.1890, 11 X 5 In. 85.00
Basket, Yurok, Burden, Geometric Design, Conical Form, 12 In. 150.00
Basket, 2-Handled, Covered, Brown Surface, Blue Design 450.00
Beaded Bag, Nez Perce, Bird Design, Contoured 165.00
Beads, Navajo, Polished, Red Clay, 28 In. 35.00
Belt, Plains, Woven Straw Base, C.1850 .... 55.00
Belt, Sioux, Beaded On Leather, 2 X 28 In. 79.50
Blanket, Germantown, Cross Design, Black, Purple, Red, 6 X 4 Ft. 4000.00
Blanket, Navajo, Diamond Design, 6 Ft. 7 In. X 4 Ft. 8 In. 270.00
Blanket, Navajo, 2 Section Design, Mountain Design, 5 Ft. X 3 Ft. 400.00
Blanket, Saddle, Multicolored Stripes, Beige Ground, 28 X 51 In. 160.00
Blanket, Saddle, Navajo, Central White Diamond, 28 X 29 In. 55.00
Blanket, Saddle, Navajo, Solid Stripes, 28 X 29 In. 25.00
Bottle, Paiute, Beaded 125.00
Bow Guard, Navajo, Silver & Turquoise, Stamped Design, 4 In. 300.00
Bowl, Acoma, Birds & Flowers, Signed, 5 In. 120.00
Bowl, Black On Black, Original Label, 7 In.Diam. 325.00
Bowl, Blue Corn, Black, 4 In. 1500.00
Bowl, Cherokee, Owls, Sitting, Signed, Amanda Swimmer, 7 In. 35.00
Bowl, Hopi, Black, Red On Cream Ground, 9 In. 150.00
Bowl, Hopi, Rain Bird, Design, Orange & Brown, 8 In. 250.00
Bowl, Hupa, Basketry, Black Zig Zag Design, Thin Bands, 4 In. 200.00
Bowl, Maricopa, Black On Red 35.00
Bowl, Marie-Santana, Black, 9 In. 2000.00
Bowl, Marie, Black, Stylized Band Design, Signed, 3 3/4 In. 475.00
Bowl, Mexico, Buff Design, Signed C.Loretto, Jemex, 3 1/2 In. 20.00
Bowl, Mission, Basketry, Geometric Design, 4 X 8 In. 100.00
Bowl, Mission, Basketry, Star Design, 4 1/2 In. 100.00
Bowl, Panamint, Basketry, Geometric Design, Black, Natural Ground 475.00
Bowl, Papago, Basketry, Human-Lizard Design, 20 In. 200.00
Bowl, Papago, Basketry, Rows Of Figures, Rams, Men, Horse, 8 1/2 In. 200.00

Bowl, Pima, 14 In.Diam. 175.00
Bowl, Pomo, Basketry, Black, Natural Ground, Feather Design, 4 In. 325.00
Bowl, Pomo, Basketry, Chevron & Deer Design, Black, 5 In. 500.00
Bowl, Pomo, Basketry, Diamond Design, Beads, Shells, Quail Feathers 325.00
Bowl, Pottery, Signed Marie & Julian 250.00
Bowl, San Ildefonso, Cream Ground, Brown Design, Signed 350.00
Bowl, Santa Clara, Black On Black, Mountain, Tree Design, 8 In. 225.00
Bowl, Tlingit, Basketry, False Embroidered Band, Swastika, 4 In. 75.00
Bowl, Tlingit, Basketry, False Embroidered Design, 4 1/4 In. 175.00
Bowl, Tlingit, Basketry, False Embroidered Design, 6 1/4 In. 200.00
Bowl, Yokuts, Basketry, 3 Bands Of Triangles, Black & Red, 16 In. 475.00
Box, Cree, Leaf Design, Birchbark, 8 X 8 X 10 1/2 In. 25.00
Box, Haida, Laced Construction, Masks, 7 3/4 X 8 1/2 In. 1725.00
Box, Navajo, Silver & Turquoise, Covered, 1 1/2 X 3 1/2 In. 300.00
Bracelet, Navajo, Turquoise & Silver 550.00
Bracelet, Watch, American, Phoenix Bird Design, Signed Lo 150.00
Canteen, Zia, Birds, Signed, 9 In. 125.00
Case, Awl, Apache, Leather, Red Pigments, Tin Cone, 12 In. 175.00
Case, Cigar, Iroquois, Moosehair, Birchbark, Pipe, Birds, Trees, 3 In. 550.00
Charger, Marie & Santana, Black, Feather Design, Signed, 13 In. 1050.00
Club, Sioux, Egg Shape, Hide Handle, 20 1/2 In. 200.00
Club, War, Plains, Gunstock, Carved Oak, 29 1/2 In. 1500.00
Club, Woodlands, Carved, Wood, Ball Head, Claw Grip, 23 In. 100.00
Costume, Parade, Chief's, Beaded Halter & Braided Reins 225.00
Coverlet, Navajo, Eagle In Center, 5 X 6 Ft. 350.00
Cradle Board, Apache, 1920 .... 200.00
Cup, Sioux, Wooden 450.00
Decoy, Curlew, Whalebone Bill, Chief Cuffie, Shinnecook, 1920s 800.00
Doll, Brave, Skookum, Black Hair, Indian Blanket, Red & Blue 65.00
Doll, Cloth, Papoose, Smoky Eyes & Teeth 125.00
Doll, Hopi, Kachina, Contemporary, 13 In. 55.00
Doll, Hopi, Kachina, Signed George Pooley, 12 1/2 In. 90.00
Doll, Maiden, Velvet Body, Felt Clothes, Painted Face, Quebec 35.00
Doll, Navajo, Cloth, Straw Feet, Wrapped Legs, Velvet Bodice, C.1920 ...... 425.00
Doll, Skookum, Man, Blanket, 11 In. 35.00
Dress, Bride, Sioux, Red & Brown Beads, Fringed, 48 In.Long 375.00
Dress, Sioux, Beaded, Fringed, 47 In.Long 400.00
Fetish, Zuni, Frog, Turquoise, 1 1/4 In. 65.00
Gloves, Crow, Floral Beaded, Buckskin, Gauntlet 195.00
Gun Case, Northern Plains, Leather, Red, Black, Beaded, 56 In. 1000.00
Hat, Hupa 175.00
Horn, Powder, Engraved Figures, Animals, Flowers, Hearts, 11 In. 100.00
Jacket, Cree, Beaded Leather, Floral Design, Pockets, 30 In. 250.00
Jacket, Northern Plains, Woolen, Beadwork, Long Sleeves 200.00
Jar, Acoma, Mexico, Open Handles, 4 1/2 In. 15.00
Jar, Black On Black, Signed Desiderio, 4 1/2 X 4 1/2 In. 275.00
Jar, Mexico, Signed Stella Teller, Isleta, White Ground, 3 3/7 In. 17.50
Jar, Olla, Acoma, Cream Ground, Red & Black Design, 7 1/2 In. 200.00
Jar, Olla, Apache, Basketry, Star Design, Dogs, 12 1/2 In. 650.00
Jar, Olla, Hopi, Blackbird Design, Orange Ground, 4 In. 150.00
Jar, Olla, Zuni, Cream Ground, Red & Brown Stylized Design, 8 In. 225.00
Jar, Pima, 5 1/2 X 5 1/2 In. 175.00
Knife Sheath, Plains, Beaded, Yellow, Green, Red, Tin Cone, 9 In. 575.00
Knife Sheath, Sioux, Beaded Leather, Green, Red, Blue, 11 In. 400.00
Knife, Woodlands, Burl, Crooked, Ball Handle, Black, 4 In. 1800.00
Ladle, Ceremonial, Austral Islands, Carved, Figures, 60 In. 625.00
Leggings, Northern Plains, Red, Blue, Beaded, Checker, 13 In. 325.00
Leggings, Plains, Beadwork Panels, Shellwork, Pair 200.00
Leggings, Sioux, Lady's, Beaded, White Ground, Tin Cones, 19 In. 325.00
Leggings, Sioux, Man's, Rawhide, Beaded, Beadwork Strip, 34 In. 425.00
Letter Opener, French Ivory Handle 10.00
Loom, Walco, Bead, 8 Tubes Of Beads, Instruction Book 65.00
Mask, Eskimo, Ninivak Island, C.1890 .... 3000.00

Mask, Senufo, Face, Oval, Human & Animal, 20 In.	175.00
Mask, Society, Iroquois, Cornhusk, False Face, Open Mouth, 12 In.	450.00
Moccasins, Apache, High Top	110.00
Moccasins, Embroidered Top, Stitched Leather Bottom	40.00
Moccasins, Multicolored Beads, Cobalt Blue, 8 In.	35.00
Moccasins, Plains	125.00
Moccasins, Plains, Child's, Beadwork	100.00
Moccasins, Sioux, Beaded, North Dakota, C.1900	175.00
Moccasins, Sioux, Fully Beaded	165.00
Model Canoe, Woodlands, Birchbark, Carved Design On Top, 32 In.	125.00
Necklace & Earrings, Zuni, Needlepoint Squash Blossom	750.00
Necklace, Turquoise, Shell Disc Beads, 26 In.	150.00
Necklace, Zuni, Squash Blossom, Several Shades Of Turquoise	800.00
Pillbox, Navajo, Sterling	27.50
Pillbox, Navajo, Turquoise Top, Sterling Silver, 1 1/2 X 4 1/4 In.	25.00
Pin, Zuni, Squaw, Petit Point	250.00
Pincushion, Mic Mac, Quillwork, Ribbon Sided, 4 In.	200.00
Pipe Bag, Knife Sheath, Sioux, White, Red, Blue, Tin Cone, 33 In.	825.00
Pipe Bag, Northern Plains, Beaded, Floral Design, Tanned, 20 In.	225.00
Pipe-Tomahawk, Beaded & Hide Handle, Iron Head, 1910, 22 In.	650.00
Pipe-Tomahawk, Hand-Forged, C.1900, 7 1/2 In.	225.00
Pipe-Tomahawk, Western Plains, Red Paint, Brass Tack Design, C.1860	650.00
Pipe-Tomahawk, Woodlands, Iron Blade, 6 Copper Studs, 20 In.	3600.00
Pipe, Sioux, Catlinite, Carved, Ring Design, 24 In.	325.00
Pipe, Sioux, Catlinite, Wood Stem, Carved Bowl, 31 In.	375.00
Pipe, Sioux, Catlinite, Wood Stem, Red Design, 37 In.	250.00
Pope Bag, Sioux, Blue, Green, Yellow, Red, Quillwork, 36 In.	300.00
Pouch, Apache, Strike-A-Light, Leather, Blue, White, Red Beaded, 5 In.	250.00
Pouch, Eastern Woodlands, Beaded, Red Cloth, Floral Design, 5 In.	100.00
Pouch, Plains, Beaded, Flap At Top, Leather Fringe, 26 In.	300.00
Purse, Pocket, Beaded	18.00
Quilt, Plains, Horsehair, Woven, Red, Yellow, Black, 18 In.	150.00
Rug, Gray With Blue, Red, & White Chimalya, 23 X 13 In.	55.00
Rug, Navajo, Banded Geometric Design, Gray, Ocher, White, And Red	120.00
Rug, Navajo, Blanket-Style Design, Peach, Brown, Beige, 5 X 3 Ft.	100.00
Rug, Navajo, Brown & Tans, 41 X 86 In.	375.00
Rug, Navajo, Cross & Diamond Design, White, Brown, Black, 4 X 3 Ft.	350.00
Rug, Navajo, Multi Colored Dazzler Design, Red Ground, 6 X 4 Ft.	625.00
Rug, Navajo, Sand Painting, Tan, Black, Blue, Yellow, 5 X 5 Ft.	2600.00
Rug, Navajo, Stripes, Black, Yellow, Pink, Zig Zag, 6 X 3 Ft.	180.00
Rug, Navajo, Tan Ground, Black Design, White Center, 50 X 35 In.	125.00
Rug, Navajo, Tan, Brown, White, Natural Ground, 5 X 3 Ft.	225.00
Rug, Navajo, Tan, Red, White, Black, Gray, 19 X 44 In.	150.00
Rug, Navajo, Transitional, 1890, 5 1/4 X 5 1/4 Ft.	1900.00
Rug, Navajo, 1930, 3 X 5 Ft.	275.00
Rug, Navajo, 2 Tray Hills, 37 X 60 In.	180.00
Sash, Chippewa, Fully Beaded	250.00
Sheath, Knife, Beaded, Black & Cobalt Blue	200.00
Sheath, Knife, Hide Handle, Rawhide, Beaded	200.00
Shield, Dance, Plains, Buffalo Hide, Ghost, Bird Design, 17 In.	550.00
Skull Cap, Hupa, Basketry, Geometric Design, Dark Ground, 7 In.	175.00
Skull Cracker, Sioux, Ceremonial, Beaded, Red, Blue, White, 29 In.	125.00
Skull Cracker, Sioux, Ceremonial, Beaded, White, Green, Yellow, 20 In.	150.00
Sword, Talwar, Gold Inlay, C.1750	300.00
Thimble, Navajo, Turquoise, Sterling Silver	45.00
Tomahawk, Ceremonial, Iron Head, Beaded, 1910, 11 1/2 In.	650.00
Tomahawk, Studded Handle, Tooled, Brass, 20 3/4 In.	660.00
Tomahawk, Western Plains, Spiked, Pewter Inlay, Head, 8 1/2 In.	375.00
Totem, Haida, Argilite Carved, 4 Figures, Hawk At Top, 14 In.	700.00
Totem, Haida, Bear Figure, Raven, Green, Black, Red, 25 In.	400.00
Tray, Apache, Basketry, Diamond Design, Black, Natural Ground, 10 In.	175.00
Tray, Apache, Basketry, Rattlesnake Design, Dog, Bird, 12 In.	425.00
Tray, Pima, Basketry, Radiating Fretted Design, 4 3/4 In.	250.00

Tray, Pima, Basketry, Radiating Fretted Design, 5 In. 400.00
Urn, Red & Black, Terra-Cotta, 2 Handles 325.00
Urn, Red, Four Mile Run, Arizona, Signed Friffon, 9 1/2 In. 475.00
Vest, Painted Chief's Portrait On Back, Hide 225.00
Vest, Sioux, Child's, Beaded, White, Multicolored, 12 In. 375.00
Vest, Sioux, Man's, Beaded, Blue Ground, Multicolored, 15 In. 450.00
Wallet, Beaded, 4 X 7 1/2 In. 12.50

INKSTAND, Baroque, Fitted With Bell & Letter Opener, C.1850, 6 1/2 In. 440.00
French, Parcel Gilt Bronze, 19th Century, 14 In. 500.00
George III, Brass Mounted, Inlaid, Mahogany, 9 1/2 In. 355.00
Gilt Bronze & Marble, Verde Antico, C.1900, 16 1/2 In. 1700.00
Glass Dome Mount, Pewter Well, Dated 1861, Brass Base 90.00
Man & Dragon Lid, Bronze & Enamel, C.1910, 7 1/2 In. 500.00
Porcelain, Floral Design, German, 9 In.Long 250.00
Ribbed, Brass Hinged Lid, Footed Base, Black Glass, 5 X 5 1/2 In. 75.00
Simpson, Hall & Miller & Co., Cut, Frosted Bottle, 7 1/2 In.Diam. 150.00
Victorian Renaissance Revival, Gilt, C.1880, 1/4 X 8 In. 95.00
Wells Flanked By Sphinxes, Allegorical Figures, Bronze, 10 3/4 In. 300.00
Winged Cherub, Glass Insert, Brass 64.00
Winged Cherubs, 2 Removable Wells, Shell Tray, Porcelain, 5 3/4 In. 50.00
With Candleholders, Wooden, C.1860 .... 120.00
2 Crystal Wells, Penholder, Sheffield, 5 X 7 In. 75.00
3-Pen Space, Cast Iron, Patent November 1879, 7 1/2 X 9 7/8 In. 44.50

INKWELL, see also Brass, Inkwell; and various porcelain categories
INKWELL, Art Deco, Lady's Head, Metal, 2 1/2 In. 115.00
Art Deco, Pen Tray, Belgian, C.1895, 9 1/2 In. 300.00
Art Nouveau, Lady's Head, Crystal & Silver Plate 45.00
Art Nouveau, Reindeer, Copper On Pewter 50.00
Bears At Table Eating Berries, Porcelain, 5 X 3 1/2 In. 225.00
Bird On Cover, Figural, Brass 45.00
Boy Standing Behind Hinged Nest With Eggs, Metal, 3 In. 65.00
Chubby Man Carving A Bird, Head Lifts For Inkwell 165.00
Deer Head Well, Marble 65.00
Dog Head, Hinged Cover, Metal, 3 1/2 In. 50.00
Dog Reading Book, Porcelain, German 75.00
Double Snail, Metal & Clear Glass 85.00
Double, 24K Gold Design, Czechoslovakia 125.00
Double, 3 Dutch Children, Bronze, Large 445.00
Dragonfly Design, Marked 65.00
Form Of Crab, Bronze, C.1900, 10 1/2 X 3 3/4 In. 325.00
Good Luck Horseshoe In Middle, Double Well, Brass, 9 1/2 In. 100.00
Hobnail, Amber 165.00
Horseshoe, Horse On Top, Single Insert, Matching Top 52.00
Jacobus, Partner's Desk, Glass In Middle, 11 1/2 X 6 1/2 In. 150.00
Ma & Pa Carter, Germany 120.00
Military Figure, Bronze & Marble, French, C.1882, 12 X 16 In. 865.00
Monument Shape, Reynolds Revolving Inkwell, Louisville, Kentucky 85.00
Ottoman With Cat, 2 Kittens On Top, Composition, 3 In. 75.00
Owl Head, Gold & Black Eyes, Bisque, Lift Top, 4 X 2 3/4 In. 195.00
Partner's, Cut Glass Insert, Wood & Brass, C.1850 .... 250.00
Revolving Glass Well, Cast-Iron Stand 95.00
Seashell Holds Brass Inkwell, Hinged Lid, Marble Base 160.00
Seated Leprechaun, Hat Lid, Signed, Cast Iron 115.00
Seated Leprechaun, Hat Lid, Signed, Cast-Iron 115.00
Sheaf Of Wheat, Sickle Closure, Carved Walnut 145.00
Sitting Bear, Head Lifts To Well, Brass-Colored Metal 42.00
Snail, Double, Metal Tray 55.00
Stoneware, Brown, 6 In. 15.00
Stylized Mistletoe Design, Art Nouveau, Copper, 9 1/2 In. 60.00
Swirl Glass, Covered With Filigree Metal 65.00
Teakettle, Glass, Opaque Blue 325.00
Teakettle, J & IE Moore, Warren, Mass., Glass, 2 1/8 In. 25.00

Tennis Racket Base, Well Is Ball, Far Rockaway Tournament, 1895 .... 135.00
   INKWELL, TIFFANY, see Tiffany, Inkwell
Traveling, Oriental 100.00
Traveling, Spring Action, Rosewood, 1 In. 20.00
Traveling, Spring Action, Rosewood, 2 In. 20.00
Wooden Shoe Shape, Hinged With A Cat, Marked Switzerland 50.00

Insulators of glass or pottery have been made for use on telegraph or
telephone poles since 1844.

INSULATOR, Am. Tel & Tel Co., Large Embossing, Bluish Aqua 2.00
   American, Rim Embossed, Light Green 27.00
   Dated 1890, Aqua 10.00
   Dated 1893, Green 10.00
   Duquesne Glass Co., Peak Top, Super Blue 25.00
   E.C. & M. Co. Sf., Short Style, Aqua 50.00
   E.C. & M. Co., Aqua With Milky Swirls 25.00
   E.C. & M. Co., Dark Green 35.00
   Embossed Prism, Light Blue 18.00
   Foster Bros., Olive Green 230.00
   G.N.W., Raised Slug Plate, Light Aqua 20.00
   Gayner, No.90, Aqua 2.00
   Hemingray, Blue 55.00
   Hemingray, No. 9, Patent Date, Jade Milk 5.00
   Hemingray, No.72a, Clear, N.M. 1.25
   Homer Brooke's, Blue 22.00
   Kimble No.820, Clear 3.00
   Knowles Cable, Patented June 17, 1890, Bluish Aqua 35.00
   Maydwell No.62, Drips, Pink 15.00
   Maydwell No.62, With Drips, Straw 12.00
   Mulford & Biddle, New York, Threadless, Teal Green 350.00
   Postal Telegraph, Purple 25.00
   Prism, Bluish Aqua, 3/4 In. 100.00
   Pyrex No.171, Clear 5.00
   Pyrex Sombrero, Dark Carnival Glass, Rainbow Colored, 10 In. 20.00
   Sombrero, Carnival Glass, Pyrex, 10 In. 25.00
   W.E. Mfg. Co., Patent December 19, 1871, Light Green 6.00
   Whitall Tatum, Light Green 2.00
   Wm. Brookfield, New York, Patent November 18, 1883, Aqua 3.00
   IRISH BELLEEK, see Belleek

   IRON, see also Kitchen; Tool; Store
IRON, Alms Box, Continental, 17th Century, 5 3/4 In. ....*Illus* 750.00
   Ashtray, Amish, Figural, Man & Woman, 3 1/2 X 2 1/2 In. 10.00

Iron, Alms Box, Continental, 17th Century, 5 3/4 In.

Ashtray, Eagle	21.00
Ashtray, Flamingo, 12 In.	32.00
Ashtray, Thermometer, T.Wright Co., 3 1/2 In.	14.00
Bell, School, Rope Driven, C.1870	250.00
Bill Hook, Lyre Shape, Embossed, C.1880	16.50
Birds, Snow, Scalloped Ends, 12 In., Pair	10.00
Bookends, Elephants, Marked A.C.W.Co.	12.00
Bookends, End Of Trail	10.00
Bookends, Indian On Horseback, Pair	20.00
Bookends, Miss Moderne, Signed	65.00
Bookends, Nudes With Wolfhounds	125.00
Bookends, Sailboats, 4 In.	18.00
Bookends, Sailing Ships, Bronzed, 3 1/2 X 4 1/2 In.	10.00
Boot Scraper, Dachshund, 21 1/2 X 8 In.	150.00
Boot Scraper, H Shaped, Hand-Forged Iron, C.1840, 8 1/2 X 1i 1/2 In.	30.00
Boot Scraper, Spaniel	30.00
Boot Scraper, Witch	75.00
Bootjack, Donkey Head	30.00
Bootjack, Naughty Nellie	23.00 To 75.00
Bowl, Hanging Handle, Button Feet, Handle, 19th Century, 6 In.Diam.	48.00
Bowl, 18th Century, 11 In.Diam.	38.00
Bracket, Shelf, Lacy, Scrolling, C.1880, 6 X 8 In., Pair	22.50
Broom Holder, Black Boy, Barefooted, Red Suit, Cast Iron, 5 In.	95.00
Buckle, Shoe, 18th Century, Pair	55.00
Candleholder, Sticking Tommy	130.00
Candlesnuffer, Hand-Forged, Scissors Type, 18th Century	75.00
Candlesnuffer, Scissors Type, 18th Century	28.00
Candlesnuffer, Tole, White Blossoms, Gold Vining, Black, 10 1/2 In.	85.00
Candlesnuffer, Wick Trimmer, 18th Century	32.00
Candlestand, Rushlight, Rhode Island, 18th Century, 29 1/4 In.	450.00
Churn, Crank, Blue Paint, Daisy, Iron, Tin, Wood, 21 X 8 X 8 In.	60.00
Coal Hod, 19th Century, Victorian	100.00 To 200.00
Cutter, Cigar, Cupples Co., Arrow, Black, 18 In.	20.00
Dispenser, String, Beehive Shape, Large	23.00
Door Knocker, Aberdeen Terrier, Brass, 4 X 6 In.	35.00
Door Knocker, Amish Girl Head	20.00
Door Knocker, Eagle	14.00
Door Knocker, Lady's Hand, Cuffed Sleeve, Nickel Plated, 4 In.	55.00
Door Knocker, Lady's Head, C.1860, 4 1/2 X 8 In.	75.00
Door Knocker, Poll Parrot, Green, Red, Yellow	25.00
Door Knocker, Woodpecker On Tree Trunk	25.00

Iron doorstops have been made in all types of designs. The vast majority of the doorstops sold today are cast iron and were made from about 1890 to 1930. Most of them are shaped like people, animals, flowers, or ships.

Doorstop, Airedale, Full Standing Figure, 10 X 11 In.	75.00
Doorstop, Aunt Jemima	75.00
Doorstop, Basket Of Flowers	25.00 To 90.00
Doorstop, Black & Yellow Worn Paint, 11 X 9 1/2 X 4 In.	100.00
Doorstop, Black Man, Colorful Livery, 8 1/2 In.	55.00
Doorstop, Boxer Dog, Brown, Original Paint, 7 1/2 In.	38.00
Doorstop, Cat	45.00 To 90.00
Doorstop, Cat, Deco, Hubley	75.00 To 90.00
Doorstop, Cat, Sitting, Black, Green Eyes, Red Mouth, Yellow Whiskers	95.00
Doorstop, Cat, Sitting, 8 1/2 In.	55.00
Doorstop, Cat, 8 In.	18.00
Doorstop, Chalet & Trees	65.00
Doorstop, Clown, Large	31.50
Doorstop, Coach, Horses & Drivers	75.00
Doorstop, Cottage, Original Paint	30.00
Doorstop, Covered Wagon, Oxen Team, 12 In.	37.50
Doorstop, Dog, Seated By Bone, 8 1/2 In.	50.00

Doorstop, Dog, Wooden Base 46.00
Doorstop, Dolly Madison, Colonial Lady, 10 X 5 1/2 X 3 In. 75.00
Doorstop, Dutch Boy & Girl, Hubley 85.00
Doorstop, Dutch Girl, With 2 Water Pails 14.00
Doorstop, Elephant, Raised Trunk 24.00
Doorstop, Falcon, Old Paint, 7 1/4 In. 60.00
Doorstop, Flower Basket, 7 In. .... 15.00 To 18.00
Doorstop, Flower Basket, 8 1/2 In. 28.00
Doorstop, Flowers 22.50
Doorstop, Frog .... 25.00 To 40.00
Doorstop, Frog, Black 65.00
Doorstop, Frog, Dark Green 65.00
Doorstop, Frog, Green Spotted 20.00
Doorstop, Galleon Ship, 3 Sails, 10 1/2 X 10 In. .... 28.00 To 45.00
Doorstop, Grapes 25.00
Doorstop, Horse .... 55.00 To 60.00
Doorstop, Horse, Pedestal Base, Parade Saddle, 7 1/2 In. 55.00
Doorstop, Jenny Lind, 4 1/2 In. 65.00
Doorstop, Lighthouse 35.00
Doorstop, Lincoln's Cabin, Green Base, Brown Cabin, 6 X 5 In. 55.00
Doorstop, Lion & Serpent 30.00
Doorstop, Lion, Rampant, 13 3/4 In. 40.00
Doorstop, Mammy, Blue Dress, 8 1/2 In. 145.00
Doorstop, Mayflower .... 32.50 To 65.00
Doorstop, Milkmaid, Blue Dress, White Apron, Blue Sunbonnet, Milk Pail 52.00
Doorstop, Old Salt 34.50
Doorstop, Parrot, On Perch .... 38.00 To 45.00
Doorstop, Parrot, Original Paint, 8 X 5 X 3 1/2 In. 40.00
Doorstop, Parrot, Polychromed, 12 In. 20.00
Doorstop, Penguin 55.00
Doorstop, Peter Rabbit, 11 3/4 In. 65.00
Doorstop, Pirate Ship, Original Paint, 10 1/4 In. 65.00
Doorstop, Pointer, Black 25.00
Doorstop, Pug, Black & White, 10 In. 75.00
Doorstop, Recumbent Lion, Oval Base, Cast Iron, 7 X 5 X 4 1/2 In. 65.00
Doorstop, Rooster, Green 25.00
Doorstop, Russian Wolfhound, Original White Paint, 15 1/2 In. 130.00
Doorstop, Scotty, Black .... 18.00 To 20.00
Doorstop, Scotty, Full Body, 10 X 8 1/2 In. 75.00
Doorstop, Scotty, White, Large 65.00
Doorstop, Setter 45.00
Doorstop, Shepherd, Full Bodies 35.00
Doorstop, Staffordshire Terrier .... 90.00 To 110.00
Doorstop, Tropical Bird 30.00
Doorstop, Twin Kittens, Side By Side, 7 1/4 In. 45.00
Doorstop, Windmill .... 25.00 To 40.00
Doorstop, Wirehaired Terrier, Tan, Black Muzzle, Hung-Down Ears 75.00
Figurine, Elk 65.00
Figurine, Fox Terrier, Blackish Brown, White Base, Standing, 3 In. 28.00
Figurine, Goat & Wagon 48.00
Figurine, Horse, Prancing, Victorian, 3 X 8 X 8 In. 25.00
Figurine, Mammy, 2 1/2 In. 40.00
Figurine, Slave Boy, Running, 30 In. 325.00
Footscraper, Dolphin, Oval Base, 9 X 10 In. 175.00
Fork, Hearth, Punch Design, Wrought, 13 In. 78.00
Frame, Lacy, 1870 .... 14.00
Frame, Picture, Stand-Up, Lacy & Gilded, 4 X 5 1/2 In. 45.00
Gong, Dinner, Hand-Forged, Triangular, Ram's Horn Design, 6 In. 30.00
Grille, Organic Design, Louis Sullivan, C.1893, 47 X 24 In. 1300.00
Hook, Beam, Hand-Forged, C.1860, 5 1/2 In. 12.50
Hook, Double Wrought 9.00
Hook, Harness, Double, 8 X 4 1/2 In. 9.00
Hook, Lantern, For Overhead Beam 18.00

Ice Skates & Key	10.00
Indicator, Wind, Mounted On Board, 12 In.	45.00
Inkstand, Desk, Glass Insert	25.00
Inkstand, Floral Design, Swirled Glass Wells, 8 In.	45.00
Iron, Doorstop, Bulldog	40.00 To 75.00
Lightning Rod, Cow Design, Arrow 22 In., Cow 9 X 6 In.	135.00
IRON, MATCH HOLDER, see also Match Holder	
Match Holder, Bird Sitting On Base, Picking Matches	35.00
Match Holder, Frog, For Wood Stove	35.00
Match Holder, Rabbit, Pheasant & Horn Figures, 8 In.	60.00
Meat Hook, With Ring, 4 Prong, 9 3/4 In.	20.00
Mold, Corn Bread, Rectangular Shape, 11 Sections, 14 X 7 1/2 In.	15.00
Mold, Corn Stick	8.50
Mortar & Pestle, Marked S.K., No.3, 4 1/2 In.	17.50
Mortar & Pestle, Marked Savery & Co.	75.00
Nutcracker, Dog, Made In England, Bronze Color, 8 1/2 In.	15.00
Ornament, Yard, Rabbit, Seated, White Paint, 12 X 12 In.	90.00
Paperweight, Gold Paint, 2 3/4 In.	5.00
Porringer, Handle, Marked Clark On Bottom, 1 1/2 Pint	75.00
Pot, Glue, Double, A.K. & Sons, 1/4 Pint	20.00
Rack, Wall, Hanging, Oak Posts, 12 Hooks, C.1900, 29 In.	90.00
Rake, Oyster, Cage With Bars, Hand-Forged, 19 X 10 In.	85.00
Roller, Cigarette, Hinged Lid, Elephant, Wind Tail, Cigarette Drops Out	175.00
Scale, Steelyard, Brass Weights, 8 1/2 In.	42.50
Scissors, Hand-Forged, Hallmarked, Large	18.00
Seat, Implement, Hocking Valley, No.241	150.00
Shoe, Mannikin's, High Top Button, 6 In., Pair	30.00
Spurs, Rowels, Cavalry	15.00
Statue, Gladiator Holding Flame, C.1860, 53 In.	1200.00
Step, Buggy, 11 X 6 X 6 In.	10.00
String Holder, Beehive Shape, Base, 4 1/2 In.	25.75
String Holder, Beehive, Dated April 11, 1862	35.00
String Holder, Claw Feet	55.00
String Holder, Inside Peg For String	14.00
Strongbox, 17th Century, Spanish, 11 1/2 In.High	*Illus* 500.00
Teakettle, Gooseneck Spout	*Illus* 175.00
Teapot, Japanese, Brass Lid, Gold & Silver Floral Sprays, 8 In.	75.00
Teapot, Japanese, Hirazogan Bird Design, Brass Lid, 8 1/4 In.	275.00
Thumb Latch, Painted Black, 11 1/4 In.	35.00
Toaster, Cut Out Heart Handle, 3 Ft. 19 1/2 In.	350.00
Tongs, Blacksmith, 20 1/2 In.	5.00
Trimmer, Wick, German	32.50
Wall Pocket, Cut Out, 9 1/2 In.	22.50

Iron, Strongbox, 17th Century, Spanish, 11 1/2 In.High

Iron, Teakettle, Gooseneck Spout

Weight, Buggy 15.50
Weight, Windmill, Bull 190.00
Whip Holder, Dated 1900 .... 750.00
Windmill, Rooster, Elgin Brand, 45 Pound, 17 X 15 X 4 1/2 In. 500.00

Ironstone china was first made in 1813. It gained its greatest popularity
during the mid-nineteenth century. The heavy, durable, off-white pottery was
made in white or was decorated with any of hundreds of patterns. Much flow
blue pottery was made of ironstone. Some of the decorations were raised.

IRONSTONE, see also Chelsea Grape; Gaudy Ironstone; Moss Rose;
Staffordshire; Wedgwood
IRONSTONE, Bedpan 5.00
Boat, Gravy, Moss Rose, Underplate 38.00
Bowl, Fruit, Impressed Adams, Pedestal, 6 X 10 In.Diam. 75.00
Bowl, John Edward, White, 3 1/2 X 9 1/2 In.Diam. 28.00
Bowl, Vegetable, Design On Cover 20.00
Bowl, Vertical Bulbous Ribs, T.Hughes, 3 X 7 1/2 In.Diam. 14.00
Bowl, White, Footed, Handled, Round, 8 1/4 X 3 1/4 In. 25.00
Bowl, White, Oval, J. & G.Meakin, 8 X 10 In. 30.00
Butter, Flower Finial, Strainer, Covered 30.00
Coffeepot, Alfred Meakin, White 58.00
Coffeepot, Corn & Oats, Corn Finial, Davenport, Large 125.00
Coffeepot, Meakin, White 75.00
Cracker Jar, Trellis, Brown On White 16.00
Cup Plate, Clementson 15.00
Cup, Feeding, Light Blue Transfer, 5 1/2 In. 40.00
Cuspidor, Lady's, Single Handle, Masked Spout, 3 X 5 1/2 In.Diam. 35.00
Dish, Dated 8, Sept.1850, White, 7 1/2 In.Diam. 9.00
Dish, Pudding, Derbyshire, 19th Century, 13 In.Diam. 60.00
Dish, Soap, Alcock's, White 10.00
Dish, Soap, Meakin 8.00
Gravy & Ladle, Covered, 15 1/2 X 7 In. 40.00
Holder, Toothbrush, Blue Shaggy Daisy Pattern 10.00
Jar, Covered, White, Woman's Face In Relief 55.00
Mold, Jelly, Rabbit, Impressed Mark, 6 1/2 X 4 In. 50.00
Pickle, Scalloped Rim, Maddock & Co. 10.00
Pitcher & Bowl, Dragon Handle, Mason, Blue, Rust, & Gold 395.00
Pitcher, Flowers & Leaves, Marked Adams & Sons, 9 1/2 In. 50.00
Pitcher, Lake Tarleton Club 32.50
Pitcher, Leaves, Berries, Watterloo Potteries, 10 1/2 In. 75.00
Pitcher, Milk, Blue & White, Cow On Sides, 1890 Mark 55.00
Pitcher, Milk, Boote 1851, Octagon, 8 In. 70.00
Pitcher, Tulips, Blue Underglaze, Copper Trim, 7 In. 40.00
Pitcher, 8-Sided, Mason's, 4 1/4 In. 58.00
Plate, Arms Of Virginia, 10 In. 20.00

Plate, Dated, Roselle J.Meir & Son, Pink, 8 1/2 In.	30.00
Plate, Deer, River, Trees, Green Border, 8 In.	12.00
Plate, Gothic Pattern, C.1850, 7 1/4 In.	28.00
Plate, Imari Pattern, Blue Transfer, Red Enamel, Marked, 9 In.	75.00
Plate, Leaf & Acorn Design, 10 Sided, 7 1/2 In.	3.50
Plate, Mason's, Blue Design, Marked, Set Of 4, 9 1/2 In.	130.00
Plate, Wheat Pattern, 10 In.	15.00
Plate, 10-Sided, 1856, Davenport, White	22.00
Platter, Burgess & Leigh, White, 10 1/2 X 12 1/2 In.	15.00
Platter, Charles Meakin, White, 8 X 11 In.	15.00
Platter, Embossed Wheat Edge, Royal St.John, 16 X 12 In.	22.50
Platter, Gaudy Spatter, Black Design, Rabbits, Frogs, 14 1/2 In.	125.00
Platter, Johnson Bros., 17 In.	14.00
Platter, Oriental, Mason's, 16 1/2 In.	100.00
Platter, Victor Shape, Elsmore & Forster, Oval, 14 X 18 In.	70.00
Platter, White, 13 1/2 In.	10.00
Platter, White, 19 In.	30.00
Spooner, Meakin, White	18.00
Sugar & Creamer, Double Phoenix, Covered, Blue & White	12.00
Sugar & Creamer, Meakin, Covered, 5 1/2 In.	16.00
Sugar & Creamer, Vista, Mason	35.00
Sugar, Covered, Meakin	60.00
Sugar, Handled, Dated May 10, 1871, White	60.00

IRONSTONE, TEA LEAF, see Tea Leaf Ironstone

Tea Set, Cobalt Blue Imari Design, Mason's, C.1890, 23 Piece	250.00
Teapot, Gold Trim, Signed Celgreave, Blue & White	20.00
Teapot, Laurel Wreath, Elsmore & Forster	130.00
Teapot, Lion, Crest, & Unicorn, Cockson & Chetwood, 9 1/4 In.	50.00
Teapot, Ribbed Body, Crimped Rim, Nut Finial, J.Edwards, 10 In.	90.00
Teapot, White, 19th Century, Burgess & Leigh, 3 1/2 In.	25.00
Tray, Fig Pattern, 1800s, White, 7 X 10 In.	40.00
Tureen, Dated April, 1902, Octagonal, 10 1/4 X 12 1/2 In.	100.00
Tureen, Log Handles & Finial, Child's, 6 X 4 1/2 In.	38.00
Tureen, Sauce, Corn & Oats, Ladle, Davenport	55.00
Tureen, Soup, White, Rectangular, Footed, Satan, Ladle, 11 In.	45.00
Tureen, Underplate & Cover, Octagon, White, 12 In.	55.00
Tureen, Underplate, Strawberry Finial, Octagon Shape, White	65.00
Tureen, Vegetable, Cockson & Chetwood Mark, Handled, 10 1/2 In.	40.00
Urn, Corinth Pattern, 8-Sided, C.1845, G.Phillips	25.00

IVORY, see also Napkin Ring; Netsuke

IVORY, Birds, Mounted On Wooden Plaque, 6 X 10 In., Pair	50.00
Bottle, Snuff, Engraved Birds, Figures, Signed, 3 In.	70.00
Bottle, Snuff, Oriental Lady On Camel	400.00
Bottle, Snuff, Oriental Lady On Elephant	450.00
Bottle, Snuff, Oriental Lady On Horse	400.00
Bottle, Snuff, Oriental Man & Woman, Side By Side, 3 In.	265.00
Box, Braiding Design, Hinged Sheffield Lid, 3 1/2 X 5 X 4 1/2 In.	165.00
Box, Cribbage, Inlaid, 3 3/4 X 9 1/2 X 2 1/4 In.	25.00
Box, Jewel, Mounted Miniatures, 19th Century, India, 17 In.	1500.00
Box, Jewel, Reticulated	600.00
Bull Elephant, With Young Tiger Attacking Mother, Signed, 9 In.	575.00
Bust, Young Black Girl, Braided Hair, Africa, 4 In.	165.00
Carving, C.1800, Teak Base, Signed, 6 In.	395.00
Case, Calling Card, Carved, Small	225.00
Case, Calling Card, Inlaid	65.00
Case, Cigar, Hand-Carved, Engraved Sterling Silver Hinges, Russian	185.00
Chess Set, Canton, Ceremonial Robes, Warrior Knights, Case, 33 Piece	800.00
Chess Set, Hand-Carved, C.1930, Original Case	595.00
Chess Set, Hand-Carved, Chinese, Boxed, King, 4 1/4 In.	1325.00
Chess Set, Hand-Carved, Original Box, King, 4 1/4 In.	1050.00
Chess Set, Nepal, Howdah, Elephant Kings, Case, C.1900, 32 Piece	550.00
Chess Set, Netsuke, Folding Wood Inlay Board	600.00
Chess Set, Wooden Box	695.00

Chopstick, Gold & Dark Blue Applied Design	10.00
Cigar Holder, Carved	40.00
Clamshell, Garden Scene, People, Trees, 1 1/2 X 3 1/2 In.	160.00
Counter, Carvings Of 11 Animals & Flowers, 2 1/2 X 3 1/2 In.	250.00
Cradle, Whalebone, Turned Spindles, Whalebone, 5 1/2 X 3 1/2 In.	475.00
Cricket Cage, Carved Dragons, Pierced Background, 4 1/4 In.	275.00
Diptych, Christ & The Magi, The Resurrection, 3 1/4 X 4 In.	200.00
Doctor's Doll, 5 In.	195.00
Doctor's Lady, Black Hair, Stand, 8 1/2 In.	225.00
Doctor's Lady, Full Figured, Movable Bracelets, 9 In.	225.00
Doctor's Lady, Movable Bracelet, 6 In.	165.00
Doctor's Lady, 12 In.	375.00
Doll, Medicine, On Stand, 12 1/2 In.	675.00
Domino Set, Prisoner Of War, Bed-Form Box, Domino, 5 1/2 In.	800.00
Elephant Bridge, On Stand, 18 In.	650.00
Etui, Carved People, Barnyard Scene On Lid, C.1760, French, 6 In.	600.00
Figurine, Angel With Flower, 9 In.	260.00
Figurine, Angel, Clasped Hands, Wings Up Over Head, C.1900, 9 In.	450.00
Figurine, Angel, Standing, 11 In.	270.00
Figurine, Apple, Stem & Leaf, Carved Garden Scene, 2 1/2 X 3 1/2 In.	160.00
Figurine, Armed Warrior, Chain Mail Garment, Spear In Hand, 8 In.	240.00
Figurine, Beauty With Bird, 11 In.	320.00
Figurine, Bishop, Robe Opens Revealing Crucifixion Scene, 10 In.	1300.00
Figurine, Boy Sitting On Tree Stump, Outstretched Frog	150.00
Figurine, Boy, Playing Pipes, 8 3/4 In.	700.00
Figurine, Christ, Flemish, 16th Century	500.00
Figurine, Crab, Japanese, 4 1/4 In.	130.00
Figurine, Cupid Kneeling, 2 1/2 In.	150.00
Figurine, Deity, Revolving Face, Kimono, Fan, 3 In.	195.00
Figurine, Eagle, 7 In.	325.00
Figurine, Elephants, 5 Graduated, Largest 5 In.	125.00
Figurine, Equestrian Warrior, Detached Spear, Case, 6 In.	450.00
Figurine, Eskimo, Whalebone	950.00
Figurine, Fisherman, 8 In.	150.00
Figurine, Fisherman, 9 In.	160.00
Figurine, Fishing Man & Lady, With Fish, Rods, 6 In.Pair	335.00
Figurine, Foo Dog, Hand-Carved, Artist's Easel, 4 In., Pair	550.00
Figurine, Foo Dog, Sitting, Head Looking To Rear, 1 3/4 In.	85.00
Figurine, Gardener In Kimono, Holding Rake & Fruit, 4 1/4 In.	225.00
Figurine, Group, An Abduction, 11 3/4 In.	1300.00
Figurine, Hunchback, 19th Century, Wooden Base, 9 In.	700.00
Figurine, Japanese Girl In Kimono, 16 In.	650.00
Figurine, King & Queen, 11 In., Pair	430.00 To 450.00
Figurine, Kuan Yin, 12 In.	285.00
Figurine, Lion Of Lucerne, Emblem Of Switzerland, 3 1/4 In.	200.00
Figurine, Longevity With Boy, 11 In.	220.00
Figurine, Man, Old, Wood Pedestal Set With Flowers, 11 In.	500.00
Figurine, Man, Seated, Wooden Leg, Ebonized Base, 7 3/4 In.	500.00
Figurine, Musician, Wood Barrel Base, German, 6 1/2 In., Set Of 7	1500.00
Figurine, Old Man With Boy, 10 1/2 In.	250.00
Figurine, Old Man, 8 In.	150.00
Figurine, Peasant Women, Hat, Holding Flower, Yoke, Basket, 6 In., Pair	320.00
Figurine, Saint Sebastian, Tied To Tree, Pierced With Arrows, 8 In.	275.00
Figurine, Supporting Puzzle Ball	120.00
Figurine, Temple Goddess	30.00
Figurine, Vendor, Man Holds Baskets, Hats, 7 1/4 In.	1000.00
Figurine, Woman Warrior, Cloak, Large Hat, Right Hand On Sword, 8 In.	250.00
Flowerpot, 17 In.	1200.00
Glove Stretcher, Deeply Carved, Chinese, 10 In.	100.00
Glove Stretcher, 9 1/2 In.	45.00
Group, Animal, Elephant Attacked By 3 Lions, 2 1/2 X 8 In.	325.00
Group, 3 Figures, 16 In.	*Illus* 7500.00
Handle, Cane, Drummer Boy, 5 1/4 In.	150.00
Holder, Cigarette, Chinese, 19th Century, Carved	45.00

Ivory, Group, 3 Figures, 16 In. *(See Page 321)*

Horn, Hunting Scenes, Medallion Of Francis II, French, 20 In.	650.00
Horse Set, Full Figural, Different Poses, Set Of 8, 2 X 2 1/2 In.	100.00
Inro, 3 Case, Seascapes, Ivory Egg, Carved Chick, C.1900	250.00
Jagging Wheel, Bird's Head, Curved Handle, 6 1/4 In.	150.00
Ladle, Coconut Shell Bowl, Ivory Handle, 12 In.	275.00
Mystery Ball, Held Up By 3 Elephants, 4 In.	75.00
Napkin Ring, Fish & Birds, Eskimo, Hand-Carved, 2 In.Wide	45.00
Necklace, Puzzle, Whalebone, Pierced & Scalloped, 29 1/2 In.	500.00
Opener, Letter, Figural, Oriental Maiden Carrying Jar, 8 In.	45.00
Paper Folder & Letter Opener, 10 1/2 X 1 1/2 In.	30.00
Plaque, Medieval Battle Scene, Rectangular, 7 X 3 1/2 In.	500.00
Pointer, Serpent Handle, Whalebone, Ivory & Wood, 32 1/2 In.	175.00
Ruler, Folding Center, Brass Fittings, 6 In.	35.00
Snuff Bottle, Dragon & Phoenix Bird, Ring Handles, 2 1/2 In.	55.00
Statue, Woman, Holding Water Lilies, Black Highlights, 26 In.	175.00
Stretcher, Glove, 6 3/4 In.	15.00
Table Screen, Cavalier Bidding Good-Bye To Family, 11 In.	850.00
Tankard, Frolicking Maids, Mermaid Handle, Silver Mounted, 10 1/4 In.	3250.00
Tusk, Birds & Bamboo Shoots, Ornate, 11 X 3 In.	70.00
Tusk, Warriors, Women, Children, Horses Climbing Mountain, 18 1/2 In.	945.00
Vase, High & Undercut Relief, Dragon Medallions, 8 3/8 In., Pair	1100.00
Vase, Hunt Scene, Wild Boar, Ebonized Base, 10 In.	1400.00
JACK ARMSTRONG, Bowl	4.00
Flashlight, Bullet Shape	18.00
Gun, Propeller, Boxed	75.00
Hike-Meter	15.00
Pedometer	11.50
Ring, Siren	24.00
Telescope	24.00

Jack-In-The-Pulpit vases were named for their odd trumpetlike shape that resembles the wild plant called jack-in-the-pulpit. The design originated in the late Victorian years.

JACK-IN-THE-PULPIT, Vase, Bark Body, Colored Spatter, Green Ground	65.00
Vase, Blue Shading On Frill, 5 In.	150.00
Vase, Chartreuse Green Opalescent, 7 1/4 In.	3.00
Vase, Cranberry Opalescent, Clear Handles, 11 In.	135.00
Vase, Enameled Bird In Flight, Gold Outlined, 10 In.	85.00

Vase, Floor, Lavender, Painted Gilt Flowers, 47 In.	750.00
Vase, Flowers, Enameled Bird, Gold Trim, 10 1/4 In.	85.00
Vase, Fluted & Pleated Top, Applied Flowers, Green, 4 In.	58.00
Vase, Green Overlay, White Outside, 8 1/4 In.	55.00
Vase, Herringbone Pattern, Amberina, 12 In.	195.00
Vase, Hobnail, Blue To Opalescent, 3 1/2 In.	35.00
Vase, Opalescent, Vaseline, 7 3/8 In.	68.00
Vase, Orange Lining, Clear Handle, Yellow, 8 5/8 In.	110.00
Vase, Pink & Yellow Opalescent Striped, 6 7/8 In.	85.00
Vase, Pink Overlay, Clear Petal Feet, 6 1/4 In.	85.00
Vase, Rainbow Striped, Rigaree Feet, 5 1/2 In.	150.00
Vase, Red & Black Shaded Lip, White Opalescent, 7 In.	125.00
Vase, Shaded Brown To Green To White, 8 In.	75.00
Vase, Swirls, Cranberry Fluted Rim, 9 In.	95.00
Vase, Tomato Overlay, Crystal Applique, 8 1/2 In.	135.00

Jackfield ware was originally a black glazed pottery made in Jackfield, England, from 1750 to 1775. A yellow glazed ware has also been called Jackfield ware. Most of the pieces referred to as Jackfield are black pieces made during the Victorian era.

JACKFIELD, Bottle, Barrel Form, 3 1/2 In.	35.00
Figurine, Spaniel, Pottery, Dark Brown, 1850-60, 8 1/2 In.	90.00
Pitcher, Cream, Pear Shape, 3 1/2 In.	30.00
Syrup, White Enamel Decor, Pewter Lid, 7 In.	50.00
Teapot, Adams Style, Relief Design	100.00
Teapot, Globular Body, Scroll Handle, Paw Feet, C.1760, 4 In.	220.00

JADE, Figurine, Bird Of Paradise, Teakwood Base, 10 In.	200.00
Figurine, Bird On Tree Stump, Teakwood Base, 7 1/2 In.	70.00
Figurine, Boy, Belted Robe, Smiling, Spinach Green, 14 1/2 In.	400.00
Figurine, Elephant, Rosewood Stand, 3 1/4 In.	245.00
Figurine, Fish, Swimming, Pop Eyed Goldfish, Green, 1 1/2 X 3 In.	115.00
Figurine, Oriental Dancer, Holding Bouquet Of Flowers, White, 7 1/2 In.	280.00
Figurine, Stork In Flight, Lotus Fronds, Wood Stand, 7 3/4 In.	425.00
Figurine, Stork On Tree, Teakwood Base, 10 In.	180.00
Figurine, Winged Beast, Reclining, Green Nephrite, 4 1/2 X 10 In.	320.00
Figurine, Zodiac Chicken, 1 X 2 1/2 In.	65.00
Figurine, 3 Birds On Tree Stump, Teakwood Base, 9 In.	110.00
Fruit, Bunch Of Grapes & Leaves, 7 X 7 In.	175.00
Fruit, Pears & Leaves, 4 X 5 In.	88.00
Hair Roller, Carved, 2 Pins, 1860	85.00
Snuff Bottle, Etched Scene, Green, 2 1/2 In.	15.00
Teapot, Mutton Fat, Mottled Brown Sides & Base, Finial, 6 X 3 1/4 In.	375.00
Tree, Gilded White Metal & Green Jade, Chinese, 3 1/2 In.	150.00
Urn, Carved Dragon, Teakwood Base, 10 1/2 In., 2 Piece	130.00
Urn, Nephite, Foo Dog Handles & Finial, Tao-Tieh Masks On Body, 7 In.	360.00
Vase, Carved Tao-Tieh Masks, Loose Ring Handles, Cover, 7 In.	1000.00

Japanese Coralene is a ceramic decorated with small raised beads and dots. It was first made in the nineteenth century. Later wares made to imitate coralene had dots of enamel.

JAPANESE CORALENE, Vase, Butterflies, Flowers, Rust Beading, 12 In.	225.00
Vase, Chrysanthemum, Leaves, Gold Beads, 10 In.	140.00
Vase, Flowers, Blue, Yellow, 8 In.	200.00
Vase, Flowers, Leaves, Pedestal Foot, Beading, 8 In.	175.00

Jasperware is a fine-grained pottery developed by Josiah Wedgwood in 1755. The jasper was made in many colors including the most famous, a light blue. It is still being made.

JASPERWARE, see also various art potteries; Wedgwood

JASPERWARE, Ashtray, Blue & White, Lady, Long Hair, Germany, 4 In.	40.00
Ashtray, White And Blue, Marked, England, 4 In.	35.00
Box, Green & White, Lady, Long Hair, Marked, 3 In.Diam.	45.00

Dish, Cheese, Classical Scenes, Covered, Blue And White, 9 In. 200.00
Hair Receiver, White And Green, Germany 25.00
Plaque, Green, White, Washington's Home, Marked, 5 1/2 In. 35.00
Toothpick, Children Dancing, Germany, Blue And White 30.00
         JEWEL TEA, see Autumn Leaf

JEWELRY, Bar Pin, Art Deco, 16 Round Diamonds, Platinum Mounting 4000.00
Bar Pin, Center Diamond, 14K White Gold, 8 X 58 Mm. 68.00
Bar Pin, 3 Gray Scottish Agates, Victorian 58.00
Beads, Jadeite, Yellow, 18 In. 950.00
Beads, Rose Quartz, Carved 175.00
Beads, Victorian, Amber, 20 In. 200.00
Belt Clip, Art Nouveau, Lavender Stone, Silver, 2 X 1 1/2 In. 75.00
Bracelet, Carved Bone, Flowers & Balls, Adjustable 33.00
Bracelet, Child's, Wrapped Gold Wire, 2 Ball Ends, Victorian 18.00
Bracelet, Embossed Flowers, Safety Chain, Yellow Gold, 3/8 In. 135.00
Bracelet, Floral Engraved, Buckle Slides, Yellow Gold, Pair 3500.00
Bracelet, 5 Large Pieces Of Gold, Colored Amber 35.00
Brooch, Cameo, Seed Pearls Outline, English, 15K Gold, 1 3/4 In. 265.00
Brooch, Gold Basket, 15 Citrine Topaz, 15K Gold Frame 190.00
Brooch, Horseshoe, 21 Round Diamonds, 15K White Gold, C.1910 .... 6500.00
Brooch, Kilt, Engraved Clan Mottos, Pair 225.00
Brooch, Profile Of Woman, C.1900, Silver & Enamel 190.00
Brooch, Spray, 101 Mine-Cut Diamonds, 18K Gold Mounting 6000.00
Brooch, Victorian Design, Sterling Silver, English Hallmarks 19.00
Brooch, 3 Classical Women, 19th Century, Gold, Enamel, & Shell Cameo 650.00
Cameo, Victorian, 14K Pink Gold Setting, Size 6 .... 65.00
Chain Slide, Opal, 14K Yellow Gold 25.00
Chain, Circular & Oval Links, 19th Century, Gold, 23 In. 800.00
Chain, Slide, 14K Gold, 30 In. 350.00
Charm, Stein, Lid Opens, 14K Yellow Gold 65.00
Chatelaine, Acanthus Foliage, Needle Case, C.1830, Gold, 21 1/2 In. 1800.00
Clasp, 3 Diamonds, Tiffany & Co., Platinum & Diamond 210.00
Cross, Rolled Gold, Hand Etched, Victorian, 2 In. 18.00
Cuff Links & Tie Tack, Square Cut Rubies, Diamond, C.1940, L.Piccard 500.00
Cuff Links, Framing 1881 & 1882 Liberty Head, 5 Dollar Gold Piece 350.00
Desk Seal, Tapered Handle, C.1845, Gold & Chalcedony, 3 1/2 In. 1300.00
Earrings, Faceted Quartz, Surrounded By Marcasites, Gold Posts 100.00
Etui, Flattened Back, Foliate Strapwork, C.1730, Gold, 3 1/8 In. 550.00
Etui, Overlaid Gold, Puti, Gold & Bloodstone, 5 1/4 In. 950.00
Hatpin, Amethyst, Sterling Overlay 35.00
Horseshoe & Riding Crop, Victorian, 10K Gold Filled 25.00
Lapel Watch, Marcasite & Enamel, C.1920, Swiss .... *Illus* 275.00
Lavaliere, 2-Color 14K Gold, Diamond, Seed Pearl, 14 X 35 Mm. 95.00
Locket, Rolled Gold, Hand Etching, Victorian, 3/4 In.Diam. 15.00
Money Clip, Spider On Gold Disc, Ruby & Diamond Body, 1 5/8 In. 400.00

Jewelry, Lapel Watch, Marcasite
& Enamel, C.1920, Swiss

Money Clip, 1883 Liberty Head, Twenty Dollar Gold Piece 550.00
Necessaire & Chatelaine, Gilt Metal & Mother-Of-Pearl, 8 1/4 In. 1100.00
Necklace & Bracelet, Indian, Silver & Turquoise, C.1900 .... 650.00
Necklace, Amber, Graduated Oval Balls, 22 In. 110.00
Necklace, Art Nouveau, Amber Orange Stones 50.00
Necklace, Brown Jade, 30 In. 600.00
Necklace, Coral, Faceted, Gold Clasp, Victorian 150.00
Necklace, Lapis, Large Round Beads, 32 In. 150.00
Necklace, Ruby Beads, 18 In. 750.00
Pendant & Brooch, Black & White Onyx, C.1890, 1i Diamonds 700.00
Pendant, Art Deco, Mother-Of-Pearl, Topaz & Pearl, 3 X 2 In. 75.00
Pendant, Memorial Scene, Dated 1796, Gold Frame, Sepia On Ivory 800.00
Pendant, Mourning Woman, Oval Frame, Braid Of Hair 95.00
Pendant, Natural Gold Nuggets, Free Form, 1 Oz., 15K Gold 1800.00
Pendant, 2 Heads, Gold Frame, Sardonyx Janus Cameo, C.1800, 1 3/4 In. 1300.00
Pin, Art Nouveau, Diamonds, Sapphires, & Peridots, C.1900, 14K Gold 500.00
Pin, Art Nouveau, Silver With Gold Wash, 2 X 2 1/2 In. 95.00
Pin, Art Nouveau, Woman's Face, Pentagram Form 50.00
Pin, Center Diamond, Marquise Shape, 14K Yellow Gold, Platinum 115.00
Pin, Paved Pearls Swordfish, Gold & Blue Enamel, 1 1/2 In. 400.00
Pin, 14 Garnets Around Large Oval Garnet 60.00
Ring, Lady's, Cluster Of Marcasites, Sterling Silver 39.00
Ring, Lady's, Emeralds, Ruby & Diamond Chips, Victorian, 14K Gold 250.00
Ring, Lady's, White Sapphires & Rubies, 18K Gold 175.00
Ring, Lady's, 3 Cut Turquoise, 14K Rose Gold 65.00
Ring, Man's Black & White Onyx Stone Cameo, 10K Yellow Gold 69.00
Ring, Masonic, 32nd Degree, 14K Gold 2000.00
Ring, Star Sapphire & Diamond, Lady's, Cabochon Sapphire, Platinum 1800.00
Ring, Thumb, Chinese, 19th Century, White Jade, 1 In.Wide 65.00
Ring, 2 Baguette Rubies, 3 Center Diamonds, 18K Gold 1200.00
Slide, Cuckoo Clock, 14K Gold 45.00
Stickpin, Abalone In Gold Bezel 12.00
Stickpin, Cabochon Sapphire, 14K Gold, Russian ....*Illus* 125.00
Stickpin, Carved Aborigine Head, Headdress, Rose Diamonds, Opal 450.00
Stickpin, Crescent, 6 Seed Pearls, 15K Gold 20.00
Stickpin, Deco, Gold Plate, White Enameling 18.00
Stickpin, Lover's Knot, With Pearl, 14K Gold 15.00
Stickpin, Shape Of Indian Chief, Savage Arms Co. 95.00
Tourmaline, Pink, Yellow Gold Mounting, Border Of Seed Pearls 400.00
     JEWELRY, WATCH, see Watch
Watch Chain, Elk Tooth, Fob Mounted, 9K Gold, 34 Dwt. 690.00
Watch Chain, Rene Lalique, Gold & Enamel *Illus*3500.00

Jewelry, Watch Chain, Rene Lalique, Gold & Enamel

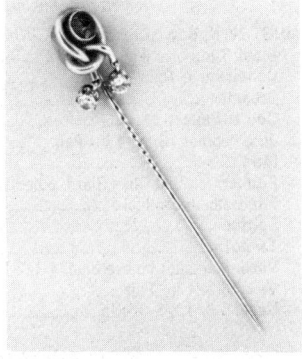

Jewelry, Stickpin, Cabochon Sapphire,
14K Gold, Russian

John Rogers statues were made from 1859 to 1892. The originals were bronze, but the thousands of copies made by the Rogers factory were of painted plaster. Eighty different figures were made.

JOHN ROGERS, Group, A Frolic At The Old Homestead, C.1880, 23 In. 200.00
Group, Checkers Up At The Farm, C.1880, 21 In. 140.00
Group, Ha, I Like Not That, C.1870, 22 In. 100.00
Group, Rip Van Winkle At Home, C.1880, 20 In. 150.00
Group, The Favored Scholar, C.1875, 21 1/2 In. 300.00

JUDAICA, Beaker, Continental, Kiddush, Moses, Aaron, Silver, 2 5/16 In. 250.00
Box, Charity, Foliage, Silver, German, Hebrew Inscribed, 4 In. 400.00
Box, Charity, Silver, Hinged Lid, 7 1/2 In. 1200.00
Box, Spice, 4 Turrets, Round Foot, Sterling Silver 265.00
Compendium, Havdalah, Silver, Polish, Filigree, 7 In. 1650.00
Container, Spice, Fish-Form, Silver, Israel, Gem-Set Eyes, 8 In. 275.00
Container, Spice, Silver, German, Fruit-Form, 6 1/2 In. 660.00
Container, Spice, Silver, Russian, Filigree, Covered, 3 1/8 In. 350.00
Crown, Torah, Silver, Hungarian, Scroll, Foliage, Beading, 15 In. 6500.00
Cup, Elijah, Silver, American, Tulip-Form, Engraved In Hebrew, 5 In. 1500.00
Cup, Kiddush, Clear, Baluster Form, Bohemian, Hebrew Engraved, 4 In. 450.00
Cup, Kiddush, Silver, Israel, Cup Inscribed, 6 3/4 In. 190.00
Figurine, Elijah Seated Beside Raven, Staffordshire, 9 1/2 In. 220.00
Havdalah Set, Trefoil Base, Silver, English, Bifurcated Handle, 4 In. 1600.00
Jug, Milk, Pear Shaped, Faience, Floral, Hebrew, 8 In. 1300.00
Lamp, Hanukah, Square Base, Silver, Polish, Foliage Border, 28 In. 1750.00
Menorah, Commandments, Lions, Sterling Silver, 10 X 8 1/2 In. 675.00
Noisemaker, Purim, Wood, Turned Wood Handle, 8 3/4 In. 150.00
Plaque, Philosopher, Medieval, Dresden, Oval Frame, 5 5/8 In. 145.00
Plate, Passover, Bezalel, Scenes Of Passover, Silver Plate, 12 3/4 In 450.00
Plate, Passover, Pewter, Order Of Seder, Wriggle Work, 16 1/2 In. 875.00
Plate, Passover, Porcelain, French, Hebrew, Passover Symbols, 16 In. 550.00
Plate, Silver, German, Jewish History, Flowers, Fruit, 18 In. 1500.00
Pointer, Torah, Silver, Italian, Cylindrical Shaft, 8 In. 875.00
Pointer, Torah, Sterling Silver 800.00
Ring, Wedding, Sterling Silver, 4 1/2 In. 650.00

Jugtown pottery refers to pottery made in North Carolina as far back as the 1750s. In 1915 Juliana and Jacques Busbee set up a training and sales organization for what they named Jugtown Pottery. In 1921 they built a shop at Jugtown, North Carolina, and hired Ben Owen as a potter in 1923. The Busbees moved the Village Store where the pottery was sold and promoted to 37 East Sixtieth Street in New York City. Juliana Busbee sold the New York store in 1926 and moved into a log cabin near the Jugtown Pottery. The pottery ended production in 1958.

JUGTOWN, Bowl, Crimped Edge, White, 2 X 6 In. 55.00
Bowl, Turquoise & Plum, 2 X 4 In.Diam. 25.00
Candlestick, Tulip 40.00
Creamer 25.00
Cup & Saucer 25.00
Jug, Pebbled, Gray, 4 In., Pair 50.00
Mug 20.00
Pitcher, Mottled Olive Glaze, Bulbous, Circle Mark, 9 1/4 In. 65.00
Pot, Bean, Individual 30.00
Spittoon 40.00
Teapot 29.00
Vase, Marked, Chinese Blue, 4 1/2 In. 75.00
Vase, 3 3/4 In., Pair 50.00
Vase, 5 3/4 X 5 3/4 In. 25.00

Kate Greenaway, who was a famous illustrator of children's books, drew pictures of children in high-waisted Empire dresses. She lived from about 1846 to 1901. Her designs appear on china, glass, and other pieces.

KATE GREENAWAY, Book, Alphabet, C.1880, Original 65.00
Candleholder, Dated 1853, Brass Handle & Feet, Signed, Pair 185.00
Doll, Pewter, Bonnet & Dress, 2 1/2 In. 30.00
Figurine, Girl, Seated, Holding Rein On Dog 185.00
Figurine, Grandpa, Gold Leather Base, 6 In. 65.00
Figurine, 7 1/2 In., Pair 75.00
Match Holder, Full Figure Girl With Muff, 6 1/4 In. 68.00
Match Safe, Copper 45.00
Napkin Ring, Child Against Ring 185.00
Napkin Ring, Girl With Muff On Each Side 125.00
Napkin Ring, Standing Boy, Grapes & Leaves On Ring 175.00
Pincushion & Tray, Figural, Lady, Tufts Silver Plate 250.00
Salt & Pepper Shaker, Boy & Girl In Basket, 3 In. 150.00
Salt & Pepper, Boy & Girl, Wire, Gold Trim 35.00
Saltshaker, Girl, Bonnet, Hands Clasped, 4 1/2 In. 65.00
Tile, 4 Seasons 350.00
Toothpick Holder, Barrel Shape, Silver Plated 100.00
Toothpick Holder, Lady In Picture Hat 85.00
Toothpick Holder, Meriden 85.00
Toothpick Holder, Top Hat, 3 Girls On Brim, Flowers & Leaves 95.00

Kauffmann refers to the type of work done by Angelica Kauffmann, a painter and decorative artist for Adam Brothers in England between 1766 and 1781. She designed small-scale pictorial subjects in the neoclassic manner. Most porcelains signed Kauffmann were made in the 1800s.

KAUFFMANN, Bowl, Bouillon, Tray, Classical Scene, Beehive Mark, Set Of 5 .... 70.00
Pitcher, Luster Finish, 8 1/2 In. 42.00
Plate, Portrait, Raised Gold, Signed, 10 In. 105.00
Tray, Cream, Gold Flowers, Burgundy Scalloped, Marked, 14 In. 75.00
Vase, Women & Child, Gold Trim, Handled, Green, Signed, 9 1/2 In. 80.00
    KAYSERZINN, see Pewter

KELVA

Kelva glassware was made by the C.F.Monroe Company of Meriden, Connecticut, about 1904. It is a pale pastel painted glass decorated with flowers, designs, or scenes.

KELVA, Box, Green Porcelain Cover, Brass Fitted, Satin Lining, 5 X 3 3/4 In. 475.00
Box, Hand-Painted White Orchids, Brass Fittings, Signed, 5 In. 395.00
Box, Hinged Cover, 7 In. 400.00
Box, Puffed, Covered, Marked, 7 In. 450.00
Planter, Mottled Green, Lilies, Ormolu Collar & Base, Signed, 8 In. 475.00

Kemple glass was made by John Kemple of East Palestine, Ohio, and Kenova, West Virginia, from 1945 to 1970. The glass was made from old molds. Many designs and colors were made. Kemple pieces are usually marked with a K on the bottom.

KEMPLE, Toothpick, Indian Head, Blue, 3 1/2 In. 20.00
Toothpick, Indian Head, Purple, 3 1/2 In. 24.00

Kew Blas is the name used by the Union Glass Company of Somerville, Massachusetts. The name refers to an iridescent golden glass made from the 1890s to 1924.

KEW BLAS, Cordial 150.00
Finger Bowl, Undertray, Fluted Rim, Marked, Gold 170.00
Salt, Ruffled & Fluted Rim, 8-Sided, Iridescent Gold, 3 In.Diam. 150.00
Vase, Allover Moire Pattern, 3 Green Shades, Signed, 8 In. 375.00
Vase, Blue & White Feathering, Butterscotch Ground, 6 1/4 In.Diam. 395.00
Vase, Pulled Feathers, Light Gold Luster Iridescence, 9 1/2 In. 1250.00
Vase, Ruffled, Gold Design Over Green Feathers, Signed, 6 In. 1250.00

Kewpies were first pictured in the "Ladies' Home Journal" by Rose O'Neill. The pixielike figures were a success, and Kewpie dolls started appearing in 1911. Kewpie pictures and other items soon followed.

KEWPIE, Bank, Souvenir, Ohio, Chalkware	15.00
Box, Soap, Kewpie In Washbasin, Signed	18.00
Buttonhole Kewpie, Original Paper Label, 2 In.	195.00
Candy Container, Barrel Candy Container, Signed	65.00
Card, Gift, Christmas, Signed, 2 1/2 X 1 In.	12.00
Creamer, Blue Jasper, 7 Kewpies, Signed Rose O'Neill	150.00
Cup & Saucer, Signed Rose O'Neill	95.00
Cup, Saucer & Plate, Fern Pattern, Action, Signed, Plate, 8 1/2 In.	150.00
Doll, Bisque, Confederate Soldier	65.00
Doll, Blue Wings, Movable Arms, Marked, 5 1/2 In.	85.00
Doll, Cameo, Composition, Socket Arms, Heart Label, Boxed, 11 1/2 In.	195.00
Doll, Celluloid, Movable Arms, 7 In.	65.00
Doll, Celluloid, 2 1/4 In.	65.00
Doll, Civil War, Action	175.00
Doll, Farmer, Action	175.00
Doll, Glassses, Original Apron, Label In Front & Back, 7 In.	395.00
Doll, Gun & Sword, Orange Hat, Bisque Feather, Label, 5 In.	325.00
Doll, Hard Plastic, Sticker, 9 In.	85.00
Doll, Impressed Nippon, 4 1/2 In.	95.00
Doll, Jointed Arms, Angel Wings, Bisque, Signed, 4 1/2 In.	175.00
Doll, Jointed Arms, Angel Wings, Paper Label, Signed, 7 1/4 In.	250.00
Doll, Jointed Shoulder, Blue Wings, Dressed, Composition, 12 In.	85.00
Doll, Labels, Signed O'Neill, 5 In.	85.00
Doll, Movable Arms, Heart Sticker, 6 1/2 In.	125.00
Doll, Pennsylvania Dutch, Red Velvet Suit, Hat, Composition, 14 In.	150.00
Doll, Pink, Holding Oar, Marked, 4 3/4 In.	125.00
Doll, Playing Guitar, Seated Next To Candlestick, 2 In.	295.00
Doll, Pouty, Action, C.1915	165.00
Doll, Red Heart Sticker, Bisque, 7 In.	175.00
Doll, Thinker, Bisque, 4 In. 235.00 To	250.00
Doll, Thinker, Painted Chalkware, Signed Rose O'Neill	85.00
Doll, Thinker, Signed Rose O'Neill, Chalkware, Germany	23.50
Doll, Traveler, Signed Rose O'Neill, 3 1/2 In.	185.00
Doll, Wedding Cake, Bride & Groom, Celluloid, 2 1/2 In.	40.00
Hugger, 4 In.	145.00
Letter Opener, Figural	30.00
Napkin Ring, Standing, Silver Plated	85.00
Napkin, Paper, Advertising, Canned Foods, 13 X 13 In.	15.00
Paper Doll, In Ville, 6 Dolls, Stand-Ups, 8 1/4 X 11 3/4 In.	15.00
Pillow, Rest Awhile, Glass Eyed	150.00
Pitcher, Action & Butterfly, Signed Rose O'Neill, Green & Pink	225.00
Pitcher, White Figures, Butterfly, Signed Rose O'Neill, 2 1/2 In.	185.00
Placecard, With Guitar	275.00
Plate, Action Kewpies, Orange & Green Luster, Signed, 8 1/2 In.	125.00
Plate, Signed Rose O'Neill	95.00
Plate, 6 Kewpies, Green Foliage, Marked, 7 3/4 In.	165.00
Plate, 7 Action Kewpies, 7 In.	75.00
Plate, 8 Action Kewpies, Signed Rose O'Neill, 7 1/2 In.	95.00
Print, 1920s, Signed Rose O'Neill, 14 X 8 In.	20.00
Sugar, Lusterware, 4 Action Kewpies, Signed Rose O'Neill, 3 1/2 In.	125.00
Thinker, Chalkware	22.00
Tie Tac	15.00
Toothpick, Figure Standing Next To Barrel	75.00
Tray, Advertising, Signed Rose O'Neill, Tin, 13 X 13 In.	165.00
Vase, Bud & Placecard Holder, The Scholar, Signed O'Neill, 2 In.	325.00
Whistle, Figural, Brass	18.50

KIMBALL, see Cluthra
KING'S ROSE, see Soft Paste

KITCHEN, see also Iron; Store; Tool; Wooden

KITCHEN, APPLE, PEELER, see Kitchen, Peeler, Apple
KITCHEN, **Basket,** Egg, Folding, Wire 18.00
 Beater, Carpet, Maple Handle, Wireware 18.50
 Board, Bread Carved On Edge, Wooden, 10 In.Diam. 45.00
 Board, Bread, Carved Bread, Round 35.00
 Board, Bread, Hanger Handle, Hardwood, 11 X 13 1/2 In. 30.00
 Board, Bread, Pig Shaped, 18 In. 10.00
 Board, Cookie, Iron, Round, Eagle Pattern 300.00
 Board, Cookie, Walnut, Eagle & Shield Design, 10 3/4 X 11 In. 375.00
 Board, Cutting, Cherry, 1 Piece, C.1860, 13 X 29 In. 85.00
 Board, Cutting, Oak Slab, Amish, 16 X 13 In. 45.00
 Board, Cutting, Pine, Pig Shape, 17 In. 15.00
 Board, Cutting, Round, 10 In. 14.00
 Bowl, Burl Figure, Wild Ash, 14 In.Diam. 110.00
 Bowl, Cheese, Pouring Lip, Handmade, Pine 65.00
 Bowl, Chopping, Red Paint 250.00
 Bowl, Dough, Tab Handles, Hand-Carved, 17 In. 55.00
 Bowl, Mixing, Green, 9 3/4 In. 7.00
 Bowl, Mixing, Yellow, 10 In. 8.00
 Bowl, Pink, 3 In. 4.00
 Bowl, Wireware, Victorian, Trellised Wire, Footed, 7 X 4 In. 45.00
 Box, Butter, Brass Studs, Swing Handles, Bentwood, 11 1/4 In. 85.00
 Box, Cake, Japanning & Stenciling, Tinware, 9 X 13 X 10 In. 30.00
 Box, Dough, Iron Nails, New Hampshire, C.1860, 25 X 27 3/4 In. 125.00
 Box, Dough, Legs, Red Paint 450.00
 Box, Dough, Lid, Pine, 28 X 12 In. 175.00
 Box, Dough, Pennsylvania, Covered, 1800s 125.00
 Box, Dough, Square Nails, Pennsylvania, Original Red, 18 1/2 X 23 In. ... 225.00
 Box, Flour, Mother Hubbard 15.00
 Box, Spice, 5 Inner Containers, Wooden, Round 150.00
 Bread Peel, Pine Handle, 49 In. 150.00
 Broiler, Footed, Rotating 230.00
 Bucket, Peach Butter, Wooden, Advertising 50.00
 Butcher Block, 6 Turned Legs, 5 Feet 500.00
          KITCHEN, BUTTER, MOLD, see Kitchen, Mold, Butter
 Cabinet, Spice, Bottom Roll-Up Lid, Lady On Front, Tin 85.00
 Can Opener, Bull's Head, Iron 28.00
 Can Opener, Figural, Ram's Head, Iron, 6 1/2 In. 65.00
 Can Opener, Figural, Unicorn, Iron, 7 In. 65.00
 Canister, Gray, Tin, Covered, Strap, C.1870, 4 1/4 X 7 In., Pair 35.00
 Canister, Tea, Dark Gray, Coned Top, 1/2 Lb. Size, 6 In. 20.00
 Carpet Beater, Woven Wicker 24.00
 Cherry Pitter, Cast Iron, Crank Type, Dated 1866 .... 25.00
 Cherry Pitter, Double, Marked Goodell, Antrim, N.H., Wood & Iron 35.00
 Cherry Pitter, Enterprise .... 22.00 To 45.00
 Cherry Pitter, Goodell Co. 15.00
 Cherry Pitter, New Standard, Legs 31.00
 Cherry Pitter, Rollman 15.00
 Cherry Pitter, 4 Legs, 1866 .... 39.00
 Cherry Pitter, 4 Spider Legs, Patent 1883, Cast Iron .... 30.00 To 45.00
 Chopper, Food, Burl Handle, 6 3/4 In. 150.00
 Chopper, Food, D-Handled, Hand-Forged Maple, Blade, C.1870 .... 30.00
 Chopper, Food, Enterprise, Tinned, Dated 1880 .... 25.00
 Chopper, Food, Griswold Puritan No.li 20.00
 Chopper, Food, Half Moon 7.50
 Chopper, Food, Harras, No.59, German 16.00
 Chopper, Food, Iron, Wooden Handles, 6 1/2 In. 35.00
 Chopper, Food, Metal, Dated 1893 .... 25.00
 Chopper, Food, Starret 450.00
 Chopper, Food, Thin Handle, Cast Iron, 7 1/4 In. 35.00
 Chopper, Food, Universal, 1897 .... 12.00
 Chopper, Food, Wooden Handles, Steel Blades, 6 In.Wide 7.50
 Chopper, Food, 6-Bladed, Bell Shape, Iron Handle, Tin, C.1890 .... 12.50

Chopper, Hand-Forged, Iron, Wooden T Handle, C.1850 .... 45.00
Chopper, Meat, Wood Handled, 6 In.Wide 7.00
Chopper, Mounted On Wood, Wall Hung, 18th Century, 16 X 11 In. 175.00
Chopper, Rattail Fold-Over Ends, Hand-Forged Iron, C.1860 .... 40.00
Chopper, Vegetable, Wooden Handle, Hand-Forged, 12 X 8 In. 35.00
Churn, Barrel Shape, Green, New England, 18th Century, 24 In. 120.00
Churn, Brass Bound, Cedar 195.00
Churn, Butter Box, Rolling, Rocker Mounted, Salmon Paint, 24 1/2 In. 250.00
Churn, Butter, Barrel, Staved Pine, Iron Bands, 12 X 48 In. 325.00
Churn, Cutout Feet & Trim, Red & Black Flame Graining, 34 In. 160.00
Churn, Cylindrical, Tin, Wooden Dasher, 15 In. 30.00
Churn, Daisy, Upright, Metal, Patent 1917, 3 Gallon 42.00
Churn, Dazey, Gallon 36.00
Churn, Dazey, Glass Jar, Wooden Paddles, Tin Cover, Iron Gears 30.00
Churn, Dazey, Wooden Lid, Tin 65.00
Churn, Gear-Driven Crank, Handled 125.00
Churn, Gem Dandy, Glass Barrel Bottom, Electric, 21 In. 30.00
Churn, Metal Bands, Old Blue 190.00
Churn, Pine Drum, Cover, 4-Bladed, 15 In.Diam. 125.00
Churn, Standing, Wrought-Iron Crank, Pine & Poplar, 15 X 33 In. 75.00
Churn, Up-And-Down, Blue-Gray, Wooden 165.00
Churn, Up-And-Down, Blue, Tin 125.00
Churn, White Cedar 125.00
Churn, Wooden, American, 19th Century, 21 In. 135.00
Churn, 2-Woman, Marked Ride-Out & Lord, C.1879, 13 In.Tall 375.00
Churn, 5 Gallon Crock 75.00
Cleaver, Meat, Keen Kutter 30.00
Cleaver, Wooden Handle 18.00
Clothes Sprinker, Elephant 20.00
KITCHEN, COFFEE GRINDER, see Coffee Grinder
Coffeepot, Nickel-Plated Copper, Gooseneck Spout 65.00
Collander, Punch Design Ribbon Border, Tin, 1830, 7 In.Deep 38.00
Collander, Side Handles, Rolled Rim, Gray, Tin, 9 3/4 X 3 3/4 In. 12.50
Cooler, Water, Blue Striped 150.00
Corer, Apple, Black Wood Handle 10.00
Corer, Apple, Carved Bone, Early 1800s, 4 In. 40.00
Cover, Pot, Copper, Handmade, 10 3/4 In. 16.50
Crimper, Pie, Chestnut Handle, Brass, 9 In. 65.00
Crimper, Pie, Melon-Ribbed Turning Wheel, Cast Aluminum, C.1900 .... 14.50
Crock, Bird & Design, Blue, 4 Gallon, 11 1/2 In. 285.00
Cup, Drinking, Gourd Shape, Orange-Rust, Holds 1 Cup 12.50
Curd Breaker, Square Nails, Iron Teeth, Original Paint, 8 X 26 In. 80.00
Cutter, Biscuit, Rotary, Dated 1892 .... 20.00
Cutter, Biscuit, Rumford, Tin 12.00
Cutter, Cabbage, Barrel Top, Wooden, 3 Blades, 42 In.Long 165.00
Cutter, Cabbage, Curly Maple, Adjustable 12.00
Cutter, Cookie, Angel, Tin 10.00
Cutter, Cookie, Bear, Dark Gray, Tin, C.1860, 1 3/4 X 3 1/2 In. 30.00
Cutter, Cookie, Bird In Flight, Perforated Flat Back 25.00
Cutter, Cookie, Bird In Flight, Tin, 1 3/4 X 3 In. 8.50
Cutter, Cookie, Bird, Tin, 4 In. 25.00
Cutter, Cookie, Cat, Sitting Up, Tin, Large 15.00
Cutter, Cookie, Cat, Sitting, Handle, Tin, 3 1/2 In. 6.00
Cutter, Cookie, Chick, Tin .... 12.00 To 15.00
Cutter, Cookie, Dog, Tin 16.00
Cutter, Cookie, Duck, Tin 15.00
Cutter, Cookie, Dutch Woman, Tin, 4 In. 10.00
Cutter, Cookie, Dutchman, Tin, 4 In. 10.00
Cutter, Cookie, Easter Cross, Tin, 2 3/4 In. 6.00
Cutter, Cookie, Fish, Tin, 4 1/2 X 1 1/2 In. 4.00
Cutter, Cookie, Full Length Ham, Tin, 5 1/2 In. 20.00
Cutter, Cookie, Ginger Boy & Girl, Tin, Set 35.00
Cutter, Cookie, Gingerbread, Figural, Tin, 3 X 5 In. 18.50

Cutter, Cookie, Goose, Tin, 3 3/4 In.	35.00
Cutter, Cookie, Hatchet, Tin	20.00
Cutter, Cookie, Heart, Punched Aluminum, Wooden Handle, 2 1/4 In.	2.00
Cutter, Cookie, Heart, Tin, Arched Handle, 3 In.	12.50
Cutter, Cookie, Hen, Standing, Tin, Large, Medium, & Miniature, Set Of 3	20.00
Cutter, Cookie, Horse, Prancing, Tin, 7 1/2 In.	105.00
Cutter, Cookie, Horse, Tin	20.00 To 30.00
Cutter, Cookie, Lady, Handmade, Tin	12.00
Cutter, Cookie, Lion, Standing, Tin	20.00
Cutter, Cookie, Man, Tin, Marked	14.00
Cutter, Cookie, Mr.Peanut, Plastic, On Display Card	35.00
Cutter, Cookie, Mr.Peanut, Plastic, Red, 6 In.	4.00
Cutter, Cookie, Peafowl, Tin	40.00
Cutter, Cookie, Rabbit, Handmade, 9 X 6 X 1 In.	45.00
Cutter, Cookie, Rabbit, Running, 7 X 4 1/4 X 1 3/4 In.	35.00
Cutter, Cookie, Rabbit, Tin, 3 X 2 In.	9.00
Cutter, Cookie, Santa Claus, Front View, Tin, 2 X 6 In.	22.50
Cutter, Cookie, Santa Claus, 3 1/4 In.	12.50
Cutter, Cookie, Santa, Tin, 5 In.	18.00
Cutter, Cookie, Santa's Boot, Figural, Tin, 2 X 3 3/4 In.	8.80
Cutter, Cookie, Star & Crescent, Tin, 2 In., Pair	10.00
Cutter, Cookie, Sugar, Dark Gray, Tin, Fluted Edge, Arched, 4 In.	12.50
Cutter, Cookie, Suite Of Cards, Tin, C.1870, Set Of 4	20.00
Cutter, Cookie, Walking Parson Reading The Good Book	25.00
Cutter, Cookie, Woodchuck, 2 3/4 In.	12.50
Cutter, Cookie, 6-Pointed Star, Tin, Point To Point, 2 1/4 In.	3.50
Cutter, Doughnut & Biscuit, Treenware, Maple, 4 1/4 In.	85.00
Cutter, Doughnut, Maple, Treenware, C.1870, 4 X 2 1/2 In.	70.00
Cutter, Doughnut, Removable Center, Aluminum, 2 3/4 In.	3.00
Cutter, Doughnut, Tin, Rumford, 1 1/2 In.	10.50
Cutter, Doughnut, Tin, Strap Handle	9.00
Cutter, Kraut, Dovetailed, Walnut	50.00
Cutter, Kraut, Indianapolis, Dated 1905	45.00
Cutter, Mushroom Shaped, Maple Handled, Sawtoothed, 2 3/8 In.	45.00
Cutter, Noodle, Green Wood Handle	5.00
Cutter, Slaw, Walnut, Heart In Crest, 7 3/4 X 20 In.	135.00
Cutter, Tobacco, P.J.Sorg	45.00
Cutter, Vegetable, Keen Kutter, Double Blade	20.00
Dipper, Metal, 13 1/2 In.	4.50
Dipper, Tubular Handle, Lapped Seams, Copper, 2 Quart	85.00
Double Boiler, Wire Bail Wooden Grip, Copper, 5 1/2 X 6 In.	70.00
Dough Box, Mustard	90.00
Dough Scraper, Long Handle, Iron, Ring Handle, 15 In.	75.00
Dough Tray, Pennsylvania, Mortised Stretcher Base	370.00
Dutch Oven, High Cover, Bail, Hanging Ring, Cast Iron, 13 1/2 In.	350.00
Eggbeater, Dated 1924	3.75
Eggbeater, Lightning, Patent, 1888	15.50
Eggbeater, Lyons, 1897	22.50 To 25.00
Eggbeater, Metal, 1820s	4.75
Eggbeater, Taplin	4.50
Eggbeater, Taplin's Dover Improved, Cast Iron, 1903	35.00
Eggbeater, Wooden Handle, Metal, 1930s	4.50
Eggbeater, 1894	25.00
Fork, 3 Tine, Wooden Handle, 1 1/2 In.	2.90
Funnel, Rolled Rim, Wire-Looped For Hang-Up, Spun Copper, 5 In.	35.00
Grater, Built Right, Tin	6.00
Grater, Cheese, Tin	6.00
Grater, Cheese, Tin, Individual Size	5.00
Grater, Crawer, Arched, Tin, 6 3/4 X 9 1/2 In.	75.00
Grater, Hand Pierced, Pine Board, Tin, 10 1/2 In.	55.00
Grater, Nutmeg	35.00
Grater, Nutmeg, Gray, Tin, 8 Pointed Star, Sliding Door, 6 In.	60.00
Grater, Nutmeg, Hinged Pocket Top, Tin	10.00

Grater, Nutmeg, Hole For Hanging, Cast Iron, Dated June 7, 1870 .... 150.00
Grater, Nutmeg, Mechanical, The Edgar, Patented, 1891 .... 42.00 To 50.00
Grater, Nutmeg, Tin & Wood, Pat. Dec. 26, 1877 .... 65.00
Grater, Nutmeg, Tin, Wooden Knob, 6 X 5 1/4 X 1 3/4 In. 45.00
Grater, Nutmeg, Wood & Tin, Square Nails 23.00
Grater, The Ideal, Gray, Tin, Washboard Shape, 7 X 11 In. 22.50
Grater, Vegetable, Crank Turned 15.00
Grater, Wall Hanging, Hinged Lid, 5 1/4 In. 7.00
Grater, 2 Drawers, Wooden, Tin Grater, 9 1/2 In. 50.00
Griddle, Pancake, Bail Handle, Cast Iron, 14 1/2 In.Diam. 20.00
Grinder, Coffee, Counter Size, Iron, Tin Drawer, Swift Mill, 13 In. 175.00
Grinder, Coffee, Maple, Dovetailed, Iron Hopper, 7 X 9 In. 110.00
Grinder, Coffee, Wall, Crystal Arcade 70.00
Grinder, Coffee, Wood Frame, Tin Sides, Dutch Design, 6 1/4 In. 50.00
Grinder, Coffee, Wooden Base, Brass Top, 6 In. 35.00
Grinder, Food, Winchester .... 18.00 To 25.00
Grinder, Meat, Enterprise No.10 .... 12.00
Grinder, Meat, Iron & Wood, Fullman Mfg.Co., 7 X 3 1/2 In. 55.00
Grinder, Meat, Keen Kutter 22.50
Grinder, Nutmeg, Crank & Wooden Handle, 4 1/4 In. 45.00
Grinder, Nutmeg, Edgar 35.00
Grinder, Poppy Seed, Brass & Iron 28.00
Hook, Pot, Swivel Arm, Joined At Top With Wrought Rivet, 11 In. 20.00
Huller, Strawberry, Patent 1900 .... 2.50
Ice Crusher, Dazey, Model 160 .... 10.00
Icebox, Brass Hardware, 3-Door, Oak 425.00
Icebox, Commercial, 8 Door, Oak 1450.00
Icebox, Lift-Top, 1 Door, Pine 195.00
Icebox, 2-Door, Golden Oak 400.00
Iron, Wafer, Brass Urn Design, Classical Figures, 5 In. 100.00
Iron, Waffle, Hand-Forged Iron, Concentric Circles & Flowers 265.00
Iron, Waffle, 5 Hearts, Alfred Anderson Co., Minneapolis 45.00
Jar, Beater, Wesson 65.00
Juice Extractor, Enterprise No.21 .... 15.00
Kettle Tilter, Forged Iron, Brass Knob, Swivel Ring 300.00
Kettle, Apple Butter, Brass, Copper Bottom 85.00
Kettle, Apple Butter, Copper, Large .... 125.00 To 350.00
Kettle, Brass Handle, Handmade, Dipper, 19th Century, 12 1/2 X 11 In. 125.00
Kettle, Brass, Iron Bail, C.1850, 8 X 11 In.Diam. 65.00
Kettle, Cylindrical, Bail Handle, Iron, 10 1/2 In. 500.00
Kettle, Doughnut, Bail Handles, Cast Iron, 10 1/4 In.Diam. 20.00
Kettle, Dovetailed, Large 225.00
Kettle, Footed, Iron, 5 1/2 In. 45.00
Kettle, Signed Waterbury, Connecticut, 1851, Brass, 8 1/2 In. 85.00
Kettle, 18th Century, Cast Iron, 5 1/2 In. 45.00
Kettle, 3-Legged, Cast Iron, Wrought Handle, 19th Century, 4 1/2 In. 48.00
Knife Holder, Cradle, Hand Carved Maple, 3 X 5 1/2 In. 45.00
Knife, Butcher, Keen Kutter 8.00
Knife, Chopping, Wrought Iron, Turned Wooden Handle, Brass Ferrule 27.50
Ladle, Agate, Blue & White 15.00
Ladle, Arrowhead Handle, Copper, 9 1/2 In. 22.50
Ladle, Brass, Forged Iron, Ring Handle, 1935 .... 350.00
Ladle, Coconut & Ivory, Shell Fitted, 19th Century, 12 In. 275.00
Ladle, Colonial, Hand Forged, Iron, Concave Bowl, 27 In. 45.00
Ladle, Hanging Hole, Handmade, Wooden, 1800s, 9 In. 8.50
Lemon Squeezer, Bird, Silver Plated Over Brass, 4 1/2 In. 39.00
Lemon Squeezer, Iron, Bottom For Pouring, C.1880 .... 30.00
Lemon Squeezer, Maple 45.00
Lemon Squeezer, Metal Hinged, Maple, C.1870, 12 In.Long 65.00
Lifter, Pie, Slide Thumb Latch, Wireware, 19 In. 16.50
Lifter, Pot, Hinged Top, 2-Arm, Wrought Iron, 11 In. 20.00
Masher, Kraut, Wooden, 27 In. 36.00
Masher, Potato, Lignum Vitae, Bell Shaped, 11 1/2 In. 65.00

Masher, Potato, Maple, 14 In.	19.50
Masher, Potato, Wooden, 9 1/2 In.	10.00
KITCHEN, MATCH SAFE, see Match Safe	
Measure, Dry, Signed Daniel Cragin, New Hampshire, 5 3/4 X 3 1/2 In.	30.00
Measure, Noggin, Handmade, Maple, Mid-19th Century, 6 X 6 X 3 1/2 In.	125.00
Measure, Old Nails, Lapped, Bentwood, 5 1/2 X 9 1/2 In.Diam.	22.50
Measuring Cup, Advertising Kelloggs, Green	16.50
Measuring Cup, Advertising Kelloggs, Pink	18.50
Measuring Cup, 3-Spout, Crystal	5.00
KITCHEN, MOLD, see also Pewter, Mold; Tin, Mold	
Mold, Baking, Santa Claus, Cast Iron, 12 In.	60.00
Mold, Bundt, Scalloped Edge, Iron, 11 X 5 In.	55.00
Mold, Butter, Acorn & Leaf, Round	60.00
Mold, Butter, Basket, Flower, & Grapes, Cast Iron, 5 7/8 In.	75.00
Mold, Butter, Cornucopia, Filled With Fruit, Cast Iron, 5 5/8 In.	75.00
Mold, Butter, Cow, Incised, Hexagonal Cylinder, Pewter Band, 4 In.	100.00
Mold, Butter, Double Acorns, Hand-Carved, 3 1/2 X 5 In., 3 Piece	65.00
Mold, Butter, Double Sheafs Of Wheat, Hand-Carved, 2 1/4 X 4 1/2 In.	95.00
Mold, Butter, Double Strawberry, Rectangular, 2 Piece	70.00
Mold, Butter, Geometric Design, Miniature	85.00
Mold, Butter, Hand-Carved Heart & Star, Pennsylvania, 5 X 9 In.	150.00
Mold, Butter, Leaves & Berries, Finger Holes, Brass, 3 1/4 X 5 In.	60.00
Mold, Butter, Petal Pattern, Square, 1 Pound	24.00
Mold, Butter, Pineapple, Cast Iron, Oval, 6 1/8 In.	75.00
Mold, Butter, Pineapple, Round	60.00
Mold, Butter, Pinwheel, Wooden Plunger, 3 In.Diam.	125.00
Mold, Butter, Sheaf Of Wheat, Hand-Carved, Wood	35.00
Mold, Butter, Swan, Hand-Carved	125.00
Mold, Butter, Swan, Round Plunger	65.00
Mold, Butter, Swan, Wooden	85.00
Mold, Butter, Wooden, Dovetailed	13.00
Mold, Cake, Lamb, Cast Iron	48.00
Mold, Cake, Mixed Fruits On Top, Gray, Tin, C.1870, 5 X 6 1/2 In.	150.00
Mold, Cake, Squirrel Design, Tin, 14 X 12 1/2 X 4 In.	65.00
KITCHEN, MOLD, CANDLE, see also Tin, Mold, Candle	
Mold, Candle, Arch Base, 12 Stands, Tin, 10 In.	145.00
Mold, Candle, Handled, Crimped Bottom, Tin, 18th Century, 10 1/2 In.	38.00
Mold, Candle, Wooden Stand, Canadian, C.1840	345.00
Mold, Candy, Easter Bunny, Sitting, C.1880, 4 In.Tall	50.00
Mold, Cheese, Pennsylvania, Tin, 4 X 4 1/2 In.Diam.	55.00
Mold, Chocolate, Banana, 3 X 7 3/4 In.	18.50
Mold, Chocolate, Bonzo, Mounted On Walnut Board, Numbered	200.00
Mold, Chocolate, Bunny, Tin, 4 1/4 X 4 1/4 X 1 1/4 In.	45.00
Mold, Chocolate, Bunny, 13 In.	65.00
Mold, Chocolate, Christmas Ornament, Figural, Tin, 3 In.	35.00
Mold, Chocolate, Clown, 11 In.	85.00
Mold, Chocolate, Crosses, 8 X 6 In.	50.00
Mold, Chocolate, Crosses, 8 1/2 X 11 X 2 In.	50.00
Mold, Chocolate, Double Puppy	65.00
Mold, Chocolate, Easter Bunny, Tin, Full Figure, 38 In.	495.00
Mold, Chocolate, Eggs, 6 X 8 1/2 In.	50.00
Mold, Chocolate, Felix The Cat, Tin, 3 1/2 X 5 1/4 In.	75.00
Mold, Chocolate, Girl With Bow	15.00
Mold, Chocolate, Halloween Cat	18.00
Mold, Chocolate, Hearts, 2 Rows Of 4, 13 X 7 1/2 In.	50.00
Mold, Chocolate, Hershey Candy, Metal	5.00
Mold, Chocolate, Kewpie, Tin, C.1930	30.00
Mold, Chocolate, Lamb, Gray, Tin, Figural, 6 1/2 X 3 X 5 In.	50.00
Mold, Chocolate, Little Girl With Big Bow	40.00
Mold, Chocolate, Man In Moon Smoking Pipe, Tin, 5 X 5 In.	33.00
Mold, Chocolate, Rabbit Sitting	75.00
Mold, Chocolate, Rabbit Sitting On Legs, 2 Rows, 7 In Row, Tin	28.00
Mold, Chocolate, Rabbit With Basket On Back, Tin, 3 1/2 X 11 1/2 In.	22.00

Mold, Chocolate, Rabbit, 18 In.	125.00
Mold, Chocolate, Santa Claus, Cast Iron, 12 In.	120.00
Mold, Chocolate, Santa Claus, 12 In.	75.00
Mold, Chocolate, Santa In Sleigh, 7 1/2 X 3 X 1 1/2 In.	40.00
Mold, Chocolate, Santa, Set Of 4, 6 In.	75.00
Mold, Chocolate, Smoking Pipe, Tin, 2 X 4 3/4 In.	45.00
Mold, Chocolate, Swan, Tin, 8 X 5 X 3 1/2 In.	60.00
Mold, Chocolate, Turkey Gobbler, Tinware, 2 3/4 X 3 In.	18.00
Mold, Chocolate, 12 Rabbits, 8 X 16 In.	55.00
Mold, Chocolate, 20 Small Turkeys	95.00
Mold, Chocolate, 24 Chicks On Nest, 8 X 13 In.	55.00
Mold, Cookie, Grapes & Floral, Cast Iron, 4 X 6 In.	80.00
Mold, Cookie, Playing Cards Suites, Boxed	5.00
Mold, Corn Bread, Iron, Dated 1920	20.00
Mold, Corn Bread, Rectangular Shape, Iron, 11 Sections, 14 X 7 In.	15.00
Mold, Cylindrical, Hinged, Tin	16.00
Mold, Food, Cabbage Rose, Copper & Tin	75.00
Mold, Food, Cornucopia, Copper, Oval, 3 X 4 X 1 1/2 In.	40.00
Mold, Food, Cornucopia, Loop, Tin Lined, Copper, C.1880, 4 X 8 In.	90.00
Mold, Food, Cow	26.00
Mold, Food, Ear Of Corn, Scalloped Skirt, Tin, 4 1/4 X 7 X 4 3/4 In.	125.00
Mold, Food, Elephant	36.00
Mold, Food, Fish Form, Marked Austria, 14 In.	27.50
Mold, Food, Fish, Embossed, C.1870, 4 1/4 X 11 In.	35.00
Mold, Food, Glass, Amber, Fleet's Fresh Fruits Jellies, 6 X 4 In.	48.00
Mold, Food, Melon Shape, Loop Hanger, Tin, 8 1/4 In.	11.00
Mold, Food, Oval, Cluster Of 5 Cherries, Tin, 4 X 6 X 2 1/4 In.	15.00
Mold, Gingerbread, Walnut Board, Vine & Floral Border, 11 In.	600.00
Mold, Hearts, 8, 2 Rows Of 4, 13 X 7 1/2 In.	50.00
KITCHEN, MOLD, ICE CREAM, see also Pewter, Mold, Ice Cream	
Mold, Ice Cream, George Washington, Hatchet Shaped, Pewter	60.00
Mold, Ice Cream, Kewpie, 1913, 7 X 6 X 2 3/4 In.	85.00
Mold, Ice Cream, Potato Shaped, Pewter, C.1910	22.50
Mold, Maple Sugar, Double Wheat Beside Flower	58.00
Mold, Maple Sugar, Heart Inside Heart, 6 X 11 In.	145.00
Mold, Maple Sugar, Heart Shape, Pine, 3 1/2 X 4 1/4 In.	45.00
Mold, Maple Sugar, Heart Shape, 2 1/2 X 2 1/2 In.	4.50
Mold, Maple Sugar, House, Large	145.00
Mold, Maple Sugar, Round Star	52.00
Mold, Maple Sugar, Santa's Boot Shape, Pine, 5 1/4 X 2 7/8 In.	35.00
Mold, Maple Sugar, Spade, Hand-Carved, 3 X 3 1/2 In.	25.00
Mold, Maple Sugar, 4 Hearts, Strips, 3 X 11 In.	115.00
Mold, Maple Syrup, Heart, Initials N & L Inside, 6 X 9 In.	135.00
Mold, Marzipan, Hinged, Germany, Tin Plated, 3 X 3 In.	30.00
Mold, Muffin, Handled, Cast Iron	15.00
Mold, Plum Pudding, Kreamer, Bail Handle, Tin	12.50
Mold, Pudding, Basket On Top, 5 1/2 In., 3 Piece	118.00
Mold, Pudding, Center Prong, Tin, 11 In.	38.00
Mold, Pudding, Fruit On Top, Pewter, 3 Piece	135.00
Mold, Pudding, Marked Great Britain, Copper, 4 X 6 X 4 1/4 In.	100.00
Mold, Pudding, Melon Shape, Tin	10.00
Mold, Pudding, Plum, Dome Top, Wire Handle, Tin, C.1880, 6 In.	12.50
Mold, Pudding, Rose Pattern, Tin	24.00
Mold, Tart, Fluted Sides, Tin, 3 X 1/2 In., Set Of 4	5.00
Mold, Tart, 6 Compartments, Tinware, 3 1/2 X 13 1/4 In.	12.50
Mop, Gears For Wringing Head, 1903, Wooden Handle	35.00
Mortar & Pestle, Wooden, 13 1/2 In.	65.00
Muffin Pan, Iron, Wagner Ware	12.00
Muffin Tin, Fruits & Vegetable, Iron	100.00
Noodle Maker, Vitatonic, Cast Iron	45.00
Paddle, Butter, Corrugated Surface, Wooden, 9 1/4 In.	4.00
Paddle, Butter, Maple, 8 3/4 X 4 In.	12.50
Paddle, Butter, Oak, 4 1/2 X 12 1/2 In.	14.50

Paddle, Butter, Wooden	10.00
Paddle, Lard, Wooden, Pine, 24 1/2 In.	18.00
Pail, Milk, Gray, Bail Handle, Tin, 4 Quart	30.00
Pail, Milk, Wire Swing Handle, Domed Cover, Gray, Tin, 2 Quart	30.00
Pan, Angel Food, Child's, Tin	4.50
Pan, Bread, Triple, St.Louis Bakery, C.1930, 12 1/2 X 18 1/2 In.	12.00
Pan, Bread, 2 Corrugated Cylinders, Hinged, Tin, 9 1/2 X 11 In.	20.00
Pan, Cake, Tube, Swansdown, Dated 1923	15.00
Pan, Cheese Drainer, Slant Sides, Handled, Tin, 14 1/2 X 8 1/2 In.	75.00
Pan, Frying, Hearth, Rattailed, Long Handled, C.1870, 23 In.	45.00
Pan, Frying, Long Handled, Cast Iron, 50 1/2 In.Diam.	165.00
Pan, Griddle, Griswold, Cast Iron, 10 In.	12.50
Pan, Milk, Gray, Slant Sided, Tin, C.1860, 4 In.Tall	22.50
Pan, Milk, Slanted Sides, Handmade, Tin	5.00
Pan, Muffin, Heart, Diamond, & Club, Cast Iron	60.00
Pan, Muffin, Shell & Maple Leaf Design, Tin, 12 1/2 X 9 1/2 In.	16.00
Pan, Muffin, Star, Hearts, Iron, 8 In.Diam.	55.00
Pan, Muffin, 8 Hole, Rectangular, Tin	12.00
Pastry Press, Stylized Pineapple, Cast Iron	75.00
Peeler, Apple, Arm & Movable Blade, On Board, Wooden	265.00
Peeler, Apple, Goodell, Cast Iron, Patent 1884	30.00
Peeler, Apple, Hand-Hewn Crank, 2 Gears, Wooden	140.00
Peeler, Apple, Hudson Parer Co., 3 Gears, Patent 1882	35.00
Peeler, Apple, Keyes, Iron, 1856	50.00
Peeler, Apple, Mechanical, Sinclair Scott Co., Heart Design	85.00
Peeler, Apple, Mechanical, Turntable, 5-Geared, Iron, 1898	75.00
Peeler, Apple, Mechanical, White Mountain No.3, Iron	45.00
Peeler, Apple, Monroe, Fitchburg, Massachusetts, Cast Iron, 1856	50.00
Peeler, Apple, Mounted On Board, Hangs On Wall, 18th Century	95.00
Peeler, Apple, On Board, 1850s	55.00
Peeler, Apple, Reading Hardware, 1868	38.00 To 45.00
Peeler, Apple, Rival No.296, 3 Gear, 1889, 11 1/2 In.Diam.	150.00
Peeler, Apple, Seat Straddler, Adjustable, Wood & Metal, 14 X 20 In.	225.00
Peeler, Apple, Table Clamp, 3 Gears, Iron, Dated 1880	48.00
Peeler, Apple, Table Clamp, 3 Gears, 1863, 12 In.	45.00
Peeler, Apple, Table Model, Cast Iron, 3 3/4 X 7 In.	145.00
Peeler, Apple, The Union, Cast Iron	55.00
Peeler, Apple, Wooden, Crank Handle, 2 Tines, 2 Size Belt Gears	150.00
Peeler, Apple, Wooden, Primitive Style	110.00
Peeler, Apple, Wooden, Shaker	250.00
Peeler, Fancy Handle	85.00
Peeler, Heart-Shaped Ram's Horn End, Signed & Dated 1823, 49 In.	195.00
Peeler, Potato, Morton Salt	3.00
Peeler, Ram's Head Handle, Iron, 46 In.	150.00
Pepper Mill, Wooden, Iron Handle, Porcelain Knob, 4 1/2 In.	15.00
Pie Bird, Duck, Pink	15.00
Pie Bird, Yellow Duck, Brown Wings	12.00
Plate Warmer, Round Wire & Iron, Wire Circles, Arched Bails, 15 In.	120.00
Plate, Griddle, Flat, Forged Iron, D Handle	130.00
Pot, Cast Iron, Long Handle	25.00
Pot, Dovetailed, Copper	200.00
Pot, Enameled Swirls Of Blue & White, Cast Iron, 11 In.Diam.	75.00
Pot, Pouring Lip, Covered, Cast Iron, C.1845, 1 Quart	85.00
Pot, Wire Bail, Cast Iron, 6 X 10 In.Diam.	53.00
Press, Garlic, Wooden	25.00
Press, Lard	25.00 To 55.00
Press, Lard, Enterprise Manufacturing Co., Philadelphia	85.00
Reflector Oven, Helmet Shape, Crank Spit, Grease Spout, Footed	250.00
Ricer, Potato, Red Handle, Metal	4.50
Roaster, Chestnut, Tin, Iron & Wooden Handle, 23 1/2 In.	75.00
Roaster, Coffee Bean, Hatch Door, Holds 2 Pounds, Tin, 21 In.	95.00
Rolling Pin, Advertising, Duvall Co., Kewanee's Best Store	165.00
Rolling Pin, Alta, Ia., Advertising In Blue, Milk Glass	90.00

Rolling Pin, Amethyst Glass, 15 In. 70.00
Rolling Pin, Bakery Shop, 2-Man, 42 In. Long 60.00
Rolling Pin, China & Wood, Springerle Board 110.00
Rolling Pin, China, Cross-Stitch Pattern 45.00
Rolling Pin, Cookie, Maple, Corrugated, 20 1/2 In. 45.00
Rolling Pin, Cornflower Design, Blue & White Stoneware 150.00
Rolling Pin, Crockery, Wesley, Iowa, Dated 1916 .... 200.00
Rolling Pin, Crystal, Wooden Handles, Embossed 1879, 20 1/2 In. 25.00
Rolling Pin, Dark Black Glass, 2 Knob Ends, Hand Made, 14 In. 80.00
Rolling Pin, Ft.Scott, Stoneware 85.00
Rolling Pin, Glass .... 8.00 To 12.00
Rolling Pin, Glass, Dark Gray Tin Cap, Embossed Handle, 16 In. 25.00
Rolling Pin, Hand Blown, Opaline 95.00
Rolling Pin, Inlaid Wood, New England 75.00
Rolling Pin, Kelvinator, Ceramic 65.00
Rolling Pin, Maple, Corrugated, Concentric Lines, 10 In. 18.50
Rolling Pin, Noodle, 2 1/4 X 16 In. 8.00
Rolling Pin, Noodles, Wooden, 13 In. 25.00
Rolling Pin, Randall, Iowa, Stoneware 160.00
Rolling Pin, Springerle, Hand-Carved, 6 Patterns, Cherry, 6 1/2 In. 120.00
Rolling Pin, Springerle, 16 Design, Red Handles, Germany 25.00
Rolling Pin, Stubby Knob Handles, 1 Piece Maple, 14 In. 18.50
Rolling Pin, Turning Handles, Birds-Eye Maple, 17 In. 35.00
Rolling Pin, 1 Piece Maple 14.00
Rolling Pin, 2-Handled, Striped Tiger Maple, 1 Piece 60.00
Rolling Pin, 19th Century, Bands Of Rosewood & Ivory, 14 1/2 In. 550.00
Rolling Pin, 32 X 13 In.Circumference 55.00
Salt & Pepper, Al Jolson, Figural, Pair 15.00
Sausage Grinder, Keen Kutter, Cast Iron 12.50
Sausage Grinder, Pegged Construction, Painted Black 50.00
Sausage Grinder, Puritan No. 122, 4-Footed 25.00
Sausage Grinder, Stuffer, Cast Iron, Dated 1855 .... 35.00
Sausage Stuffer & Lard Press, Cast Iron 75.00
Sausage Stuffer, Copper 35.00
Sausage Stuffer, Copper Bands, Wooden Plunger, Tin, 20 In. 70.00
Sausage Stuffer, Glass & Tin 12.00
Scale, Columbia Family Scales, Black, Brass Face 45.00
Scale, Prudential Family Scale, White, Round Dial, 1913 .... 25.00
Scale, Stillyard, Iron, 22 In.Long 35.00
Scoop, Blueberry, Tin 35.00
Scoop, Butter, Hook Handle, Maple, 6 X 9 1/2 In. 75.00
Scoop, Butter, Maple 12.00
Scoop, Butter, Wooden, 9 In. 30.00
Scoop, Cranberry, Handmade 95.00
Scoop, Hand-Carved, Red Stained, 1860-70, 15 X 6 X 2 In. 60.00
Scoop, Ice Cream, Dated 1894 .... 29.00
Scoop, Ice Cream, Nickel Over Brass 29.00
Scoop, Ice Cream, Tin 20.00
Scoop, Maple Butter, Concave Bowl, C.1860, 9 1/2 In. 30.00
Scrub Stick, Corrugated, Hand Hewn Wood, 18th C., 28 X 5 In. 150.00
Seeder, Raisin, Everett Patent, Wood Handle, Wire, 1880s .... 20.00 To 42.00
Sheller, Corn, Little Giant, Cast Iron 18.00
Sieve, Birch Laced, Norwegian, 20 In.Diam. 35.00
Sieve, Screen, Wooden 28.00
Sieve, Tin & Wire, Round, 10 In. 8.00
Sifter, Flour, Agitator Handle, 5 Cup, C.1930 .... 8.50
Sifter, Flour, Nesco 6.50
Sifter, Flour, Stenciled June 2, 1883, Hunters New Lightning 295.00
Sifter, Flour, 2 Cup 3.00
Sifter, Graniteware, Gray, 10 In. 15.00
Sifter, Nailed Lappings, Wire Mesh Screening, Bentwood, 13 In.Diam. 25.00
Sifter, Wooden, Dovetailed Hopper, Wooden Roller, Iron Crank 60.00
Skewer Set, Hand-Forged, Flat Shaft, Ring Top, Set Of 5 .... 995.00
Skillet, Cooking, Hearth, Iron, 3 Legged, 11 X 5 In. 35.00

Skillet, Indentations For Making Muffins, Iron, 10 In.Diam.	18.00
Skimmer, Brass, Wrought-Iron Handle, C.1830, 18 In.	110.00
Skimmer, Cast-Iron Handle, Brass, 20 In.	62.00
Skimmer, Initials LR, Cast Iron	110.00
Skimmer, Ladle, Handled, Sheet Iron, 18 3/4 In.	22.50
Skimmer, Tin, 6 1/2 In.	5.00
Skimmer, Wooden Handle, Tin, 24 In.	20.00
Slicer & Corer, Lawe's Dandy Apple, 1913	10.00
Slicer, French Bean, Harras	35.50
Slicer, Vegetable, Wood, 21 X 3 In.	35.00
Spatula, Tall, Skinny, Wooden Handle, C.1860, 16 In.	15.00
Spice Chest, Hanging, 6 Drawer, Old Blue & White Paint, 8 X 13 In.	200.00
Spice Chest, Lady Pictured, Moshier Bros., Tin	500.00
Spice Chest, Slide Top, Old Mustard Paint, Wooden, 4 X 3 1/2 X 6 In.	30.00
Spice Chest, Wooden, 8 Tin Containers, Dated 1858, 9 In.Diam.	375.00
Spice Chest, 4-Drawer, Brown On Buff Sponge, 18 1/2 X 13 1/2 In.	265.00
Spice Chest, 6 Compartments, Tin, Brass Knobs, 1900s	48.00
Spice Chest, 7-Drawer, Signed & Dated Maine 1874	195.00
Spice Chest, 8-Drawer	145.00
Spice Chest, 8-Drawer, Arch Top, Pine, C.1860, 10 X 17 1/2 In.	185.00
Spice Chest, 8-Drawer, Painted White, Tin	135.00
Spice Chest, 8-Drawer, Porcelain Knobs, Pine	130.00
Spice Chest, 8-Drawer, Wood Knobs, Tin Skirt, 13 1/2 X 8 In.	175.00
Spice Chest, 9-Drawer, 9 X 12 In.	85.00
Spoon, Tasting, Hollow Handle, Copper, C.1830, 8 1/4 In.	65.00
Spoon, Tasting, 1 Piece Stock, Maple, C.1860, 13 1/4 In.	65.00
Stamp, Butter, Beaver, Cased Wood, 3 1/8 In.Diam.	210.00
Stamp, Butter, Bluebird, Leafy Branch, Wooden, 3 In.	225.00
Stamp, Butter, Cow, Folk Art	130.00
Stamp, Butter, Cow, Hand-Carved, Maple, 3 1/2 X 3 In.Diam.	250.00
Stamp, Butter, Cow, Serrated Edge, Wooden, 3 1/2 In.	150.00
Stamp, Butter, Cow, Stylized Leaf, Wooden, 4 1/4 In.	100.00
Stamp, Butter, Deeply Carved, Pineapple Design	45.00
Stamp, Butter, Eagle Holding Leafy Branch In Beak, Wooden, 3 In.	200.00
Stamp, Butter, Fern Leaf & Twig, Hand-Carved, 4 1/2 In.Diam.	80.00
Stamp, Butter, Flower Design, 4 In.Diam.	40.00
Stamp, Butter, Fox, Running, Tree, Wooden, 2 1/2 In.	150.00
Stamp, Butter, Geometric Dentil Design, Star, Wooden, 4 1/2 In.	80.00
Stamp, Butter, Grouse, Standing, Carved Rim, Wooden, 3 1/4 In.	300.00
Stamp, Butter, Heart Within Geometric Design, Wooden, 4 1/4 In.	150.00
Stamp, Butter, Incised Deer, Branch Of Leaves, Wooden, 4 In.	300.00
Stamp, Butter, Masonic Design, Hand-Carved, 5 1/2 X 1 1/4 In.	20.00
Stamp, Butter, Peaceful Heart, Wreath Reserve, Wooden, 4 In.	200.00
Stamp, Butter, Pelican, Standing, Wooden, 3 1/4 In.	175.00
Stamp, Butter, Pine Leaf & Fronds, Knob Handle, 3 1/4 In.Diam.	35.00
Stamp, Butter, Pineapple	28.00
Stamp, Butter, Plunger Type, Leaf	25.00
Stamp, Butter, Primitive Tulip, Pennsylvania	125.00
Stamp, Butter, Ram, Stylized Flowers, Wooden, 4 1/2 In.	350.00
Stamp, Butter, Singing Bird, Folk Art	95.00
Stamp, Butter, Strawberry & Leaves, 3 1/2 In.	25.00
Stamp, Butter, Swan, Folk Art	98.00
Stamp, Butter, Swan, Hand-Carved, Wooden, 4 In.	150.00
Stamp, Butter, Wheat Pattern	30.00
Stamp, Butter, Wheat Shaft, Knob Handle, 3 Circles, 2 1/4 In.Diam.	40.00
Stamp, Butter, 3 Leaves, Concentric Circles, Hand-Carved, 2 1/4 In.	65.00
Stamp, Eagle, Facing Left, Shield Center, Hand Cut	125.00
Steamer, Plum Pudding, Tin	40.00
Stirrer, Apple Butter, Primitive, 35 In.Handle	23.50
KITCHEN, STOVE, see Stove	
Strainer Dipper, Rattail Handle, Hand-Forged Iron, 18 1/2 In.	80.00
Strainer, Cottage Cheese, Maple, 8 X 8 In.	100.00
Strainer, Tea, Brass Screen, Metal Handle	2.00
Strainer, Wrought-Iron Handle, Hook, Brass, 19 1/2 In.	40.00

Sugar Nipper, Handle Latch, Steel, 9 3/4 In.	25.00
Teakettle, Folding Strap Handle, Copper Base, Tin, 10 X 10 In.	65.00
Teakettle, Wirebail Handle, Nickel Over Copper, C.1900, 1/2 Gal.	40.00
Tenderizer, Meat, Stoneware, Wooden Handle, Dated 1877	69.00
Tenderizer, Steel Spikes, 19th Century, Round, 6 1/2 In.	25.00
Tin, Muffin, Kellogg's All-Bran	20.00
Toaster, Bannock, Tripod Arched Grid, Horseshoe Shape	400.00
Toaster, Hand Held, Iron Wire, Wooden Handle	15.00
Toaster, Hearth, Iron, Tree Trunk Handle, 30 In.	65.00
Toaster, Hearth, Rotating, Twisted Arches, Tree Of Life, Forged Iron	350.00
Toaster, Iron, Whirling, Tripod Base, 3 Pieces, 19 In.	192.00
Toaster, Marshmallow, Angelus, 3 Forks	37.50
Toaster, Swivel, Wrought Iron, 3 Legged Stand, 17 X 15 In.	225.00
Tongs, Ice, Cast Iron, Opens To 18 In.	18.50
Tongs, Pickle, Victorian	17.50
Tongs, Sugar, Spring Knob, Wrought Iron, 6 3/4 In.	68.00
Tongs, Toast, Wooden, C.1870	50.00
Tray, Knife, Hand-Hole Center, Pine, 7 X 11 In.	10.00
Tub, Butter, Hand-Rubbed Wood, 8 X 18 In.	95.00
Utensil Rack, Lintel, Open Heart Uprights, 14 In.	300.00
Vessel, Drinking, Honey Colored, Treenware, Stemmed, 5 In.	12.50
Wafer Iron, Hand-Forged, Norwegian, Copper Plate, 32 In.Long	135.00
Waffle Iron, Heart & Star, Erie, Pennsylvania, Dated 1920	60.00
Wash Stick, Pine, Contoured, 25 In.Tall	18.50
Washboard, Brass, National Washboard Co., The Brass King	10.00
Washboard, Glass	29.00
Washboard, Pine, Corrugated, Soap Pocket, 15 X 23 1/2 In.	87.00
Washboard, The Brass King, National Washboard Co., Brass	10.00
Washing Machine, Rocket No.155, Wood Cradle, Rocking	155.00
Whipper, Cream, Tin, Embossed Label Fries, 9 1/2 In.	30.00
Wrench, Jar, Fruit, Wood Handle	4.00
KNIFE, B.P.O.E., Brass	75.00
Belt, American Revolution, Hand-Forged, Iron, 7 1/2 In.	195.00
Bolo, 1913	40.00
Boot, Bowie, Joseph Allen & Sons, England, Mother-Of-Pearl Handle	150.00
Boot, Bowie, Manhattan Cutlery, Bone Handle	150.00
Boot, Bowie, Stars & Moon In Blade, Coral Set In Handle	200.00
Bowie, Civil War, Silver Handle, Shell Design, Etched Blade, 8 1/2 In.	225.00
Bowie, German Silver Guard, Marked L.F. & Co., 5 3/4 In.	145.00
Bowie, Ivory Grip, C.1860, 6 In.	135.00
Bowie, Marked G.Beardshaw, Red Leather Sheath, C.1860, 10 1/2 In.	650.00
Bowie, Wostenholm & Sons, England, Silver Cross Guard, 12 1/2 In.	195.00
Clasp, C.1750, Hand-Forged, Incurved Blade, Hooked Point, Closed, 12 In.	175.00
Dated 1915, 10K Gold, Pocket	30.00
Fascine, American Revolution, For Building Fortification, 13 In.	185.00
Fleshing, Curved Hand Wrought Steel, Double Wooden Handle, 18 In.	25.00
Hay, Short Handled, Partial Label, 25 1/4 In.	8.50
Hunting, German Royalty, Proverb, Dated 1763	650.00
Hunting, Jean Cast Cutlery Company	40.00
Hunting, Staghorn & Enameled Silver, 10 In.	80.00
Kukri, India, Horn Grips, Sheath, C.1890, 12 1/2 In.	37.50
Pen, Mother-Of-Pearl Sides, End Ring, 2 Blades, 1 In.	25.00
Pocket, Arrow Co., Germany, Miniature, Brass Color Handle	24.00
Pocket, Craftsman, No.9491	18.00
Pocket, Figural, Shoe, Germany	28.00
Pocket, Golden Wedding Whiskey	20.00
Pocket, Guarantee Life Insurance, Bullet Shape, U.S.A., 3 1/2 In.	12.00
Pocket, Ivory Handles, Brass Bolsters	32.00
Pocket, Keen Kutter	50.00
Pocket, Picture Of Saint & Church, Germany, Pearl Handle, 3 In.	12.00
Pocket, Pruning, Southington, Ebony Handle	12.50
Pocket, Remington Acorn, Punch Ground Down	15.00
Pocket, Remington, Advertising Coca-Cola	75.00

Pocket, Remington, Quick Point	60.00
Pocket, Remington, 2 Blade	15.00
Pocket, Shriners, 1956, Ambassador, Pearl Handle, 2 In.	15.00
Russell Green River Works, 24 In.	40.00
Sharpener, Winchester	35.00
Skinning, Buffalo Hunter's, C.1870, Wooden Grip, Brass Studs, 7 In.	45.00
Spanish Artillary, Pistol Grip, 12 In.	32.50
Trench, World War I, Italian	47.50
United Staes Navy, Stag Handle, Sheffield, England, 4 1/2 In.	225.00
Woodsman, Case XX, 15 In.	40.00
1 Piece Bone Grip, Carved Woman, Silver Ferrule, Italian, 11 1/2 In.	275.00

KNOWLES, TAYLOR & KNOWLES, see KTK; Lotus Ware

KOCH, Bowl, Apple Design, Shaded, Signed, 10 In.	40.00
Plate, Grapes, Colored Sprigs, Signed, 6 1/4 In.Diam.	15.00
Plate, Grapes, 8 1/2 In.	58.00

Korean ware is a heavy-glazed pottery usually featuring three-dimensional figures of people and animals as decorations. Dull orange and gray-blue are favored colors. Korean ware is still being made.

KOREAN WARE, Pitcher, Signed Sumida, 12 3/4 In.	*Illus*	175.00
Vase, 2 Boys, Bucket On Rope, Black, Artist Seal, 11 3/4 In.		235.00
Water Set, 7 Piece		575.00

Korean Ware, Pitcher, Signed Sumida, 12 3/4 In.

K.P.M   *Most dealers and collectors use the term "KPM" to refer to Berlin porcelain but the same initials were used alone and in combination with other symbols by several German porcelain makers. They include the Konigliche Porzellan Manufaktur of Berlin, initials used in mark 1823-1847; Meissen, 1723-1724 only; Krister Porzellan Manufaktur in Waldenburg, after 1831; Kranichfelder Porzellan Manufaktur in Kranichfeld, after 1903; and the Kister Porzellan Manufaktur in Scheibe, after 1838.*

KPM, Bottle, Figural, Court Jester, Hat Stopper, 1830, 4 1/2 In.	125.00 To 185.00
Candlestick, Female Cupid Form, Triform Base, Scepter Mark, 8 1/2 In.	200.00
Cup & Saucer, Royal Ivory, Demitasse, The Claridge	27.50
Dessert Set, Summer Flowers, Gilded, Coffeepot, 10 In., 22 Piece	475.00
Figure, Classical, Marked, C.1840	650.00
Figurine, Cleopatra	2000.00
Figurine, Diana, 19th Century	*Illus* 1200.00
Figurine, Shepherd Boy Carrying Lamb Over Shoulder, White, 4 1/4 In.	70.00
Figurine, Tiger Cat, Paws On Cracked Egg, Marked, 4 1/2 In.	70.00
Figurine, Woman, Black & Gold Designs, Marked, 8 1/2 In., Pair	495.00

KPM, Figurine, Diana, 19th Century   *(See Page 339)*

KPM, Plaque, Cleopatra

KPM, Plaque, Madonna
& Child

Painting On Porcelain, Seminudes, Framed, 11 X 14 In., Pair	2500.00
Painting, Young Woman With Bird, Gold Leaf Frame, 6 1/2 X 10 In.	1700.00
Plaque, Cleopatra	*Illus* 2000.00
Plaque, Innocence, C.1900, Scepter Mark, 10 1/2 In.	4000.00
Plaque, Madonna & Child	*Illus* 700.00
Plaque, Ruth, Standing In Wheat Field, Scepter Mark, 13 X 7 7/8 In.	1700.00
Plaque, Springtime, Maiden, Pastoral, Scepter Mark, 9 3/8 X 6 3/8 In.	1700.00
Plaque, Three Fates, Scepter Mark, Label, 10 X 7 5/8 In.	3000.00
Plate, Castle In Paretz Center, Gilded Border, 9 1/2 In.	150.00
Plate, Cherries, Open Handles, 1/ 1/2 In.	35.00
Plate, Painted Fruit, C.1915, Scepter Mark, 7 1/2 In., Set Of 11	1300.00
Platter, Man With Horn, Lady With Bird In Cage, 12 1/2 X 17 3/4 In.	495.00
Platter, Seafood, 6 In.	18.00
Tray, Lady's Head With Scarf, Signed, Oval, 8 X 10 In.	950.00
Vase, Art Deco, Procession Of Egyptians All Around, 10 In.	85.00
Vase, Lovers In Garden, Spray Of Flowers, Covered, Marked, 17 In., Pair	1900.00
Wall Pocket, Sculptured Flutings, Ribbon & Bow, Hand-Painted, 9 In.	90.00
Wall Pocket, 3-Dimensional Cupids, Crossed Sword Mark, 5 X 8 In., Pair	950.00

K.T.&K.
CHINA   *KTK are the initials of the Knowles, Taylor and Knowles Company of East Liverpool, Ohio, founded by Isaac W.Knowles in 1853. They made Lotus Ware. The firm merged with American China Corporation in 1928. The company closed in 1934.*

KTK LOTUS WARE, see Lotus Ware

KTK, Jar, Open Work Lid & Sides, Turquoise-Tipped White Balls, 6 In.	800.00
Mug, Little Boy Blue, Porcelain, Scene On Both Sides, Marked, 3 1/4 In.	28.00
Planter, Cornell Pattern, Flowers	85.00
Sugar & Creamer, Embossed Flowers, All White	325.00
Syrup, Metal Knob	38.50

KU KLUX KLAN, Box, Ballot, Wooden	55.00
Music, Sheet, March, Red Klansman On Horse, 1924	15.00
Ribbon, Provisional Klonvocation, Detroit, Michigan, 1925	12.00

Kutani ware is a Japanese porcelain made after the mid-seventeenth century. Most of the pieces found today are nineteenth century.

KUTANI, Bowl, Pink & Red Roses, Gold Trim, 9 In.	200.00
Cracker Jar, Geisha Girl	55.00
Inkstand, Sterling Silver Crab Well, Porcelain Base, 12 1/4 In.	550.00
Pitcher, C.1890	65.00
Pitcher, Floral Designs, Curved Handle, 19th Century, 12 In.	100.00
Tea Set, Oriental Scene, Grays, Pink, Gold Beading, Cups & Saucers	95.00
Tea Set, White Dragons, Gold Trim, 13 Piece	195.00
Teapot, Sugar, & Creamer, Allover Floral	100.00
Tray, Dresser, & Bowl, Red Trim, Geishas, 10 In.	65.00
Vase, Club Shaped, 12 In.	325.00
Vase, Flared Top, Ruffled Rim, Polychrome Birds & Flowers, 36 1/2 In.	150.00
Vase, Girls & Scenery, 2 Handles, 7 In.	75.00
LACQUER, Box, Cigar, Russian, 19th Century	49.00
Box, Sewing, Inlaid Polychrome Mother-Of-Pearl, China, C.1900	50.00
Inro, Pagoda Form, Geese Inside, Ground Eggshell, 9 1/2 In.	250.00
Tray, Floral, 18 1/2 In.	5.00

R. LALIQUE

LALIQUE

Lalique glass was made by Rene Lalique in Paris, France, between the 1890s and his death in 1945. The glass was molded, pressed, and engraved in Art Nouveau and Art Deco styles. Pieces were marked with the signature "R. Lalique." Lalique glass is still being made. Pieces made after 1945 bear the mark "Lalique."

LALIQUE, Atomizer, Frieze Of Women, Bronze Atomizer, Marked, 5 In.	250.00
Atomizer, Nude Females Holding Flowers, Signed, 6 X 2 In.	350.00
Atomizer, 6 Nudes	210.00
Bottle, Cologne, Black Enamel, Dahlia Design, Signed, 5 In.	130.00
Bottle, Cologne, Nude Children In Relief, Signed, Pair	675.00
Bottle, Perfume, Enfants, C.1925, Stamped, 4 In.	250.00
Bottle, Perfume, Female Figures, Stopper, Marked, Black, 5 1/2 In.	1350.00
Bottle, Perfume, Robin's-Egg Blue Stopper, Flask Shape	85.00
Bottle, Perfume, Smoke Glass, Embossed Stars, 4 3/4 In.	265.00
Bottle, Perfume, Stylized Blades Of Grass, Signed, Base, 8 1/4 In.	800.00
Bottle, Perfume, Stylized Woman's Face, Brown Stain, 4 In.	280.00
Bottle, Perfume, 4 Draped Females, Sienna Brown, Enamel, 6 In.	300.00
Bowl, Beaded Circles, Art Deco, 8 In.	260.00
Bowl, Embossed Angels, Opalescent & Clear, 14 1/2 In.	3150.00
Bowl, Finger, Underplate, Blue, Signed	75.00
Bowl, Flower Circles Over All, Opalescent, Marked, 10 In.	335.00
Bowl, Fruit, Coquilles Pattern, Signed	450.00
Bowl, Fruit, Frosted Rose, 3 Cherubs, Signed Block Letters, Pair	450.00
Bowl, Ivy, Scalloped Rim, 9 In.	250.00
Bowl, Lilies-Of-The-Valley Border, 12 3/4 In.	250.00
Bowl, Lily Pads, Signed, 6 X 11 In.Diam.	245.00
Bowl, Lion Finial, Lion On Each Side, Signed, 9 X 8 In.	285.00
Bowl, Madagascar, Band Of Monkey Faces, Marked, 12 In.Diam.	650.00
Bowl, Mistletoe Pattern, Blue Cast, Signed, 9 1/2 In.	675.00
Bowl, Opalescent Leaves & Berries, Block Letter, 3 1/2 In.	350.00
Bowl, Relish & Underplate, Squares In Center, Signed, 4 1/2 In.	75.00
Bowl, Relish, Underplate, Center Raised Design, Signed, Plate, 6 In.	75.00
Bowl, Scalloped, Opalescent Leaves, Raised Boughs, Signed, 9 In.Diam.	240.00
Bowl, Sprinting Greyhounds, Block Signature, 9 1/2 In.Diam.	575.00
Bowl, Thistle Pattern, Clear Frosted, Flared Top, 4 3/4 In.	150.00
Bowl, 12 Fish In Whirlpool Design, Signed, 2 X 11 3/4 In.Diam.	395.00
Box, Cigarette, Glass Beads, Scale Design, Signed, 5 1/4 X 4 In.	450.00
Box, Cigarette, Long-Haired Cat On Lid, Clear, Signed, 4 In.	165.00
Box, Glass, Covered, Frosted, Seashells, Blue, Signed, 2 3/4 In.	350.00
Box, Powder, 3 Dancing Nudes On Lid, Signed, 1 1/2 X 3 3/4 In.Diam.	250.00
Bracelet, Green, Link Inscribed, 8 1/2 In.	1350.00
Chandelier, Stylized Sunflowers, Signed, Frosted Yellow, 12 In.	700.00
Clock, Semicircular Form, Molded Birds, Stamped Face, Signed, 6 In.	2250.00
Clock, Two Figurines, Clear & Frosted, Marked, C.1925, 15 In.	4400.00

Dish, Design Around Body & Knob Of Cover, 3 X 5 3/4 In.Diam. 450.00
Fernery, Ball Shape, Signed & Numbered, 7 In. 1000.00
Figurine, Angelfish, Blue, Signed, 1 3/4 X 2 In. .... 65.00 To 120.00
Figurine, Cat, Sitting, Lavender, Signed, 3 1/2 In. 65.00
Figurine, Female, Nude, Arms Behind Head, Frosted, 9 In. 165.00
Figurine, Owl, Black Onyx Base, Signed, 7 In. 285.00
Figurine, Partridge, Frosted White, Bird Standing, Signed, 5 In. 135.00
Figurine, Rooster Head 200.00
Figurine, Sirene, Opalescent, Blue & Ocher, Signed, 4 1/8 In. 1100.00
Figurine, Suzanne, Milky Opalescent, Signed, 9 In. 3300.00
Goblet, Duncan, Nude Figures For Stem, Signed, 6 1/2 In .... 85.00 To 195.00
Goblet, Marienthal Pattern, Grapes & Vines, Signed, 5 In., Pair 200.00
Goblet, Vines & Berries, Signed, Brown Stain, Clear, 7 In. 420.00
Holder, Placecard, Flower Basket, Signed, 2 X 1 1/2 In., Set Of 4 .... 325.00
Hood Ornament, Kneeling Nude Female, Signed, 5 In. 850.00
Hood Ornament, Profile Of Team Of Horses, Signed, C.1932, 5 1/2 In. 1500.00
Inkstand, 3 Papillons, Cover, Signed, 3 In. 300.00
Jar, Powder, Petals Form Flower Lid, Signed, 2 1/4 X 3 3/8 In. 98.00
Lemonade Set, Berries, Signed, Pitcher, C.1930, 7 1/4 In., 11 Piece 700.00
Menu Card, Frosted, Menu At Top, Grapes On Vine, Signed, 6 X 3 In. 300.00
Pail, Champagne, Frolicking Nymphs, Leafage, Signed 700.00
Paperweight, Conical Shape, Berries, Frosted & Clear, Signed 235.00
Paperweight, Sanglier, Gray, Boar, Charcoal, Marked, 3 1/2 In. 1200.00
Paperweight, Sirene, Sea Nymph In Crouching Pose, Signed, 4 In. 1950.00
Pendant, Berries In High Relief, Frosted & Clear, Signed, 1 3/4 In. 495.00
Pendant, Fioret 325.00
Pendant, Kneeling Nymph, Flowering Branches, Signed, 1 1/4 In.Diam. 250.00
Pendant, Triangular, Berries In Relief, Signed, 1 3/4 X 1 1/2 In. 495.00
Perfume, Intaglio Butterflies, Globular Form, Signed, Stopper 495.00
Perfume, Sea Urchin Design, Enameled Boss, Signed, 4 X 4 1/2 In. 295.00
Perfume, 4 Butterflies, Stylized Geometric Design, Signed 495.00
Plaque, Woman, Frosted Glass, Surrounded By Fishes, Marked, 12 In. 2200.00
Plate, Annual, 1976, Eagle 110.00
Plate, Bubbles Radiating Out Of Center, 11 In. 195.00
Plate, Coquille Pattern, Signed, 8 In.Diam. 195.00
Plate, Coquille Pattern, Signed, 12 In.Diam. 375.00
Plate, Molded Tree, Matte Black, Signed, 10 1/2 In. 125.00
Plate, Vases Filled, Overflowing Flowers, Signed, 11 3/4 In. 175.00
Plate, Wheat Design, Signed, 9 1/2 In. 125.00
Plate, 6 Raised Nudes, 10 1/2 In. 695.00
Rose Bowl, 8 Crimped, Pale Blue To Mediterranean Blue, 3 1/2 In. 65.00
Shade, Lamp, Hanging, Molded Leaves, 13 In. 385.00
Tray, Thorn Design, Frosted Glass, Oval, Signed, 4 1/2 X 3 In. 150.00
Tumbler, Hesperides, Marked, Amber, 5 In. 395.00
Vase, Acanthus Design, Blue Stain, Signed, 8 1/2 In. 165.00
Vase, Archers, Frosted Clear Glass, Signed, C.1925, 10 1/4 In. 800.00
Vase, Archers, Signed, Amber, 10 1/4 In. 1600.00
Vase, Brambles Pattern, Blue, Incised Signature, 8 7/8 In. 2500.00
Vase, Bud, Vertical Ribs, Clear, Marked, 9 In. 500.00
Vase, Champagne Pattern, Gunmetal Color, Signed, 7 In. 585.00
Vase, Charmilles, Frosted, Inscribed, 13 3/4 In. 1500.00
Vase, Cherries & Leaves, Footed, Signed, 5 1/2 In. 200.00
Vase, Cherry Design, Frosted, Bulbous Top, 7 In. 185.00
Vase, Courges, Marked, Purple, 7 3/4 In. 3200.00
Vase, Danaides, Trace Of Green, Frosted, Signed, C.1925, 7 1/4 In. 450.00
Vase, Druides, Green, Marked, 7 1/2 In. 775.00
Vase, Druides, Satiny Opalescent, Marked, 7 In. 360.00
Vase, Escargot, Ridges Of Matte Ground, Blue, Marked, 8 In. 2200.00
Vase, Esterel, Ovoid, Blossoms, Brown Wash, Signed, C.1932, 5 3/4 In. 250.00
Vase, Female Figures, Green Wash, Spherical, Marked, 8 1/4 In. 475.00
Vase, Fern Leaves, Blue Cast, Frosted, Signed, 7 1/2 X 6 In. 450.00
Vase, Ferrieres, Green, Marked, 6 3/4 In. 950.00
Vase, Fish, Frosted, Seahorse Handles, Signed, 7 1/4 In. 425.00
Vase, Formose, Molded Goldfish, Signed, 6 3/4 In. 320.00

Vase, Gold-Amber, Massive Handles, Signed Block Letters, 6 In. 2700.00
Vase, Gray, Spherical, Stylized Leafage, Signed, 14 In. 1875.00
Vase, Gros Scarabees, Beetles, Mint Green, Marked, 11 1/2 In. 4500.00
Vase, Heard Of Deer Feeding, Fruit Tree, Frosted, Signed, 6 1/2 In. 550.00
Vase, Leaf Pattern, Bulb Shape, Flat Flared Rim, Signed, C.1925, 9 In. 375.00
Vase, Medusa, Molded Octopus Arms, Signed, Red, 6 1/2 In. 950.00
Vase, Milan, Massive, Deep Amber, Signed, 11 In. 450.00
Vase, Mistletoe Buds, Leaves, Blue Wash, Marked, 6 In. 350.00
Vase, Mistletoe, Opalescent Block, 6 1/2 In. 595.00
Vase, Molded Fish Around, Oberon, Frosted, Signed, 3 1/2 In. 375.00
Vase, Nivernais, Green, Marked, 6 1/2 In. 600.00
Vase, Nudes, Arm In Arm, Signed, 7 1/2 X 9 3/4 In. 2300.00
Vase, Ormeaux, Allover Leaves, Amber, Signed, 6 1/2 In. 2000.00
Vase, Ornis, Gray To Charcoal, Marked, 7 1/2 In. 725.00
Vase, Perles Design, Signed In Black Letters, 5 In. 250.00
Vase, Poissons, Pearly Opalescent, Marked, 9 1/2 In. 900.00
Vase, Rampillon, Molded Flowers & Diamonds, Signed, 5 1/4 In. 400.00
Vase, Sauge, Green, 11 In. 2500.00
Vase, Scalloped, Olive-Gray, Acid Etched, 7 In. 525.00
Vase, Sea Forms, Seahorse, Jellyfish, Frosted, Signed, 10 In. 400.00
Vase, Serpent, Frosted Colorless Glass, Marked, 10 In. 2750.00
Vase, Sophora, Leaves, Amber, Marked, 10 In. 3000.00
Vase, Soudan, Milky Opalescent, Blue Wash, Marked, 7 In. 225.00
Vase, Thistle Pattern, Blown-Out, White, Marked & Numbered, 9 In. 1150.00
Vase, Tournai, Stylized Trees, Signed, Green, 5 In. 350.00
Vase, Vine Design, 12 Roosting Birds, Signed, 7 In. 650.00
Vase, Vines & Leaves, Marked, 5 3/4 In. 135.00
Vase, Waves, Frosted, Clear Top, 7 1/2 In. 325.00
Vase, 24 Molded Fish, Frosted, Signed, 3 1/2 X 3 3/4 In. 380.00
Wine, Duncan Pattern, Nude Stem, Signed, 5 1/2 In. 85.00

**LAMP, see also Bradley & Hubbard, Lamp; Burmese, Lamp; Handel,
Lamp; Pairpoint, Lamp; Tiffany, Lamp**
LAMP, Aladdin, Amberina Base & Burner 350.00
Aladdin, B-40 .... 65.00
Aladdin, B-41 .... 57.00
Aladdin, B-51 .... 65.00
Aladdin, B-80 .... 35.00
Aladdin, B-88 .... 250.00
Aladdin, B-125 .... 80.00
Aladdin, B-131 .... 45.00
Aladdin, Beehive, Amber 85.00
Aladdin, Beehive, Red 275.00
Aladdin, Beehive, Red, Green, & Clear 375.00
Aladdin, Coolidge Drape 75.00
Aladdin, Country Store, Hanging, Brass & Tin 125.00
Aladdin, Design On Base, Reverse Painted Glass Shade, 14 1/2 In. 145.00
Aladdin, Lincoln Drape, Alacite, Scalloped Base 175.00
Aladdin, Lincoln Drape, Scalloped Cobalt Blue Shade 500.00
Aladdin, Little Buttercup, Amethyst 100.00
Aladdin, Milk Glass, Art Nouveau Styling, Opalescent 95.00
Aladdin, Moonstone, Pink 95.00
Aladdin, No.B-27, Simplicity, Ivory, Alacite .... 95.00 To 200.00
Aladdin, No.B-30 .... 80.00
Aladdin, No.B-40, With Burners 55.00
Aladdin, No.B-48 .... 150.00
Aladdin, No.B-49 .... 150.00
Aladdin, No.B-53, Clear, Washington Drape 30.00
Aladdin, No.B-60, Short Lincoln Drape, Yellow 230.00
Aladdin, No.B-62, Short Lincoln Drape, Amber 300.00
Aladdin, No.B-75, Alacite, Ivory 75.00
Aladdin, No.B-75, With Burners 65.00
Aladdin, No.B-85, White, Moonstone 100.00
Aladdin, No.B-86, Table, Green 100.00

Aladdin, No.B-98, Green 95.00
Aladdin, No.B-115, With Burners 65.00
Aladdin, No.G-22, Alacite, 11 1/2 In. 45.00
Aladdin, No.G-24, Tall Pink 90.00
Aladdin, No.G-163 .... 350.00
Aladdin, No.M-123, Figurine 135.00
Aladdin, No.2, Mantel 425.00
Aladdin, No.4, Gallery 200.00
Aladdin, No.6, Mantel 80.00
Aladdin, No.11, Mantel 70.00
Aladdin, No.12, Mantel 60.00
Aladdin, No.104, Clear 75.00
Aladdin, No.105, Green 120.00
Aladdin, No.106, Amber 150.00
Aladdin, No.109, Cathedral, Amber 58.00
Aladdin, No.1214n, With No.616s 375.00
Aladdin, Red Beehive 150.00
Aladdin, Shade, No.401, Clear 80.00
Aladdin, Table, Ivory Scroll Base, Original Shade, 24 In., Pair 45.00
Aladdin, Vertical Ribbed Glass, Burner 65.00
Aladdin, Vertique Rose, Moonstone 90.00
Aladdin, Wall Bracket, Brass 85.00
Aladdin, Washington Drape, Round Base, Complete 65.00
Alcohol, Brass, Floral Embossed Finger Loop, 3 1/2 In. 30.00
Alcohol, Embossed Finger Loop, Tin Bottom, Brass, 3 1/2 X 3 1/2 In. 30.00
Angel, Double Hanging Type, Embossed Copper Font, Frosted Globe 550.00
Apex, Yellow Cased Globe, Gold Dragon Design, 15 1/2 In. 250.00
Applesauce, Frosted Leaf Font, Etched Shade, Dated 800.00
Argand, Double Arm, B.Gardiner, N.Y., Bronze & Gilt, 17 1/2 In. 475.00
Astral, Cut & Etched Globe, Brass Stem & Base, 24 In. 475.00
Astral, Cut Glass Shade, Grapes, Leaves, 2-Tier Marble Base, 1871 .... 495.00
Banquet, Figural Cherub Stem, Flowered Globe, Wired, 32 In. 450.00
Banquet, Floret, Consolidated Glass, Frosted, Green 195.00
Banquet, Globe Shade, Onyx Shaft, American, C.1880, Brass, 30 In. 140.00
Barn, Reflector, Chimney, Tin 40.00
Berry, Pennsylvania 185.00
Betty, American, Brass, 4 In. 45.00
Betty, Brass, Chain, Wick, 4 In. 45.00
Betty, Hinged Cover, Hanging Hook, 19th Century, American, Tin, 4 3/4 In. 175.00
Betty, Pick & Chain, Tin, 5 1/2 X 6 3/4 In. 175.00
Betty, Tin 130.00
Bicycle, C.T.Ham, C.1900, 5 3/4 In. 65.00
Bicycle, Carbide, Brass 65.00
Bicycle, Carbide, Hawthorne, Brass 65.00
Bicycle, Carbide, Nickel 55.00
Bicycle, Carbide, Old Sol, Hawthorne, Nickel Over Brass 55.00
Bicycle, Demon, Candle 37.50
Blue Bristol, Bracket, White Enameled Design, Art Glass, 6 In. 35.00
Boudoir, Reverse Painted, Handle On Base, 16 X 7 In. 185.00
LAMP, BRADLEY & HUBBARD, see Bradley & Hubbard, Lamp
Bronzed Elephant Forms Base, Art Deco, Electric 35.00
Candelabra, Victorian, Removable Finials, Bronze, 13 In. 190.00
Candelabra, 3-Light, Blue & White Jasperware, 29 1/2 In. 1760.00
Candelabra, 5-Light, Burnished, Black Onyx Base, Brass, 20 In. 750.00
Candelabra, 6-Light, French, C.1900, Gilt Bronze, 29 In., Pair 2200.00
Candle, Finger, Prism Pattern Base, Glass 48.00
Carbide, Old English 37.50
Chamber, Pressed Glass, Clear, Brass Collar, 8 1/4 In. 20.00
Chandelier, Canopied Drop, S-Scrolled Branches, Cut Glass, 4 Ft. 5 In. 3300.00
Chandelier, Cut Prisms, 7 Rows, Cut Beaded Top, 7 Bulb, 36 In. 850.00
Chandelier, Gold Caramel Glaze, 42 In. 295.00
Chandelier, Petalware Monax Shades, 5-Light 135.00
Chandelier, Rococo, 6-Light, C.1850, Gilt Bronze, 3 Ft. 8 In. 700.00
Chandelier, Wrought Iron, 2-Light, C.1860 .... 275.00

Coach, U.P.R.R., Tin	80.00
Coal Oil, Embossed Flowers On Flared Base	85.00
Coin Dot Base, Ruby Cut To Clear, Brass Fittings, Bohemian, 22 In.	60.00
Cologne, Red & Clear	7.00
Coreopsis, Pink Flowers, Green Trim, Miniature	245.00
LAMP, COSMOS, see Cosmos, Lamp	
Cresoline, Complete	30.00
Desk, Partner's, Double, Signed, Emeralite	400.00
Dirk Van Erp, Copper, Marked, C.1915, 23 1/2 In.	1650.00
Dragon Head Handles, Teak Base, Cloisonne & Bronze, 14 In.	150.00
Embossed Head Of Will Rogers & Wiley Post, Airplane, 16 In., Pair	250.00
Emeralite, Desk, Signed & Dated	395.00
Emeralite, Double Knuckle	250.00
English Hobnail, Wired, Crystal, 9 1/2 In.	62.50
Fairy, Bristol, Green, Pink Flowers, Gold Trim	125.00
Fairy, Chalet Red Windows, Cast Iron	245.00
Fairy, Cranberry Verre Moire Shade, Clear Base, 5 In.	170.00
Fairy, Cricklite, Cut Standard, Gilt Fittings, 15 3/4 In., Pair	425.00
Fairy, Diamond Point, Base Marked Clarke, Apple Green	62.00
Fairy, Diamond-Quilted Pattern, Yellow & Clear, 2 Piece	80.00
Fairy, Verre Moire Cranberry, Clear Base, Clarke, Signed	185.00
Fairy, Verre Moire, Ruffled Base, Marked Clarke, 4 7/8 In.	425.00
Figural, Cockatoo, Red Crest, On Stump, Milk Glass Base, 13 In.	250.00
Filler, Whale Oil, Gooseneck, Brass Cap, C.1850, Tin	75.00
Finger, Aquarius, Pedestal, Apple Green	125.00
Finger, Brass, Floral Embossed, Loop Handle, 3 3/4 In.	20.00
Finger, Coolidge Drape	60.00 To 65.00
Finger, Octagonal Front, Aquamarine, 6 1/2 In.	120.00
Finger, Oil Guard, Dated 1870	38.00
Finger, One-O-One Pattern	65.00
Finger, Peacock Feather Pattern	46.50
Floor, G.Stickley, Oak, Lined Willow Shade	*Illus* 3000.00
Frosted Crystal Shades, Bronze, Argand, Pair	500.00
Girandole, George III, Carved Gilt Wood & Gilt Metal, 24 In.	605.00
Girandole, Queen Anne, Brass Candleholder, Walnut, 20 In., Pair	950.00
Gone With The Wind, Blown-Out Children's Heads, Electrified	375.00
Gone With The Wind, Cranberry Coin Spot Shade & Font, 8 1/4 In.	2000.00
Gone With The Wind, Delft, Blue, 24 In.	375.00
Gone With The Wind, Drape & Cord Pattern, Red Satin Glass	125.00
Gone With The Wind, Enameled Floral Design, Multicolored Ground	395.00
Gone With The Wind, Flowers, Eggshell Ground, Dated 1895, 18 1/2 In.	225.00
Gone With The Wind, Fruit Pattern, White Satin	360.00
Gone With The Wind, Kerosene, Hand-Painted Iris	365.00
Gone With The Wind, Maple Leaf Pattern, Red Satin	675.00
Gone With The Wind, Pale Green, Violet Decor, Electrified, 24 In.	275.00
Gone With The Wind, Pillar & Chain Pattern	490.00
Gone With The Wind, Red Satin, Puffed Out Maple Leaf, 1897, 24 1/2 In.	795.00
Gone With The Wind, White, Blown White Face, 24 1/4 In.	650.00
Gone With The Wind, Yellow, Pink Roses, 30 In.Tall	625.00
Gorham, Bronze, Ionic Column Shape, Marked, 20 In.	95.00
Hall, Hanging, Cranberry Glass	60.00
Hand, Buttercup, Glass, Blue	140.00
Hand, Sandwich, Blue Clambroth, Ribbed Daisy Design	195.00
LAMP, HANDEL, see Handel, Lamp	
Hanging, 45 Jewels, Openwork Brass Filigree	350.00
Jefferson, Painted Glass, Patinated Metal, Landscape	*Illus* 800.00
Jefferson, Table, Full Floral, Hand-Painted, 18 In.	1775.00
Kerosene, Atterbury Ribbed Loop Font, Gem Base, Opaque White	110.00
Kerosene, Blue Enameled Flowers, Vaseline Glass, Germany, 13 In.	125.00
Kerosene, Cathedral, Blue Font, Clear Base, 12 3/4 In.	185.00
Kerosene, Clear, Bracket, Blown Chimney, Brass Burners, 14 In.	23.00
Kerosene, Cobalt Blue, Lincoln Drape Pattern, 8 1/2 In.	70.00
Kerosene, Cobalt Blue, Lincoln Drape Pattern, 9 1/2 In.	85.00
Kerosene, Floral Design, Milk Glass, Miniature	27.50

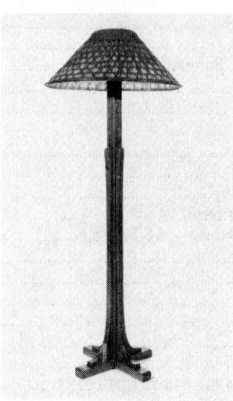

Lamp, Floor, G.Stickley, Oak, Lined Willow Shade

(See Page 345)

Lamp, Jefferson, Painted Glass,
Patinated Metal, Landscape

Kerosene, Grape Harvest Figural Stem, Dated 1872 .... 65.00
Kerosene, Honeycomb Font, Opalescent Blue 127.00
Kerosene, Jefferson, Reverse Painted Shade, Signed 975.00
Kerosene, Open Rose, Clear 30.00
Kerosene, Pedestaled, Glass, Snowflake Design, 8 1/2 In. 35.00
Kerosene, Victorian, Cupid On Base, Pink Floral Shade 350.00
Lady, Amber & Green Shade, A.Sechrist Co., Art Nouveau, 22 In. 3500.00
Lantern, Justrite Bull's-Eye Acethylene, Brass 99.00
Lard Oil, Kinnear's Patent, 1851 .... 75.00
Lard, Pump, Maltby-Neal Type, Tin 225.00
Lavender Slag Dome, Art Nouveau, 20 In. 275.00
Library, Kerosene, Pull-Down, Dated 1880, Cast-Iron Frame 395.00
Library, Pull-Down, Hand-Painted Shade, Prisms 300.00
Library, Pull-Down, Prisms, Roses On Pink & Yellow Ground, Brass 695.00
Lincoln Drape, Amber, Miniature 135.00
Marble, Signed La Selbe, 25 In., 45 Pounds 8500.00
Mechanical, Hitchcock, Nickel On Brass 350.00
Mercury Reflector On Adjustable Post, Triangular, Tin 45.00
Milk Glass, Orange, Embossed Frills & Tassels, 9 In. 110.00
Miller, Ornate Base, Purple Poppies On Globe, 1895, Signed, 30 1/2 In. 375.00
Miner's, Sunshine, Teapot 60.00
Miner's, Sunshine, Tin 65.00
Miniature, Lincoln Drape Pattern 115.00
Musical Jesters, Frosted Globe, Art Nouveau 95.00
Night-Light, Figural, Long-Eared Begging Puppy, Glass Eyes 40.00
Night, Figural, Long-Eared Puppy, Glass Eyes 40.00
Nouveau Girl On Side, Gilded, Bronze, French, Signed L.Potet, C.1890 .... 1300.00
Nutmeg, Brass Handle & Band, Embossed Nutmeg, Blown Chimney, 6 1/2 In. 125.00
Nutmeg, Cobalt Blue, 8 1/2 In. 165.00
Oil, Coolidge Drape 75.00
Oil, Coolidge Drape, Cobalt Blue 200.00
Oil, Feather Duster & Sawtooth, Yellow, 21 1/2 In. 85.00
Oil, Garfield Drape, Cobalt Blue, 9 In. 135.00
Oil, Miniature, Brass, 2 In. 10.00
Oil, Nellie Bly, Floral Sprays, Matching Shade, Miniature 135.00
Oil, One-O-One Pattern, 10 In. 75.00
Oil, Princess Feather Pattern, 12 In. 45.00
Oil, Rayo, Nickel Plated, Brass Burner, Milk Glass Shade, 21 In. 135.00
Oil, Signed Miller Light Co., Nickel Over Brass, Scroll Allover 95.00
Oil, Wall Bracket, Tin Reflector, Dated 1898, Black, 13 1/2 In. 60.00
Oil, 2-Light, Nude God With Staff, French, 19th Century, Bronze, 12 In. 450.00
Oil, 4 Blown-Out Lions, Head On Font, Clear Glass, 8 1/4 In. 105.00

Opalescent Coin Spot Font, Spatter Glass Stem, 9 3/4 In.	395.00
Opalescent, Sheldon Swirl	125.00
Oven, Candle Socket, Wooden Handle, Wrought Iron, England, 45 In.	265.00

LAMP, PAIRPOINT, see Pairpoint, Lamp

Parlor, Milk Glass, Pink, Ball Shade, Iron Base, Raised Design	350.00
Parlor, Milk Glass, Umbrella Type Shade, Iron Base, 25 In.	180.00
Peg, Enamel Floral Design, Rose Satin Glass, Fluted Shade, Pair	2450.00
Peony, Stained Glass, Patinated Metal, Wilkinson & Co. ....Illus	2400.00
Petticoat, Japanned, Tin, 4 1/4 In.	85.00
Petticoat, Original Asphaltum Finish, Burners, 4 1/2 In.	65.00
Petticoat, Original Parts & Finish, Tin	65.00
Pioneer, Dietz	225.00
Plume Pattern, Red Satin, Miniature, 7 1/2 In.	300.00
Reverse Painted Shade, Bronze Adjustable Base, Pittsburgh, 1i In.Diam.	875.00
Sandwich, Blue, Stars, Plumes, Original Burner, 4 1/2 In.	325.00

LAMP, SATIN GLASS, see Satin Glass, Lamp

Shade, Aladdin, Swiss Mountain	450.00
Sinumbra, Hanging, H.N.Hooper & Co., C.1840, Gilt Bronze, 26 1/2 In.	3750.00
Snake Charmer Holding Lamp, Art Deco, Czechoslovakia, Bronzed	150.00
Snow Scene, Hand-Painted, Art Glass, Signed Peynaud, 8 In.	290.00
Solar, Boston, C.1830, Frosted & Cut Shade, Gilt Bronze, 18 1/4 In.	175.00
Solar, Damascene Shade, Cornelius & Co., C.1850, Bronze, 22 1/4 In.	650.00
Sparking, Blown Camphene Glass, Pewter & Brass Fittings, 3 3/4 In.	35.00
Sparking, Sandwich, Knop Stem, Single Wick, C.1850, 4 1/4 In.	650.00
Sparking, Separate Standard, Blown, 6 1/4 In.	325.00
Spider Web, Milk Glass, Miniature	295.00
Stained Glass, Gilt Metal, Art Nouveau ....Illus	1200.00
Student, Brass Frame, Milk Glass Shade, 1871, Library Lamp, 21 In.	350.00
Student, Cast Brass Base, Green Shade, Signed Miller, C.1890, 21 In.	795.00
Student, Dated 1870, Signed C.A.Kleeman, N.Y., Brass	495.00
Student, Double Light, Adjustable, Electrified, Brass, 25 In.	275.00
Student, Double Light, Victorian, Brass, 29 In.	550.00
Student, Green Cased Shade, Dated 1871, Signed C.Argand, 21 In.	550.00
Student, Nickel Plated Brass, Shade, C.F.A.Henricks, 21 1/4 In.	250.00
Student, Rose Satin Quilted Shade, Adjustable, Brass, Signed, 21 In.	1200.00
Student, Single, All Original	275.00
Student, Single, Manhattan Brass Co., 1879	275.00
Sunshine, Miner's, Tin	30.00
Table, Cameo Glass, Acid Cut Cherry Tree Design, Ledoux	2300.00
Table, Filigree Border, Slag Glass Panels, 20 In.	450.00

Lamp, Peony, Stained Glass, Patinated
Metal, Wilkinson & Co.

Lamp, Stained Glass, Gilt Metal, Art Nouveau

Table, Gone With The Wind, Victorian, 19th Century, 22 In. 160.00
Table, Victorian, Globular Shape, White Glass Shade, 21 In. 80.00
Table, Wicker 150.00
    LAMP, TIFFANY, see Tiffany, Lamp
Torchere, Bellflower Pendant, Silver Bronze, 5 Ft. 7 1/2 In., Pair 9500.00
Tulip Form Shade, Footed Spherical Body, Victorian, 12 3/4 In. 200.00
Turkey Foot Pattern, Oil, Cobalt Blue 150.00
Urn Shape, Cambridge, Crown Tuscan, 11 In., Pair 140.00
Vapo Cresline, 6 1/2 In. 65.00
Wedding, Clear Base, Fonts, & Match Holder, Ripley & Co., Dated 1870 .... 1350.00
Whale Oil, Acorn Shape Font, Single Burner, Brass, 7 In. 120.00
Whale Oil, American, Tin, Pair 295.00
Whale Oil, Blown Font, Pewter Collar, Sandwich Glass, 7 1/4 In. 95.00
Whale Oil, Blown Glass, Twin Pewter Burners, Chain, C.1840 .... 160.00
Whale Oil, Bull's-Eye Pattern, Sandwich Glass & Clear, 6-Sided 45.00
Whale Oil, Candlestick, Blue Shade, Hand-Painted Flowers, 27 In., Pair 645.00
Whale Oil, Floral Cut, Clear, 9 1/2 In. 40.00
Whale Oil, Heart & Thumbprint, Sandwich Glass, C.1830, 8 1/2 In., Pair 395.00
Whale Oil, Hexagonal Base, Block Font, Flint, 10 In. 85.00
Whale Oil, Inverted Pear Font, Pressed Glass Base, 11 1/4 In. 75.00
Whale Oil, Loop On Column Base, Pewter Top, C.1835, Vaseline Glass, Pair ... 550.00
Whale Oil, Overlay With Clambroth Base, White Cut To Opaque Green 950.00
Whale Oil, Peg, Pewter Burners, Blown Glass, 7 In. 160.00
Whale Oil, Pewter Collar & Burner, Glass Stopper 95.00
Whale Oil, Pewter Collar, Bulbous Shape, Bown-In Mold, 2 3/4 In. 25.00
Whale Oil, Saucer Base, Handled, Brass, 6 1/2 In. 185.00
Whale Oil, Sparking, Pewter Collar, Blown-In Mold, 2 3/4 In. 25.00
Whale Oil, Three Face Pattern 225.00
Whale Oil, Tin 225.00
Whale Oil, 1 Wick Burner, Pewter, 4 3/4 In. 365.00
Whale Oil, 2 Brass Spouts, 11 In. 110.00
LANTERN, Buggy, Simmon's, Bull's-Eye Inside Globe, Clamp 45.00
Canal, N.Y.State, Onion Glass Globe, 12 X 18 In. 220.00
Candle, Givens, Corpus Christi, Texas, Marked 1894 .... 35.00 To 65.00
Candle, Pierced, Conical Top, Hinged Door, Tin, 14 In. 195.00
Dietz, No.40, Traffic Guard, Red Globe 26.00
Dietz, Tubular, Brass, 11 In. 68.00
Farm, Dietz, Amber Globe 60.00
Fire Department, Dietz King 125.00
Free-Blown Glass Globe, Circular Brass Handle, 13 1/2 In. 140.00
Frosted Cylindrical Shade, Battery Operated, Brass 28.00
Inspector's, Dietz Acme, Hooded 75.00
Inspector's, Dietz Acme, Mercury Glass Reflector, Tin, 13 1/2 In. 50.00
Punchwork, Cone Shape, Hinged Opening, Tin, Pair 40.00
    LANTERN, RAILROAD, see Railroad, Lantern
Ship, Port & Starboard, Handmade, Brass, 9 In., Pair 185.00
Signal, Candle, Tin, Small 22.00
Skater's, Brass, 7 In. 79.00
Skater's, Green Globe, Brass 65.00
Skater's, Tin .... 25.00 To 45.00
Skating, Wick, Brass 40.00
Wrist Ring, Blown-In Glass Globe, Oil Burner, 19th Century, 13 In. 185.00

Le Verre Francais

    Le Verre Francais cameo glass was made in France between 1920 and 1933
    by the C. Schneider factory. It is mottled and usually
    decorated with floral designs, and bears the incised signature
    Le Verre Francais.

LE VERRE FRANCAIS, Pitcher, Signed, 12 1/2 In. 850.00
    Vase, Mottled Design, Orange Ground, Signed, 5 1/2 In. 650.00

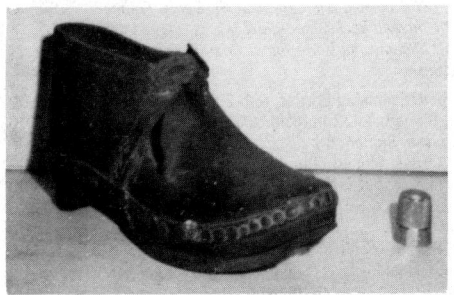

Leather, Shoe, Buckle Top, Wooden Plank Bottom,
Iron Heel & Toe

Leather, Shoe, High-Top, Salesman's Sample

LEATHER, Belt, Cartridge, Brass Buckle	22.50
Billy Club, Police	22.50
Box, Collar, 12 Dollars	20.00
Case, Calling Card, Mother & Child Embossed On Front	12.50
Flask, Powder, Pair	60.00
Helmet, Police, Mettendorf	200.00
Leggins	6.50
Net, Fly, Horses	7.50
Robe, Buggy, Cowhide	27.50
Saddle, American Western, Hand-Tooled, With Bridle	50.00
Saddle, Side	225.00
Shoe, Buckle Top, Wooden Plank Bottom, Iron Heel & Toe .... *Illus*	60.00
Shoe, High-Top, Salesman's Sample .... *Illus*	50.00

LEEDS POTTERY,

*Leeds pottery was made at Leeds, Yorkshire, England, from 1774 to 1878.
Most Leeds ware was not marked. Early Leeds pieces had distinctive
twisted handles with a greenish glaze on part of the creamy ware. Later ware
often had blue borders on the creamy pottery.*

LEEDS, Bowl, Floral, Pink, 10 3/4 In.Diam.	28.00
Cup Plate, Blue Feather Edge, 4 1/2 In.Diam.	58.00
Mug, Milk, Kakiemon-Style Branches, C.1775, Iron Red, 4 3/4 In.	385.00
Plate, Strawberry Center, Orange, Green, Brown, Blue Border, 5 In.	60.00
Teapot, Rose, Floral Sprays, Floral Knop, 4 3/4 In.	375.00
Teapot, Spray	35.00
Teapot, Yellow, Brown & Orange Design, 8 In.	210.00

*Geo. Zoltan Lefton Company has imported porcelains to be sold in
America since 1940. The pieces are often marked with the Lefton name.*

LEFTON, Creamer, Pink Roses, No.C-6198	7.00
Figurine, Pixie, Lying Down & Seated, No.305, Pair	20.00
Figurine, Pixie, Seated On Brown Squirrel, No.H-758	5.00
Figurine, Pixie, Seated, Yellow & Brown Dog, No.Es-8526	5.00
Pitcher, Cream, Figural, Lincoln Bust	25.00
Salt & Pepper, Cooking Pot Shape, Red	5.00

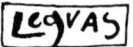

Legras was founded in 1864 by Auguste Legras at St. Denis, France.
It is best known for Art Nouveau and cameo glass wares. Legras merged
with Pantin in 1920 and became the Verreries et Cristalleries de St.
Denis et de Pantin Reunies.

LEGRAS, Bowl, Amber Acid Etched, Scalloped, Enameled Berries, 4 1/2 In.Diam. 85.00
Bowl, Basket-Shaped, Cherries, Leaf Rim, Signed, 8 1/2 In.Diam. 415.00
Bowl, Enamel, Basket Shape, Cherries, Leaves, Signed, 8 In. 335.00
Bowl, Scalloped Rim, Multicolor Leaves, Berries, Signed, 3 In. 85.00
Bowl, Scalloped, Enameled Leaves & Berries, Amber Etched, 4 1/2 In. 85.00
Cookie Jar, Leaves & Single Red Flower, Brass Lid & Handle, 7 In. 600.00
Cracker Jar, Cameo, Brass Fittings, Burgundy 895.00
Decanter, Frosted Body, Yellow Trim, Signed, 7 1/2 In. 395.00
Lamp, Birds In Flight, White & Pink Ground, Signed, 12 1/2 In. 995.00
Rose Bowl, French Cameo, Winter Scene, Orange Ground, Snow, Signed 175.00
Vase, Acid Cut Back, Geometric, 5 1/2 In. 350.00
Vase, Birds Cut Out In Flight, Red Ground 625.00
Vase, Cameo, Enameled Red Poppy On Orange-Yellow, Signed, 12 1/2 In. 650.00
Vase, Cameo, Lavender To Green, Lake, Trees, Acid Cut, Signed, 14 In. 895.00
Vase, Deco Floral, Acid Cut Back, 10 1/2 In. 400.00
Vase, Enameled Multicolored Flowers, Signed, 9 1/2 In. 250.00
Vase, Morning Glories, Enameled, 7 In. 120.00
Vase, Overlaid Lake Scene, Mottled Ground, 13 3/4 In. 350.00
Vase, Pink & White Apple Blossoms, Green Ground, 19 1/2 In. 1250.00
Vase, Quatrefoil, Leaves, Fruit, Signed, 5 In. 350.00
Vase, Scenic, Enameled, Trees & Mountains, 6 In. 345.00
Vase, Seaweed Design, Cream, Tan, & Brown, 14 In. 1375.00
Vase, Winter Scene, Signed, 5 In. 195.00
Vase, Winter Scene, Signed, 9 1/2 In. .... 350.00 To 355.00
Vase, Winter Scene, Woman Walking In Snow, Signed, 14 1/4 In. 320.00

Lenox china was made in Trenton, New Jersey, after 1906. The firm also
makes a porcelain similar to Belleek.

    LENOX, see also Ceramic Art Co.
LENOX, Ashtray, Gold Mark, 8 In. 25.00
Bonbon, Handled, Green Wreath Mark 35.00
Bottle, Hattie Carnegie, White Figural Stopper .... 100.00 To 125.00
Bottle, Perfume, Figural, Fish, Signed De Vilbiss 125.00
Bowl, Ming, Handled 60.00
Bowl, Pinehurst, 5 1/2 In. 15.00
Bowl, Raised Peacocks, Leaf & Scroll Trim, Gadrooned Top, 8 1/2 In. 85.00
Bowl, Yale, 3-Dimensional, 7 X 5 1/2 In. 195.00
Box, Cigarette, World's Fair, Coral 65.00
Box, Powder, Art Deco Head Finial, Hattie Carnegie, 3 3/4 In. 75.00
Cake Stand, Ming, Low Footed, Black Mark 50.00
Candleholder, Abstract Shape, Green Mark, 8 In. 45.00
Candleholder, Lyre Shape, Abstract Design, Green Mark, 8 In. 40.00
Candleholder, Stylized Horn Shape, White, Green Mark, 8 In. 45.00
Coffee Service, Gold Greek Key Band, Green Mark, 3 Piece 75.00
Coffeepot, Sterling Silver Ship Design, Marked, 6 1/2 In. 100.00
Compote, Boat Shape, Gold Handles, Grape Design, Palette Mark 120.00
Creamer, Chocolate Brown, Silver Overlay 55.00
Creamer, Hand-Painted Pink Roses, Marked 100.00
Creamer, Washington Wakefield, Covered, Marked 195.00
Cup & Saucer, Coral, Demitasse 22.00
Cup & Saucer, Fawn, Demitasse 40.00
Cup & Saucer, Green, Demitasse .... 25.00 To 40.00
Cup & Saucer, Historical China, 1933, Green Wreath Mark 25.00
Cup & Saucer, Ivory, Flying Geese, Green Palette, Demitasse 50.00
Cup & Saucer, Lowell 25.00
Cup & Saucer, Ming .... 22.00 To 37.50

Cup & Saucer, Tiffany Silver Holder, 6	175.00
Cup & Saucer, Yellow, Demitasse	30.00 To 40.00
Cup, Bouillon, Sterling Silver Holder, 12	400.00
Cup, Chocolate, Ivory, Gold Trim, Blue Trim, Marked	50.00
Cup, Gold Paste Stars & Floral, Gold Dragon Handle, Demitasse	25.00
Cup, Tea, Autumn, Black Mark	50.00
Dish, Candy, Blue Mark, 6 In.	27.00
Dish, Candy, Shell Shaped, Gold Trimmed, 6 In.	50.00
Dish, Imperial Council Session, Atlantic City, 1927, Green Wreath	95.00
Dish, Leaf Shape, White Scroll Handle, Green Wreath, 6 X 3 In.	30.00
Dish, Leaf, Exterior Design, Brushed Gold Rim, Palette Mark, 6 In.	265.00
Dish, Sage Green, 4 1/2 In.	20.00
Dish, Shell, Green Wreath, 9 1/2 In.	45.00
Dish, Shell, Pink, 6 In.	30.00
Dish, Sterling Silver Overlay, White, Green Mark, Oval, 5 1/2 In.	125.00
Ewer, Rose Decor, Green Wreath Mark, 6 1/4 In.	95.00
Figurine, Bird, White, Green, Marked, 6 1/4 In.	30.00
Figurine, Leda & Swan, White, Dated 1929, 11 In.	260.00 To 275.00
Figurine, Mistress Mary	315.00
Figurine, Penguin Atomizer	90.00
Figurine, Robin, Green Back, 5 1/2 In.	30.00 To 45.00
Figurine, Swan, Ivory, Green Wreath Mark, 4 1/2 In.	35.00
Figurine, Swan, Pink, 4 1/2 In.	25.00 To 30.00
Figurine, Swan, 5 1/4 In.	35.00
Honey Pot, Gold Gilt Trim, White, Green Wreath Mark	55.00
Jar, Jam, Grapes, Palette Mark	55.00
Jar, Jam, Green & Gold Band Of Bees, Covered	65.00
Jug, Cider, Silver Overlay Fruit & Leaves, Marked	325.00
Loving Cup, Russet & Lavender Grapes, Artist Signed, 12 In.	575.00
Mask, Art Nouveau Lady's Face, 9 In.	355.00
Mug, Deer Portrait, Dragon Handle, 6 In.	125.00
Mug, Dragon Handle, Portrait Of Dog, 6 In.	125.00
Mug, Elk's Head, Gold Dragon Handle, Fruit Design, 6 In.	95.00
Mug, Gooseberries, Signed	95.00
Mug, Jovial Monk, Sterling Silver Rim, Base, & Handle, Marked	165.00
Pitcher, Cider, Blackberries, 8 X 6 1/2 In.	125.00
Pitcher, Indian In Full Headdress, Palette Mark, 14 In.	495.00
Pitcher, Lemonade, Hand-Painted, Signed, Green Mark, 6 In. *Illus*	90.00
Plate, Bread & Butter, Autumn, Black Mark	12.00
Plate, Chop, Wheat Pattern	35.00
Plate, Dinner, Autumn, Black Mark	30.00
Plate, Fish, Acid Etched Gold Border, Green Wreath Mark, 6	480.00
Plate, Fish, Brook Trout, Signed Morley, 9 In.	85.00

Lenox, Pitcher, Lemonade, Hand-Painted, Signed, Green Mark, 6 In.

Plate, Fish, Weak Fish, Signed Morley, 9 In. 85.00
Plate, Grenable Ivory Pattern, Black Mark, 10 1/2 In. ....
Plate, Hot, Ming 35.00
Plate, Orleans Pattern, 8 In. 10.00
Plate, Pheasants, Signed W.Morley, 9 In. 85.00
Plate, Rhodora, 10 1/2 In. 15.00
Plate, Service, Gold Border, Black & Gold Leaves, Green Mark, Set Of 12 .... 275.00
Salt & Pepper, Gold, Metal Holder, Tray, Green Mark 30.00
Salt & Pepper, His Master's Voice .... 18.50 To 35.00
Salt & Pepper, Pheasants Flying, 6 In. 22.00
Salt & Pepper, Swan, Gold Trim, Spoon, 3 Pieces 30.00
Salt & Pepper, 1939 World's Fair Emblem, Yellow & White 65.00
Salt, Hand-Painted Rose Design, 1 1/2 In. 7.50
Salt, Shell & Coral Pattern, Green Mark, 3 X 2 In., 4 .... 35.00
Salt, Swan, Green Wreath Mark, 2 1/2 In. 27.00
Salt, Swan, Ivory, Green Wreath Mark, 5 In. 35.00
Shade, Lamp, Torch, Ivory, Fluted, Green Wreath Mark, 8 X 10 In. 45.00
Soup, Cream, Imperial, Underliner, Green Mark, 7 In. 16.00
Stein, Monk Drinking Wine, Copper Lid, Dated 1902 .... 210.00
Stein, Monk, Monochromatic Brown, Sterling Silver Lid, Wreath Mark 325.00
Sugar & Creamer, Brown Betty Ware, Silver Overlay 195.00
Sugar, Hawthorne, Covered 95.00
Sugar, Sweets To The Sweet, Gold Lettering, Brown Glaze, Wreath Mark 58.00
Tea Set, Medallion Of Pink Roses, Green Palette Mark, 3 Piece 195.00
Tea Set, Piano Key Design, Black & White, Green Wreath, 3 Piece 225.00
Tea Set, Pink Handle, Pink Knobs, Green Mark, 3 Piece 145.00
Tea Set, Royal Blue, Sterling Overlay, 3 Piece 425.00
Toby Jug, George Washington, Dated 1896, Signed 575.00
Toby Jug, William Penn, Indian Handle, Green Wreath Mark .... 120.00 To 185.00
Tray, Plume Shape, Embossed Center, Green Wreath Mark, 7 1/4 In. 40.00
Urn, Green, Swan Handles, White, Green Wreath Mark, 10 In., Pair 135.00
Urn, Presentation, Silver Medallion, Wreath, 5 1/4 In. .... 110.00 To 135.00
Vase, Art Deco Floral Design, Raised Enamel, Palette Mark, 6 In. 65.00
Vase, Beaker Shaped, Gold Trim, Blue, Palette Mark, 8 1/4 In. 78.00
Vase, Blue Top, White Bulbous Bottom, Green Mark 26.00
Vase, Blue, White Flowers, 9 In. 125.00
Vase, Bud, Brown Pheasants, 10 3/4 In. 20.00
Vase, Bud, Gold Mark, 10 3/4 In. 20.00
Vase, Coral, Floral, Ribbed, Green Mark, 6 In. 45.00
Vase, Embossed Flowers, Pink, Ribbed, Green Wreath 65.00
Vase, Figural, Colonial Lady 155.00
Vase, Gold Center Handle, Green Mark 35.00
Vase, Hand-Painted Squirrel, Grays & Black, Palette Mark, 10 In. 225.00
Vase, Shades Of Pink, 13 In. 225.00
Vase, Silver Overlay, 10 In. 90.00

LETTER OPENER, Advertising, Welsback Mantel Lamp, San Jose, California 35.00
Alligator, Celluloid .... 6.00 To 7.50
Art Deco, Rooster End, Sterling Silver 23.00
Bone, Figural Indian, Souvenir Montiou Springs, Colorado 15.00
Century Of Progress, Brass, 1934 .... 12.00
Chip-Carved Handle, Whalebone, 9 1/2 In. 100.00
Dog Bringing Duck To Master, English, Brass, 10 1/4 In. 75.00
Egyptian, Sheath, Brass 18.00
Geisha Girl Holding Fan On Top, Celluloid, 7 1/2 In. 10.00
Hand-Carved Ivory, Victorian 75.00
International Motors Trucks & Tractors 20.00
Ivory, Rabbit Top 17.00
Mr.Peanut, Enamel, Printed Planters, Metal 200.00
Scrimshaw Ship & Lighthouse, Ivory Handle, 8 1/2 In. 50.00
Spear Shape, Hole For Hanging, Jones & McDuffie, Celluloid 8.00
Texas Centennial, Brass 12.00
Uneeda Biscuit Slicker Boy, Box, 8 1/2 In. .... 50.00 To 75.00

Walrus Ivory, Reindeer On Back, Signed	30.00
Washington, D.C., Shield, 7 In.	25.00
Weber Implement & Auto Co., St.Louis, Brass	7.50
Whalebone, Sterling Silver Handle, Beaded Trim, 1820, 9 In.	45.00

The Libbey Glass Company has made glass of many types from 1892 to the present.

LIBBEY, Banana Bowl, Kimberly Pattern, 13 X 9 1/4 In.	695.00
Basket, Engraved Floral, C.1911, Signed, 9 3/4 X 12 In.	600.00
Bowl, Brilliant Cut, Old Sword Mark, 7 1/2 In.	175.00
Bowl, Fruit, Gloria, 9 In.Diam.	295.00
Bowl, Rajah Pattern, 8 In.Diam.	395.00
Bowl, Regis Pattern, Signed, 8 In.	145.00
Bowl, Wedgemere Pattern, 1891, W.Anderson Design, 3 1/2 X 8 In.Diam.	795.00
Bread Tray, Hobstar, Fan & Strawberry, Signed, 12 X 6 In.	285.00
Bucket, Champagne, Hobstars, 32 Point Star Base, 6 1/2 X 6 In.	480.00
Candlestick, Teardrop Stem, Hobstars, Diamonds, & Cane, 9 In.	295.00
Celery, Colonna, Signed	245.00
Claret, Beer, Menagerie, Opalescent	75.00
Claret, Royal Fern Pattern, High Stem, C.1920, Set Of 8	395.00
Cologne, No.42, Signed	98.00
Compote, Hobstar & Cane, Knobbed Base, Signed, 5 X 7 In.Diam., Pair	795.00
Compote, Turquoise Dots, Ribbed, Twisted Stem, Signed, 6 3/4 In.	350.00
Decanter, Harvard Pattern, Matching Stopper, 13 In., Pair	1095.00
Dish, Candy, Amberina & Amber To Ruby, Signed, 7 In.	325.00
Dish, Cheese, Harvard Pattern, Covered	550.00
Dish, Relish, Sultana Pattern, 1906 Signature, 3 1/2 X 7 1/2 In.	95.00
Flower Center, Empress, Signed, 10 In.Diam.	575.00
Glass, Juice, Footed, Engraved Band, Signed, Amber, Set Of 4	65.00
Goblet, Silhouette, Black Cat Stem, Signed, 7 In.	195.00
Ice Tub, Harvard Pattern, Tab Handles, 5 X 7 In.Diam.	295.00
Pitcher, Middlesex Pattern	695.00
Plate, Ellsmere Pattern, Saber Mark, Signed, 6 3/4 In.	95.00
Relish, Hobstars, Hobnail, & Split Vesicas, 8 3/4 X 5 In.	125.00
Rose Bowl, Corinthian, Signed, 5 In.	325.00
Saltshaker, Dice Pattern, Original Top	100.00
Sherries, Moonbeam Cut, Set Of 6, Signed	125.00
Syrup, Hinged Lid & Handle In Silver Plate On Copper, C.1901	175.00
Tray, Bread, Hobstar, Fan, & Strawberry, Signed, 12 X 6 In.	285.00
Tray, Colonna, Signed, 8 In.	175.00
Tray, Colonna, Signed, 12 In.	650.00
Tumbler, Intaglio Cut, Signed	35.00
Vase, Allover Flowers, Fishscale Design, 5 3/4 X 8 1/2 In.	65.00
Vase, Colonna Pattern, Saber Mark, 7 1/2 In.	135.00
Vase, Corinthian, 1869-1906, 18 Pointed Star Base, Signed, 12 In.	250.00
Vase, Corset Shape, Brilliant Cut, Signed, 12 In.	375.00
Vase, Flat Knop, Amberina, Signed, 8 1/2 In.	395.00
Vase, Leaves & Flowers, Swirls, Signed, 14 In.	350.00
Vase, Trumpet, Allover Cut, Signed, 10 In.	150.00
Vase, Trumpet, Hobstar, Fan, & Crosshatching, 10 In.	150.00
Wine, Opalescent Polar Bear Stem, Signed	155.00

LIGHTING DEVICES, see Candleholder; Candlestick; Lamp; etc.

Lightning rod balls are collected for their variety of shape and color. These glass balls were at the center of the rod that was attached to the roof of a house or barn to avoid lightning damage.

LIGHTNING ROD & BALL, Full-Bodied Cow, 9 1/4 X 6 3/4 In.	150.00
Full-Bodied Horse, 9 X 8 In.	150.00
LIGHTNING ROD, Animal, Circus Horse	70.00
Animal, Cow	75.00
Ball, Milk Glass, Blue	18.00
Ornament, Snowflake Pattern Cut In Ruby Glass, 18 X 5 In.	55.00

Limoges porcelain has been made in Limoges, France, since the mid-nineteenth century. Fine porcelains were made by many factories, including Haviland, Ahrenfeldt, Guerin, Pouyat, Elite, and others.

LIMOGES, see also Haviland

LIMOGES, Ashtray & Match Holder, Pall Mall Cigarettes	25.00
Atomizer, Reclining Nude, Blue Ground, 2 3/4 X 2 3/4 In.	110.00
Base, Bluebird, White, Blue & Gold, Satin Finish, 2 Handles, 7 In.	80.00
Basket, Purple Flowers, Gold Handles, Artist Signed, 9 X 5 In.	60.00
Biscuit Jar, Underplate	125.00
Bone Dish, J.Pouyat, Green, White, & Gold, Set Of 5	35.00
Bottle, Cologne, Flower, Gold Design, Pair	45.00
Bowl, Hand-Painted Shells, 6 In.Diam.	17.50
Bowl, Ice Cream, Hand-Painted, C.1854	75.00
Bowl, Vegetable, Pouyat, Covered, Green & Rust Design	20.00
Box, Handkerchief, Purple Violets, Square	85.00
Box, Pill, Blue, Forget-Me-Nots, Signed, Covered	26.00
Box, Pink Ground, Artist Signed, Covered, 6 In.	159.00
Box, Powder, Forget-Me-Nots, Blue	35.00
Box, Sardine, Fish On Cover, Gold Finial, Marked, 4 3/8 X 2 3/4 In.	32.00
Box, Scenic, Covered, Pink Ground, Artist Signed, 6 In.	159.00
Box, Stamp, Red Roses, Blue Ground, Gold Trim, 3 1/2 In.	15.50
Bread Tray, Blue, Green, & Gold, 9 X 9 In.	30.00
Bust, Maria De Medici, Puffed Sleeves, Lace Collar, Signed, 22 In.	440.00
Butter Dish, Gold Encrusted	65.00
Button, Portrait, Signed	20.00
Charger, Fish, Victorian With Gold Border, Signed, 13 In.	250.00
Charger, Gold Flowered Handles, Signed, 1o 1/2 X 12 In.	155.00
Charger, Hand-Painted, Negro Fortune-Teller, Signed, 13 In.	16.00 To 160.00
Charger, Red & Pink Roses, Scalloped Edge, Artist Signed	350.00
Charger, 3 Kittens Watching Goldfish Bowl, Gold Trim	135.00
Chocolate Pot, Florals, Gold Outlining	215.00
Chocolate Pot, Gold Rim & Handle	45.00
Chocolate Pot, Roses, Gold Trim	64.00
Chocolate Pot, Yellow Roses & Ground, Gold Trim, Square	95.00
Chocolate Set, Art Deco, Geometric Design, Marked, 6 Piece	155.00
Chocolate Set, Dogwood Flowers, Gold Bands, 5 Cup & Saucers	229.00
Chocolate Set, Floral Design, Gold Bands, 9 Piece	230.00
Chocolate Set, Water Lily Design, Signed, 8 Cups & Saucers	250.00
Cider Set, Blackberry Design, 3 Glasses	165.00
Cider Set, Cluster Purple Grapes & Green Leaves, Signed	249.00
Cider Set, Crab Apples, Foliage, Rust To Green, Marked, 5 Piece	285.00
Cider Set, Purple Grapes, Green Leaves, Signed, 16 In. Tray	249.00
Cider Set, Soft Yellow Roses, Gold Trim, Set Of 5 Mugs	225.00
Compote, Courting Couple, Garland, Signed, 9 In.	79.00
Cracker Jar, Russet Poppies, Barrel Shape, Gold Sunburst	75.00
Creamer, Butterfly With Basket Weave Design, 4 1/2 In.	48.00
Creamer, Red Block	100.00
Cruet, Hand-Painted Blue & White Flowers	48.00
Demitasse Set, Gingko Leaf Design, 12 Cups & Saucers, Case, C.1880	110.00
Dish, Cheese, Mice On Rope Design, Platinum Trim	75.00
Dish, Enameled Copper, Lovers Kissing, Red & Gold Accents, 6 In.	300.00
Dish, Nappy, Roses, Pink & Red, Green Leafing, Artist Signed	25.00
Dish, Vegetable, Gold Handles, Covered	45.00
Dish, Young Girl Chasing Butterflies, 11 1/4 In.	80.00

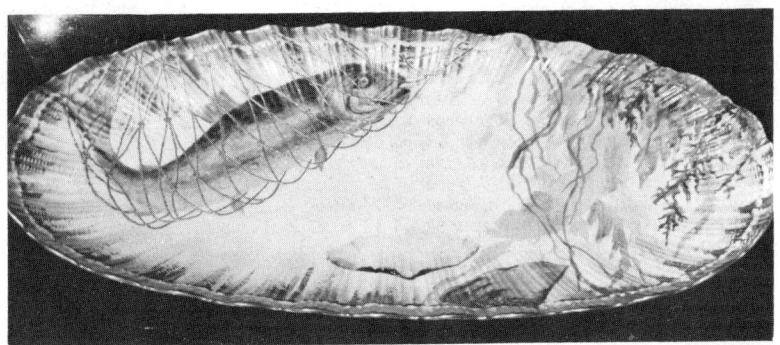

Limoges, Fish Set, Carrie Draper, Artist, 16 Piece

Ewer, Cherries & Foliage, 12 In.	115.00
Ewer, Clover Blossoms, Dated 1903, Initialed, Marked, 12 3/4 In.	140.00
Ewer, Embossed Design, Sponged Gold Interior, Signed, 12 3/4 In.	75.00
Ewer, Wine, Grape Design, Dated 1901, Cover	145.00
Ewer, Wine, Grapes, Gold Trim & Finial, Marked, Covered, 11 3/4 In.	175.00
Fish Set, Carrie Draper, Artist, 16 Piece ....*Illus*	400.00
Fish Set, Gold Overlay, Dated 1896, 15 Piece	700.00
Fish Set, Pastel Colors, C.1900, Set Of 12 Plates	450.00
Fish Set, Signed Purvis, 13 Piece	250.00
Fish Set, Signed Roche, Set Of 12	190.00
Fish Set, Various Shells, Hand-Painted, Pink, Purple, Brown, 7 Piece	185.00
Game Plate, Gold Border, Artist Signed, 9 1/4 In.Diam., Set Of 7	875.00
Game Plate, Gold Border, 9 In.	45.00
Game Plate, Guinea Fowl, Artist Signed, 10 In.	68.00
Game Plate, Quail, Gold Rococo Border, Signed, 9 1/4 In.	85.00
Game Set, Forest Scene Platter, 11 Plates, Gold Rims, Platter 19 In.	750.00
Game Set, Game Birds, Floral Border, Pink & Brown, Signed, 6 Plates	700.00
Game Set, Yellow Border With Gold, Artist Signed, 5 Piece	350.00
Game Set, 6 Plates, Platter, Artist Signed	265.00
Goblet, Portrait Of Man, Pedestal, Signed, 10 In.	225.00
Hair Receiver, Allover Roses	60.00
Hair Receiver, Yellow Pansies, Green-Blue Ground	38.00
Hatpin Holder, Pink & Blue Flowers, Gold Leaves & Trim, 5 In.	65.00
Hatpin Holder, Portrait, Girl & Peacock, Marked, 3 5/8 In.	135.00
Honey Pot, Pink Roses, Green Ground, 2-Handled, Lidded, Underplate	70.00
Honey Pot, Underplate, Pink Roses, Green Ground, Gilded, 6 In.	70.00
Jar, Powder, Cream, Gold Design, Angels At Play, 5 In.	175.00
Jar, Powder, Pink Roses, Gold Trim, Green Ground, 4 1/2 In.Diam.	95.00
Jar, Rose, Red & Gold, Flowers, 4 1/4 In.	50.00
Lemonade Set, Pearlized Luster, Gold Handle, Marked, 7 Piece	200.00
Mug, Dated 1911, Artist Signed	35.00
Mug, Friendship, Auld Lang Syne, Grapes, Leaves, Signed	35.00
Mug, Indian Girl, Brown Ground, Hand-Painted, Marked, 5 1/4 In.	150.00
Oyster Plate, Elite, Gold Trim, Scalloped, 5 Sections, 8 3/4 In.	30.00
Oyster Plate, Gold & White, Set Of 8	150.00
Pin Tray & Candleholders, Birds & Flowers, 11 X 5 3/4 In., 1 Piece	140.00
Pitcher, Allover Floral, Gold Handle & Rim, Signed, 13 In.	90.00
Pitcher, Allover Roses, Artist Signed, Small	162.00
Pitcher, Cider, Clover, Pink & Green	200.00
Pitcher, Cider, Cream Ground, Fruit & Floral, Blossoms, Signed	165.00
Pitcher, Cider, Grape Design, Luster Trim, Set Of Cups	175.00
Pitcher, Cider, Hand-Painted Water Lilies, Coin Gold Trim, 1908 Mark	95.00
Pitcher, Cider, Painted Grapes, Leaves, Green Ground	65.00

Pitcher, Cider, Portrait, Signed	90.00
Pitcher, Cream, Flowers, Gold Trim, Impressed	50.00
Pitcher, Hand-Painted Windmills, Blue Base & Crown, 7 In.	35.00
Pitcher, Helmet Thistle, 7 In.	65.00
Pitcher, Lemonade, Lemons & Leaves, Artist Signed, 6 1/2 In.	160.00
Pitcher, Purple Plum & Leaves, Gold Handle, 8 In.	65.00
Pitcher, Purple Plums, Green Ivy, Green Ground, Gold Trim, 5 In.	75.00
Pitcher, Rope Handle, 1880 Mark, 5 1/2 In.	30.00
Pitcher, Roses, Gold Trim, Signed, 7 1/4 In.	145.00
Pitcher, Tankard, Green, Purple Iris, Signed, 14 1/2 X 6 In.	175.00
Pitcher, Tankard, Lilac & Purple Grapes, Signed, 13 In.	139.00
Pitcher, Thistle, Helmet	65.00
Planter, Footed, Purple Irises, Elephant Handles, 8 1/2 X 8 In.Diam.	275.00
Planter, Yellow Body, Purple Floral, Gold Trim, 7 In.	75.00
Plaque, Cavalier Leaning On Chair, 5 X 4 In.	500.00
Plaque, Cavalier Serenading Woman, Brass Frame, 2 1/2 X 4 In.	250.00
Plaque, Cavaliers Seizing A Maiden, 5 3/4 X 4 1/4 In.	575.00
Plaque, Mallard In Flight, Scalloped, Hand-Painted, 16 In.Diam.	235.00
Plaque, Snipes, Rococo Gold Border, Signed, 13 1/2 In.	250.00
Plaque, Thistle, Purple, White, & Pink, 13 In.	95.00
Plaque, Venus Standing By Cupid, Basket, Grapes, 8 X 5 In.	750.00
Plaque, Wall, Roses, Medallion Center, Gold Trim, 14 X 10 In.	125.00
Plaque, 2 Maidens In Garden, 13 1/2 In.	250.00
Plate, Cake, Lilacs & Roses, Gold Trim, Open Handles, 11 3/4 In.	35.00
Plate, Cake, Roses, Artist Signed	65.00
Plate, Chop, Enameled Corn, Artist Signed	70.00
Plate, Chop, Game Birds, Gold Rococo Edge, Signed, 13 In.	215.00
Plate, Chop, Hand-Painted Grape Design, Signed, 1i 1/2 In.	125.00
Plate, Crossed Tennis Racquets & Balls, Gold Edge, 8 3/8 In.	35.00
Plate, Fish, Artist Signed	60.00
Plate, Fish, Dated 1882, Oblong	35.00
Plate, Fish, Lake Scene, 7 In.Diam.	37.00
Plate, Game, Bird Design, Rococo Border, Signed, 12 1/2 In.	250.00
Plate, Game, Ducks, Scalloped Gold Rim, Signed, 11 In.	46.00
Plate, Game, Robust Bird, Gold Edge, Marked, 10 1/2 In.	85.00
Plate, Game, 3 Rabbits In Woodland, Gold Border, 12 In.	135.00
Plate, Hand-Painted, Woman On Tree Limb, Gold Trim, Signed, 11 In.	125.00
Plate, Hanging, Fruit, Gold Border, 11 3/7 In., Pair	295.00
Plate, Hanging, Game, Birds, Natural Colors, 11 In.	185.00
Plate, Hanging, Lady On Bench, Basket, Signed, 10 In.	75.00
Plate, Hanging, Spanish Cavalier, Guitar, 10 In.	75.00
Plate, Lady On Bench, Coronet, Signed Luc, 10 In.	75.00
Plate, Mallard Duck, Signed, 10 In.	250.00
Plate, Oyster, Forget-Me-Not Design	30.00
Plate, Pale Blue Ground, Roses, Signed	45.00
Plate, Pink & Deep Red Carnations, 9 In.	40.00
Plate, Poppies & Buds, Scalloped, Pink & Green, 14 In.Diam.	85.00
Plate, Portrait Of Lady Of The Night, Signed, 7 1/2 In.	40.00
Plate, Portrait, 3 Cherubs Drink Wine, 8 3/4 In.	85.00
Plate, Purple & Blue, Gold Scalloped Border, 8 1/2 In.	35.00
Plate, Spider Web, Ivy, Scalloped Gold Border, 9 In.	38.00
Plate, Sweet Pea Bouquet, Open Handled, Signed	47.50
Plate, Wild Boars In Snow, Rococo Gold Edge, Signed, 9 7/8 In.	107.00
Platter, Blue Flowers, Roses, Scroll Rim, Gold Bamboo Handles	32.00
Platter, Turkey, Roses, Gold Trim, 19 In.	95.00
Punch Bowl, Blackberry Leaves & Blossoms Inside, Footed, Marked	450.00
Ramekin & Liner, Pink Roses, Blue Medallions	65.00
Ramekin, Roses, Gold Border, 2 Piece	14.00
Ring Tree, Gold & Violets Design	30.00
Ring Tree, Hand, Pansies	50.00
Salad Set, Leaf-Shaped, Rose Design, 9 Piece ....*Illus*	340.00
Salad Set, Roses, Leaf Shape, 9 Piece	340.00
Sugar & Creamer, Floral, Garden Scene, Man, Woman, Lots Of Gold	135.00

Limoges, Salad Set, Leaf-Shaped, Rose Design, 9 Piece

Sugar & Creamer, Roses, Artist Signed, Gold & Green	40.00
Sugar & Creamer, Violets, Gold Trim	45.00
Sugar, Covered, Red Block	125.00
Tankard, Grapes In Green, Purple, Brown, Blue, Fuchsia, Signed, 11 In.	185.00
Tankard, Multicolored Grapes, 11 In.	189.00
Tankard, Purple Berries, Flowers, 11 In.	190.00
Tankard, Sgraffito Work Of Monk Pouring Wine Into Mug, 13 1/2 In.	125.00
Tea Set, Green Ground, Gold Handled, Rose Bouquets, 4 Cups	245.00
Teapot, Floral Trim, White With Gold Spout & Handle	30.00
Tray, Bread, Floral, Gold Trim, Tree Form	20.00
Tray, Cake, White Ground, Flowers, Gold Edge, Marked, 9 1/2 In.	35.00
Tray, Celery, Branches, Berries, Scalloped Edge, 12 1/2 In.	45.00
Tray, Dresser, Black-Eyed Susan Design, 11 1/2 X 4 1/4 In.	45.00
Tray, Dresser, Castle Scene, Fluted, 12 In.	35.00
Tray, Dresser, Diamond Shape, Violets, Gold, Signed, 8 X 10 In.	75.00
Tray, Dresser, Hand-Painted Yellow Roses, 9 X 12 In.	42.00
Tray, Dresser, Irregular Rim, Garlands, Gold Trim, 11 1/2 X 7 3/4 In.	18.00
Tray, Dresser, Kidney Shaped, Pink Flowers, 13 X 9 In.	45.00
Tray, Ice Cream, Pink Asters, Gold Trim, 12 3/4 In.	125.00
Tray, Tea, White, Floral Design, Open Handles, 15 X 23 In.	55.00
Vase, Arabian Scene, 11 1/2 In.	50.00
Vase, Asters, Artist Signed, 10 In.	145.00
Vase, Cottage Scene, Signed, 8 3/4 In.	175.00
Vase, Double Gourd Form, Blue, Gold, White, Signed, 6 1/2 In.	660.00
Vase, Enamel On Copper, Flowerheads, Leaves, Signed, 8 In.	2200.00
Vase, Orchids, Green Leaves, Gold Head Handles, 9 In.	95.00
Vase, Pastel Enamel, Random Dribble, Signed, 4 1/2 In.	445.00
Vase, Red-Purple Roses, Green Leaves, Bulbous, 12 In.	165.00
Vase, Reticulated Collar, Hand-Painted Roses & Vines, 7 In.	150.00
Vase, Stylized Iris, Flowers, Green & Black Stems, Marked, 16 In.	165.00
Vase, White, Violet, Sky Blue, Black Geometric Design, Marked, 13 In.	3200.00
LINDBERGH, Bookends, Bronze	65.00
Box, Pencil, Spirit Of St.Louis, Ruler, Tin	25.00
Box, Photograph Of Lindbergh & Plane, Tin, Covered	45.00
Card, Perfume Display, Lucky Lindy, 1927, 15 X 10 In.	20.00
Figurine, 1820s, Celluloid, 6 In.	32.00
Watch Fob, With Compass	35.00
Watch, Pocket, New York To Paris, Fob	600.00

Lithophanes are porcelain pictures made by casting clay in layers of various thicknesses. When a piece is held to the light, a picture of light and shadow is seen through it. Most lithophanes date from the 1825 to 1875 period. A few are still being made.

LITHOPHANE, Candle Shield, Daniel In The Lion's Den, Iron Holder 300.00
Dish, Scallop Shell Shape, Cathedral Scene Center, 7 In.Diam. 55.00
Lampshade, 5-Panel, All Signed 700.00
Mug, Butterfly & Floral, Family Scene, 4 1/2 In. 45.00
Panel, Cupid String Trap For Young Ladies, 4 1/4 X 5 1/4 In. 225.00
Panel, Lady & Gentleman, Crossing Stream, 2 1/2 X 3 3/4 In. 65.00
Panel, Pair Of Lovers On Swing In Woods, 4 1/4 X 5 1/4 In. 225.00
Panel, Scheherazade, Framed, 6 X 6 3/4 In. 375.00
Plaque, The Storm, Running Boy & Girl, 4 1/4 X 5 1/8 In. 90.00
Shade, 5 Panel, Candlestick Base, 3 Panels Of Children, Signed 850.00
Shade, 6-Trapezoid, Bronze Base 1200.00
Shield, Candle, Wooden Frame, Ivory Thumbscrew, 16 1/2 In. 375.00
Stein, Floral Front, Soldier Bidding Farewell, 1/2 Liter 135.00
Stein, Floral Front, Zum Andenken, Pewter Top, 1/4 Liter 110.00
Stein, Occupational, World War I German Soldier, 1/2 Liter 160.00
Tea Set, Blown-Out Dragon, Satsuma, 15 Piece 155.00
Tea Warmer, 1 Piece Panel, Holder, Cast Metal Legs 350.00
Tea Warmer, 4 Panels, Brass Holder, 4 1/2 X 5 In. 295.00
Tea Warmer, 4 Panels, Silver Plated, Square 1600.00
Toddy Warmer, 4-Colored, Tin Frame 220.00
Tray, Pin, Fox Hunt Scene, Rococo Border, C.1890, 5 3/4 X 2 In. 45.00

Liverpool, England, has been the site of several pottery and porcelain factories from 1716 to 1785. Some earthenware was made with transfer decorations. Sadler and Green made print-decorated wares from 1756. Many of the pieces were made for the American market and featured patriotic emblems such as eagles, flags, and other special-interest motifs.

LIVERPOOL, Jug, Sailing Ship And Motto, C.1800, 15 In. 450.00
Jug, Sailors Return, 8 In. 350.00

LOCKE ART, Champagne, Poppy Pattern, 6 In. 50.00
Cookie Jar, Repousse Leaves, Gold Buds, Cover Hallmarked, 6 In. 245.00
Muffineer, Worcester, Acanthus Leaf, Silver Plated, Marked, 6 In. 75.00
Plate, Etched Poinsettias, Signed, 7 In. 125.00
Tray, Ice Cream, Engraved Flowers, 16 X 8 In. 200.00
Tumbler, Engraved Sheaths Of Wheat, 2 3/4 In. 75.00
Vase, Flared Top, Etched Rose Design, Signed, 6 1/4 In. 325.00
Vase, Intaglio Cut Panels, Facet Cut Bottom, 7 1/2 In. 110.00
Vase, Ruffled Shape, Peonies, Signed, 5 In. 425.00

Johann Loetz-Witwe bought a glassworks in Austria in 1840. He died in 1848 and his widow ran the company, then in 1879 his grandson took over. Loetz glass was varied. Most collectors recognize the iridescent gold glass similar to Tiffany but many other types were made. The firm was closed in World War II.

LOETZ, Basket, Art Nouveau Brass Holder, Silver Coin Spots, 6 1/2 In. 350.00
Bowl, Each Side Forming Lip, Iridescent Amber Dribbled, 9 X 4 1/2 In. 575.00
Bowl, Fruit, Cobalt Blue Mottling, 3 Dimples, 4 X 10 In.Diam. 495.00
Bowl, Ruffled, Green With Gold & Blue, 8 In. 120.00
Bowl, Ruffled, Iridescent Salmon, Silvery Blue Oil Spots, Signed, 6 In. 450.00
Ewer, Flared Mouth, Sterling Silver Overlay, Florals, 5 1/4 In. 1050.00
Inkwell, German Legend, 1900s, Brass Hinged Top, Purple, 5 1/4 In. 350.00
Inkwell, Hinged Brass Lid, Green Iridescent Insert In Pewter Frame 175.00
Rose Bowl, Bold, Rose, Lavender, Pink, & Blue Highlights, 4 In. 425.00
Rose Bowl, Purple Ground, Silver Swags 150.00
Rose Bowl, Rose, Lavender, Pink & Blue, Silver Overlay, 4 In. 425.00
Rose Bowl, Silver Overlay, Gold, Iridescent Highlights, 4 In. 382.50
Shade, Red Flames, Yellow Zippers 85.00
Shade, Yellow, Blue, & Green, 3 3/4 In. 325.00
Vase, Allover Trailings Of Oil Spots & Gold, Amber & Green, 10 In. 100.00
Vase, Blue & Gold Iridescent, Black Spots, Bulbous, 4 1/4 In. 200.00

Vase, Blue Design, Amber Ground, 6 1/2 In. 375.00
Vase, Blue Green Iridescent Mottling, Green Ground, 7 In. 395.00
Vase, Blue Iridescent, Twisted, Cylindrical, 12 In. 100.00
Vase, Blue On Amber, Flared Top, 4 1/2 In. 140.00
Vase, Clear & Sky Blue, Iridescent Gold Waves, Marked, 8 1/4 In. 750.00
Vase, Copper Frame Of Orange Trees, 14 1/2 In. 395.00
Vase, Double Gourd Shape, Blue Iridescent, Crossed Arrows, 7 In. 500.00
Vase, Formosa Pattern, Blue Threadware, Metallic Ground, 3 1/2 In. 160.00
Vase, Green Iridescent, Bronze Art Nouveau Holder, 14 In. 395.00
Vase, Green-Gold To Bright Red, 9 In. 310.00
Vase, Green, Blue & Purple, 9 1/2 In. 425.00
Vase, Green, Crackle Glass, Ruffled Top, Austria, Signed, 3 1/2 In. 350.00
Vase, Green, Gold Dust, Dimples & Swirled, 14 X 7 In. 392.00
Vase, Green, Gold, Corset Shape, 6 In. 75.00
Vase, Greenish-Blue Iridescence, Amber Spots, Pinched, 4 1/4 In. 148.00
Vase, Iridescent Blue Dragons, Signed, 8 In. 325.00
Vase, Iridescent Green Swirl, Arranger Top, White Ground, 6 In. 250.00
Vase, Iridescent Green, Signed, 4 1/4 In. 270.00
Vase, Iridescent Purple, Red, Gold Overlay Flowers, 10 In. 150.00
Vase, Leaf & Berry Design, Purple, Sterling Silver Overlay, 8 3/4 In. 1195.00
Vase, Lily Pads, Conical, Iridescent Gold, Marked, 9 In. 2200.00
Vase, Papillon Pattern, Cobalt Iridescence, Ribbed Handles, 6 In. 300.00
Vase, Phenomenon, Quatrefoil Mouth, 8 In. 165.00
Vase, Pinched Sides, Lavender, Aqua, & Green Mottling, 7 In. 75.00
Vase, Pulled Feather, Purple, 5 In. 500.00
Vase, Rose, Silvery Blue, Olive Iridescence, Signed, 7 In. 1500.00
Vase, Ruffled Neck, Green Iridescent, Signed, 4 1/4 In. 265.00
Vase, Silver Overlay, Blue Green Iridescent, 7 In. 1200.00
Vase, Silver Overlay, C.1900, Apricot & Amber, 10 1/4 In. ....*Illus* 1450.00
Vase, Silver Overlay, C.1900, Green & Blue, 9 1/2 In. ....*Illus* 725.00
Vase, Silver Overlay, Mottled Surface, Signed, 7 In. 1195.00
Vase, Silver Overlay, 10 In. 900.00
Vase, Sterling Silver Overlay, Ruby, Signed, 7 In. 1095.00
Vase, Treebark Texture With Knots, Green, 7 In. 75.00
Vase, Trumpet, Green, Flaring Top, 12 In. 120.00
Vase, Violet, Green, & Silver Dots & Striations, Apricot, 8 In. 750.00
Vase, White Ground, Green Swirl Design, Flower Top, 6 In. 250.00
Vase, Yellow Threads, Blue Iridescence, 4 In. 225.00
Vase, 3-Handled, 6 In. ....*Illus* 70.00
Vase, 4-Cornered, Green Iridescent, 4 3/4 In. 55.00
Vase, 4-Sided Turned-Down Lip, Burgundy Strips, Gray Ground, 10 In. 400.00

Loetz, Vase, Silver Overlay, C.1900, Apricot & Amber, 10 1/4 In.

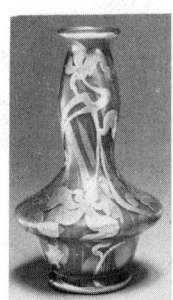

Loetz, Vase, Silver Overlay, C.1900, Green & Blue, 9 1/2 In.

Loetz, Vase, 3-Handled, 6 In.

LONE RANGER, Bank, TV 60.00
  Book, Gold Robbery, Hardcover, 1939 .... 4.00 To 5.00
  Book, Lone Ranger & Tonto, 1940 .... 7.00
  Book, Paint, Never Used 45.00
  Brush, Clothes 1939 .... 15.00 To 22.00
  Comics, 1950's, Set Of 5 .... 20.00
  Doll, Boxed 250.00
  Doll, Mask & Hat 80.00
  Figurine, On Silver, C.1938, 4 1/2 In. 20.00
  Flashlight Ring 35.00
  Game, Hi Ho Silver 37.50
  Game, Playset Rodeo, Original Box 75.00
  Game, Target 40.00
  Harmonica, Original Display 22.00
  Hat, Cowboy, Red Trim, Black, 1966 .... 10.00
  Kit, Aurora Model, 1967, Sealed Box 15.00
  Kit, First Aid, 1938 .... 25.00
  Knife, Black, Silver, Bullet On Back 25.00
  Knife, Pocket, Red Handle 18.00
  Lantern, Chuck Wagon 52.00
  Lithograph On Platform, Windup, Marx, Boxed 165.00
  Lunch Box, Tonto Coin 40.00
  Paint Box 10.00
  Pedometer .... 20.00 To 27.00
  Pen, Silver Bullet, Original Card .... 18.00 To 25.00
  Pencil Box 20.00
  Pistol, Clicker, Decal, Gray 45.00
  Record Player, Wood Case 100.00
  Ring, Airplane 30.00
  Ring, Film Strip 30.00
  Ring, Flashlight .... 25.00 To 26.00
  Ring, Silver Bullet 20.00
  Ring, Six-Shooter .... 25.00 To 48.00
  Silver Bullet 28.00
  Snow Globe 30.00
  Spoon, 1938 .... 12.00
  Target Practice Game, Boxed 37.00
  Toothbrush Holder 30.00
  Toy, Guitar 22.50
  Toy, Windup, 1938, Tin, Boxed 225.00
  Wristwatch 125.00

LONGTON HALL, Plate, C.1755, Vine Leaves & Sprigs, 8 1/4 In.Diam. 465.00

*Longwy Workshop of Longwy, France, first made ceramic wares in 1798.
The workshop is still in business. Most of the ceramic pieces found today
are glazed with many colors to resemble cloisonne or other enameled metal.*

LONGWY, Ashtray, Floral, Blue Ribbed Base, Elevated Gold Section 50.00
  Box, Bird In Flight, Crackle Blue Ground, Marked, 4 1/2 In.Diam. 100.00
  Enameled Blossom, Cobalt Blue Ground, Signed, 10 1/4 In. 170.00
  Muffineer, Blue Ground, Yellow, Green, Cream & Mauve, 5 In. 95.00
  Pin Tray, Multicolored Floral, Scalloped, 5 3/4 X 4 In. 40.00
  Plate, Woodland Scene, Hunting Dogs, 9 In. 45.00
  Tile, Bird Among Flowers, 8 X 8 In. 175.00
  Vase, Multicolored Floral, Bulbous, 8-Sided, 6 In. 85.00
  Vase, Multicolored Floral, Cylindrical, 3 1/2 In. 32.00
  Vase, 8-Sided, Cobalt Blue, Multicolored Floral, Blue Ground, 5 In. 95.00

Lonhuda Pottery Company of Steubenville, Ohio, was organized in 1892 by
William Long, W.H. Hunter, and Alfred Day. Brown underglaze
slip decorated pottery was made. The firm closed in 1896.

LONHUDA, Feeder, Invalid, Violet Design, Artist Signed, 6 In.	150.00
Vase, Cinnamon Design On Body & Up Neck, Flare Top, 8 In.	255.00
Vase, High Glaze, Floral, Artist Signed, 8 In.	225.00

Lotus Ware was made by the Knowles, Taylor & Knowles Company of
East Liverpool, Ohio, from 1890 to 1900.

LOTUS WARE, Creamer, White, Floral & Bamboo Design, Marked, 4 In.	75.00
Pitcher, Overlaid Fishnet Pattern, Gilt Trim, 5 X 4 In.	450.00
Pitcher, White Fishnet, Signed, 3 1/2 In.	350.00
Rose Bowl, Beaded & Ruffled, Medallion Handles, 4 In.	525.00
Vase, Gargoyle Faces, Flowers, Leaves, 2-Handled	150.00
Vase, Morning Glories, Gold Insect, 8 In.	675.00

J.&J.G.LOW

Low art tiles were made by the J. and J.G. Low Art Tile Works
of Chelsea, Massachusetts, from 1877 to 1902. A variety of art and other
tiles were made.

LOW, Ashtray, Lady's Profile In Brass Rim, 4 1/2 In.	75.00
Box, Pill, Lady's Profile On Cover	85.00
Tile, Lady With Turban, Olive Glaze, Signed	120.00
LOY-NEL-ART, see McCoy	

Luneville, a French faience factory, was established in 1731 by Jacques
Chambrette. It is best known for its fine biscuit figures and groups and
for large faience dogs and lions. The early pieces were unmarked. The firm
was acquired by Keller and Guerin and is still working.

LUNEVILLE, Bowl, Salad, Corner Designs, 11 In.Square	20.00
Butter Tub, Hand-Painted Flowers, Covered	20.00
Tureen, Hand-Painted Flowers, Embossed Leaf Base, 8 1/4 X 7 In.	40.00
Vase, Hand-Painted Irises, Tricorn Shape, 7 X 6 In.	115.00
Vase, Mottled Amber Shading To Burgundy, Pewter Overlay, Signed	300.00
Vase, White & Gold Enameled Flowers & Bee, Cobalt Blue, 8 In.	155.00

Lusterware was meant to resemble copper, silver, or gold. It has been used
since the sixteenth century. Most of the luster found today was made during
the nineteenth century.

LUSTER, Copper, Bowl, Rice, White Cherubs In Relief, 6 In.	55.00
Copper, Bowl, 4 X 3 In.	40.00
Copper, Bowl, 6 1/4 In.	40.00
Copper, Creamer, Blue & Cream Stripes, 4 1/2 In.	35.00
Copper, Creamer, Tan Band	25.00 To 35.00
Copper, Creamer, Yellow Band, Pink Luster Flowers, 4 In.	55.00
Copper, Cup, Handleless, Yellow Band	50.00
Copper, Pitcher, Ballet Scene, Blue Scrolls, 7 1/2 In.	145.00
Copper, Pitcher, Blue Band, Girl & Cat, 3 1/2 In.	75.00
Copper, Pitcher, Blue Band, 4 1/4 In.	40.00
Copper, Pitcher, Blue Flowers, 5 In.	65.00
Copper, Pitcher, Boar Hunt, C.1820, 7 1/2 In.	225.00
Copper, Pitcher, Children On Side, Mask Spout, Green Trim, 6 In.	65.00
Copper, Pitcher, Entwined Circles In Relief, 5 1/2 In.	130.00
Copper, Pitcher, Figural Spout, Embossed Figures, 5 1/2 In.	50.00

Copper, Pitcher, Hand-Painted Floral Bands, 3 In.	35.00
Copper, Pitcher, Impressed Dancers, Blue Scrolls, 8 In.	65.00
Copper, Pitcher, Mandarin Design, 6 1/2 In.	27.50
Copper, Pitcher, Pink Flowers, Signed Lancaster, 2 In.	30.00
Copper, Pitcher, Pink Flowers, 6 In.	55.00
Copper, Pitcher, Raised Baskets Of Flowers, C.1850, 6 1/2 In.	55.00
Copper, Pitcher, Raised Figures, Blue Band	25.00
Copper, Pitcher, Sand Band, 4 1/2 In.	55.00
Copper, Pitcher, 2 Raised Red Roses, Yellow Band & Beading	42.00
Copper, Pitcher, 3 Rows Of Beading, Bulbous Bottom, Gold Band, 5 In.	85.00
Copper, Pitcher, 7 3/4 In.	48.00
Copper, Sugar & Creamer, Tray, Handled	30.00
LUSTER, COPPER, TEA LEAF, see Tea Leaf, Ironstone	
Copper, Teapot, Enameled Design, 6-Footed, 7 1/2 In.	300.00
Copper, Teapot, Ribbed Georgian Style, C.1820, 6 1/2 X 6 1/2 In.	125.00
LUSTER, FAIRYLAND, see Wedgwood	
Gold, Tea Set, Child's, Hand-Painted Birds, Box	55.00
Lavender, Vase, Marked Germany, 5 3/4 In.	20.00
Pink, Bowl & Liner Plate, Pink, Blue, & Green, Bowl 6 1/2 In.Diam.	90.00
Pink, Bowl, Serving, House Pattern, 6 1/2 X 3 1/2 In.	42.00
Pink, Cup & Saucer, Demitasse, Schoolhouse	0.00
Pink, Cup & Saucer, Eagle Mark, Letters C.T.	8.00
Pink, Cup & Saucer, Feather Design, Green	42.00
Pink, Cup & Saucer, Feather Pattern, White Ground	25.00
Pink, Cup & Saucer, Fruit & Blues	22.00
Pink, Cup & Saucer, Leaf & Flower Design	75.00
Pink, Cup & Saucer, Thistle Pattern	24.00
Pink, Cup & Saucer, Wishbone Handles, Floral Design	42.00
Pink, Cup & Saucer, Woman & Child	25.00
Pink, Cup, Saucer, & Plate, Girls Posing In Flowers	29.00
Pink, Mug, Shaving, Ladies, Lily-Of-The-Valley Design	48.00
Pink, Pitcher, Bulbous, Stripes & Floral Panel, C.1840, 8 In.	135.00
Pink, Pitcher, Embossed Leaf Rim, Grape Bunch Each Side, C.1820, 5 In.	165.00
Pink, Pitcher, School Pattern	30.00
Pink, Plate, Bubble Pattern, Ribbed, 6 1/2 In.	22.00
Pink, Plate, Leaves & Border, Floral, 7 In.	15.00
Pink, Plate, Pink Band, Luster Leaf & Flower, C.1820, 7 In., Set Of 4	95.00
Pink, Plate, 8 In.	35.00
Pink, Sugar, Covered	75.00
Pink, Sugar, Double Handles, Cover, 7 1/2 In.	85.00
Silver, Loving Cup, Copper Luster Inside, 5 X 4 1/2 In.	50.00
Silver, Loving Cup, 2-Handled, Copper Luster Inside, 4 1/4 In.	55.00
Silver, Pitcher, Covered, Pair	45.00
Silver, Teapot, Painted Silver Scene, Staffordshire Mark	60.00
LUSTER, SUNDERLAND, see Sunderland	

Lustre Art Glass Company was founded in Long Island, New York, in 1920 by Conrad Vahlsing and Paul Frank. The company made lampshades and globes that are almost indistinguishable from those made by Quezal.

LUSTRE ART, Candlestick, Signed, Blue Iridescent, 9 In.	185.00
Shade, Feather Design, Gold Threading, Scalloped	140.00
Shade, Gold Threading Over Green & Gold Leaves, Signed, Set Of 6	750.00
Shade, White Feathers, Gold Ribbing, Signed, 5 1/4 In., Pair	250.00

Lustres are mantel decorations, or pedestal vases, with many hanging glass prisms. The name really refers to the prisms, and it is proper to refer to a single glass prism as a lustre. Either spelling, luster or lustre, is correct.

LUSTRES, Bohemian, Red, Pair	275.00
Girl And Dog, Gilded Brass, Ruby Prism, Set Of 3	250.00
Gold Trim, Bristol, Pink Satin Glass, 10 5/8 In., Pair	425.00
Hunter, Gilded Brass, Clear Prism, Set Of 2	150.00

Lady's Portrait, Bristol, Prisms, 12 In., Pair 225.00

> *Lutz glass was made in the 1870s by Nicholas Lutz at the Boston and Sandwich Company. He made a delicate and intricate threaded glass of several colors. Other similar wares are referred to as Lutz.*

LUTZ, Bowl, Pink Opalescent Luster, Ruffled Underplate, 2 3/4 X 5 In. 70.00
Plate, Pink & White Swirl, Iridescent Gold Flecks 60.00
Vase, Applied Handle, 8 In. 125.00

> *Petrus Regout established the De Sphinx pottery in Maastricht, Holland, in 1836. The firm was noted for its transfer-printed earthenware. Many factories in Maastricht are still making ceramics.*

MAASTRICHT, Bowl, 7 1/2 In. 10.00
Bowl, 8 In. 35.00
Plate, Abbey Pattern, Blue, 8 1/4 In. 15.00
Plate, Blue & White 7.50
Plate, Hong Pattern, 7 1/2 In. 15.00

> *Maize glass, sold by the W.L.Libbey & Son Company of Toledo, Ohio, was made by Joseph Locke in 1889. It is pressed glass formed like an ear of corn. Most pieces were made for household use.*

MAIZE, Berry Bowl, Green Leaves, White Ground, Libbey, 8 In.Diam. 130.00
Carafe, Water, Custard, Green Trim 225.00
Celery, Blue Leaves, Iridescent 85.00
Celery, Custard 85.00
Finger Bowl, Custard 135.00
Mustard, Covered 125.00
Saltshaker, Green Leaves, Original Lid 75.00
Sugar Shaker, Opaque White Body, Yellow Gold Leaves, C.1890 .... 60.00
Sugar Shaker, Yellow & Gold Leaves, Custard Glass .... 175.00 To 195.00
Syrup, Green Husks, Opaque White 275.00
Toothpick, Custard Glass 225.00
Tumbler, Blue Leaves, Gold Trim, Cream Opaque, 4 In. 195.00
Tumbler, Blue Leaves, Gold Trim, Opaque Cream, 4 In. 195.00
Tumbler, Yellow Leaves, Barrel Shape, Gold Trim, 4 In. 195.00

> *Majolica is any pottery glazed with a tin enamel. Most of the majolica found today is decorated with leaves, shells, branches, and other natural shapes and in natural colors. It was a popular nineteenth-century product.*

MAJOLICA, see also Wedgwood
MAJOLICA, Ashtray, Forest Scene, 4 In. 15.00
Ashtray, Turkish Man 18.00
Basket, Applied Flowers, 3 Birds On Branch Handle, French, 18 In. 700.00
Basket, Bird Center, Vase Type, 10 3/4 In. 100.00
Biscuit Barrel, Engraved Flowers On Cover, Brass Bail 110.00
Bowl, Lemon Yellow, Brown Trim, White Flowers, 8 3/4 In. 60.00
Box, Pin, Original Sticker 40.00
Butter Pat, Shell & Seaweed Pattern 18.00
Cake Set, Maroon Basket Weave, Yellow Flowers, 7 Piece 85.00
Cake Stand, Tree Trunk Base, Raised Leaves, Pink Ground, 9 1/2 In. 85.00
Charger, Urbino Style, 2 Ladies, 2 Cherubs, Clouds, Marked, 20 In. 125.00
Coffeepot, Shell & Seaweed Pattern 215.00
Compote, Green Leaves, Pink Ground, Footed, 9 1/2 In. 75.00
Creamer, Butterfly 55.00
Creamer, Pink Flowers, Green Ivys, Branch Handle, 4 1/2 In. 45.00
Cup & Saucer, Seaweed Pattern 110.00
Cup & Saucer, Shell & Seaweed Pattern 150.00
Dish, Blue, Yellow, Ocher, Cupid Holding Staff, 8 1/2 In. 550.00

Dish, Center, Candleholder, Brown, Blue, Yellow, Signed	76.00
Dish, Leaf, 7 X 9 In.	33.00
Dish, Reticulated, 17th Century, Center Cupid, Savona, 8 1/2 In.	550.00
Dish, Sardine	75.00
Figurine, Black Boy With 3 Baskets Of Flowers	115.00
Figurine, Gypsy Man & Woman, 18 In., Pair	500.00
Humidor, Figural, Friar, Covered, 6 1/2 In.	22.50
Humidor, Men & Grapes	85.00
Humidor, Pipe On Cover	45.00 To 65.00
Jardiniere, Forest Mold, 8 1/2 X 10 In.	85.00
Jardiniere, High Relief Dragons Around Bowl, 34 In., 2 Piece	350.00
Lamp, Oil, Ferns, Yellow & Green, Brass Base	115.00
Match Holder, Castle, 5 X 7 In.	95.00
Match Holder, Indian, Striker, 10 1/2 In.	125.00
Mug, Ear Of Corn, Green, White, & Yellow Glaze, 5 1/2 In.	45.00
Mug, Tankard, Maize, Ear Of Corn, Marked, 5 1/2 In.	22.00
Oyster Plate, Signed Minton & Registry Mark, March, 1867	55.00
Pitcher, Basket Weave, Peas	50.00
Pitcher, Cat, Handled, 11 In.	125.00
Pitcher, Corn, Small	35.00
Pitcher, Maize Pattern, Lavender Lining, 7 In.	38.00
Pitcher, Pine Tree Pattern, Cobalt Blue & White, Gold Trim, 7 In.	85.00
Pitcher, Pink Flowers, Green Basket Weave, 6 In.	45.00
Pitcher, Seaweed & Shell, 6 In.	150.00
Pitcher, Water Lily	87.00
Pitcher, Woodbark, 7 1/2 In.	60.00
Pitcher, Yellow, Water Lilies, Lavender Lining, 7 In.	37.50
Planter, Avocado Glaze, Molded Decoration, Austria, 4 X 8 In.	30.00
Planter, 4-Footed, Busts Of Women In Relief, 8 1/2 X 7 In.	135.00
Plate, Apples, Etruscan	25.00
Plate, Berries, Green Ground	15.00
Plate, Cauliflower	60.00
Plate, Corn Pattern, 9 In.	55.00
Plate, Dog Next To Doghouse, Leaf Border, C.1870, 11 In.	70.00
Plate, Leaf Design, 8 In.	25.00
Plate, Leaf, Green, Pink, Yellow, 9 X 7 In.	15.00
Plate, Oyster	38.00
Plate, Oyster, George Jones	95.00
Plate, Pink, Green Leaves, Pedestal, Etruscan, 5 1/4 In.	78.00
Plate, Shaggy Dog House, 10 1/2 In.	55.00
Platter, Shell & Seaweed Pattern, 13 1/2 X 9 1/4 In.	85.00
Stein, Man With Pipe, Geschutzt Mark, 1/2 Liter, 7 In.	225.00
Stein, Nudes & Grapes	69.00
Sugar, Cauliflower	80.00
Syrup, Blackberry	25.00
Syrup, Sunflower Pattern, Pewter Lid	40.00
Tea Set, Bamboo, Etruscan, Marked, 3 Piece	250.00
Teapot, Bamboo, English	68.00
Teapot, Pineapple	75.00
Umbrella Stand, 20 In.	160.00
Urn, Carp, Tail Handle, Green, Blue Ground, 11 1/2 In., Pair	345.00
Vase, Cream Ground, Multicolored Design, Marked, 5 3/4 In.	15.00
Vase, Floral Design, Sanded, Large	50.00
Vase, Iris Handles, Art Nouveau, 12 In.	88.00

MAP, Atlas, School, 1856, California Gold Fields & Territories	35.00
Dublin, New Hampshire, Dated 1907, Corrected 1906, Oilcloth, 36 X 28 In.	50.00
England, Scotland, Wales, Amy Young, Sampler, 1813	750.00
Ireland, Family Names, County Of Origin, Framed, 16 X 20 In.	40.00
Maryland, Highways, Railways, & Steamboat Lines, 1920, 36 X 52 In.	15.00
Piano, Brass, Slag Glass Shade, Caramel, Floral Design, Cherubs, 28 In.	275.00
Richmond, La., 1882, Railroad, 28 X 50 In.	45.00

Marbles of glass were made during the nineteenth century. Venetian swirl, clear glass, sulfides, and marbles with frosted white animal figures embedded in the glass were popular. Handmade clay marbles were made in many places, but most of them came from the pottery factories of Ohio and Pennsylvania. Occasionally, real stone marbles of onyx, carnelian, or jasper can be found.

MARBLE CARVING, Dog, Renaissance Style, Black & Green, 1i X 12 In. 600.00
   Maiden, Classical, Seated, C.1881, 21 1/4 In. 1000.00
   Nymph & Satyr, Carrier-Belleuse, 19th Century, White, 28 In. 4000.00
   Nymph, C.1900, Inscribed Carli, 28 In. 900.00
   Satyr & Bacchante, Sits On Wine Cup, 23 In. 375.00
   Venus De Milo, 19th Century, Polished, 34 In. 800.00

MARBLE, Agate, 5/8 In., 1 Dozen 35.00
   Agate, 7/8 In. 4.50
   Carmel, 1 In. 25.00
   Carmel, 1 1/4 In. 55.00
   Comic, Betty Boop 22.50
   Comic, Emma 30.00
   Comic, Orphan Annie 40.00
   Comic, Smitty 32.00
   Mr.Peanut, Logo On Label, Packet Of 40 .... 6.75
   Purple, 5/8 In. 15.00
   Sulfide, Annie, Comic Strip 35.00
   Sulfide, Bear .... 45.00 To 60.00
   Sulfide, Bear, Standing, 1 3/4 In. 90.00
   Sulfide, Boar, 1 1/2 In. 68.00
   Sulfide, Cow, 1 3/4 In. 70.00
   Sulfide, Dog .... 35.00 To 65.00
   Sulfide, Eagle, 1 1/4 In. 100.00
   Sulfide, Eagle, 1 5/8 In. 148.00
   Sulfide, Elephant, 1 1/2 In.Diam. 45.00
   Sulfide, Grazing Sheep, 1 1/2 In. 125.00
   Sulfide, Onion Mica, 1 15/16 In. 95.00
   Sulfide, Parrot 95.00
   Sulfide, Picking Hen, 1 3/4 In. 85.00
   Sulfide, Poodle, 1 5/8 In. 135.00
   Sulfide, Rabbit, 1 1/2 In. 20.00
   Sulfide, Rearing Horse, 1 3/4 In. 125.00
   Sulfide, Rearing Horse, 1 7/8 In. 125.00
   Sulfide, Squirrel 85.00
   Sulfide, Squirrel Eating A Nut, 2 In. 90.00
   Sulfide, Squirrel, Standing, 2 3/8 In. 250.00
   Sulfide, Swirl, 2 5/16 In. 725.00
   Swirl, Candy Stripe, Large 85.00
   Swirl, Peppermint, 7 7/8 In. 55.00
   Swirl, 1 7/8 In. 55.00
   Swirl, 7 7/8 In. 55.00

The Marblehead Pottery was founded in 1905 as a rehabilitative program for the patients of a Marblehead, Massachusetts, sanitarium by Dr. J. Hall. Two years later it was separated from the sanitarium, and it continued operations until 1936. Many of the pieces were decorated with marine motifs.

MARBLEHEAD, Berry Set, Yellow, Bowl, 9 3/4 In., 5 Piece 160.00
   Bottle, Perfume, Figural, Egyptian Mummy, Label 250.00
   Bowl, Banded Design At Top, Blue Semiglass Ground, Signed 350.00
   Bowl, Black Luster, 6 In. 78.00
   Bowl, Blue, 5 1/2 In. 25.00
   Vase, Beige, 3 In. 75.00
   Vase, Blue, 7 In. 78.00

Vase, Bulbous, Blue Matte, 7 1/2 In. 50.00
Vase, Cylinder, Blue Matte, 8 In. 55.00
Vase, Cylindrical, Gray, Signed, 4 1/2 In. 35.00
Vase, Green, 4 1/2 In. 60.00
Vase, Slants Inward, Small Shoulder, Pink Mauve, 5 In. 95.00
Vase, Squatty, Blue, 4 1/2 In. 60.00
     MARINE, see Nautical

*Martinware is a salt-glazed stoneware made by the Martin Brothers of
Middlesex, England, between 1873 and 1915. Many figural jugs and vases
were made.*

MARTIN BROTHERS, Bird, Detachable Head, 1903, Stoneware .... *Illus* 5000.00
  Figurine, Bird, Green, Gray, Blue, Detachable Head, 11 In. 5000.00
  Pitcher, Flowering Lotus, 7 1/2 In. 200.00
  Salamanders Attacking Tadpoles, 10 In. 400.00
  Vase, Bottle, Flowers, 6 In. 125.00
  Vase, Bottle, Flowers, 7 In. 175.00
  Vase, Fish, Grotesque, 10 In. 500.00
  Vase, Fish, Grotesque, 9 In. 300.00
  Vase, Flowers, 6 In. 125.00

*Mary Gregory glass is identified by a characteristic white figure painted
on dark glass. It was made from 1870 to 1910. The name refers to any glass
decorated with a white silhouette figure and not just the Sandwich glass
originally painted by Miss Mary Gregory.*

MARY GREGORY, Bottle, Amber, Pastoral Scene, Girl, Stopper, 8 1/4 In. 150.00
  Bottle, Barber, Amethyst 150.00
  Bottle, Barber, Cobalt Blue, Boy Chasing Butterfly 185.00
  Bottle, Barber, Emerald Green, Butterfly Net, Boy, 7 In. 125.00
  Bottle, Cologne, Beveled Sides, Girl With Umbrella, Blue, 8 In. 225.00
  Bottle, Cordial, Optic Ribbed, White Angel, Stopper, 9 In. 140.00
  Bottle, Perfume, Blue, White Figures, 5 3/4 In., Pair 250.00
  Bowl, Boy & Girl, White Enamel, Ormolu Feet, Lime Green, 6 In. 225.00
  Box, Jewel, Girls Feeding Bird, Sapphire Blue, Footed, 5 In. 395.00
  Box, Patch, Girl Picking Flowers, Ruby, 1 X 2 In. 195.00
  Box, Patch, Girl, Hinged Top, Sapphire Blue, 1 1/4 X 2 In.Diam. 175.00
  Box, Powder, Green, Covered, Girl With Bird, 4 1/2 In. 150.00
  Chest, Jewelry, Black, Children, Moth, Brass Feet, 5 X 3 In. 495.00

Martin Brothers, Bird, Detachable Head,
1903, Stoneware

Cruet, Vinegar, Lime Green, Boy, Pack On Back, 7 1/4 In. 165.00
Cruet, White Girl, Blue Handle, Sapphire Blue, 10 In. 225.00
Decanter, Girl With Watering Can, Trefoil-Shaped Lip 145.00
Ewer, Mountaineer, White On Green, C.1850 .... 175.00
Goblet, Boy & Girl, White Enamel, Sapphire Blue, 5 1/4 In., Pair 110.00
Goblet, Footed, Facing Boy & Girl, Sapphire Blue, 5 1/8 In., Pr. 110.00
Jug, Green, Mountaineer, 1850, 15 In. 225.00
Mug, Boy, Clear Handle, 2 3/4 In. 90.00
Pickle Caster, Ruby 495.00
Pitcher, Boy In White Suit, Plated Top, 8 In. 95.00
Pitcher, Boy With Sailboat, Sapphire Blue, 6 1/8 In. 235.00
Pitcher, Emerald Green, Young Boy, 4 1/4 In. 95.00
Pitcher, Mountaineer, 1875, 14 In. 115.00
Pitcher, Sapphire Blue, Boy & Sailboat, 6 In. 235.00
Pitcher, Water, Amber 125.00
Salt & Pepper, Shaker, Amber, Square, Original Tops 225.00
Stein, Lady's, Girl Flying Kite, Amber, Pewter Top, 3 In. 195.00
Sugar Shaker, Blue 65.00
Sugar Shaker, Cranberry 65.00
Tumbler, Boy & Girl, White, Clear Glass, Pair 180.00
Tumbler, Boy Sitting, Sapphire Blue, White Enamel, 4 1/2 In. 65.00
Tumbler, Boy, White Enamel, Emerald Green, 3 7/8 In. 50.00
Tumbler, Boy, White Enamel, Tinted Features, Sapphire Blue 42.00
Tumbler, Juice, Girl Playing With Ball, Gold Rim 40.00
Tumbler, Water, Apple Green, Girl, Basket Of Flowers, 2 3/4 In. 35.00
Tumbler, White Figure, Vaseline 40.00
Tumbler, Young Boy, White Enamel, Sapphire Blue, 3 3/4 In. 40.00
Vase, Blue, Honey Amber, Boy, Sailboat, 9 In. 165.00
Vase, Boy & Girl Picking Flowers, Cranberry, 8 1/4 In. 310.00
Vase, Boy & Girl With Flowers, Cranberry, Crystal Foot, 8 In. 295.00
Vase, Boy With Butterfly, Cranberry, 4 3/4 In. 100.00
Vase, Boy With Ship, Cranberry, 5 In. 100.00
Vase, Boy With Stick, Cranberry, White Enamel, 8 1/2 In. 165.00
Vase, Boy, Girl, White Enamel, Sapphire Blue, 9 1/4 In., Pair 395.00
Vase, Boy, White Enamel, Sapphire Blue, 6 In. 85.00
Vase, Brass Collar, Ormolu Feet, Girl Blowing Trumpet, 6 In. 135.00
Vase, Bud, Female On Green Glass, 3 Ormolu Feet, 3 In. 95.00
Vase, Cherub Head, Enameled, Atlantic City, 6 In., Pair 400.00
Vase, Cobalt Blue, Cylinder Shape, Girl, Hat, 9 5/8 In. 75.00
Vase, Cobalt, Boy Chasing Bird, Gold Trim 165.00
Vase, Cranberry, Boy With Whip, 5 In. 100.00
Vase, Cranberry, Fluted, Hand-Painted, Girl 125.00
Vase, Cut Scalloped Top, Facing Girls, Blue, 13 1/2 In., Pair 550.00
Vase, Emerald Green, Boy, Hat, 7 3/4 In. 88.00
Vase, Facing Boy & Girl, All White, Cranberry, 9 In., Pair 365.00
Vase, Facing Boy & Girl, Gold Trim, Cobalt Blue, 9 5/8 In., Pr. 145.00
Vase, Girl & Butterflies In White, Amber, 8 In. 85.00
Vase, Girl At Pump, Young Man, Medium Green, 13 3/4 In. 295.00
Vase, Girl Blowing Horn, Bird On Hand, Pink Overlay, 10 1/4 In. 195.00
Vase, Girl Feeding Bird, Green Satin, White Enamel, 6 1/4 In. 150.00
Vase, Girl Feeding Birds, Lime Green, 4 1/2 In. 110.00
Vase, Girl Feeding Birds, Lime Green, 9 1/4 In. .... 110.00 To 118.00
Vase, Girl Holding Basket, Lavender, Scalloped, 12 1/2 In. 195.00
Vase, Girl In White Enamel, Brass Rim, Brass Handles, 6 In. 110.00
Vase, Girl Picking Flower, Opaque Taupe, 10 1/2 In. 135.00
Vase, Girl Seated, Holding Sprig, Cranberry, 3 7/8 In. 95.00
Vase, Girl Standing By Post, Tan Bristol, 11 1/2 In. 135.00
Vase, Girl Tinted Face, Cobalt, 7 1/2 In. 135.00
Vase, Girl With Apron Of Flowers, Emerald Green, 9 In. 145.00
Vase, Girl With Balloon, Cranberry, 5 In. 100.00
Vase, Girl With Hat, White Enamel, Cobalt Blue, 9 3/4 In. 75.00
Vase, Girl With White Flower, Cranberry, 4 In. 100.00

Vase, Lime Green, Boy In Riding Habit, 1 7/8 In.	88.00
Vase, Lime Green, Crackle, Girl With Hat, 6 1/8 In.	135.00
Vase, Opaque Tan, Girl, Flowers, Garden, 11 3/8 In.	125.00
Vase, Painted Face, Pale Pink, 6 1/2 In.	65.00
Vase, Pink Overlay, Bristol, Boy With Hoop, 9 1/8 In.	175.00
Vase, Pink Overlay, Bristol, Girl & Bird, 10 1/4 In.	195.00
Vase, Ruffled, Girl, Cobalt Blue, 12 In.	195.00
Vase, Sailor Boy & Girl, Tinted Faces, C.1880, 12 In., Pair	195.00
Vase, Sapphire Blue, Boy, Hat, Cylinder, 9 1/2 In.	75.00
Vase, Tinted Face Girl, Cobalt Blue, 7 1/2 In.	135.00
Vase, Triple Bulbous Base, Girl, Amber, 6 1/4 In.	58.00
Vase, White Facing Boy & Girl, Cranberry, 9 In., Pair	365.00
Vase, White Figure On Green Glass, 3 In.	75.00
Vase, White Girl With Hat & Butterfly Net, Lime Green, 7 In.	135.00
Wine, Amber, Girl, White Enamel, 5 3/8 In.	95.00

Masonic Shrine glassware was made from 1893 to 1917. It is occasionally called Syrian Temple Shrine glassware. Most pieces are dated.

MASONIC, Bookends, Emblem, Metal	15.00
Chalice, Shrine, Pittsburgh, St.Paul, 1908, Cranberry	65.00
Chalice, St.Paul, Minn., 1908, Black Bottom, Gold Wheat, Emblem	75.00
Champagne, Pittsburgh, 1911, Gold Scepters	75.00
Champagne, Shriner's Syria, April, 1910, Alligators, King Neptune	65.00
Champagne, Shriner's, Rochester, Pittsburgh, 1911	65.00
Champagne, Shriner's, 1909.Swords & Tobacco Leaf Base	75.00
Fez, Shriner's, Marked Oriental	8.00
Goblet, Shrine, Scimitar & Moon, Syria Temple, June 1899	100.00
Goblet, Washington, D.C., 1900	85.00
Goblet, 1908, Louisville, Kentucky, Emblem, Gold-Leaf Base	75.00
Hourglass, Ohio Lodge Symbol, Wooden, 9 5/8 In.	85.00
Mirror, Pocket, Veiled Prophet, Dated October 6, 1896	32.00
Mug, Hand-Painted River & Bridge, Pittsburgh, Penn., Sword Handles	68.00
Mug, Knights Templar, Dated June, 1909, Blue	30.00
Pencil, Mechanical, Order Of Eastern Star, Bullet Shape	10.00
Pin, Eastern Star, Seed Pearls	10.00
Pin, Lapel, Shriner's Fez, Enameled	17.50
Pitcher, 60th Anniversary, 1853-1913, No. 25, F. & A.M., 12 1/2 In.	75.00
Plate, Lodge No.130, Haddonfield, New Jersey, C.1911	25.00 To 35.00
Plate, Wheeling Commandery No.UK.T., May 17 & 18, 1911, 10 In.	30.00
Sign, 3 Martyred Presidents, Carved Horn	65.00
Slides, Degree, Color, Projector, Slide, 3 1/4 X 4 In.	175.00
Tumbler, Grand Consistory Of Kentucky, 1917, Frosted, 3 In.	30.00
Tumbler, Temple, Governor O.Jones, 1893, Diamond Zipper Base, Ruby	35.00
Watch Fob, Square & Compass, Mother-Of-Pearl Buckle, Leather Strap	125.00
Watch Fob, Strap, Terre Haute, Indiana, July, 1912	15.00
Watch Fob, 91st Grand Lodge, Porcelain	25.00

J.Massier fils

Massier pottery is iridescent French art pottery made by Clement Massier in Golfe-Juane, France, in the late nineteenth and early twentieth centuries. It is characterized by a metallic luster glaze.

MASSIER, Jardiniere, Chinese Art Nouveau Floral, Signed, 17 1/2 In.	400.00

MATCH HOLDER, see also Iron, Match Holder; Staffordshire, Match Holder; Store, Match Holder

MATCH HOLDER, Baby Chick, Striker Plate, Silver Plated	22.50
Bingal Bluing, Cardboard & Tin	40.00
Bird Sitting On Base, Picking Up Matches, Cast Iron	35.00
Bulldog Tobacco	285.00
Colonial Couple, Bisque	42.00
Cone Shape, Brass	26.00

Corrugated Striking Surface, Pedestal, Ironstone, White, 3 In. 20.00
DeLaval Separator, Tin .... 55.00 To 85.00
Dog, Sterling Silver 125.00
Double-Handled, Ashtray Base, Cast Iron 36.00
Eagle & Star Design, Cast Iron 18.00
Girl With Muff, Bisque, Striker 45.00
Kettle Shape, Tin, 3 1/4 X 4 In. 8.00
Kool's, Picture Of Penguin 20.00
Open Satchel Form, Sapphire Blue 40.00
Pocket, Arched Crimped Top, Tin, 4 X 7 In. 65.00
Rabbit, Pheasant, & Horn, Cast Iron, 5 X 8 In. 60.00
Sharples 175.00
Slippers, Tin, 3 1/2 In. 18.00
Slippers, Twisted Ribbon Bows, Wood Backplate, Brass, 3 3/4 In. 22.00
Striking Surface, Original Red & Green Paint, Tin 30.00
Wall, Flip Lid, Dated 1899, Brass 35.00
Wrigley's Juicy Fruit 65.00

       MATCH SAFE, see also Silver-Sterling, Match Safe
MATCH SAFE, A With Eagle, Scroll Sides, Anheuser Busch, Silver Plated 45.00
Columbian Exposition, 1892, Silver Soldered 35.00
Columbus, Silver Plated 125.00
Compliments Of Silas Peirce & Co., Boston, Brass 24.00
Dutch Boy 115.00
Hanging, Swing Lid, Signed Parker, Patented, 1869, Cast Iron 65.00
Hoof, Silver Plated 75.00
Impressed Eagle, Outspread Wings, Nickel Over Brass 20.00
Incurved Sides, Engraved Flowers, C.1900, 14K Gold, 2 3/8 In. 375.00
Juicy Fruit Gum 150.00
Marble's, 1900, Cylinder 20.00
Nude In Color, 1900, Celluloid & Metal 110.00
Pair Of Jeans Shape, Tin 115.00
Pedestal Base, Tiger Maple, 3 1/2 In. 75.00
Pointer Dog On Lid, Patented 1862, Cast Iron 65.00
Ridgewood Tobacco Co., Suitcase Shape, Nickel Plated Brass 90.00
Rochester Brewing Co., Brass 20.00
Running Horse, Metal 11.00
Shamrock Cover, Engraved, Sterling Silver 38.00
Silver Plate Over Brass 32.00
Souvenir, Union Station, St.Louis, 1904, Attached Cutter 38.00
St.Louis World's Fair, 1904, Brass .... 18.00 To 34.00
Table, Slant Sides, Wooden, Black Paint 35.00
Union Station, St.Louis, Dated 1904, Attached Cigar Cutter 38.00
Val Blatz Brewing Co. 95.00
Wall, American Stores Co., Blue Paint 35.00
Wall, Urn Shape, Dated 1867, Cast Iron 35.00
Waterproof, Marked Marbles, Brass 22.00

MATT MORGAN
—CIN. O—
ART POTTERY CO

*Matt Morgan opened an art pottery company in Cincinnati, Ohio, in 1883.
It lasted in business for only a year, closing because of money problems.*

MATT MORGAN, Ewer, Handle, Bat Design 550.00
Vase, Geometric Raised Pattern, 4 In. 350.00

McCoy

*McCoy pottery is made in Roseville, Ohio. The J.W. McCoy
Pottery was founded in 1899. It became the Brush McCoy Pottery
Company in 1911. The name changed to the Brush Pottery in 1925. The
Nelson McCoy Sanitary and Stoneware Company was founded in
Roseville, Ohio, in 1910. This firm made art pottery after 1926. In 1933*

it became the Nelson McCoy Pottery. Pieces marked McCoy were made by the Nelson McCoy Company.

MC COY, Ashtray, Free Form, Turquoise, 6 X 4 In.	5.00
Bowl, C.1930, 8 In. To 5 In., Nest Of 4	25.00
Bowl, Dog's, Green, 2 1/2 X 7 1/2 In.	10.00
Bowl, Mixing, Pineapple Design, Green, 8 In.	12.50
Bowl, Pink Bird Perched On Side, Aqua, Large	15.00
Cachepot, Double, Yellow Bird, Green	12.00
Candleholder, Dark Green & Purple, Marked, 3 In., Pair	10.00
Candleholder, Glossy Onyx Drizzle, 3 X 6 In., Pair	12.00
Casserole, Blue Green, Signed, Covered, 1 Pint	10.00
Cookie Jar, Alice In Wonderland	40.00
Cookie Jar, Apple, Basket Weave	20.00
Cookie Jar, Bananas	20.00
Cookie Jar, Bean Pot	20.00
Cookie Jar, Bear	12.00 To 25.00
Cookie Jar, Beehive & Kitten	20.00
Cookie Jar, Bell, Ring For Cookie	20.00
Cookie Jar, Boy & Girl Dancing, Barrel Shaped	12.00
Cookie Jar, Bushel Basket	25.00
Cookie Jar, Cabin	35.00
Cookie Jar, Chef	35.00 To 40.00
Cookie Jar, Chinese Lantern	30.00
Cookie Jar, Circus Horse	30.00
Cookie Jar, Clown	12.00
Cookie Jar, Clown In Barrel	25.00
Cookie Jar, Cook Stove	15.00
Cookie Jar, Cookie Bank	30.00
Cookie Jar, Cookie Barrel	10.00
Cookie Jar, Cookie Cabin	25.00
Cookie Jar, Cookie Jug	10.00
Cookie Jar, Covered Wagon	18.00
Cookie Jar, Cow	8.00
Cookie Jar, Cow, Purple, Cat On Back	35.00
Cookie Jar, Dalmatians	55.00
Cookie Jar, Davy Crockett	40.00 To 65.00
Cookie Jar, Donkey	35.00
Cookie Jar, Drum	25.00
Cookie Jar, Dutch Boy	10.00 To 30.00
Cookie Jar, Dutch Girl, White	22.50
Cookie Jar, Fortune Cookie	25.00
Cookie Jar, Friendship 7	25.00 To 40.00
Cookie Jar, Frontier Family	15.00 To 20.00
Cookie Jar, Grandfather Clock	25.00
Cookie Jar, Granny	25.00
Cookie Jar, Hobbyhorse	30.00 To 40.00
Cookie Jar, Honey Bear	25.00
Cookie Jar, Indian	65.00
Cookie Jar, Kissing Penguins	45.00
Cookie Jar, Kitten In Basket	25.00
Cookie Jar, Kookie Kettle	12.00
Cookie Jar, Lantern	20.00
Cookie Jar, Little Clown	15.00 To 25.00
Cookie Jar, Locomotive	40.00 To 45.00
Cookie Jar, Lollipop	15.00
Cookie Jar, Mammy	50.00
Cookie Jar, Mickey & Minnie	70.00
Cookie Jar, Mother Goose	35.00
Cookie Jar, Mr.& Mrs.Owl	22.00
Cookie Jar, Oaken Bucket	10.00
Cookie Jar, Old Car	35.00
Cookie Jar, Old-Fashioned Auto, Touring Car	35.00
Cookie Jar, Owl	15.00

Cookie Jar, Picnic Basket .... 25.00 To 35.00
Cookie Jar, Pig .... 15.00 To 20.00
Cookie Jar, Pig, Red Bandana 25.00
Cookie Jar, Pilsbury Doeboy 26.00
Cookie Jar, Pineapple 15.00
Cookie Jar, Potbelly Stove 15.00
Cookie Jar, Puppy 25.00
Cookie Jar, Raggedy Ann 35.00
Cookie Jar, Rocking Chair 55.00
Cookie Jar, Rooster .... 25.00 To 28.00
Cookie Jar, Sack Of Cookies .... 15.00 To 20.00
Cookie Jar, Squirrel, Metlox 30.00
Cookie Jar, Stove, Black 15.00
Cookie Jar, Stove, Potbelly, Gold & Red Trim, White .... 22.50 To 25.00
Cookie Jar, Teakettle, Black .... 15.00 To 25.00
Cookie Jar, Teapot, Copper Luster 20.00
Cookie Jar, Tepee .... 55.00 To 65.00
Cookie Jar, Touring Car .... 25.00 To 35.00
Cookie Jar, Train 45.00
Cookie Jar, Treasure Chest 20.00
Cookie Jar, Wedding Jar 20.00
Cookie Jar, Western Saddle, With Blackboard 20.00
Cookie Jar, Wishing Well .... 12.00 To 45.00
Creamer, Pinecone, Green & Brown, Marked 4.75
Decanter, Whiskey, Locomotive, Lid 32.00
Flower Frog, Duck, Glossy, 4 X 2 In. 15.00
Jar, Pretzel, Green 37.00
Jug, Olympia, Ear Of Corn 165.00
Jug, Onyx, Stopper, Blue, 10 In. 25.00
Match Holder, Double Turtle 15.00
Mug, Beer, Barrel Shaped 5.00
Mug, El Rancho, 3 1/2 In. 5.00
Picnic Basket 30.00
Pitcher Set, Man Molded In Relief, Green, 6 Mugs 145.00
Pitcher, Milk, Brown Glaze 25.00
Pitcher, Windmill, C.1916, Blue & White 115.00
Planter, Beer Glass Shape, Pedestal, Aqua 5.00
Planter, Boy & Girl, Light Green 2.50
Planter, Figural, Frog, Open Back, Green 15.00
Planter, Figural, Spinning Wheel 12.00
Planter, Figural, Turtle 11.00
Planter, Frog & Lily, Aqua 56.00
Planter, Frog, Reclining, 10 In. .... 10.00 To 12.00
Planter, Gondola 10.00
Planter, Goose Cart 10.00
Planter, Green, Birds On Nest, 4 X 6 In. 6.00
Planter, Minstrel 20.00
Planter, Parrot, Marked, Blue Green, 7 1/2 In. 4.00
Planter, Pelican 10.00
Planter, Spinning Wheel 12.00
Planter, Swan, White, 7 In. 12.00
Planter, Tulips, Attached Saucer, 4 In. 6.00
Planter, Wishing Well, With Chain, Brown & Green, Marked 8.50
Stein, Dated December, 1964 .... 15.00
Stein, Schlitz 25.00
Sugar & Creamer, Pinecone .... 14.00 To 15.00
Tankard Set, Buccaneer, Blue Gray, 6 Mugs 85.00
Tankard, Green, 8 In. 45.00
Tea Set, Daisy, Pink & Green 25.00
Tea Set, Ivy, 3 Piece 25.00
Tea Set, Pinecone, 3 Piece 17.50
Teapot, Daisy, 1942 .... 15.00
Teapot, Gooseneck, Marked, 6 Cup Size 10.00

Teapot, Green	15.00
Teapot, Maroon, 6 Cup	10.00
Teapot, Pinecone, 1942	15.00
Umbrella Stand, Woodland, Green	350.00
Vase, Amaryllis & Leaves, Bottle Shaped, Green Ground, 4 In.	5.00
Vase, Brownish Green, 6 1/2 X 3 1/2 X 3 In.	5.00
Vase, Bud, Garden Club, Green	12.00
Vase, Bunch Of Grapes, Green, Brown, & Beige, 9 1/2 In.	25.00
Vase, Chrysanthemum, Lavender, 8 In.	18.00
Vase, Dark Green, Footed	4.75
Vase, Double Tulip, 8 In.	12.00
Vase, Fluted Center, Handles, Scroll Ending In Dots, 7 X 9 In.	35.00
Vase, Iris, Yellow, Brown Glaze, 7 In.	75.00
Vase, Lily, Yellow	18.00
Vase, Navarre, 6 1/2 In.	185.00
Vase, Salmon Pink, Ribbed, Flared Top, Square Handled, 9 In.	8.00
Wall Pocket, Banana	6.00
Wall Pocket, Cuckoo Clock	19.00
Wall Pocket, Flower	6.00
Wall Pocket, Grapes	6.00
Wall Pocket, Pear	6.00
Wall Pocket, Umbrella Shape	18.00

PRESCUT

The McKee name has been associated with various glass enterprises in the U.S. since 1836, including J. & F. McKee (1850), Bryce, McKee & Co. (1850-1854), McKee and Brothers (1865), and National Glass Co. (1899). In 1903 the McKee Glass Company was formed in Jeanette, Pennsylvania. It became McKee Division of the Thatcher Glass Co. in 1951, and was bought out by the Jeanette Corporation in 1961. Pressed glass, kitchenware, and tableware were produced.

MC KEE, Bowl, Autumn, Jade	20.00
Bowl, Coach, Blue Cane Design, 1886	65.00
Reamer, Custard	30.00
MECHANICAL BANK, see Bank, Mechanical	
MEDICAL, Bag, Leather	11.50
Bellows, Dental, Leather, Foot Operated	45.00
Bleeder, Case Marked Chas.Lentz, Philadelphia, 2 1/4 In.	90.00
Bleeder, Horn Handle, 2 Blades, Arnold, Smithfield, London	85.00
Bleeder, Single Blade, Folding Brass Case, Revolutionary War	45.00
Bleeder, 3 Blades, Brass	50.00
Bottle, 3 Spout, Hand Blown	18.50
Box, Dental, Gold Crown Making, Oak	200.00
Cabinet, Instrument, Plate Glass Back, Door, Sides, Iron	475.00
Cabinet, Labels, 70 Tin Drawers, Oak, 19 X 17 1/4 In.	425.00
Cabinet, 3 Shelves & Drawers, Oak, 5 Ft.	700.00
Chair, Dental, Ritter, 1921	500.00
Chair, Doctor's, Tole Painting, Iron Base, Carved, Oak	700.00
Chair, Gynecological Examining	300.00
Eyecup, John Bull, 1917	9.00
Feeder, Invalid, Floral On Porcelain	25.00
Forceps, T.Hawksley, London, Chrome Plated Metal, Wood Handles	30.00
Knife, Bleeder, Veterinarian's, Spring-Loaded Blade, Case	90.00
Lens, Trial, Walnut Slant Front Case, Extras In Drawer	875.00
Magneto Electric Machine, Walnut Box, Brass Works, Pat.4-18-1854	85.00
Mallet, Fleam, Solid Ebony, 8 1/2 X 1 1/2 In.Diam.	65.00
Microscope, Bausch & Lomb, Patent 1915, Case, 5x & 10x, Large	280.00
Microscope, Henry Crouch, London, Dovetailed Wooden Box, Brass	165.00
Saw, Orthopedic Surgeon's, Civil War, Ebony Handle, Steel Blade	45.00
Scapel, Surgeon's, Oval Bone Handle, Steel Blade, Civil War, English	25.00
Surgical Kit, Indian Wars Period, Patent Leather Pouch, 8 Tools	60.00

Syringe Kit, Stamped 1915, Broad Arrow, British Military, Needles 65.00
Syringe, Parke Davis, Dated 1901, Case, Oval 11.00
Table Mortician's, Folding, Dated 1886 .... 165.00
Tool, Dentist, Mother-Of-Pearl Handle, Gold Band 20.00
Trumpet, Ear, Brass Overlaid With Shiny Black Finish 65.00

Meerschaum pipes and other carved pieces of meerschaum date from the nineteenth century to the present time.

MEERSCHAUM, Figurine, Guardian Angel, Holding Lute, 5 1/2 In. 150.00
Holder, Cigar, Carved Bulldog On Top Of Case 75.00
Holder, Cigar, Carved Full-Size Lady, Case, Amber 48.00
Holder, Cigar, Carved Hand Holding Egg 10.00
Holder, Cigar, Carved Horses, Valvet Case, Amber 48.00
Holder, Cigar, Carved, Original Box 40.00
Holder, Cigar, Cheroot, Carved Labrador Retriever, Case 60.00
Holder, Cigarette, Seated Woman With Wings, 5 X 2 1/2 In. 160.00
Pipe, Bacchus Head, Coverd With Grapes & Vines, 19 In. 250.00
Pipe, Buxom Lady, Case, 3 1/2 In. 60.00
Pipe, Carved Elk In Front Of Bowl, Amber Stem, Case, 10 In. 500.00
Pipe, Carved Horned Goat, Case 85.00
Pipe, Carved Skull Bowl, Case 85.00
Pipe, Claw Foot, Amber Stem, Case 125.00
Pipe, Dragon Claw, Carved 175.00
Pipe, Eagle Claw Holding Bowl, Yellow Stem, Velvet Case 125.00
Pipe, Horse, Leather Case, 5 1/4 In. 80.00
Pipe, Horses Around Flower, Amber Stem, Case, 19th Century, 7 In. 125.00
Pipe, Lion's Head, 7 X 2 1/2 In. 175.00
Pipe, Nude Girl, Legs Wrapped Around Bowl, 6 In. 350.00
Pipe, Nude Lady, Arms Folded Over Head, Flower Bowl 175.00
Pipe, Stallion, Back Biting Action, Amber Stem, 3 3/4 In. 110.00
Pipe, 2 Fighting Stallions, Miniature 95.00

Meissen is a town in Germany where porcelain has been made since 1710. Any china made in that town can be called Meissen, although the famous Meissen factory made the finest porcelains of the area.

MEISSEN, see also Dresden; Onion
MEISSEN, Basket, Applied Flowers, Marcolini Mark, 11 X 7 X 7 In. 500.00
Basket, Pedestal, Reticulated, Crossed Swords Mark, 8 1/4 In. 250.00
Bottle, Scent, Double-Gourd, Panels, Crossed Swords, 4 1/4 In. 300.00
Bowl, Bowl, Cobalt Ground, Floral Relief, Signed, Marked, 12 In. 359.00
Bowl, Courtship Scene, Polychrome Sprays, 11 In.Diam. 175.00
Bowl, Deep Pink Ground, Gold Baroque Design, C.1860, 12 In. 329.00
Bowl, Gold & Ivory Garland, Blue Ground, Crossed Swords, 12 In. 295.00
Bowl, Gold Design, Blue Crossed Swords, Pink, C.1860, 12 1/4 In. 330.00
Bowl, Gold Floral Relief, Cobalt Ground, Sword Mark, Signed, 12 In. 359.00
Bowl, Hand-Painted Flower Groups Allover, Gold Edge, Square, 9 In. 60.00
Bowl, Hausmaler, Marked, C.1740, 6 1/4 In. 2000.00
Bust, Maiden, Claret Bodice, Lace Collar, Blue Mark, 13 In. 950.00
Cachepot, Applied Flowers, Pastoral Scene 165.00
Caddy, Tea, White With Roses, Crossed Swords 99.50
Cane Handle, Painted Equestrian Battle Scene, C.1745, 2 3/4 In. 1320.00
Charger, Blue & White, Pegasus, Marked, 16 In. 800.00
Charger, Gold Trim, White Ground, Crossed Swords, 11 In. 295.00
Charger, Vermilion Ground, White Center, Crossed Swords, 11 In. 195.00
Chocolate Pot, Scattered Flowers, White, Crossed Swords, 9 1/2 In. 95.00
Compote, Gold Tracery, Floral Design, Meissen Incised, 7 In. 210.00
Cracker Jar, Gold Scrolls & Flowers, White Ground, 7 In. 100.00
Cup & Saucer, Demitasse, Lozenge Shape, Crossed Swords, Set Of 12 .... 1500.00
Cup & Saucer, Gold Relief, Leaf Edge, 19th Century 145.00
Cup, Coffee, Painted Reserves, Gilt & Floral, Pair 65.00
Cup, Feeding, Blue & White, Gilt, 6 In. 37.50

Dish, Nut, Shell-Shaped, Gold Edge, Roses, Crossed Swords	50.00
Dish, Oyster Shell, Blue Floral, Crossed Swords Mark, 4 X 5 In.	95.00
Dish, Pierced Handles, Flowers, Square, 16 X 16 In.	225.00
Figurine, Allegorical, Envy, Crossed Swords Mark, 5 3/4 In.	325.00
Figurine, Aurochs, C.1761, Spotted Coat, Gray Hooves, 5 1/2 In.	600.00
Figurine, Ballet Dance	175.00
Figurine, Boy With Wings On Horse, Girl, Riding Stick, Marked, Fair	500.00
Figurine, Boy, Turkish, Red Cap, Blue Pants, Tree Stump, 4 In.	800.00
Figurine, Child, Dressed As A Miner, Yellow, Gray Hat, 5 In.	800.00
Figurine, Child, Dressed As Miner, C.1760, Crossed Swords, 5 1/2 In.	800.00
Figurine, Colonial Gentleman, Crossed Swords Mark, 6 1/2 In.	495.00
Figurine, Couple, Dancing, Blue Dress, Pink Jacket, Marked, 6 In.	600.00
Figurine, Cupid Sharpening Arrows, C.1850, Crossed Swords, 7 In.	495.00
Figurine, Cupid, Offering Heart, Crossed Swords, 7 1/4 In.	750.00
Figurine, Cupid, Seated On Draped Base, 19th Century, Marked, 7 In.	550.00
Figurine, Farmer, C.1740, By Tree Trunk, Crossed Swords, 4 1/4 In.	1100.00
Figurine, Girl, Holding Toy Lamb, Crossed Swords, 6 1/4 In.	950.00
Figurine, Girl, Kneeling, Yellow Cap, White Skirt, Tan Apron, 4 In.	150.00
Figurine, Harlequin With Tankard, C.1900, Crossed Swords, 10 3/4 In.	800.00
Figurine, Harlequin, Brown Mask, Crossed Swords, 5 3/4 In.	375.00
Figurine, Harlequin, Playing Bagpipes, C.1745, 5 5/8 In.	950.00
Figurine, Huntsmen, Stages Of Hunt, Crossed Swords, 3 In., Set Of 12	1800.00
Figurine, Lady In Lace On Love Seat, Signed	75.00
Figurine, Maiden, Barefoot, Grapes In Hand, Crossed Swords, 5 In.	195.00
Figurine, Maiden, Lifted Skirt, Spider On Derriere, Marked, 8 In.	375.00
Figurine, Mandarin Boy, Nodding, Puce Cap, Green Leaf Hat, 9 In.	1800.00
Figurine, Musician, Strumming Lute, Crossed Swords	450.00
Figurine, Organ-Grinder, Crossed Swords Mark, 5 3/4 In.	325.00
Figurine, Owl, White, Blue Crossed Swords Mark, 6 In.	75.00
Figurine, Penguin, Blue Crossed Swords Mark, 6 3/4 In.	115.00
Figurine, Philomele, Marked, 17 In.	955.00
Figurine, Plump Girl, Basket, Flowers, Marked, 5 In.	295.00
Figurine, Rustic Lovers, Crossed Swords Mark, 5 1/8 In.	650.00
Figurine, Shepherd, Lamb & Woman Under Tree, Sword Mark, 10 In.	850.00
Figurine, Strolling Musican, Blue, 19th Century	650.00
Figurine, Swan, 7 3/4 In.	300.00
Figurine, The Beggar Boy, C.1890, 7 1/2 In.	575.00
Figurine, Turkish Boy, C.1760, Crossed Swords Mark, 4 3/4 In.	800.00
Flatware Handle, Set Of 22	*Illus* 325.00
Group, Love Flaming Eternally, Allegorical, Crossed Swords, 9 In.	1000.00
Group, Maiden & Her Lap Dog, Crossed Swords, 5 7/8 In.	600.00
Handle, C.1900, Cobalt Blue, Set Of 17	*Illus* 175.00
Handle, Cane, Equestrian Battle Scene, Yellow Banding, 2 In.	1320.00
Handle, Flatware, Pistol-Shaped, Blue Onion, Set Of 12	*Illus* 900.00
Handle, Flatware, Set Of 24	*Illus* 500.00
Knife & Spoon, Pistol-Shaped Handle, C.1900, Set Of 15	*Illus* 225.00
Knife Handle, C.1900, Set Of 6	*Illus* 250.00
Mirror, Dressing, Putti & Flowers, 19th Century, 15 In.	150.00
Pitcher, European Scene, Gilt Ground, Porcelain, 8 7/8 In.	275.00
Plaque, The Sistine Madonna, Virgin, Child, Host, , Marked, 11 In.	1200.00
Plate, Bird, Blossom, 18th Century, Marked, 8 3/4 In.	550.00
Plate, Blossoms & Fences, Central Flower, Blue, C.1730, 13 1/4 In.	1650.00
Plate, Game, Fish, 9 1/2 In.	45.00
Plate, Hand-Painted Flower Center, Scalloped Gold Rim, 9 In.	40.00
Plate, Ivory & Gold, Cobalt, Enameled, Blue Swords Mark, 9 In.	169.00
Plate, Leaves & Florals In Relief, Gold On White, 10 1/2 In.	145.00
Plate, Maiden Pouring Water, Gilded, Crossed Swords, 9 1/8 In.	900.00
Plate, Red Tiger Pattern, 19th Century, Marked, 9 1/2 In.	165.00
Plate, Soup, Hand-Painted Florals, Crossed Swords, Pair	45.00
Plate, Watteauesque Scene, Pink, Gold Scroll, Marked, 10 1/4 In.	850.00
Platter, Crossed Swords Mark, Pierced Insert, 10 1/4 X 22 1/4 In.	300.00
Platter, Flowers, C.1900, 20 In.	1400.00
Platter, Rose Design, Plain Edge, Marked, 16 1/4 In.	50.00

Meissen, Cutlery and Flatware Handles, C. 1900

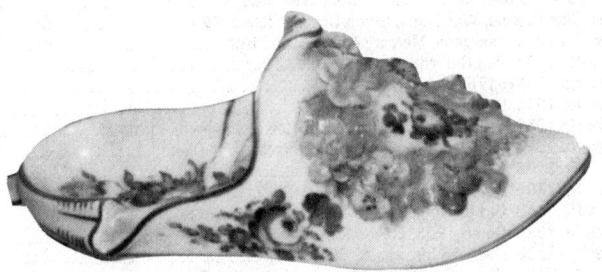

Meissen, Slipper, Hand-Painted & Gilded, Crossed Swords Mark

Salt, Flowers, Painted Bugs, 3-Cornered, Crossed Swords, 1 1/2 In. 150.00
Slipper, Hand-Painted & Gilded, Crossed Swords Mark ....*Illus* 45.00
Tea Caddy, White, Roses, Crossed Swords, 5 1/4 In. 99.50
Tea Set, Floral Design, White Ground, Pot 10 1/2 In., 3 Piece 600.00
Tureen, Vegetable, Floral Design, Blue, Gold Trim, 10 In. 300.00
Urn, Snake Handles, Cobalt Blue & Gold, 16 In. 2500.00
Urn, Stand, Acorn Finial, Shepherd, Cupid, & Maiden, 16 In. 175.00
Vase, Campana For, Serpent Handles, Covered, C.1900, 24 1/4 In., Pair 1100.00
Vase, Garden Scene, Applied Putti, Crossed Swords, 18 3/4 In., Pair 5000.00
Vase, Gilt Details, Crossed Swords, 19 5/8 In. 400.00
Vase, Top & Bottom Gold Rim, Rose & Bud, Crossed Swords, 10 In. 50.00
Vase, Watteau Painting, Blue Crossed Swords, 4 In. 495.00

Mercury, or silvered, glass was first made in the 1850s. It lost favor for a while but became popular again about 1910. It looks like a piece of silver.

MERCURY GLASS, Candlestick, 6 1/2 In., Pair	75.00
Dish, Candy, Etched, Covered, 7 In.	85.00
Goblet, Engraved Grapes & Leaves, Seal, 7 1/2 In.	135.00
Rose Bowl	25.00
Salt, 6-Footed	15.00
Spooner, Vintage Pattern	60.00
Tieback, Embossed Floral, Pewter Shank, 3 1/2 In.Diam., Pair	55.00
Toothpick	15.00
Vase, Gold, 9 In.	38.00

Mettlach, Germany, is a city where the Villeroy and Boch factories worked. Steins from the firm are known as Mettlach steins. They date from about 1842. PUG means painted under glaze.

METTLACH, Bowl & Underplate, Raised Leaves, Green & Brown, White Ground	120.00
Bowl, Octagonal Shape, Signed, 5 1/2 X 3 1/2 In.	250.00
Charger, No.1382, Strolling Knight, Castle Mark, 14 1/2 In.	550.00
Charger, No.1425, Bust Of Lady	475.00
Charger, No.2805, Standing Deer In Forest, Marked, 15 1/8 In.	300.00
Flagon, Gray, Blue, Vegetables, Domed, No.2076, 10 5/8 In.	275.00
Mug, Barrel Shape, Drink Hires Root Beer, Picture Of Hires Boy	120.00
Pitcher, Green Leaves, Brown Branches, Twig Handle, 8 1/2 In.	255.00
Pitcher, No.171, Dancing Figures, Marked, 15 1/8 In.	250.00
Pitcher, No.1169, Famous German Busts, Marked, 14 3/4 In.	250.00
Pitcher, No.2085, Border Of Trophies, Marked, 15 5/8 In.	250.00
Pitcher, No.2107, 2 Liter, King Gambremus, 1895, Castle Mark	800.00
Pitcher, No.2210, White Figures, Terra-Cotta Body, Gargoyle Lip	950.00
Planter, Birds, Brown Ground, Gold Trim, Castle Mark, 4 X 9 In.	325.00
Plaque, Blue Ground, War Ships, Green Ocean, Signed, 12 In.	180.00
Plaque, No.426a, Seascape, Mercury Mark, 15 In.Diam.	220.00
Plaque, No.1003, Pug Girl With Cockatoo, 8 1/2 In.	166.00
Plaque, No.1044/5176, Blue Castle Scene	275.00
Plaque, No.1044/5177, Blue Castle Scene	275.00
Plaque, No.1652, Maiden Carrying Basket Of Flowers, Signed, 11 In.	695.00
Plaque, No.2041, Man, Woman, & Jumping Horses, 15 In.Diam.	750.00
Plaque, No.2196, Castle, 13 1/4 In.	1150.00
Plaque, No.2305, Boat Scene, Matte Finish, 10 In.	110.00
Plaque, No.2542, Girl In Profile, Castle Mark, 15 1/2 In.	900.00
Plaque, No.2626, Dated 1903, Etched, Castle Mark, 7 3/4 In.	300.00
Plaque, No.2805, Deer, 16 In.	595.00
Plaque, No.3131, Ducks On Stream, Mercury Mark, 11 1/2 In.	170.00
Plaque, No.5041, Man With The Flute, Signed, 12 In.	165.00
Plaque, No.7071, Blue, Signed, 7 3/4 X 5 7/8 In.	375.00
Plaque, No.7071, White On Blue, 5 7/8 X 7 3/4 In.	450.00
Plaque, No.7072, Cameo, 8 X 8 In.	895.00
Plate, No.3096, Beige, Navy Blue Design, Hexagonal, 7 In.	50.00
Plate, Octagonal, Signed, 6 3/4 In.Diam., Pair	200.00
Punch Bowl, No.2087, Underplate, 16 In.Diam.	175.00
Punch Bowl, No.2234, Grapes, Birds, Dwarf Knob, Cover, 15 1/2 In.	500.00
Stein, 1/4 Liter, Sad Radish	300.00
Stein, 4/10 Liter, Bartholomay's, Rochester, 5 1/2 In.	110.00
Stein, 1/2 Liter, Rich Man, Salt Glaze	235.00
Stein, 1/2 Liter, World War I Machine Gun, Dated 1920	335.00
Stein, 1/2 Liter, World War II Machine Gun	375.00
Stein, No.6, 3 Liter, Raised Figure, Man With Scales	550.00
Stein, No.6, 6 Liter, Justice With Scales, Noah, Relief	550.00
Stein, No.24, 1 Liter, Old Man In Panels, Verse	375.00
Stein, No.171, 1/4 Liter, Fine Raised Figures, White & Blue	210.00
Stein, No.675, 1/2 Liter, Barrel, Inlaid Lid, Brown, Tan	160.00 To 175.00

Stein, No.1005, 1 Liter, White Relief Figures In 3 Panels 375.00
Stein, No.1028, 1/2 Liter, Woman Holding Bundle Of Hops 225.00
Stein, No.1184, 1/4 Liter, Pedestal Base, Scrolled 195.00
Stein, No.1370, 1/2 Liter, Raised Figures Ad Motto 295.00
Stein, No.1370, 1/2 Liter, Raised Figures, Motto 295.00
Stein, No.1395, 1/2 Liter, Cards, Etched 430.00
Stein, No.1403, 1/2 Liter, Tavern Scene With Bowling .... 495.00 To 550.00
Stein, No.1476, 1/2 Liter, Dwarfs, Etched 465.00
Stein, No.1526/588, 1/2 Liter, Maiden In Oval Panel, PUG 175.00
Stein, No.1526/589, Drinking Scene, PUG 175.00
Stein, No.1526, 1/2 Liter, Plain Beige 100.00
Stein, No.1527, 1 Liter, Inlaid Lid, Knights Drinking, Etched 600.00
Stein, No.1530, 1/2 Liter, Man Smoking Pipe, Etched 100.00
Stein, No.1786, 1/2 Liter, St.Florian, Mercury Mark, Etched 800.00
Stein, No.1789, 1/2 Liter, Mosaic, Geometric Flowers 340.00
Stein, No.1796, 1/2 Liter, Musketeer, Etched 650.00
Stein, No.1863, 1/2 Liter, Stuttgart, Village Scene, Etched 480.00
Stein, No.1909-727, 3/10 Liter, 3 Bowling Scenes, False Bottom 195.00
Stein, No.1914, 1/2 Liter, 4-F, Athletic Scenes 625.00
Stein, No.1932, 1/2 Liter, Cavaliers .... 300.00 To 450.00
Stein, No.2001, Lawyer 450.00
Stein, No.2001, 1/2 Liter, Book, Architect 500.00
Stein, No.2012, 1/4 Liter, State Shield, Mosaic 450.00
Stein, No.2024, 1/2 Liter, Berlin, View Of City, Glazed .... 500.00 To 600.00
Stein, No.2025, 3/10 Liter, Nude Cherubs, Etched 300.00
Stein, No.2050, 1/2 Liter, Man, Maid, Castle Mark 500.00
Stein, No.2182, 1/2 Liter, Bowling, Figures In Relief, Castle Mark 245.00
Stein, No.2184, 1/2 Liter, Elves, Scrolls In Relief 275.00
Stein, No.2184, 3/10 Liter, Elves, Scrolls In Relief 195.00
Stein, No.2231, 1/2 Liter, Knights & Cavaliers Drinking, Etched 550.00
Stein, No.2285, 1/2 Liter, Lovers, Inlaid Lid, Etched 485.00
Stein, No.2324, 1/2 Liter, Football Game, Etched 800.00
Stein, No.2363, 1/2 Liter, Egyptian Drinking Scene 200.00
Stein, No.2373, 1/2 Liter, St.Augustine, Florida .... 485.00 To 650.00
Stein, No.2382, 1/2 Liter, Thirsty Rider, Etched .... 550.00 To 685.00
Stein, No.2394, 1/2 Liter, Siegfried, Etched 575.00
Stein, No.2419, 5 Liter, Courtroom Scene, PUG 800.00
Stein, No.2440, 1/2 Liter, Ten Girls In Relief 500.00
Stein, No.2557, 1/2 Liter, Men, Cards In Relief 425.00
Stein, No.2631, 3 Liter, Running Man Chasing Animal 1600.00
Stein, No.2632, 1/2 Liter, Bowling, Etched 265.00
Stein, No.2652, 1/4 Liter, Three Scenes, Men In Sailboat 675.00
Stein, No.2754/6129, 3 Liter, Pewter Lid, Three Panels 495.00
Stein, No.2796, 3 Liter, Heidelburg Scene, Etched, Inlaid Lid 1600.00
Stein, No.2809, 1/2 Liter, Giant With Children In Forest, Etched 485.00
Stein, No.2823, 1 Liter, Bavarian Girl With Gun, Etched 475.00
Stein, No.2829, Castle Top, Houses, Towns, 1 Liter, C.1905 .... 375.00
Stein, No.2830, 1/2 Liter, Bavarian Girl In Mountains, Etched 415.00
Stein, No.2832, 1/2 Liter, Girl In Window, Etched 425.00
Stein, No.2893/1197, 3 Liter, German Eagle, Crown, State Shields 180.00
Stein, No.2921, 3 Liter, Hunters With Steins By Fire 1150.00
Stein, No.2931, 1/2 Liter, Hunter Taking Stein From A Maiden 350.00
Stein, No.2958, 3 Liter, Boy Bowling, Etched 985.00
Stein, No.2959, 1 Liter, Boy Bowling, Etched .... 675.00 To 750.00
Stein, No.3136, 1 Liter, American Eagle, Wreath, Etched Geometric 600.00
Tile, Rosy Finch, Bittersweet Branch, Brass Footed 45.00
Tumbler, No.2327, Boy & Duck 50.00
Vase, Applied Florets, Etched, Incised Mark, 7 In., Pair 429.00
Vase, Cameos On Blue Ground, Perforated Handles, Signed, 10 In. 210.00
Vase, Diana Pouring Water, Stars, Marked, 13 In., Pair 300.00
Vase, Elephant Trunk, 14 In. 800.00
Vase, Etched, Castle Mark, C.1899, 13 In. 400.00
Vase, No.1749, Girls, Dated 1912, 12 3/4 In. 600.00

Vase, No.2435, Flower Design, Marked, Gray & Dark Blue, 6 X 4 In. 150.00
Vase, Strawberries, Flowers, & Birds, Castle Mark, 12 1/2 In., Pair 650.00
    MICKEY MOUSE, see Disneyana

Milk glass was named for its milky white color. It was first made in England during the 1700s. The height of its popularity in the United States was from 1870 to 1880. It is now correct to refer to some colored glass as blue milk glass, black milk glass, etc. The letter B before the numbers xx refers to the book "Milk Glass" by E. Belknap. The letter F before the numbers xx refers to the book "Yesterday's Milk Glass Today" by Regis F. and Mary F. Ferson.

    MILK GLASS, see also Cambridge; Cosmos

MILK GLASS, Banana Stand, Openwork, Triple Stem 42.00
Basket, Open Rope Handle, Blue, 4 X 5 1/4 In.Diam. 14.00
Bathtub, Souvenir, Atwood, Kansas 24.50
Berry Set, Openwork Rim, Chrysanthemum Pattern 75.00
Boot, Cowboy, Black 28.00
Boot, With Spur 30.00
Bottle, Actress 30.00
Bottle, Barber, Osiris Dandruff Cure, Cartoon Of Bird 145.00
Bottle, Hand-Painted Pansies, Gold Trim, Stopper, White, 10 In. 25.00
Bowl, Arch Border, 8 1/2 In.Diam. 30.00
Bowl, Atterbury, Apple Blossoms 85.00
Bowl, Atterbury, Crinkled Lacy Edge 28.50
Bowl, Banana 20.00
Bowl, Brown & Yellow Ground, Pink Blossoms 25.00
Bowl, Daisy & Tree Of Life, Round, B-106c, 8 In. 30.00
Bowl, Honey, Beehive, Pink, Figural 9.00
Bowl, Scroll & Eye, 9 In. 55.00
Bowl, Seashell Pattern, Gold Trim, 3-Toed, 9 In. 95.00
Box, Fluted, Woolly Lamb Lid, Black, 5 1/2 X 3 3/4 In. 22.00
Box, Love Laughs At Looks, Heart Shaped 15.00
Butter, Coreopsis, Green Band, Covered, White 67.50
Butter, Crossed Ferns, Ball & Claw Feet, Covered 25.00
Butter, Flattened Diamond & Sunburst, Covered 12.00
Butter, Purple Slag, Covered, 8 X 9 In., B-293 .... 180.00
Cake Stand, Hand-Painted Wild Roses 35.00
Candleholder, Black, 9 In., Pair 22.00
Candleholder, Crucifix 40.00
Candleholder, Daisy & Button, 2-Light, Pair 20.00
Canoe, Souvenir, Rockland, Me. 10.00
Celery, Jeweled, Purple Slag, B-295b 105.00
Celery, Purple Slag, Fluted, B-295a 90.00
Compote, Atlas, Green, Open Edge, F-385 .... 250.00
Compote, Atlas, Lacy Edge, 8 1/2 X 9 In.Diam. 98.00
Compote, Atlas, Open Edge, F-385 .... 125.00
Compote, Atlas, Open, Bearded Man 68.00
Compote, Atterbury, Crimped Edge, Open 22.00
Compote, Green, Scroll, F-383 .... 175.00
Compote, Hobnail, Pink, 5 1/2 In. 25.00
Compote, Jenny Lind, Flint 95.00
Compote, Lattice Edge 38.00
Compote, Loop, Sandwich Glass, 8 X 4 3/4 In. 95.00
Compote, Raindrop Pattern, Italian Blue, 5 1/2 X 8 In. 65.00
Compote, Scroll, F-383 .... 100.00
Compote, Scroll, Hexagonal, 8 X 8 In. 48.00
Compote, Thousand Eye, F-292 .... 70.00
Condiment Set, Cosmos 325.00
Cornucopia, Pink, 5 In. 20.00
Cracker Jar, Roses, Draping, Covered 30.00
Creamer, Block Pattern, Blue, 3 In. 21.00
Creamer, Cosmos, Applied Handle, Pastel Colors, White 125.00
Creamer, Feather, Covered, Blue 26.00

Creamer, Figural, Owl, Blue, 3 1/2 In.	35.00
Creamer, Flattened Diamond & Sunburst	10.00
Creamer, Little Boy, F-267	160.00
Creamer, Owl, Block Pattern, Blue, 3 In.	21.00
Creamer, Owl, 3 1/2 In., B-91	38.00
Cruet, Grape Design, Blown	25.00
Cup & Saucer, Beaded Edge Saucer, C.1942	6.00
Cup, Fleur-De-Lis & Drape, 2 3/4 In.	15.00
Dish, Bird Cover, Sleigh	25.00
Dish, Blue Hen Cover	150.00
Dish, Blue Hen Cover, Signed Vallerysthal	75.00
Dish, Blue Hen Cover, White Lacy Base	150.00
Dish, Blue Setter Dog Cover, Signed Vallerysthal	135.00
Dish, Boar's Head Cover, Dated, F-332	700.00
Dish, Candy, Seashell Pattern, Gold Trim, Footed, Covered, Label	75.00
Dish, Chick & Egg Cover	65.00
Dish, Chick & Eggs Cover, Eyes, Dated, B-141	135.00
Dish, Chick Emerging From Egg Cover, Sleigh Base	50.00
Dish, Chick In Egg On Sleigh, Covered	45.00
Dish, Chicks On Round Basket, B-1426	45.00
Dish, Closed Neck Swan Cover, Basket Base	35.00
Dish, Dog Cover, B-174d	35.00
Dish, Dog Cover, McKee Signed, F-71	175.00
Dish, Dove Cover, McKee, Signed, F-61	250.00
Dish, Duck Cover, Atterbury, All White, Dated, F-46	125.00
Dish, Duck Cover, Atterbury, Amethyst Head, Dated, F-4	225.00
Dish, Duck Cover, Atterbury, Blue, Dated, F-82	500.00
Dish, Duck Cover, Atterbury, Dated, No Eyes, Blue	500.00
Dish, Duck Cover, Atterbury, Dated, No Eyes, White	125.00
Dish, Duck Cover, Wave Base, Blue, 8 1/2 In.	26.00
Dish, Eagle On Nest Cover, 3 Eggs	60.00
Dish, Entwined Fish Cover, Dated Lacy Base	150.00
Dish, Fish Cover, Atterbury	165.00
Dish, Fish Cover, Entwined, Dated, F-51	125.00
Dish, Fox Cover, Lacy Base, Dated	100.00
Dish, Hand & Dove Cover, Dated, F-52	125.00
Dish, Hand & Dove Cover, Lace, Dated Base	150.00
Dish, Hen Cover, American, F-567	45.00
Dish, Hen Cover, Black Eyes	42.00
Dish, Hen Cover, Blue Marble, F-8	150.00
Dish, Hen On Chick Base, Flaccus	145.00
Dish, Hen On Nest Cover, Miniature	8.00
Dish, Hen On Nest Cover, Vallerystahl, 2 1/2 In.	35.00
Dish, Hen With Chicks Cover, McKee, F-47-320	200.00
Dish, Lion Cover, Lacy Base, Dated	100.00
Dish, Lion Cover, Ribbed, Lacy, Dated, F-47	100.00
Dish, Moses In Bulrushes Cover	135.00
Dish, Pickle, Fish, Dated 1872	30.00
Dish, Pope Leon Cover	95.00
Dish, Rabbit Cover, Dated March 3, 1886, Blue, 9 In.	375.00
Dish, Rabbit Cover, Dated March 9, 1886, White	75.00
Dish, Reclining Camel Cover, Opalescent	150.00
Dish, Rectangular Handled, 6 X 11 In., M-228	80.00
Dish, Remember The Maine Cover, Green	50.00
Dish, Robin On Nest, B-157a	75.00
Dish, Robin On Nest, Eyes, B-157b	90.00
Dish, Sandwich, Pekingese, Covered	100.00
Dish, Soap, Blue	5.00
Dish, Swan Cover, McKee, F-59	175.00
Dish, Swan Cover, Raised Wing, Lacy Base, F-179	125.00
Dish, Turkey Cover, McKee, F-58	175.00
Dish, White Hen, Blue Head, Lacy Base, Eyes, B-146, 7 In.	75.00
Dish, Woolly Recumbent Dog Cover	50.00

Dish, Yellow Hen Cover, White Lacy Base	150.00
Dresser Bottle, Actress Pattern	55.00
Egg, Easter, Hand-Painted Yellow Chick, Turkey Size	30.00
Egg, Embossed Florals & Easter	15.00
Egg, Goose	10.00
Eggcup, Blackberry Design	85.00
Eggcup, Chicken Claw On Egg	26.00
Eggcup, Painted Chick	12.00
Eggcup, Swan At Base	10.00
Eggcup, Yellow Chick Coming Out Of Side	45.00
Epergne, 3 Bud, 10 In.Diam.	60.00
Epergne, 3-Lily, Pink	45.00
Figurine, Boar's Head, B-176	985.00
Figurine, Elephant With Mahout, French, Deep Blue	290.00
Figurine, Entwined Fish, B-163a	195.00
Figurine, Hand & Dove, B-163b	135.00
Figurine, Hen, Plated Sapphire Blue Head, B-146	175.00
Figurine, Owl, Atterbury	225.00
Figurine, Pekingese Dog, B-173b	190.00
Figurine, Steer's Head, RWL	1185.00
Fish Set, Fish Shape, Dated Patent June 4, 1872, 9 Piece	295.00
Globe, Poolroom, Pair	100.00
Goblet, Blackberry	45.00
Goblet, Block & Palm	35.00
Goblet, Circle	20.00
Goblet, Diamond, Blue	8.50
Goblet, Lacy Dewdrop	20.00
Goblet, Strawberry	30.00
Hat, Daisy & Button, 2 1/2 In.	6.50
Hat, Threaded, Blue	45.00
Hatpin Holder, Floral, Tree Trunk Shape	2.50
Honey Dish, Blackberry Design	45.00
Jar, Cabin, Westmoreland Mustard	65.00
Jar, Covered, Queen Victoria	90.00
Jar, Eagle, B-178a	110.00
Jar, Owl, B-182	145.00
Jar, Powder, Palmette Pattern, Octagonal, Lid, 3 X 3 1/2 In.	35.00
Lamp Base, Miniature, Embossed Painted Cosmos	45.00
Lamp Base, Miniature, Fleur-De-Lis Pattern	40.00
Lamp, Drape Pattern, Electric, Pair	110.00
Lamp, Molded Scallops, Stylized Floral Design, Red, 9 1/4 In.	50.00
Lamp, Swan Based, Blue, C.1869, 10 1/2 In.	300.00
Lamp, Versailles, Enamel, Pair	90.00
Lavabo, Hobnail	50.00
Match Holder, Hand & Fan	15.00
Match Holder, Purple Slag, B-297h	48.00
Mug, Bird On Nest, Purple Slag, B-298c	50.00
Mug, Bull & Elk, 2 In.	22.00
Mug, Heron & Peacock, Child's	45.00
Mug, Liberty Bell	175.00
Mug, Swan & Cattail	45.00
Mustard, Bull's Head	55.00 To 60.00
Napkin Ring, Atlas, Blue & Gold Design	15.00
Paperweight, Rabbit	12.00
Paperweight, Washington Monument, F-389	110.00
Pipe, Souvenir, Elmore, Minn.	24.50
Pitcher, Cream, Sawtooth Pattern	12.00
Pitcher, Dolphin	65.00
Pitcher, Owl, B-80, 7 1/2 In.	175.00
Pitcher, Syrup, Pewter Top, Poppies, Fishnet Ground, 7 In.	90.00
Pitcher, Water, Cosmos, B-83	250.00
Pitcher, Water, Guttate, Gold Rim & Handle	100.00
Plate, Black, Heart Border, 6 In.	10.00

Plate, Columbus, 1492-1892, 9 1/2 In.	45.00
Plate, Contrary Mule, Hand-Painted Border	25.00
Plate, Cupid's Head, Lacy Border, 9 1/2 In.	28.00
Plate, Easter, Chicks, Egg In Basket	30.00
Plate, Fruit Design, Westmoreland, 8 In.	5.00
Plate, Gothic & Chain Border	25.00
Plate, Gothic, Open Edge, White, 8 1/2 In.	17.50
Plate, Half-Pinwheel Pattern, 7 1/2 In.	45.00
Plate, Hearts & Anchors	30.00
Plate, Hen On Nest, Ribbed Base	45.00
Plate, Lattice Border, Apple Blossom Center, 10 1/2 In.	45.00
Plate, Leaf & Branch Border	35.00
Plate, Picture Of General Lee	15.00
Plate, Pinwheel, 7 1/4 In.	22.00
Plate, Serenade, 6 In.	35.00
Plate, Three Kittens, 7 In.	25.00
Plate, Tri S, Black, 8 1/2 In.	12.00
Plate, 13 Star, Washington Bicentennial, C.1932, Black	35.00
Platter, Retriever, B-53	130.00
Platter, Rock Of Ages, Clear Rim, F-569	140.00
Reamer, Sunkist	12.00
Reamer, Sunkist, Green	22.00
Relish, Blackberry	55.00
Rolling Pin, Painted Ship	38.00
Rolling Pin, Sailor's Farewell	48.00
Rolling Pin, White, 14 In.Long	75.00
Rolling Pin, Wooden Handles	38.00
Rooster, Standing, Covered, Large	18.00
Salt & Pepper, G.E.Refrigerator Shape	30.00 To 40.00
Salt & Pepper, Scroll, Green, Pair	40.00
Salt & Pepper, Shaker, Ribbed Design, 5 1/2 In.	20.00
Salt, Blackberry Design, Footed	65.00
Salt, Master, Purple Slag, Handled	40.00
Salt, Strawberry, Footed, Flint	20.00
Salt, Swan, Open, M-276	50.00
Saltshaker, Cosmos, Pink Band, 3 1/2 In.	40.00
Saltshaker, Grape, 4-Sided	20.00
Saltshaker, Guttate, Original Lid, Pink	45.00
Sauce, Blackberry	30.00
Shoe, Bow, Blue	25.00
Slipper, On Skates	32.00
Spooner, Blackberry Design	85.00
Spooner, Flattened Diamond & Sunburst	10.00
Spooner, Honeycomb	15.00
Spooner, Little Girl, F-270	130.00
Spooner, Paneled Daisy	25.00
Spooner, Sandwich Loop, F-266	75.00
Spooner, Wild Rose, Child's	25.00
Stein, Buttermilk, Serenade	25.00
Sugar & Creamer, Crown Top, Covered	22.00
Sugar & Creamer, Fruit Pattern, Flint	25.00
Sugar & Creamer, Strutting Peacock, Westmoreland, Blue	75.00
Sugar Shaker, Grape & Leaves, Original Top, Northwood	21.00
Sugar Shaker, Iris, Pastel Design	45.00
Sugar Shaker, Netted Oak	35.00
Sugar Shaker, Parian Swirl, Rose Design	30.00
Sugar Shaker, Scrolled Rib, Blue	35.00
Sugar, Blackberry Finial, Covered	40.00
Sugar, Covered, Lacy Edge, Marbleized Green	85.00
Sugar, Flattened Diamond & Sunburst	10.00
Sugar, Princess Feather, Covered, B-215	90.00
Sugar, Rose Leaf, Covered, Flint	69.00
Sugar, Swan Covered, Blue	50.00

Sugar, Wild Rose, 2-Handled, Open, Child's	50.00
Syrup, Catherine Anne	30.00
Syrup, Netted Ribbons	65.00
Syrup, Swan & Stork	80.00
Syrup, Washington Centennial	95.00
Syrup, Wild Iris, Design	45.00
Table Set, Roman Cross, 4 Piece	155.00
Table Set, Sawtooth, 4 Piece	175.00
Table Set, The Family, No Eyes, 5 Piece	650.00
Tankard, Scroll, B-78a	125.00
Tankard, Scroll, Green, B-78a	125.00
Toothpick, Horseshoe & Clover	20.00
Toothpick, Scrolled Shell, Enamel Design	28.00
Toothpick, Strawberry Pattern, Footed, Signed	17.00
Tray, Embossed Scrolls, Blue, 6 X 8 In.	18.00
Tray, Lady & Fan, Painted Red, Gold, & Blue	50.00
Tray, Leaf Shape, Stippled, 5 1/2 X 7 1/2 In.	14.00
Tray, Moses In The Bullrushes	45.00
Tumbler, Fruit Design, Footed, 5 In.	7.00
Tumbler, Louisiana Purchase Pattern	15.00
Tumbler, Scroll, Blue, F-48	35.00
Vase, Flared & Crimped Rim, Bulbous Base, 10 1/2 In.	38.00
Vase, Floral Design, Blue & Gold, 9 In.	25.00
Vase, Grape & Cable, 9 3/4 In.	25.00
Vase, Panels Of Oriental Figures, C.1880, Signed, Blue, 4 1/2 In.	45.00
Vase, 3-Mold Roses, 8 In.	25.00

*Millefiori means many flowers. It is a type of glasswork popular in
paperweights. Many small flowerlike pieces of glass are grouped
together to form a design.*

MILLEFIORI, see also Paperweight

MILLEFIORI, Cruet, Dark Canes, Applied Camphor Handle & Stopper	195.00
Cruet, Frosted Handle & Stopper, 8 In.	95.00
Cup & Saucer	35.00
Sugar Shaker, Original Top, 5 In.	72.50
Tumbler, Pastel Colors	95.00
Vase, Bulbous, Slender Neck, Crimped Ruffled Top, 8 In.	80.00

*Minton china has been made in the Staffordshire region of England
from 1793 to the present. Many marks have been used; the one shown
dates from c. 1873 to 1911.*

MINTON, Cadogan Pot, Floral & Fruit, Green, White, & Maroon	325.00
Candlestick, Floral Transfer Design, White Ground, 6 In., Pair	115.00
Coffeepot, Demitasse, 6 1/2 In.	45.00
Cup & Saucer, Demitasse, Indian Tree, Marked	35.00
Cup & Saucer, Impressed S, 1889	45.00
Ewer, Cherubs, Brown Branch Handle, 1864 Mark, 15 In.	325.00
Flask, Moon, Plum Ground, Chinese Design, Marked, 8 1/4 In.	100.00
Medallion, White, Blue Ground, Pate-Sur-Pate, Signed, 2 In., Set Of 3	390.00
Plate, Chinese Tree, 1843 Factory Mark, 7 In.	30.00
Plate, Hand-Painted, Seashells, Signed, 10 In.Diam., Pair	395.00
Plate, 2 Tiger Kittens, 1 With Rat In Mouth, C.1870, 7 In.	35.00
Salt, With Spoon, Gold Etched Interior	20.00
Seat, Garden, Pierced Round Top, Polychrome Floral, C.1870, 18 In., Pr.	175.00
Slop Jar, Trelliswork & Florets, Dated 1881, Liner, Cover, 11 In.	440.00
Tankard, Dancers On Stone Wall, C.1860, Majolica & Pewter, 13 In.	105.00
Teapot, Floral, C.1864	80.00
Tile, Crown Transfer, Goat In Mountain Scene, C., 1873, 6 In.	35.00
Tile, Goats In Mountain, Brown Transfer, C.1873, Framed, 6 In.Square	35.00
Tile, Victoria Jubilee, 1897	35.00

Urn, Painted Birds & Flowers, Gilded Handles, 7 1/2 In., Pair 100.00
Urn, Scrolled Handles, Chinoiserie Design, Marked, 22 In. 60.00
Vase, Arts & Crafts Design, Dated 1909, Pottery, Blue & Purple 95.00
Vase, Butterflies, Grapes, Blue Ground, Marked, 57 In., Pair 9500.00
Vase, Classical Maiden & Cupid, 1913, Signed, Covered, 13 3/8 In., Pair 2250.00
Vase, Earthenware, Burgundy, Olive Green, Cream Design, 9 In. 70.00
Vase, Floral & Fruit Panels, Blue Ground, Bird Knob, 13 In., Pair 3750.00
Vase, Gold Insects, Blue Floral, Gold & Rust Design, Marked, 7 In. 150.00
Vase, Polychrome Neck, 1872, Signed L.Solon, 13 1/4 In. 2500.00
Vase, Trophy-Shape, Pink Ground, Floral Medallion, 10 In. 565.00
Vase, 3 Monkey's Heads Ring Vase, Poppy Leaves, C.1965, 12 In. 250.00
      MIRROR, see Furniture, Mirror

> *Mocha ware is an English-made product that was sold in America during*
> *the early 1800s. It is a heavy pottery with pale coffee and cream*
> *coloring. Designs of blue, brown, green, orange, or black or white*
> *were added to the pottery.*

MOCHA, Beaker, Sienna, White, Green Incised Top Band, 4 In. 230.00
  Beaker, Vellum, Brown, Mustard, Green Incised Top & Bottom Band, 2 In. 330.00
  Bowl, Banded, Mustard, Brown, White Bands, Seaweed, 5 1/2 In.Diam. 320.00
  Bowl, Blue, Ocher & White Bands, 2 3/4 In. 95.00
  Bowl, Brown, Beige, White, Greentop Band, 2 1/2 In. 280.00
  Bowl, Covered, Earthworm, Tan & Yellow Ground, 13 1/8 X 6 In.Diam. 325.00
  Bowl, Dark Mustard Band, Seaweed, Brown Band, Blue Band, 2 3/4 In. 190.00
  Bowl, Earthworm, Light Tan, Yellow Ground, Covered, 5 1/4 In. 325.00
  Bowl, Leaf, Mustard, Brown Top Band, 6 In. 950.00
  Bowl, Mixing, Yellowware, Blue Feathering Seaplants On Band, 11 1/2 In 90.00
  Bowl, Mustard Band, Seaweed, White & Brown Band, Green Incised Top 190.00
  Bowl, Seaweed, Gray Band, Black & White Band Bottom, 3 In. 150.00
  Bowl, Seaweed, Green, 14 In.Diam. 135.00
  Bowl, Seaweed, Mustard, Blue Band, Green Band Top, 6 In.Diam. 210.00
  Bowl, Seaweed, Terra-Cotta Band, Brown Stripes, Cream, 5 1/2 In.Diam. 215.00
  Bowl, Seaweed, White & Mustard Band, Green Top, 7 In. 200.00
  Cup & Saucer, Demitasse, Marbleized Swirl 390.00
  Cup & Saucer, Demitasse, Speckled, Brown, Blue, White, Mustard 210.00
  Cup & Saucer, Sienna, White, White Top & Bottom Band 160.00
  Cup & Saucer, Speckled, Handleless, Black & White Checkered Band 240.00
  Cup & Saucer, Vellum, Brown, Sienna, White, Green Band Top & Bottom 425.00
  Cup, Brown & Beige, Large 58.00
  Cup, Caudle, Banded, Mustard Band, Looped Worm, Brown, White 290.00
  Cup, Caudle, Leaf, Mustard, Incised Yellow Band Top, White Handle 500.00
  Humidor, Checkerboard Banded, Black & White, Brown, Blue, Acorn 1300.00
  Jug, Blue Band, Looped Worm, Black Band, Green Band, 5 In. 400.00
  Jug, Bulbous, Gray-Blue Band, Worm Circling, 6 In. 275.00
  Jug, Cream, Covered, Brown, Beige, White, White Spout, 6 In. 300.00
  Jug, Cream, Vellum, Brown, Mustard, White, Green Band Top, 6 1/2 In. 330.00
  Jug, Dark Mustard Body, Blue Band Rim, White Spout, 4 1/2 In. 650.00
  Jug, Flames In Brown, Blue, & Bronze, C.1820, 5 1/8 In. 175.00
  Jug, Leaf, Blue Ground, 6 1/2 In. 475.00
  Jug, Leaf, Bulbous, Blue Ground, 3 1/2 In. 150.00
  Jug, Leaf, Reddish Mustard Body, Green Band Top & Bottom, 8 In. 3600.00
  Jug, Marbleized Leaf, Blue Ground, 6 1/2 In. 475.00
  Jug, Ribbed At Top, C.1790, Marbleized, Terra-Cotta Ground, 6 1/2 In. 850.00
  Jug, Standing Seaweed, Gray-Tan Band, White, Blue, Black, Blue Band Top 170.00
  Jug, Standing Seaweed, Green Band, Black & White Band, 6 1/2 In. 160.00
  Mug, Black, Blue, Sienna, White Bands, Green Incised Band, 5 In. 220.00
  Mug, Blue Band, Cat's-Eye, Blue & White Band, 3 1/2 In. 160.00
  Mug, Blue Band, Looped Worm, White Top Band, 4 In. 210.00
  Mug, Blue, White, Brown Scroddle Tan Band, Black Design, 4 In. 360.00
  Mug, Brown, Yellow, White Swag Top, 6 In. 400.00
  Mug, Gray-Green Top Band, Brown, Tan, White Cat's-Eye, 4 1/2 In. 520.00
  Mug, Green Band Top & Bottom, White Handle, 2 1/2 X 2 1/2 In. 250.00
  Mug, Seaweed, Blue Band, Black, White Band, Blue Top Band, 85 In. 200.00

Mug, Seaweed, Tan Band, Black, White Band, Blue Top Band, 4 In. 160.00
Mug, Squat, Brown, Sienna, Blue, White, Blue Band, Blue Band, 4 In. 330.00
Mug, Squat, Marbleized, Brown, Mustard, White, Green Incised Band, 4 In. 210.00
Mug, Standing & Prone Seaweed, Blue Band, Black, White Blue, 6 In. 130.00
Mug, Standing Seaweed, Beige Band, Brwon & White, Blue Top, 5 In. 140.00
Mug, Standing Seaweed, Blue Band, Blue & White Band, 6 In. 160.00
Mug, Standing Seaweed, Gray Band, Black & White, Blue, 6 In. 120.00
Mug, Standing Seaweed, Gray-Green Band, Black & White Band, 5 In. 210.00
Mug, Tan Paste, Wavy Blue & Brown Worm & Cat's-Eye Design, 3 In. 120.00
Mug, 1 Cream & Gray Bands, Tan Ground 75.00
Mustard Pot, Speckled, Covered, Flower Design On Cover 190.00
Pitcher, Blue & Green 180.00
Pitcher, Seaweed, Footed, Blue, 7 1/2 In. 175.00
Pot, Enameled Flowers, Shield Mark 55.00
Potty, White Ringlets To Waist, C.1850, 2 1/8 X 2 3/4 In.Diam. 125.00
Punch Pot, Blue, Black, White, Sienna, Geometric Bands, 12 In. 650.00
Salt, Open, Brown Band, Flowers & Foliage 250.00
Saucer, Banded, Black, Blue, Sienna, White, 6 In, ... 160.00
Shaker, Cat's-Eye, Blue Ground, Brown & Mustard Stripes, 4 1/2 In. 150.00
Spill, Banded, Incised, Cream, Brown, Tan, 3 1/2 In. 190.00
Spill, Geometric Banded, 5 1/2 In. 170.00
Tea Caddy, Brown, Beige, White Top & Bottom Bands, 5 1/2 In. 310.00
Teapot, Individual, Marbleized, Brown, Sienna, White, 3 1/2 In. 310.00
      MOLD, ICE CREAM, see Pewter, Mold, Ice Cream

MONART, Vase, Mottled Orange, Dark Top, 11 In. 235.00
Vase, Urn Shape, Orange Mottled, Dark Top, Label, 8 X 10 1/2 In. 300.00

MONMOUTH, Pitcher, Fan-Shaped Design Around Bottom, Glossy Brown, 6 In. 8.00
Vase, Stylized Leaf Design, Side Handles, 7 1/2 In. 10.00
      MONT JOYE, see Mt.Joye

William Moorcroft managed the art pottery department for James Mac Intyre & Company of England from 1898 to 1913. In 1913 he started his own company, Moorcroft Pottery, in Burslem, England. The earlier wares are similar to those made today, but color and marking will help indicate the age.

MOORCROFT, Biscuit Barrel, Florian, Blue Floral, Silver Plated Fittings 400.00
Bowl, Blue-Green Ground, Flowers, 4 1/4 In. 40.00
Bowl, Center Flower, Blue-Green Ground, 2 X 4 In.Diam. 40.00
Bowl, Fruit, Iris, Flambe Glazed, 9 In. 195.00
Bowl, Green Iridescent, 9 1/4 In.Diam. 55.00
Bowl, Punch, Pomegranate Design Inside & Out, Signed, 14 1/2 In. 250.00
Bowl, Wisteria, Green Leaves Inside & Out, Signed, 11 In.Diam. 165.00
Bowl, Yellow & Green, Purple & Red Orchids, 3 1/2 In. 65.00
Candlestick, Pink Floral, Green Leaves, 4 In., Pair 60.00
Console Set, Salmon Hibiscus On Green, Marked, Bowl 9 3/4 In. 80.00
Cup & Saucer, Demitasse, Florian, Blue & White 300.00
Cup & Saucer, Wisteria & Green Leaves, Cobalt Blue, Signed 145.00
Dish, Poppies On Cobalt Blue, Covered, Marked, 6 3/4 In. 135.00
Ginger Jar, Burslem, Iridescent Orange Luster, 21 1/4 X 8 3/4 In. 100.00
Tea Service, Art Nouveau, 3 Piece ....*Illus* 750.00
Trivet, Mushrooms, Green Sign, 5 1/2 In.Diam. 175.00
Vase, Bulbous, Flambe, Paper Label, 2 3/4 In. 75.00
Vase, Design On Cobalt Blue, Sticker, 3 1/2 In. 85.00
Vase, Floral, Cobalt Blue, Signed, 3 1/4 In. 60.00
Vase, Flowers & Leaves, 6 1/2 In. 85.00
Vase, Orchids On Cobalt Blue, Royal Mark, 3 1/2 In., Pair 145.00
Vase, Pansy, Blue, 3 In. 50.00
Vase, Pink & Yellow, Flowers, Green Ground, 4 1/2 In. 45.00
Vase, Pink, Magnolia, 6 In. 50.00
Vase, Pomegranate & Grape Design, Blue Ground, Green Mark, 7 In. 150.00

Moorcroft, Tea Service, Art Nouveau, 3 Piece

Vase, Pomegranate Design, 4 X 3 1/2 In.	95.00
Vase, Poppies, Green Stems On Cobalt Blue, Signed, 6 1/4 In.	145.00
Vase, Red & Blue Pansies, Imperial Mark, Burslem, 3 1/2 In.	135.00
Vase, Red Fruit, Yellow Leaves, Marked Potter To Queen, 7 1/4 In.	145.00
Vase, Rose Panels, Streaky Blue, 2-Handled, C.1915, 10 In.	200.00
Vase, Sang De Boeuf, 1945, 9 1/2 In.	395.00
Vase, Yellow & Red Freesia On Cobalt Blue, Marked, 5 In.	95.00
Vase, Yellow Luster, Bulbous, 3 1/2 In.	70.00
Vase, Yellow Luster, Signed, 1916, 9 In.	50.00

Moriage is used to identify Japanese pottery to which a raised overglaze decoration has been added. This relief ornamentation may be elaborate. The term applies to the style or technique.

MORIAGE, Ashtray, Scenic, Marked	35.00
Basket Shape, Pink & Yellow Roses, Gold Stippled, 10 1/2 In.	175.00
Basket Tray, Handled, 8 1/2 In.	125.00
Box, Powder, Jewels, Pinks, Gold	75.00
Candlestick, Blue With White Slip, 6 1/2 In.	135.00
Chocolate Pot, Green Ground, Floral Design, 9 1/2 In.	249.00
Chocolate Pot, Hand-Painted Medallions	110.00
Chocolate Pot, Red & Pink Roses, Green Ground	250.00
Chocolate Set, Cobalt Ground, Birds & Florals, 6 Cups	550.00
Cracker Jar, Orchids, Green Ground, Double Handle, 8 In.Diam.	229.00
Cup & Saucer, Allover Leaves, Gold Ground, Signed	125.00
Cup & Saucer, Ivy, Green, Cup Footed	82.00
Decanter, Elephant Design, Dragon Motif, Barrel Shape	175.00
Dish, Green, Fluted, Floral, Gold, 5 In.	35.00
Dish, Raised Slipware, Fluted, Green & Red Floral, 5 1/4 In.	38.00
Ewer, Beaded Base, Pink & Green, 8 1/2 In. ....*Illus*	100.00

Moriage, Ewer, Beaded Base, Pink & Green, 8 1/2 In.

Ewer, Pierced Opening, Pink, Orchid, & Yellow Flowers, 7 1/2 In.	225.00
Hair Receiver, Green, Gold, Butterflies	85.00
Hatpin Holder, Raised Enameling, Pink & Purple Flowers	70.00
Hatpin Holder, Red Roses, Turquoise, Beaded	40.00
Jar, Overall Design, Teal Blue, 6 1/2 X 6 1/2 In.	150.00
Mustache Cup, Roses, 2 Piece	95.00
Plate, Dragon, Gray	17.00
Plate, Floral Medallions, 10 In.	45.00
Rose Bowl, Melon Ribbed, Oval Mark, Crown On Base	135.00
Rose Bowl, Peonies, Lacy Slip, Jeweled, Signed	195.00
Sugar, Creamer, & Teapot, Violets, Medallions, Putti Work	150.00
Tankard, Red, Gold, Yellow, Purple Roses, Green Slip Work, 13 In.	350.00
Tea Set, Flying Dragons, Green Enamel Eyes, 17 Piece	129.00
Tea Set, 6 Cups & Saucers, Pagoda Mark	250.00
Tray, Beading, Floral Center, Scalloped, 12 In.Diam.	180.00
Tray, Calling Card, Turquoise Dragons, Slip Trailing, Signed	50.00
Vase, Allover Jewels, Floral, 3-Handled, 11 In.	70.00
Vase, Bead, Hand-Painted Florals, 9 1/4 In.	260.00
Vase, Floral Medallions, Pastel Enameling, 7 3/4 In.	210.00
Vase, Florals On Front & Back, Pierced Handles, 8 1/4 In.	110.00
Vase, Hand-Painted Roses In Center Medallion, Green Ground, 9 In.	225.00
Vase, Marbleized Ground, Red Roses, 4 1/2 In.	179.00
Vase, Mauve Ground, Red Mums, Double Handle, 9 In.	239.00
Vase, Red Mums, Mauve Ground, 9 1/2 In.	230.00
Vase, Roses, Leaves, Blue Maple Leaf, Signed, 9 In.	195.00
Vase, Roses, Leaves, Slip Work, Signed, Blue Maple Leaf, 9 In.	195.00
Vase, Slip Trailed Dragons, Enamel Beads, Pink, 6 In.	150.00

Mosaic Tile Company of Zanesville, Ohio, was started by Karl Langenbeck and Herman Mueller in 1894. Many types of plain and ornamental tiles were made until 1959. The company closed in 1967.

MOSAIC TILE CO., Paperweight, Lincoln Portrait, 3 1/2 In.	20.00

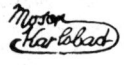

Moser glass was made by Ludwig Moser and Sohne, a Bohemian glasshouse founded in 1857. Art Nouveau type glassware and iridescent glassware were made. The firm is still working.

MOSER, Atomizer, Amethyst To Clear, Frosted Rings, 5 1/2 In.	175.00
Atomizer, Bulb, Cameo Beads On Each Of 6 Panels, 5 1/2 In.	175.00
Bottle, Cologne, Malachite, 6 1/2 In.	225.00
Bottle, Perfume, Cranberry, Enamel Floral Work, 3 1/4 In.	65.00
Bowl, Fleur-De-Lis Design, 22 Ruby Jewels, Gold Fields, Signed, 9 In.	235.00
Bowl, Floral Garland, Panel Cut, Signed, 6 X 4 In.	290.00
Bowl, Light Blue, Flowers & Ivys, 4 1/2 In.	165.00
Bowl, Multicolored Enameled Leaves, Glass Acorns, Signed, 5 5/8 In.	1150.00
Bowl, Signed, Amber, 8 In.Diam.	100.00
Compote, Blue, Acorns & Fern Design, Tri Cornered, 5 X 7 In.	385.00
Compote, Etruscan Warriors, Acid Cut Back Design, Purple, Signed	285.00
Cup & Saucer, Demitasse, Amber, Gold Dot & Leaves, Grapes	75.00
Cup & Saucer, Gold Overlay, Enameled, Emerald Green	130.00
Dish, Sweetmeat, Enameled, Rubena, Signed	325.00
Ewer, Multicolored Enameled, Gold Vines, Gold Trim, Signed, 13 3/4 In.	395.00
Ewer, Olive, Polychrome Flowering Branch, Blue Handle, Marked, 11 In.	400.00
Jar, Jam, Cranberry To Clear, Daisy Design, Signed	295.00
Jar, Powder, Emerald Green, Enameled	175.00
Pitcher & Bowl, Blossoms & Leaves, Gold Filigree, Signed, Miniature	245.00
Pitcher, Amber, Clear Reeded Handle, Flowers, Ivys, Signed, 7 In.	225.00
Pitcher, Amethyst To Cranberry, Leaves, Dragonflies, 10 In.	950.00
Pitcher, Raised Acorns, Colored Enameling, Dragonfly, 5 In.	475.00

Pitcher, Snake Handle, Amethyst To Cranberry, 10 1/4 In. 950.00
Sweetmeat, Rubena, Enameled, Signed 325.00
Toothpick, Rib Design, Signed 45.00
Tumbler, Light Blue, Enameled Flowers & Ivys, Signed 60.00
Vase, Alexandrite, Scalloped, Faceted Honeycomb Body, Signed, 8 In. 245.00
Vase, Amber, Frosted, 4 Elephants, Palm Trees, Signed, 11 1/2 In. 585.00
Vase, Amethyst To Clear, Engraved, Floral, 12 In. 195.00
Vase, Applied Bees, Gold & Enameled Design, Signed, 11 In., Pair 725.00
Vase, Band Of Cameo, Ruby & Amber, Jungle Scene, Signed, 13 1/2 In. 1485.00
Vase, Barrel Shape, Fern Pattern, Gold Over Large Area, 5 X 5 1/2 In. 265.00
Vase, Birds & Floral, Enameled, 14 In., Pair 275.00
Vase, Blue Cut Back, Clear, Gilt Design, 4 1/4 In. 155.00
Vase, Bud, Enameled Flowers & Leaves, Signed, 15 In. 200.00
Vase, Butterfly Design, Overshot, Signed, 16 In. 230.00
Vase, Crystal Icicle Drippings At Top, Gold Design, 4 Feet, 9 1/8 In. 695.00
Vase, Elephants & Jungle Scene, Gold Enamel, Signed, 8 In. 1200.00
Vase, Embossed Spider Mums, Crimped Top, Green To Clear, 11 1/2 In. 95.00
Vase, Emerald Green, Gold Flowers, Stripes, Signed, 4 X 9 In. 225.00
Vase, Enameled, Pedestal Shaped Bottom, Ruby, Signed, 8 3/4 In., Pair 395.00
Vase, Engraved, Enameled Flowers, Amethyst To Clear, 12 In. 195.00
Vase, Gold & Enamel, 15 1/2 In. 150.00
Vase, Gold Cameo, 4 Elephants, Birds In Flight, Signed, 11 1/2 In. 585.00
Vase, Gold Floral Design, 14 In. 67.50
Vase, Icicles On Top, Enameled Bird, Scrolls, Sapphire Blue, 9 In. 695.00
Vase, Intaglio, Corset Shape, Emerald Green To Clear, Signed, 6 In. 200.00
Vase, Pedestal, Figures Impressed In Gold, Purple, Signed, 20 In. 395.00
Vase, Pedestal, Mitered Cuts, Frieze Above Foot, Carlsbad, 20 In. 495.00
Vase, Purple Paneled, 5 X 4 In. 80.00
Vase, Ruby Jewels, Gold, Blue Top, Amethyst Base, Signed, 15 In. 250.00
Vase, Shaded Green Intaglio, 12 In. 250.00
Vase, White, Green, Amber, & Gold, Signed, 17 1/2 X 6 In. 325.00
Vase, Wild Rose, Applied Bees, Gold Trim, Signed, 11 X 4 1/2 In. 725.00
Wine, Intaglio Cut, Signed, Pair 160.00

Moss rose china was made by many firms from 1808 to 1900. It refers to any china decorated with the moss rose flower.

MOSS ROSE, Bowl, Ironstone, 6 In. 12.00
Coffeepot, Ironstone 68.00
Gravy Boat 30.00
Plate, Cake, Open Handles, Ironstone 20.00
Plate, 7 In. 15.00
Plate, 9 In. 30.00
Platter, Ironstone, 7 X 11 In. 23.00
Saucer, Fruit, 5 In. 10.00
Tureen, With Lid, Ironstone, 12 In. 60.00

Mother-of-pearl glass, or pearl satin glass, was first made in the 1850s in England and in Massachusetts. It was a special type of mold-blown satin glass with air bubbles in the glass, giving it a pearlized color.

MOTHER-OF-PEARL, see also Pearl
MOTHER-OF-PEARL, Biscuit Jar, Pink & White Stripes, Satin, 6 1/2 In. 750.00
Bowl, Pale Yellow, Floral Sawtooth Rim, 9 1/2 In. 560.00
Bowl, Rose, White, Pearl Stripes, Crimped Top, 2 1/4 In. 95.00
Bowl, Satin Glass, Diamond-Quilted, Apple Green, 4 7/8 In. 695.00
Bowl, Zipper Pattern, Pink Lining, Numbered, Green, 4 3/4 In. 595.00
Box, Jewelry, Victorian, Floral Design, 4 X 11 In. 170.00
Cheese Dish, Herringbone, Clear Knob & Finial, Pink 525.00
Cruet, Diamond-Quilted, Cut Stopper, Frosted Handle 295.00
Cruet, Diamond-Quilted, Triangular Handle 585.00
Ewer, Herringbone Pattern, Cranberry To White, 6 1/2 In. 195.00
Ewer, Pink Quilted Design, 5 1/2 In. 175.00
Jar, Diamond-Quilted, Silver Top, Rim, & Handle, 5 1/8 In. 425.00
Jar, Sweetmeat, Diamond-Quilted, Ribbed, White Lining 395.00

Jar, Sweetmeat, Diamond-Quilted, Rose Satin, 5 1/2 In. 295.00
Lamp, Fairy, Diamond-Quilted, Blue Satin, Marked, 3 1/2 In. 150.00
Lamp, Fairy, Diamond-Quilted, Rose Satin, Marked S.Clarke 275.00
Lamp, Fairy, Diamond-Quilted, Rose, Clarke Base, 3 1/2 In. 165.00
Pitcher, Herringbone, Raspberry To Pink, Square Mouth 425.00
Rose Bowl, Blue Herringbone, 3 In. 195.00
Rose Bowl, Coin Dot Pattern, Blue To White, 3 In. 145.00
Rose Bowl, Dark Gold, Gold Stripes, Wafer Base, 3 1/4 In. 95.00
Rose Bowl, Herringbone Pattern, Blue To White, 3 3/4 In. 165.00
Rose Bowl, Rose Herringbone, White Lining, 3 1/2 In. 225.00
Rose Bowl, Satin, Pink, Blue & Yellow, 6 In. 385.00
Rose Bowl, Striped Pattern, Mocha, Pinched Top, 3 In. 135.00
Rose Bowl, White Satin Striped, Crimped, 2 3/4 In. 120.00
Rose Bowl, 8 Crimps, Blue Satin, Herringbone, 4 In. 125.00
    MOTHER-OF-PEARL, SATIN GLASS, see also Satin Glass; Smith
    Brothers; Tiffany Glass; etc.
Sugar & Creamer, Satin Glass, Creamer 2 1/2 In. 350.00
Tumbler, Diamond-Quilted, Blue Enameled Flowers, Pink 225.00
Tumbler, Diamond-Quilted, Satin Glass, 3 3/4 In. 110.00
Tumbler, Diamond-Quilted, Square Top, Deep Rose, 3 3/4 In. 145.00
Tumbler, Diamond-Quilted, Yellow 95.00
Vase, Concentric Diamonds, Applied Camphor, 10 1/2 In. 500.00
Vase, Diamond-Quilted Pattern, Butterscotch, 6 In. 235.00
Vase, Diamond-Quilted, Blue, Footed, Narrow Neck, 11 In. 225.00
Vase, Diamond-Quilted, Ruffled, Mocha, 6 1/2 In., Pair 325.00
Vase, Drape, Ruffled, Pink, 5 3/4 In. 280.00
Vase, Fan Shape, Frosted Wafer Foot, Blue, 3 1/2 In. 235.00
Vase, Green Flower & Acorn, Pinched, 3-Way Top, 4 In. 425.00
Vase, Herringbone, Bulbous, Ruffled, Blue, 5 1/2 In. 150.00
Vase, Herringbone, Thorn Handle, 3-Petal Top, 6 3/4 In. 275.00
Vase, Peach Herringbone, Ruffled, White Lining, 5 1/2 In. 165.00
Vase, Pink Bottom To Rose Top, Cased, 6 In. 125.00
Vase, Pink, Herringbone, Pleated Top, 5 1/2 In. 125.00
Vase, Raindrop Pattern, Cranberry, White Lining, 7 1/2 In. 190.00
Vase, Raindrop Pattern, Turned-Down Top, 7 1/2 In. 185.00
Vase, Raindrop, Butterfly & Flowers, Signed, Blue, 12 In. 495.00
Vase, Raindrop, Butterscotch, 8 1/2 In. 150.00
Vase, Ribbon Swirl, Shaded Red To White, 5 1/2 In. 325.00
Vase, Rose Ribbon Design, Gold Prunus Blossoms, 3 In. 395.00
Vase, Striped Pattern, White Lining, Gold, 4 In. 120.00
Vase, Yellow Coralene Fleur-De-Lis, Diamond-Quilted, 9 In. 465.00
    MOUSTACHE CUP, see Mustache Cup

Mont Joye is an enameled cameo glass made in the late nineteenth and the twentieth centuries by Saint-Hilaire Touvoir de Varraux and Co. of Pantin, France. This same company produced De Vez glass.

MT.JOYE, Basket, Handled, Carved Poppies & Leaves, 6 X 6 In. 550.00
Rose Bowl, Stippled Ground, Gold Enamel, 3 In. 110.00
Rose Bowl, Violets, Gold Rim, Signed, 4 1/2 In. 250.00
Vase, Blue & Gold Floral, Purple Cut To Light Gray, 8 In. 575.00
Vase, Cameo, Vine & Flowers, Gold, Silver, & Bronze, Signed, 14 In. 325.00
Vase, Deep Amethyst, Enameled, Floral, 11 In. 135.00
Vase, Embossed Flowers & Leaves, Brass Holder, Cranberry, Signed 325.00
Vase, Enameled Flowers, 12 In. 375.00
Vase, Gold Oak Leaves, Silver Acorns, Logo In Gold 495.00
Vase, Iris, Amethyst, 12 In., Pair 195.00
Vase, Irises, Gold Leaves, Purple, Signed, 13 1/2 In. 270.00
Vase, Roman Gold Enameled Leaves, Ice Green Ground, Signed, 13 In. 415.00

Mt.Washington Glass was made at the Mt.Washington Glass Co. located in New Bedford, Massachusetts. Many types of art glass were made there from 1850 to the 1890s.

MT. WASHINGTON, see also Burmese; Crown Milano

MT.WASHINGTON, Biscuit Jar, Melon, Ribbed	395.00
Bottle, Dresser Floral Design	35.00
Bowl, Blooming Pansies, Quilted, 2 1/4 X 4 In.	275.00
Bowl, Tricornered, Fuchsia, 5 In.	285.00
Bride's Basket, Enameled, Pulled-Down Plated Edge	525.00
Bride's Bowl, Acid Cut, Pairpoint Base, 9 X 5 In.	995.00
Cracker Jar, Flowers, Yellow To Orange Body, Signed, 7 In.	395.00
Cracker Jar, Swirled Satin, Enameled & Jeweled, 4 In.	175.00
Creamer, Flowers On Handle	175.00
Cruet, Enameled Flowers, Gold Trim, Beige Ground	700.00
Cruet, Shading, Ribbed, Acid Finish, 7 In.	925.00
Egg, Allover Strawberry Diamonds, Star Base, Egg Lid	185.00
Hatpin Holder, Floral, Mushroom Shape	145.00
Jar, Oak Leaf & Acorn Design, Silver Plated Top, C.1890, 6 In.	90.00
Muffineer, Forget-Me-Not Blossoms, Blue Ground	285.00
Muffineer, Melon	140.00
Pickle Caster, Inset Of Diamond-Quilted Cranberry	425.00
Pitcher, Ewer Shape, Satin Finish Hobnail, Opaque Green	75.00
Plate, Burmese, Salmon To Yellow, 9 1/4 In.	295.00
Rose Bowl, Heron & Seaweed	175.00
Salt & Pepper, Floral	65.00
Saltshaker, Egg Shape, Columbian Exhibition, 1893	85.00
Saltshaker, Egg, Flat End	50.00
Saltshaker, Egg, Forget-Me-Nots, Blue	40.00
Saltshaker, Egg, Forget-Me-Nots, Green	40.00
Saltshaker, Egg, Pansies, Yellow	40.00
Saltshaker, Figural, Original Top	90.00
Saltshaker, Melon Ribbed, Floral Design, Pair	65.00
Saltshaker, Swirled Base, Flowers, Pewter Top, 3 In.	45.00
Saltshaker, Tomato, Original Top, Blue & White	45.00
Shaker, Salt, Melon	60.00
Shaker, Sugar, Tomato, Florals, White Ground	135.00
Spooner, Diamond-Quilted, Scalloped Rim, 4 3/4 In.	395.00
Sugar Shaker, Egg, Blue	235.00
Sugar Shaker, Enameled Tropical Leaves, Insects On Cover	175.00
Sugar Shaker, Ostrich Egg	245.00
Sugar Shaker, Tomato, Acid Cut, Butterfly On Lid	175.00
Sugar, Peachblow, 3 3/4 In.	500.00
Sugar, Shaker, Egg Shape, Enameled Flowers, 4 1/2 In.	150.00
Syrup, Loop & Daisy, 3 1/2 In.	235.00
Tumbler, Diamond-Quilted, Amberina	110.00
Tumbler, Yellow Top Edge, 3 5/8 In.	225.00
Vase, Blossoms, Panels Of Birds, Red Ground, 12 1/4 In., Pair	300.00
Vase, Bud, Bronzed Metal Crane & Dragonfly, Ruby, 13 1/2 In.	385.00
Vase, Dimpled Bottom, Cylinder Top, Yellow	185.00
Vase, Double, Turquoise, Rosette On Each, 3 In.	145.00
Vase, Flared & Scalloped Rim, 9 In.	250.00
Vase, Flowers, 12 In., Pair	95.00
Vase, Jack-In-The-Pulpit, White To Rose Interior	122.00
Vase, Lily, Salmon To Yellow, Acid Finish, 9 In.	450.00
Vase, Pedestal, Oval Mouth, White Lusterless, 3 X 7 In.	52.50
Vase, Ruffled Top, Signed, 14 In.	450.00

Mud figures are small Chinese pottery figures made in the twentieth century. The figures usually represent workers, scholars, farmers, or merchants. Other pieces are trees, houses, and similar parts of the landscape. The figures have unglazed faces and hands but glazed clothing. The figures were originally made for fish tanks or planters.

MUD FIGURE, Man, 4 In. 40.00
    Woman Sitting, Holding Prayer Beads, Green, Yellow, 5 1/2 In. 45.00
    Woman Water Carrier, 5 In. 65.00
    Fish 90.00
    Vase, Floral, Triangular, 6 In. 85.00
    Man, 10 In. 125.00
    Man, 14 In. 150.00

*Mulberry ware was made in the Staffordshire district in England from,
about 1850 to 1860. The dishes were decorated with a transfer design of a
reddish brown, now called mulberry. Many of the patterns are similar to
those used for flow blue and other Staffordshire transfer wares.*

MULBERRY, Basin, Wash, The Temple 120.00
    Bowl, Vegetable, Footed, Finial On Lid, Octagonal, Covered 75.00
    Coffeepot, Wreath Pattern, C.1845 .... 110.00
    Cup & Saucer, Handleless, Pelew 45.00
    Cup & Saucer, Handleless, Shapoo 45.00
    Cup Plate, Corean .... 35.00 To 40.00
    Cup, Handleless, Corean 60.00
    Gravy Boat, Pelew 95.00
    Pitcher, Milk, Kyber, 1 1/2 Pint 115.00
    Plate, Corean, Podmore, Walker & Co.8 In. .... 21.25 To 25.00
    Plate, Corean, 9 1/2 In. 50.00
    Plate, Corinthia, Castle Scene In Medallions, Challinor, 8 1/2 In. 75.00
    Plate, Cyprus, 7 1/4 In. .... 17.00 To 22.00
    Plate, Cyprus, 9 In. 45.00
    Plate, Hong, C.1850, 10 In. 40.00
    Plate, Panama, Davenport, 10 In. 21.25
    Plate, Swiss Scenery, 10 In. 35.00
    Platter, Corean, P.W. & Co., 13 1/2 X 10 1/2 In. 95.00
    Platter, Corean, P.W. & Co., 16 In. 35.00
    Platter, Leipzig, Clementson, C.1850, 14 In.Diam. 78.00
    Platter, Strawberry, Walker, 16 X 12 In. 125.00
    Vase, Washington, Ironstone, P.W. & Co., 9 3/4 In. 45.00
    Vase, Washington, 8 7/8 In. 45.00

MULLER FRES
LUNÉVILLE

*Muller Freres, French for Muller Brothers, made cameo and other art
glass from the early 1900s to the late 1930s. Their factory was first located
in Luneville and later moved to Croismaire, France.*

MULLER FRERES, Vase, Cameo, Luneville, Trees, River, Gold Ground, Signed, 5 In. 795.00
    Vase, Cameo, Pink Flowers, Green Frosted Ground, 5 3/4 In. 1195.00
    Vase, Cameo, Red & Pink Roses, Carved, Cream Ground, 7 1/2 In. 1500.00
    Vase, Cameo, Red Orchid, 3 Cuttings, 8 In. 825.00
    Vase, Gray, 3 Blown-Out Swallows In Flight, Signed, 9 In. 560.00
    Vase, Luneville, Mottled Brown To Orange, Signed, 6 1/2 In. 150.00
    Vase, Poppies, Pink Shading To Burgundy, 6 In. ....*Illus* 1425.00
    Vase, Windmill Scene, Yellow Ground, Signed, 13 3/4 In. 1395.00

MUSIC, Accordion, Honer, 12 Bass Piano 150.00
    Accordion, Lestor, 10 Keys One Side, 2 On Other, Germany, 10 X 10 In. 45.00
    Accordion, Milano Organetto, 21 Trebles, 8 Bass, C.1920 .... 85.00
    Accordion, Rosewood, Brass, & Mother-Of-Pearl, 1880 .... 150.00
    Autoharp, Mother Maybelle Carter, Instructions 38.00
    Automata, Lute Player, French 4500.00
    Banjo-Mandolin, 8 String, C.1903, Ivory Keys 175.00
    Banjo-Mandolin, 8 String, Inlaid Mother-Of-Pearl, Bird's-Eye Maple 110.00
    Banjo, Mandolin Neck, Inlaid, American 125.00
    Banjo, Maxitone, Dated 1901, 21 In. 65.00
    Banjo, Pearl Inlay, 30 In. 75.00
    Banjo, Supertone, 5 String, Inlaid Neck 125.00

Muller Freres, Vase, Poppies, Pink Shading
To Burgundy, 6 In.

Banjo, Tenor, Bacon & Day, Special Edition No.2, With Case 250.00
Banjo, Tenor, Lyon & Healy, Resonator 125.00
Banjo, Vega, Boston, Mass., Style N, Original Case, 33 X 12 In. 285.00
Banjo, Vega, Tenor 250.00
Banjo, Waverly, Tenor 45.00
Banjo, Waverly, 4 String, Hand-Painted Head, Case 125.00
Bird Box, C.1900, Hinged Cover, Semi Precious Stones, Austrian, 4 In. 750.00
Bird In Cage, Animated Bird On Perch, Brass Cage, German, 13 In. 275.00
Bird In Cage, Mechanical, 3 Birds, Nest, Limb, 1890, 9 Movements, 22 In. 2400.00
Box, Bell, Regina, 15 Discs, 15 1/2 In.Disc 5495.00
Box, Boudoir, Plays Blue Danube, Old Folks At Home, 5 1/4 X 3 1/2 In. 465.00
Box, Calliope, 13 Discs, 6 Saucer Balls, 9 1/8 In.Disc 1100.00
Box, Carola, Roll Operated Clarinet, 3 Rolls 200.00
Box, Criterion, No.8-100, 10 1/2 In.Disc 1200.00
Box, Freres, Interchangeable Cylinders, Drawer, Soprano 3495.00
Box, German, 2 Rows Red & Green Diamonds, Tin, 3 X 4 1/2 In. 65.00
Box, Hurdy-Gurdy, Movable Wheels, Sterling Silver, 2 X 2 3/4 In. 395.00
Box, Imperial Symphonion, 2-Comb, Coin Operated, 18 1/4 In.Disc 1950.00
Box, Inlaid Medallions, 10-Tune, Swiss, C.1880, 27 3/4 X 5 1/4 In. 925.00
Box, Italian Organ Grinder & Monkey, 2 Children, Large 200.00
Box, Japanese Doll, Sankyo Orgel, 1920s, 13 In.Tall 85.00
Box, Key Wind, Cylinder, 8 Tune, 10 1/2 In.Cylinder 1100.00
Box, L'pee, Brass Works, Rosewood, Marquetry 1395.00
Box, LeCoultre, Brass Bedplate, Inlaid 1800.00
Box, Lithographed Scenes, German, Windup, Tin, C.1900 .... 75.00
Box, Manivelle Symphonion, 6 Discs 225.00
Box, Mermod Freres, Coin Operated, 8 Tunes 625.00
Box, Mermod Freres, Soprano, 3 Cylinders In A Drawer 3495.00
Box, Mira, Console, Mahogany, 15 3/4 In.Disc 3800.00
Box, Mira, 6 3/4 In.Disc 900.00
Box, Nicole Freres, American Tunes, C.1860, Fruitwood Case 3500.00
Box, Nicole, Pietro Dura Stone Inlay, 8 Tunes, Cylinder 11 In. 2000.00
Box, Olympia, Double Comb, Twelve 15 1/2 In.Discs 2850.00
Box, Paillard, 2 Cylinder, Carved Mahogany Case 3500.00
Box, Polyphon, Bells, Upright Model, 22 1/2 In.Disc 4000.00
Box, Polyphon, Disc, Walnut Case, Coin Operated, 43 In. 3500.00
Box, Polyphon, Upright, Disc Storage Cabinet 6900.00
Box, Regina, Bell Box, 15 1/2 In.Disc 5495.00
Box, Regina, Bow Front, 15 In.Changer, Mahogany 9000.00
Box, Regina, Coin Operated, Oak, 33 Discs, 15 1/2 In. 320.00
Box, Regina, Double Comb, Storage Cabinet, 50 Discs 3000.00
Box, Regina, Hexaphone, Mahogany 5000.00
Box, Regina, No.59128, Double Comb, 22 Discs, Walnut Case, 15 In.Disc. 6800.00

Box, Regina, Orchestral, Style 5, Upright, 27 In.Disc .... 8500.00 To 8900.00
Box, Regina, Table Model, Double Comb, 15 1/2 In.Disc 2795.00
Box, Regina, 1890, 22 Discs 5000.00
Box, Reuge, Cylinder, 2-Tune, Jewel Case, Artist Signed Plaque, 7 In. 85.00
Box, Seeburg, Art Deco, Chrome, Plastic, & Blue Mirrors, 1940 .... 1400.00
Box, Stella, Console Model, Oak, 37 X 25 X 19 In. 1250.00
Box, Stella, 53-Tune, Mahogany, Stand With Drawer, 31 X 42 X 24 In. 4250.00
Box, Swiss, Cylinder, Jewel Case, Brass Center Plaque, Footed, 7 1/2 In. 95.00
Box, Swiss, Manivelle Type, Portrait Of Young Women, Round, 3 In. 75.00
Box, Swiss, 10-Tune, Inlaid Medallion, C.1890, 23 1/4 X 10 1/4 In. 900.00
Box, Swiss, 3-Tune, Color Lithograph On Cover, Brass Hand Crank, 5 In. 115.00
Box, Swiss, 8-Tune, Rosewood Veneer, 26 1/2 In. 425.00
Box, Symphonion, Imperial, C.1900, Stand, 15 In.Disc *Illus*4750.00
Box, Symphonion, 8 In.Cylinder, 7 Discs, Mahogany Cased 990.00
Box, Walting, Musical Upright, Coin Operated, 5 Cent 8500.00
Box, Watling, Musical Upright, Coin Operated, 5 Cent 8500.00
Box, Zither-Guitare, Bronze Side Handles, 10 Tunes, 13 1/2 In.Cylinder 850.00
Bugle, Army, Philadelphia Depot, 1916 .... 50.00
Bugle, 7th Cavalry, Brass 42.00
Calliope, Tangley 43 Note, Manual Or Roll, 10 Rolls 7500.00
Calliope, Wurlitzer, Double Tracker Style, Organette Foto Player 5500.00
Cello, Tiger Maple, Spruce, Brass Keys, Abraham Prescott, 50 In. 575.00
Clarinet, Selmer Contrabass, Rosewood, Silver Plated Case 750.00
Clavichord, George Iii, Schoene & Insen, London 1796, 31 X 23 In. 125.00
Flute, Gemeinhardt, Closed Hole, Sterling Silver 275.00
Flute, 6 Key, Ivory Mouthpiece, Rosewood 80.00
Guitar-Zither, Menzenhauer, St.Louis World's Fair Model 58.00
Guitar, Gibson, L-5, 1932 .... 1150.00
Guitar, Gibson, 1938, Black & Ivory 1000.00
Guitar, John C.Haynes & Co., Rosewood Fingerboard, Pine Table, 36 In. 125.00
Guitar, Martin, D-41 .... 1100.00
Harmonica, Hohner, Echo, Boxed 18.00
Harmonica, Hohner, No.147, Marine Band Tremolo, Germany 22.50
Harmonica, Shenandoah, Zeppelin, Miniature 29.00
Horn, Phono, Edison, 14 In. 50.00
Hurdy-Gurdy, 16 Note Paper Roll, German 1100.00

Music, Box, Symphonion, Imperial,
C.1900, Stand, 15 In.Disc

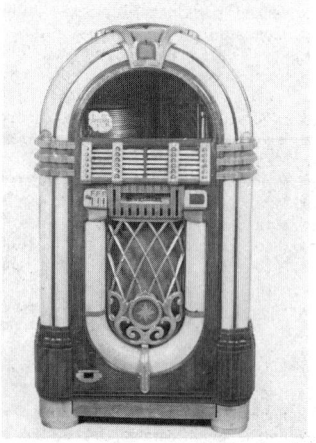

Music, Jukebox, Wurlitzer, Multi-
Selector, No.1015, Art Deco

Lamp, Gone With The Wind, Yellow, C. 1900, 21 In.

Silver Plate, Castor Set, Reed & Barton, C. 1875, 5 Piece, 8¾ In.

Wedgwood, Pitcher, Majolica, Etruria, Ribbed Fans, 1879, 7 In.

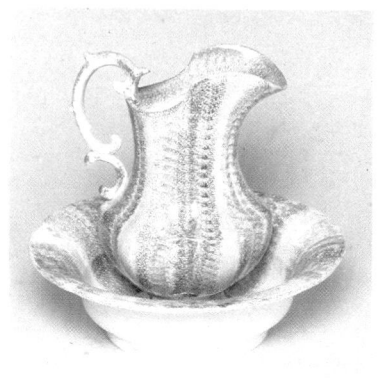

Spatterware, Bowl And Pitcher,
C. 1825

Buffalo Pottery Deldare, Pitcher, A
Noble Hunting Party, 1911, 9½ In.

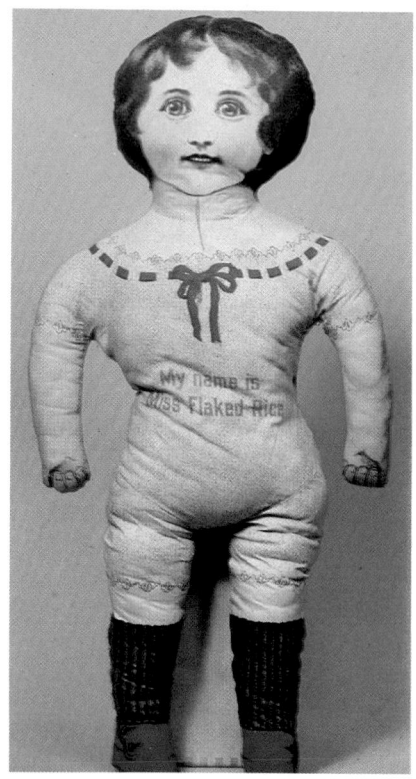

Doll, Cloth, Miss Flaked Rice, Copyright
1899, 21 In.

Dolls, Jumeau, Bebe, Bisque,
Paperweight Eyes, Pierced Ears,
19 In.; 18 In.

Doll, Marque, Bisque, Blue Glass
Eyes, Blonde Mohair Wig, 1916,
22 In.

Disneyana, Dolls, Snow White & The Seven Dwarfs, Merrythought Manufacturing Co., 1938

Bank, Mechanical, Punch & Judy, Shepard And Adams, C. 1895, 7½ In.

Doll, Lenci, Felt, 17½ In.

Toy, Cast Iron, Carriage, Horse And Driver, Pratt & Letchworth, C. 1892, 15½ In.

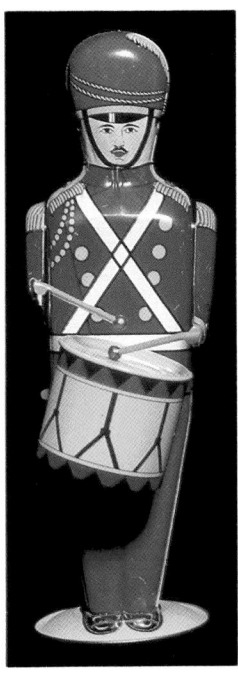

Toy, Furniture, Chest Of Drawers, 1870–80

Toy, Drum Major, Wolverine, Spring Wound, 1935, 13 In.

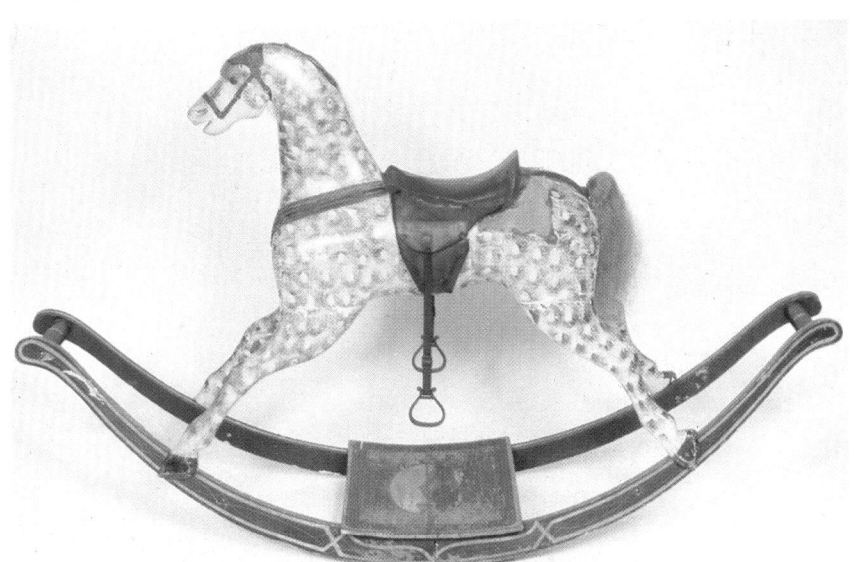

Toy, Rocking Horse, Wood, 3 Ft. 6½ In.

Toy, Horses and Wagon, Pull Toy, German, C. 1915,
30½ In.

Toy, Merry-Go-Round, Lithographed Paper On
Wood, 28 In. Diam.

Toy, Bowling Game, Wood And Lithographed Paper,
C. 1900

Toy, Dollhouse,
Mansion, Bliss, 1900,
2 Ft. 4 In.

Toy, Dollhouse, German, Elevator, 1900, Open; Closed

Carousel, Horse, Armitage-Herschell,
1890s, 3 Ft. 2½ In.

Clock, Turkish Numerals, Winged Griffins Surround Face, 24¼ In.

Sailor's Valentine, Trinidad, 1905

Cloisonne, Basin, Lily Pond And Flowers, 18th Century, 16 In.

Music, Organ, Concert Roller, American, 19th Century

Jukebox, Gables, 2-Knob, 1932	650.00
Jukebox, Rock Ola, Model 1422, 1946	1250.00
Jukebox, Rock Ola, Model 1426	1695.00
Jukebox, Rock Ola, Model 1432	395.00
Jukebox, Seeburg, With Xylophone, Art Glass	5500.00
Jukebox, Wurlitzer, Model 750	1700.00
Jukebox, Wurlitzer, Model 1050	4500.00
Jukebox, Wurlitzer, Model 1080	4500.00
Jukebox, Wurlitzer, Multi-Selector, No.1015, Art Deco	*Illus* 2800.00
Mandolin Harp, 1894 Patent	35.00
Mandolin, Gibson, Model A	450.00 To 495.00
Mandolin, Gibson, Model A2, C.1925, Case	600.00
Mandolin, Leather Design, Gilt Paint, 8 In.	50.00
Mandolin, Washburn Sticker & Logo, Case	150.00
Marxophone, Original Cardboard Box, C.1912, Sheet Music	55.00
Melodeon, Dated 1864, Rosewood	700.00
Melodeon, Spang	500.00
Nickelodeon, Coin Operated, Stained Glass Front, 10 Tunes, 25 Cent	1500.00
Nickelodeon, Link 2e, With Xylophone	8900.00
Nickelodeon, Pipes, Link Style, C Keyboard	9500.00
Nickelodeon, Seeburg, Cabinet Model, Stained Glass & Oak	5000.00
Nickelodeon, Western Electric Mascot, Piano & Mandolin	6250.00
Nickelodeon, Wurlitzer, Style SA, Piano, Mandolin, Flute Pipes	8500.00
Nickelodeon, 1980 Coinola Style O, Art Glass, 2 Rolls	2700.00
Organ, Artizan, Military Band, Plays Wurlitzer 125 Rolls	7650.00
Organ, Band, Artizan, 181 Pipes	6000.00
Organ, Barrel, Monkey, Reed Type	2500.00
Organ, Carousel, Wurlitzer, Barrel Operated, Oak Case	6000.00
Organ, Concert Roller, American, 19th Century	*Illus* 450.00
Organ, Eastlake, Dated 1885, Walnut	1600.00
Organ, Estey, Church	800.00
Organ, Estey, Electrified, Wooden Works, 2 Banks, 15 Stops, 1890s	2000.00
Organ, Farrand, Oak Reed, Exposed Pipes	900.00
Organ, Gem Roller, 4 Cobs	300.00
Organ, Limonaire, Child's Carousel, 34 Key, 8 Music Books	7500.00
Organ, Mason & Hamlin, Reed, Walnut	1000.00
Organ, Pipe, Moller, 40 Rolls	500.00
Organ, Pump, W.W.Putnam & Co., Cathedral Top, Beveled Glass, Oak, 1903	425.00
Organ, Roller, Concert, Hand Crank, 5 Cobs, Patent 1887, 17 X 15 In.	675.00
Organ, Street, Molinary, Brass Pipes	6000.00
Organ, Street, Poirot Barrel, 35 Key, 65 Flute Pipes	4750.00
Organette, Galley Orchestrone, Floor Model, 48 Note, 22 Rolls	1500.00

The phonograph, invented by Thomas Edison in the 1880s, has been made by many firms.

Phonograph, Amberola, IA Chassie	585.00
Phonograph, B.F.Columbia, Aluminum Horn	600.00
Phonograph, Banner Triumph, 11-Panel Signet Horn	800.00
Phonograph, Carola, Child's, Original Finish	225.00
Phonograph, Columbia, BD, Spruce Horn	1650.00
Phonograph, Columbia, Eagle, C.1900	200.00
Phonograph, Columbia, Home Grand, Cylinder 5 In.	2200.00
Phonograph, Columbia, No Horn, Cylinder, 5 In.	1300.00
Phonograph, Columbia, Oak Horn	1100.00
Phonograph, Edison, Amberola VI	450.00
Phonograph, Edison, Amberola, Model No 30, Cylinder, Windup, 35 Records	349.00
Phonograph, Edison, Black Gem	200.00
Phonograph, Edison, Cylinder, Small Horn	495.00
Phonograph, Edison, Gem, Morning Glory Horn, 3 & 4 Minute	550.00
Phonograph, Edison, Maroon Gem, Model D, Original 2-Piece Horn	700.00
Phonograph, Edison, Model 30	250.00
Phonograph, Edison, Opera, Matching Mahogany Cylinder Cabinet	4000.00
Phonograph, Edison, Standard, Cygnet Horn	475.00
Phonograph, Edison, Standard, Morning Glory Horn	350.00
Phonograph, Edison, Standard, 2-Minute Play, Small Horn	368.00
Phonograph, Edison, Standard, 30 In.Brass Horn	450.00
Phonograph, Edison, Standard, 4-Minute Records	240.00
Phonograph, Edison, Triumph, 50 Cylinders	595.00
Phonograph, Gramophone, American Berliner	2200.00
Phonograph, Gramophone, Columbia, Model A O	525.00
Phonograph, Gramophone, Columbia, Table Model, C.1900	1500.00
Phonograph, Gramophone, Edison Fireside, Model A, Morning Glory Horn	550.00
Phonograph, Maroon Gem, Original Horn	700.00
Phonograph, Mira, Double Comb, 12 In., 18 Discs	2300.00
Phonograph, Reginaphone, Double Comb, 15 1/2 In., Inside Horn, 12 Discs	4100.00
Phonograph, Rosenfield, Coin Operated	3700.00
Phonograph, Sonora, Chippendale Console, Carved Tone Arm	1000.00
Phonograph, Victor I	500.00 To 575.00
Phonograph, Victor III, Large Oak Horn	1300.00 To 1350.00
Phonograph, Victor V, Oak Music Master Horn	1500.00 To 1600.00
Phonograph, Victor VI, Mahogany Horn	2600.00
Phonograph, Victor, Orthophonic, 6 Records, Walnut Cabinet	4000.00
Phonograph, Victor, Schoolhouse	1250.00
Phonograph, Victor, 4 Brass Bell Horn	700.00
Piano, Aeolian, Player, 25 Cent Coin Operated, 10 Tunes	3500.00
Piano, Ampico Symphonique, Player Grand, Rolls	5995.00
Piano, Broadwood, Pre-1820, Square	1800.00
Piano, Chickering B, Square Legs, Mahogany, 5 Ft. 4 In.	8500.00
Piano, Chickering, Ampico, Baby Grand, 1927, Reproducing	*Illus* 1500.00
Piano, Chickering, Ampico, Grand, Walnut	9800.00
Piano, Chickering, C.1840, Rosewood	6000.00
Piano, Chickering, Concert Grand, Rosewood Case	5600.00
Piano, Chickering, Upright Grand	500.00
Piano, Everett, Baby Grand, Carved	2500.00
Piano, Grand, Steinway & Sons, Rosewood, Fruit & Foliage	2200.00
Piano, Haynes, Reproducing Baby Grand	6000.00
Piano, J.Broadwood & Sons, Grand, 1860s, Rosewood	3000.00
Piano, Jesse French, Art Glass Panels, Electrified, Tiger Oak	2000.00
Piano, Knabe, Ampico A, Art Case, Louis XVI Legs, Walnut, 5 Ft. 8 In	9000.00
Piano, Knabe, Ampico, Model A, Lacquer Finish, 5 Ft. 8 In.	9500.00
Piano, Mahogany, Federal, Inlaid Flowers, C.1790, 33 X 62 In.	5200.00
Piano, Marshall & Wendell, Ampico Reproducing, Baby Grand	3100.00
Piano, Moore & Moore, London, C.1880, Cottage	4000.00
Piano, Player, Aeolian Duo-Art, Bench, Rolls	3950.00
Piano, Player, Aeolian, Bellows, 1903 Advertising Literature	475.00
Piano, Player, Angelus	150.00

Music, Piano, Chickering, Ampico, Baby
Grand, 1927, Reproducing

Piano, Player, Chickering Ampico Grand, 100 Rolls, Bench, 6 Ft. 6000.00
Piano, Player, George Steck, Duo-Art, Bench, Walnut 2500.00
Piano, Spanish Barrel, On Cart, Blocks, Cymbal & Bells 550.00
Piano, Spinet, Jessie French, Fruitwood, Mid-1800s 1500.00
Piano, Square Back, Rosewood Veneer, G & B Barmore, C.1851 .... 2165.00
Piano, Steinway, Duo-Art Player Grand, Model Or 4500.00
Piano, Steinway, Grand, Duo-Art No.222, 1924, 50 Rolls, 6 Ft. 1 In. 9800.00
Piano, Steinway, Square Grand, Carved Legs, 1879 .... 8500.00
Piano, Steinway, Square Grand, Rosewood, C.1872 .... 3500.00
Piano, Steinway, Upright, C.1903, Ebonized Wood, 62 X 52 In. 300.00
Piano, Weber, Duo-Art, Louis XV, Grand 7200.00
Piano, Woodward & Brown, Square, Grand 2800.00
Rolmonica, Paper Roll 60.00
Sheet, A Little Bit O' Honey, Oval Black Mother & Baby 10.00
Sheet, A Trip To Niagara, Railroad Theme, 1904, Engine Picture 7.50
Sheet, Amos & Andy 12.00
Sheet, Babes On Broadway, Judy Garland 10.00
Sheet, Back To Carolina, 1913 .... 10.00
Sheet, Brownies On Parade, 1908 .... 12.00
Sheet, Casey Jones, 1909 .... 15.00
Sheet, Chocolate Drops, 1902 .... 10.00
Sheet, Dis Ain't No Time For An Argument, 1906 .... 10.00
Sheet, Ev'ry Darkey Had A Raglan On, 1901 .... 10.00
Sheet, Fall River Line, 1913 .... 10.00
Sheet, Good Ship Lollipop, You Gotta Smile, Shirley Temple 12.00
Sheet, I Want To Hold Your Hand, The Beatles 12.00
Sheet, Know Nothing Polka, 1855, Black & White Lithograph Cover 15.00
Sheet, Like An Angel You Flew Into Everyone's Heart, Lindbergh's 10.00
Sheet, Little Orphan Annie, 1931, Ovaltine 18.00
Sheet, Mickey Mouse's Birthday Party, 1936 .... 22.00
Sheet, Monarch Of The Air, 1927, Lindbergh, Photograph On Cover 4.00
Sheet, Moxie Song, 1921 .... 12.00
Sheet, Napoleon's Last Charge, E.T.Paull 10.00
Sheet, Our Little Girl, Shirley Temple 20.00
Sheet, Over The Rainbow, Judy Garland 15.00
Sheet, Strenous Life, 1901, Theodore Rossevelt Cover 25.00
Sheet, The Minstrel Show Parade, 1913 .... 10.00
Sheet, Wizard Of Oz, Judy Garland 15.00
Stand, Fruitwood, Adjustable, 27 In. 110.00
Ukulele, Carrying Case, Wooden, 21 In. 45.00
Ukulele, Maxitone 28.00
Violano, Mills, Mahogany Case, Violin & Piano By Roll, Coin Operated 7500.00
Violin, Lindblad, Fiddleback, 1899, Case 125.00
Violin, Signed Schweitzer, Plush Case 87.00

Mustache cups were popular from 1850 to 1900. A ledge of china or silver held the hair out of the liquid in the cup.

MUSTACHE CUP & SAUCER, Budded Roses, Blue Ground, Gold Trim, Porcelain 28.00
  Father, Gold Trim, Germany 45.00
  Flow Blue Flowers, Gold Trim 95.00
  Flowers, Cobalt Blue Leaves, 6 1/4 In. 65.00
  Moriage Palm Scene, Blue Maple Leaf, Nippon 125.00

MUSTACHE CUP, Floral, Austrian, White Ground 15.00
  Fruit Pattern, Webbed Shape Saucer, 3 Crown Mark 38.00
  Matching Saucer, Sailing Ship, Prayer, Sunderland Luster 95.00
  The Race Of The Century, Horses, Cheering Spectators 45.00
  Wilcox, Silver Plated 88.00

MZ Austria is a mark used by Moritz Zdekauer from about 1900. The firm worked in the town of Alt-Rohlau, Austria.

MZ AUSTRIA, Chocolate Pot, 4 Cups & Saucers 55.00
  Plate, Pink & White Roses, Muted Aqua Ground, 9 In. 30.00
  Sugar & Creamer, Covered 15.00
  Sugar & Creamer, Floral 10.00

Nailsea glass was made in the Bristol district in England from 1788 to 1873. Many pieces were made with loopings of colored glass as decorations.

NAILSEA, Candlestick, 7 In. 65.00
  Flask, Hand Blown, Red, White, & Blue Swirls, C.1820 .... 150.00
  Flask, White Loopings, Cobalt Blue Tooled Lip, Leather Holder 175.00
  Lamp, Blue Threaded Base & Rim Of Shade, White Loops, 13 1/2 In. 1000.00
  Lamp, Fairy, Red & White, 4 In. 350.00
  Pitcher, Amber Handle, White On Amber, 7 In. 210.00
  Pitcher, Water, Bulbous, Opaque, White Loopings, Red Ground, 8 1/8 In. 175.00
  Rose Bowl, Cranberry, White Loopings, 5 X 3 In. 95.00
  Vase, Blue, White Loops, 8 In. 235.00
  Vase, White Loops, Peacock Blue, 5 X 4 1/2 In. 35.00

NAKARA

Nakara is a trade name for a white glassware made around 1900 that was decorated in pastel colors. It was made by the C.F. Monroe Company of Meriden, Connecticut.

NAKARA, Box, Bishop's Hat Shape, Hinged Cover, Pink & White Azaleas, 8 In. 350.00
  Box, Blue Iris, Beige To Brown, Octagonal, Signed, 6 1/2 In. 550.00
  Box, Cigar, Covered, Green & Pink Florals, Signed 665.00
  Box, Flowers, 3 1/2 In.Diam. 235.00
  Box, Green To Yellow, Blue Iris, Octagonal, Hingeo Cover, 6 1/2 In. 350.00
  Box, Irises, Hinged Cover, Octagonal, 6 1/2 In. 550.00
  Box, Jewelry, Painted Flowers On Lid, Green, Signed3 1/4 In.Diam. 190.00
  Box, Olive Green With Flowers, Cut Corners, Marked, 6 1/2 In.Square 150.00
  Box, Purple Blossoms, Orange, Ormolu Frame, Signed, 5 1/2 In.Diam. 650.00
  Box, Salmon, Pink & Green, Round, 6 In. 225.00
  Dish, Open, Blue, 3 1/2 In.Diam. 135.00
  Dish, Pin, Beaded, Ormolu Handles, Signed, Green 125.00
  Humidor, Florals, Gold Letters, Green Ground, Signed 600.00
  Humidor, Pink Flowers, Cigars Written In Gold 450.00
  Smoke Set, Cigarette & Match Holder Attached, Flowers, 6 In. 650.00
  Vase, Baluster Form, Ormolu Stand, Florals, Signed, 13 1/2 In. 100.00
  Vase, Raised Scrolls, Pink Roses, Green Ground, Signed, 16 In. 300.00

Nanking china is a blue-and-white porcelain made in China for export during the eighteenth century.

NANKING, Bowl, Tea, With Saucer, 1790-1810 .... 135.00
  Cup & Saucer, Blue & White, Gold Rim, Pair 70.00
  Platter, Oval, Blue & White, Pavilion, Fisherman, Boat, 13 In. 150.00
  Platter, Oval, Blue & White, Reticulated Border, 11 1/2 In. 280.00
  Platter, Pavilions, Covered Boat, Blue & White, 13 In. 110.00
  Pot, Cream, Sparrow Beak Spout, 1790-1810 .... 265.00

Napkin rings were popular from 1869 to about 1900.

NAPKIN RING, Detroit Scenic, Gilt 15.00
  Figural, Baby Chick On Oval Base, Silver Plate, Rogers Smith 125.00
  Figural, Barrel On Curly Feet, Engraved Comin Thru The Rye 42.00
  Figural, Baseball Player At Bat, Silver Plated 175.00
  Figural, Bird, Holding Ring, Left Side, 1 On Right Side, Pair 195.00
  Figural, Bird, In Flight On Side Of Ring, Silver Plated, Marked 95.00
  Figural, Bird, On Nest, Eggs On Top Of Ring, Twig Feet 65.00
  Figural, Bird, Sits Beside Etched Ring 65.00
  Figural, Book With Clasp 80.00
  Figural, Boomerang, Marked 85.00
  Figural, Boy, Playing Ball With Cat 79.00
  Figural, Boy, Pulling Off Socks, Silver Plated 215.00
  Figural, Boy, Riding Dog Beside Ring, Silver Plated 215.00
  Figural, Boy, Standing By Fence 149.00
  Figural, Bulldog, Guarding Doghouse, Silver Plated 275.00
  Figural, Cat, In Tuxedo, Standing, Silver Plated 110.00
  Figural, Cat, On Top, Dog, Front Paws On Ring, Silver Plated 225.00
  Figural, Cat, Pulling Ring, Wheels, Silver Plated 195.00
  Figural, Cat, Pushing Hoop Ring, Silver Plated 125.00
  Figural, Chick & Whishbone, New Amersterdam, Silver Plated 25.00
  Figural, Chick & Wishbone, A Sterling Wish, Sterling Silver 95.00
  Figural, Chick & Wishbone, WR Mark, Silver Plated 36.00
  Figural, Chinaman, Pigtail, Flower At Feet, Basket Weave Ring 275.00
  Figural, Cow In Pasture, Sheaf Of Wheat, Wilcox, Silver Plate 250.00
  Figural, Cow, Standing Behind Ring, Silver Plated 165.00
  Figural, Crossed Rifles, Filigree Ring, Silver Plated 225.00
  Figural, Cupid & Wishbone On Heart Shaped Base, Silver Plated 95.00
  Figural, Dachshund, Ring On Back, Silver Plated 185.00
  Figural, Dog, Pulling Cart, Wheels Go Around 159.00
  Figural, Dog, Pulling Ring, Wheels, Girl Driving, Silver Plated 215.00
  Figural, Dog, Sits Beside Barrel, Silver Plated 145.00
  Figural, Eagle, Spread Wings, Silver Plated, Meriden, Pair 60.00
  Figural, Eagles, Holding Ring, Silver Plated, Meriden, Britannia 95.00
  Figural, Fawn, Garland Around Neck, Guards Ring, Square Foot 145.00
  Figural, Four-Leaf Clovers, Copper 7.50
  Figural, Fox, Pulling Cart, Wheels Move, Silver Plated 159.00
  Figural, French Maid, Silver Plated 215.00
  Figural, Frog 67.00
  Figural, Girl, Large Hat, Pushing Ring, Silver Plated 215.00
  Figural, Girl, Playing With Dog, Silver Plated 185.00
  Figural, Girl, With Fawn, Silver Plated 195.00
  Figural, Goat Pulling Ring, Wheels, Silver Plated .... 150.00 To 195.00
  Figural, Griffin, On Top Of Ring, Silver Plated 195.00
  Figural, Grizzly Bear 125.00
  Figural, Horse, Prancing, Ring On Back .... 195.00 To 210.00
  Figural, Horse, Pulling Cart, Movable Wheels, Rogers 275.00
  Figural, Kangaroo, Marked 85.00
  Figural, Kangaroo, Ostrich Hold Ring With Boomerang 95.00
  Figural, Kewpie 95.00
  Figural, Lady, Barefoot, Watering Flowers, Silver Plated 275.00
  Figural, Leaf, Long-Tailed Bird On Stem, Meriden 95.00
  Figural, Leaf, Ostrich & Kangaroo Ball Feet, 5 In. 95.00

Figural, Lily Bud, Curling Stem On Lily Leaf, Signed	85.00
Figural, Lily Pad & Flower, Ring Center, Rogers	55.00
Figural, Man, Bowtie, Highhat, Lady In Red Coat, Pair	22.00
Figural, Monkey & Dog, Dressed, Silver Plated	215.00
Figural, Ostrich On Side, Kangaroo Other, On Leaf	99.00
Figural, Peacock	135.00
Figural, Peasant Girl, Hands On Hip, Signed, 3 1/2 In.	150.00
Figural, Rifle In Front Of Ring, Kate Greenaway, Silver Plated	195.00
Figural, Sailor With Anchor, Silver Plated	215.00
Figural, Squirrel Eating Nut, Silver Plated	65.00
Figural, Squirrel, Pushing Ring, Silver Plated	195.00
Figural, Stag, Ring On Back, Silver Plated	210.00
Figural, Starfish & Flowers, 1 3/4 In.	28.00
Figural, Turtle, Crawling On Base, Silver Plated	125.00
Figural, Twin Eagles On Rectangular Base, Wilcox	50.00 To 75.00
Figural, Violin, Leaning Against Elevated Base	65.00
Figural, Water Lily Pad Base, Toronto Silver Plate Co.	95.00
Floral Design, Corset Shape, Initialed	12.50
Floral, Cloisonne	35.00
Gott Mit Uns, Brass	9.50
Pembroke Pattern, Sterling Silver, 1 1/2 In.High	60.00

*Nash glass was made in Corona, New York, by Arthur Nash and his sons
after 1919. He worked at the Webb factory in England and for the
Tiffany Glassworks in the United States.*

NASH, Candlestick, Red Chintz Design, Signed, 4 1/2 In., Pair	425.00
Compote, Chintz, Blue & Green On Clear Ground, Signed, 6 In.Diam.	135.00
Dish, Nut, Ribbed Body, Gold Iridescent, Signed, 4 In.Diam.	165.00
Vase, Chintz, Blue & Green, 10 1/4 In.	200.00
Vase, Flower Form, Florals Around Stem, Luster Gold, 5 1/2 In.	395.00
Vase, Gold Iridescent, Purple Iridescent Interior, 4 In.	275.00
Vase, Notched Rim, Molded Rib Design, Gold Iridescent, Signed, 4 1/2 In.	145.00
Vase, Red Opaque Luster, Blue Chintz Design, Signed, 10 1/4 In.	650.00

NATZLER, Bowl, C.1950, Red Reduction Glaze, 9 1/4 In Diam.	3100.00

NAUTICAL, see also Scrimshaw

NAUTICAL, Barometer, Admiral Fitroy's, Walnut Case, Hanging, 36 X 6 1/2 In.	375.00
Bell, Brass, Iron Clapper, Hang-Up Ring, 5 In.	50.00
Bell, Brass, 12 X 17 In.	250.00
Bell, Cast-Iron Hanger, 16 X 18 In.	500.00
Bell, Mounted In Carved Wood Stand, Bronze, 30 1/4 In.	150.00
Binnacle, John Bliss, New York, 1840-70, All Brass, 24 In.	175.00
Binnacle, Mahogany Base, Side Weights & Lights, Ireland	2750.00
Binnacle, Sharman D.Neil, Ltd., Belfast, Mahogany	2750.00
Chart, Washington State, 24 X 44 In.	6.50
Chest, American, C.1860, Lift-Out Tray, Pine, 11 X 15 X 9 In.	550.00
Chest, Apothecary, Mahogany, Brass Handles, 11 X 19 In.	300.00
Chest, Locking Drawers, Bottle Compartment, Gray, 19 X 1, 1/2 In.	425.00
Clock, Chelsea, U.S.Marine Corps, Silvered Dial, Nickel, 7 In.Diam.	225.00
Compass, Bronze, Compensating Balls, USNL	135.00
Compass, Dry, Dent, London, Gimbaled, Cover, Octagonal, 8 In.	1000.00
Compass, Gimbaled, Boxed, 5 In.Square	65.00
Compass, Gyro, Bronze	750.00
Compass, J.Bliss & Co., N.Y., 1840-70, Original Gimbal, Brass, 7 In.	1000.00
Compass, Walnut Box & Instructions, Brass	325.00
Compass, Wet, J.E.Hand & Sons, American, Cover, Copper Box, 7 1/2 In.	125.00
Compass, Wilcox, Crittenden & Co., Inc., Box 7 1/2 X 5 1/4 In.	125.00
Cronometer, Brass, Corcoran Witt & Co., C.1820, 7 1/2 X 12 In.	690.00
Door, With Porthole, Solid Teak	225.00
Eardrum, Whale, Good Color	15.00

Fid, For Sail Making, Wooden, 16 In. 16.00
Figurehead, Polynesian Girl, 19th Century 1300.00
Foghorn, Bellows, C.1850, Norwegian, Copper & Brass, 8 X 14 1/2 In. 325.00
Harpoon, Brass, 1844, 25 In. 125.00
Lamp, Signal, 19th Century, Copper Pins, Marked EGS, Brass, 14 In. 275.00
Lantern, Corner, Curved Lens, Brass Handle, Copper 105.00
Lantern, Handmade, Wick Lights, Port & Starboard, 9 In., Pair 175.00
Lantern, Masthead, Kerosene, Fresnel Lens, Galvanized 125.00
Lantern, Starboard & Port, Brass, 10 1/4 In., Pair 300.00
Log, Walker No. 23776, Rotars & Dials, Brass, 10 In. 175.00
Model, Lights Inside, People On Deck, C.1930, Paper, Wood, & Canvas 1250.00
Model, Santa Maria, Sails, Anchor, & Rigging, German 235.00
Model, 3-Masted Ship, Ivory Sailors, Whalebone & Wood, 37 X 24 In. 2700.00
Octant, J.L.Liscomb, Cased 700.00
Octant, Ramsden, London, 18th Century, Marked, Brass, 17 In. 2100.00
Parallel Rule, Ebony & Brass, 18 In. 42.00
Portholes, Brass, 12 In., Pair 135.00
Pulley, Sailing Vessel, Wooden 50.00
Pulley, Wrought-Iron Hook, Wooden, 15 In.Diam. 55.00
Pump, Wooden Plunger, Patent 1884, Rubber Hose, Brass, 30 In. 40.00
Rope Becket, Red, White, & Blue, 19th Century, 7 In. 80.00
Rule, Parallel, Rolling, Keuffer & Esser Co., N.Y., Box, 16 In. 175.00
Sailor's Valentine, Wax Figure Of Lady, Bouquet Of Roses, 1800s 150.00
Sextant, English Brass, 1943 Certificate, Mahogany Case 285.00
Sextant, Spencer & Co., London, Ebony, Ivory, & Brass, 14 In. 755.00
Ship's Wheel, Bronze, 12 In. 38.00
Sign, Kelvin, Bottomley & Baird Ltd., Engraved, Brass, 12 X 36 In. 395.00
Spotlight, Bronze 950.00
Steam Gauge, Bronze, 6 In.Diam. 24.00
Sternboard, From The Greenleaf 2100.00
Sundial & Compass, Equinoctial, A.Abraham Co., England, Case 800.00
Taff, Towed Behind Tall Ships To Measure Mileage, Brass, C.1830 .... 350.00
Telescope, Brass, Extends To 12 1/2 In. 58.00
Telescope, Day & Night, Doland, London, Brass, Extends To 35 In. 275.00
Telescope, H.E.Vincent, Charleston, Brass & Mahogany, Closed 24 In. 800.00
Telescope, Queen Anne Tripod, E.G.King, Boston, C.1850, 31 In.Long 1300.00
Telescope, Signed Miller, Extra Lens, Tripod, Boxed 1300.00
Telescope, 4-Section, American, Signed, Brass 235.00
Whistle, Boatswain's, Marked Tiffany 75.00
     NEEDLEWORK, see Textile, Picture; Textile, Sampler

> *Netsuke are small ivory, wood, metal, or porcelain pieces used as the button on
> the end of a cord holding a Japanese money pouch. The earliest date from
> the sixteenth century.*

NETSUKE, Bone, Gamma Sonnin, Holds Staff, Toad On Shoulder, 2 7/16 In. 80.00
  Bone, Shi-Shi Sitting Up, Front Paws On Ball, 1 1/2 In. 125.00
  Ivory & Wood, Whale, Inlaid Eyes, 19th Century 1700.00
  Ivory, Bamboo Shoot, Snail Crawling Up, Signed Masatsugu 550.00
  Ivory, Carpenter, Seated Cross Legged, Holding Mallet, Signed 2600.00
  Ivory, Chick In Egg, 1 1/2 In. 40.00
  Ivory, Coiled Snake, Eating Mouse, Mouse Behind Snake, 2 In. 65.00
  Ivory, Dog, Resting On Legs, Collar, Bell, Fur Details, Fur 800.00
  Ivory, Dog, Seated, Black Patches, Paw On Shell, Signed, Mitsubaru 750.00
  Ivory, Dragon, Tan Patina, 2 In. 55.00
  Ivory, Fish In Basket, 1 1/2 X 1 1/4 In. 75.00
  Ivory, Flowering Camellia, Full Bloom, On Twig, Signed Shubi 3500.00
  Ivory, Fox, 18th Century 2500.00
  Ivory, Icho Nuts, 3-Sided Type 700.00
  Ivory, Lady With 2 Faces, Signed, 2 In. 40.00
  Ivory, Man Riding A Kneeling Elephant 125.00
  Ivory, Man Seated On Crab, Hands In Front Of Face 110.00
  Ivory, Man Seated With Arms Folded, Standing Tiger 125.00
  Ivory, Man Standing, Wearing Kimono, Holding Pipe 100.00

Ivory, Man Wrestling With Dragon	125.00
Ivory, Man, Robe, Foot On Turtle, Holding Cloth, 2 In.	100.00
Ivory, Man, Seated, Smoking Pipe, Child Kneeling By Side, 2 In.	70.00
Ivory, Man, Sitting, Beating Drums With Drumsticks, 2 In.	40.00
Ivory, Man, Squatting On Large Crab, Wearing Kimono	110.00
Ivory, Man, Woman, Seated, Bench, Pouring Wine, Smoking Pipe, 2 In.	70.00
Ivory, Mice Playing In Rice Bale, 19th Century	200.00
Ivory, Monkey, Seated, Holding Frog, Pink Polychrome Details, Signed	900.00
Ivory, Monkey, Sitting, Holding Baby, Arm Outstretched, 2 In.	40.00
Ivory, Mother & Child, Standing, Bare Breasts, Shell Combs, Signed	2000.00
Ivory, Old Man, Nodding Head, 2 1/2 In.	60.00
Ivory, Rabbit Resting On Larger Rabbit, 2 In.	55.00
Ivory, Rat & Gourd, Extended With Stems, Rat On End, Inlaid Eyes	450.00
Ivory, Rat, Seated, Legs Under Body, Tail Curled, Inlaid Eyes	450.00
Ivory, Rats, 7, Stained Black, 3 White, Signed Kangyoku	900.00
Ivory, Samurai Carrying Bell, Signed	375.00
Ivory, Seated Man, Arms Enfolding Snarling Tiger	125.00
Ivory, Snake, Wrapped Around Monkey, Mouth Open, Teeth, Tongue	2500.00
Ivory, Standing Man, Robed, Holding Pipe To Ear	100.00
Ivory, Swan, Nesting, 2 Young In Her Wings, Signed Bisbue	1000.00
Ivory, Tiger & 2 Cubs, Seated On Log, Cub Biting Mother, Signed	400.00
Ivory, Tiger Killing Ram, Signed, 2 1/2 In.	565.00
Ivory, Tiger, Seated, Head Turned, Fur Details, Signed Masakazu	650.00
Ivory, Tiger, Seated, Licks Hind Paw, Eyes Inlaid, 19th Century	1800.00
Ivory, Toad With Smaller Toad On Back, 2 In.	32.00
Ivory, Toad, 2, Crouching On Lily Pad, Signed Osai	350.00
Ivory, Two Wrestlers Standing Side By Side, 2 In.	40.00
Ivory, Upside-Down Basket, Pair Of Mice, 2 In.	40.00
Ivory, Warrior, Standing, Sword, Crouching Figure On Hat, 2 In.	65.00
Ivory, Warrior, Wrestling Serpent, Holding Red Apple, 2 In.	110.00
Ivory, Wild Boar, Signed, 2 In.	50.00
Ivory, Woman & Child Carrying Huge Vase Up Stairs	45.00
Ivory, Woman & Child Carrying Vase Up Stairs	50.00
Ivory, Wrestler, Standing, Holding Open Kimono, Signed Bisbu	700.00
Ivory, Wrestlers, Waistbands, Aprons, Standing, Arm Around Neck	650.00
Wood, Boar & Dog, Running Side-By-Side, Signed Yasufusa	800.00
Wood, Boar, Head Raised, Inlaid Eyes, Signed Harumitsu	3000.00
Wood, Eagle, Grasping A Tengu Chief In Claws, Inlaid Eyes	650.00
Wood, Frog On Basket, Climbing Over Edge, Wickerwork, Signed	350.00
Wood, Frog, Seated, Wrapped In Leaf, 19th Century	45.00
Wood, Horse, Recumbent, Signed	160.00
Wood, Man, Kneeling, Arms Folded, Hair Dressed, Signed Sosui	1800.00
Wood, Monkey, With Young, Mother Seated, Signed Masanao	400.00
Wood, Mushrooms, Cluster Of 3, Stalk	500.00
Wood, Sleeping Dog, 18th Century	1000.00
Wood, Snake, Several Coils, Head Peering, Signed Minko	650.00
Wood, Wolf, 19th Century, Signed	1200.00

*New Martinsville Glass Manufacturing Company was established in 1901
in New Martinsville, West Virginia. It was bought and renamed the
Viking Glass Company in 1944 and is still producing fine glasswares.*

NEW MARTINSVILLE, see also Peachblow

NEW MARTINSVILLE, Basket, Janice, Blue, 10 X 13 In.	75.00
Bookends, Elephant	55.00 To 145.00
Bookends, Horse, Glass	39.00
Bookends, Nautilus, Crystal	50.00
Bookends, Sailing Ship, Paper Label, Pair	75.00
Bookends, Starfish, Crystal	60.00
Bottle, Perfume, Amber, Pair	19.00
Bottle, Perfume, Queen Anne, Blue	20.75
Bowl, Bride's, Peachblow, Crimped, Rose, Fuchsia, 10 1/2 In.	155.00
Candleholder, Figural, Seal, 7 In.	50.00
Candleholder, Green, Pair	45.00

Candleholder, Heart Shaped Swan, Pair	30.00
Figurine, Baby Bear	35.00 To 45.00
Figurine, Chick, Crystal	35.00
Figurine, Elephant, 7 In.	65.00
Figurine, Hunter, Pair	35.00
Figurine, Police Dog	45.00
Figurine, Rabbit	45.00
Figurine, Rooster, Crystal, 7 1/2 In.	55.00
Figurine, Ruby Heart Swan, 7 1/2 In.	20.00
Figurine, Russian Wolfhound	55.00
Figurine, Seal With Ball, 4 1/2 In.	35.00
Figurine, Squirrel, On Base, 6 In.	55.00
Figurine, Swan, Emerald, Heart, 5 In.	15.00
Figurine, Swan, Emerald, 7 1/2 In.	18.00 To 20.00
Figurine, Swan, Janice	25.00
Figurine, Wolfhound, Frosted	66.00
Jar, Dresser, Green, Covered, Signed	20.00
Mustard, Janice, Covered, Spoon	25.00
Pitcher, Red, Set Of 5 Tumblers	225.00
Rose Bowl, Janice, Crimped	15.00
Salt & Pepper Shaker, White Pillar, Flowers	25.00
Sugar & Creamer, Dark Green	13.50

Newcomb Pottery was founded by Ellsworth and William Woodward at Sophie Newcomb College, New Orleans, Louisiana, in 1896. The work continued through the 1940s. Pieces of this art pottery are marked with the letter N inside the letter C.

NEWCOMB, Bowl, Carved Jonquils, C.1915, Sadie Irvine, Blue Ground, 5 1/2 In.	660.00
Bowl, Carved Lilies, C.1915, Matte Glaze, Marked, 5 1/4 In.Diam.	385.00
Bowl, Pink Floral, Vines, Blue Ground, Artist HB, 7 In.Diam.	425.00
Swirls, Firm's Marks, Violet Ground, 2 3/4 In.	320.00
Toothpick, Deep Blue, Brown Specks	175.00
Vase, Band Of Leaves & Flowers, Marked, Matte Blue Ground, 5 In.	220.00
Vase, Bud, Geometric Design, 6 1/2 In.	375.00
Vase, Bud, Marked, Matte Blue, 2 1/2 X 6 1/4 In.	100.00
Vase, Bud, Thumb-Formed Spiral, Marked, Matte Black, 6 1/4 In.	150.00
Vase, Cylindrical, Carved Stylized Floral, C.1910, Marked, 6 1/2 In.	500.00
Vase, Dimpled, Green, Lavender, & Rose, 2 3/4 X 4 In.	230.00
Vase, Dimples, Green, Lavender, Rose, High Glaze, 4 X 2 3/4 In.	250.00
Vase, Gourd Shape, Marked, 3 3/4 X 4 3/4 In.	125.00
Vase, Leaves & Flowers, Marked, Blue Ground, 8 1/4 In.	400.00
Vase, Moon Shining On Spanish Moss, Signed H.Bailey, Blue, 6 In.	1400.00
Vase, Oak Tree, Moss & Moon, Sadie Irvine, 6 In.	800.00
Vase, Trees & Spanish Moss, Cylindrical, Paper Label, 5 3/4 In.	440.00
Vase, White Flowers, Signed Henrietta Bailey, Blue, 6 In.	700.00

Newhall Porcelain Manufactory was started at Newhall, Shelton, Staffordshire, England, in 1782. Simple decorated wares were made. Between 1810 and 1825, the factory made a glassy bone porcelain marked with the factory name.

NEWHALL, Cup & Saucer, Chinese Figures, Orange	100.00
Dish, Black & Gray Floral Spray Design, 18th Century, 8 1/2 In.	110.00
Teapot, Flower's Sprigged, C.1790	175.00

Niloak Pottery (Kaolin spelled backwards) was made at the Hyten Brothers Pottery in Benton, Arkansas, between 1909 and 1946. Although the factory did make cast and molded wares, collectors are most interested in the marbleized art pottery line.

NILOAK, Bowl, Flower, Pastel Blue To Pink, Signed, 7 1/2 X 3 1/2 In. 30.00
   Candlestick, Swirl, 8 1/2 In., Pair 225.00
   Cornucopia, Olive-Green, Pedestal, 6 In. 16.00
   Ewer, Winged Eagle On Side, Semimatte Glaze, 10 In. 30.00
   Ewer, 7 In. 15.00
   Frog, Figural 15.00
   Pitcher, Eagle, 10 In. 20.00
   Pitcher, Marked, Foil Sticker, Green Over Tan, 4 X 5 In. 5.00
   Pitcher, Milk, Pink 15.00
   Planter, Figural, Frog 15.00
   Sugar & Creamer, Blue To Pink 35.00
   Sugar & Creamer, Signed, Blue 45.00
   Vase, Cornucopia & Leaf, Green, 3 In. 15.00
   Vase, Fan, Matte Blue, 6 3/4 In. 25.00
   Vase, Green, Silver Sticker, 8 In. 28.00
   Vase, Matte Blue, 6 1/4 In. 18.50
   Vase, Pink, Twisted With Wings, 7 In. 12.00
   Vase, Scalloped Top, Double Handle, Rose To Blue, 8 In. 45.00
   Vase, Swan, Blue 20.00
   Vase, Swirl, Hourglass Shape, Impressed Mark, 7 1/2 In. 95.00
   Vase, Swirl, 4 In. 38.00
   Vase, Swirl, 5 In. 25.00
   Vase, Swirl, 8 1/4 In. .... 60.00 To 80.00
   Vase, Swirl, 9 1/4 In. 50.00
   Vase, Swirl, 10 1/2 In. 85.00

Nippon-marked porcelain was made in Japan from 1891 to 1921. "Nippon" is the Japanese word for "Japan."

NIPPON, Ashtray & Matchbox Holder, White Rock Soda, Green Letters, Marked 35.00
   Ashtray, Black Cat On Fence 125.00
   Ashtray, Dogs On Both Sides, Blown Out, Rectangular 325.00
   Ashtray, Elk In Woods 125.00
   Ashtray, Matchbox Holder, Fatima Cigarettes 48.00
   Ashtray, Scenic, Beaded, Bisque 60.00
   Ashtray, Windmill Scene, 5 1/4 In. 50.00
   Basket, Butterfly Design, Gold Trim, Signed 28.50
   Basket, Floral, Gold Handle, 8 In. 50.00
   Basket, Floral, Gold Trim, Pink, 4 In. 40.00
   Basket, Gold Relief, Handled, White, 5 X 5 In. 50.00
   Basket, Pink Roses, Gold, Signed, 9 In. 24.00
   Basket, Raspberries, Gold Handle & Edge, 5 1/2 In. 22.50
   Basket, Sailboat, Enameled Design, Handled, 9 In.Long 125.00
   Basket, Yellow Flowers, Gray Leaves, Marked 38.00
   Berry Set, Lake, Forest, White Swan, Dark Ground, 7 Piece 350.00
   Berry Set, Multifloral Roses, Green Ground, Marked, 7 Piece 45.00
   Berry Set, Painted Pansies, Gold Trim, Maple Leaf Mark, 13 Piece 225.00
   Berry Set, Rose Trim, Gold, 6 Piece 125.00
   Berry Set, Swan Scene, Beading, Gold, Signed, 5 Piece 110.00
   Berry Set, Violets & Leaves, Scalloped Rim, Marked, 6 Piece 85.00
   Birdbath, Bird On Rim, Signed, 6 1/2 In. 375.00
   Bottle, Cologne, Blue Flowers 35.00
   Bottle, Cologne, White, Cobalt Band, Gold Beading, Pink Flowers, 4 In. 70.00
   Bottle, Perfume, Beaded Top, Sailboat On Pink, Green Wreath Mark 30.00
   Bottle, Perfume, Violets, Gold Trim, White Ground, Green Mark 55.00
   Bottle, Perfume, Yellow With Turquoise Ground, Green M, 4 1/2 In. 120.00
   Bowl, Acorn, Bisque Finish, Scalloped Edges, Marked, 5 3/4 In. 35.00
   Bowl, Bluebirds & Flowers, Shallow, Green Wreath Mark, 9 In. 30.00
   Bowl, Floral Border, Gold Trim, Flared, Marked, 7 1/2 In. 38.00
   Bowl, Floral, Footed, 6 In.Diam. 75.00
   Bowl, Fruit, Grapes & Leaves, Gold Design, Footed, M In Wreath, 7 In. 85.00

Bowl, Grape, Bluebirds, Blossoms, Underplate, 7 In. 75.00
Bowl, Hand-Painted Floral Interior, Green M In Wreath, 10 In.Diam. 319.00
Bowl, House, Trees, Lake, Beaded Handle, 9 In. 48.00
Bowl, Medallions, Gold Edge, 3-Legged, 8 1/2 In. 30.00
Bowl, Molded Brazil Nuts, 2-Handled, Signed, 7 1/2 In. 125.00
Bowl, Nut, Brazil, Beading & Jeweling, Earth Tones, Marked, 9 In. 95.00
Bowl, Nut, Slip Work On Feet, Marbleized Effect, 7 1/2 In. 85.00
Bowl, Orange Sunset, Trees, Lake, Bull Elk, 7 In. 40.00
Bowl, Peanut, Ball Feet, Heavy Moriage, Blown Out, 7 In.Diam. 80.00
Bowl, Peanut, Molded Peanut Bottom, 3 Peanut Feet, Marked, 8 In. 95.00
Bowl, Pierced Handles, Pink Roses, Gold Trim, Artist Signed, 8 In. 60.00
Bowl, Pink & Magenta Clover, Pastel Ground, Gold Trim, Marked, 8 In. 32.00
Bowl, Pink Floral, Gold Trim, Scalloped, 6 In. 15.00
Bowl, Poinsettia, Design, Footed, Green Mark, 6 In.Diam. 45.00
Bowl, Punch, Scenic Medallion, Swans, Lake, Green Ground, Marked 375.00
Bowl, Raised Chestnuts, Footed, 7 1/2 In. 65.00
Bowl, Red, Blue, Green, & Gold, Center Medallion, 10 In. 55.00
Bowl, Scenic, 10 In.Square 70.00
Bowl, Swan In Lake, Trees, Sprig Handles, 8 In. 50.00
Bowl, Swan, Scenic, Square, 8 In. 115.00
Bowl, Triangle Of Flowers, Blue Morning Glory, 6 1/2 In. 12.00
Bowl, White, Gold Swags, Flowers, Signed, 9 In 75.00
Bowl, Windmill, House, Beaded Rim & Handles, Green Mark, 7 1/2 In. 65.00
Bowl, 2-Handled, Blue Mark, Square, 9 1/2 In.Diam. 60.00
Box, Flower Design, Green, Yellow, Blue, Gold Trim, 4 In. 38.50
Box, Grand Piano Shape, Covered, Signed 175.00
Box, Pin, Leaves & Flowers, Green Wreath Mark, 3 1/4 In. 25.00
Box, Powder, Floral Border, Green Wreath Mark, 4 In. 40.00
Box, Powder, White Ground, Pink Roses, Footed, M In Wreath 40.00
Box, Ring, Floral, Pedestal, Covered, 3 In. 25.00
Box, Spade Shape, Pink Roses, Gold Trim, 2 3/4 In. 15.50
Box, Trinket, Butterfly Shape, Floral 40.00
Butter Pat, Azalea 15.00
Butter Pat, Floral & Gold, Open Handles, Set Of 6 .... 35.00
Butter Pat, Red Flowers, Green & Blue Trim, 3 1/4 In. 13.00
Butter, Orange Flowers, Gold Beading, Covered, Marked 80.00
Butter, White Opalescent Jewel & Flowers, Gold Trim 145.00
Cake Plate, Allover Design, 11 In.Diam. 80.00
Cake Set, Flying Egrets, Gold & Jeweled Edge, 7 Piece 225.00
Cake Set, Hand-Painted, Violets, 7 Piece 55.00
Cake Set, Scenic, House & Trees, 6 Plates, 7 Piece 135.00
Cake Set, Turquoise Ground, Flying Egrets, Gold & Jeweled Border 225.00
Cake Set, Windmill Center, Gold Trim, Cobalt Blue 245.00
Candlestick, Black & White Design, Pink Ground, 5 In., Pair 25.00
Candlestick, Enameled, Red & Blue Design, C.1900, 9 In. 175.00
Candlestick, Iris Outlined In Gold, Marked, 5 1/4 In. 40.00
Candlestick, Moriage, Marked, 8 In. 175.00
Candlestick, Pink, Black & White Design, Pair 70.00
Candlestick, White, Flowers & Gold Trim, Marked, 5 In. 20.00
Casserole, Birds & Flowers, Covered, Handles, Signed, 8 In. 20.00
Celery Set, Blue Flowers & Butterflies, Marked, 7 Piece 60.00
Celery Set, Floral, Marked, Tray, 12 3/4 X 5 In. 45.00
Celery Set, Rural Scene, Shaded Greens, 7 Piece 95.00
Celery Set, Yellow Roses, 6 Piece 115.00
Chamberstick, Cobalt & Floral, Marked 40.00
Charger, Floral, Paneled, Yellow Ground 30.00
Charger, Lobster, Shells, Celery, Pierced, 12 In. 195.00
Cheese Dish, Domed Cover, Orange Flowers, M In Green Wreath 65.00
Cheese Dish, Pink Flowers, Beige Banding, Gold Outlining, M In Wreath 55.00
Chocolate Pot, Bluebirds 200.00
Chocolate Pot, Floral Medallion, Gold, Maple Leaf Mark, 11 In. 205.00
Chocolate Pot, Flying Swallows & Flowers, Marked, 9 1/2 In. 180.00
Chocolate Pot, Gold Beading, Roses, Gold Ground 275.00

Nippon, Chocolate Set, Floral Design,
Pot, 6 Cups & Saucers

Chocolate Pot, Gold Beads & Jewels, Farm Scene	285.00
Chocolate Pot, Moriage Dragon, Green Eyes, Red Tongue, Signed, 10 In.	210.00
Chocolate Pot, Moriage, Roses, Green Ground	250.00
Chocolate Pot, Raised Gold Jewels, Gold Ball Feet	375.00
Chocolate Pot, Roses, Pink & Lavender Flowers, Green Trim, Marked	125.00
Chocolate Pot, Royal Blue, Red & Pink Roses, Nagoya, Signed	140.00
Chocolate Pot, White, Bands Of Pink Roses, Gold Design	40.00
Chocolate Set, Cobalt & Floral, 14 Piece	265.00
Chocolate Set, Cobalt Border, Floral Design	245.00
Chocolate Set, Deco Style, Floral, Jeweled Border, Marked	165.00
Chocolate Set, Floral Border Top, Blue Rising Sun Mark, 10 Piece	125.00
Chocolate Set, Floral Design, Pot, 6 Cups & Saucers *Illus*	300.00
Chocolate Set, Floral, Cobalt Blue, 14 Piece	175.00
Chocolate Set, Raised Gold Florals, Imperial Nippon	375.00
Chocolate Set, Rose Floral, Brown Ground, Marked, 6 Cups & Saucers	165.00
Chocolate Set, Royal Koga-Geisha Girls Design, Gold Trim	250.00
Chocolate Set, Scenes Of San Francisco, 6 Piece	400.00
Chocolate Set, Swans On Lake, Green Mark, 6 Piece	285.00
Chocolate Set, White, Gold Floral Design, Green Wreath Mark	185.00
Cider Set, Ducks On Lake, 5 Mugs	275.00
Cider Set, Large Roses, 4 Mugs	175.00
Cocoa Pot, Red Poppies & Gold Trim, Marked	165.00
Compote, Jeweled, 3 1/2 X 5 1/4 In.Diam.	30.00
Compote, Pineapple, Grapes, Large Matte	125.00
Compote, Red & Blue, Butterflies & Floral, 10 In.	75.00
Compote, Red Banding, Gold Lace Flowers, Marked, 10 In.	75.00
Compote, Scenic, Gold Beading & Trim, Blue Maple Leaf Mark, 4 1/2 In.	55.00
Compote, Wreaths Of Pink Roses, Gold Trim, Green M Wreath Mark	45.00
Condiment Set, Florals, Yellow Bands, Gold Beaded, 4 Piece	40.00
Cookie Jar, Blue & White Cranes	200.00
Cookie Jar, Floral, Gold Trim, Marked	135.00
Cookie Jar, Gold & Pink Roses, 6-Sided, Royal Crown Mark	155.50
Cookie Jar, Lavender, Pink & Yellow Flowers, Green Edging, 7 In.	88.00
Cookie Jar, Melon Rib, Beaded Tassels, Gold Trim, Lid	150.00
Cookie Jar, Melon Rib, Scenic, 3 Gold Feet, Cobalt Blue, Gold Trim	275.00
Cookie Jar, Scenic Medallion With Swans & Jewels, Cobalt Blue Trim	250.00
Cookie Jar, Scenic, Swans, Jeweled, Cobalt Blue Trim	275.00
Corn Set, Hand-Painted, 7 Piece	350.00
Cracker Jar, Allover Gold Design, Roses, Gold Beading, Handled	145.00
Cracker Jar, Floral & Geometric Design, 6-Sided, Gold Trim	42.00
Cracker Jar, Floral, Cobalt Blue Trim	65.00
Cracker Jar, Fox Hunt, Handled, Marked	45.00
Cracker Jar, Gilt & Pink Rose Band, M Wreath, 2 Handles	55.00
Cracker Jar, Melon Shape, Raised Enameling, Blue & Gold	150.00
Cracker Jar, Moriage Dragon	265.00
Cracker Jar, Pink & Lilac Flowers, Cobalt Blue Rim	175.00
Cracker Jar, Red Roses, Gold Trim, 3 Feet, Green Mark	75.00

Cracker Jar, Red, Gaudy, Gold Trim, 3-Handled 225.00
Cracker Jar, Swelling Shoulders, 6 Panels Of Flowers, Shrine Mark 110.00
Creamer & Sugar, Bluebirds, Gold Edging, Marked 90.00
Creamer & Sugar, Windmill, Trees, Lake, Gold Trim 24.00
Creamer, Egyptian Design, Palm Trees, Boat, Lake, Marked 25.00
Creamer, Gold & Beaded 28.00
Cricket Jar, Silhouette Pattern 65.00
Cup & Saucer, Fuchsia & Lilac Flowers, Green Crown Mark, Set Of 5 .... 100.00
Cup & Saucer, Gold Beading, Maple Leaf Mark 25.00
Cup & Saucer, Orange Roses, Green Ground 18.00
Cup & Saucer, Phoenix Bird, Rising Sun Mark 15.00
Cup & Saucer, Pink & Green Scenic, Black Beading, Marked 28.00
Cup & Saucer, Pink Floral, Blue Ground, Marked 10.00
Cup & Saucer, Violets, Rising Sun Mark 20.00
Cup & Saucer, Yellow, Blue, Orange, Sailboat, Marked 30.00
Cup, Lemonade, Blackberry 15.00
Cup, Lemonade, Strawberry Design, Hand-Painted, Miniature 13.00
Cup, Pedestal Base, Eggshell Procelain, Gold & Floral, Signed 125.00
Decanter, Whiskey, Moriage, Covered, Multicolored, 8 In. 295.00
Dish, Basket, Pink & Blue Morning Glories, 7 X 5 In. 55.00
Dish, Basket, Tree Of Life Design, Marked, 7 1/2 In. 28.00
Dish, Candy, Nile Scene, Blown-Out Coconuts, Signed 40.00
Dish, Candy, Pink Roses, Ivy, Gold Lace, Signed, 7 In. 30.00
Dish, Candy, Roses, Outlined In Gold, Footed, Open, Signed, 7 In. 35.00
Dish, Celery, Blue, Yellow, Orange, Sailboat, Gold Band, Marked, 5 In. 45.00
Dish, Celery, Cottage, Lake, & Boat Scene, Beaded 28.00
Dish, Celery, Gray Birds 30.00
Dish, Cheese, Azalea 75.00
Dish, Cheese, Black Stripes & Roses 48.00
Dish, Cheese, Green Border, Pink Florals, Golds 42.50
Dish, Cheese, Rising Sun, Slant Top, Pink Roses 40.00
Dish, Cheese, Slant Top, Floral & Gold Trim, Marked, 7 3/4 X 3 In. 55.00
Dish, Dresser, Shamrock Shaped, Flowers, Gold Trim, Marked 35.00
Dish, Jiggs Cartoon Character, Blown Out, Signed 65.00
Dish, Palm Trees, Heart Shaped, 4 3/4 In. 35.00
Dish, Palm Trees, Heart Shaped, 5 In. 35.00
Dish, Pancake, Brown & Beige, Geometric Design, Marked 50.00
Dish, Pancake, Cobalt Blue & Gold On White, Cover, Maple Leaf Mark 110.00
Dish, Pancake, Floral, White Ground 40.00
Dish, Pickle, Floral, 7 1/2 In. 10.00
Dish, Pin, Dresser, 3-Footed, Orange Flowers, Black Ground, 2 1/4 In. 45.00
Dish, Roses, Green Border, Gold Lacing, Marked, 9 In. 48.00
Dish, Warm Sunset Scene, Handled, 6 In. 12.00
Dish, White, Pink Flowers, Green Ivys, Yellow Border, 6 1/4 In. 24.00
Doll Head, Bisque, Ball Jointed, Blue Eyes, 21 In. 275.00
Dresser Set, Azalea Pattern, 6 Piece 160.00
Dresser Set, Gold Feet, Green Wreath Mark 150.00
Dutch Shoe, Green Mark 65.00
Eggcup, Blown-Out Doll Face, Signed 85.00
Ewer, Cobalt & Roses, Gold, 10 1/2 In. 185.00
Ewer, Gold With Purple, Iris Green Ground, Marked, 11 1/2 In. 125.00
Ewer, Green, Gold & Violet, Leaf Mark, 11 In. 195.00
Ewer, Moriage, Enameled Design Panels, Signed, 8 In. 110.00
Ewer, Portrait Of Madame Recamier, Olive Green, Gold Trim, 12 In. 575.00
Ewer, Raised Gold Mums, Red, Royal Kinran, 12 In. 495.00
Ewer, Roses, Blue & Gold Handle, Spout, & Pedestal, Marked, 9 1/4 In. 210.00
Ewer, Royal Kinran, Red, Raised Gold Mums, 12 In. 495.00
Fernery, Floral Medallions, Dots, Blue Maple Leaf Mark, 5 In.Square 135.00
Fernery, Lake, Trees, Autumn Shades, Footed, Marked, 7 In. 185.00
Fernery, Moriage Trim, 5 1/2 In. 50.00
Fernery, Scenic, Jeweled Feet, Square, 6 In. 75.00
Fernery, Scenic, Lake, Trees, Autumn Shades, Jeweled Sides, Marked, 7 In 185.00
Fruit Set, Gold Gilding Florals, Blue Leaf Mark, 7 In., Set Of 6 .... 95.00

Ginger Jar, Cobalt Panels, Gray Flowers, Marked	150.00
Goblet, Allover Violets, Leaves, Ivys, Gold Trim, Marked, 6 In.	85.00
Gravy Boat & Underplate, Scrolls, Gold Beading, Blue Trim	75.00
Gravy Boat, Underplate, Hand-Painted, Blue & Gold Scrolling	98.00
Hair Receiver, Blue & Purple Violets, White Beading, Gold Trim	27.00
Hair Receiver, Encrusted Gold & Beading, Lattice Design	40.00
Hair Receiver, Gold, Pink Squares	22.00
Hair Receiver, Lake Scene, Swans, Browns, Marked	16.00
Hair Receiver, Pink Flowers, Gold Trim, Blue Mark	45.00
Hair Receiver, Rose, Gold Netting, Blue, Rose, Flowers, 5 In.	35.00
Hair Receiver, Violet Flowers, Hand-Painted, Covered	35.00
Hair Receiver, 3 Gold Feet, Gold Leaves, White Enamel Flowers	35.00
Hatpin Holder, Airplane Design	85.00
Hatpin Holder, Floral, White Ground	25.00
Hatpin Holder, Flowers, Beading, Green Maple Leaf	30.00
Hatpin Holder, Multicolored, Marked	37.00
Hatpin Holder, Purple Flowers, Open Top	22.50
Hatpin Holder, Roses, Gold, RC Mark	35.00
Humidor, Automobile Design, Signed	400.00
Humidor, Collie Dog Blown-Out	550.00
Humidor, Deer, Scenic, 4 1/2 In.	175.00
Humidor, Dogs, Blown-Out	600.00
Humidor, Flowers & Gold, Lavender Ground, Hexagon	225.00
Humidor, Geometric Design, Beer & Woods, Blue Wreath, 5 1/2 In.	125.00
Humidor, Moose, Hand-Painted	225.00
Humidor, Playing Cards & Poker Chips	275.00
Humidor, Reindeer, Marked	95.00
Humidor, Sailboat & Palm Trees	185.00
Humidor, Sailboat Scene, Raised Beading, Green Wreath Mark, 6 In.	200.00
Humidor, Scenic, Trees, Leaves, Green Mark, 2 1/2 X 4 In.	125.00
Humidor, Scenic, 4-Sided, Green M In Wreath, 5 In.	225.00
Humidor, Wooded Scene, Green M Mark, 5 1/2 In.	125.00
Inkwell, Pen Rest	175.00
Jar, Cricket, Roses, Gold Overlay & Finial, Covered, 4 1/4 In.	75.00
Jar, Jam, Flowers, Gold Trim, Underplate	125.00
Jar, Jam, Jeweled, 3 Piece	85.00
Jar, Jam, Scenic, Royal Kaga	55.00
Jar, On Plate, Pink Roses, Gream Ground, Spoon, Blue Rising Sun	25.00
Jar, Powder, Roses, Gold Edge, Green Mark	75.00
Jar, Powder, Roses, Gold Trim, Marked, 4 1/2 In.	35.00
Jar, Scenic Design, Indented Corners, Green Wreath Mark, 4 3/4 In.	70.00
Jug, Wine, Ear Of Corn & Husks, Brown, Green, Yellow	245.00
Jug, Wine, Fox Hunt Scene	325.00
Jug, Wine, Green Ground, Clusters Of Purple Flowers	375.00
Jug, Wine, Portrait Of Monk, Green Ground, 8 In.	325.00
Jug, Wine, Scenic, Moriage Design	365.00
Lamp, Fairy, Owl, Bisque	*Illus* 2000.00
Lazy Susan, Orange & Yellow Roses, Marked	30.00
Lemonade Set, Purple Violets, Gold Border, Marked, Set Of 4 Mugs	125.00
Match Holder, Flowers, Outlined In Gold, Marked	40.00
Match Holder, Green, Blue, Jeweling & Gold Beading, 2 3/4 In.	95.00
Match Holder, Striker Attached Plate, Heart Shaped	58.00
Matchbox Holder, Souvenir, U.S.Capitol Building, 4 In.Long	65.00
Mayonnaise Set, Green & Yellow, 3 Piece	65.00
Mayonnaise Set, Multifloral, Gold Trim, 3 Piece, Marked	42.00
Mayonnaise, Azalea Pattern, 2 Piece	15.00
Mayonnaise, Pink Roses, Gold Lines, Marked, 3 Piece	30.00
Mug, Blown-Out Doll Face, Marked, 3 In.	115.00
Mug, Boats On River At Dawn, Signed, Green Mark, 3 1/2 In.	120.00
Mug, Drinking Monk, Moriage Design, Signed	350.00
Mug, Fisherman, Blown Out, Green Mark	850.00
Mug, Googly-Eyed Boy	55.00
Mug, Indian In Canoe, Gray Matte Ground, Wreath Mark	165.00

Nippon, Lamp, Fairy, Owl, Bisque

Mug, Moriage Dragon, Green Mark, 5 1/2 In.	185.00
Mug, Violets, Gold Trim, Handled, 4 In.	12.50
Mustard & Underplate, Floral Roses, Gold Beading, Green M In Wreath	18.00
Mustard & Underplate, Yellow, Beige, & Brown Decoration, Ladle	40.00
Mustard Pot, Attached Tray, Floral Band, Covered	26.00
Mustard Pot, Pink Flowers, Green & Gold Decorations	27.00
Mustard Pot, Pink Roses, Gold Trim, Covered, Spoon	20.00
Mustard Pot, Spoon, Florals & Golds	29.00
Mustard Set, Tray, Salt & Pepper, Jar, Spoon, Rising Sun Mark	36.00
Napkin Ring, Blue, Green, Gold Floral, Marked	50.00
Napkin Ring, Triangular Shaped, Pair	75.00
Nappy, Pink & Green, Ivy, Gold Lacing, Marked, 7 In.	30.00
Nappy, Roses, Green Ground, Gold Lacing, Square, 5 In.	25.00
Nappy, Western Scene Of Cowboy, Horse, Lariat, Handled	50.00
Nappy, White, Band Of Pink & Yellow Flowers	15.00
Nappy, Yellow Flowers, Artist Signed	45.00
Nut Set, Flowers, Gold Rim, 7 Piece	75.00
Nut Set, Gold & Violets & Greenery, Blue E-Oh Mark	100.00
Nut Set, Green, White, Gold, Scalloped, 6 In.Bowl, 5 Cups, Marked	115.00
Nut Set, Melon Shape, White, Gold Lacing, Marked	35.00
Nut Set, Sailboat, Pedestal, Cobalt Blue & Gold, 6 Piece	160.00
Nut Set, White & Purple Flowers, Scalloped Edge, Marked, Set Of 5	85.00
Pincushion Doll, Dutch Girl	100.00
Pitcher, Berries, Florets, Gold Neck, Geometric Design, 10 In.	159.00
Pitcher, Gold, Green, Gold Beading, Marked, 7 In.	70.00
Pitcher, Lemonade, Pink Flowers, Cherry Blossom Mark	45.00
Pitcher, Milk, Azalea	115.00
Pitcher, Milk, Flower Border, Raised Gold & Beading, Covered, 7 In.	55.00
Pitcher, Milk, Scenic, Gold Panel, Blue	100.00
Pitcher, Milk, White, Green With Gold, 7 1/2 In.	55.00
Pitcher, Portrait, Raised Gold, Beading, Blue Maple Leaf, 6 In.	225.00
Pitcher, Roses, Gold Trim, Green Ground, 8 In.	75.00
Pitcher, Syrup, Turquoise & Brown, Scene Of Tree, House, Sea	59.00
Pitcher, Syrup, Underplate, Floral	65.00
Pitcher, Water, Red Roses, Cobalt Blue	125.00
Pitcher, Water, Rising Sun, Suns Are Gold	35.00
Planter, Egyptian Scene, 3-Pillared	130.00
Planter, Gold Borders, Jade Jewels, Cobalt Blue, 9 1/2 In.	235.00
Planter, Scenic, 8 In.Diam.	160.00
Plaque, Basket Of Grapes, Framed	130.00
Plaque, Boat Scene, Blue Maple Leaf Mark, 9 In.	95.00
Plaque, Forest Scene, Lavender, Brown, Chocolate Border, Marked, 9 In.	75.00
Plaque, Hand-Painted White Orchids, Gold Bead Trim, Leaf Mark, 10 In.	95.00
Plaque, Hanging, Bisque, Moriage Bird, Berries, Yellow Ground, 8 In.	65.00

Plaque, Hanging, House, Trees, Water, 9 In.	55.00
Plaque, Hanging, Orange Sunset, Trees, Creek, Bridge, 8 1/2 In.	75.00
Plaque, Hanging, Sunset, Birch Trees, 7 1/2 In.	65.00
Plaque, Lion, Bas Relief, 10 1/2 In.	600.00
Plaque, Moose, Blown-Out	475.00
Plaque, Scenic, Bisque, 10 In.	140.00
Plaque, Spring Scene, 11 In.	200.00
Plaque, Wall, Fish, Scallions, 12 1/2 In.	225.00
Plaque, Wall, Hunting Scene, Marked, 9 In.	85.00
Plaque, Wall, Stylized Owl In Sunset, 10 In.Marked	105.00
Plaque, Woodland Scene, Green M Wreath Mark, Bisque Finish	55.00
Plate, Azalea, 10 In.	15.00
Plate, Bird & Floral, 6 In.	15.00
Plate, Blown-Out Indian On Horseback, 10 1/2 In.	595.00
Plate, Cake, Black & White Scenic, Gold Trim, Blue Leaf Mark	35.00
Plate, Cake, Daisy Design, 10 1/2 In.	30.00
Plate, Camel Rider, Tent, Rised Gold Border	175.00
Plate, Capitol At Washington, Pink Poppy, 8 1/2 In.	50.00
Plate, Chestnuts, 8 1/2 In.	50.00
Plate, Chinese Pattern, Gold, 10 In.	70.00
Plate, Cobalt, Gold, Lace Design, Marked, 8 1/2 In.	58.00
Plate, Desert Island, Palm Trees, 8 In.	12.00
Plate, Flowers, Peacock, Black Ground, Blue Border, 8 1/2 In.	30.00
Plate, Gaudy Roses, Marked, 10 In.	75.00
Plate, Grape Design, Scalloped, 13 In.	125.00
Plate, Hand-Painted, Pierced Handle, 6 1/2 In., Pair	25.00
Plate, House & Chickens, 7 1/2 In.	70.00
Plate, Mums, Green M, 10 In.	45.00
Plate, Pink & Red Roses, 8 In.Diam.	18.00
Plate, Pink Carnations, Marked, 8 In., Set Of 4	200.00
Plate, Snow Goose, 4 Birds, Beading, 9 In.	45.00
Plate, Soup, Bouillon, Underplate, Azalea	17.50
Plate, Swags Of Roses, Gold Trim, Signed, 10 In.	45.00
Plate, Tree Design, 8 1/2 In.	40.00
Plate, Washington, D.C., Roses, Marked, 8 1/2 In.	30.00
Platter, Azalea, 11 1/2 In.	35.00
Platter, Lorraine Design, Signed, 16 1/4 In.	16.00
Punch Bowl, Purple & Green Grapes, Matte Finish, Green M In Wreath	335.00
Punch Set, Scenic, Gold Trim, 7 Piece	600.00
Relish, Azalea, 4-Part	75.00
Relish, Cobalt, Floral	28.00
Relish, Egyptian Boat Scene, 7 In.	24.00
Relish, Gold, Magenta Flowers, Signed, 7 In.	16.00
Relish, Green, Aqua, Navy Stylized Design, Marked	20.00
Relish, Lake, Trees, 2-Handled, M In Wreath, Hand-Painted	20.00
Relish, Scenic, Divided, Pedestal, 10 1/2 In.	60.00
Ring Tree, Hand, Florals	40.00
Ring Tree, Pink Flowers, Gold Trim, Gold Beading, Marked	60.00
Rose Jar, Covered, Gold & Floral, Signed	65.00
Rose Jar, Covered, Maple Leaf Mark, 6 In.	65.00
Salt & Pepper, Azalea	16.00 To 40.00
Salt & Pepper, Birds On Tree, Blue Imperial	15.00
Salt & Pepper, Handled, Floral & Gold Bands, Pair	18.50
Salt & Pepper, Pink Floral, Marked	12.00
Salt & Pepper, Pink Flowers, White Ground, Gold Band, Signed	25.00
Salt & Pepper, Portrait, Beading, Footed, Green	125.00
Salt & Pepper, Royal Satsuma, Figures, Houses, Gold	20.00
Salt, Cobalt Blue, Gold Trim, Set Of 7	40.00
Shaker, Sugar, Gold On Cream, Green Wreath Mark, 3 1/2 In.	55.00
Shaker, Sugar, Morning Glory Design, Signed	55.00
Shaker, Sugar, White Netting, Purple Violets	37.50
Shaving Mug, Floral & Gold, Green M In Wreath Mark	70.00
Shaving Mug, Rose Design, Gold Trim, Green M In Wreath	110.00

Shoe, Dutch, Floral	65.00
Smoke Set, Humidor, Scenic, Cigarette Holder, Tray	165.00
Smoke Set, Indian Pattern Border, Horse's Head Center	575.00
Spittoon, Lady's Hand, Violet & Turquoise Beading, Marked	145.00
Stein, Dutch Scene, 9 In.	250.00
Stein, Enameled Turquoise Dots, Gold Bands, 2 Oval Scenes, 5 1/2 In.	135.00
Strainer, Tea, Cobalt, Roses, Gold Trim	70.00
Strainer, Tea, Pink & Blue Floral, Marked	33.00
Sugar & Creamer, Azalea	45.00
Sugar & Creamer, Cobalt Blue Medallion	70.00
Sugar & Creamer, Gold & Green Repousse	50.00
Sugar & Creamer, Green Ground, Floral, Beaded, Marked	80.00
Sugar & Creamer, Hand-Painted, Gold Trim, Footed	35.00
Sugar & Creamer, Hand-Painted, Windmill, Trees, & Lake, Gold Trim	29.00
Sugar & Creamer, Pink Roses, Gold Beading	22.00
Sugar & Creamer, Pink, Blue, Gray, Gold Trim	18.00
Sugar & Creamer, Red Camellias, Gold Design, Marked	16.00
Sugar & Creamer, Scenic, Footed	40.00
Sugar & Creamer, Tree, Cottage, Sailboat, Blue Rising Sun Mark	35.00
Sugar & Creamer, Trees & Water, Beige To Red, M In Wreath	58.00
Sugar & Creamer, Violet, Copper Luster, Marked	20.00
Sugar & Creamer, Wild Rose, Covered, Footed, Green M Wreath	38.00
Sugar & Creamer, Windmill Design, Rising Sun Mark	20.00
Sugar & Creamer, Windmill Scene, Marked	70.00
Sugar Shaker, Azalea	85.00
Sugar Shaker, Enameled & Floral	60.00
Sugar, Cobalt Blue & Gold	145.00
Syrup & Underplate, Floral Gold & Blue Bands	60.00
Syrup, Floral, Gold Trim	65.00
Syrup, Roses, Gold Trim, Liner, 6-Sided, Cover	85.00
Syrup, Underplate, Orange Flowers, Gold Trim, Rising Sun Mark	45.00
Syrup, White Ground, Green Border, Covered	45.00
Syrup, 6-Sided, Pink Roses & Gold On Lid & Liner, Blue, M In Wreath	85.00
Tankard, Hand-Painted, Royal Nishiki Mark, 12 1/2 In.	160.00
Tazza, Lavender Ground, Green M Wreath, 7 X 5 1/2 In.	400.00
Tea Set, Black, White Flowers, Gold Trim, Marked	155.00
Tea Set, Cream Ground, Blue Floral Design, Set Of 4 Cups & Saucers	195.00
Tea Set, Flying Egrets, Gold & Jeweled Edge, 7 Piece	350.00
Tea Set, Flying Geese, Apple Green, Imperial Mark, 15 Piece	225.00
Tea Set, Jeweled, Green Satin Ground, White Flying Geese	350.00
Tea Set, Lake Scene, Gold Grapes, Leaves, Set Of 5 Cups	225.00
Tea Set, Pink, Yellow Roses, Blue Ground, Signed, 13 Piece	325.00
Tea Set, Red, Blooming Cherry Trees, 17 Piece	295.00
Tea Set, White, Cobalt Trim, Jeweling, 17 Piece	350.00
Tea Strainer, Green, Gold & Floral Bands	45.00
Tea Strainer, Roses, Maple Leaf Mark, 2 Piece	50.00
Tea Strainer, Underbowl, Hand-Painted Roses, Blue	65.00 To 70.00
Tea Strainer, Violets, Gold, Green Tracing	35.00
Tea, Strainer, Violet & Pink Roses, Marked, 2 Piece	50.00
Teapot, Floral, Gold Trim, Beading, Signed, 5 1/2 In.	69.00
Teapot, Gold Relief, Tobacco Jar, Egyptian Scene, Jeweled, Signed	300.00
Teapot, Roses, Bluebirds	45.00
Teapot, Roses, Cobalt Blue Trim	25.00
Teapot, Scenic Medallions, Gold Matte, Jewels, Blue Mark	90.00
Teapot, Tan, Gold Work Allover, Scene Panels, Green Mark	95.00
Tile, Portrait Egyptian Princess	50.00
Tobacco Jar, Allover Scenic, 5 1/2 In.	120.00
Tobacco Jar, Cloisonne Design	70.00
Tobacco Jar, Devil Design *Illus*	425.00
Tobacco Jar, Floral, Moriage Squirrel On Lid, 8 X 5 In.Diam.	300.00
Tobacco Jar, Lava Skull	450.00
Tobacco Jar, Playing Cards *Illus*	300.00
Tobacco Jar, Scenic, Sailboat	225.00

Nippon, Tobacco Jars, Devil Design;
Playing Cards *(See Page 409)*

Toothpick, Acorns, 2 Gold Handles	20.00
Toothpick, Azalea	85.00
Toothpick, Boat Scene, Green Mark	15.00
Toothpick, Desert Scene, 3 Jeweled Handles, M In Wreath	55.00
Toothpick, Floral & Gold, 3-Handled, Rising Sun Mark	22.00
Toothpick, Sailing Ships, Water	75.00
Toothpick, Scenic, Pedestal, Yellow	48.00
Tray, Blue & Brown Flowers, Green Leaves, Marked, 4 X 8 In.	35.00
Tray, Floral, Gold Trim, White, 12 In.	25.00
Tray, Floral, Pink, Bold Trim, 9 1/2 In.	55.00
Tray, Flowers, Gold Edging, 17 1/2 In.	45.00
Tray, Gold Dragons, Square, 5 1/2 X 5 1/2 In.	25.00
Tray, House, Meadow, Jeweled Handles, Green Wreath Mark, 7 X 5 1/2 In.	28.00
Tray, Multicolored Butterflies, Black & Gold Border, Signed, 10 In.	85.00
Tray, Pin, Shamrock Shape, Matte Scene, Brown Rim	45.00
Tray, Pink, Shamrock Shape, Palm Tree & Water, Marked	45.00
Tray, Portrait, Egyptian Ladies, Jewel In Hair, 9 X 12 In.	335.00
Tray, Raised Gold Branches & Leaves, 10 X 7 In.	22.00
Tray, Scenic, Bisque, Green Wreath, 9 1/2 In.	70.00
Tray, White Ground, Roses, Blue, Marked, 9 1/2 X 6 In.	32.00
Tray, Woodland Scene, 10 In.	200.00
Urn, Coral, Jade Trim, Incised Flower, Pedestal, 6 In.	150.00
Urn, Pink & Yellow Peonies, Blue Maple Leaf, 23 1/2 In., 3 Piece	650.00
Urn, Roman Ruins Scene, Gold & Enamel Trim, Covered, 15 In.	475.00
Vase, Allover Design, 9 In.	30.00
Vase, Allover Floral, Gold Trim, White Ground, 2-Handled, 8 In.	65.00
Vase, Allover Gold Dots, 11 In.	435.00
Vase, Basket, Yellow, Purple Grapes, 5 1/4 In.	45.00
Vase, Birds, 6 In.	25.00
Vase, Blue Ground, Flowers On Black, Gold Outline, Marked, 10 In.	140.00
Vase, Blue Roses, Cased White Satin, 8 In.	35.00
Vase, Boat Scene, Handled, 16 In.	30.00
Vase, Bulb, Black Ground, Mixed Flowers, Marked, 12 1/2 In.	140.00
Vase, Butterfly & Flowers, Nishiki, 13 In.	149.00
Vase, Cherry Blossom Design, 5 1/2 In.	80.00
Vase, Cherry Tree, Gold Trim, Green Mark, 8 In.	95.00
Vase, Cobalt, Floral, Gold Trim, 14 In.	295.00
Vase, Cobalt, Lake Scene, Woods, Gold Trim, 7 In.	125.00
Vase, Cottage Scene, Buff Ground, Gold Handles, 6 1/4 In.	70.00
Vase, Cream Ground, Allover Gold Crewel, Signed, 5 In.	50.00
Vase, Daffodil, Farmhouse In Background, 6 1/2 X 8 1/2 In.	325.00
Vase, Desert Scene, Man, Camel, Sands, Skies, 8 1/2 In.	625.00
Vase, Desert Scene, Melon Shape, Cobalt, Browns & Orange, 8 1/2 In.	185.00
Vase, Dogwood Blossoms, Gold Eagles, Cobalt Blue Band, 6 1/2 In.	325.00
Vase, Dragon, Double Handle, 3 1/2 In.	25.00
Vase, Eagle Front & Back, Gold & Floral, 6 1/2 X 8 1/2 In.	325.00
Vase, Egyptian Scenic, Sunset Colors, Marked, 8 In.	119.00
Vase, Farm & Pond Scene, Double Mark, 12 In.	75.00

Vase, Farmer, 2 Oxen, Gold Design & Handles, 8 1/2 In. 245.00
Vase, Floral & Gold, Green Wreath Mark, 7 1/2 In. 40.00
Vase, Floral Ground, Scenic Medallion, Marked, 8 In. 140.00
Vase, Floral, Black Ground, 12 In. 50.00
Vase, Floral, Blue Ground, Lots Of Gold, Marked, 6 In. 80.00
Vase, Floral, Brown Satin & Yellow, 9 In. 70.00
Vase, Floral, Imperial Mark, 8 5/8 In. 125.00
Vase, Floral, Marked, 6 In. 30.00
Vase, Floral, Purple, Gold Beading, Covered, Marked, 9 In. 295.00
Vase, Floral, Roses, Blue Green, Russet Trim, Marked, 7 In. 195.00
Vase, Floral, White, Orange, Blue, Lavender, Green Wreath Mark, 5 In. 35.00
Vase, Florals All Around, Black Ground, Green M In Wreath, 11 1/2 In. 145.00
Vase, Florals, Gold, & Jeweling, 10 1/2 In. 325.00
Vase, Flowers, Gold & Jeweled Top, 3 Gold Handles, 11 1/2 In. 195.00
Vase, Flowers, Gold Bottom, Royal Dinran, Cobalt Blue, 9 1/2 In. 150.00
Vase, Flowers, Gold Dragon Border, Handled, Marked, 11 In. 175.00
Vase, Flowers, Gold Outline & Beading, Handled, 5 3/4 In. 40.00
Vase, Flowers, Hand-Painted, Green M Mark, 10 1/2 In. 195.00
Vase, Geese In Flight, Gold Border, Italian Blue Ground, 6 In. 100.00
Vase, Geese On Lake, 2-Handled, Blue Maple Leaf, 11 In. 375.00
Vase, Gold & Silver Panels, Mums, Black Ground, Green Mark, 17 1/2 In. 275.00
Vase, Gold Beaded Medallions, Raised Gold, Handled, 8 In. 95.00
Vase, Gold Handles, Jeweled, Signed, 8 In. 265.00
Vase, Gold Medallions, Gold Beads, Handled, 8 1/2 In. 325.00
Vase, Gold Roses, Marked, 7 1/2 In., Pair 300.00
Vase, Gold Tracery Around Roses, Blown-Out, Geometric Rim, 9 In. 310.00
Vase, Gold Vine & Leaves, Grapes, Marked, 6 1/2 In. 137.00
Vase, Gold, Blue Ground, Scenic Panels, Green M In Wreath, 9 In. 185.00
Vase, Gray Ground, Bird Perched On Limb, Maple Leaf Mark, 9 In. 185.00
Vase, Greek Scene, Jeweled, 10 1/2 In. 250.00
Vase, Green, Trumpet Shape, Green M, 8 In. 92.00
Vase, Indian In Canoe, Handled, 7 In. 125.00
Vase, Indian, 10 In. 110.00
Vase, Iris Design, Gold Handles, Dark Blue Ground, Marked, 12 1/4 In. 75.00
Vase, Lady On Bridge, Ring Handles, Gold Trim, 9 1/2 In. 335.00
Vase, Lake & Boat Scene, 9 X 16 In. 450.00
Vase, Lake Scene, Jeweled, Hand-Painted, Green M Mark, 11 In. 115.00
Vase, Lake, Boats, & Trees, Green Ground, Gold Trim, Green Wreath, 8 In. 260.00
Vase, Landscape, Beaded Rim, Handles, 6 In. 35.00
Vase, Lava Dragon, 4 1/2 In. 35.00
Vase, Lilies, Matte Finish, 2-Handled, 10 In. 170.00
Vase, Man On Camel, Gold & Cobalt, Bisque, 8 1/4 In. 525.00
Vase, Monkey Design, 11 In. ....*Illus* 475.00
Vase, Oasis, Handled, Green Wreath Mark, 4 1/2 In. 38.00
Vase, Palm Trees, Flowers, Boat, Sunset Colors, Marked, 9 In. 185.00
Vase, Parrot, High-Gloss Glaze, 8 1/2 In. 190.00
Vase, Pastel Flowers, Gilt Trim, Handled, Green M Mark, 11 1/2 In. 125.00

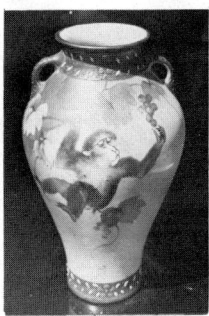

Nippon, Vase, Monkey Design, 11 In.

Vase, Pastel Roses, Gold Overlay, Pinch Top, Marked, 9 In.	130.00
Vase, Pink On Pink Design, Satin Glass, Footed, 10 In.	55.00
Vase, Portrait, 2 Maidens, Gold & Red, Signed, 10 1/2 In.	370.00
Vase, Queen Louise Portrait, Golds, 12 In.	495.00
Vase, Red & White Roses, Green Ground, Gold Trim, Long Handles, 8 In.	125.00
Vase, Red Flowers, Striped Ground, Marked, 6 In.	55.00
Vase, Red Roses, Raised Gold, Green Ground, 10 In.	295.00
Vase, Rose Medallion, Gold Trim, Red, 9 In.	100.00
Vase, Rose, Gold Ground, Bulbous, 11 In.	495.00
Vase, Roses, Artist Signed, 7 In.	35.00
Vase, Roses, Floral, Blue Roses, Marked, 10 In.	170.00
Vase, Roses, Gold Design, Grecian, Green Wreath Mark, 10 In.	235.00
Vase, Roses, Pink & Yellow, Maple Leaf Mark, 8 1/4 In.	325.00
Vase, Roses, White Beads, Bulbous, Fluted Top, Marked, 7 1/2 In.	220.00
Vase, Scene, Paneled, Dark Ground, Square, 9 In.	60.00
Vase, Scenic Medallions, Handled, Green Wreath Mark, 7 In.	45.00
Vase, Scenic, Gold Handles & Legs, 13 In.	300.00
Vase, Scenic, Gold Trim, 10 1/4 In.	355.00
Vase, Scenic, Leaf Gold Outline, 11 In.	185.00
Vase, Scenic, Pedestal, 5 1/2 In., Pair	85.00
Vase, Scenic, 15 X 8 In.	210.00
Vase, Ship Scene, Light Blue Ground, Gold Handles, 8 In.	120.00
Vase, Sunset Scene With Ship, 2-Handled, Flowers On Neck, Marked	140.00
Vase, Swan Scene, Bisque, 12 3/4 In.	200.00
Vase, Tapestry, Pink & Yellow Roses, Turquoise Ground, Marked, 8 In.	475.00
Vase, Tapestry, Roses, Pastel Ground, Ear Handles, Marked, 6 In.	395.00
Vase, Tapestry, Scenic, Bottle Neck, Man In Boat, Marked, 9 In.	575.00
Vase, Turquoise Ground, Red Roses, Gold Trim, 13 In.	350.00
Vase, White Ground, Birds, 9 1/2 In.	395.00
Vase, Windmill Scene, 6 In.	30.00
Vase, Windmill, 2-Cottages, 2-Handled, 7 In.	85.00
Vase, Woodland Scene, 10 1/2 In.	285.00
Vase, Yellow Ground, Purple Violets, Blue & Gold Top, 11 X 5 In.	145.00
Vase, Yellow Roses, Green & Beige Ground, Jeweled, Marked, 11 In.	165.00
Vase, Yellow, Pink Roses, 2-Handled, 6 3/4 In.	35.00
Vase, 2 Pheasants, Gold Trim, Cobalt Blue & Gold, Signed, 12 1/2 In.	385.00

Nodders or nodding figures, or pagods, are porcelain figures with heads and hands that are attached to wires. Any slight movement causes the parts to move up and down. They were made in many countries during the eighteenth and nineteenth centuries.

NODDER, Andy Gump, 3 3/4 In.	75.00
Chester Gump, 3 3/4 In.	75.00
Chin Chin, 3 1/2 In.	85.00
Chinoiserie, Man & Woman, Head, Tongues, & Arms Nod, Bisque, 6 In.	495.00
Cleveland Indians, Indian Face	20.00
Denny, Character, 11 In., 1940	65.00
Figurine, Head, Arms & Tongue Nod, Bisque, Man & Woman, 6 In., Pair	450.00
Girl In 1890 Costume, Bisque, 4 1/4 In.	195.00
Lady, Dress & Cape, Field Glasses, Blue & White, German, 6 In.	140.00
Man With Cigar & 1 Glass Eye, Papier-Mache	38.00
Man With Hat, Blue & White, Staffordshire	145.00
Man, Oriental, Sitting, Green, White Kimono, Holding Fan, 7 In.	345.00
Matchbook Holder, Sitting Dog, Cigar In Mouth	45.00
Monk, Raised Arm, Hidden Pitcher Of Wine, Numbered, Germany, 5 3/4 In.	125.00
Mr.Peanut, Papier-Mache	65.00
Oriental Man, Head & Both Hands Nod, Gold Dot Trim, French, 6 1/4 In.	375.00
Oriental Man, Holds Knife & Sheath, Bisque, 6 In.	165.00
Oriental Man, Seated, Fan In Hand, Matte Green Bisque, 7 X 6 1/2 In.	295.00
Oriental Man, Seated, Green & White Kimono, Open Fan, German, 7 In.	345.00
Oriental Sage, Dagger In 1 Hand, Sheath In Other, Germany, 5 1/2 In.	135.00

Oriental, Seated Man, Head & Hands Move, 5 1/2 In.	475.00
Rachel, 3 3/4 In.	85.00
Scotsman In Beret, Bisque, Germany, 3 1/2 In.	25.00
Triple, German Porcelain, 5 In.	435.00

Noritake-marked porcelain was made in Japan after 1904 by Nippon Toki Kaisha.

NORITAKE, Ashtray, Lake House Scene	30.00
Ashtray, Matchbox Holder, Hand-Painted Roses, 6-Sided, Footed	85.00
Ashtray, Portrait, Horse, 4 1/2 In.	38.00
Asparagus Set, Pearlized Green & Peach, 7 Piece	85.00
Basket, Boat Shape, Florals	34.00
Berry Set, Tree In Meadow, Pierced Handles, 6 Saucers	65.00
Bonbon, Azalea	35.00
Bowl, Azalea, 5 1/4 In.Diam.	6.50
Bowl, Azalea, 6 In.	15.00
Bowl, Azalea, 10 In.Diam.	30.00
Bowl, Cobalt Blue, Gold Beading	30.00
Bowl, Duck In Flight, Scenic, 1 Handle	20.00
Bowl, Ear Handles, Allover Flowers, Green M In Wreath, 8 In.	35.00
Bowl, Flower Clusters, Gold Beading, 8 In.	40.00
Bowl, Luster Ware, Floral, Oval, 1925	20.00
Bowl, Nut, Figural Squirrel	90.00
Bowl, Nut, Molded Chestnuts All Around, Blown-Out, 10 1/4 In.	95.00
Bowl, Pink Water Lily Shape, Blown-Out	40.00
Bowl, River With Swan, House & Tree, Handled, 8 3/4 In.	25.00
Bowl, Salad, Azalea	140.00
Bowl, Salad, Open Handle, Tree In Meadow, 11 In.Diam.	25.00
Bowl, Tree In Meadow, Open Handled, Oval, 7 In.	20.00
Bowl, Tree In Meadow, Oval, 9 In.	25.00
Bowl, Vegetable, Azalea, 9 In.Diam.	25.00
Bowl, Water Lily Design, Gold, Scalloped, Footed, 7 In.	35.00
Box, Trinket, Lady On Top, Greek Key Border, Red M In Wreath	50.00
Bread Tray, Azalea, 12 1/2 In.	32.00
Bread Tray, Tree In Meadow	35.00
Butter Tub, Azalea	28.00 To 60.00
Butter Tub, Tree In Meadow, Insert	25.00
Butter, Covered, Azalea, Gold Finial, Drain, Round	150.00
Cake Plate, Azalea	30.00
Cake Plate, Tree In Meadow, 10 In.	20.00
Cake Set, Tree At Lake Pattern, 6 Plates, Green Mark, 7 Piece	55.00
Cake Set, Tree In Meadow, 7 Piece	75.00
Candleholder, Double, Handled, Blue, Green M Wreath, 4 3/4 In., Pair	14.00
Casserole, Azalea, Covered	55.00
Celery, Azalea, 12 1/2 In.	32.00
Celery, Tree In Meadow, 12 In.	28.50
Child's Set, Azalea, Complete, 15 Piece	1350.00
Chocolate Cup & Saucer, Tree In The Meadow	18.00
Chocolate Pot, Scenic	45.00
Chocolate Set, Pink Flower, Yellow Center, Gray Leaves, Marked	130.00
Chocolate Set, Red Roses, Blue Ground, 12 Piece	210.00
Cocoa Set, Parrot Among Flowers, 5 Cups & Saucers	155.00
Coffee Set, White, Pink Flowers, Marked, 5 Piece	130.00
Coffeepot, Demitasse, Tree In Meadow	350.00
Coffeepot, Tree In Meadow, Demitasse	225.00
Coffeepot, 4 Cups & Saucers, Tree In Meadow, Demitasse	280.00
Compote, Tree In Meadow, Footed, 6 1/2 In.	25.00
Condiment Set, Azalea, 5 Piece	32.00 To 40.00
Condiment Set, Tree In Meadow, 5 Piece	32.50
Creamer, Azalea, Helmet Shape, Open	40.00

Creamer, Underplate, Roses, Gold Rim, Marked 26.00
Cruet, Azalea .... 115.00 To 190.00
Cruet, Tree In Meadow 85.00
Cup & Saucer, Azalea .... 11.00 To 15.00
Cup & Saucer, Patricia 7.50
Cup & Saucer, Tree In Meadow 13.50
Dish, Azalea, Artist Signed, 12 In. 30.00
Dish, Candy, Geometrics, Handled, M In Wreath, 5 1/2 X 5 1/2 In. 16.00
Dish, Floral, Gold Feet, Signed, 7 In. 20.00
Dish, Lemon, Azalea 15.00
Dish, Lemon, Tree Behind House Pattern 15.00
Dish, Lemon, Tree In Meadow, Handled, 5 1/2 In. 15.00
Dish, Shell, Azalea 235.00
Dish, Vegetable, Azalea, Oval, 10 1/2 In. 26.00
Dish, Vegetable, Pierced Handled, Oval, 10 1/2 In. 35.00
Egg, Easter, First Edition 1971 .... 75.00
Eggcup, Azalea .... 30.00 To 35.00
Fruit Set, Gold Beads On White Ground, Cobalt Blue, 7 Piece 215.00
Gravy Boat, Azalea .... 25.00 To 30.00
Humidor, Floral, Square Top, Round Bottom, Green Wreath, 6 1/4 In. 95.00
Humidor, Hand-Painted Sailing Scene, Green Wreath Mark, 6 In. 35.00
Humidor, Scenic, 6-Sided, Enameled Finial 80.00
Jam Set, Tree In Meadow, Underplate & Spoon 35.00
Jar, Tobacco, Azalea 550.00
Jug, Milk, Azalea .... 100.00 To 135.00
Match Holder, Art Deco, Flapper Girl's Head 10.00
Mayonnaise Set, Azalea, 3 Piece 25.00
Mayonnaise Set, Red, Blue, Yellow Flowers, Blue Ground, 3 Piece 25.00
Mayonnaise Set, Tree In Meadow, Underplate & Spoon 22.00
Mustard, Attached Underplate, Floral Medallions, Blue & Gold, Lid 25.00
Mustard, Azalea, Handled .... 40.00 To 48.00
Mustard, Scalloped Tray, Original Spoon, Fruit & Foliage, 3 In. 25.00
Napkin Ring, Floral With Butterfly 12.00
Nappy, Scenic, 6 In. 6.50
Planter, 4 Gold Feet, All Around Scene, Green Mark, 6 1/4 X 5 In. 70.00
Plate, Azalea, 6 1/4 In. .... 6.00 To 7.50
Plate, Azalea, 7 1/2 In. .... 6.50 To 8.50
Plate, Azalea, 8 1/2 In. 15.00
Plate, Azalea, 10 In.Diam. 12.00
Plate, Cake, Azalea, 10 In. 30.00
Plate, Flying Turkey 20.00
Plate, Lemon, Fork, Azalea 18.00
Plate, Orange Roses, Gold Trim, Handled, 6 1/4 In. 27.50
Plate, Soup, Azalea, Handled 40.00
Plate, Tree In Meadow, 6 1/2 In.Diam. 4.50
Plate, Tree In Meadow, 7 1/4 In.Diam. 6.00
Plate, Tree In Meadow, 8 1/2 In. .... 7.00 To 12.00
Platter, Azalea, 10 1/4 In. 110.00
Platter, Azalea, 12 In. 35.00
Platter, Azalea, 14 In. .... 32.00 To 40.00
Platter, Azalea, 16 In. 295.00
Platter, Tree In Meadow, Oval, 11 1/2 In. 15.00
Platter, Turkey, Azalea, Large 400.00
Relish, Azalea, Handled, Oval, 7 1/4 In. 35.00
Relish, Azalea, Loop Handle, 2-Compartment 200.00
Relish, Azalea, 4-Section 85.00
Salt & Pepper, Azalea, 3 1/2 In. .... 18.00 To 20.00
Salt, Swan, Red Mark 8.00
Sauce, Azalea, 5 1/4 In. 7.50
Server, Lemon, Green & Orange 10.00
Shaker, Sugar, Fruit, Marigold Ground 16.50
Sherbet, House In Meadow, Gold Band, Set Of 6 .... 85.00
Spooner, Flat 65.00

Strainer, Tea, Orange Border, Florals 10.00
Sugar & Creamer, Azalea .... 6.50 To 28.00
Sugar & Creamer, Tree In Meadow .... 20.00 To 50.00
Sugar & Creamer, Winthrop 39.00
Sugar Shaker & Creamer, Azalea 100.00
Sugar Shaker & Creamer, Gold Design, Trees, Pagoda, & Birds, 6 In. 45.00
Sugar Shaker & Creamer, Tree In Meadow .... 5.00 To 95.00
Sugar Shaker, Tree In Meadow 25.00
Sugar, Gold Trim & Flowers, Red Wreath Mark 8.00
Syrup Set, Tree In Meadow 45.00
Syrup, Azalea, Underplate .... 58.00 To 110.00
Syrup, Roses, Red & Gold 30.00
Tea Strainer, Orange Luster, Florals 12.00
Teapot, Azalea .... 55.00 To 80.00
Teapot, Tree In Meadow 65.00
Tile, Azalea .... 28.00 To 40.00
Tile, Garland, Orange & Black Trim, Footed 10.00
Toothpick, Azalea .... 70.00 To 120.00
Toothpick, Tree In Meadow, 6-Sided, Green Mark, 2 1/2 In. 60.00
Tray, Aqua, Flowers, Gold Trim, 4 Sections, 8 3/4 In. 22.00
Tray, Pin, Clown Sits On Edge, Pearl Luster Finish, 4 In. 40.00
Tray, Sandwich, Tree In Meadow, Indented For Cup 25.00
Vase, Cherry Blossoms, Black, 9 1/2 In. 17.50
Vase, Lake Scene, Gold Beading, Handles, 5 In. 35.00
Vase, Phoenix Bird, Florals, Gold Handles, Green Wreath, 11 1/2 In. 375.00
Vase, Wall, Black, White Flowers 35.00
Waffle Set, Tree In Meadow 45.00
Wall Pocket, Black Rim, Blue With Orange Luster, 5 1/2 X 8 In. 25.00
Wall Pocket, Lake Scene, 7 In. 20.00
Wall Pocket, Swan On Lake, Luster 18.00

The Norse Pottery Company started in Edgerton, Wisconsin, in 1903. In 1904 the company moved to Rockford, Illinois. The company made a black pottery, which resembled early bronze relics of the Scandinavian countries. The firm went out of business in 1913.

NORSE, Bowl, Cupped, Footed, 9 In. 95.00
Bowl, 8 Full Figure Owls, Bronze Metallic Finish, 4 In. 250.00

The North Dakota School of Mines was established in 1892 at the University of North Dakota.

NORTH DAKOTA SCHOOL OF MINES, Bowl, Finger Indents Inside, 5 1/2 In.Diam. 39.00
Bowl, Signed Chuck Gowran, Blue, 5 In. 42.00
Curtain Pull Ring & Coaster 50.00
Pitcher, Lip, Handle 35.00
Vase, Lavender, Cable, 5 In. 75.00

Northwood Glass Company worked in Martins Ferry, Ohio, in the 1880s to c. 1923. They marked some pieces with the underlined letter N. Many pieces of carnival glass were made by this company.
    NORTHWOOD, see also Carnival Glass; Custard Glass; Goofus Glass; Pressed Glass
NORTHWOOD, Beverage Set, Cut, Gold Trim, Green, 7 Piece 300.00
Bonbon, Butterfly, Amethyst 50.00
Bowl, Blooms & Blossoms, Goofus Paint, 7 1/4 In. 22.50
Bowl, Emerald Green Holly, Gold Trim, 8 3/4 In.Diam. 75.00

Bowl, Fruit & Flowers, Fluted, Spiked Edges, 7 1/4 In.Diam.	100.00
Bowl, Grape Frieze, Cobalt Blue, 3-Footed, Allover Gold	335.00
Bowl, Inverted Fan & Feather, Footed, 4 1/2 In.	75.00
Bowl, Oriental Poppy, 3-Footed, Allover Gold, Amethyst, 10 1/2 In.	335.00
Bowl, Roulette Pattern	65.00
Butter, Beaded Circle, Covered	350.00
Butter, California, Covered, Green	110.00
Butter, Colorado, Covered, Green	145.00
Butter, Covered, Gold Rose, Signed	110.00
Butter, Covered, Iridescent Amber	55.00
Butter, Peach Pattern, Gold Trim, Covered, Green	175.00
Compote, Jelly, Cable & Strawberry, Signed	48.00
Compote, Jelly, Nestor Green	35.00
Compote, Singing Bird, Covered, Signed, Clear	165.00
Compote, Sweetmeat, Grape Pattern, Covered, Purple	225.00
Cracker Jar, Cherry & Cable, Clear & Gold, Signed	165.00
Creamer, Colorado, Green	50.00
Creamer, Drapery, Blue Opalescent	42.00
Creamer, Gold Rose, Signed	75.00
Creamer, Green, Teardrop Flowers	25.00
Creamer, Regent, Green & Gold	75.00
Cup, Punch, Cherry & Cable, Pedestal, Clear, Set Of 3	120.00
Goblet, Singing Bird, Signed, Clear	150.00
Peach, Spooner, Green, Marked	55.00
Plate, Sunflower, Marked, Green	30.00
Saltshaker, Argonaut Shell, Script Signed	175.00
Sauce, Footed, Intaglio, Blue Opalescent	22.50
Spooner, Regent, Green & Gold	75.00
Sugar & Creamer, Colorado, Individual, Green	60.00
Sugar, Paneled Cherry, Open	23.00
Syrup, Daisy & Button With Thumbprint Panels, Blue	135.00
Table Set, Cherry & Cable, Clear With Gold, Signed	295.00
Table Set, Cherry Lattice, Gold Trim, 4 Piece	225.00
Table Set, Chrysanthemum Sprig, Custard, Signed, 3 Piece	350.00
Table Set, Drapery, Blue Opalescent, 4 Piece	370.00
Table Set, Singing Bird, Clear & Blue	300.00
Toothpick, Flute	20.00
Tumbler, Cherry & Lattice, Gold Trim, Signed	15.00
Tumbler, Coin Spot, Green, Signed	22.00
Tumbler, Colorado, Handled, Green	30.00
Tumbler, Green Opalescent, Coin Spot, Signed	22.00
Tumbler, Oriental Poppy, Gold Trim, Green	18.00
Tumbler, Tiger Lily, Gold Trim, Green	21.00
Vase, Diamond Point, Green Carnival, Signed	44.00
Vase, Lily, Scalloped Top, Green, 10 7/8 In.	12.00
Vase, Pink, Yellow Pull-Ups On White, Crimped Top, Satin, 8 1/4 In.	750.00
Water Set, Drapery, Blue Opalescent, 7 Piece	485.00
Water Set, Jewel & Flower, 7 Piece	550.00
Water Set, Lily Of The Valley, Crimped, Amethyst, 7 Piece	325.00
Water Set, Regal, 4 Tumblers, Blue Opalescent, 5 Piece	500.00
Wine, Singing Bird, Signed, Clear	125.00

Nu-Art was a trademark registered by the Imperial Glass Co. of Bellaire, Ohio, about 1920.

NUART, Vase, Signed, Gold, Green, & Blue Aurene, 7 In.	180.00

NUTCRACKER, Alligator, Old Green Paint, Cast Iron, 14 X 3 1/2 In.	65.00
Bronze, 1/2 Walnut, Screw Top Handle, Vienna, 6 1/2 In.	125.00
Dazey, St.Louis, Missouri, Ratchet Type	22.50
Dickens, Brass	35.00
Dog, Cast Iron, Made In Chicago	60.00
Dog, Iron	35.00
Double, Pearl Handle	38.00

Female, Wooden	20.00
Man Thumbing Nose, Iron, Screw On Counter	25.00
Man, Gray Hair, Ruddy Complexion, Hand-Carved	175.00
Parrot, Green, Orange & Gold, Iron, 10 X 6 X 3 In.	50.00
Perfection, Patent 1914, Screw Type	22.50
Sargeant's No.10, New Haven, Japanned, Cast Iron	35.00
Squirrel, Ratchet Type, Patent 1925, Alex Woldert	22.50
Squirrel, Tray, Black	50.00
St.Bernard, Cast Iron	60.00
St.Bernard, Old Gold Paint, Cast Iron, 11 X 6 1/2 In.	56.00
Walnut Pedestal, Hammer, Silver Plated, 6 1/2 In., 2 Piece	28.00
Woman's Legs Form Handles, Brass, 4 1/2 In.	38.00

Nymphenburg, a German porcelain factory, was established at Neudeck-ob-der-Au in 1753 and moved to Nymphenburg in 1761. The company is still in existence. Modern marks include a shield superseded by a star or crown, and a crowned CT with a checkered shield.

NYMPHENBURG, Figurine, Lady, Holding Vase, Pink Skirt, Shawl, Marked, 6 3/4 In.	155.00
Figurine, Mule, 5 X 4 1/2 In.	125.00

Occupied Japan is the mark used on pieces of pottery and porcelain made during the American occupation of Japan after World War II, from 1945 to 1952. Collectors are now buying these pieces. The items were made for export to the United States.

OCCUPIED JAPAN, Ashtray, Alligator, Mouth Open, Tail Curled, Marked, 5 1/2 In.	4.50
Ashtray, Jockey, Riding On Racehorse, Pot Metal	39.00
Ashtray, Niagara Falls	6.00
Basket, Dainty Flowers, Miniature, 2 1/2 In.	20.00
Basket, Straw, Hinged Cover, Handle, 7 1/2 X 5 X 3 In.	30.00
Blue Willow, Service For 8	150.00
Bookends, Figural, Dog, 4 In.	15.00
Bottle Opener, Happy Hooligan, Iron	8.00
Box, Overlayed With Gold, Flower Design, 5 X 4 In.	32.00
Butter, House Shape, Covered	25.00
Cigarette Box, Oriental, Bird, Flower, 4 1/4 X 2 1/4 In.	25.00
Cigarette Lighter, Piano Shape, Porcelain	20.00
Coaster Set, Chinese Red, Set Of 6 Coasters	45.00
Cup & Saucer, Demitasse, Square, Scenic, Brass Stand, Marked	75.00
Deer, 2 In.	5.00
Dish, Green Curled Leaf, Rust, Gold Decoration	24.00
Figurine, Ballerina, Net Skirt, 4 1/2 In.	18.00
Figurine, Blackamoor Man & Woman, White, Brown, Gold, 8 In.	30.00
Figurine, Boy Playing Banjo, With Dog, 4 1/2 In.	20.00
Figurine, Boy Playing Drum, Bisque, Green & Blue, 4 3/4 In.	17.50
Figurine, Boy, Knapsack On Back, 5 In.	30.00
Figurine, Boy, Standing By Fence, 6 1/2 In.	15.00
Figurine, Cat, Sitting, Black Stripes, 2 In.	9.00
Figurine, Children, Oriental, Chubby, 3 In., Pair	12.00
Figurine, Colonial Boy Pushing Wheel Barrow, 6 X 6 In.	38.00
Figurine, Colonial Boy, Basket Of Flowers, Gondola Shape	48.00
Figurine, Colonial Couple, Stand, 8 In.	20.00
Figurine, Colonial Lady, 9 1/2 In.	25.00
Figurine, Colonial Pair, Each On Own Bench, 2 3/4 In.	6.50
Figurine, Girl & Boy, Musicians, 18th-Century Costumes, 6 In.	45.00
Figurine, Girl Dancing, Wide Brim Hat, 6 1/2 In.	25.00
Figurine, Girl Looking Down At Duck, 5 In.	15.00
Figurine, Girl, Blue Delft, Holding Tambourine, 5 In.	25.00
Figurine, Girl, Blue Delft, Pink Skirt, 5 1/4 In.	25.00
Figurine, Girl, In Bandana, Shoes, Gold Castle, 5 In.	20.00
Figurine, Globe Trotter	15.00
Figurine, Little Black Musicians, 3 In.	15.00
Figurine, Little Shoppers	25.00

Figurine, Man, Accordion, 4 1/2 In.	6.00
Figurine, Man, Umbrella, 4 In.	6.00
Figurine, Monks, Each Playing An Instrument, 3 In.	20.00
Figurine, Oriental Man & Woman, 6 In., Pair	20.00
Figurine, Santa, 5 In.	20.00
Figurine, Squirrel, Salt & Pepper	10.00
Figurine, Uncle Sam	20.00
Figurine, Woman & Man With Mandolin, Hands Extended	25.00
Figurine, Woman Musician Holding Mandolin, 5 In.	10.00
Lamp, Colonial Couple Dancing, 11 In.	22.50
Match Holder, Double Basket, Bisque	95.00
Match Holder, Wall Mount, Double Bisque Figures, Marked	98.00
Mug & Saucer, Blue Willow	30.00
Mug, Figural, Old Charley, 3 1/2 In.	20.00
Piano & Player, China	16.00
Planter, Boy On Stump Of Cut Tree, 4 1/2 In.	12.50
Planter, Camel Lying Down, 7 1/2 In.	15.00
Planter, Donkey & Cart, 3 1/2 X 7 1/2 In.	22.00
Planter, Donkey & Sleeping Mexican, 6 X 3 3/4 In.	12.00
Planter, Donkey Pulling Cart, Marked, 7 In.	7.50
Planter, Duck, Wearing Hat, 6 1/2 In.	12.00
Planter, Elf	7.00
Planter, Hanging, Parrot	25.00
Planter, Head Of Mama & Baby Deer, 7 1/2 In.	25.00
Planter, Oriental Girl, Coolie Hat, 5 In.	9.00
Planter, Shoe, With Bird	12.00
Plaque, Colonial Lady In Relief, Bisque	20.00
Plaque, Colonial Man & Lady, Pair	30.00
Plaque, Dutch Boy	8.50
Plaque, Gentleman	20.00
Plate, Blue Willow, 6 In	10.00
Plate, Blue Willow, 7 In.	12.50
Range Set, Tomato Pattern, 3 Piece	42.50
Salt & Pepper, Bride & Groom	15.00
Salt & Pepper, Yellow Birds, Orange Beaks, Green Wings, 3 In.	8.50
Salt, Master, Swan	18.00
Shoe, Pink Roses, Gold Trim, White	6.00
Tea Set, Blue Willow, Miniature, 15 Piece	68.00
Tea Set, Burnt Orange, Ivys, Gold Trim, 4 Cups & Saucers	95.00
Tea Set, Child's, Floral Border, White Ground, 26 Piece	155.00
Tea Set, Cottage Style, Thatched Roof, 3 Piece	50.00
Teapot, Hand-Painted Florals, Dark Brown Ground	18.50
Teapot, House Shape	25.00
Teapot, Impressed Floral Design, 2 Cup	6.00
Teapot, Red, Yellow Green Flowers	35.00
Toothpick, Birdhouse On Side, Bird On Perch, 3 1/2 In.	10.00
Toothpick, Crane, Standing Beside Holder	10.00
Toothpick, Zebra	5.00
Toy, Duck Sitting On Cracked Egg	20.00
Vase, Blown-Out Flowers, Orange	8.00
Vase, Colonial Boy, Tree, Girl With Bird On Shoulder, 6 In.	38.00
Vase, Colonial Man, Basket Of Flowers, Oval, 7 In.	55.00
Vase, Flower Shape, 3 Cherubs, 5 In.	45.00
Vase, Magenta Floral, Gold Trim, Saji Crown Mark, 11 In.	55.00
Vase, Man's Face & Upper Torso, 3 3/4 In.	10.00
Wall Pocket, Ballerina In Net Skirt, 5 In.	20.00
Wall Pocket, Colonial Man & Woman, Pair	35.00
Wall Pocket, Duck	30.00
Wall Pocket, Flying Ducks	30.00
Wheel Barrow, Flower, Blue, 2 X 3 In.	5.00

G. E. OHR, BILOXI.

Ohr pottery was made by George E. Ohr in Biloxi, Mississippi, between 1883 and 1918. The pieces were made of very thin clay and were twisted, folded, and dented into odd, graceful shapes.

OHR, Bowl, Bulbous, Pinched Rim, Blackberry, Porous Lumps, Signed, 3 1/2 In. 130.00
Bowl, Crumpled On One Side, Speckled Glaze, Marked, 2 5/8 In. 440.00
Bowl, Green & Brown, Scalloped Rim, Signed, 3 In. 150.00
Bowl, Mottled Tan & Green, Crimped Rim, Signed, 2 1/2 X 3 In.Diam. 165.00
Bowl, Ruffled, Brown-Green Interior, Flecked Glaze, Marked, 7 In. 330.00
Bowl, Truncated-Cone Shape, Tan Glaze, Marked, 3 1/2 In. 110.00
Bowl, White, Brown, & Blue, Unglazed, 4 1/4 X 5 1/4 In. 95.00
Inkstand, Artist's Palette Form, C.1900, Green Glaze, Marked, 6 1/4 In. 275.00
Mug, Bulging Side, Crimped Handle, Mustard & Brown, Marked, 6 In. 360.00
Mug, Iridescent Dark Brown, Pale Orange Inside, Marked, 3 3/4 In. 125.00
Mug, Speckled Red Interior, Dated 3-18-96, Incised, 3 3/8 In. 165.00
Mug, Spherical Form, Molded Handle, Ocher & Brown, Marked, 4 1/2 In. 110.00
Pitcher, Ovoid Body, Blue, Green, 3 1/2 In. 105.00
Rose Bowl, Tiny Sawtooth Rim, Green & Tan Glossy, Incised In Base 235.00
Teapot, Thumbprint Design, Crimped Handle, Marked, 3 3/4 In. 990.00
Vase, Baluster Body, Amber, Speckled Gray, Green, Marked, 7 In. 400.00
Vase, Bulbous Form, Streaky Mustard Glaze, Marked, 2 In. 275.00
Vase, Bulbous, Folded Rim, C.1900, Gun-Metal Glaze, Marked, 4 3/4 In. 110.00
Vase, Crimps & Twist, Handled, Green Glaze, Orange Blush, 7 In. 725.00
Vase, Crumpled, Crimped, Gun-Metal Finish, Marked, 4 1/8 In. 220.00
Vase, Cylindrical Form, Rose & Green Glaze, Marked, 3 3/4 In. 225.00
Vase, Flaring Rim, Greenish Orange Glaze, Marked, 5 1/4 In. 195.00
Vase, Flattened & Crimped Rim, Marked, Gun-Metal Glaze, 2 3/4 In. 300.00
Vase, Gun Metal, 4 1/2 X 4 1/2 In. 160.00
Vase, Hourglass Form, Charcoal, Yellow, Green, Brown, Marked, 4 In. 95.00
Vase, Lizard Around Top, Ribbed Brown Glaze, 3 X 3 In. 250.00
Vase, Ovoid Body, Twisted Shoulder, Purple, Marked, 4 3/4 In. 350.00
Vase, Ovoid Form, Green & Gun-Metal Glaze, Marked, 2 3/4 In. 140.00
Vase, Pinched Side, Olive Mustard Glaze, Marked, 6 1/8 In. 275.00
Vase, Pinched, Pleated, Dark Brown, 3 1/4 X 5 1/4 In. 200.00
Vase, Pulled Center, Gun Metal Lead Matte Finish, Incised Script 255.00
Vase, Ruffled Rim, Streaked, Signed, Mottled Salmon, 4 3/4 In. 400.00
Vase, Ruffled, Chartreuse-Streaked Navy Glaze, 5 1/4 In. 380.00
Vase, Ruffled, Fuchsia & Green, Marked, 4 1/4 In. 380.00
Vase, Speckled Brown, Mustard, Pleated Rim, 5 X 4 In. 210.00
Vase, Twisted Neck, Notched Rim, Mottled Glaze, Marked, 3 5/8 In. 250.00

OLD IVORY
84
*Old ivory china was made in Silesia, Germany, at the end of the nine-
teenth century. It is often marked with a crown and the word Silesia.
The pattern numbers appear on the base of each piece.*

OLD IVORY, Berry Set, No.16, 7 Piece 195.00
Berry Set, No.76, 7 Piece 200.00
Berry Set, 2-Tone Brown, Scroll Trim, Silesia, Gold Trim, 7 Piece 130.00
Bowl, Holly Pattern, 2 X 9 1/2 In.Diam. 65.00
Bowl, No.7, Pierced Handles, 9 1/2 In.Diam. 65.00
Bowl, Soup, No.28 .... 85.00
Bowl, Vegetable, No.16, Large 45.00
Box, German, Powder, Lid 10.00
Cake Plate, No.16, 10 In. 60.00
Cake Plate, Ohme Mark, 10 In. 68.00
Cake Plate, Pierced Handle, 10 3/4 In. 75.00
Cake Set, No.84, 7 Piece 195.00
Celery, No.16, Silesia, 11 1/2 In. 50.00
Celery, Oval, 12 X 5 In. 50.00
Chocolate Pot, No.11 .... 355.00
Chocolate Pot, No.15 .... 75.00
Creamer, No.15 .... 20.00 To 40.00
Cup & Saucer, Brown & Ivory Poppy Design, Demitasse 25.00
Cup & Saucer, No.15 .... 50.00
Cup & Saucer, No.84 .... 50.00
Dish, Bone, No.200, 9 In. .... 60.00 To 95.00

Dish, Candy, No.15	65.00
Hair Receiver, 2 Piece	225.00
Mustard, No.84	125.00
Plate, Chop, No.82, 13 In.	125.00
Plate, Dinner, No.30	80.00 To 85.00
Plate, No.15, 8 1/2 In.	40.00
Plate, No.16. 6 1/4 In.	23.00
Plate, No.16. 7 1/2 In.	35.00
Plate, No.16. 8 1/2 In.	29.00
Plate, No.28, 8 1/4 In.	45.00
Plate, No.84, 7 3/4 In.	38.00
Plate, No.84, 8 1/2 In.	45.00
Plate, No.118, Open Handles	52.00
Plate, No.200, 7 1/2 In.	25.00
Relish, No.16, Oval	42.00
Relish, No.84, 8 1/4 X 5 In.	55.00
Relish, No.200	40.00
Salt & Pepper, No.11	90.00
Salt & Pepper, No.16	100.00
Salt & Pepper, No.75	70.00
Sugar & Creamer, La Touraine, Pair	95.00
Sugar & Creamer, No.15, Set	100.00
Sugar & Creamer, No.84	110.00
Sugar & Creamer, Thistle Pattern	62.50
Sugar, Covered, No.15	50.00
Tray, Celery, Silesia, No.16, 11 1/2 In.	50.00
Tray, Oval, 11 1/2 X 8 In.	95.00
Waste Bowl, Scalloped Rim, No.84, 5 1/2 In.	75.00

OLD SLEEPY EYE, see Sleepy Eye

Onion, originally named "bulb pattern," is a white ware decorated with cobalt blue or pink. Although it is commonly associated with Meissen, other companies made the pattern in the late nineteenth and twentieth centuries.

ONION, Bowl, Meissen, 9 3/4 In.	35.00
Bowl, Vegetable, Oval, Meissen, 9 In.	95.00
Canister Set, Paper Label, Japan, 4 Piece	60.00
Chamberstick, Blue, Marked, 2 1/2 In.	55.00
Cheeseboard, Meissen, Crossed Swords, Blue, 6 X 10 In.	175.00
Creamer, Meissen, Crossed Swords, Blue, 3 1/2 In.	65.00
Crimper, Meissen	135.00
Cup & Saucer, Blue, Marked, 5 1/2 In.	20.00 To 25.00
Cup & Saucer, Crossed Swords	55.00
Cup & Saucer, Demitasse, Blue, 3 1/4 In.	30.00
Cup & Saucer, Demitasse, Meissen	30.00
Darner, Wooden Handle, Blue	75.00
Dipper, Wooden Handle, Bowl 3 3/4 In.	95.00
Dish, Blue, Rose Design, Marked, 3 1/2 In., Pair	40.00
Dish, Bone, Meissen, Crossed Swords	55.00
Dish, Pinched Sides & Corners, Crossed Swords, 6 1/2 In.Square	110.00
Feeder, Pap, Blue, Marked, 6 X 3 1/2 In., Pair	30.00
Funnel Strainer, Pierced, Meissen, Pink	235.00
Gravy Boat, Attached Underplate, Meissen	125.00
Gravy Boat, Pouring, Meissen, Crossed Swords	45.00
Masher, Meissen, Blue	135.00
Masher, Meissen, Pink	185.00
Meat Tenderizer, Porcelain	75.00
Mortar & Pestle, Meissen, Pink	350.00
Mustard, Covered, Blue & White, 3 In.	22.50
Pitcher, 3 1/8 In.	45.00
Plate, Blue, Marked, 10 In.	10.00
Plate, Chop, Deep Center, Meissen, Crossed Swords, 12 1/4 In.	255.00
Plate, Feather Design, Meissen, Crossed Swords, 11 1/2 In.	335.00
Plate, Meissen, 7 1/2 In.	20.00

Plate, Scalloped Rim, Floral Reserves, Meissen, 8 In., Set Of 8	220.00
Platter, Meissen, Crossed Swords, 1o 1/2 In.	185.00
Platter, Meissen, Crossed Swords, 11 1/2 In.	165.00
Platter, Meissen, Crossed Swords, 16 In.	195.00
Platter, Meissen, 13 1/2 In.	75.00
Platter, Meissen, 13 1/2 X 9 In.	85.00
Platter, Meissen, 17 In.	175.00
Platter, Meissen, 19 In.	200.00
Rolling Pin, Meissen	185.00
Rolling Pin, Meissen, Pink	235.00
Salt & Pepper, Blue, Metal Screw Top, Marked, 3 In.	30.00
Salt Box, Hanging, Wood Lid, Meissen, Pink	385.00
Spoon, Design In Bowl, Meissen, Blue	145.00
Spoon, Mixing, Meissen, Blue	135.00
Spoon, Pierced, Meissen, Pink, 4 1/4 In.	245.00
Strainer, Meissen, Wooden Handle, Pink, 6 X 3 In.	185.00
Strainer, Meissen, 3 In.Diam.	135.00
Strainer, Pink, Wooden Handle, Meissen, 6 X 3 In.	185.00
Strainer, Tea, Blue, 4 In.	25.00
Sugar & Creamer, Gold Trim	45.00
Sugar, Melon Shape, Covered, Meissen, Crossed Swords, Blue	95.00
Teapot, Blue, Covered, Ribbed, 4 In.	60.00
Tenderizer, Meat, Meissen, Blue	135.00
Tenderizer, Meat, Meissen, Pink	195.00
Tile, Ball Footed, Meissen, Crossed Swords, 5 In.Square	125.00
Tray, Serving, Meissen, 11 X 10 In.	285.00
Vase, Blue, Spill Type Scroll Feet, Oval Base, Marked, 4 In., Pair	70.00

Opalescent glass is translucent glass that has the bluish-white tones of the opal gemstone. It is often found in pressed glassware made in Victorian times. Some dealers use the terms opaline and opalescent for any of the bluish-white translucent wares.

OPALESCENT, Atomizer, Perfume, Coin Dot, Blue	65.00
Banana Boat, Argonaut Shell, White, 8 1/2 In.	58.00
Basket, Hobnail, Blue, 5 1/2 In.	25.00
Basket, Old Man Winter, Handle, White, 7 1/2 X 7 1/2 In.	40.00
Berry Set, Beaded Heart, Green To Custard, 7 Piece	95.00
Berry Set, Flower & Jewel, 6 Individual Bowls, Vaseline	325.00
Berry Set, Flower & Vine, 7 Piece	215.00
Berry Set, Idyll, Green, 7 Piece	295.00
Berry Set, Iris With Meander, 6 Sauces, Vaseline	225.00
Berry Set, Jeweled Heart, Clear, 5 Piece	65.00
Berry Set, Leaf Medallion, Amethyst, 7 Piece	295.00
Berry, Wild Bouquet, Master, White	65.00
Biscuit Jar & Plate, White Enameled Flowers, 8 1/4 In.Diam.	225.00
Bonbon, Beaded Fan, Ruffled, Blue	35.00
Bonbon, Blossom & Palms, White	30.00
Bonbon, Water Lily With Cattails, Handled, Persian Blue	28.00
Bottle, Perfume, Plumes, Blue, 3 In.	25.00
Bottle, Wine, Rib Optic, Stopper, Cranberry, 13 1/2 In.	85.00
Bowl, Basket Weave, Green	25.00
Bowl, Beaded Fan, Ruffled, Footed, Blue	35.00
Bowl, Beaded Star, Crimped, Pedestal, Blue, 8 1/2 In.	28.00
Bowl, Berry, Alaska, Northwood, Master, Blue	95.00
Bowl, Berry, Chrysanthemum Sprig, Master, Blue	295.00
Bowl, Berry, Iris Meander, Amethyst, Large	50.00
Bowl, Berry, Swag With Brackets, Vaseline	85.00
Bowl, Blossoms & Web, Blue	60.00
Bowl, Daisy & Plume, Green	45.00
Bowl, Daisy & Plume, 3-Footed, White	35.00
Bowl, Grape & Cherries, Blue	40.00
Bowl, Greek Key & Ribs, Green, Domed, Footed	45.00
Bowl, Green Ruffled Top, 3-Footed, 8 1/2 In.	45.00

Bowl, Hobbs, Vaseline, 5 X 3 In.	100.00
Bowl, Hobnail, Folded In On 2 Sides, Blue, 10 1/2 In.	50.00
Bowl, Honeycomb & Clover, Blue, 8 1/2 In.Diam.	38.00
Bowl, Honeycomb & Clover, Flared, Green, 9 In.	35.00
Bowl, Honeycomb & Clover, Master, Green	40.00
Bowl, Meander Shell With Dots, Green, 9 In.Diam.	32.00
Bowl, Meander, Footed, Blue	65.00
Bowl, Meander, Ruffled, 3-Footed, Green, 9 In.	25.00
Bowl, Meander, 3-Footed, White	30.00
Bowl, Nested Roses, Fluted, Signed, Green, 9 In.	35.00
Bowl, Palm & Scroll, Fluted, 3-Footed, White, 8 In.	30.00
Bowl, Raindrop Bands, Threaded Ground, Vaseline, 7 1/4 In.Diam.	28.00
Bowl, Reflecting Diamonds, Blue	40.00
Bowl, Ribbed Spiral, Fluted Edge, Blue, 8 1/4 In.	48.00
Bowl, Ruffles & Rings, White & Clear, 10 In.Diam.	30.00
Bowl, Ski Star, Ruffled, Peach, Large	70.00
Bowl, Water Lily With Cattails, Amethyst, 8 In.	37.50
Bowl, Water Lily With Cattails, Green, 4 1/2 X 8 1/2 In.Diam.	37.00
Bowl, Wheel & Block, Blue To White, 9 1/2 In.	35.00
Butter, Covered, Tokyo, Green	135.00
Butter, Diamond Spearpoint, Covered, Vaseline	250.00
Butter, Drapery, Covered, Blue	125.00
Butter, Everglades, Covered, Blue	325.00
Butter, Fluted Scroll, Covered, Vaseline	225.00
Butter, Regal, Covered, Northwood, Blue	250.00
Butter, Regal, Northwood, Covered, Green	175.00
Butter, Scroll & Acanthus, Gold & Enameling, Blue	120.00
Butter, Seaweed, Covered, Blue	225.00
Butter, Swag & Bracket, Covered, Blue	165.00
Butter, Wreath & Shell, Covered, Vaseline	200.00 To 210.00
Candlestick, Rope & Skirt, Blue, Handled	40.00
Celery, Alaska, Enameled, Blue	235.00
Celery, Block, Northwood, Blue	55.00
Celery, One Thousand Eyes, Opaque	50.00
Chandelier Globe, Honeycomb Optic, Melon Ribs, 16 X 10 In.	300.00
Compote, Intaglio, Blue, Small	25.00
Compote, Jelly, Blue Ribbed Spiral	40.00
Compote, Jelly, Brackets, Blue	30.00
Compote, Jelly, Intaglio	28.00
Compote, Jelly, Intaglio, Vaseline	68.00
Compote, Jelly, Iris With Meander, White	28.00
Compote, Jelly, Maple Leaf, Blue	45.00
Compote, Jelly, Ribbed Spiral, Vaseline	45.00
Compote, Jelly, Swag With Brackets, Blue	46.00
Compote, Jelly, Swag With Brackets, White	22.00 To 30.00
Creamer, Alaska, Northwood, Blue	75.00
Creamer, Alaska, Vaseline	62.00
Creamer, Beaded Ovals In Sand, Green	40.00
Creamer, Circled Scroll, Blue	85.00
Creamer, Classic, Log Foot, Blue	85.00
Creamer, Drapery, Blue	45.00
Creamer, Everglades, Blue	45.00
Creamer, Fluted Scrolls, Blue	40.00 To 50.00
Creamer, Hobnail In Square, White	16.00
Creamer, Hobnail, Clear	45.00
Creamer, Intaglio, Blue	45.00
Creamer, Iris With Meander, Blue	55.00
Creamer, Iris, Green	80.00
Creamer, Jackson, Blue	45.00
Creamer, Jewel & Flower, White	40.00
Creamer, Reverse Swirl, Burlington Mark, Blue	70.00
Creamer, Swirl, Blue	55.00
Creamer, Tokyo, Green	95.00

Creamer, Water Lily & Cattails, Blue	40.00
Creamer, Wreath & Shell, Blue	50.00
Cruet, Alaska, Blue	295.00
Cruet, Alaska, Enameled Forget-Me-Nots, White	68.00
Cruet, Cone, Blue Cased	125.00
Cruet, Fern & Daisy, Blue	40.00
Cruet, Fern, Branberry	220.00
Cruet, Fine Cut, Blue	65.00
Cruet, Fluted Scroll, Clear Stopper, Vaseline	120.00
Cruet, Hobnail, Cranberry	45.00
Cruet, Hobnail, Fenton, Yellow	30.00
Cruet, Hobnail, White	26.00
Cruet, Intaglio, Clear Northwood Stopper, Blue	145.00
Cruet, Intaglio, White	44.00 To 95.00
Cruet, Jackson, Blue	75.00 To 85.00
Cruet, Medallion Sprig, Green	115.00
Cruet, Ribbed Lattice, Clear Stopper, Blue	125.00
Cruet, Seaweed, Blue	115.00
Cruet, Swag With Brackets, Green	225.00
Cruet, Swirl, Chrysanthemum Base, White	65.00
Cup, Ribbed Spiral, Vaseline	35.00
Dish, Button Panels, Northwood, Vaseline	40.00
Dish, Candy, Wishbone Pattern, Blue, 4 X 5 1/2 In.	40.00
Dish, Hobnail, Green, 5 In.	12.00
Dish, Jackson, 3-Footed, Blue	35.00
Dish, Treebark, Footed, Yellow	38.00
Goblet, Dahlia, Vaseline	65.00
Goblet, Diamond-Quilted, Blue	32.00
Hat, Coin Dot, Blue, 3 In.	28.00
Ice Cream Set, Hobnail, Vaseline, C.1880	225.00
Jar, Powder, Hobnail, Blue	30.00
Jelly, Intaglio, Blue	39.00
Lamp, Finger, Swirled Stripes, Blue Handle, Blue & White	145.00
Lamp, Little Duchess, Milk Glass	125.00
Lamp, Snowflake, Brass Connector, Blue	225.00
Lamp, Swirl, Flat Finger, Vaseline	235.00
Lamp, Table, Coin Dot, Brass Fittings, Crystal	150.00
Mug, Stork In Rushes, Blue	38.00
Pitcher, Beatty Honeycomb, Blue	295.00
Pitcher, Child's, Hobb's Hobnail, Vaseline	195.00
Pitcher, Christmas Snowflake, Blue	300.00
Pitcher, Coronation, Blue	95.00
Pitcher, Daisy & Fern, Blue, 8 1/2 In.	100.00
Pitcher, Drape, White, 9 1/2 In.	75.00
Pitcher, Fluted Scrolls, White	95.00
Pitcher, Hobnail, Footed, White, 8 1/2 In.	40.00
Pitcher, Juice, Hobnail, Cranberry	65.00
Pitcher, Milk, Hobnail, Clear Feet, Bull's-Eye, Blue ....*Illus*	85.00
Pitcher, Milk, Hobnail, Square Mouth, Blue	65.00
Pitcher, Milk, Hobnail, White, 7 In.	55.00
Pitcher, Swirl, Applied Handle, White, 4 1/4 In.	35.00
Pitcher, Swirl, Blue	145.00
Pitcher, Thousand Eye, Scalloped Base, White	115.00
Pitcher, Water, Alaska, Blue	350.00 To 390.00
Pitcher, Water, Alaska, Vaseline	350.00
Pitcher, Water, Beatty Rib Swirl, Blue	200.00
Pitcher, Water, Bull's-Eye Button, Gold Trim, Green	95.00
Pitcher, Water, Buttons & Braids, Blue	135.00
Pitcher, Water, Buttons & Braids, Green	150.00
Pitcher, Water, Coin Dot, Fenton, Blue	150.00
Pitcher, Water, Cranberry Swirling Maze	200.00
Pitcher, Water, Daisy & Fern, Blue	110.00
Pitcher, Water, Drapery, Blue	200.00

Opalescent, Pitcher, Milk, Hobnail,
Clear Feet, Bull's-Eye, Blue

(See Page 423)

Pitcher, Water, Drapery, Cranberry	275.00
Pitcher, Water, Fluted Scroll, Blue	195.00
Pitcher, Water, Fluted Scrolls, White	75.00
Pitcher, Water, Hobnail, Cranberry	175.00
Pitcher, Water, Intaglio, Blue	220.00
Pitcher, Water, Intaglio, White	75.00
Pitcher, Water, Poinsettia, Blue	95.00
Pitcher, Water, Poinsettia, Burlington Mark, Blue	150.00
Pitcher, Water, Reverse Swirl, Clear	110.00
Pitcher, Water, Reverse Swirl, White	110.00
Pitcher, Water, Seaweed, Bulbous, White	185.00
Pitcher, Water, Swag With Brackets, White	135.00
Pitcher, Water, Swirl, Blue	110.00
Pitcher, Water, Windows, Burlington, Blue	175.00
Plate, Iris With Meander, Clear, 7 In.	15.00
Plate, Plymouth, Fenton, White, 6 In.	6.00
Plate, Ribbed Spiral, Blue, 7 1/2 In.	30.00
Plate, Water Lily & Cattails, 10 1/2 In.	35.00
Relish, Jewel & Fan, Blue, 8 3/4 X 5 1/2 In.	30.00
Rose Bowl, Oval Hobs, Vaseline	55.00
Rose Bowl, Wreath & Shell, Vaseline	65.00
Salt & Pepper, Idyll, Gold Trim, Green	85.00
Salt, William & Mary, Vaseline	45.00
Saltshaker, Alaska, Vaseline	55.00
Saltshaker, Swirl, Cranberry, 3 3/4 In.	60.00
Salver, Tokyo, 8 1/2 In.	30.00
Sauce, Drape, Blue	20.00
Sauce, Everglades, Blue	22.50
Sauce, Jewel & Flower, Gold Trim, Vaseline	35.00
Sauce, Ribbed Spiral, Yellow	18.00
Sauce, Wild Bouquet, Green	25.00
Sauce, Wild Bouquet, White	20.00
Sauce, Wreath & Shell, Vaseline	22.50
Shade, Gas, Polka Dot, Blue, 5 In.	75.00
Soup, Cream, Beaded Block, Blue	22.00
Spooner, Alaska, Blue	55.00 To 80.00
Spooner, Alaska, Northwood, Blue	75.00
Spooner, Alaska, White	25.00
Spooner, Block, Northwood, Blue	45.00
Spooner, Bubble Lattice, Blue	32.00 To 50.00
Spooner, Dahlia, Vaseline	30.00
Spooner, Fluted Scrolls, Blue	42.00
Spooner, Fluted Scrolls, Vaseline	60.00

Spooner, Fluted Scrolls, White	35.00
Spooner, Idyll, Green	75.00
Spooner, Intaglio, Blue	75.00
Spooner, Iris With Meander, Gold Trim, Blue	45.00
Spooner, Iris, Green	85.00
Spooner, Leaf Medallion, Gold Trim, Amethyst	135.00
Spooner, Reverse Swirl, Burlington Mark, Blue	55.00
Spooner, Scroll With Acanthus, White	30.00
Spooner, Tokyo, Green	40.00 To 80.00
Spooner, Water Lily & Cattails, Green	40.00
Spooner, Wild Bouquet, Green	68.00
Spooner, Wild Bouquet, White	30.00
Spooner, Wreath & Shell, Blue	75.00
Spooner, Wreath & Shell, Yellow	80.00
Sugar & Creamer, Beaded Ovals In Sand, Gold & Enamel, Clear	110.00
Sugar & Creamer, Hobnail, Child's, Blue	12.00
Sugar Shaker, Argus Swirl, Pink	135.00
Sugar Shaker, Coin Spot, 9 Panel, Blue	65.00
Sugar Shaker, Fern, Blue	90.00
Sugar Shaker, Forget-Me-Not, Green	115.00
Sugar Shaker, Quilted Phlox, Green	78.00
Sugar Shaker, Reverse Swirl, Blue	90.00 To 110.00
Sugar Shaker, Reverse Swirl, Vaseline	115.00
Sugar Shaker, Ribbed Lattice, Blue	60.00
Sugar Shaker, Ribbed Lattice, Cranberry	95.00
Sugar Shaker, Swirl	65.00
Sugar Shaker, Swirl, Blue	100.00
Sugar Shaker, Twist, Clear	40.00
Sugar Shaker, Windows, Blue	125.00
Sugar, Alaska, Clear	38.00
Sugar, Covered, Bubble Lattice, Blue	85.00
Sugar, Creamer, & Spooner, Leaf Medallion, Gold Trim, Green	200.00
Sugar, Everglades, Covered, Blue & Gold	55.00
Sugar, Flora, Covered, Vaseline	100.00
Sugar, Fluted Scrolls, Covered, White	40.00
Sugar, Idyll, Open, Green	45.00
Sugar, Iris With Meander, Gold Trim, Blue	65.00
Sugar, Jewel & Flower, Covered, White	60.00
Sugar, Reverse Swirl, Burlington Mark, Blue	100.00
Syrup, Beatty Swirl, Clear	90.00
Syrup, Bubble Lattice, Bulbous, Blue	195.00
Syrup, Chrysanthemum, Swirl Base, Blue	150.00
Syrup, Coreopsis, Blue	185.00
Syrup, Currier & Ives, Amber	135.00
Syrup, Daisy & Fern, Blue	95.00
Syrup, Daisy & Fern, Bulbous, Blue	70.00
Syrup, Daisy In Criss Cross, White	165.00
Syrup, Diamond Spearhead, Green	160.00
Syrup, Polka Dot, Clear	60.00
Syrup, Reverse Swirl, Collared, Clear	120.00
Syrup, Reverse Swirl, Vaseline	100.00
Syrup, Ribbed Lattice, Blue	155.00
Syrup, Seaweed, Blue	185.00
Syrup, Swirl, Squatty, Blue	125.00
Syrup, Windows, Clear	75.00
Table Set, Fluted Scrolls, Vaseline, 4 Piece	250.00
Table Set, Intaglio, White, 4 Piece	275.00
Table Set, Leaf Medallion, Amethyst, 4 Piece	750.00
Table Set, Repeat S, Amethyst With Gold, 4 Piece	385.00
Table Set, Stippled Fleur-De-Lis, Amethyst With Gold	335.00
Table Set, Swag With Brackets, Green, 4 Piece	350.00
Table Set, Tokyo, Blue, 4 Piece	485.00
Toothpick, Beatty Honeycomb, White	25.00

Toothpick, Diamond Spearhead, Northwood, Green	58.00
Toothpick, Hobnail, White	25.00
Toothpick, Hobnail, 4 Rounded Feet, Vaseline	15.00
Toothpick, Idyll, Blue	75.00
Toothpick, Iris With Meander, Blue	50.00
Toothpick, Iris With Meander, Vaseline	78.00
Toothpick, La Belle	65.00
Toothpick, Ribbed Spiral, White	55.00
Toothpick, Swirl, Chrysanthemum Base, Cranberry	110.00
Toothpick, Wreathed Shell, Vaseline	135.00
Top Hat, Hobnail, Blue	35.00
Tray, Card, Argonaut Shell, White	29.00
Tray, Hobnail, Fan Shape, White	18.00
Tray, Water, Beatty Swirl, Blue	110.00
Tray, Water, Swirled, Blue	55.00
Tumbler, Alaska, Blue	70.00
Tumbler, Arabian Nights, Blue	40.00
Tumbler, Beatty Swirl, White	20.00
Tumbler, Circled Scroll, Blue	85.00
Tumbler, Criss Cross, Rubena	110.00
Tumbler, Double Ring Excelsior Pattern	150.00
Tumbler, Drape, Blue	20.00
Tumbler, Hobnail, Cranberry	45.00
Tumbler, Hobnail, 10 Row, Blue	95.00
Tumbler, Hobnail, 10 Row, Blue, 3 3/4 In.	88.00
Tumbler, Hobnail, 10 Row, Cranberry, 3 7/8 In.	95.00
Tumbler, Inverted Fan & Feather, Blue	45.00
Tumbler, Jackson, Blue	36.00
Tumbler, Palm Beach, Blue	85.00
Tumbler, Poinsettia, White	35.00 To 45.00
Tumbler, S-Repeat, Blue	40.00
Tumbler, Stars & Stripes, Cranberry	45.00
Tumbler, Swag With Brackets	35.00
Tumbler, Swirl, Blue	45.00
Tumbler, Swirl, White	20.00
Tumbler, Wreath & Shell, Collared, Blue	40.00
Vase, Canterbury, Pink, 3 In.	18.00
Vase, Diamond Quilted, Blue, 11 In.	42.50
Vase, Hobnail, Blue, Miniature	12.00
Vase, Hobnail, Handkerchief, Plum	85.00
Vase, Hobnail, Pink, 7 3/4 In.	45.00
Vase, Hobnail, Stretched Top, Crimped, Vaseline, 13 In.	35.00
Vase, Open Windows, White, 7 1/2 In.	65.00
Vase, Pulled Loop, Peach, 10 In.	50.00
Vase, Spiral Optic, Cranberry, 12 In., Matched Pair	235.00
Vase, Spiral Optic, Flared, Partial Foil Label, Green	35.00
Vase, Tree Trunk, Blue, 11 In., Pair	55.00
Vase, White Corn	35.00
Water Set, Bubble Lattice, Blue, 6 Piece	335.00
Water Set, Buttons & Braids, Blue, 7 Piece	248.00
Water Set, Buttons & Braids, Green, 7 Piece	200.00
Water Set, Cromwell, Clear, Gold & Amethyst Stain, 7 Piece	150.00
Water Set, Daisy & Fern, Cranberry, 7 Piece	365.00
Water Set, Drapery, Blue, 6 Piece	290.00
Water Set, Hobnail, Vaseline, 7 Piece	195.00
Water Set, Intaglio, White, 7 Piece	275.00
Water Set, Jewel & Flower, 5 Piece Illus	850.00
Water Set, Paneled Holly, Gold Trim, Green, 7 Piece	345.00
Water Set, Regal, Northwood, Blue, 7 Piece	685.00
Water Set, Swirl, Rubena, 7 Piece	395.00
Whiskey Taster, Lacy, Amethyst	125.00

Opalescent, Water Set, Jewel & Flower, 5 Piece

Opaline, or opal glass, was made in white, green, and other colors. The glass had a matte surface and a lack of transparency. It was often gilded or painted. It was a popular mid-nineteenth-century European glassware.

OPALINE, Bottle, Cologne, White & Gold Trim, Stopper, Blue, 7 3/4 In. 95.00
  Vase, Town Pump, Spigot & Handle, Footed, 6 1/2 In. 65.00

OPERA GLASSES, French, Brass & Mother-Of-Pearl, Paris 25.00
  Lemaire, Paris, Brass 45.00
  Lemaire, Paris, Mother-Of-Pearl, Case 40.00
  Mother-Of-Pearl, France 25.00
  Snail Shell 42.00
  Telescopic, Hand Holder, Gold Filled 125.00
      ORGAN, see Music, Organ

ORPHAN ANNIE, Ashtray, Sandy Standing, 1930s 125.00
  Badge, Decoder, 1936 .... 25.00
  Badge, Secret Society 22.00
  Bank, Dime Register 135.00
  Book, Big Little, With The Circus, 1934 .... 20.00
  Book, Pop-Up 85.00
  Cards, Trading, 1937 .... 25.00
  Decoder, 1935 .... 25.00
  Decoder, 1936 .... 25.00
  Decoder, 1938 .... 19.00
  Decoder, 1939 .... 14.00 To 25.00
  Figurine, Bisque, 4 Piece 165.00
  Game, Travel, Milton Bradley 30.00
  Holder, Toothbrush, Sandy, On Sofa, Bisque, 1930 .... 95.00
  Manual, 1937 .... 28.00
  Medal, Good Luck, Secret Society 12.50
  Mug, Ovaltine, Stoneware 28.00
  Mug, Red Shaker Top, Ovaltine, Plastic 35.00
  Pastry Set, Boxed 55.00
  Pin, Secret Society .... 12.50 To 15.00
  Plate 20.00
  Radio, Sandy, Daddy Warbucks 275.00
  Saucer, Sandy 15.00
  Stove, Cream & Red, 7 1/2 X 4 In. .... 25.00 To 27.50
  Stove, Electric 65.00
  Stove, Green & Buff 24.00
  Toy, Jumping Rope 400.00
  Toy, Sandy, Windup 175.00
  Tumbler & Shaker, Beetleware, Pair 25.00
  Tumbler, Red Shaker Top, Decal 25.00
  Vase, Wall Pocket, Sandy 25.00

Watch, Sun .... 22.00 To 45.00
Wristwatch, Red Leather Band 65.00

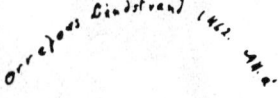

Orrefors Glassworks, located in the Swedish province of Smaaland, was
established in 1916.

ORREFORS, Bowl, Crimped Base, Signed, 11 In.Diam. 45.00
   Bowl, Crystal, Half Moon Cutout Design, 5 1/4 In. 55.00
   Bowl, Green, Maroon Swirls, Artist Signed, 4 1/4 In. 30.00
   Bowl, Intaglio Cut Topless Dancer, Frosted, Signed, 11 3/4 In. 350.00
   Ewer, Landberg Exposition, Amber, 13 In. 125.00
   Figurine, Elephant 60.00
   Goblet, Mushroom Shape Bowl, Spatter Top, Blue & White Stem 25.00
   Vase, Bud, Ariel, Steel Gray Shading, Ivory Base, Marked, 10 In. 800.00
   Vase, Bud, Edvin Ohrstrom, C.1960 ....*Illus* 800.00
   Vase, Engraved Glass, Simon Gate, C.1933 ....*Illus* 725.00
   Vase, Engraved, Maiden In Field, Marked, 6 In. 25.00
   Vase, Engraved, Mermaid, Black Foot, Marked, 8 1/2 In. 725.00
   Vase, Paperweight, Fish Swimming, Signed, 6 In. 345.00

Ott & Brewer Company operated the Etruria Pottery at Trenton,
New Jersey, from 1863 to 1893. It was under the direction of
William Bromley, Sr., from the Belleek factory at Belleek, Ireland,
from 1883.

OTT & BREWER, Cracker Jar, Blue & Gold On White, 6 In. 75.00
   Creamer, Flower Sprays, Gold Handle 150.00
   Creamer, Pansy Nosegays, 3 1/2 In. 135.00
   Cup & Saucer, Demitasse, Glossy White, Cream Interior, Signed 165.00
   Cup & Saucer, Tea, Tridacna, Pink Interior 85.00
   Dish, Nut, Shell Shaped, Twig Handle, Gold Trim 90.00
   Pitcher, Cobalt, Flower Design, 9 In. 45.00
   Saucer, Gold Pastel Flower, Cream Ground, 4 In.Diam. 60.00
   Sugar & Creamer, Cactus Pattern, Nacreous Finish, Bronze Trim 285.00

OVERBECK, Figurine, Little Lady, Pink Shawl 170.00

OWENS UTOPIAN

Owens Pottery was made in Zanesville, Ohio, from 1891 to 1928. The
first art pottery was made after 1896. Utopian Ware, Cyrano, Navarre,
Feroza, and Henri Deux were made. Pieces were usually marked with a form
of the name Owens. About 1907 the firm began to make tile and gave up the
art pottery wares.

OWENS, Base, Lamp, Soudanese, Floral 250.00
   Bowl, Lotus, White Blossoms, 4 3/4 X 3 1/2 In. 140.00
   Ewer, Utopian, Signed Steele, 3 In. 175.00
   Ewer, Utopian, Signed Steele, 6 In. 175.00
   Jardiniere, Art Nouveau 225.00
   Jardiniere, Lotus, Butterflies, 7 1/2 X 10 1/2 In. 200.00
   Jardiniere, Nasturtiums, 8 1/4 X 7 In. 60.00
   Jardiniere, Orange & Yellow Zinnias, Brown To Yellow Glaze, 11 In. 150.00
   Jardiniere, Utopian, Matte, Pedestal 350.00
   Jug, Opalesce, Pansies, Green Design, 6 In.Diam. 600.00
   Jug, Whiskey, Corn Design 225.00
   Mug, Blackberries, T.Steele, 4 1/2 In. 105.00
   Mug, Floral, High Glaze, 5 1/4 In. 90.00
   Mug, Utopian, Fruits & Leaves Design, 5 In. 150.00
   Pitcher, Berry Design, 12 In. 160.00

Orrefors, Vases, Engraved Glass, Simon Gate,
C.1933; Bud, Edvin Ohrstrom, C.1960

Pitcher, Purple Fruit & Green Leaves, Blue Ground, Signed, 5 1/2 In. 150.00
Pitcher, Utopian, Orange Floral, Signed, 4 In. 135.00
Tankard Set, 4 Mugs, Leaf & Berry Design, Tankard, 9 1/2 In. 425.00
Tankard, Hand-Painted Stalks Of Wheat, Brown & Yellow, 11 1/2 In. 175.00
Tankard, Utopian, Cherries & Leaves, 12 In. 175.00
Tankard, White, Brown, Berries, Pale Green, Green Ground, 12 In. 175.00
Vase, Aborigine, 6 In. 65.00
Vase, Bud, Utopian, 9 1/2 In. 295.00
Vase, Cyrano, Pillow, 4 X 6 In. 65.00
Vase, Floral, Opalescent, 10 In. 275.00
Vase, Gray Leaves, Flowers, Brown Ground, 9 1/2 In. 125.00
Vase, Ovoid, Owensart, 10 3/4 In. 350.00
Vase, Utopian, Berries, 8 In. 150.00
Vase, Utopian, Bright Leaves, S.Timberlake, 7 1/2 In. 125.00
Vase, Utopian, Brown High Glaze, Pansies, 13 In. 140.00
Vase, Utopian, Clover, 4 1/2 X 3 1/2 In. 70.00
Vase, Utopian, Currants, 8 In. 160.00
Vase, Utopian, Matte, Twisted, Floral, 14 In. 175.00
Vase, Utopian, Nasturtium Design, Swirled, 14 In. 175.00
Vase, Utopian, Pillow, Baby Chick In Reeds, Signed, 4 1/4 In. 500.00
Vase, Utopian, Swirled, Nasturtium Design, 14 In. 135.00
Vase, Utopian, Swirled, 14 In. 135.00
Vase, Venetian, 10 In. 165.00
Vase, Yellow Roses, Bulbous, Signed Timberlake, 8 In. 225.00
Wall Pocket, Figural, Acorn, Large 85.00

OYSTER PLATE, Gold Webbing, Scalloped Gold Border, French, 9 In.Diam. 55.00
    Haviland, Green, Brown, & White 49.50

> Paden City Glass Manufacturing Company was established in 1916 at
> Paden City, West Virginia. It is best known for glasswares but also
> produced a pottery line. The firm closed in 1951.

PADEN CITY, Box, Powder, Military Cap, Amber 15.00
    Cup & Saucer, Ivy Design, Set Of 7 .... 35.00
    Figurine, Pony, Light Blue, 11 1/2 In., Pair 300.00
    Figurine, Pouter Pigeon 40.00
    Plate, Pink & Yellow Nasturtiums, 6 In. 2.00
    Plate, Princess, 10 In. 14.00
    Platter, Oval, 14 In. 55.00

PAINTING, On Ivory, Court Lady, Brass Frame, 4 X 5 In. 140.00
    On Ivory, Court Woman, Ormolu Frame, Signed B.Kokier, 6 1/2 X 4 In. 260.00
    On Ivory, Gentleman, Locket, Gold Filled Case, C.1810 .... 250.00
    On Ivory, Interior With 3 Women, P.Meunier, France, 3 5/8 X 3 In. 90.00
    On Ivory, Man On Horseback, Signed Dimarc, 3 1/2 X 2 1/2 In. 165.00

Painting, On Porcelain, Poesie, Wagner, 4 X 6 In.

On Ivory, Plaque, Diana & Her Servant, Framed, 6 In.	850.00
On Ivory, Portrait, Lady, French, Signed J.Rigaule, 2 1/2 In., Pair	250.00
On Ivory, Victorian Lady, Brass Frame, Boxed, 2 In.	100.00
On Ivory, Woman, Violeau, Signed, Framed, Oval, 5 1/4 X 6 In.	125.00
On Ivory, Young Court Woman, Signed G.Kodier, 6 1/2 X 4 1/2 In.	260.00
On Porcelain, Christ As A Youth	135.00
On Porcelain, Gypsy Girl, Signed Emile, Papier-Mache Frame	250.00
On Porcelain, Maiden In Crypt Kisses Image, Germany, 7 X 5 In.	375.00
On Porcelain, Maria Louise, Signed Wagner, 3 1/2 X 2 1/2 In.	160.00
On Porcelain, Melon Eater, Marked Germany, 3 1/2 In.Diam.	45.00
On Porcelain, Poesie, Wagner, 4 X 6 In.	*Illus* 950.00
On Porcelain, Renaissance Prince, Framed	150.00
On Porcelain, Woman, Dore Bronze Frame, 9 X 12 1/2 In.	425.00
On Tin, Oil, Vase Of Flowers, C.1909, 9 1/2 X 13 1/2 In.	50.00

Pairpoint Corporation was a silver and glass firm founded in New Bedford, Massachusetts, in 1880. Although the company went through many reorganizations and name changes, it is still working.

PAIRPOINT, Bell, Amethyst Glass	125.00
Biscuit Jar, Fan Design On Lid That Folds, Pale Green, Gold Gilt	450.00
Bottle, Perfume, Ribbed, Pear Shape, Long Ribbed Stopper, 7 In., Pr.	125.00
Bottle, Perfume, Teadrop Ground Stopper	149.00
Bottle, Perfume, 8-Ribbed Stopper, 6 In., Pair	145.00
Bowl, Cabbage Leaf Pattern, Marked, 9 1/2 In.	125.00
Bowl, Console, Coleus Pattern, Green Pedestal, 4 X 14 In.Diam.	325.00
Bowl, Nut, Cabbage Leaves, Head Form Feet, 7 1/2 X 10 3/4 In.	115.00
Bowl, Pedestal, Green, 12 In.	190.00
Bowl, Puffy Inserts, Silver Plated Base, Marked, 10 1/2 In.	160.00
Box, Cigarette, Signed, Porcelain & Silver Plated	195.00
Candleholder, Held Up By Cupid, 7 1/4 In.	25.00
Candlestick, Bubble Base, Blue, 6 In., Pair	150.00
Candlestick, Canaria, Vintage Engraved, 10 1/2 In.	75.00
Candlestick, Controlled Bubble Connector, Amber, 12 In., Pair	125.00
Candlestick, Cranberry To Clear, Sunburst Pattern, 10 In., Pair	519.00
Candlestick, Crystal, Onyx & Silver, Pineapple Stem, 15 In., Pr.	400.00
Candlestick, Topaz, Bubble Ball, 4 1/2 In., Pair	85.00
Castor, Pickle, Lid & Tongs, Silver Plated	95.00
Chalice, Bubble Stem, 12 In.	185.00
Compote, Amethyst, Bubble Ball, 8 X 8 In.	50.00
Compote, Bubble Ball In Stem, Ruby, 6 X 5 3/4 In.	175.00
Compote, Peppermint Stick, Teardrop Stem, 10 X 8 1/2 In.	400.00
Compote, Victoria, 7 1/4 X 8 1/4 In.	100.00

Pairpoint, Lamp, Painted Glass,
Puffy, Pewter

Pairpoint, Lamp, Puffy Lilac Blossom,
Early 20th Century

Console Set, Green, Bubble Ball, 9 In. Candlestick	170.00
Cracker Jar, Burmese Coloring, Signed	325.00
Cracker Jar, Green, Flowers & Leaves, Signed, 8 1/2 In.	425.00
Cup Plate, Amber	6.00
Cup Plate, Amethyst	7.00
Cup, Shaving, Brush Rest	42.50
Dish, Candy, Viscera Pattern, Pedestal, Covered, Clear Cut	135.00
Dish, Ruby, Heart Shaped, Handled, 7 1/2 In.	45.00
Knife, Fruit, Allover Fruit Design	23.00
Lamp, Acid Cut-Back Scenic Shade, Brass Base, Signed, 13 In.	350.00
Lamp, Clipper Ship On Dolphin Base, Signed	3400.00
Lamp, Coralene Finish Shade, Fleur-De-Lis Pattern, Signed, 22 In.	650.00
Lamp, Delft Design, Signed, Miniature	435.00
Lamp, Directoire, Textured Shade, Double Arm, Marble Base, 19 In.	1700.00
Lamp, Dome Shape Globe, Silver Plated Dolphin, Marble Base, 20 In.	50.00
Lamp, Fairy, Coralene Flowers, Blue Ground	350.00
Lamp, Fairy, Pansy Design, Blown-Out Shade, Wooden Base, 8 In., Pr.	375.00
Lamp, Hummingbirds & Roses Shade, Sticker, Signed, Shade 14 In.	3500.00
Lamp, Kerosene, Oriental Design, Mice Feet	325.00
Lamp, Painted Glass, Puffy, Pewter	Illus 2300.00
Lamp, Puffy Lilac Blossom, Early 20th Century	Illus 5775.00
Lamp, Puffy Lilac Blossom, Orange, Yellow, Butterfly, 23 In.	5775.00
Lamp, Puffy Rose Tree Pattern, Shade, Signed, 14 1/2 In.	975.00
Lamp, Puffy, Apple Blossoms, Butterflies, Ivory Ground, 15 In.	725.00
Lamp, Reverse Painted Shade, 8-Sided Standard, Signed, 23 In.	1150.00
Lamp, Reverse Painted, Brass, Landscape Painting, Signed, 23 In.	1500.00
Lamp, Reverse Painted, Exeter Shade, Bronze Base Signed	1200.00
Lamp, Scenic Carlisle Shade, Parrots, Signed, 18 In.	3100.00
Lamp, Table, Grape Leaves, Clusters, Green Base, 19 In.	3400.00
Lamp, Table, Harvest Scene, Signed, 20 In.	2850.00
Lamp, Table, Rose Bouquet, Floral Base, Signed, 12 In.	3975.00
Lamp, Venetian Harbor, Full Ships All Around, Blues, 20 In.	2650.00
Paperweight & Ring Holder, Teapot Shape, Label	95.00
Paperweight, Well For Penpoints & Erasers, 3 In.	175.00
Pitcher & Basket, Floral Engraving, Roping Edge, Swing Handle	35.00
Planter, Brass, Glass Liner	75.00
Plate, Hooked Center Handle, Buckingham Pattern, 10 In.Diam.	95.00
Shade, 3 Reverse Painted Scenes, Silver Plated Base, 15 In.	1950.00
Toothpick, Ruffled Edge, Silver Footed, Handled	35.00
Urn, Deep Red, Bubble Ball Base, 12 X 10 In.	250.00
Vase, Bubble Ball Stem, Canaria Color, 14 In.	225.00
Vase, Charissa, Engraved, 12 In.	160.00
Vase, Coleus Pattern, 9 3/4 In.	200.00

Vase, Deer & Deco Design, Ruffled, Sterling Silver Overlay, 9 In.	225.00
Vase, Etched, Clear Bubble Ball, Blue, 13 In.	135.00
Vase, Green Base, Clear Bubble Knob, Green Top, 8 In.	85.00
Vase, Hand-Painted, Brass Holder, 7 In.	150.00
Vase, Jack-In-The-Pulpit, Purple, Enameled Daisies, Sticker, 7 In.	85.00
Vase, Twist Glass, Cobalt Blue, 9 X 10 In.	175.00
Vase, Vintage Pattern, Signed, Green, 9 In.	65.00
Water Set, Engraved Star Of David, 4 Pedestal Glasses, 5 Piece	375.00
Wine, Flambeau, Black Stems, Red, 5 1/4 In.	32.00

PAPER DOLL, Alice Faye, C.1941, 3 Dolls, Merrill, Uncut	90.00
Amy Carter, Uncut	8.00
Arnold Printworks Rabbit, Uncut	65.00
Ava Gardner, Cut	20.00
Baby Bonnie, Whitman, 1960	18.00
Baby Brother & Baby Sister, C.1932, 2 Dolls, Whitman, Cut	35.00
Benny Goodman & Peggy Lee, 1942, 4 Cut Dolls, 6 Uncut Pages	60.00
Betsy McCall, Life-Size, Gabriel 1955	65.00
Betsy McCall, 32 Pages	25.00
Blondie, 1940	20.00
Bottle, Perfume, Lucky Lindy, Authentic, C.1927, 2 3/4 In.	12.00
Boy & Girl On Swing, 1910, Uncut	5.00
Boy In Academy Dress Uniform, 1904, 7 In.	12.50
Boy On Swing, 1910, Uncut	5.00
Boy, Military Uniform, American Color Type Co., 7 In.	12.50
Boy, Military Uniform, C.1904, Uncut, 7 In.	13.00
Bridal Party, 5 Dolls, 1940s, Boxed, Uncut	18.00
Bride & Soldier Groom, 1947	12.00
Brownie Scout, Uniforms Of Many Nations, Uncut, Boxed	24.00
Charlie McCarthy, Cut	20.00
Cinderella Coach, Other Characters, Uncut	7.50
Circus, Sideshow, Uncut	6.00
Claudette Colbert, Uncut	35.00
Colleen Moore, Dollhouse, 8 Pages	50.00
Connie Francis, Uncut	18.00
Cyd Charisse	15.00
Daisy Mae & L'il Abner, Uncut	22.00
Debbie Reynolds	15.00
Dinah Shore, Uncut	30.00
Ding Dong, Puss's In The Well	3.00
Dinky Dog & Freckles Frog, Kelloggs, Uncut	20.00
Dionne Quints, Yvonne, C.1940, Merrill, Cut	22.00
Dionne Quintuplets, Let's Play House	75.00
Dolly Dingle & Her Dollies, 1926	15.00
Dolly Dingle, Sheet, Uncut	15.00
Dolly Dingle, Travels, Series 2, 1921	25.00
Douglas Fairbanks & Mary Pickford, Uncut, Delineator, 1917	22.00
Elizabeth Taylor, Cut	15.00
Eve Arden, Uncut	18.00 To 20.00
Fashion, C.1890, Willa Wright, 2 Costumes, 5 1/2 In.	45.00
Flying Marvels, Precut, 1944	18.00
Gale Storm, Uncut	35.00
Gibson Girl, Black & White, Pen & Ink, Handmade, C.1890	30.00
Girl, Folding Stand-Up Base, Raphael Tuck, 12 In.	27.50
Girl, Moving Arms & Legs, C.1880, Die Cut, 6 Changes	30.00
Gloria Jean, 1941	20.00
Gone With The Wind, C.1940, 18 Dolls, Merrill, Cut	160.00
Grace Kelly, Uncut	45.00
Hedy Lamarr, C.1942, 2 Dolls, Merrill, Cut	65.00
High School Paper Dolls, C.1940, 16 Dolls, Merrill, Cut	18.00
History Of Little Fanny, 5th Edition, London, 1810, 7 Figures	500.00
Jane Russell, Uncut	25.00
Jeanette MacDonald, C.1941, 2 Dolls, Merrill, Cut	65.00

Jockey, Racehorses, Dated June 21, 1895, Racetrack, Uncut	6.50
Jones Family, 1958, Uncut	10.00
June Allyson, Uncut	35.00
Lady, Gowns, Hand Cut, Hand-Colored Paper, Wynna Wright, 5 1/2 In.	27.50
Lana Turner, 2 Dolls, C.1942, Whitman, Cut	45.00
Lennon Sisters, Uncut	25.00
Lettie Lane, C.1908, 13 Dolls, Clothes, Cut	25.00
Little Folk's Play Friends, Patent 1919, Helping Mother, Uncut	3.00
Liz Taylor, Folder, 1954	11.00
Lost Horizons, Uncut	15.00
Marie Osmond, Uncut	12.00
Marilyn Monroe, Saalfield, 1953, Uncut	45.00
Mary Poppins, Magic Paper, 1964, Boxed, Set Of 5	15.00
Mistress Mary, 1917	12.50
My Pet, 2 Uncut Dresses	15.00
My Twins, Sue, Pam, & Baby Brother, Uncut	6.50
Natalie Wood	15.00
Natalie Wood, Uncut	18.00
Old Woman In The Shoe, Uncut	35.00
Organ-Grinder, Uncut	35.00
Our Gang, October, 1925	20.00
Palmer Cox Brownies, Jointed, Uncut, Dated 1895	60.00
Partridge Family, Uncut	12.00
Pat Boone, Uncut	18.00
Polly & Peter Perkins, 1934, Uncut	5.00
Pollyanna, Uncut	18.00
Queen Elizabeth & Family, Coronation, Uncut	29.00
Rita Hayworth, Carmen, 1948, Uncut	20.00
Rosemary Clooney, Uncut	25.00
Roy Rogers, Uncut	25.00
Royal Reggie, Outfits	25.00
Sailor, McLoughlin Bros., Uncut Sheet Of 10	35.00
Shirley Temple, 5 Outfits, 1936, Cut, 34 In.	58.00
Snow White, 7 Dwarfs, 1937, Cut	30.00
Sonia Henie, 3 Dolls, C.1939, Cut	65.00
Sunshine Family, Uncut	12.00
Tableaux Battle Of New Orleans, 1896, 7 1/2 X 10 In., 8 Piece	15.00
Teddy Bear, 5 Outfits, Ottmon Lithograph, 1900s, 10 1/2 In.	235.00
Texas Tom, 1920s, Uncut	5.00
Trips To Mother Gooseland, Stand-Ups, H.A.Hart, 10 X 15 In.	3.00
Twiggy, Wearable Dress, Uncut	15.00
Ziegfeld Girl, 6 Famous Movie Stars, 10 Models, C.1941, Cut	150.00
Zimmerman Bicyclist	35.00
PAPER, Almanac, Kickapoo Indian Medicine, 1873	22.50
Almanac, Piso's Cure-All, Hazeltine's For 1894, 1 3/8 X 2 In.	10.00
Band, Cigar, Set Of 100	10.00
Book, Big Big, Mickey Mouse, 1935	65.00
Book, Big Little Book, Alley Oop	18.00
Book, Big Little Book, Betty Boop	18.00
Book, Big Little Book, Buffalo Bill	20.00
Book, Big Little Book, Dan Dunn, Operator 48	9.00
Book, Big Little Book, Desert Eagle Rides Again	9.00
Book, Big Little Book, Flash Gordon	18.00
Book, Big Little Book, Men Of The Mounted	9.00
Book, Big Little Book, Smitty	12.00
Book, Big Little Book, Tarzan	7.00
Book, Black Beauty, 1894, Gild Design Cover	5.00
Book, Coloring, Fifty States, Mr.Peanut	6.00
Book, Dolly Dingle, Original	600.00
Book, Fruit & Candies Recipes, Published By Lydia Pinkham, C.1920	4.50
Book, Golden, Zorro, 1958	5.00
Book, Little Big Book, Tarzan	8.00

Book, Little Black Sambo, 1948, 29 Illustrations, Cardboard Cover 7.00
Book, Three Little Pigs, 1918 .... 17.50
Book, U.S.Atlas, 1835, Hand-Colored Maps 32.00
Bookmark, Mennen's Violet Talcum Powder, Die Cut, Lake Medallion 2.00
Bookmark, Victorian, Floral, Silk Ends, Set Of 3 .... 7.50

PAPER, CALENDAR, see Calendar Paper

Catalog, French Hollowware, Lalance & Grosjean Co., New York, 1867 .... 30.00
Envelope, Acme Cubana Cigars, Holds 2 Cigars, Patented 1898 .... 2.00
Figural, Bird, Die Cut, 7 Birds On Branch, Germany, C.1880, 4 1/2 In.Sq. 7.50
Handbill, Anna Christie, Greta Garbo, 6 X 9 In. 25.00
Handbill, Forbidden, Stanwyck & Menjou, Sepia Design, 8 X 21 In. 15.00
Handbill, Movie, The Invisible Man, Claude Rains, 9 1/2 X 14 In. 95.00
Handbill, Polly Of The Circus, Clark Gable, Marion Davies, 6 X 9 In. 10.00
Label, Food Tin, Seward Salmon 15.00
Stock Certificate, Katser, Frazer Corp., Nevada, 1946, Brown 6.00
Telegram, American Telegraph Co., 1866 .... 4.00

PAPERWEIGHT, see also Baccarat, Paperweight

PAPERWEIGHT, Blossom, Green Leaves, Emil Stanger, Dated 1910 ....2300.00
Blue Bell, 3 X 3 1/4 In. 46.00
Blue Flower, Faceted Top, 3 1/4 In. 55.00
Bohemian, Scattered Millefiori, Silhouettes, Butterfly, 2 In. 500.00
Bohemian, Silhouette Canes, Hourse, Butterfly, & Eagle, 3 1/8 In. 785.00
Bubble Ring, Clear, 3 1/2 In. 55.00
Bulldog, Clear, Oval, 2 7/8 In. 8.00
Caithness, Artic Night 135.00
Caithness, Asteroid 125.00
Caithness, Floral Fountain, Red 225.00
Caithness, Sea Crab, 1974 .... 125.00
Chinese Flower, 6 Inner & 6 Outer Petals, 2 3/8 In. 45.00
Chinese Peacock 12.50
Civil War Soldier Pictured, Clear 110.00
Clichy, Chequer, Circles, Pink, Green, 3 In. 900.00
Clichy, Red Ground, Scattered Millefiori, 3 In. 750.00
Clichy, Scattered Millefiori, Pink Rose, 2 3/4 In. 400.00
Clichy, White Ground, Millefiori, 3 1/4 In. 700.00
Columbian World's Fair, State Building 45.00
Columbus, Christopher, D'Albret 115.00
Dome Shape, Glass Worker's Union, 1917, Columbus, Ohio 35.00
Dome, Crossed Ax & Hammer 25.00
Eagle, 6-Inch Wingspan, Bronze 75.00
Empire State Building, 1940s 20.00
Figural Bulldog, Clear Glass Eyes, Orange, 2 3/4 In. 17.50
Figural, Cowboy Hat, Kansas City Dressed Beef Co. 45.00
Figural, Crocodile, Independent Stove Co., Owosso, Michigan 10.00
Figural, Green Glass Turtle, 6 X 4 In. 135.00
Figural, Red Lobster, Cast Iron 15.00
Ghandi, D'Albret, 2 Color 100.00
Glass, Snowbaby In Center 75.00
Hemingway, Ernest, D'Albret 60.00
High Dome, Central Bubble, Crimped Splatter, American, 3 In. 75.00
Hills Brothers Coffee 15.00
Home Sweet Home, C.1910, Large 35.00
Home Sweet Home, 3 1/2 In.Diam. 65.00
Horseshoe, Bronze, Union Station, Kansas 20.00
Independent Stove Co., Crocodile 10.00
I've Got My Eye On You, Semi Porcelain, 1880, 3 In.Diam 60.00
King Of Sweden, D'Albret 50.00
Looped Garland, Canes, Turquoise Ground, Clichy, 3 1/8 In. 750.00
Millefiori, Circles In Red, White, Blue, & Green, 1 3/4 In. 150.00
Millefiori, Facets, Blue & Yellow Circles, Whitefriar 150.00
Napoleon Bonaparte, Clear, Pale Green Ground, Sulphide, 2/3 In. 300.00

Pansy, Purple, Yellow & Brown, Green Leaves, 2 7/8 In. 1400.00
Perthshire, Christmas Mistletoe, 2 5/8 In. 95.00
Perthshire, Clematis, On Latticinio Basket, 2 5/8 In. 135.00
Perthshire, Flat Bouquet Of Flowers, Dragonfly, 3 1/2 In. 475.00
Perthshire, Millefiori Garland, Red Flower, Colored Canes, 3 In. 135.00
Perthshire, Pansy, Garland Of Canes, 2 5/8 In. 250.00
Planters Peanuts, Glass, Rectangular, 1938 .... 19.00
Remember The Maine, Ship, Multifloral Ground 50.00
River Barge, Bronzed Metal 18.00
Royal Order Of Moose 25.00
Sandwich Glass, Cane & Filigree Twists, 2 3/8 In. 50.00
Sandwich, Poinsettia, Cobalt Blue Flower, 12 Petals, 3 In. 450.00
Shack Amaxon Worsted Co., Glass, 1900s 22.00
Silhouette Of Lady, Green, Blue, Coral, White, Bacchus, 2 3/4 In. 700.00
Sodden Snow Center, Bacchus, 3 1/2 X 2 1/4 In. 385.00
St.Louis, Amber, Green Leaves, Clear Glass, 1 7/8 In. 700.00
St.Louis, Concentric Millefiori, Green, Blue, Red, White, 2 In. 375.00
St.Louis, Dahlia, Purple, Yellow Stamen, 2 3/4 In. 1800.00
St.Louis, Faceted Central Punty, Filigree Twists, 2 1/2 In. 250.00
St.Louis, Fruit On Latticinio, 1979, France 390.00
St.Louis, Green, Pink, White Florets, White Ground, 1 3/4 In. 400.00
St.Louis, Piedouche, 1953 .... 525.00
Stourbridge, Mushroom, Concentric, White, Blue, Green, 3 In. 275.00
Sulfide, Llazlo Kossuth, C.1851 .... 350.00
Victor Spring Beds, 1900s 23.00
Washington Insurance Co., Bronze 20.00
Whitefriars, Concentric, Blue, Pink, Green, Red, White, 3 In. 250.00
Whittemore, Holly, White Jasper Ground, Dated 1958 .... 275.00
World's Fair, 1893, Acid Etched 85.00

Papier-mache is a decorative form made from paper mixed with glue, chalk, and other ingredients, then molded and baked. It becomes very hard and can be decorated. Boxes, trays, and furniture were made of papier-mache. Some of the early nineteenth-century pieces were decorated with mother-of-pearl.

PAPIER-MACHE, Bottle Opener, Fat Waiter Carrying Mugs, Hand-Painted, 1920 .... 35.00
Bowl, 7 In. 8.00
Box, Mother-Of-Pearl Inlay, Black 65.00
Box, Pencil, Inlaid Silver, Black, 8 In. 15.00
Candy Container, Black Cat, Germany 22.50
Candy Container, Rabbit 15.00
Case, Spectacle, Hinged Cover, Purple Lining, Gold Design 25.00
Coaster, Japan, 4 1/2 In.Diam. 3.00
Dish, Candy, Chicken Shape, Yellow Beak, White, 4 1/2 In. 55.00
Egg, Easter, Child's, Florals, Red Ground, 3 1/2 X 5 In. 13.00
Figurine, Duck, Blue & Gray 23.00
Figurine, Indian, Sitting, White 100.00
Figurine, Lincoln, Black Broadcloth Suit, 13 In. 80.00
Figurine, Rabbit, Pink, 2 In. 3.00
Figurine, Sheep, Woolly Coat, White, 2 1/2 In. 22.00
Figurine, Turkey, 12 In. 325.00
Jar, Tobacco, Figural, Mandarin 65.00
Mask, Japanese, Frowning Man, Open Mouth, Hair, 6 1/2 In. 50.00
Nodder, Clown, C.1900, 8 In. 85.00
Picture, Castle In Landscape, Mother-Of-Pearl, Oval, 20 In. 130.00
Roly Poly, Happy Hooligan, 5 In. 100.00
Roly Poly, Happy Hooligan, 9 In. 225.00
Roly Poly, Musical, 5 In. 70.00
Stand, Bonnet, Female Bust, Kidskin Head, Green Dress, 16 In. 350.00
Tea Caddy, Victorian, Mother-Of-Pearl Inset 65.00
Toy, Horse, Pull, Gray, Wood, German, 9 1/2 X 12 X 3 1/4 In. 145.00
Tray, C.1850, Stenciled Gilt Flowers, Bamboo Stand, England 750.00
Tray, Gilt Chinoiserie, C.1810, Table Mounted, 30 1/2 In. 770.00
Tray, Polychrome Figures, Stand, 23 1/2 X 31 In. 2750.00

Tray, Sprays & Birds, 19th Century, Stand, 32 X 19 In. 1790.00
    PARASOL, see Umbrella

> Parian is a fine-grained, hard-paste porcelain named for the marble it
> resembles. It was first made in England in 1846 and gained in favor in the
> United States about 1860. Figures, tea sets, vases, and other items were
> made of Parian at many English and American factories.

PARIAN, Bonbon, Shape Of Lady's Hand, 1870 Registry Mark, 8 In.Long 195.00
    Bust, Chopin, 2 3/4 In. 22.50
    Bust, Clytie, Impressed Copeland, Art Union Of London, 1863 .... 400.00
    Bust, Maid Of Athens, J. & T.B. 75.00
    Bust, Wagner, 2 3/4 In. 22.50
    Figurine, Child, Bundle Of Wheat Forms Vase On Back, 7 In. 75.00
    Figurine, Classical Maiden, Holds Mask Next To Face, 14 In. 145.00
    Figurine, Draped Woman, 19th Century, Glass Dome, 14 3/4 In. 100.00
    Figurine, Farm Boy, Sheaf Of Wheat Behind, Carrying Jug, 10 1/2 In. 65.00
    Figurine, Girl Holding Mandolin In Front, 7 In. 48.00
    Figurine, Young Girl On Tasseled Cushion Playing Harp, 8 1/4 In. 75.00
    Match Holder, Dog Seated, Scratcher, Shell-Shaped Saucer 45.00
    Pitcher, Hound Handle 150.00
    Pitcher, Stiff Acanthus Molding, Marked 45.00
    Vase, Hand Holding Lily, 6 1/2 In. 37.50
    Vase, 2 Cupids, 9 In. 65.00

> Vieux Paris, or Old Paris, is porcelain ware that is known to have been
> made in Paris in the eighteenth or early nineteenth century but has no
> identifying manufacturer's mark.

PARIS, Cachepot, Floral & Figural Scenes, Green, Gilding, 9 1/2 In., Pair 1450.00
    Candleholder, Rococo Form, Figures & Goats, 12 1/2 In., Pair 115.00
    Jardiniere, Ruffled Rim, Molded Satyr's Mask Handles, Bowl, 19 In. 400.00
    Tea Set, Hand-Painted Bright Flowers, White, C.1815, 12 Piece 275.00
    Tea Set, Hand-Painted Garland, Gilt, C.1815, Miniature, 9 Piece 75.00
    Tea Set, Hand-Painted Garlands, Gilt, C.1815, 23 Piece 350.00
    Tea Set, Lavender, White & Gold Trim, C.1810, 14 Piece 295.00
    Tea Set, White, Gold Trim, Miniature, C.1850, 11 Piece 65.00
    Vase, Campana Shape, Le Chatelain & Le Depard, 11 1/2 In., Pair 550.00
    Vase, Flair, Vignette Gold & Blue 149.00
    Vase, Floral, Cobalt Blue, Gold Trim, 2-Handled, 12 In. 195.00
    Vase, Hand-Painted Flowers, Cobalt Blue, Gold Trim, Handled, 12 In. 195.00
    Vase, Pillow, 2 Birds, Foliage, 4 Gold Feet, 8 1/2 X 11 In. 325.00
    Vase, Portrait, Maroon, Gold, & Green, 13 X 8 In. 179.00
    Vase, Side-By-Side, Applied Foot & Floral Design, 3 1/2 In. 45.00

> Pate-de-verre is an ancient technique in which glass is made by blending and
> refining powdered glass of different colors into molds. The process was
> revived by French glassmakers, especially Galle, around the end of the
> nineteenth century.

PATE-DE-VERRE, Ashtray, Medallion, Red, Purple, Signed, 6 1/4 X 3 1/2 In. 1305.00
    Atomizer, Green Leaves, Red Berries, Signed H.Berg, 5 3/4 In. 1000.00
    Base, Lamp, 48 Red Poppies, Windows, Brass Base, Signed, 9 In. 1995.00
    Bowl, Emerald, Violet & Aquamarine Streaks, Marked, 8 In. 3900.00
    Bowl, Mottled Pink & Clear, Signed & Dated, Decorchemont 895.00
    Dish, Figural, Green, Yellow, Black Bumblebee, Signed, 4 In. 1000.00
    Figurine, Bird, C.1900, Turquoise Blue, Signed, 3 3/4 In., Pair 1000.00
    Figurine, Female Dancer, Flowing Robe, A.W., Nancy, 10 1/4 In. 3000.00
    Figurine, Fish, Green, Yellow, & Orange, Signed, 3 1/2 In. 1950.00
    Figurine, Woman, Yellow To Ocher, Signed, 9 1/4 In. 4500.00
    Lamp, 48 Poppies Peeking Out Of Windows, Brass Base, 9 In. 1495.00
    Paperweight, Sailing Ship On Ocean, Amber, Partly Frosted 55.00
    Pendant, Bee Mold, Yellow, Black, Signed, 1 1/3 In. 450.00
    Pendant, Yellow, Brown, Blue Butterfly, Marked, 2 1/2 In. 400.00
    Pitcher, Yellow Ground, Butterfly, Flowers, Green Leaves, 8 In. 500.00

Vase, C.1925, Purple Streaked, G.Argy-Rousseau, 8 5/8 In. 1000.00
Vase, Cranberry Masks, Violet To Gray, Marked, 9 In. 3300.00
Vase, Dogwood Blossoms, Cobalt Blue Branches, Ovoid, 5 3/4 In. 3300.00
Vase, Pinecones, Gray Ground, Red, Yellow, Marked, 7 In. 2450.00
Veilleuse, Green & Purple Ground, Flowers, Marked, 6 In. 2500.00
Veilleuse, Purple Ground, Cobalt Blue Bands, 3 Flowers, 7 In. 1400.00

Pate-sur-pate means paste on paste. The design was made by painting layers of slip on the ceramic piece until a relief decoration was formed. The method was developed at the Sevres factory in France about 1850. It became even more famous at the English Minton factory about 1870.

PATE-SUR-PATE, Box, Dresser, Art Nouveau, Female 125.00
Chocolate Pot, Raised Scene Of Seminude Maiden, 9 1/4 In. 95.00
Lamp, Flowers & Bird, Etched Shade, Brass Base, 20 1/2 In. 650.00
Tile, Figure Of Nude Dancer, Baron-Limoges, 5 1/2 X 6 1/2 In. 275.00
Tile, Figure Of Nude Dancer, Blue 250.00
Tile, Nude Dancer 190.00
Vase, Blue, Lavender, Dancing, Lady, 2-Handled, 5 1/2 In. 295.00
Vase, Cherubs, Panels, Covered, Crossed Swords, 15 1/2 In., Pair 2300.00
Vase, Cupid Panels, Scrolled Feet, Covered, Meissen, 15 In. 900.00
Vase, Cupid, Cobalt Blue, 6 In. 295.00
Vase, Fan Shape, Beige, White Angelfish, Swimming, 6 1/2 In. 80.00
Vase, Orange Ground, White Cupids, Vines, 13 In., Pair 2250.00
Vase, Parian Body, Teal Blue, White Figures, Cupid, 8 In. 2250.00
Vase, Parian Body, White Head Of Maiden, Warrior, 8 In., Pair 650.00
Vase, White Sea Gulls, Rust Ground, 9 In. 110.00

Paul Revere pottery was made at several locations in and around Boston between 1906 and 1942. The pottery was operated as a settlement-house type of program for teen-aged girls. Many pieces were signed S.E.G. for Saturday Evening Girls. The firm concentrated on children's dishes and tiles. Decorations were outlined in black and filled in with color.

PAUL REVERE, Lantern, Candle, Tin, Original Condition, 10 In. 195.00
Pitcher, Mottled Cobalt Blue & Green, Marked, 7 In. 75.00

Peachblow glass originated about 1883 at Hobbs, Brockunier and Company of Wheeling, West Virginia. It is a glass that shades from yellow to peach. It was lined in white. New England peachblow is a one-layer glass shading from red to white. Mt. Washington peachblow shades from pink to blue. Reproductions of peachblow have been made, but they are of poor quality and can be detected.

PEACHBLOW, Basket, Applied Camphor Handle, Raised Swirls, Sandwich, 5 1/2 In. 895.00
Bowl, New England, Square Top, Fluted, 8 1/4 X 4 1/2 In. 325.00
Caster, Pickle, Wheeling, Fuchsia To Yellow 895.00
Creamer, Wheeling, 3 3/4 In. 750.00
Cup, Punch, New England .... 325.00 To 385.00
Darner, Rose To White, 6 In. 225.00
Ewer, Wheeling, Twisted Amber Handle, C.1890, 7 In. 150.00
Fruit, Pear, New England 145.00
    PEACHBLOW, GUNDERSON, see Gunderson
Pitcher, Hobnail Pattern, Ribbed Camphor Handle, 6 1/2 In. 480.00
Rose Bowl, Satin Finished, 4 In. 90.00
Salt & Pepper, Guttate Pattern 125.00
Salt & Pepper, Wheeling, Pewter Tops, 2 In. 295.00
Sugar Shaker, Wheeling 795.00
Table Set, Wheeling, Silver Plated Holder, 3 Piece 1850.00
Toothpick, New England, Square 375.00
Toothpick, New England, Square Mouth 350.00
Toothpick, Ruffled 85.00
Toothpick, Shiny Pink Enamel Flowers 295.00
Tumbler, Acid Finish 118.00

Tumbler, Gold Flowers, Bee, Rose To White, 4 1/2 In. 195.00
Tumbler, New England, Glossy, Raspberry To White, 3 3/4 In. 295.00
Tumbler, Wheeling 352.00
Tumbler, Wheeling, Red Shading To Yellow, Opaque Lining, 3 3/4 In. 350.00
Tumbler, Wheeling, White Lining, Red Shaded To Yellow, 3 7/8 In. 350.00
Vase, Cased Blue Interior, 6 1/4 In. 95.00
Vase, Coralene Coral Design, Bulbous, Marked, 12 In. 250.00
Vase, Enameled Red Cherries & Leaves, Gold Trim, 10 1/2 In., Pair 760.00
Vase, Mt.Washington, 4 1/2 In. 1075.00
Vase, New England, Lily Form, 8 1/4 In. 295.00
Vase, New England, Ovoid, Flaring Rim, 19th Century, 14 1/2 In. 675.00
Vase, Red Cherries, Flowers, Green & Gold Leaves, 10 1/2 In., Pair 895.00
Vase, Wheeling, Stick, Acid Finish, 19th Century, 12 1/2 In. 200.00
Vase, Wheeling, Stick, 8 1/2 In. .... 650.00 To 750.00
   PEACHBLOW, WEBB, see Webb Peachblow
Whimsy, Wheeling, Pear 395.00

PEARL, Charger, Pigeons, Tree, Lacquer, 18 In. 350.00
   PEARL, OPERA GLASSES, see Opera Glasses
Shell, Last Supper Scene, Hand Carved, 6 In. 75.00
Toothpick, Penknife Shape, 2 Blades, 2 1/2 In. 20.00

Peking glass is a Chinese cameo glass of the eighteenth and nineteenth centuries.

PEKING GLASS, Bottle, Snuff, Red Overlay, Carved Both Sides, 18th Century 235.00
Bottle, Snuff, Red To Clear, 2 1/4 In. 100.00
Bottle, Snuff, Reverse Painted Scenes Of Women, 4 1/2 In. 265.00
Candleholder, Iron Cock's Foot Base, Yellow 40.00
Vase, Butterfly & Flowers, C.1865, Yellow On White, 8 In. 295.00
Vase, Cameo, Cut Blue To White, 8 3/4 In. 350.00
Vase, Cameo, Hibiscus, Butterfly, Red Carved To White, 6 In. 180.00
Vase, Cameo, Red & White, 10 In., Pair 650.00
Vase, Cranes Flying Over Green Foliage, White, 12 In., Pair 735.00
Vase, Empress & Mandarin, Logo, Blue, Pair 60.00
Vase, White To Red, Red Base & Collar, Peonies, 10 In. 320.00

Peloton glass is European glass with small threads of colored glass rolled onto the surface of clear or colored glass. It is sometimes called spaghetti, or shredded coconut glass.

PELOTON, Basket, Folded-Over Top, Applied Feet, Colored Strings, 8 In.Diam. 300.00
Epergne, 3-Handled, Ruffled Trumpet, Fluted Base 1250.00
Finger Bowl, Multicolored Threads, Crystal 145.00
Rose Bowl, Blue & Yellow Filaments, White & Rose, 2 1/4 In. 225.00
Rose Bowl, White Cased, Crystal Feet, 83 3/4 In. 295.00
Vase, Bulbous Base, Narrow Neck, Amethyst, 5 In. 200.00

PEN & PENCIL SET, Parker, Orange Duofold 100.00
Sheaffer, Gold Plated, Ivory Case 29.00
Waterman, No.494, 1930s, Full Size, Sterling Silver 350.00

PEN, Agate, Overlaid Openwork, Turquoise Terminal, Leather Case, 5 7/8 In. 350.00
Aiken Lambert, Capital Cabinet, 1918, Black 15.00
Bob Turley, New York Yankee 10.00
Charles Keene Matchstick Filler, Gold Nib, 1905 .... 8.00
Conklin, 1920s, Baby Blue 30.00
Desk Set, Parker, Lady Duofold, Marble Base, Dated April 25, 1911 .... 30.00
Dip, Mother-Of-Pearl .... 15.00 To 25.00
Dip, Mother-Of-Pearl, Gold Tip 27.00
Dr.Faber's Self-Filler, 1904, Gold Nib 22.00
Dunn, Black With Red End, 1923 .... 15.00
Eversharp, Doric, Adjustable Nib 20.00
Eversharp, Gold Seal Art Deco, 1928, Full Size, Jade Green 125.00

Eversharp, Skyline	15.00
Holder, Ivory Handle, Marked J.Gillott, Pen Maker To The Queen, 1856	28.00
Mabie Todd Swallow, 1933, Bronze & White Marble, Presentation Box	55.00
Marxton, 14K Gold Point	8.00
Mason, Engraved Half Moon & Face, Worn On Chain, 3 1/2 X 4 1/2 In.	50.00
Mont Blanc Diplomat, No.149, 1979, Boxed	135.00
Parker Parkette, Maroon Marble	15.00
Parker, Challenger	10.00
Parker, Duofold Deluxe, Jr., 1929	55.00
Parker, Duofold Jr., Red	75.00
Parker, Duofold Sr., Red Lacquer, 1928	75.00
Parker, Duofold Sr., 1930, Mandarin Yellow	225.00
Parker, Duofold, Large	39.00
Parker, Duofold, 1916 Patent, Orange	26.00
Parker, Green Bamboo, 1927	90.00
Parker, Lady Duofold, Yellow	125.00
Parker, Lucky Curve, No.28, 1912, Red & Black Wood Grain Eyedropper	600.00
Parker, 21, Blue & Silver	10.00
Parker, 61, Turquoise & Silver	40.00
Sheaffer, Lifetime Triumph, 1940s, Gold Filled Band, Black	15.00
Swan, 1918, Medium Point, Black	16.00
Swan, 1920, Fine Point, Sterling Silver	35.00
Wahl Eversharp, 1930s, Black & Cream	70.00
Waterman, No.12	25.00
Waterman, No.12, Silver Overlay, Hard Rubber, Orange Red	700.00
Waterman, 14K Gold, Box, 3 Piece	35.00
Wiper, George Washington Figure Sewn On, Mid-19th Century	200.00
PENCIL, Babe Ruth, Baseball On Top	15.00
Budweiser	12.00
Case, Lacquer, Oriental	50.00
Century Of Progress, 1934, Lady's	10.00
Chicago & Northwestern, R.R.	14.00
Cross, Sterling Silver, Box	30.00
Dixcel Gasoline	10.00
Eversharp, Sterling Silver	19.00
Herringbone Design, Gold Filled	38.00
Mickey Mouse, Head On Top	60.00
Mr.Peanut	10.00
Parker, No.51, 1950s	10.00
Perfect Point, Gold Filled	16.00
Sterling Silver, Engraved	22.00
Wahl Eversharp, Mechanical, Silver Plated	6.00
PENNSBURY, Mug, Eagle & Flag	60.00
Sugar & Creamer, Hex Mark, Brown Inside, Glossy Brown, 4 In.	18.00

Peters and Reed Pottery Company of Zanesville, Ohio, was founded by John D. Peters and Adam Reed in 1897. Chromal, Landsun, Montene, Pereco, and Persian are some of the art lines that were made until the company closed in 1920.

PETERS & REED, see also Zane

PETERS & REED, Jardiniere, Moss Aztec, Grapes, Signed	60.00
Jug, Applied Sprigs, Little Handle, 7 In.	55.00
Jug, Cavalier Heads & Flowers, Pinch Spout	90.00
Jug, Grape Applique, Brown, 7 In.	45.00
Mug, Grapes, Leaves & Vine, Handled, 5 1/2 In.	85.00
Mug, Portrait, 5 In.	38.00
Pitcher, Cameo Design, 5 In.	85.00
Pitcher, Water, Sprigged-On Heads, Brown Glaze	80.00
Vase, Moss Aztec, 11 1/2 In.	55.00
Wall Pocket, Moss Aztec, Grape & Leaf, Signed, Pair	75.00
Wall Pocket, Moss Aztec, Ivy & Berry, 9 1/2 In.	50.00

PETROUS REGOUT, see Maastricht

Pewabic Pottery was founded by Mary Chase Perry Stratton in 1903 in Detroit, Michigan. Pewabic type pottery is still being made.

PEWABIC, Tile, Bronze Iridescent	165.00
Tile, Indian Maiden	135.00
Vase, Shield Shaped, C.1910, Blue Flecked Tan Glaze, Label, 7 1/2 In.	140.00
Vase, Squat, Blue Maple Leaf Mark, 6 In.	160.00

Pewter is a metal alloy of tin and lead. Some of the pewter made after 1840 has a slightly different composition and is called Britannia metal.

PEWTER, Basin, D.Melville, Newport, 1776-93, 8 In.Diam.	475.00
Basin, E.Danforth, Conn., 1786-95, 9 In.Diam.	550.00
Basin, English Touchmark, 9 1/4 In.Diam.	105.00
Basin, English, Samuel Ellis, London, 10 1/2 In.	110.00
Basin, German, 11 1/2 In.Diam.	100.00
Basin, Nathaniel Austin, Mass., 1763-1807, Touchmark, 8 In.	375.00
Bowl, Footed, Marked Boardman & Hall, 5 In.	235.00
Bowl, Poppies In Relief, Art Nouveau, Handles, Germany, 6 In.	75.00
Bowl, Waste, American, Roswell Gleason, 5 1/2 In.	125.00
Box, Almond Shape, Cast Feet & Handles, 3 Angel Marks, 9 In.	125.00
Box, Jewelry, Apple Pattern, Art Nouveau, 9 X 5 X 2 1/2 In.	80.00
Candlestick, C.1865, 8 In., Pair	125.00
Candlestick, Freeman Porter, Westbrook, Maine, Pair	550.00
Candlestick, Nordic Lady Holding 2 Candles, 3 In.	400.00
Candlestick, Removable Bobeche, 7 3/4 In., Pair	180.00
Candlestick, T.B.M. & Co., 8 In., Pair	1000.00
Charger, American, Joseph Danforth, 13 In.Diam.	525.00
Charger, Dated 1784, German, 13 1/8 In.	250.00
Charger, Double Reeded Rim, London Mark, 18 1/4 In.	300.00
Charger, James Spackman, London, C.1730, 15 In.Diam.	200.00
Charger, Marked With 2 Crowned A's, 15 In.	175.00
Charger, Nathaniel Austin, Main, 1763-1800, 15 In.	325.00
Charger, Samuel Hamlin, Connecticut, 1767-1801, 13 1/2 In.	425.00
Charger, Townsden & Compton, C.1800-10, English	190.00
Coffeepot, Baluster, Roswell Gleason, 12 1/2 In.	230.00
Coffeepot, Double Belly, Sellew & Co., Ohio, 1830-60, 12 In.	275.00
Coffeepot, English, James Dixon, 11 1/2 In.	160.00
Coffeepot, Lighthouse Form, Hiram Yale, 10 1/2 In.	300.00
Coffeepot, Lighthouse Form, Roswell Gleason, 11 In.	500.00
Coffeepot, Lighthouse, F.Porter, Maine, 1835-60, 11 In.	270.00
Coffeepot, Ribbed, Baluster, Allen Porter, Maine, 1830-40 .... 300.00 To	450.00
Coffeepot, Signed Parr, 12 In.	165.00
Creamer, English, C.1800, Scroll Handle & Spout, Mark EV, 3 3/4 In.	250.00
Dish, Deep, Benjamin & Joseph Harbeson, Philadelphia, 11 In.	650.00
Dish, Deep, Joseph Spackman, London, C.1760, 12 In.Diam.	180.00
Dish, Deep, Thomas Danforth Boardman, 1805-50, 9 In.	500.00
Dish, Hot Water, James Dixon, 8 In.	80.00
Dish, Kayserzinn, Leaf Shape, Chrysanthemums, Handled, Footed, 10 In.	110.00
Dish, Samuel Ellis, London, 1721-48, 12 1/8 In.	130.00
Dish, Victorian, Stamped London, George Inn, 4 1/2 In.Diam.	20.00
Flagon, Cherub Head Thumblift, Crown Rose Mark, 13 1/2 In.	400.00
Flagon, Communion, Sheep Thumblift, Pear Shape, 13 7/8 In.	200.00
Flagon, Covered, English, 19th Century, 8 1/4 In.	120.00
Flagon, Domed Lid, Berry Finial, Heart Spout, Marked, 11 1/2 In.	250.00
Flagon, Heart Shaped Lid, Double Acorn Thumbpiece, 11 In.	600.00
Flagon, Scottish, Heart Shaped, Ball Thumb Latch, 9 In.	175.00
Flagon, Thomas Danforth Boardman & Co., 1805, 11 In.	950.00
Flagon, 12 1/4 In.	200.00

Flask, Pocket, Sneaky, Made In England, 4 1/2 X 8 1/2 In.	25.00
Flask, Spirit, Blue Flowers, Rectangular, 14 In.	350.00
Kettle, Hot Water, Brass Base, Wooden Feet, European, 18 In.	300.00
Ladle, American, I.Brown & Co.	50.00
Ladle, Basin Form, Wooden Handle, America, 19th Century, 15 In.	60.00
Ladle, Turned Wooden Handle, 15 1/4 In.	75.00
Lamp, Oil, Blown Fount, Tells Hours, 13 In.	475.00
Lamp, Sparking, Snuffer Cap, 4 In.	110.00
Lamp, Whale Oil, Capen & Malineux, New York, 1848, 8 In., Pair	575.00
Lamp, Whale Oil, Double, 10 In.	200.00
Measure, Baluster, Heart Shaped Lid, Acorn Thumbpiece, 10 In.	325.00
Measure, Graduated, Set Of 6	250.00
Mold, Candle, Single Tube, 15 In.	67.50
Mold, Candy, Kewpie, C.1930, 2 1/2 X 6 3/4 X 1 1/2 In.	8.50
Mold, Candy, 3 Cannon, Lititz, Pennsylvania	17.00
Mold, Candy, 5 Hands, Lititz, Pennsylvania	18.00
Mold, Chocolate, Bird	12.50
Mold, Ice Cream, Ace Of Hearts, Tiny Spot Medallion	15.00
Mold, Ice Cream, Airplane	34.00 To 37.00
Mold, Ice Cream, American Beauty Rose, 2 1/4 X 2 3/4 X 1 1/4 In.	40.00
Mold, Ice Cream, American Flag, Hinged	110.00
Mold, Ice Cream, American Flag, Marked S & Co., 282, 4 X 2 1/2 In.	75.00
Mold, Ice Cream, Apple, With Stem	16.00
Mold, Ice Cream, Automobile	52.00
Mold, Ice Cream, Baby	37.00
Mold, Ice Cream, Ball	8.00
Mold, Ice Cream, Banjo	48.00
Mold, Ice Cream, Barrel	29.00
Mold, Ice Cream, Baseball Player	48.00
Mold, Ice Cream, Basket, Oval	20.00
Mold, Ice Cream, Battleship With Waves	40.00
Mold, Ice Cream, Bear, Lying Down	49.00
Mold, Ice Cream, Bear, Seated	52.00
Mold, Ice Cream, Beet	28.00
Mold, Ice Cream, Bell, New Year's	22.00
Mold, Ice Cream, Bell, Wedding, With Cupid	32.00
Mold, Ice Cream, Bomb	24.00
Mold, Ice Cream, Book, Dated 1888	39.00
Mold, Ice Cream, Boy Washington, Hatchet Over Shoulder	55.00
Mold, Ice Cream, Bride & Groom Plaque	56.00
Mold, Ice Cream, Bull, Head To Side	48.00
Mold, Ice Cream, Bunch Of Grapes	32.00
Mold, Ice Cream, Calla Lily, 3 Piece	28.00
Mold, Ice Cream, Canary	36.00
Mold, Ice Cream, Cannon	49.00
Mold, Ice Cream, Carnation	24.00
Mold, Ice Cream, Cherries, 4 In Mold	18.00
Mold, Ice Cream, Chick In Egg	26.00
Mold, Ice Cream, Chick, Hatching	37.50
Mold, Ice Cream, Christmas Tree	55.00
Mold, Ice Cream, Christmas Wreath, 4 1/2 X 4 1/2 In.	85.00
Mold, Ice Cream, Cigar	20.00
Mold, Ice Cream, Circle & Star, 3 3/4 In.	25.00
Mold, Ice Cream, Club Shape, Marked C.C., 3 X 3 In.	60.00
Mold, Ice Cream, Cotton Bale	26.00
Mold, Ice Cream, Cow, Lying Down	43.00
Mold, Ice Cream, Cradle, 3-Part	28.00
Mold, Ice Cream, Cucumber	18.00
Mold, Ice Cream, Cup, Fancy	23.00
Mold, Ice Cream, Cupid Heart	34.00
Mold, Ice Cream, Cupid In Rose	24.00
Mold, Ice Cream, Cupid On Shell	37.00
Mold, Ice Cream, Cupid, Seated	32.00

Mold, Ice Cream, Daisies, 3 In Mold	34.00
Mold, Ice Cream, Dog, St.Bernard	38.00
Mold, Ice Cream, Donkey	45.00
Mold, Ice Cream, Dove Of Peace	41.00
Mold, Ice Cream, Doves Cooing	36.00
Mold, Ice Cream, Eagle, Trophy	65.00
Mold, Ice Cream, Ear Of Corn, 6 3/4 In.	45.00
Mold, Ice Cream, Egg, Goose	12.00
Mold, Ice Cream, Egg, Poached	21.00
Mold, Ice Cream, Eggs, Whippoorwill, 4 In.	21.00
Mold, Ice Cream, Engagement Ring	16.00
Mold, Ice Cream, Equitable Life Insurance Co., Des Moines	90.00
Mold, Ice Cream, Flying Stork With Baby	36.00
Mold, Ice Cream, Football Player	52.00
Mold, Ice Cream, Football, 3-Part	29.00
Mold, Ice Cream, Four-Leaf Clover, Dated 1889	40.00
Mold, Ice Cream, George Washington Bust	50.00
Mold, Ice Cream, Glass, 3-Part	34.00
Mold, Ice Cream, Golfer, Female	52.00
Mold, Ice Cream, Golfer, Male	52.00
Mold, Ice Cream, Gourd	22.00
Mold, Ice Cream, Hand, Directing	39.00
Mold, Ice Cream, Harp	48.00
Mold, Ice Cream, Heart, To Be Pierced By Arrow	26.00
Mold, Ice Cream, High Hat	36.00
Mold, Ice Cream, Horn Of Plenty	32.00
Mold, Ice Cream, Horse, Rearing	58.00
Mold, Ice Cream, Horseshoe, Good Luck	34.00 To 37.00
Mold, Ice Cream, Indian Chief, Dated 1896	55.00
Mold, Ice Cream, K Of C Emblem	20.00
Mold, Ice Cream, Kewpie	52.00 To 68.00
Mold, Ice Cream, Knight Templar	34.00
Mold, Ice Cream, Lady's Shoe	40.00
Mold, Ice Cream, Lamb	46.00
Mold, Ice Cream, Lemon	20.00
Mold, Ice Cream, Lily Pond	22.00
Mold, Ice Cream, Lily-Of-The-Valley Leaves	24.00
Mold, Ice Cream, Lily, Calla, 3-Part	22.00
Mold, Ice Cream, Lincoln Plaque	54.00
Mold, Ice Cream, Lincoln, Bust	54.00
Mold, Ice Cream, Lion, Lying Down	56.00
Mold, Ice Cream, Locomotive, Streamlined	70.00
Mold, Ice Cream, Maltese Cross	25.00
Mold, Ice Cream, Mandolin	48.00
Mold, Ice Cream, Martha Washington	48.00
Mold, Ice Cream, Masonic Emblem, Letter G	28.00
Mold, Ice Cream, Mother Scroll	49.00
Mold, Ice Cream, Napoleon	75.00
Mold, Ice Cream, Nest Of Eggs	39.00
Mold, Ice Cream, Number 6	22.00
Mold, Ice Cream, Number 9	22.00
Mold, Ice Cream, Palette, Artist's	48.00
Mold, Ice Cream, Pansy	29.00
Mold, Ice Cream, Passionflower	28.00
Mold, Ice Cream, Peach, Half, Stone Out	25.00
Mold, Ice Cream, Pear	15.00
Mold, Ice Cream, Peas-In-A-Pod	45.00
Mold, Ice Cream, Pig	25.00
Mold, Ice Cream, Plymouth Rock	65.00
Mold, Ice Cream, Poinsettia	43.00
Mold, Ice Cream, Pomegranate	19.00
Mold, Ice Cream, Pond Lily, 3-Part	26.00
Mold, Ice Cream, Potato	16.00

Mold, Ice Cream, Pumpkin .... 18.00 To 30.00
Mold, Ice Cream, Puss 'n Boots 75.00
Mold, Ice Cream, Question Mark 32.00
Mold, Ice Cream, Rabbit, Crouching 32.00
Mold, Ice Cream, Rabbit, Sitting Up 36.00
Mold, Ice Cream, Roast Turkey 18.00
Mold, Ice Cream, Rose, American Beauty 34.00
Mold, Ice Cream, Rose, 3 In Mold 32.00
Mold, Ice Cream, Rotary Club Emblem 18.00
Mold, Ice Cream, Sailboat, 3-Masted Clipper Ship 75.00
Mold, Ice Cream, Sailor 46.00
Mold, Ice Cream, Santa With Pack 38.00
Mold, Ice Cream, Shamrock 34.00
Mold, Ice Cream, Shoe 45.00
Mold, Ice Cream, Slipper, 3 Piece 29.00
Mold, Ice Cream, Snowball 24.00
Mold, Ice Cream, Soldier, National Guard 55.00
Mold, Ice Cream, Squirrel 65.00
Mold, Ice Cream, Steamer 38.00
Mold, Ice Cream, Stork & Baby 48.00
Mold, Ice Cream, Strawberry, 2 In Mold 28.00
Mold, Ice Cream, Sweet Potato 22.00
Mold, Ice Cream, Teakettle 45.00
Mold, Ice Cream, Tenpin 30.00
Mold, Ice Cream, Tiger, 3-Part 75.00
Mold, Ice Cream, Tomato 18.00
Mold, Ice Cream, Top Hat 40.00
Mold, Ice Cream, Tree Stump 22.00
Mold, Ice Cream, Trunk, Bon Voyage 39.00
Mold, Ice Cream, Tulip, 3-Part 20.00
Mold, Ice Cream, Turkey, Standing 25.00
Mold, Ice Cream, Waffle 18.00
Mold, Ice Cream, Washington, Bust 49.00
Mold, Ice Cream, Wishbone 29.00
Mold, Ice Cream, Yellow Kid 85.00
Mold, Spoon, Colonial, Hand-Forged Rivets, 5 X 6 In.Square, 2 Piece 225.00
Mug, Carnarvon Castle, Marked, English, 1 Pint 45.00
Mug, English, Crowned X Stamped Inside, 1/2 Pint 55.00
Mug, English, Pint 85.00
Mug, Marked J.B. & Co. Ltd., 1 Pint 32.00
Mug, Measure, 1/2 Gill 9.00
Pitcher, Bellied, Hinged Lid, 7 1/2 In. 105.00
Pitcher, Elderberry Blossoms, Kayserzinn, 9 1/2 In. 120.00
Pitcher, Mephistopheles, Kayserzinn, Signed, 10 In. 250.00
Pitcher, Syrup, Acorn Thumb Latch, Hallmarked 125.00
Pitcher, Tappit Hen Shape, Cover, 7 In. 110.00
Plate, Alms, Marked London, 4 5/8 In. 22.50
Plate, B.Barns, 8 7/8 In. 325.00
Plate, Blakeslee Barns, Phila., 1812-17, 8 7/8 In. 250.00
Plate, Central Crest, Foliage, Knight's Head, 13 In. 105.00
Plate, Coat Of Arms, Edmund Harvey, 1700, English, 9 1/4 In. 150.00
Plate, Crown On Medallion, Lettering, Scalloped, 1 3/4 In. 45.00
Plate, David Melville, Newport, 1776-93, 8 1/4 In.Diam. 150.00
Plate, Domed Center, Rosette Motif, Embossed Floral Band, 13 In. 50.00
Plate, Double Eagle, Thomas Danforth Mark, 8 3/4 In. 260.00
Plate, Floral Design, Dated 1904, 10 In. 100.00
Plate, Hot Water, English, Hallmarked 180.00
Plate, Jacob Whitman, Connecticut, 1758-90, 7 In. 210.00
Plate, Lovebird, Philadelphia, 1800-50, 7 7/8 In.Diam. 220.00
Plate, Melville 4-Mark Touch, David Melville, 1755-93, 8 1/4 In. 250.00
Plate, N.Austin, Charlestown, Mass., 1763-1807, 8 5/8 In.Diam. 250.00
Plate, Nathaniel Austin, Charlestown, Mass., 1763-1800, 15 In.Diam. 925.00
Plate, Nathaniel Austin, Charlestown, Mass., 1793-1807, 8 3/4 In. 225.00

Plate, Richard Austin, 8 1/2 In. 150.00
Plate, Richard King, London, C.1775, 9 1/4 In. 90.00
Plate, Samuel Leats, English, C.1725, 12 In. 70.00
Plate, Samuel Pierce, Greenfield, Mass., 1792-1830, 8 In.Diam. 200.00
Plate, Scene Of Building, Trees, Birds, Marked, 8 In. 45.00
Plate, Signed Boardman, Pair 400.00
Plate, Stamped With 3 Crowns, Set Of 6, 7 In. 210.00
Plate, T.Danforth II, Connecticut, 1855-82, Touchmark, 12 1/4 In. 375.00
Plate, Thomas Danforth II, Connecticut, 1755-82, 8 In.Diam. 200.00
Plate, Thomas Danforth III, Philadelphia, 1807-13, 7 3/4 In. 150.00
Plate, Thomas Danforth, III, 8 In. 150.00
Platter, Kayserzinn, Pond Fish Design, Water Swirls, 24 1/2 X 11 In. 165.00
Porringer, Cast Handle, 3 1/2 In. 195.00
Porringer, Crown Handle, New England, 5 1/4 In.Diam. 225.00
Porringer, Deep Bowl, Pierced Flowered Handle, Hamlin, 6 1/2 In. 650.00
Porringer, Domed Center, Flowered Handle, Marked, 6 1/2 In. 650.00
Porringer, Pierced Hearts, Circular Bowl, 4 3/4 In. 100.00
Porringer, Richard Lee, Vermont, 1795-1816, 3 3/4 In.Diam. 500.00
Porringer, S.Pennock, Chester County, C.1800, Tab-Handled, 5 1/2 In. 2000.00
Porringer, Samuel E.Hamlin, Jr. 800.00
Porringer, T.D. & S.Boardman, Conn., Old English Handle, 4 1/2 In. 500.00
Porringer, T.D. & S.Boardman, Hartford, 1810-50, Crown Handle, 5 In. 400.00
Porringer, T.D. & S.Boardman, Hartford, 1810-50, 4 1/2 In.Diam. 500.00
Pot, Punce, English, C.1800 .... 85.00
Salt, Footed, 3 1/4 In. 10.00
Salt, Lion's Heads, Footed, 19th Century, 2 1/2 In., Pair 55.00
Shaker, Israel Trask, Mass., 1813-56, Beaded Rim, 2 1/2 In. 500.00
Spoon, Claw End Handle, 6 7/8 In. 15.00
Spoon, Figural Handle, 4 1/2 In. 12.50
Spoon, Shellback Handle, Hall's Patent, C.1800, 7 In. 22.00
Strainer, Tea, Hinged Cover, Latch Over Strainer, 5 1/2 In.Diam. 75.00
Sugar & Creamer, Crescent 25.00
Sugar & Creamer, Footed, Marked Winthop, American 42.00
Sugar & Creamer, Nekrasoff, Covered Sugar, Original Spoon 30.00
Sugar Shaker, New England, Baluster Body, Pierced Top, C.1800, 6 In. 75.00
Sugar, Ashbil Griswold, Conn., 1807-35, Ball Finial, Molded Feet, 6 In. 325.00
Sugar, Covered, Rosewell Gleason, 7 1/2 In. 260.00
Sugar, Eagle Touch With Griswold, 6 In. 355.00
Syrup, Angel Touchmark 95.00
Tablespoon, Raised Design On Reverse, Set Of 6 .... 50.00
Tankard, Dome Top, Incised Shell, Scroll Handle, Marked, 8 1/2 In. 475.00
Tankard, English, Domed, Scrolled Thumbpiece, Pint 200.00
Tankard, English, Half Pint, 3 1/2 In. 45.00
Tankard, Scroll Handle, Ball Finial, Dated 1827, German, 7 1/4 In. 325.00
Tankard, Tapered Form, Strap Handle, Crown Over WR, 6 In. 150.00
Tea Set, Green Glass Liner, Jade Inserts, Florals, 9 In.Pot 250.00
Teapot, A.Potter, Maine, 1830-40, 7 In. 350.00
Teapot, American, Roswell Gleason, 9 In. 100.00
Teapot, Austrian, Marked Bee On Bottom, C.1800, 7 In. 75.00
Teapot, Baluster Form, Roswell Gleason, 9 1/2 In. 125.00
Teapot, Bulbous, Dixon & Smith, 12 X 6 In. 225.00
Teapot, Calder, Spherical Body, Domed Cover, 8 In. 325.00
Teapot, Engraved Body, Late 19th Century 125.00
Teapot, Federal, Ebonized Handle, American, 10 1/2 X 4 1/2 In. 135.00
Teapot, Floral Design, Flower Finial, Marked Homan & Co., 10 1/2 In. 55.00
Teapot, Fuchsia Flowers In Relief, 5 1/2 In. 90.00
Teapot, Inverted Pear-Shaped Body, Animal Spout, Dolphin, 7 In. 90.00
Teapot, J.H.Palethorp, Philadelphia, 1820-40, 8 1/2 In. 225.00
Teapot, James Dixon & Son, Birmingham, 19th Century, 13 In. 75.00
Teapot, Kayserzinn, Embossed Floral 68.00
Teapot, Locke & Carter, New York, 1837-45, Marked, 7 1/2 In. 160.00
Teapot, Marked A. Porter, 6 1/2 In. 385.00
Teapot, Marked Cincinnati Britannia Co., 9 In. 70.00

Teapot, Morey & Ober, Boston, 7 3/4 In. 70.00
Teapot, Scrolling Handle & Spout, Dome Lid, Gleason, 12 In. 375.00
Teapot, Signed Daniel Curtis, New York City 250.00
Teapot, Smith & Co., Boston, 7 1/4 In. 200.00
Teapot, Smith & Co., Boston, 8 In. 110.00
Teapot, Swan Spout, Spreading Foot, Hinged Cover, Marked, 10 In. 75.00
Teapot, Tankard Shape, G.Richardson 500.00
Teapot, William McQuilkin, Philadelphia, 1845, 8 In. 310.00
Teaspoon, Shell Design, C.1800, 5 3/4 In. 22.50
Urn, Fish Design, 2-Handled, Kayserzinn 135.00
Vase, French, A.Ledru, Face Of Neptune, Bottle Form, 9 In. 1200.00
Vase, Kayserzinn, Raised Flowers & Leaves, 13 In. 195.00

PEYNAUD, Vase, Cameo, Floral & Anemones, Rose & Magenta, Signed, 10 In. 275.00

> *Phoenix Bird, or flying Phoenix, is the name given to a blue and*
> *white chinaware made between 1900 and World War II. A variant*
> *is known as Flying Turkey.*

PHOENIX BIRD, Bowl, Rice, 5 In. 15.00
Eggcup, Flying Turkey, Ironstone 12.00
Ginger Jar, Covered, 5 In. 40.00
Jar, Ginger, Flying Turkey, Ironstone, 7 In. 58.00
Nut Set, Melon Shaped, 5 Matching Bowls 45.00
Plate, Leaf Shaped, 10 In. 35.00
Plate, 7 3/8 In. 10.00
Platter, Bird, Japan, Oblong, 12 In. 22.00
Salt & Pepper 15.00
Saucer, Turkey 5.00
Tumbler, Nippon 25.00
Vase, Birds, White, Mint Green Ground, 10 In. 165.00

> *Phoenix Glass Company was founded in 1880 in Pennsylvania. The firm*
> *made commercial products such as lampshades, bottles, and glassware.*
> *Collectors today are interested in the sculptured glassware made by the*
> *company from the 1930s until the mid-1950s.*

PHOENIX, Base, Lamp, Green & Brown Pinecone Embossed Pattern 28.00
Bowl, Blue Parrots, 11 X 10 In. 325.00
Bowl, Frosted Green Flowers, Pedestal, 8 In. 95.00
Bowl, Green Sculptured Lemons, White Ground, 8 In. 85.00
Bowl, Open Rose, Green, 10 In. .... 68.00 To 70.00
Bowl, Red, Brown, Custard, Owl, 6 In. 105.00
Figurine, Owl, Clear, 5 1/4 In. 45.00
Fruit Stand, Daffodil, Green, 11 In. .... 48.00 To 50.00
Glass, Vase, Molded Flowers, Figure 8 Shape, Paper Label, 7 1/2 In. 80.00
Lamp, Bluebell, White Ground, Pair 65.00
Lamp, Dogwood, 3 Colors 178.00
Lamp, Mint Green, White, Berries & Foliage, Marked 195.00
Lamp, Orange Berries, Green Foliage, 21 1/2 In. 145.00
Lamp, Praying Mantis, Amber 235.00
Lamp, Sculptured Green Berries & Foliage On White, 22 In. 295.00
Plate, Kumquats, Green, 8 1/4 In. 30.00
Plate, Kumquats, Yellow, 8 1/4 In. 30.00
Vase, Acorns, Orange & Cream, 7 In. 65.00
Vase, Birds Of Paradise, White Ground, 6 3/4 In. 95.00
Vase, Birds, Orange, Green, & White, 7 In. 85.00
Vase, Blue Berries, Leaves, Opaque White Ground, 9 1/2 In. 75.00
Vase, Bluebell, Blue & White, 7 In. 90.00
Vase, Bluebell, White Ground, 11 In. 90.00
Vase, Bluebell, Yellow Ground, White Bells, 7 In. 80.00
Vase, Bluebell, Yellow Ground, White Bells, 8 In. 82.00

Vase, Bluebell, White, Pink Ground, 7 In. 79.00
Vase, Bluebell, 3 Colors, 10 1/2 In. 112.00
Vase, Bluebirds, Pink & Green, 6 1/2 In. 135.00
Vase, Bubble, Tricornered, Lavender, 6 In. 24.00
Vase, Catalonian, Aqua, 11 3/4 In. .... 38.00 To 45.00
Vase, Cattails, 2-Color Dragonflies, White Ground, 6 In. 60.00
Vase, Dancing Nudes, White Relief, Blue Ground, 12 In. .... 175.00 To 325.00
Vase, Deco Head, Both Sides, White Ground, 10 In. 170.00
Vase, Dogwood, Blooming White Flowers, Purple Ground, 7 In. 130.00
Vase, Dragonfly & Leaves In Relief, Pillow, Green, 7 In. 85.00
Vase, Fern, Frosted, 6 In. 35.00
Vase, Ferns, Blue & Clear, 7 1/2 In. 35.00
Vase, Ferns, Opalescent & Cream, 7 1/2 In. 65.00
Vase, Ferns, Paper Label, Blue & White, 7 In. 65.00
Vase, Florals, White Frosted, Aqua Ground, 7 1/2 In. 125.00
Vase, Flowers, Blown-Out, Blue With White, 7 1/2 X 6 1/2 In. 85.00
Vase, Flowers, Ice Finish, Blue & Clear, 10 3/4 In. 95.00
Vase, Flowers, Ivys, White Luster, 7 In. 50.00
Vase, Flowers, Orange, Green Leaves, 10 1/2 In. 85.00
Vase, Flying Geese, Cinnamon, 9 1/2 In. 225.00
Vase, Flying Geese, Moon-Shaped, 12 X 10 In. 140.00
Vase, Flying Geese, Pillow, Beige & White, 9 1/2 In. 135.00
Vase, Flying Geese, Pillow, Blue, 9 1/2 X 11 1/2 In. 155.00
Vase, Hummingbirds, Green, 6 In. 40.00
Vase, Hummingbirds, Purple, 5 1/2 In. 55.00
Vase, Hummingbirds, Turquoise & Cream, 6 In. 60.00
Vase, Leaves, Acorns, Cinnamon, White Ground, 7 In. 100.00
Vase, Lovebirds, Blue, Rose, & White, 7 In. 135.00
Vase, Lovebirds, Butterscotch, Retangular, 6 1/2 X 6 In. 75.00
Vase, Lovebirds, Flowers & Leaves, Purple, 6 1/2 In. 75.00
Vase, Lovebirds, Pink Birds, White Ground, 6 1/2 In. 115.00
Vase, Lovebirds, Translucent Blue, 10 In. 130.00
Vase, Lovebirds, Yellow, Green, Coral, 10 In. 135.00
Vase, Madonna, Blown-Out, Blue & White, 10 In. 150.00
Vase, Madonna, Opaque Ground, Ribbed Sided, Paper Label, 10 1/4 In. ... 245.00
Vase, Owls, Red, Custard Ground, 6 In. 75.00
Vase, Pan, With Frolicking Nudes, Pink & Blue, 11 3/4 In. 250.00
Vase, Praying Mantis, Pearlized, Ovoid, 7 In. 185.00
Vase, Praying Mantis, 3-Color, Fan, 8 1/2 In. 155.00
Vase, Roses, Brown, Yellow Ground, 9 1/2 In. 50.00
Vase, Roses, Oblong, Amber, 12 In. 85.00
Vase, Trumpet Vine, Custard, Blue, 10 1/2 In. 99.00
Vase, Vines, White, Blue Ground, Label, 11 In. 159.00
Vase, Wild Geese, Blue, 9 1/2 In. 100.00
Vase, Wild Geese, White, 9 1/2 In. 85.00
       PHONOGRAPH, see Music, Phonograph
PHOTOGRAPHY, Ambrotype, Children, Girl Holding Baby, Gilt Frame 12.50
   Ambrotype, Civil War Trooper 37.50
   Ambrotype, Civil War, 2 X 2 1/2 In. 25.00
   Ambrotype, Fireman Rescuing Baby, 3 1/4 X 3 3/4 In., Pair 100.00
   Ambrotype, Man Smoking Pipe, Holding Hammer 118.00
   Ambrotype, Man, Half Plate 27.50
   Ambrotype, Niagara Falls, Canadian Side, 19th Century 125.00
   Cabinet Card, Clergyman 7.50
   Cabinet Card, General Grant & Family, 1885 .... 20.00
   Cabinet Card, General Logan, Civilian Clothes 15.00
   Cabinet Card, General Sheridan 13.50
   Cabinet Card, Horses, Buggies, & Riders 7.50
   Cabinet Card, Men In Front Of Clothing Store 19.50
   Cabinet Card, Prince & Princess Henry Of Prussia 8.00
   Cabinet Card, Red Cross Worker 10.00
   Cabinet Card, Small Child With Big Horn & Violin 15.00

Cabinet Card, Tattooed Man, 2 Poses, Pair	46.50
Cabinet Card, Two Giants	11.00
Camera, Ansco, Vest Pocket, No.0	20.00
Camera, Argus, C44, Case	42.50
Camera, Autographic Brownie, No.2A, Folding	23.00
Camera, Autographic Jr., 1914	25.00
Camera, Baby Brownie Special	15.00
Camera, Blair No.2 Weno	20.00
Camera, Brownie, Folding, ECK No. 3	19.50
Camera, Bull's-Eye Kodak No.2, Manual	55.00
Camera, Buster Brown, No.2a, Box	25.00
Camera, Ciroflex, Case	25.00
Camera, Conley, Folding Glass Plate, Red Bellows, Cherrywood	120.00
Camera, Conley, Folding, Case, Rosewood	80.00
Camera, Conley, 6 Plate Holders, Tripod, Leather Case, Brass	500.00
Camera, Fairchild Aerial	75.00
Camera, Folding Gem, Poco, Box, Plates	70.00
Camera, Keystone Radiopticon	35.00
Camera, Kodak Duaflex	15.00
Camera, Kodak Medalist I, C.1943, F3.5 Lens	45.00
Camera, Kodak, Folding Hawkeye, Rainbow Model	15.00
Camera, Kodak, Folding, No.3-A, 1913, Postcard Size Pictures	15.00
Camera, Kodak, Target Hawkeye, 6-16	18.00
Camera, Kodak, Vest Pocket, Folding, No.127, 1913	10.00
Camera, Kodak, Vigilant 6-16, Boxed	27.00
Camera, Mentor Reflex	95.00
Camera, No.2 Bull's-Eye	20.00
Camera, Pathex Motion Picture, Original Leather Case	47.50
Camera, Popular Pressman, Aldis Butcher Lens, 3 1/4 X 4 1/4 In.	80.00
Camera, Revere Eye-Matic, 8 MM., 1950s	16.00
Camera, Seneca, No.2a, Scout	70.00
Camera, Univex, Model A, Box & Instructions	25.00
Camera, Vive No.1	65.00
Camera, Weno Hawkeye, No.7, Wooden Shipping Box	50.00
Camera, Zeiss Contaflex IV	55.00
Camera, Zeiss-Ikon, Leather Case	43.00
Carte De Visite, Album, Gold Hinge, Gold Lettering, 5 X 7 In.	16.50
Carte De Visite, Alexander Dumas	15.00
Carte De Visite, Civil War Soldier	5.00
Carte De Visite, Civil War, Set Of 6	35.00
Carte De Visite, Hunter Posed With Dog & Gun	20.00
Carte De Visite, James Lowell	10.00
Carte De Visite, Lincoln, Seated, Looking At Watch, Brady	35.00
Carte De Visite, Pauline Cushman	7.00
Carte De Visite, Schyler Colfax	14.50
Carte De Visite, Surveyor With Transit, Tripod, & Target	15.00
Carte De Visite, Tom Thumb, Wife & Child	8.50
Carte De Visite, William Cullen Bryant	10.00
Carte De Visite, 2 Girls Holding Doll	7.50
Daguerreotype Case, Gutta-Percha, Bonneted Baby, 9th Plate	65.00
Daguerreotype Case, Gutta-Percha, Child, Framed, 3 X 2 1/2 In.	85.00
Daguerreotype Case, Gutta-Percha, Civil War Soldier	75.00
Daguerreotype Case, Gutta-Percha, Girl With Lamb	65.00
Daguerreotype Case, Gutta-Percha, Picture Of Woman, 3 In.	55.00
Daguerreotype Case, Gutta-Percha, The Beggar, 2 1/2 X 3 In.	85.00
Daguerreotype Case, Gutta-Percha, The Huntress, 3 1/2 X 4 In.	75.00
Daguerreotype Case, Gutta-Percha, The Tryst, C.1857, 4 X 5 In.	85.00
Daguerreotype Case, Gutta-Percha, Victorian Girl, Black	75.00
Daguerreotype Case, Oval, 2 1/4 X 3 1/4 In.	45.00
Daguerreotype, Christian Woman, Red Velvet Lined Case	22.50
Daguerreotype, Man Holding Newspaper, Lady With Umbrella, 1/6	35.00
Daguerreotype, Man With Compass	175.00
Daguerreotype, Nude, Tinted & Etched	1650.00

Daguerreotype, Postmortem Of Man	55.00
Daguerreotype, Terrier, Signed Vancle, 1/6 Plate	300.00
Daguerreotype, Whitin Family, Maine, 1/6 Plate	295.00
Enlarger, Sunray, Black Crackle Finish	35.00
Glass, Measuring, Eastman Kodak	7.50
Lamp, Darkroom, Kodak, Kerosene	15.00
Lamp, Kerosene, Dark Room, Tin	27.50
Lens, Cooke, Portrait, Wood & Brass	125.00
Lens, Portrait, Brass, Large	100.00
Magic Lantern, Electric, Box	20.00
Magic Lantern, German, 26 Slides	55.00
Magic Lantern, 15 Slides, Tin	65.00
Megaletoscope, Charles Ponti Label & Instructions	150.00
Photograph, Fish, Spun Glass Tail, 1900s, 4 3/4 In.	35.00
Photograph, Nude, String Of Pearls, 1907, 4 X 5 1/2 In.	19.00
Projector, Excel, Moxie, 200-Foot Capacity	300.00
Projector, Postcard, Red Finish	55.00
PHOTOGRAPHY, STEREO, see Stereo	
Tintype, Bearded Union Officer, Gilt Frame, 2 1/2 X 3 In.	64.50
Tintype, Black Baby In Crib, Full Plate	125.00
Tintype, Civil War Officer, C.1863, 1/2 Case	80.00
Tintype, Civil War, Infantryman, Framed, 2 1/2 X 3 1/4 In.	34.50
Tintype, Grizzled Infantryman, Gilt Frame, 2 1/2 X 3 1/4 In.	29.50
Tintype, Indian, White Girls, Beaded Frame	55.00
Tintype, Lady, Half Plate	3.75
Tintype, Man On Donkey, 1/4 Plate	14.50
Tintype, Men, Women, Couples, 2 1/2 X 3 1/2 In.	3.75
Tintype, People Behind Comical Screen	12.00
Tintype, Railroad Conductor, Wife, 1870s, Half Plate	225.00
Tintype, Soldier, Uncle John Brower, Leather Case	37.50
Tintype, Woman, Walnut Frame, C.1880, 2 1/2 X 2 3/4 In.	45.00
Tintype, 2 Carpenters	20.00
Tintype, 2 Ice Cutters	24.00
Tintype, 4 Men, Copper Frame, 4 1/4 X 3 1/2 In.	9.00
Tintype, 27 People Outdoors, Half Plate	18.00
PIANO, see Music, Piano	

About 1880 the well-decorated home had a shawl on the piano. The bisque piano baby was designed to help hold the shawl in place. They range in size from 6 to 18 inches. Most of the figures were made in Germany.

PIANO BABY, Alpine Clothes, Seated, 12 In.	95.00
Bisque, 9 In.	120.00
Blonde Girl, Pink Dress, Arms Raised, 9 1/2 In.	395.00
Boy, Green & White Shift, Gold Beading, Holds Puppy, 7 1/2 In.	175.00
Boy, Holding Dog, 3 1/2 X 5 In.	65.00
Boy, Limbs Wire Tied, Blue Eyes, Crocheted Suit, 5 1/2 In.	90.00
Bubble Blower Girl, Marked, Bisque, 13 In.	425.00
Crawling Blonde, 2 Front Teeth, Marked, 6 1/2 In.	280.00
Crawling On Tummy, Marked, 4 1/4 In.Long	145.00
Crawling, Heubach, 12 In.	225.00 To 450.00
Crawling, Knit Hat, Playing With Bear, Heubach, 10 In.	450.00
Crawling, White Nightgown, Sunburst, 8 In.	175.00 To 195.00
Crawling, White Nightie, Trimmed In Blue, Heubach, 4 In.	135.00
Crawling, White Shift, Marked, Intaglio Eyes, 4 In.	65.00
Hands Up, Blonde Curls, Rattle, Green Dress	175.00
On Stomach, Marked Heubach, 5 In.	225.00
On Stomach, With Cat, 7 In.	225.00
Playing With Feet, Nightgown, Sunburst, 7 1/2 In.	185.00
Playing With Toes, Seated, White Gown, Green Trim, 8 In.	265.00
Seated Boy, Pink Trimmed Nightie, Hands Raised, Marked, 3 1/2 In.	145.00
Seated Girl, Green Dress With Bows, Heubach, 10 In.	125.00
Seated, Heubach, 9 In.	295.00

Seated, White Dress, Hand Up Holding Pink Flower, 6 1/2 In. 195.00
Seated, 14 In. 250.00
Sitting In Open High Shoe, Hand Above Head, Marked, 5 In. 160.00
Sitting Position, Playing With Toes, Pair 300.00
Sitting, Holding Apple, Greenish Yellow Gown, 4 1/2 In. 65.00
Sitting, Red Painted Shoes, Heubach, 5 In. 200.00
Squatting Nude, Heubach, 9 In. 375.00

*Pickard china was started in 1898 by Wilder Pickard. Hand-painted china
was a featured product. The firm is still working in Antioch, Illinois.*

PICKARD, Bonbon, Scalloped, Red Poppies, Signed, Handled 55.00
Bottle, Cologne, Paper Label, Artist Signed 37.50
Bowl, Acorn & Leaf Design, Footed, Signed, 8 X 7 In. 90.00
Bowl, Fruit, Reddish Orange Poppies, Artist Signed, 7 In. 95.00
Bowl, Green & Black Geometrics, Flowers, Gold Trim, Signed, 9 5/8 In. 100.00
Bowl, Open Handles, Berries, Signed, 8 In. 125.00
Bowl, Shamrocks, Gold Trim, Footed, 9 In. 325.00
Celery, 1930, Gold 60.00
Charger, Berries, Blossoms, Leaves, Gold Border, 12 1/2 In. 250.00
Coffee Set, Aura Argenta Linear, Gold & Silver Design, Marked, 3 Pc. 325.00
Coffeepot, Allover Floral, Gold Trim, 1905 Mark, 8 1/2 In. 155.00
Compote, Flowers, Pink Roses, Gold Trim, Artist Signed, 4 3/4 In. 135.00
Creamer, Black & Orange Luster, Scrolls, Signed 47.00
Creamer, Blue Leaves, Orange Band, Signed, Marked 68.00
Creamer, Gold, Black, & Orange Luster, Scrolls, Circle Mark 60.00
Cup & Saucer, Art Deco Design, Demitasse, Signed 45.00
Dish, Relish, Gold Center, Band Of Fruits, Signed, 12 1/2 In. 89.00
Hatpin Holder, Iris Design 75.00
Jug, Corn, Artist Signed, C.1898, 6 1/4 In. 245.00
Marmalade Set, Metallic Grape Pattern, C.1905, 6 In., 3 Piece 295.00
Pitcher, Aura Argenta Linear, Podlaha, 8 In. 200.00
Pitcher, Cider, Hops, Wheats, Leaves, Marked, 5 1/2 X 7 1/2 In. 325.00
Pitcher, Claret, Fruit Design, Signed Challinor, 10 1/2 In. 245.00
Pitcher, Lemonade, Scenic, Signed E.Challinor 525.00
Pitcher, Lemonade, Strawberries, Gold 275.00
Pitcher, Lemonade, Trees, Fruits, & Blossoms, 6-Sided, 9 1/4 In. 285.00
Pitcher, Milk, Currants, Artist Signed, 4 1/4 In. 195.00
Pitcher, Milk, Gooseberries, Brown Tones, Signed 155.00
Pitcher, Oranges & Orange Blossom, Gold Rim, Signed, 5 In. 75.00
Pitcher, Oriental Poppies, Gold Trim, 1898-1904 Mark, 10 1/2 In. 450.00
Pitcher, Pink & Green, Gold Trim, Artist Signed, Circle Mark, 5 In. 145.00
Pitcher, Water, Metallic Grapes, Artist Signed, Circle Mark.8 In. 225.00
Plate, Art Deco, Geometrics, Flowers, & Leaves, 10 1/2 In. 75.00
Plate, Autumn Scene, Artist Signed, Circle Mark, 8 1/2 In. 125.00
Plate, Cake, Purple Flowers, Gold Border, Handled, 1905 Mark 65.00
Plate, Century Of Progress, 1933 .... 18.00 To 30.00
Plate, Daisies, Gold Raised Flowers, Signed, 1905 Mark, 8 In. 60.00
Plate, Fruits, Gold Trim, Signed, 10 3/4 In. 155.00
Plate, Gold Border, Floral Design, 7 1/2 In. 28.00
Plate, Gold Scalloped Edge, Flowers, Signed, 9 In. 85.00
Plate, Iris, Gold Leaves & Border, Artist Signed, 8 1/2 In. 65.00
Plate, Italian Gardens, Purple Iridescence, Signed, 11 In. 125.00
Plate, Orchids, 8 In. 75.00
Plate, Palm Scenes, 9 In. 125.00
Plate, Peaches, Signed, 8 1/2 In. 40.00
Plate, Scenic, Pastels, Artist Signed 160.00
Plate, Shield Medallions, Rampant Lion, Floral, Signed, 9 In. 115.00
Plate, Transfer, Young Lady, 1919-22, Marked, 7 In. 125.00
Plate, Violets, Circle Mark, Signed, 8 1/2 In. 55.00

Plate, Wild Rose, 7 In.	65.00
Plate, Woodland Scene, Signed Challinor, Maple Leaf Mark, 11 In.	300.00
Relish, Handled, Pink & Green Flowers, Gold Trim, C.1905, 5 1/2 In.	25.00
Salt & Pepper, Currants, Signed	40.00
Salt, Pedestal, Gold Floral, Pair	15.00
Sugar & Creamer, Blue & Green, Bellflower Design, Gold Trim	50.00
Sugar & Creamer, Gold Allover, RS Prussia, Pickard Marks	80.00
Sugar & Creamer, Gold Floral, Square, Signed	45.00
Sugar & Creamer, Hand-Painted Bellflower, Gold Trim	50.00
Sugar & Creamer, Squirrel Design, Flowers, Pedestal	110.00
Sugar, Gold Encrusted, Handled, Large, 1919	45.00
Syrup, Aura Argenta, Signed, 1905 Mark	95.00
Tea Set & Tray, Gold, 4 Piece	125.00
Tea Set, Dutch Girl Scene, Artist Signed, Bisque Finish	275.00
Tea Set, Pink Floral, Green Leaves, Marked, 15 Piece	135.00
Tray, Floral, Gold Handles, Open, Oblong, Signed, 14 In.	85.00
Tray, Gold & Orange Trees, C.1912, Signed, Oblong, 9 3/4 In.	95.00
Tray, Gold Center & Frame, Landscape, 1912-19 Mark, 15 In.	135.00
Tray, Metallic Grape Pattern, C.1910, Signed, Oblong, 8 1/2 In.	95.00
Tray, Oval, Signed, 11 1/2 In.	135.00
Tray, Poppies, C.1910, Artist Signed, Oval, 12 3/4 In.	195.00
Tray, Scenic, Moonlight, Artist Signed, C.Marker, 8 3/4 In.	195.00
Vase, Amphora, Gold Upper, Black Bottom, Peacock, Signed, 8 In.	425.00
Vase, Art Deco, Poppy, Signed King, 11 In.	250.00
Vase, Black & Pink Floral, Gold Trim, Signed, C.1910, 4 1/4 In.	50.00
Vase, Chinese Enamel Peony & Plum Bossoms, Signed, 9 In.	300.00
Vase, Garden Scene, Fountain, Matte Finish, Signed Challinor, 7 In.	350.00
Vase, Gold Flowers, Pink Roses, Medallion, Handled, 10 In.	235.00
Vase, Gold Handles, White, Cobalt Bands, Old Mark, 7 In.	200.00
Vase, Gold, Riverside Scene, Pink Roses, Marked, 14 In.	395.00
Vase, Green & Gold, 8 In.	42.00
Vase, Large Tulip, Artist Signed, 12 1/4 In.	225.00
Vase, Moon Scene Over Lake, Handles, Signed, 9 In.	285.00
Vase, Moonlight & Palm Trees, Double Handled, Leaf Mark, 6 1/4 In.	285.00
Vase, Palm Trees, Surrounding Lake, 2 Handles, 7 In.	180.00 To 235.00
Vase, Peacock, C.1919, 7 In.	235.00
Vase, Poppy, Signed King, 11 In.	250.00
Vase, Red Flowers & Ground, Gold Neck & Handles, Signed, 6 In.	145.00
Vase, Wildwood Pattern, Pastels, Signed James, 8 1/4 In.	395.00

PICTURE, see also Painting; Print	
PICTURE, Floral, Human Hair, Shadowbox Frame	100.00
Silhouette, Bird In The Window, Hand Cut	30.00
Silhouette, Gentleman, C.1840, R.Dummings	200.00
Silhouette, Mistletoe Ball, Hand Cut	30.00
Silhouette, Spring Flowers, Hand Cut	30.00
Silhouette, Woman, High-Collar Dress, Gilt Frame, 4 1/2 X 5 1/2 In.	60.00
Silk & Hair, Georgian Scene Of Ship & Building, C.1790	95.00

PIGEON BLOOD, see Cranberry Glass; Ruby Glass	
PILKINGTON, Vase, Fleur-De-Lis, Gold Ground, Signed, 6 In.	400.00

PINCUSHION DOLL, Arms Away From Body	135.00
Blonde Flapper, Blue Dress, Japan	30.00
Blonde Hair, Papier-Mache, Germany, 6 In.	12.50
Blonde, Band Around Top Chignon, Goebel Mark, 4 1/2 In.	185.00
Blonde, One Arm Away, Dated 1925, Germany	27.00
Bonneted, Long Sleeve Blouse, Lavender Feather Trim	75.00
Brush, Japan, 5 3/4 In.	20.00
China Brush, Yellow Hat, 5 1/2 In.	15.00
Colonial Lady, Arms & Hands Away, Orange Bow, 5 1/2 In.	195.00
Colonial Lady, Hand Bending Toward Face	22.50

Colonial Lady, Marked Germany	35.00
Dark Hair, Blue Comb, Both Arms Away, Germany	37.00
Dutch Girl, Gold Trimmed Bodice, Dutch Hat, 3 3/4 In.	165.00
Dutch Girl, 2 1/2 In.	45.00
Feathered Hat, Gray Hair, Germany, 6 1/2 In.	30.00
Flapper, Arms Flexed Outward, Hand-Painted, Germany, 3 In.	35.00
Flapper, Blonde Hair, Red Beads In Hair, Arms On Hip, 3 In.	30.00
Flapper, Hat, Brown Hair, Dotted Blouse	23.00
German, Blonde Hair, Pink Roses & Necklace	22.50
Girl, Holding A Flower, Germany	45.00
Girl, Holding Basket With Cushion, Japan	12.50
Girl, Pink Dress, Fan To Bodice, Ecru Lace On Bottom	25.00
Gray-Haired Lady, Curled Bun Over Ears, 2 1/2 In.	55.00
Hand At Head, Other At Breast, High Hair, Germany, 3 1/2 In.	26.00
Hand Holding Fan, Red Hat With Feather, Germany, 2 1/2 In.	22.00
Hand-Painted, Pottery, Germany, 6 In.	45.00
Hands At Breasts, Blonde Hair, Germany, 3 1/2 In.	26.00
Hands Holding Rim Of Green Hat, 6 X 2 In.	24.00
Kneeling Baby, Full-Figured, Outstretched Arms	145.00
Lady, Black Molded & Painted Dress, Bonnet, 4 1/4 In.	50.00
Lady, Blonde Hair, One Hand On Hip, 3 In.	30.00
Lady, Brown Hair, Blue Bow On Top, Incised Number	60.00
Lady, Holding Fan, Germany	25.00
Lady, Ruffled Collar, Opaque Ceramic, Germany, 4 In.	45.00
Lady, Wig, Heubach, 4 In.	500.00
Lady, With Love Letter, 4 3/4 In.	250.00
Molded Hair, Hands Clasped To Bosom, Germany, 3 3/4 In.	30.00
Movable Arms, Silk Gown, Bisque, Germany, C.1880, 8 1/4 In.	45.00
Open Arms, Golden Hair, 1 3/4 In.	30.00
Open Arms, One Hand Holding Fan, White Wig, Germany, 5 In.	100.00
Pansy, 1/2 Face Bisque, Blue Glass Eyes, Silk Petals	75.00
Pink Hair Comb, Taffeta Flowers, Germany, 2 In.	30.00
Plumed Hat, Molded Hair, Arm Extended, Holding Fan, Germany	35.00
Porcelain, Beaded Headband, Germany	32.50
Porcelain, Bent Elbows, Bun Hairdo, Germany, 2 In.	15.00
Silver Head, Arm Behind Head	23.00
Spanish Dancer, Hand-Painted Features, Germany, 3 3/4 In.	30.00
PINK SLAG, see Slag, Pink	
PIPE, Black Forest, Spiked Helmet Lid, Painted Bowl, Tassel, 50 In.	150.00
Briar, Tom Thumb, 3 In.	8.00
Camp Grant, Clambroth	12.00
Case, Match Safe, Tobacco, & Pipe, Ridgewood Tobacco, Patent 1872	65.00
China, German, Deer Scene, Wood Stem, Bone Mouth, 40 In.	65.00
Clay, German	5.00
Copper Lined Bowl, 18th Century, Pewter, 4 1/2 In.	75.00
Deer In Mountains, China, No Stem	30.00
Eagle & American Flag On Bowl, Handmade, Maple, 6 X 4 1/4 X 2 1/2 In.	70.00
French, Lady's, Rhinestone Trim	15.00
Gorilla Family, Briarwood, Carved, 14 In.	950.00
Hand-Carved & Painted Bowl, Bavarian, 37 1/2 In.	60.00
Hand-Painted Stags, China & Brass, 22 In.	65.00
Hunter & Turkey, Brass Capped, Porcelain, 7 In.	75.00
Indians On Horseback, Looking For Killed Buffalo, Briarwood, 11 In.	750.00
Mallard Duck Bowl, Porcelain	100.00
PIPE, MEERSCHAUM, see Meerschaum, Pipe	
Opium, Bamboo & Sterling, 22 In.	140.00
Opium, Bamboo, Sculptured Sterling Silver Band, No Bowl	125.00
Opium, Cloisonne, Blue, White, Gold, & Red, 8 In.	210.00
Porcelain, Bow, Scene, Boy, Man, Rabbit, Snow, 28 In.	55.00
Revolver Shape	30.00
Silver Cap Screen, Bone	35.00
Trumpet, Nickel Over Brass, 1901, Boxed	50.00

Woman's Hand Holding Bowl, Case, 3 1/2 In. 75.00

Pirkenhammer is a porcelain manufactory started in 1802 by Friedrich
Holke and J.G. List.

PIRKENHAMMER, Plate, Gold Birds, Butterflies, Flowers 25.00

Pisgah pottery pieces that are marked "Pisgah Forest Pottery" were
made in North Carolina from 1926 until the present. Vases, teapots, jugs,
candlesticks, and many other items were made.

PISGAH FOREST, Bowl, Turquoise, 1959, 2 3/4 In. 47.00
Cup & Saucer, Turquoise 13.00
Jar, Turquoise, Rose Lining, 1942 .... 47.00
Pitcher, Turquoise, 10 In. 35.00
Plate, Grape Ground, 1946, Stephen, 10 In. 50.00
Sugar & Creamer, Cameoware, Signed Stephen 250.00
Sugar & Creamer, 1942 .... 60.00
Vase, Blue, 9 In. 40.00
Vase, Crystalline, 4 In. 125.00
Vase, Green Flowing To Beige, Signed & Dated, 9 1/4 In. 265.00
Vase, Maroon Design On Blue Ground, Signed, 4 1/2 In. 52.00
Vase, 3-Handled, Turquoise, 5 In. 40.00

PISTOL, Dart, Wyandotte, Steel 15.00
Luger, Case Marked K.B.A.G. 1916, German 7500.00

PLANTERS PEANUTS, Ashtray, Ceramic 60.00
Ashtray, Figural, 50th Anniversary 25.00
Barrel, Label 185.00
Canister, 1916, 10 Pound 35.00
Clock, Masonite, 13 X 17 In. 35.00
Glass, Cocktail, Mr.Peanut, Figural, Plastic 16.50
Jacket, Planters Worker's, Embroidered Mr.Peanut & Figure 65.00
Jar, Barrel, Decal 125.00
Jar, Embossed, 8-Sided, Peanut Finial 29.00
Jar, Fishbowl, Embossed, Label On 1 Side 55.00
Jar, Football 150.00
Jar, Football Shape 165.00
Jar, Hexagon, Peanut Man In Yellow 65.00
Jar, Leap Year, 1940, Original Box 45.00
Jar, Mr.Peanut, Yellow, Embossed Peanut Top 90.00
Jar, Peanut Corners, 11 1/2 In. 90.00
Jar, Pennant, 10 Pound .... 25.00 To 145.00
Jar, 4-Sided Square, Embossed 45.00
Jar, 5 Cent, Octagonal 95.00
Jar, 8-Sided, Embossed, Peanut Finial 135.00
Knife, Folding, Mr.Peanut For President 15.00
Knife, Fold-Out, 1960 .... 4.00
Mirror, 14 X 17 In. 30.00
Mug, Mr.Peanut 7.00
Olympic Set, Bow, 4 Coasters, Metal 40.00
Pail, Red Pennant, 10 Pound 25.00
Postcard, Mr.Peanut Showing Different Stores, Set Of 3 .... 10.00
Salt & Pepper, Mr. Peanut, Cork Bottom, Plastic, Blue 8.00
Spoon, Mr.Peanut, Silver Plated, Perforated Bowl, 5 1/4 In. 18.50
Tape Measure, Mr.Peanut, Round 2.00
Towel, Beach, Mr.Peanut, Large 25.00

Toy, Mr. Peanut, Windup, Walker 125.00
    PLATE, see under special types such as ABC; Calendar

> *Plated amberina was patented June 15, 1886, by Edward D. Libbey and made by the New England Glass Works. It is similar to amberina, but is characterized by a cream-colored or chartreuse lining (never white) and small ridges or ribs on the outside.*

PLATED AMBERINA, Vase, 5 In. 1600.00
    PLATED SILVER, see Silver Plate

> *Plique a jour is an enameling process. The enamel was laid between thin raised metal lines and heated. The finished piece has transparent enamel held between the thin metal wires.*

PLIQUE A JOUR, Spoon, Demitasse, Original Box, Set Of 6 .... 400.00

POLITICAL, Bandana, Teddy Roosevelt, 1912 .... 75.00 To 100.00
    Bandana, W.H.Harrison 850.00
    Beanie, Hoover For President 20.00
    Book, Cartoon, Roosevelt & Roosevelt, Organ-Grinder Herbie & Pals 25.00
    Book, Harrison Log Cabin Song, 1840, 64 Pages 30.00
    Box, Collar, Garfield, 1880 .... 125.00
    Bread Plate, Teddy Roosevelt 200.00
    Bust, Wendell Willkie, Frosted Glass 135.00
    Bust, Woodrow Wilson, 1916, Life-Size, Plaster 46.50
    Button, Adlai Stevenson For President, 4 In. 15.00
    Button, Bryan, Sewell, Portraits, 7/8 In. 17.00
    Button, Coolidge & Dawes 29.00
    Button, Coolidge, Portrait 10.00
    Button, Cox, Roosevelt, Jugate, 1920, 7/8 In. .... *Illus* 1800.00
    Button, Elihu Root, 1916, President Hopeful, Picture 8.00
    Button, Embossed Head Of Hoover, 1932, Brass, 1 In.Diam. 12.50
    Button, Franklin Roosevelt, Picture 5.00
    Button, Franklin Roosevelt, Raised Profile, Porcelain 40.00
    Button, Get Right With Ike, Picture, 5/8 In.Diam. 4.00
    Button, Hoover & Curtis 4.50
    Button, Housewives For Ike, Red, White, & Blue, 3 In. 14.00
    Button, LaFolette, Wheeler, Bronze, 1 In. 25.00
    Button, Landon & Knox 5.00
    Button, Landon, Sunflower On Celluloid, Picture, 1936 .... 10.00
    Button, Lapel, Hoover Elephant 30.00
    Button, McKinley & Roosevelt, Brass Color, 3 In.Diam. 45.00
    Button, McKinley & Wife 15.00
    Button, McKinley, Roosevelt, Jugate, Portraits 20.00
    Button, McKinley, Roosevelt, Portraits 12.00
    Button, McKinley, 1900, Hobbyhorse .... *Illus* 825.00
    Button, Missouri's Minutemen For Roosevelt 22.50

Political, Button, Cox, Roosevelt,
Jugate, 1920, 7/8 In.

Political, Button, McKinley,
1900, Hobbyhorse

Political, Button, T.Roosevelt,
Return From Africa

Political, Button, Wilson, 1912,
Multicolored

Button, Ohio For Carter, 1976, 4 In.	12.00
Button, Progressive Policies, Law Under Wilson, 7/8 In.	20.00
Button, Roosevelt, Garner, Bronze	5.00
Button, Roosevelt, Wallace, Jugate	10.00
Button, Roosevelt, Wallace, 1 In.	10.00
Button, Sunflower, Landon & Knox, Felt	3.00
Button, T.Roosevelt, Portrait, 7/8 In.	13.00
Button, T.Roosevelt, Return From Africa *Illus*	275.00
Button, Taft, Portrait, 1 1/4 In.	20.00
Button, Vote Socialist, Thomas, Maurer, 3/4 In.	9.00
Button, William Henry Harrison, Log Cabin Scene, 1840	150.00
Button, William Howard Taft, Picture, 1908-12, Color	10.00
Button, Willkie Clubs Of Illinois	5.00
Button, Wilson, Portrait	12.00
Button, Wilson, 1912, Multicolored *Illus*	1250.00
Button, Wm.Howard Taft, New Hampshire Choice For 1912	15.00
Cane Head, Our Next President, William McKinley, 1896	37.50
Cane, Inauguration Of W.Wilson, 1917, Golf Club Shape	85.00
Clip, Name, Hoover, Blue & Gold, 1 X 1/4 In.	7.50
Commission, Army, 1910, William H.Taft, Full Signature	84.50
Flag, Garfield, Arthur	185.00
Gloves, I Like Ike	20.00
Handkerchief, Democratic Presidents To Johnson	8.00
Hat, Straw, Wallace For President	25.00
Lantern, Picture Of Garfield & Arthur	200.00
Medal, Our President, Grover Cleveland, 1887, Pewter	10.00
Mirror, Pocket, Where Our President Fell, 1901	45.00
Mirror, Pocket, William J.Bryan For President, Sepia	38.00
Mug, F.D.Roosevelt, New Deal	12.50
Mug, Figural, Elephant, 1968, G.O.P., Frankoma	40.00
Mug, Happy Days, Pottery, Green	20.00
Mug, Howard Taft, 5 In.	85.00
Music, Sheet, Keep Cool & Keep Coolidge, 1924	5.00
Music, Sheet, Wilson's Inaugural March	5.00
Necktie, Truman	30.00
Necktie, Wallace	30.00
Pen, Harding For President, Picture	6.50
Pin, Willkie, Enameled Eagle	12.00
Pipe, Harrison, Protection For American Labor, Clay	125.00
Pitcher, Al Smith, China	45.00
Plate, For President Grover Cleveland, Ironstone, 8 In.	30.00
Postcard, Calvin Coolidge, Getting Off Train	10.00
Postcard, Calvin Coolidge, Wife & Old Car	10.00

Political, Ribbon, Lincoln, Kansas Statehood

Political, Ribbon, Lincoln, Johnson, Union & Victory

Political, Ribbon, Lincoln, Inauguration, 1861, Swiss

Political, Ribbon, Fillmore & Donelson, 3 X 7 1/4 In.

Political, Ribbon, Lincoln, 3 1/2 X 8 1/2 In.

Political, Ribbon, Lincoln & Hamlin, 1860, 5 1/4 In.

Political, Ribbon, Lincoln, 3 1/2 X 8 1/2 In.

Political, Ribbon, Lincoln, 1860, Wide Awakes, 6 1/2 In.

(See Page 456)

Postcard, Roosevelt Bear, Set Of 2	16.00
Postcard, Roosevelt Family, Souvenir, C.1903, Pach Bros.	10.00
Postcard, Taft & Sherman, 1908	20.00
Postcard, Woodrow Wilson, Flag Above, Oval Wreath	8.00
Poster, Nixon, Crowds Of People, Red Ground, 24 X 30 In.	25.00
Poster, President Grover Cleveland & Adlai Stevenson, 1892	88.00
Razor, Straight, Wilson, Marshall, Pictures	225.00

Ribbon Fob, Teddy Roosevelt	240.00
Ribbon Fob, William Jennings Bryan	140.00
Ribbon, Fillmore & Donelson, 3 X 7 1/4 In. ....*Illus*	130.00
Ribbon, Lincoln & Hamlin, 1860, 5 1/4 In. ....*Illus*	300.00
Ribbon, Lincoln, Inauguration, 1861, Swiss ....*Illus*	300.00
Ribbon, Lincoln, Johnson, Union & Victory ....*Illus*	425.00
Ribbon, Lincoln, Kansas Statehood ....*Illus*	130.00
Ribbon, Lincoln, 1860, Wide Awakes, 6 1/2 In. ....*Illus*	400.00
Ribbon, Lincoln, 3 1/2 X 8 1/2 In. ....*Illus*	475.00
Ring, Hoover, Figural G.O.P. Elephant, Silver Plated	35.00
Shot Glass, Happy Days	9.00
Sign, Bumper, We Need Roosevelt	22.00
Sign, Levander For Governor, Cardboard, 44 X 25 In.	30.00
Stickpin, Death To Rum, Hatchet Shape	25.00
Stickpin, Elephant, Hoover	10.00
Stickpin, Teddy Roosevelt, Moose	10.00
Thimble, Coolidge, Dawes	12.00
Ticket, Guest, Republican National Convention, 1900	15.00
Torch, Turned Wooden Poster, Pewter Fonts, 30 In., Pair	170.00
Torch, 3 Wicks Joined Over Air Tube	85.00
Tray, John F.Kennedy, 1964, Full Color	2.50
Tray, Pictures T.Roosevelt & McKinley, Dated 1900	75.00
Tumbler, Our Martyr President, W.McKinley	27.50
Watch Fob, Harry S.Truman, Inauguration, January 20, 1949	40.00
Watch Fob, Teddy Roosevelt, Ribbon	240.00
Watch Fob, William Jennings Bryan	140.00

*Pomona glass is clear with a soft amber border decorated with pale blue or
rose-colored flowers and leaves. The colors are very, very pale. The
background of the glass is covered with a network of fine lines. It was made
from 1885 to 1888 by the New England Glass Company.*

POMONA, Bowl, Cornflower, Crimped, 2nd Grind, 8 X 3 1/2 In.	300.00
Bowl, Crimped, Cornflowers, 1st Grind, 5 In.	140.00
Bowl, Finger, Ruffled Amber Top, 1st Grind	45.00
Bowl, Ruffled Cornflowers, 2nd Grind, 5 1/2 In.	98.00
Bowl, 2nd Grind, 4 1/2 X 2 1/2 In.	57.00
Cup, Punch, Amber Stained Leaf Rim & Handle, 2 1/2 In., Set Of 5	50.00
Cup, Punch, Cornflower Design, C.1885, 2 5/8 In., Pair	65.00
Pitcher, Amber Stained Rim, Cornflowers, Square Top, 6 1/2 In.	350.00
Pitcher, Water, Inverted Bull's-Eye, 2nd Grind, Square Mouth	150.00
Toothpick, Tricornered	140.00
Tumbler, Blue Cornflowers, Amber Stain, 2nd Grind	135.00
Tumbler, Cornflower, Blue & Amber Staining, 2nd Grind, 3 3/4 In.	150.00
Tumbler, Cornflower, 1st Grind, Set Of 4	900.00
Tumbler, Cornflower, 2nd Grind, 6 1/2 In.	60.00
Tumbler, Diamond Optic, Scalloped Border, Amber Top	115.00
PONTYPOOL, see Tole	
POO WARE, see Banko	

POPEYE, Alarm, Clock, C.1929, New Haven	675.00
Ashtray, Lithograph Tin Insert, Wooden	135.00
Bank, Dime, 1950s	55.00
BB Game, Bar Zim, Boxed	45.00
Bell, Cover For Christmas Tree Bulb, Plastic, Blue	10.00
Box, Crayon, Tin, 1933	28.00
Box, Pencil, 1930s	18.00 To 40.00
Box, Sunshine Biscuit, 1935	28.00
Bubble Set, 1936	15.00
Cover, Pillow, Embroidered, 1930s, Characters, 15 X 15 In.	75.00
Cutter, Cookie, Animals, 1930s, Boxed	45.00
Doll, Original Clothes, Pipe, All Cloth, 18 In.	150.00
Doll, Squeaker, King Features, 11 1/2 In.	50.00
Doorstop, Original Paint, 1930s, Wooden, 15 In.	45.00

Figure, Wood, Jointed, 1930, 5 1/2 In. 95.00
Figure, Wood, Jointed, 1930, 8 1/2 In. 275.00
Fork & Spoon, Silver Plate, Original Box 15.00
Game, Juggler .... 45.00 To 55.00
Game, Pipe Toss 30.00
Game, Popeye The Juggler, Glass Top, 1929, 3 1/2 X 5 In. 50.00
Game, Target, Complete In Original Box 110.00
Jigsaw Puzzle, 1932 .... 45.00
Juggler Game 60.00
Lamp, Figural, Pot Metal, Hand-Painted, 1930 .... 145.00
Lantern, Boxed 125.00
Night-Light 125.00
Olive Oyl, Figure, Rubber, 9 In. 45.00
Olive Oyl, Figure, Wood, Jointed, 1930, 4 3/4 In. 65.00
Olive Oyl, Puppet, Hand 24.00
Pencil, Mechanical, 10 In. 20.00
Pipe, Wooden 22.50
Pistol, Pirate, 1936 .... 125.00
Punching Bag 550.00
Record, Popeye Pirate Treasure, 45 RPM, 1943 .... 35.00
Salt & Pepper, 1 Is Olive 45.00
Spoon & Fork, Silver Plate, Original Box 15.00
Sprinkling Can 75.00
Toy, Brutus & Popeye, Ride In Tin Wagon, Celluloid 275.00
Toy, Brutus & Ride In Tin Wagon, Celluloid 275.00
Toy, Carrying Caged Parrot, Windup, Tin .... 50.00 To 275.00
Toy, In Airplane 350.00
Toy, Jack-In-The-Box 65.00
Toy, Juggles, Spinach Can, Wooden, Holgate 20.00
Toy, On Roof, Windup 300.00
Toy, On Unicycle, Linemar 650.00
Toy, The Champ, Marx, Boxed 1500.00
Toy, With Olive Oyl On The Roof 650.00
Whimpey, Figure, Rubber, 9 In. 45.00
Whistle 25.00
Wristwatch, 7 Jewels, Swiss 120.00

PORCELAIN, see also Copeland; Nippon; RS Prussia; etc.
PORCELAIN, Ashtray, Pinecone Design, 3-Cornered, Signed, Silesia 25.00
Bank, Pig, German, Smiling Head, Orange In Ears & Mouth 40.00
Bottle, Oriental, Blue & White Kara Kosa, 11 In. 50.00
Bottle, Perfume, German, Floral, 4 3/4 In. 30.00
Bowl, Center Arhats, Warrior, Scalloped, Signed Kinkozan, 9 In. 700.00
Bowl, Cherubs & Flowers, Handled, Covered, 13 1/4 X 7 1/4 In. 200.00
Bowl, Flowers & Roses, Silesia, 9 1/2 In.Diam. 95.00
Bowl, Fruit, French, Blossoms, Fruits, Multicolored, 13 In. 80.00
Bowl, Fruit, Gold Openwork, Yellow & Peach Roses, 11 In.Long 55.00
Bowl, Gilded Foliate Handles, Gilded Feet, 16 X 11 3/4 In. 300.00
Bowl, Reticulated, Maidens & Cherubs On Base, 18 1/2 In. 325.00
Box, Hinged Cover, Plume Feet, French, Gilt Metal Mounted, 8 In. 50.00
Box, Patch, French, Bird & Dragonflies, 1 3/4 X 2 1/8 In. 115.00
Bust Of Catherine II, Puce Robe, Laurel Wreath, Marked, 4 In. 3850.00
Cachepot, Woman Sitting In Garden, C'hing Period, 5 1/4 In., Pair 125.00
Cake Plate, Water Lilies, Scalloped, Pearlized, Silesia, 12 In. 62.00
Chocolate Pot, Green Leaves, Silesia 65.00
Chocolate Pot, Roses, Shamrocks, Gold Trim, Silesia, 9 1/4 In. 30.00
Crocus Pot, Fingernail Design, Enameled, 4 X 7 1/4 In., Pair 175.00
Cup & Saucer, Dejeuner, 19th Century, 5 Sets 300.00
Cup & Saucer, Handleless, Pink & Purple Luster Floral Design 27.50
Cup & Saucer, Purple, Man, Woman, Sea, English 15.00
Dish, Nut, Chinese, 4 Medallions, Yellow, Green, 3 1/4 In. 5.00
Dish, Powder, Covered, All White, Silesia 4.00
Dish, Soap, Hanging, Rose Florals, Green Leafing, C.1880 .... 25.00

Ewer, Duck Handle, Crest Mark, 4 1/2 In. .... *Illus* 35.00
Figurine, Bird, Brown Mark, 6 In., Pair 70.00
Figurine, Buddha, Enamel Floral Robe, Prayer Beads, C'hing, 9 In. 185.00
Figurine, German Shepherd, White Base, Gray, Pink Ears, 10 In. 75.00
Figurine, Girl, Holding Basket Of Florals, 5 In. 6.00
Figurine, Goddess Hebe, Holding Amphora In Hand, 10 7/8 In. 60.00
Figurine, Ice Cream Seller, Russian, Bucket On Shoulder, 8 In. 3300.00
Figurine, Man & Woman Dancing, Polychrome Enameling, 6 1/4 In. 35.00
Figurine, Napoleon Bonaparte, Standing, Military, 17 In. 300.00
Figurine, Napoleon, Standing, Full Uniform, German, 9 In. 165.00
Figurine, Nude Boy On Ibex Antelope, C.1905, Fasold & Stauch 125.00
Figurine, Parrot, Tree Stump Base, German, 6 In. 100.00
Figurine, Samoyed, Russian, Tonic, Hood, Mittens, 8 1/2 In. 3250.00
Figurine, Sitting Hoeti, Flowered Robe, C'hing Period, 10 X 10 In. 345.00
Figurine, Takasago Couple, Blue & White, Japanese, 14 In., Pair 350.00
Figurine, Whippet Family, Mother & 2 Pups, Grassy Terrain, 9 In. 145.00
Figurine, 2 Peasant Gardeners, Long Gray Coats, Russian, 8 In. 660.00
Figurine, 2 Russian Wolfhounds, Brown, White, Germany, 10 In. 135.00
Hair Receiver, Hand-Painted Pink & White Roses, Silesia 15.00
Hatpin Holder, Floral Design, Marked, Silesia 40.00
Hatpin Holder, Pink Rose, Green Leaves, White Ground, 4 1/4 In. 30.00
Holder, Bulb, Chinese Shape, Pink, Fingernail Design, 4 In., Pair 165.00
Jar, Ginger, Oxblood, Original Lid, C.1870, 14 In. 375.00
Jardiniere, Prunus Blossoms & Phoenix Bird, Japan, 10 In. 300.00
Jardiniere, Rocaille Handles, Painted Flowers, German, 7 1/4 In. 300.00
Mortar & Pestle, French 33.00

PORCELAIN, NAPKIN RING, see Napkin Ring

Plaque, Madonna & Child, 19th Century, Framed, 4 1/2 X 6 In. 300.00
Plaque, Queen Louise, Oval, 4 X 3 In. 435.00
Plaque, Young Woman With Pink Roses, Brass Frame, 6 X 5 1/2 In. 300.00
Plate, Center Portrait, C.1900, French, Gilt Mounted, 9 1/2 In. 70.00
Plate, Floral, Blue Mark, Silesia, Octagonal 37.50
Plate, Game, Rhinoceros, African Landscape 575.00
Plate, Rooster & Hen, Gold Trim, 6 1/2 In. 30.00
Shoe, Bulldog, Trying To Get Mouse Going In Toe 40.00
Sugar & Creamer, Bluebird Pattern, Victorian, Austria 30.00
Sugar, Pink & Purple Luster, Green Floral, 6 3/4 In. 20.00
Tankard, Orchid Base, Yellow Top & Handle, 18 In. .... *Illus* 110.00
Toast Holder, Bamboo Shapes, Gold Trim, England, 7 X 4 In. 35.00
Tray, Spoon, Landscape Border, Scalloped Sides, Chinese, 5 In. 100.00
Urn, Floral, C.1900, French, Gilt Bronze Mounted, 10 1/2 In. 60.00
Urn, Scenes Of Mother & Children, C.1850, French, 10 In., Pair 150.00
Vase, Baluster Form, Bird, Floral, Tree Design, China, 4 5/8 In. 1300.00
Vase, Chinese, C.1900, Powder Blue, 20 1/2 In. 1300.00

Porcelain, Ewer, Duck Handle, Crest
Mark, 4 1/2 In.

Porcelain, Tankard, Orchid
Base, Yellow Top &
Handle, 18 In.

Vase, Chrysanthemums, Gold Outline, German, 11 1/2 In., Pair 360.00
Vase, Flambe, Lavender-Blue Glaze, Purple Mottling, 12 In. 130.00
Vase, Globular Body, Applied Flowers & Figures, German, 19 In. 150.00
Vase, Moon Flask, Chinese, Blue & White, 12 1/2 In. 525.00
Vase, Owls Perched In Tree, Full Moon, Signed Winton, 7 In. 195.00
Vase, Polychrome Orchids, Square Foot, Marked Rozenburg, 4 In. 1700.00
Vase, Rustic Figures, C.1900, H.Wolfsohn, Marked, 12 1/4 In., Pair 850.00
Vase, Samurai In Armor, Bats, Moon, Signed Kinkozan, 30 1/2 In. 850.00

Postcards were first legally permitted in Austria on October 1, 1869.
The United States passed postal regulations allowing the card in 1873.
Most of the picture postcards collected today date after 1910.

POSTCARD, A Heavy Snowfall, Tuck, Glass Beading, 1907, Color 1.75
Abraham Lincoln At The Civil War Front, Set Of 12 .... 3.00
Aerial Swing, Luna Park, Night Scene, C.1905 .... 8.95
Angel Leads Child To Christmas Tree, Germany, Color 3.95
Angels Pouring Basket Of Toys On Christmas Tree, 1906, Color 2.50
Babe Ruth, Set Of 12 .... 6.00
Baker's Chocolate Lady 10.00
Bird's-Eye View Of Rapid City, S.D., 1918 .... 3.00
Broadway South From 1st St., Los Angeles, Trolley & Buggies 3.00
Buffalo Bill Wild West Show, Set Of 4 .... 16.00
Calendar, 1912 .... 10.00
Christmas, Angels, Trees, & Children, Set Of 119 .... 85.00
Christmas, Love One Another, Child With 2 Dogs, Tuck, Color 4.00
Christmas, Winter An Der Spree, Tuck, Color 2.50
Christmas, With Golliwog, Agnes Richardson, Tuck, Color 9.00
Christmas, 1930, Kansas City, Mo., Stagecoach, Stamp 12.00
Decoration Day, Set Of 25 .... 50.00
Double-Decker Bus On 5th Ave., New York City 4.00
Easter, Art Nouveau 5.00
Easter, Set Of 5 .... 3.00
Expositions & Fairs, Set Of 30 .... 30.00
Glove Shape, Leather 6.00
Horse Racing, Man's Best Friend, Tuck 4.00
Horse-Drawn Fire Engine Going To Fire, Decatur, Illinois, Set Of 3 .... 30.00
In The Hunting Field, Tuck, Hounds, Horses, & Fox Hunt 3.00
Indian Chief Buckskin Charlie, Embossed, H.H.Tammen, 1903 .... 7.00
July 4th, Set Of 12 .... 24.00
Labor Day, Nash 55.00
Leap Year, Set Of 19 .... 28.00
Lincoln, Including Memorial Car, Set Of 1o 35.00
Main Street, Doon, Iowa 5.00
Mary, Joseph, & Baby, Angel Handing Wreath To Baby, Glossy, Germany 3.50
Michigan Central R.R. Depot, Kalamazoo, 1913 .... 3.50
Mickey Mouse, 5 X 7 In. 2.00
Monongahela Wharves, Pittsburgh, 1902, View Of Packet Boats 3.50
Mount Vernon, Embossed, 1912 .... 5.00
Mouseketeers, 5 X 7 In. 3.00
Navajo Blanket Weaver, Embossed, H.H.Tammen, 1904 .... 7.00
New York To Paris Auto Race In Thomas Flyer 20.00
Panama, Pacific International Expo., 1914, Entire Expo. 10.00
Patriotic Greeting, July 4th, Girl Drummer 10.00
Plymouth, 1957, Front Of Car 3.50
President Washington, Set Of 45 .... 90.00
Proposal To Baby, Harrison Fisher, Set Of 6 .... 35.00
Public Square West, Bucyrus, Ohio, 1914 .... 4.00
Public Square, Boonveille, Indiana 2.50
Railroad Yard, Fremont, Nebraska, Wreath 5.00
Rapid Transit In Kentucky, Black Man On 2-Wheeled Cart, 1910 .... 5.00
S.S.Merion, Woven Silk 10.00
Santa Claus, Toasting With Champagne Glass, 1910, Color 4.50
Santa, In Balloon, Dropping Toys, Ullman, 1907, Color 5.00

Shooting The Chutes, Coney Island, C.1908, Night Scene	9.50
St.Louis World's Fair, 1904, Varied Industries Building	6.00
Steamer Minneapolis On Lake Minnetonka, Minn.	5.00
Sunday School, Postmarked St.Louis, Mo., 1932, 1 Cent	12.00
Taft & Sherman, Pair	6.00
Teddy Roosevelt, Set Of 6	15.00
Valentine, 1 Cent	5.00
Waiting For Birth, Doll Attached	5.00
Warships At Anchor, Hotel Chamberlin, Fort Monroe, Va.	12.00
Woodward Ave., Looking Toward River, 1911	2.75
3 Children Seated On Log, Signed Ellen Clapsaddle, Color	5.00
3 Dead Bandits, 1900	12.00
POSTER, Amos 'n Andy, 1930s, 20 X 13 In.	75.00
Barnum & Bailey, Midgets, Bagonghi, 3-Foot-High Rider, 30 X 40 In.	280.00
Barnum & Bailey, Strobridge, C., 1896, Male Hurdle Race, 26 X 28 In.	300.00
Barnum & Bailey, 1892, 10 X 15 In.	45.00
Be A Sea Soldier, Underwood	75.00
Be A U.S. Marine, World War I, Flagg	150.00
Blue Jacket Revolvers, 14 Different Guns, 1870s, Framed, 23 X 27 In.	160.00
Briar Pipe, Man Smoking, 1910, Framed, 31 X 23 In.	195.00
Careless Word, A Needless Sinking, 1942, Anton Fischer, 37 X 28 In.	25.00
Chicago World's Fair, Weimer Purcell, Lithograph, Framed	300.00
Circus, Ringling Brothers, 1940s, Clown & Elephant, 6 1/2 X 10 In.	85.00
Cole Bros., Circus Trains Unloading, Animals, C.1930, 20 X 30 In.	95.00
Cunard New Steamers, Boston To Europe, C.1923, Tugs, 28 X 40 In.	350.00
Cycle Francaise, C.1900, Patriotically Attired Woman, 45 X 62 In.	150.00
Firestone, Barney Oldfield, Motto	1000.00
Girl With Flag, Harrison Fisher	60.00
Hitler As Monkey, Uncle Sam As Organ-Grinder, 1943, 20 X 15 In.	20.00
I Was A Teenage Werewolf, 27 X 41 In.	40.00
If You Want To Fight, Christy	250.00
Keep These Off The U.S.A., Norton	45.00
King's Row, Original Linen Back	800.00
Lindbergh Welcome Home, Framed, 14 X 18 In.	22.00
Little Rascals, 1952, 27 X 41 In.	18.00
Lobby, Blood & Sand, Valentino In Toreador Dress, 11 X 14 In.	325.00
Lobby, Casablanca, Original	1250.00
Lobby, Check & Double Check, Amos 'n Andy, 5 Scene Cards, 11 X 14 In.	150.00
Lobby, Klondike Annie, Mae West In Feathered Hat, 11 X 14 In.	135.00
Lobby, Sins Of The Fathers, Emil Jannings, 11 X 14 In.	75.00
Marines In Khakis, Leyendecker	75.00
Marlow Coaster Brakes, Boys On Bikes, 1930s	95.00
Movie, Awakening Of Spring, 1917, Hungarian, Framed, 38 1/2 In.	850.00
Movie, Little Rascals, 1930s, 42 X 26 In.	50.00
Movie, Tim McCoy In Phantom Ranger, 4 Cowboys, 41 X 26 In.	50.00
Movie, Traffic In Souls, 1913, Laid On Linen, Lithograph	225.00
Munson Panamerican Lines, C.1925, On Linen, 21 X 31 In.	200.00
New England Fair, Worcester, Mass., Horses, 19th Century, 30 X 40 In.	175.00
New York Life Insurance Co., C.1896, Father Time, 15 X 19 In.	95.00
New York World's Fair, 1939, Sphere, Pylon, Cardboard, 8 1/2 X 10 In.	7.00
Red Belt Cigar, Girl In Red Outfit, 1895, Framed, 22 X 17 In.	375.00
Red Cross Nurse, Coffin	30.00
Red Cross Nurse, H.Fisher	60.00
Red Cross, Jessie Wilcox Smith	50.00
Remington Arms, Hunter Shooting Ducks, 1920s, Framed, 16 X 20 In.	195.00
S.S.France, New Concept In Luxury For All, 1962, 30 X 45 In.	145.00
Tell That To The Marines, Flagg	100.00
Victory, Flagg, 20 X 28 In.	60.00
Winchester, 3 Young Hunters Shooting, 1900s	175.00
World War I, I Want You, Flagg	750.00

POTTERY, see also Buffalo Pottery; Staffordshire; Wedgwood; etc.

Pottery, Shoe, Bulldog Trying To Get
Mouse Entering Toe

POTTERY, Brick, Embossed Profile Of Abe Lincoln, C.1860 .... 75.00
Figurine, Austrian, Boy, Girl, Seated, Whimsical, 7 1/2 In., Pair 775.00
Jar, Cookie Jar Printed On Front, Bricker, Blue & White 225.00
Jar, Galena, Impressed Mark, Buff, Green Clear Glaze, 11 3/4 In. 95.00
Jug, Grotesque, Smiling Visage, Insiced Lanier Meaders 65.00
Plaque, French, Woman, Lily, Ivory, Yellow, Blue, Marked, 11 X 15 In. 450.00
Shoe, Bulldog Trying To Get Mouse Entering Toe ....*Illus* 40.00
Tile, Art Deco, Draped Cherub, 12 X 6 In. 85.00
Vase, Birds, Wisteria Branches, Cobalt Blue, Japanese, 3 3/4 In. 275.00
Vase, Figural, Austrian, Putto Clutching Vase, Black, White, 15 In. 600.00
Vase, French, Gray-Blue Scrolls, Nudes, Gild Ground, 9 In. 950.00
Vase, Geometric Design, Ovoid, C.1924, Maria M.Martinez, 3 1/2 In. 160.00
Vase, Multicolored Stylized Flowers, Hancock & Sons, 10 1/2 In., Pr. 485.00

POWDER FLASK, Cap Is Measure, Tole 37.50
Carved Cow Horn, Brass Top & Spout, Figure Of Soldier, Germany 795.00
Cow Horn, C.1840, Brass Spout, Removable Base, 9 In. 37.50
Cow Horn, German, 17th Century, Carved Maiden & Soldier 850.00
Embossed Hunter With Gun & Dog, Brass, Copper Stem, 7 In. 60.00
Embossed Ribbed Melon, Brass, 8 In. 72.50
French, Boar Head, Hare, & Hunting Bubble, Copper, 7 1/2 In. 97.50
German Wheel Lock, Geometric Carving, Horn Body 195.00
Hunter With Sword, On Horse, Wounded Boar, Lanthorn, Circular 195.00
Navy, KM Mark, Colt's Patent 275.00
Panel Design, Copper 39.50
Relief Dead Game, American Flask & Co., Copper, 8 1/4 In. 95.00
Relief Double-Headed Russian Imperial Eagle, Brass 250.00
Rifle, Shell Design Both Sides, Copper, 8 In. 44.50
Stag In Center, Oakleaf Wreath, Copper, 8 1/2 In. 74.50
Standing Stag Center, Oakleaf Wreath, Copper 110.00
Telescopic Spout, Marked Paris, Copper, 7 1/2 In. 74.50

POWDER HORN, American Revolutionary, Initialed I.C.A., For Peace 55.00
Carved Wood Plug, Leather Strap, 12 In. 27.00
Engraved Map Of Great Lakes, Eagle & Shield, 13 In. 750.00
Engraved Primitive Animals & Birds, European, 9 1/4 In. 220.00
French & Indian War, Dated 1764, Map Of Hudson & Mohawk River 1450.00
French & Indian War, Signed John Tyall, Dated 1765, 13 In. 1000.00
Gosport Navy Yard, 1842, Copper, 11 1/2 In. 595.00
Overlapping Leaf Design, Copper, Lacquer Finish, 7 In. 54.50
Pennsylvania, C.1760, Carved Spout, Wooden Base, Owner's Name 875.00
Primitive Engraved Scrolls & Inscription, Dated 1748, 6 In. 60.00
Revolutionary War, Signed 1776, Church, Weather Vase, 13 In. 1400.00
Signed W.W., 1775, Marching Soldiers, Wood Plug, 12 In. 1100.00

PRATT
FENTON

Pratt ware means two different things. It was an early Staffordshire pottery, cream colored with colored decorations, made by Felix Pratt during the late eighteenth century. There was also Pratt ware made with transfer designs during the mid-nineteenth century in Fenton, England.

PRATT, Bowl, 2-Handled, Oakleaf, Acorn Border, Signed Sir David Wilkie, R.A.	325.00
Cup & Saucer, Pastoral Scene, Lilac Ground, C.1860	70.00
Cup & Saucer, Scenes, Green Ground	155.00
Jar, Mustard, Boar Hunting Scene, 1850s, 5 In.	35.00
Jar, Pomade, Boar Hunting Scene, Blue Glaze	18.50
Pitcher, Embossed Figures Making Wine, C.1820, 5 In.	230.00
Pitcher, Roman Scenes, Pink Luster	125.00
Pitcher, Sporting Innocence In Heart Frame, C.1800, 7 1/2 In.	185.00
Plate, Brown, Green, Classic Figures Border, 9 In.	125.00
Plate, Linlithgow Palace, Blue Transfer, Colors, C.1830, 9 1/2 In.	95.00
Plate, Preparing For The Ride, Pink Border, 7 In.	75.00
Plate, The Skewbald Horse, Apple Green Border, 7 In.	75.00
Potlid, Dog, Butcher's Block, Boat, Wooden Frame, 6 In.	100.00
Potlid, Dog, Table, Bust Of Shakespeare, Book, Inkwell, 6 In.	100.00
Potlid, Fox	37.00
Potlid, Pigeon	37.00
Potlid, Rustic Lovers, Saying Around Edge	75.00
Potlid, Shakespeare Village, Framed	62.00
Potlid, Weasel	37.00
Potlid, 2 Cries Of London	37.00
Tea Set, Old Greek Pattern, 3 Piece	150.00

Pressed glass was first made in the United States in the 1820s after the invention of pressed glass machines. Hundreds of patterns of pressed glass were made in complete table settings. Although the Boston and Sandwich Works was the most famous of the pressed glass factories, there were about sixteen other factories making pressed glass from 1830 to 1850, and still more from 1850 to 1900, when pressed glass reached its greatest popularity. It is now being widely reproduced.

PRESSED GLASS, Aberdeen, Goblet	22.00
ACANTHUS, see Ribbed Palm	
ACME, see Butterfly With Spray	
ACORN MEDALLION, BEADED, see Beaded Acorn Medallion	
Acorn Band, Goblet	35.00
Acorn, Compote, 6 1/2 In.	25.00
Acorn, Goblet	20.00 To 36.00
Acorn, Sauce, Flint	12.00
Acorn, Spooner, Paneled	30.00
Actress, Cake Stand, Frosted	65.00
Actress, Compote, Frosted, Covered, 8 In.	190.00
Actress, Creamer	60.00
Actress, Creamer, Clear	35.00
Actress, Dish, Maud Granger, 5 1/2 X 9 In.	40.00
Actress, Goblet	75.00
Actress, Goblet, Frosted Foot & Rim	70.00
Actress, Sauce	15.00
Actress, Sauce, Pedestal, 4 1/2 X 2 1/2 In.	16.00
Admiral Dewey, Pitcher, Water	75.00
Admiral Dewey, Pitcher, Water, 4 Tumblers	250.00 To 300.00
Adonis, Butter, Covered, Green	45.00
Adonis, Celery	18.00 To 20.00
Adonis, Sugar	22.00
Aegis, Creamer	15.00
Aegis, Wine	6.00
Aida, Creamer	15.00
Alabama, Creamer	28.00 To 35.00
Alaska, Butter, Green, Gold, Covered	110.00
Alaska, Creamer, Green	35.00

Alaska, Cruet, Green With Enameling, Original Stopper	235.00
Alaska, Spooner, Vaseline	50.00
Albany, Cruet, Original Flat Stopper	20.00
All Over Diamond, Spooner	16.00
Almond Thumbprint, Wine	10.00
Almond, Wine	17.00
Amazon, Butter, Covered	55.00
Amazon, Compote, Octagonal, Open, 6 In.	20.00
Amazon, Compote, Open, 5 1/2 In.	35.00
Amazon, Creamer, Child's	35.00
Amazon, Syrup, Clear	44.00
Amazon, Wine	16.50
AMBERETTE, see Klondike	
American Beauty, Cake Plate, Child's, Pedestal, 5 In.Diam.	32.00
Amulet, Wine, Gold	14.00
Anthemion, Creamer	21.00
Anthemion, Pitcher, Water	50.00
Anthemion, Plate, Rolled Edge, 10 In.	20.00 To 30.00
Anvil, Salt, Master, Sapphire Blue	38.00
Apollo, Goblet, Etched	50.00
Apollo, Tumbler, Etched	25.00
Aquarium, Pitcher, Water	180.00
Arched Fleur-De-Lis, Banana Stand	46.00
Arched Forget-Me-Not Bands, Creamer	20.00
Arched Grape, Goblet	30.00 To 35.00
Arched Ovals, Goblet	35.00
Argosy, Wine, Flint	34.00
Argus, Eggcup	20.00
Argus, Eggcup, Flint	24.00 To 25.00
Argus, Saucer, Scalloped Rim, 5 1/2 In.Diam.	5.00
Argus, Toothpick, 4 Row	22.00
Argus, Tumbler	20.00
Argus, Wine, Flint	45.00
Arrowhead In Oval, Table Set, Child's, 4 Piece	95.00
ART NOVO, see Dogwood	
Art, Cake Plate	50.00
Art, Cake Stand	60.00
Art, Goblet	18.00

Pressed Glass, Actress, Creamer

Pressed Glass, Arched Fleur-De-Lis, Sugar

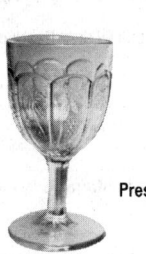

Pressed Glass, Arched Grape, Goblet

Art, Spooner .... 22.00 To 29.00
Art, Sugar, Covered 42.50
Artichoke, Butter, Covered, Frosted 65.00
Ashburton With Sawtooth, Tumbler 60.00
Ashburton, Celery, Scalloped Top 125.00
Ashburton, Decanter, Bar Lip, 1 Quart 55.00
Ashburton, Eggcup, Flint .... 14.00 To 18.00
Ashburton, Goblet, Barrel Shape 35.00
Ashburton, Goblet, Flaring Top 49.00
Ashburton, Goblet, Flint .... 22.00 To 40.00
Ashburton, Whiskey, Handled 75.00
Ashburton, Wine, Flint .... 20.00 To 25.00
Atlanta, Butter, Covered 55.00
Atlanta, Cake Stand 115.00
Atlanta, Celery, Clear, 7 In. 35.00
Atlanta, Goblet 75.00
Atlanta, Sauce 22.50
Atlanta, Sauce, Set Of 4 .... 36.00
Atlanta, Toothpick 35.00
Atlanta, Toothpick, Frosted 45.00
Atlas, Cake Stand, 9 In. 25.00
Atlas, Celery 28.00
Atlas, Creamer, Flat, Etched 23.00
Atlas, Salt, Master 10.00
Atlas, Toothpick 15.00
Aurora, Spooner 8.00
Aztec, Bonbon, Footed, 4 1/2 In. 13.00
Aztec, Creamer 26.00
Aztec, Tumbler 6.00
Aztec, Wine 14.50
Baby Face, Goblet, Frosted 75.00
Baby Lion, Cake Salver 82.00
    BABY THUMBPRINT, see Dakota
Bakewell Block, Goblet, Flint 82.00
Bakewell Block, Tumbler, Flint 45.00
Bakewell Block, Whiskey, Handled 100.00
    BALDER, see Pennsylvania
    BALKY MULE, see Currier & Ives
Ball & Swirl, Creamer .... 22.50 To 25.00
Ball & Swirl, Creamer, Footed 15.00
Ball & Swirl, Goblet, Flint 20.00
Ball & Swirl, Mug 10.00
Ball & Swirl, Mug, Child's 20.00
Ball & Swirl, Spooner 20.00
Baltimore Pear, Butter, Covered .... 50.00 To 65.00
Baltimore Pear, Celery 47.00
Baltimore Pear, Creamer 40.00
Baltimore Pear, Pitcher, Water 80.00
Baltimore Pear, Plate, 9 1/4 In. 35.00
Baltimore Pear, Sugar & Creamer 60.00
Baltimore Pear, Sugar, Covered 45.00
    BAMBOO, see Broken Column
    BANDED BEADED GRAPE MEDALLION, see Beaded Grape Medallion,
    Banded
Banded Buckle, Creamer, Applied Handle 45.00
Banded Buckle, Goblet 22.00
Banded Buckle, Spooner .... 13.00 To 26.00
Banded Buckle, Sugar, Covered 45.00
Banded Buckle, Tumbler, Clear 30.00
    BANDED PORTLAND, when flashed with pink, is sometimes called Maiden
    Blush
Banded Portland, Celery 32.00
Banded Portland, Compote, High Standard 42.50

Banded Portland, Compote, Open, 8 1/2 In. 42.00
Banded Portland, Dish, Olive, Maiden Blush 28.00
Banded Portland, Goblet 30.00
Banded Portland, Pitcher, Water, Child's .... 32.00 To 38.00
Banded Portland, Pitcher, Water, Gold Trim 175.00
Banded Portland, Pitcher, Water, 8 In. 110.00
Banded Portland, Sauce, 5 In. .... 11.50 To 16.00
Banded Portland, Saucer 8.00
Banded Portland, Toothpick .... 14.00 To 39.50
Banded Portland, Tumbler 29.50
Banded Portland, Tumbler, Gold Trim .... 29.00 To 50.00
Banded Portland, Vase, 6 In. 14.00
Banded Prism Bar, Goblet 20.00
    BANDED RAINDROP, see Candlewick
Banded Star, Creamer .... 20.00 To 40.00
    OTHER BANDED PATTERNS, see under name of basic pattern
    BAR & DIAMOND, see Kokomo
Barberry, Creamer 25.00
Barberry, Cup, Plate 10.00
Barberry, Goblet 25.00
Barberry, Syrup, Pewter Lid, Dated 130.00
    BARLEY & OATS, see Wheat & Barley
    BARLEY & WHEAT, see Wheat & Barley
Barley, Goblet 25.00
Barley, Goblet, Flint 20.00
Barley, Pitcher, Water 32.00
Barley, Wine 18.00
Barred Forget-Me-Not, Bread Plate, Canary 45.00
Barred Forget-Me-Not, Spooner 20.00
    BARRED OVALS, see Banded Portland
Barred Star, Goblet 14.00
Barrel Argus, Goblet, Flint 39.00
Barrel Argus, Tumbler 45.00
    BARREL HONEYCOMB, see also Honeycomb
    BARRELED BLOCK, see Red Block
Basket Weave, Cup & Saucer, Amber 22.00
Basket Weave, Cup & Saucer, Blue 25.00
Basket Weave, Goblet, Amber 25.00
Basket Weave, Pitcher, Water, Amber 40.00
Basket Weave, Pitcher, Water, Canary 38.00
Basket, Leaf Pattern, 13 1/2 In. 45.00
Bead & Scroll, Cruet, Etched 45.00
Bead & Scroll, Goblet 17.00
Bead & Scroll, Pitcher, Green 100.00
Bead & Scroll, Wine 22.00
Beaded Acorn, Goblet, Leaf Band 25.00
Beaded Arch Panels, Creamer 18.00
Beaded Band, Cake Stand, 7 1/2 In. 28.00
Beaded Band, Dish, Relish 12.50
Beaded Band, Wine 18.00
    BEADED BULL'S-EYE & DRAPE, see Alabama
Beaded Chain, Salt 23.00
Beaded Chain, Spooner 16.00
Beaded Circle, Creamer, Green, Gold, Enamel 35.00
Beaded Dart Band, Spillholder 18.00
Beaded Dewdrop, Bowl, Oblong, Flint, 8 1/2 In. 25.00
Beaded Dewdrop, Cake Stand, 8 1/2 In. .... 42.00 To 45.00
Beaded Dewdrop, Compote, Pedestal, 6 1/4 In. 25.00
Beaded Dewdrop, Creamer 65.00
Beaded Dewdrop, Dish, Pickle 15.00
Beaded Dewdrop, Dish, 6 1/4 X 4 1/4 In. 20.00
Beaded Dewdrop, Relish, 8 1/4 X 4 1/4 In. .... 24.00 To 35.00
Beaded Dewdrop, Saucer, 5 In. 35.00

Beaded Dewdrop, Sugar Shaker	85.00
Beaded Dewdrop, Wine	75.00
Beaded Ellipse And Fan, Creamer	17.00
Beaded Ellipse, Pitcher, Milk	25.00
Beaded Grape Medallion, Creamer	48.00
Beaded Grape Medallion, Eggcup	20.00
Beaded Grape Medallion, Goblet	20.00
Beaded Grape Medallion, Spooner	18.50 To 30.00
Beaded Grape Medallion, Spooner, Banded	28.00
Beaded Grape, Bowl, Green, 3 3/4 In.	16.00
Beaded Grape, Bowl, Green, 4 1/2 In.	18.00
Beaded Grape, Bowl, Green, 4 1/2 X 7 In.Diam.	25.00
Beaded Grape, Bowl, Green, 5 1/2 In.	20.00
Beaded Grape, Bowl, Green, 6 1/2 In.	40.00
Beaded Grape, Bowl, Green, 6 1/4 X 8 1/4 In.Diam.	35.00
Beaded Grape, Bowl, Green, 8 In.	30.00
Beaded Grape, Bowl, Square, 8 In.	20.00
Beaded Grape, Bread Tray, Green	40.00
Beaded Grape, Butter, Covered, Green	85.00
Beaded Grape, Cake Stand, Green, 9 In.	75.00 To 90.00
Beaded Grape, Celery, Green, 11 In.	50.00 To 65.00
Beaded Grape, Compote, Jelly	55.00
Beaded Grape, Creamer, Gold Trim	40.00
Beaded Grape, Cruet, Original Stopper, Green	95.00 To 105.00
Beaded Grape, Pitcher, Green, 6 In.Square	85.00
Beaded Grape, Pitcher, Water, Green	125.00
Beaded Grape, Plate, Green, 8 1/2 In.	45.00
Beaded Grape, Salt & Pepper, Green	85.00
Beaded Grape, Spooner, Green	50.00
Beaded Grape, Sugar, Covered, Green	75.00
Beaded Grape, Toothpick, Gold Trim, Green	55.00
Beaded Grape, Tumbler, Green	45.00
Beaded Grape, Vase, Green, 7 In.	50.00
Beaded Loop, Cake Stand, 9 In.	35.00
Beaded Loop, Compote, Open, 5 In.	15.00
Beaded Loop, Cruet	32.00
Beaded Loop, Goblet	24.50
Beaded Loop, Spooner	22.00
Beaded Loop, Tumbler, Set Of 5	75.00
Beaded Loop, Wine, Flint	40.00
BEADED MEDALLION, see Beaded Mirror	
Beaded Mirror, Compote, Open	35.00
Beaded Mirror, Spooner	25.00
Beaded Oval & Scroll, Sugar & Creamer, Covered	90.00
Beaded Ovals In Sand, Creamer, Apple Green	45.00
BEADED STAR, see Shimmering Star	
Beaded Swirl, Creamer, Child's	14.00
Beaded Swirl, Creamer, Green	37.00
Beaded Swirl, Cruet, Blown Discs	22.00
Beaded Swirl, Cup, Custard, Emerald	15.00
Beaded Swirl, Eggcup	12.50
Beaded Swirl, Saltshaker, Green, Pair	30.00
Beaded Swirl, Sugar, Child's, Covered	25.00
Beaded Swirl, Tumbler, Green	25.00
Beaded Tulip, Creamer	45.00
Beaded Tulip, Goblet	25.00 To 27.00
Beaded Tulip, Pitcher, Water	45.00
Beaded Tulip, Wine	25.00
BEARDED MAN, see Viking	
Beatty Rib, Dish, Oblong	24.00
Beatty Rib, Sauce, Flat	16.50
Beehive, Jug, Impressed William Darst, Omaha, Neb.	70.00
Belcher Loop, Celery, Knobbed Stem, 5 X 10 In.	70.00

Belcher Loop, Compote, Footed, Flint, 8 1/4 X 10 1/2 In.	70.00
Belfast, Goblet	12.00
Bellflower, Bowl, 8 In.	95.00
Bellflower, Cordial, 4 In.	68.00
Bellflower, Creamer, Footed, 6 1/2 In.	60.00
Bellflower, Eggcup	20.00 To 28.00
Bellflower, Goblet	24.00 To 32.00
Bellflower, Goblet, Flint	48.00
Bellflower, Plate, 6 In.	60.00
Bellflower, Spooner	20.00
Bellflower, Spooner, Single Vine	27.00
Bellflower, Tumbler	35.00 To 50.00
Bellflower, Wine, Knob Stem, Flint	55.00
Belmont, Butter, Covered	80.00
BELTED WORCESTER, see Worcester, Belted	
BENT BUCKLE, see New Hampshire	
BERKELEY, see Blocked Arches	
Berry Cluster, Creamer	16.00 To 25.00
Bethlehem Star, Butter	55.00
Bethlehem Star, Compote, Covered, 5 1/4 In.	50.00
Beveled Diamond & Star, Creamer	15.00
Beveled Diamond & Star, Pitcher	35.00 To 36.50
Beveled Diamond & Star, Plate, 10 In.	15.00
Beveled Diamond & Star, Tankard	35.00
Beveled Diamond & Star, Wine	15.00
Beveled Star, Celery, Green	75.00
Beveled Star, Jelly, Green	30.00
Beveled Star, Sugar, Covered, Green	55.00
Beveled Star, Toothpick	25.00
Bicycle Girl, Pitcher, Water	350.00
BIG BLOCK, see Henrietta	
Bigler, Wine	36.00
Bilikin Flute, Wine	22.00
Birch Leaf, Goblet	16.50
Birch Leaf, Salt, Pedestal, White, Flint	30.00
Bird & Strawberry, Bowl, Fruit, Ruffled, Large	60.00
Bird & Strawberry, Bowl, 4-Legged, Oval, 9 1/2 In.	58.00
Bird & Strawberry, Butter, Covered	65.00 To 85.00
Bird & Strawberry, Cake Stand, 6 1/2 In.	50.00
Bird & Strawberry, Creamer	45.00
Bird & Strawberry, Creamer, Gold Rim	135.00
Bird & Strawberry, Cup, Punch	15.00 To 35.00
Bird & Strawberry, Dish, Candy, Heart Shaped, 5 3/4 In.Diam.	28.00
Bird & Strawberry, Pitcher, Water	165.00
Bird & Strawberry, Spooner	40.00
Bird & Strawberry, Sugar, Covered	75.00
Bird & Strawberry, Tumbler	18.00 To 40.00
BIRD IN RING, see Butterfly & Fan	
Bismarc Star, Goblet	18.50
Blackberry, Pitcher, Buttermilk	15.00
Bleeding Heart, Cake Stand	48.00
Bleeding Heart, Compote, Covered, 8 1/4 In.	70.00
Bleeding Heart, Creamer, Applied Handle, 1870-80	65.00
Bleeding Heart, Goblet	12.00 To 29.00
Bleeding Heart, Spooner	24.50 To 36.00
Block & Circle, Champagne	22.00
Block & Circle, Goblet	10.00
Block & Circle, Wine	17.50
Block & Fan, Cake Stand, Amber, 10 1/4 In.	25.00
Block & Fan, Celery	18.00
Block & Fan, Decanter, Water	30.00
Block & Fan, Ice Tub	55.00
Block & Fan, Wine	37.50

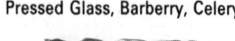

Pressed Glass, Barberry, Celery

Pressed Glass, Ashburton, Champagne,
Presentation Piece

Pressed Glass, Beaded
Grape, Toothpick

Pressed Glass, Bellflower, Compote

Pressed Glass, Bleeding Heart, Goblet

Pressed Glass, Bigler, Vase

Pressed Glass, Broken Column, Goblet

Pressed Glass, Bull's-Eye, Creamer

Pressed Glass, Buckle, Goblet

BLOCK & FINE CUT, see Fine Cut & Block	
Block & Honeycomb, Goblet	16.00
Block & Iris, Goblet	12.50
Block & Pleat, Celery	18.00
BLOCK & STAR, see Valencia Waffle	
Block & Sunburst, Sugar	34.00
BLOCK WITH STARS, see Hanover	
Block With Thumbprint, Celery, Flint	35.00
Block, Butter, Covered	42.00
Block, Tumbler, Amber	22.00
Block, Water Set, Amber, 7 Piece	210.00
Block, Wine, Footed, 4 In.	6.00
Blocked Arches, Syrup	32.00
BLOCKHOUSE, see Hanover	
BLUEBIRD, see Bird & Strawberry	
Bouquet, Bowl, 8 1/2 In.	22.00
Bouquet, Goblet	15.00
Bow Tie, Cake Stand, 9 In.	45.00
Bow Tie, Compote, High Standard	55.00
Bow Tie, Compote, Open	52.00
Bow Tie, Goblet	36.00 To 50.00
Bow Tie, Jar, Jam, Covered	38.00 To 55.00
Bow Tie, Pitcher, Juice	55.00
Bow Tie, Punch Bowl, Footed, 10 X 10 In.	100.00
Bow Tie, Spooner	15.00 To 25.00
Bow Tie, Sugar, Covered	52.00 To 55.00
BRADFORD BLACKBERRY, see Bradford Grape	
Bradford Grape, Goblet, Flint	35.00
Bradford Grape, Tumbler	95.00
Branched Tree, Pitcher, Milk	65.00
Branched Tree, Pitcher, Water	58.00
Brazilian, Toothpick	25.00
Bringing Home The Cows, Pitcher, Water	350.00
Britanic, Compote, Open, 9 In.	28.00
Broken Column, Bowl, 5 In.Square	67.50
Broken Column, Cake Stand, 9 In.	55.00
Broken Column, Celery	33.00 To 35.00
Broken Column, Compote, Flared Rim, 6 In.	55.00
Broken Column, Cracker Jar	55.00 To 65.00
Broken Column, Creamer	32.50
Broken Column, Spooner	25.00
Broken Column, Spooner, Red Dot	45.00
Brooklyn Flute, Champagne, Flint	35.00
Brooklyn Flute, Goblet, Flint	20.00
BRYCE, see Ribbon Candy	
Buckle & Star, Creamer	24.00 To 30.00
Buckle & Star, Spooner	24.00
Buckle & Star, Wine	26.00
Buckle, Bowl, Flint, 10 In.	60.00
Buckle, Compote, Open, 8 1/2 In.	38.00
Buckle, Goblet	15.00 To 28.50
Buckle, Spooner	36.00
Buckle, Tumbler	35.00
Budded Ivy, Spooner	25.00
Bull's-Eye & Bar, Goblet, Flint	55.00
Bull's-Eye & Daisy, Goblet, Red Eyes	26.50
Bull's-Eye & Daisy, Nappy, Green Eyes	17.50
Bull's-Eye & Daisy, Wine, Cranberry Eyes	26.50
Bull's-Eye & Drape, Sugar, Open, 4 In.	32.00
BULL'S-EYE & FAN, see Daisies in Oval Panels	
Bull's-Eye & Pillar, Wine, Flint	45.00
Bull's-Eye & Rosette, Tumbler	45.00
BULL'S-EYE BAND, see Reverse Torpedo	

BULL'S-EYE VARIANT, see Texas Bull's-Eye

Bull's-Eye, Celery, Flint	72.00
Bull's-Eye, Decanter, Bar Lip, Flint, Quart	110.00
Bull's-Eye, Goblet	50.00 To 95.00
Bull's-Eye, Grape & Bead, Lamp, 9 1/2 In.	95.00
Bull's-Eye, Lamp, Green, 8 1/2 In.	130.00
Bull's-Eye, Sugar, Covered, Flint	105.00
Bull's-Eye, Toothpick, Beaded Panel, Gold Trim	17.00
Bull's-Eye, Tumbler	75.00
Bull's-Eye, Wine, Flint	40.00
Bunker Hill, Bread Plate	60.00
Butterfly & Fan, Creamer	35.00
Butterfly & Fan, Plate	35.00
Butterfly With Spray, Mug, 2 1/2 In.	20.00
Butterfly, Compote, Stemmed, Hartley Co., 1881	58.00
Button & Star, Toothpick	18.00
Button Arches, Creamer, Clear, 4 In.	17.00
Button Arches, Sugar, Covered	25.00
Button Panel, Butter, Child's, Covered	65.00 To 68.00
Button Panel, Butter, Covered	55.00
Button Panel, Sugar, Covered, Gold Trim	45.00
Button Panel, Tumbler, Clear, Gold Trim	15.00
Buzz Star, Goblet	9.00
Cabbage Rose, Cake Stand	65.00
Cabbage Rose, Celery	38.00 To 60.00
Cabbage Rose, Goblet	32.00
Cabbage Rose, Wine	40.00 To 43.00
Cable With Ring, Sugar, Covered, Flint	68.00
Cable, Eggcup	28.00
Cable, Goblet, Flint	38.00 To 45.00
Cable, Honey	15.00
Cable, Plate	55.00
Cable, Salt, Master, Pedestal	24.00
Cable, Spooner	45.00
Cadmus, Toothpick	22.00

CALIFORNIA, see Beaded Grape
CAMEO, see Ceres
CANADIAN DRAPE, see Garfield Drape

Canadian, Compote, Scenes, Open, C.1880	50.00
Canadian, Goblet	65.00
Canadian, Pitcher, Water	85.00 To 95.00
Canadian, Wine	35.00 To 38.00
Candlewick, Cake Stand	35.00
Candlewick, Compote, 8 In.	38.50
Candlewick, Cup & Saucer	25.00

CANDY RIBBON, see Ribbon Candy

Cane & Fan, Soup Tureen	30.00
Cane & Rosette, Creamer	26.00
Cane Horseshoe, Tumbler, Gold Rim, Star & Rayed Base	18.00
Cane Shield, Tumbler, Green	22.00
Cane, Goblet	22.50
Cane, Honey	15.00
Cane, Pitcher, Water	25.00 To 28.50
Cane, Plate, Toddy, Apple Green	16.50
Cane, Sugar, Covered	40.00
Cane, Tumbler, Blue	22.00 To 25.00
Cape Cod, Cruet	18.50
Capitol Building, Champagne	25.00
Cardinal Bird, Creamer	25.00 To 50.00
Cardinal Bird, Goblet	28.50 To 42.00
Cardinal Bird, Honey, 3 1/2 In.Diam.	32.50
Cardinal, Sauce, Footed	15.00

CARMEN, see Paneled Diamond & Finecut

Pressed Glass, Bull's-Eye & Daisy, Goblet

Pressed Glass, Cable, Spooner

Pressed Glass, Button Arches, Spittoon

Pressed Glass, Cabbage Rose, Mug

Pressed Glass, Cable With Rings,
Footed Bowl

Pressed Glass, Canadian, Compote

Pressed Glass, Cardinal, Spooner

Carolina, Goblet, Wine, Ruby Stain, Souvenir 26.00
Carolina, Pitcher, Water .... 12.00 To 47.50
Cathedral, Compote, High Standard, Amber 42.00
Cathedral, Creamer 28.00
Cathedral, Cruet, Original Stopper, Amber 65.00
Cathedral, Goblet, Amber 40.00
Cathedral, Spooner 25.00
Cathedral, Tumbler .... 12.00 To 24.00
Cathedral, Wine 29.00
    CENTENNIAL, see also Liberty Bell; Washington Centennial
Centennial, Bread Plate 65.00
Centennial, Goblet 30.00
Centennial, Mug 30.00
Ceres, Pitcher, Milk, Small 15.00
Ceres, Sugar, Covered 45.00
Chain & Shield, Creamer .... 18.00 To 23.00
Chain & Shield, Goblet 25.00
    CHAIN WITH DIAMONDS, see Washington Centennial
Chain With Star, Creamer 26.00
Chain With Star, Goblet .... 15.00 To 23.00
Chain With Star, Pitcher 50.00
Chain With Star, Relish 10.50
Chain With Star, Spooner .... 15.00 To 29.00
Chain, Butter, Covered .... 16.00 To 20.00
Chain, Compote, With Cover, 12 In. 45.00
Chain, Creamer .... 16.00 To 20.00
Chain, Goblet 22.00
Chain, Spooner 15.00
Chain, Sugar, Covered 25.00
Chain, Wine 19.00
Champion, Butter, Covered, Gold Trim 25.00
Champion, Spooner 18.00
Champion, Sugar, Covered 25.00
Champion, Wine 10.00
Chandelier, Celery 27.00
Chandelier, Goblet 55.00
Checkerboard, Butter 45.00
Checkerboard, Cruet, Blown 25.00
Cherry & Fig, Goblet 25.00
Cherry, Spooner, Frosted 10.00
Chestnut Oak, Sugar 32.00
Chicken, Celery 30.00
    CHURCH WINDOWS, see Tulip Petals
Circle, Compote, Jelly 14.50
Clambroth, Eggcup, Cable, Flint 550.00
Classic Medallion, Bowl, Footed, Low 35.00
Classic Medallion, Creamer 15.00
Classic, Celery .... 150.00 To 165.00
Classic, Compote, Covered, Log Feet 150.00
Classic, Creamer, Log Feet 185.00
Classic, Goblet .... 185.00 To 250.00
Classic, Pitcher, Open Log Feet, 10 In. 275.00
Classic, Sauce, Log Feet 32.50
Classic, Spooner 95.00
Classic, Spooner, Frosted 78.00
Classic, Spooner, Log Feet 125.00
Clear & Diamond Panels, Butter, Covered, Blue 70.00
Clear & Diamond Panels, Goblet 15.00
Clear & Diamond Panels, Table Set, Child's, Blue, 4 Piece 210.00
Clear Panels With Cord Band, Compote, Covered, 8 X 13 1/2 In. 35.00
Clear Panels With Cord Band, Relish, Handled, 8 1/2 In. 9.00
Clear Panels With Cord Band, Wine 15.00
Clematis, Goblet 34.00

Coarse Ribs, Butter, Covered	13.50
Coarse Zig-Zag, Cake Stand	25.00
Coarse Zig-Zag, Plate, 8 1/4 In.	12.00
Coin & Dewdrop, Goblet	28.50
COIN SPOT, see Coin Spot Category	
Colonial Panel, Punch Bowl, 16 In.Diam.	45.00
Colonial, Sherbet, Footed	8.00
Colonial, Water Set, Child's, 7 Piece	90.00
Colonial, Whiskey, Handled	45.00
Colonial, Wine	45.00
Colorado, Banana Boat	25.00
Colorado, Berry Bowl, Footed, 9 In.	42.00
Colorado, Berry Set, Green, 5 Piece	95.00 To 115.00
Colorado, Berry Set, 5 Piece	125.00
Colorado, Bowl, Fluted, Green, Gold Trim, 9 In.	40.00
Colorado, Bowl, Green, Crimped, 7 In.	35.00
Colorado, Bowl, Ruffled, 7 In.	15.00
Colorado, Butter, Clear Dome Cover	60.00
Colorado, Butter, Covered, Green	145.00
Colorado, Cake Stand	18.00
Colorado, Compote, Crimped, Footed, 6 X 4 1/2 In.	20.00
Colorado, Creamer, Emerald, Souvenir, Gold Trim	30.00
Colorado, Creamer, Gold Trim, Souvenir, Dated 1901	110.00
Colorado, Creamer, Green	50.00
Colorado, Creamer, Green, Gold Trim, Large	40.00
Colorado, Dish, Candy, Green	20.00
Colorado, Match Holder, Gold Trim, Green	35.00
Colorado, Mug, Maggie Colgan 1902, Green	25.00
Colorado, Mug, Souvenir, Green, Miniature	18.00
Colorado, Nappy, Blue, Tricornered	30.00
Colorado, Sauce, Gold Trim, Flint, Green	22.00
Colorado, Sugar, Covered, Green	85.00
Colorado, Toothpick, Blue	35.00
Colorado, Toothpick, Gold Trim, Green	28.00
Colorado, Toothpick, Green	30.00
Colorado, Toothpick, Merry Christmas, Green	35.00
Colorado, Toothpick, Souvenir, Buffalo Exposition, 1901	25.00
Colorado, Toothpick, Souvenir, Lebanon, N.H., Green	40.00
Colorado, Tray, Card, Imperial Fair, 1905, Green	28.00
Colorado, Tray, Footed, Round, Clear	22.50
Columbia, Creamer, Miniature	25.00
Columbia, Sugar	40.00
Columbian Coin, Celery, Frosted	35.00 To 48.00
Columbian Coin, Creamer	85.00
Columbian Coin, Creamer, Frosted	85.00
Columbian Coin, Epergne, Gilded Coins	135.00
Columbian Coin, Goblet, Frosted	65.00
Columbian Coin, Pitcher, Milk, Gold Trim	165.00
Columbian Coin, Syrup, Frosted	135.00
Columbian Coin, Tray, Water, Frosted	115.00
Comet, Goblet, Flint	65.00
COMPACT, see Snail	
Continental, Bread Plate	65.00
Cord & Tassel, Compote, Covered, Oval, 5 X 8 In.Diam.	65.00
Cord & Tassel, Goblet	18.50 To 20.00
Cord Drapery, Butter, Green	150.00
Cord Drapery, Compote	55.00
Cord Drapery, Compote, Covered, 4 In.	60.00
Cord Drapery, Cruet	35.00
Cord Drapery, Relish, 9 1/4 In.	25.00
Cord Drapery, Sauce	4.00
Cord Medallion, Goblet	22.50
Cord Rosette, Goblet	35.00

Pressed Glass, Cathedral, Compote

Pressed Glass, Ceres, Covered Bowl

Pressed Glass, Classic, Covered Compote

Pressed Glass, Columbian Coin, Salt & Pepper

Pressed Glass, Chain & Shield, Pitcher

Pressed Glass, Chicken, Mustard Jar

Pressed Glass, Croesus, Toothpick

Cordova, Bottle, Perfume	15.00
Cordova, Toothpick	35.00
Cornucopia, Pitcher	60.00
Cornucopia, Pitcher, Water	50.00
Cornucopia, Wine	25.00
PRESSED GLASS, COSMOS, see Cosmos	
Cottage, Creamer	19.00 To 20.00
Cottage, Cup & Saucer	35.00
Cottage, Sugar, Covered	28.00
CRANE, see Stork	
Crescent & Fan, Decanter	58.00
Crescent & Fan, Rose Bowl	20.00
Croesus, Berry Set, Amethyst, 5 Piece	175.00
Croesus, Berry Set, Gold Trim, Green, 5 Piece	140.00
Croesus, Butter, Green	185.00
Croesus, Condiment Tray, Green & Gold	45.00
Croesus, Cruet, Original Stopper, Gold Trim, Green	225.00
Croesus, Pitcher, Water, Gold Trim, Green	115.00
Croesus, Saltshaker	50.00
Croesus, Spooner, Green, Gold Trim	55.00
Croesus, Spooner, Purple, Gold Trim	85.00 To 120.00
Croesus, Sugar, Covered	165.00
Croesus, Sugar, Covered, Green, Gold Trim	95.00
Croesus, Tray, Condiment, Emerald Green	48.00
Croesus, Tumbler, Green, Gold Trim, Set Of 6	350.00
Croesus, Tumbler, Purple, Gold Trim	68.00 To 75.00
Croesus, Water Set, Amethyst, Gold Trim, 8 Tumblers, 9 Piece	295.00
Crossbar, Creamer	12.00
Crossed Block, Goblet	25.00
Crossed Ovals, Wine	10.00
Crossed Pressed Leaf, Spooner	22.00
Crowfoot, Creamer	27.50
Crowfoot, Pitcher, Water	38.00 To 45.00
Crowfoot, Spooner, Footed	26.00
CROWN JEWELS, see Chandelier	
Crusader Cross, Goblet	12.00
Crystal Wedding, Butter, Covered	45.00
Crystal Wedding, Cake Stand, Clear	35.00
Crystal Wedding, Celery, Etched	39.00
Crystal Wedding, Pitcher, Milk, 7 In.	110.00
CUBE & DIAMOND, see Milton	
CUBE & FAN, see Pineapple & Fan	
Cube, Goblet, Square Stem, Etched	12.00
CUPID & PSYCHE, see Psyche & Cupid	
Cupid & Venus, Bread Plate	32.00 To 42.00
Cupid & Venus, Bread Plate, Amber	55.00
Cupid & Venus, Celery	22.00 To 45.00
Cupid & Venus, Champagne	95.00
Cupid & Venus, Compote, High Standard, Covered, 8 3/4 In.	100.00
Cupid & Venus, Creamer, Footed	50.00
Cupid & Venus, Cruet, Original Stopper	85.00
Cupid & Venus, Goblet	45.00 To 52.50
Cupid & Venus, Jar, Jam, Covered	38.00
Cupid & Venus, Mug, Miniature, 2 In.	28.00
Cupid & Venus, Mug, 3 1/2 In.	18.00
Cupid & Venus, Pitcher, Milk, Amber	95.00 To 195.00
Cupid & Venus, Pitcher, Water	38.00 To 70.00
Cupid & Venus, Plate, Amber, 10 1/2 In.	75.00
Cupid & Venus, Plate, Clear, 10 1/2 In.	15.00
Cupid & Venus, Sauce, Footed, 3 1/2 In.	7.00 To 14.00
Cupid & Venus, Spooner	24.00
Cupid & Venus, Wine	65.00
Currant, Cake Plate, 11 In.	52.50
Currant, Creamer	60.00

Currant, Goblet .... 22.00 To 25.00
Currant, Spooner 27.00
Currier & Ives, Goblet 28.00
Currier & Ives, Pitcher, Milk 38.00
Currier & Ives, Pitcher, Water 38.00
Currier & Ives, Spooner 22.00
Currier & Ives, Tray, Water, Clear 35.00
Currier & Ives, Wine .... 16.00 To 28.00
Curtain Tieback, Compote, Covered, 7 1/2 In. 28.00
Curtain Tieback, Goblet 12.50
Curtain, Celery .... 24.00 To 27.00
Curtain, Spooner 22.00
Cut Block, Wine 30.00
Cut Log, Bowl, Curved, 7 X 3 In. 15.00
Cut Log, Butter, Covered 75.00
Cut Log, Cake Stand, Pedestal, 10 In. 75.00
Cut Log, Cake Stand, 8 1/2 In. 65.00
Cut Log, Celery .... 50.00 To 65.00
Cut Log, Compote, Covered, 8 In. 90.00
Cut Log, Compote, Jelly, Covered, 6 In. 65.00
Cut Log, Compote, Scalloped, 6 In. 35.00
Cut Log, Creamer .... 6.00 To 50.00
Cut Log, Creamer, Individual 10.00
Cut Log, Creamer, 3 In. 15.00
Cut Log, Goblet .... 50.00 To 55.00
Cut Log, Honey, Covered, Large 160.00
Cut Log, Mug .... 13.50 To 14.00
Cut Log, Mug, C.1880 .... 17.00
Cut Log, Nappy 18.50
Cut Log, Nappy, Handled 15.00
Cut Log, Pitcher, Water 85.00
Cut Log, Pitcher, Water, 12 1/2 In. 135.00
Cut Log, Spooner 45.00
Cut Log, Sugar & Creamer, Individual, Covered 55.00
Cut Log, Sugar, Covered 70.00
Cut Log, Wine .... 18.50 To 30.00
Dagger, Goblet, Etched 35.00
Dahlia With Leaves, Creamer 30.00
Dahlia With Petal, Relish 20.00
Dahlia With Petal, Sugar, Gold Trim 25.00
Dahlia, Cake Plate .... 17.00 To 25.00
Dahlia, Cake Stand, Amber, 9 In. 65.00
Dahlia, Goblet 35.00
Dahlia, Goblet, Etched 32.00
Dahlia, Mug, Vaseline, Handled 38.00
Dahlia, Pitcher, Blue 150.00
Dahlia, Pitcher, Water .... 42.00 To 55.00
Dahlia, Plate, Blue, Closed Handles, 9 In. 50.00
Dahlia, Plate, Handled, 9 In. 24.00
Dahlia, Spooner 22.00
Dahlia, Wine 35.00
Daisies In Oval Panels, Berry Bowl 15.00
Daisies In Oval Panels, Cup, Custard 9.00
Daisies In Oval Panels, Goblet 16.00
Daisies In Oval Panels, Mug 11.50
Daisies In Oval Panels, Parfait, Handled 24.00
Daisies In Oval Panels, Spooner 11.00
Daisies In Oval Panels, Spooner, Green, Gold Trim 30.00
Daisies In Oval Panels, Toothpick .... 18.50 To 75.00
Daisies In Oval Panels, Tumbler, Green Eyes 18.50
Daisies In Oval Panels, Wine, Gold Trim 18.50
Daisy & Block, Goblet 12.50
    DAISY & BUTTON, see also Paneled Daisy & Button

Daisy & Button With Amber Panels, Bowl, 8 In.	50.00
Daisy & Button With Crossbar, Goblet, Amber	35.00 To 38.00
Daisy & Button With Crossbar, Pitcher, Water, Vaseline	90.00
Daisy & Button With Narcissus, Goblet	22.50
Daisy & Button With Narcissus, Wine	11.00
DAISY & BUTTON WITH OVAL PANELS, see Hartley	
Daisy & Button With Thumbprint, Syrup, Blue	120.00
Daisy & Button With V-Ornament, Celery	26.00
Daisy & Button With V-Ornament, Creamer	26.50
Daisy & Button With V-Ornament, Creamer, Amber	45.00
Daisy & Button With V-Ornament, Toothpick, Amber	25.00
Daisy & Button With V-Ornament, Tumbler, Amber	25.00
Daisy & Button, Bowl, Berry, Amber, 11 In.Diam.	85.00
Daisy & Button, Bowl, Berry, Single Amber Panel	47.00
Daisy & Button, Bowl, 2 X 5 X 9 In.Diam.	45.00
Daisy & Button, Butter, Amber Panel, Covered	135.00
Daisy & Button, Canoe, Amber, 14 In.	55.00
Daisy & Button, Canoe, 1 Pointed End, 14 In.	18.00
Daisy & Button, Celery, Triangular	28.00
Daisy & Button, Goblet	24.00
Daisy & Button, Goblet, Amber	20.00
Daisy & Button, Hat, Blue	22.00
Daisy & Button, Pitcher, Milk, Blue	49.00
Daisy & Button, Shoe, Original Perfume Bottle Inset, Blue	45.00
Daisy & Button, Shot Glass, Blue, 1 1/2 Ounce	30.00
Daisy & Button, Slipper, Dated 1886, 4 In.	35.00
Daisy & Button, Spooner, Amber Panel	60.00
Daisy & Button, Sugar, Amber Panel	40.00
Daisy & Button, Toothpick, Bucket With Bail, Amber	30.00
Daisy & Button, Toothpick, Hat Shape	15.00
Daisy & Button, Toothpick, Metal Rim, Amber	35.00
Daisy & Button, Toothpick, Tumbler Shape, Blue	45.00
Daisy & Button, Wine, Blue	20.00
Dakota, Cake Stand	45.00
Dakota, Celery, Etched	33.50 To 38.00
Dakota, Celery, Red Fern & Berry Trim	25.00
Dakota, Compote, Jelly, Covered, Etched	60.00 To 62.50
Dakota, Compote, 6 In.	35.00 To 42.00
Dakota, Creamer	55.00
Dakota, Goblet, Clear	28.50
Dakota, Goblet, Etched	36.00
Dakota, Goblet, Etched, Ruby Stain	75.00
Dakota, Goblet, Wide Band	25.00
Dakota, Goblet, 3 Row	18.00
Dakota, Mug	22.00
Dakota, Pitcher, Milk, Etched	78.00
Dakota, Sauce, Etched	26.00
Dakota, Sauce, Etched, Footed, 4 1/4 In.	8.00
Dakota, Spooner	28.00
Dakota, Spooner, Etched	35.00
Dakota, Sugar, Covered	39.00
Dakota, Table Set, Etched, 5 Piece	175.00
Dakota, Tankard	95.00
Dakota, Wine	16.00 To 30.00
Dakota, Wine, Etched	36.00
Darling Grape, Tumbler	13.00
Dart, Compote, Jelly	10.00
Deer & Dog, Celery	55.00 To 65.00
Deer & Dog, Compote, Etched, Covered, 9 X 15 In.	235.00
Deer & Dog, Pitcher, Water	260.00
Deer & Dog, Wine	75.00
Deer & Oak Tree, Pitcher, Water	95.00 To 145.00
Deer & Pine Tree, Bread Plate, 13 X 8 In.	35.00 To 45.00

Deer & Pine Tree, Celery, Footed 95.00
Deer & Pine Tree, Creamer 65.00
Deer & Pine Tree, Dish, Vegetable 9 X 5 3/4 In. 55.00
Deer & Pine Tree, Mug, Large 45.00
Deer & Pine Tree, Relish, 7 X 4 In. 35.00
Deer & Pine Tree, Spooner 35.00
Deer & Pine Tree, Sugar, Open 18.00
Deer & Pine Tree, Tray, Bread Plate, Amber 55.00
Deer, Dog & Hunter, Goblet, Etched 75.00
Deer, Dog & Hunter, Tankard, Water 175.00
Delaware, Banana Bowl, Gold Trim, Rose 55.00
Delaware, Berry Bowl, Green, 9 In. 35.00
Delaware, Berry, Green With Gold, Small 22.00
Delaware, Bowl, Green, Gold, 8 In. 40.00
Delaware, Bowl, Oval, Emerald, 12 In. 40.00
Delaware, Butter, Green 165.00
Delaware, Celery, Emerald Green, Gold Trim 65.00
Delaware, Creamer, Green 50.00
Delaware, Pitcher, 6 Tumblers, Rose 325.00
Delaware, Spooner 32.00
Delaware, Spooner, Green, Gold Trim .... 40.00 To 45.00
Delaware, Spooner, Rose 45.00
Delaware, Spooner, Rose, Gold Trim .... 55.00 To 75.00
Delaware, Tray, Dresser, 9 In. 30.00
Delaware, Tumbler, Amethyst 35.00
Delaware, Tumbler, Green, Gold Trim .... 32.00 To 40.00
Delaware, Tumbler, Rose, Gold Trim .... 35.00 To 45.00
Dew & Raindrop, Berry Set, 9 Piece 60.00
Dew & Raindrop, Cordial 12.00
Dew & Raindrop, Cup, Punch .... 5.00 To 6.00
Dew & Raindrop, Goblet 30.00
Dew & Raindrop, Sugar, Covered 50.00
Dew & Raindrop, Tumbler 7.00
Dewdrop Bands, Goblet 15.00
Dewdrop In Points, Bread Plate, Vine Border, 9 In. 25.00
Dewdrop In Points, Goblet 25.00
    DEWDROP WITH FLOWERS, see Quantico
Dewdrop With Star, Salt, Footed, Set Of 3 .... 20.00
Dewdrop With Star, Sauce, Footed, 4 1/2 In. 6.50
Dewdrop, Dish, Relish 8.50
Dewdrop, Goblet 16.00
Dewdrop, Wine 15.00
    DEWEY, see also Admiral Dewey
Dewey, Creamer, Canary 41.00
Dewey, Pitcher, Gridley, You May Fire When Ready 95.00
Dewey, Pitcher, Milk .... 45.00 To 65.00
Dewey, Pitcher, Water .... 38.00 To 79.00
Dewey, Pitcher, Water, Patriotic, Dewey At Manila, 9 In. 60.00
Dewey, Pitcher, Water, Sailor 115.00
Diagonal Band & Fan, Goblet 32.00
Diagonal Band & Fan, Wine 12.50
Diagonal Band, Bread Plate, Motto Eureka, 11 1/2 X 9 In. 32.50
Diagonal Band, Bread Plate, 13 In. 21.00
Diagonal Band, Butter, Covered .... 30.00 To 35.00
Diagonal Band, Celery 22.00
Diagonal Band, Celery, Clear .... 18.50 To 22.00
Diagonal Band, Champagne, Clear 15.00
Diagonal Band, Creamer .... 17.00 To 19.00
Diagonal Band, Creamer, Clear 20.00
Diagonal Band, Goblet .... 15.00 To 22.00
Diagonal Band, Relish, 8 In. 10.00
    DIAMOND & SUNBURST, see also Flattened Diamond & Sunburst
Diamond & Sunburst Zippers, Wine 8.00

Pressed Glass, Psyche &
Cupid, Creamer

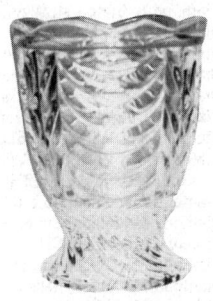

Pressed Glass, Curtain, Spooner

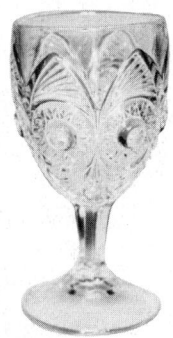

Pressed Glass, Daisies In Oval
Panels, Goblet

Pressed Glass, Cupid &
Venus, Bread Plate

Pressed Glass, Daisy & Button
With Crossbar, Goblet

Pressed Glass, Daisy & Button
With Thumbprint, Goblet

Pressed Glass, Delaware, Pitcher

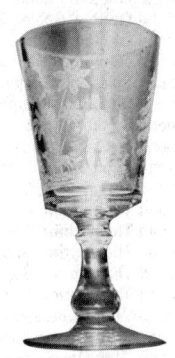

Pressed Glass, Deer &
Dog, Goblet

Diamond & Sunburst, Goblet	12.00
Diamond & Sunburst, Sugar	24.00
Diamond & Sunburst, Wine	15.00
Diamond Band, Mug	25.00
Diamond Bar & Block, Spooner	10.00
Diamond Block, Decanter, Flint	125.00
Diamond Cut With Leaf, Creamer, Blue	45.00
Diamond Cut With Leaf, Goblet	15.00
Diamond Cut With Leaf, Sugar, Covered, Amber	65.00
Diamond Cut With Leaf, Wine	20.00
DIAMOND HORSESHOE, see Aurora	
Diamond Medallion, Butter, Covered	29.00
Diamond Medallion, Butter, Covered, Clear & Gold	35.00
Diamond Medallion, Celery	25.00
Diamond Medallion, Goblet	15.00 To 17.00
Diamond Medallion, Relish	8.00
Diamond Medallion, Spooner	19.00 To 30.00
Diamond Mirror, Creamer	15.00
Diamond Panel, Spooner, Child's, Green	25.00
DIAMOND POINT DISCS, see Eyewinker	
Diamond Point Heart, Toothpick, Green	18.00
DIAMOND POINT WITH PANELS, see Hinoto	
Diamond Point, Bowl, Flint, 6 1/4 In.Diam.	20.00
Diamond Point, Celery, Flared Top, Flint	62.00
Diamond Point, Champagne, Flint, 5 3/8 In.	75.00
Diamond Point, Claret, Flint	87.50
Diamond Point, Compote, Flared Top, Flint, 10 1/2 X 8 1/2 In.	70.00
Diamond Point, Eggcup, Flint	29.00
Diamond Point, Goblet, Flint	45.00 To 65.00
Diamond Point, Salt & Pepper	35.00
Diamond Point, Spooner, Flint	40.00
Diamond Point, Sugar, Covered, Flint	80.00
Diamond Point, Sugar, Flat Scalloped Base, Open, Flint	25.00
Diamond Point, Whiskey, Handled, Flint	75.00
Diamond Point, Wine, Flint	50.00 To 52.00
Diamond Quilted, Celery, Footed, Amber	38.00
Diamond Quilted, Creamer, Amethyst	55.00
Diamond Quilted, Goblet	15.00
Diamond Quilted, Goblet, Amber	30.00
Diamond Quilted, Goblet, Blue	30.00 To 65.00
Diamond Quilted, Goblet, Sapphire Blue	26.00
Diamond Quilted, Tumbler, Amethyst	38.00
Diamond Quilted, Wine, Footed, Amethyst	28.00
Diamond Splendor, Goblet, Gold Trim	18.00
Diamond Sunburst, Compote, Clear, 7 1/4 In.	12.50
Diamond Sunburst, Creamer, Hobbs	26.00
Diamond Sunburst, Wine	14.00 To 19.00
Diamond Thumbprint, Butter, Covered	160.00
Diamond Thumbprint, Celery, Petal Scalloped, Flint, 9 1/2 In.	200.00
Diamond Thumbprint, Champagne	350.00
Diamond Thumbprint, Compote, Flint, 8 1/2 In.Diam.	45.00
Diamond Thumbprint, Spooner	75.00
Diamond Thumbprint, Sugar, Covered	135.00
Diamond Thumbprint, Tumbler, Flint	95.00
Diamond With Double Fans, Goblet	18.50 To 22.50
Diamond With Double Fans, Sugar, Child's, Covered	20.00
Diamond With Double Fans, Wine	15.00
Diamond, Cake Stand, Blue	55.00
Diamonds In Diamonds, Creamer	12.00
Diapered Flower, Sugar, Covered, Opaque Blue	40.00
Diasy & Button With Crossbar, Creamer, Amber	45.00
Diasy & Button With Thumbprint, Goblet, Amber	25.00 To 30.00
Dice & Block, Cruet, Original Stopper, Amber	75.00

Dog With Rabbit In Mouth, Goblet, Etched 65.00
Dogwood, Berry, Master, Green, Paneled 65.00
Dogwood, Bowl, Green, Gold, Oval, Paneled 48.00
Dogwood, Bowl, Green, Paneled 75.00
Dogwood, Lamp, Paneled, 9 1/2 In. 55.00
Dolphin, Candlestick, Clambroth, Petal Socket 550.00
Dolphin, Candlestick, Clear, 10 3/4 In. 117.50
Dolphin, Compote, Frosted, 8 In. 65.00
Dolphin, Compote, Jelly, Frosted, 4 3/4 X 6 In.Diam. 75.00
Dolphin, Goblet, Footed, Frosted 95.00
    DORIC, see Feather
Dot & Dash, Goblet 12.00
Dot & Dash, Saucer, Footed 5.00
Dotted Loop, Wine 12.00
Double Beaded Band, Goblet 12.50
Double Beetle Band, Spooner, Blue 45.00
Double Dahlia & Lens, Toothpick, Traces Of Color 25.00
    DOUBLE DAISY, see Rosette Band
Double Fan, Bowl, 7 X 9 In. 35.00
Double Fan, Wine 8.00
    DOUBLE LOOP, see Double Loop & Dart
Double Loop & Dart, Goblet 15.00
Double Loop & Dart, Tumbler 20.00
Double Spear, Creamer 28.00
Double Spear, Sugar, Covered 22.50
Doyle's 500, Table Set, Child's 95.00
Dragon, Sauce 45.00
Draped Red Block, Tumbler 36.50
Drapery, Creamer 29.00
Drapery, Goblet .... 18.00 To 24.50
Drapery, Pitcher, Buttermilk 25.00
Drapery, Sugar 12.00
Drapery, Sugar, Covered 42.00
Drapery, Tumbler, Blue To Opalescent 30.00
Drum, Butter, Child's, Covered 125.00
Drum, Butter, Covered 80.00
Drum, Spooner 38.00
Duchess Loop, Wine, Flint 14.00
    EARL, see Spirea Band
Early Moon & Star, Tumbler 95.00
Early Moon & Star, Tumbler, Footed 75.00
Early Thumbprint, Tumbler, Footed, 4 1/4 In. 45.00
Early Thumbprint, Tumbler, 4 1/2 In. 48.00
Egg & Dart, Creamer 12.00
Egg In Sand, Bread Plate 25.00
Egg In Sand, Goblet 24.50
Egg In Sand, Lemonade Set, 5 Goblets, Tray, 7 Piece 210.00
Egg In Sand, Plate 30.00
Egg In Sand, Spooner, Amber 55.00
Egg In Sand, Sugar, Covered, Amber 65.00
Egg In Sand, Tray, Water 45.00
Egyptian, Bread Plate .... 30.00 To 48.00
Egyptian, Butter, Covered 75.00
Egyptian, Compote, Sphinx At Base, Covered, 8 In. 145.00
Egyptian, Creamer .... 27.50 To 33.00
Egyptian, Goblet .... 25.00 To 39.00
Egyptian, Sauce, Footed 8.00
Egyptian, Spooner 35.00
Elaine, Bread Plate, Frosted, 9 In. 50.00
Elk Medallion, Goblet 50.00
Empress, Cruet, Gold Trim, Original Stopper 50.00
Empress, Table Set, Green, Gold Trim, 4 Piece 375.00
    ENGLISH HOBNAIL CROSS, see Klondike

English Hobnail, Condiment Set, Child's, 4 Piece	35.00
Esther, Berry Set, Master, Set Of 4 Berries	250.00
Esther, Dish, Relish, Emerald Green, 11 X 5 1/2 In.	45.00
Esther, Pitcher, Amber Stain, Daisies	250.00
Esther, Tumbler	30.00

ETCHED BAND, see Dakota
ETCHED DAKOTA, see Dakota
ETCHED PATTERNS, see under main pattern: e.g., Etched Dakota, see Dakota

Eureka, Goblet, Flint	17.00 To 27.00
Eureka, Wine, Flint	25.00
Everglades, Berry Set, Gold Opalescent, 4 Piece	95.00
Excelsior Variant, Sugar	38.00
Excelsior With Maltese Cross, Goblet	52.00
Excelsior, Champagne	68.00
Excelsior, Creamer, Flint	45.00
Excelsior, Tumbler, Double Ring, Footed	55.00
Excelsior, Wine, Flint	48.00
Eyewinker, Butter, Covered	65.00
Eyewinker, Butter, Covered, Amber	85.00
Eyewinker, Butter, Covered, Green	65.00
Eyewinker, Cake Stand, 6 1/2 X 9 In.Square	68.00
Eyewinker, Compote, Covered, 6 X 10 In.	60.00
Eyewinker, Goblet	65.00
Eyewinker, Pitcher, Milk	60.00

FAGOT, see Vera

Faith, Hope & Charity, Plate	65.00
Falling Leaves, Pitcher, Water	35.00

FAN, see also Butterfly & Fan

Fan & Star, Compote, Clear, 6 X 8 In.	32.00
Fan With Diamond, Creamer	19.00
Fan With Diamond, Goblet, Buttermilk	24.00
Fan With Diamond, Pitcher, Buttermilk	20.00
Fan With Diamond, Wine	19.50
Fancy Cut, Pitcher, Water, Child's	30.00
Fancy Cut, Table Set, Child's, 4 Piece	90.00
Fancy Diamonds, Wine	12.00
Fancy Loop, Bowl, Punch, 12 In.Diam.	95.00
Fancy Loop, Toothpick	35.00
Feather Duster, Cake Stand	12.00
Feather Duster, Creamer	10.00
Feather Duster, Spooner, Green	28.00
Feather Duster, Water Set, Emerald Green, 7 Piece	145.00
Feather, Bowl, Oval, 9 1/4 In.	15.00
Feather, Butter, Covered	45.00 To 47.50
Feather, Cake Plate, 8 1/2 In.	25.00 To 26.00
Feather, Cake Stand, Pedestal, 4 1/2 X 8 1/2 In.Diam.	35.00
Feather, Cake Stand, 10 3/4 In.	40.00
Feather, Celery	20.00 To 23.50
Feather, Compote, Jelly	22.00
Feather, Cordial	18.00
Feather, Creamer	26.00
Feather, Cruet	22.00 To 26.00
Feather, Dish, Candy, Gold Trim, 2 X 5 1/2 In.	14.00
Feather, Dish, Pickle, Gold Trim, 7 1/4 X 4 1/2 In.	14.00
Feather, Goblet	25.00 To 35.00
Feather, Honey, 3 1/2 In.	15.00
Feather, Pitcher	30.00
Feather, Pitcher, Water, Green	185.00
Feather, Sauce, Flat	10.00
Feather, Spooner	12.00 To 18.00
Feather, Spooner, Green	75.00
Feather, Sugar, Covered	32.50 To 45.00

Pressed Glass, Diagonal Band, Goblet

Pressed Glass, Diamond Cut With Leaf, Plate

Pressed Glass, Diamond Point

Pressed Glass, Diamond Thumbprint,

Pressed Glass, Egg In Sand, Goblet

Pressed Glass, Egyptian

Pressed Glass, Excelsior, Bitter Bottle

Pressed Glass, Fern
Burst, Goblet

Feather, Syrup, Emerald Green	195.00
Feather, Wine, Plain Top	30.00 To 36.00
Feathered Arches, Punch Bowl, Child's	20.00 To 22.50
Fern Burst, Celery	14.00

Fern Garland, Wine	15.00
Fernland, Creamer, Child's	12.00 To 15.00
Fernland, Creamer, Child's, Green	28.00
Fernland, Sugar, Child's, Covered	15.00
Fernland, Sugar, Child's, Covered, Green	30.00
Fernland, Table Set, Child's, 4 Piece	85.00
FESTOON & GRAPE, see Grape & Festoon	
Festoon, Bowl, 9 1/4 In.	24.00
Festoon, Cake Stand, 10 In.	24.00 To 40.00
Festoon, Creamer	21.00
Festoon, Spooner	25.00
Fickle Block, Compote, Fruit	18.00
Fickle Block, Goblet	9.00
Fickle Block, Pitcher, Water	15.00
Fine Cut & Block, Compote, Covered, 5 1/2 In.	30.00
Fine Cut & Block, Creamer	30.00
Fine Cut & Block, Tumbler	25.00
Fine Cut & Diamond, Celery	20.00
Fine Cut & Panel, Compote, Covered, 7 X 10 In.	35.00
Fine Cut & Panel, Decanter & 6 Wines, Green	15.00
Fine Cut & Panel, Pitcher	25.00
Fine Cut & Panel, Tray, Water, Blue	55.00
Fine Cut & Panel, Wine	10.00
Fine Cut & Panel, Wine, Amber	18.00
Fine Cut, Bowl, Amber On 6 Panels, Footed, 8 In.	45.00
Fine Cut, Creamer, Blue	48.00
Fine Cut, Goblet	15.00 To 50.00
Fine Cut, Goblet, 6 Panel	16.00
Fine Cut, Pitcher, Water, Blue	95.00
Fine Cut, Toothpick, Canary	28.00
Fine Cut, Tray, Ice Cream, Amber	40.00
Fine Cut, Tray, Lion's Head Handles, Amber	45.00
Fine Cut, Wine	10.00
Fine Cut, Wine Set, Green, 7 Piece	135.00
Fine Diamond Point, Spooner, Flint	43.00
Fine Rib With Cut Ovals, Goblet	195.00
Fine Rib, Tumbler	39.00
Fine Rib, Wine, Flint	38.00 To 45.00
Fishscale, Bowl, Covered, 7 3/4 In.	37.50
Fishscale, Butter, Covered	40.00
Fishscale, Cake Stand	28.00 To 30.00
Fishscale, Compote, High Standard	25.00
Fishscale, Compote, Jelly	12.50 To 16.50
Fishscale, Compote, Open	25.00
Fishscale, Compote, 7 X 6 In.	45.00
Fishscale, Goblet	20.00 To 33.00
Fishscale, Jar, Pickle, Pear Shape	16.50
Fishscale, Pitcher, Water	35.00
Fishscale, Pitcher, Water, Flint	40.00
Fishscale, Plate, 8 In.	24.00 To 30.00
Fishscale, Plate, 9 In.Square	26.00
Fishscale, Relish, Pear Shape	16.00
Fishscale, Sauce	6.00
Fishscale, Sauce, 4 In.Square	8.00
Fishscale, Sherbet, 4 1/2 In.	18.00
Fishscale, Spooner	24.50
FLAT DIAMOND & PANEL, see Lattice & Oval Panels	
Flat Diamond, Cordial	18.00
Flattened Diamond & Sunburst, Bowl, Punch, Child's	24.00
Flattened Diamond & Sunburst, Butter, Child's, Covered	20.00
Flattened Diamond & Sunburst, Butter, Covered	12.00
Flattened Diamond & Sunburst, Creamer	10.00
Flattened Diamond & Sunburst, Punch Bowl, 4 Cups, Child's	50.00

Fleur-De-Lis & Drape, Cordial	35.00
Fleur-De-Lis & Tassel, Plate, Green, 8 In.	32.00 To 35.50
Fleur-De-Lis, Cake Stand	28.00
Flora, Creamer	32.00
Flora, Creamer, Green	25.00
Flora, Pitcher, Water	35.00
Flora, Pitcher, Water, Green, Gold Trim	85.00
Flora, Sugar, Covered	25.00
Flora, Tumbler, Green, Gold Trim	25.00
Florette, Condiment Set, Pink	135.00
Florette, Cracker Jar, Pansies, White	85.00
FLORIDA, see Herringbone	
Florida Palm, Creamer	10.00
Flower & Pleat, Bowl, Pastel Shading, 8 1/2 In.	26.00
Flower & Pleat, Creamer, Chevron On Applied Handle	45.00
Flower Band, Goblet, Clear	48.00
Flower Band, Sugar, Frosted, Covered	150.00
FLOWER FLANGE, see Dewey	
Flower Medallion, Tumbler, Clear With Pink & Gold	18.00
FLOWER PANELED CANE, see Cane & Rosette	
Flower Pot, Berry Dish, 4 Corner Feet, 2 Handles, Green	15.00
Flower Pot, Cake Stand, High Standard, 10 1/2 In.	60.00
Flower Pot, Compote, Covered, 7 In.	55.00
Flower Pot, Creamer	31.00
Flower Pot, Sauce, Square	8.00
Flower Pot, Sugar, Creamer, Spooner	70.00
Flower Pot, Sugar, Open	16.00
Flower With Cane, Berry, Master, Pink, Gold Trim	35.00
Flower With Cane, Sauce	10.00
Flower With Cane, Tumbler	20.00
Flower With Cane, Tumbler, Pink	15.00
Flute, Decanter, Bar Lip, Flint	65.00
Flute, Eggcup, Flint	24.50 To 26.50
Flute, Goblet	11.50
Flute, Pitcher	28.00
Flute, Wine, Flint	13.00
Fluted Scrolls, Creamer	18.50 To 22.00
Fluted Scrolls, Creamer, Blue	48.00
Fluted Scrolls, Spooner, Vaseline	45.00
Flying Birds, Goblet	110.00
FLYING ROBIN, see Hummingbird	
Forest Fantasy, Goblet	65.00
Forget-Me-Not In Scroll, Goblet	8.50
FORGET-ME-NOT IN SNOW, see Stippled Forget-Me-Not	
Forget-Me-Not, Compote, High Standard, Covered, 8 In.	65.00
Forget-Me-Not, Creamer	28.00
Forget-Me-Not, Cup & Saucer, Ribbed	31.00
Forget-Me-Not, Goblet, Barred	29.50
Forget-Me-Not, Spooner	22.00
Four Petal, Sugar, Covered	68.00
Fox & Crow, Pitcher, Water	175.00
Fringed Drape, Cordial	15.00
Fringed Drape, Cruet, Original Stopper, Gold Trim	15.00
FROSTED PATTERNS, see also under name of main pattern	
Frosted Block, Sugar	22.00
Frosted Circle, Butter, Covered	55.00
Frosted Circle, Compote, Covered, 6 In.	43.00
Frosted Circle, Cruet, Original Stopper	35.00
Frosted Circle, Spooner	35.00
Frosted Circle, Sugar, Covered	55.00
FROSTED CRANE, see Frosted Stork	
Frosted Dog, Compote, Covered, 8 In.	175.00
Frosted Dog, Compote, Low Standard, Covered, 8 1/2 In.Diam.	235.00

Frosted Dolphin, Compote, 7 1/2 X 6 1/2 In.	60.00
Frosted Eagle, Butter, Etched	190.00
Frosted Eagle, Sugar, Covered, Etched	225.00
FROSTED FLOWER BAND, see Flower Band, Frosted	
Frosted Fruits, Pitcher, Water	90.00
Frosted Hand, Cake Stand	82.50
Frosted Leaf, Goblet, Flint	20.00
Frosted Leaf, Salt, Footed, Flint, Master	48.00
Frosted Lion, Bread Plate	36.00
Frosted Lion, Bread Plate, Give Us This Day	75.00
Frosted Lion, Celery, Etched	145.00
Frosted Lion, Compote	140.00
Frosted Lion, Compote, Covered	70.00
Frosted Lion, Compote, Oval, 9 In.Long, 9 In.High	95.00
Frosted Lion, Creamer	59.00 To 62.00
Frosted Lion, Goblet	48.00
Frosted Lion, Jar, Jam, Clear & Frosted	55.00
Frosted Lion, Jar, Jam, Rampant Lion Finial	85.00
Frosted Lion, Paperweight, Round	70.00 To 1350.00
Frosted Lion, Pitcher, Water	195.00
Frosted Lion, Relish, Lion Handles	45.00
Frosted Lion, Sauce, Footed	20.00 To 24.00
Frosted Lion, Sauce, 4 In.	20.00
Frosted Lion, Spooner, Etched	75.00
Frosted Lion, Sugar, Head Finial, Covered	50.00
Frosted Magnolia, Goblet	60.00 To 82.00
Frosted Oak Band, Goblet	95.00
Frosted Oak, Butter, Covered	40.00
Frosted Ribbon With Double Bars, Goblet	12.00 To 22.50
Frosted Ribbon, Celery	42.00
Frosted Ribbon, Creamer	25.00
Frosted Roman Key, Champagne	65.00
Frosted Stork, Bread Plate, 11 1/2 X 8 In.	43.50 To 65.00
Frosted Stork, Pickle Castor	85.00
Frosted Stork, Plate, Iowa City	65.00
Frosted Stork, Spooner	48.00
FROSTED WAFFLE, see Hidalgo	
Fruit Panels, Goblet	27.00
Fuchsia, Spooner	24.00
Gaelic, Compote, 5 1/4 X 5 1/4 In.	27.00
Gaelic, Creamer, Green Leaves, Etched	40.00
Gaelic, Goblet	25.00
Galloway, Bowl, 5 1/2 In.Diam.	10.00
Galloway, Butter, Covered	45.00
Galloway, Creamer	12.00
Galloway, Creamer, Oval, Gold Trim	20.00
Galloway, Creamer, 1000 Islands, 1904, Cranberry Trim	28.00
Galloway, Cruet	30.00
Galloway, Pitcher, Water	45.00 To 58.00
Galloway, Pitcher, Water, Child's	20.00 To 23.00
Galloway, Relish	18.50
Galloway, Spooner	26.00
Galloway, Toothpick	23.00
Galloway, Vase, 14 1/2 In.	18.00
Galloway, Wine	36.00
GARDEN OF EDEN, see Lotus & Serpent	
Garfield Drape, Butter, Covered	52.50
Garfield Drape, Celery	43.00
Garfield Drape, Compote, Covered	125.00
Garfield Drape, Creamer	32.50 To 52.00
Garfield Drape, Goblet	18.00 To 32.00
Garfield Drape, Honey	16.00
Garfield Drape, Pitcher, Milk	55.00 To 57.50

Garfield Drape, Pitcher, Water 70.00
Garfield Drape, Spooner .... 17.00 To 46.00
Garfield Memorial, Bread Plate 60.00
Garfield, Bread Plate 60.00
Gathered Knot, Celery 32.00
George Peabody, Cup & Saucer, Toddy 75.00
Georgia Gem, Toothpick 18.00
Georgia Gem, Tumbler, Green 25.00
Georgia, Compote, Open 30.00
Georgia, Sugar, Covered .... 39.00 To 40.00
Giant Bull's-Eye, Goblet, Flint 45.00
Giant Prism With Thumbprint Band, Tumbler 50.00
Giant Prism, Whiskey 40.00
Gladstone, Dish, Rose, Clover, & Thistle, 1869 Mark 25.00
Gladstone, Mug, Blue 45.00
Gladstone, Mug, Clear 40.00
    GOOD LUCK, see Horseshoe
Gooseberry, Creamer .... 29.50 To 30.00
Gooseberry, Goblet .... 25.00 To 30.00
Gooseberry, Sauce, Flint 7.00
Gooseberry, Sugar & Creamer 80.00
Gothic Arch, Salt, Opaque Blue 135.00
Gothic Arch, Spooner 18.00
Gothic, Champagne 72.50
Gothic, Champagne, Flint 125.00
Gothic, Eggcup, Flint 32.00
Gothic, Goblet, Flint .... 32.00 To 40.00
Gothic, Sauce, Flint 14.50
Gothic, Sugar, Covered .... 25.00 To 75.00
Gothic, Wine, Flint 95.00
    GRACE, see Butterfly & Fan
    GRAND, see Diamond Medallion
    GRAPE, see also Beaded Grape; Beaded Grape Medallion; Magnet &
    Grape; Magnet & Grape With Frosted Leaf; Paneled Grape Band
Grape & Festoon With Shield, Creamer, Applied Handle 42.00
Grape & Festoon With Shield, Goblet 38.00
Grape & Festoon With Shield, Mug 25.00
Grape & Festoon, Celery 38.00
Grape & Festoon, Creamer 27.50
Grape & Festoon, Creamer, Stippled 28.00
Grape & Festoon, Goblet .... 18.00 To 45.00
Grape & Festoon, Sauce 7.00
Grape & Festoon, Spooner .... 15.00 To 22.00
Grape & Festoon, Spooner, Clear Leaf 20.00
Grape & Festoon, Sugar, Covered 40.00
Grape Band, Goblet .... 18.00 To 28.00
Grape Vine With Ovals, Creamer 40.00

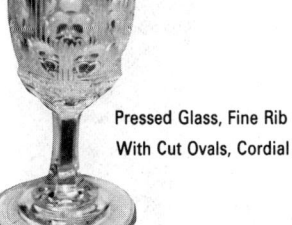

Pressed Glass, Fine Rib
With Cut Ovals, Cordial

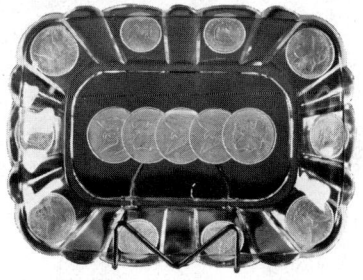

Pressed Glass, U.S.Coin Frosted

Pressed Glass, Frosted
Eagle, Compote

Pressed Glass, Frosted Dolphin, Compote

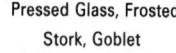

Pressed Glass, Frosted
Stork, Goblet

Pressed Glass, Fruit Panels, Goblet

Pressed Glass, Grape & Festoon, Cup

Pressed Glass, Garfield Drape,
Water Pitcher

Pressed Glass, Grape &
Festoon With Shield,
Goblet

Pressed Glass, Hamilton, Compote

Pressed Glass, Harp, Spill Holder

Grape Vine With Ovals, Creamer, Child's .... 40.00 To 55.00
Grape Vine With Ovals, Creamer, Child's, Amber 20.00
Grape Vine With Ovals, Creamer, Child's, Blue .... 20.00 To 68.00
Grape With Gothic Arches, Creamer, Green 45.00
Grape With Panels, Pitcher, Water, Cover 65.00
Grape With Thumbprint Band, Goblet 9.00
Grape With Thumbprint Band, Sauce, Green 30.00
Grape With Thumbprint, Bowl, Berry 20.00
Grape With Vine, Pitcher, Water 38.00
Grasshopper With Insect, Sugar, Covered 25.00
Grasshopper, Butter, Covered 22.50
Grasshopper, Compote, Covered, 7 3/4 In. 65.00
Grasshopper, Pitcher, Water, Clear 55.00
Grasshopper, Spooner, Amber 55.00
Greenfield Swirl, Goblet, Canary 34.00
Gridley, Pitcher, Water .... 85.00 To 95.00
Group Thumbprint, Pitcher, Water, Gold 20.00
Hairpin, Decanter, Bar Lip 55.00
Hairpin, Whiskey, Handled 42.00
Halley's Comet, Goblet 18.00
Halley's Comet, Tankard 75.00
Halley's Comet, Wine .... 20.00 To 25.00
      HAMILTON WITH CLEAR LEAF, see Hamilton with Leaf
Hamilton With Leaf, Compote, High Standard, Flint 85.00
Hamilton With Leaf, Whiskey, Handled 85.00
Hamilton, Creamer, Flint 25.00
Hamilton, Goblet, Flint 37.00
Hamilton, Spooner .... 20.00 To 42.00
Hamilton, Wine, Flint 55.00
      HAND, see Pennsylvania Hand
Hanover, Creamer 23.00
Hanover, Sugar, Covered 24.50
Hanover, Tumbler, Amber 25.00
Harp, Spooner 95.00
Hartley, Butter, Covered 28.00
Hartley, Celery 22.00
Hartley, Creamer 23.00
Hartley, Wine 24.00
Harvard Yard, Wine 25.00
Harvard, Sugar, Green 30.00
Hawaiian Lei, Cake Stand 38.00
Hawaiian Lei, Compote, Jelly, Bee 17.50
Hawaiian Lei, Compote, 8 In. 35.00
Hawaiian Pineapple, Tumbler 105.00
Heart & Thumbprint, Celery, Clear 45.00
Heart Band, Toothpick 22.00
Heart Band, Toothpick, Ruby Top 22.00
Heart Stem, Celery 45.00
Heart Stem, Compote, Covered, High Standard, 7 In. 135.00
Heart Stem, Creamer 45.00
Heart Stem, Sugar, Covered 55.00
Heart With Thumbprint, Banana Bowl 45.00
Heart With Thumbprint, Bowl, 8 In. 25.00
Heart With Thumbprint, Goblet .... 18.50 To 42.00
Heart With Thumbprint, Goblet, Green 35.00
Heart With Thumbprint, Lamp, Green, 9 In. 150.00
Heart With Thumbprint, Nappy, Gold Handled, Green 40.00
Heart With Thumbprint, Plate, Green, 6 1/4 In. 65.00
Heart With Thumbprint, Rose Bowl 48.00
Heart With Thumbprint, Salt & Pepper Shakers 95.00
Heart With Thumbprint, Sugar & Creamer 24.00
Heart With Thumbprint, Sugar & Creamer, Green 85.00
Heart With Thumbprint, Tray, Card, Folded Sides 25.00

Heart With Thumbprint, Tumbler	30.00
Heart With Thumbprint, Tumbler, Gold Trim	30.00
Heart With Thumbprint, Vase, Green, 6 In.	45.00
Heart With Thumbprint, Vase, 6 In.	22.00
HEARTS OF LOCH LAVEN, see Shuttle	
Heavy Gothic, Berry, Master	110.50
Henrietta, Pitcher, Water	38.00
Henrietta, Syrup	49.50
Hercules Pillar, Syrup, Amber	75.00
Heron, Celery, Blue	85.00
Heron, Creamer	45.00
Heron, Sugar, Covered, Flint	40.00 To 45.00
Herringbone, Berry Set, Green	85.00
Herringbone, Goblet, Buttermilk	18.00
Herringbone, Goblet, Emerald Green	25.00 To 35.00
Herringbone, Pitcher, Water, Emerald Green	65.00
Herringbone, Sugar, Green	35.00
Herringbone, Syrup, Green	165.00
Hexagon Block, Nappy, Etched, 7 1/2 In.	126.00
Hexagon Star, Toothpick, Clear With Gold	28.00
Hickman, Compote, Jelly	16.00
Hickman, Condiment Set, Child's, Green	120.00
Hickman, Creamer	25.00
Hickman, Pitcher	38.00
Hickman, Spooner	12.00 To 27.00
Hickman, Sugar, Covered	28.50 To 34.00
Hidalgo, Celery, Frosted	25.00
Hidalgo, Goblet	18.00 To 30.00
Hidalgo, Goblet, Etched	16.00
Hidalgo, Pitcher, Milk	38.50
Hinoto, Tumbler, Footed	38.00
Hinoto, Whiskey, Footed	38.00
Hobnail With Thumbprint Base, Butter, Covered, Blue	65.00
Hobnail With Thumbprint Base, Creamer, Child's	18.00 To 25.00
Hobnail, Butter, Ruffled Edge, Amber, Covered	35.00
Hobnail, Cake Stand, 10 In.	35.00
Hobnail, Mug, Child's, Dark Amber	14.00
Hobnail, Pitcher, Amber	65.00
Hobnail, Pitcher, Blown, Square Top, 8 In.	35.00
Hobnail, Pitcher, Water, Blue	50.00
Hobnail, Pitcher, Water, Double Eye	55.00
Hobnail, Spooner	18.50
Hobnail, Spooner, Ornamental Band	24.00
Hobnail, Sugar, Open	18.50
Hobnail, Toothpick, Amber	30.00
Hobnail, Tray, Child's, Amber	15.00
Hobnail, Tray, Water	15.00
Hobnail, Tumbler, Frosted Canary	45.00
HOLBROOK, see Pineapple & Fan	
Holly, Celery	45.00
Holly, Goblet	80.00
Holly, Pitcher, Water, Applied Handle	87.50
Holly, Sauce, Amber	45.00
Honeycomb With Flower Rim, Creamer, Amber	32.00
Honeycomb With Ovals, Goblet, Flint	17.00
Honeycomb, Butter, Child's, Covered	35.00
Honeycomb, Compote, Engraved New York, 8 In.	50.00
Honeycomb, Compote, Scalloped, Open, 7 1/2 X 5 1/2 In.	35.00
Honeycomb, Flint, 6 1/4 In.	20.00
Honeycomb, Goblet	12.00 To 15.00
Honeycomb, Goblet, Flint, 6 In.	20.00
Honeycomb, Sauce, Flint	15.00
Honeycomb, Spooner	15.00

Honeycomb, Tumbler, Daisy & Button Base, Blue 25.00
Honeycomb, Wine .... 5.00 To 20.00
Horn Of Plenty, Compote, Flint, Open, Scalloped Rim, 9 In. 60.00
Horn Of Plenty, Compote, 7 1/2 X 6 1/2 In. 85.00
Horn Of Plenty, Eggcup 26.00
Horn Of Plenty, Eggcup, Flint 38.00
Horn Of Plenty, Goblet, Flint 65.00
Horn Of Plenty, Honey 22.50
Horn Of Plenty, Sauce, Flint 14.50
Horn Of Plenty, Sugar, Covered 100.00
Horn Of Plenty, Sugar, Flint 125.00
Horn Of Plenty, Sugar, Open 45.00
Horn Of Plenty, Tumbler 95.00
Horseheads Medallion, Celery 75.00
Horseheads Medallion, Spooner 35.00
Horsemint, Cake Stand 23.00
Horsemint, Wine 12.00
Horseshoe, Bowl, Cereal 15.00
Horseshoe, Bowl, Vegetable, Oval 20.00
Horseshoe, Bread Plate .... 32.00 To 45.00
Horseshoe, Cake Stand .... 40.00 To 65.00
Horseshoe, Celery 45.00
Horseshoe, Creamer .... 20.00 To 40.00
Horseshoe, Cup & Saucer, Green 10.00
Horseshoe, Dish, Cheese, Covered 175.00
Horseshoe, Goblet 35.00
Horseshoe, Goblet, Knob Stem 30.00
Horseshoe, Pitcher, Water 65.00
Horseshoe, Pitcher, 8 1/2 In. 195.00
Horseshoe, Plate, Portland, 10 In. 40.00
Horseshoe, Plate, 9 1/2 In. 10.00
Horseshoe, Plate, 11 In. 12.00
Horseshoe, Relish 15.00
Horseshoe, Spooner 20.00
Horseshoe, Sugar & Creamer 20.00
Horseshoe, Sugar Shaker, Amber 40.00
Horseshoe, Tumbler, Footed, Yellow, 9 Ounce 15.00
Horseshoe, Tumbler, Footed, 9 Ounce 15.00
Huber, Whiskey, Handled, Flint 47.50
      HUCKLE, see Feather Duster
Hummingbird, Celery 20.00
Hummingbird, Compote, 7 In. 48.00
Hummingbird, Creamer .... 25.00 To 32.00
Hummingbird, Pitcher, Blue 100.00
Hummingbird, Pitcher, 5 1/2 In. 22.00
Hummingbird, Wine, Flint 38.00
Hundred Eye, Goblet 15.00
Hundred-Leaved Rose, Spooner 16.00
      IDA, see Sheraton
      IDAHO, see Snail
Idyll, Pitcher, Green With Gold 300.00
Idyll, Table Set, Jefferson Glass, Gold Trim, 3 Piece 175.00
Illinois, Celery, Green 65.00
Illinois, Toothpick .... 25.00 To 45.00
Illinois, Toothpick, Gold Trim 30.00
Illinois, Toothpick, Square 24.00
      INDIANA SWIRL, see Feather
Intaglio Sunflower, Toothpick, Green Stained Flowers 35.00
Intaglio, Compote, Jelly, Blue 35.00
Intaglio, Creamer, Custard 75.00
Interlocked Hearts, Creamer .... 25.00 To 27.00
Inverted Fan & Feather, Pitcher, Water, Gold Trim, Green 145.00
Inverted Fern, Eggcup, Flint 28.00

Inverted Fern, Goblet, Buttermilk 35.00
Inverted Fern, Goblet, Flint .... 26.00 To 28.50
Inverted Fern, Tumbler 65.00
Inverted Heart, Mug 27.50
    INVERTED THISTLE, see Late Thistle
Inverted Thumbprint & Star, Goblet 10.00
Inverted Thumbprint, Cordiel, Amber 35.00
Inverted Thumbprint, Goblet .... 10.00 To 14.00
Inverted Thumbprint, Pitcher, Clear Twist Handle, Blue, 7 In. 160.00
Inverted Thumbprint, Spooner, Amber 17.00
Inverted Thumbprint, Syrup, Amber 60.00
Inverted Thumbprint, Syrup, Emerald Green 75.00
Iowa, Cruet, Original Stopper 35.00
Iris & Herringbone, Goblet, Footed 14.00
Iris & Herringbone, Orange Bowl, 8 In. 20.00
Iris & Herringbone, Sugar & Creamer 12.00
Iris & Herringbone, Tumbler, 4 In. 24.00
Iris With Meander, Spooner, Blue 55.00
Iris With Meander, Toothpick, Amethyst 40.00
Iris With Meander, Toothpick, Blue 45.00
Iris, Creamer 9.50
Iris, Pitcher, Water 23.00
Iris, Pitcher, Water, Amber 30.00
Iris, Tumbler 8.50
Isis, Pitcher, Water, Jubilee 24.00
Ivy In Snow, Celery 32.00
Ivy In Snow, Cup, Blue 28.00
Ivy In Snow, Plate, 7 In. 12.00
Ivy In Snow, Plate, 10 In. 20.00
Ivy In Snow, Tumbler, Gold Trim 18.00
Jacob's Ladder, Cake Stand 28.00
Jacob's Ladder, Cake Stand, Pedestal, 10 1/2 In.Diam. 65.00
Jacob's Ladder, Celery .... 30.00 To 40.00
Jacob's Ladder, Compote, Open 29.00
Jacob's Ladder, Compote, 7 In. 14.00
Jacob's Ladder, Compote, 8 In. 38.00
Jacob's Ladder, Creamer .... 28.50 To 45.00
Jacob's Ladder, Goblet 75.00
Jacob's Ladder, Pitcher, Water, Applied Handle 175.00
Jacob's Ladder, Plate, 6 In. 22.50
Jacob's Ladder, Plate, 6 1/2 In. 25.00
Jacob's Ladder, Relish 18.00
Jacob's Ladder, Salt, Master .... 31.00 To 32.50
Jacob's Ladder, Sauce 7.00
Jacob's Ladder, Wine .... 25.00 To 38.50
    JASPER, see Late Buckle
Jefferson Optic, Pitcher, Lemonade, Cobalt Blue 85.00
Jenny Lind, Compote 150.00
Jenny Lind, Compote, Milk Glass 85.00
Jenny Lind, Match Safe 65.00
Jersey Swirl, Jar, Jam, Glass Lid 50.00
Jersey Swirl, Plate, Amber, 6 1/4 In. 20.00
Jersey Swirl, Plate, 10 In. 22.00
Jersey, Wine 40.00
Jewel & Dewdrop, Cake Stand 37.50
Jewel & Dewdrop, Compote, Open, 6 In. 65.00
Jewel & Dewdrop, Compote, 8 1/2 X 5 1/2 In. 27.00
Jewel & Dewdrop, Mug, Handled 18.50
Jewel & Dewdrop, Pitcher, Water .... 35.00 To 40.00
Jewel & Dewdrop, Toothpick 25.00
Jeweled Heart, Creamer, Gold 18.00
Jeweled Heart, Cruet, Green 135.00
Jeweled Heart, Pitcher, Water 65.00

Pressed Glass, Holly, Compote

Pressed Glass, Hobnail,
Tumbler & Pitcher

Pressed Glass, Horn Of
Plenty, Whiskey

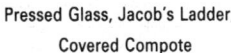

Pressed Glass, Horseshoe,
Covered Compote

Pressed Glass, Inverted Fern, Creamer

Pressed Glass, Jacob's Ladder,
Covered Compote

Pressed Glass, Jeweled Heart, Pitcher

Jeweled Heart, Tumbler 20.00
Jeweled Moon & Star, Compote, 6 3/4 X 8 In. .... 45.00 To 55.00
    JOB'S TEARS, see Art
    JUBILEE, see Hickman
Jumbo, Creamer, Man Under Handle 175.00
Jumbo, Goblet, C.1870, Etched 65.00
    KAMONI, see Pennsylvania
    KANSAS, see Jewel & Dewdrop
Kentucky, Tumbler, Green 25.00
Kentucky, Water Set, 5 Piece 55.00
Keystone Grape, Goblet 24.00
King's Crown, Bowl, Fruit, 10 1/2 In. 25.00
King's Crown, Champagne, Cobalt Blue 15.00
King's Crown, Compote, Jelly 45.00
King's Crown, Creamer, Green Thumbprint, 3 In. 40.00
King's Crown, Cruet Set, Clear 325.00
King's Crown, Dish, Preserve, Oval, 10 1/2 X 8 1/4 In. 24.00
King's Crown, Goblet 12.00
King's Crown, Goblet, Flint, Amethyst Spots 20.00
King's Crown, Goblet, Souvenir, Corinna, Maine, Green 25.00
King's Crown, Mustard, Covered 35.00
King's Crown, Tray, Ice Cream 40.00
King's Crown, Wine 20.00
King's Curtain, Cake Stand 18.00
King's Rose, Plate, Luster Vine Border, 6 1/4 In. 115.00
King's Rose, Plate, 8 1/4 In. 150.00
King's 500, Cruet, Original Stopper .... 10.00 To 28.00
King's 500, Nappy, Handled, Blue, Gold Trim, 5 In. 36.00
King's 500, Sugar, Covered, Cobalt Blue 55.00
Klondike, Berry Set, 4 Bowls 325.00
Klondike, Bread Plate 135.00
Klondike, Goblet, Clear 125.00
Knights Of Labor, Mug, 6 In. 45.00
Knights Of Labor, Platter, Blue 300.00
Kokomo, Butter 20.00
Kokomo, Wine .... 17.00 To 18.00
    LACE, see Drapery
Lacy Daisy, Creamer .... 22.50 To 25.00
Lacy Dewdrop, Banana Stand 45.00
Lacy Dewdrop, Goblet 45.00
Lacy Dewdrop, Goblet, Gold Trim 36.00
Lacy Dewdrop, Pitcher, Water, Emerald Green 37.50
Lacy Dewdrop, Syrup 85.00
Lacy Medallion, Toothpick, Gold Trim, Green 30.00
Lacy Medallion, Tumbler, Green, Souvenir Of Pittsburgh 27.00
Lacy Medallion, Tumbler, Hampton Beach, N.H., Green 15.00
Ladders, Cordial 18.00
Lakewood, Goblet 10.50
Laredo Honeycomb, Celery 45.00
Laredo Honeycomb, Wine 22.00
Late Buckle, Relish 11.00
Late Buckle, Relish, 9 3/4 In. .... 11.00 To 13.00
Late Butterfly, Sugar, Covered 25.00
Late Thistle, Pitcher, Water, Green 85.00
Late Thistle, Tumbler, Gold Trim, Green 24.00
Lattice & Oval Panels, Goblet, Flint 55.00
Lattice & Oval Panels, Tumbler 85.00
Lattice & Oval Panels, Wine, Flint 55.00
Lattice, Cake Stand, 12 In. 47.50
Lattice, Cordial 28.00
Lattice, Goblet .... 20.00 To 25.00
Leaf & Dart, Creamer 38.00
Leaf & Dart, Goblet .... 18.50 To 45.00

Leaf & Dart, Sugar, Covered .... 25.00 To 33.00
Leaf & Dart, Tumbler, Footed 12.00
Leaf & Dart, Wine 20.00
Leaf & Flower, Berry Bowl, Clear & Frosted, Amber 65.00
Leaf & Flower, Creamer, Amber 50.00
Leaf & Flower, Spooner 29.00
Leaf & Flower, Tankard, Water, Amber 95.00
Leaf & Star, Sugar, Gold Trim, Covered 32.00
Leafy Scroll, Goblet 23.00
Lee, Wine, Flint 95.00
   LEVERNE, see Star in Honeycomb
Liberty Bell, Bread Plate 30.00
Liberty Bell, Butter, Covered 225.00
Liberty Bell, Creamer .... 125.00 To 155.00
Liberty Bell, Creamer, Applied Reeded Handle 125.00
Liberty Bell, Creamer, Child's 65.00
Liberty Bell, Goblet .... 20.00 To 45.00
Liberty Bell, Goblet, Knob Stem .... 38.00 To 45.00
Liberty Bell, Goblet, Straight Stem 45.00
Liberty Bell, Pitcher, Water, Smooth Applied Handle 495.00
Liberty Bell, Plate, 6 In. 90.00
Liberty Bell, Plate, 8 In. 110.00
Liberty Bell, Platter, Signers, 9 1/4 X 13 In. .... 85.00 To 125.00
Liberty Bell, Saltshaker, Original Lid 55.00
Liberty Bell, Saltshaker, Pewter Lid, 1776 Liberty 1876, Clear 80.00
Liberty Bell, Sauce, Footed 25.00
Liberty Bell, Spooner 65.00
Liberty Bell, Sugar Shaker, Pewter Top 75.00
Liberty Bell, Sugar, Covered 110.00
Liberty Bell, Sugar, Open 90.00
Liberty Bell, Table Set, Child's, 4 Piece 450.00
Liberty Glass, Spooner 145.00
Lightning, Celery 22.00
Lily Of The Valley, Celery 42.00
Lily Of The Valley, Creamer .... 49.00 To 58.00
Lily Of The Valley, Creamer, 3-Footed 85.00
Lily Of The Valley, Goblet .... 28.00 To 48.00
Lily Of The Valley, Pitcher, Water 64.00
Lily Of The Valley, Wine 135.00
Lincoln Drape, Eggcup, Flint .... 26.00 To 32.00
Lincoln Drape, Goblet 57.00
   LION, see also Frosted Lion
Lion, Bread Plate, Gillinder 105.00
Lion, Bread Plate, 12 1/2 In. 55.00
Lion, Butter, Child's 100.00
Lion, Celery, Etched, Gillinder 110.00
Lion, Celery, Swirl Base, Handled, 8 In. 27.50
Lion, Celery, 9 In. 45.00
Lion, Compote 45.00
Lion, Compote, Covered, Oval, Gillinder 105.00
Lion, Cup, Child's 18.00
Lion, Dish, Pickle, Crouching Lion Handles, Frosted 48.00
Lion, Goblet, Etched 45.00
Lion, Goblet, Gillinder 69.00
Lion, Spooner, Child's 100.00
Lion, Sugar 100.00
Lion, Sugar, Child's, Covered 100.00
Lion, Sugar, Covered, Gillinder 55.00
   LION'S LEG, see Alaska
   LIPPMAN, see Flat Diamond
Log Cabin, Creamer .... 125.00 To 130.00
Log Cabin, Dish, Relish 85.00
Log Cabin, Sauce 40.00

Log Cabin, Spooner .... 85.00 To 110.00
Log Cabin, Sugar, Covered 90.00
Loop & Dart With Diamond Ornament, Creamer 35.00
Loop & Dart With Round Ornament, Goblet .... 12.00 To 19.00
Loop & Dart, Celery 30.00
Loop & Dart, Celery, Flint 45.00
Loop & Dart, Champagne 30.00
Loop & Dart, Goblet .... 18.50 To 27.00
Loop & Dart, Relish, Flint 22.50
Loop & Dart, Spooner .... 25.00 To 32.00
Loop & Dart, Sugar, Covered .... 35.00 To 42.00
Loop & Dart, Wine, Barrel Shape 35.00
Loop & Pillar, Celery 6.00
Loop With Dewdrops, Creamer .... 22.00 To 25.00
Loop With Dewdrops, Goblet 22.00
Loop With Dewdrops, Sugar, Covered 32.00
Loop With Fisheye, Goblet .... 21.00 To 23.00
    LOOP WITH STIPPLED PANELS, see Texas
    LOOP, see also Seneca Loop; Yuma Loop
Loop, Celery, 10 1/4 In. 55.00
Loop, Compote, 9 1/2 X 7 In. 33.00
Loop, Eggcup, Flint 26.00
Loop, Goblet .... 22.00 To 28.00
Loop, Spooner 15.00
    LOOPS & DROPS, see New Jersey
Loops & Fans, Goblet 12.00
Lotus & Serpent, Bread Plate 45.00
Lotus & Serpent, Butter, Covered 75.00
Lotus & Serpent, Creamer 25.00
Lotus & Serpent, Mug 38.00
Lotus & Serpent, Pitcher, Water 40.00
Lotus & Serpent, Relish, 7 In. 22.00
Lotus, Compote, High Standard, 8 X 8 In. 38.00
Louisiana, Compote, Scalloped, 5 1/4 In. 20.00
Madison, Sauce 10.00
Magnet & Grape With Frosted Leaf, Compote, Covered, 9 In. 165.00
Magnet & Grape, Goblet .... 18.00 To 65.00
Magnet & Grape, Plate, Anchor & Yacht 29.00
    MAIDEN BLUSH, see Banded Portland
Maine, Cake Stand, Pedestal 53.00
Maine, Compote, Open, 5 In.Diam. 20.00
Maine, Creamer 23.00
Maine, Pitcher, Milk, Green, 7 1/2 In. 125.00
Majestic, Creamer .... 10.00 To 15.00
Manhattan, Dish, 1 Handle, 4 1/2 In. 8.00
Manhattan, Plate, 6 In. 6.00
Manhattan, Toothpick, Clear, Gold Trim 35.00
Maple Leaf, Bowl, Amber, Oval 50.00
Maple Leaf, Bread Plate, Canary, Diamond Center 60.00
Maple Leaf, Pitcher, Footed, Oval, 7 1/2 In. 40.00
Mardi Gras, Cup, Punch 4.00
Mardi Gras, Toothpick, Scalloped Top 25.00
Marquisette, Spooner 25.00
Maryland, Compote, Jelly 15.00
Maryland, Goblet .... 19.00 To 55.00
Maryland, Salt & Pepper 85.00
Maryland, Tumbler 18.00
Mascotte, Butter, Etched, Covered 48.00
Mascotte, Cake Basket, Metal Handle 36.00
Mascotte, Celery 24.00
Mascotte, Creamer 18.00
Mascotte, Goblet .... 12.00 To 22.50
Masonic, Pitcher, Buttermilk 12.50

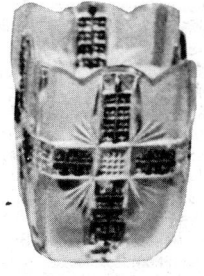

Pressed Glass, Leaf
& Dart, Goblet

Pressed Glass, Klondike, Tumbler

Pressed Glass, Jumbo,
Marmalade Jar

Pressed Glass, Liberty
Bell, Goblet

Pressed Glass, Lily Of
The Valley, Goblet

Pressed Glass, Lincoln Drape, Compote

Pressed Glass,
Beaded Grape Medallion

Pressed Glass, Loop With
Fisheye, Goblet

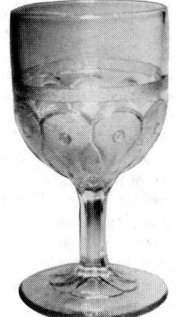

Massachusetts, Bottle, Bar 50.00
Massachusetts, Butter, Covered 55.00
Massachusetts, Decanter 49.00
Massachusetts, Toothpick 50.00
McKinley, Bread Plate, It Is God's Way, His Will Be Done 60.00
Medallion Sprig, Pitcher, Blue 200.00
Medallion Sprig, Pitcher, Green 200.00
Medallion Sprig, Saltshaker, Green To Clear 40.00
Medallion Sunburst, Creamer, 3 In. 18.00
Medallion Sunburst, Creamer, 6 In. 18.00
Medallion, Bowl, Green, 9 X 6 In. 30.00
Medallion, Cake Stand, Blue 80.00
Medallion, Cordial Set, Ruby Applied 35.00
Medallion, Creamer, Amber 32.00
Medallion, Mug, C.1870 .... 30.00
Medallion, Pitcher, Water, 1880s, Blue 98.00
Medallion, Wine 15.00
Melrose, Compote, Jelly 14.50
Melrose, Goblet 16.00
Melrose, Spooner .... 24.00 To 28.00
Melrose, Sugar, Covered 32.00
Melrose, Wine 21.00
Memphis, Creamer, Green 35.00
Memphis, Tumbler, Green 15.00
Memphis, Water Set, Green, Gold Trim, 7 Piece .... 175.00 To 225.00
Michigan, Creamer 20.00
Michigan, Creamer, Child's 32.00
Michigan, Cup & Saucer 28.00
Michigan, Cup, Punch .... 10.50 To 12.00
Michigan, Eggcup 25.00
Michigan, Goblet 40.00
Michigan, Goblet, Gold Trim 32.50
Michigan, Pitcher, Water, Child's 22.00
Michigan, Relish 14.00
Michigan, Salt & Pepper 30.00
Michigan, Spooner, Child's .... 18.00 To 28.00
Michigan, Sugar, Individual 24.00
Michigan, Syrup 30.00
Michigan, Syrup, Original Clamp-On Lid 65.00
Michigan, Toothpick 25.00
Michigan, Toothpick, Enameled Red Flower, Yellow Stained 45.00
Michigan, Toothpick, Gold Loops 48.50
Michigan, Toothpick, Lemon Flashing, Pink Carnations 55.00
Michigan, Tumbler 28.00
Michigan, Waste Bowl 32.00
Michigan, Water Set, Ruby & Gold, 6 Tumblers 325.00
Millard, Candy, Covered 85.00
Milton, Celery, Tall 15.00
Milton, Goblet, Plain Stem 10.00
Minerva, Butter 60.00
Minerva, Cake Stand, 8 In. 70.00
Minerva, Compote, Pedestal, 7 In. 65.00
Minerva, Creamer .... 39.50 To 40.00
Minerva, Goblet 85.00
Minerva, Jar, Jam, Original Cover 165.00
Minerva, Relish, Oblong 25.00
Minnesota, Butter, Covered 20.00
Minnesota, Creamer 24.00
Minnesota, Goblet .... 17.00 To 26.00
Minnesota, Toothpick .... 22.00 To 24.50
Minnesota, Toothpick, 3-Handled 20.00
Minnesota, Wine 16.00
Mirror & Loop, Eggcup, Flint 40.00

Mirror, Compote, Scalloped Rim, 10 1/2 X 9 1/4 In.	90.00
Mississippi, Sugar, Covered	80.00
Missouri, Sauce, Green	15.00
Missouri, Sugar & Creamer, Green, Covered	40.00
Mitered Bars, Celery	22.00
Mitered Bars, Goblet	22.50
MITERED DIAMOND POINT, see Mitered Bars	
Mitered Frieze, Celery	24.00
Mitered Prisms, Cake Stand	38.00
Monkey Climber, Goblet, C.1870	70.00
Monkey, Mug, Amethyst	135.00
Monkey, Spooner	110.00
Monkey, Sugar, Open	65.00
Moon & Star, Berry Bowl	40.00
Moon & Star, Bowl, Large	20.00
Moon & Star, Champagne	22.00
Moon & Star, Compote, Covered, 9 1/2 In.	42.00 To 45.00
Moon & Star, Compote, Open, 9 In.	45.00
Moon & Star, Compote, 6 3/4 X 8 In.	55.00
Moon & Star, Compote, 8 1/2 In.	45.00
Moon & Star, Compote, 10 X 11 In.	135.00
Moon & Star, Goblet	35.00
Moon & Star, Spill	30.00
Moon & Star, Sugar & Creamer	45.00
MOON & STORK, see Ostrich Looking at the Moon	
Morning Glory, Tumbler, Flint, Footed, 4 3/4 In.	335.00
Nail, Goblet, Etched	29.00
Nail, Pitcher, Water	40.00
Nail, Sauce, Pedestal	12.00
Nail, Spooner, Ruby, Etched	60.00
Nailhead, Compote, Open, 7 3/4 In.	25.00
Nailhead, Plate, 9 In.	12.00
Nailhead, Sugar, Open	15.00
Nailhead, Wine	16.00
Near Cut, Vase, 11 1/2 In.	72.00
NEBRASKA, see Bismarc Star	
Nellie Bly, Bread Plate	165.00
Nestor, Berry Set, Green	250.00
Nestor, Compote, Jelly, Blue	20.00
Nestor, Creamer, Blue	45.00
Nestor, Creamer, Green	60.00
Nestor, Spooner, Green	50.00
Nestor, Sugar, Covered, Green	75.00
New England Flute, Champagne, Flint	25.00
New England Pineapple, Goblet, Flint	35.00 To 65.00
New Hampshire, Bowl, Pink Flashing	15.00
New Hampshire, Goblet, Applied Gilt, Set Of 4	75.00
New Hampshire, Sugar, Covered	12.00
New Hampshire, Sugar, Ruby Stain	35.00
New Hampshire, Toothpick, Fuchsia	25.00
New Hampshire, Wine	18.00
New Hampshire, Wine, Flaring Rim	15.00
New Jersey, Butter, Covered	45.00
New Jersey, Butter, Sugar, & Creamer, Gold Trim, Covered	140.00
New Jersey, Goblet	12.50 To 38.00
New Jersey, Plate, 10 1/2 In.	26.00
New Jersey, Plate, 12 In.	22.00
New Jersey, Relish	21.50
New Jersey, Salt & Pepper	35.00
New Jersey, Spooner	28.00
New Jersey, Sugar, Covered	38.00
New Jersey, Sugar, Covered, Gold Trim	35.00 To 38.00
New Jersey, Toothpick, Gold Trim	55.00

New Jersey, Wine, Flaring Rim, Gold Trim	24.00
New York, Dish, Heart Shaped, Handle	25.00
Niagara Falls, Platter, 11 X 16 In.	125.00
Nursery Rhymes, Creamer, Child's	45.00
Nursery Rhymes, Pitcher, Child's	95.00
Nursery Rhymes, Pitcher, Water, Child's	110.00
Nursery Rhymes, Pitcher, 4 Tumblers, Child's	195.00
Nursery Rhymes, Plate, Bopeep	28.00
Nursery Rhymes, Punch Bowl, Child's	125.00
Nursery Rhymes, Punch Set, Child's, 5 Piece	180.00
Nursery Rhymes, Sugar, Child's	55.00
Nursery Rhymes, Sugar, Child's, Covered	65.00
Nursery Rhymes, Table Set, Child's, 4 Piece	230.00 To 265.00
Nursery Rhymes, Toothpick	50.00
Nursery Rhymes, Water Set, Child's, 7 Piece	260.00
Oak Leaf Band, Goblet	28.00
Oak Wreath, Spooner	15.00
Oak Wreath, Sugar, Open	15.00
Oaken Bucket, Creamer	28.00
Oaken Bucket, Sugar, Covered, Yellow	48.00
Oaken Bucket, Tumbler	16.00
Olympia, Tumbler, Dewey With Ship, Eagle, & Cannon	45.00
ONE HUNDRED ONE, see One-O-One	
One-O-One, Bread Plate, Sheaf Of Wheat, Farm Implement, 11 In.	65.00
One-O-One, Celery	39.00
One-O-One, Creamer	28.00
One-O-One, Toothpick, Pink	55.00
ONE-THOUSAND EYE, see Thousand Eye	
Open Rose, Canoe, 8 In.Long	12.00
Open Rose, Creamer, Applied Handle	45.00
Open Rose, Goblet	16.50 To 17.00
Open Rose, Pitcher, Water	175.00
Open Rose, Spooner	18.50 To 22.00
Opposing Pyramids, Goblet	9.00
OREGON, see also Beaded Loop	
Oregon, Celery	23.00
Oregon, Dish, Pickle	16.00
Oregon, Goblet	15.00 To 32.00
Oregon, Tumbler	44.50
Oriental Fan, Goblet	25.00
ORION, see also Cathedral	
Orion Thumbprint, Pitcher, Water	85.00
Ostrich Looking At The Moon, Goblet	65.00
Oval Star, Butter, Child's, Covered	10.00
Oval Star, Creamer, Child's	10.00
Oval Star, Sugar, Child's	10.00
Owl & Possum, Goblet	50.00 To 55.00
Paddlewheel, Creamer	13.00
Palm & Scroll, Cake Stand	28.00
Palm & Scroll, Salt & Pepper	25.00
Palm Beach, Wine	12.00
Palm Leaf Fan, Celery	22.00
Palm Leaf Fan, Compote, Jelly	12.50
Palm Leaf Fan, Pitcher	41.50
Palm Leaf Fan, Pitcher, Water	42.00
Palm Stub, Goblet	12.50
Palm, Eggcup, Set Of 6	90.00
Paneled Acorn Band, Sugar, Covered	40.00
Paneled Anthemion, Creamer	16.00
Paneled Apple Blossom, Goblet	18.00 To 27.00
Paneled Cane, Goblet	15.00
Paneled Cane, Sugar, Covered	30.00
Paneled Cherry, Goblet	25.00 To 27.00

Pressed Glass, Maine, Syrup

Pressed Glass, Moon &
Star, Covered Bowl

Pressed Glass, New England
Flute, Goblet

Pressed Glass, Open
Rose, Goblet

Pressed Glass, New England
Pineapple, Pitcher

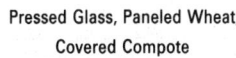

Pressed Glass, Paneled Wheat,
Covered Compote

Pressed Glass, Ostrich Looking
At The Moon, Goblet

Pressed Glass, Paneled Forget-
Me-Not, Marmalade

Paneled Cherry, Toothpick 24.00
Paneled Cherry, Tumbler 16.50
    PANELED DAISY & BUTTON, see also Daisy & Button With Amber
      Panels
Paneled Daisy & Button, Creamer 24.00
Paneled Daisy, Bowl, Oblong, 5 1/2 X 8 In. 20.00
Paneled Daisy, Bowl, Square, 7 1/4 In. 15.00
Paneled Daisy, Bowl, Square, 8 In. 15.00
Paneled Daisy, Butter, Covered 45.00
Paneled Daisy, Cake Stand, 9 In. 30.00
Paneled Daisy, Celery .... 25.00 To 35.00
Paneled Daisy, Compote, Covered, 5 In. 40.00
Paneled Daisy, Creamer 46.00
Paneled Daisy, Goblet 28.00
Paneled Daisy, Mug 22.00
Paneled Daisy, Pitcher, Water 45.00
Paneled Daisy, Plate, Square, 9 1/2 In. 25.00
Paneled Daisy, Relish 18.00
Paneled Daisy, Spooner 25.00
Paneled Daisy, Sugar Shaker 38.00
Paneled Daisy, Wine 10.00
Paneled Dewdrop, Cordial, 3 1/4 In. 30.00
Paneled Diamond & Finecut 35.00
Paneled Diamond Band, Sugar 15.00
Paneled Diamond-Cut & Fan, Spooner 17.50
Paneled Diamonds & Flowers, Goblet 26.00
Paneled Diamonds, Goblet 16.00
    PANELED DOGWOOD, see Dogwood
Paneled Forget-Me-Not, Cake Stand 29.00
Paneled Forget-Me-Not, Compote, Open 40.00
Paneled Forget-Me-Not, Compote, 7 1/2 In. 35.00
Paneled Forget-Me-Not, Goblet .... 22.00 To 40.00
Paneled Forget-Me-Not, Marmalade 30.00
Paneled Forget-Me-Not, Pitcher, Water 65.00
Paneled Forget-Me-Not, Relish 16.50
Paneled Grape Band, Goblet, Flint 28.00
Paneled Heather, Bowl, Gold Trim, 8 1/4 In.Diam. 24.00
Paneled Heather, Bowl, 9 1/2 In. 16.00
Paneled Heather, Butter, Covered 45.00
Paneled Heather, Compote, Jelly, Gold Trim, 5 X 5 In. 18.00
Paneled Heather, Compote, Jelly, 5 X 5 In. 18.00
Paneled Heather, Cruet, Original Stopper 28.00
Paneled Heather, Goblet, Gold Trim 22.50
Paneled Heather, Sugar & Creamer, Frosted, Green 20.00
Paneled Heather, Sugar, Covered 35.00
Paneled Heather, Tumbler 14.00
Paneled Herringbone, Celery, Emerald Green 28.00
Paneled Herringbone, Creamer, Emerald 25.00
Paneled Herringbone, Match Holder, Attached Plate, Green 28.00
Paneled Herringbone, Pitcher, Water, Emerald Green 75.00
Paneled Hexagons, Compote, Jelly, Blue .... 31.50 To 32.00
Paneled Hexagons, Goblet 9.00
Paneled Honeycomb, Pitcher, Milk 34.50
Paneled Iris, Wine 14.00
Paneled Jewels, Goblet 15.00
Paneled Long Jewels, Goblet 12.00
Paneled Ovals, Goblet, Flint 35.00
Paneled Palm, Sugar 24.00
Paneled Sawtooth, Sugar, Open, Flint 22.00
Paneled Smocking, Spooner 15.00
Paneled Smocking, Sugar, Covered 15.00
    PANELED STAR & BUTTON, see Sedan
    PANELED STIPPLED BOWL, see Stippled Band

Paneled Stippled Scroll, Creamer 7.50
Paneled Strawberry, Tumbler 20.00
Paneled Thistle, Butter, Covered 45.00
Paneled Thistle, Cake Stand .... 28.00 To 45.00
Paneled Thistle, Rose Bowl, 6 1/2 In. 35.00
Paneled Thistle, Salt & Pepper 40.00
Paneled Thistle, Toothpick 32.00
Paneled Wee Blossoms, Goblet 24.00
Paneled Wheat, Sugar 18.00
Paneled Wild Daisy, Creamer 20.00
Paris, Cake Stand 15.00
Pavonia, Goblet .... 21.50 To 32.50
Pavonia, Goblet, Etched 25.00
Pavonia, Pitcher, Water, Applied Handle 60.00
Pavonia, Pitcher, Water, Maple Leaf Etching 65.00
Pavonia, Tumbler, Etched 16.00
Pavonia, Wine, Fern & Berry Etched 25.00
Peacock Feather, Bowl, 8 1/4 In.Diam. 20.00
Peacock Feather, Celery 29.50
Peacock Feather, Compote, Candy 28.00
Peacock Feather, Cruet 24.00
Peacock Feather, Cruet, Bulbous Stopper 35.00
Peacock Feather, Pitcher, Water .... 48.00 To 85.00
Peacock Feather, Sauce, Flint 14.50
Peacock, Tumbler 25.00
    PEACOCK'S EYE, see Peacock Feather
Peerless, Bread Plate 25.00
Peerless, Salt, Footed 10.00
    PENNSYLVANIA, see also Pennsylvania Hand
    PENNSYLVANIA HAND, see also Pennsylvania
Pennsylvania Hand, Butter, Covered 85.00
Pennsylvania Hand, Celery .... 38.00 To 45.00
Pennsylvania Hand, Compote, Covered, High Standard 95.00
Pennsylvania Hand, Goblet 65.00
Pennsylvania, Celery, Flat 27.00
Pennsylvania, Cracker Jar 42.50
Pennsylvania, Creamer, Child's 30.00
Pennsylvania, Goblet .... 15.00 To 22.00
Pennsylvania, Juice 12.00
Pennsylvania, Juice, Green 22.00
Pennsylvania, Spooner 22.00
Pennsylvania, Spooner, Child's 12.00
Pennsylvania, Toothpick, Green 85.00
Pennsylvania, Tumbler 15.00
Pennsylvania, Wine .... 10.00 To 17.00
Pentagon, Table Set, Butter, Creamer, Spooner, & Open Sugar 100.00
Pentagon, Wine 16.00
Philadelphia Centennial, Goblet 35.00
Picket, Bread Plate, 13 X 8 In. 65.00
Picket, Goblet .... 25.00 To 35.00
Pigs In Corn, Goblet .... 170.00 To 195.00
    PILLAR & BULL'S-EYE, see Thistle
Pillow & Sunburst, Creamer 10.00
Pillow Encircled, Celery 19.50
Pillow Encircled, Celery, Etched 22.00
Pillow Encircled, Creamer 32.00
    PINAFORE, see Actress
Pineapple & Fan, Butter, Covered 20.00
Pineapple & Fan, Celery 28.00
Pineapple & Fan, Creamer, Squat, Gold Trim, Green 32.00
Pineapple & Fan, Cruet, Stopper, 1900s 30.00
Pineapple & Fan, Decanter, Open 12.00
Pineapple & Fan, Spooner .... 15.00 To 30.00

Pineapple & Fan, Sugar & Creamer 30.00
Pineapple & Fan, Tankard 40.00
Pineapple & Fan, Tumbler 12.50
Pineapple, Saltshaker, Original Lid, Pink 20.00
Pioneer's Victoria, Pitcher, Water, 9 3/4 In. 45.00
Pioneer's Victoria, Wine 13.00
   PITT HONEYCOMB, see Honeycomb
Pittsburgh, Pitcher, Pillar-Molded, 8-Ribbed, 8 In. 225.00
Pittsburgh, Whiskey, Emerald Green 95.00
Pleasant To Labor, Bread Plate 42.00
Pleat & Panel, Bread Plate .... 32.00 To 45.00
Pleat & Panel, Butter Pat 25.00
Pleat & Panel, Cake Stand, 9 In. .... 45.00 To 50.00
Pleat & Panel, Celery .... 33.00 To 40.00
Pleat & Panel, Creamer .... 26.00 To 29.00
Pleat & Panel, Goblet .... 12.00 To 18.00
Pleat & Panel, Plate, 7 In. 15.00
Pleat & Panel, Relish 15.00
Pleat & Panel, Sugar, Covered 38.50
Pleat & Panel, Water Tray 65.00
Pleating, Pitcher, Water 30.00
Plume & Block, Celery 28.00
Plume & Block, Pitcher, Water 32.00
Plume, Berry Set, Adams Glass Co., 1874 .... 85.00
Plume, Butter, Covered 48.00
Plume, Compote, Covered 45.00
Plume, Plate, Cake, 5 3/4 X 9 1/4 In. 35.00
Pogo Stick, Pitcher, Water 47.50
Pointed Hobnail, Wine 10.50
Pointed Jewel, Goblet 15.00
Pointed Jewel, Tumbler 20.00
   POINTED PANELED DAISY & BUTTON, see Queen
   POINTED THUMBPRINT, see Almond Thumbprint
Polar Bear, Goblet 80.00
Polar Bear, Pitcher, Water 225.00
Polar Bear, Tray, Frosted, Oval 125.00
Polar Bear, Tumbler 95.00
Popcorn, Goblet, Line Ears 31.00
Popcorn, Spooner 35.00
Popcorn, Wine 11.50
Portland Petal, Goblet 14.00
   PORTLAND WITH DIAMOND POINT BAND, see Galloway; Virginia
Portland, Boat, Relish, 12 In. 16.00
Portland, Creamer .... 12.00 To 15.00
Portland, Creamer, Clear, 2 3/4 In. 17.00
Portland, Cruet, Original Stopper 34.00
Portland, Goblet 24.00
Portland, Pitcher, Water, Clear, 9 In. 29.00
Portland, Sugar, Covered 30.00
Portland, Toothpick .... 16.00 To 22.00
Portland, Toothpick, Gold Trim 20.00
Portland, Tumbler, Child's 5.00
Portland, Tumbler, Gold Trim 18.50
Portland, Vase, Bud 12.00
Post, Celery 28.00
   POTTED PLANT, see Flower Pot
Powder & Shot, Goblet, Flint 65.00
Powder & Shot, Goblet, Girl With Fan 45.00
Powder & Shot, Spooner, Flint 18.00
   PRAYER RUG, see Horseshoe
President Taylor, Bread Plate, Etched 350.00
Pressed Diamond, Celery 27.00
Pressed Diamond, Compote, 6 1/2 In. 10.00

Pressed Diamond, Creamer, Blue 40.00
Pressed Diamond, Cruet, Amber 75.00
Pressed Diamond, Spooner, Amber 30.00
Pressed Diamond, Spooner, Blue 25.00
Pressed Diamond, Tumbler, Amber 30.00
Pressed Leaf, Pitcher, Water 68.00
Primrose, Celery 19.00
Primrose, Plate, Amber, 7 In. 28.00
Primrose, Wine, Amber .... 25.00 To 36.00
    PRINCESS FEATHER, see also Lacy Medallion
Princess Feather, Goblet .... 20.00 To 29.50
Princess Feather, Goblet, Buttermilk 60.00
Princess Feather, Spooner .... 20.00 To 35.00
Printed Hobnail, Eggcup 28.00
Priscilla, Butter 70.00
Priscilla, Cake Stand 40.00
Priscilla, Mug 35.00
Priscilla, Syrup 35.00
Priscilla, Table Set, 4 Piece 175.00
Prism & Bull's-Eye, Wine, Flint 80.00
Prism & Crescent, Tumbler 47.00
Prism & Daisy Bar, Wine 18.00
Prism & Diamond Band, Creamer 15.00
Prism & Flattened Sawtooth, Pitcher 75.00
Prism Arc, Creamer 12.00
Prism, Eggcup, Double, Flint 45.00
Prism, Eggcup, Flint 25.00
Prism, Goblet, Flint 20.00
Psyche & Cupid, Celery .... 38.50 To 40.00
Psyche & Cupid, Creamer .... 37.50 To 67.50
Psyche & Cupid, Goblet 35.00
Psyche & Cupid, Plate, Milk Glass 35.00
Psyche & Cupid, Sauce, Footed, 2 1/4 X 3 3/4 In. 10.00
Psyche & Cupid, Spooner 37.50
Psyche & Cupid, Sugar, Covered 40.00
Psyche & Cupid, Sugar, Covered, Flint 45.00
Psyche & Cupid, Table Set, 4 Piece 210.00
Quantico, Creamer .... 28.00 To 30.00
    QUEEN ANNE, see Viking
Queen, Goblet .... 18.00 To 20.00
Queen, Pitcher, Water .... 40.00 To 45.00
Queen, Pitcher, Water, Amber .... 70.00 To 75.00
Queen, Spooner, Amber 30.00
Queen, Wine 18.50
Raindrop, Compote, Blue, 5 1/2 X 8 In. 65.00
Raindrop, Creamer, Blue 30.00
Raindrop, Saucer, Blue 10.00
Raspberry & Grape, Creamer 38.00
Raspberry, Goblet 28.50
Rayed Flower, Tumbler, Clear & Pink 10.00
Reardon, Goblet, Etched 14.00
Rebecca At The Well, Compote, Frosted Ribbon Design 200.00
    RECESSED OVALS WITH BLOCK BAND, see Recessed Ovals
Recessed Ovals, Goblet 14.00
Red Block, Cup, Punch 5.00
Red Block, Goblet .... 12.00 To 48.00
Red Block, Rose Bowl, Small 8.00
Red Block, Spooner .... 30.00 To 38.00
Red Block, Sugar, Covered 58.00
Red Block, Tumbler 12.00
Red Block, Wine .... 30.00 To 38.00
Reeding, Cordial 18.00
    REGAL, see Paneled Forget-Me-Not

Pressed Glass, Pennsylvania, Goblet

Pressed Glass, Pleat &
Panel, Footed Bowl

Pressed Glass, Princess
Feather, Spooner

Pressed Glass, Pressed
Leaf, Cordial

Pressed Glass, Primrose, Pitcher

Pressed Glass, Rose In Snow, Goblet

Pressed Glass, Roman Rosette, Creamer

Reticulated Cord, Creamer	26.00
Reverse Torpedo, Banana Stand	95.00
Reverse Torpedo, Saucer	10.00
Reverse 44, Creamer, Gold Trim	25.00
Reverse 44, Pitcher, Gold Trim, Amethyst, 12 In.	55.00
Reverse 44, Sugar, Open, Footed, Handles, Signed US	40.00
Reverse 44, Syrup	40.00
Reverse 44, Tumbler, Clear, Silver Trim	25.00
Ribbed Ellipse, Cake Stand, 8 3/4 In.	24.00
Ribbed Forget-Me-Not, Mug, Child's, 3 In.	22.50
Ribbed Forget-Me-Not, Sugar, Open	22.00
Ribbed Grape, Goblet, Flint	55.00
Ribbed Grape, Plate, Flint, 6 In.	45.00
Ribbed Grape, Spooner, Flint	29.50
Ribbed Ivy, Bowl, Low, 8 In.Diam.	25.00
Ribbed Ivy, Eggcup, Flint	28.00
Ribbed Ivy, Goblet, Flint	16.00 To 42.00
Ribbed Ivy, Honey	15.00
Ribbed Ivy, Tumbler	85.00
Ribbed Ivy, Tumbler, Whiskey	78.00
Ribbed Ivy, Whiskey, Handled	85.00
Ribbed Ivy, Wine	75.00
Ribbed Ivy, Wine, Flint	80.00
RIBBED LEAF, see Bellflower	
RIBBED OPAL, see Beatty Rib	
Ribbed Palm, Creamer	78.00
Ribbed Palm, Eggcup, Flint	25.00 To 28.00
Ribbed Palm, Goblet, Flint	26.00 To 42.00
Ribbed Palm, Tumbler	85.00
Ribbed Palm, Wine, Flint	40.00 To 45.00
RIBBED PINEAPPLE, see Prism & Flattened Sawtooth	
Ribbed Sawtooth, Pitcher	42.00
Ribbed Thumbprint, Cruet	18.00
Ribbed Thumbprint, Toothpick	15.00
Ribbon Candy, Bowl, 8 In.	15.00
Ribbon Candy, Compote, High Standard	22.50
Ribbon Candy, Compote, Open, 7 1/2 In.	15.00
Ribbon Candy, Compote, 6 1/2 In.	25.00
Ribbon Candy, Creamer	15.00
Ribbon Candy, Dish, 8 1/4 In.	23.00
Ribbon Candy, Pitcher, Milk	40.00
Ribbon Candy, Plate, 8 In.	12.50 To 13.00
Ribbon Candy, Spooner	18.00 To 22.00
Ribbon, Bottle, Cologne, Stopper, Frosted	59.00
Ribbon, Bowl, Oblong, 5 3/8 X 8 In.	16.00
Ribbon, Bowl, Waste	39.00
Ribbon, Goblet	28.00
Ribbon, Goblet, Clear	28.50
Ribbon, Pitcher, Milk	20.00
Ribbon, Pitcher, Water, Large	62.00
Ribbon, Spooner, Frosted	22.00
Right Swirl, Goblet	16.00
Rising Sun, Bowl, 9 3/4 In.	20.00
Rising Sun, Goblet	18.00 To 22.00
Rising Sun, Goblet, Green Sun	19.50
Rising Sun, Tumbler, Green & Clear	14.00
ROCHELLE, see Princess Feather	
Rock Crystal, Plate, Clear, 12 3/4 In.	18.00
Rock Of Ages, Bread Plate, Milk Glass Center	150.00
Roman Cross, Goblet	12.00
Roman Key, Goblet, Flint	48.00
Roman Key, Spooner, Flint	30.00
Roman Rosette, Butter, Covered	50.00

Roman Rosette, Cordial	25.00 To 30.00
Roman Rosette, Creamer	15.00 To 32.00
Roman Rosette, Goblet	35.00
Roman Rosette, Salt & Pepper, Original Tops	25.00
Romeo, Goblet	18.00
Rooster, Table Set, Child's, 4 Piece	350.00
Rope & Thumbprint, Butter, Covered, Blue	65.00
Rope & Thumbprint, Compote, 8 In.	100.00
ROPE BANDS, see also Clear Panels with Cord Band	
Rope Bands, Relish, Handled, 8 1/2 In.	9.00
Rose In Snow, Butter	65.00
Rose In Snow, Creamer	42.00
Rose In Snow, Creamer, Amber	45.00
Rose In Snow, Creamer, Round	30.00
Rose In Snow, Creamer, Round, Vaseline	65.00
Rose In Snow, Creamer, Square	35.00 To 55.00
Rose In Snow, Jar, Powder, Lid	18.00
Rose In Snow, Mug, In Fond Remembrance	24.00
Rose In Snow, Perfume, Original Top	40.00
Rose In Snow, Pitcher, 5 In.	50.00
Rose In Snow, Plate, 7 In.	12.00
Rose In Snow, Plate, 9 1/2 In.	30.00
Rose In Snow, Sauce, 4 In.	6.00
Rose Leaves, Goblet	12.50 To 28.50
Rose Point Band, Creamer	22.00
Rose Point Band, Creamer, Flat Bottom	18.00
Rose Point Band, Sugar, Handled, 3 1/2 In.	18.00
Rose Sprig, Bowl, Footed, 8 1/ X 9 In.	35.00
Rose Sprig, Dish, Vaseline, 9 X 6 In.	23.00
Rose Sprig, Goblet	25.00
Rose Sprig, Goblet, Yellow	32.00
Rose Sprig, Tumbler	30.00
Rose Windows, Water Set, 6 Tumblers, 7 Piece	500.00
Rosette Band, Tumbler, Faceted, Ruby & Clear, Souvenir	27.00
ROSETTE MEDALLION, see Feather Duster	
Rosette With Palms, Plate, 9 In.	10.00
Rosette With Palms, Sugar, Covered	31.00
Rosette With Palms, Wine	12.00 To 15.00
Rosette, Butter, Covered	40.00
Rosette, Compote, Jelly	14.50
Rosette, Creamer	19.00
Rosette, Goblet	26.00
Rosette, Plate, Handled, 9 In.	22.00
Rosette, Relish	13.50
Rosette, Spooner	14.00 To 23.00
Royal Crystal, Butter, Ruby	55.00
Royal Crystal, Goblet, Ruby Top	40.00
Royal Ivy, Butter	
Royal Ivy, Rose Bowl	39.00
Royal Ivy, Rose Bowl, Frosted To Deep Cranberry	125.00
Royal Ivy, Spooner	65.00
Royal Ivy, Syrup, Northwood, Frosted & Clear	125.00
Royal Ivy, Toothpick	110.00
Royal Ivy, Toothpick, Ruby	75.00
Royal Lace, Tumbler, Blue	25.00
Royal Oak, Pitcher, Water, Milk Glass	150.00
Royal Oak, Sugar Shaker, Clear To Pink, Frosted	155.00
Royal Oak, Sugar, Frosted Lid	65.00
RUBY ROSETTE, see Pillow Encircled	
RUBY THUMBPRINT, see King's Crown	
S Repeat, Creamer, Gold Trim	58.00
S Repeat, Cruet, Original Knob Stopper, Blue	55.00
S Repeat, Saltshaker, Sapphire Blue	20.00

S Repeat, Syrup, Clear 25.00
S Repeat, Tray, Water, Light Green 80.00
Sandwich Heart, Creamer 85.00
    SANDWICH LOOP, see Hairpin
Sandwich Star, Spooner, Flint 40.00
Sawtooth & Star, Goblet, Ruby Top, Etched Holly & Leaves 45.00
    SAWTOOTH BAND, see Amazon
    SAWTOOTH WITH PANELS, see Hinoto
Sawtooth, Celery 32.00
Sawtooth, Champagne 14.00
Sawtooth, Compote, Open, 10 In. 80.00
Sawtooth, Creamer 70.00
Sawtooth, Goblet, Large 86.50
Sawtooth, Pitcher, Water 85.00
Sawtooth, Spooner 50.00
Sawtooth, Spooner, Flint 53.00
Sawtooth, Sugar, Covered 35.00
Sawtooth, Table Set, Milk Glass 65.00
Sawtooth, Tumbler 40.00
Sawtooth, Wine 60.00
Sawtooth, Wine, Knob Stem .... 16.00 To 35.00
Saxon, Goblet 12.50
Scalloped Lines, Creamer 35.00
Scalloped Lines, Spooner 22.00
Scarab, Goblet .... 85.00 To 95.00
Scroll With Acanthus, Berry Set, Floral Enameling, 7 Piece 190.00
Scroll With Acanthus, Compote, Jelly, Stemmed, Green 87.50
Scroll With Cane Band, Bowl, 8 In. 12.50
Scroll With Cane Band, Butter, Amber 150.00
Scroll With Cane Band, Cake Stand, 8 In. 13.00
Scroll With Cane Band, Tumbler 10.00
Scroll With Cane Band, Tumbler, Amber 28.00
Scroll With Cane Band, Tumbler, Gold Trim 20.00
Scroll With Flowers, Cake Plate, Clear 30.00
Scroll With Flowers, Creamer .... 22.00 To 32.00
Scroll With Flowers, Eggcup 26.00
Scroll With Flowers, Goblet .... 23.00 To 29.00
Scroll With Flowers, Pickle, Open Handled 18.00
Scroll With Flowers, Relish, 2-Handled, 9 In. 11.00
Scroll With Flowers, Spooner 32.00
Scroll With Flowers, Sugar, Covered 45.00
Scroll, Goblet .... 15.00 To 16.00
Scroll, Pitcher, Buttermilk 10.00
Scroll, Spooner .... 14.00 To 25.00
Scroll, Sugar & Creamer, Green 10.00
Sedan, Creamer 21.00
Sedan, Relish, 10 In. 10.00
Sedan, Wine .... 15.00 To 18.00
Semi-Loops, Goblet 18.00
Seneca Loop, Compote, Flint, 8 In. 30.00
Seneca Loop, Creamer, Applied Handle 65.00
Seneca Loop, Spooner, Clear 28.00
Sequoia, Goblet 12.00
Serrated Band & Prisms, Goblet 12.00
Serrated Band & Prisms, Mug, Handled 15.00
Sheaf & Block, Cake Stand, 12 In. 30.00
    SHEAF & DIAMOND, see Fickle Block
Sheaf Of Wheat, Bread Plate 26.00
Sheaf Of Wheat, Pitcher, Water 48.00
Shell & Jewel, Bowl, Clear, 8 In. 22.00
Shell & Jewel, Creamer, Clear 24.00
Shell & Jewel, Pitcher .... 22.00 To 65.00
Shell & Jewel, Pitcher, Jewels 45.00

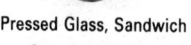
Pressed Glass, Sandwich
Star, Spill Holder

Pressed Glass, Rose Sprig, Goblet

Pressed Glass, Sawtooth, Pomade

Shell & Jewel, Pitcher, Water	30.00 To 40.00
Shell & Jewel, Pitcher, 6 Tumblers	110.00
Shell & Jewel, Tumbler	16.00
Shell & Jewel, Tumbler, Blue	32.00
Shell & Jewel, Tumbler, Frosted	17.50
Shell & Tassel, Bowl, Oval, 10 In.	30.00 To 45.00
Shell & Tassel, Bowl, 12 X 6 1/2 In.	45.00
Shell & Tassel, Bread Plate	60.00
Shell & Tassel, Butter, Dog Finial, Covered	87.50 To 88.00
Shell & Tassel, Cake Stand, 10 In.	68.00
Shell & Tassel, Pickle	22.00
Shell & Tassel, Platter, Square, 9 X 13 In.	59.00 To 65.00
Shell & Tassel, Spooner	15.00 To 35.00
Sheraton, Bread Plate, Octagonal, Blue	30.00
Sheraton, Butter, Covered	32.00
Sheraton, Celery	29.00
Sheraton, Compote, High Standard	22.00
Sheraton, Compote, Open, Amber, 7 In.	27.50
Sheraton, Creamer	18.00 To 22.50
Sheraton, Creamer, Amber	28.00
Sheraton, Goblet, Blue	25.00
Sheraton, Spooner	19.00
Sheraton, Spooner, Blue	30.00
Sheraton, Wine	23.00
Shield & Anchor, Goblet	45.00
Shimmering Star, Bowl, Fluted, Blue, 8 1/2 In.	30.00
Short Ribs, Goblet	18.00
Short Tidy, Goblet	15.00
Shoshone, Banana Stand	24.00
Shoshone, Cake Stand, Green & Clear	22.00
Shoshone, Cruet, Emerald Green	69.00 To 75.00
Shrine, Butter	49.00
Shrine, Compote, Jelly	18.00
Shrine, Mug, 3 1/4 In.	35.00
Shrine, Pitcher, Water	48.00
Shrine, Relish	14.50 To 30.00
Shrine, Salt & Pepper	45.00
Shuttle, Cordial	12.00
Shuttle, Cup, Punch	8.00
Shuttle, Wine	12.00
Simple Scroll, Toothpick, Gold Trim	21.00
Singing Birds, Sauce, Footed	45.00
Six Panel Finecut, Goblet	21.50
Snail, Bowl, 9 In.	38.00
Snail, Celery	32.00

Pressed Glass, Shell & Tassle, Compote

Pressed Glass, Scroll With
Flowers, Goblet

Snail, Cracker Jar, Covered, 8 In.Diam.	125.00
Snail, Creamer, Etched	25.00
Snail, Relish, Oval	20.00
Snail, Sauce, 4 3/4 In.Diam.	15.00
Snail, Spooner	25.00
Snake Drape, Goblet	17.00
Snakeskin & Dot, Cup Plate	12.00
Snow Drop, Tray, Ice Cream, 6 Saucers, Portland Glass	110.00
Snowflake, Table Set, Child's, 4 Piece	70.00
Snowflake, Tumbler	9.00
Southern Ivy, Sauce	8.00
SPANISH AMERICAN, see Admiral Dewey	
SPANISH COIN, see Columbian Coin	
Spirea Band, Creamer, Blue	28.00
Spirea Band, Goblet	25.00
Spirea Band, Goblet, Amber	20.00 To 35.00
Spirea Band, Spooner	9.00
Spirea Band, Spooner, Blue	35.00
Spirea Band, Tumbler, Blue	35.00
Spirea Band, Wine, Amber	32.00
Spirea Band, Wine, Blue	32.00
Spirea Band, Wine, Vaseline	25.00
Sprig, Celery	36.00 To 40.00
Sprig, Compote, Covered, 11 3/4 In.	50.00
Sprig, Compote, Open	30.00
Sprig, Goblet	27.00 To 28.50
Sprig, Pitcher, Water	40.00
Sprig, Sauce, Footed	12.00

Pressed Glass, Shrine, Bowl

Sprig, Spooner	25.00
Squirrel In Bower, Pitcher, Water	210.00
Squirrel, Pitcher, Water, 8 In.	190.00
Stag, Goblet, Etched	45.00
Star & Dart, Butter, Flint, Covered	58.00
Star & Fan, Spooner, Child's	18.00
Star & Lens, Tumbler	12.50
STAR & PUNTY, see Moon & Star	
Star In Bull's-Eye, Bowl, Oval, 8 1/2 X 6 3/4 In.	22.00
Star In Bull's-Eye, Water Set, Gold Trim, 7 Piece	135.00
Star In Bull's-Eye, Wine	23.00
Star In Diamond, Cordial	16.00
Star In Honeycomb, Pitcher, Water	34.00 To 45.00
Star In Honeycomb, Sugar	37.00
Star Of Bethlehem, Cordial	10.00
Star Of Bethlehem, Toothpick	20.00
Star Of David, Tumbler	11.00
Star Rosetted, Bread Plate	45.00
Star Rosetted, Bread Plate, A Good Mother	40.00
Star Rosetted, Compote, Covered, 8 1/2 In.	48.00
Star Rosetted, Wine	6.00
Star, Creamer, Clear, 4 5/8 In.	15.00
Star, Goblet	18.00
Starred Scroll, Wine	7.00
Stars & Bars, Celery	24.00
Stars & Bars, Cordial	18.00
Stars & Bars, Goblet	14.00 To 15.00
Stars & Bars, Goblet, Dog	45.00
Stars & Bars, Goblet, Moose Family	45.00
Stars & Bars, Goblet, Mountain Scenery	45.00
Stars & Bars, Saltshaker	10.00
Stars & Stripes, Creamer	22.00
Stars & Stripes, Toothpick	25.00
Stars & Stripes, Wine	11.00 To 15.00
Stedman, Goblet, Flint	12.00
Stedman, Tumbler	40.00
Stippled Band, Goblet	12.00
Stippled Band, Spooner	14.00
Stippled Chain, Goblet	26.00
Stippled Chain, Spooner	18.00 To 28.00
Stippled Cherry, Berry Bowl, 6 X 8 1/4 In.Diam.	23.00
STIPPLED DAHLIA, see Dahlia	
Stippled Daisy, Creamer	22.00
Stippled Diamond Band, Goblet	18.00
Stippled Double Loop, Goblet	12.00
Stippled Fans, Bread Plate, Deep Blue	50.00
Stippled Fleur-De-Lis, Tumbler, Green	15.00
Stippled Forget-Me-Not, Wine	40.00
Stippled Fuchsia, Goblet	24.00
Stippled Grape & Festoon, Compote, Acorn Finial, Covered	115.00
Stippled Grape & Festoon, Compote, Covered, 8 X 8 In.	49.00
Stippled Grape & Festoon, Creamer, Clear Leaf	40.00
Stippled Grape & Festoon, Goblet	21.00 To 28.00
Stippled Grape & Festoon, Spooner	20.00 To 35.00
Stippled Ivy, Goblet	18.00 To 22.50
Stippled Medallion, Eggcup	22.50
STIPPLED PANELED FLOWER, see Maine	
Stippled Peppers, Goblet	20.00
Stippled Sandbur, Compote, Jelly	16.50
Stippled Sandbur, Sugar	15.00
STIPPLED SCROLL, see Scroll	
STIPPLED STAR VARIANT, see Stippled Sandur	
Stippled Star, Creamer, 1870	28.00

Stippled Star, Goblet	25.00
Stippled Star, Spooner	26.00
Stippled Woodflower, Creamer, Sandwich	25.00
STORK LOOKING AT THE MOON, see Ostrich Looking at the Moon	
Stork, Creamer	15.00
Stork, Relish, One-O-One Border	18.00
Straight Banded Worchester, Goblet	32.00
Strawberry & Currant, Goblet	28.00 To 32.00
Strawberry With Roman Key Band, Goblet	29.50
Strawberry, Goblet	18.00 To 25.00
Strawberry, Tumbler	16.00
Strigil, Bowl, Oval, 10 In.	19.00
Strigil, Celery	26.00
Strigil, Creamer	20.00
Sunbeam, Goblet, Stemmed, Blue, Gold	23.00
Sunburst, Creamer	30.00
Sunburst, Cup, Punch	10.00
Sunburst, Spooner	25.00
Sunburst, Wine	15.00
Sunk Daisy, Toothpick	25.00
Sunk Diamond & Lattice, Pitcher, Water	24.00 To 25.00
Sunk Honeycomb, Butter, Covered	45.00
Sunk Honeycomb, Dish, Cheese, Ruby Trim, 7 1/4 In.	150.00
Sunk Prism, Creamer	22.00
Sunken Primrose, Bowl, Frosted & Clear, 10 In.	22.00
SUNRISE, see Rising Sun	
Swag With Brackets, Berry Bowl, Master, Blue	40.00
Swag With Brackets, Creamer, Green	50.00
Swan With Tree, Pitcher, Water	110.00
Swan, Goblet, Mesh Ground, Canary	65.00
Swimming Swan, Pitcher, Water	185.00
Swirl, Butter, Child's, Covered	22.00 To 28.00
Swirl, Candleholder, Pendant Drop, 14 1/2 In., Pair	100.00
Swirl, Creamer, Child's	18.00
Swirl, Tumbler	8.00
Swirled Star, Butter, Child's, Covered	23.00 To 25.00
Sylvan, Toothpick	24.00
Tacoma, Cordial	12.00
Tailored, Wine, Etched Morning Glories	12.00
Tarentum's Victoria, Tumbler, Gold Trim, Green	20.00
Teardrop & Tassel, Berry Set, 5 Bowls, Blue, 6 Piece	175.00
Teardrop & Tassel, Pitcher, Blue	200.00
Teardrop & Tassel, Pitcher, Water	55.00
TEARDROP & THUMBPRINT, see Teardrop	
Teardrop, Banana Stand, Scalloped Rim	85.00
Teardrop, Celery	20.00
Teardrop, Wine	15.00 To 15.50
Teardrop, Wine, Etched	32.50
Tennessee, Mug, Goofus Paint	25.00
Tennessee, Pitcher, Water, Clear	75.00
Texas Bull's-Eye, Goblet	22.50
Texas Bull's-Eye, Wine	15.00
Texas Star, Sugar, Open	15.00
Texas, Cake Stand, 11 In.	50.00
Texas, Creamer	12.00
Texas, Creamer, Miniature	17.00 To 19.50
Texas, Sherbet	6.00
Texas, Sugar, Small	15.00
Texas, Toothpick	12.00 To 20.00
Texas, Vase, 7 1/2 In.	33.00
The States, Butter, Covered	35.00
The States, Pitcher, Water	85.00
Theodore Roosevelt, Bread Plate, Dancing Bear Border	110.00

Thistle, Goblet .... 24.00 To 30.00
Thistle, Relish 22.00
Thistle, Tumbler 49.00
Thistle, Wine, Flint 35.00
Thousand Eye Band, Goblet 28.00
Thousand Eye, Bowl, Amber Knob Stem, Footed, 7 In. 25.00
Thousand Eye, Bread Plate, Apple Green 37.00
Thousand Eye, Celery, Footed .... 35.00 To 36.00
Thousand Eye, Champagne 9.00
Thousand Eye, Compote, Amber, 7 1/2 X 5 In. 45.00
Thousand Eye, Compote, Open, Amber 22.50
Thousand Eye, Compote, 3-Knob, Open 25.00
Thousand Eye, Cruet, Apple Green, Stirrup Handle 120.00
Thousand Eye, Eggcup 35.00
Thousand Eye, Eggcup, Blue 29.00
Thousand Eye, Goblet, Amber 30.00
Thousand Eye, Goblet, Blue .... 30.00 To 38.00
Thousand Eye, Goblet, Green 30.00
Thousand Eye, Inkwell, Original Cover, Amber 45.00
Thousand Eye, Jug, Stopper 15.00
Thousand Eye, Pitcher, 3 Knob Stem, Blue 100.00
Thousand Eye, Salt & Pepper, Banded, Apple Green 55.00
Thousand Eye, Toothpick 15.00
Thousand Eye, Toothpick, Blue .... 29.00 To 35.00
Three Face, Compote, Covered, 6 In. 135.00
Three Face, Compote, 8 1/4 In. 80.00
Three Face, Salt & Pepper, Original Tops 85.00
Three Face, Spooner, Etched 75.00
Three Panel, Berry Set, Amber, 7 Piece 75.00
Three Panel, Bowl, Fruit, Amber, 10 7/8 In. 50.00
Three Panel, Bowl, Fruit, Blue, 10 3/4 X 4 In. 65.00
Three Panel, Bowl, Fruit, 10 In. 22.00
Three Panel, Creamer, Blue 40.00
Three Panel, Creamer, Vaseline 32.00
Three Panel, Goblet, Amber 37.00
Three Panel, Goblet, Blue 42.00
Three Panel, Pitcher, Milk, 7 In. 45.00
Three Panel, Spooner 20.00
Three Panel, Spooner, Amber .... 22.00 To 35.00
Three Panel, Sugar, Covered, Amber 21.00
Three Panel, Tumbler, Blue 40.00
Three Presidents, Bread Plate 48.00
Three Presidents, Bread Plate, Frosted 50.00
Three Presidents, Goblet 350.00
    THREE SISTERS, see Three Face
Thrush & Apple Blossoms, Goblet 45.00
Thumbprint, Celery, Pattern In Base, Flint 125.00
Thumbprint, Goblet 48.00
Thumbprint, Goblet, Amber 12.50
Thumbprint, Goblet, Flint 42.00
Thumbprint, Sauce, Flint 14.50
Thumbprint, Tumbler, Ship's, Footed, 3 1/2 In. 30.00
Thumbprint, Wine 38.50
    TOBIN, see Leaf & Star
Tokyo, Berry Bowl, Master, Green 40.00
Torpedo, Bowl, 9 In. 24.00
Torpedo, Celery .... 34.50 To 45.00
Torpedo, Compote, Covered, 8 In. 115.00
Torpedo, Compote, Open, 8 In. 25.00
Torpedo, Creamer 30.00
Torpedo, Goblet 90.00
Torpedo, Goblet, Etched 35.00
Torpedo, Pitcher 45.00

Pressed Glass, Squirrel, Creamer

Pressed Glass, Strawberry, Creamer

Pressed Glass, Three Face,
Covered Compote

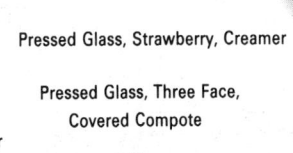

Pressed Glass, Tree Of Life, Compote

Pressed Glass, Thistle, Goblet

Pressed Glass, Thumbprint, Pitcher

Pressed Glass, Waffle &
Thumbprint, Glass

Pressed Glass, Tulip &
Sawtooth, Decanter

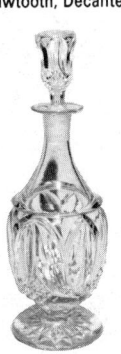

Torpedo, Pitcher, Milk, Bulbous, Applied Handle, 7 In. 135.00
Torpedo, Pitcher, Water, Applied Handle 95.00
Torpedo, Spooner .... 30.00 To 35.00
Torpedo, Sugar, Open 30.00
Torpedo, Syrup .... 72.00 To 95.00
Torpedo, Tray, Water, 9 1/2 In.Diam. 115.00
Torpedo, Tumbler, Etched Floral 45.00
Torpedo, Waste Bowl, Etched 45.00
Tree Bark, Pitcher, Water 40.00
Tree Of Life, Bowl, 8 In. 24.00
Tree Of Life, Bread Plate, Oval 30.00
Tree Of Life, Butter Pat, Blue 28.00
Tree Of Life, Butter, White 35.00
Tree Of Life, Compote, Frosted Base, Hand On Pedestal, 10 In. 139.00
Tree Of Life, Compote, Handled, 5 In. 50.00
Tree Of Life, Compote, With Hand 100.00
Tree Of Life, Creamer & Sugar, Covered, Marked 142.00
Tree Of Life, Creamer, Portland, Signed 45.00
Tree Of Life, Pitcher, Water, Applied Handle 175.00
Tree Of Life, Plate, Shell Shaped, 3-Footed, 12 1/2 In. 55.00
Tree Of Life, Sauce, Leaf Shaped, Set Of 6 .... 55.00
Tree Of Life, Spooner, Pittsburgh Glass 30.00
Tree Of Life, Toothpick, Pedestal, Blue 35.00
Tree Of Life, Tumbler, Footed, Signed 45.00
    TRILBY, see Valentine
Triple Band, Goblet.. 25.00
Triple Triangle, Goblet 40.00
Triple Triangle, Mug 42.50
Tulip & Honeycomb, Compote, Square, Child's 45.00
Tulip & Honeycomb, Punch Bowl, Child's 22.00
Tulip & Honeycomb, Punch Set, 6 Cups, Child's 85.00
Tulip & Honeycomb, Spooner, Child's 10.00
Tulip & Honeycomb, Sugar, Covered, Child's .... 17.00 To 20.00
Tulip & Honeycomb, Table Set, Child's, 4 Piece .... 45.00 To 65.00
Tulip Petals, Toothpick 30.00
Tulip With Sawtooth, Compote, Open 50.00
Tulip With Sawtooth, Decanter, Original Stopper 60.00
Tulip With Sawtooth, Tumbler, Footed .... 48.00 To 52.00
Tulip With Sawtooth, Wine 29.50
Tulip, Celery, 7 1/2 In. 27.00
Tulip, Goblet, Flint 40.00
Tulip, Tumbler, Footed 45.00
Tulip, Vase, Clear, 8 7/8 In. 17.50
Tulip, Whiskey, Handled 45.00
Twin Snowshoes, Creamer, Child's 15.00
Twin Teardrops, Bowl, 8 In. 12.00
Twin Teardrops, Bowl, 9 In. 20.00
Twin Teardrops, Plate, 9 1/2 In. 18.00
Twinkle Phlox, Butter 30.00
    TWINKLE STAR, see also Utah
Twinkle Star, Pitcher, Milk 35.00
Two Band, Compote, Covered, 7 X 7 1/2 In. 35.00
Two Band, Table Set, Child's, 4 Piece 160.00
Two Panel, Butter, Covered, Green 50.00
Two Panel, Creamer 12.00
Two Panel, Creamer, Blue 40.00
Two Panel, Goblet 22.00
Two Panel, Salt, Green 10.00
Two Panel, Spooner, Canary 30.00
Two Panel, Tumbler, Amber 35.00
Two Panel, Waste Bowl, Amber 31.00
Two Panel, Wine, Blue 40.00
U.S.Coin, Bread Tray 100.00

U.S.Coin, Cake Stand	365.00
U.S.Coin, Compote, Coins Dated 1892, Covered, 9 1/4 In.	265.00
U.S.Coin, Compote, Open, 7 X 7 In.	325.00
U.S.Coin, Compote, Quarters, 20 Cent Pieces, Covered, 7 1/4 In.	195.00
U.S.Coin, Compote, 25 Cent & 1 Dollar, Covered, 9 X 6 In.	425.00
U.S.Coin, Goblet, Dime	275.00
U.S.Coin, Pickle, Oblong	185.00
U.S.Coin, Sauce, Flat	110.00
U.S.Coin, Sugar	440.00
U.S.Coin, Toothpick, Frosted, Dollars Dated 1892	125.00
U.S.Coin, Toothpick, 1892	75.00
U.S.Rib, Butter, Covered, Emerald Green, Gold Trim, Square	48.00
U.S.Rib, Toothpick, Gold Trim, Green	25.00
Utah, Butter, Covered	30.00
Utah, Goblet	12.00
Utah, Pitcher, Water	30.00
Utah, Salt & Pepper	33.00
Valencia Waffle, Compote, C.1880, Blue, 8 X 7 In.Square	55.00
Valencia Waffle, Goblet, Square Base, Canary	35.00
Valencia Waffle, Salt & Pepper, Square, Apple Green	45.00
Valencia Waffle, Syrup, Blue	65.00
Valentine, Goblet	95.00
Venus, Sugar, Open	20.00
Vera, Bowl, Frosted, 5 In.	8.00
Vera, Bowl, Fruit, Frosted, 11 In.	16.00
Vermont, Berry Set, Green, 6 Piece	60.00
Vermont, Eggcup, Green & Gold	28.00
Vermont, Goblet, Green	55.00
Vermont, Pickle, Gold Trim, Green	22.00
Vermont, Sauce, Green	12.00
Vermont, Toothpick, Gold Trim, Green	25.00 To 50.00
Vermont, Tumbler, Green, Gold Trim	35.00
Victoria, Sugar, Gold Trim, Covered, Green	55.00
Victoria, Wine	8.00
Viking, Bowl, Footed, 6 1/2 In.	25.00
Viking, Butter, Covered	55.00
Viking, Compote, Covered	72.00
Viking, Compote, Low Standard, Covered	75.00
Viking, Creamer	22.50 To 49.00
Viking, Jar, Apothecary	45.00
Viking, Pitcher	70.00
Viking, Pitcher, Water, Bearded Face At Spout	50.00 To 90.00
Viking, Sugar & Creamer, Clear	40.00
Viking, Sugar, Covered	45.00 To 55.00
VIRGINIA, see also Galloway	
Virginia, Butter, Gold Trim, Covered	22.50
Virginia, Creamer	12.00
Waffle & Star Band, Toothpick	25.00
Waffle & Thumbprint, Claret	110.00
Waffle & Thumbprint, Decanter, Bar, 1 Quart	45.00 To 75.00
Waffle, Eggcup, Flint	30.00
Waffle, Sugar, Covered, Flint	135.00 To 140.00
Waffle, Tumbler	48.00
Waffle, Whiskey, Handled	65.00
Warrior, Bread Plate, Frosted, Signed Jacobus	195.00
WASHBOARD, see Adonis	
Washington Centennial, Cake Stand, 8 1/2 In.	45.00
Washington Centennial, Celery	42.00 To 55.00
Washington Centennial, Compote, Open, 7 In.	30.00 To 36.00
Washington Centennial, Sauce	10.00
Washington, Eggcup, Flint	65.00
Washington, Tumbler	98.00
Washington, Whiskey	55.00

Pressed Glass, Wedding
Ring, Goblet

Pressed Glass, Washington Centennial, Relish Dish

Pressed Glass, Wildflower,
Goblet

Pressed Glass, Westward Ho, Covered Compote

Water Lily, Creamer, Flat Bottom	18.00
Waterford, Goblet	9.00
Wedding Bells, Tumbler	20.00
Wedding Ring, Goblet	25.00 To 55.00
Wedding Ring, Syrup	35.00
Wellsburg, Celery	45.00
Westmoreland, Celery	14.50
Westmoreland, Rose Bowl, 6 In.	26.00
Westmoreland, Sugar, Covered	26.50
Westmoreland, Syrup	35.00
Westmoreland, Tankard	49.00
Westward Ho, Butter	145.00
Westward Ho, Celery, Frosted	100.00
Westward Ho, Compote, Covered	70.00
Westward Ho, Compote, Covered, 9 In.	165.00
Westward Ho, Compote, Covered, 16 In.	420.00
Westward Ho, Compote, Jelly	95.00
Westward Ho, Compote, Open, 9 In.	155.00
Westward Ho, Creamer	255.00
Westward Ho, Dish, Covered, Rectangular, 6 1/4 X 4 1/2 In.	245.00
Westward Ho, Pitcher, Milk	235.00
Westward Ho, Pitcher, Water	140.00 To 320.00
Westward Ho, Pitcher, Water, Clear & Frosted	195.00
Westward Ho, Sauce, Footed	37.50
Westward Ho, Spooner	87.00
Westward Ho, Sugar & Creamer, Covered	265.00 To 275.00
Wheat & Barley, Creamer	16.00 To 25.00
Wheat & Barley, Creamer, Amber	29.50
Wheat & Barley, Creamer, Blue	32.00
Wheat & Barley, Pitcher, Water, Amber	78.00

Wheat & Barley, Spooner .... 12.00 To 14.00
Wheat & Barley, Sugar, Covered .... 24.00 To 32.00
Wheat & Barley, Sugar, Covered, Amber 45.00
Wheat & Barley, Tumbler, Amber 30.00
Wheat Sheaf, Bread Plate, 11 In. 45.00
Whirligig, Butter, Child's, Covered 22.50
Whirligig, Butter, Covered 30.00
Whirligig, Punch Bowl, 6 Cups, Child's 55.00
Whirligig, Table Set, Child's, 4 Piece 60.00
Wild Bouquet, Creamer, Green 75.00
Wild Rose With Bowknot, Water Set, Frosted, Clear, 7 Piece 75.00
Wild Rose, Punch Set, Child's, 7 Piece 230.00
Wildflower, Bread Plate, Amber, 9 3/4 In.Square .... 32.00 To 42.00
Wildflower, Butter 30.00
Wildflower, Butter, Covered, Amber 35.00
Wildflower, Cake Stand, Blue 45.00
Wildflower, Celery 33.50
Wildflower, Creamer 28.00
Wildflower, Goblet, Amber .... 17.50 To 35.00
Wildflower, Goblet, Vaseline 35.00
Wildflower, Pitcher 15.00
Wildflower, Pitcher, Water, Green 65.00
Wildflower, Salt & Pepper, Amber 35.00
Wildflower, Spooner, Yellow, Footed, 5 In. 12.00
Wildflower, Tumbler, Amber .... 30.00 To 45.00
Willow Oak, Bowl, 7 In. 22.00
Willow Oak, Butter 45.00
Willow Oak, Cake Stand, 10 In.Diam. 28.00
Willow Oak, Compote, High Standard, Blue 60.00
Willow Oak, Compote, Scalloped, 6 In. 28.00
Willow Oak, Creamer .... 22.00 To 34.00
Willow Oak, Creamer, Amber .... 23.00 To 28.00
Willow Oak, Goblet .... 32.50 To 40.00
Willow Oak, Pitcher, Milk 48.00
Willow Oak, Plate, Handled, 11 In. 24.00
Willow Oak, Plate, 10 1/2 In. 20.00
Willow Oak, Tumbler 30.00
Windflower, Goblet 30.00
Windflower, Tumbler 45.00
  WISCONSIN, see Beaded Dewdrop
Wooden Pail, Creamer, Child's 28.00
Wooden Pail, Spooner, Amber 30.00
Worcester, Belted, Tumbler, Footed, Flint 30.00
Wyoming, Butter, Covered 35.00
Wyoming, Compote, 8 In. 38.00
X-Ray, Bowl, Emerald Green, With Gold, 8 1/8 In. 45.00
X-Ray, Creamer 35.00
X-Ray, Sugar, Covered 50.00
X-Ray, Sugar, Green, Covered 50.00
X-Ray, Toothpick, Green, Gold Trim 60.00
X-Ray, Water Set, Gold Trim, Green, 6 Piece 160.00
  YALE, see Crowfoot
Yoke & Circle, Tumbler 15.00
Yoke Band, Goblet, Cut Flowers 10.00
Yoked Loop, Whiskey, Footed 30.00
York Herringbone, Sugar, Ruby Stained, Covered 50.00
Yuma Loop, Goblet, Flint 32.00
Zigzag, Pitcher, Water 30.00
Zipper Slash, Toothpick, Mt.Vernon 30.00
Zipper, Candlestick, Etched, 10 In. 45.00
Zipper, Humidor 45.00
Zipper, Pitcher, Applied Handle, 8 1/2 In. 19.50
Zipper, Pitcher, Milk, Amber 55.00

100-EYE, see Hundred Eye
100-LEAVED ROSE, see Hundred Leaved Rose
101, see One-O-One
1,000-EYE, see Thousand Eye

The size of the print is given, not the overall size with frame.
PRINT, see also Store, Sign
PRINT, Annie Benson Muller, Chubby Baby With Bottle & Bunny, 13 X 15 In. 32.00
Audubon, American Coot, 12 1/2 X 19 1/2 In. 425.00
Audubon, Baltimore Orioles, C.1840 .... 110.00
Audubon, Meadowlarks, C.1840 .... 110.00
Awakening, Bessie Gutmann, 15 X 19 In. 28.00
Bartlett, Ballson Springs, People & Oxen In Village Street, 1838 .... 18.00
Bartlett, Little Falls, Railroad Scene, Valley Of The Mohawk 35.00
Bartlett, Niagara Falls From The Ferry, 1837 .... 22.00
Bowen, Little Chief Hare, Lithograph, 21 1/4 X 27 1/4 In. 350.00
Charlotte Becker, Little Miss Mischief, 15 X 18 In. 35.00
Christy, Looking Backward, 1903, 13 X 16 In. 35.00
    PRINT, CURRIER, see Currier
    PRINT, CURRIER & IVES, see Currier & Ives
Eider Duck, Male, Hand-Colored Copper Plate Engraving, Marked 385.00
Flagg, Say When, Framed, 13 X 17 In. 20.00
Flagg, What More Do You Want, Framed, 13 X 17 In. 20.00
Flagg, With This Ring I Thee Wed, Framed, 13 X 17 In. 20.00
Fran Truxsess, Morning Glory, Signed & Framed, 7 X 9 In. 50.00
Gilbert, Allan, Victorian Lady, Signed, Lithograph, 7 X 9 In. 35.00
Gutmann, A Little Bit Of Heaven, Original Frame 35.00
Gutmann, Awakening, Original Frame 35.00
Gutmann, Cherub Poolside With Butterfly, Framed, 15 X 20 In. 40.00
Gutmann, Excuse My Back, Unframed, 7 1/2 X 12 1/2 In. 18.00
Gutmann, Falling Out, Framed, Oval Glass 15.00
Havell, Broad-Winged Hawk, Engraving, 38 X 25 In. 1600.00
Havell, Crested Grebe, Engraving, 21 3/4 X 30 1/2 In. 425.00
Havell, Prairie Warbler, Engraving, 19 5/8 X 12 1/4 In. 425.00
Humphrey, Miss Muffet's Christmas Party, Framed, 17 X 9 1/2 In. 95.00
Icart, Buddha, Blue, Rectangular 775.00
Icart, France And America, Allegory, C.1918, 21 X 16 In. 1450.00
Icart, Kittens, 1925, Signed, Oval Frame 575.00
Icart, La Nuit Et Le Moment, 11 X 9 In. 2200.00
Icart, Lilies 138.50
Icart, Nude Eve 950.00
Icart, Retour De Promenade, Windmill Mark, Signed, 18 X 14 1/2 In. 595.00
Icart, Three Women, One Wading, 20 1/2 X 17 1/4 In. 1050.00
J.W.Smith, Beauty & Beast, 9 X 11 1/2 In. 15.00
J.W.Smith, Girl By Ocean, 7 1/2 X 10 In. 15.00
J.W.Smith, Girl Picking Grapes, 7 X 10 In. 15.00

Japanese prints are listed as follows: Print, Japanese, name of artist,
title or description, type, size. The following terms are used to denote type:
Tate-e is a vertical composition. Yoko-e is a horizontal composition.
The words Aiban, Chuban, Hosoban, Oban, and Koban denote size.
The sizes are 13 x 9 inches, 10 x 7 1/2 inches, 12 x 6 inches,
15 x 10 inches, and 7 x 4 1/2 inches respectively.
Japanese, Goyo, Seated Woman, Kimono Falling Open, Signed 935.00
Japanese, Hasui, Scene & Beach At Shihiri-Ga-Hama In Sagami Province 325.00
Japanese, Hasui, Spring Rain At Gokolkuji 350.00
Japanese, Hoshida, Fujiyama From Niho 250.00
Japanese, Kuniyoshi, Celebrated Places In The Eastern Capital 700.00
Japanese, Triptych, 3 Geishas, Cherry Tree, 15 X 10 In. 150.00
Japanese, Yeizan, Children Playing The Seven Gods Of Good Luck, 1830 .... 70.00
Japanese, Yoshida, View Of Fuji, C.1937, 10 X 15 In. 120.00
Kellogg, Gertrude, 3/4 Length Woman Holding Gan 30.00
Kellogg, Washington, Trenton, April 1789, Lithograph, 16 X 12 1/2 In. 60.00

Lindsay, Martin, Cleveland, Showing Public Square, Lithograph 35.00
Lithograph, The Highland Shepherd Boy, Dated 1880, 15 X 19 In. 40.00
Lithograph, Wooden Horse Pulling 2-Wheel Cart, 13 1/2 X 5 1/2 In. 165.00
McCarthy, Lone Sentinel, Signed & Numbered, Framed 200.00
Nutting, Afternoon Tea, Framed, 17 3/4 In.Square 85.00
Nutting, Bean Porridge Hot, 7 1/2 X 9 1/2 In. 59.00
Nutting, Day In June, Bride Near Trees, Gilt Frame, Signed, 17 In. 70.00
Nutting, Honeymoon Cottage, 12 X 18 In. 40.00
Nutting, Panoramic Water Scene, Down The Lake, Signed, Framed, 19 In. 39.00
Nutting, Red Eagle Lake, Framed, 18 X 22 In. 50.00
Nutting, Shaded Bridge, 7 1/2 X 9 1/2 In. 25.00
Palmer, The Old Homestead, Animals In Barnyard 345.00
Parrish, Air Castles, 1906 .... 68.00
Parrish, Daybreak 160.00
Parrish, Daybreak, Original Frame, 10 X 18 1/2 In. 125.00
Parrish, Fisk Tire, Advertising 40.00
Parrish, Garden Of Allah 200.00
Parrish, Interlude 175.00
Parrish, Romance 375.00
Parrish, Under Summer Skies 85.00
Prang, Sunlight In Winter, Gilded Frame, 30 X 30 In. 150.00
Rockwell, Shuffleton's Barbershop, Autographed 350.00
Rockwell, The Jockey, Autographed 250.00
Rockwell, Tired But Happy, Autographed 295.00
Rockwell, Walking To Church, Autographed 295.00
Rockwell, You've Got To Be Kidding, Autographed 225.00
Underwood, Four Men Playing Poker, 8 1/4 X 10 1/4 In. 50.00
     PURPLE SLAG, see Slag, Purple
PURSE, Alligator 12.00
Beaded, Cobalt Blue Carnival Beads, 4 3/4 X 7 3/4 In. 47.00
Beaded, Floral Design, Green Leaves, Blue, 10 3/4 X 6 In. 45.00
Beaded, German Silver Top, Large 30.00
Beaded, Jet Black, Drawstring Closure 28.00
Beaded, Lined, Evening 12.00
Chain Link, German Silver 30.00
Chatelaine, Sterling Silver 175.00
Clutch, Gold Cord Design Of Butterfly, Black, Red, & Green, Tokyo, 1945 .... 15.00
Crochet, 1900 .... 10.00
Double Chained, Jet Beads Design, Sterling Silver Handle 125.00
Drawstring, Beaded, Blue 30.00
Drawstring, Flapper's, Beaded Edges, Black Suede 18.00
Evening, 7 Change Slots, Bill Clip, Rouge, & Powder, German Silver 35.00
Gold Mesh, Set Jewels, C.1910, Tiffany, Sapphire Clasp, 5 3/8 In. 1900.00
Gold, Cartouche Cover, Flowers, Blonde Tortoiseshell, 4 3/8 In. 100.00
Leather, Hand-Tooled, 1910 .... 30.00
Mesh, Art Deco, Whiting & Davis 35.00
Mesh, Enameled, Whiting & Davis 28.00
Mesh, French, C.1890, Granulated Ground, 14K Gold & Citrine 375.00
Mesh, German Silver 35.00
Mesh, Hues Of Blue, Fringe, Clasp & Chain 40.00
Mesh, Metal, Art Deco Design, Painted 40.00
Mesh, Whiting & Davis, 10K Gold & Sterling Silver, 6 X 3 1/2 In. 300.00
Miser's, Art Nouveau, Silver Beads, 14 X 2 1/2 In. 55.00
Petit Point, Bird, Roses, Deco Design, Lined 125.00
Petit Point, Brass Framed, Dated 1928 .... 45.00
Silver Beaded, Victorian, Blue 275.00
Silver Mesh, Art Deco Opening, Green Stones, 5 X 8 In. 75.00
Silver Mesh, German 21.00
Silver Mesh, German, Chain Handle, 6 X 7 1/2 In. 35.00
Slide Chain, Amber Glass Beads 65.00
Tin, Art Deco, Lithograph, Child's, 4 1/2 In. 60.00
Velvet, Brass Trim 12.00
Vitruvian Scrolls, Tassel, 18K 2-Color Gold, Sapphire Clasp 1100.00

Quartz, Box, Gourd Form, Leaf Knop On
Cover, Rose, 5 1/4 In.

QUARTZ, Box, Gourd Form, Leaf Knop On Cover, Rose, 5 1/4 In. ....*Illus* 550.00
    Figurine, Bird, On Tree Stump, Rose, 12 3/4 In., Pair ....*Illus* 1400.00

Quezal

Quezal glass was made from 1901 to 1920 by Martin Bach, Sr. He made
iridescent glass of the same type as Tiffany.

QUEZAL, Bowl, Blue Scrollwork, Gold Iridescent, Marked, 10 In. 600.00
    Bowl, Punch, Iridescent, Ocher, Inverted Foot, Signed, 13 In. 300.00
    Bowl, Signed, Gold, 10 1/2 In. 80.00
    Compote, Gold Iridescent, Slender Stem, Signed, 5 In. 275.00
    Compote, Orange Iridescent, Signed, 5 X 5 In. 375.00
    Dish, Nut, Iridescent Gold, Fluted Rim, 1 1/2 In. 175.00
    Lamp, Gold Ribbed Shade & Base, Marked The Twilight, 10 In. 1500.00
    Lamp, Original Base, Signed Shade, 15 In. ....*Illus* 2600.00
    Salt, Gold Iridescent, Blue Highlights, 3 In. 65.00
    Shade, Blue Feather, No Ruffles 250.00
    Shade, Blue Hearts & Vines 135.00
    Shade, Blue, Feather, Signed 250.00
    Shade, Brown Pulled Design On Yellow 275.00
    Shade, Gold & White Fishnet On Gold 175.00
    Shade, Gold Feather On Calcite, Gold Lined, Signed, 7 In., Set Of 4 .... 860.00
    Shade, Gold Feather On Opalescent, Signed, Pair 250.00
    Shade, Gold Hearts & Threading, Gold Lining, Signed, Pair 260.00
    Shade, Gold Hooked Feather On White, Gold Lined, Set Of 3 .... 575.00
    Shade, Gold Iridescent Feather Design, Ruffled, Signed, 6 In., Pair 275.00
    Shade, Gold Iridescent, Pulled Feathers, 6 X 4 1/2 In. 350.00
    Shade, Gold Panel 85.00
    Shade, Gold Spider Webbing Over Green & Gold Leaves, Set Of 3 .... 465.00
    Shade, Gold With Green Feather, Signed 120.00
    Shade, Gold, 5 1/2 In. 75.00
    Shade, Green Feather Bullet, 8 In. 325.00
    Shade, Green Pulled Feather, Gold Edge & Lining, 5 1/4 In. 95.00
    Shade, Hook Feather, Gold Lined, Gold, 7 In. 210.00
    Shade, Iridescent, Orange Scrolling Design, Signed, 4 1/2 In. 115.00
    Shade, Leaves On Beige Ground, Gilt Interior, Pair 300.00
    Shade, Orange Drape, Green Border, Chartreuse Ground 185.00
    Shade, Pulled Feather, Random Gold Threading, Signed, Pair 350.00
    Shade, Pulled Feathers On Calcite, Gold Inside, Signed, 6 In., Pair 320.00
    Shade, Pulled Feathers, Gold Iris Interior, Signed, Pair 350.00
    Shade, Pumpkin, Signed 120.00
    Shade, Ribbed, Flaring Mouth, Amber, Signed, 6 In. 125.00
    Shade, Ruffled Edge, Gold Ribbed, Signed, 5 1/2 In., Pair 165.00
    Shade, Ruffled Gold Fishnet Pattern, Signed, 8 In. 1350.00
    Shade, White & Yellow, 5 1/4 In., Pair 450.00

Quartz, Figurine, Bird, On Tree Stump,
Rose, 12 3/4 In., Pair

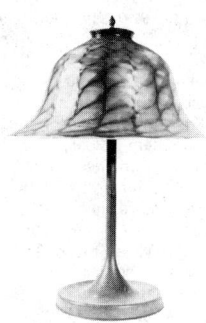

Quezal, Lamp, Original Base,
Signed Shade, 15 In.

Quezal, Vase, Jack-In-The-Pulpit, 1905-25

Toothpick 200.00
Vase, Agate, Ocher, Brown, Green, Signed, 4 1/4 In. 525.00
Vase, Bud, Orange Iridescent, Ruffled Top, Signed, 10 1/4 In. 250.00
Vase, Easter Lily Shape, Gold Iridescent, Signed, 8 1/2 In. 450.00
Vase, Gold Iridescent, Classic Shape, Signed, 7 In. 275.00
Vase, Gold Lacing Design, Gold Luster Lining, Signed, 8 In. 1175.00
Vase, Green Pulled Feather On Blue, 7 1/2 In., Pair 975.00
Vase, Green Sides, Amber, Yellow, Amber Iridescent, Signed, 8 In. 1875.00
Vase, Green, Gold Feathering, Gold Interior, 6 1/2 In. 1000.00
Vase, Iridescent Gold, Fine Ribbed, Signed, 2 1/2 In. 300.00
Vase, Jack-In-The-Pulpit, Amber, Concentric Waves, Signed, 6 In. 420.00
Vase, Jack-In-The-Pulpit, Iridescent Amber, Signed, 7 1/2 In. 650.00
Vase, Jack-In-The-Pulpit, 1905-25 ....*Illus* 2000.00
Vase, King Tut Design, Blue, Gold Trim, 3-Footed, Signed, 8 1/2 In. 2200.00
Vase, King Tut, Gold, Signed, 12 1/2 In. 1250.00
Vase, Oviform, Yellow, Floral Silver Overlay, 6 1/4 In. 650.00
Vase, Pulled Gold Feathers, Opalescent Ground, Signed, 3 1/2 In. 475.00
Vase, Pulled Green Lattice Design, Gold Interior, Signed, 6 1/2 In. 1000.00
Vase, Ribbed, Platinum, 8 1/4 In. 450.00
Vase, Striated Feathers, Palmettes, Signed, C.1905, 11 In. 1800.00

QUILT, Amish, Bars, Green, Purple, Green Border, 76 X 80 In. 2500.00
Amish, Bowtie Pattern, Kalona, Iowa, C.1820, Hand-Died, 78 X 69 In. 500.00
Amish, Child's, 9-Patch Pattern, Yellow, Green, Gray, Blue, 40 X 62 In. 200.00
Amish, Crib, Corn & Beans Pattern, Blue & Lavender, 61 X 44 In. 210.00

Amish, Crib, Crazy Squares Design, Multicolored, 71 X 54 In. 550.00
Amish, Crib, Friendship, Blue, Lavender, Purple, 56 X 50 In. 450.00
Amish, Flower Garden, Queen Size 165.00
Amish, Monkey Wrench Pattern, Blue, Lavender, Gray, Green, 69 X 41 In. 450.00
Amish, Purple, Black, Green, Gray, Leaf Design, Pennsylvania, 68 X 83 In. 450.00
Amish, Sawtooth Framing, X Shapes, 1920s, 82 X 66 In. 700.00
Amish, Single Patch Pattern, Kalona, Iowa, C.1920, 80 X 66 In. 450.00
Amish, Squares Into Smaller Swares, Homespun, 66 X 70 1/2 In. 225.00
Applique Alphabet, Vine Border, Dated 1894, 76 X 74 In. 900.00
Applique Flowers, Quilted Feather Wreath, C.1870, 83 X 94 In. 350.00
Applique In Green, Brown, & Yellow, Crewel Embroidery, 68 X 82 In. 425.00
Applique, Rose Design, White Ground, Scalloped, C.1870, 81 X 78 In. 350.00
Appliqued Flower Design, Pink Ground, 72 X 99 In. 135.00
Appliqued Sunbonnet Baby, Scalloped Border, 69 X 87 In. 120.00
Appliqued, 20 Stitches Per Inch, C.1867, Full Size 350.00
Bar, Multicolored Woolens, Taffetas, 70 X 75 In. 145.00
Barn-Raising Pattern, Wool 400.00
Black Silk Patches, Color Feather Stitching, 1890 .... 285.00
Bowtie, Blue, Red, & Earth Tones, Ivory Ground, C.1910, 84 X 80 In. 250.00
Brick Pattern, C.1900, Lined, 96 X 100 In. 45.00
Brown, Blue, White, Geometric Squares, Purple Ground, 72 X 74 In. 105.00
Calico, Pieced, Brown, Pink, White, Orange Peel Design, 80 X 88 In. 302.00
Calico, Pieced, Green, White Irish Border, 68 X 72 In. 165.00
Checked Squares, Autographed By Maker, Diamond Pattern, 80 X 81 In. 100.00
Crazy, Silk & Velvet, Hand-Stitched, 19th Century, 30 X 30 In. 150.00
Crazy, Victorian, Embroidery Stitches, 67 X 82 In. 160.00
Crazy, Wool, Silk, Cotton, & Linen, Feather Stitching, Twin Size 85.00
Crib, Patchwork, Pink & White, C.1940, 42 X 44 In. 90.00
Crib, Star Center, Floral Corners, Sawtooth Border 180.00
Diamond Overall Pattern, Reversible, 83 X 70 In. 95.00
Double Monkey Wrench, C.1820, American, Shell Quilting, 72 X 88 In. 400.00
Double Wedding Ring, Scalloped Edge, Hand-Stitched, Double Bed 125.00
Double Wedding Ring, Scalloped Edge, 82 X 65 In. 90.00
Embroidered, Black Bands, Silk, 66 X 60 In. 375.00
Feather Stitch, Child's, 2 X 3 Ft. 20.00
Flower Design In Center, Pink, Blue, & Green, White Ground, 72 X 99 In. 185.00
Flower Garden Pattern, Yellow Trim, 66 X 84 In. 110.00
French Knot, Pennsylvania, 20th Century, Fruits & Leaves, 76 X 84 In. 1800.00
Friendship, Feather Stitching, 499 Names, 1913, 84 X 84 In. 240.00
Friendship, Red, Green, Yellow, Blue, Dated, 1830 .... 1200.00
Grandmother's Flower Garden, 72 X 79 In. 135.00
Hand-Sewn Chintz, Florals, Beige Ground, Lined, 84 X 93 In. 135.00
Hudson Valley, Green & Pink, White Ground, Pieced Border 400.00
Hudson Valley, Pink & Green, Initialed, Dated 1860 .... 375.00
Indiana Puzzle, Blue & White Calico, 1910-20, 71 X 80 In. 150.00
Irish Chain, Red & White, Double Size 150.00
Irish Chain, 4 Hearts, Hand-Sewn, C.1900, 86 X 72 In. 125.00
Log Cabin Design, Brown, Beige, C.1880, 86 X 86 In. 350.00
Log Cabin Design, Pieced, 82 X 82 In. 175.00
Lone Star Pattern, Crazy Quilt Border, New England, Wool, 1880s 385.00
Mennonite, Red, Green, Pennsylvania, C.1930, 68 X 76 In. 295.00
Multicolor, Hand Made, Scalloped Edge, 82 X 65 In. 90.00
Multicolored Patch, Scalloped Edges, C.1930, 68 X 78 In. 150.00
Paisley & Calico, Red, Brown, & Blue, C.1850, 69 X 89 In. 100.00
Patchwork & Block, Reversible, Stripes, Prints, Cotton, 80 X 84 In. 70.00
Patchwork, French Bouquet, Gold, Green, Floral Prints, 99 X 85 In. 300.00
Patchwork, Hand Made, Blue, Green, Brown, Pink, Double 95.00
Patchwork, To Outside Borders, Machine Sewn, 76 X 96 In. 45.00
Penny, Cut Corner Patchwork, Silk & Velvet, American, 96 X 50 In. 110.00
Pieced Calico, American, Shell Quilting, 19th Century, 81 X 81 In. 475.00
Pieced Calico, Bowtie Pattern, American, 19th Century, 76 X 68 In. 325.00
Pink On White, Drunkard's Path Design, 80 X 80 In. 170.00
Pinwheel-In-Square, Calico, Orange, Brown, Yellow, 77 X 68 In. 230.00

Schoolhouse, Maroon & Blue, Pieced Cotton, 68 X 60 In.	500.00
Squares Of Various Colors, Checkered Homespun Back, 78 X 68 In.	195.00
Star Of Bethlehem Pattern, White Ground, C.1870, 72 X 70 In.	500.00
Sunbonnet Babies, 41 Squares, 1920s, 83 X 80 In.	270.00
Sunbonnet, Blue Dividers, Double Bed	125.00
To The Brave Soldiers Of New Hampshire, 68 X 88 In.	450.00
Top, Triangle Design, Black Field, Victorian, Silk, 71 X 74 In.	100.00
Trip Around The World Pattern, Pink Flowers, 83 X 90 In.	230.00
Wedding Ring Pattern, Hand-Quilted, White, Double, C.1930	125.00
Wedding Ring Pattern, Pink & Green, 1920s, 71 X 71 In.	250.00
Wedding Ring, 84 X 66 In.	115.00
Windmill Pattern, Pink & Red Calico, 68 X 82 In.	85.00
4-Patch Squares Of Calico, White & Gray Ground, 1920s, 63 X 70 In.	120.00
8-Pointed Ohio Stars In Squares, Calico, C.1880, 79 X 70 In.	185.00

HR.
Quimper

Quimper pottery was made in Quimper, France. Most of the pieces found today were made during the nineteenth and twentieth centuries. A Quimper factory has worked in France since the eighteenth century.

QUIMPER, Bell, Figural, Peasant Lady, Skirt Is Bell, Signed	75.00
Bell, Pinecone Design, Marked HD, 5 X 4 In.	55.00
Bowl, Handles, Red Flowers, Half Circles, Covered, 6 In.	125.00
Bowl, Hanging, Porringer, Peasant Man, Signed.5 In.	42.00
Bowl, Peasant Design, Scalloped, Oval, 3 In.Deep, 6 X 4 In.	35.00
Bowl, Peasant, Star Signature, 12 In.	65.00
Creamer, Pink Daisies, Marked, 3 1/4 In.	70.00
Cup & Saucer, Demitasse, Hexagon Shape, Florals In Panels, Marked	28.50
Cup & Saucer, Lady, Foliage, Fluted	75.00
Cup & Saucer, Peasant Girl Center Front, Circles, Trademark	45.00
Cup & Saucer, Yellow, Cobalt Trim, Man, Staff, Marked	35.00
Cup & Saucer, 6-Sided, Yellow, Marked	28.00
Dish, Breton Hat Shaped, Covered, Signed, 6 In.	120.00
Dish, Portrait Of Man, 6 5/8 In.	65.00
Dish, Salt, 5 Red Tulips, Green Leafing, Marked, 3 5/8 In.	18.00
Dish, 3-Compartment, Cobalt Blue & Yellow Trim, Signed, 11 In.Wide	325.00
Eggcup & Saucer, Signed	35.00
Eggcup, Basket Of Flowers In Colors, Yellow Ground	45.00
Eggcup, Blue, Green, & Rose, Yellow Ground, Signed	45.00
Eggcup, Swan	48.00
Eggcup, 6-Sided, Signed, 2 1/2 In.	28.00
Figurine, Dutch Girl, Signed, Berthe Savigny, 6 1/2 X 6 In.	475.00
Figurine, Man, Seated Between Baskets, Signed	210.00
Inkwell, Figural, Lady	88.00
Jugs, Portrait Of Man & Woman, 2-Sided, 7 1/2 X 5 In.	175.00
Knife Rest, Peasant Design	75.00
Pitcher, Floral, Signed, Large	135.00
Pitcher, Flowers, 4 1/2 In.	35.00
Pitcher, Green, 8 In.	125.00
Pitcher, Lady, 4 Panels, Cobalt Blue Trim, Sepia, Ovoid, 8 5/8 In.	350.00
Pitcher, Peasant Man & Florals, Green, Blue, Orange, Signed, 5 1/2 In.	65.00
Pitcher, Peasant Woman, Pinch Lipped, Marked, 5 In.	65.00
Pitcher, Woman Underneath, Green, 7 1/2 In.	130.00
Plate, Flowers, Blue Rims On White, Cut Corners, Marked, 4 1/4 In.	55.00
Plate, Flowers, Woman, & Tree Center, Signed, 6 3/4 In.	22.00
Plate, Man With Pipe, 2-Flower Band Border, 11 1/4 In.Diam.	110.00
Plate, Man, Fence, & Trees Center, Signed, 6 3/4 In.	22.00
Plate, Nun & Rosary Scene, Floral Edge, 8 In.	80.00
Plate, Peasant, White Ground, Signed, 9 1/2 In.	125.00
Plate, Rooster & Foliage Center, Multicolored Border, Marked, 10 In.	115.00
Plate, Soup	48.00
Plate, 4 1/2 In.	20.00

Plate, 8 3/4 In.	28.00
Porringer, Peasant Design, Blue Spongeware Border, 5 In.	55.00
Porringer, Yellow, Bird Design, Covered, Signed, 4 In.	50.00
Sugar, Florals Around Male Figure, Yellow Ground, Signed, Covered	60.00
Vase, Lady, White & Blue Designs, Tricornered, 7 In.	135.00
Vase, Peasant Girl, Cross Hatch Design, Signed, 11 1/2 In.	185.00
Vase, Vines, Metal Ball Top & Metal Rim Base, Signed, 9 In., Pair	250.00
Wall Pocket, Man & Foliage, Trademark, 10 1/2 In.	42.00
Wall Pocket, Woman Holding Bouquet, Marked, 10 1/2 In.	150.00

RADFORD
JASPER

Radford pottery was made by Alfred Radford in Broadway, Virginia, Tiffin and Zanesville, Ohio, and Clarksburg, West Virginia, from 1891 until 1912. Jasperware, Ruko, Thera, Radera, and Velvety Art Ware were made.

RADFORD, Vase, Lincoln Head, Jasperware	250.00

RADIO, Airline, Cabinet, Heavily Carved	675.00
Atwater Kent, Horn & Battery Eliminator, 4 Tubes	300.00
Atwater Kent, Model 10, Breadboard	325.00 To 365.00
Atwater Kent, Model 19	250.00
Atwater Kent, Model 20	75.00
Atwater Kent, Model 40, Tubes	65.00
Atwater Kent, No.10c, Breadboard	450.00
Atwater Kent, Outside Speaker	90.00
Atwater Kent, Speaker	25.00
Baseball Shape, 1930s	250.00
Clarion, 5 Tube, Battery, Wood Cabinet, Table Model	95.00
Crosely, Pup, 1 Tube	325.00
Crystal Set, Howe, Headphones	125.00
Crystal, Marvel, Freed-Eisemann, Earphones	35.00
Crystal, Philmore, Boxed	35.00
Dr Pepper, Store Cooler Shape, 1930s, Wooden	395.00
Freshman Masterpiece	65.00
Get Smart, Pen-Shaped, Boxed	17.50
Kolster, Battery	45.00
Pepsi Cola	250.00
Philco, Portable, Transitone, Battery Or Electric, Bakelite Front	15.00
R.C.A.Electrola Radiola	200.00
Radiola, Portable	275.00
Shaped Like Baseball, 1930s	200.00
Stromberg Carlson, Table Model, Wooden	50.00
Victrola Radiola	200.00
Zenith, Wood Table Model, 1930s	85.00

RAILROAD, Ashtray, Northern Pacific R.R., Glass, Black, Red, & Clear	18.00
Ashtray, Santa Fe R.R., 3 3/4 In.	10.00
Badge, Blue Ridge Lines, Hat	15.00
Badge, Hat, Brakeman, M.C.R.R.	27.00
Bell, Baldwin Locomotive Works, Brass, March, 1921, 18 In.	850.00
Bell, Brass, Yoke, 500 Pounds	550.00
Bell, Crossing, 12 In.Diam.	95.00
Bell, Steam Engine	350.00
Blanket, Great Northern Railway, Maroon Logo, 83 X 59 In.	78.00
Blanket, Pullman Logo	45.00
Bottle Opener, Pennsylvania R.R.	4.00
Bottle, Pullman	35.00
Bowl & Underplate, Wabash, Silver Plate, 5 1/4 In.	50.00
Bowl, Berry, Southern Pacific	22.00
Bowl, Bouillon, Milwaukee, Chicago R.R., Covered	20.00
Bowl, Cereal, B. & O., Warwick, 5 3/4 In.Diam.	17.00
Bowl, Cereal, Northern Pacific, Yellowstone	40.00
Bowl, Cereal, Pacific Railroad	18.00

Bowl, Prairie Mountain Wildflower Pattern, S.P.R.R., 6 In.	20.00
Bowl, Salad, Milwaukee Road Traveler	15.00
Bucket, Fire, Collapsible, Boston & Maine, Canvas, Bail Handle	35.00
Burlington R.R., Pagoda Style, Reed & Barton	65.00
Butter Chip, P.R.R., Silver Plated, 4 1/2 In.Diam.	35.00
Butter Pat, Chicago & Northwestern, Flambeau Pattern	18.00
Butter Pat, U.P.R.R.	12.50
Button, Great Northern R.R.	3.50
Caboose, Wooden, 10 X 30 Feet	3500.00
Can, Oil, Denver & Rio Grande, Copper, 2 Gallon, Bail Handle	195.00
Can, Watering, P.R.R.	20.00
Can, Watering, Southern California R.R.	35.00
Cards, Playing, Chessie In Gold Band, Double Deck, Plastic Box	23.00
Cards, Playing, Denver & Rio Grande Canyon Scene	25.00
Cards, Playing, G.N.R.R., Double Deck	35.00
Cards, Playing, Kittens, C. & C., Double Deck	25.00
Cards, Playing, Penn Central, Boxed	14.00
Cards, Playing, Rock Island	20.00
Celery, C. & O.Capital	150.00
Celery, Cheat River Scene, B. & O., 12 X 6 In.	125.00
Celery, P.R.R. Keystone	50.00
Celery, Platinum Blue, N.Y.N.H. & H., 10 1/2 X 5 In.	65.00
Chair, Collapsible, Pullman, Upholstered, B. & O.	150.00
China, Bowl, Cereal, Desert Flower, Union Pacific	22.50
China, Dinner & Breakfast Plate & Cup & Saucer, N.Y.C.R.R., 1927	128.00
Chocolate Pot, Santa Fe	42.00
Creamer, B. & O.R.R., Blue, 4 In.	56.00
Creamer, Penn., Silver Soldered, 6 In.	42.00
Cup & Saucer, B. & O. Centennial, Demitasse, 1st Series, 1927	65.00
Cup & Saucer, B. & O., 1927, Demitasse	65.00
Cup & Saucer, Centennial, B. & O., Squat	45.00
Cup & Saucer, Chesapeake & Ohio, Silhouette, Demitasse	150.00
Cup & Saucer, Chessie, Syracuse	85.00
Cup & Saucer, Floral Ground, Thomas Viaduct In Saucer	65.00
Cup & Saucer, Wild Flower, Southern Pacific	60.00
Cup, Bouillon, B. & O., Scammell, 4 In.Diam.	28.00
Cup, Bouillon, Centennial Pattern, Lamberton	30.00
Cup, Bouillon, Dewitt Clinton, N.Y.C., Syracuse	6.00
Cup, Bouillon, N. & W.Ry.	25.00
Desk, Map, Territory Information & Maps In Drawers, Oak	1500.00
Dish, Nut, C. & O., Silver	40.00
Eggcup, Centennial, C. & O., 3 1/4 X 3 1/4 In.	35.00
Eggcup, Desert Flower, Union Pacific	18.00
Eggcup, Double, BR Aristocrat	90.00
Extinguisher, B. & O.R.R.Co., Brass, 13 In.	65.00
First Aid, New York City, Tin Box, 8 1/2 X 4 1/2 In.	25.00
Fixture, Light, Dining Car, Converted To Electric, Metal	135.00
Glass, Union Pacific R.R.	7.00
Gravy Boat, P.R.R. Keystone	50.00
Handbook, Electrical Engineer's, Black Leather Bound, 1912	25.00
Hanger, Clothes, Pullman, Wooden	8.00
Hat, Conductor's, Boston & Maine	45.00
Hat, Conductor's, N.Y.Central	35.00
Hat, Pullman	40.00
Jack, Boston & Maine, Iron, 10 In.Tall	7.50
Jug, Stoneware, B. & O.	60.00
Key, C. & O., Brass	15.00
Key, N.Y.O. & W.Ry.Brass	125.00
Key, Switch, C. & N.W.R.R.	20.00
Knife, Pocket, L. & N.R.R.	30.00
Lamp, Caboose, Aladdin, Nickel Plated Font, Tin Shade	165.00
Lamp, Inspector, P.R.R., Dietz, Complete	65.00
Lamp, Model A, Union Carbide	40.00

Lamp, Oil, Coach, Brass, Pair	150.00
Lamp, Oil, Wall Bracket, Marked N.Y.C.	47.00
Lamp, Side, Coach, Kerosene, 2 Wicks, Brass, Marked	175.00
Lamp, Switch, Adlake	63.00
Lamp, Switch, Red, Green Lens	120.00
Lantern, A.T.& S.F., Amber Globe	65.00
Lantern, Adlake, C.T.R.	30.00
Lantern, Adlake, Red Globe, N.Y.C.S.	38.00
Lantern, B. & O., Capitol Dome Globe	80.00
Lantern, Caboose, Pair	300.00
Lantern, CCC & STL	63.00
Lantern, Clear Globe, Frosted Letters D & H, 1921	30.00
Lantern, D. & H., Bell Bottom	80.00
Lantern, D.L. & W.R.R., Armspear	54.00
Lantern, D.L. & W.R.R., Tall Globe	110.00
Lantern, Delta Electric	15.00
Lantern, Dietz No.39, N.H.Ry., Bell Bottom	100.00
Lantern, Dietz Supreme, Boston Elevated Railway	35.00
Lantern, Dietz, Boston & Maine, Clear Etched	32.00
Lantern, Dietz, Little Wizard, Red Globe	28.00
Lantern, Dietz, N.Y.C. Lines, Globe	35.00
Lantern, Flagman's, Red Globe, Adlake Kero, Canada, U.S.A.	30.00
Lantern, G.M.O. R.R.	35.00
Lantern, Hand, Embossed Globe, P.R.R.	35.00
Lantern, Inspector's Dietz Acme, N.Y.C. R.R.	75.00
Lantern, Inspector's, Dietz, Hood & Reflector, P.R.R.	60.00
Lantern, Inspector's, P.R.R.	40.00
Lantern, Kerosene, B & M, Patented 1928, 10 In.Tall	30.00
Lantern, M.K.T., Bell Bottom	125.00
Lantern, New Haven R.R., Battery, Brass, 1920, 8 In.	35.00
Lantern, New York Central Wireguard, 10 In.Tall	26.50
Lantern, New York Central, Red Glass Globe, Tin	55.00
Lantern, Pere Marquette	35.00
Lantern, Wabash R.R.	42.50
Lantern, Wright Glass Fount, G.T.R.	88.00
Lock & Key, Southern Railroad	40.00
Lock, B. & M.R.R., Brass	25.00 To 30.00
Lock, B. & O., Heart Shaped, Brass	20.00
Lock, Boston & Main Sheet Iron	22.50
Lock, C.B.& Q. R.R.	10.00
Lock, D. & H.R.R., Heart Shaped, Key, Brass	100.00
Lock, Embossed N. & W., Brass	40.00
Lock, Heart Shaped, N. & W.Ry., Co., Brass	65.00
Lock, Keen Kutter, Emblem Shape	70.00
Lock, Key, Santa Fe	25.00
Lock, N. & W., Heart Shaped, Brass	45.00
Lock, Ry.Express Agency, Key, Marked	47.50
Lock, Signal, L. & N., Steel	10.00
Lock, Southern Pacific R.R., Brass	45.00
Lock, Switch, Kansas City, Brass	30.00
Lock, Union Pacific Roadway & Bridge Dept., Brass	65.00
Lock, Wabash R.R., Key, Brass	45.00
Menu, Erie & Chicago Line, , C.1870	12.50
Oilcan, B. & O., Galvanized Steel, 23 In.	25.00
Oilcan, Rear Base Strap, D.R. & G.R.R., 2 Gallon	185.00
Oiler, Marked D.L. & W. R.R.	50.00
Paperweight, C. & H., Stourbridge Lion, Bronze, Dated 1929	12.00
Pin, Lapel, Southern Pacific, SP In Red, Screw Back, Pair	12.00
Pitcher, N.Y.Central, DeWitt Clinton	50.00
Plate, B. & O. Lamberton, 10 In.	85.00
Plate, Compartment, Clockwise Border Scenes, B. & O., 11 In.	125.00
Plate, Country Gardens, N.Y.C., 11 In.Diam.	75.00
Plate, Gotham, P.R.R., 10 1/2 In.Diam.	40.00

Plate, New York City Mohawk, 9 In.	60.00
Plate, Santa Fe R.R., Stamped Ancient Mimbreno	85.00
Plate, Soup.B. & O.R.R., Wood, Dark Blue, 10 In.	400.00
Plate, Southern R.R., Piedmont Pattern, 7 1/2 In.	18.00
Plate, Steam, Missouri Pacific	175.00
Plate, Yellow Bird, Powhatan, Norfolk & Western, 6 1/4 In.	30.00
Platter, Atlantic Coastline, Marked, 11 X 7 In.	75.00
Platter, Centennial, B. & O., Indian Creek, 15 3/4 X 11 In.	60.00
Platter, Cumberland Narrows, B. & O., Oval, 11 1/2 X 8 In.	75.00
Platter, Cumberland Narrows, B. & O., 15 X 10 1/2 In.	110.00
Platter, Eagle, Missouri Pacific, Syracuse, 10 1/2 X 7 1/4 In.	20.00
Platter, Flambeau Pattern, Chicago & Northwestern, 7 1/2 X 5 In.	15.00
Platter, Maddox Trenton China, Blue, 8 X 13 In.	55.00
Platter, Union Pacific, Overland Historical Pattern, 14 In.	195.00
Platter, Union Pacific, Overland, Western Scenes, 8 In.	85.00
Poster, N.Y.Central, Thoroughbreds, LaSalle Street Station	75.00
Poster, Night Freight, England, C.1946, 40 X 50 In.	225.00
Puncher, Ticket	12.00
Recess Light, Pullman Car, 1899	15.00
Relish, Piedmont, Southern R.R., Octagonal, 3 1/2 X 7 In.	13.00
Safe, N.Y.Central System, LaSalle Station, Chicago, Gold Leaf	5000.00
Saucer, B. & O., Centennial, 5 In.	28.00
Saucer, Demitasse, B. & O.R.R., Blue & White	15.00
Saucer, Streamliner Pattern, Union Pacific	3.50
Schedule, Rock Island, Suburban, Train, 1939	1.50
Shovel, Stove, Caboose, Cast Iron	8.50
Sign, Express Agency, Printed On Both Sides, 14 X 14 In.	27.50
Sign, Ga.R.R., Porcelain, Red & White, 11 X 16 In.	65.00
Sign, Pea, Red, White Porcelain, 12 In.Square	45.00
Sign, Union Pacific, Stainless Steel, 27 X 10 1/2 In.	65.00
Sign, Women's Toilet, Gold Leaf, Wooden, 4 X 26 In.	125.00
Sledgehammer, P.R.R., Bronze, C.1933, 8 Lb.	30.00
Sledgehammer, Penn Central, Bronze, Signed, 1900	15.00
Spike Hammer, Marked B & M R.R., Oak Handle	18.50
Spittoon, Pullman, Brass	35.00
Spittoon, Stamped Pennsylvania R.R., Keystone	55.00
Step Stool, Pullman, Yellow Base, Gray Metal, 14 1/2 X 12 In.	110.00
Step, Platform, Conductor's, Great Northern	125.00
Stock Certificate, Chicago, Burlington, & Quincy R.R., 1880-1900	11.00
Stock Certificate, Green Bay & Western R.R., 1940s	9.00
Stool, Pullman, Wood Top	80.00
Stove, Caboose, M.K.& T.Ry., Marked	225.00
Sugar, Burlington Route, Covered, Silver Plated, 3 1/4 In.	45.00
Switch Lock & Key, B. & O. R.R., Brass	30.00
Switch Lock, Kansas City R.R., Brass	30.00
Syrup, Attached Tray, Chicago & Northwestern, Silver Plate	75.00
Tablecloth, Damask, Missouri Central	32.00
Tablecloth, Linking 13 States With Nation, B. & O., 52 X 42 In.	30.00
Teapot, B. & O.Centennial	350.00
Teapot, Rock Island, Silver Plated	50.00
Tie Bar, Brass, Figural, Locomotive	4.50
Timetable, Tricolored Map Inside, 1897, Open, 17 X 47 In.	28.00
Tongs, Sugar, Missouri Pacific	42.00
Torch, Hand, P.R.R., Metal	10.00
Torch, L.V.R.R., No.6, Pair	15.00
Tray, Serving, Great Northern, Oval, 1920s	20.00
Tumbler, Water, Flag & Initial Center, Lehigh Valley, 5 1/2 In.	18.00
Tumbler, Water, Purple Logo, Atlantic Coastline R.R., 5 In.	6.00
Tureen, Soup, B. & O., Silver Plated, 4 X 7 1/2 In.	125.00
Uniform, Conductor's, Southern R.R.	150.00
Wagon, Baggage, Steel Frame, C. & E.I.R.R.	250.00
Whistle, Backup, C. & O.R.R., Peanut Type, Brass, 3 In.	45.00
Whistle, Brass, Northeastern Lines, C.1880, 9 1/2 In.	125.00

Whistle, Lukenheimer, Steam, Brass	80.00
Whistle, Steam, Brass, 8 1/2 X 1 3/4 In.	45.00
Whistle, Steam, Brass, 13 In.	125.00

RAINBOW, see Mother-of-Pearl; Satin Glass

RAZOR, Amco Soligen, Straight, Germany, Bone Handle, Gold Gilt Blade	10.00
Castle Scene On Ivory Celluloid, Germany, Straight	30.00
Ever-Ready, Brass, 1912	8.00
Ever-Ready, Safety, Original Case	5.00
Geometric Carved Ivory Handle, Straight	12.00
George Wosfenholm & Sons, Straight	8.00
Griffen Cutlery	8.00
Hone, Colorful Tin Box	18.00
Ivory Celluloid Handles	4.00
Ivory Handle, Straight	15.00
K.T.Barber's, Straight, Set Of 12	165.00
Keen Kutter, Original Box	8.50
Keen Kutter, Straight	45.00
Kriss Kross, Safety	10.00
Litts, Straight	7.00
Rolls-Royce, Box With Instructions	25.00
Ship Etched On Blade, Straight	27.00
Strop, Double Leather, Brass Fittings	15.95
Strop, Wooden Handle, Case, 11 1/2 In.	6.00
Superwedge, Straight, Red Handle	15.00
The Improved Eagle, Straight, Spread Eagle Figure On Blade	10.00
William Elliot, Germany	9.00
Winchester, With Strop	110.00

Reamers, or juice squeezers, have been known since 1767, although most of those collected today date from the twentieth century.

REAMER, All Wooden	55.00
Amber	16.00
Brown, 3 Piece	35.00
California Fruit Growers Assoc., Sunkist, Crystal	18.00
California Fruit Growers, Yellow Opaque Glass, McKee	35.00
Cast Iron	22.50
Clown, Full-Bodied, New Sigma	17.00
Clown, Green, 7 1/2 In.	40.00 To 45.00
Clown, Hand-Painted, Japan, 2 Piece	35.00
Clown, Nu Sigma, Full Bodied	17.00
Clown, Orange & Green Design, Japanese, 7 In., 2 Piece	125.00
Crisscross, Glass, Green	14.00
Duck, Gold Trim, Ceramic, 2 Piece	45.00
Fry Ovenware, Blue	45.00
Glass, Pink	10.00
Green & White, Flower In Center	30.00
Green Custard, Marked McKee	28.00
Jadite, Jeanette Glass	18.50
Lemon, Figural, China, Yellow & Green, 2 Piece	23.00
McK Skokie, Green	12.00
Milk Glass, Blue, Marked Sunkist	50.00
Milk Glass, Green, Embossed McKee	22.00
Peach Luster & Green	35.00
Pink Jenny	75.00
Puddinhead, Figural	120.00
Saucer Type, Yellow, Green Leaf	15.00
Sunkist Juice, Yellow Opaque Glass	25.00 To 30.00
Sunkist Oranges & Lemons, Clear Handle	25.00
Sunkist, Milk Glass	5.00 To 10.00
Sunkist, Milk Glass, Green	13.00
Sunkist, Opaque Green	25.00
Sunkist, Pink	15.00

Ultramarine, Jeanette	50.00
Westmorland, Pink	65.00
Wooden, 11 In.	65.00

The Red Wing Pottery of Red Wing, Minnesota, was a firm started in 1878. It was not until the 1920s that art pottery was made. It closed in 1967. Rumrill pottery was made for George Rumrill by the Red Wing Pottery Company and other firms. It was sold in the 1930s.

RED WING, Ashtray, Minnesota Twins, 1965 World Series	35.00
Ashtray, 75th Anniversary	50.00
Basket, Pink	18.00
Basket, Pink, 10 In.	20.00
Bean Pot, Advertising, Saffron Ware, 2 Quart	40.00
Bean Pot, R.W.Union, Wire Handle, 1 Quart	60.00
Bean Pot, Sponge Band	125.00
Bowl, Beater	65.00
Bowl, Beater, You Beat Eggs, We Beat Prices	45.00
Bowl, Blue Sponge On Tan, 4 3/8 X 7 In.Diam.	58.00
Bowl, Bobwhite, 12 In.	25.00
Bowl, Green & Brown, 2-Handled, 9 1/2 X 4 In.	35.00
Bowl, Marked, Brown, 7 In.	15.00
Bowl, North Star Co., Brown Slip Inside, Unglazed Outside, 7 In.	22.00
Bowl, Petal Rim, Scalloped Daisies Inside, 5 1/2 X 10 In.Diam.	42.50
Bowl, Rust, Blue Sponge Ovenware, 7 In.	47.50
Bowl, Spongeware Band, 8 In.Diam.	60.00
Casserole, Blue Advertising Inside, Pierre, South Dakota, 7 1/4 In.	100.00
Casserole, Greyline, 7 In.	125.00
Casserole, Spongeware Band	145.00
Churn, Drop 8 Pattern, 5 Gallon	110.00
Churn, Leaf Pattern, 6 Gallon	210.00
Churn, Wood Dasher, Original Lid	150.00
Cookie Jar, Acorn, Leaf On Lid, Basket Weave Bottom, Signed	12.50
Cookie Jar, Apple	20.00
Cookie Jar, Baker, Blue	35.00
Cookie Jar, Baker, Yellow	20.00
Cookie Jar, Bobwhite	38.00
Cookie Jar, Cat In Basket	12.50
Cookie Jar, Chef, Blue	20.00
Cookie Jar, Chief, Yellow	25.00
Cookie Jar, Dog In Basket	12.50
Cookie Jar, Dutch Girl, Blue	30.00
Cookie Jar, Dutch Girl, Yellow	25.00 To 26.00
Cookie Jar, Monk, Blue	30.00 To 45.00
Cookie Jar, Saffron, Lid, Signed, 8 In.	65.00
Cookie Jar, Spongeware Band, Cover	350.00
Cookie Jar, Turnabout Bears	35.00
Cookie Jar, Winking Lion	12.50
Cooler, Iced Tea, 2 Gallon	295.00
Cooler, Leaf Pattern, 4 Gallon	400.00
Cooler, Water, Barrel Shape, White & Blue Banding, Spigot, 3 Gallon	128.50
Cooler, Water, 2 Gallon	750.00
Crock, Birch Leaves, 4 Gallon	30.00
Crock, Canning, 1/2 Gallon	115.00
Crock, Double P Pattern, MSW__Co., 2 Gallon	60.00
Crock, Double P Pattern, 4 Gallon	42.50
Crock, Lace 8 Pattern, 3 Gallon	42.50
Crock, With Wing, 2 Gallon	15.00
Crock, 15 Gallon, Marked	30.00
Dish, Divided, Iris, 26 X 12 1/2 In.	5.00
Dish, Hors D'oeuvre, Figural, Bobwhite	30.00
Ewer, Matte Ivory, Dolphin Handled, 10 In.	20.00
Figurine, Cowboy, 11 In., Pair	30.00
Hot Plate, 1958	30.00

Jar, Beater	65.00
Jar, Chocolate, Bowery's Hot, Tan Cattail Design, Lid	125.00
Jar, Fruit, Blue Lettering, 1 Gallon	325.00
Jar, Fruit, Mason, Blue Lettering	275.00
Jar, Fruit, Mason, 1/2 Gallon	85.00
Jar, Fruit, Mason, 1 Gallon	160.00
Jar, Fruit, Mason, 1 Quart	100.00
Jar, Pantry, Advertising, No Cover	245.00
Jug, Brown Top, Marked, 1 Gallon	40.00
Jug, Elks	300.00
Jug, Gold Wing, Paper Label, Miniature	50.00
Jug, Green, 8 1/2 In.	35.00
Jug, Lithia Spring Water, Londonberry, N.H., 3 Gallon	395.00
Jug, Minnesota State Fair, Miniature	115.00
Jug, Postal Convention, Miniature	300.00
Jug, With Wing, 1/2 Gallon	135.00
Juicer, Cup	55.00
Keg, Mustard, McLaughlin's	100.00
Mug, Hamms Beer	65.00
Pitcher, Cherries & Leaves, Blue & Gray, 6 In.	65.00
Pitcher, Cherry Band, Advertising	120.00
Pitcher, Cherry Band, Blue & Gray	70.00
Pitcher, Gross Mercantile Co., Bridgewater, S.Dakota	80.00
Pitcher, Spongeware Band, Small	135.00
Pitcher, Titonka, Iowa, Spongeware Band, Gray Line	135.00
Pitcher, Water, Bobwhite, 11 1/2 In.	24.00
Pitcher, Water, Brown	40.00
Planter, Deer Flower Frog, Ivory, 16 In.	30.00
Planter, Figural, Swan, 6 In.	10.00
Plate, Apple, 12 In.	7.00
Plate, Lexington, Rose, 7 1/2 In.	6.00
Plate, Lotus	5.00
Platter, Zinnia, 11 X 12 In.	5.00
Reamer, Pedestal, Yellow, 7 In.	125.00
Reamer, 7 In.	75.00
Salt & Pepper, Bobwhite, Boxed	25.00
Saucer, Bobwhite, Set Of 6	20.00
Sugar & Creamer, Aqua	12.00
Teapot, Bird	20.00
Toothpick, McKinley	225.00
Tray, Bread, Bobwhite, 23 In.	50.00
Vase, Brown, Green Interior, Shell Shape, Original Label, 8 In., Pair	15.00
Vase, Bulbous Bottom, Flared Mouth, Marked, Dark Green, 3 X 7 In.	12.00
Vase, Cattails, Brown Ground, 7 In.	40.00
Vase, Green Interior, Brown	12.00
Vase, Molded Lions, Matte Gray Green, Marked, 8 In.	48.00
Vase, Pinched Top, White Interior, Baby Blue, 8 In.	25.00
Vase, Roman Figures	16.00
Wall Pocket, Turquoise, Violin, 13 In.	25.00
Wall Pocket, Violin Shape, White	15.00
Water Cooler, Last Of The Butterflies, Salt Glaze, 8 Gallon	350.00

Redware is a hard red stoneware that originated in the late 1600s and continues to be made. The term is also used to describe any common clay pottery that is reddish in color.

REDWARE, Bank, Figural, Grinning Male Head, 3 1/8 In.	110.00
Bedpan, 18th Century, Manganese Splotching	75.00
Bowl, Coggled Edge, Pennsylvania, Yellow Slip Design, 13 1/2 In.	500.00
Charger, Yellow Slip Design, Coggled Edge	300.00
Crock, D.M.Baker's Pottery, Waynesboro, Pennsylvania	50.00
Crock, John Bell, Waynesboro	90.00
Dish, Yellow Highlights, Green, Clear Glaze, 7 In.	155.00
Figurine, Head, Military Man, White Details, 8 In.	195.00

Flowerpot, Stamped Geometric Design, C.1850, 7 1/2 X 7 In.	75.00
Humidor, J.G.Dill's, Embossed Rings & Staves, Barrel Shape, 7 In.	75.00
Jar, Dark Green, Orange Glaze, 21 In.	175.00
Jar, Galena, Brown Glaze, 11 1/2 In.	65.00
Jar, John Bell, Waynesboro	525.00
Jar, Sweetmeat, Shakespeare Design, Pair	95.00
Jug, Bulbous, Black Glaze, 8 In.	75.00
Jug, Bulbous, Handled, Black Glaze, 4 1/2 In.	75.00
Jug, Bulbous, Handled, Black Glaze, 8 1/4 In.	75.00
Jug, Dark Brown Glaze, 8 1/2 In.	55.00
Mold, Cake, Bundt, 12 In.Diam.	75.00
Mold, Food, Flight Into Egypt, 5 In.Diam.	65.00
Mold, Pudding, Turk's Turban, Speckled, 3 X 7 In.	55.00
Mold, Turk's Head, Orange Glaze, Brown Spotches, 7 1/2 In.Diam.	50.00
Pan, Milk, Brownish Green Glaze, 18 1/2 In.	60.00
Paperweight, Book Shape, Marbleized Yellow & Tan, 5 1/2 X 3 1/2 In.	110.00
Pitcher, Masked Spout, Marked, 8 In.	85.00
Pitcher, White Dots Around Shoulder, Salmon Glaze, 4 1/2 In.	45.00
Planter, Hanging, Crimped Rim, 4 1/2 X 9 In.Diam.	25.00
Plate, Pie, Yellow Slip Design, Coggled Edge, 9 3/4 In.	295.00
Plate, 9 3/4 In.	75.00
Pot, Herb, Dark Brown Glaze, 6 In.	38.00
Teapot, Enameled Design, Oriental Mark	20.00

    REGOUT, see Maastricht

Richard was the mark used on acid-etched cameo glass vases, bowls, night-lights, and lamps in Lorraine, France, during the 1920s.

RICHARD, Lamp, Cameo, Scenic, Signed, 30 In.	2400.00
Vase, Chateau Scenic, Orange Ground, Signed, 10 5/8 In.	895.00
Vase, 9 In.	*Illus* 1200.00

Ridgway pottery has been made in the Staffordshire district in England since 1808 by a series of companies with the name Ridgway. The transfer-design dinner sets are the most widely known product. They are still being made.

    RIDGWAY, see also Flow Blue

RIDGWAY, Bowl, Coaching Days, Paying Toll, 8 1/2 In.	30.00
Bowl, Coaching Days, Post Boys, 8 1/2 In.	30.00
Calendar Plate, 1928, Pickwick	55.00
Cup & Saucer, Apple Blossom	15.00
Cup & Saucer, Coaching Days, Silver Trim, Marked	50.00
Mug, Coaching Days, Breakdown Taking On The Mails, 5 In.	50.00
Mug, Coaching Days, Silver Trim, 4 3/4 In.	40.00
Mug, Coaching Days, 4 In.	30.00
Pitcher, Dated 1885, Gold Rope Bands At Top, Gray, 12 X 6 In.	90.00
Pitcher, St.Albans, Roses, Gold & Black	175.00
Pitcher, Tam O'Shanter, Tan, Dated 1835, 10 In.	220.00
Plaque, Coaching Days, A Cast Shoe, 9 In.	35.00
Plate, Coaching Days, 10 In.	30.00
Plate, Coaching Days, 12 In.	40.00
Plate, Medina, Blue & White, 10 5/8 In.	25.00
Platter, Blue Willow, 13 1/2 X 11 In.	35.00
Platter, Wadham College, Figures, C.1825, 16 5/8 In.	275.00
Tankard, Coaching Days, 5 In.	38.00
Tankard, Coaching Days, 6 Mugs, Silver Rims, Handles	250.00
Tea Set, Child's, Hair Fern Pattern, 1888, Marked, 6 Cups & Saucers	195.00
Teapot, Coaching Days, Covered, Racing The Mail, 5 In.	95.00

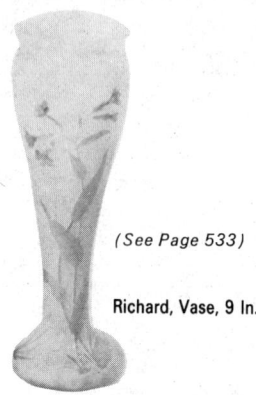

(See Page 533)

Richard, Vase, 9 In.

Teapot, Coaching Days, Racing The Mail, Silver Trim, 5 1/4 In.	95.00
Tray, Coaching Days, Christmas Visitor, Scalloped, 12 1/2 In.	70.00
Trivet, Coaching Days, Silver Trim	43.00
Tumbler, Coaching Days, Silver Trim, 4 In.	30.00

Riviera Ware was made by the Homer Laughlin Co. from 1938 to 1950. Plates were square and cup handles were squared.

RIVIERA, Bowl, Mauve, 5 1/4 In	6.00
Bowl, Soup, Flat, Mauve	6.50
Fruit, Green, 5 1/2 In.	3.00
Plate, Mauve, 10 In.	10.00
Platter, Oval In Center, Rectangular, Green	100.00
Platter, Oval, Mauve, 11 1/4 In.	12.50
Sauceboat, Red	10.00
Teapot, Covered, Green	32.50

Rockingham in the United States is a brown glazed pottery with a tortoiseshell-like glaze. It was made from 1840 to 1900 by many American potteries. Mottled brown Rockingham wares were first made in England at the Rockingham factory. Other wares were also made by the English firm.

ROCKINGHAM, Bedpan, Figural Bird	125.00
Bottle, Shoe, Embossed Laces, Impressed Victoria, 6 In.	30.00
Bowl, Dark Amber Glaze, 6 1/4 In.	10.00
Bowl, Flat Milk Pan Style, 7 3/4 In.Diam.	45.00
Bowl, Shallow, 2 1/2 In.	55.00
Bowl, 8 1/2 In.	20.00
Coffeepot, Grape Pattern	250.00
Coffeepot, 11 In.	65.00
Cup & Saucer, Gold Scrolls, White	30.00
Cup, Custard	25.00
Dish, Embossed Rim, 8 1/2 X 8 3/4 In.	60.00
Dish, Soap, Oval, 5 1/4 In.	95.00
Figurine, Poodle, 18 In.	360.00
Flask, Book Shape	375.00
Knob, Door, Includes Lock & Key	35.00
Mug, Powder Horn & Indian Handle	31.00
Pan, Milk	165.00
Pitcher, Embossed Dancers, 6 In.	55.00
Pitcher, Embossed Scene, Children & Goat, 7 In.	90.00
Pitcher, Hound Handle, C.1880	125.00

Pitcher, Surprise, Medallion Design, Frog Figure Bottom, 9 In. 175.00
Plate, Armorial, Lemon Ground, Floral Design, Set Of 12 .... 325.00
Plate, Pie, 8 1/2 In. 85.00
Plate, Pie, 10 1/2 In. 49.00
Plate, Scalloped, 19th Century, 8 1/2 In.Square 85.00
Platter, Crows-Foot, Oval, 13 In. 105.00
Teapot, 5 1/2 In. 65.00
    ROGERS, see John Rogers

Rookwood pottery was made in Cincinnati, Ohio, from 1880 to 1960. All of this art pottery is marked, most with the famous flame mark. The R is reversed and placed back to back with the letter P. Flames surround the letters.

ROOKWOOD, Ashtray, Boss Stoves 37.00
Ashtray, Cow Design 75.00
Ashtray, Eagles, 1935, Aqua 30.00
Ashtray, Frog, Aqua, 1939 .... 68.00
Ashtray, Glossy Light Blue, 6 In.Diam. 35.00
Ashtray, Nude Lady, Ivory, 1940, 4 1/2 In. 110.00
Ashtray, Owl Perched On Side, 1939, 5 1/2 X 6 1/2 In. 85.00
Ashtray, Western Southern Ins., Anniversary, 1938, 5 1/2 In. 50.00
Base, Lamp, Wax Matte, Blue & Black Florals, 10 In. 175.00
Basket, Pansies, Painted By W.P.McDonald, 1892, Marked, 10 1/4 In. 440.00
Bookends, Basket, 5-Color Floral, 1927 .... 225.00
Bookends, Birds, Pink Matte, Pair 110.00
Bookends, Dog, Cream 165.00
Bookends, Dutch Boy & Girl, Signed, 1929 .... 145.00
Bookends, Elephants, Blue, 1923 .... 150.00
Bookends, Elephants, White, 1944 .... 95.00
Bookends, Flower Bouquet 72.00
Bookends, Flowers, Green, 1945, 9 1/4 X 5 1/2 In. 85.00
Bookends, Girl Seated, Reading, Pink 250.00
Bookends, Lady Reading 200.00
Bookends, Owl .... 36.00 To 75.00
Bookends, Owl, Blue, High-Gloss 105.00
Bookends, Rooks, Blue Matte, 1946, 5 1/2 In., Pair 135.00
Bookends, Rooks, Blue, 1921 .... 125.00
Bookends, Rooks, Green, 1928, 5 1/4 X 4 1/4 In. 135.00
Bookends, Rooks, 1950, McDonald 150.00
Bookends, Trees, Red-Brown, 1930, 5 1/2 In., Pair 155.00
Bookends, Water Lilies, 1919 .... 125.00
Bowl, Berry, 1917, Pink Matte, 7 X 3 In. 39.00
Bowl, Flat Globular Form, Sara Toohey, 1889, Marked, 3 1/2 In. 165.00
Bowl, Lincoln, Wax Matte, 1928, 9 X 3 In. 245.00
Bowl, Pink, Brown, 1926, 7 In. 35.00
Bowl, Shell Shaped, 5 1/2 In. 150.00
Bowl, Signed Charles Todd, 1920, 7 In. 200.00
Bowl, Slat-Blue, 4-Footed, 1921, Signed 25.00
Bowl, Turquoise High Glaze, 1922, 10 In.Diam. 40.00
Bowl, Turquoise Interior, White Outside, 1922, 8 In. 40.00
Bowl, Turquoise, Lotus, 13 In. 135.00
Bowl, Yellow, 1921, 3 X 5 In. 12.50
Candleholder, Brown, White Raised Flowers, 5 In. 38.00
Candleholder, Green.Gold, Sea Horses In Corner, 4 In. 50.00
Candleholder, 1918, Yellow, 5 In. 25.00
Candlestick, Blue Matte, 20 In. 40.00
Candlestick, Blue-Gray, Gold Flecks, 1923 .... 38.00
Candlestick, Molded Cherubs & Wreaths, Matte Brown, 24 In., Pair 1050.00
Centerpiece, Female Form, Turquoise Interior, Dated 1927 .... 475.00
Chamberstick, With Dragon, Blue 160.00
Coffeepot, Double Gourd Form, Bird, 1894 Mark, 9 In. 1900.00

Creamer, Rose Pattern, Cameo Glaze, 1891 .... 185.00
Creamer, 1886, Bisque, Grace Young, 4 In. 197.50
Dish, Nut, Shell Shape, Signed 475.00
Ewer, Berried Branches, C.A.Baker, 1899, Marked, 8 1/2 In. 550.00
Ewer, Handled, Tricornered Lip, Sweet Peas, Dated 1898, Signed, 6 In. 340.00
Ewer, Nasturtiums On Body, Sage Green, Signed, 1900, 8 1/2 In. 425.00
Ewer, Pansy Design, 1899, 6 1/2 In. 375.00
Ewer, Sara Toohey, 1889, 7 1/2 In. 350.00
Ewer, Shaded Rose Sprays, 1891, 9 1/2 In. 95.00
Ewer, Yellow Flowers, Leafed Twig, Brown Glaze, 1907, Signed, 6 In. 265.00
Figurine, Bust Of Young Woman, White, 1925, 8 X 7 In. 170.00
Figurine, Donkey, Louis Abel, 1935 .... 125.00
Figurine, Dutch Girl On Pedestal, Brown, 6 In. 160.00
Figurine, Madonna & Child, Cream Glaze, 7 1/2 In. 115.00
Figurine, Nude On Rock, Blue 150.00
Figurine, Nude, White Matte Glaze, 1928, Signed 125.00
Flask, Pilgrim, Olive Green, Bamboo Shoots, Black, Marked, 6 In. 325.00
Flower Frog, Turquoise Figural Lotus, 13 In. 140.00
Honey, Green Jewel Porcelain Glaze, 1883, Kiln Mark, 4 In. 347.50
Inkstand, Rook Standing On Edge Of Lily Pad Inkwell, 1925, Blue 595.00
Jar, Shield On Cover, Dated 1940, Chartreuse, 10 In. 40.00
Jardiniere, Floral Design, Pansy, Silver Overlay, Signed, 5 In. 1500.00
Jug, Carved Branches, Blossoms, J.Wenderoth, 1884, Marked, 5 1/4 In. 425.00
Jug, Cherries, 1903, 6 In. 220.00
Jug, Honey, Incised Painted Clover, 1883, 4 3/4 In. 195.00
Jug, Honey, Signed, 1882 Mark, Round 475.00
Jug, Honey, 1883, Carved Floral Design, Harriet Wenderoth 290.00
Jug, Incised Wheat Leaves, Brown 515.00
Jug, Whiskey, Hops & Leaves Design, L.Ashbury, 1896, Brown Glaze 250.00
Jug, 1893, Artist Olga Geneva Reed, 6 In. 400.00
Lamp Base, Pink & Yellow, Green Molded Gladiolus, C.1929, 15 In. 395.00
Lamp Base, 3 Sea Horse Form, 1905, Brown-Green Matte, 12 In. 220.00
Letter Holder, 1847 Postage Stamp 35.00
Mask, Comedy, Green 125.00
Mug, Ashbury Corn, 1902 .... 215.00
Mug, Corn Design, Rothenbush, 1899 .... 475.00
Mug, Indian Brave, Marked, Sadie Markland, 1898, 5 1/4 In. 1200.00
Mug, Matte Green, Brown & White, 1905, 5 1/2 In. 235.00
Mug, 1882 Ribbon Mark, 7 In. 500.00
Paperweight, Dog 85.00
Paperweight, Elephant, Blue, 1926, 3 1/4 X 4 In. 95.00
Paperweight, Fruit In Basket, Artist Signed 95.00
Paperweight, Girl, Ivory, 1929, 4 X 4 1/4 In. 125.00
Paperweight, Girl, Turquoise, 1943, 4 X 4 1/4 In. 100.00
Paperweight, Monkey 60.00
Paperweight, Rabbit, Ivory, 1946, 3 X 3 In. 65.00
Paperweight, Rook, Navy, 1915, 3 X 4 In. 125.00
Paperweight, Seated Nude, 1932, White 125.00
Paperweight, Squirrel, Ivory, 1933, 4 X 4 In. 85.00
Pitcher, Clover Design, Trefoil Mouth, Butterfly Handle, 16 X 4 In. 295.00
Pitcher, Floral With Butterfly, Side Spout, 1884, 6 1/4 In. 350.00
Pitcher, Heart Shaped Rim, Flower Form Handle, Dated 1896, 4 In. 235.00
Pitcher, Poppies, 1898, Signed, 4 1/2 In. 295.00
Pitcher, Tri Corner, Red Cherries, Green Ground, 5 1/2 In. 195.00
Plaque, Along The River, Lenore Asbury .... *Illus* 850.00
Plaque, Blue & White, Lady In Center, 9 In. 300.00
Plaque, Christ Child In Swaddling Clothes, Signed, 14 X 19 In. 780.00
Plaque, Christ Child, Oval, Signed In Black, 21 In. 480.00
Plaque, Country Scene, 1914, Artist Signed, 14 X 9 In. 2000.00
Plaque, Mountains, McLaughlin, 9 X 7 In. 1125.00
Plaque, R.Earl Menzel, Dated 1904, A.M.Valentien, 10 In.Diam. 298.00
Plaque, The Poplars, Pastoral Scene, Lake, 6 X 8 In. 1350.00
Plate, Souvenir, Indiana State College, Blue, 8 In. 45.00

Rookwood, Plaque, Along The River,
Lenore Asbury

Pot, Blue Pennants At Top, Gray, 1901, Signed, 3 In.	210.00
Smoking Set, Elephant, 1935, 5 In.	70.00
Sugar & Creamer, High Gloss, Green, Individual	35.00
Sugar & Creamer, Sailing Ship, Blue	235.00
Sugar & Creamer, Vellum Glaze, Yellow	45.00
Sugar & Creamer, 1924, Pink	45.00
Tea Caddy, Green Sweet Clover Design, 1905	475.00
Tea Caddy, Standard Glaze, Artist Signed	450.00
Teapot, Band Of Grape Leaves, Marked, Unglazed, 8 3/4 In.	80.00
Teapot, Painted By W.Klemm, 1900, Holly Berries, Marked, 6 In.	525.00
Tile, Scenic, Framed, 6 X 6 In., Pair	1000.00
Tile, 3 Geese, 1925, 6 In.Square	110.00
Trivet, Grapes, 1924, 6 X 6 In.	80.00
Trivet, Molded Ducks Border, Round	40.00
Trivet, Sea Gulls In Flight, 1918, Circular	105.00
Vase, Abstract Floral, 1920, 11 1/2 In.	300.00
Vase, Amber & Cream, 1901, 34 In.	65.00
Vase, Amber, 1911, 9 1/2 In.	45.00
Vase, Art Nouveau, Iris Glaze, 1945, Jens Jensen, 6 1/2 In.	295.00
Vase, Berried Branch, C.C.Lindeman, 1902, Marked, 4 1/2 In.	165.00
Vase, Bird & Floral Design, White Ground, 1946, 6 In.	500.00
Vase, Black Boy In Ragged Hat, 1895, B.Horsfall, Marked, 7 In.	1300.00
Vase, Blue & Green Floral, Matte Finish, Small Relief, 7 1/2 In.	185.00
Vase, Blue Matte, 1921, 5 1/2 X 4 1/2 In.	40.00
Vase, Blue Rooks, 5-Sided, 1923, 5 1/2 In.	45.00
Vase, Blue To Green, Cartoonlike Characters, 1911, 5 1/2 In.	100.00
Vase, Blue, Fish Design, Bulbous, Signed, 4 1/2 In.	90.00
Vase, Bottom Band Of Rooks, Matte, Butterscotch, 6 1/2 In.	65.00
Vase, Brown To Light Gray, Pink Roses, 6 1/2 In.	585.00
Vase, Brown, Cream Spatter, 1924, 8 1/2 In.	45.00
Vase, Burgundy, 1923, 3 1/4 In.	30.00
Vase, Butterflies, Light Blue Gloss, 4 1/2 In.	75.00
Vase, Cantalope Shape, Pink, Green Top, Berry On Branch, 4 In.	45.00
Vase, Caramel Glaze, Over Ivory, 6 In.	65.00
Vase, Cattails, 1922, 5 In.	50.00
Vase, Celery Green, Man Playing Flute, 7 In.	55.00
Vase, Cream Ground, Purple Flowers, Gray Rims, 1929, 6 In.	295.00
Vase, Crocuses & Leaves, Marked, 1902, J.Zettel, 6 1/4 In.	380.00
Vase, Crystalline, Beige Tone, 8 In.	95.00
Vase, Cylindrical, Flowers, 1910, Olive & Blue Ground, 8 3/4 In.	650.00
Vase, Daffodils, Copper Overlay, K.Shirayamadani, 1901, 4 In.	2400.00
Vase, Dark Blue Matte, Green Florals, 1904, 6 In.	200.00
Vase, Dark Blue, 2 Roses, Green, & Yellow Flowers, 1905, 5 1/2 In.	295.00
Vase, Deep Orange, Black, Pink Dogwood, 1918, 9 In.	550.00
Vase, Elizabeth Lincoln, Vellum, Floral, 4 3/4 In.	385.00
Vase, Fish Design, Bulbous, Signed, Blue, 4 1/2 In.	90.00
Vase, Fish, 1885, Albert Valentien, Marked, Matte Blue, 20 In.	3000.00
Vase, Flaring Neck, Geometric Designs, Dated 1927, Drip Glaze, 5 In.	30.00
Vase, Floral Edge, Yellow To Yellow Green, 1917, 5 1/2 In.Diam.	26.00

Vase, Floral Vellum, 1917, Signed P.C., 8 In. 425.00
Vase, Floral, Iris Glaze, 1906, 7 X 5 In. 750.00
Vase, Floral, Nasturtiums, 1903, 7 1/2 In. 750.00
Vase, Floral, Standard Glaze, Dated 1887, Signed, 18 In. 750.00
Vase, Floral, Tiger Lilies, 1905, Grace Hull, 6 In. 575.00
Vase, Flowers, Carl Schmidt, 1911, Marked, Iris Glaze, 8 3/4 In. 750.00
Vase, Flowers, Elizabeth Lincoln, 1894, Brown Ground, Marked, 4 In. 165.00
Vase, Flowers, Green, 1922, 5 3/4 In. 20.00
Vase, Flowers, Yellow, 1931, 6 1/2 In. 40.00
Vase, Forest Scene, River, Geese, Orange Sky, Signed, 8 In. 950.00
Vase, Ginkgo Trees, 1921, Arthur Conant, Marked, 9 1/4 In. 450.00
Vase, Grapes & Leaves, 1907, 6 1/2 In. 475.00
Vase, Green, Molded Sea Gulls, 1945, 9 In. 90.00
Vase, High Glaze Turquoise, 1946, 12 1/4 In. 135.00
Vase, Holly & Berries, W.P.McDonald, 1892, Brown, Marked, 9 1/2 In. 550.00
Vase, Holly Leaf Pattern, 1921, 6 3/4 In. 40.00
Vase, Impressionistic Flowers, 1922, E.T.Hurley, Marked, 8 3/4 In. 420.00
Vase, Incised Floral, 1913, Matte Brown, Hentshel, 9 In. 85.00
Vase, Iris Glaze, I.Bishop, 1906, Blue To White Ground, 7 In. 525.00
Vase, Iris, Bulbous, 1901, 4 In. 425.00
Vase, Jewel, 1944, Tan, 6 1/2 In. 30.00
Vase, Kingfisher, Trees, Jeweled, 12 In. 750.00
Vase, Lavender, 1915, 5 3/4 In. 35.00
Vase, Lorinda Epply, 1929, 9 In. 290.00
Vase, Louwelsa, Orange Carnation, Signed Lillie Mitchel, 6 In. 195.00
Vase, Magnolia Blossoms, Signed, 1904, 8 1/2 In. 575.00
Vase, Man Playing Flute, Sheep & Dog, 7 In. 55.00
Vase, Molded Flower, 9 In. 93.00
Vase, Moonlit Landscape, , 1908, Clara Lindeman, Marked, Green, 7 In. 550.00
Vase, Night Scene, Gourd Shape, Rust & Olive Green, Marked, 9 In. 800.00
Vase, Olive Green Trim, Burnt Orange Ground, Signed, 8 In. 145.00
Vase, Ovoid, Flowers, C.Steinle, 1908, Green Ground, Marked, 4 1/4 In. 140.00
Vase, Ovoid, Flowers, Leafage, Green, Rose, Blackberry, 1922, 9 In. 400.00
Vase, Pink & Blue, 1922, 11 In. 180.00
Vase, Pink Carnations, Ivory Ground, 7 In. 265.00
Vase, Pink Dogwood, Gray Ground, 5 In. 195.00
Vase, Pink, Cherubs, Dancing, Garland, 6 In. 42.00
Vase, Pink, Geometric Relief On Bottom, 1928, 5 1/2 In. 40.00
Vase, Pink, Green Top, Tulip Design, 1931, 7 1/2 In. 60.00
Vase, Pink, 1929, 6 1/2 In. 45.00
Vase, Plant & Olive Leafage, 1902, O.G.Reed, Marked, 9 In. 2000.00
Vase, Poppies, Buds, K. Shirayamadani, 1906, Marked, 12 1/4 In. 3850.00
Vase, Poppy, R.Valentien, 1886, Brown Ground, Marked, 13 1/2 In. 1250.00
Vase, Raised Butterflies, High Glaze, 4 1/2 In. 65.00
Vase, Religious, 1934, 5 In. 98.00
Vase, Rook, 5-Panel, 4 1/2 In. 65.00
Vase, Rooks, Blue, 1920, 7 1/2 In. 95.00
Vase, Roses, 1895, Toohey, 8 1/2 In. 200.00
Vase, Ruffled & Beaded Neck, Flowers, Gray Ground, Signed, 4 3/4 In. 325.00
Vase, Sadie Markland, 1893, 5 In. 225.00
Vase, Scenic Vellum Glaze, L.Ashbury, 1815, Marked, 8 1/4 In. 770.00
Vase, Scenic, Vellum, 1905, E.Diers, 9 In. 750.00
Vase, Sea Horse Design, 1915, Brown Ground, 8 3/4 In. 120.00
Vase, Shirayamadani, Cherries & Leaves On Blue, 1929, 8 1/2 In. 395.00
Vase, Silver-Mounted Lip, Bottle Form, Nasturtium, Marked, 10 In. 440.00
Vase, Stand, Yellow Wild Roses, Yellow To Brown Ground, 6 In. 300.00
Vase, Stylized Poppies, Grace Hall 1903, 5 1/2 In. 375.00
Vase, Swans, Gray Matte, 3 1/2 In. 35.00
Vase, Swollen Cylinder, Geraniums, M.A.Daly, 1887, Marked, 12 In. 880.00
Vase, Swollen Cylinder, Tulips, J.D.Wareham, 1902, Marked, 15 In. 770.00
Vase, Trees, 1920, Edward Diers, Marked, 8 X 4 In. 480.00
Vase, Trumpet Neck, Japanese Style Birds, Signed, 11 In. 1500.00
Vase, Turquoise, Glossy, 1949, 5 3/4 In. 30.00

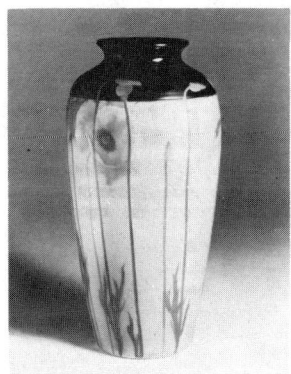

Rookwood, Vase, 1906, Kataro Shirayamadani

Vase, Turquoise, Tulips, 10 In.	69.00
Vase, Valentien, 1885, Floral, Glaze, 12 In.	595.00
Vase, Vellum, Floral Panels, 1915, 7 In.	275.00
Vase, Vellum, Floral, 1906, 4 3/4 In.	265.00
Vase, Vellum, Scenic, 1905, 9 In.	750.00
Vase, Vellum, Scenic, 1925, 7 1/2 In.	525.00
Vase, Vellum, Scenic, 1946, S Mark, 8 In.	1250.00
Vase, Vellum, Snow Scene, Dated, Artist Signed, 13 In.	1100.00
Vase, Vellum, White To Light Gray, White Roses, 1905, 7 1/2 In.	625.00
Vase, Venetian Scene, Maria L.Storer, 1894, 7 1/4 In.	1295.00
Vase, Wax Matte, Signed Elizabeth Lincoln, 1926, 8 In.	225.00
Vase, Wax Matte, Signed K.S., 1940, 7 In.	140.00
Vase, Yellow Flowers, E.N.Lincoln, 1901, Brown Ground, Marked, 9 In.	330.00
Vase, 1906, Kataro Shirayamadani	*Illus* 3850.00
Wall Pocket, Medium Green Glaze, Foliage Design, 1900, 9 X 15 In.	270.00
RORSTRAND, Vase, Floral, Purple & Green, 4 1/2 X 8 In.	325.00

Rosaline glass is a rose-colored jade glass that was made by the Steuben Glass Works in Corning, New York.

ROSALINE, Bowl, Basket Weave	20.00
Bowl, Console, Alabaster Base	500.00
Bowl, Rolled Rim, 14 1/2 In.	150.00
Box, Candy, Water Lily, Covered	32.00
Compote, Alabaster Base, Stem, & Finial, Pink, 20 In.Diam.	610.00
Compote, Alabaster Foot, 12 X 3 In.	475.00
Compote, Alabaster, 10 X 5 In.	395.00
Figurine, Happiness Bird	20.00
Finger Bowl & Plate, Bowl 9 3/4 In.	1000.00
Lamp, Fairy, Owl	22.50
Plate, Copper Wheel Design, 9 In.	200.00
Plate, Leaf Shape	22.00
Swan, Open	20.00
Vase, Cut To Ivorene, Butterfly & Coin Design, 7 1/2 In.	2450.00
Vase, Drape Effect Pattern, Taper Shape, Signed, 6 In.	70.00
Vase, Rolled Over Top, Alabaster Wafer Base, 3 In.	125.00

Rose bowls were popular during the 1880s. Rose petals were kept in the open bowl to add fragrance to a room. The glass bowls were made with crimped tops, which kept the petals inside. Many types of Victorian art glass were made into rose bowls.

ROSE BOWL, Ruffled, White Spatter Bottom, Pink To Raspberry Top, 18 1/4 In.	95.00
Yellow Satin, 5 Embossed Shells Around Base	85.00

Rose Canton china is similar to Rose Medallion except no people are pictured in the decoration. It was made during the nineteenth and twentieth centuries in greens, pinks, and other colors.

ROSE CANTON, Bowl, 2 X 4 1/2 In.Diam.	24.00
Chocolate Pot, Allover Gold Design, 10 In.	45.00
Plate, 8 1/2 In.	85.00

Rose Medallion china was made in China during the nineteenth and twentieth centuries. It is a distinctive design picturing people, flowers, birds, and butterflies. They are colored in greens, pinks, and other colors.

ROSE MEDALLION, Ashtray, 7 1/2 In.	85.00
Bowl, C.1890, Footed, 3 1/2 In.	35.00
Bowl, Figures, Pavilions, Birds, Flowers, Butterflies, 11 In.	1200.00
Bowl, Flange Rim, Shallow, 8 1/2 In.	35.00
Bowl, Fruit, Reticulated, Oval, 11 X 10 X 4 1/2 In.	350.00
Bowl, Genre Scene, Floral Panels, Birds, 14 1/2 In.	600.00
Bowl, Kidney Shape, 10 1/4 X 8 3/4 In.	265.00
Bowl, Lemon Peel Glaze, Oval, 8 1/2 X 3 1/2 In.	175.00
Bowl, Oblong, 6 3/4 X 9 In.	210.00
Bowl, Punch, C.1890, 15 X 6 In.	950.00
Bowl, Scalloped, Oval, 6 X 7 1/2 In.	50.00
Bowl, Serving, Low, 11 In.Diam.	145.00
Bowl, 10 3/4 In.	375.00
Bowl, 19th Century, Oval, 8 1/2 X 10 1/2 In.	275.00
Box, Footed, 4 In.Diam.	235.00
Box, Portrait On Lid & Sides, Signed, 1 1/2 X 1 1/4 In.	55.00
Butter, Gold & Enamel Trim, Insert, Covered	450.00
Butter, With Liner, Birds, Butterflies, Floral Panels, 7 In.	225.00
Charger, Center Bird, Fan Shape, Floral Panels, 15 In.	350.00
Cup & Saucer	60.00 To 75.00
Cup & Saucer, Butterflies & Birds	65.00
Cup & Saucer, Demitasse, Butterflies & Birds	40.00
Cup, Bouillon, Cover & Underplate	45.00
Dish, Leaf Shape, 6 1/2 X 5 In.	45.00
Dish, Orange Peel Color, Oval, 11 1/4 In.	210.00
Dish, Scalloped, 4 1/4 In.Diam.	37.50
Dish, Serving, Covered, Water Scene, Gold Ground, 9 1/2 In.	350.00
Dish, Serving, Flowers, Figures, Gold Ground, Covered, 10 In.	200.00
Dish, Serving, Genre & Floral Design, Butterflies, 9 In.	150.00
Dish, Shell Shape, C.1870, Signed, 11 In.	80.00
Dish, Vegetable, Covered, 8 1/2 In.	300.00
Dish, Vegetable, Nut Finial, 8 1/2 X 7 In.	250.00
Flower Arranger, C.1830, 9 In.	1250.00
Garden Seat, Barrel Form, Floral, Birds, 18 In.	2500.00
Jar, Covered, C.1860, 17 In.	1400.00
Pitcher, Pinch Spout, 4 1/2 In.	255.00
Plate, C.1900, 10 In.	65.00
Plate, Cut Corners, 7 In.Square	55.00
Plate, Footed, Oval, C.1880, 11 In.	95.00
Plate, Lattice Edge, Signed, 8 1/2 In.	75.00
Plate, Marked, 6 In.	22.00
Plate, Octagonal	32.50
Plate, Oval, C.1860, 9 1/2 In.	75.00
Plate, People & Birds, 10 In., Pair	225.00
Plate, People, Floral, & Birds, 6 1/8 In.	21.00
Plate, People, Scenic, & Birds, 9 1/2 In.	55.00
Plate, Scalloped, 7 In.Diam.	70.00
Plate, 7 In.	45.00
Plate, 7 1/4 In.	25.00 To 45.00
Plate, 8 In.	65.00
Plate, 8 3/8 In.	48.00 To 55.00
Plate, 11 In.	85.00

Platter, Fish, Scenic & Floral Panels, Pierced Liner, 18 In. 600.00
Platter, Octagonal, 8 1/4 In. 120.00
Platter, Oval, 11 X 8 1/4 In. 150.00
Platter, Oval, 13 X 10 1/2 In. 285.00
Platter, Triangular, C.1850.10 In. 195.00
Punch Bowl, C.1790, 15 X 6 In. 1400.00
Saucer, 4 1/2 In.Diam. 30.00
Seat, Garden, Oriental Domestic Scene, 19 In. 1900.00
Spoon, Rice, Old People In Bowl, Flowers On Handle 35.00
Sugar, Covered .... 65.00 To 95.00
Sugar, Genre Scene, Domed Cover, Knob Finial, 5 In. 275.00
Tea Set, 4 Piece 500.00
Teapot, Bird & Butterfly Design, Entwined Handle, 6 1/4 In. 125.00
Teapot, Cylinder Shape, White Spout, Wicker Handle, 5 In. 150.00
Teapot, Floral, Birds & Butterflies, Domed Cover, 9 In. 375.00
Teapot, Original Wicker Basket, Cozy, Brass Hardware 200.00
Teapot, Pear Shape, Gold Design, C.1900, 6 In. 115.00
Teapot, Urn Shaped Body, Footed, Floral Panels, 10 In. 500.00
Teapot, 2 Small Cups, Flat Lid, Teapot 5 1/4 In. 150.00
Teapot, 5 1/2 In. 200.00
Tray, Clover Leaf, 11 1/2 In.Wide 225.00
Tray, Lemon Peal Glaze, Reticulated, 10 In. 185.00
Tray, Oval, 6 3/4 In. 75.00
Tray, 19th Century, 10 1/2 In.Diam. 110.00
Umbrella Stand, Oriental Scene, Gold Ground, Flowers, 24 In. 750.00
Vase, Birds, Butterflies, Floral Design, Flaring Top, 13 In. 375.00
Vase, C.1890, 7 1/2 In. 45.00
Vase, Cylinder, 10 1/2 X 4 3/8 In.Diam. 375.00
Vase, Flare Form, Raised Central Rib, 10 In. 250.00
Vase, Floral, Birds And Butterflies, Flared Top, 13 1/2 In. 375.00
Vase, Mandarin, 14 In., Pair 4200.00
Vase, 10 In. 245.00
Vase, 12 In. 385.00
     ROSE O'NEILL, see Kewpie

*Rose Tapestry porcelain was made by the Royal Bayreuth factory of
Germany during the late nineteenth century. The surface of the ware feels
like cloth.*

ROSE TAPESTRY, Ashtray, 3-Color Roses, 4 Rests, Square 250.00
    Basket, Lavender Flowers, Handle, Green Mark, 3 1/2 In. 300.00
    Basket, Pink Roses, Handle, Blue Mark, 6 1/2 X 3 3/4 In. 475.00
    Basket, Shadow Roses, 3-Color, Handle, Blue Mark, 3 X 5 In. 375.00
    Basket, 3-Color Roses, Pinched-In Sides, Miniatures 275.00
    Berry Bowl, Pink Roses, 5 1/2 In. 110.00
    Bowl, Fruit, 3-Color Roses, Rolled Edge, Gold Trim, 10 1/2 In. 315.00
    Bowl, Sugar, Yellow, White Roses, Covered, 2 1/2 In. 75.00
    Box, Kidney Shape, 3-Color Roses, Large 375.00
    Box, Powder, Covered, Gold Legs, 4 In. 235.00
    Box, Powder, Gold, Footed, Signed 100.00
    Box, Powder, Pink Roses, Footed 165.00
    Box, Ring, Pink Roses, Square 225.00
    Box, 3-Color Roses, Pinched-In Sides, Oval, 3 1/2 In. 275.00
    Box, 3-Color Roses, Square Ends, Blue Mark, 4 X 4 3/4 In. 350.00
    Cake Plate, Open Handles, Pink Roses, 11 In. 235.00
    Cake Plate, 3-Color Roses, 6 In. 110.00
    Celery, Pink Roses, Open Handles, 8 In. 145.00
    Chocolate Pot, Scenic, Mountain Goats, Blue Mark 865.00
    Clock, 3-Color Roses, Royal Bayreuth, 4 1/8 In. 375.00
    Cracker Jar, Gold Finial, Handled, Covered 585.00
    Creamer, Corset Shape, Bands Of Leaves & Pink Roses 150.00
    Creamer, Pinched Nose Shape, Pink Roses 125.00
    Creamer, Pinched Spout, Blue Mark, 3 1/2 In. 195.00
    Creamer, Straight-Sided, Pink Roses 125.00

Creamer, 3-Color, Blue Mark	110.00
Dish, Berry, Blue Mark, 5 In.	125.00
Dish, Candy, Clover Shape, 3-Color Roses	150.00
Dish, Candy, Heart Shaped Leaf, Pink Roses	175.00
Dish, Candy, 3-Color Roses, 8 In.	175.00
Dish, Maple Leaf, Bands Of Leaves & Pink Roses, 6 X 6 In.	200.00
Dish, Maple Leaf, 3-Color Roses	165.00
Dish, Pin, Yellow & Pink Roses, Open, 3 In.	85.00
Hair Receiver, 3 Gold Feet, Blue Mark	295.00
Hair Receiver, 3-Color Roses, Footed	135.00
Hatpin Holder, 3-Color, 4 1/2 In.	200.00
Humidor, Pink Roses	875.00
Humidor, Woman Leaning Against Horse, Mushroom Finial, 6 In.	335.00
Match Holder, Pink Roses, Hanging	175.00
Match Holder, 3-Color Roses	250.00
Match Safe, 3-Color Roses, Wall	225.00
Pitcher, Corset Shape, 3 3/4 In.	239.00
Pitcher, Lemonade, Pink Roses, 8 X 7 In.	700.00
Pitcher, Milk, Don Quixote, Blue Mark, 6 In.	395.00
Pitcher, Milk, Pink Roses, Pinched Nose	150.00
Pitcher, Pinched Spout, Blue Mark, 4 1/4 In.	235.00
Pitcher, Pinched Spout, 3-Color Roses, Blue Mark, 3 1/2 In.	165.00
Pitcher, Water, Corset Shape, Pink Roses, 7 In.	450.00
Pitcher, White Roses, 5 In.	295.00
Planter, Pink Roses, Rose Bowl Style, Insert, Large	250.00
Planter, 3-Color Roses, Green Mark, 2 3/4 In.	145.00
Planter, 3-Color Roses, Insert, Handled, Small	150.00
Plaque, Roses, Molded Gold Trim Border, Blue Mark, 9 1/2 In.	475.00
Plate, Gold Trim, 7 1/2 In.	115.00
Plate, Molded Edge, C.1880, 7 1/4 In.Diam.	100.00
Plate, 3-Color Roses, Blue Mark, 7 1/2 In.	195.00
Ring Tree, Pink Roses, Green Mark	450.00
Shoe, Lady's	210.00
Slipper, Lady's, Portrait Toe, Blue Mark	260.00
Sugar, Bulbous, Pink Roses, Covered	175.00
Sugar, 3-Color Roses, Covered	175.00
Teapot, Blue Mark	595.00
Toothpick, Footed, Double Handled, Signed	325.00
Toothpick, Pink Roses, 4 Feet, 2 Handles	175.00
Toothpick, 3 Openings, 3-Color Roses	250.00
Toothpick, 3-Color Roses, Handled, Squat	225.00
Tray, Dresser, Canted Sides, Rectangular, 11 1/2 X 8 1/4 In.	200.00
Tray, Dresser, 3-Color Roses, Blue Mark	375.00
Tray, Dresser, 3-Color Roses, Green Mark, 11 1/2 In.	225.00
Vase, Bud Shape, Pink Roses, 4 1/2 In.	185.00
Vase, Bud, Bulbous, 3-Color Roses, 5 1/2 In.	250.00
Vase, Castle & Mountains, Royal Bayreuth, 4 In.	185.00
Vase, Castle, Forest Scene, Blue Ground, Blue Mark, 5 In.	265.00
Vase, Chrysanthemums, 5 1/2 X 12 In.	260.00
Vase, Cylinder, 3-Color Roses, Gold Trim, 4 1/4 In.	185.00
Vase, Cylindrical, Flared Base, Pink Roses, Footed, 5 In.	225.00
Vase, Handled, Lady With Horse, Blue Mark, 8 1/2 In.	395.00
Vase, Pink Roses, 8 In.	475.00
Vase, Ruffled Top, Pink Roses, Footed, Squat, 4 In.	250.00
Vase, Scenic, Ruffled, Footed, 4 In.	400.00
Vase, Urn Shape, 3-Color Roses, 4 1/2 In.	185.00
Vase, Victorian Lady, Woods, Ground, Blue Mark, 7 1/2 X 5 In.	275.00
Vase, Yellow & Pink Roses, Blue Mark, 4 1/2 In.	210.00
Wall Pocket, 3-Color Roses, 9 In.	500.00

MARKE

Rosenthal porcelain was established in Selb, Bavaria, in 1880. The German factory still continues to make fine-quality tableware and figurines.

ROSENTHAL, Berry Bowl, Luster, Hand-Painted	7.00
Bowl, Border Design, 8 In.Diam.	75.00
Candleholder, Triple	12.00
Candlestick, Designed Ground Base, Signed, 7 1/2 In.	40.00
Celery, Premier Pattern, 9 1/2 In.	22.50
Chocolate Pot, Roses On White Ground	55.00
Coffeepot, Winifred Pattern, Floral	90.00
Cup & Saucer, Demitasse, Flowers	17.50
Cup & Saucer, Floral, Signed	12.00
Cup & Saucer, Gold Sprays & Trim, White	15.00
Cup & Saucer, Silver Overlay, Maria Pattern, Marked	65.00
Demitasse Set, Flowers, Crown Mark, Set Of 6	110.00
Demitasse Set, Roses, Sterling Base, 3 Piece	125.00
Dish, Serving, Irregular Rim, Leaf Shape, Berries	100.00
Dish, Serving, Strawberries, Pink, Gold Handle, Signed, 11 In.	75.00
Figurine, Ballerina, Dying Swan	550.00
Figurine, Bird, Signed T.Karne	95.00
Figurine, Birds On Branch, Signed & Numbered	85.00
Figurine, Bunny Rabbit, White Porcelain, Pink Accents, 6 1/4 In.	85.00
Figurine, Dachshund, Doxie Begging, 7 In.	210.00
Figurine, Dachshund, 3 X 5 1/2 In.	210.00
Figurine, Dog, Dachshund, Laying On Stomach, Green Collar, Signed	385.00
Figurine, Finch On Leafy Stump, Artist Signed	35.00
Figurine, Girl With Geese, No. 256	80.00
Figurine, Kitten, Signed	75.00
Figurine, Kneeling Nude, Modeled By L.Friedrich-Gronau	250.00
Figurine, Pouter Pigeon, White Fan Tail, Puffed Chest, 6 In.	145.00
Figurine, Raven, Seated, 9 1/2 In.	95.00
Figurine, Reclining Sheep, No. 196	75.00
Figurine, Robin, Pedestal, Artist Signed, 5 1/4 In.	80.00
Figurine, Rooster, Signed Heidenreich, 6 In.	120.00
Figurine, Squirrel, 7 X 7 In.	135.00 To 150.00
Figurine, Turtle, Porcelain, 1 X 2 1/2 In.	70.00
Figurine, 3 Birds On Branch, Artist Signed & Numbered	85.00
Fish Set, Fish In Underwater Scene, Gold Trim, 6 Plates, Platter	125.00
Hatpin Holder, Pale Green, Pink Roses	39.00
Plaque, Wedding Party, Terrace, Marked, 9 X 13 In.	450.00
Plate, Cake, Portrait Of Apollo, Gold Dots, Violet Ground, 10 In.	50.00
Plate, Chop, Nymph & Flute Player, Gold Trim, Green, 13 In.	50.00
Plate, Fruit, Hand-Painted, Gilt Embossed Edge, 8 1/2 In., Pair	85.00
Plate, Ivory, 11 In., Set Of 7	265.00
Plate, Phoenix, Plate, 6 In.	12.00
Plate, Phoenix, 9 1/2 In.	18.00
Saltshaker, Rosebuds, Sterling Silver Pedestal, 2 In., Pair	35.00
Sugar & Creamer, Donatello Pattern, Hand-Painted, Blue, 3 1/2 In.	75.00
Teapot, Silver Overlay, Light Blue	125.00
Tray, Purple & Yellow Pansies, Gold Handles, 7 In.Diam.	35.00
Vase, Berries, Leaves, & Vines In White, Ovoid, 11 1/2 In.	185.00
Vase, Cameo Pattern, Roman Soldier Head, Lilac Medallion	48.00
Vase, Hand-Painted Orchids, Black Ground, Signed, 5 In.	95.00
Vase, Hand-Painted, Scalloped Top, Nasturtiums, 7 1/2 In.	25.00
Vase, Hand-Painted, Scalloped Top, Wisteria, Square Base, 7 1/2 In.	25.00

Roseville
U.S.A.

Roseville Pottery Co. was organized in Roseville, Ohio, in 1890. Another plant was opened in Zanesville, Ohio, in 1898. Many types of pottery were made. The firm closed in 1954.

ROSEVILLE, Ashtray, Creamware	40.00
Ashtray, Donatello, 4 3/4 In.	95.00 To 125.00
Ashtray, Florentine, Brown & Green	42.00
Ashtray, Mayfair, White, 3 1/2 In., Set Of 4	35.00

Ashtray, Ming Tree	38.00
Ashtray, Peony, Gold Trim, 3 X 5 In.	45.00
Ashtray, Peony, Green	26.00
Ashtray, Pine Cone, Blue, 2 1/2 X 5 In.	42.00
Ashtray, Pine Cone, Green	15.00
Ashtray, Silhouette	25.00
Ashtray, Snowberry, Rose	30.00
Ashtray, Wincraft, Brown	35.00
Bank, Apple Shape	95.00
Base, Bud, Dahlrose, Double, 6 In.	30.00 To 32.00
Basket, Apple Blossom, Blue, 8 In.	50.00
Basket, Apple Blossom, Pink, 8 In.	48.00
Basket, Bushberry, Brown, 8 In.	45.00
Basket, Bushberry, Green, 6 1/2 In.	30.00
Basket, Clematis, Blue, 6 In.	30.00
Basket, Clematis, Yellow Flower, Burnt Orange To Green, 10 In.	60.00
Basket, Columbine, Blue, 7 In.	46.00
Basket, Dogwood, Flower Frog, Green, 8 In.	55.00
Basket, Donatello, 12 3/4 In.	129.00 To 165.00
Basket, Foxglove, Light To Dark Green, 8 In.	35.00
Basket, Freesia, Blue, 8 In.	42.00
Basket, Freesia, Green, 7 In.	35.00
Basket, Freesia, Green, 8 In.	40.00 To 45.00
Basket, Hanging, Apple Blossom, Pink	55.00 To 65.00
Basket, Hanging, Bushberry, Brown, Glazed	47.00
Basket, Hanging, Columbine, Brown, Large	85.00
Basket, Hanging, Florentine, Brown, 9 In.	55.00
Basket, Hanging, Florentine, 7 In.	60.00 To 70.00
Basket, Hanging, Fuchsia, Brown, 5 In.	125.00
Basket, Hanging, Futura, Pink & Gray, 5 In.	125.00
Basket, Hanging, Matte Green	27.00 To 45.00
Basket, Hanging, Peony, Green	60.00
Basket, Hanging, Peony, Pink	75.00
Basket, Hanging, Snowberry, Green	70.00
Basket, Hanging, Water Lily, Blue	47.00
Basket, Hanging, Zephyr Lily, Green	45.00 To 55.00
Basket, Iris, Pink, 10 In.	60.00
Basket, Magnolia, Brown, 8 In.	45.00
Basket, Ming Tree, Green	60.00
Basket, Peony, Gold Trim, 7 In.	40.00
Basket, Snowberry, Green, 7 In.	42.50
Basket, Water Lily, Blue, 12 In.	70.00
Basket, Wincraft, Orange, 8 In.	35.00
Basket, Wincraft, Orange, 12 In.	60.00
Basket, Wisteria, Hanging, Brown	300.00
Bookends, Wincraft, Brown	35.00
Bowl & Candlesticks, Freesia, Blue, Bowl 14 In.	50.00
Bowl, Apple Blossom	19.00
Bowl, Baneda, Green, 7 3/4 In.	60.00
Bowl, Baneda, Pink, 6 In.	50.00
Bowl, Bittersweet, Gray, 8 In.	32.00
Bowl, Bittersweet, Handled, Yellow, 12 In.	40.00
Bowl, Blackberry	125.00
Bowl, Bleeding Heart, Green, 5 In.	25.00
Bowl, Bushberry, Blue, 4 1/2 In.	25.00
Bowl, Carnelian I, Handle, Beige & Blue, 10 1/2 In.	50.00
Bowl, Carnelian I, 2 1/4 X 4 In.Diam.	18.00
Bowl, Carnelian II, Green, 9 In.	95.00
Bowl, Carnelian, Mottled Pink, Handled, 9 X 3 In., 2 Piece	17.50
Bowl, Cereal, Juvenile, Chicks On Green Band	30.00
Bowl, Cherry Blossom, 4 In.Diam.	95.00
Bowl, Columbine, Dark Rose, 3 In.	22.00
Bowl, Columbine, Pink, 3 In.	25.00

Bowl, Console, Apple Blossom, Green	60.00
Bowl, Console, Blackberry, Silver Paper Label, 13 In.	100.00
Bowl, Console, Freesia, Brown, Oval, 14 In.	62.00
Bowl, Console, Luffa, Green, 4 X 13 In.	45.00
Bowl, Console, Magnolia, Blue	42.50
Bowl, Console, Magnolia, Orange, 14 In.	35.00
Bowl, Console, Ming Tree, Green	33.00
Bowl, Console, Peony, Handled, Yellow Ground, Signed, 11 X 5 1/2 In.	65.00
Bowl, Console, Silhouette, Blue	23.00
Bowl, Console, Tuscany, Gray, 11 In.	22.00
Bowl, Console, White Rose	50.00
Bowl, Corinthian, 6 X 3 In.	55.00
Bowl, Cornelian, Spongeware, 6 X 8 3/4 In.	40.00
Bowl, Dogwood, 7 In.	48.00
Bowl, Donatello, 7 X 4 In.	45.00
Bowl, Donatello, 10 X 3 In.	50.00
Bowl, Donatello, 12 X 3 In.	70.00
Bowl, Falline, Blue & Tan, 6 1/4 In.	85.00
Bowl, Florane, 7 In.	37.50
Bowl, Foxglove, Green, 3 In.	17.00
Bowl, Freesia, Handled, Green, 6 In., Pair	40.00
Bowl, Gardenia, Green, 6 In.	20.00
Bowl, Gardenia, Handled, Gray, 8 In.	40.00
Bowl, Imperial I, 2 1/2 In.	30.00
Bowl, Iris, 5 In.	15.00
Bowl, Jonquil, Black Sticker, 8 X 2 3/4 In.	55.00
Bowl, Jonquil, 4 In.	28.00 To 40.00
Bowl, Magnolia, Blue, Handled, 4 In.	22.00 To 25.00
Bowl, Magnolia, Brown, 3 In.	20.00
Bowl, Magnolia, Green, 6 In.	22.00
Bowl, Ming Tree, Green Glaze, 14 1/4 X 5 1/4 In.	28.00
Bowl, Ming Tree, Handled, Green, 10 In.	40.00
Bowl, Moss, Pink To Green, 4 In.	25.00
Bowl, Moss, 4 X 2 In., Diam.	45.00
Bowl, Mostique, Geometric Flower, Green Glaze, 9 In.	42.00
Bowl, Mostique, 5 1/2 X 3 In.	40.00
Bowl, Mostique, 6 1/2 X 3 In.	45.00
Bowl, Peony, Handled, Yellow, 6 In.	40.00
Bowl, Pine Cone, Green, 10 In.	50.00
Bowl, Pine Cone, Green, 12 In.	35.00
Bowl, Poppy, Handled, Yellow To Pink, 10 In.	40.00
Bowl, Rosecraft Vintage, 8 X 2 In.	35.00
Bowl, Rozane, Ivory, 4 In.	32.50
Bowl, Silhouette, White, 8 In.	20.00
Bowl, Snowberry, Blue, Footed, 11 In.	45.00
Bowl, Snowberry, Console, Blue, 12 In.	40.00
Bowl, Snowberry, Console, Green, 10 In.	35.00
Bowl, Snowberry, Green, 11 In.	45.00
Bowl, Spittoon, Brown, Panel	40.00
Bowl, Sunflower, 9 In.	45.00
Bowl, Velmoss Scroll, 3 X 8 In.	60.00
Bowl, Velmoss Scroll, 9 X 3 In.	35.00
Bowl, Water Lily, Brown & Yellow Flowers	45.00
Bowl, Water Lily, 3 In.	18.00
Bowl, White Rose, Green, 3 In.	16.00
Bowl, Wincraft, Blue, 5 In.	40.00
Bowl, Wincraft, Italian Green, 8 In.	37.50
Bowl, Wisteria, Blue, 5 1/2 In.	60.00
Bowl, Wisteria, Brown, 2 X 5 In.	50.00
Bowl, Wisteria, Brown, 4 In.	43.00 To 60.00
Bulb Dish, Freesia, Brown, 6 In.	20.00
Candleholder, Apple Blossom, Blue	12.00
Candleholder, Apple Blossom, Blue, 4 1/2 In., Pair	45.00

Candleholder, Apple Blossom, Pink, 4 In.	50.00
Candleholder, Apple Blossom, Rose, 2 In., Pair	27.50
Candleholder, Cherry Blossom, 4 1/2 In., Pair	155.00
Candleholder, Clematis, Brown, 4 In., Pair	30.00
Candleholder, Freesia, Brown, 2 In., Pair	18.50
Candleholder, Snowberry, Blue, Pair	18.00
Candleholder, Water Lily, Pair	15.00
Candlestick, Bushberry, Brown, 2 In., Pair	29.00
Candlestick, Carnelian I, Pair	43.00
Candlestick, Dahlrose, Paper Label	30.00
Candlestick, Dawn, Pair	30.00
Candlestick, Florentine, Double	40.00
Candlestick, Freesia, Pair	20.00
Candlestick, Fuchsia, Brown, 2 In., Pair	25.00
Candlestick, Lotus, Blue, Pair	30.00
Candlestick, Mock Orange, Yellow, 2 In., Pair	30.00
Candlestick, Rozane, Floral Design, Medallion Mark, 9 1/4 In.	185.00
Candlestick, Silhouette, Green, 3 In., Pair	20.00
Candlestick, Snowberry, Blue, 4 1/2 In., Pair	40.00
Candlestick, Tuscany, Pair	35.00
Candlestick, White Rose, Pink, 2 In., Pair	20.00
Candlestick, Wincraft, 2 In., Pair	27.50
Candlestick, Zephyr Lily, Blue, 2 In., Pair	20.00
Candlestick, Zephyr Lily, Green, 4 1/2 In., Pair	40.00
Cigarette Box, Silhouette, Cover, Blue Green	32.00
Compote, Donatello, 6 X 7 In., Pair	55.00
Compote, Florentine, Ivory, 5 In.	43.00
Compote, Lustre, Pink Glaze, 12 In.	125.00
Compote, Rozane Mongol, Partial Label, Red, 8 In.Diam.	500.00
Compote, White Rose, Handled, Blue, 8 In.	38.00
Compote, Zephyr Lily, Green	50.00
Conch Shell, Ming Tree, Aqua, 8 In.	40.00
Conch Shell, Peony, Green, 9 In.	45.00
Console Set, Gardenia, Gray, Bowl 10 In.	70.00
Console, Apple Blossom	40.00
Console, Clematis, Blue, 10 In.	45.00
Cookie Jar, Clematis, Brown	75.00
Cookie Jar, Freesia	60.00
Cornucopia, Bittersweet	28.00
Cornucopia, Bleeding Heart, 8 In.	32.00
Cornucopia, Bushberry, Green, 8 In., Pair	60.00
Cornucopia, Clematis, Blue, 6 In.	30.00
Cornucopia, Freesia, Blue, 6 In., Pair	35.00
Cornucopia, Freesia, Brown, 8 In.	30.00
Cornucopia, Magnolia, Green, 9 In., Pair	100.00
Cornucopia, Snowberry, Green, 8 In.	35.00
Creamer & Plate, Juvenile	35.00
Creamer, Bittersweet, Gray	14.00
Creamer, Medallion, Mercury, 3 In.	47.50
Cup & Saucer, Snowberry, Pink	30.00
Dish, Feeding, Tom The Piper's Son, Green, 8 In.	55.00 To 57.50
Dish, Mayfair, Green, Chartreuse Lining, 10 In.	45.00
Ewer, Bleeding Heart, 6 In.	50.00
Ewer, Clematis, 6 1/2 In.	42.00
Ewer, Fuchsia, Bleeding Heart, Pair	125.00
Ewer, Gardenia, Brown, 15 In.	85.00
Ewer, Gardenia, Green, 10 In.	50.00
Ewer, Imperial II, 5 1/2 In.	105.00
Ewer, Pine Cone, Green, 15 In.	125.00
Ewer, Poppy, 18 In.	225.00
Ewer, Snowberry, Rose, 10 In.	50.00
Ewer, Snowberry, Rose, 15 In.	100.00
Ewer, Snowberry, 16 In.	100.00
Ewer, Wincraft, Blue, 8 In.	35.00

Ewer, Zephyr Lily, Blue, 10 In.	50.00
Fan, Brown, Paneled, Dancing Nude, Marked, 8 In.	150.00
Figurine, Nude, Silhouette	150.00
Flower Frog, Donatello, 5 X 3 In.	65.00
Flower Frog, Rosecraft, 3 1/2 In.	12.00
Flower Holder, Clematis, Green, 5 In.	30.00
Flowerpot & Tray, Pine Cone, 5 1/2 In.	17.00
Flowerpot, Bleeding Heart, Blue, 6 In.	37.00
Flowerpot, Freesia, Green	35.00
Flowerpot, Mostique, 6 3/4 X 8 In.	25.00
Flowerpot, Snowberry, Green	20.00
Flowerpot, White Rose, Blue	32.00
Hair Receiver, Medallion	50.00
Jardiniere, Artcraft, Brown, 7 In.	65.00
Jardiniere, Artcraft, Ivory, 5 In.	58.00
Jardiniere, Baneda, Pink, 7 In.	135.00
Jardiniere, Blackberry, 4 In.	115.00
Jardiniere, Blackberry, 7 In.	75.00
Jardiniere, Cherry Blossom, Brown, Tan, Red, 9 In.	165.00 To 275.00
Jardiniere, Clematis, Pedestal, Brown, 25 In.	275.00 To 325.00
Jardiniere, Columbine, 6 In.	32.00
Jardiniere, Corinthian, 5 In.	40.00
Jardiniere, Corinthian, 11 1/2 X 9 In.	95.00
Jardiniere, Corinthian, 7 In.	55.00
Jardiniere, Dahlrose, Pedestal, 24 1/2 In.	450.00
Jardiniere, Dahlrose, 6 In.	48.00
Jardiniere, Dogwood, Pedestal, 28 1/2 In.	650.00
Jardiniere, Donatello, 4 In.	30.00 To 40.00
Jardiniere, Earlam, Blue, 4 In.	40.00
Jardiniere, Freesia, Burnt Orange To Brown, Stand, 24 1/2 In.	225.00
Jardiniere, Laurel, Orange, 6 1/2 X 7 In.	85.00
Jardiniere, Magnolia, Green, Pedestal, 31 In.	450.00
Jardiniere, Normandy, 8 1/2 In.	85.00
Jardiniere, Normandy, 9 In.	155.00
Jardiniere, Pine Cone, Pedestal, Blue, 8 In.	385.00
Jardiniere, Primrose, Pedestal, Brown, 27 In.	375.00
Jardiniere, Snowberry, 8 In.	37.50
Jardiniere, Topeo, Mahogany, 6 In.	125.00
Jardiniere, White Rose, Green To Pink, Handled, 4 In.	42.00
Jardiniere, Wisteria, Blue, 5 1/2 In.	70.00
Jardiniere, Wisteria, 4 X 6 In.	90.00
Jug, Cherry Blossom, Brown, 5 1/2 X 4 In.	125.00
Jug, Cherry Blossom, 7 In.	150.00
Lamp, Tuscany, Red	150.00
Lemonade Set, Bushberry, 2 Mugs, 5 Piece	140.00
Letter Holder, Rozane	190.00
Mug, Bushberry, Green	48.00
Mug, Dutch, Geese	33.00
Mug, Indian Chief, Creamware	160.00
Mug, Magnolia, Brown	23.50
Mug, Raymor, Brown, Handled	40.00
Mug, Rozane, Artist's Initials	97.50
Mug, 2-Handled, Juvenile, Rabbit	45.00
Pan, Bake, Venetian, 9 In.	34.00
Pitcher, Blackberry, Water	96.00
Pitcher, Blended, C.1890, 7 In.	135.00
Pitcher, Bridge Scene, Bassford & Peterson Clothing, 1912	65.00
Pitcher, Cow	140.00
Pitcher, Freesia, 10 In.	60.00
Pitcher, Juvenile, Side Spout, Chicks On Green Band	35.00
Pitcher, Landscape, 7 1/2 In.	24.00 To 85.00
Pitcher, Medallion, Side Pour	55.00
Pitcher, Tulip	65.00
Planter, Apple Blossom, Blue, 12 In.	35.00

Planter, Apple Blossom, Brown, 12 In.	24.00
Planter, Apple Blossom, Green, 8 In.	40.00
Planter, Apple Blossom, Green, 12 In.	35.00
Planter, Apple Blossom, Handled, Pink, 9 X 2 1/2 In.	22.50
Planter, Apple Blossom, Pink, 6 X 2 1/2 In.	22.50
Planter, Apple Blossom, Pink, 12 In.	50.00
Planter, Apple Blossom, 12 In.	30.00 To 32.50
Planter, Apple Blossom, 15 In.	38.00
Planter, Artwood, Aqua	45.00
Planter, Basket, Water Lily, 6 In.	18.00
Planter, Bleeding Heart, 8 In.	42.00
Planter, Double, Silhouette, Aqua, 5 1/2 In.	47.50
Planter, Earlam, Aqua & Blue, 5 1/2 X 10 1/2 In.	65.00
Planter, Lotus, Green & Yellow	85.00
Planter, Magnolia, Sleigh, Blue, 6 In.	29.00 To 35.00
Planter, Matte Green, Beetles	75.00
Planter, Mayfair, Pink Lining, Blue, 10 In.	32.50
Planter, Ming Tree, 8 In.	40.00
Planter, Mock Orange, 4-Footed	38.00
Planter, Pasadena, Brass Frame, Green	37.50
Planter, Zephyr Lily, Hanging, Green	60.00
Planter, Zephyr Lily, 6 In.	30.00
Plate, Baby Bunting, Child's	75.00
Plate, Juvenile, Rabbit, 7 In.	30.00
Plate, Raymor, Gray, 7 In.	10.50
Pocket, Wall, Florentine	40.00
Rose Bowl, Dawn, Aqua, 4 In.	40.00
Rose Bowl, Jonquil, Paper Label, 5 1/2 In.	27.50
Sand Jar, Florane, Green, 10 In., Pair	150.00
Sign, Dealer	500.00
Spittoon, Blue & Gold	100.00
Sugar & Creamer, Apple Blossom, Green	45.00
Sugar & Creamer, Magnolia, Brown	35.00
Sugar & Creamer, Snowberry, Blue, Pair	33.00
Sugar & Creamer, Wincraft, Blue	22.00
Sugar, Wincraft, Tan	14.00
Tankard, Creamware, Indian, Full Headdress	225.00
Tankard, Snowberry, Green, 10 In.	48.00
Tea Set, Freesia, 3 Piece	115.00
Tea Set, Landscape, 3 Piece	250.00
Tea Set, Snowberry, Blue, 3 Piece	70.00
Tea Set, Wincraft, Blue	80.00
Teapot, Clematis, Blue	60.00
Teapot, Magnolia, Blue	60.00
Teapot, Sugar, & Creamer, Magnolia	105.00
Teapot, Zephyr Lily, Blue, 7 In.	50.00
Tray, Foxglove, Cranberry, 11 In.	35.00
Umbrella Stand, Aztec, Green, 24 In.	275.00
Umbrella Stand, Blended	250.00
Umbrella Stand, Irises In Panels, Green Drip On Brown	175.00
Umbrella Stand, Rozane, 1917, 9 X 19 In.	375.00
Urn, Clematis, Green, 6 In.	25.00
Urn, Cosmos, Green, 4 In.	42.50
Urn, Cremona, Pink, 4 In.	52.00
Urn, Freesia, Blue, 8 In.	40.00
Urn, Jonquil, 4 In.	30.00
Urn, Wisteria, Gold Sticker, 5 X 7 In.	87.50
Urn, Wisteria, 5 In.	50.00
Vase, Apple Blossom, Twig Handles, Pink, 9 1/4 In.	35.00
Vase, Artwood, 6 In.	14.00
Vase, Aztec, 3 1/4 In.	80.00
Vase, Baneda, Green, 4 In.	45.00 To 54.00
Vase, Baneda, Green, 5 1/4 In.	60.00

Vase, Baneda, Handle, Deep Rose, 9 1/2 X 12 In. 200.00
Vase, Baneda, With Hand, Silver Label, 5 1/2 In. 62.50
Vase, Baneda, 6 In. 48.00
Vase, Bittersweet, Gray, 6 In. 24.00
Vase, Bittersweet, Green, 7 In. 35.00
Vase, Bittersweet, Unmatched Handles, Green, 9 In. 75.00
Vase, Blackberry, Handled, 5 In. 130.00
Vase, Blackberry, 4 In. .... 85.00 To 110.00
Vase, Blackberry, 5 In. 115.00
Vase, Blackberry, 8 In. 195.00
Vase, Bleeding Heart, 10 In. 70.00
Vase, Bud, Clematis, Gold & Brown, 7 In. 37.50
Vase, Bud, Corinthian, Double, 6 In. .... 30.00 To 35.00
Vase, Bud, Donatello, Double, 7 X 4 In. .... 55.00 To 75.00
Vase, Bud, Double, Dogwood II, 8 In. 65.00
Vase, Bud, Florentine, Double, 5 In. .... 30.00 To 45.00
Vase, Bud, Imperial I, Handled, 9 In. 35.00
Vase, Bud, Imperial, Triple 28.00
Vase, Bud, Magnolia, Handled, Blue, 7 In. 33.00
Vase, Bud, Peony, Double, Green, 5 In. 25.00
Vase, Bud, Snowberry, Green, 7 In. 30.00
Vase, Bud, Snowberry, Rose, 7 In. 35.00
Vase, Bud, Wincraft, Light Green, 6 In. 20.00
Vase, Bushberry, Ball Shaped, Blue, 9 3/4 X 6 1/2 In. 45.00
Vase, Bushberry, Blue, 4 In. 20.00
Vase, Bushberry, Green, 4 In. 20.00
Vase, Bushberry, Handled, Blue, 8 In. .... 32.00 To 40.00
Vase, Bushberry, Handled, Brown, 8 In. 65.00
Vase, Bushberry, 6 In. .... 28.00 To 35.00
Vase, Carnelian II, Pink, Gray, Brown, 10 In. .... 65.00 To 100.00
Vase, Carnelian II, Rose With Purple Overglaze, 9 In. 78.50
Vase, Carnelian II, 12 In. 100.00
Vase, Cherry Blossom, Blue & Rose, 7 In. 165.00
Vase, Cherry Blossom, Blue, 5 In. 90.00
Vase, Cherry Blossom, Number 618 Under Glaze, 5 1/2 In., Pair 180.00
Vase, Clematis, Blue, 7 In. 28.00
Vase, Clematis, Blue, 12 In. 45.00
Vase, Clematis, Brown, 7 1/2 In. 26.00
Vase, Clematis, Brown, 12 In. 55.00
Vase, Clematis, Brown, 15 In. 155.00
Vase, Clematis, Green With Pink, 8 In. 55.00
Vase, Clematis, Green, 7 In. 28.00
Vase, Clematis, Green, 9 In. 25.00
Vase, Clematis, Pink, Green, 8 In. 55.00
Vase, Clematis, White Flower On Blue, Handled, Footed, 10 1/2 In. 38.00
Vase, Columbine, Brown, 3 In. 15.00
Vase, Columbine, Handled, Blue, 6 In. 20.00
Vase, Columbine, 12 In. 75.00
Vase, Corinthian, 6 In. 43.00
Vase, Cremona, Green, 4 In. 30.00
Vase, Dahlrose, Flare Top, 8 In. 65.00
Vase, Dahlrose, 2-Handled, 8 In. 55.00
Vase, Dahlrose, 6 In. 38.00
Vase, Dahlrose, 12 In. 75.00
Vase, Dawn, Ivory, 8 1/2 In. 55.00
Vase, Dawn, White, 6 In. 45.00
Vase, Dawn, 10 In. 65.00
Vase, Dogwood, Pink, 18 1/2 In. 135.00
Vase, Donatello, 7 1/2 In. 50.00
Vase, Double, Clematis, 5 In. 18.00
Vase, Fan Shape, Panel Nude, 8 In. 165.00
Vase, Ferrella, Red, 6 In. 125.00
Vase, Floor, Fuchsia, Blue, 15 In. 155.00

Vase, Florentine, Handled, 10 In.	45.00
Vase, Florentine, 9 In.	33.00
Vase, Florentine, 12 1/2 In.	135.00
Vase, Foxglove, Green, 4 1/2 In.	18.00
Vase, Foxglove, 6 In.	25.00
Vase, Freesia, Fan Shape, Brown, Handled, 7 In.	40.00
Vase, Freesia, Handled, Green, 9 In.	45.00
Vase, Freesia, Orange, 7 1/4 In.	25.00
Vase, Fuchsia, Blue, 6 In.	37.00
Vase, Fuchsia, Blue, 12 In.	95.00
Vase, Fuchsia, Brown, 9 In.	55.00
Vase, Fuchsia, Rust, 6 In.	30.00
Vase, Futura, Fan Shape, 6 In.	40.00
Vase, Futura, Terra-Cotta, Green Leaves & Flowers, 5 In.	85.00
Vase, Gardenia, Gray, 8 In.	37.00
Vase, Imperial I, 9 In.	42.00
Vase, Imperial I, 14 In.	110.00
Vase, Ixia, Sticker, 8 1/4 In.	55.00
Vase, Jonquil, Handled, 6 In.	46.00
Vase, Jonquil, 4 In.	30.00
Vase, Jonquil, 4 1/2 In.	45.00
Vase, Jonquil, 8 In.	75.00
Vase, Jug, Imperial I, 8 In.	52.00
Vase, La Rose, 6 In.	50.00
Vase, Laurel, Green, 9 In.	45.00
Vase, Laurel, Green, 10 In.	100.00
Vase, Laurel, 6 In.	38.00
Vase, Laurel, 8 In.	65.00
Vase, Luffa, Brown & Green, Gold Sticker, 7 1/4 In., Pair	115.00
Vase, Luffa, Brown, 6 1/4 In.	65.00
Vase, Luffa, 2-Handled, 4 In.	28.00
Vase, Luffa, 6 In.	65.00
Vase, Luffa, 8 1/2 In.	45.00
Vase, Magnolia, Handled, Brown, 6 In.	25.00
Vase, Ming Tree, Celestial Blue, 14 1/2 In.	180.00
Vase, Ming Tree, Handled, 6 In.	37.00
Vase, Mock Orange, Green, 10 In.	25.00 To 40.00
Vase, Moderne, White, 7 In.	30.00
Vase, Monticello, Blue & Tan Stripes, 11 1/2 In.	200.00
Vase, Moss, 9 In.	50.00
Vase, Mostique, 6 In.	20.00
Vase, Mostique, 8 In.	16.00
Vase, Mostique, 10 In.	45.00
Vase, National Conference Of Catholic Charities, 1934, Blue, 5 In.	65.00
Vase, Orian, Aqua, 10 1/2 In.	85.00
Vase, Orian, 7 1/2 In.	55.00
Vase, Panel Nude, 6 In.	145.00
Vase, Panel, 12 1/2 In.	165.00
Vase, Pauleo, Red, 16 1/2 In.	950.00
Vase, Peony, Handled, Gray, 9 In.	30.00
Vase, Peony, Pink & Green With Yellow, 9 In.	55.00
Vase, Pillow, Bleeding Heart, Blue, 8 In.	32.00
Vase, Pillow, Bleeding Heart, 9 In.	45.00
Vase, Pillow, Fuchsia, Brown, 8 In.	47.00
Vase, Pillow, Snowberry, Handled, Blue, 6 In.	28.00
Vase, Pillow, White Rose, Brown, 8 In.	40.00
Vase, Pillow, Zephyr Lily, Green, 7 In.	30.00 To 40.00
Vase, Pine Cone, Pedestal, Brown, 10 In.	160.00
Vase, Pine Cone, 6 In.	40.00
Vase, Primrose, Blue, 8 In.	35.00
Vase, Primrose, Brown	115.00
Vase, Primrose, Pink, 8 In.	45.00
Vase, Raised Thornapple & Leaf Pattern, Handled, 9 1/2 In.	80.00

Vase, Rosecraft Vintage, 6 In.	65.00
Vase, Rosecraft Vintage, 12 In.	95.00
Vase, Rosecraft, Blue, 12 In.	50.00
Vase, Rozane Royal, Wafer & Banner Mark, 6 1/2 In.	145.00
Vase, Rozane, Handled, Green, 1917, 6 1/2 In.	40.00
Vase, Rozane, Oriental Rust, 10 In.	26.00
Vase, Russco, Ball Shaped, Gold Crystal	55.00
Vase, Russco, Blue, 6 In.	30.00
Vase, Russco, Brown, 9 In.	55.00
Vase, Scroll, Velmoss, 10 In.	70.00
Vase, Silhouette, Blue, 6 In.	30.00
Vase, Silhouette, Nude, Cream & Green, 10 In.	95.00
Vase, Silhouette, Nude, White, 7 In.	75.00
Vase, Snowberry, Green	45.00
Vase, Sunflower, Handled, 5 In.	85.00
Vase, Sunflower, 2-Handled, 5 1/2 In.	55.00
Vase, Sunflower, 5 In.	55.00
Vase, Teasel, Tan, 6 In.	52.50
Vase, Thornapple, Pink & Green, 9 In.	60.00
Vase, Topeo, Aqua & Blue, 7 In.	80.00
Vase, Topeo, Green & Black, 6 In.	75.00
Vase, Topeo, Red, 9 1/2 In.	48.00
Vase, Tourmaline, Aqua, 4 1/2 In.	57.50
Vase, Tourmaline, Handled, Blue, 6 In.	40.00 To 45.00
Vase, Tourmaline, 6 In.	45.00
Vase, Tuscany, Mottled Pink, Green Leaf Handles, 7 1/4 In.	60.00
Vase, Tuscany, 4 1/2 In.	22.00
Vase, Velmoss	35.00
Vase, Velmoss II, Handled, Green, 6 In.	30.00 To 45.00
Vase, Vista, 15 1/2 In.	185.00
Vase, Water Lily, Blue, 4 1/2 In.	17.00
Vase, Water Lily, Blue, 18 In.	145.00
Vase, Water Lily, Double Handle, 6 In.	18.00
Vase, Water Lily, 2-Handled, Blue, 8 1/2 In.	30.00
Vase, Water Lily, 6 In.	18.00
Vase, Wincraft, Brown, 8 1/2 In.	20.00
Vase, Windsor, Geometric Red Brown, 6 In.	225.00
Vase, Wisteria, Blue, 10 In.	100.00
Vase, Wisteria, Brown, 4 1/2 In.	70.00
Vase, Wisteria, Brown, 8 In.	70.00
Vase, Wisteria, Brown, 10 In.	157.00
Vase, Yellow Flowers, Brown Ground, 12 1/2 In.	95.00
Vase, Zephyr Lily, Blue, 6 1/2 In.	26.00
Vase, Zephyr Lily, Blue, 8 In.	28.00
Vase, Zephyr Lily, Dated 3-5-47, 8 In.	65.00
Vase, Zephyr Lily, Green, 7 In.	28.00 To 30.00
Vase, Zephyr Lily, Terra-Cotta, 6 In.	37.50
Vase, Zephyr Lily, 2 Bow Handles In Center, Green, 12 1/2 In.	60.00
Wall Pocket, Apple Blossom, Green	35.00
Wall Pocket, Blackberry	250.00
Wall Pocket, Bleeding Heart, Blue	48.00
Wall Pocket, Carnelian I, 8 In.	65.00
Wall Pocket, Carnelian II	40.00 To 80.00
Wall Pocket, Clematis, Green	40.00
Wall Pocket, Columbine, Pink-Gray	90.00
Wall Pocket, Corinthian, 9 1/2 In.	55.00
Wall Pocket, Florentine, Marked, 9 1/2 In.	55.00
Wall Pocket, Florentine, 7 In.	45.00
Wall Pocket, Florentine, 12 1/2 In.	40.00 To 70.00
Wall Pocket, Freesia, Blue	40.00
Wall Pocket, Freesia, Brown	40.00
Wall Pocket, Freesia, Green, 8 In., Pair	90.00
Wall Pocket, Gardenia, Gray	58.00

Wall Pocket, Iris, Pink 60.00
Wall Pocket, Jonquil 235.00
Wall Pocket, Panel Daisy, Dark Brown 85.00
Wall Pocket, Silhouette, Blue 48.00
Wall Pocket, Silhouette, Burgundy 48.00
Wall Pocket, Snowberry, Blue 25.00
Wall Pocket, Tuscany, Gray 70.00
Wall Pocket, Velmoss Scroll, 8 In. 125.00
Wall Pocket, Velmoss, Raspberry, 8 In. 63.00
Wall Pocket, Wincraft, Blue 50.00
Wall Pocket, Zephyr Lily, Green, 8 In. .... 25.00 To 40.00
Wall Pocket, Zephyr Lily, Rust, Green 65.00
Water Set, Magnolia, 4 Mugs, Brown 225.00
Window Box, Donatello, 16 X 6 1/4 X 7 In. 275.00
Window Box, Rosecraft, 44 1/2 X 6 X 5 1/2 In. 95.00

Rowland and Marsellus Company is a mark which appears on historical Staffordshire dating from the late nineteenth and early twentieth centuries. Rowland and Marsellus is believed to be the British Anchor Pottery Co. of Longton, England. Many American views were made.

ROWLAND & MARSELLUS, Plate, Brooklyn, N.Y., Rolled Edge 20.00
Plate, Souvenir, Cleveland, O., Vignette Rim, 10 1/2 In. 45.00
Plate, Views Of Asbury Park, N.J., Dark Blue, 8 1/2 In. 30.00

ROY ROGERS, Badge & Whistle, Deputy Sheriff, Embossed Roy & Trigger 45.00
Badge, Deputy Sheriff 30.00
Bank, Figural, Boot, Metal 12.00
Camera, Pictures Roy & Trigger .... 12.00 To 18.00
Clock, Alarm, Animated, Ingraham .... 100.00 To 165.00
Doll, Nodder 30.00
Flashlight, With Siren Signal 25.00
Game, Horseshoe 46.00
Gloves, Name In Script 35.00
Guitar .... 15.00 To 50.00
Gun & Wrist Holster 15.00
Gun, Cap, Boxed, 7 In. 14.00
Gun, Cap, Boxed, 9 In. 20.00
Harmonica, Risers, Roy's Picture, Boxed .... 8.00 To 25.00
Holster, Silver Belt Buckle 75.00
Horseshoe, Lucky, Rubber .... 12.00 To 18.00
Lantern, Boxed 20.00
Lincoln Logs, Cabin Construction Set, Boxed 38.00
Lunch Box .... 10.00 To 13.50
Mug .... 5.00 To 12.00
Poster, Stand-Up, Autographed 18.00
Ring, Photograph Of Hero, 1950 .... 35.00
Shootin' Iron, Boxed 50.00
Spyglass 15.00
Thermos .... 8.00 To 8.50
Toy, Stagecoach, With Wagon Train, Windup, Marx, Boxed 65.00
Wristwatch, Move The Dial & Horse & Rider Appear Animated 45.00

The Royal Bayreuth factory was founded in Tettau, Bavaria, in 1794. It has continued to modern times. The marks have changed through the years. A stylized crest, the name "Royal Bayreuth," and the word "Bavaria" appear in slightly different form from 1870 to about 1919. Later dishes include the words "U.S. Zone," the year of the issue, and do not have the word "Bavaria."

ROYAL BAYREUTH, see also Rose Tapestry; Sand Babies; Snow Babies; Sunbonnet Babies

ROYAL BAYREUTH, Ashtray, Black Corinthian, White Center Figure, Blue Mark 42.00
  Ashtray, Clown, Red, Blue Mark 90.00
  Ashtray, Corinthian 35.00
  Ashtray, Devil & Card, Blue Mark 65.00
  Ashtray, Devil's Head, Blue Mark 170.00
  Ashtray, Elk .... 110.00 To 120.00
  Ashtray, Goats, Scenic 38.00
  Ashtray, Goose, Green Frog In Beak, Blue Mark 375.00
  Ashtray, Hunter With Gun, Heart Shaped, Blue Mark 55.00
  Ashtray, Pastoral Cows, Blue Mark 50.00
  Ashtray, Picture Of Bulldog, Captioned Come On, Green Mark 35.00
  Ashtray, Spur, Leather Like Handle, Moose Scene Interior 75.00
  Basket, Dancing Couple, Gold Band, Marked, 4 1/4 In. 239.00
  Basket, Donkeys & Man, Trees, 6 In. 190.00
  Basket, Floral Inside & Out, Gold Trim, Marked, 4 1/2 In. 329.00
  Basket, Scenic, Donkey, Man 175.00
  Bell, Original Clapper, Beach Babies 285.00
  Berry Bowl, Pink Roses, Blue Mark, 5 1/2 In. 110.00
  Bonbon, Enameled Roses, Blue Mark, 9 1/2 X 3 3/4 In. 175.00
  Bonbon, Men In Sailing Ship, Leaf Shape, 6 1/2 In.Diam. 80.00
  Bowl, Blown-Out Grapes, 10 3/4 In. 200.00
  Bowl, Jeweled, White Ground, Yellow Roses, Blue Mark, 10 In. 175.00
  Bowl, Lettuce, Blue Mark, 4 X 10 In.Diam. 245.00
  Bowl, Little Boy Blue, Blue Mark, 4 In. 115.00
  Bowl, Musicians, Scalloped, 3 Feet, Blue Mark, 6 7/8 In. 110.00
  Bowl, Reticulated Border, Roses, 10 1/2 In.Diam. 145.00
  Box, Covered, Fishing Scene, Blue Mark, 4 X 2 1/2 In. 65.00
  Box, Cuff Links, Dogs Attacking Stag, Blue Mark 65.00
  Box, Heart Shaped, Pastoral Scene, Covered, Blue Mark 95.00
  Box, Kidney Shaped, 3-Color Roses, Insert, Blue Mark 375.00
  Box, Pin, Jack & Jill, Heart Shaped, Covered, Blue Mark 60.00
  Box, Powder, Melon Shape, 3 Gold Feet, Marked, 4 In. 195.00
  Box, Powder, Pink Roses, Footed, Blue Mark 165.00
  Box, Ring, Pink Roses, Square, Blue Mark 225.00
  Box, 3-Color Roses, Oval, Blue Mark, 2 In. 190.00
  Box, 3-Color Roses, Oval, Pinched Sides, Blue Mark, 3 In. 275.00
  Butter, Arabs & Horses, Covered, Rectangular, 4 1/2 X 6 In. 115.00
  Butter, Scenic, 3 Men Mounted On Horses, 1 1/2 X 6 1/4 In. 140.00
  Cake Plate, Bopeep 140.00
  Cake Plate, Brittany Girls, Blue Mark, 10 1/2 In. 95.00
  Cake Plate, Little Bopeep, Open Handled, 10 1/2 In. 175.00
  Cake Plate, Pink Roses, Blue Mark, 6 In. 110.00
  Cake Plate, Pink Roses, Open Handles, Blue Mark, 11 In. 235.00
  Cake Plate, 3-Color Roses, Blue Mark, 6 In. 110.00
  Candleholder, Cape Cod, Fishing 275.00
  Candleholder, Man In Boat Fishing, Blue Mark, 4 In. 69.00
  Candleholder, Mounted Rider & Hounds, Blue Mark, 4 In. 69.00
  Candlestick, Art Nouveau, Handled, Rose Design, Pair 135.00
  Candlestick, Corinthian, Blue Mark 75.00
  Candlestick, Devil & Card, Blue Mark 195.00
  Candlestick, Girl In White Dress, Dog, Shield Back, Blue Mark 245.00
  Candlestick, Jack & Jill 140.00
  Candlestick, Storks, Black & White Enamel, Green, 4 In. 90.00
  Chamberstick, Boy, Blue 130.00
  Chamberstick, Corinthian, Blue Mark, 5 1/2 In. 90.00
  Chamberstick, Jack & Jill 125.00
  Chocolate Set, Poppy Shape, Red & Green, Pot 7 1/2 In., 3 Pc. 190.00
  Compote, Poppy, Leaves Form Stem, Blue Mark, 5 1/2 In.Diam. 295.00
  Compote, Poppy, Pastel 250.00
  Cracker Jar, Tomato 285.00
  Creamer Mountain Goat 155.00
  Creamer, Alligator, Blue Mark, 4 1/2 In. .... *Illus* 75.00

Royal Bayreuth, Creamer, Sand Babies, Blue Mark, 3 1/4 In.; Pitcher, Devil & Cards, Blue Mark, 5 In.; Creamer, Alligator, Blue Mark, 4 1/2 In.

(See Pages 553, 555, 556)

Creamer, Apple, Blue Mark, 3 3/4 In. .... 60.00 To 95.00
Creamer, Apple, Green, Touch Of Red, Blue Mark 100.00
Creamer, Arab Riding Camel In Desert, Blue Mark 175.00
Creamer, Baby's, Green Mark 110.00
Creamer, Bell Ringer, Blue Mark 245.00
Creamer, Bopeep, Blue Mark .... 80.00 To 90.00
Creamer, Bouquet Of Roses, Pearlized, Covered, 4 1/4 In. 215.00
Creamer, Boy Blue 55.00
Creamer, Bull, Black, Red Horns, Blue Mark .... 60.00 To 145.00
Creamer, Bull, Brown, Marked .... 135.00 To 145.00
Creamer, Bull, Gray .... 125.00 To 135.00
Creamer, Butterfly, Open, Blue Mark .... 165.00 To 185.00
Creamer, Cat, Black .... 95.00 To 135.00
Creamer, Cat, Gray 65.00
Creamer, Chicken, Yellow 65.00
Creamer, Chimpanzee, Washington, D.C., On Side, 4 In. 185.00
Creamer, Clown, Red, Blue Mark, 3 3/4 In. 145.00
Creamer, Coachman, Blue Mark .... 100.00 To 145.00
Creamer, Coachman, Red Coat, Blue Mark, 4 1/4 In. 150.00
Creamer, Cockatoo 130.00
Creamer, Conch, Lobster Handle 67.00
Creamer, Corinthian, Blue Mark, Black, 4 1/2 In. .... 40.00 To 65.00
Creamer, Corinthian, Rust Lining, Yellow, Blue Mark, 3 3/4 In. 85.00
Creamer, Corset Shape, Leaves & Pink Roses, Blue Mark 150.00
Creamer, Cow, Black 145.00
Creamer, Cows On Side, 3 1/2 In. 65.00
Creamer, Crow, Black 95.00
Creamer, Devil & Cards, Blue Mark .... 75.00 To 150.00
Creamer, Duck, Blue Mark .... 125.00 To 135.00
Creamer, Eagle .... 125.00 To 145.00
Creamer, Elk, Blue Mark .... 70.00 To 85.00
Creamer, Fish 55.00
Creamer, Fish Head, Blue Mark 150.00
Creamer, Fox Hunt, 5 In. 95.00
Creamer, Frog 68.00
Creamer, Frog, Green, Blue Mark .... 75.00 To 120.00
Creamer, Girl, With Candle 75.00
Creamer, Girl, With Dog, Blue Mark 85.00
Creamer, Grape Design, Signed, 3 3/4 In. 59.00
Creamer, Green Base, Scenic, Girl, Puppy, Marked 95.00

Creamer, Hunter & Dog, Blue Mark, 4 1/2 In. 95.00
Creamer, Jack & The Beanstalk, Blue Mark .... 80.00 To 115.00
Creamer, Jack Horner, Blue Mark, 3 1/2 In. 80.00
Creamer, Lamplighter, Blue Mark .... 150.00 To 165.00
Creamer, Lobster & Lettuce Leaf, Signed .... 55.00 To 80.00
Creamer, Lobster, Blue Mark .... 55.00 To 85.00
Creamer, Man Of The Mountain, Blue Mark 110.00
Creamer, Melon, Pink Floral Spout, Blue Mark 145.00
Creamer, Milkmaid With Jug, Blue 200.00
Creamer, Miss Muffet, 4 1/2 In. 80.00
Creamer, Monk, 4 1/2 In. 90.00
Creamer, Mountain Goat, Blue Mark, 3 3/4 In. .... 155.00 To 170.00
Creamer, Murex Shell, Blue Mark 35.00
Creamer, Musicians, Hand-Painted, 3 1/2 In. 89.00
Creamer, Oakleaf, Blue Mark, 4 In. .... 75.00 To 100.00
Creamer, Old Man Mountain 60.00
Creamer, Pansy, Orchid, Pink, Yellow, 4 In. .... 125.00 To 145.00
Creamer, Parakeet 175.00
Creamer, Pearlized, Signed, Blue Mark, 5 In. 65.00
Creamer, Pearls, Brown 110.00
Creamer, Pelican 75.00
Creamer, Penguin, Black, Yellow, Square 95.00
Creamer, Pheasant, Blue Mark, 4 1/4 In. 79.00
Creamer, Pinched Rose Shape, Pink Roses, Blue Mark 125.50
Creamer, Platypus, Blue Mark 550.00
Creamer, Polar Bears, Moonlight Scenic, Blue Mark, 3 1/2 In. 150.00
Creamer, Poodle, Black, Blue Mark .... 120.00 To 135.00
Creamer, Poodle, Gray .... 135.00 To 180.00
Creamer, Poppy, Green-Yellow 110.00
Creamer, Poppy, Red, Blue Mark, 3 1/2 In. .... 65.00 To 100.00
Creamer, Robin, Blue Mark, 4 In. .... 100.00 To 130.00
Creamer, Rooster .... 155.00 To 195.00
Creamer, Sand Babies, Blue Mark, 3 1/4 In. ....*Illus* 75.00
Creamer, Scenic, Basket Girl, Claming, Marked 85.00
Creamer, Scenic, Girl, Wheat, Rooster, Chickens, Marked 85.00
Creamer, Scenic, Goats 75.00
Creamer, Seal On Seashore, Blue Mark 70.00
Creamer, Seal, Gray, Blue Mark, 4 In. 165.00
Creamer, St.Bernard .... 145.00 To 185.00
Creamer, Storks, Green Ground, Blue Mark, 4 3/4 In. 70.00
Creamer, Straight Side Shape, Pink Roses, Blue Mark 125.00
Creamer, Tankard, 2 Cows In Green Field, Blue Mark, 3 3/4 In. 65.00
Creamer, Toby Coachman 145.00
Creamer, Tomato, Blue Mark, 3 3/4 In. .... 45.00 To 58.00
Creamer, Turtle, Blue Mark 250.00
Creamer, Water Buffalo, Black & White 115.00
Creamer, Watermelon 150.00
Cup & Saucer, Bopeep, Girl, Dog, Marked 105.00
Cup & Saucer, Brittany Girl, Blue Mark 68.00
Cup & Saucer, Devil & Cards, Marked, Demitasse .... 65.00 To 145.00
Cup & Saucer, Goose Girl, Blue Mark 55.00
Cup & Saucer, Poppy, Red, Demitasse 160.00
Cup & Saucer, Poppy, Yellow, Pearlized, Demitasse 55.00
Cup & Saucer, Scene Old Mill, Waterfall, Church, Demitasse 35.00
Cup & Saucer, Yellow & Pink Roses, Blue Mark 195.00
Cup, Dice, Devil & Card, Blue Mark 85.00
Desk Set, Pink, Gold Trim, Gold Mark, 4 Piece 395.00
Dish, Berry, Blown-Out Panels, Gold Outlining, 6 In., Set Of 6 .... 100.00
Dish, Candy, Clover Shaped, 3-Color Roses, Blue Mark 150.00
Dish, Candy, Devil & Cards, Blue Mark 75.00
Dish, Candy, Lobster, 5 In. 79.00
Dish, Candy, Maple Leaf, 3-Color Roses, Blue Mark 165.00
Dish, Celery, Lobster, Blue Mark 125.00

Dish, Cheese, Cover, Hunt Scene	75.00
Dish, Feeding, Boy Blue, Blue Mark, 7 1/2 In.	80.00
Dish, Lobster, Covered, 5 In.	85.00
Dish, Nut, Mother-Of-Pearl, Poppy Pink, Blue Mark, 6 In.Diam.	125.00
Dish, Poppy, Blue Mark, 5 1/2 In.	48.00
Dish, Poppy, Pink, Green Leaves, Handled, 4 In.	18.00
Dish, Tomato, Covered, Blue Mark, 4 1/4 In.	24.00 To 25.00
Fernery, Rose Design, Blue Mark, 6 In.	95.00
Figurine, Water Buffalo, Red Horns, Marked	139.00
Flower Holder, Hunt Scene, Covered, Blue Mark, 3 1/2 In.	85.00
Frame, Picture, Scenic, Hunting Scene, 10 In.	175.00
Hair Receiver, Oyster & Pearl, Gold Lid	175.00
Hair Receiver, Sheep, Hand-Painted	75.00
Hair Receiver, Tapestry, Footed, 3 In.	175.00
Hair Receiver, 3-Color Roses, Footed, Blue Mark	135.00
Hatpin Holder, Dachshund, Blue Mark	325.00
Hatpin Holder, Hunter With Dog, Blue Mark, Square, 4 1/2 In.	275.00
Hatpin Holder, Owl	235.00
Hatpin Holder, 3-Color Roses	200.00
Humidor, Chimpanzee, Covered	400.00
Humidor, Corinthian	135.00 To 225.00
Humidor, Hunt Scene, Blue Mark	195.00
Humidor, Pink Roses, Blue Mark	875.00
Humidor, Troubadours, Signed Dixon, Blue Mark	295.00
Jar, Jam & Plate, Grape, Green	185.00
Jar, Powder, English Hunting Scene	95.00
Jar, Powder, Farmer & Turkeys, Covered	95.00
Jug, Farm Scene, 5 In.	65.00
Lobster Set, Red & Green, Set Of 6 Plates	300.00
Loving Cup, Corinthian Ware, Colored Figures, Large	95.00
Match Holder, Clown, Wall, Red	185.00 To 215.00
Match Holder, Devil Card, Wall	235.00
Match Holder, Monkey, Wall	235.00 To 325.00
Match Holder, Musicians, Holds Box Matches	100.00
Match Holder, Wall, Devil & Card	195.00
Match Holder, Wall, Pink Roses, Blue Mark	175.00
Mayonnaise Set, Goosegirl, Blue Mark	105.00
Mayonnaise Set, Jack & Jill, Blue Mark	115.00
Mayonnaise Set, Man Fishing, Blue Mark	105.00
Mayonnaise Set, Red Poppy, 3 Piece	55.00
Mug, Beer, Playing Scene, Yellow Bottom, Blue Mark	97.00
Mug, Corinthian, Greek Key, Grecian Figure, Blue Mark, 5 In.	40.00
Mug, Devil & Cards, Blue Mark, 5 In.	85.00 To 125.00
Mug, Drum, Child's	27.50
Mug, Humpty-Dumpty, Child's	45.00
Mug, Tavern Scene, Script Inside, Blue Mark	65.00
Mustard & Spoon, Rose, Figural, Blue Mark	145.00
Mustard & Spoon, Shell, Blue Mark	55.00
Mustard & Spoon, Tomato	30.00 To 40.00
Mustard, Farm Scene, Blue Mark, Signed	45.00
Mustard, Goosegirl, Handles, Footed, Blue Mark	75.00
Mustard, Lobster, Ladle, Green Leaf Underplate	79.00
Mustard, Poppy, Red	75.00
Mustard, Shell	40.00
Nappy, Little Boy Blue, Tricornered, Handle	130.00
Pitcher, Cavalier, Blue Mark, 3 1/2 In.	85.00
Pitcher, Child's, Ring Around The Rosie, 3 1/4 In.	130.00
Pitcher, Cows, Pink & Green Ground, Blue Mark, 6 1/2 In.	70.00
Pitcher, Dachshund, 5 1/4 In.	550.00
Pitcher, Devil & Card, Blue Mark, 7 1/4 In.	420.00 To 495.00
Pitcher, Devil & Cards, Blue Mark, 5 In.	*Illus* 180.00
Pitcher, Fisherman Scene, Blue Mark, 5 1/4 In.	65.00
Pitcher, Floral & Duck Design, Enamel Beading, 6 3/4 In.	110.00

Pitcher, Girl In Hat, Handled, Blue Mark, 9 1/2 In. 275.00
Pitcher, Hand-Painted, Ivory, Blue Mark, 5 1/2 In. 110.00
Pitcher, Hunt, 4 3/4 In. 110.00
Pitcher, Milk, Apple, 4 1/4 In. 100.00
Pitcher, Milk, Coachman 185.00
Pitcher, Milk, Corinthian, Red Lining, Blue Mark 85.00
Pitcher, Milk, Devil & Cards, Blue Mark 265.00
Pitcher, Milk, Eagle, Marked 260.00
Pitcher, Milk, Elk 175.00
Pitcher, Milk, Fish Head 155.00
Pitcher, Milk, Melon, Blue Mark 105.00
Pitcher, Milk, Monkey, Green 225.00
Pitcher, Milk, Pinched Nose, Pink Roses, Blue Mark 150.00
Pitcher, Milk, Poppy, Apricot, Blue Mark 165.00
Pitcher, Milk, Roses, Pink, Straight Sides, Blue Mark 150.00
Pitcher, Milk, Speckled Trout, Blue Mark 225.00
Pitcher, Mouse, Gray & Orange, Blue Mark, 7 3/8 In. 575.00
Pitcher, Pinched Nose, Pastoral Scene, 8 1/2 In. 255.00
Pitcher, Pinched Nose, 4 Cows, 9 X 8 In. 175.00
Pitcher, Tomato, Blue Mark, 4 1/2 In. .... 61.00 To 75.00
Pitcher, Washerwoman, Pinched Nose, Blue Mark, 3 3/4 In. 65.00
Pitcher, Water, Corset Shape, Pink Roses, Blue Mark, 7 In. 450.00
Pitcher, Water, Elk, Blue Mark .... 225.00 To 295.00
Pitcher, Water, Goosegirl, Pinched Nose, Blue Mark 225.00
Pitcher, Water, Gray & Green, Sailboat Scene, 7 3/4 In. 250.00
Pitcher, Water, Lobster, Blue Mark 325.00
Pitcher, Water, Shell, Coral Handle 200.00
Pitcher, Water, Tomato, Blue Mark 250.00
Planter, Chicken Farmer Scene, Insert 75.00
Planter, Murex Shell, 9 1/2 In. 295.00
Planter, Reticulated Side, Ship Scenes, Insert, Blue Mark 110.00
Planter, Round, Pink, Blue Mark, Insert 250.00
Planter, 3-Color Roses, Handled, Small 145.00
Plate, Arab On Horse, Green Mark, 9 In. 85.00
Plate, Bopeep, Blue Mark, 6 In. 75.00
Plate, Boy Blue, Blue Mark, 6 In. .... 75.00 To 105.00
Plate, Cows In Pasture, Blue Mark, Pair 75.00
Plate, Devil & Cards, Blue Mark, 7 In. 175.00
Plate, Dog, Girl, Blue Mark, 9 In. 75.00
Plate, Dutch Children On Pier, Open Handled 98.00
Plate, Geranium, Pearlized, 7 3/4 In.Diam. 65.00
Plate, Girl With Dog, Blue Mark, 9 In. .... 75.00 To 85.00
Plate, Grapes, Gold Scalloped Rim, Yellow Ground, 10 In. 155.00
Plate, Jack & Jill, 6 In. .... 48.00 To 49.00
Plate, Jack Horner, 7 3/4 In. 75.00
Plate, Man In Boat Fishing, Ducks Overhead, Blue Mark, 11 In. 260.00
Plate, Miss Muffet 45.00
Plate, Oakleaf, Pearlized 95.00
Plate, Poppy, Blue Mark, 6 In.Diam. 30.00
Plate, Poppy, Orange, Blue Mark, 7 In. 35.00
Plate, Poppy, Pearlized, White, Blue Mark, 8 1/4 In. 80.00
Plate, Roses, Blue Mark, 7 In. 150.00
Reamer, Spiky Shell 39.00
Relish, Tomato 65.00
Rose Bowl, Boy Blue, Blue Mark, 3 X 4 1/2 In.Diam. 80.00
Salt & Pepper, Elk, Blue Mark, Pair 125.00
Salt & Pepper, Lamplighter, Blue Mark 175.00
Salt, Grape, Purple, Pair 30.00
Saltshaker, Devil & Cards 85.00
Sauceboat, Lobster 65.00
Shoe, Man's, High, Tan, Black Stitching, Gold Trim 75.00
Shoe, Oxford, Man's, Cinnamon 85.00
Slipper, Portrait Of Man & Lady Toe 350.00

Stein, Elk 150.00
Stein, Wood Nymph, Bare Bosom, Wings, Water, Green, 7 In. 300.00
Striker, Match, Blue Mark, 3 1/2 In. 60.00
Sugar & Creamer, Boy Blue, Boat Shape, Blue Mark 195.00
Sugar & Creamer, Coral Shell, Blue Mark 85.00
Sugar & Creamer, Corinthian Pattern 95.00
Sugar & Creamer, Jester, Blue Marked 125.00
Sugar & Creamer, Lobster, Covered, Signed .... 50.00 To 175.00
Sugar & Creamer, Poppy, Red, Blue Mark, Signed 210.00
Sugar & Creamer, Purple Grape, Covered, Signed .... 149.00 To 235.00
Sugar & Creamer, Ring Around Rosie, Girl & Dog, Blue Mark 95.00
Sugar & Creamer, Tomato, Marked .... 85.00 To 125.00
Sugar & Creamer, 3-Color Roses, Gold Handles 395.00
Sugar, Grape, Purple .... 72.00 To 85.00
Sugar, Jack & Jill, Blue Mark 85.00
Sugar, Little Bopeep, Cornered, Blue Mark 90.00
Sugar, Lobster 72.50
Sugar, Pansy, Open 125.00
Sugar, Pineapple, Blue Mark 12.00
Sugar, Pink Roses, Bulbous, Covered, Blue Mark 175.00
Sugar, Ring Around Rosie, Blue Mark 185.00
Sugar, Tomato, Covered, 3 In. .... 35.00 To 50.00
Sugar, Tomato, Lettuce Leaf Underplate .... 38.00 To 47.50
Sugar, 3-Color Roses, Covered, Blue Mark 175.00
Tankard, Green, Cavalier Scene, Blue Mark 70.00
Tea Set, Scenes With Cows, Rams, & Sheep, Signed, 3 Piece 250.00
Teapot, Pansy, Blue Mark 485.00
Teapot, Poppy, Red 160.00
Teapot, Sheep Scene 195.00
Teapot, Tomato .... 95.00 To 125.00
Toothpick, Bell Ringer, Blue Mark 160.00
Toothpick, Brittany Girl, 3-Handled, Blue Mark 98.00
Toothpick, Cavalier Scene, Scuttle Shape, 3 1/2 In. 80.00
Toothpick, Conch Shell, Pearlized, Souvenir, Blue Mark 35.00
Toothpick, Corinthian, 3-Handled, Orange, 2 1/4 In. 43.00
Toothpick, Corinthian, 3-Handled, 4 In. 43.00
Toothpick, Devil 75.00
Toothpick, Elk, Red Mark .... 85.00 To 110.00
Toothpick, Hen & Rooster, 3-Handled 140.00
Toothpick, Open Rose, Pink 175.00
Toothpick, Poppy, Marked, White 145.00
Toothpick, Stork, Tricornered, Yellow, Blue Mark 65.00
Tray, Card, Blue Mark, 3 3/4 In.Square 85.00
Tray, Dresser, Devil & Cards, Signed, Blue Mark 350.00
Tray, Dresser, 3-Color Roses, Green Mark, 11 1/2 In. 225.00
Tray, Jack & Jill, 4 In.Square 75.00
Tray, Pin, Dutch Girl 50.00
Tray, Pink Roses, Signed, 8 X 11 In. 85.00
Vase, Band Of Cattle, Roses, Enameled Dots, Green Mark, 4 In. 95.00
Vase, Bud, Bulbous, 3-Color Roses, Blue Mark .... 200.00 To 250.00
Vase, Bud, Pink Roses, Narrow, Blue Mark, 4 1/2 In. 185.00
Vase, Castle Scene, Gold Handles, 2 3/4 In. 185.00
Vase, Cattle, Roses On Foot & Rim, Green Mark, 4 1/2 In. 95.00
Vase, Cavaliers, 10 In. 225.00
Vase, Cherries & Grapes, Reds & Greens, Blue Mark, 9 3/4 In. 110.00
Vase, Cows, Rams, & Sheep, Signed, 7 In. 210.00
Vase, Game Birds, Top Section, Square Mouth, Blue Mark, 5 In. 75.00
Vase, Hunt Scene, 5 In. 60.00
Vase, Hunt, Round, Footed, 2 1/2 In. 75.00
Vase, Mountain Goats, Blue Mark, 6 In. 150.00
Vase, Mountain Goats, Blue Mark, 7 X 5 1/2 In. 95.00
Vase, Musicians, Hallmarked Silver Rim, Blue Mark, 3 5/8 In. 48.00
Vase, Musicians, Sterling Rim, 2-Handled, Miniature, Pair 95.00

Royal Berlin, Vase, Gold Leaf,
C.1800, Griffin Handles, 18 In.

Vase, Oakleaf Luster, Green, Blue Mark, 3 X 2 3/4 In.	58.00
Vase, Pastoral Scene, 5 1/2 In.	85.00
Vase, Pink Poppies, 7 1/2 In.	55.00
Vase, Pink Roses, Squat, Footed, Ruffled Top, Handles, 4 In.	250.00
Vase, Ring Around Rosie, Silver Rim, 3-Handled	80.00
Vase, Ring Around Rosie, Sterling Silver Top, 2-Handled	75.00
Vase, Seal On Seashore, Blue Mark, 3 3/4 In.	95.00
Vase, Sheep, Sterling Silver Collar, Signed, 3 1/2 In.	60.00
Vase, Sheepherder, Blue Mark, 4 1/2 In.	60.00
Vase, Swans, 4 In.	54.00
Vase, Urn, 3-Color Roses, Blue Mark, 4 1/2 In.	185.00
Vase, 2 Gibson Girl Busts At Top, Green, 4 1/2 In.	145.00
Wall Pocket, Blown-Out Grapes, Luster Rim, 9 1/2 X 5 1/2 In.	325.00
Wall Pocket, Grape, Pink, Green Leaves	225.00
Wall Pocket, Yellow Grapes	175.00 To 195.00

ROYAL BERLIN, see also KPM
ROYAL BERLIN, Vase, Gold Leaf, C.1800, Griffin Handles, 18 In. ....*Illus* 850.00

Royal Bonn is the nineteenth-century trade name for the Bonn China Manufactory established in 1755 at Bonn, Germany. A general line of porcelain dishes was made.
ROYAL BONN, see also Flow Blue

ROYAL BONN, Clock, Blue Floral, Gargoyles Front, Ansonia Works	600.00
Clock, China Case, Flowers, Gold Trim, Scrolls, Blue, Marked, 6 1/2	135.00
Compote, Scenic Sailboat At Dock, 9 1/2 X 3 1/2 In.	85.00
Lamp, Oil, Urn Style, China Font, Green, Gold Trim, Signed	165.00
Plate, Fish In Center, 9 In.	85.00
Vase, Allover Floral, Raised Gold, Handled, 1755 Mark, 8 In.	93.00
Vase, Dandelions & Leaves, Brown Ground, 5 In.	95.00
Vase, Floral Front & Back, Raised Gold Scrolls, Handled, 10 In.	135.00
Vase, Floral, Tapestry, 8 1/2 In.	195.00
Vase, Flowers, Signed, Lilac, 8 In.	85.00
Vase, Hand-Painted Portrait Of Woman, Artist Signed, 7 1/2 In.	425.00
Vase, Hand-Painted Portrait, Gold Handles, Signed, 10 1/2 In.	285.00
Vase, Maiden Portrait, 1900, Signed, 12 1/2 In.	700.00
Vase, Orange, Green, Lavender Flowers, Signed, 12 In.	85.00
Vase, Pink Flowers, Beige Ground, 7 In.	125.00
Vase, Tapestry, Alternating Floral, Rose Panels, 9 In.	235.00
Vase, Tapestry, Flowers, Trees, & Leaves, 12 1/2 In., Pair	425.00
Vase, Windmill & Cottage, Birds, Artist Signed, 8 1/2 In.	135.00
Vase, 3 Birds, On Limb, Gold Flowers, 9 1/2 In.	265.00

Royal Copenhagen porcelain and pottery have been made in Denmark since 1772. They are still being made. One of their most famous wares is the Christmas Plate Series.

ROYAL COPENHAGEN, Bowl, Center, 3 Classical Maidens, Cupid, Purple, 10 In. 80.00
  Box, Gold & Floral Design, Covered, 1894 Mark 60.00
  Dish, Dated 1906, Commemorative, Signed, 7 7/8 X 8 In., Pair 50.00
  Figurine, Cat, Siamese, Sitting, 7 1/2 In. 165.00
  Figurine, Cockerel & Hen, 1930, 10 In. .... 200.00 To 225.00
  Figurine, Goose Girl, 6 In. 145.00
  Figurine, Lovebirds, 5 1/2 In. 95.00
  Figurine, Mermaid, On Stomach, 1920, 7 In.Long 150.00
  Figurine, Polar Bear, Stalking, 11 In. 225.00
  Figurine, Sandman, 8 In. 750.00
  Figurine, Siamese Cat, Sitting, 7 1/2 In. .... 135.00 To 165.00
  Figurine, Siamese Cat, 7 3/4 In. 90.00
  Figurine, Sitting Siamese Cat, No.2851/3281, 7 1/2 In. 140.00
  Gravy, Blue & White, Attached Underplate 95.00
  Plaque, Dragon, Signed Krog, 1889, 12 In. 85.00
  Plate, Christmas, 1963 .... 60.00
  Plate, Christmas, 1965 .... 85.00
  Plate, Christmas, 1970 .... 22.00
  Plate, Flora Danica Pattern, 7 5/8 In., Set Of 12 .... 3100.00
  Plate, Little Mermaid, Summer 22.50
  Tray, Pen, Flying Bat, Gray, Brown, Lavender, Marked, 9 In. 50.00
  Vase, Cactus, 4 1/2 In. 60.00
  Vase, Dahl-Jensen Landscape, Signed, 12 In. 350.00
  Vase, Dutch Windmill Scene, 6 1/2 In. 55.00
  Vase, Marsh Grass & Butterfly, No.542/235, 6 1/2 In. 50.00

Royal Copley was produced by the Spaulding China Company of Sebring, Ohio, from 1939 to 1960.

ROYAL COPLEY, Figurine, Bird, 8 In. 30.00
  Figurine, Deer & Fawn, Heads, Browns, 10 In. 18.00
  Pitcher, Flowers, Yellow To Blue, 8 In. 14.00
  Planter, Bluebird, Open Center 10.00
  Planter, Deer Head, Open Center, 6 1/2 X 7 In. 10.00
  Planter, Elephant, Bail & Howdah, 7 1/2 In. 12.50
  Planter, Leaping Gazelles, Green, 6 1/2 X 6 In. 8.50
  Planter, Rooster, In Relief 12.00
  Planter, Rooster, Multicolored, 8 In. 7.50
  Planter, Row Of Flower Forms, Turquoise, Rose, Yellow, 3 X 7 In. 6.00
  Vase, Brown, Raised Leaves, Flat Sides, Handled, 7 1/2 In. 6.00
  Vase, Figural, Chinese Girl, Standing, Pot In Hand, 8 In. 5.00
  Vase, Horsehead, Light Brown, Yellow Mane, 8 In. 9.00
  Vase, Indian Boy, Standing By Pot, Brown, Yellow, Green Label 10.00
  Wall Pocket, Chinese Girl, Big Yellow Hat, Rose, Green Dress 12.00
  Wall Pocket, 2 Oriental Girls 14.00

Royal Crown Derby Company, Ltd., was established in England in 1876.
ROYAL CROWN DERBY, see also Derby
ROYAL CROWN DERBY, Cigarette Lighter, Ronson, Imari, 3 1/2 In. .... 50.00 To 95.00
  Cup & Saucer, Rose, Pansy, & Lily 15.00
  Dessert Set, 22 Piece 300.00
  Figurine, Sealyham Dog .... 45.00 To 65.00
  Lamp Base, Marine Scene, Blue & White, Artist Signed, 1937 .... 135.00
  Plate, Gold Scrolls, Marked, 10 In. 12.00
  Plate, Japan Design, 1939, Marked, 10 1/2 In. 75.00
  Tureen, Sauce, Waves, Covered, Red 85.00

Royal Doulton was the name used on pottery made after 1902. The Doulton factory was founded in 1815. Their wares are still being made. For a more complete listing see "Kovels' illustrated Price Guide to Royal Doulton."

ROYAL DOULTON, Ash Pot, Old Charley	100.00
Ashtray, Farmer John, A Mark	125.00
Ashtray, Flambe, Country Scene, Noke, 4 1/2 In.	35.00
Ashtray, The Major	30.00
Bottle, Bell's Scotch Whiskey, Back Label, Stopper	20.00
Bottle, Liqueur, Flambe, Silver Overlay, Marked, 7 1/4 In.	400.00
Bottle, Liqueur, Flambe, Silver Overlay, 8 1/2 In.	695.00
Bottle, Whiskey, Highland	70.00
Bottle, Zorro, A Mark, 10 1/2 In,	50.00
Bottle, Zorro, Black, 4 In.	35.00
Bowl, Auld Mac, A Mark	100.00
Bowl, Coaching Days, Silver Plated Rim, 8 In.	85.00
Bowl, Farmer John, A Mark	125.00
Bowl, Kirkwood, 9 1/2 In.	40.00
Bowl, Nursery Rhyme Series, Old Mother Hubbard	40.00
Bowl, Robert Burns, Scenes Outside, 7 1/2 In.	135.00
Bowl, Robin Hood, King Of The Archers, 6 1/2 In.Diam.	50.00
Bowl, Sir Roger De Coverley Series, Scalloped, 8 X 11 In.	85.00
Bowl, Woodland Silhouette, Footed, 9 In.Diam.	125.00
Candleholder, Witches All Around, Brown Glaze, 2 1/4 In., Pair	165.00
Candlestick, Dutch Scene, 6 X 2 In.	125.00
Candlestick, Yellow, Black Sailboat, Signed, 9 In.	125.00

Character jugs are modeled of the head and shoulders of the subject. They were made in four sizes: large - 5 1/4 to 7 inches, small - 3 1/4 to 4 inches, miniature - 2 1/4 to 2 1/2 inches, and tiny - 1 1/4 inches. Toby jugs depict a full seated figure.

Character Jug, 'ard Of 'earing, Miniature	1195.00
Character Jug, 'ard Of 'earing, Small	675.00
Character Jug, 'arriet, Large	175.00
Character Jug, 'arry, A Mark, Large	175.00
Character Jug, 'arry, A Mark, Small	85.00
Character Jug, Auld Mac, Music, Large	375.00
Character Jug, Barleycorn, Miniature	75.00
Character Jug, Captain Hook, Miniature	250.00
Character Jug, Clown, White Hair, Large	950.00
Character Jug, Drake, Small	65.00
Character Jug, Farmer John, A Mark, Small	90.00
Character Jug, Fat Boy, Small	75.00
Character Jug, Fat Boy, Tiny	100.00
Character Jug, Fortune Teller, Large	265.00
Character Jug, Fortune Teller, Small	290.00
Character Jug, Frair Tuck, Large	350.00
Character Jug, Gladiator, Small	375.00
Character Jug, Jockey, Large	175.00
Character Jug, John Peel, A Mark, Miniature	65.00
Character Jug, John Peel, Tiny	175.00
Character Jug, Johnny Appleseed, Large	150.00 To 275.00
Character Jug, Lord Nelson, Large	250.00
Character Jug, Mikado, Small	285.00
Character Jug, Mr.Micawber, Tiny	90.00
Character Jug, Old Charley, Music, Large	375.00
Character Jug, Old Charley, Tiny	100.00
Character Jug, Old King Cole, Small	110.00
Character Jug, Paddy, Large	125.00
Character Jug, Paddy, Tiny	110.00

Character Jug, Sam Weller, A Mark, Small	75.00
Character Jug, Samuel Johnson, Small	175.00
Character Jug, Scaramouche, Large	500.00
Character Jug, Scaramouche, Miniature	375.00
Character Jug, Simple Simon, Large	475.00
Character Jug, Smuts, Large	1900.00
Character Jug, St.George, Small	75.00
Character Jug, Touchstone, Large	225.00
Character Jug, Town Crier, Large	130.00 To 135.00
Character Jug, Uncle Tom Cobbleigh, Large	350.00
Character Jug, Vicar Of Bray, A Mark, Large	190.00 To 210.00
Coffee Set, Reynard The Fox, Hand-Painted, Covered Pot	238.00
Cream Soup, Kirkwood, 2-Handled, Stand	29.50
Creamer, Sam Weller, 3 In.	95.00
Creamer, Watchman, 2 In.	40.00
Cup & Saucer, Blue Crisscross Design	15.00
Cup & Saucer, Coaching Days	40.00
Cup & Saucer, Demitasse, English Renaissance, Green & Gold	15.00
Cup & Saucer, Glamis Thistle, Demitasse	25.00
Cup & Saucer, Jackdaw Of Rheims	55.00
Cup & Saucer, Kirkwood	22.50
Cup & Saucer, Mr.Micawber	65.00
Cup & Saucer, Rosell, Roses, Gold Trim	15.00
Cup, Beaker, King Edward VII, Queen Alexandra	90.00
Cup, Coronation, Handleless, 1911, 4 In.	30.00
Cup, Loving, Coronation, King Edward, Mary, 1937, 10 1/2 In.	565.00
Dish, Baby, Bunnykins	75.00
Dish, Cereal, Pan Playing Pipes	25.00
Dish, Pin, Winston Churchill Portrait, 4 In.	75.00
Figurine, A La Mode, HN 2544	195.00
Figurine, Affection, HN 2236	60.00
Figurine, Alexandra, HN 2398	135.00
Figurine, Alsatian, HN 1115	300.00
Figurine, Annabella, HN 1872	495.00 To 525.00
Figurine, Apple Maid, HN 2160	375.00
Figurine, At Ease, HN 2473	135.00
Figurine, Autumn Breezes, HN 1911, Pink	125.00 To 145.00
Figurine, Autumn Breezes, HN 1913, Green	135.00
Figurine, Bachelor, HN 2319	195.00 To 225.00
Figurine, Ballad Seller, HN 2266	250.00
Figurine, Ballerina, HN 2116	210.00 To 295.00
Figurine, Basket Weaver, HN 2245	450.00
Figurine, Bedtime Story, HN 2059	140.00
Figurine, Beggar, HN 2175	460.00
Figurine, Belle O' The Ball, HN 1977	170.00 To 225.00
Figurine, Belle, HN 2340	45.00
Figurine, Bernice, HN 2071	795.00
Figurine, Bess, HN 2002	235.00 To 275.00
Figurine, Biddy, HN 1513	150.00
Figurine, Blithe Morning, HN 2065	200.00
Figurine, Bo-Peep, HN 1811	74.00
Figurine, Bon Appetit, HN 2444	190.00
Figurine, Bonnie Lassie, HN 1626	225.00 To 310.00
Figurine, Bride, HN 2873	95.00
Figurine, Bridesmaid, HN 2148	225.00
Figurine, Bridesmaid, HN 2196	70.00
Figurine, Bridget, HN 2070	275.00
Figurine, Broken Lance, HN 2041	695.00
Figurine, Bunny, HN 2214	100.00
Figurine, Buttercup, HN 2309	90.00
Figurine, Calumet, HN 1689	600.00
Figurine, Calumet, HN 2068	650.00
Figurine, Camellia, HN 2222	225.00 To 260.00

Figurine, Captain MacHeath, HN 464 .... 750.00
Figurine, Carmen, HN 2545 .... 225.00
Figurine, Carpet Seller, HN 1464 .... 210.00 To 300.00
Figurine, Cat, Flambe, 12 In. 260.00
Figurine, Celeste, HN 2237 .... 225.00
Figurine, Chelsea Pair, HN 577, Female 495.00
Figurine, Chloe, HN 1476 .... 285.00
Figurine, Chloe, HN 1765 .... 240.00
Figurine, Christmas Morn, HN 1992 .... 110.00 To 125.00
Figurine, Christmas Time, HN 2110 .... 375.00
Figurine, Clarinda, HN 2724 .... 150.00 To 199.50
Figurine, Clarissa, HN 1525 .... 495.00
Figurine, Cleopatra, HN 2868 .... 895.00 Ro 1095.00
Figurine, Clockmaker, HN 2279 .... 200.00 To 250.00
Figurine, Coachman, HN 2282 .... 450.00
Figurine, Cobbler, HN 1706 .... 295.00
Figurine, Cocker Spaniel, HN 1187, Copper Coat, 5 1/2 In. 83.00
Figurine, Dachshund, Black, HN 1129 .... 110.00
Figurine, Daffy-Down-Diliy, HN 1712 .... 260.00 To 350.00
Figurine, Dainty May, HN 1639 .... 295.00
Figurine, Darby, HN 2024 .... 265.00
Figurine, Darling, HN 1319 .... 110.00
Figurine, Debutante, HN 2210 .... 290.00 To 300.00
Figurine, Delight, HN 1772 .... 170.00 To 495.00
Figurine, Denise, HN 2273 .... 245.00
Figurine, Diana, HN 1986 .... 135.00
Figurine, Dimity, HN 2169 .... 300.00
Figurine, Dorcas, HN 1558 .... 425.00
Figurine, Easter Day, HN 1976 .... 600.00
Figurine, Easter Day, HN 2039 .... 250.00
Figurine, Eliza, HN 2543 .... 195.00
Figurine, English Setter & Pheasant, HN 2529 .... 235.00
Figurine, Ermine Coat, HN 1981 .... 225.00 To 250.00
Figurine, Esmeralda, HN 2168 .... 325.00
Figurine, Fair Maiden, HN 2211 .... 60.00
Figurine, Family Album, HN 2321 .... 325.00
Figurine, Figurine, Seashore, HN 2263 .... 250.00
Figurine, Fiona, HN 2694 .... 105.00 To 149.50
Figurine, Fortune Teller, HN 2159 .... 395.00 To 450.00
Figurine, Forty Winks, HN 1974 .... 200.00 To 225.00
Figurine, Fox, Flambe, No.14 .... 54.00
Figurine, French Peasant, HN 2075 .... 375.00
Figurine, Gay Morning, HN 2135 .... 275.00 To 300.00
Figurine, Genevieve, HN 1962 .... 200.00
Figurine, Geraldine, HN 2348 .... 135.00
Figurine, Girl With Yellow Frock, HN 588 .... 1100.00
Figurine, Good King Wenceslas, HN 2118 .... 325.00
Figurine, Good Morning, HN 2671 .... 130.00 To 132.00
Figurine, Goody Two Shoes, HN 2037 .... 65.00
Figurine, Gossips, HN 2025 .... 395.00
Figurine, Grace, HN 2318 .... 100.00 To 139.50
Figurine, Grandma, HN 2052 .... 295.00
Figurine, Granny's Shawl, HN 1647 .... 390.00
Figurine, Griselda, HN 1993 .... 400.00
Figurine, Gypsy Dance, HN 2230 .... 245.00
Figurine, Harlequin, HN 2186 .... 180.00
Figurine, Harmony, HN 2824 .... *Illus* 140.00
Figurine, Heart To Heart, HN 2276 .... 300.00 To 310.00
Figurine, Her Ladyship, HN 1977 .... 285.00 To 295.00
Figurine, Hilary, HN 2335 .... 149.50
Figurine, Honey, HN 1909 .... 345.00
Figurine, Huntsman, HN 2492 .... 125.00 To 140.00
Figurine, Hurdy Gurdy, HN 2796, Musical 565.00

Royal Doulton, Figurine, Harmony, HN 2824

(See Page 563)

Royal Doulton, Figurine, Jane, HN 2014

Figurine, In The Stocks, HN 2163	650.00
Figurine, Indian Temple Dancer, HN 2830	625.00
Figurine, Innocence, HN 2842	85.00
Figurine, Irene, HN 1621	325.00
Figurine, Ivy, HN 1768	74.00
Figurine, Jane, HN 2014	*Illus* 350.00
Figurine, Janet, HN 1737	300.00
Figurine, Janet, HN 1916	200.00 To 250.00
Figurine, Janice, HN 2022	285.00
Figurine, Jean, HN 2032	265.00 To 300.00
Figurine, Jersey Milkmaid, HN 2057	325.00
Figurine, Jolly Sailor, HN 2172	560.00
Figurine, Karen, HN 1994	350.00
Figurine, Kate Hardcastle, HN 1719	575.00
Figurine, Katrina, HN 2327	280.00 To 285.00
Figurine, Lady April, HN 1958	325.00
Figurine, Lady Betty, HN 1967	275.00 To 310.00
Figurine, Lady Charmian, HN 1948	200.00
Figurine, Lady Charmian, HN 1949	225.00
Figurine, Lady Fayre, HN 1557	675.00
Figurine, Lady Pamela, HN 2718	125.00 To 159.50
Figurine, Lambing Time, HN 1890	120.00 To 149.50
Figurine, Leisure Hour, HN 2055	475.00
Figurine, Lilac Time, HN 2137	290.00
Figurine, Lisa, HN 2310	110.00
Figurine, Little Boy Blue, HN 2062	150.00
Figurine, Little Lady Make Believe, HN 1870	350.00
Figurine, Little Mistress, HN 1449	295.00
Figurine, London Cry, Strawberries, HN 749	700.00
Figurine, Long John Silver, HN 2204	450.00
Figurine, Loretta, HN 2337	100.00 To 139.50
Figurine, Love Letter, HN 2149	295.00
Figurine, Lucy Lockett, HN 524	595.00
Figurine, Lunchtime, HN 2485	184.50
Figurine, Make Believe, HN 2225	60.00
Figurine, Mantilla, HN 2712	210.00
Figurine, Marguerite, HN 1928	280.00 To 310.00
Figurine, Marietta, HN 1341	375.00

Figurine, Mary Had A Little Lamb, HN 2048	60.00
Figurine, Mary Jane, HN 1990	475.00
Figurine, Masquerade, HN 600, Female	350.00
Figurine, Matilda, HN 2011	600.00
Figurine, Maureen, HN 1770	255.00
Figurine, Maureen, M 84	210.00
Figurine, Mayor, HN 2280	425.00
Figurine, Maytime, HN 2113	275.00
Figurine, Melanie, HN 2271	149.50
Figurine, Melody, HN 2202	300.00
Figurine, Midsummer Noon, HN 1899	550.00
Figurine, Minuet, HN 2019	265.00 To 295.00
Figurine, Miss Demure, HN 1402	170.00
Figurine, Modern Piper, HN 756	1395.00
Figurine, Mr.Micawber, HN 2097	310.00
Figurine, Nell Gwynn, HN 1887	475.00
Figurine, Newsboy, HN 2244	625.00
Figurine, Noelle, HN 2179	350.00 To 375.00
Figurine, Old Balloon Seller, HN 1315	115.00
Figurine, Old King Cole, HN 2217	695.00
Figurine, Old Lavender Seller, HN 1492	625.00
Figurine, Old Meg, HN 2494	250.00
Figurine, Olga, HN 2463	200.00
Figurine, Omar Khayyam, HN 2247	115.00
Figurine, Orange Lady, HN 1953	210.00 To 225.00
Figurine, Owd Willum, HN 2042	200.00 To 235.00
Figurine, Paisley Shawl, HN 1987	235.00 To 275.00
Figurine, Pamela, HN 1469	475.00
Figurine, Patchwork Quilt, HN 1984	350.00
Figurine, Patricia, HN 1414	400.00 To 500.00
Figurine, Pearly Boy, HN 1482	210.00
Figurine, Pecksniff, HN 2098, 7 1/2 In.	325.00
Figurine, Penelope, HN 1901	290.00 To 500.00
Figurine, Penguin, Flambe, No.4	62.00
Figurine, Penny, HN 2338	40.00
Figurine, Phyllis, HN 1420	575.00
Figurine, Picnic, HN 2308	60.00
Figurine, Pierrette, HN 644	525.00
Figurine, Pierrette, HN 732, White & Black	925.00
Figurine, Poacher, HN 2043	245.00
Figurine, Poke Bonnet, HN 612	950.00
Figurine, Polly Peachum, HN 549	500.00
Figurine, Polly Peachum, HN 550, Potted	345.00
Figurine, Polly Peachum, HN 589, Potted	350.00
Figurine, Potter, HN 1518	550.00
Figurine, Primrose, HN 1617	650.00
Figurine, Priscilla, HN 1337	385.00
Figurine, Professor, HN 2281	164.50
Figurine, Rabbit, Flambe, No.113	55.00
Figurine, Rag Doll, HN 2142	50.00
Figurine, Rhinoceros, Flambe, 19 In.Long	445.00
Figurine, Romance, HN 2430	145.00
Figurine, Rose, HN 1368, Potted	75.00
Figurine, Roseanna, HN 1926	340.00 To 350.00
Figurine, Rosebud, HN 1580	150.00
Figurine, Rosebud, HN 1983	300.00
Figurine, Rosina, HN 1364, Potted	485.00
Figurine, Sabbath Morn, HN 1982	260.00
Figurine, Sandra, HN 2275	85.00
Figurine, Schoolmarm, HN 2223	164.50
Figurine, Seafarer, HN 2455	200.00
Figurine, Simone, HN 2378	119.00
Figurine, Sir Walter Raleigh, HN 1751 _Illus_	650.00

Figurine, Sir Walter Raleigh, HN 2015 .... 560.00 To 650.00
Figurine, Southern Belle, HN 2229 .... 100.00
Figurine, Spanish, Dancers Of The World, HN 2831 .... 325.00
Figurine, Spring Flowers, HN 1807 .... 320.00
Figurine, St.George, HN 2067 .... 2500.00
Figurine, Stitch In Time, HN 2352 .... 125.00 To 144.50
Figurine, Stop The Press, HN 2683 .... 145.00
Figurine, Summer, HN 2086 .... 340.00 To 390.00
Figurine, Suzette, HN 2026 .... 300.00
Figurine, Sweet & Twenty, HN 1298 .... 230.00
Figurine, Sweet & Twenty, HN 1589, Potted, Small 350.00
Figurine, Sweet Anne, HN 1496 .... 200.00
Figurine, Sweet Sixteen, HN 2231 .... 225.00
Figurine, Teenager, HN 2203 .... 235.00 To 280.00
Figurine, Tete-A-Tete, HN 798, Potted 1150.00

Royal Doulton, Figurine,
Sir Walter Raleigh,
HN 1751
(See Page 565)

Royal Doulton, Figurine, Young Love, HN 2735

Figurine, Thanksgiving, HN 2446 .... 180.00
Figurine, Tinkle Bell, HN 1677 .... 45.00
Figurine, Tony Weller, HN 684 .... 950.00
Figurine, Tooties, HN 1680 .... 65.00
Figurine, Top O' The Hill, HN 1833, Pink 145.00
Figurine, Town Crier, HN 2119 .... 225.00 To 265.00
Figurine, Toymaker, HN 2250 .... 375.00
Figurine, Uriah Heep, HN 554 .... 275.00
Figurine, Uriah Heep, HN 2101 .... 310.00
Figurine, Veneta, HN 2722 .... 159.50
Figurine, Veronica, HN 1517 .... 275.00
Figurine, Victorian Lady, HN 728 .... 250.00
Figurine, Victorian Lady, HN 1452 .... 350.00
Figurine, Vivienne, HN 2073 .... 250.00
Figurine, Wee Willie Winkie, HN 2050 .... 375.00
Figurine, Wendy, HN 2109 .... 74.00
Figurine, Windflower, HN 2929 .... 325.00
Figurine, Winter, HN 2088 .... 350.00 To 395.00
Figurine, Wood Nymph, HN 2192 .... 165.00
Figurine, Young Love, HN 2735 .... *Illus* 540.00
Fish Plate, Gray Mullet, Gold Scroll Rim, 1907, Signed, 9 In. 165.00
Fish Plate, Impressed Date Code, 8 3/4 In., Set Of 11 .... 600.00
Gravy Boat, Countess, 3 Pieces, 11 In. 65.00
Group, White Horse & Pale Brown Foal, Pedestal, 7 X 5 In. 300.00

Humidor, Applied Relief Toby Figures, Tan & Brown, 6 In. 90.00
Humidor, Jackdaw Of Rheims 195.00
Jug, Cobalt Blue Ground, Crosses, Scrollwork, Signed, 9 In. 475.00
Jug, Columbian Exposition 250.00
Jug, Commemorative, Dickens Characters, 1936 .... 750.00
Jug, Concord, Bayeux Tapestry, 6 In. .... 90.00 To 110.00
Lamp, Town Crier, Original 375.00
Match Holder, Dewars Scotch Advertising, Pebbly Finish 47.50
Match Holder, Mr.Squeers, Scenic, 2 In. 95.00
Match Holder, Welsh Ladies, Scenic, Square, 2 1/2 In. 95.00
Mug, Flow Blue Scenic, 4 1/2 In. 65.00
Mug, Fox Hunt Scene, 3-Handled 65.00
Mug, Ugly Duchess, 7 1/2 In. 200.00
Pitcher, & Bowl, Fishnets Outside, Boats Inside, Marked 250.00
Pitcher, Aldin's Dog 75.00
Pitcher, Applied Stag Hunt, Marked, 6 In. 95.00
Pitcher, Authors Series, Chaucer Ye Tabard, Marked, 7 1/2 In. 110.00
Pitcher, Baggy Trousered Golf Players, C.1890, Ditty, 7 In. 300.00
Pitcher, Classical Figures, Blue & White, 8 In. 85.00
Pitcher, Coaching Days, 6 1/2 In. 135.00
Pitcher, Curiosity Shop, Square 150.00
Pitcher, Fagin, 7 In. 175.00
Pitcher, Flow Blue Scenic, 5 1/4 In. 75.00
Pitcher, Fox Hunt Scene, Signed R.Gough, Green, Gold Trim 200.00
Pitcher, Gaffers, Man Smoking Pipe, Black Hat, 5 3/4 In. 95.00
Pitcher, Gay Lady 46.00
Pitcher, Good Is Not Good Enough, Flowers, 7 1/2 In. 155.00
Pitcher, Moorish Gate Series, Marked, 4 5/8 In. 85.00
Pitcher, Mustard & Brown Trim, 8 In. 50.00
Pitcher, Old London, Square 225.00
Pitcher, Oliver Twist, Square 150.00
Pitcher, Pickwick Papers, Square 160.00
Pitcher, St.Louis World's Fair, 1934, Dutch Scene, 2 1/2 In. 45.00
Pitcher, White, Egyptian Design 60.00
Plaque, Treasure Island Series, Long John Silver, 15 In.Diam. 135.00
Plate, Anne Hathaway's Cottage, 10 1/2 In. 25.00
Plate, Cavalier, Blue & White, 10 In. 45.00
Plate, Child's, Oranges & Lemons 25.00
Plate, Country Cottage Scene, 10 In. 65.00
Plate, Doctor, 10 1/2 In. 55.00
Plate, English Cottage Scene, 10 In. 62.00
Plate, Falconer, 10 In. 65.00
Plate, Floral Center, Red Rims, Signed, 10 1/2 In., Set Of 10 .... 595.00
Plate, Forest Silhouette, 10 In. 65.00
Plate, Garden Scene, 10 1/2 In. 25.00
Plate, George V & Queen Mary Coronation, 7 In. 25.00
Plate, George V & Queen Mary Coronation, 8 In. 37.50
Plate, Gnomes & Toadstools, Worms, Cobwebs, 8 1/2 In. 225.00
Plate, Hand-Painted Ring-Necked Pheasant, Signed, 9 In. 365.00
Plate, Hurtsmonceaux Castle, 10 In. .... 62.00 To 65.00
Plate, Jackdaw Of Rheims Series, Marked, 10 1/4 In. 55.00
Plate, Jester, 10 1/2 In. 60.00
Plate, Kirkwood, 7 1/2 In. 14.00
Plate, Kirkwood, 10 1/2 In. 18.00
Plate, Kookaburra Bird, 10 In. 65.00
Plate, Mayor, 10 1/2 In. 55.00
Plate, Muckrose Abbey, 10 1/2 In. 35.00
Plate, Mythical Pan, 10 In. .... 62.00 To 65.00
Plate, Old Mother Hubbard, 7 In. .... 30.00 To 35.00
Plate, Oriental Figures Among Ruins, 10 In. 62.00
Plate, Pink Rim, Hand-Painted Orchids, Gilding, 10 1/2 In. 695.00
Plate, Ploughing Scene, 10 In. 62.00
Plate, Queen Elizabeth At Old Moreton Hall, 10 In. 75.00

Plate, Robin Hood Series, Scalloped, 10 3/8 In. 70.00
Plate, Rochester Castle, Blue & White, Oval 40.00
Plate, Sam Weller, 7 1/2 In. 105.00
Plate, Sir Roger De Coverley Series, 10 In. 70.00
Plate, Soup, Kirkwood, 8 1/2 In. 16.00
Plate, Tempest, 10 In. 55.00
Plate, Titanian Ware, Bird & Leaf Design, 8 1/2 In. 55.00
Plate, Washington Mansion, Mt.Vernon, Blue On White, 9 3/4 In. 48.00
Plate, White Setter, Full Portrait, 10 In. 35.00
Plate, 1978, Valentine, Boxed 29.00
Platter, Kirkwood, Oval, 13 In. 75.00
Platter, Kirkwood, 17 1/2 In. 115.00
Shaker, Salt, Sheep In Meadow, Sunset, Pedestal, Pear Shape 25.00
Sugar & Creamer, Swirl Pattern, White 18.00
Sugar, Sam Weller, Rectangular Handled, 6 1/8 In. 50.00
Tankard, Eglinton Tournament, 6 1/2 In. 65.00
Tankard, Oliver 200.00
Teapot, Bluebirds, Florence Barlow 750.00
Teapot, Dutch Scene, Noke, 8 1/2 In. 275.00
Teapot, Kingsware, Witch, Cat & Cauldron, Brown Glaze 250.00
Tile, Coaching Days, 6 1/2 In.Square 20.00
Tobacco Jar, Monks, 5 1/2 In. 230.00
Tobacco Jar, Windsor Castle 95.00
Toby Jug, Cliff Cornell, Large 350.00
Toby Jug, Lambeth, C.1925, 4 In. ....*Illus* 250.00
Toby, Old Charley, Large 150.00
Toby, Winston Churchill, 5 1/4 X 9 In. 100.00
Tray, Robin Hood, Friend Of The Poor, 5 X 10 1/2 In. 85.00
Tray, The Fighting Cocks, Old English Inn Series, 4 X 6 In. 31.00
Vase, Art Nouveau, C.1900, Glazed, 15 In. 175.00
Vase, Babes In Woods, Dog In Front Of Little Girls, 5 In. 259.00
Vase, Babes In Woods, Handled, Gold Trim, 2 3/4 X 4 1/4 In. 250.00
Vase, Babes In Woods, Mother, 2 Girls, Dog Under Tree, 9 In. 325.00
Vase, Babes In Woods, Woman Picking Berries, 5 1/4 In. 235.00
Vase, Brangwyn Ware, 12 In. 120.00
Vase, Burns' Cottage Home, 8 In. 75.00
Vase, Children, Blue, 2 Waist Handles, 7 In. 325.00
Vase, Cobalt Blue & Beige, Slater, 7 In., Pair 195.00
Vase, Cobalt Blue Top & Bottom, Beige Tapestry Center, 9 In. 75.00
Vase, Deer, Hannah Barlow, 9 1/2 In. 595.00
Vase, Flambe, Fish Design, Artist Signed FM, 8 1/2 In. 995.00
Vase, Flambe, Harbor Scene, Sailing Vessels, 8 X 5 In. 165.00
Vase, Flambe, Pumpkin Shape, 7 1/2 In. 525.00
Vase, Flambe, Veined Sung Design, Ovoid, 10 In. 235.00

Royal Doulton, Toby Jug, Lambeth, C.1925, 4 In.

Vase, Friar Tuck Joins Robin Hood, 9 In. 125.00
Vase, Gold Tapestry, 9 1/2 In. 145.00
Vase, Gray Green Parakeets, Sparrows, C.1895, Signed, 13 In. 220.00
Vase, Jackdaw Of Rheims Series, Handled, Marked, 5 1/4 In. 85.00
Vase, Pressed Leaf Ware, Leaves, Gold & Blue Ground, 5 1/8 In. 75.00
Vase, Raised Design On Top, Hanging Flowers, 10 1/2 In. 145.00
Vase, Rouge Flambe, Countryside Scene, Barrel Shape, 5 In. 85.00
Vase, Rouge Flambe, Scenic, 8 1/2 In. 280.00
Vase, Sheep, Hannah Barlow, 9 In. 485.00
Vase, Silicon, 3 1/4 In. 45.00
Vase, Stag, 3 Small Deer, Meadow, Daisies, Signed, 7 In. 185.00
Vase, Tan, Beige, Eggshell Design, Hearts & Flowers, 8 In. 265.00
Vase, Umbrella, Blue, Children, Lady, Guitar, 22 In. 450.00
Vase, Veined, Sung Design, Flambe, 10 In. 195.00
Vase, White Flowers, Green Ground, 8 1/2 In. 185.00

Royal Dux is a porcelain made by Duxer Porzellanmanufaktur, a
factory established in 1860 in Dux, Bohemia (now Czechoslovakia).
Reproductions are being made.

ROYAL DUX, Bowl, Girl On Side Holding Flowers, Open Handles, 15 X 12 In. 610.00
Bowl, Leaves & Flowers, Gilded Handles, 10 In.Diam. 60.00
Centerpiece, Figural, Mauve, Ivory, Ocher, 15 3/4 In. .... 250.00 To 525.00
Centerpiece, Lily Pad Bowl, 2 Nymphs, Marked, 15 1/2 In. 250.00
Figurine, Arabian Horse, 6 In. 45.00
Figurine, Bear, Polar, Walking, Signed, 12 X 8 In. 95.00
Figurine, Bear, Polar, White, 15 X 10 In. 180.00
Figurine, Beetle, Huge Pinches, 3 Dimensional, 8 In. 150.00
Figurine, Bird, On Tree, Blue-Gray, Black, 7 X 8 In. 66.00
Figurine, Bisque Woman, Blue Skirt, Red Hair, Pink Triangle, 22 In. 450.00
Figurine, Bohemian Peasant, Satin Fish, Marked, 11 1/2 In., Pair 595.00
Figurine, Boy At Spring Filling Wooden Pitchers, 24 In. 300.00
Figurine, Boy, Breeches, Girl, Planter, Triangle Mark, 5 1/2 In. 325.00
Figurine, Dog, Sitting, Setter Type, Reddish Brown, 6 X 3 In. 37.00
Figurine, Donkey, Saddle, Eye Guards, Next To Cactus, 5 In. 315.00
Figurine, Elephant, Trunk Raised, Exposed Tusks, 13 In. 175.00
Figurine, Elephant, Trunk Up, Beige & Brown, Signed, 8 X 6 In. 65.00
Figurine, Elephant, White, 6 1/2 X 6 1/2 In. 65.00
Figurine, Fisher Boy & Girl, Green & Gold, Signed, 10 1/2 In., Pair 485.00
Figurine, German Shepherd & Collie, Triangle Mark, 8 X 9 In. 235.00
Figurine, Horse, Roaring, Brown, White Face, Signed, 13 X 7 1/2 In. 165.00
Figurine, Hunter With Arrows On Back, Large Bird In Hand, 14 In. 395.00
Figurine, Hunter, Carrying Horn, 2 Dogs, 28 In. 650.00
Figurine, Hunter, Pheasant, Bird In Hand, 14 In. 325.00
Figurine, Laboring Father, Mother, Child, 24 In. 425.00
Figurine, Lady In Blue Dress, 10 In. 150.00
Figurine, Lion, Lioness, & Deer, White, Marked, 17 X 12 1/2 In. 995.00
Figurine, Mother Helps Child Reach Father's Arms, 25 In. 375.00
Figurine, Nymph With Harp, On Rock Formation, 12 1/4 In. 225.00
Figurine, Penguin, 6 X 3 1/2 In. 33.00
Figurine, Polar Bear, Seated, White, Black Eyes, 14 In. 95.00
Figurine, Princess, Seated, Ruffled Skirt, Pink Triangle, 9 In. 190.00
Figurine, Roman Lady Closing Cape, Pink Triangle Mark, 14 1/4 In. 395.00
Figurine, Setter With Duck, Triangle Mark, 14 X 7 In. 90.00
Figurine, Water Carrier, C.1910, Marked, Pair .... *Illus* 650.00
Figurine, Water Carrier, Gold, Lavender & Beige, Tab, 10 In. 250.00
Figurine, Wild Turkey, On Stump, Black Feathers, 8 In. 56.00
Jardiniere, Moss Green Ground, Pink & Yellow Roses 125.00
Pitcher, Girl Handle, 7 In. 399.00
Seated Princess, Book, Blue Jacket, White Dress, 14 In. 160.00
Vase, Cream Base, Gold Cherries, Pink Blossoms, Marked, 16 In. 150.00
Vase, Figural, Olive, Ivory, Rust, Gilding, Marked, 26 In. 725.00

Royal Dux, Figurine, Water Carrier, C.1910,
Marked, Pair

(See Page 569)

Vase, Handles, Raised Apples, Gold Trim, Triangle Mark, 15 In., Pr.	390.00
Vase, Open Handles, Gold, Pink Triangle Mark, 11 In., Pair	145.00
Vase, Oriental Figures, Green & Pink Dress, Marked, 7 1/2 In., Pair	275.00
Vase, Strawberries, Pair, 15 In.	595.00
Vase, 3 Orange Poppies, Green Ground, 15 In.	125.00

Royal Flemish glass was made during the late 1880s in New Bedford, Massachusetts, by the Mt. Washington Glass Works. It is a colored satin glass decorated in dark colors with gold designs.

ROYAL FLEMISH, Biscuit Jar, Patented February 27, 1894, 7 In.	500.00
Biscuit Jar, Roman Coins, Medallions, Silver Plated Lid, 9 In.	1950.00
Ewer, Circlets Of Dark Blue, Crosses, Gold Lines, 12 In.	3500.00
Vase, Jeweled, Gold, Black, Rust, & Tan Enameling, 12 1/2 In.	2250.00
Vase, Pastel Chrysanthemum Blossoms, 12 In.	1450.00
ROYAL HAEGER, Vase, Swans, Blue, 8 1/4 In.	20.00
Wall Pocket, Sheik's Head, 7 In.	10.00

      ROYAL IVY, see Pressed Glass, Royal Ivy
      ROYAL OAK, see Pressed Glass, Royal Oak
      ROYAL RUDOLSTADT, see Rudolstadt

ROYAL SAXE, Dish, Lobster, Gold Lobster, Reticulated Rim, Marked, 12 In.	125.00
Plate, Scenic, House & Mountains, Crown Mark, 8 1/2 In.	75.00
Vase, Gold Designs, Maiden Reading, Cupid, Crown Mark, 8 1/4 In.	75.00

Royal Vienna was established in Vienna by Claude Innocentius du Paquier in 1719. The factory closed in 1865. Since then, various German and Austrian factories have reproduced Royal Vienna wares, complete with the original beehive mark.

      ROYAL VIENNA, see also Beehive

ROYAL VIENNA, Base, Lamp, Musical Scene Medallion, Gold, Marked, 14 In.	245.00
Cake Plate, Portrait In Center, Signed Kauffmann, 9 In.	21.00
Candlestick, Green, Gold Trim, 12 In.	125.00
Charger, Blossom, Rose & White Drape, Marked, 14 In.	1900.00
Charger, Mercury & Horse, Minerva's Temple, 19 In.	1200.00
Charger, Rape Of Leucippus' Daughters, Marked, 15 3/8 In.	2250.00
Cocoa Pot, Woman & Child Design, Signed Wagner, 6 1/5 In.	450.00
Coffee Set, Gold & Magenta, C.1900, Medallions, 7 Piece	425.00
Coffeepot, Queen Louise Design, Signed Kronller, 10 In.	500.00

Royal Vienna, Plaque, Hand-Painted

Cracker Jar, Bulbous, 4-Footed, Lily-Of-The-Valley Design	110.00
Cup & Saucer, Beehive Mark, Blue	75.00
Cup & Saucer, Demitasse, Medallion Of Greek Scene, Footed	60.00
Cup & Saucer, Portrait, Encrusted Gold, Blue, Signed Wagner	150.00
Game Plate, Grouse, Rim Medallions, Beehive Mark, 9 1/2 In.	65.00
Jar, Covered, Grecian Lady, Cobalt Blue, Beehive Mark, 7 1/2 In.	225.00
Jardiniere, Donatello, Marked, 7 3/4 In.	95.00
Mug, Friar Tuck, Full Bee, 5 In.	55.00
Pitcher, Oriental, Gilt Design, 4 In.	95.00
Plaque, Hand-Painted	*Illus* 2500.00
Plaque, Maiden & 7 Cupids, C.1910, Marked, 16 1/2 In.	1800.00
Plaque, Mignon, C.1910, Marked, 12 X 6 In.	650.00
Plate, Bacchante, Naked, Flower, Garland, Blue Border, 10 In.	850.00
Plate, Game, Deep Red, Gold Trim, Beehive Mark, 9 In.	100.00
Plate, Gentleman, Maidens, Cobalt Blue Edge, Beehive Mark, 9 In.	175.00
Plate, Graciosa, Paneled Border, C.1910, Marked, 9 1/2 In.	1100.00
Plate, Green, Pink, & Gold, Cupid In Cart, 3 Ladies, 8 In.	40.00
Plate, Jeweled Border, Gilded, C.1910, Marked, 34 1/4 In.	450.00
Plate, Maiden On Cloud, Bird On Finger, Crown Mark, 6 1/2 In.	65.00
Plate, Maiden With Long Hair, Raised Gilding, Signed, 9 1/2 In.	700.00
Plate, Monk Drinking Beer, Gold & Maroon Trim, Marked, 12 In.	185.00
Plate, Ophelia, Floral Bouquet, C.1910, Marked, 9 1/2 In.	650.00
Plate, Portrait, Brunette, Gold Trim, Beehive Mark, 8 In.	145.00
Plate, Portrait, Gold, Signed, 10 In.	650.00
Plate, Portrait, Ruth, Blue & Gold Border, 9 1/2 In.	485.00
Plate, Portrait, Salome, Blue & Gold Border, 9 1/2 In.	485.00
Plate, Reflection, C.1900, Green Border, Marked, 9 5/8 In.	1000.00
Plate, Scenic, Musick, Signed, 10 3/4 In.	300.00
Plate, Service, Classical Vignettes, C.1900, 11 In., Set Of 12	1600.00
Plate, The Departure Of Paris, Warrior, Mother, 9 In.	450.00
Plate, 2 Maidens, Green Border, Beehive Mark, 9 1/2 In.Diam.	250.00
Pokal, Pink & Burgundy Ground, 15 In.	1450.00
Urn, Classic Scene, Open Gold Handles, Signed Kauffmann, 15 In.	295.00
Urn, Lid, Triangular Base, Scene Of Juno, C.1856, Signed	550.00
Urn, 3 Maidens, Covered, Beehive Mark, Signed, 15 1/2 In.	325.00
Vase, Amor & Psyche Front, Idyll Back, Beehive, 10 1/2 In.	625.00
Vase, Bird, Eagle, & Flowers, Gold & Silver, Beehive Mark, 13 In.	325.00
Vase, Blue & White, Cloud Sky Ground, Woman, Signed, 8 In.	425.00
Vase, Bullet Shape, 5 1/2 In.	110.00
Vase, Chalice Shape, 8 In.	150.00
Vase, Double-Handled, Marked, 10 1/2 In.	135.00
Vase, Floral, Fluted, 12 X 8 In.	80.00
Vase, Flowers & Gold Trim, Miniature	185.00
Vase, Full Figure Woman, Signed Wagner, 10 In.	595.00
Vase, Hero & Leander, Jeweling, Stand, Marked, 38 3/4 In.	5000.00

Vase, Man & Woman Panel, Gold Handle, Blue Beehive, 6 3/4 In.	145.00
Vase, Marguerite, Sheer Gown, C.1910, Marked, 6 In.	600.00
Vase, Portrait Of Young Lady With Lilacs, Marked, 9 3/4 In.	150.00
Vase, Portrait, Wagner, Handled, 9 In.	450.00
Vase, Serpentine, 3 Figure, Green, Magenta, Beehive Mark, 10 In.	175.00
Vase, Victorian Lady, Green Coronet, Blue Beehive, 12 1/2 In.	295.00
Vase, Worship Of Cora, 7 In.	195.00
Vase, 3 Graces & Cupid, Claret Border, Covered, 29 In.	3000.00

Royal Worcester porcelain was made in the later period of Worcester pottery, which was originally established in 1751. The Royal Worcester trade name has been used by Worcester Royal Porcelain Company, Ltd., since 1862.

ROYAL WORCESTER, Basket, Basket Weave Design, Blue, Gold Trim, 7 In.	180.00
Basket, Basket Weave Design, Marked, 5 In.	110.00
Basket, Bird's Nest Shape, Handle, C.1890, Marked, 6 In.	250.00
Basket, Cream, Gold, & Green, Dated 1905, Handled, 9 X 7 In.	159.00
Basket, Wicker, Yellow & Green, Gold Trim, C.1903, 5 1/4 In.	85.00
Bowl, Basket Weave, Hand-Painted Flowers, 8 3/4 In.	285.00
Bowl, Beige Satin, Grape Leaves, Marked, 8 In.	350.00
Bowl, Butterfly, Gilded, Dated 1918, 10 1/8 In.	225.00
Bowl, Leaf Pattern, 9 In.	230.00
Bowl, Scalloped, Latticework & Rosettes, C.1887, 8 In.Long	400.00
Box, Apples, Grapes, Flowers, Round, Covered, 2 X 2 1/2 In	65.00
Candlesnuffer, Figural, Japanese Lady, Purple Mark	125.00
Candlesnuffer, Monk, Brown, Carries Bible, Mark, 4 3/4 In.	85.00
Candlesnuffer, Monk, Feathered Hat, Black Mark	20.00
Candlesnuffer, The Cook, White, C.1895	125.00
Candlesnuffer, Woman Holding Fan, Marked, 4 In.	275.00
Candlestick, Dated 1889, 4 3/8 In.	65.00
Candlestick, Figural, Cherub Blowing Horn, 7 3/4 In.	365.00
Chocolate Pot, Green To Light Tan, 1897, 9 In.	375.00
Coddler, Egg, Fruit Design, Black Berries, Pair	30.00
Coffeepot, Gold Handle, Gold Flowers, C.1887, 10 In.	150.00
Coffeepot, Lighthouse Shape, Gold Banding, 7 1/4 In.	45.00
Compote, Raised Border In Gold, Green Mark, 9 X 5 In.	375.00
Cracker Jar, Gadrooned Body, Gold Band, 1888, Signed, 7 In.	175.00
Creamer, Barrel Shape, Gold Bamboo Handle, C.1890, 5 1/2 In.	130.00
Creamer, Floral Design, Bamboo Handle, Ivorene, Purple Mark	135.00
Cup & Saucer, Demitasse, Black, Gold Lines, Purple Mark	60.00
Cup & Saucer, Demitasse, Marked 1887	50.00
Cup & Saucer, Jeweled, Sunflower Design, Blue, Marked	150.00
Cup & Saucer, Polychrome Floral, C.1891, 2 1/2 In.	75.00
Dish, Shell, Cream To Pink Beige, Gold Edge, 4 1/4 In.	48.00
Dish, Shell, 3 Feet, Polychrome Floral Design, 1900, 4 In.	190.00
Ewer, Beige Ground, Gold Tracery, Relief Neck, 8 1/2 In.	395.00
Ewer, Double Gourded, Wrapped Dragon On Body, 11 1/2 In.	425.00
Ewer, Elves Laying Brick, Florals, Ribbon Handle, 10 1/4 In.	695.00
Ewer, Flowers, Lizard Form Handle, Circle Mark, 11 1/4 In.	600.00
Ewer, Gilt Reptile Handle, Polychrome Design, 11 1/2 In.	550.00
Ewer, Lemon & Coral, Gold Design, 7 1/2 In.	195.00
Ewer, Pink Flowers, Roped Gold Handle, 1897 Mark, 8 3/8 In.	175.00
Ewer, Salamander Handle, 1880 Mark, 11 1/2 In.	495.00
Ewer, Simulated Bamboo Around Body, Forms Spout, 8 1/2 In.	50.00
Figurine, African, Boy & Girl, Water Vessel, 17 In., Pair	3000.00
Figurine, African, C.1885, 17 1/4 In., Pair	3000.00
Figurine, Against The Wind, C.1870, 12 In.	495.00
Figurine, Blue Parakeet, 7 In.	119.30
Figurine, Bluebird, No.2664, On Tree Trunk Base, 5 1/2 In.	120.00
Figurine, Bluebirds, 1965, Pair	1750.00
Figurine, Boy, Thursday's Child	120.00
Figurine, Burma	50.00

Figurine, Cairo Water Carrier, No.1250, C.1887, 8 In. 475.00
Figurine, Calves, 2 Calves Together, 4 In. 65.00
Figurine, Castinet Dancer, Gold Coloring, C.1880, Signed 1000.00
Figurine, Child Of World, Burmah 50.00
Figurine, Children, Sleep Boy 125.00
Figurine, Classical Woman, Holding Bird, C.1890, 9 1/2 In. 200.00
Figurine, Cook, C.1894 .... 85.00
Figurine, Countries Of The World, Ireland 50.00
Figurine, Dog, Dated 1938, Doris Lindner 243.00
Figurine, Dutch Boy & Dutch Girl, Pink Mark, Pair 350.00
Figurine, Elephant, Gilded & White, C.1865, Marked, 8 In. 390.00
Figurine, Elephant, Jardiniere On Back, C.1882, 6 In. 150.00
Figurine, English Queen Mary, 8 In. 495.00
Figurine, Fisher Boy & Girl, Rustic Dress, 17 In., Pair 1500.00
Figurine, Foals, 2 Small Ponies Playing, 5 1/2 In. 100.00
Figurine, Fox Terrier, No.2870, White, Marked, 3 3/4 In. 195.00
Figurine, Friday's Child 75.00
Figurine, Grandmother's Dress, 7 In. 295.00
Figurine, Hedge Sparrow 50.00
Figurine, Indian Brave & Squaw, With Child, 1932, 6 1/2 In. 325.00
Figurine, Italy, No.3067, 3 3/8 In. 135.00
Figurine, Johnnie, No.3433 .... 175.00
Figurine, Kneeling Oriental Lady, No.3397, 5 7/8 In. 225.00
Figurine, Little Jack Horner 125.00
Figurine, March, No.3454, F.G.Doughty, 5 1/2 In. 135.00
Figurine, Mischief, Purple Mark, Signed 125.00
Figurine, Monday's Child, Doughty, 6 1/2 In. 135.00
Figurine, Monday's Child, No.3257, 6 1/2 In. 125.00
Figurine, Mother Machree, 1894, Signed 175.00
Figurine, Munnasall The Clay Figure Maker, 7 3/4 In. 450.00
Figurine, Native Boy, Signed, 5 In. 95.00
Figurine, Nude Lady Bather, No.3689, 5 3/8 In. 165.00
Figurine, Parakeet Boy, No, 3087, Red 175.00
Figurine, Putto, Water Vessel, Stone Wall, Marked, 5 In. 175.00
Figurine, Sabrina, Leaning On Ledge, Marked, 10 In. 600.00
Figurine, Sea Breeze, Signed Doughty 175.00
Figurine, Sleepy Boy, Doughty 77.00
Figurine, Sunday's Child, Sitting On Sand Pail 85.00
Figurine, Swan, Jardiniere On Back, C.1894, 7 1/2 In. 350.00
Figurine, Sweet Anne 125.00
Figurine, Tommy, No.2913, Red Shirt, Blue Pants, 4 1/8 In. 135.00
Figurine, Tuesday's Child, No.3534 .... 125.00
Figurine, Veiled Lady, Ivory Porcelain, 1867 Mark, 11 In. 1575.00
Figurine, Water Carrier, Boy & Girl, Pouring Water, 17 In. 1500.00
Figurine, Wine, 1918, 6 In. 150.00
Figurine, Woman In 12th Century Costume, Signed, 9 In. 450.00
Figurine, Woman Mourning Death Of Bird, C.1890, 10 1/4 In. 225.00
Figurine, Yankee, Impressed C, 7 In. 325.00
Figurine, Yankee, No.1231, 7 In. .... 240.00 To 325.00
Holders, Menu, Down & Out, Brickwork Base, Marked, 6 In. 1400.00
Jar, Multicolored Florals, Beige Ground, Purple Mark, 6 In. 360.00
Jug, Green To Light Tan, 1895, 7 In. 360.00
Jug, Raised Gold Salamander, Branch Handle, 1917 Mark, 6 In. 225.00
Jug, Ruby Ground, Gilt Vine Design, 6 1/2 In. 285.00
Jug, Tan & Gilded, 5 1/4 In. 150.00
Ladle, Soup, Blue Ivy Leaves, Brown Handle, Blue Mark 65.00
Pitcher, Butterflies, Flowers, Marked 35.00
Pitcher, Cabbage Leaf, Dated 1901, Signed, 3 1/2 In. 85.00
Pitcher, Classical Profile, Gold & Polychrome, C.1889 .... 250.00
Pitcher, Cream, Flowers, Handled, Signed, Purple Mark, 5 In. 155.00
Pitcher, Flat Back, Multicolored Flowers, Cream, 5 In. 100.00
Pitcher, Floral Design, Cream Ground, Purple Mark, 5 In. 195.00
Pitcher, Floral Design, Cream Ground, 7 1/2 In. 300.00

Royal Worcester, Pitcher, Green Mark, 2 1/2 In.

Pitcher, Floral, Gold Trim, 1903 Mark, 4 3/4 In.		165.00
Pitcher, Flowers, Gold Trim, Cream Ground, 9 In., Pair		300.00
Pitcher, Gold Handle, Flower Spray, C.1886, 8 In.		70.00
Pitcher, Gold Handle, Multicolored Floral, Beige, 5 In.		165.00
Pitcher, Gold Lion, Shell Pouring Lip, C.1880, 9 In.		325.00
Pitcher, Gold Ram's Head Handle, Morning Glories, 9 In.		225.00
Pitcher, Green Mark, 2 1/2 In.	*Illus*	40.00
Pitcher, Horn, Purple Mark, 11 3/4 In.	*Illus*	160.00
Pitcher, Ivorene, Florals, Bamboo Handle, Marked, 4 In.		110.00
Pitcher, Ivory Ground, Dragon Handle, Marked, 10 In.		850.00
Pitcher, Multicolored Floral, Beige Ground, Marked, 5 In.		165.00
Pitcher, Tankard Shape, Ice Lip, Fern, Beige, Marked, 7 In.		165.00
Planter, Bird, Floral, Blue Ground, Green Bands, 4 In.		150.00
Plate, Birds, Dated 1879, 9 In.		139.00
Plate, Blue Pagoda, Gold Border, C.1878, 7 3/4 In.		35.00
Plate, Cameo Inserts, Gold Trim, Roses, Signed, Pair		595.00
Plate, Pastel Flowers, Gold Trim, Scalloped, 1891		20.00
Plate, Pink Ground, Enameled Purple Flowers, 9 In.		95.00
Plate, Rosemary, Date 1929, 9 1/4 In.		15.00
Platter, C.1878, 13 X 15 In.		100.00
Rose Bowl, Dragonfly & Roses, Green Mark		125.00
Salt, Master, Dolphin Holding Shell, Beige, 4 X 3 1/2 In.		185.00
Salt, Shell Shaped, Open		65.00
Shell, On Coral Branch, White, Green Mark		250.00
Spill Vase, Figures Of Girls, Dated 1908, 5 1/4 In., Pair		495.00
Spill Vase, Gilt Owl On Bamboo, Crown Mark, 7 3/4 In.		450.00
Sugar & Creamer, Gold Lid & Handles, C.1890, 4 1/2 In.		150.00
Sugar & Creamer, Yellow Ground, 1918 Mark		95.00
Sugar, Floral Design, Beige Ground, Purple Mark, 4 In.		110.00

Royal Worcester, Pitcher, Horn,
Purple Mark, 11 3/4 In.

Sugar, Gold Leaf Handles, Covered, Purple Mark, 4 3/4 In.	110.00
Tazza, Figural, Blue Border, Gilt Trim, C.1880, 7 In., Pair	1300.00
Tea Caddy, Ivorine Ground, Flowers, Berries, Green Mark, 4 In	100.00
Teapot, Flowers, Dated 1890, Purple Mark, 5 X 6 In.	350.00
Teapot, Gold Flecks, Blue, 6 3/4 In.	200.00
Teapot, Green To Light Tan, 1896, 6 In.	310.00
Teapot, Japanese Design, Blue Flowers, Marked, 6 In.	300.00
Teapot, Purple & Pink Flowers, Gold Trim, Signed, 9 In.	200.00
Tureen, Brown Willow Pattern, Elephant Handles, 12 In.	145.00
Urn, Gilded Snake Handles, Marked, 5 In.	400.00
Urn, Gilding On Body, C.1889, 16 1/4 In.	450.00
Urn, Porcelain, Children Skating, Pink Ground, C.1895	425.00
Vase, Amphora Shape, Gold Rim, Triangle Mark, C.1890, 7 In.	325.00
Vase, Bamboo Shape, Floral Design, Bamboo Handle, 10 1/2 In.	110.00
Vase, Biscuit Ground, Pear Shape, Polychromed, Marked, 10 In.	175.00
Vase, Blackberries, Foliage, Fruit & Flower, 5 1/2 In.	160.00
Vase, Bowl Shape, Castle Scene On Front, 3 In.	99.50
Vase, Bud, Hand-Painted Flowers, C.1908, Signed, 3 In.	145.00
Vase, Bulbous, Flowers, C.1889, Signed	320.00
Vase, Castle, Cattle, Gold Handles, 8 In.	300.00
Vase, Chrome Morning Glories, Gold Leaves, 14 In.	250.00
Vase, Cornucopia, White, 2 3/4 In.	39.00
Vase, Cream Ground, Polychrome, Wildflowers, Marked, 9 In.	150.00
Vase, Curved Bamboo Design, Double Ended, C.1888, 5 1/2 In.	100.00
Vase, Daisies & Leaves, Gilt & Silvered, 1882, 12 1/4 In.	350.00
Vase, Double, Bamboo Leaf, Twig Handle, Marked	300.00
Vase, Flask Form, Yellow Ground, Pilgrim, Marked, 7 In.	250.00
Vase, Floral & Blackberries, Signed, Black Mark, 4 1/2 In.	75.00
Vase, Floral Design, Bird & Butterfly, Green Mark, 9 1/2 In.	100.00
Vase, Floral, Fig Shape, Openwork Base, 1900 Mark, 4 1/4 In.	195.00
Vase, Flowers & Leaf Design, Narrow Neck, C.1862, 15 In.	1250.00
Vase, Gargoyled Knees, Gold Outlining, C.1880, 4 3/4 In.	250.00
Vase, Gilt Dog, 19th Century, Crown Mark, 9 3/4 In.	650.00
Vase, Gold Heron & Butterfly, Serpent Handles, 8 3/4 In.	525.00
Vase, Gold Satyr Masque At Handle, Dated 1888, 10 3/4 In.	325.00
Vase, Gold Scalloped Base, C.1891, 3 1/2 In.	97.00
Vase, Hand-Painted Blackberries, Signed, 4 3/4 In.	85.00
Vase, Highland Cattle Scene, Signed, 16 In., Pair	585.00
Vase, Ivory, Gold & Bronze Mums, 1888, 6 In.	470.00
Vase, Ivory, Gold Trim, 12 Sided, Acorn Top, Marked, 11 In.	750.00
Vase, Japanese Design, Dragonflies, Marked, 8 In., Pr.	325.00
Vase, Jeweled, Urn Form, 3 Eagle Talons, Blue, Marked, 6 In.	225.00
Vase, Masks At Neck & Collar, Dolphin Handles, 9 1/4 In.	365.00
Vase, Molded Woven Body, Gold Handles, Green, Marked, 8 In.	400.00
Vase, Outlined Polychrome Panels, Signed, C.1900, 4 1/2 In.	60.00
Vase, Oviform, Wildflowers, Pink Ground, Marked, 10 In.	240.00
Vase, Peacock On Branch, Artist Signed, Marked, 4 In.	265.00
Vase, Pierced Neck, Fern Design, Purple Mark, 13 1/2 In.	995.00
Vase, Pierced Top, Gold Outlined Florals, Handles, 12 In.	475.00
Vase, Pierced, Geese Flying, Sky, Marsh, Marked, 18 In.	750.00
Vase, Pierced, Morning Landscape, Metallic, Marked, 6 In.	900.00
Vase, Pink & Yellow Flowers, Cream Ground, 9 In.	155.00
Vase, Rose Bowl Shape, Scene Of Castle, 3 In.	99.50
Vase, Shell, Roman Gold Trim, 1888 Mark, 5 1/2 X 8 In.	475.00
Vase, Shell, Roman Gold, Marked, 8 1/2 In.	475.00
Vase, Spider Amid Foliage, Loop Handles, C.1880, 12 1/2 In.	350.00
Vase, Urn Shape, Profile In Scroll Handles, C.1895, 12 In.	200.00
Vase, Yellow Ground, Floral Design, 8 1/4 In.	525.00
Vase, 2-Toned Gold, Hand-Painted Dahlias, C.1880, 12 In., Pr.	435.00
Vase, 3 Gold Serpent Handles, Red Leaves, Green Mark	325.00
Wall Pocket, Drawn Pouch Form, Gilt Cord, Marked, 6 In., Pr.	300.00
Wall Pocket, Orchid, Gold, Brown, & Beige, Pair	500.00
Wall Pocket, Orchid, Gold, Dark Brown, Pair	450.00

Wall Pocket, Shell-Shaped, White, Brown Trim, Pair 375.00

Roycroft products were made by the Roycrofter community of East Aurora, New York, in the late nineteenth and early twentieth centuries. The community was founded by Elbert Hubbard. The products included furniture, metalware, leatherwork, and jewelry.

ROYCROFT, Andirons, Iron, Roycroft Emblem, C.1905, 30 In., Pair 3250.00
  Bookends, Crimped Edges, 4 X 3 In. 38.00
  Bookends, Door & Knocker Design 38.00
  Bookends, Elephant, Copper With Leather Inserts 95.00
  Bookends, Owl, Copper 25.00
  Bookends, Round, Marked, 4 1/4 X 3 3/4 In. 33.00
  Bookends, Viking Ships 60.00
  Bowl, 6 X 2 In. 45.00
  Bowl, 8 In.Diam. 43.33
  Calendar, Perpetual, Hammered Copper 28.00
  Candelabra, 2-Light, C.1920, Marked, 10 In., Pair 220.00
  Candlestick Holder, 6 Holes, 15 1/2 In.Long 65.00
  Candlestick, Circle Design, Marked, 6 X 3 1/2 In. 85.00
  Candlestick, Silvered 85.00
  Crumb Set 30.00
  Desk, Oak, Hammered Copper Pulls, Marked, 40 X 40 In. 1200.00
  Doll, Bean Bag, Clownie 65.00
  Inkwell, Brass, With Glass, 4 1/2 In. 45.00
  Jug, Brown, 5 In. .... 23.00 To 39.00
  Lamp, Bridge, Parrot Design 375.00
  Lamp, Stamped Mark, C.1915, 13 1/2 In. 400.00
  Letter Opener 35.00
  Mustard, Cover, Brown, 4 1/2 In. 25.00
  Pencil Holder 60.00
  Tray, Calling Card, Copper, 7 1/4 In. 50.00
  Tray, Pen, With Letter Opener, Signed 45.00
  Tray, Pencil, 6 X 4 In. 20.00
  Tray, Stylized Floral Design, Handled, Marked, 21 3/4 In. 100.00
  Tray, 6 Cups, Tray 8 1/2 In. 75.00
  Vase, American Beauty Shape, 6 In. 55.00
  Vase, Arts & Crafts, Copper & Pewter 145.00
  Vase, Hammered Copper, 4 1/2 In. 35.00
    ROZANE, see Roseville

RRP is the mark used by the firm of Robinson-Ransbottom. The firm was founded by the Ransbottom brothers in 1900 in Ironspot, Ohio. In 1920 they merged with the Robinson Clay Product Company of Akron, Ohio, to become Robinson-Ransbottom. Pieces are often confused with those of the Roseville Pottery. The factory is still working.

RRP CO., Cookie Jar, Pig 35.00
  Vase, Leaves, Blue, 8 In. 35.00

RS Germany porcelain was made at the factory of Rheinhold Schlegelmilch after 1869 in Tillowitz, Germany. It was sold decorated or undecorated.

RS GERMANY, Ashtray, Orange Poppies On Shaded Ground, 4 In. .... 15.00 To 32.00
  Ashtray, Poppy Design, Orange 30.00
  Berry Set, Floral, Glossy, Set Of 6 Bowls 85.00
  Bonbon, Pink Roses, Pedestaled 34.00
  Bone Dish, Gold Trim 15.00
  Bowl, Beige Pearlized Sides, Center Flowers, Blue Mark, 9 1/4 In. ... 38.00
  Bowl, Boat Shape, Open Handle, Orange Floral, Green Mark, 8 In. ... 60.00

Bowl, Copper Luster, Florals, Butterflies, Signed, 8 In.	59.00
Bowl, Cream To Green, Pink & White Blossoms, 8 In.	45.00
Bowl, Floral, White Poppies, Loop Handles, 10 In.	45.00
Bowl, Florals, Footed, Green, 7 1/4 In.	65.00
Bowl, Iris, Blue Mark, 9 1/2 In.	35.00
Bowl, Multicolor Flowers, Blue Mark, 9 1/4 In.	27.00
Bowl, Peonies, Double Handles, Hand-Painted, Green Mark, 8 In.	58.00
Bowl, Pierced Ends, Pink To Gray, Green Mark, 8 1/2 X 3 In.	72.00
Bowl, Pink Roses, Tan & Orange, 4 Footed, 5 7/8 In.	55.00
Bowl, Poppies & Lilacs, Whtie To Tan, 10 1/2 In.	135.00
Bowl, Poppy Design, Orange Luster, Ball Feet, 5 3/4 In.	35.00
Bowl, Purple Cream Pearl Glaze, Roses, 8 In.	155.00
Bowl, Robin Design, 9 1/2 In.Diam.	110.00
Bowl, Sugar, Floral, Orchid Flower, Yellow-Brown Ground	22.00
Bowl, White Poppies, Colored Florals, Loop Handles, 10 In.	45.00
Box, Collar Button, Gold Trim, White	22.00
Box, Flowers, Porcelain, Covered, 3 1/2 In.Diam.	25.00
Box, Petal Shaped, White, 4 X 2 In.	20.00
Box, Powder, Floral, Gold & Green, Green Mark, 4 1/2 In.	28.00
Box, Powder, Green Ground, Poppies	48.00
Cake Plate, Poppy, Handled, 10 In.	30.00
Cake Set, Leaf Design, Olive Green, Gold Trim, 5 Piece	145.00
Cake Set, Open Handled, 4 Plates, Tray 10 3/4 In., 5 Piece	160.00
Celery, Blown-Out Iris, Steeple Mark, 9 1/2 In.	90.00
Celery, Green, White Flowers, Gold Trim, Green Mark, 14 In.	75.00
Chocolate Pot, Art Deco Motif, Gold Trim	68.00
Chocolate Pot, Molded Iris Edge, Red Steeple Mark, 9 1/2 In.	80.00
Chocolate Pot, Pink Roses, Green & Cream Ground, Marked, 9 In.	110.00
Chocolate Pot, Roses, Luster Finish, Steeple Top, 6-Sided, 9 In.	65.00
Chocolate Set, Floral Roses & Daisies, Cream Ground, 4 Cups	195.00
Chocolate Set, Roses, Green Ground, 9 Piece	235.00
Chocolate Set, 4 Cups & Saucers, Florals, Gold Trim, 5 Piece	260.00
Compote, Strawberry, Gold Trim, Green, Pink Orchids, Signed	89.00
Condiment Set, Blue Flowers, Gold Trim, 5 Piece	75.00
Cracker Jar, Hydrangeas	95.00
Cracker Jar, Painted Violets, Cream Ground, Gold Bands & Handles	130.00
Cracker Jar, Poppies	90.00
Cracker Jar, Red, Yellow Roses, Covered, Green Mark	93.00
Cracker Jar, Roses, Green Mark	75.00 To 115.00
Creamer, Purple Violets, Blue Mark	18.00
Creamer, Roses	15.00
Creamer, White & Pink Mums, Green Mark	28.00
Cup & Saucer, Chocolate, Plate 6 1/2 In.	48.00
Cup & Saucer, Cotton Plant	25.00
Cup & Saucer, Demitasse, Blown, Swirled	31.00
Cup, Nut, Pearlized Sides, Gold Bowl, Signed	15.00
Demitasse Set, Tulip Design, Blue Mark	500.00
Dish, Black Speckles, Orange Luster, Pierced Handles, 7 1/2 In.	85.00
Dish, Boat Shape, Pink Flowers, Open Handles, 8 1/2 X 4 1/2 In.	30.00
Dish, Boat Shape, Pink Flowers, 8 1/2 In.	25.00
Dish, Candy, Floral Pattern, Handle Over Top, Marked	45.00
Dish, Candy, Footed, Flowers, Steeple Mark	40.00
Dish, Candy, Leaf Shape, Calla Lily, 5 1/2 In.	18.00
Dish, Cheese & Cracker, Poppies, Orange Luster, Tiered	48.00
Dish, Nut, Fluted, Marked, Orange & Multicolored, 4 3/4 In.	25.00
Dish, Pickle, Orange Poppy, Blue Flowers, 2 Handled, 9 In.	25.00
Dish, Pickle, White Roses, Green Ground	45.00
Dish, Sauce, Tulips, Scalloped, Blue Mark	16.00
Dish, Scenic, Blue & White Pheasant, 10 Sided, 5 1/2 In.	38.00
Fernery, Flowers, Green	125.00
Hair Receiver, Roses, Cream & Brown Ground, Marked, 2 1/2 In.	50.00
Hair Receiver, White, Gold Trim, Blue Mark	32.50
Hatpin Holder, Blue Forget-Me-Nots, Gold Top, Green Mark	55.00
Hatpin Holder, Calla Lily Design, Green Ground	50.00

Hatpin Holder, Green Poppies, Green Mark, 4 3/4 In. 30.00
Hatpin Holder, Peach Roses, Gold Trim, Footed, Marked 45.00
Hatpin Holder, Roses 69.00
Hatpin Holder, White & Gold 110.00
Inkwell, Hand-Painted Dragon, Porcelain, 3 1/2 In.Square 72.00
Jar, Powder, Water Lily, White 35.00
Mayonnaise Bowl, Gold Clover Roses 50.00
Mug, Large Red Roses 40.00
Mustard, Covered, Red Steeple Mark 56.00
Mustard, Pink Rose, Shaded Ground, Covered 37.00
Nail Buffer Set, White Roses, Gold Trim, Signed 75.00
Nut Set, Beige Ground, Roses, 4-Footed, Set Of 6 Bowls 90.00
Pitcher, Pickard Gold Design, Blue Mark, 6 1/2 In. 175.00
Plaque, Mill Scene, Steeple Mark 450.00
Plate, Blue Star, Green, Pink, Rose Flowers, Signed 39.50
Plate, Daffodils, Gold Rim, 8 1/2 In. 38.00
Plate, Gardenia, Gold Trim, Marked, 8 In. 28.00
Plate, Mill Scene, 7 3/4 In. 75.00
Plate, Pink & Salmon Fish, Gold Leaves, 8 1/2 In. 55.00
Plate, Pond Scene, 10-Sided, 8 In. 42.00
Plate, Roses, 8 In. 55.00
Plate, White Rose, Gray Shading, 8 1/2 In. 42.00
Plate, White Tulips, 6 1/2 In. 10.00
Plate, 2 Cherub Center, Reticulated Rim, Blue Mark, 7 1/4 In. 165.00
Relish, Applied Acorns, Open End, 5 X 4 In. 13.50
Relish, Boat Shape, Gold Border, Green Mark, 4 1/4 In. 38.00
Relish, Roses, Green Ivy, Peach, Open, 10 In. 35.00
Salt & Pepper, Daffodils, Marked 60.00
Salt & Pepper, Rose Design 40.00
Sauce, Forget-Me-Nots, Petal Rim, Gold Trim, 8 In. 12.00
Sugar & Creamer, Brown Tones, Orange Flowers 29.00
Sugar & Creamer, Cottage Scene, Covered 65.00
Sugar & Creamer, Floral 48.00
Sugar & Creamer, Hand-Painted Iris, Blue Mark 38.00
Sugar & Creamer, Peach, Orange, Pink Nasturtiums 50.00
Sugar & Creamer, Satin Lily-Of-The-Valley, Square 43.00
Sugar, Covered, Roses, Shaded Green, Blue Mark 20.00
Syrup, Underplate, Pale Blue Border, Pink Roses, Covered 40.00
Tankard, Art Nouveau, Blown-Out Flowers, Gold & White, 9 In. 200.00
Teapot, Tan, White, Gray, Black Trim 65.00
Toothpick, Floral, Gold Trim, Open Handle 35.00
Toothpick, Pink Roses, 3 Handles 82.00
Toothpick, Roses, 4 Scalloped Feet, 2 Handles, Green Mark 55.00
Toothpick, Violets, 3 Handles, Blue Mark 55.00
Tray, Bread, Beige, Gold, White, Roses, 15 In. 70.00
Tray, Bun, Green & White Flowers, Gold Trim 80.00
Tray, Coral & White, Fuchsia, Green Leaves, Cream Ground, Signed 55.00
Tray, Grosbeak, Sterling Overlay 105.00
Tray, Relish, Beige, Yellow Roses 50.00
Tray, Scenic, Open Handle, Round, Marked, 7 In. 175.00
Tree, Ring, Pink, Daisies, Hand-Painted 28.00
Tumbler, Pink & White Rose, Blue Mark 25.00
Vase, Apricot Poppies, 4 In. 45.00
Vase, Basket With Roses, Cylinder Shape, 7 3/4 In. 72.00
Vase, Blue Ground, Parrots, Gold Trim, 8 In. 70.00
Vase, Country Cottage Scene, Brown, Cylindrical Shape, 8 In. 110.00
Vase, Lilies, Red Panel Top & Bottom, 8 1/2 In. 65.00
Vase, Nightwatch Scene, Gold Trim, Double-Handled, 5 1/2 In. 295.00
Vase, Parrots On Front Panel, Gold Trim, Blue Ground, 8 In. 70.00
Vase, Winter Scene, Artist Signed, Blue Mark, 5 In. 85.00

RS POLAND, Cup & Saucer, Bells Of Ireland 50.00
Cup & Saucer, Shadow Foliage, White Flowers, Green, Marked 50.00

RS Prussia, Berry Set, Floral, Red
Mark, 7 Piece

Vase, Peach Roses, Floral Handled, Gray Ground, Marked, 6 1/8 In.	65.00
Vase, Pheasants, Scenic, 2-Handled, Red Mark, 3 1/2 In.	245.00
Vase, Pheasants, Signed, Red Mark, 5 X 6 In.	185.00
Vase, Roses, Swags Of Golden Chains, Red Mark, 7 1/4 In.	150.00
Vase, White Lilies, Yellow Ground, Gold Handles, 8 1/4 In.	125.00

*RS Prussia porcelain was made at the factory of Rheinhold Schlegelmilch
after 1869 in Tillowitz, Germany. It was sold decorated or undecorated.*

RS PRUSSIA, Basket, White, Foliage Design, Red Star Mark	95.00
Berry Bowl, Castle Scene	450.00
Berry Bowl, Fruit Design, Pearlized, Gold Edge, Red Mark, Set Of 6	250.00
Berry Bowl, Yellow Rose Design, Molded Rim, C.1870, 10 In.	175.00
Berry Set, Blown-Out Iris, Pink, Poppies, Red Mark, 6 Piece	485.00
Berry Set, Floral, Red Mark, 7 Piece ....*Illus*	1650.00
Berry Set, Gold Rim, Floral Center, Pearlized, Signed, Marked	345.00
Berry Set, Iris Mold, Wild Rose Design, 7 Pieces	300.00
Berry Set, Lilies On Green Ground, Red Mark, 6 Piece	215.00
Berry Set, Petal Mold, Roses, Daisies, Gold Beading, 7 Piece	385.00
Berry Set, Pond Lilies, Red Mark, Bowl 11 In., 7 Piece	425.00
Berry Set, Roses & Daisies, Gold Beading, Red Mark, 7 Piece	385.00
Berry Set, Roses, Side Scoops, Glossy, Gray, Moss, Red Mark, 6 Piece	285.00
Berry Set, Starfish, Master Bowl 9 1/4 In., 7 Piece	325.00
Bonbon, Blown-Out Poppies, Pearlized, Red Mark, 7 1/4 In.	95.00
Bonbon, Carnation Mold, 3-Footed, Red Mark	90.00
Bonbon, Footed, Gold Medallion, Flower Bouquet, Magenta, Red Mark	125.00
Bonbon, Leaf Shape, Twig Handle	85.00
Bonbon, Pink Roses, Green & Gold, Red Mark, 5 1/2 In.	125.00
Bowl, Blown-Out Carnations, Red Mark, 12 In.	450.00
Bowl, Blown-Out Flowers Around Rim, Water Lilies, 10 1/2 In.	225.00
Bowl, Blown-Out Flowers, Scalloped, Red Mark, 10 3/4 In.	120.00
Bowl, Blown-Out Green Flowers & Leaves, Red Mark, 10 In.	100.00
Bowl, Blown-Out Iris, Footed, Red Mark, 5 1/2 In.	90.00
Bowl, Blown-Out Iris, Hand-Painted Roses, Red Mark, 9 1/2 In.	450.00
Bowl, Blown-Out Roses, Pink, Orange, & Blue, Red Mark, 10 1/2 In.	145.00
Bowl, Blue & Pink Floral, Blue Edge, 8 1/2 In.	120.00
Bowl, Blue, Orchids, 11 In.	85.00
Bowl, Bluebirds, Swans, Lily Of The Valley, Roses, Marked, 10 In.	650.00
Bowl, Cabbage, Green With Roses, Red Mark, 7 In.	225.00
Bowl, Cabbage, Iridescent, Purple Iris, Red Mark, 10 In.	375.00
Bowl, Canterbury Bells, Footed, 6 In.	90.00
Bowl, Carnations, Green, Pink & White Roses, Red Mark, 10 In.	365.00
Bowl, Christmas Holly, Satin, Lavender Border, 10 1/2 In.	150.00
Bowl, Console, Blown-Out Carnation, Red Mark, 15 In.	1100.00

Bowl, Cottage Scene, Gold Border, 10 1/4 In.Diam. 250.00
Bowl, Cream, Pink Roses, Red Mark, 10 In. 150.00
Bowl, Crown Shaped Center Handle, Red Mark, Large 750.00
Bowl, Dice Players, 11 In. 900.00
Bowl, Embossed Arrows, Flower Forms, Red Mark, 8 1/4 In. 147.00
Bowl, Embossed Irises On Rim, Center Flower, Red Mark, 10 In. 260.00
Bowl, Floral Bouquet Center, Red Mark, 10 1/2 In. 210.00
Bowl, Floral Bouquet Center, Scalloped Rim, Marked, 10 1/2 In. 210.00
Bowl, Floral Center, Blown-Out Rim, Gold Trim, Red Mark, 10 In. 155.00
Bowl, Floral Center, Gold & Yellow Edge, Red Mark, 10 1/2 In. 240.00
Bowl, Floral Center, Painted Arches, Red Mark, 10 In.Diam. 150.00
Bowl, Floral Design, Scalloped, 9 1/2 In. 145.00
Bowl, Floral Rim, Open Handles, Blue To Yellow, 11 In. 68.00
Bowl, Floral Rose Design, Marked, 13 1/2 In. 100.00
Bowl, Floral, Red Mark, 12 3/4 & 11 In.Diam., Pair 450.00
Bowl, Floral, Scalloped Edge, Marked, 11 In. 150.00
Bowl, Flower Center, Gold Scalloped Border, Marked, 10 1/2 In. 165.00
Bowl, Flowers In Glass Bowl, Red Mark, 10 3/4 In. 275.00
Bowl, Flowers, Green, Gray, Gilt Edge, 10 1/2 In. 165.00
Bowl, Fruit Design, Marked, 10 1/2 In. 300.00
Bowl, Gold Fluted Rim, Roses Inside & Out, Red Mark, 9 In.Diam. 259.00
Bowl, Green, Pink Roses, Red Mark, 10 1/2 In. 195.00
Bowl, Icicle Mold, Pond Lilies, Red Mark, 9 1/4 In.Diam. 195.00
Bowl, Iridescent Flowers, Gold Tracery, Pearlized, 10 3/4 In. 295.00
Bowl, Iris Mold, Winter Scene, Red Mark, 10 1/2 In. 1000.00
Bowl, Iris, Blown-Out, Red Mark, 10 1/2 In. 250.00
Bowl, Iris, Satin, Floral Center, Roses, Marked, 10 1/2 In. 250.00
Bowl, Jeweled, Red Mark, 11 In.Diam. 135.00
Bowl, Magnolia Blossoms, Gold, White, & Tan, Red Mark, 1/ 1/2 In. 285.00
Bowl, Melon Boy, Green, 10 1/2 In. 345.00
Bowl, Melon Eaters, 11 In. 875.00
Bowl, Mill Scene, Red Mark, 9 1/2 In. 525.00
Bowl, Molded Jewels, Roses, & Snowballs, Green, 11 In.Diam. 165.00
Bowl, Molded Rim, Swans & Pond Lilies, Red Star, 11 In.Diam. 250.00
Bowl, Nut, White & Green Ground, Pink Roses, Marked, 6 In. 95.00
Bowl, Pastel Roses, Red Mark, 9 In. 135.00
Bowl, Pink & White Roses, Red Mark, 9 In. 120.00
Bowl, Pink & Yellow Roses, Gold Crimped, Red Mark, 11 In.Diam. 175.00
Bowl, Pink Asters, Green, 10 In. 88.00
Bowl, Pink Carnation, Red Mark, 10 In. 110.00
Bowl, Pink Flowers, Water, Molded Rim, 10 3/4 In. 250.00
Bowl, Pink, Yellow, Roses, Gold Beading, Marked, 11 In. 195.00
Bowl, Poppies, Lilies Of The Valley, Green Trim, Red Mark, 10 In. 250.00
Bowl, Poppy Reflection, Gold Trim, Red Mark, 8 1/2 In. 125.00
Bowl, Poppy, Satin, Marked, 11 In. 225.00
Bowl, Purple Violets, Inverted Panels, Red Mark, 10 In. 159.00
Bowl, Quiet Cove, Red Mark, 10 1/4 In. 550.00
Bowl, Quiet Cove, Red Mark, 11 In. 695.00
Bowl, Raised Jewels, Beige, Blue, Roses, Red Mark, 10 In. 195.00
Bowl, Rose Center, Gold Border, Marked, 10 1/2 In. 250.00
Bowl, Rose Design Inside & Out, Footed, Marked, 6 3/4 In. 150.00
Bowl, Rose Design, Gold Trim, Marked, 10 1/2 In. 100.00
Bowl, Roses In Center, Fluted, Gold Band, 8 In. 95.00
Bowl, Roses, Green Ground, White Ribbed Trim, 10 In., Pair 195.00
Bowl, Roses, Red Mark, 10 3/4 In.Diam. 185.00
Bowl, Roses, Scalloped, Gold Rim, 11 In. 195.00
Bowl, Roses, Shaded Green Ground, Pink, 11 In. 155.00
Bowl, Ruffled, Green, White Blossoms, 10 In. 229.00
Bowl, Sailboat, Castle On Mountain, Red Mark, 10 1/4 In. 95.00
Bowl, Satin, Flowers Outside & Inside, 3-Footed, Marked, 8 In. 150.00
Bowl, Satin, Red, White, Carnation, Acanthus Leaves, Marked, 10 In. 195.00
Bowl, Triple Flower Form, Floral & Leaves, Red Mark, 9 3/8 In. 155.00
Bowl, Turkey, Red Mark, 11 In. 850.00

Bowl, Water Lilies, 10 1/2 In. 225.00
Bowl, Winter Scene, Iris Mold, Red Mark, 8 1/2 In. 950.00
Bowl, Winter Scene, Satin Iris Mold, Marked, 10 1/2 In. 1050.00
Bowl, 5 Iris In Green, Cream, Pink Poppies, Marked, 10 In. 195.00
Bowl, 5 Portraits Of Victorian Ladies, Footed, 6 1/2 In. 250.00
Bowl, 12 Roses, Cream Ground, Gold Trim, Red Mark, 10 1/2 In. 225.00
Box, Pin, Leaf Shape, Covered, Red Mark, 4 X 2 1/2 In. 98.00
Box, Powder, Flowers & Leaves, Beaded, Red Mark, 2 1/2 X 4 In. 90.00
Butter Pat, Green & Yellow Flowers, Gold Edge, Red Mark 59.00
Cake Plate, California Poppy, Open Handle, Red Mark, 11 1/2 In. 150.00
Cake Plate, Castle Scene, Brown Tones 500.00
Cake Plate, Center Roses, Blue Border, Iris, Red Mark, 10 In. 150.00
Cake Plate, Clematis 125.00
Cake Plate, Dice Players 675.00
Cake Plate, Embossed Iris, Wheelock Gesetzlich, Cobalt Blue 750.00
Cake Plate, Fall Seasons, Green Tones, Open Handled, 9 1/2 In. 495.00
Cake Plate, Floral Design, Gold Trim, Marked, 11 In. 220.00
Cake Plate, Floral Rose Design, Marked, 11 In. 220.00
Cake Plate, Floral, Iris Mold, 11 In. 178.00
Cake Plate, Flower Basket, Medallion Border, Pearlized, Red Mark 235.00
Cake Plate, Fruit Design, Open Handles, Red Mark, 11 In. 195.00
Cake Plate, Fruit Icicle Mold 150.00
Cake Plate, Gold Rim, Pink Ground, Red Mark, Signed 250.00
Cake Plate, Hand-Painted Flowers, Embossed Rim, 11 In. 125.00
Cake Plate, Hanging Basket Center, Red Mark 325.00
Cake Plate, Melon Boys, Red Mark, Green, Gold, 11 In. 850.00
Cake Plate, Melon Eaters, Ruffled, 12 In. 350.00
Cake Plate, Molded Flowers, Gold Rim, Open Handles, Red Mark 159.00
Cake Plate, Molded Flowers, Leaves Border, Rose Center, 9 In. 169.00
Cake Plate, Molded Flowers, Roses Center, Open Handled, 9 In. 90.00
Cake Plate, Newport Belle, Hand-Painted, 12 1/2 In. 75.00
Cake Plate, Pearlized Finish, Calla Lilies, Green Wreath, 11 In. 125.00
Cake Plate, Pearlized, Blown-Out Rim, Handle, Red Mark, 11 In. 235.00
Cake Plate, Peonies, Open Handle, Red Mark, 9 1/2 In. 175.00
Cake Plate, Pink & White, Gold Trim, 10 In. 150.00
Cake Plate, Purple, Pink Roses, Open Handle, 11 In. 260.00
Cake Plate, Roses, Blue Border, Iris, Red Mark, 10 1/2 In. 150.00
Cake Plate, Roses, Gold Rim, Handle, Green Wreath Mark, 10 In. 75.00
Cake Plate, Roses, Gold Trim, 3-Handled, Red Mark .... *Illus* 410.00
Cake Plate, Satin, Pink & Yellow Roses, Red Mark 175.00
Cake Plate, Scalloped, Florals, Red Mark, 11 1/2 In. 165.00
Cake Plate, Snowballs & Roses 100.00
Candlestick, Cottage Scene, 2-Handled 195.00

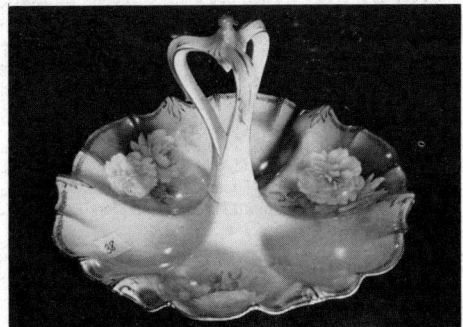

RS Prussia, Cake Plate, Roses, Gold Trim,
3-Handled, Red Mark

Celery, Basket Of Roses, Glazed, Red Mark, 12 In. 100.00
Celery, Castle Scene, Brown & Yellow, Gold Trim, Mark, 12 In. 775.00
Celery, Florals, Beaded Gold, Floral Edge, 12 In. 45.00
Celery, Flowers, Handled, Red Mark, 9 1/2 In. 125.00
Celery, Mill Scene, Brown Tone, 9 1/2 In. 185.00
Celery, Open Handles, Blown Edges, Flowers, Red Mark 135.00
Celery, Pink & Gold, Pink Roses, Open Handle, 13 1/2 X 6 1/4 In. 150.00
Celery, Poppies, Green Ground, Red Mark, 12 1/4 In. 150.00
Celery, White Flowers, Green Ground, Red Mark 145.00
Charger, Floral Medallion On Edge, Yellow Ground 185.00
Chocolate Cup & Saucer, Green, White Flowers, Gold Beading 85.00
Chocolate Cup, Lily Of The Valley, Red Mark 50.00
Chocolate Pot, Blown-Out, Pearlized 395.00
Chocolate Pot, Bluebirds On Lid, Red Mark 545.00
Chocolate Pot, Carnations & Roses, Red Mark, Pink 225.00
Chocolate Pot, Castle, Scene, Red Mark, 8 In. 1050.00
Chocolate Pot, Floral On Satin Finish, Beaded Edging, Red Mark 235.00
Chocolate Pot, Hand-Painted Roses, Blown-Out Base, Red Mark 245.00
Chocolate Pot, Pink & Rose Florals, Satin Finish 425.00
Chocolate Pot, Poppies, Blending Orange & Cream, Marked, 10 In. 285.00
Chocolate Pot, Red Floral, Red Mark 200.00
Chocolate Pot, Roses & Flowers, Red Mark, 10 1/2 In. 450.00
Chocolate Pot, Roses, Golds, Floral, Icicle Mold, 9 1/2 In. 315.00
Chocolate Pot, Roses, 8 Ball Feet, Red Mark, 8 1/2 In. 195.00
Chocolate Pot, Scallopeo Rim & Shoulder, 9 3/4 In. 50.00
Chocolate Pot, Urn On Portica, Bluebirds On Lid, Marked 545.00
Chocolate Pot, Violet Luster, Gold Fleur-De-Lis, Red Mark 98.00
Chocolate Pot, 2 Lebrun Portrait Medallions, Cobalt Blue 525.00
Chocolate Set, Floral Rose Design, Gold Trim, 10 1/2 In. 800.00
Chocolate Set, Florals, Blue Raspberries, Red Mark 1050.00
Chocolate Set, Jeweled, Florals, Green & Gold, Red Mark 800.00
Chocolate Set, Summer Season, Blown-Out Poppy Mold 7500.00
Chocolate Set, Summer Season, 13 Piece .... *Illus* 7500.00
Chocolate Set, Sunflower Mold, Red Mark 550.00
Chocolate Set, Violets, Red Star, 13 Piece 550.00
Cocoa Pot, Floral, Blown-Out Ladies' Heads 285.00
Cocoa Pot, Swan Scene, Cream Tones 285.00
Coffeepot, Demitasse, Blown-Out Iris, Spring Season 1100.00
Coffeepot, Swan & Forest Scene, Satin Finish, Signed, 7 1/4 In. 395.00
Compote, Footed, Red Mark, 6 1/2 In. 125.00
Condiment Set, White Floral On Green Ground, Red Mark, 3 Piece 135.00
Cookie Jar, Flying Bluebirds, Cover 250.00
Cracker Jar, Blown-Out Iris, Flower Finial, Red Mark 235.00
Cracker Jar, Flowers, Footed 225.00
Cracker Jar, Flowers, Pearlized, Green Ground, Red Mark, 8 1/2 In. 275.00
Cracker Jar, Ivy Trim, Matte Finish 210.00
Cracker Jar, Lily Pattern, Pearlized, Red Mark 190.00
Cracker Jar, Melon Eaters 1500.00
Cracker Jar, Pink, White Flowers, Green Ground, Red Mark, 8 In. 275.00
Cracker Jar, Pink, Yellow, & White Roses, Yellow Gold & White 295.00
Cracker Jar, Rose Design, Covered, 9 X 5 1/2 In. 525.00
Cracker Jar, Rose Design, Gold Trim, Marked, Covered, 5 1/2 In. 525.00
Cracker Jar, Roses, Blown-Out, Green On White, Red Mark 215.00
Cracker Jar, Satinized Jeweled, 2 Handles, 8-Footed 350.00
Cracker Jar, Scalloped Top & Bottom, Satinized Flowers, Red Mark 365.00
Cracker Jar, Turquoise, Florals, Red Mark 395.00
Cracker Jar, White, Rose Floral, Marked 175.00
Cracker Jar, Winter Season, Red Mark 1150.00
Creamer, Blown-Out Carnation, Red Mark 85.00
Creamer, Castle Scene, Green, Red Mark 225.00
Creamer, Covered, Bouquets Of Pink, Yellow Roses, Underplate 145.00
Creamer, Mill Scene, Footed, Green Ground 135.00
Creamer, Pheasant & Pine Tree, Red Mark 300.00

RS Prussia, Chocolate Set, Summer Season, 13 Piece

Cup & Saucer, Floral Design, Demitasse, Red Mark	60.00
Cup & Saucer, Fruit On Cup, Red Mark	70.00
Cup & Saucer, Holly Design, Raised Gold	85.00
Cup & Saucer, Melon Boy, Red Mark	400.00
Cup, Court Scene, Man & Lady, Shaded Gold, Demitasse	95.00
Cup, Loving, Melon Boys, Jeweled, Boy On Back	1400.00
Cup, Tea, Pink Flower, Blue Ground, Gold Trim, Footed	60.00
Cup, White Iris, Red Feet, Old Mark, Signed	35.00
Dessert Set, Pink Roses, Gold Trim, Four 6 In.Plates, 5 Piece	250.00
Dish, Beige To Green Ground, Pink Roses, Marked, 8 X 4 In.	55.00
Dish, Berry, Iris Mold Edge, Colored Roses, Red Mark, 5 1/2 In.	62.00
Dish, Condiment, Flowers, Gold Stems, Ruffled, 5 1/2 X 12 In.	165.00
Dish, Pin, Leaf Shape, Flowers, Red Mark	100.00
Dresser Set, Aqua Floral, 4 Piece	235.00
Ewer, Portrait, Autumn Scene, Handled, Red Mark, 6 In.	550.00
Ewer, Summer, Marked, 9 In.	1500.00
Ewer, White Satin Bird Of Paradise, Red Mark	950.00
Fernery, Cottage Scene, Brown, Footed, Insert	350.00
Fernery, Floral, 4 Dark Green Floral Feet, Marked, 9 In.	545.00
Hair Receiver, Butterflies, Red Mark, Footed	65.00
Hair Receiver, Gold, Green, Red Mark	129.00
Hair Receiver, Lily Design, Handkerchief Mold, Gold Beaded Rim	149.00
Hair Receiver, Pale Green, Yellow & Pink Roses, Gold Trim	235.00
Hair Receiver, Rococo, Diamond Form, Red Mark	80.00
Hatpin Holder, Attached Pin Tray, Pink & Blue Florals, White	175.00
Hatpin Holder, Floral Design, 6-Sided, Red Mark	145.00
Hatpin Holder, Mill Scene, Brown Tones	225.00
Hatpin Holder, Pink Roses Design, Red Mark, 5 In.	115.00
Hatpin Holder, Roses & Daisies Reflected In Pond, Red Mark	125.00
Hatpin Holder, Scalloped Base	149.00
Hatpin Holder, Water Lily	90.00
Hatpin Holder, White, Purple, Green, Red Mark	195.00
Humidor, Jewels, Three-Leaf Clovers, Red Mark	325.00
Ice Cream Set, Red Steeple Mark, 5 Piece	250.00
Jar, Condiment, Melon Blossom, Spoon, Aqua To Pink	85.00
Jar, Jam, Cabbage Rose, Covered, Red Mark	168.00

RS Prussia, Pitcher, Lemonade, Pastel Floral, 7 1/2 In.

Mug, Scuttle, Portrait Of Potocka 300.00
Mustard, Beige & Pink Water Lilies, 8 Feet, Red Mark 90.00
Mustard, Flowers, Pedestal, Cover 225.00
Mustard, Ladle, Melon Blossom Shape, Lavendar, Green, Gold 58.00
Mustard, Swallows, Ladle, Red Mark 200.00
Pitcher, Cider, Floral, Pink Ground, Red Mark 385.00
Pitcher, Lemonade, Pastel Floral, 7 1/2 In. .... *Illus* 375.00
Pitcher, Milk, Basket Of Flowers On Front, Red Mark 125.00
Pitcher, Milk, Lily Design, Red Mark 450.00
Pitcher, Pink Rose, Scalloped Rim, Red Mark, 5 1/4 In. 30.00
Pitcher, Swan, Red Mark 135.00
Pitcher, Syrup, Pearlized Green, Pink Roses, Red Mark 85.00
Pitcher, Tankard, Melon Eaters, Red Mark 3700.00
Pitcher, Water Lily Design, Gold Trim, C.1890, 10 In. 350.00
Planter, Fluted, Pink Roses, Red Mark 140.00
Plaque, Old Man Of The Mountain, Swans, 8 In.Diam. 550.00
Plate, Allover Roses, Gold Ground, 11 In. 225.00
Plate, Art Nouveau Figures, Gold Trim, Red Mark, 10 1/4 In. 240.00
Plate, Blown-Out Carnations, Pink, Yellow, Green, Red Mark, 11 In. 200.00
Plate, Blown-Out Iris Panels, Open Handle, Red Mark, 10 3/4 In. 80.00
Plate, Blown-Out Leaf Border, Flower Center, Red Mark, 6 In. 25.00
Plate, Bouquet Of Flowers, Red Mark, 8 1/2 In. 145.00
Plate, Bronze Leaves, 2 Roses, Scalloped Border, 7 1/2 In. 85.00
Plate, Brown, Green, White Hydrangas, Red Mark, 8 In. 95.00
Plate, Castle Scene, Dark Green Ground, Red Mark, 8 1/2 In. 550.00
Plate, Deep Crimson, Pink, Mauve, Marked, 8 5/8 In. 147.00
Plate, Embossed Iris Border, Floral Center, Red Mark, 10 1/2 In. 195.00
Plate, Floral Embossed, Green, 8 In. 100.00
Plate, Flower Forms, Scroll Center, Red Mark, 7 1/2 In. 60.00
Plate, Girl Holding Basket Of Fruit, 8 In. 1050.00
Plate, Gold & Yellow, Brown Edge, Floral Center, Scalloped, 8 In. 45.00
Plate, Green Flowers, Water, 9 1/2 In. 155.00
Plate, Green Leaves, Pink Accent, Raised Points, Red Mark, 8 In. 95.00
Plate, Green, Gold Roses, 8 In. 125.00
Plate, Hand-Painted Flowers In Glass Bowl, Red Mark, 8 1/2 In. 135.00
Plate, Hand-Painted Flowers, Gold Border, Lily Border, 8 1/4 In. 55.00
Plate, Iris Rim, Floral, Open Handled, Marked, 10 1/2 In. 275.00
Plate, Keyhole, Cobalt Blue Fleur-De-Lis, Portrait, 10 In. 895.00
Plate, Leaves & Shadow Flowers, Beaded Rim, Red Mark, 8 1/2 In. 95.00
Plate, Melon Boys, Jeweled, Green, Red Mark, 6 In. 395.00
Plate, Mill Scene, Open Handle, 10 In.Diam. 175.00
Plate, Molded Flowers, Gold Border, Red Mark, 8 1/2 In. 90.00
Plate, Pink Design, Crystal Bowl, 8 1/2 In. 85.00

RS Prussia, Plate, Satin, 8 In.

Plate, Plume Mold, Green Ground, Gold Trim, Poppies, 8 In.	85.00
Plate, Portrait Medallion, Red Mark, 11 1/4 In.	125.00
Plate, Portrait, Autumn Scene, Keyhole, Red Mark, 9 In.	950.00
Plate, Portrait, Male, Le Brun, Peacock, Daffodils, 12 In.	700.00
Plate, Puffed-Out Fleur-De-Lis, Multicolor, Red Mark, 10 7/8 In.	215.00
Plate, Roses, Gold Trim, Red Mark, 7 In.	65.00
Plate, Roses, Scalloped Border, 7 3/4 In.	95.00
Plate, Satin, 8 In.	*Illus* 1050.00
Plate, Solid Gold Blown-Out Carnation, Red Mark, 8 1/2 In.	130.00
Plate, Swan, Red Mark, 8 In.	475.00
Plate, Winter Scene, 8 1/2 In.	865.00
Plate, 5 Blown-Out Iris, Roses, Gold, Magenta Rim, Red Mark, 9 In.	135.00
Plate, 5 Medallions Of Women, Cobalt Blue Trim, Red Mark, 6 In.	385.00
Relish, Floral Design, Gold Trim, Red Mark, 13 1/2 In.	50.00
Relish, Jeweled, Open, Red Mark, 9 X 4 3/4 In.	185.00
Relish, Jewels, Cobalt Blue, Red Mark, 9 In.	125.00
Relish, Rose Design, Marked, 13 1/2 In.	50.00
Relish, Scalloped Rim, Pink, Yellow Roses, Open Handle, 9 1/2 In.	70.00
Relish, Swan Scene, Beaded Rim, Red Mark, 9 3/4 In.	230.00
Relish, 3 Swans, Beaded, Scenic, Open Handles, Red Mark	227.00
Salt & Pepper, Purple Violets, White Ground, Red Mark	145.00
Shaker, Sugar, Floral, Ornate, 5 1/2 In.	150.00
Shaving Mug, Blue, Red Roses, Gold Trim, Red Mark	150.00
Shaving Mug, Hanging Basket Of Flowers	150.00
Shaving Mug, Lily Design, Footed, Red Mark	225.00
Shaving Mug, Scalloped, Red Roses, Gold Trim, Blue Ground	150.00
Shaving Mug, Scuttle, Blown-Out Flowers	88.00
Shaving Mug, Soap Drain, Cottage Scene, Bluebirds	288.00
Strainer, Tea, Roses, Red Mark	100.00
Sugar & Creamer, Castle Design, Red Mark, Set	495.00
Sugar & Creamer, Castle Scene, Cottage, Green, Marked	350.00
Sugar & Creamer, Child's, Hanging Basket Of Flowers	125.00
Sugar & Creamer, Cottage Scene, Red Mark	350.00
Sugar & Creamer, Dogwood, Red Star	85.00
Sugar & Creamer, Floating Lilies, Red Mark	275.00
Sugar & Creamer, Floral	60.00 To 145.00
Sugar & Creamer, Hand-Painted Flowers, Satin Finish	185.00
Sugar & Creamer, Leaf Design	75.00
Sugar & Creamer, Luster, Pearl Ground, Covered	235.00
Sugar & Creamer, Mill Scene, Brown Tones	350.00 To 500.00
Sugar & Creamer, Scalloped Flowers, Red Mark	140.00
Sugar & Creamer, Swallows Over Pond Of Lilies, Marked	385.00
Sugar & Creamer, Swans, Urn, Portico, Red Mark	525.00

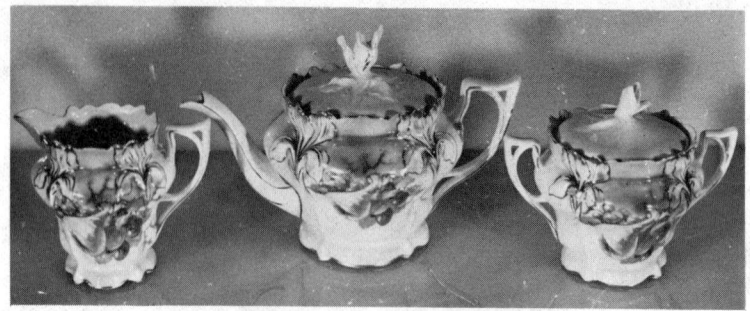

RS Prussia, Sugar, Creamer, & Teapot, Blown-Out Iris Mold

RS Prussia, Tankard, Dice Players,
Jeweled, Red Mark

RS Prussia, Tankard, Fall
Season, Red Mark

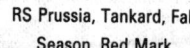

RS Prussia, Tankard, Fall Season

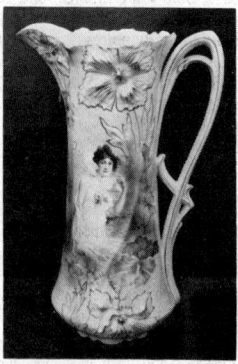

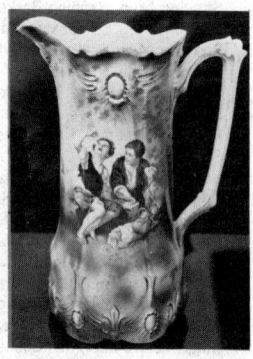

RS Prussia, Tankard, Melon
Eaters, Jeweled

Sugar & Creamer, Vines & Roses, Scalloped Body, Red Mark 250.00
Sugar & Creamer, Violets, Covered 130.00
Sugar & Creamer, Yellow & Red Roses, Ball Feet, Covered, Red Mark 125.00
Sugar Shaker, Victorian Man & Woman, Red Mark 295.00
Sugar, Creamer, & Teapot, Blown-Out Iris Mold .... *Illus* 850.00
Sugar, Molded Shell, Turquoise & Yellow, Pedestal, Marked 90.00
Sugar, Swans In Forest, Covered, Red Mark 149.00
Syrup, Satinized 110.00
Tankard, Acorn Mold, Winter Season, Satin Finish 5000.00
Tankard, Blown-Out Poppies, Gold Flowers, Red Mark, 11 In. 895.00
Tankard, Blown-Out Roses, Blue Ground, Double Handles 500.00
Tankard, Dice Players, Jeweled, Red Mark .... *Illus* 4000.00
Tankard, Fall Season .... *Illus* 2800.00
Tankard, Fall Season, Red Mark .... *Illus* 4750.00
Tankard, Floral, 12 In. 450.00
Tankard, Green, White Flowers, Gold, 6-Sided, Red Mark, 11 1/2 In. 695.00
Tankard, Melon Eaters, Jeweled .... *Illus* 3100.00
Tankard, Mill Scene, Acorn Mold, Marked, Brown 1800.00
Tankard, Roses, Green Shading, Red Mark 425.00
Tankard, Roses, Olive Green Ground, Red Mark, 10 3/4 In. 650.00
Tankard, Roses, Yellow Ground, Stipple Mold, Signed, 13 1/4 In. 430.00
Tankard, Ship, Marked, 11 In. 1800.00
Tankard, Summer Season .... *Illus* 3100.00
Tankard, Summer Season, Red Mark .... *Illus* 4900.00
Tankard, Swan, 10 In. 425.00
Tankard, Vertical Ribs, Floral, Gold Trim, Red Mark, 11 1/2 In. 595.00
Tankard, Winter Season, Acorn Mold, Red Mark .... *Illus* 5000.00
Tankard, 6-Paneled, Raised Gold Scrolling, Pedestal, 11 1/2 In. 589.00
Tea Set, Child's, Cottage Scene, 6 Cups & Saucers, 17 Piece 350.00
Tea Set, Melon Eaters, 3 Piece 1450.00
Teapot, Bunches Of Lilacs, Squatty 65.00
Teapot, Fuchsia, Green Daisies, Marked 190.00
Teapot, Mill Scene, Brown Tones 400.00
Teapot, Roses, Gold Trim, Beading, Footed, Red Mark, 6 1/2 In. 290.00
Toothpick, Scalloped, Turquoise & Yellow, 2-Handled, Red Mark 125.00
Toothpick, Water Lily Scene 85.00
Tray, Bread, Portrait, Autumn, Red Mark, 13 1/4 X 6 1/4 In. 950.00
Tray, Bun, Castle Scene, Handled, Red Mark 110.00
Tray, Bun, Floral Border, Celery Green Ground, Oblong, Marked 220.00

RS Prussia, Tankard, Summer
Season, Red Mark

RS Prussia, Tankard, Summer
Season

RS Prussia, Tankard, Winter
Season, Acorn Mold, Red Mark

Tray, Bun, Hand-Painted Roses, Red Mark, 12 1/2 In.	139.00
Tray, Bun, Icicle Design, Lilies In Water, Red Mark	375.00
Tray, Bun, Poppies, Green Ground, Red Mark, 13 X 9 In.	500.00
Tray, Bun, Roses, Red Mark, 12 1/2 In.	125.00
Tray, Bun, Schooner, Brown, Orange, Gold, Open Handled, Marked	750.00
Tray, Bun, Swans, Trees, Open Handled, Red Mark	800.00
Tray, Bun, Water Lilies, Handled, 13 In.	195.00
Tray, Dresser, Barnyard Scene, Icicle Mold	925.00
Tray, Dresser, Iris Mold, Green & Gold, 11 X 7 1/2 In.	259.00
Tray, Dresser, Melon Boy, Jeweled, Red Mark	1150.00
Tray, Dresser, Schooner, Red Mark, 11 1/4 In.	875.00
Tray, Dresser, Sheepherders, Red Mark	725.00
Tray, Dresser, Snowbird Pattern	475.00
Tray, Floral, Luster, Open Handled, Red Mark, 11 X 7 1/2 In.	150.00
Tray, Frosted Platinum Floral Edge, Red Mark, 12 X 6 In.	185.00
Tray, Green, Cream, Yellow, Brown, Red Mark	250.00
Tray, Mill Scene, Oval, Red Mark, 12 1/2 X 6 In.	550.00
Tray, Mill Scene, Red Mark, 11 1/2 X 7 In.	595.00
Tray, Pink, Yellow Roses, Green Ground, Satin, Red Mark, 12 1/2 In.	185.00
Tray, Portrait, Allegory Series, Signed, Marked, 7 3/4 X 4 In.	425.00
Tray, Summer Season, Scenic Ground, Iris Border	875.00
Tray, Swan, Red Mark, 12 3/4 X 7 1/2 In.	350.00
Tray, Yellow Roses, Feathery Border, Open Handled, Red Mark	189.00
Urn, Melon Eaters, Jeweled, 2 Handles	950.00
Vase, Bonnet Girl, Double Handled, 6 X 10 In.	385.00
Vase, Bud, Old Man Of The Mountain Scene, 4 5/8 In.	55.00
Vase, Cottage Scene, Red Mark, 4 In.	260.00
Vase, Farmyard Scene, Red Mark, Red Pheasant On Back, 10 In.	725.00
Vase, Floral, Jeweled, Footed Base, Marked, 10 In.	355.00
Vase, Floral, 2-Handled, Red Mark, 9 In.	350.00
Vase, Gold Handles, Prussia Mold, Vivid Design, 7 In.	239.00
Vase, Green, Red & Pink Roses, Marked, 8 In., Pair	295.00
Vase, Handled, Melon Boys, Jeweled, Red Mark, 6 In.	1100.00
Vase, Jeweled, Gold & Beading, Red Mark, 8 1/2 In.	425.00
Vase, Madame Le Brun Portrait, Marked, 7 1/2 In.	225.00
Vase, Medallion Of Pink Roses, Jeweled, Handled, Red Mark, 9 In.	400.00
Vase, Melon Eaters, Jeweled, Handles At Bottom, Red Mark, 10 In.	1375.00
Vase, Mill Scene, 6 In.	90.00
Vase, Old Man Of The Mountain, Bluebirds, Marked, 9 In.	700.00
Vase, Pheasant, 8 In.	210.00
Vase, Red & Green Floral, Red Mark, 6 In.	190.00
Vase, Rococo, Gold Handles, Flowers, Red Mark, 4 1/4 In.	235.00
Vase, Swan, Gold Footed, Double Handle, Red Mark, 10 In.	700.00
Vase, The Cage, Red, Gold Trim, 5 In.	155.00
Vase, Vivid Design, Gold Handles, 7 In.	239.00
White Satin, Flowers, Cherries, Marked, 10 1/2 In.	250.00
RS SUHL, Plate, Orange Poppies, Gold Border, 7 1/2 In., Pair	65.00

R.S.Tillowitz porcelain factory was started at Tillowitz near Silesia in 1869 by Rheinhold Schlegelmilch. Table services and ornamental pieces were made.

RS TILLOWITZ, Cake Plate, 2-Handled	35.00
Cake Set, Art Deco, 7 Piece	150.00
Dish, Candy, Poppies, Footed	28.00
Sugar & Creamer, Pheasant, Gold Design, Black	225.00
Sugar, Silesia, Covered	13.50
Teapot, Flowers, Orange	35.00
Tray, Pin, Silver Luster, Dated 1924, 9 1/2 X 7 1/4 In.	29.00
Vase, Yellow, White, & Lavender, 9 In., Pair	295.00

Rubena Verde is a Victorian glassware that was shaded from red to green. It was first made by Hobbs, Brockunier and Company of Wheeling, West Virginia, about 1890.

RUBENA VERDE, Bowl, Overshot Pattern, Ruffled, 10 In.	77.50
Bowl, 10 In.	135.00
Cruet, Inverted Thumbprint, Cut Stopper, 6 1/2 In.	295.00
Epergne, Center Trumpet In Bowl, Hanging Basket, 22 In.	325.00
Pitcher, Corset Shape, Enameled Flowers, Scalloped Rim	200.00
Pitcher, Inverted Thumbprint, 8 In.	250.00
Rose Bowl, White Florals, Gold Scrolls, 4 1/2 X 4 In.	88.00
Tumbler, Inverted Thumbprint, 4 In.	50.00
Vase, Egg Shape, Petal Feet, Enameled Chicks, 6 In.	185.00
Vase, Enameled Flowers, Ruffled Rim, Ribbed, 12 In.	235.00

Rubena is a glassware that shades from red to clear. It was first made by George Duncan and Sons of Pittsburgh, Pennsylvania, about 1885.

RUBENA, see also Pressed Glass, Royal Ivy; Pressed Glass, Royal Oak

RUBENA, Bottle, Perfume, Mistletoe Design, Frosted, Gold Trim, 3 1/4 In.	110.00
Bottle, Wine, Hallmarked Sterling Silver Rim & Lit, 12 1/2 In.	185.00
Bowl, Dessert, Serving Spoon, Hobnail, S.P.James Tufts Frame, 14 In.	450.00
Bowl, Footed, Pillar Effect, 6 1/4 In.	95.00
Bowl, Hobnail, Strawberry, Silver Plated Frame, Spoon, 14 1/2 In.	425.00
Bowl, Honeycomb, 10 In.	125.00
Butter, Artichoke Finial, Frosted Crackle, Covered	65.00
Castor, Pickle, Diamond-Quilted Pattern, White Flowers	375.00
Celery, Diamond Quilted	55.00
Cruet, Hobnail	165.00
Cruet, Inverted Thumbprint	80.00
Decanter, Wine, Swirl, Hallmarked Silver Rim & Lip, 12 1/4 In.	195.00
Dish, Sweetmeat, Ferns & Butterflies, Acid Cut	145.00
Pickle Castor, Inverted Thumbprint, Enameled Daisies, 11 In.	350.00
Pitcher, Clear Applied Handle, Overshot Glass, 5 1/2 In.	95.00
Pitcher, Cranberry To Clear, Coin Spot Design, 7 In.	135.00
Pitcher, Cranberry To Clear, Ribbed, Clear Handle, 8 In.	145.00
Pitcher, Etched Deer, Forest Scene	135.00
Pitcher, Inverted Melon Paneled, Trefoil Rim, 8 1/2 In.	165.00
Pitcher, Inverted Thumbprint, Bulbous, 6 X 7 1/2 In.	110.00
Pitcher, Water, Clear Applied Handle, Bulbous, 8 In.	115.00
Pitcher, Water, Hobb's Optic, Clear	95.00
Rose Bowl, Applied Flower, Stem, & Leaves, Overshot	95.00
Rose Bowl, Ribbed, 4 In.	60.00
Sugar Shaker	95.00
Syrup, Hobb's Optic, Etching	100.00
Syrup, Threaded	125.00
Tumbler, Embossed Swirl, Overshot Glass, 3 3/4 In.	58.00
Tumbler, Hobnail, 10-Row, Frosted, 6 1/4 In.	125.00
Tumbler, Hobnail, 10-Row, Frosted, 6 3/4 In.	110.00 To 125.00

Ruby glass is a dark red color. It was a Victorian and twentieth-century ware. The name means many different types of red glass.

RUBY GLASS, see also Cranberry Glass; Pressed Glass; Souvenir

RUBY GLASS, Basket, Coney Island, Handled, 3 1/2 X 2 1/2 In.	20.00
Berry Bowl, Nail Pattern, 8 1/2 In.Diam.	85.00
Berry Bowl, Thumbprint, Small	20.00
Berry Bowl, Thumbprint, 7 3/4 In.	52.00
Berry Set, Pleating, Pedestal Base, 5 Piece	125.00
Berry Set, Scroll With Cane Band, 6 Piece	110.00
Berry Set, Spearhead, Gold & Frosted Band, 7 Piece	100.00
Berry Set, Thumbprint, 7 Piece	195.00
Berry, Master, Thumbprint, Boat Shape, Engraving	135.00
Bottle, Castor, Thumbprint, Original Mustard Top	40.00

Bottle, Condiment, Thumbprint	60.00
Bottle, Wine, Loop & Block, Original Stopper	95.00
Bowl, Pioneer's Victoria, 7 In.	45.00
Bowl, Punch, King's Crown Pattern	250.00
Bowl, Radiant Daisy & Button, 7 In.	42.00
Box, Jewel, White Enameled Flowers, Bug, Footed, 6 X 5 1/2 In.	250.00
Butter, Beaded Swag, Covered	95.00
Butter, Block & Lattice, Covered	95.00
Butter, Button Arches, Frost Band, Gold Trim, Covered	100.00
Butter, Late Block, Covered	95.00
Butter, Loop & Block, Covered	55.00
Butter, Spearpoint Band, Covered	60.00
Candlestick, Pavonia, Gold Trim, Souvenir	45.00
Canoe, Souvenir, Springhill, N.S.	16.00
Celery, King's Crown	55.00
Celery, Thumbprint	68.00
Compote, Jelly, Sunk Honeycomb, 6 X 6 1/2 In.	110.00
Compote, Thumbprint, Etching, Scalloped Rim, 8 1/2 In.	135.00
Cordial, Louise, 1909	22.00
Cracker Jar, Melon Shape, Silver Plated Top & Handle	190.00
Creamer, Beading, Gold Trim, Lebanon, N.H., 2 3/4 In.	19.00
Creamer, Bethelem Star	28.00
Creamer, Block & Lattice	55.00
Creamer, Button Arches, Frost Band, Gold Trim	55.00
Creamer, Child's, Truncated Cube, 3 In.	13.00
Creamer, Child's, Truncated Cube, 6 In.	13.00
Creamer, Flat Diamond Box	50.00
Creamer, Heart Blank, Stained	22.50
Creamer, Hexagon Block	45.00
Creamer, Lewis & Clark	30.00
Creamer, Loop & Block	55.00
Creamer, Nail, Etched	70.00
Creamer, Pavonia	50.00 To 55.00
Creamer, Pillow Encircled	40.00
Creamer, Printed Diamond, Springfield, Mass., 4 1/4 In.	17.00
Creamer, Radiant Daisy & Button	49.00
Creamer, Red Block	45.00
Creamer, State Fair, 1914	20.00
Creamer, The Prize	45.00
Creamer, Triple Triangle	55.00
Creamer, Winona	45.00
Cruet, Beaded Swirl, With Oval Lenses	85.00
Cruet, Block & Lattice	95.00
Cruet, Block & Lattice, Ruby Bottom	125.00
Cruet, Blocked Thumbprint, Souvenir, Charles City	125.00
Cruet, Cut Flowers, Swan Head Handles, Stopper	360.00
Cruet, Sunken Honeycomb, Etched	80.00
Cruet, Vintage Pattern, Engraved To Clear, Matching Stopper	65.00
Cup & Saucer, Sea Nymphs, Gold Trim	75.00
Cup & Saucer, Thumbprint	25.00
Cup, Punch, White City, Chicago, 1905	18.00
Decanter, Cut Neck Ring, Cut Flutes, Original Stopper, 13 In.	85.00
Decanter, Looped Red Block, Matching Stopper	80.00
Decanter, Red Block Variant	110.00
Decanter, Victorian Pioneer, World's Fair, 1893	65.00
Dish, Divided, Handled	47.50
Goblet, Beaded Dart Band	23.00
Goblet, Bleeding Heart	12.00
Goblet, Block & Lattice	32.00
Goblet, Loop & Block	38.00
Goblet, Red Block	28.00 To 35.00
Goblet, Red Block, Souvenir, Battle Creek, Michigan	28.00
Goblet, Roanoke	30.00 To 35.00
Goblet, Scalloped Yoke	28.00

Goblet, Short Panel Diamonds	22.00
Goblet, Thumbprint	30.00
Goblet, Truncated Cube	30.00
Honey, Beehive	42.00
Jar, Powder, Diamond Optic, Crystal Lid	40.00
Jardiniere, Gold Design, 12 In.	95.00
Lamp, Hanging, Hall, Brass Frame	285.00
Match Holder, Royal Crystal	18.00
Mug, Button & Arches, Christmas, 1909, Lillian, 3 In.	18.50
Mug, Inverted Diamond, 3 In.	14.00
Mug, Lebanon Fair, 1916	26.00
Mug, Mosinee, Wisconsin, 4 1/2 In.	45.00
Mug, Near Cut, Coleman, Michigan, 3 In.	18.00
Mug, Pineapple Fan	65.00
Mug, Pointed Hobstar, Montreal, 2 1/2 In.	16.00
Mug, Thumbprint Base, Concord, N.H., 3 1/2 In.	18.00
Pitcher, Block & Double Bar, 2 Tumblers	185.00
Pitcher, Bulbous, Ruffled, Clear Reeded Handle	90.00
Pitcher, Milk, Hobnail	100.00
Pitcher, Milk, Job's Tears	135.00
Pitcher, Milk, King's Crown	55.00
Pitcher, Milk, The Bridge In The Glen, Sparta, New Jersey	30.00
Pitcher, Milk, Thumbprint, 8 In.	80.00
Pitcher, Tankard, Truncated Cube	95.00
Pitcher, Thumbprint, With Leaf & Berry	110.00
Pitcher, Water, Loop & Block	110.00
Pitcher, Water, Lorraine	150.00
Pitcher, Water, Nail	150.00 To 175.00
Pitcher, Water, Pillow Encircled	115.00
Pitcher, Water, Pleating Pattern	75.00
Pitcher, Water, Plume	125.00 To 155.00
Pitcher, Water, Roanoke	135.00
Pitcher, Water, Valentine	250.00
Potty, Souvenir, Brooks, Maine	18.00
Rose Bowl, Majestic	55.00
Salt & Pepper, Roman Rosette	90.00
Saltshaker, Dakota, Souvenir	20.00
Saucer, Cottage	20.00
Saucer, Thumbprint, Pair	19.00
Slipper, Gold Rim, 4 1/2 In.	40.00
Spooner, Bethlehem Star	28.00
Spooner, Button Arches, Frost Band, Gold Trim	50.00
Spooner, Pavonia	50.00
Spooner, Red Block	38.00 To 60.00
Spooner, Spearpoint, Frosted Band	50.00
Spooner, The Prize	50.00
Spooner, Thumbprint	65.00
Spooner, Zipper	15.00
Sugar & Creamer, Leaf & Star, Gold Trim	70.00
Sugar, Arched Ovals, Kutztown Fair, 1917, Open	20.00
Sugar, Checkerboard Pattern, Gold Trim	35.00
Sugar, Nail, Open	30.00
Sugar, Pavonia, Covered	65.00
Sugar, Red Block, Covered	45.00 To 56.00
Sugar, Triple Triangle, Covered	70.00
Syrup, Hexagon Block	135.00 To 185.00
Syrup, Majestic	155.00 To 165.00
Syrup, Reverse Torpedo	165.00
Syrup, Torpedo, Ruby Band	155.00
Syrup, Truncated Cube	145.00
Syrup, Zipper Borders	145.00
Table Set, Pavonia, 4 Piece	255.00
Table Set, Red Block, 4 Piece	255.00 To 265.00
Table Set, Tacoma, 4 Piece	295.00

Table Set, York Herringbone, 4 Piece 210.00
Tankard, Water, 12 In. 60.00
Toothpick, Button Arches, Gold Trim 45.00
Toothpick, Button Arches, Sadie, 1906 .... 18.00
Toothpick, Cordova 38.00
Toothpick, Elwood, Indiana 10.00
Toothpick, Heart Band .... 21.00 To 22.00
Toothpick, Iris & Meander 35.00
Toothpick, Scroll With Cane Band 45.00
Toothpick, Summit 38.00
Toothpick, Thumbprint, Etched 24.50
Toothpick, Truncated Cube 30.00
Toothpick, York Herringbone, Engraved 40.00
Toothpick, Zanesville, Chautauqua Lake 20.00
Tray, Engraved Vintage, 9 In.Diam. 25.00
Tumbler, Arches, Crozier, Iowa 27.50
Tumbler, Atlantic City, 1906 .... 22.00
Tumbler, Button Arches, Souvenir, 1909 .... 23.00
Tumbler, Diamond & Sunburst Variant 22.00
Tumbler, Frosted Leaves 25.00
Tumbler, Loop & Block .... 27.00 To 35.00
Tumbler, Nail 28.00
Tumbler, Red Block 25.00
Tumbler, Roanoke 24.00
Tumbler, Savin Rock, Connecticut, Clear Block Base, 1904 .... 35.00
Tumbler, Spearpoint Band, Frost Band, Gold Trim 32.00
Tumbler, Strawberry .... *Illus* 35.00
Tumbler, Three Story 32.00
Tumbler, Thumbprint .... 23.00 To 35.00
Tumbler, Triple Triangle 35.00
Tumbler, Whiskey, Engraved Vintage, 2 1/2 In., Set Of 4 .... 48.00
Tumbler, Whiskey, Engraved Vintage, 5 1/2 In., Set Of 4 .... 48.00
Vase, Bud, Metal Crane, C.1890, 13 3/4 In. 350.00
Vase, Globe, Rough Pontil, 10 1/4 X 10 1/4 In. 105.00
Water Set, Block & Double Bar, 5 Piece 215.00
Water Set, Block & Lattice, Bulbous Pitcher, 7 Piece 295.00
Water Set, Button Arches, Frosted Band, 7 Piece 345.00
Water Set, Checkerboard, Trace Of Gold, 5 Piece 235.00
Water Set, Dakota, Etched, 5 Piece 210.00
Water Set, Pavonia, Etched, 5 Piece 235.00
Water Set, Red Block, 7 Piece 265.00
Water Set, Thumbprint 285.00
Wine, Bull's-Eye Band, Souvenir 18.00
Wine, Button Arches .... 19.50 To 25.00
Wine, Mt.Clemens, 1900 .... 18.00
Wine, Red Block, Single Row 35.00
Wine, Teardrop 30.00
Wine, Thumbprint, Souvenir, Brainerd, Mn. 45.00
Wine, World's Fair 1893 .... 18.50
Wine, 6 Flutes 10.00

Rudolstadt was a faience factory in the Thuringia region of Germany from 1720 to about 1791. In 1854, Ernst Bohne began working in the area and in 1882, L Straus & Sons began production of luxury decorative porcelain at Rudolstadt. Collectors often refer to late pieces as Royal Rudolstadt. Late nineteenth- and early twentieth-century pieces are most commonly found today.

RUDOLSTADT, see also Kewpie
RUDOLSTADT, Bust, Lady With Crown, Jeweled Center, Blue, Royal, Mark, 15 In. 550.00
Cracker Jar, Pansies, Florals, Swirled Rib, Royal 150.00
Creamer 15.00
Creamer, Roses In Vining Design, Gold Trim, Signed, Royal 85.00

Ruby Glass, Tumbler, Strawberry

Rudolstadt, Ewer, Textured
Design, Applied Mark,
9 1/2 In.

Rudolstadt, Pitcher, Reticulated
Top, Flowers, Blue Mark, 10 In.

Ewer, Cream, Floral, Royal, 10 In.	130.00
Ewer, Multicolor Raised Flower Sprays, Ivory, Gold Trim, 7 In.	75.00
Ewer, Raised Flower Sprays, Gold Trim, Marked, Royal, 7 In.	75.00
Ewer, Textured Design, Applied Mark, 9 1/2 In. .... *Illus*	50.00
Mug & Saucer, Elf	10.00
Pitcher, Hand-Painted Flowers, Gold Handle, Royal	75.00
Pitcher, Reticulated Top, Flowers, Blue Mark, 10 In. .... *Illus*	55.00
Plate, Floral, 8 1/2 In.	45.00
Plate, Roses, Gold Rim, 8 1/2 In.	38.00
Plate, Yellow Chrysanthemums, Gold Trim, Royal, 8 1/2 In.Diam.	35.00
Teapot, Gold With Roses, Marked, Royal, 5 1/2 In.	30.00
Teapot, Individual, White Roses, Leaves, Royal, 3 1/2 In.	42.00
Tete-A-Tete, Crowned N Marks .... *Illus*	1100.00

Rudolstadt, Tete-A-Tete, Crowned N Marks

Vase, Cavaliers, Royal, 7 In. 285.00
Vase, Classical Figures, Gilt Details, Marked, 18 In., Pair 475.00
Vase, Figural, Widespread Wings, Scalloped, Gold Crest, 4 In. 85.00
Vase, Floral Design, Cobalt Blue Ground, Royal, 13 In. 195.00
Vase, Floral Design, 8 In. 45.00
Vase, Green, Lady & Dove, Royal, 7 1/2 In. 55.00
Vase, Morning Glory Tapestry, 1882-91 .... 96.00
Vase, Morning Glory, Royal, 1882 .... 96.00
Vase, Scenic, Lady Holding Dove, Royal, 7 1/2 In. 50.00

RUG, Abadeh, Bar Medallion Center, Geometric Forms, 4 1/4 X 5 1/2 Ft. 450.00
Afghan, Rust Field, 7 X 10 Ft. 625.00
Afshar, Botehs In Rust, Ivory Field, 4 Ft. 2 In. X 6 Ft. 2 In. 550.00
Afshar, Botehs, Indigo Ground, 5 Ft. 2 In. X 7 Ft. 5 In. 550.00
Aubusson, Bouquet Medallion, Buff, 12 Ft. 8 In. X 16 Ft. 1600.00
Aubusson, Petal Medallion, 15 Ft. 10 In. X 13 Ft. 7 In. 1800.00
Aubusson, Rose Bouquet Medallion, Celery Field, 7 3/4 X 8 1/4 Ft. 1800.00
Aushak, Medallion, Ivory Field, 8 Ft. 11 In. X 11 Ft. 8 In. 2800.00
Belouch, Medallions, Brown, Blue, Cream, 2 Ft. 7 In. X 5 Ft. 425.00
Bessarabian, 8 Floral Sprays, Ivory Border, 8 Ft. 10 In. X 5 Ft. 11 In. 1600.00
Bijar, Geometric Design, Blue, Ivory Trim, 3 X 8 Ft. 400.00
Bijar, Geometric Design, Ivory Trim, 4 X 8 Ft. 525.00
Bijar, Herati Design, Indigo Field, 3 Ft. X 24 Ft. 5 In. 1500.00
Bijar, 3 Ft. 5 In. X 5 Ft. 2 In. 1250.00
Cabistan, Bird Figures, 3 Ft. 2 In. X 5 Ft. 11 In. 200.00
Chinese, Floral Bouquet Corners, Rose Beige Field, 11 X 10 3/4 Ft. 550.00
Chinese, Multicolored Blossoms, Yellow Field, 3 Ft. 10 In. X 5 3/4 Ft. 325.00
Chinese, Single Dragon, Taupe Ground, 4 Ft. 2 In. X 5 3/4 Ft. 250.00
Daghestan, Prayer, Stylized Flowers, Ivory, 3 Ft. 5 In. X 4 1/2 Ft. 250.00
Fereghan, Green, Indigo, Orange, & Ivory, 9 Ft. 11 In. X 5 Ft. 3 1/2 In. 1500.00
Hamadan Kurd, Runner, 5 Ft. 4 In. X 16 Ft. 10 In. 1200.00
Hamadan, Boteh Design, Indigo Ground, 3 1/2 Ft. X 6 Ft. 5 In. 475.00
Hamadan, Camel Hair, Blue, Geometric Design, 4 X 9 Ft. 750.00
Hamadan, Camel Hair, Floral, Leaf, Brown, Gold, 10 X 10 Ft. 1900.00
Hamadan, Connected Flowerheads, Red Field, 10 Ft. 2 In. X 5 1/2 Ft. 300.00
Hamadan, Detached Sprays, Red Field, 9 1/4 X 12 Ft. 475.00
Hamadan, Floral Sprays, Red Field, 3 Ft. 8 In. X 6 Ft. 8 In. 100.00
Hamadan, Floral Sprays, Turtle Border, 8 Ft. 10 In. X 11 3/4 Ft. 500.00
Hamadan, Geometric Florals, Indigo Ground, 2 Ft. 7 In. X 5 Ft. 405.00
Hamadan, Palmettes, Rust Ground, 2 Ft. 5 In. X 3 Ft. 10 In. 175.00
Hamadan, White Medallion & Spandrels, Blue Field, 5 1/2 X 3 1/2 Ft. 160.00
Hamadan, 3 Ft. 5 In. X 5 Ft. 8 In. 500.00
Hand-Woven Birds, Trees, Llama Wool, 47 X 68 In. 55.00
Heriz, Blue Medallions, Rust Field, Ivory, Blue, 8 X 11 Ft. 2000.00
Heriz, Geometric Medallions, 2 Ft. 8 In. X 8 Ft. 4 In. 650.00
Heriz, Medallion, Red, Blue, Cream, Gold, 11 X 9 Ft. 1800.00
Hooked Center, Braided Rows Outside, Oval, 37 X 54 1/2 In. 50.00
Hooked, Abstract Design, 35 X 26 In. 95.00
Hooked, American Pictorial, Green, Brown, Beige, Horse, 24 X 39 In. 475.00
Hooked, Clamshell Edge, Multicolors, Star Center, 53 X 26 In. 135.00
Hooked, Frost Pattern, Dog On Carpet, Floral Around Center, 32 X 61 In. 225.00
Hooked, Geometric, Pinwheels, Brown & Red, Beige Ground, 65 X 35 1/2 In. 125.00
Hooked, Green & Rose, 22 1/2 X 42 1/2 In. 40.00
Hooked, Indian Brave, Brown Rib, Feathers In Hair, 19 X 29 In. 175.00
Hooked, Nautical Theme, 20th Century, Wool, 29 X 54 In. 255.00
Hooked, Pattern Of Leaves In Blue, Green Edge, 1920s, 34 X 50 1/2 In. 75.00
Hooked, Red Flower, Buds, & Stars, Gray Field, 24 X 32 In. 225.00
Hooked, Santa Claus & Reindeer Center, 31 1/2 X 39 In. ....*Illus* 450.00
Hooked, Table, Tree Of Life Design, On Burlap, American, 14 X 20 In. 165.00
Hooked, Tan Ground, Blue Border, Maine, 19th Century, 67 X 36 1/2 In. 225.00
Kapoutrang, Center Floral Medallion, Spandrels, 12 Ft. X 8 Ft. 7 In. 500.00
Kashan, Arabesque Pattern Center, Vine Border, 4 3/4 X 7 Feet 1300.00
Kashan, Mohtashem, Silk, 4 Ft. 2 In. X 6 Ft. 8 In. ....*Illus* 8500.00
Kashan, 10 1/2 X 15 1/2 Ft. 8000.00

Rug, Hooked, Santa Claus & Reindeer
Center, 31 1/2 X 39 In.

Rug, Kashan, Mohtashem, Silk,
4 Ft. 2 In. X 6 Ft. 8 In.

Kazak, Diamond Design, Blue, Rust Trim, 3 X 16 Ft.	550.00
Kazak, Hexagon Design, Green, Blue, Rust, 3 Ft. X 8 Ft. 6 In.	600.00
Kazak, Hexagon Design, Ivory Trim, 3 Ft. 8 In. X 11 Ft.	925.00
Khorasan, Petal-Formed Medallion, 10 1/3 Ft. X 13 Ft. 7 In.	1600.00
Kirman, Center Medallion, Rose, 13 Ft. 10 In. X 9 Ft. 10 In.	3500.00
Kirman, Directional Medallion, 13 Ft. 7 In. X 9 Ft. 10 In.	1500.00
Kirman, Floral Medallion Center, Salmon Border, 6 3/4 X 6 3/4 Ft.	1500.00
Kirman, Floral Medallion, Green, 8 Ft. 2 In. X 8 1/4 Ft.	625.00
Kirman, Floral Medallion, Ivory Field, 2 Ft. 10 In. X 5 Ft.	250.00
Kirman, Floral Medallion, Tan Field, 9 Ft. 8 In. X 14 Ft.	1900.00
Kirman, Flowering Sprays, Buff, 9 Ft. X 14 Ft. 2 In.	1700.00
Kirman, Ivory Ground, Blue Border, C.1855, 8 X 11 Ft.	5000.00
Kirman, Medallions, Ivory Ground, 5 Ft. 8 In. X 8 Ft. 6 In.	800.00
Kirman, Millefleurs, Ivory, 17 Ft. 4 In. X 2 Ft. 7 In.	700.00
Kirman, Overall Florals, Blue Field, 2 1/2 Ft. X 5 Ft. 2 In.	475.00
Kirman, Rose Medallion Center, Ivory Field, 10 Ft. 7 In. X 4 Ft. 11 In.	850.00
Kirman, 2 Ft. 3 In. X 4 Ft. 2 In.	160.00
Kurdish, Abstract Designs, Persimmon Ground, 6 1/2 X 6 Ft.	550.00
Kurdish, Geometric Medallions, 3 Ft. 5 In. X 15 Ft. 11 In.	900.00
Lillihan, Floral Design, Wine Ground, 5 Ft. 11 In. X 9 Ft. 7 In.	375.00
Lillihan, Floral Sprays Center, Pink Field, 5 Ft. 1 In. X 6 Ft.	100.00
Lillihan, Vines, Burgundy Field, 2 Ft. 7 In. X 6 Ft. 5 In.	300.00
Log Cabin Pattern, Geometric Multicolors, 66 X 34 1/2 In.	185.00
Mahal, Floral Design, Salmon Field, 9 Ft. X 11 Ft. 4 In.	600.00
Mahal, Floral, Rust Field, 7 Ft. 2 In. X 10 Ft. 2 In.	625.00
Needlepoint, Floral Panels, 8 Ft. 7 In. X 6 Ft. 7 In.	800.00
Oushak, Red, Green, Floral Design, Turkish, 11 Ft. 4 In. X 12 In.	1000.00
Peking, Floral Medallion, Indigo Field, 8 1/3 X 11 1/3 Ft.	800.00
Persian, Octagonal Medallion, Blue Herati Field, 5 1/2 X 3 1/2 Ft.	300.00
Portuguese, Flowering Urns, 8 Ft. 5 In. X 5 Ft. 8 In.	1200.00
Portuguese, Overall Design, 12 1/2 Ft. X 8 Ft. 10 In.	2000.00
Prayer, Oriental, 2 X 6 Ft.	750.00

Prayer, Yuruk, Brick Red, White, & Brown, 4 Ft. 7 In. X 3 Ft. 3 In. 400.00
Qasvin, Latch Hook Medallions, Rust Ground, 3 Ft. 5 In. X 6 Ft. 575.00
Qasvin, Red Field, Blue, Floral, Dark Blue Border, 18 X 10 Ft. 5800.00
Raveled Yarn, 43 X 25 In. 110.00
Rerab, Medallions, Floral Ground, 2 Ft. 11 In. X 9 Ft. 7 In. 650.00
Runner, Rag, Multistriped, 54 X 29 In. 50.00
Saraband, Boteh Design, Blue, Ivory Trim, 4 X 10 Ft. 450.00
Sarouk, Center Medallion, Russet, 8 Ft. 7 In. X 10 3/4 Ft. 1300.00
Sarouk, Floral Bouquets, Rose, 10 1/3 Ft. X 15 Ft. 10 In. 4400.00
Sarouk, Floral Sprays Center, Mulberry, 11 Ft. 5 In. X 9 Ft. 2 In. 425.00
Sarouk, Floral Sprays, Angular Border, 4 Ft. 2 In. X 6 Ft. 5 In. 1800.00
Sarouk, Floral Sprays, Burgundy, 9 Ft. X 11 Ft. 8 In. 2100.00
Sarouk, Floral Sprays, Magenta Field, Blue Border, 5 X 3 1/2 Ft. 1300.00
Sarouk, Floral Sprays, Rose Field, 7 3/4 X 9 3/4 Ft. 600.00
Sarouk, Flowering Vase, Rose Field, 4 Ft. 1 In. X 6 Ft. 4 In. 850.00
Sarouk, Red Field, Blue & Yellow, Medallion, 6 X 4 Ft. 2000.00
Sarouk, Runner, Dark Wine Red, 2 Ft. 4 In. X 22 In. 725.00
Sarouk, Wine Field, Floral, C.1925, 3 Ft. 5 In. X 4 Ft. 10 In. 2200.00
Senneh, Diamond-Shaped Medallions, Blue Field, 6 3/4 Ft. X 4 Ft. 5 In. 1150.00
Senneh, Ivory, Indigo, Mustard, & Gray, 4 1/2 X 6 1/3 Ft. 2400.00
Serab, Blue Center Medallion, Grid Design Border, 5 Ft. 2 In. X 3 Ft. 275.00
Serab, Medallions, Tan Field, 2 Ft. 11 In. X 9 Ft. 7 In. 650.00
Serabend, Boteh Design, Indigo Field, 3 1/2 X 15 1/4 Ft. 500.00
Serapi, Blue Medallion, Rust Field, Blue Trim, 9 X 12 Ft. 2800.00
Shiraz, Diamond Medallion, Ivory, Green, Blue, 6 X 8 Ft. 800.00
Shiraz, 3 Cross Medallions, 3 Ft. 11 In. X 4 Ft. 11 In. 550.00
Shirvan, Prayer, Stylized Flowers, 3 Ft. 10 In. X 5 Ft. 900.00
Shirvan, 3 Ft. 5 In. X 5 Ft. 6 In. 1900.00
Soumak, Saddlebag, Pile, & Kilim, 2 Ft. 11 In. X 4 Ft. 8 In. 125.00
Sparta, Medallions, Blue Field, 4 Ft. 7 In. X 11 Ft. 5 In. 150.00
Sparta, 6 Medallions, Dusty Rose, 11 Ft. 9 In. X 2 Ft. 8 In. 100.00
Sultanabad, Palmettes, Orange Field, 12 X 18 Ft. 2300.00
Tabriz, Allover Paisley Design, 5 Ft. 10 1/2 In. X 8 Ft. 10 In. 2500.00
Tabriz, Floral Designs, Buff Field, 3 Ft.8 In. X 6 Ft. 5 In. 475.00
Tabriz, Floral Medallion Design, Green, Beige, & Rose, 10 X 13 Ft. 5500.00
Tabriz, Hand-Woven Wool, Rumanian, 6 Ft. 5 In. X 4 Ft. 7 In. 750.00
Tekke Bokhara, 3 Ft. 3 In. X 4 Ft. 450.00
Turkoman Style, Tekke Guls On Red, 6 Ft. 7 In. X 3 Ft. 10 In. 175.00
Two Gray Hills, C.1920, Woven By Rose Arizona, 7 Ft. 5 In. X 5 1/2 Ft. 1295.00
Yomud, Stylized Gulls, Plum, 6 Ft. 7 In. X 10 Ft. 8 In. 1900.00

 *Rumrill Pottery was designed by George Rumrill of Little Rock, Arkansas. From 1930 to 1933, it was produced by the Red Wing Pottery of Red Wing, Minnesota. In 1938, production was transferred to the Shawnee Pottery, Zanesville, Ohio.*

RUMRILL, Ewer, Orange & Mottled Brown, 6 In., Pair 55.00
Vase, Art Deco Spiral Form, C.1930, 2-Handled, Green 45.00
Vase, Brown Inside, Handled, Marked, Beige Ground, 7 In. .... 25.00 To 35.00
Vase, Swan Handles, Sea Green, 8 In. 17.00

Ruskin Pottery was established in 1898 at West Smethwick, Birmingham, England. The factory worked until 1935.

RUSKIN, Bowl, Blue Glaze, Very Lightweight, 8 In.Diam. 200.00
Saltshaker, Iridescent Blue, 2 1/2 In. 45.00
Saltshaker, Mauve, 2 1/2 In. 35.00
Vase, Mottled Glaze, Blue, Cream, Purple, 14 In. 150.00

Russel Wright designed dinnerwares in modern shapes for four companies. Iroquois China Company, Harker China Company, Steubenville Pottery, and Justin Therod and Sons made dishes marked Russel Wright. The Steubenville wares, first made in 1938, are the most common today.

RUSSEL WRIGHT, Bowl, Oval, Coral, 10 In.	16.00
Casserole, Handled, Gray, Covered	35.00
Clock, Mustard Yellow Face, White Numerals, 8 X 8 In.	85.00
Cup & Saucer, American Modern, Seafoam	6.00
Cup & Saucer, Coral	6.00
Cup, Seafoam, Set Of 12	55.00
Dish, Nut, Coral, Pair	4.00
Pitcher, Chartreuse	18.00
Pitcher, Steubenville, Blue	24.00
Pitcher, Water, Gray & Green, 10 1/2 In.	10.00
Plate, Dinner, Coral	5.00
Platter, Round, Coral, 13 In.	16.00
Shaker, Coral	10.00
Sugar, Covered, Brown	30.00
Sugar, Covered, Rust	30.00
Teapot, Coral	20.00

Sabino glass was made in the 1920s and 1930s in Paris, France. Founded by Marius-Ernest Sabino, the firm was noted for Art Deco lamps, vases, nudes, figures, and animals in clear, colored, and opalescent glass. Production stopped during World War II, but resumed in the 1960s with manufacture of nudes and small opalescent glass animals. The new pieces are a slightly different color and can be recognized.

SABINO, Bowl, Seaweed & Shell Design, Marked, Two 4 In.Bowls, 12 In.	225.00
Figurine, Christ, Sacred Heart, 8 In.	300.00
Lamp, Boudoir, Art Deco, Frosted, 1930	95.00
Perfume, Opalescent, 5 Dancing Ladies, 6 3/4 In., Pair	135.00 To 155.00
Vase, Topaz, Leaves, Art Deco, Signed, 5 In., Pair	235.00

Salopian ware was made by the Caughley factory of England during the eighteenth century. The early pieces were in blue and white with some colored decorations. Many of the pieces called Salopian are elaborate color-transfer decorated tablewares made during the late nineteenth century.

SALOPIAN, Cup & Saucer, Turquoise Ground, Transfer Pattern	150.00
Plate, Green, View Of Bridge, 8 In.	100.00
SALT & PEPPER, see Pressed Glass; Porcelain; etc.	

Salt glaze is a hard, shiny glaze that was developed for pottery during the eighteenth century. It is still being made.

SALT GLAZE, Bowl, Milk, Flowers, 19th Century, Cobalt Blue, 9 3/4 In.Diam.	105.00
Butter, Stenciled, Covered, Blue & White, 10 Pound	75.00
Candleholder, Gray & Blue, 3 In.	18.00
Crock, Cobalt Blue Chick, New York, 19th Century, 6 1/2 In.	195.00
Figurine, Cat, Hand-Painted Cobalt Blue, 4 1/2 In.	9.50
Figurine, Rooster, Hand-Painted, 5 1/2 In.	11.00
Jar, Cracker, Maple Leaf Design, Blue & White	110.00
Jar, R.F.Reppert, Greensboro, Pa., Cobalt Blue, 8 In.	90.00
Jug, Vermont Spring Company, 5 Gallon	95.00
Pitcher, Flowers & Leaves, Pennsylvania, Cobalt Blue, 10 1/2 In.	140.00
Pitcher, Good Samaritan Scene, Pewter Lid, Marked, 6 In.	250.00
Salt Box, Blue & White	220.00
Strainer, Blue & White	75.00
SAMPLER, see Textile, Sampler	

Samson and Company, a French firm specializing in the reproduction of collectible wares of many countries and periods, was founded in Paris in the early nineteenth century. Chelsea, Meissen, Famille Verte, and Oriental Lowestoft are some of the wares that have been reproduced by the company. The company uses a variety of marks to distinguish its reproductions. It is still in operation.

SAMSON, Box, Hunt Scene, Pink, White Interior, Signed, 1 1/8 X 1 3/4 In. 385.00
  Jar, Temple, Chinoiserie Reserve, Claret Ground, Marked, Pair 1100.00
  Plateau, Mirrored, Reflecting Pool, Garden, Wooden Base, 32 In. 600.00

Sand babies were used as decorations on a line of children's dishes made by the Royal Bayreuth China Company. The children are playing at the seaside. Collectors use the names "sand babies" and "beach babies" interchangeably.

SAND BABIES, Bell, Original Clapper 285.00
  Bowl, Cereal, Blue Mark, 7 1/2 In. 125.00
  Creamer, Blue Mark, 3 1/4 In. ....*Illus* 75.00
  Tray, Pin, Blue Mark, 3 1/2 X 5 In. 90.00
  Tray, Pin, 6-Sided, Blue Mark 65.00
  Tray, Pin, 8-Sided, Small 75.00
  Vase, Blue Mark, 4 1/2 In. 95.00

Sandwich glass is any one of the myriad types of glass made by the Boston and Sandwich Glass Works in Sandwich, Massachusetts, between 1825 and 1888. It is often very difficult to be sure whether a piece was really made at the Sandwich factory because so many types were made there and similar pieces were made at other glass factories.
  SANDWICH GLASS, see also Pressed Glass, etc.
SANDWICH GLASS, Bottle, Cologne, 12 Panel, Emerald Green, 4 1/4 In. 90.00
  Bottle, Scent, Amethyst, Pewter Stopper, 2 5/8 In. 70.00
  Bottle, Scent, Lay Down Sea Horse, Trailings, 2 1/2 In. 125.00
  Bottle, Scent, Peacock, Original Screw Top, 2 1/4 In. 65.00
  Bottle, Whimsey, Applied Rigaree, Spiral Rosette, C.1840 .... 500.00
  Cake Stand, Amethyst Smocking, Low, 8 1/2 In.Diam. 750.00
  Candlestick, Amethyst, Single, 7 1/2 In. 450.00
  Candlestick, Dolphin, Double Step, Canary Yellow, Pair 975.00
  Candlestick, Double Step, Vaseline Yellow, 9 3/4 In., Pair 650.00
  Candlestick, Grecian Column, Double Step, Clambroth, Pair 375.00
  Candlestick, Hexagonal Form, 1835, Amethyst, 7 1/2 In., Pair 750.00
  Candlestick, Petal & Loop, Clambroth, 1800s, 7 In. 295.00
  Candlestick, Petal & Loop, Light Blue, C.1850, 7 In. 295.00
  Candlestick, Petal & Loop, Vaseline Yellow, 7 In., Pair 425.00
  Candlestick, 6 Knobs On Cup Rim, Loop, C.1840, 7 In. 100.00
  Compote, Crackle Glass, 4 1/2 X 5 3/4 In. 45.00
  Compote, Fern Pattern, Sunburst Ribbed Center, 4 1/2 In. 25.00
  Compote, Shields & Pine Trees, Knob Stem, 5 In. 50.00
  Creamer, Lacy, Miniature 60.00
  Darner, Opaque Lavender & Blue, 5 In. 155.00
  Decanter, Ribbed Ivy, Original Tulip Stopper, Flint 75.00
  Decanter, Shell & Ribbing, C.1840, 6 In., Pair 220.00
  Decanter, Stippled, Frosted 110.00
  Goblet, Bull's-Eye Pattern, Flint 70.00
  Goblet, Cable Pattern, Flint 45.00
  Goblet, Diamond Point Pattern, Flint 40.00
  Goblet, Honeycomb, Opalescent, Flint, 6 In. 225.00
  Goblet, Paneled Ovals Pattern, Flint 35.00
  Jar, Pomade, Basket Weave Pattern, Covered, Opaque Blue 295.00
  Jar, Pomade, Figural, Muzzled Bear, C.1845, Amethyst, 3 In. 200.00
    SANDWICH GLASS, LAMP, see Lamp
  Lemonade Set, Engraved Water Lilies & Heron, Threaded, 7 In. 400.00
  Mantelpiece, Amber Bowl, Cameo Opalescent, 14 In. 175.00

Pitcher, Amber Reeded Handle, Blue Overshot, 5 1/2 In.	90.00
Pitcher, Hobnail, Applied Handle, Clear, C.1850, 9 In.	125.00
Pitcher, Overshot, Bulbous, Reeded Handle	110.00
Pitcher, Rope Handle Encircles Body, Square Top, Amber	495.00
Salt, Christmas, Original Top & Agitator, Dated 1877	95.00
Saucer, Peacock Eye, Flint, 4 1/2 In.	30.00
Spill, Star, Flint	35.00
Spooner, Beaded Mirror	55.00
Tieback, Curtain, Opalescent, 3 In.Diam., Pair	50.00
Tray, Lacy Butterfly, 8 X 5 1/4 In.	225.00
Tumbler, Tapered, Hearts Around Top, Amethyst, 3 1/2 In.	120.00
Vase, Bigler Pattern, Vaseline Yellow, 9 3/4 In.	325.00
Vase, Block & Punty, 1835-45, Amethyst, 9 1/2 In., Pair	500.00
Vase, Hyacinth, Cobalt Blue, 8 3/4 In.	65.00
Vase, Hyacinth, Free-Blown, Infolded Rim, Sapphire Blue, 8 In.	145.00
Vase, Icicle, 3-Footed Metal Stand, Blue, 12 1/2 In.	70.00
Vase, Loop Pattern, Footed, C.1840, 5 3/4 In.	425.00
Vase, Loop, Marble Base, Gauffered Rim, Blue, 9 1/2 In.	375.00
Vase, Melon Ribbed, Scalloped, Clear, 8 1/2 In.	265.00
Vase, Tulip, 8 Petals On Sides, Opalescent Blue	750.00
Whiskey Taster, Lacy, Scalloped Foot, Emerald Green	175.00

Sarreguemines

Sarreguemines pottery was first made in Lorraine, France, about 1770. Most of the pieces found today date from the late nineteenth century.

SARREGUEMINES, see also Kate Greenaway

SARREGUEMINES, Girl & Geese, Signed H.Loux, 8 In.	32.00
Plate, Calendar, July, Boys Fishing	20.00
Plate, Comical Monkey, Pierced, 8 In.	28.50
Plate, Lime To Brown Latticework, Grapevines, Marked, 7 In.	28.00
Plate, Nursery, Each Different, Set Of 6	69.00
Vase, Lilies, Snake & Apple Design, 15 3/8 In., Pair	295.00

Satin glass is a late nineteenth-century art glass. It has a dull finish that is caused by a hydrofluoric acid vapor treatment. Satin glass was made in many colors and sometimes had applied decorations.

SATIN GLASS, Basket, Turquoise Ground, Gold Design, Silver Rim, 5 X 5 In.	195.00
Biscuit Jar, Blown-Out Sections, Metal Lid	110.00
Biscuit Jar, Blown-Out Sections, Silver Plated Lid	145.00
Biscuit Jar, Flowers, Silver Plated Cover, Bail, & Rim, Blue	175.00
Biscuit Jar, Silver Plated Top & Handle, Pink	165.00
Bottle, Perfume, Hand-Painted Flower, Blue, 5 In.	75.00
Bowl, Blue, 3 1/2 In.	73.00
Bowl, Rainbow Mother-Of-Pearl, Crimped, 4 3/8 X 6 In.	995.00
Box, Diamond-Quilted, Blue, 4 3/4 In.	70.00
Bride's Bowl, Frosted Edging, Enameled & Coral Cherries, 12 In.	395.00
Compote, Blue, White Outside, Silver Plated Base	135.00
Compote, Ruffled, Pink Overlay, Silver Plated Foot, 5 5/8 In.	125.00
Cracker Jar, Beaded Drape, Red	235.00
Cracker Jar, Molded Shell & Seaweed Design, Pink, Silver Top	210.00
Cruet, Pink, Quilted	45.00
Dish, Flowers, Gold & Green Foliage, Purple, 10 3/4 In.Diam.	235.00
Ewer, Enameled Birds, Camphor Handle, Blue, 9 In.	245.00
Ewer, Forget-Me-Nots, Melon Sections, Pink, 8 1/4 In.	95.00
Ewer, Melon-Ribbed, Aqua, Gold & Brown Enameling, 9 In.	135.00
Ewer, Pink To White, Frosted Thorn Handle, 8 1/4 X 5 In.	165.00
Ewer, Robin's-Egg Blue, C.1885, Lined In White, 8 In.	135.00
Ewer, Rose & Orange Shading To Pink, Thorn Handle, 9 In.	175.00
Ewer, 2 Birds, Frosted Handles, Shaded Pink, 8 1/2 In., Pair	195.00
Inkwell, Swirl Design, Blue, Butterflies, 3 1/4 In.	225.00
Jar, Sweetmeat, Diamond-Quilted, White Lining, Pink, 5 1/4 In.	295.00

Item	Price
Lamp, Fairy, Diamond-Quilted Mother-Of-Pearl, Marked, 3 3/4 In.	295.00
Lamp, Fairy, Ratching Ruffled Base, Mother-Of-Pearl, 5 In.	425.00
Lamp, Fairy, Ruffled Top, Lemon Yellow, Clarke Base, 6 In.	225.00
Lamp, Fairy, White	35.00
Lamp, Mauve, Scrolled Leaf Pattern, Nutmeg Burner, 8 In.	225.00
Lamp, Rose & White, 9 In.	250.00
Mustard, Ruffle & Bead Design, Pink	100.00
Pitcher, Amber, Polka Dot, Applied Threaded Handle, 9 1/2 In.	250.00
Pitcher, Hobnail, Raspberry Ruffled Top, Caramel Handle, 9 In.	180.00
Pitcher, Quilted, Pink, 7 1/2 In.	190.00
Rose Bowl, Apple Green Overlay, Enameled Flowers, 3 3/4 In.	110.00
Rose Bowl, Blue Overlay, Embossed Flowers, White Lining, 4 In.	110.00
Rose Bowl, Blue Overlay, White Lining, Leaf Feet, 4 1/2 In.	135.00
Rose Bowl, Crimped, Yellow, 3 1/2 In.	45.00
Rose Bowl, Diamond-Quilted, Cut Velvet, White Lining, 3 1/4 In.	165.00
Rose Bowl, Enameled, Gold Trim, Pink Case, 6 In.	165.00
Rose Bowl, Italian To Dark Blue, 3 1/2 In.	50.00
Rose Bowl, Pinching In Ruffled Top, 3 1/4 In.	50.00
Rose Bowl, Pink Ribbon, Gold Prunus, Wafer Foot, 3 1/8 In.	335.00
Rose Bowl, Pink, 3 1/2 In.	73.00
Rose Bowl, Shaded Yellow	55.00
Rose Bowl, Shell & Seaweed, Blue To Dark Blue	175.00
Rose Bowl, Tree Of Life Pattern, Berry Pontil, 5 1/2 In.	100.00
Rose Bowl, Yellow Ruffled Top, Cream Body	79.00
Rose Bowl, Yellow, 4 1/4 X 4 3/4 In.	75.00
Salt & Pepper, Egg Shape, Columbian Exposition, 1893, Pink	135.00
Salt & Pepper, Scroll & Bulge	50.00
Sugar & Spooner, Fleurette Pattern, Silver Plated Tops	395.00
Sugar Shaker, Melon Ribbed, Original Lid	75.00
Sugar, Coreopsis, Enameled Flowers, Silver Plated Top	145.00
Syrup, Guttate, Pink	185.0C
Vase, Balustrade Shape, Butterscotch To Pale Yellow, 9 In.	160.00
Vase, Bud, Rose To Pink, 5 3/4 X 3 1/2 In., Pair	185.00
Vase, Burnt Orange, Random Markings, 9 X 5 In.	138.00
Vase, Butterscotch To Pale Yellow, 8 In.	175.00
Vase, Camphor Feet, Ruffled, Enameled Flowers, Apricot, 9 In.	210.00
Vase, Cut Velvet Ruffled Top, Diamond-Quilted, 7 In.	195.00
Vase, Diamond Gilded, Medium Blue, Ruffled Top, 9 In.	185.00
Vase, Diamond Pattern, Pinched, Pink, 7 1/4 In., Pair	170.00
Vase, Diamond-Quilted, Applied Camphor Petal Feet, 8 In.	95.00
Vase, Diamond-Quilted, Blue, 10 1/4 X 5 1/4 In.	195.00
Vase, Diamond-Quilted, Floral Enamel Design, 4 1/4 In.	70.00
Vase, Diamond-Quilted, White & Yellow, 7 1/2 In.	150.00
Vase, Diamond-Quilted, White Interior, 4 3/4 In.	90.00
Vase, Enameled Flowers, White Inside, Blue & Yellow, 9 1/2 In.	95.00
Vase, Enameled Flowers, 3-Petal Top, Peach Overlay, 10 In.	110.00
Vase, Herringbone Quilted, Light Blue, 7 In.	150.00
Vase, Herringbone, Applied Rigaree Tie, Apricot, 6 In.	115.00
Vase, Herringbone, Ruffled, Original Price Label, 7 In.	225.00
Vase, Melon Ribbed Base, Pink To Raspberry At Top, 12 1/4 In.	185.00
Vase, Moss Rose Enameling, Fluted, Peach Overlay, 10 1/2 In.	195.00
Vase, Mother-Of-Pearl, Pink Moire, 7 3/4 In.	165.00
Vase, Peachblow, Lace De Boheme Cameo, C.1880, 9 In.	275.00
Vase, Pinch Sided, Shaded Blues, Yellow Floral, 10 In.	340.00
Vase, Pink Diamond, Ruffled Top, 13 In.	128.00
Vase, Ruffled & Flared, Fluted Sides, 11 In.	60.00
Vase, Trumpet, Thorn Overlay, Pink Liner, 14 1/2 In.	650.00
Vase, White To Yellow, Quilted, Footed, 7 1/4 In.	55.00
Water Set, Herringbone, 5 Mother-Of-Pearl Tumblers, Blue	725.00

SATIN GLASS, WEBB, see Webb

Satsuma is a Japanese pottery with a distinctive creamy beige crackled glaze. Most of the pieces were decorated with blue, red, green, orange, or gold.

Almost all the Satsuma found today was made after 1860. Japanese faces are often a part of the decorative scheme.

SATSUMA, Bowl, Center Kuanyu Surrounded By Arhats, 19th Century, 9 3/4 In. 400.00
Bowl, Deep Blue, Gold Scenes, Trees, Blue Leaves, Signed, 4 In. 150.00
Bowl, Design Outside & Inside, C.1880, 7 X 12 In.Diam. 425.00
Bowl, Diaper & Flowers, Mountain Scene, 4 1/2 X 3 In. 490.00
Bowl, Priests, Warriors, 1870-80, Signed, 7 X 5 1/2 In. 150.00
Bowl, Thousand Faces, C.1900, 10 In.Diam. 145.00
Bowl, 2 Warriors, Crackle, Gold Trim, 9 3/4 In.Diam. 150.00
Box, Women, Men, & Temples, 1 3/4 X 4 1/2 In.Diam. 375.00
Caddy, Bird On Prunus, Brocade Work On Lid & Handles, 5 1/2 In. 165.00
Cake Server, Signed, 8 Signed Plates, Server 7 1/2 In. 750.00
Charger, Figural, Designed Border, C.1880, 8 1/2 In. 110.00
Charger, Landscape Scene, Diaper Design, 13 In. 250.00
Cocoa Pot, Gaudy Cobalt, Red Designs, Oriental Man, Fan 85.00
Cocoa Set, Groups Of Children, Tan, Gold, & Red, 13 Piece 275.00
Cocoa Set, Tan, Gold & Red Design, Group Of Children 275.00
Coffeepot, Cobalt Blue, Gold Design, Figural Scene, 10 In. 225.00
Cracker Jar, Blown-Out, Scenic, 11 In. 155.00
Cracker Jar, Melon Shape, Oriental Figures, Gold Trim 200.00
Cup & Saucer, Thousand Faces 115.00
Cup & Saucer, White Dragon Handle, Men On Cup & Saucer 159.00
Cup, Chocolate, Warrior, Geishas, Footed 13.00
Demitasse Set, Dragon Spout & Finials, Green Wreath, 6 Piece 80.00
Dish, Warriors At Combat, Riverbank, Shell Form, 6 3/4 In.Long 400.00
Dragon Boat, Seven Gods Of Happiness, Blue & Gold, 11 X 5 X 11 In. 480.00
Ewer, Roses, Gold Trim, 9 1/4 In. 175.00
Figurine, Bijin, Kimono, Left Arm Raised, 19th Century, 13 In. 1600.00
Figurine, Ebisu 1350.00
Incense Burner, Long Legs, 3 1/2 In. 325.00
Incense Burner, Scene Of Flowers & Trees, Gold, Signed, 5 3/4 In. 700.00
Incense Burner, 3 Samurai, Landscape, Gilt Trim, Marked, 5 In. 650.00
Jar, Bird On Prunus Tree, Brocade On Lid, 2-Handled, 5 1/2 In. 160.00
Jar, Rose Petal, Figural Scene, Diaper Pattern, 5 In. 125.00
Jar, Temple, Laughing Face Handle, Dragon Form, Red, Black, 12 In. 250.00
Lamp, Figural, Coach, Man, & Horse, Silk Shade 35.00
Luncheon Set, C.1855, 14 Piece 250.00
Pitcher & Bowl, Gold & Green Chrysanthemums, Swan's Neck Handle 750.00
Pitcher, Duck Head Handle, Gold & Enamel, 6 In. ....*Illus* 250.00
Pitcher, Figural, Cat-Shaped, Crouching, Brown, Blue Collar 225.00
Plate, Gilded & Painted Flowers, Tan Ground, C.1880, Signed, 10 In. 125.00
Plate, Kwannon & 2 Arhats, Gold Crest Mark, 7 1/4 In., Set Of 4 .... 38.00
Plate, Taisho Period, House Of Satsuma Mark 35.00

Satsuma, Pitcher, Duck Head Handle,
Gold & Enamel, 6 In.

Stand, Vase, Lion's Head On 3 Legs, 1880, Signed, 4 1/2 In.Wide 75.00
Tea Caddy, Beige Ground, Diaper & Figural Design, C.1885 .... 165.00
Tea Set, Bamboo Trees In Gold Leaf, 21 Piece 295.00
Tea Set, Blue & White Prunus, Vines, Leaves, 6 Cups & Saucers, 16 Pc. 235.00
Tea Set, Dragon Spouts, 1920-30, 18 Piece 150.00
Tea Set, Garden Scene, Gold Scrollwork, 2 Cups & Saucers 145.00
Tea Set, People At Various Tasks, Gold Work, 2 Cups & Saucers 135.00
Tea Set, Pink Flowers, Blue Ground, 6 Cups & Saucers, 15 Piece 235.00
Tea Set, Showa Period, Dragon Finials & Spouts, 18 Pieces 175.00
Teapot, Bamboo Handle & Spout, Bird, Butterfly, C.1886, 5 In. 150.00
Teapot, Elephant, Pagoda Finial 30.00
Teapot, Funnel Shape, Side Handle, Figures, 4 In. 110.00
Teapot, Pink & White Enameled Flowers, Gold Trim 50.00
Tureen, Soup, Matching Underplate, C.1880, Gilded, 15 In.Long 870.00
Urn, Winged Griffins, Beige, Peonies, Orange, Signed, 10 In. 135.00
Vase, Awata, Large Lilies, 14 In., Pair 260.00
Vase, Cobalt & Gold, Flowers & Scenes, Figures 90.00
Vase, Cobalt Panels, Geisha Front, 12 In. 140.00
Vase, Courtyard Scene, Blue, Brown, Green, 1915, 12 In. 150.00
Vase, Diaper Pattern, Figural Geisha, Gold Blossoms, 9 In. 130.00
Vase, Dragon Among Frieze Of Arhats, Pear Shape, Signed, 7 1/2 In. 300.00
Vase, Enameled Wisteria, Gold Leaves, Birds, C.1900, 9 3/4 2 In. 160.00
Vase, Figural Handle, Floral Ground, Signed, 23 X 11 In. 500.00
Vase, Figural, Golds, 25 In. 450.00
Vase, Figures & Flowers, C.1920, Gold Trim, 11 1/2 In. 100.00
Vase, Figures, Beading, 2-Handled, 16 X 8 In. 298.00
Vase, Figures, Flowers, C.1920, Gold Trim, 11 1/2 In. 100.00
Vase, Figurines, Elephants, High Relief, 12 In., Pair 425.00
Vase, Fish Decoration, Rust, Gold Branches, 12 1/4 In. 75.00
Vase, Floral Design, Gold Accents, Green Ground, 17 1/2 In. 225.00
Vase, Floral Rim, Diaper Design, Warrior Scene, 15 1/2 In., Pair 600.00
Vase, Flower Design, Double Handled, 19 In. 245.00
Vase, Foo Dogs On Bulbous Part, Dragon On Neck, Olive, 15 1/2 In. 195.00
Vase, Footed, Handles, C.1915, 9 1/2 In. 95.00
Vase, Garden Scene, Men & Woman, 4 In. 395.00
Vase, Geisha Holding Basket, Green, Rust, Gold, 12 1/2 In. 85.00
Vase, Gosu Blue Rim, Blue Mums, Edo Period, 8 3/4 X 6 1/4 In. 150.00
Vase, Ladies On Front & Back, Blue & Gold Trim, 6 1/2 In., Pair 695.00
Vase, Leaves Outline In Gold Beading, C.1915, Cobalt Blue, 15 In. 125.00
Vase, Man & Woman In Cartouches, Floral, 7 1/2 In. 695.00
Vase, Moriage Design, C.1870, 15 In. 110.00
Vase, Niskikide Diaper Pattern, Teacher, Scholars, Beige, 9 In. 175.00
Vase, One Thousand Butterflies, 2 1/2 X 3 1/2 In., Pair 395.00
Vase, Oriental Men, Burnt Orange & Blue, Ivory Ground, 10 In. 135.00
Vase, Ovoid Form, Chrysanthemum Design, 8 3/4 In., Pair 140.00
Vase, Priest Riding Dragon Over Waves, Gold Trim & Beading, 6 In. 24.00
Vase, Rings On Neck, Gold Trim, 1890, 7 1/2 In. 65.00
Vase, Roses, Enameled, Handled, 14 3/4 In. 75.00
Vase, Scenes Of Men & Women, Cartouches, Floral & Diaper, 7 1/2 In. 695.00
Vase, Scenic With Figurines, Golds, 1890, 23 1/2 X 10 In. 650.00
Vase, Seashells & Stylized Wave, Coral Forms, Signed, 12 In. 150.00
Vase, Seated Arhats & Kwannon, Gold & Enamel, 12 1/2 In., Pair 1250.00
Vase, Star-Shaped Medallions, Gilt Foliate Ground, 6 In. 220.00
Vase, Students & Scholar, 2 1/2 In. 385.00
Vase, Temple, Oviform Body, Bale Handles, 24 In., Pair 900.00
Vase, Warriors & Poet, Signed, 12 X 7 In. 300.00
Vase, Warriors Design, 4 3/4 In. 275.00
Vase, Waterfowl Design, 3 1/2 In. 300.00
Vase, Wisteria Design, 12 In. 495.00
Vase, Wisteria Leaves, Gold, Butterflies, Red & Gold, 2 1/2 In. 300.00
Vase, Wisteria Vine & Flowers, Red Reign Mark, 6 In., Pair 650.00
Vase, Woman & Man, Florals, Beading, Handled, 12 In. 125.00
Vase, Women In Garden, Blue, Gold, Signed, 25 In. 550.00

Vase, Women Scene, Gold On Cobalt Blue, 12 In., Pair 1200.00

SCALE, Apothecary, Brass Fulcrum Arm, Pans, Brass, Iron, & Tin, 17 1/4 In. 225.00
Apothecary, Iron Beam Balance, Glass Pans, Civil War, Box 85.00
Assay Pans, Calibration, Control Marks, C.1850, California Gold Rush 40.00
Balance, Diamond, Weights, Tweezers, Scoop, Teakwood Case, 1 Pt.Thru 200 .... 134.50
Balance, Frary Improved Spring, Calibrated To 50 Pounds, 12 In. 30.00
Balance, Marked J.M.Dow, New York 350.00
Balance, Marked Pelouze Mfg.Co., Chicago, 9 In. 25.00
Balance, Penna. & N.Y.C., Nickel Plated Brass Top, 13 1/2 X 5 1/2 In. 45.00
Brass Pan, Buffalo Brand, Cast Iron, 29 X 14 X 22 In. 125.00
Butter, Handmade, Hangs On Nail, All Wood, 37 In. 95.00
Candy Store, Buffalo, Polished Brass Tray & Measuring Bar 69.50
Candy, Marked Pelouze, 1915, Cast Iron 35.00
Chatillon, Brass Face, 1892 .... 80.00
Chatillon, Heavy-Duty, Ironclad 12.00
Columbia, Candy Store, Glass Front, Walnut, 6 1/2 X 1 3/4 Ft. 575.00
Counter, Stimpson, Large 135.00
Cradle Type, Scoop, Brass, 11 X 18 In. 30.00
Egg, Jiffy Way, Lithograph, Tin 22.50
Egg, Oakes Mfg.Co., Tipton, Indiana, Black, Tin 15.00
Fairbanks, Brass Weight, Pan, & Measure Bar 60.00
Fairbanks, Fishtail, P.O.Dept. 40.00
Fairbanks, U.S.Post Office, Brass Pan, Arm, & Weight, Cast-Iron Base 165.00
Hanging, Salter's Improved Spring Balance, Brass Face, 24 Pounds 18.00
Howe, Porcelain Tray, Brass Bar Weight Face, Old Red Paint 95.00
Huckster, Brass, 8 1/2 In. 15.00
Jockey, C.1860, English 4500.00
Kitchen, Chatillon, Grams 15.00
Letter, Inkstand, Victorian, English, Brass, 9 1/2 X 4 1/2 In. 350.00
Letter, 2 Sets Of Weights, English, Mahogany Base, 6 X 10 In. 245.00
Map, Boxwood, 3 X 6 In. 55.00
Medicine, Separate Gram Weights, Counter Type 95.00
Nude Child, Scales Attached To Head, Brass, 6 1/2 X 6 1/2 In. 40.00
Paper, Arc-Shaped, Marked Cornelius Kahlen, N.Y., Brass & Iron 175.00
Parcel Post, Lander, Frary & Clark, Connecticut, To 20 Pounds 50.00
Parcel Post, Pelouze Mfg.Co. 10.00
Pendulum Balance, Letter Clip, Small 100.00
Pocket, Balance, Brass 55.00
Postage, 1904 .... 23.00
Postal, Fairbanks, Dated 1888, Cast Iron & Brass, 3 1/4 X 4 1/2 In. 85.00
Postal, Ideal, Zone & Cost Schedules 42.00
Postal, Marvel, Cents, Olive Green, Metal 25.00
Postal, Platform, Spring 16.00
Postal, The Precision, Several Schedules 60.00
Postal, 2 Cents Per Ounce 40.00
Potato, Original Green Paint, Large 165.00
Prescription, 18 Assorted Brass Weights 120.00
Rocker Balance, Harrison 85.00
Spring Balance, Brass Face, Calibrated To 24 Pounds, Iron, 10 3/4 In. 22.50
Spring, Chatillon, 18 Ounce 4.00
Spring, Eagle, Brass Faced, Hanging 14.00
Spring, Hanging, Brass Faced, Star Touchmark, Brass, 8 1/2 In. 20.00
Spring, Landers, New York, 40 Pounds 15.00
Steelyard, Bennis & Call Co. 15.00
Steelyard, Weight & Hooks, 16 1/4 In. 12.50
Steelyard, 2 Weights & Hooks, Cast Iron 17.00
Store, Copper Pans, Weights, 10 X 5 1/2 X 6 In. 65.00
Store, Trefoil Base, 2 Weights, Cast Iron, 10 X 20 In. 65.00
Tea, Counter Top, Pan, Brass Base, C.1880, Base 4 1/4 X 11 1/4 In. 75.00
Trener, Weighs To 4 Pounds, Brass Arm & Scoop 90.00
Weighs & Tells Fortune 175.00
650 Kilo Calibrated, Upright, Round Porcelain Face 65.00

Schafer & Vater, makers of small ceramic items, are best known for their amusing figurals. The factory was located in Volkstedt, Germany, from 1890 to 1917.

SCHAFER & VATER, Bottle, Merry Christmas, Santa Claus Holding Tree	125.00
Bottle, One Of The Boys, Man On Bar Stool, 7 In.	95.00
Bottle, Poison, Skeleton In Cloak, Brown, 3 Skulls	138.00
Bottle, Uncle Sam, Standing Profile, Multicolor, 6 In.	125.00
Box, Trinket, Bisque, Pink, White Cupid, Green Ground, 2 In.	55.00
Box, Trinket, Pink, White Cupid, Green Relief, 2 1/4 In.	55.00
Creamer, Godmother, Fairy, Blue, 4 In.	55.00
Creamer, Maid, Blue, 4 In.	65.00
Creamer, Maid, Multicolor, 3 1/2 In.	55.00
Creamer, Mother Goose, Multicolor, 3 1/2 In.	125.00
Creamer, Oriental Bird, Multicolor, 5 In.	115.00
Hair Receiver, Ladies' Faces, Jeweling, Triangular	90.00
Hatpin Holder, Bisque, Ladies' Faces In Relief, Jeweling	150.00
Match Holder, Man With Violin, Multicolor, 4 In.	125.00

Schneider

Schneider Glassworks was founded in 1903 at Epinay-sur-Seine, France, by Charles and Ernest Schneider. Art glass was made between 1903 and 1930. The company still produces clear crystal glass.

SCHNEIDER, Bowl, Bulbous, White & Orange, 4 1/4 X 3 1/4 In.	65.00
Bowl, Centerpiece, Mottled, Wrought-Iron Holder, Signed, 10 In.	295.00
Bowl, Mottled Sides, C.1925, Magenta Ground, Signed, 9 1/4 In.	150.00
Compote, Hollow Standard, Amethyst Base, 6 In.	600.00
Pitcher, Pink, White, & Dark Maroon, Label	290.00
Vase, Bubbly, Orange, Signed, 12 In.	395.00
Vase, Mottled, Hammered Iron Cagework, 11 In.	300.00
Vase, Orange, Grape Center, Green Bottom, Signed, 10 In.	150.00
Vase, Pillow Shape, Pink, Amethyst, & Yellow, Signed, 7 1/4 In.Wide	265.00
Vase, Powder Blue Shading To Plum, Signed, 8 In.	295.00
Vase, Red & Brown, Tortoiseshell Exterior, Signed, 7 In.	135.00
Vase, Signed, Moss Agate, 18 In.	160.00

Scrimshaw is bone or ivory or whale's teeth carved by sailors and others for entertainment during the sailing-ship days. Some scrimshaw was carved as early as 1800.

SCRIMSHAW, see also Nautical

SCRIMSHAW, Battle Of Bunker Hill, 8 In.	200.00
Cane, Whalebone, Turk's Head Knob, Brass Base, 36 1/2 In.	230.00
Cribbage Board, Elephant Tusk, Engraved Ship, 22 In.	400.00
Cribbage Board, Walrus Tusk, Engraved With Seals, 20 1/2 In.	500.00
Hunting Horn, French & Indian War, Bird, Cannon, Flags, 9 1/2 In.	325.00
Mounted, Brass Socket, Dated 1818, 3 1/2 In.	145.00
Spoon, Salt, Ivory	15.00
Tooth, Woman, Victorian Dress, Holding Fan, Red Highlights, 7 In.	300.00
Tray, Pen, Whalebone, Engraved, 6 In.	125.00
Turtle Shell, Flags, Eagle, Washington, Mottoes, Signed, 24 X 18 In.	3000.00
Walrus Tusk, Game, Cribbage, Alaskan Coastline On Reverse, 16 In.	1000.00
Whale's Tooth, Bull In The Woods, Signed J.Schpuyle	550.00
Whale's Tooth, Miss Liberty & The Whaler, Signed J.A.	300.00
Whale's Tooth, Sea Captain Talking To Cabin Boy, 4 In.	80.00
Whale's Tooth, Victorian Lady, Fan & Shawl, Red Highlights, 7 In.	300.00
Whale's Tooth, Whaling Scene, Ships Pursuing Whale, 3 1/2 In.	55.00
Whale's Tooth, Whaling Scene, 5 1/4 In.	235.00
Wheel, Jagging, Horse's Foreleg Holds Jagging Wheel, 6 In.	550.00

SCUTTLE MUG, see Shaving Mug, Scuttle

SEG, see Paul Revere Pottery

 Sevres porcelain has been made in Sevres, France, since 1769. Many copies of the famous ware have been made. The name originally referred to the works of the Royal porcelain factory. The name now includes any of the wares made in the town of Sevres, France.

SEVRES, Base, Bronze Mounted, Covered, Lovers, Marked, 28 In., Pair 3750.00
   Bottle, Perfume, 8-Sided Body, Hand-Painted, Signed, 7 In., Pair 350.00
   Bowl, Art Nouveau Border Design, Silver Rim, Signed, 7 In.Square 195.00
   Box, Lovers & Landscape, Gilt Border, Marked, Blue, Oval, 11 In. 300.00
   Box, Painted Garden Scene, Rose Ground, Covered, 7 X 4 In. 80.00
   Bust, Marie Antoinette, L Mark, 5 1/2 In. 100.00
   Bust, Marie Antoinette, White Glaze, Set On Column, Marked, 15 In. 325.00
   Case, Jewel, Hinged Lid, Pastoral Lovers, Signed, 4 1/2 X 2 1/2 In. 225.00
   Chamberstick, Ormolu Mounted, C.1840, 5 In.Long 95.00
   Chocolate Pot, Paneled, Floral, Gold Trim 20.00
   Clock & Candelabra Set, Bronze On Pink Porcelain, C.1760, 18 1/2 In. 9750.00
   Clock Garniture, Bronze Candlesticks, Marked, Raingo, Clock, 21 In. 3250.00
   Compote, Clouds, Putti, Polychrome, Grapevine, 7 1/2 In. 275.00
   Cracker Jar, Cameo, Purple Irises, Clambroth Ground, Signed, 6 3/4 In. 595.00
   Cup & Saucer, Fluted Body, Gros Bleu, C.1755, 3 In. 1100.00
   Cup & Saucer, Portrait, Enameled, Blue Turquoise 120.00
   Cup & Saucer, Rose Pompadour, Scene Of Figures By Port 200.00
   Figurine, Bear, Polar, Red, Black Base, Marked, 13 In. 1600.00
   Jardiniere, Musician & Maidens, Gilt Border, Marked, Oval, 14 In. 850.00
   Jardiniere, Painted Lovers Each Side, Gilt & Turquoise, 4 7/8 In. 350.00
   Jardiniere, 18th Century, Medallions, Blue Ground, 7 3/4 In. 950.00
   Mug & Saucer, Yellow Ground, Farmyard Scene, Exotic Birds, Marked 1300.00
   Patch Box, Shell Shape, Gold Scrolls & Medallion, Flower Closure 110.00
   Pitcher, Raspberry Pattern, Signed, 9 In. 125.00
   Plaque, Napoleon & Josephine, Imperial Dress, Signed, 5 X 7 In., Pair 300.00
   Plate, Blackberry Pattern, Embossed Bows, Gold Rim, 10 1/2 In. 25.00
   Plate, Duc De Bourgogne, 1846 Blue Mark, Signed 210.00
   Plate, King L.Phillip, C.1846, 10 In., Set Of 12 .... 875.00
   Plate, Louis XV, Cobalt Blue Border, Gilded, 10 In. 260.00
   Plate, Madame Lavalliere, Green & Gold Border, Signed 195.00
   Plate, Peach Blossoms, Artist Signed 65.00
   Plate, Peasants In Pursuits, Set Of 4, 9 1/4 In. 500.00
   Plate, Princess De Lamballe, 1844 Series, Gold Rim, Signed, 9 1/4 In. 225.00
   Plate, Rustic Lovers, Panels Of Flowers, N Mark, 9 In., Set Of 6 .... 1200.00
   Plate, Scalloped Blue Edge, Enameled Scroll, Marked, C.1880, Set Of 8 .... 825.00
   Salt Cellar, Painted Cluster, Amorous, Blue Celeste, 3 1/4 In., Pair 175.00
   Urn, Bellflower Design, Brass Leaves, Village Scenes, Signed, 17 In. 1000.00
   Urn, Bronze Mounted, Covered, Female Figure, Blue Luster, 16 In. 375.00
   Urn, Coat Of Arms In Gold, Bronze Handles, 1837 Mark, 10 In., Pair 950.00
   Urn, Gilt Metal, 43 In. .... *Illus* 6000.00

Sevres, Urn, Gilt Metal, 43 In.

Urn, Portrait, Lady, Ormolu Base & Top, 14 In. 225.00
Vase, Bleu-Du-Roi, Covered, 26 In. 400.00
Vase, Classical Maidens, Gilt Bronze Mounts, 35 1/4 In., Pair 2000.00
Vase, Green, Beige, Mauve, Blue Spots, Marked, 7 1/4 In. 450.00
Vase, Jeweled, Maiden & Cupids, Covered, Marked, 35 In. 3750.00
Vase, Military Trophy Design, Handled, Marked, 12 In., Pair 800.00
Vase, Mother With Children, Covered, Crossed Swords, 19 3/4 In., Pair 2250.00
Vase, Mustard, Brown, Blue, C.1907, Marked, 7 1/2 In. 530.00
Vase, Nymph Riding Dolphin, Gilt Bronze Mounts, Signed, 31 In. 290.00
Vase, Ormolu, Landscape, Trophy Reserves, Figural Handles, 24 In. 1700.00
Vase, Panels Of Lovers, Gilt Bronze Mounted, 24 1/4 In., Pair 2750.00
Vase, Pastels, Italian Blue Ground, Dore Mounts, 16 In., Pair 1250.00
Vase, Pastoral Panels, Gilt Bronze Mounted, Blue, 18 1/2 In., Pair 4000.00
Vase, Ruffled Rococo Form Body, Gilt Whorl Feet, 9 1/4 In., Pair 525.00
Vase, Shepherdess Spinning Wool, Covered, Blue Border, 79 In. 9800.00
Vase, Turquoise & Crimson, Lilies, Gold Ground, Marked, 10 In. 425.00

Sewer tile figures were made by workers in the sewer tile factories in the
Ohio area during the late nineteenth and early twentieth centuries.

SEWER TILE, Pig, Sitting, Large, Ohio 135.00
Pig, Standing, Ohio, Small 120.00

SEWING, Basket, Victorian, 2 Tier, 38 1/2 In. 60.00
Basket, Wicker, Japanese Coins, 9 In.Diam. 8.00
Bird, Brass & Iron, Patented 1853, 5 1/4 In. 155.00
Bird, Burgundy Cushion, Brass 125.00
Bird, Clamp, Wooden, 4 In. 85.00
Bird, Dated 1853 On Wing, Silver Plated 125.00
Bird, Dated 1887, Brass 140.00
Bird, Fat Robin, Clamp, Brass 175.00
Bird, Heart End On Clamp, 18th Century, Cast Iron 185.00
Bird, Patented 1858, Brass 110.00
Bird, Velvet Pincushion, Marked Patented 1858, Brass 125.00
Bird, 2 Cushions, Dated, Silver Plated 125.00
Board, Tape Loom, 18th Century, American, Pine, 10 X 31 1/2 In. 350.00
Box, Clark ONT, Pegs For 8 Spools, Thimble & Needles 20.00
Box, Fitted, C.1860, Hinged Top, Ebony & Mother-Of-Pearl Inlay 650.00
Box, Lift-Off Top, 22 Spool Holders, Pincushion, Oak, 12 X 12 X 3 In. 55.00
Box, Oriental, Lacquer, Claw Shaped Feet, Ivory Grills, 10 X 17 In. 200.00
Box, Tunbridge Ware, Inlaid With Stained Woods, 10 1/2 In. 130.00
Box, Walnut, Bird's-Eye Maple Veneer, Dovetailed Drawers 155.00
Case, Needle & Thread, Sandalwood, Egg Shape, Pierced Knob 65.00
Case, Needle, Boye, Wooden Base, Drawer 125.00
Case, Thimble, Parcel Gilt Silver, Pearls, Ruby Chip Knob, 2 In. 115.00
Case, Thimble, Polished Bamboo, Acorn Shape 55.00
Chatelaine, Fitted Etui, Notebook, Sterling Silver, Hallmarks, 1880s 450.00
Clamp, Hemming, Swinging Arm, Iron, Screw Clamp 45.00
Darner, Each End Different Size, Double Ended, 7 1/4 In. 10.00
Darner, Egg, Knob Handle, Handmade, Wooden, 4 In. 22.00
Darner, Egg, Ruby Red, Handled 25.00
Darner, Glove, Sterling Silver 25.00
Egg, Needle Case, The Columbian Egg .... 32.00 To 48.00
Holder, Needle, Prudential 6.00
Holder, Thimble, Figural, Umbrella, Hand-Painted Lacquer 32.00
Iron, Charcoal, Bird On Front 85.00
Iron, Charcoal, Pagoel, Cast Iron 22.00
Iron, Flat, Child's, Dover, Green Handle, 1 1/2 X 3 1/2 In. 22.50
Kit, Calvert Whiskey, Bottle Shape, Plastic, 1943s 6.00
Kit, Lydia Pinkham, Chrome 9.00
Kit, With Brush, Needlepoint Top, Austrian Leather 15.00
Machine, Improved S. & E.Hand Sewing Machine, Hand Crank, Dated 1897 .... 75.00
Machine, Singer, Hemstitcher 75.00
Machine, Singer, Portable, Electric, Oak Case, Gold Stenciling 75.00
Machine, Treadle, Folding, Attachment Box, Dated 1889, Oak 12.00

Machine, Wilcox & Gibbs, Portable, Dated 1882	75.00
Marker, Pattern, Rotating Disk, Brass Ferrule, 6 1/4 In.	6.50
Needle Book, Powder Compact Shape, Bead Design Of Roses, Dated 1834	85.00
Needle Book, Shrimpton's, Folding Advertising Case, C.1880, 4 In.	4.50
Needle Holder, Figural, German Stein	3.00
SEWING, PINCUSHION DOLL, see Pincushion Doll	
Pincushion & Tape Measure, Monkey, Stuffed	25.00
Pincushion, Adolf Hitler Bending Over, Cast Plaster, 1941	55.00
Pincushion, Art Nouveau, Grape & Leaves	8.50
Pincushion, Beaded Edges, Beaded Song Bird Center, Fuchsia, 3 X 4 In.	33.00
Pincushion, Black Mammy .... 22.00 To 40.00	
Pincushion, China Lady	20.00
Pincushion, Crocheted, Baby Bootie Shape	5.00
Pincushion, Doll, Gray Hair, Pink Satin Dress, German, 3 In.	45.00
Pincushion, Figural, Cat, Head Moves, White Metal	20.00
Pincushion, Figural, Rabbit, Pot Metal	15.00
Pincushion, Footed, Urn Shape, Cast Iron	12.00
Pincushion, Heart Shape, Crossed Flags, Beaded	45.00
Pincushion, Parrot Shape, Yellow, Green, & Gray Green	15.00
Pincushion, Patchwork, Hand-Sewn, Gray & White, 4 In.Square	4.00
Pincushion, Rabbit, Pot Metal	15.00
Pincushion, Slipper	12.50
Pincushion, Teddy Bear, Tape Measure Tongue, 7 In.	65.00
Pincushion, Victorian, Br ⌐ Shoe	50.00
Scissors, Larkin	9.00
Scissors, Stork, Original Case	15.00
Shears, Tailor's, C.1840, Hand-Forged Iron, 12 In.	38.00
Shuttle, People Scene, Carved Ivory	40.00
Tape Measure & Pincushion, Telephone Shape, Porcelain	18.50
Tape Measure, Bear, Celluloid .... 12.00 To 25.00	
Tape Measure, Black Man, Celluloid	100.00
Tape Measure, Bottle, Whiskey, Stopper Is Tape, Embossed Kentucky	15.00
Tape Measure, Chicken, Worm In Bill Turns, Brass	25.00
Tape Measure, Converse Bridge Co., Celluloid	15.00
Tape Measure, Embossed Owl Glass Eyes, Brass, Germany	40.00
Tape Measure, French Costumed Girl, Celluloid	30.00
Tape Measure, Harlequin Lady, Occupied Japan, Porcelain	45.00
Tape Measure, Head, English Butler, Fly On Head Is Tape, Porcelain	40.00
Tape Measure, John Deere, Multicolored	45.00
Tape Measure, Lady, Victorian, Costume, Metal	15.00
Tape Measure, Lydia Pinkham	32.00
Tape Measure, Modern Dairy, Wisconsin, Celluloid	15.00
Tape Measure, Mr.Peanut, Round	2.00
Tape Measure, Owl, Glass Eyes, Germany, Brass & Silver Plated	22.00
Tape Measure, Owl, Round, Metal Embossed	12.00
Tape Measure, Parrot, Celluloid	27.50
Tape Measure, Pennsylvania Central R.R.	12.50
Tape Measure, Pig, Brass	28.00
Tape Measure, Pig, Turn Tail To Wind, White Metal .... 25.00 To 45.00	
Tape Measure, Pincushion, Monkey, Stuffed	25.00
Tape Measure, Round, Scene Of White House, Capital, Washington	15.00
Tape Measure, Scene With Child, Dated 1906	28.00
Tape Measure, Sears, Roebuck & Co., Plows	35.00
Tape Measure, Sunflower, Flat, Round, Metal	12.00
Tape Measure, Tire Shape, Goodyear Tire Co.	2.50
Tape Measure, Trojan Ice Cream	28.00
Tape Measure, Turtle, Pull My Head, Silver Plated	25.00
Thimble Holder, Tree, 3-Tiered, Revolving Carousel, 8 1/2 In.	49.50
Thimble, Advertising, Calvert	5.00
Thimble, Gold Washed Sterling Silver, Raised Roses	21.00
Thimble, Gold, Wide Band Of Leaves, Size 7	80.00
Thimble, Grape Design, Sterling Silver	30.00
Thimble, Greek Key Banding, Sterling Silver	35.00

Thimble, House Scene, Dated 1908, Sterling Silver	35.00
Thimble, Scrimshaw, Ivory	15.00
Thimble, Star Brand Shoes, Metal	6.00
Thimble, Winter Sleighing Scene, Sterling Silver	10.00
Thimble, 3 Churches, 14K Gold	125.00
Thread Holder, Sterling	65.00
Threader, Needle, Prudential, Strength Of Gibralter	6.50
Winder, Thread, Flower Shape	20.00
Yarn Holder, Cutout Sterling Top, Gorham 1899 Mark	165.00

Shaker-produced items are characterized by simplicity, functionalism, and orderliness. There were many Shaker communities in America from the eighteenth century to the present day.

SHAKER, Bag, Flour	155.00
Basket, Berry, Vertical Splint Worksides, Pine Base, 6 1/4 In.	80.00
Basket, Bread, Handle, 7 X 10 X 3 In.	40.00
Basket, Cheese	110.00
Basket, Desk	45.00
Basket, Feather	210.00
Basket, New England, 19th Century, Handle, Covered, 14 X 12 1/2 In.	220.00
Basket, Sewing, Tufted Lining, Fitted, Cover, Ash Splint, 5 X 3 1/2 In.	65.00
Basket, Signed Alonzo Little	450.00
Basket, Storage, Splint	295.00
Basket, Swing Handle, Enfield, Conn., 19th Century, 13 1/2 X 14 In.	255.00
Basket, Top Handle, Dark Natural Color, 9 7/8 In.Diam.	95.00
Basket, Woven On Covers, Top Handle, Gathering Feathers, 8 1/2 In.	65.00
Beater, Carpet, Wire Fittings Around Joints	35.00
Bell, House, Dwelling, Brass, Iron Axis, Rope Cord, 11 In.	715.00
Bin, Flour, Hancock	225.00
Board, Cutting, Folding Legs, 19th Century, Pine, 48 X 29 1/2 In.	350.00
Book, Hymnal, Canterbury Shakers, First Edition, 273 Pages	80.00
Book, Original Shaker Music, North Family, Mt.Lebanon, 1893, 271 Pages	80.00
Bookmark, E.J.Neale & Co., Mount Lebanon, Black, White, & Gray Silk	155.00
Bowl, Burlwood, Cutout Handholds, Wood Yoke, 3 Pieces, 16 In.	1045.00
Box, Alfred Colony, Painted Powder Blue	95.00
Box, Bentwood, Oval, Finger Construction, Copper Tacks, 6 In.	175.00
Box, Cutlery, Bentwood, Classic Style	65.00
Box, Fingered, Storage	395.00
Box, Glove, Woven Poplar, Sabbath Day Lake, Maine, 12 1/4 In.	105.00
Box, Harvard, Nest Of 5, Largest 6 1/8 In.	495.00
Box, Knife, Bentwood, 13 X 8 1/8 In.	65.00
Box, Oval, Old Red Paint	320.00
Box, Pantry, Bentwood, Harvard, Hand-Forged Nails, 5 1/2 In.	75.00
Box, Pantry, Harvard, Oval V Lap, 5 5/8 In.	68.00
Box, Pantry, Harvard, Oval V Lap, 6 1/4 In.	68.00
Box, Sewing, One Fitted Inside Other, 19th Century	200.00
Box, Sewing, Pink Satin Lining, Sabbath Day Lake, Signed, 7 In.	125.00
Box, Sewing, 8-Sided, Pink Silk Lined, Alfred, Maine Mark	160.00
Box, Spit, Circular Form, 4 Tapered Fingers, Yellow, 11 In. Diam.	2530.00
Box, Utensil, Double Section, Center Handle, Hickory, 12 3/4 X 8 In.	115.00
Box, Utility, Oval, Fitted Lid, Ocher-Yellow, 3 X 8 1/4 In.	440.00
Box, Utility, Oval, Fitted Lid, 4 Fingers, 1 1/4 X 12 In.	440.00
Box, Utility, Oval, Lid, 4 Tapered Fingers, 3 1/2 X 8 1/4 In.	350.00
Box, V-Lap, Harvard Type, Natural Wood, 5 1/2 In.Diam.	68.00
Box, V-Lap, Harvard Type, Natural Wood, 5 7/8 In.Diam.	68.00
Box, V-Lap, Harvard Type, Natural Wood, 9 1/4 In.Diam.	68.00
Box, 4-Fingered, Painted, Oval	1550.00
Brush, Dyed Lavender Horsehair, Honey Maple, Trim Turnings, 8 In.	75.00
Brush, Hearth, Curvy Black Wooden Handle, Black Bristles, 21 3/4 In.	80.00
Brush, Horsehair, Curvy Maple Handle, 11 In.	65.00
Bucket, Iron Bands, Bail Handle, Wooden Grip, Old Green, Wooden, 13 In.	35.00
Bucket, Metal Hang-Up, Wooden, Tin Band, Red & White, Signed	110.00
Bucket, Sugar, Covered, 9 1/2 X 10 1/2 In.	85.00

Canteen, Buttonhole Lap, Unpainted, 10 1/4 In. 78.00
Carrier, Wooden, Hancock, Natural With Green Trim 700.00
Chopper, Food 25.00
Coffeepot, Side Spout, Pewter Finial, 9 1/4 In. 65.00
Coffeepot, Tin 85.00
Coffeepot, 2 Layer, Wooden Finial, Tin 55.00
Comb, Scalp, Maple, Round Brush, 2 X 1 1/4 In. 75.00
Comb, Shampoo, Notched Teeth, 2 In.Diam. 32.00
Darner, Ball Rotates Within The Case, Dark & Light Wood 38.00
Darner, Egg, Turned Hardwood 35.00
Darner, Maple, Removable Needle Holder, 6 In. 75.00
Darner, Treen, Removable Handle, Wooden Finule To Top, 2 3/4 In. 45.00
Dipper, Tin, Dark Gray, 7 In.Tubular Handle, 7 In.Rim 65.00
Dustpan, Child's, Tin, Dark Gray, Hang-Up Loop, 8 X 9 In. 130.00
Dustpan, Original Finish, Black 45.00
Ember Carrier, Sheet Tin, Wooden Handle, Hinged Top, 18 1/2 In. 180.00
Flax Wheel, Saxony, Attached Yarn Winder, 3 Legs, 4 Ft. X 39 In. 550.00
Funnel, Tin, Black, Looped End Clip, Tubular Tin Handle, 7 In. 50.00
SHAKER, FURNITURE, see Furniture
Grinder, Herb, Twirled Between Palms, 6 1/4 In. 22.00
Knife, Hand-Dovetailed, Walnut, Straight-Sided, Cutout Grip 95.00
Ladder, Household, Pine, Carved & Painted Brown-Red, 5 Ft. 7 In. 825.00
Lifter, Pie, 2-Tined, Wooden Handle 35.00
Measure, Bentwood, Oak, Marked Sabbath Day Lake, Me., 7 1/2 In.Diam. 180.00
Mirror, Hand, Maple, Marked No.10, 11 1/2 In.Long, 4 X 6 In.Mirror 95.00
Mold, Box, Sabbath Day Lake, Theodore Johnson 20.00
Napkin Ring, Treenware, Wood Inlays, Corset Waisted, 1 5/8 In.Diam. 75.00
Pincushion, Base Edged In Deerskin, Velvet Crown, 2 3/4 In.Diam. 70.00
Pincushion, Signed Sabbath Day Lake, Signed, Wooden 125.00
Pincushion, Velvet, Wood, 2 In.Diam. 45.00
Rolling Pin, Clothespin Handles, 20 1/2 In. 65.00
Rolling Pin, Clothespin Knobs, 17 In. 55.00
Rolling Pin, Stick Handles 36.00
Rug, Rag, Braided, Navy Blue, Green, Brown, Black, 10 X 7 Ft. 880.00
Rule, Hand-Notched Scoring, 8 Panel Sides, Scribed Numbers, Maple 60.00
Saucepan, Tin, 13 In.Diam. 30.00
Sewing Roll, Tan Leather, Pincushion End, Floral Satin Lining 75.00
Sieve, Horsehair, 13 In. 65.00
Spool Holder, Pincushion, Maple, 7 Spool Spindles, 5 In.Diam.Base 110.00
Straw Braider, Rotated By Wooden Crank, Maple, 29 In. 180.00
Textile, Cloak, Black Wool, Ribbons, Full Length 300.00
Tin, Blue-Green Paint, 2 3/4 In. 15.00
Tool, Basket Making, Canterbury, Tin Teeth, 7 X 1 In. 45.00
Tray, Bean Sorting 48.00
Tub, Syrup, Finger Lapped 95.00
Wash Basket 135.00
Washtub, Old Yellow Paint, Hancock 185.00

Shaving mugs were popular from 1860 to 1900. Many types were made, as
including occupational mugs featuring pictures of the man's job. There were
scuttle mugs, silver-plated mugs, glass-lined mugs, and others.

SHAVING MUG, Fish Scuttle, Gold Trim 25.00
Floral, Gold Trim, Cobalt Blue, 2 Piece 35.00
Floral, R.S.Poland 85.00
Hand-Painted Bluebirds, Signed & Dated 37.50
Lily-Of-The-Valley, Pink Luster 30.00
Mephistopheles, Milk Glass 20.00
Name Joe Robinson 35.00
Occupational, Barbershop, Barbers & Customers 190.00
Occupational, Bartender, Man Drinking 155.00
Occupational, Bartender, 2 Customers 195.00
Occupational, Blacksmith, Shoeing Horse 175.00
Occupational, Buggy Driver, 2 Horses 180.00

Occupational, Butcher, Steer & Tools	100.00
Occupational, Cabdriver, Coach & Horse	180.00
Occupational, Carpenter, At Bench	160.00
Occupational, Dentist Pulling False Teeth	125.00
Occupational, Doctor's Name, Banner On Horizontal Pole, Limoges	90.00
Occupational, Dr.A.S.Burton, Dental Tools	75.00
Occupational, Dry Goods Salesman & Customer	190.00
Occupational, Express Driver, Wagon & Horses	185.00
Occupational, Farmer, Plowing With 2 Horses	190.00
Occupational, Grocery Store & Clerk	135.00
Occupational, Iron Puddler, Name In Gold	195.00
Occupational, Locomotive, Wood Burner	75.00
Occupational, Milk Wagon, 3 Horses	175.00
Occupational, Pharmacist, Mortar & Pestle	150.00
Occupational, Printer, At Printing Case	190.00
Occupational, Railway Conductor, Caboose	125.00
Occupational, Tobacconist, With Brush	90.00
Partitioned Insert Brush Rest, Hartford Silver Plate	45.00
Portrait, Long-Haired Beauty, Crown Germany, 3 In.	25.00
Remember Me	22.00
Rose Design, Gold Trim, Nippon	30.00
Scuttle, Floral	30.00
Scuttle, Hand-Painted	17.00
Scuttle, Sailor's Poem, Mariner's Compass	30.00
St.Bernard Dog	60.00

Shawnee
USA

Shawnee pottery was made in Zanesville, Ohio, from 1935 until 1961.
Shawnee also produced pottery for George Rumrill during the late 1930s.

SHAWNEE, Casserole, Corn King, Covered, 11 1/2 In.	35.00 To 45.00
Cookie Jar, Cookie Stories	35.00
Cookie Jar, Hey Diddle Diddle	38.00
Cookie Jar, Muggsy Dog	30.00
Cookie Jar, Pink Elephant	35.00
Cookie Jar, Puss 'n Boots	25.00 To 35.00
Cookie Jar, Smilin' Pig	20.00
Cookie Jar, Winnie The Pig	45.00
Creamer, Cat, Yellow	15.00
Creamer, Corn King	10.00 To 12.00
Creamer, Duck	10.00
Creamer, Elephant	10.00 To 12.00
Creamer, Puss 'n Boots	7.00 To 13.00
Dish, Butter, Corn, Covered	20.00
Dish, Relish, Corn King	8.00
Mug, Corn	20.00
Pitcher, Bopeep, Large	18.00
Pitcher, Corn, 8 1/2 In.	15.00 To 44.50
Pitcher, Little Boy Blue	22.00
Pitcher, Milk, Corn	40.00
Pitcher, Milk, Little Bopeep	22.00
Pitcher, Milk, Little Boy Blue & Little Bopeep	30.00
Pitcher, Milk, Pig	15.00
Pitcher, Milk, Smiling Pig	35.00 To 45.00
Pitcher, Smiley	22.00
Planter, Corn	20.00
Planter, Elephant, Black, Marked Shawnee Usa	45.00
Planter, Elf	6.00
Planter, Giraffe	12.00
Planter, Globe, Green & Yellow	14.00 To 18.00
Planter, Reclining Deer	18.00
Planter, Scalloped, White Underglaze, Blue, 9 In.	22.00

Planter, Squirrel	5.00
Planter, Water Wheel	15.00
Planter, Wishing Well, Green	16.00
Plate, Corn On Cob	7.00
Salt & Pepper, Corn, 3 1/2 In.	8.00 To 15.00
Salt & Pepper, Farmer Pig, 3 In.	7.50
Salt & Pepper, Figural, Lamb	10.00
Salt & Pepper, Man & Woman Pig, 5 In.	12.50
Salt & Pepper, Milk Can Shape	6.50
Salt & Pepper, Puss 'n Boots	12.50
Salt & Pepper, Red Riding Hood	13.00
Salt & Pepper, Winking Owl	10.00
Shaker, Corn King	10.00
Shaker, Dutch Boy & Girl	12.00
Shaker, Winnie Pig, Pair	8.50
Shoe, Green	8.00
Sugar & Creamer, Corn, Covered	25.00
Sugar, Lid, King Corn	18.00
Teapot, Corn	15.00 To 35.00
Teapot, Corn Queen, 1 Cup Size	30.00 To 45.00
Teapot, Granny	35.00
Teapot, Tom The Piper's Son	20.00 To 35.00
Vase, Pink, 9 3/4 In.	10.00
Vase, Swirl Design, Handles Near Base, Green, 5 1/2 In.	10.00

SHEFFIELD, see Silver Plate; Silver-English

Shirley Temple dishes, blue glassware, and any other souvenir-type objects with her name and picture are now collected. Cobalt blue glassware decorated with Shirley Temple's picture was made by the Hazel Atlas Glass Company from 1934 to 1942.

SHIRLEY TEMPLE, Book, Big Little Book, 1935, Little Colonel	15.00
Book, My Crayon	27.00
Cards, Playing, Complete	75.00
Creamer, Blue Glass, Picture	32.00 To 38.00
Doll, Composition Body, 13 In.	200.00
Doll, Composition Body, 18 In.	265.00
Doll, Composition, Curly-Top, 1930s, 20 In.	650.00
Doll, Composition, 1934, Original Clothes, 13 In.	400.00
Doll, Flirty, Original Clothes, 25 In.	545.00
Doll, Jointed, Composition, Sleep Eyes, Marked Ideal, 16 In.	250.00
Doll, Original Dress, 1957, 19 In.	200.00
Doll, Pink Dress, All Original, Ideal, 1937, 11 In.	495.00
Doll, Red, White Dress, Shoes, Panties, 1972	30.00
Figurine, Cat & Dog, Puffed Sleeves, Dimples, Saltstone	45.00
Figurine, With Dog, Saltstone	17.50
Flirty Eyes, Original Wig & Dress, 25 In.	500.00
Ideal, Jointed Wrists, Blue Organdy Dress, 36 In.	950.00
Mug, Blue Glass, Picture	45.00 To 60.00
Music, Sheet, The Bluebird, 1940, Photograph On Cover	15.00
Paper Dolls, 18 In., Uncut	60.00
Pitcher, Blue Glass, Picture	30.00 To 36.50
Pocket Watch	150.00
Postcard, Dressing Room	7.00
Punchboard, Miss Charming	10.00
Sleep Eyes, Marked Head, Body, & Clothes, 13 In.	325.00
Tea Set, Salmon Colored, Cameos Of Shirley, Plastic	40.00
Toy, Trunk, Wooden	100.00
Vinyl, 36 In.	950.00

SILHOUETTE, see Picture, Silhouette

SILVER CHINESE, Coffee Set, Oriental Figures, C.1890, 5 Piece	950.00

Silver deposit glass was made during the late nineteenth and early twentieth centuries. Solid sterling silver was applied to the glass by a chemical method so that a cutout design of silver metal appeared against a clear or colored glass. It is sometimes called silver overlay.

SILVER DEPOSIT, Plate, Flowers, 7 In. 35.00
Vase, Flowers, Cobalt Blue, 8 In. 50.00

Silver plate is not solid silver. It is a ware made of a metal such as nickel or copper, then covered with a thin coating of silver. The letters EPNS are often found on American and English silver plated wares. Sheffield silver is a type of silver plate.

SILVER PLATE, Biscuit Box, Beaded Base, Cover, I.C. & Co., C.1870, 7 In. 175.00
Box, Collar Button, Engraved Floral, Marked Poole 18.50
Butter, Gadrooned Border, Liner, Covered, 8 X 5 1/2 In. 100.00
Butter, Knife Rest, Engraved Birds & Butterflies, Insert 48.00
Cake Basket, Art Nouveau, Swing Handle, Fluted, 10 1/4 In.Diam. 95.00
Candelabra, 3-Light, Reeded Arms, Flame Finial, 12 1/2 In., Pair 150.00
Candelabra, 3-Light, 2 Section Each, 18 1/2 In., Pair 300.00
Candelabra, 4-Light, Rococo Leaf & Scroll Stems, 20 In., Pair 550.00
Candelabra, 5 Arms, Intertwining Arms, Embossed Design, 10 In. 60.00
Candlesnuffer, Bell Shaped, Wooden Handle 21.00
Candlestick, Beaded Base Rim, Middletown Plate Co., 10 1/4 In. 25.00
Candlestick, Circular Base & Shaft, 2 Section, 11 1/2 In., Pr. 80.00
Candlestick, Grape Clusters, 9 In., Pair 75.00
Coffee & Tea Set, Elkington & Co., C.1859, 4 Piece 500.00
Coffin Marker, Our Baby 20.00
Compote & Basket, Dolphin Stem, Meriden, C.1930 .... 100.00
Compote, Oystershell Design, Tiered, English, 7 1/4 In. 195.00
Cooler, Wine, Pedestal Base, Grapevine Band, Liner, 12 In., Pair 1200.00
Cracker Jar, Fluted, Bail Handle, Engraved Crackers, Empire 42.00
Creamer, Art Nouveau, Reed & Barton 85.00
Dish, Chafing, Domed Cover, Footed, 9 In. 45.00
Dish, Cheese, Hinged Cover, Sheffield, M.Boulton, C.1815, 13 In. 250.00
Dish, Entree, Gadroon Rim, Sheffield, C.1830, 12 1/4 In., Pair 425.00
Dish, Entree, Scalloped, Covered, Sheffield, C.1830, 12 1/4 In. 300.00
Dish, Entree, Scroll Rim, Covered, Warming Pan, 13 1/2 In., Pair 1000.00
Dish, Figural, Swan, Marked J.B., 6 X 4 1/2 In. 48.00
Dish, Vegetable, Double, 2-Handled, Warming Tray, Covered, 17 In. 175.00
Dish, Vegetable, Gadrooned Borders, English, Covered, 11 In. 120.00
Dish, Venison, Tree & Well Tray, Hot Water Base, 27 X 15 In. 1100.00
Epergne, Engraved Crest, Cut Glass Finial, C.1810, 12 In. 400.00
Epergne, 4 Arm Supports, Barker-Ellis, 12 X 22 In.Diam. 325.00
Epergne, 4 Vaseline Lilies, English, 14 1/2 X 3 1/2 In. 300.00
Ewer, Rodgers, Hinged Cover, Wood Handle, English, 10 1/4 In. 90.00
Ewer, Vase-Shaped Body, Figural Handle, 19th Century, 15 In. 140.00
Holder, Watch, Old-Fashioned Full-Figured Girl, Bonneted 175.00
Knife Rest, Cherubs Each End, Rope Rest, Roger Smith & Co. 30.00
Knife Rest, Figural, Fox 29.00
Ladle, Art Deco, Monroe Silver Co. 5.00
Ladle, Punch, Savoy, Gold Wash Bowl, 1847 Rogers, 15 In. 50.00
Match Safe, Lady's Profile 55.00
Mirror, Plaque, Pierced Gallery, Paw Feet, 19 X 32 1/2 In. 425.00
      SILVER PLATE, MUSTACHE CUP, see Mustache Cup
      SILVER PLATE, NAPKIN RING, see Napkin Ring
Pitcher, Applied Acorns & Leaves, Beading, Marked Colonial 65.00
Pitcher, Ice Water, Reed & Barton 1867, 13 In. 65.00
Pitcher, Porcelain Lined, Tilt, Goblet, Meriden, 20 In. 245.00
Pitcher, Tankard, Art Nouveau, Marked Tufts, 10 1/2 In. 75.00
Pitcher, Tilting, Porcelain Lined, Dated 1879, Reed & Barton 325.00
Salver, Scalloped Rim, Foliate Feet, 19th Century, 24 1/2 In. 475.00
Salver, Shell & Scroll Border, English, 14 In.Diam. 155.00
Samovar, Victorian, Reed & Barton 185.00
Sauceboat, Oval Bowl, 4 Paw Feet, Reeded Border, 4 1/2 In. 50.00

Server, Fish, Silver Ferrule, Bone Handle, Pair	50.00
Shaker, Cocktail, Cylindrical Form, Gorham Mfg. Co., 13 1/2 In.	40.00

SILVER PLATE, SPOON, SOUVENIR, see Souvenir, Spoon, Silver Plate

Spooner, Animal Finial, 12 Spoons	115.00
Stand, Card, Dolphin Stem	15.00
Sugar & Creamer, Drink Moxie	200.00
Sugar & Spoon Holder, Squirrels In Handles, Bird Lid	100.00
Table Service, Elkington & Co., C.1875, Covered, 5 Piece	750.00
Tea Caddy, Ladies & Child, Barbour Co., 3 1/2 X 2 1/4 In.	48.00

SILVER PLATE, TOOTHPICK, see Toothpick

Tray, Art Deco, Woman In Tropical Setting, 12 In.Square	180.00
Tray, Engraved Surface, 4 Scroll Feet, 2-Handled, 31 In.	175.00
Tray, Foliate Scrolls, 2-Handled, Covered, C.1830, 28 In.	500.00
Tray, Gadrooned Border, Center Armorials, English, 14 In.	100.00
Tray, Geometric Design, Art Deco, Bakelite Handles, 17 1/4 In.	150.00
Tray, Pen, Feather Shape, Owl On End, Glass Eyes, 8 In.	185.00
Tray, 2-Handled, 4 Paw Feet, Gadrooned Edges, 20 In.	140.00
Tureen, Collus & Co., London, Beaded Rims, 13 1/4 X 9 1/2 In.	275.00
Urn, Hot Water, Stand, Reed & Barton, 12 In., Pair	70.00
Urn, Tea, Inverted Pear-Shaped, Flower Finial, 16 1/2 In.	375.00
Urn, Tea, Lobed Circular Form, English, 14 1/2 X 15 In.	550.00
Vase, Cylindrical, Flowers, Foliage, Scrollwork, 17 In.	95.00
Vase, Molded Chrysanthemums, Reed & Barton, 3 1/4 X 10 In.	175.00
Wagon, Wine, 2 Coaster, Openwork Sides, 18 1/2 In.	115.00
Wine Cooler, Campana Form, M.Boulton & Co., C.1830, 10 1/4 In.	650.00
Wine Cooler, Sheffield, C.1830, Detachable Liner, 9 1/2 In., Pr.	1200.00
Wine Cooler, Urn Form, Pedestal, Engraved Crest, 10 In., Pair	550.00

American silver was usually marked with the name or initials of the silversmith or silver company. The word "Sterling" was not in general use until about 1860.

SILVER-AMERICAN, see also Tiffany Silver; Silver-Sterling

SILVER-AMERICAN, Basket, Cake, Scrolling Design, Beading, Swing Handle, 12 In	950.00
Basket, Cake, Whiting Mfg.Co., Providence, C.1910, 16 In.	475.00
Basket, Flower, Reed & Barton, Taunton, Mass., C.1915, 19 In.	550.00
Basket, Lion's Paw Feet, Trelliswork, 16 1/4 In.	1400.00
Basket, Nouveau Chasing Allover, Unger Brothers, Footed	125.00
Basket, Oval Form, Howard Sterling Co., Providence, C.1900	200.00
Beaker, E.Jaccard & Co., C.1840, Tapered Cylinder, 3 3/4 In.	300.00
Beaker, Hunting Scene, 1820-30, 3 1/2 In.	550.00
Beaker, Joel Sayre, Southampton, C.1800, 3 In., Pair	1760.00
Beaker, John McFarlane, Boston, C.1805, 3 1/2 In.	330.00
Beaker, Reeded Border, Smith Silver Co., Set Of 6	300.00
Beaker, Scovil & Co., C.1835, Tapered Cylinder, 3 1/2 In.	375.00
Beaker, Willey & Blaksley, C.1835, Triple Rim, 3 5/8 In.	450.00
Bonbon, G.W.Shiebler & Co., C.1877, 14K Gold, 11 In.	650.00
Bonbon, Pierced, Oval Form, Foliage, Fruit Swags, 6 In.	175.00
Bowl, Branches & Berries, Whiting Mfg.Co., C.1905, 10 In.	600.00
Bowl, Chased Fruits, Covered, Gorham, C.1915, 12 1/2 In.	1500.00
Bowl, Circular Form, Flared Sides, Monogram, 10 In.	175.00
Bowl, Engraved, The Randahl Shop, Chicago, C.1920, 9 In.	100.00
Bowl, Foliage, C.1900, Shiebler & Co., 12 In.	525.00
Bowl, Fruit, Pierced Scrolls, Oval Form, 15 1/2 In.	1000.00
Bowl, Joel Sayre, New York, C.1800, Ball Feet, 5 In.	990.00
Bowl, Lobed Sides, Whiting Mfg. Co., 1911, 10 1/4 In.Diam.	200.00
Bowl, Mulberry & Vine Design, Footed, 13 1/2 In.	600.00
Bowl, Poppy Form, Reed & Barton, 13 1/2 In.	450.00
Bowl, Punch & Ladle, Grape Leaves, 18 In.	2500.00
Bowl, Sea Flora, C.1880, Whiting Mfg. Co., 10 In.	1550.00
Bowl, Waste, Spherical Form, Geometric Pattern, 4 In.	225.00
Bowl, William Moulton IV, Massachusetts, C.1800, 6 In.	1430.00

Box, Stamp, Unger Bros.	65.00
Brush, Cupid Astride, Unger Bros., Small	115.00
Butter, Pierced Liner, Dome Cover, Reed & Barton, 5 In.	60.00
Cake Basket, Handled, Ball, Black, & Co., C.1870, 11 3/4 In.	950.00
Cake Stand, Pierced Bowl, Whiting, Providence, 3 1/4 In.	120.00
Candelabra, Floral Design, Detachable Nozzle, 16 In.	3100.00
Candelabra, S-Form Branches, C.1910, 13 1/4 In., Pair	650.00
Candleholder, Geometric, Grape & Vine Feet, C.1780, Signed	95.00
Candlestick, Blue Enamel, Thomas Co., C.1925, 8 In., Pair	550.00
Cann, Abraham Carlile, Philadelphia, 1791-94, 4 In.	1540.00
Cann, Baluster, Form, Crest, C.1770, Quart, 6 1/2 In.	800.00
Cann, Baluster, Form, Leaf Handle, C.1760, 5 In.	600.00
Case, Card, Engine Turned Design, Gorham	95.00
Case, Card, Etched Jaguar Head, Scrolled, 3 1/7 In.	100.00
Case, Cigarette, Engraved Cover, Rectangular, 4 In.	30.00
Casket, Jewel, Ovoid Body, Figures, Covered, 12 In.	950.00
Castor, R.Peaston, 1774, 5 1/4 In.	325.00
Chalice & Paten, W.Van Erp, California, 7 1/8 In.	800.00
Chalice, Female Figure Stem, C.1864, Gorham, 9 1/2 In.	275.00
Cheese Scoop, Grape Lead, N, Harding & Co., Boston, C.1865	75.00
Chocolate Pot, Flower Panels, Ivory Finial, 9 In.	550.00
Chocolate Pot, Trumpet Base, Side Spout, 8 1/4 In.	325.00
Coaster, Repousse Floral Border, S.Kirk & Son, Set Of 6	95.00
Coffee & Tea Set, Leaf-Capped Handles, Gorham, 5 Piece	3000.00
Coffee & Tea Set, Mt.Vernon Silver Co., C.1913, 7 Piece	4100.00
Coffee Service & Tray, Foliate Scrolls, 5 Piece	3750.00
Coffee Service, Foliate Scrolls & Flower Heads, Set	1400.00
Coffee Service, Pyriform Body, Leafage, C.1900, 6 Piece	4500.00
Coffee Service, Shield Form, Bone Knops, 5 Piece	750.00
Coffee Set, Gorham & Co., C.1865, Greek Style, 7 Piece	4400.00
Coffeepot, Moorish Design, Tapering Spout, 10 In.	450.00
Coffeepot, National Silver Co., Meriden, C.1930, 8 In.	125.00
Coffeepot, Turkish, Engraved Birds In Flight, 11 In.	850.00
Coffeepot, Urn Shape, S.Kirk & Son, C.1850, 10 3/8 In.	1400.00
Compote, Draped Woman Stem, Parrot Form Handles, Pair	1000.00
Compote, Figural, Draped Woman Standing Stem, 13 In.	750.00
Compote, Howard & Co., New York, C.1905, 3 1/2 In., Pair	650.00
Compote, National Silver Co., New York, C.1930, 4 1/2 In.	30.00
Compote, Whiting Co., Rhode Island, C.1900, 5 3/4 In.	700.00
Creamer, Cow, Figural, Standing, 3 X 4 1/2 In.	265.00
Creamer, Dominick & Haff, 1888, Waved Rim, 4 1/8 In.	125.00
Creamer, Gelston & Co., New York, C.1840, Pear Form, 4 In.	250.00
Creamer, Helmet Form, John Vernon, New York, C.1790, 7 In.	750.00
Creamer, Helmet Form, William Holmes, Jr., Boston, C.1800	600.00
Creamer, Philip Garrett, Philadelphia, C.1830, 5 In.	140.00
Creamer, Vase Form, Dome Lid, Engraved, 8 1/2 In.	225.00
Crumber, Henry Hebbard, C.1860, Coin, 12 1/4 In.	150.00
Cup, Julep, For Best Grade Yearling Heifer, 1850, Coin	300.00
Cup, Trophy, Floral Clusters, Scroll Handles, 14 In.	2000.00
Dessert Service, Baltimore Rose Pattern, 17 Pieces	1500.00
Dessert Spoon, Benjamin Gurnee, N.Y.C., C.1824, 7 In.	60.00
Dish, Asparagus, Floral Design, Paw Feet, 2-Handled, 15 In.	1600.00
Dish, Baltimore Rose Design, Everted Border, 12 In.	475.00
Dish, Bread, Oval Form, C.1910, International Silver Co.	190.00
Dish, Bread, 2-Handled, Pierced Border, Pair, 14 In.	935.00
Dish, Butter, Violets & Foliage, Covered, 7 1/2 In.	400.00
Dish, Candy, Oblong, C.1924, Whiting Mfg. Co., 6 In.	45.00
Dish, Circular Form, Molded Rim, 11 In.	175.00
Dish, Condiment, Clover Form, Glass Liner, 10 In.	250.00
Dish, Entree, Fleur-De-Lis, Covered, C.1860, 14 In.	950.00
Dish, Entree, Palmete Design, Ring Handle, 9 In.	1100.00
Dish, Flower Border, Gorham Mfg., C.1899, 15 In.	525.00
Dish, Jacobi & Jenkins, C.1870, 6 3/4 In.	245.00

Dish, Leaves & Hazelnuts, Teardrop Form, 15 1/4 In.	750.00
Dish, Muffin, Pierced Quatrefol Design, Covered, 9 In.	200.00
Dish, Sweetmeat, Scroll Design, Swags, Pierced Border, 10 In.	250.00
Dresser Set, Love's Dream, Unger Brothers, 4 Piece	575.00
Ewer, John C. Moore, New York, C.1840, 11 In.	220.00
Ewer, Presentation, Vase Form, Horseshoe At Neck, 18 In.	4250.00
Ewer, Pyriform Body, Gelston & Treadwell, C.1845, 15 1/4 In.	1400.00
Ewer, 2 Landscapes, S.Kirk & Son, 16 1/8 In.	2300.00
Flask, Cut Glass, Unger Bros.	125.00
Flask, Hip, Shovel Shape, Grapevine Design, 6 1/2 In.	350.00
Food Pusher, Shield & Ribbon Design, Monogram C	25.00
Fork, Baby, Mary Had A Little Lamb, Scene On Handle, Rogers	38.00
Fork, Beaded Edge, Vanderslice & Co., Set Of 8	650.00
Fork, Dessert, Old English Thread, W.Chawner II, Set Of 6	300.00
Fork, Dinner, Ivy Design, Duhme & Co., Coin	30.00
Fork, Erickson, Gardner, Massachusetts, Set Of 9	485.00
Fork, Fiddle Thread, Bailey & Co., 1848, Marked	375.00
Fork, Fiddle Thread, Benjamin Burnee, Marked, 7 5/8 In.	80.00
Fork, Fiddle Thread, J. Stockman, Phila., C.1828, 7 In.	75.00
Fork, Fish, Versailles, Gorham, Set Of 12	600.00
Fork, Olive, W.Kendrick, Louisville, 1824-80, Coin	30.00
Fork, Prince Albert, Lincoln & Reed, Marked, Set Of 6	420.00
Fork, Serving, Strasbourg, Gorham	85.00
Gadrooned Shoulder, Leaf Shaped Handle, 1869, 11 In.	250.00
Goblet, Cylindrical Form, Classical Design, 7 In.	275.00
Goblet, J.H.Bowie, Maryland, C.1810, Bell Form, 7 In., Pair	1200.00
Gravy Boat, Underplate, Gorham Co., Rhode Island, C.1915	110.00
Handle, Cane, Foliate Scrolls, Engraved In Script	10.00
Ice Tongs, Chrysanthemum, Gold Wash, Durgin, 8 In.	295.00
Jug, Milk, Greek Key Pattern, C.18656 1/2 In.	200.00
Knife, Erickson, Gardner, Massachusetts, 9 Piece	225.00
Knife, Fish, Hepplewhite Pattern, Reed & Barton, 10 7/8 In.	55.00
Ladle, B.C.Frobisher, Boston, 1792-1862, 6 1/4 In.	50.00
Ladle, Buttercup Pattern, Gorham, 13 In.	300.00
Ladle, C.1857, Shreve, Brown & Co.	70.00
Ladle, Cream, F.Kinsey, Coin	75.00
Ladle, Engraved, R. & W.Wilson, C.1845, Coin, 11 In.	200.00
Ladle, Fiddle Handle, Wood & Hughes, New York, C.1850, 12 In.	120.00
Ladle, Fiddle Thread, J, Conning, Alabama, Coin, 13 In.	250.00
Ladle, Gravy, Medici, Gorham	95.00
Ladle, Mustard, Medallion, Bust Of Washington, Harding	95.00
Ladle, Oval Twist Pattern, Whiting Mfg. Co., 12 1/2 In.	250.00
Ladle, Punch, Louis XV, Whiting Mfg. Co., 10 3/4 In.	175.00
Ladle, Punch, Maryland, Gilt Wash Bowl, Gorham, 12 7/8 In.	225.00
Ladle, Punch, Medallion Pattern, Gilt Bowl, C.1865	250.00
Ladle, Punch, Oval Medallion, Duhme & Co., Cincinnati, Coin	175.00
Ladle, Punch, Oval Thread, Shell Bowl	225.00
Ladle, Soup W.P.Jones, C.1840, Coin, 12 3/4 In.	225.00
Ladle, Soup, Fiddle Terminal, Maltby Pelletreau, C.1815	175.00
Ladle, Soup, Frederick Marquand, Savannah, C.1823, 13 In.	800.00
Ladle, Soup, Henry Salisbury & Co., 1835-39, 13 In.	160.00
Ladle, Soup, John McMullin, Philadelphia, C.1800, 13 In.	320.00
Ladle, Soup, Les Six Fleurs Pattern, Reed & Barton, C.1901	440.00
Ladle, Soup, Prince Albert, Caldwell & Co., C.1850	325.00
Ladle, Soup, Samuel C.Brown, N.Y., 1824-30, 13 1/2 In.	275.00
Ladle, Tomato Vine Pattern, Oval Bowl, Bowed Handle, 10 In.	500.00
Loving Cup, 2-Handled, Gorham, 4 3/8 In.	55.00
Mirror, Toilet, Heart Form Frame, Gorham, 1895, 15 In.	800.00
Mug, Greek Key Design, Gorham Mfg., Providence, 1874, 3 In.	165.00
Mug, 10 Brownies, Children Marching, Gorham, 2 1/4 In.	140.00
Narrow Scoop, Script Engraving, Twisted Section, Coin	345.00
Pincushion, Heart Shaped, Reed & Barton	65.00
Pitcher, Adolphe Hummel, New Orleans Mark, Coin, 9 7/8 In.	2750.00

Pitcher, Harris & Schafer, Washington, C.1890, 16 In., Pair 3080.00
Pitcher, Helmet Shape, Gorham, 15 3/8 In. 500.00
Pitcher, Water, & Underplate, Flowers & Scrolls, 10 In. 1800.00
Pitcher, Water, Bailey & Kitchen, Philadelphia, 1847, 15 In. 1100.00
Pitcher, Water, Baldwin Gardiner, New York, C.1845, 32 Ounce 520.00
Pitcher, Water, Baltimore Rose Design, Vine Handles, 8 In. 1400.00
Pitcher, Water, Chantilly Pattern, Gorham, 1907, 9 3/4 In. 1300.00
Pitcher, Water, E. Stebbins & Co., New York, C.1840, 9 In. 1320.00
Pitcher, Water, Floral Bouquets, Spherical Form, 7 In. 600.00
Pitcher, Water, Japanese Style, Whiting Mfg., 7 In. 5300.00
Pitcher, Water, William Gales, Son & Co., C.1858, 10 In. 660.00
Pitcher, Water, Wood & Hughes, New York, C.1850, 14 In. 660.00
Pitcher, Whiting Mfg. Co., C.1880, 7 1/4 In. .... *Illus* 5300.00
Porringer & Stand, Martele, Gorham Co., 1898, 5 1/2 In. 1300.00
Porringer, Hays & Byers, New York, C.1770, 8 In. 1750.00
Porringer, William Cowell, Sr., Boston, C.1730, 7 1/2 In. 1400.00
Ramekin, Reed & Tie Rim, Shell Handles, Set Of 10 .... 1200.00
Salt & Pepper Castor, Vase Shape, S.Kirk & Son, 4 3/4 In. 80.00
Salt, Egyptian Design, Curled-Up Snake Center, Pair 150.00
Salver, Foliate Edge, Diaper Pattern, 10 In. 550.00
Sauceboat, Fish Form, Gorham, 1891, 6 In. 800.00
Server, Pie, King's, Bailey & Co., C.1850, Coin, 11 1/8 In. 150.00
Shaker, Pepper, Flowers & Foliage Design, 5 In., Pair 175.00
Shaker, Pepper, Owl Form, Dominick & Haff, 1882, Set Of 4 .... 350.00
Shears, Grape, Gorham, 6 1/2 In. 110.00
Shears, Grape, Unger Bros. 70.00
Shovel, Salt, Coin, 3 5/8 In. 16.00
Snuffer, Candle, Gorham, Chantilly 50.00
Snuffer, Candle, Shell Design, Tray, Footed, Coin 750.00
Spectacles, Adjustable Sides, Maker's Mark 75.00
Spectacles, C.Storrs, Utica, New York, 4 1/2 In. 130.00
Spoon, A.Henderson, Philadelphia, 1835, Set Of 6 .... 240.00
Spoon, Abraham Patton, Baltimore, 1795-1815, Set Of 5 .... 200.00
Spoon, Basket Of Flowers, G.Giffing, 1815-35, Set Of 6 .... 300.00
Spoon, Basket Of Flowers, J.Stevens, 1797, Set Of 5 .... 200.00
Spoon, Bright Cut, J.Walraven, C.1795, 5 3/8 In., Set Of 5 .... 500.00
Spoon, Coffin Corner, I.A.Shaw, C.1795, 5 1/4 In., Set Of 3 .... 300.00
Spoon, Coffin End, Saunders Pitman, 1732-1804 .... 40.00
Spoon, Dessert, Fiddle, Shepherd & Boyd, C.1810, Set Of 6 .... 1400.00
Spoon, Dessert, Flared Handle, Jones, Ball & Poor, Boston 28.00
Spoon, Egg, Olive, R. & W.Wilson, Phila, C.1850, Set Of 6 .... 295.00
Spoon, J.Dorsey, Philadelphia, C.1794, Set Of 6 .... 240.00
Spoon, Master Salt, Fiddle Handle, Lumsden & Shop 18.00
Spoon, Mustard, Fiddle Tipped, Wilson, C.1850 .... 45.00
Spoon, Paul Revere, Jr., Boston, C.1790 .... 1650.00
Spoon, Pointed Tip, James Musgrave, C.1795, 9 3/8 In., Pair 400.00
Spoon, Rattail, C.A.Burnett, Alexandria, Virginia, Coin 35.00
Spoon, Salt, B.Gardiner, New York, 1827-38, Coin 25.00
Spoon, Salt, Baldwin Gardiner, Philadelphia & N.Y., 1830s 25.00
Spoon, Salt, Bright Cut, John Burger, N.Y.C., 1725, Pair 200.00
Spoon, Salt, Fiddle Thread, B.B. & Co., C.1850, Coin, Set Of 4 .... 150.00
Spoon, Salt, Fiddle, Johnson & Godley, Albany, 1843 .... 45.00
Spoon, Salt, Shell Bowl, P.Garrett, C.1825, Coin, Pair 75.00
Spoon, Salt, Tayler & Hinsdale, Newark & New York, Pre 1820 .... 35.00
Spoon, Salt, Thomas J.Megear, C.1830, Coin, Pair 150.00
Spoon, Serving, Bright Cut, G.Cannon, Warwick, R.I., C.1795 .... 175.00
Spoon, Serving, Coffin End, A.Denilt, N.Y.C., C.1805 .... 85.00
Spoon, Serving, Double Construction, W.Brown, 1845-49, Coin 45.00
Spoon, Serving, Fiddle Thread, Gale, Wood, & Hughes, C.1836 .... 95.00
Spoon, Serving, G.Cannon, Pointed, C.1795, 9 1/4 In. 175.00
Spoon, Serving, King's Pattern, F.Marquand, C.1830 .... 150.00
Spoon, Serving, Marcus Merriman, New Haven, C.1790 .... 80.00
Spoon, Serving, Oval End, Isaac Hutton, Albany, C.1790 .... 125.00

Spoon, Serving, Pointed End, John Vernon, N.Y.C.1795	175.00
Spoon, Serving, Richard Clayton, Cincinnati, C.1834	40.00
Spoon, Serving, Shell Back, W.Walker, Phila., C.1810	125.00
Spoon, Serving, Ward & Bartholemew, 1804-09, Coin	50.00
Spoon, Serving, Warriors, C.1900, Shiebler & Co., Pair	412.00
Spoon, Sieve, J.E.Caldwell, Scalloped Bowl, 7 In.	50.00
Spoon, Tea Caddy, J.Bird, Fiddle, 1825-35, 4 In.	400.00
Spreader, Butter, Cottage Pattern, C.1840, 7 11/16 In., Pair	70.00
Sugar & Creamer, E.Stebbins & Co., New York, C.1835	700.00
Sugar Shell, Flared Handle, McKay, Spear & Brown	45.00
Sugar Tongs, Bird Feet Nippers, Hoyt, Albany, C.1830	225.00
Sugar Tongs, Bright Cut, Roe, Kingston, N.Y., 1800	185.00
Sugar Tongs, Fiddle Shell, Stodder & Forbisher, 1816-25	95.00
Sugar Tongs, J.Shoemaker, 1810, 6 1/4 In. ....*Illus*	1700.00
Sugar Tongs, Openwork, Feather Edge, Arnold, C.1760	450.00
Sugar Tongs, Oval Grips, Joshua Weaver, Penna., C.1790, Pair	250.00
Sugar, Bird Finial, Abraham Schuyler, Albany, C.1765, 5 In.	4000.00
Sugar, Covered, John Leacock, Philadelphia, C.1770, 6 In.	5225.00
Sugar, Vase Form, Geometric Design, C.1805, 8 In.	190.00
Tablespoon, Acanthus, C.1850, Set Of 12	175.00
Tablespoon, Daniel Parker, C.1840	135.00
Tablespoon, Fiddleback, W.Moulton, Mass., C.1772, Coin, Pair	100.00
Tablespoon, Fiddleback, Ziba Ferris & Son, C.1830, Coin	125.00

Silver-American, Pitcher, Whiting Mfg. Co.,
C.1880, 7 1/4 In.

Silver-American, Sugar Tongs, J.Shoemaker, 1810, 6 1/4 In.

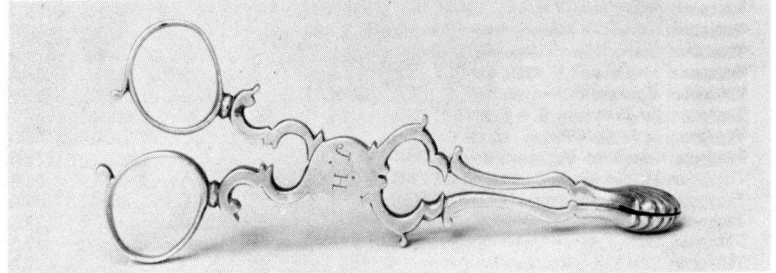

Tablespoon, Hand-Engraved, Touchmark A.B., Coin, 8 1/4 In. 30.00
Tablespoon, I.Hutton, Albany, C.1800, Set Of 12 .... 2200.00
Tablespoon, Joseph Clark, Lynn-Saugus, Boston, C.1765 .... 140.00
Tablespoon, Medallion Pattern, C.1865, Set Of 12 .... 425.00
Tazza, Country Scene, C.1900, Samuel Kirk & Sons, 6 In. 600.00
Tea Service, Cooper & Fisher, New York, C.1850, 6 Piece 3800.00
Tea Service, Engraved, C.1860, Gorham, 5 Piece 3600.00
Tea Service, Gorham Manufacturing Co, C.1909, 5 Piece 900.00
Tea Service, John Targee, New York City, C.1812, 3 Piece 3000.00
Tea Set, Beaded Edges, Theodore B.Starr, N.Y., 3 Piece 225.00
Tea Set, Beading, Chicken Leg Feet, C.1862, Gorham, 3 Piece 550.00
Tea Set, Henry Salisbury & Co., New York, C.1855, 3 Piece 715.00
Tea Set, John Ward, Philadelphia, C.1815, Marked, Coin, 3 Piece 1900.00
Tea Set, Loring Andrews Co., Kettle On Lampstand, 7 Piece 3300.00
Tea Set, Lows, Ball & Co., Boston, C.1845, 3 Piece 1760.00
Tea Set, S.Kirk & Son, Baltmore, C.1880, 4 Piece 1650.00
Tea Set, Straight Sides, Frank W.Smith Silver Co., 3 Piece 250.00
Tea Set, Thomas Whatenby, Philadelphia, C.1825, 5 Piece 2600.00
Tea Set, William Forbes, New York, C.1845, 4 Piece 1760.00
Teaspoon, Bird Back, G.Walker, Philadelphia, 1793-1816, 6 In. 45.00
Teaspoon, Bird Back, M.Richardson, Jr., C.1795, 5 In. 170.00
Teaspoon, Bird Back, Pointed, J.David, Jr., Phila., C.1790, Pr. 175.00
Teaspoon, Bright Cut, B.Cleveland, Newark, N.J., C.1790 .... 65.00
Teaspoon, Bright Cut, Eoff & Howell, N.Y.C., C.1806 .... 45.00
Teaspoon, Bright Cut, Ezekiel Burr, Providence, C.1790 .... 65.00
Teaspoon, C.1850, Wm, Durgin, Concord, N.H., Coin 18.50
Teaspoon, Coffin End, A. & C.Brandt, Phila., C.1800, 6 In. 50.00
Teaspoon, Coffin End, C.Babbit, Taunton, Ma., C.1815, Set Of 4 .... 200.00
Teaspoon, Coffin End, D.Greenleaf, Hartford, Ct., C.1800 .... 45.00
Teaspoon, Coffin End, Davis & Brown, Boston, C.1810 .... 40.00
Teaspoon, Coffin End, F.Curtis, Woodbury, Ct., C.1845, Coin 18.50
Teaspoon, Coffin End, Geer Terry, Maine, C.1800, 5 1/8 In. 40.00
Teaspoon, Coffin End, H.Prescott, Keeseville, N.Y., C.1828 .... 40.00
Teaspoon, Coffin End, Joseph Hall, Albany, C.1800, 5 3/8 In. 35.00
Teaspoon, Coffin End, S.Mumford, Newport, 1817-20, Set Of 6 .... 150.00
Teaspoon, Coffin End, S.Mumford, 1815-20, Coin, Set Of 6 .... 150.00
Teaspoon, Coffin End, S.Sargeant, Middlebury, Ct., C.1800 .... 45.00
Teaspoon, Coffin End, Smith & Chamberlain, C.1830, Coin 18.50
Teaspoon, Coffin End, Wm. McDougal, N.H., C.1825, Coin 20.00
Teaspoon, Coffin End, Wm.Stinson, N.Y., 1813, Coin 16.50
Teaspoon, F. & D.Kinsey, Coin 55.00
Teaspoon, Fiddle Tipped, W.Gennet, N.Y., C.1850, Set Of 6 .... 120.00
Teaspoon, Fiddle, C.Kendall, N.Y., 1780-97, Coin 18.50
Teaspoon, Fiddle, Easton & Sanford, Nantucket, C.1835 .... 65.00
Teaspoon, Fiddle, Goodwin & Dodd, Hartford, C.1812, 5 3/4 In. 30.00
Teaspoon, Fiddle, Littleton & Dunn, Boston, Coin 15.00
Teaspoon, Fiddle, M.Merriman, New Haven, C.1820, Engraved 20.00
Teaspoon, Fiddle, Pratt, Caps In Rectangular Punch 16.00
Teaspoon, Fiddle, Zahm & Jackson, Lancaster, C.1845, Set Of 6 .... 210.00
Teaspoon, Foliate Design Handle, J.McMullin, C.1795 .... 45.00
Teaspoon, Garland Of Flowers, P.Fries, Philadelphia, C.1837 .... 60.00
Teaspoon, George Elliott, Delaware, C.1855, Coin 125.00
Teaspoon, J.H.Carleton, C.1850, Set Of 5 .... 65.00
Teaspoon, Japanese Pattern, Gorham, 5 3/4 In., Set Of 12 .... 225.00
Teaspoon, King's Pattern, B. & S.Demilt, C.1839 .... 45.00
Teaspoon, La Fantasia Pattern, Unger Bros., 6 In. 85.00
Teaspoon, Long Drop, Zachariah Brigden, Boston, C.1780 .... 80.00
Teaspoon, Marked Hutchinson & Connell, Coffin End, Coin 22.50
Teaspoon, Mattias Haverstick, Lancaster, Pa., C.1780 .... 95.00
Teaspoon, Nautilus, Benedict, N.Y.C., C.1840 .... 16.00
Teaspoon, Olive, Beggs & Smith, Cincinnati, 6 1/8 In. 18.00
Teaspoon, Oval End, Barnabus Webb, Boston, C.1755 .... 110.00
Teaspoon, Pointed Drop, M.Gorham, New Haven, C.1790 .... 45.00

Teaspoon, Prince Albert, Stauffer & Harley, Set Of 6 .... 125.00
Teaspoon, Raised Shell, William Homes, Boston, C.1760 .... 175.00
Teaspoon, S.T.Crosby, Boston, 1850, Initialed, Coin 18.50
Teaspoon, S.Wadsworth & Co., Oval Tipped, Coin, Set Of 12 .... 175.00
Teaspoon, Script Initialed, Nathaniel & Thomas, 1860, Coin 16.50
Teaspoon, Shell Above Drop, J.Patterson, Annapolis, C.1761 .... 165.00
Teaspoon, Shell Back, Benjamin Burt, Boston, C.1760 .... 195.00
Teaspoon, Shell Back, Stilliman, New Haven, C.1760 .... 195.00
Teaspoon, Shell Back, Thomas Edwards, Boston, C.1750, Marked 180.00
Teaspoon, Shell, Pointed End, F.Bicknell, Rome, N.Y., C.1818 .... 35.00
Teaspoon, Stowell, Baltimore, C.1855, Initialed Back, Coin 18.50
Teaspoon, Wakefield, Great Falls, N.H., C.1830, Coin 20.00
Teaspoon, Ward & Bartholemew, 1804-09, Coin, Pair 35.00
Toilet Set, Roses, Cupid, Maidens, C.1900, 8 Piece 675.00
Tongs, Asparagus, T.Fletcher, Philadelphia, C.1840, 11 In. 170.00
Tongs, Sugar, Hughes & Hall, 1840s 35.00
Tongs, Sugar, Joseph Shoemaker, Philadelphia, C.1810, 6 In. 140.00
Tongs, Sugar, M.Taber & Co., Providence, R.I., Coin, 5 3/4 In. 65.00
Tray, Foliate Scrolls, Oval Form, 26 1/2 In. 1800.00
Tray, Nursery Rhyme, Wm. B. Kerr & Co., New Jersey, C.1920 .... 1000.00
Tray, Serving, Gorham, New York, C.1929, 14 In. 600.00
Tray, Tea, Watson Co., Attleboro, Mass., C.1930, 24 In. 1200.00
Tray, 2-Handled, Gorham Mfg.Co., C.1900, 28 In. 275.00
Tray, 2-Handled, Kirk & Son, Inc., C.1900, 26 1/8 In. 1900.00
Tureen, Sauce, Covered, Gorham Co., C.1899, 11 In., Pr. 1320.00
Tureen, Soup, Covered, Whiting Mfg.Co., C.1865, 16 In. 2640.00
Tureen, Soup, Covered, 2-Handled, Pedestal Foot, 13 1/2 In. 1800.00
Urn, Tea, Vase Form, Ball Feet, Loop Handles, C.1800, 17 In. 1045.00
Vase, Bud, Kirk & Son, Inc., C.1930, 7 1/2 In. 55.00
Vase, Floral Swags, C.1900, Marked B.S.C., 11 In. 715.00
Vase, Greek Design, Urn Form, Footed, Loop Handles, 8 In. 200.00
Vase, Trumpet Form, Foliate Design, 20 In., Pair 950.00
Vase, Trumpet Form, Spreading Foot, 20 In. 900.00
Vase, Trumpet Form, 4 Scroll Feet, Mum Design, 19 In. 1700.00
Vase, Trumpet, International Silver Co., C.1920, 13 In. 160.00
Waiter, Bailey & Co., Philadelphia, C.1850, 7 In. 275.00
Whistle, Bos'n's, Engraved Top, Naval Anchor Design 175.00

SILVER-AUSTRIAN, Bowl, E.Riemer, C.1920, Repousse & Chased, 7 1/2 In.Diam. 200.00
Bowl, Sweetmeat, Ruby Glass, Vienna, C.1866, 5 1/4 In. 275.00
Candelabra, C.1870, Nude Stem, 14 In., Pair 900.00
Case, Cigarette, Crest On Front, Black Trim, 5 X 3 In. 200.00
Casket, Blue Enamel Lid & Sides, C.1920, 5 3/8 In. 475.00
Ewer, Applied Scrolling, C.1870, 10 In. 275.00
Plate, Lobed Rim, Jc.Klinckosch, C.1900, 10 In., Set Of 6 .... 850.00
Tea & Coffee Set, S.T.M., Vienna, 1833-34, Case, 11 Piece 3500.00

SILVER-CANADIAN, Fish Slice, George Savage & Sons, Montreal, C.1835 .... 350.00

SILVER-CHINESE, Bowl, Applied Bamboo, Birds, Wang, Hing & Co., C.1900, 10 In. 1500.00
Bowl, Punch, Chrysanthemums, Marked WH 90, 10 1/4 In. 550.00
Bowl, Punch, 2 Dragons Chasing Sun, 12 In.Diam. 1400.00
Card Case, Dragon, Bamboo Design 230.00
Cocktail Shaker, Raised Dragon, Artist Signed, 8 1/2 In. 290.00
Compote, Footed, Wang Hing, Hong Kong, C.1890, 9 1/2 In. 300.00
Compote, Pierced Floral Design, Genre Scene, 12 In. 350.00
Fork, Pickle, Gold Wash, Lacquer Handle, 18th Century 40.00
Goblet, Tulip Form, Animals, Luen Wo, Shanghai, C.1890, 10 In. 750.00
Mug, Covered, Battle Scene, Khecheong, Canton, C.1845, 6 In. 850.00
Relish, 4 Ball Feet, Wang Hing, Hong Kong, C.1890, 19 In. 250.00
Ship, Sampan, 3 Masts, Sail, Rigging, 4 5/8 In. 100.00
Tablespoon, Fiddle Pattern 75.00
Tray, Pin, Wang Hing, Pierced, Footed 150.00

Silver-Danish, Bowl & Servers, Salad, Georg Jensen, Footed

SILVER-CONTINENTAL, Bag, Birds, Scrolls, Frogs, Chain Handle, 13 In. 100.00
   Basket, Fan Form, Glass Liner, C.1910, 10 In. 700.00
   Basket, Fruit, Grape Clusters, Vine Handle, 11 In. 600.00
   Basket, Fruit, 2-Handled, Vine Trim, Leaves, 13 In. 225.00
   Bowl, Centerpiece, Glass Liner, FR Mark, 1890, 15 In. 650.00
   Bowl, Fruit, Pierced, Foliate Scrolls, 8 In., Pair 400.00
   Bowl, Rococo Revival, Handled, 15 3/4 In. 325.00
   Bowl, Sweetmeat, Cut Glass Container, Lid, 13 In., Pair 1400.00
   Centerpiece, Table, Maiden With Dove, Flowers, 19 In. 1300.00
   Chamberstick, Merman, Vase Form Sconce, 6 In. 600.00
   Container, Spice, Tower Form, C.1910, 10 In. 900.00
   Cordial Service, Scrollwork, Frolicking Putti, Set 225.00
   Dagger, Sheath, Mythological Ladies, Clip, 12 1/2 In. 125.00
   Decanter, Pheasant Form, Removable Head, 9 1/2 In., Pair 1500.00
   Decanter, Rectangular Form, Musical Design, 11 In. 225.00
   Dish, Leaf Form, Oak, Putto Design, Pair 250.00
   Dresser Set, Ivory Paginator, FR Mark, C.1880, 9 Piece 1700.00
   Ewer, Inverted Teardrop Form, C.1875, 15 1/2 In., Pair 1100.00
   Frame, Photograph, Embossed, Pierced, Fruit, Lions, 16 In. 225.00
   Jardiniere, 4 Scroll Feet, Floral Swags, 10 In. 350.00
   Ornament, Table, Bird Form, Male & Female Pheasant 2250.00
   Platter, Chased Foliate Design, 20 In.Long 495.00
   Sauceboat, On Stand, Scrollwork, Leaves, Berries, 8 In. 550.00
   Tablespoon, Rattail Bowl, C.1727, Rib Handle 95.00
   Tray, Tea, Foliate Handle, Scrolling Design, 24 In. 800.00

SILVER-DANISH, Bowl & Servers, Salad, Georg Jensen, Footed .... *Illus* 2400.00
   Bowl, Berry Stem, Georg Jensen, C.1945, 6 3/4 In. 1200.00
   Bowl, Footed, Bell Shape, Georg Jensen, C.1931, 5 1/2 In. 550.00
   Bowl, Fruit, Center Column, Dated 1921, 5 1/2 X 9 1/2 In.Diam. 225.00
   Bowl, Georg Jensen, Silver Beads, Marked, 6 1/4 In. 280.00
   Bowl, Openwork Ring & Ball, Georg Jensen, 5 1/4 X 4 In. 250.00
   Bowl, 4-Footed, 3 1/2 X 7 In.Diam. 225.00
   Bracelet, Melon Shape Bosses, Clasp Stamped, 8 In. 260.00
   Brooch, Hand-Wrought Floral, Georg Jensen 48.00
   Case, Cigarette, Lady's, Georg Jensen, 5 Ounce 265.00
   Cocktail Set, Georg Jensen, Coats Of Arms, 12 Glasses 2200.00
   Coffee Set, Blossom Pattern, Georg Jensen .... *Illus* 2550.00
   Coffeepot, Domed Cover, Bone Finial, Simon Groth, 1837, 11 In. 500.00

Silver-Danish, Coffee Set, Blossom Pattern, Georg Jensen

Silver-Danish, Dish, Shell Shaped,
Georg Jensen, 7 1/2 In.

Compote, Boat Form, Lobed Stem, Copenhagen, C.1919, 8 In. 650.00
Decanter & Plate, Elongated Windows, Georg Jensen, 10 1/2 In. 600.00
Dish, Shell Shaped, Georg Jensen, 7 1/2 In. .... *Illus* 1875.00
Pin, Art Nouveau, Bird Design, Jensen, 2 1/2 In. 300.00
Pitcher, Art Deco, Georg Jensen, Copenhagen, 17 In. 1900.00
Pitcher, Water, Bow Handle, C.1935, Georg Jensen, 11 3/4 In. 1200.00
Pitcher, Water, Georg Jensen, C.1940, 8 3/4 In. 725.00
Plate, Gadroon Rim, Chased Hunting Scene, H.B.Mark, 11 1/8 In. 440.00
Salt & Pepper Shaker, Georg Jensen, 2 In. 250.00
Spoon, Sugar, Classic Pattern, Georg Jensen 45.00
Tea & Coffee Set, Copenhagen, 1910, Coffeepot, 9 In., 4 Piece 800.00
Tea Urn, Copenhagen, 1893-94 .... *Illus* 900.00
Tie Bar, Applied Horsehead, Georg Jensen 38.00
Toothpick, Chicken Perched On Wishbone Base 45.00
Tray, Art Deco, Georg Jensen, Copenhagen, 17 1/4 In. 1500.00
Tray, Circular, Scalloped Edge, Georg Jensen, 11 In. 550.00
Tray, 2-Handled, Oval, Vertical Cuts, Georg Jensen, 24 In. 3750.00

SILVER-DUTCH, Basket, Fruit, Street Scene, Musicians, 12 In. 400.00
  Belt, People Links 450.00

Silver-Danish, Tea Urn, Copenhagen, 1893-94   *(See Page 621)*

Silver-English, Chamberstick, Paul Storr, 1828, 2 1/2 In.

Box, Tobacco, Scene Of Peasants Drinking, C.1850, 4 1/2 In.	350.00
Chocolate Pot, Baluster Form, Flowers	425.00
Fork & Spoon, Serving, Openwork Twist Handles, 12 In.	140.00
Jug, Figural, Napoleon, C.1910, 4 1/2 In.	350.00
Nef, Frolicking Putti, 3 Masts, C.1910, 12 In.	2400.00
Shoe, Baroque Scrolls, Scenes Of Suitors, C.1897, 10 In.	1100.00
Windmill, Thatched Dome, Wooden Base, 1951, 10 1/2 In.	650.00

English silver is marked with a series of 4 or 5 small hallmarks. The standing lion mark is the most commonly seen sterling quality mark.

SILVER-ENGLISH, Basket, Cake, Henry Chawner, London, 1790	2800.00
Basket, Embossed, 1827, R.Gainsford, 49.3 Ounces	4500.00
Basket, Flowers & Scrolls, Lobed, Charles Harris, 1890, 9 In.	1100.00
Basket, Peter & Ann Bateman, 8 7/8 X 3 7/8 In., Pair	2000.00
Basket, Reticulated, Gadrooned Edge, Twisted Handle, 3 In.	1500.00
Basket, Sugar, William Abdy, London, 1787	412.00
Beaker, Gilded Interior, Nathan Smith & Co., 1802, 3 1/2 In.	275.00
Bonbon, C.1892, W.Comyns, London, Cherubs, 6 1/2 In.	175.00
Bowl, Indian Style, Fruit, Foliate, 3 1/4 In.	500.00
Bowl, Isaac Cookson, Newcastle, C.1732, 3 7/8 In.	450.00
Bowl, Ladle, Masks On Rim, H.E. & Co., 1901, 12 1/2 In.Diam.	2300.00
Bowl, Oval, Pierced Floral Design, Footed, 4 In.	220.00
Box, Cigarette, Cedarwood Liner, 3 Sections, 8 In.	275.00
Box, Cigarette, Rectangular Form, Hinged, 8 In.	275.00
Box, Maiden In Profile, Covered, C.1902, 6 In.	350.00
Box, Thread, Detachable Cover, Chased, W.Comyns, 1892, 3 In.	265.00
Candelabra, George III, Shell & Scroll Design, 18 In., Pr.	1900.00
Candelabra, 3-Light, S-Scroll Arms, E.J.G., 1923, 9 In.	900.00
Candlestick, Chamber, Adam Style, Square Base, 5 In., Pr.	150.00
Candlestick, Chamber, Ribbon Tied Swags, 5 In., Pair	150.00
Candlestick, Detachable Sconce, T.J. & N.Creswick, 1838, 6 In	
Candlestick, John Parsons & Co., 1792, 7 1/2 In., Pair	1150.00
Candlestick, Removable Sconce, T.J. & N.Creswick, 1838, 6 In.	400.00
Castor, Wine, Pierced Holder, Sheffield, 1835, 17 1/8 In.	275.00
Chamberstick, Paul Storr, 1828, 2 1/2 In. *Illus*	2090.00
Chamberstick, Taper, Sheffield, C.1810	325.00

Chatelaine, Link Chain, London, 1889-90, W.Comyns, 7 In. 1450.00
Coaster, George III, John Roberts, 1813, 5 3/4 In., Pair 1300.00
Coaster, Wine, George III, Thomas & Jas. Creswick, 1813, Pr. 900.00
Coffee & Tea Set, Celtic Design, 1874, Pot, 11 In., 4 Piece 3000.00
Coffee & Tea Set, Chased Pear Form, Barnards, 1869, 5 Piece 4000.00
Coffee Set, Fruit Clusters, Gilt Interior, 6 Piece 7000.00
Coffee Set, Pear Form, Fruit Cluster, Marked, 6 Pece 7000.00
Coffeepot & Teapot, D. & S., 1926, Gadroon Border, 7 1/2 In. 500.00
Coffeepot, Baluster Form, J.E.Terry, 1829, 8 In. 800.00
Coffeepot, Chased To Resemble Barrel, C.S.Harris, 1884, 8 In. 750.00
Coffeepot, D. & G.Holy, C.1830, Pear Shape, 8 1/2 In. 175.00
Creamer, Beaded Edge, Cut Central Band, Sheffield, 4 In. 110.00
Creamer, Cow, Hinged Lid, George Fox, 1883, 4 In. 1100.00
Creamer, George V, Bullet Form, Hoop Handle, 7 In. 225.00
Cup, George IV, 2-Handled, Paul Storr, 1825 .... *Illus* 2200.00
Cup, Stephen Ardesoif, London, 1775, 5 In. 300.00
Cup, Trophy, Benjamin Smith, 1831, 19 In. 3000.00
Dish, Cellini Pattern, George Angell, 1870, 12 3/4 In. 1200.00
Dish, Nut, Wheelbarrow Form, Cut Glass, 7 1/2 In. 600.00
Dish, Ring, GeorgeIII, Latticework, Dolphin Swag, 7 In. 1100.00
Dish, Stylized Fruits, Crichton, 1910, Handled, 8 In. 200.00
Dish, Well & Tree, 3 Crest Border, Oval, 25 In. 3000.00
Dish, 3 Chased Napkins, Mortimer & Hunt, 1842, 11 In. 3750.00
Egg Warmer, C.1790, Harp Shape Handled, Sheffield, 11 1/2 In. 225.00
Epergne, 3 Baskets, Winged Griffin Supports, 1865, 31 In. 6000.00
Ewer, Cellini Pattern, Animal, Foliate Design, 12 In. 1600.00
Ewer, Flowers & Acanthus Design, Bamboo Handle, 10 In. 500.00
Ewer, M.Hall & Co., 1879, Hinged Cover, 10 3/4 In., Pair 600.00
Figurine, Equestrian, Richard Comyns, 1940, 12 In. 1700.00
Figurine, Grenadier Pikeman, Carrington & Co., 1969, 9 In. 400.00
Figurine, Highlander, Carrington & Co., 1871, 15 3/4 In. 1200.00
Figurine, Queen's Guard, Carrington & Co., 1967, 6 7/8 In. 450.00
Fish Slice, Grillwork On Blade, Dated 1818, 11 3/4 In. 275.00
Fish Slice, Pierced, Hester Bateman, 1789, 11 3/4 In. 750.00
Flagon, Victorian, Hands & Son, London, C.1874, 7 In. 1000.00
Fork, Roast, Fearn & Chawner, 1813 .... *Illus* 1400.00
Funnel, Wine, London, Henry Hyde, 1844 .... 800.00
Goblet, J.E.Terrey, 1828, Campana Form, Hunt Scene, 8 3/4 In. 325.00
Grater, Nutmeg, George Pearson, 1817, Hinged Cover, 1 1/2 In. 325.00
Grater, Nutmeg, Nutmeg Shape, H. & T., 1853, 1 5/8 In. 500.00
Holder, Placecard, Assorted Animal Forms, Set Of 11 .... 100.00

Silver-English, Cup, George IV,
2-Handled, Paul Storr, 1825

Silver-English, Fork, Roast, Fearn & Chawner, 1813

(See Page 623)

Inkstand, Cut Glass Insert, Martin & Hall, 1868, 10 In.	700.00
Inkstand, George III, Oval, Cut Glass Pounce Pot, 3 3/4 In.	650.00
Inkstand, Pond Form, Broom Penholders, W.M. & S., 1898, 8 In.	400.00
Inkstand, 2-Well, Joseph & John Angel, 9 X 5 1/4 In.	450.00
Inkstand, 3-Bottle, William Plummer, 1784, 9 1/2 In.	525.00
Jug, Cream, Circular Form, Scroll Handle, 3 1/8 In.	45.00
Kettle, Hot Water, Queen Anne, C.1925, L.A.Crichton, London	1750.00
Ladle, Gravy, S, Hennell, London, C.1804	125.00
Ladle, Sauce, Hester Bateman, 1788, Pair	350.00
Ladle, Sauce, Samuel Hennel, London, 1807-08	65.00
Ladle, Toddy, Ralph Maidman, 1731, Hallmarks, 12 In.	490.00
Match Holder, Mappin & Webb, 1926, 2 1/2 X 1 3/4 In.	65.00
Mug, Child's, E.S.B., 1914, S-Scroll Handle, 3 1/8 In.	100.00
Mug, Fuller, White, London, C.1761, 5 In.	450.00
Mug, Hester Bateman, London, C.1788, 5 In.	425.00
Nutmeg Grater, Engraved Edges, L. & A.Mark, C.1800, 1 7/8 In.	275.00
Nutmeg Grater, Engraved Leaves, S.Pemberton, 1809, 1 3/8 In.	425.00
Papboat, Greek Key Band, John Emes, 1806-07, 5 1/16 In.	275.00
Plaque, Medieval Battle, Banqueting Scene, 16 In., Pr.	2500.00
Plate, Engraved Motto, W.Stroud, 1905, 9 1/2 In., Set Of 12	8000.00
Punch Bowl, C.1895, 7 X 11 1/4 In.Diam.	750.00
Rattle, C.1810, Marked M.C., Coral Teether ......*Illus*	500.00
Rattle, Faceted Whistle, Hung With Seven Bells, 5 3/8 In.	500.00
Salt & Pepper, Bright Cut, J.S. & T., 1931, 4 In.	325.00
Salt, Glass Eyes, Hallmarked 1885, 3 1/2 In.	150.00
Salt, Pierced Rims, Inserts, George Fox, 1885, 2 1/2 In., Pair	375.00
Salt, Pierced, Original Spoon & Pepper, Cobalt Blue Liner	89.00
Salt, Triform Base, 3 Dolphins, 3 1/2 In.	900.00
Salver, Engraved Crest, 3-Footed, Marked, 8 1/4 In.	475.00
Salver, Robert Salmon, Footed, C.1871, 7 In.	200.00
Salver, S.C.Younge & Co., Sheffield, 1822, 14 3/8 In.Diam.	700.00
Salver, 4 Fox Hunting Scenes, Animal Motifs, 12 In.	1400.00
Sauceboat, Reeded Rim, Crighton Bros., 1823	425.00
Sauceboat, Shell & Hoof Feet, William & James Priest	225.00
Scissors, Grape, Regency, Paul Storr, 1816 ......*Illus*	2200.00
Scissors, Reily & Storer, 1832, Branch Grips, 6 7/8 In., Pair	250.00
Scoop, Cheese, Paul Storr, 1820, 9 1/8 In. ......*Illus*	1540.00
Scoop, Cheese, W.Kingdon, 1821, Ivory Handled, 8 1/4 In.	265.00
Scoop, Cheese, Wooden Handle, 1831, Wm. Kingdon, London	95.00
Scoop, Marrow, Thos.Ollivant, London, C.1801	195.00
Server, Salad, Chased Chicken Foot, Bone Handles, 13 In., Pair	500.00
Slice, Fish, Hester Bateman, London, C.1789	775.00
Snuff Bottle & Vinaigrette, 1871, Ruby Glass ......*Illus*	400.00
Snuffbox, Basket Weave Top, F.Clark, 1835, 2 1/2 X 1 3/8 In.	100.00
Snuffbox, Cowrie Shell, Phipps & Robinson, 1807, 3 1/4 In.	500.00

Silver-English, Snuff Bottle & Vinaigrette, 1871, Ruby Glass

Silver-English, Scissors, Grape, Regency, Paul Storr, 1816

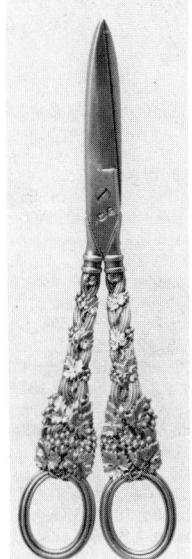

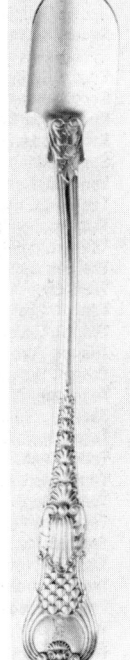

Silver-English, Scoop, Cheese, Paul Storr, 1820, 9 1/8 In.

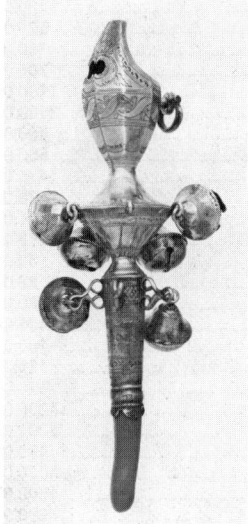

Silver-English, Rattle, C.1810, Marked M.C., Coral Teether

Snuffbox, Dated 1823, Birmingham, Hinged Lid, 2 1/2 In.	155.00
Spoon Warmer, Shell Form, Wrigglework Engraving, 5 In.	475.00
Spoon, Berry, Chased Grapes & Leaves, 1798, Marked, Pair	330.00
Spoon, Berry, D.Urquhart & N.Hart, 1806	175.00
Spoon, Berry, Georgian, Marked 1827, 8 In.	145.00
Spoon, Berry, Hallmarked, W.Eley & W.Fearn, 1802, 8 1/2 In.	125.00
Spoon, Berry, Serving, Coat Of Arms, 1810, 8 1/4 In.	125.00
Spoon, Crested, Christian Reid, Newcastle, C.1803, Pair	300.00
Spoon, Fruit, Hallmarked, 1792, Set Of 6	310.00

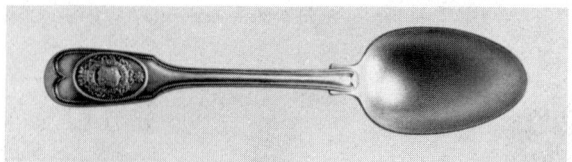

Silver-English, Spoon, Regency, Paul Storr, 1819, Set Of 6

Spoon, Gravy, D.Urquhart & Hart, 1804, Pair	350.00
Spoon, Kings Pattern, Charles Eley, 1827, 11 1/4 In., Pair	425.00
Spoon, Marmalade, London, Newcastle 1828, 5 In., Pair	90.00
Spoon, Marrow, Georgell, Deer's Head On Back, Marked	125.00
Spoon, Regency, Paul Storr, 1819, Set Of 6 .... *Illus*	440.00
Spoon, Salt, Robert Cruickshank, London, C.1786, 4 In., Pair	75.00
Spoon, Serving, Hester Bateman, C.1785, 9 In., Pair	450.00
Spoon, Serving, John Wren, London, Crested, C.1801, 9 In., Pair	300.00
Spoon, Stuffing, Reverse Tip, C.1839, 12 In.Long	155.00
Spoon, Sugar Sifter, Fiddleback, E.Eaton, 1849, Falcon Crest	200.00
Spoon, Tea Caddy, Gilt, Birmingham, Joseph Taylor, 1821, Pair	575.00
Strainer, Lemon, George III, Edward Aldridge, London, 6 In.	325.00
Sugar Caster, Octagonal, Goldsmith & Silversmith, 1909, 8 In.	300.00
Tankard, Covered, Thomas Farren, London, C.1740	500.00
Tankard, Gurney & Cook, London, C.1748, 7 In.	750.00
Tea Set, Benoni Stephens, 1826, Leaf-Capped Handle, 3 Piece	700.00
Tea Set, Peter, Ann, & William Bateman, 1801, 3 Piece	1700.00
Tea Set, Spherical Form, Celtic Design, 5 Piece	2250.00
Teakettle, Lampstand, C. & R.Comyns, 1923, 13 1/2 In.	750.00
Teapot, Oval Form, Wood Knop, John Edwards, 1807, 6 1/4 In.	500.00
Teapot, Queen Anne Style, Hemming, London, C.1905	475.00
Teapot, Scrolls, Flowers, Bird Head Spout, Marked, 6 In.	425.00
Teapot, Wooden Handle & Finial, William Plummer, 1790, Oval	700.00
Teaspoon, Bright Cut, C.Hougham, 1755-89, Small, Set Of 10	250.00
Teething Ring, Wishbone With Chick, Out Of Egg	50.00
Toast Rack, Scrolled Feet, 6 Slice, Hutton & Sons, Hallmarked	38.00
Toast Rack, Victorian, Robert Garrand, 1853, 6 1/2 In.	650.00
Tongs, Asparagus, Joseph & Albert Savory, 1834, 10 1/2 In.	475.00
Tongs, Sugar, Peter & Ann Bateman, 1794, 5 1/2 In., Pair	150.00
Top, Decanter, Grotesque Head, Movable Ears, 1882, 2 1/2 In.	125.00
Tray, Maiden Head, Mark W.M.Chester, C.1901, 11 In.	525.00
Tray, S.C.Younge & Co., Handled, 1820, 2. 1/4 In.	3200.00
Tray, Shell & Shield Design, Sheffield, C.1930, 31 In.	2000.00
Trowel, Beaded Border, Barnards, 1870, 16 1/2 In.	475.00
Tureen, James Young, 1792, Covered, 21 In. .... *Illus*	5000.00
Tureen, Soup, W.Hutton & Sons, Ltd., Covered, 1908, 11 3/4 In.	1500.00
Urn, Hot Water, James Hobbs, London, 1831, 152 Ounces	5600.00
Urn, Hot Water, 1784-85, 83 Troy Ounces .... *Illus*	2000.00
Vinaigrette, Cathedral, Edward Smith, 1844, 1 1/2 In.	600.00
Vinaigrette, Matthew Linwood, 1804 .... *Illus*	600.00
Vinaigrette, Windsor Castle, Gervase Wheeler, 1839, 1 3/4 In.	950.00
Waiter, John Robinson, London, 1748, 6 In.	700.00
Waiter, Thomas Bradbury, London, C.1899, 8 In.	225.00
SILVER-FRENCH, Bonbon, Cut Glass, Ivy Vine Frame, 10 In.	275.00
Box, Pill, Applied Poppies, Hallmarked, 1 3/4 In.Diam.	48.00
Candlestick, Table, Paris 1809-19, Leaf Tips, 10 In., Pair	1200.00
Case, Enamel Design On Lid, Marked, C.1930, 3 5/16 X 2 1/8 In.	90.00
Ciborium, Gilt & Enamel, Gothic Design, 9 In.	200.00
Ciborium, Religious Symbols, Gilt Interior, 9 In.	250.00
Coffee & Tea Set, Chased, Floral Finial, C.1870, 5 Piece	3200.00

Silver-English, Tureen, James Young, 1792, Covered, 21 In.

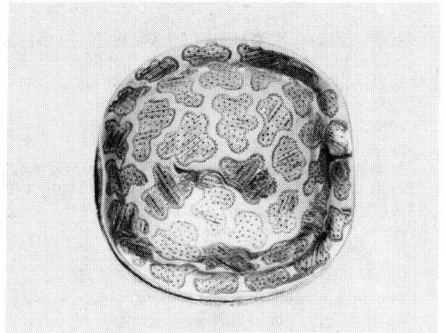

Silver-English, Urn, Hot Water,   Silver-English, Vinaigrette, Matthew Linwood, 1804

1784-85, 83 Troy Ounces

Coffee Service, Pear Form, Regency Design, 5 Pieces	4750.00
Coffeepot, Louis XV, Elongated Pear Form, 8 1/2 In.	375.00
Coffeepot, Regence Style, Cardeilhac, 1800s, 10 In.	1700.00
Communion Set, Glass Cruet, 3 Pieces	450.00
Dessert Service, Tallois Mayenol, 2-Color Gilding, 48 Piece	1800.00
Ewer, Cut Glass, Spiral Mounts, Scroll Handle, 10 In.	400.00
Goblet, Tulip Form, Flowers, Scrolls, 4 In., Pair	225.00
Jug, Claret, C.1890, Silver Overlay, Iris Etched, 13 In.	650.00
Ladle, Punch, Fiddle Thread Pattern, 19th Century	55.00
Mustard, Figural, Owl, Swags & Acanthus, C.1875, 5 1/2 In.	650.00
Plate, Portrait Medallion, Puiforcat, C.1900, 11 3/4 In.	1500.00
Spurs, Husks, Foliage, Serpentine Mount, C.1820, Pair	385.00
Sugar Caster, Lobed Form, Trim Foot, Pierced Cover, 7 In.	475.00
Sundial & Compass, Pocket, Chapotot, 18th Century, Case	1540.00
Taster, Wine, Grapevine, Snake Handles, 3 1/4 In., Pair	250.00
Tongs, Sugar, Hallmarked	50.00
Tray, Foliate Scrolls, Shellwork, Flowers, 14 In.	400.00
Wine Taster, S.S.T.L., 1819-38, Ring Handle, 3 1/8 In.	250.00

SILVER-GERMAN, Beaker, Double, Gilded Inside, I.K.Mark, 5 In.	1600.00
Beaker, Pineapple Lobes, Cherubs, 5 In.	150.00
Bowl, Centerpiece, Oval Form, Cartouches, 17 In.	700.00
Bowl, Divided, Paw Feet, Birds, Flowers, 1900, 10 1/2 In.	475.00

Silver-Irish, Coconut Cups, George III

Candlestick, L.A.K., C.1810, Putti Masks, 9 1/4 In., Pair 1500.00
Chalice, Commemorative, Gothic Design, 8 In. 250.00
Creamer, Cow, Loop Tail Forms Handle, Hinged Cover, 6 In. 633.00
Dipper, Holy Water, Christ Child & Angels, 2 Piece 225.00
Ladle, C.1840, Bone Handle, Conch Shell Bowl 325.00
Ladle, Punch, Marked Bartels, C.1830, 13 1/2 In. 150.00
Pheasant, Male, Hinged Wings, C.1900, 13 1/2 In. 375.00
Tea & Coffee Set, Spritzer & Funhmahn, C.1930, 4 Piece 2000.00
Tray, Inset Prussian Coins, C.1915, Coin, 13 In. 400.00
Warmer, Muffin, Putto Design, 13 In. 900.00

SILVER-IRISH, Coconut Cup, George III, C.1790 .... Illus 350.00
Coconut Cup, George III, C.1790, Pair .... Illus 225.00
Coconut Cup, George III, William Bond, 1791 .... Illus 225.00
Sauceboat, George III, R.Calderwood, 6 In., Pair .... Illus 3600.00
Spoon, Dessert, Engraved Crest, James LeBass, 1835, Set Of 10 .... 250.00
Spoon, Egg, C.1820, Dublin 45.00
Spoon, Strainer, Divided, Richard Sawyer, Dublin, 12 3/4 In. 325.00
Tongs, Sugar, S. Neville, Dublin, C.1805 .... 175.00

SILVER-ITALIAN, Case, Cigarette, Applied Gold Husks, C.1900, 3 3/4 In.Long 325.00
Dish, 3 Paw Feet, 6 Scroll Design, 13 In. 200.00
Ewer, Underplate, Inverted Pear Form, 20 1/2 In. 2200.00
Lamp, 4 Satyr Mask Spouts, Center Figure, C.1830, 21 1/4 In. 1650.00

SILVER-JAPANESE, Bowl, Sea Creatures, Footed, C.1880, 7 1/2 In. 360.00
Box, Cigarette, Dragons Design, C.1900, 4 3/4 In. 360.00
Tea Set, Tray, Dragons, Clouds, Dragon Handle, 5 Piece 2300.00
Tea Set, Wood Tray, Spherical Form, 5 Piece 600.00

SILVER-MEXICAN, Butter Pat, Shaped Rim, Maciel, 3 1/2 In.Diam., Set Of 8 .... 50.00

SILVER-ORIENTAL, Box, Cigarette, Siam, Elephant Design, Wood Interior, 3 In. 50.00

SILVER-PERUVIAN, Bowl, Curved Hexagonally Paneled Sides, Flat Rim, 12 In. 240.00
Box, Cigarette, Convex Top, Incan Figural Panel 140.00
Cocktail Shaker, Double Domed Top, 11 1/4 In. 160.00
Dish, Scalloped Leaf Shape, Wooden Handle, 14 In. 45.00
Figurine, Game Cock, 1 Crouching, 1 Attacking, 7 1/2 X 7 In 475.00
Pitcher, Water, Hand-Hammered, Spherical Bowl, 8 In. 195.00
Tray, Hand-Hammered, Scalloped Rim, 20th Century, Pair 450.00

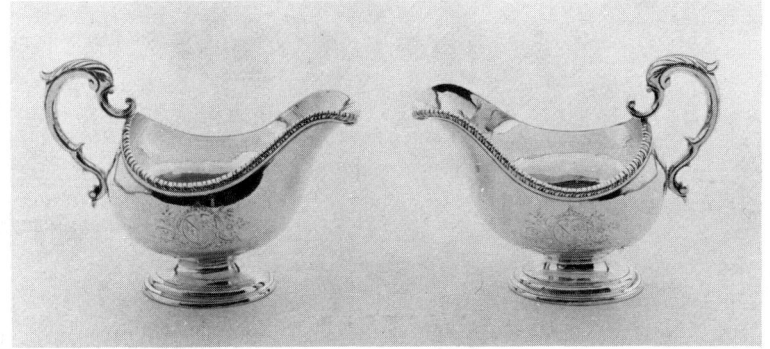

Silver-Irish, Sauceboat, George III, R. Calderwood, 6 In., Pair

SILVER-POLISH, Candlestick, C.1925, Neoclassical, 13 In., Pair 750.00
   Gadroon Rim, Elongated Oval, Malsz, Warsaw, C.1840, 30 In. 1100.00
   Tea Caddy, C.1800, Lead Liner, 5 1/4 In. 600.00

SILVER-PORTUGUESE, Candlestick, Firn, Oporto, C.1850, 7 7/8 In., Pair 400.00
   Candlestick, J.F.D.G., Oporto, 19th Century, 6 5/8 In., Pr. 425.00
   Tea & Coffee Set, Mass, Oporto, C.1860, 4 Piece 1200.00

     Russian silver is marked with the cyrillic or Russian alphabet. The numbers 84, 88, or 91 indicate the content of solid silver pieces. Russian silver may be higher or lower than sterling standard. Other marks indicate maker, assayer, or city of manufacture.

SILVER-RUSSIAN, see also Faberge
SILVER-RUSSIAN, Bottle, Scent, Enameled, Moscow 1894, Red, White, Blue, 6 In. 2310.00
   Box, Sugar, Crowned Monogram, C.A.S., St.Petersburg, 1867 .... 825.00
   Cake Basket, A.Markolua, 1840, Lobed, Oval Form, 13 1/4 In. 500.00
   Case, Cigarette, Gold Script, Cabachon Blue Gem Thumbpiece 245.00
   Compact, Leaves & Stripes, C.1900, Blue Enamel, 4 1/4 In. 225.00
   Cup, Vodka, Lobed Form, Flowers, Flaring Lip, 3 In., Pair 440.00
   Decanter, Cranberry Glass, Ovchinnikov, Moscow, 1879, 16 In. 990.00
   Dish, Art Nouveau, Chased Floral, Handled 95.00
   Fork, Serving, Moscow, 1896-1908, 8 1/4 In. 70.00
   Goblet, Chalice Shape, Hallmarked, 1881, 4 In., Set Of 6 .... 285.00
   Ladle, Fiddle Pattern, Shyalovtsi, 1894, 9 Ounce 165.00
   Mug, Barnyard Scene, Paramonov, Moscow, 1876, 6 In. 550.00
   Salt, Throne, Enameled, N.V.Alekseyev, 1896, 4 1/2 In. 1760.00
   Snuffbox, Peter The Great, C.1838, 3 In. 300.00
   Spoon, Demitasse, Gilt, Enameled, Dmitri Nicholaev, C.1910 .... 1540.00
   Spoon, Demitasse, Teardrop Bowl, Red, White & Blue Accents 50.00
   Spoon, Serving, Shaded Enamel, Moscow, C.1910, 6 1/8 In. 1870.00
   Spoon, Snake & Rat Stem & Handle, Flower Bowl, 5 In. 150.00
   Strainer, Tea, Gilt & Enamel, Ivan Khlebnikov, C.1900 .... 550.00
   Sugar, Boat Shaped, Melon Ribbed, Dated 1827, Savoref 595.00
   Tankard, Cylindrical Form, Anton Kuzmichev, 1888, 6 In. 880.00
   Teapot, A.S., St.Petersburg, 1840, Lobed Oval Form, 5 3/4 In. 450.00

SILVER-SCANDINAVIAN, Dish, Meat, Marked G.G., 18th Century, 18 In.Long 1200.00

SILVER-SCOTTISH, Goblet, Ovoid Body, Knop Stem, Round Base, 6 1/4 In., Pair 900.00
   Goblet, Patrick Robinson, Edinburgh, 1779, Pair .... *Illus* 1500.00

(See Page 629)

Silver-Scottish, Goblet, Patrick Robinson, Edinburgh, 1779, Pair

Ladle, Sauce, Alex Zeigler, C.1800, 6 In.	150.00
Spoon, Egg, C.1838, R & S Aberdeen	65.00
SILVER-SIAMESE, Bowls, Peasants Working In Field, 5 In., Pair	200.00
Plate, Niello, Scrolling Foliage, Set Of 6, 8 In.	800.00
SILVER-SOUTH AMERICAN, Mate Cup, Chased Foliage Bowl, Knop Stem, 9 1/4 In.	165.00
Stirrup, Side Saddle, 18th Century, Chiseled Design	595.00
SILVER-SPANISH, Nef, Galleon Style, 3 Masts, Sailors, Dolphin Feet, 13 1/4 In.	1100.00

Sterling silver is made with 925 parts of silver out of 1,000 parts of metal. The word sterling is a quality guarantee used in the United States after about 1860.

SILVER-STERLING, see also Silver-American; Silver-English; etc.

SILVER-STERLING, Bowl, Circular Form, Curved Sides, Embossed Rim, 8 7/8 In.	90.00
Box, Cigarette, Curved Back, Nude Woman On Repousse Cover	160.00
Box, Colonial Dancing Couple, 3 1/4 X 3 1/4 In.	250.00
Box, Spice, Chased Scrolling & Foliage, C.1810, 2 3/4 In.	250.00
Brush, Clothes, Art Nouveau, Lady With Flowing Hair	12.50
Buttonhook, Art Nouveau, Handle Embossed With Head, 7 In.	22.00
Candelabra, 5-Light, Twisted Candles, 1 1/2 In.	80.00
Candlestick, Beaded Top & Base, DeMatteo, 5 3/4 In., Pair	165.00
Case, Card, Allover Engraving, Coin.3 1/2 X 2 1/2 In.	150.00
Case, Flexible Chain Links To Secure Cigarettes	88.50
Chalice Cup, Applied Grapes, Lid, Gold Wash Interior, 14 In.	600.00
Collar Button, Profile Of Roman Warrior	18.00
Collar, Cat, Horseshoe Shape, Medallion Cat Face On Chain	175.00
Comb, Mustache, Chased Checked Design, 5 5/8 In.	55.00
Creamer, Figural, Cow, Insect On Lid, 4 1/4 X 7 In.	590.00
Crucifix, Vienna, 1854, 18 1/4 In.	415.00
Curler, Mustache, Handled	24.00
Cutter, Cigar, Spring Loaded	65.00
Decanter, Lacy Design On Black, Glass Pedestal	150.00
Decanter, Overlay, Grape Cluster Stopper, 13 1/4 In.	225.00
Dresser Set, Art Nouveau, 12 Piece	1450.00
Dresser Set, Repousse Floral Deco, 13 Piece	300.00
Figurine, Buffalo, Standing, 3 X 5 In.	530.00
Figurine, Cow, Standing, Horned, 1925, 3 1/2 In.	255.00
Figurine, Pig, Seated, 2 X 1/2 In.	88.00
Figurine, Retriever, Sitting, With Collar, 4 In.	240.00
Figurine, Stallion, Standing, 1925, 3 1/2 X 3 1/2 In.	265.00

Flask, Whiskey, Art Nouveau 275.00
Food Pusher, Shield & Ribbon Design, C Monogram 25.00
Fork, Lettuce, Thistle Pattern, Dated 1901 .... 48.00
Fork, Serving, Cherub On Handle, 7-Tined, 4 3/4 In. 30.00
Humidor, 3-Tiered, Cover On Each, 9 3/4 X 7 4/8 In. 300.00
Iron & Brush, Curling, Mustache 49.00
Iron, Mustache, Pearl Button On Handle 75.00
Knife Rest, Elongated Dog 18.00
Knife, Butter, Hallmarked, 7 In. 15.00
Knife, Cuticle 12.00
Ladle, Punch, Repousse, Single Lip, 14 In. 450.00
Ladle, Water, Continental, C.1890, 14 In.Long, 6 1/2 Ounces 150.00
Match Safe, Art Nouveau, 3 X 1 1/2 In. 80.00
Match Safe, Butterfly-Winged Figure Of Nude In Bower 85.00
Match Safe, Fishing Scene 46.00
Match Safe, Hunt Scene 85.00
Match Safe, Inscribed 1857-1903 .... 16.00
Match Safe, Masonic Emblem & Monogram, Embossed 60.00
Match Safe, Oriental Warrior 65.00
Match Safe, Ornate Design, Vase Shape 75.00
Match Safe, Totally Ribbed, Raised Leaf On Front, 1 3/4 In. 28.50
Match Safe, Victorian Design, Monogram 55.00
Match Safe, Woman's Head, Flowing Hair 65.00
Mirror, Oval Beveled Glass, Hand, 13 In. 45.00
Pipe Set, Spoon, Cleaner, & Tamper 48.00
Pitcher, Water, Graphic Cut, Overlaid 125.00
Rattle, Acorn Shape Bells, Whistle 145.00
Rosette, Bridle, Pair 15.00
Salt & Pepper Shaker, 1 1/2 In. 40.00
Salt, Figural, Donkey Carrying 2 Dips, Beaded Base, 3 In. 38.00
Seal, Art Nouveau Handle, Blank Seal 14.00
Server, Cucumber, Grapes & Leaves On Handle 25.00
Shoehorn 22.00
Spoon, Baby, Handle Curves To Form Stork, Marked 800 .... 35.00
Spoon, Baby, Pussycat 30.00
Spoon, Engraved Indian Head 25.00
       SILVER-STERLING, SPOON, SOUVENIR, see Souvenir, Spoon, Sterling Silver
Stretcher, Glove 24.00
Tankard, Leaves, Flowers, & Stems, Repousse, 8 1/2 In. 1000.00
Tea Ball, Japanese Lantern Shape, Chain With Ring 110.00
Tea Drop, Egg Shape, Basket Weave Of Roses, 2 In. 115.00
Tea Set, Mission Style, Wood Handled, 3 Piece 375.00
Teaspoon, Lidded, Repousse Basket Weave, 6 In. 110.00
Toothpick, Trash Can Shape, 2-Handled 25.00
Whistle, Bosun Mate, With Ring, 5 1/2 In. 58.00

SILVER-SWEDISH, Beaker, Hellberg, 1818, Gilt Band, Engraved, 8 1/8 In. 1200.00
Snuffbox, Stone Set Cover, August Ahnstrom, 1845, 3 1/2 In. 412.00
Snuffbox, 2 Chased Figures, Matte Ground, 1838, 2 7/8 In. 225.00

SILVER-TIBETAN, Dagger, Shou Medallions, Bats, Bosses Of Coral & Jade, 20 In. 700.00
       SILVER, SHEFFIELD, see Silver Plate; Silver-English

*Sinclaire cut glass was made by H.P.Sinclaire and Company of
Corning, New York, between 1905 and 1929. Pieces were made of crystal as
well as amber, blue, green, or ruby. Only a small percentage of Sinclaire
glass is marked.*

SINCLAIRE, Bowl, Amber, Rolled Rim, Intaglio Flowers, Signed, 10 1/2 In. 50.00
Bowl, Fruit, Brilliant Cut, Signed, 8 X 5 In. 245.00
Candlestick, Amethyst, Signed, 13 In., Pair 350.00

Candlestick, Crystal Stem & Bobeche, Green Base, Signed, 3 In. 70.00
Candlestick, Spiral Rib Hollow Stem, Amber, Signed, 10 In., Pair 175.00
Pitcher, Cut & Engraved, Pedestal, Signed, 9 In. 1150.00
Plate, Amber, Leaf Design, Set Of 6, 8 1/2 In. 120.00
Teapot, Roses Pattern, Signed 800.00
Tray, Georgian Pattern, 13 In. 195.00
Tray, Greek Key & Laural Pattern, Signed, 13 In.Diam. 195.00
Tray, Hobstar, Fans, Crosscuts, Oval, 10 X 7 In. 150.00
Vase, Adams No.2, Signed, 20 In. 775.00
Vase, Stratford Pattern, Signed, 16 In. 275.00
Vase, 3 Roses, Hobstars, 24-Rayed Star Bottom, Signed, 10 1/2 In. 175.00

> Slag glass is streaked with several colors. There were many types made from
> about 1880. Pink slag was an American Victorian product of unknown
> origin. Purple and blue slag were made in American and English factories.
> Red slag is a very late Victorian product. Other colors are known, but
> are of less importance to the collector.

SLAG, Amber, Lamp, Table 395.00
    Blue, Spooner, Bird 15.00
    Blue, Vase, 6 In. 105.00
        SLAG, CARAMEL, see Chocolate Glass
    Green, Bowl, Pedestal, Oval, 7 X 12 In. 35.00
    Green, Toothpick 8.00
    Orange, Ashtray, Marked, 4 In. 12.00
    Pink, Cup, Punch, Inverted Fan & Feather 125.00
    Pink, Saucer, Inverted Fan & Feather, Footed, 5 1/2 X 4 5/8 In.Diam. 225.00
    Pink, Spooner, Inverted Fan & Feather 235.00
    Pink, Toothpick, Inverted Fan & Feather 275.00
    Pink, Tumbler, Inverted Fan & Feather, 3 7/8 In. 395.00
    Purple, Bowl, Footed, 4 1/2 X 3 3/4 In. 70.00
    Purple, Butter Dish, Cow, Covered 125.00
    Purple, Celery, Fluted Pattern 45.00
    Purple, Hanging, Hall, 4-Sided, Cathedral Shape, 10 In. 175.00
    Purple, Plate, Closed Lattice Edge Plate, 10 3/4 In. 75.00
    Purple, Plate, 10 1/2 In. 70.00
    Purple, Salt, Horseshoe On Sides, Square Base 36.00
    Purple, Shot Glass, Just A Thimblefull, C.1880, Geo.Davidson & Co. 55.00
    Purple, Spooner, Oval Medallion 65.00
    Purple, Sugar & Creamer, Figural, Owl, Imperial 10.00
    Purple, Sugar, Scroll With Acanthus, Open 75.00
    Purple, Vase, 10 In. 65.00
    Purple, Vase, 1930s, 11 In. 45.00
    Red, Basket, Floral Pattern, Fenton 42.00
    Red, Bowl, Pedestal, 7 1/4 X 4 In. 50.00
    Red, Compote, Jefferson, Bicentennial 150.00
    Red, Mug, Shaving, Orange Tree 75.00
    Red, Urn, Grecian, Satin Finish 35.00

> Sleepy Eye pottery was made to be given away with the flour products of
> the Sleepy Eye Milling Co., Sleepy Eye, Minnesota, from about
> 1882 to 1952. It is a heavy stoneware with blue decorations, usually the
> famous profile of an Indian.

SLEEPY EYE, Bowl, Salt 325.00
    Cookbook, Loaf Of Bread .... 150.00 To 175.00
    Crock, Butter, Blue Gray 750.00
    Crock, Salt, Blue Gray .... 325.00 To 650.00
    Mug, Blue On White, 4 1/2 In. .... 160.00 To 235.00
    Mug, Blue On Yellow, 4 1/2 In. .... 700.00 To 800.00
    Pitcher, Blue On Gray, 8 In., 1/2 Gallon .... 175.00 To 235.00
    Pitcher, Blue On Gray, 9 In., 1 Gallon 225.00
    Pitcher, Blue On White, 4 1/2 In., 1/2 Pint 120.00
    Pitcher, Blue On White, 5 1/4 In., 1 Pint .... 165.00 To 200.00

Pitcher, Blue On White, 6 1/2 In., 1 Quart	250.00
Stein, All Cobalt Blue	1000.00
Stein, Blue & White	800.00
Stein, Yellow & Brown	580.00 To 700.00
Sugar Bowl, Blue On Yellow	700.00 To 800.00
Vase, Blue & Gray, 8 1/2 In.	225.00 To 325.00

Slip is a thin mixture of clay and water, about the consistency of sour cream, that is applied to the pottery for decoration.

SLIPWARE, Plate, Pennsylvania, 6 In.	95.00
Plate, Perry County, Pennsylvania, 10 In.	195.00

SLOT MACHINE, see Coin-Operated Machine

Smith Bros. Co. *Smith Brothers glass was made after 1878. The owners had worked for the Mt. Washington Glass Company in New Bedford, Massachusetts, for seven years before going into their own shop.*

SMITH BROTHERS, Bowl, Melon Ribbed, Cream Ground, Apricot Pansies, 3 In.	225.00
Bowl, Pansy, Red Rampant Lion, Melon Ribbed, Signed, 2 1/2 In.	135.00
Bowl, Trailing Gold Strands, Enamel Drops, Signed, 9 In.	360.00
Bowl, White Flower, Green Leaves, Lion Trademark, 9 In.	500.00
Box, Powder, Lid, Rampant Lion, Ribbed, Signed, 5 1/2 In.Diam.	225.00
Cracker Jar, Art Nouveau Woman's Portrait In Gold	500.00
Creamer, Sterling Silver Holder	125.00
Jar, Pumpkin Shape, Enameled Daisies, Beige Ground, 2 1/4 In.	50.00
Lamp, Hand-Painted Stork & Cattails	225.00
Muffineer, Cream Ground, Yellow Daisies, Signed, 4 1/4 In.	275.00
Rose Bowl, Daisy & Leaf Design, Red Rampart Lion, 4 1/2 In.	250.00
Sugar & Creamer, Blue Pansies, Signed	185.00
Sugar Shaker, Flower, Sterling Silver Top, White, 6 In.	70.00
Vase, Hand-Painted Birds, Foliage, & Berries, Blue, 11 1/2 In.	150.00
Vase, Hummingbird, Pink, Silver Plated Holder, 10 1/4 In.	125.00
Vase, Log Cabin Scene, Gold Holder, 8 1/4 In.	185.00
Vase, Pairpoint Holder, 4 1/4 In., Pair	140.00
Vase, Swirled Bulbous Body, Enameled Daisies, 6 3/4 In.	130.00

Snow Babies, made from bisque and spattered with glitter sand, were first manufactured in 1864 by Hertwig and Company in Thuringia. Other German and Japanese companies copied the Hertwig designs. Originally, Snow Babies were made of candy and used as Christmas decorations. There are also Snow Babies tablewares made by Royal Bayreuth.

SNOW BABIES, Arms Outstretched, Sitting, 2 1/2 In.	95.00
Boy Skater, Molded Clothes, 2 In.	125.00
Cup & Saucer, Demitasse, Blue Mark	135.00
Doll, Baby Falling Over Ball, 1 3/4 In.	32.50
Doll, Dogs Pulling Red Sled With Baby, 3 1/4 In.	32.50
Figurine, Seated, Legs Bent, Outstretched Arms, Marked, 3 In.	125.00
Girl On Sled, Molded Skirt, 2 In.Long	125.00
Girl Skater, Molded Clothes, 2 In.	125.00
Girl, One Hand Raised, Sitting, Sweater & Cap, 1 1/2 In.	35.00
Girl, Seated, Molded Skirt, Pink, 1 1/4 In.	75.00
Group, One Seated, One On Side, One Standing, 1 In.	40.00
Polar Bear On Back, Legs Crossed Over Yellow Ball, 1 1/2 In.	95.00
Polar Bear, Germany, 1 1/4 In.	40.00
Polar Bear, Standing On Sled, 2 In.	100.00
Reclining On Side, One Arm Up, 2 3/4 In.	48.00
Seal & Ball, 2 In.	40.00
Seated, Holding Snowball, 2 1/2 In.	125.00
Snow Church, Bisque, 3 In.	150.00
Snow Globe, Glass	12.00

Snowman, Seated, Arms & Legs Extended, 2 1/4 In.	135.00
Tile, Tea, Blue Mark	150.00
Toothpick, Pedestal, Blue Mark	150.00
Toothpick, Silver Rim, Royal Bayreuth	125.00
SNUFF BOTTLE, see Bottle, Snuff	

SNUFFBOX, Classical Woman & Youth, Marked H.L. & Co., C.1800, Gold & Enamel	8500.00
Double Wall, Hen Engraved, 18th Century, Copper, Presentation	450.00
Dragonflies, Lady's, Porcelain, French, 1 3/4 X 2 1/8 In.	69.00
Engraved Allover, Edward Smith, Birmingham, 1850, Sterling Silver	275.00
Figural, Lady's Square Toed Shoe, Hinged, Papier-Mache, 3 3/4 In.	58.00
Figural, Shoe, Hinged Cover, Dragonfly, Papier-Mache, 3 1/4 In.Long	65.00
Flower Swags, Birds, Diamonds, & 1 Cameo, Gold & Bloodstone	5500.00
French Court Scene Cover, Swiss, C.1840, Gold & Enamel, 3 3/8 In.	6500.00
Heart Form, C.1840, Copper, 3 In.	165.00
Marked Eley, London, C.1860, Japanned, Tin, 1 1/2 X 1/2 In.	10.00
Musical, Tortoiseshell Lid Depicts New York City Hall, C.1826	2000.00
Musical, Tortoiseshell, Hand-Cut, C.1800	1800.00
Musical, Tortoiseshell, 2 Tune, C.1825	1600.00
Outdoor Scene Of People, Cover, Silver Plate, 7 7/8 In.	17.00
Slender, Heart Form, C.1840, Copper, 3 In.	165.00
White Ware, Hand-Painted Scene, Limoges, Marked, 2 1/2 X 3 1/2 In.	38.00
Wire Hinged Top, Convex Top & Bottom, Signed C.J.Hauck, 3 1/4 In.	65.00

Soapstone is a mineral that was used for foot warmers or griddles because of its heat-retaining properties. Soapstone was carved in many countries in the nineteenth and twentieth centuries.

SOAPSTONE, Bed Warmer, Wire Bail Handle, Initial R N, 8 1/2 X 8 1/4 In.	22.50
Bookends, Dragons, Pair	48.00
Box, Jewelry, Casket Shape	40.00
Box, Rose Quartz Elephant Finial	68.00
Figurine, Buddha, Soapstone Base, 9 In.	37.50
Figurine, Cow, Monkey On Back, 1920s	35.00
Figurine, Horse, Rearing, 6 X 7 In.	32.00
Figurine, Two Old Men, Seated, Wood Stand, 2 1/2 X 2 1/2 In.	75.00
Hand Warmer, Used In Lady's Muff, 6 X 1 1/2 In.Square	12.50
Holder, Paint, Artist's, 5 Holders, Leaves & Flowers, C.1900, 9 In.	100.00
Inkwell, Bull's-Eye Top, C.1830, Beveled Corners, 2 1/2 In.Square	45.00
Inkwell, Curved Shoulders, C.1790	45.00
Mold, Bullet, Single Cavity, Hardwood Handles	110.00
Planter, Cut-Out Birds, 3 1/2 In.	22.50
Vase, Carved Wolf & Man, 6 In.	40.00
Vase, Double, Openwork Flowers, Birds, Leaves, 8 In.Long	65.00
Vase, Dragon & Clouds, 2-Handled, 5 1/2 X 4 X 8 In.	95.00
Vase, Floral Carving, 2 Openings, 6 1/2 In.	75.00
Vase, Floral Shape, Flower & Leaf, Brown, 12 In.	120.00
Vase, Marbleized Rust, Mutton & Black, C.1900, 8 1/4 X 5 1/4 In.	220.00
Vase, Mountain Scenery, 6 1/2 In.	35.00
Vase, Peony & Leaves, 4-Footed Base, 12 In.	90.00
Vase, Rust & Green, 5 1/4 X 3 1/2 In.	103.00
Warming Stone, New Hampshire, C.1860, 4 3/4 In.Diam.	12.50

SOFT PASTE, Bowl, Woman & Children, Halo Of Roses, Cobalt Blue Rim, 5 In.	22.50
Cup & Saucer, Demitasse, Blue Flower, Gold Outlining, C.1850	20.00
Cup & Saucer, Handleless, Adams Rose	110.00
Cup & Saucer, Handleless, Floral	24.00
Plate, Strawberry Luster Design, 7 1/2 In.	15.00
Saucer, King's Rose	*Illus* 250.00

SOUVENIR, Cup, Macy's Employees Drum Corp., Brass & Gold	250.00
Spoon, Silver Plate, Berlin Brandenburgertor, Figural Gate	12.50
Spoon, Silver Plate, Boston, Horseshoe Shaped Handle, Beanpot	12.50
Spoon, Silver Plate, Canada, Figural, Indian's Head, 4 3/4 In.	12.50

Soft Paste, Saucer, King's Rose

Spoon, Silver Plate, Century Of Progress, Chicago, 1933	15.00
Spoon, Silver Plate, Douglas Fairbanks	6.50
Spoon, Silver Plate, Fiji, Embossed Grasshouse, 4 1/4 In.	12.50
Spoon, Silver Plate, Floral Handle, Vines & Thistle Shank	10.00
Spoon, Silver Plate, Gloria Swanson	6.50
Spoon, Silver Plate, Grand Bahama, Pirate & Ship, Twist Shank	10.00
Spoon, Silver Plate, La Sagrada Familia, Barcelona, Cathedral Shank	12.50
Spoon, Silver Plate, Mae Murray	6.50
Spoon, Silver Plate, Mexico, Gaucho Playing Guitar, 5 In.	12.50
Spoon, Silver Plate, Niagara Falls, Canada, Enameled Maple Leaf	14.50
Spoon, Silver Plate, Niagara Falls, Canada, Maple Leaf Handle	12.50
Spoon, Silver Plate, Oberammergau, Figural Handle, Austria	10.00
Spoon, Silver Plate, Oregon, Beaver State, Seal, Twist Shank	14.50
Spoon, Silver Plate, Ramon Navarro	6.50
Spoon, Silver Plate, Shield Handle, Wyoming, Cowboy On Bronco	12.50
Spoon, Silver Plate, Suffolk County Whaling Museum, Sag Harbor	12.50
Spoon, Sterling Silver, Actor's Fun Fair, Round Bowl	275.00
Spoon, Sterling Silver, Agnes Booth, Gold Wash Bowl, Gorham	125.00
Spoon, Sterling Silver, Alaska-Yukon	30.00
Spoon, Sterling Silver, Albuquerque, New Mexico, Hotel Alvarado	25.00
Spoon, Sterling Silver, Atlantic City, Boardwalk	60.00
Spoon, Sterling Silver, Bison Hunt, North Platte-Black Hill	125.00
Spoon, Sterling Silver, Boston Tea Party, State Insignia	35.00
Spoon, Sterling Silver, Boston, Paul Revere, Demitasse	20.00
Spoon, Sterling Silver, Buffalo, N.Y., Hudson River	20.00
Spoon, Sterling Silver, Cadillac, Founder Of Detroit	30.00
Spoon, Sterling Silver, California, Oranges In Bowl	32.00
Spoon, Sterling Silver, Catalina Island, Cal., Fish Top Handle	39.00
Spoon, Sterling Silver, Catskill, Mountain House, Gilt Bowl	85.00
Spoon, Sterling Silver, Champlain, Canada, City Hall, Toronto	100.00
Spoon, Sterling Silver, Chicago Art Institute, Indian Finial	65.00
Spoon, Sterling Silver, Chicago World's Fair, Heart Bowl, Demitasse	40.00
Spoon, Sterling Silver, Christmas, Santa Claus Entering Chimney	150.00
Spoon, Sterling Silver, Colorado Skyline, Denver Etched In Bowl	48.00
Spoon, Sterling Silver, Colorado Springs, In Bowl	15.00
Spoon, Sterling Silver, D.A.R.	32.00
Spoon, Sterling Silver, Elk City, Sunflower Handle	20.00
Spoon, Sterling Silver, Eureka, California, 2 Teddy Bears	70.00
Spoon, Sterling Silver, Evangeline, Figural, Demitasse	120.00
Spoon, Sterling Silver, First Baptist Church, Glenwood, Iowa	16.00
Spoon, Sterling Silver, Forest & Stream, Rifle, Fishing Rod Stem	50.00
Spoon, Sterling Silver, Fort George, Canada, Enameled Crest	12.50
Spoon, Sterling Silver, George Washington, City, Eagle Top	35.00
Spoon, Sterling Silver, Golden Gate, San Francisco	35.00
Spoon, Sterling Silver, Homestake Mills, South Dakota	50.00
Spoon, Sterling Silver, Hotel Chamberlin, Point Comfort, Virginia	35.00
Spoon, Sterling Silver, Indian Bust, Denver In Gold Washed Bowl	42.00

Spoon, Sterling Silver, Indian, Full-Bodied 85.00
Spoon, Sterling Silver, Indian, Niagara Falls Bowl 30.00
Spoon, Sterling Silver, Kansas, Engraved Sugar Beet, Garden City 38.00
Spoon, Sterling Silver, Kentucky, Gibson Girl On Top, Louisville 80.00
Spoon, Sterling Silver, Los Angeles, California In Bowl 15.00
Spoon, Sterling Silver, Los Animas, Colorado In Bowl 15.00
Spoon, Sterling Silver, Louisiana Purchase, Pan-American, 1901 .... 33.00
Spoon, Sterling Silver, Manitou, Colorado, Pike's Peak 40.00
Spoon, Sterling Silver, Miner, Colorado Springs, Colorado, Demitasse 37.00
Spoon, Sterling Silver, Missouri State Seal, Mendon In Bowl 18.00
Spoon, Sterling Silver, Mormon Temple, Indian Finial 75.00
Spoon, Sterling Silver, Mormon Temple, Salt Lake City, Indian 85.00
Spoon, Sterling Silver, Nantucket, Demitasse 20.00
Spoon, Sterling Silver, Nebraska Seal On Handle, Lincoln In Bowl 18.00
Spoon, Sterling Silver, New Auditorium, Milwaukee, Kneeling Indian 65.00
Spoon, Sterling Silver, New Orleans, Skyline, Shepard Mark 100.00
Spoon, Sterling Silver, New York, Skyline, Statue Of Liberty 80.00
Spoon, Sterling Silver, Ohio, Design On Handle 20.00
Spoon, Sterling Silver, Old Church Of San Felipe, New Mexico 87.50
Spoon, Sterling Silver, Oregon, Sagajawea Statue In Bowl 20.00
Spoon, Sterling Silver, Pan-American Exposition, Official 48.00
Spoon, Sterling Silver, Pan-Pacific International Exposition 40.00
Spoon, Sterling Silver, Pere Marquette, Last Landing, Dated 1675 .... 145.00
Spoon, Sterling Silver, Pikes Peak, Colorado, Indian .... 75.00 To 85.00
Spoon, Sterling Silver, Pittsburgh, 1894, G.A.R. 35.00
Spoon, Sterling Silver, Ponce De Leon, St.Augustine, Demitasse 85.00
Spoon, Sterling Silver, Portland, Oregon, Gold Wash Bowl 28.00
Spoon, Sterling Silver, Prospector, Mining Scene, Boulder, Colorado 80.00
Spoon, Sterling Silver, Quebec, Samuel De Champlain, Demitasse 70.00
Spoon, Sterling Silver, Railroad Engine, Letter Down Handle 90.00
Spoon, Sterling Silver, Rainbow Girls, Plain Bowl 20.00
Spoon, Sterling Silver, Rebus, Kansas, Concordia Engraved In Bowl 65.00
Spoon, Sterling Silver, Robert E.Lee Monument 48.00
Spoon, Sterling Silver, Rutland, Vermont, 1910, Demitasse 15.00
Spoon, Sterling Silver, Salem Witch, Cat, & Moon 115.00
Spoon, Sterling Silver, Salt Lake City, Demitasse 20.00
Spoon, Sterling Silver, Salt Lake City, Temple In Bowl 50.00
Spoon, Sterling Silver, Santa & Bell, Bowl Scene Of Fireplace 100.00
Spoon, Sterling Silver, Savannah, Georgia, Black Boy, Demitasse 115.00
Spoon, Sterling Silver, Setting Sun, Indian 30.00
Spoon, Sterling Silver, Sheboygan, Wisconsin 18.00
Spoon, Sterling Silver, Soldier, U.S.A. In Bowl, Seaside, Oregon 95.00
Spoon, Sterling Silver, Southern Belle, Flowered Handle, Illinois 75.00
Spoon, Sterling Silver, St.Augustine, Florida, Alligator 42.00
Spoon, Sterling Silver, Statue Of Liberty, Demitasse 60.00
Spoon, Sterling Silver, Stork In Flight, St.Louis In Bowl 55.00
Spoon, Sterling Silver, Taft Spade, Round Bowl 125.00
Spoon, Sterling Silver, Toledo, Ohio 40.00
Spoon, Sterling Silver, U.S.Mint, Denver, Colorado 35.00
Spoon, Sterling Silver, Unadilla Cutout, Twisted Shank, 4 In. 18.50
Spoon, Sterling Silver, Virginia 25.00
Spoon, Sterling Silver, W.C.T.U., World Globe Top, Demitasse 28.00
Spoon, Sterling Silver, Washington Irving's Home, Demitasse 25.00
Spoon, Sterling Silver, Wichita, Kansas, Cutout Horses & Plow 45.00
Spoon, Sterling Silver, World's Fair, 1934, Buildings 18.50
Spoon, Sterling Silver, Wyoming, Shield Handle, Cowboy, 3 1/2 In. 12.50

*Spangle glass is multicolored glass made from odds and ends of colored glass
rods. It includes metallic flakes of mica covered with gold, silver, nickel, or
copper. Spangle glass is usually cased with a thin layer of clear glass over
the multicolored layer.*
SPANGLE GLASS, see also Vasa Murrhina
SPANGLE GLASS, Basket, Silver Mica, Crimped Edges, Clear Handle, Aqua 65.00

Mica Flakes, Maroon, Green, & White, 5 X 4 1/4 In.	70.00
Rose Bowl, Opaque White, Pink, Yellow, Maroon & Blue	78.00
Vase, Mica Flecks, White Lining, Crimped, Blown, 8 3/4 In.	48.00
Vase, Ribbed Neck, Pinched Body, Blue & Gold Mica, 5 In.	50.00

Spanish lace is a Victorian glass pattern that seems to have white lace on a colored background. Blue, yellow, cranberry, and clear glass was made with this distinctive white pattern. It was made in England and the United States after 1885.

SPANISH LACE, Bride's Basket, Vanbergh Holder, Blue	65.00
Celery, White	30.00
Cruet	65.00 To 95.00
Pitcher, Cranberry	275.00
Pitcher, Water, Blue	195.00
Pitcher, Water, Ruffled Top, Blue Opalescent	165.00
Spooner, Cranberry Opalescent	73.00
Syrup, Metal Top, White On Clear, 5 1/2 In.	95.00
Vase, Ruffled Rim, Opalescent Lemon, 11 1/2 In.	85.00
Water Set, Blue & White, 7 Piece	325.00

Spatter glass is a multicolored glass made from many small pieces of different colored glass. It is sometimes called End-Of-Day glass.

SPATTER GLASS, Basket, Orange & White, 6 1/2 In.	17.00
Basket, Orange Stripes, Yellow, Rope Handle, 9 X 12 In.	95.00
Birds, Multicolored, 2 X 5 In.	60.00
Bowl, Yellow, Clear, Orange, White, Maroon, Pinched, 3 X 4 In.	40.00
Box, Cigar, 6 X 3 In.	75.00
Candlestick, Pink & Green, Mica Flecks, 8 1/2 In.Pair	135.00
Cruet, Applied Handle & Stopper, Blue & White	75.00
Darner, Stocking, 11 1/2 In.	75.00
Ewer, Pink & Green, Mica Flecks, 10 In.	85.00
Jar, Sweetmeat, Rainbow Colors, Barrel Shape, 7 1/2 In.	85.00
Lamp, Fairy, Cased, Yellow & White, Icicle Trim, 4 In.	235.00
Lamp, Fairy, Clarke Cup, Velvet Holder, 5 1/2 In.	195.00
Pitcher, Pink & White, Clear Handle, 7 In.	88.00
Pitcher, Swirl & Ribbed, Ruffled Top, White Inside, 8 In.	195.00
Pitcher, Swirl Design, Pink, Maroon, Yellow, Blue, Green, 7 In.	195.00
Pitcher, Tricornered, Reeded Handle, Green & White	85.00
Rolling Pin, Blues & Reds	118.00
Sugar Shaker, Cranberry & White	55.00
Sugar Shaker, Pink & White, Original Top	50.00
Vase, Brown, Blue & Yellow, Mica Flecks, 8 1/2 In.	85.00
Vase, Fluted, Pink, 6 In.	20.00
Vase, Paperweight Base, Blue & Cranberry	45.00
Vase, Red, Blue, Green, & Brown, Cased Over White, 10 In.	65.00

Spatterware is a creamware or soft-paste dinnerware decorated with spatter designs. The earliest pieces were made during the late eighteenth century, but most of the wares found today were made from 1800 to 1850. The spatterware dishes were made in the Staffordshire district of England for sale in America.

SPATTERWARE, see also Spongeware

SPATTERWARE, Bowl, Green & Brown, 8 In.	17.50
Bowl, Mixing, Green & White, 5 X 9 In.	65.00
Creamer, Pink & Blue Rainbow, Octagonal, 4 1/4 In.	210.00
Creamer, Red Rose, Brush Enamels, C.1835, 3 3/4 In.	235.00
Cup & Saucer, Handleless, Double Ogee Shape, C.1840, Red & Blue	125.00
Cup Plate, Peafowl, Red Edge, Red Feathers, 4 1/4 In.	250.00
Pitcher & Basin, Lavender & Dark Green	1300.00
Plate, Adam Rose Center, Blue, 8 1/4 In.	190.00
Plate, Blue, Peafowl In Red, Green, Black, Marked, 8 In.	225.00
Plate, Blue, 10 1/4 In.	75.00

Plate, Castle Center, Blue Spatter Border, 9 3/4 In. 210.00
Plate, Castle Scene, Blue, 5 In. 150.00
Plate, Peafowl, Impressed Mark, Dated 1879, Red, 8 In. 125.00
Plate, Peafowl, Pink, 8 In. 100.00
Plate, Peafowl, Red, Purple, Blue Rainbow, 8 1/4 In. 600.00
Plate, Red & Yellow Bull's-Eye 185.00
Plate, Soup, Flower Center 150.00
Plate, Soup, Peacock, Pink, 10 1/2 In. 285.00
Pot, Honey, Tulip Design, No Lid 175.00
Salt & Pepper, Leaf Mold, Original Tops, Pair 115.00
Tea Set, Castle Pattern, Creamer, Sugar, & Teapot, Covered 1350.00
Tea Set, Child's, Peafowl, 4 Piece 310.00
Teapot, Pink, Peafowl, Covered 650.00

Spelter is a synonym for a zinc alloy. Figurines, candlesticks, and other
pieces were made of spelter and given a bronze or painted finish.

SPELTER, Candlestick, Man & Woman Holding Torches, C.1865, 15 In., Pair 298.00
Figurine, Horse With Rider, Signed W.Wolff, 1862, 25 In. 795.00
Figurine, Nude Man Wrestling Eagle, Chicks At Feet, Signed, 24 In. 975.00
Figurine, Woman, Classical, Standing, 14 In. 75.00

SPINNING WHEEL, American, 19th Century, 34 1/2 In. 125.00
Chip-Carved Ends, Initialed J.A., Chestnut, 58 In. 250.00

Spode pottery, porcelain, and bone china were made by the Stoke-on-Trent
factory of England founded by Josiah Spode about 1770. The firm
became Copeland and Garrett from 1833 to 1847, then W.T.Copeland or
W.T.Copeland and Sons until 1976. It then became Royal Worcester
Spode. The word Spode appears on many pieces made by the Copeland
factory. Most collectors include all the wares under the more familiar
name of Spode.

SPODE, see also Copeland
SPODE, Bowl, Black & White Scene, Gold & Gray, 8 In. 165.00
Bowl, Vegetable, Irene, Oval 45.00
Coffeepot, Primrose Pattern 75.00
Dish, Leaf, Creamware, Blue Design, C.1796, 5 X 5 In. 65.00
Dish, 967 Pattern, Beaded Rim, Marked, C.1810, 6 3/8 In. 715.00
Plate, Celadon Rim, Blossoms, Hexagonal, Marked, C.1815, 9 1/4 In., Pair 225.00
Platter, Bridal Rose, 13 In. 30.00
Platter, Willow Pattern, C.1790 ....*Illus* 250.00
Tureen, Soup, Underplate, Blue, White, & Gold, 12 In. 325.00

Spongeware is very similar to spatterware in appearance. The designs were
applied to the ware by daubing the color. Many dealers do not differentiate
between the two wares and use the names interchangeably.

SPONGEWARE, Bowl, Bale, 4 Round Molded Feet, Deep Blue, 5 X 10 1/4 In. 245.00
Bowl, Blue & White, 9 In. 90.00
Bowl, Brown On Yellow, 7 X 2 1/8 In. 45.00
Bowl, Cereal, 5 In., Pair 25.00
Bowl, Crimped, Blue On Cream, 3 1/2 X 7 In.Diam. 85.00
Bowl, Florets, Stamped Baker & Co., England, 3 3/4 In. 25.00
Bowl, Green On Cream, 8 In. 45.00
Bowl, Green Sponging On Yellow Ground, 6 X 10 1/2 In.Diam. 80.00
Bowl, Linked Medallion Rim, Red & Green Wreath Center, 6 3/4 In. 110.00
Bowl, Mixing, Blue & White, 6 1/2 X 12 In.Diam. 150.00
Bowl, Mush, C.1865, Blue 77.00
Bowl, Mush, Tan & Green, Cream Ground, 6 In. 39.00
Bowl, Pudding, Indented In 8 Places, Blue & White, 10 1/2 In. 240.00
Bowl, Pudding, 8 Indents, Blue & White, 10 1/2 In.Diam. 240.00
Bowl, Rust-Blue Redwing, 7 In. 38.00
Bowl, Yellow, Blue, Raised Scroll Border, 7 1/2 In. 45.00

Spode, Platter, Willow Pattern, C.1790

Butter, Good Luck, Covered	90.00
Casserole, Covered	55.00
Chamber Pot, 4 3/4 X 9 1/4 In.Diam.	110.00
Commode Jar	165.00
Cookie Jar, Stenciled Cookies, Brown & Black On White	295.00
Creamer, Goose-Spouted, Blue Design, Green, 4 In.	125.00
Crock, Butter, Cover, Blue & White	250.00
Crock, Butter, Indian Good Luck Sign, Blue & White	85.00
Crock, Butter, Lid	250.00
Cup, Batter, Basket Weave, Blue & White	60.00
Cup, Custard	23.00
Cuspidor, Blue & White, 5 X 1 1/2 In.	95.00
Cuspidor, Blue, 7 1/2 In.	89.00
Cuspidor, Copper Luster Bands, Brown On White, 6 1/2 In.	50.00
Dish, Baking, Blue & White, Round	95.00
Dish, Pierced Cover, Red & Gold, 7 1/2 In.Diam.	35.00
Dish, Pudding, Marked 19, U.S.A., Yellow, 5 In.Diam.	22.00
Dish, Soap, Blue & White	180.00
Dish, Soap, Green Diamond Border, 3 3/4 X 5 In.	48.00
Dish, Soap, Rectangular, Blue	175.00 To 195.00
Dish, Soap, Sponge Sides, Ribbed Rim, Multicolor, 4 X 6 3/8 In.	235.00
Dish, Vegetable, Blue, Oval	165.00
Holder, Toothbrush	70.00
Jug, Spaced Design, 1800s, Deep Blue, 9 In.	315.00
Jug, Wine, Blue	225.00
Mug	75.00
Pitcher & Bowl, Blue & Cream, 11 1/2 In.	90.00
Pitcher & Bowl, Blue & Green, C.1830	350.00
Pitcher & Bowl, Blue & Tan, Small	50.00
Pitcher & Bowl, Bowtie & Blue Decal	225.00
Pitcher, Advertising On Side, Green, Tan, & Brown	25.00
Pitcher, August Becker	160.00
Pitcher, Barrel, Brown, Yellow, & Green, 8 In.	60.00 To 80.00
Pitcher, Blue & White, Brown Interior, 8 In.	70.00
Pitcher, Blue & White, 5 In.	*Illus* 45.00
Pitcher, Blue & White, 9 In.	165.00
Pitcher, Brown, Green On Beige, 5 In.	75.00
Pitcher, Brown, 7 In.	65.00
Pitcher, Dark Blue & Yellow, 6 1/2 In.	85.00
Pitcher, Embossed Carlock Farmers Elevator Co.	45.00
Pitcher, Girl With Dog, 9 In.	250.00
Pitcher, Grape, 9 In.	90.00
Pitcher, Kissing Dutch, 9 In.	100.00

Spongeware, Pitcher, Blue & White, 5 In.

(See Page 639)

Pitcher, Middle Stripe, Bulbous, Wide Lip, 9 In.	240.00
Pitcher, Scroll, 8 In.	85.00
Pitcher, Tan & Green, Cream Ground, 4 1/2 In.	48.00
Pitcher, Windmill At The Bush, 8 In.	90.00
Planter, Copper Luster Around Scalloped Rim, 9 1/2 In.Diam.	65.00
Plate, Blue Border & Florets, Green Leaves, Plums, 10 In.	140.00
Plate, Red Florets, Green Leaves, 9 In.	35.00
Plate, Tulip	65.00
Plate, Virginia Pattern, Stamped Adam & Co., Tunstall, 9 In.	60.00
Root Beer Set, Pitcher & 4 Mugs, Buckeye	100.00
Salt, Butterfly	150.00
Salt, Daisy	80.00
Salt, Raspberry	85.00
Saucer, Green Circles, Red Centers, 6 1/4 In.	23.00
Spittoon, Blue Band Around Pinched-In Waist, Blue & White	79.00
Spittoon, Blue, 6 1/2 In.	115.00
Spittoon, Brown	40.00 To 55.00
Spittoon, Cream, Embossed Pattern	225.00
Spittoon, Medium Blue, 6 X 4 In.	125.00
Spittoon, White & Blue	75.00
Syrup, Advertising, Blue & White, 2 Quart	650.00
Teapot, Brown & Green Daubing On Tan	175.00
Toothpick, Swan	35.00

      SPOOL CABINET, see Store, Spool Cabinet

ST.LOUIS, Bottle, Perfume, Floral Design, Cameo, Signed, 2 1/4 In. 295.00

*Staffordshire is a district in England where pottery and porcelain have
been made since the 1900s. Thousands of types of pottery and porcelain have
been made in the hundreds of factories that worked in the area. Some of the
most famous factories have been listed separately. See Royal Doulton,
Royal Worcester, Spode, Wedgwood, and others.*

      STAFFORDSHIRE, see also Flow Blue; Mulberry

STAFFORDSHIRE, Basket, Brown, White Swan Cover, 3 In.	58.00
Bowl, Fruit, Blue Design, Pastoral Scene, 12 In.	135.00
Bowl, India Pattern, Pierced, Blue & White, 10 In.	145.00
Bowl, Inside Transfer Of Men Playing Quoits, 6 X 3 1/4 In.	88.00
Bowl, Park Scene, C.1840, 12 1/2 In.	110.00
Bowl, Soup, Panoramic Scenery, Stevenson	100.00
Bowl, Wash, Green Leaves, Black Strawberries, 12 1/2 In.	125.00
Breakfast Set, Child's, Red Server, Creamer, & Sugar	56.00
Bust, Clyte, Off-White, 13 X 21 In.	490.00

Bust, George Washington, C.1840, Square Plinth, 7 7/8 In. 375.00
Bust, John Locke, Pink Toga, Brown Hair, Green Plinth, 7 In. 180.00
Bust, Neptune, Sponged Plinth, 11 3/4 In. 665.00
Chocolate Set, Birds In Medallion, 4 Cups & Saucers, 11 Piece 185.00
Coffeepot, Late General Washington, Red, Blue Bands 325.00
Coffeepot, View Of Franklin's Tomb, Blue & White 1250.00
Cradle, Sleeping Doll, Bedclothes, 4 1/8 In. 285.00
Creamer, Cow & Milkmaid, In Hat, Out Cow's Mouth, 7 In. 210.00
Creamer, Forget-Me-Not, Pink 65.00
Creamer, Soldier's Return, Blue 95.00
Cup & Saucer, Handleless, Archery Pattern, Black & White 30.00
Cup & Saucer, Handleless, White, Plum-Colored Leaves In & Out 25.00
Cup & Saucer, Lombardy, Handleless, Italian Blue 35.00
Cup & Saucer, Nursery Rhyme, 3 Red Transfer Scenes, C.1860 .... 48.00
Cup & Saucer, Palestine, Handleless, Pink 45.00
Cup & Saucer, Woman, Child, Garden, Purple Luster Border 25.00
Cup Plate, Adelaide's Bower, Black 30.00
Cup Plate, Ancient Ruins, C.1830, Green Transfer 25.00
Cup Plate, Chantilly, Blue 25.00
Cup Plate, Embossed Daisy Rim, Red Transfer, 4 1/4 In. 30.00
Cup Plate, Friburg, Blue 25.00
Cup Plate, Light Blue, Canova 30.00
Cup Plate, Lily, Brown Transfer, Wood & Challinor, 4 1/4 In. 35.00
Cup Plate, Marino, Italian Blue 20.00
Cup Plate, Rhine River Scene, Brown 32.00
Cup Plate, Rousillon, Blue 25.00
Cup Plate, Ship Anchored, Wood, Dark Blue 295.00
Cup Plate, Tuscan Rose, Brown 34.00
Cup, Stirrup, Fox Head, 1820-23, Iron Red Coat, 5 1/4 In. 800.00
Cup, Tea, Blue Willow Pattern, Miniature 18.00
Dish, Hen On Nest Cover 250.00
Dish, Hen On Nest Cover, White, Eggs Showing, 5 X 7 In. 100.00
Dish, Hen On Nest Cover, Yellow Basket Weave, Marked WK 120.00
Dish, Maids & Shepherd, C.1825, Blue, 9 3/4 In. 110.00
Figurine, Accordion Player, Spaniel At Side, 10 3/4 In. 110.00
Figurine, Amish Couple, Standing, Grassy Mound, 8 In. 55.00
Figurine, Bower, Two Girls Holding Blue Grapes, 4 In. 225.00
Figurine, Brigand & Companion With Boat, 1850, 11 In. 165.00
Figurine, Brigand With Rifle, 1850, 9 1/4 In. 85.00
Figurine, Cat, Seated, C.1780, Ocher Spotted, 2 7/8 In., Pair 550.00
Figurine, Cat, Seated, C.1785, Redware Ears & Muzzle, 4 1/4 In. 550.00
Figurine, Child Astride A Large Dog, 10 In. 250.00
Figurine, Cobbler & Wife, Pink Luster, 6 1/2 In. 125.00
Figurine, Cottage, Court Couple Against Tree, 9 In., Pair 100.00
Figurine, Dick Turpin On Horse, 1850, 10 In. 140.00
Figurine, Dog, Gold Collar, Lock, & Chain, 9 1/2 In., Pair 120.00
Figurine, Dog, Marked, 11 In., Pair 115.00
Figurine, Dog, White, Black Trim, 4 In., Pair 99.50
Figurine, Dog, Yellow Eyes, Gold Lock & Chain, 9 In., Pair 100.00
Figurine, Dog, 10 In., Pair 110.00
Figurine, Elephant, 2 1/2 In. 28.00
Figurine, English, Welsh, & Scottish Drinkers 125.00
Figurine, Girl Gathering Fruits, 1900, 7 1/2 In. 65.00
Figurine, Girl With Spaniel, 7 1/2 In. 110.00
Figurine, Huntsman On Horse, 1850, 7 In. 115.00
Figurine, Husband & Wife, Standing Arm-In-Arm, 6 1/2 In. 110.00
Figurine, Jackfield Spaniel, 14 In., Pair 295.00
Figurine, John Liston, Actor, 1825-30 .... 1750.00
Figurine, Lady Seated Holding Basket, Man Standing, 9 In. 75.00
Figurine, Lady, Fur Boa, Boy, Hat, C.1820, 8 1/4 In. 425.00
Figurine, Lady, Hand On Hip, Brown Hat, Yellow Dress, 3 5/8 In. 325.00
Figurine, Lions, Tan Brown, Glass Eye, Pair 195.00
Figurine, Lovers, 10 In. 80.00

Figurine, Milkmaid & Swain, 10 In. 125.00
Figurine, On Tree Stump, Brown, Grassy Mound, 10 3/4 In. 300.00
Figurine, Poodles, 4 1/2 In., Pair 95.00
Figurine, Prodigal's Return, Man Caped, Bearded, 14 In. 175.00
Figurine, Queen Victoria & Prince Of Wales, Jubilee, 18 In. 550.00
Figurine, Red Riding Hood & The Wolf, 8 In. 125.00
Figurine, Scottish Couple, Holding Hands, Tree, Grass, 9 In. 85.00
Figurine, Seated Cat, Black Spots, 3 1/2 In. 80.00
Figurine, Shepherd, Blue Kilt, Rock, 2 Sheep, 10 3/4 In. 90.00
Figurine, Souter Johnnie, Seated, Hold A Mug, 8 1/4 In. 15.00
Figurine, Spaniel, Glass Eyes, 12 In., Pair 100.00
Figurine, Steeplechaser, Chestnut Horse, Yellow Coat, 8 In. 90.00
Figurine, Swain, Cobalt Blue Jacket, 8 1/4 In. 48.00
Figurine, Turkey Fowl, Pearlware, Strutting, 6 3/4 In. 300.00
Figurine, Widow, Signed Walton, 11 1/2 In. 275.00
Figurine, Woman, Yellow Dress, Fruit, C.1820, 8 1/2 In. 230.00
Figurine, Zebra, Standing, Oval Mound, Prancing, 5 In. 50.00
Flower Holder, C.1900, Nursing Calf, Oval Base, 11 In., Pair 250.00
Group, Hound Chasing Hare, 9 1/2 In. 125.00
Inkwell, Figural, Boy Feeding 2 Birds, Gold & White 125.00
Jar, Apothecary, Pink & White, Gilt Label, 11 1/2 In. 105.00
Jug, Lafayette & Cornwallis, Luster, 4 5/8 In. .... *Illus* 325.00
Jug, Lafayette & Cornwallis, Luster, 6 5/8 In. .... *Illus* 425.00
Jug, Lafayette At Tomb Of Franklin, C.1825, 9 1/4 In. 600.00
Match Holder, Children Selling Vegetables, Pastel 45.00

Staffordshire, Jugs, Lafayette & Cornwallis, Luster, 6 5/8 In.; 4 5/8 In.

Match Holder, Figural, Boot, Lace, Pink Base, 3 1/2 In. 30.00
Match Holder, 2 High Boots, Boot Jack For Striking, 4 In. 35.00
Mug, Black Transfer, Hunt Scene, Silver Trim, Marked 65.00
Mug, Child's, Harbor Scene, Pink Transfer, 2 1/2 In. 45.00
Mug, Child's, Harbor Scene, Red Transfer, 2 1/4 In. 48.00
Mug, Child's, This Is The House Jack Built 65.00
Mug, Luster, Seated Lady, Child, Garden, Blue Ground, 6 In. 75.00
Mug, Shaving, Grayish Green, White Inside, Pink Flowers, 3 In. 35.00
Mug, Turpin's Ride To York, Pink Transfer 56.00
Mustard, Flowers, Gold Trim, White 15.00
Pitcher & Bowl, Lake, Gray Transfer 450.00
Pitcher, Bark & Ivy, 2 Sleeping Children, 6 In. 20.00
Pitcher, Canova, T.Mayer, Pink & Green Transfer, 1 1/2 Quart 75.00

Pitcher, Gypsy, Cobridge, Earth Tone, 9 1/2 In. 225.00
Pitcher, Gypsy, Cobridge, Lavender & White, 9 1/2 In. 225.00
Pitcher, Hunting Dogs & Bird, Pink Luster Trim, 5 3/4 In. 120.00
Pitcher, Mica, Cobalt Blue, 8 In. 135.00
Pitcher, Milk, Abbeyville Pattern, Blue & White 105.00
Pitcher, Milk, Grecian Figures, Tarboote, Blue, 6 1/2 In. 80.00
Pitcher, Pink & Purple Luster, Polychrome, 5 1/2 In. 40.00
Planter, Wild Rose Pattern, Blue, 8 1/2 X 14 In. 90.00
Plate, Arms Of New York, C.1840, Blue Eagle Mark, 9 7/8 In. 495.00
Plate, Boston State House, C.1830, Floral Border, 10 1/8 In. 325.00
Plate, Boy Selling Papers, C.1860, 6 1/2 In. 68.00
Plate, Brown, Swan Design, Pedestal 45.00
Plate, Caledonia, Purple, 9 1/2 In. 35.00
Plate, Canova, Green Transfer, 8 1/2 In., Pair 36.00
Plate, Clyde Scenery, Red & White, 9 In. 20.00
Plate, Corinthia, Pink, 8 1/2 In. 52.00
Plate, Coronation, Blue & White Transfer, Marked, 10 In. 165.00
Plate, Dark Blue, Castle Of Lavenza, Wood, 10 1/4 In. 95.00
Plate, Falls Of Montmorency, Blue, 9 In. 255.00
Plate, Formosa, 1879, 9 1/2 In. 30.00
Plate, Gaudy Rose Design, Impressed Mark, 8 3/4 In. 95.00
Plate, Grand Erie Canal, Legend Praising De Witt Clinton 390.00
Plate, Grecian Pattern, Ridgway, Green, 9 1/2 In. 14.00
Plate, Hall's Picturesque Scenery, 8 1/2 In. 70.00
Plate, Hartford, Connecticut, Black, 10 In. 125.00
Plate, Hartford, Connecticut, Pink, 10 In. 125.00
Plate, Landing Of Lafayette At Castle Garden, 10 In. 350.00
Plate, Light Blue, Landing At Plymouth, Marked, 10 In. 45.00
Plate, Lost, Crying Child, Doll, Street, 5 5/8 In. 50.00
Plate, Marine Railway Station, C.1870, 7 1/2 In. 68.00
Plate, Musketeer Pattern, Cobalt Blue, 7 In. 28.00
Plate, New York City Hall, Dark Blue, 9 In. 80.00
Plate, Oriental Tent Scene, 9 In. 17.00
Plate, Oriental Toddy, Blue, 4 1/2 In. 60.00
Plate, Oriental, W.R.& Co., 9 In. 22.00
Plate, Palestine, Marked, Red Transfer, 9 1/2 In. 40.00
Plate, Peach & Cherry Pattern, C.1822, Blue & White, 6 1/2 In. 85.00
Plate, Peacock Pattern, Blue, Yellow, Brown, C.1810, 8 In. 200.00
Plate, Persian, Blue Transfer, 5 1/4 In. 15.00
Plate, Peruvian Horse Hunt, Brown Transfer, 9 3/4 In.Diam. 35.00
Plate, Public Library, Boston, Blue & White 20.00
Plate, Punch & Judy, 7 In. 25.00
Plate, R. Hall's Select Views, Hospital, Blue, 6 5/8 In. 55.00
Plate, Residence Of Marquis Lafayette, Blue 120.00
Plate, Rhode Island, Blue, Marked, 8 1/2 In. 425.00
Plate, Rugby Players, 7 1/2 In. 48.00
Plate, Sancho & The Priest & The Barber, Blue, 7 5/8 In. 75.00
Plate, Shanghai 15.00
Plate, Sicilian, Black & White, 7 In., Pair 25.00
Plate, Soup, Blue, Steamboat, 10 In. 175.00
Plate, Soup, Renown Pattern, 9 In. 11.00
Plate, Soup, Windsor Castle, Blue Transfer 165.00
Plate, Temperance Meeting, Polychrome, 5 1/4 In. 25.00
Plate, Texas Centennial, Pink, 10 In. 10.00
Plate, The Baltimore & Ohio R.R., 10 In. 450.00
Plate, Union Line, Wood, Dark Blue, 10 In. 375.00
Plate, Venetian Scenery, Black, 10 In. 35.00
Plate, View Near Conway, N.H., Red, 9 In. 85.00
Plate, View Of Canterbury Cathedral, Clews, 10 In. 60.00
Plate, View Of Trenton Falls, Shell Border, 7 1/2 In. 255.00
Plate, Views Of Daytona Beach, Souvenir 53.00
Plate, Views Of Providence, R.I., Blue 22.00
Plate, Water Works, Philadelphia, Blue, 10 1/4 In. 400.00

Plate, Windmill & Scenery, Holland, Mich., 10 3/8 In. 25.00
Plate, Winter View Of Pittsfield, Mass., Marked, Blue, 8 In. 175.00
Plate, 3-Story Building & Observatory, 1818, Clews, 10 5/8 In. 300.00
Platter, Cape Coast Castle, Africa, Blue 525.00
Platter, Child's, Fishers, Cork, Edge, & Malkin 38.00
Platter, Chinese Marine Pattern, Gadrooned Rim, 14 X 11 In. 75.00
Platter, Mendenhall Ferry, C.1825, Cows & Sheep, 16 5/8 In. 375.00
Platter, Millennium, Pink, 1832, 14 1/2 In. 135.00
Platter, Oriental Scenery, Blue, 14 X 11 In. 110.00
Platter, Rhine River Pattern, C.1840, 17 1/2 X 15 In. 95.00
Platter, Turkey Center, Harvest Ground, 18 X 14 1/4 In. 75.00
Platter, Washington Vase, Italian Blue, 11 X 8 In. 30.00
Platter, Windsor Castle, Signed Clews, 17 X 13 In. 385.00
Salt & Pepper, Toby Men, Hats, Holding Mug, Pair 110.00
Sauceboat, Bologna, Italian Blue 50.00
Spill Vase, Poodles Flank Holder, Pink, Pair 200.00
Sugar & Creamer, Flowers & Leaves, Gold Trim, White 45.00
Sugar & Creamer, Lozere, E.Challinor 80.00
Tea Set, Child's, Cinderella Scenes, C.1889, 24 Piece 435.00
Tea Set, Girl With Dog, Building, C.1850 .... 150.00
Tea Set, Red Blossoms, C.1851, Miniature, 15 Piece 175.00
Teapot, Brown, Sardinia 115.00
Teapot, Lavender, Lady, Child, & Dog, 9 1/2 In. 135.00
Teapot, Scenic Pattern, Light Blue Transfer, C.1840 .... 85.00
Teapot, Scenic, Blue Transfer, C.1840 .... 85.00
     STAFFORDSHIRE, TOBY JUG, see Toby Jug
Toothpick, Scaleby Castle, Blue, 7 3/4 In. 55.00
Tray, Canova, Pink & Green, 8 1/2 In. 35.00
Vase, Couple Seated On Bench, Bird In Tree, 11 In. 115.00
Vase, Fantasy Ware, Art Deco, Floral & Butterflies, 8 In., Pr. 100.00
Vase, Little Red Riding Hood, 9 1/4 In. 80.00
Vase, Red Riding Hood & Wolf, 10 X 6 X 2 1/2 In. 125.00

Stangl pottery was organized in 1929, succeeding the Fulper Pottery
Company. Stangl porcelain birds are popular collectibles.

STANGL, Ashtray, No.3914, White 20.00
Ashtray, No.5067, Green & Gold 5.00
Basket, Terra Rose, Applied Handle, 11 In. 30.00
Bird, Allen Hummingbird, No.3634, Oval Mark, 3 1/2 In. 60.00
Bird, Bird Of Paradise, No.3408, 5 1/2 In. .... 55.00 To 64.50
Bird, Black Throated Warbler, No.3814 .... 60.00
Bird, Blackpoll Warbler, No.3810 .... 45.00
Bird, Blue Headed Vireo, No.3448, 4 1/2 In. .... 42.50 To 50.00
Bird, Bluebird, No.3216 .... 47.50
Bird, Bluebird, No.3276, 5 In. .... 50.00 To 55.00
Bird, Bluebirds, Double, No.3276d .... 135.00 To 140.00
Bird, Bobolink, No.3595, 4 3/4 In. 50.00
Bird, Brewer's Blackbird, 3 1/2 In. 45.00
Bird, Cardinal, No.3444, 6 1/2 In. 65.00
Bird, Cerulean Warbler, No.3456 .... 46.50 To 60.00
Bird, Chat, No.3590 .... 55.00
Bird, Chestnut Sided Warbler, No.3812 .... 45.00
Bird, Chestnut-Back Chickadee, No.3811, Oval Mark, 5 In. 80.00
Bird, Chickadees, Group, No.3581, Oval Mark, 8 1/2 In. .... 100.00 To 140.00
Bird, Cockatoo, No.3405, 6 In. .... 35.00 To 60.00
Bird, Cockatoo, No.3505s, 6 In. 35.00
Bird, Cockatoo, No.3580, 8 7/8 In. 125.00
Bird, Cockatoo, No.3584, 11 3/8 In. 200.00
Bird, Evening Grosbeak, No.3813, 5 In. .... 55.00 To 100.00

Bird, Flying Duck, No.3443 .... 150.00 To 200.00
Bird, Gold Crowned Kinglet, Group, 5 1/2 X 5 In. 95.00
Bird, Gold Crowned Kinglet, 4 1/8 In. 35.00
Bird, Gray Cardinal, No.3596 .... 30.00
Bird, Hen, No.3446 .... 46.00
Bird, Hummingbird, No.3585, Signed 45.00
Bird, Hummingbird, No.3599d, Oval Mark, 8 X 10 1/2 In., Pair 200.00
Bird, Kentucky Warbler, No.3598 .... 18.00 To 50.00
Bird, Key West Quail Dove, No.3454 .... 195.00 To 250.00
Bird, Kingfisher, No.3406, 3 1/2 In. .... 25.00 To 40.00
Bird, Lovebird, No.3400 .... 28.00 To 55.00
Bird, Lovebirds, No.3408 .... 75.00
Bird, Oriole, No.3402 .... 34.50 To 50.00
Bird, Oriole, No.3402s, 3 1/4 In. 23.00
Bird, Orioles, Double, No.3402d, 5 1/2 In. .... 65.00 To 125.00
Bird, Parakeet, No.3582, Blue 195.00
Bird, Parakeets, No.3582d, Green .... 130.00 To 150.00
Bird, Parula Warbler, No.3583, 4 1/2 In. .... 28.00 To 30.00
Bird, Prothonotary Warbler, No.3447, 5 In. .... 44.50 To 50.00
Bird, Prothonotary Warbler, No.3447, 6 In. 95.00
Bird, Red Faced Warbler, No.3594, 3 In. 30.00
Bird, Redstarts, Double, No.3490, 9 In. .... 95.00 To 165.00
Bird, Rivoli Hummingbird, No.3627 .... 65.00 To 90.00
Bird, Rooster, No.3445, Yellow .... 55.00 To 100.00
Bird, Rufous Hummingbird, No.3585, 3 In. .... 35.00 To 40.00
Bird, Swan, Black & Gold 30.00
Bird, Titmouse, No.3592, 2 1/2 In. 30.00
Bird, Warbler, No.3447 .... 40.00 To 45.00
Bird, Warbler, No.3456 .... 35.00
Bird, Warbler, No.3598 .... 35.00
Bird, Wild Fowl, No.4454, 10 X 9 1/2 In. 125.00
Bird, Wilson Warbler, No.3597 .... 20.00 To 35.00
Bird, Wren, No.3401, 3 1/2 In. 35.00
Bird, Wren, No.3401, 4 3/4 In. 27.50
Bird, Wren, No.3401d, 6 3/4 In. 55.00
Bird, Wrens, Double, No.3401d, 8 In. .... 60.00 To 85.00
Bird, Yellow Warbler, 4 In. 45.00
Bowl, Cereal, Fruit & Flowers 3.50
Bowl, Handled, Bittersweet 3.00
Bowl, Tab Handled, Festival 3.00
Bowl, Wisteria, Seascape, Blue, 9 1/4 In.Diam. 139.50
Candle Cube, Green 15.00
Coffee Set, Holly Pattern 150.00
Creamer, Orchard Song 4.00
Cup & Saucer, Colonial, Demitasse, Green 8.00
Cup & Saucer, Golden Harvest 5.50
Eggcup, Colonial, Blue 12.00
Eggcup, Country Garden 6.00
Mug, Festival 3.50
Pitcher, Ball Shape, Green 12.00
Pitcher, Terra Rose, White & Tan, 5 1/2 In. 12.00
Pitcher, Water, Yellow 6.50
Pitcher, 22K Gold Trim, Sticker, 6 In. 15.00
Plate & Cup, Child's, Kitten Capers, Plate Divided 15.00
Plate, Daisy, Blue, 8 In. 3.50
Plate, Daisy, Blue, 10 1/2 In. 5.00
Plate, Golden Harvest, 10 In. 12.00
Plate, Kumquat, 8 In. 4.00
Platter, Shape Of Woman's Head, White, 7 In. 20.00
Platter, Terra Rose Garden Flower, Green, Yellow Border, 14 In. 38.00
Salt & Pepper, Bittersweet 5.00
Salt & Pepper, Town & Country 14.00
Saucer, Magnolia 2.00

Server, Festival, Handled, 6 In.	3.50
Server, Hand, Country Garden	6.00
Server, Tidbit, 10 In.	15.00
Sign, Dealer	45.00
Sugar & Creamer, Prelude, Covered	7.50
Sugar & Creamer, Star Flower, Covered	6.00
Tray, Relish, Orchard Song	6.00
Vase, Double Handled, 22K Gold, Beige, 7 1/2 In.	12.00
Vase, Green & Gold, 7 In.	10.00
Vase, Marked, Gold Over Tan, 5 1/2 In.	7.00
Vase, Pink & Gold, 8 In.	12.00
Vase, Terra Rose, Blue, 7 1/4 In., Pair	35.00

Star Holly is a milk glass type of glass made by the Imperial Glass Company of Bellaire, Ohio, in 1957. The pieces were made to look like Wedgwood jasperware. White holly leaves appear against colored borders of blue, green, or rust. It is marked on the bottom of every piece.

STAR HOLLY, Plate, Green, 6 In.	45.00
Sherbet, Blue	85.00

Steins have been used for over 500 years. They have been made of ivory, porcelain, stoneware, faience, silver, pewter, wood, or glass in sizes up to nine gallons. Although some were made by Meissen, Capo-Di-Monte, and other famous factories, most were made in Germany. The words "Geschutz" or "Musterschutz" on a stein are the German for patented or registered design, not company names.

STEIN, Art Nouveau Design, Incised, Pewter Lid, Germany, 6 In.	100.00
B.P.O.E., German, 1/2 Liter	145.00
Beer, German, Crown Mark	75.00
Black Boy Portrait, Lithophane Bottom, Porcelain	250.00
Crystal, Pewter Filigree, Cranberry Lined, Pedestal Base	600.00
Deer & Rabbit, Pewter Lid, Dated 1886, Glass Liner, 1/2 Liter	50.00
Embossed Figures, Dwarf Finial, Musicians & Peasants, 7 3/4 In.	195.00
Figural, Gaudeamus Skull, Pottery, 1/2 Liter, 5 1/2 X 4 X 6 In.	295.00
German, Blue Stoneware, 1890, 1 Liter	50.00
Glass, Paperweight Lid, Pewter Handle, German, 1/2 Liter	60.00
Gnomes, Figural Gnome Finial, Simon Peter Gerz, 1/2 Liter	225.00
Hand-Painted, Art Deco, C.1900, Signed Jul.H.Brauer	115.00
Lithophane, Figural, Bowling Pin, Musterschutz, 1/2 Liter	665.00
Lithophane, Pewter Hinged Lid, Floral, Banner, Fur Erinnerling	135.00
STEIN, METTLACH, see Mettlach, Stein	
Ninepins Design, Wood Grain Glaze	150.00
Occupational, Telegrapher, Cavalier With Bugle, 1/2 Liter	225.00
Regimental, World War II Machine Gunner, 1/2 Liter	265.00
Stoneware, Hunter Theme, Blue & Gray Glaze, Embossed Pewter Lid	110.00
Stoneware, Hunting Scene, Pewter & Enamel Top, Gray, 1/2 Liter	50.00

Stereo cards that were made for stereopticon viewers became popular after 1840. Two almost identical pictures were mounted on a stiff cardboard backing so that, when viewed through a stereoscope, a three-dimensional picture could be seen.

STEREO, Card, Barker, Niagara In Winter—Coasting On The Ice Mountain	4.00
Card, By The Side of Still Water, On The Plain of Jezreel, A Shepherd	2.00
Card, Happy New Year, No.657, Dated 1875	4.00
Card, Kilburn, Lizzie Bourne Monument, Railway Train, Mt.Washington	4.00
Card, Kilburn, The Great Bridge, New York, Beige Curved View	5.00
Card, Lady Holding A Bouquet Of Flowers, Tinted	5.00
Card, Life On The Shore Of Galilee At Tiberias, Palestine	2.00
Card, London Stereoscopic, Gray Mount, Lady Laying Out Playing Cards	6.00

Card, Lovejoy & Foster, Madison St., Chicago 2.00
Card, Maid Of The Mist In The Whirlpool Rapids, White Mount Curtis 3.00
Card, Rescue Dogs, Swiss Alps, William England 5.00
Card, Soule, Boston Harbor And East Boston From State Street 8.00
Card, Tissue, Royal Horse-Drawn Coach, Voiture De Gala A Trianon 5.00
Card, Totherick, Pennsylvania Avenue And Capitol, Yellow 5.00
Card, Valentine, Allegorical Series, Weller, N.H., No.602, Dated 1876 .... 5.00
Card, Vallee, Wolfe's Monument, Quebec City, Canada 6.00
Card, W.Notman, Montmorency Falls Near Quebec, No.520 .... 15.00
Card, West Shore Of Galilee, Plain Of Gennesaret & Mt. Of Beatitudes 2.00
Glass, Bolton Hall, Bolton Abbey, England, C.1900 .... 15.00
Glass, Lake Como, Italy 11.00
Glass, Saint Anthony's Falls, Minnesota, Ferrier, Soulier, Levy 40.00

Stereoscopes, or stereopticons, were used for viewing the stereo cards. The hand viewer was invented by Oliver Wendell Holmes, although more complicated table models were used before his was placed in production in 1859.

STEREOSCOPE, Burl Walnut, 2 Fold, View Cards, 14 X 9 X 12 In. 150.00
Viewer, Bickers-Type, Table Model, 42 Cards, Walnut 150.00
Viewer, J.W.Cadwell, Revolving ....*Illus* 500.00
Viewer, World War I, 100 Cards, Oak Carrying Case 140.00

STERLING SILVER, see Silver-Sterling

Steuben glass was made at the Steuben Glass Works of Corning, New York. The factory, founded by Frederick Carder and T.C.Hawkes, Sr., was purchased by the Corning Glass Company. They continued to make glass called Steuben. Many types of art glass were made at Steuben. The firm is still producing glass of exceptional quality.

STEUBEN, see also Aurene
STEUBEN, Ashtray & Cigarette Holder, Aurene, C.1905, Signed, 2 3/8 In. 375.00
Basket, Clear, Signed, 7 X 6 In. 85.00
Bonbon, Green Jade & Alabaster, Footed, Signed, 5 In. 85.00
Bottle, Perfume, Verre De Soie, Flame Stopper, Dark Blue 150.00
Bowl, Acid Cutback Jade To Alabaster, Natzu, 12 In. 680.00
Bowl, Airtrap, Crystal, Pedestal, Green Handles, Oval, 14 In. 460.00
Bowl, Alabaster Handle & Foot, Fleur-De-Lis, Jade, 16 In.Diam. 695.00
Bowl, Blue Base, Clear, 10 In. 65.00
Bowl, Calcite, 10 In.Diam. .... 70.00 To 125.00
Bowl, Centerpiece, Punty & Swirl Design, Signed, 8 X 5 In. 185.00
Bowl, Centerpiece, Ribbed, Light Amber, Signed, 13 3/4 X 5 1/2 In. 115.00
Bowl, Cranberry, Fleur-De-Lis, 8 In. 140.00
Bowl, Flared, Signed, Green Jade, 9 7/8 In. 135.00
Bowl, Grotesque Form, Signed, 11 3/4 X 6 In. 85.00

Stereoscope, Viewer, J.W.Cadwell, Revolving

Bowl, Ivorene, Gold Aurene Rim, 10 X 4 In.	145.00
Bowl, Ivorene, Grotesque, Signed, 10 In.	350.00
Bowl, Pedestal, Crystal Air Trap, Clear Green Handles, Signed, 14 In.	460.00
Bowl, Ribbed & Swirled, Underplate, Signed, Celeste Blue	55.00
Bowl, Ribbed Topaz, Aquamarine Rim, Blue Pedestal, Signed, 12 In.	125.00
Bowl, Ribbed, Marine Blue, Signed, 2 1/4 X 4 3/4 In.	35.00
Bowl, Rippled Sides, Bubble Glass, C.1930, Pale Green, 11 3/4 In.	100.00
Bowl, Verre De Soie, Green Threading, Signed, F.Carder, 4 In.	65.00
Bowl, Verre De Soie, Loops Of Floral, Amber Rim, 3 1/2 In.	155.00
Box, Patch, Gold & White Florals On Cover, Green, 2 1/2 In.Diam.	98.00
Candlestick, Alabaster & Jade, Signed, Pair	125.00
Candlestick, Amber, Reddish Glow, 13 3/4 In., Pair	140.00
Candlestick, Double Ball Stem, Marina Blue, Signed, 12 In., Pair	250.00
Candlestick, Engraved Calcite Gold, 6 X 6 In., Pair	750.00 To 950.00
Candlestick, Green Threading, Signed, 10 In., Pair	225.00
Candlestick, Green, 6 In., Pair	225.00
Candlestick, Pearl To Pink, 4 1/2 In.	40.00
Candlestick, Pomona Green, Waffle Pontil, Signed, 4 In., Pair	125.00
Champagne, Applied Threads On Bowl, Flemish Blue, Signed, 7 1/4 In.	70.00
Champagne, Bristol Yellow, Swirl Ribbed Purple Stem, 5 1/2 In.	60.00
Champagne, Speckled Lavender Twisted Stem, Signed	95.00
Cocktail, Teardrop Stem, C.1930, Set Of 12	600.00
Compote, Alabaster & Jade, 7 1/4 In.	375.00
Compote, Black Base, Ivory, Signed With Fleur-De-Lis, 7 In.Diam.	375.00
Compote, Bubbled Top, Green, Signed, 7 X 4 1/2 In.	125.00
Compote, Controlled Bubbles, Reeded Rim, Blue, Signed, 5 1/4 In.	115.00
Compote, Gold Aurene Lining, 7 X 8 1/4 In.	725.00
Compote, Jade & Alabaster, Pedestal, 3 X 8 1/4 In.Diam.	147.00
Compote, Pedestal, Celeste Blue, Signed, 7 X 6 In.	325.00
Compote, Ribbed Amethyst Crystal, Clear, Stem, Signed, 7 3/4 In.	65.00
Compote, Stemmed, Covered, Purple, 14 In.	325.00
Compote, Teardrop Stem, Reeded Ruffled Rim, Blue, Signed, 5 In.	95.00
Console Set, Elfin Green, Twisted Candlestick, 4 Pieces	495.00
Console Set, Green, Signed, Bowl 14 In., 3 Piece	125.00
Console Set, Pink Threading, Diamond Optic, Signed, Bowl 12 In.	400.00
Cornucopia, Crystal, Signed, Pair	70.00
Cruet, Aurene Shading To Platinum, Signed, 5 In.	2250.00
Decanter, Allover Reeding & Bubbling, Green, Signed, 10 1/2 In.	175.00
Decanter, Figural, Fish, Gray, 17 In., Pair	1150.00
Decanter, Teardrop, Burnt Amber, Purple Base, Stopper, Signed, 9 In.	165.00
Dish, Calcite, Amber Iridescent, 5 3/4 In.	75.00
Epergne, Tricornered, Alabaster Base, Signed, 10 1/4 In.	595.00
Figurine, Gazelle, Signed, Clear	300.00
Figurine, Horsehead, 5 In.	135.00
Figurine, Owl, Art Deco, Frosted Large Eyes, Signed, 5 1/2 In.	225.00
Goblet, Celeste Blue & Topaz Stem, Ribbed, Signed, 8 1/2 In.	95.00
Goblet, Clear Bowl, Twist Amethyst Stem	85.00
Goblet, Flemish Blue, 5 3/4 In.	40.00
Goblet, Green Bowl, Intaglio Cut Thistles, Signed, 6 In.	258.00
Goblet, Green Jade, Jade Stem On Alabaster Base, 7 In.	30.00
Goblet, Inner Spiral Stem, 5 In.	40.00
Goblet, Jade, Green	120.00
Goblet, Jade, Twisted Alabaster Stem	140.00
Goblet, Leaf Etching, Blue, Signed Steuben & Carder, 9 1/2 In.	200.00
Goblet, Ribbed Bristol Yellow, Ribbed Purple Stem, 8 1/2 In.	70.00
Goblet, Ribbed Stem, Selenium Red, 6 1/2 In., Pair	120.00
Goblet, Teardrop Stem, 9 7/8 In.	45.00
Goblet, Twisted Alabaster Stem, Jade	125.00
Goblet, Wine, Optic Rib, Signed, 8 1/2 In.	55.00
Goblet, Wine, Random Threading, Flemish Blue, Signed, 7 1/2 In.	75.00
Holder, Flower, Calcite, Iron Stand, Gold Lining, 9 In.	245.00
Jar, Diagonal Swirl, Bulbous Stopper, Pomona Green, Signed, 7 In.	125.00
Jar, Dresser, Alabaster Lid, Flowers, Leaves, & Swags, 4 3/8 In.	245.00

Jar, Dresser, Diagonal Swirl, French Blue, Signed, 4 In., Set Of 3	295.00
Jar, Dresser, Pink Crystal, Square, Flower Petal Stopper, 5 In.	110.00
Jar, Puff, Acid Cutback	595.00
Lamp, Green Jade & Alabaster, Acid Cut, Oriental Scenes, 30 In.	850.00
Lamp, Green Jade To Alabaster, Acid Cut, 6 X 12 1/2 In.	890.00
Lamp, Night Table, Amber Shade, Bronze Footed, Marked, 6 1/4 In.	150.00
Lamp, Oriental Scenes, Jade & Alabaster, Original Shade, 30 In.	950.00
Lamp, Perfume, Gold Loop, Ivorene, Bronze Base, Signed, 7 1/2 In.	625.00
Mug, Ivory Yellow Jade & Marbleized, 4 In.	45.00
Parfait, Alabaster Wafer Base, Jade Green, 4 1/2 In.	120.00
Perfume, Jade, Alabaster Stopper, Signed	185.00
Pitcher, Black Threading, Black Faceted Stopper, Signed, 10 1/4 In.	150.00
Pitcher, Diamond-Quilted, Fluted Rim, 4-Cornered Top, Signed, 9 In.	175.00
Pitcher, Water, Clear, Drawstring Pouch, Signed	85.00
Plate, Black Reeding Under Rim, Clear, Signed, 8 In.Diam.	38.00
Plate, Fleur-De-Lis, Copper Wheel Design, Amethyst, 8 1/2 In.	200.00
Plate, Floral, Leaves, & Ovals, Border Bands, Signed, 7 1/4 In.	95.00
Plate, Green Jade, Signed F.Carder, 9 In.	65.00
Plate, Pomona Green, Signed, 8 In.	20.00
Plate, Sherbet, Calcite	125.00 To 195.00
Plate, Signed, Selenium Red, 8 1/2 In.	125.00
Salt, Clear To Black Threading, Signed, 2 In.	125.00
Salt, Pedestal, Signed, 2 In., Set Of 6	250.00
Salt, Verre De Soie, Pedestal	35.00
Shade, Acid Etched Design, Calcite	80.00
Shade, Calcite, Ivory Outside, Gold Inside, 2 1/4 In., Pair	250.00
Shade, Chartreuse & Gold, Signed	115.00
Shade, Dome-Shaped, Calcite, Greek Key Design, 7 In.Diam.	90.00
Shade, Drag Loop, Gold Border, Gold Lined, Dark Green, Set Of 4	670.00
Shade, Gold Drape, Gold Hook Border, Gold Lined	135.00
Shade, Gold Fishnet On White, Signed	200.00
Shade, Gold Leaf & Vine, Calcite, Gold Lined	200.00
Shade, Pulled Feather, Flared Rim, Gold Ground, Signed, 6 In.	115.00
Shade, Pulled Feather, Gold Lined, Blue & Gold, Signed	155.00
Shade, Signed, 5 3/4 X 5 1/2 In.	90.00
Shade, Snakeskin, Gold Lined	155.00
Shade, White Pulled Feathering, Signed, 6 1/2 In.	150.00
Sherbet & Underplate, Optic-Ribbed Bowl, Amber Stem & Foot	75.00
Sherbet & Underplate, Purple	95.00
Sherbet, Calcite	125.00
Sherbet, Green, 6 In.	65.00
Sherbet, Underplate, Jade	125.00
Sherbet, Underplate, Ribbed, Clear Stem, Blue, 4 In.	55.00
Sherbet, Yellow Stemmed, Yellow Rimmed Underplate, Signed	85.00
Shot Glass, Fleur-De-Lis, Footed, Green Threading, Signed, Set Of 3	150.00
Tumbler, Amberina	125.00
Tumbler, Green, 7 In.	17.50
Tumbler, Pink Threaded	39.00
Vase, Acid Cutback, Jade, Alabaster, Maplewood, 12 In.	950.00 To 1200.00
Vase, Alabaster Handles, Green Jade, Ovoid, 12 In.	500.00
Vase, Alabaster, Double Gourd, Signed, 6 In.	165.00
Vase, Amber Reeding, Clear, Bubbly, Ruffled Neck, Signed, 7 In.	95.00
Vase, Blue, Random Bubbles, Threading, 8 In.	675.00
Vase, Bud, Amethyst, Signed, 6 1/2 In.	275.00
Vase, Bud, Flowers, Leaves, & Swags, Bulbous Base, 10 1/2 In.	395.00
Vase, Bulbous Swirled Form, Silenium Red, C.1925, 6 3/4 In.	120.00
Vase, Bulbous, Turned-Over Rim, Bristol Yellow, Signed, 3 1/2 In.	65.00
Vase, Cluthra, Pink & Red, Signed, 8 1/2 In.	850.00
Vase, Crackled Pink, Etched Mums, Signed, 12 3/4 In.	1400.00
Vase, Diagonal Swirl, 4-Sided, Signed, 5 1/2 In.	150.00
Vase, Double Ball Stem, Green Top, Topaz Feet, Signed, 10 In.	170.00
Vase, Fan Shaped, Amber Ribbed Top, Green Ball Stem, Signed, 8 1/4 In.	95.00
Vase, Fan Shaped, Ribbed, Topaz Base, Pomona, Green Top, Signed, 10 In.	160.00

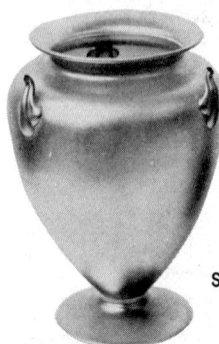

Steuben, Vase, Gold, Iridescent

Vase, Fan, Amber Ribbed Top, Green Ball Stem & Foot, Signed, 9 In.	95.00
Vase, Fan, Amber Ribbed, Crystal, Signed, 6 In.	95.00
Vase, Fan, Ball Stem, Green, 6 3/4 In.	75.00
Vase, Fan, Jade Green, Alabaster Ball Stem, Signed, 9 In.	165.00
Vase, Fan, Knob, Celeste Blue, Signed, 6 1/4 In.	105.00
Vase, Flask Shape, Engraved Floral Pattern, Signed, 10 X 10 In.	375.00
Vase, Fleur-De-Lis, Strawberry, Signed, 11 X 9 In.	950.00
Vase, Gold, Iridescent *Illus*	300.00
Vase, Green Jade, Alabaster Handles, Signed, 10 1/4 In.	550.00
Vase, Green Jade, Alabaster Lion's Head Prunts, Fleur-De-Lis, 7 In.	275.00
Vase, Grotesque Folded Handkerchief Shape, Pedestal, Signed, 9 In.	175.00
Vase, Grotesque, Black Glass Base, Ivory, 6 1/4 In.	160.00
Vase, Grotesque, Blue Shading To Clear, Signed, 8 In.	195.00
Vase, Grotesque, Clear To Amethyst, Signed, 9 In.	175.00
Vase, Grotesque, Pedestal Foot, Clear To Green, Signed, 9 In.	125.00
Vase, Handkerchief, Cranberry To Clear, Signed, 11 In.	185.00
Vase, Hyacinth, Blue, Swirl, Signed, 7 In.	125.00
Vase, Inverted Teardrop, Wide Base, Signed, 7 In.	105.00
Vase, Ivorene, Flared, Ruffled, & Stretched, Signed, 4 1/2 In.	170.00
Vase, Ivorene, Signed, 5 1/2 X 5 3/4 In.	180.00
Vase, Ivorene, 7 1/2 X 8 1/2 In.	285.00
Vase, Jack-In-The-Pulpit, Label, Signed, 12 1/4 In.	90.00
Vase, Jade, Alabaster Raised Foot, 6 1/2 In.	85.00
Vase, Leaf & Vine Design, Off-White Millefiori, Signed, 12 In.	2950.00
Vase, M Handles, Numbered, 7 3/4 In.	125.00
Vase, Optical Ribbing, Greenish Blue, Signed, 5 In.	150.00
Vase, Oriental Poppy, Signed, 5 In.	1375.00
Vase, Ovoid, Green Jade, Alabaster Handles, 12 In.	500.00
Vase, Pink Cast, 3 Blue Shell Feet, Clear, Signed, 8 In.	85.00
Vase, Pink Cluthra, 5 X 4 3/4 In.	275.00 To 325.00
Vase, Pomona, Hexagonal, Diagonal Swirls, Green, Signed, 8 In.	95.00
Vase, Pomona, 3-Branch Thorn, Signed, Green, 6 1/2 In.	175.00
Vase, Ribbed Amethyst, Clear Ring Handles, Signed, 6 In.	250.00
Vase, Rose, Pink, Blossoms, Ovoid, C.1925, Signed, 9 In.	1100.00
Vase, Rounded Shoulder, Footed, Moss Agate, C.1920, 10 3/4 In.	800.00
Vase, Spaced Vertical Ribs, Jade Green, Trademark, 6 5/8 In.	127.00
Vase, Swirl Ribbed, Blue Crystal, Signed, 7 In.	85.00
Vase, Trumpet Shape, Controlled Bubbles, French Blue, 9 7/8 In.	85.00
Vase, 3-Branch Thorn, Pomona Green, Signed, 6 1/2 In.	175.00
Whiskey, Applied Handle, Black Reeding, Clear, Signed, 2 1/2 In.	40.00
Wine Decanter, 4 Pinched Sides, Gold, Stopper, 11 In.	550.00
Wine Set, Dimpled, 6 Wines, Signed	1275.00
Wine, Blue & Topaz Stem, Ribbed, Signed, 6 1/2 In.	95.00
Wine, Clear, Diamond-Quilted, Green Threading, Signed, 4 1/4 In.	40.00
Wine, Green, 4 1/2 In.	20.00
Wine, Optic Rib, Green Bowl & Wafer, Clear Stem, 4 1/2 In.	20.00

Wine, Ribbed, Marine Blue, Yellow Stem, Signed, 3 3/4 In. 40.00
Wine, Twisted Stem, Pomona Green, Signed, 5 1/2 In. 45.00

*Stevengraphs are woven pictures made like ribbons. They were manufactured
by Thomas Stevens of Coventry, England, and became popular in 1862.*

STEVENGRAPH, Bookmark, Birthday Wishes 55.00
Bookmark, Daughter 55.00
Bookmark, Friend 55.00
Bookmark, Happy Birthday 55.00
Bookmark, Many Happy Returns 50.00
Bookmark, New Years Greeting, Tassle, 2 X 9 In. 40.00
Bookmark, Remember Me 45.00
Bookmark, Washington Centennial 125.00
Bookmark, World's Fair 1893, Mrs.Palmer, Woman's Bldg., Tassel 140.00
Bookmark, 1893 Columbian Expostion, Mrs.Potter Palmer 150.00
Called To The Rescue, Framed 375.00
Dick Turpin's Last Ride On Bonnie Black Bess 395.00
Full Cry 250.00
Full Cry, Original Frame 350.00
George Washington Centennial, 1876, Original Paper Backing 85.00
Landing Of Columbus, Columbian Exposition, 1893 .... 250.00
The Death 225.00
The Finish 150.00
The Last Lap, Men On Highwheel Bicycles, Framed .... 295.00 To 395.00
The Meet 225.00
The Water Jump 200.00

*Stevens & Williams of Stourbridge, England, made many types of glass,
including layered, etched, cameo, and art glass, between the 1830s and
the 1930s. Some pieces are signed "S and W."*

STEVENS & WILLIAMS, Bottle, Cologne, Green Striped, Clear Cut Stopper, 9 In. 165.00
Bottle, Cologne, Intaglio Cut, Ball Stopper, 8 In. 245.00
Bowl, Blue Liner, Enamel Flowers, Footed, 6 X 5 In. 425.00
Bowl, Gold & Silver Colored Acorns, 5 3/4 In. 275.00
Bowl, Marquetry Handles, Applied Roses, 14 X 9 In. 1250.00
Inkwell, Applied Cherry, Hinged Cover, 3 In. 225.00
Mug, Blue Feet & Handle, Amber 75.00
Pitcher, Rose To Amber, Fluted Rim, 7 X 6 In. 249.00
Rose Bowl, Arboresque, White Craquelle, 4 1/4 In.Diam. 125.00
Rose Bowl, Box Pleated Top, Cream Lining, 4 3/8 In.Diam. 195.00
Rose Bowl, Box Pleated Top, Deep Rose, 4 1/2 In.Diam. 195.00
Rose Bowl, Diamond-Quilted Mother-Of-Pearl, 4 In. 235.00
Rose Bowl, Zipper, Crimped, C.1886, 5 1/2 X 4 1/2 In. 385.00
Spittoon, Green 95.00
Vase, Applied Amber Plums, White Lining, 7 1/4 In. 375.00
Vase, Applied Gooseberry, Vaseline Opalescent, 4 In. 195.00
Vase, Applied Work In Green, 6-Footed, Handled, 11 In. 275.00
Vase, Cherries & Amber Leaves, Rigaree, 5 In., Pair 275.00
Vase, Engraved Flowers & Whiplash Leaves, 13 1/2 In. 125.00
Vase, Gilded, Silvered Prunus Blossoms, Marked, 9 In., Pr. 950.00
Vase, Green Floral Cameo, Opaque Ground, 4 1/2 In. 790.00
Vase, Jewel Ware, Green Base & Feet, C.1866, 5 In. 125.00
Vase, Lime Green, Opalescent Pink, 6 In. 135.00
Vase, Pink To White Floral, Ruffled Rim, 7 1/2 In. 185.00
Vase, White Passionflowers, Ruffled, Signed, 8 In. 1000.00
Vase, White, Turquoise, White & Pink Flowers, 8 1/4 In. 375.00

*Henry William Stiegel started his first factory in Pennsylvania in
1763. He remained in business until 1774. Glassware in the Stiegel style*

has been made by many factories. The wares are made in clear or colored glass and are decorated in various styles.

STIEGEL TYPE, **Bottle,** Enameled, Handled, Stopper, 14 1/2 In. 125.00

Stoneware is a coarse glazed and fired potter's ware that is used to make crocks, jugs, etc.

STONEWARE, Bedpan, White	20.00
Bottle, Blob Top, Incised & Blued, Gray Glaze, 9 In.	35.00
Bottle, Canteen Shape, Wire Handle, Drinking Scene, 7 3/4 In.	195.00
Bottle, Canterbury, New Hampshire, Brown & Tan, 5 1/2 In.	95.00
Bottle, Eureka House, Hotel Of Suffern, New York, 1 Quart	22.00
Bottle, Evil Eye & Forked Tongue, R. Burge	575.00
Bottle, Figural, Pig, Anna Pottery, Albany	600.00
Bottle, Incised Hancock's Beer, Blue Neck & Top, 10 In.	38.00
Bottle, Root Beer, Dark Brown Slip, 1 Quart	16.00
Bottle, Thick Lip, D.W.Tarr & Co., Blue, 1 Quart	28.00
Bottle, Water, Blue & White	225.00
Bowl Set, Diamond Point, Blue & Tan, Set Of 5	125.00
Bowl Set, Diamond Point, Blue & White, Set Of 4	155.00
Bowl, Basketlike Handle, White Salt Glaze, 13 In.	55.00
Bowl, Blue, 12 In.	80.00
Bowl, Brown, 6 7/8 In.	8.00
Bowl, Daisy & Bow, Blue, 6 1/2 In.Diam.	100.00
Bowl, White, 2 Blue Bands, 9 In.	85.00
Bowl, Yellow Slip Glaze, 12 In.	270.00
Butter, Ackley, Iowa	75.00
Butter, Basket Weave, Covered, Blue & White	80.00
Butter, Blue & Gray, Cherry Lid, 6 In.	48.00
Butter, Blue & White, Original Lid	65.00
Butter, Butterflies, Blue & White	80.00
Butter, Butterflies, Covered, Blue & White	70.00
Butter, Columbian Exposition, 1893	300.00
Butter, Covered, Green	55.00
Butter, Cream, Chocolate Brown, Brown Interior, 7 In.	15.00
Butter, Daisy & Waffle, Blue & White, Covered	80.00 To 95.00
Butter, Daisy, Covered, Blue & White	49.00
Butter, Dragonfly, Covered, Blue & White	100.00
Butter, Farm Scene, Covered, Blue & White	135.00
Butter, Freehand Leaf Design	390.00
Butter, Geometric Design, White	75.00
Butter, Grayish Tan, Brown Inside	13.50
Butter, Scroll, Blue & Tan, Covered	55.00 To 65.00
Butter, Scroll, Blue & White	110.00
Butter, Scroll, Blue & White, Covered	85.00 To 110.00
Butter, Standing Cow, Blue & White, Covered	225.00
Butter, Waffle & Sunflower, Blue & White, Covered, 6 In.	65.00
Butter, Wild Flower, Wooden Lid	95.00
Canister Set, Basket Weave Pattern, Gray & Blue, 12 Piece	1500.00
Canister Set, Wheat Pattern, Green Glaze, 3 Piece	45.00
Canteen, Tavern Scene, Blue & Gray	295.00
Chamber Pot, Rose With Fishscale, Child's	100.00
Chamber Pot, Wildflower, Lid	100.00
Churn, Albany Slip, Wooden Top, 7 1/4 In.	25.00
Churn, Butter, Albany Slip	85.00
Churn, Butter, Cobalt Daffodils, Marked Harrington & Burger	325.00
Churn, Deer With Tree, J. Burger Jr., 5 Gallon	2000.00
Churn, Tooled Lines, Boston Mark, Dated 1804, 2 Gallon	325.00
Cookie Jar, Floral Decal, Black	20.00
Cookie Jar, Floral Decal, Italian Blue	15.00
Cooler, Lemonade, Barrel Shape, Spigot, Yellow Glaze	65.00
Cooler, Nickel-Plated Faucet, Lid, Blue Stripes, 2 Gallon	25.00
Cooler, Water, Barrel Shape, Dragonfly & Tulip Design, 6 Gallon	175.00

Cooler, Water, Barrel Shape, 8 Blue Bands, Spigot, 6 Gallon	98.00
Cooler, Water, Blue & White, Cover, 2 Gallon	60.00
Cooler, Water, Blue Ribbon Band, Buckeye Pottery, Cover, 3 Gallon	175.00
Cooler, Water, Jeffords & Co., Phila., 1869, Metal Cover, 12 1/2 In.	55.00
Cooler, Water, Original Spigot, Marked Crown & 2, Blue Banded	70.00
Cooler, Water, Stag Scene, Cream, Green Shading, 12 1/4 In.	350.00
Cooler, Water, White, Blue Bands, Brass Spigot, 3 Gallon	68.00
Cooler, Wishing Well Design, Robinson Clay Products, Blue, White	450.00
Creamer, Lincoln, Marked UHL, Blue, 4 1/2 In.	85.00
Crock, Apricot Pattern, Cover	69.00
Crock, Beck's, Parish, Iowa, 5 Gallon	110.00
Crock, Bird Design, Cobalt Blue, Marked, 2 Gallon	300.00
Crock, Bird In Cornstalk, Signed Bangor Stoneware Co., 1 Gallon	275.00
Crock, Bird, Peabody, 3 Gallon	275.00
Crock, Black & Cream, 1 Gallon	24.00
Crock, Cheese, Hand-Thrown Ear Handles, Covered	25.00
Crock, Cheese, Producers Creamery	35.00
Crock, Cobalt Blue Design, Gray Glaze, 7 1/4 In.	90.00
Crock, Cobalt Blue Design, Stylized Fish, 3 Gallon	250.00
Crock, Cobalt Blue Floral Spray, Design, 1 Gallon	75.00
Crock, Cobalt Blue Flower, Rolled Rim, Marked, 4 Gallon, 11 In.	100.00
Crock, Cobalt Blue Flowers, Wm.Rowley, Middlebury, Ohio, 3 Gallon	155.00
Crock, Cobalt Blue Flowers, 4 Leaves, 5 Gallon, 13 In.	55.00
Crock, Cobalt Blue Glaze, Eared Handles, 3 Gallon	50.00
Crock, Cobalt Blue Spike Tail Bird, White's Utica, 3 Gallon	385.00
Crock, Cobalt Bluebird On Branch, A.A. & C.G.Herwood, 2 Gallon	185.00
Crock, Cobalt Bluebird, Crossed Double, Marked, 10 In.	350.00
Crock, Crowden & Wilcox, Harrisburg, Pa., 4 Gallon	360.00
Crock, Engraved Cow, Marked Gardiner, Blue, 3 Gallons	400.00
Crock, Eyeglasses & Eyes, West Troy Pottery, Blue, 2 Gallon	150.00
Crock, Gray, Eared Handles, Incised Line, Brown, 1 Gallon	30.00
Crock, Hubbel & Chesebro, N.Y., Flowers Out Of Beehive, 3 Gallon	195.00
Crock, Impressed Oak Tree, Barnabas Edmands, C.1835, Blue, 7 In.	125.00
Crock, Impressed Swan, Earred, Blue Wash, 10 1/2 X 1/ 1/2 In.	95.00
Crock, Impressed Swan, Outstretched Wings, On Flag, Lid, 12 In.	200.00
Crock, J. & E.Norton, Bennington, Vt., 2 Gallon	190.00
Crock, Leaf & Flower, Ear Handle, Cowden & Wilcox, 2 Gallon	195.00
Crock, Lily Pattern, Western, 5 Gallon	40.00
Crock, Marked Penn Yan, Cobalt Blue, Rearing Stag, 4 Gallon	220.00
Crock, Michigan Cottage Cheese Co., Oswego, 6 1/4 X 9 1/4 In.	62.50
Crock, New York Stoneware Co., Fort Edward, Floral, 4 Gallon	175.00
Crock, Parish, Iowa, 2 Gallon	55.00
Crock, Parish, Iowa, 3 Gallon	65.00
Crock, Parish, Iowa, 5 Gallon	110.00
Crock, Revolutionary Soldier, Fife & Drum, 3 Gallon	2400.00
Crock, Running Bird, 2 Gallon	195.00
Crock, Sanford's Inks, Bail & Lid, Blue & White	95.00
Crock, Stenciled, Williams & Reppert, 2 Gallon	135.00
Crock, Storage, Handled, Cover, Cobalt Blue, Burger & Lang, 2 Gallon	160.00
Crock, Stylized Deer, Fence, & Trees, Edmonds & Co., 3 Gallon	2150.00
Crock, Stylized Leaf Bouquet, N.Y.Stoneware Co., Ft.Edward, 5 Gal.	125.00
Crock, West Troy Pottery, Chicken Pecking Corn, 3 Gallon	375.00
Crock, Western, Blue Fruit, 12 Gallon	150.00
Crock, White, Blue, Indian Head Within Concentric Circle, 19 In.	60.00
Crock, Whites Stoneware, Utica, NY, Flower Basket, 1860s, 2 Gallon	165.00
Crock, 2-Handled, Fruit, Hanging Vine, 25 In.	250.00
Crock, 3-Flower Design, 4 Gallon	85.00
Crock, 3-Winged Butterfly, Geddes, N.Y., 2 Gallon	150.00
Cuspidor, Chocolate Brown, Incised Vertical Lines	35.00
Cuspidor, Green	55.00
Custard, Fishscale, Blue & White	65.00
Dish, Soap, Beaded Rose, Blue & White	95.00
Dish, Soap, Cat Head	75.00

Dish, Soap, Covered, Apple Blossom, Liner	125.00
Dish, Soap, Rose, Blue & White	90.00
Dish, Soap, White, Green Bands, 5 1/2 X 2 1/4 In.	65.00
Ewer, Grape Pattern, White	55.00
Flask, Brown, 8 In.	78.00
Holder, Toothbrush, Rose Decal	85.00
Humidor, Cigar, Utica, Snake Lid	200.00
Humidor, Tobacco, Blue & Gray	185.00
Inkwell, Schoolhouse, Thick Collar, C.1870, 2 In.Diam.	14.50
Jar, Apothecary, Pure Mustard, White Medallion, 7 1/2 X 13 In.	350.00
Jar, Beater, Wesson Oil, Blue & White	60.00
Jar, Bird, Pebbly Cobalt Blue, Impressed Mark, 11 In.	135.00
Jar, Canning, Bail Handle, Pat.Feb.11, 1896	35.00
Jar, Canning, Blue Stenciled Label, Greensboro, Pa., 9 In.	55.00
Jar, Canning, Blue Stenciled Label, Wheeling, W.Va., 9 In.	65.00
Jar, Canning, Brown, Squatty, 4 X 5 In.	16.00
Jar, Canning, Union Stoneware, 1 Gallon	225.00
Jar, Cobalt Blue Design & Label, Richmond, Va., 11 1/2 In.	75.00
Jar, Cobalt Blue Flower, 9 1/2 In.	85.00
Jar, Cobalt Label, Greensboro, Pa., 2 Gallon, 12 In.	85.00
Jar, Cobalt Label, New Geneva, Pa., 6 Gallon, 18 In.	105.00
Jar, Cobalt Stenciled Label, Eagle, Brushed, 10 Gallon, 20 In.	590.00
Jar, Cylindrical, Sloping Shoulders, Tan, Label, 14 1/4 In.	45.00
Jar, Design, Pennsylvania, 4 Gallon	125.00
Jar, Dilliner & Stautaz, New Geneva, Pa., Cobalt Blue Label, 2 Gal.	95.00
Jar, Hand, With Pointing Finger, Blue Cuff, 3 Gallon	725.00
Jar, I Framed By Blue Wreath, Lyons, 1 Gallon	150.00
Jar, Jas.Hamilton & Co., Greensboro, Pa., Blue, 2 Gallon	55.00
Jar, Man With Hat & Shovel, Smoking A Pipe, 2 Gallon	3300.00
Jar, Preserving, I.Seymour, Tray, Glaze Shades To Amber, 9 In.	15.00
Jar, R.T.Williams, New Geneva, Pa., Cobalt Label, 1 1/2 Gallon	30.00
Jar, Slop, Bowtie, Blue & White	85.00
Jar, Snuff, Incised Fish & Cherries, Shiny Blue, 1/2 Gallon	350.00
Jar, Solomon Bell, Cobalt Blue, Floral Rim, 1 Gallon, 9 In.	185.00
Jar, Stenciled Cobalt Label, 2 Gallon, 11 1/2 In.	60.00
Jar, T.F.Reppert, Greensboro, Pa., Blue, 2 Gallon	65.00
Jar, Tobacco, Gray's Pottery, Victorian Smoking Scene	40.00
Jug, A.B.Wheeler & Co., Boston, 3 Gallon	175.00
Jug, Batter, Bird & 4's, 4 Quart	560.00
Jug, Batter, Blue Around Ears, Spout, & Handle, Wire Bail	75.00
Jug, Batter, Circles, Tin Covered, Cobalt Blue Design	275.00
Jug, Batter, White, Circles, Tin Covered, Cobalt Blue Design	275.00
Jug, Bird On Branch, J. Burger Jr., 4 1/2 Gallon	725.00
Jug, Bird On Branch, Norton & Co., Bennington, Vt., Blue, 10 1/2 In.	220.00
Jug, Bird On Branch, 3 Blue Leaves, Charlestown, Gray, 2 Gallon	240.00
Jug, Bird, West Troy, N.Y.Pottery, 2 Gallon	205.00
Jug, Blue Fern, 11 1/4 In.	45.00
Jug, Blue Flower, Stamped L.& B., B.Chace-Somerset, 11 1/2 In.	95.00
Jug, Blue Flowers, 3 Gallons	145.00
Jug, Blue Leaf, E. & L.P.Norton, Bennington, Blue & Gray, 1 Gallon	98.00
Jug, C. & W., Bird Reaching For Grapes, 3 Gallon	1550.00
Jug, Cider, Reddish Brown Glaze, 11 In.	15.00
Jug, Cobalt Bird Design, 2 Gallon	160.00
Jug, Cobalt Blue Daisy Design, Cowden & Wilcox, 2 Gallon	235.00
Jug, Cobalt Blue Design, Bird, 2 Gallon, Norton	230.00
Jug, Cobalt Blue Floral Spray, Rolled Lip, Marked, 13 In.	90.00
Jug, Cobalt Blue Flower, Haxston & Co., New York, 1 Gallon	155.00
Jug, Cobalt Blue Grape & Foliage, Signed Edmunds & Co., 1 Gallon	225.00
Jug, Cobalt Blue Handle & Front, Gray Glaze, Ovoid, 11 1/2 In.	85.00
Jug, Cobalt Blue Tree, Norton, Bennington, Vermont, 1 Gallon	135.00
Jug, Cowden & Wilcox, 5 Tulips, 4 Gallon	1000.00
Jug, Cowden, Harrisburg, Blue On Handle, 2 Gallon	150.00
Jug, D.Goodale, Hartford, Blue Wash On Name & Handle, 3 Gallon	95.00

Jug, Design, Signed W.Hart, Ogdensburgh, 2 Gallon 265.00
Jug, Devil, Black, Red & White Design, 12 In. 25.00
Jug, Dove, Signed Geo. F.Hewett, Worcester & Boston, 2 Gallon 195.00
Jug, E. & L.P.Norton, Bennington, Cobalt Blue Flower, 1 Gallon 235.00
Jug, Floral Design, Cobalt Blue, 2 Gallon, 14 1/4 In. 85.00
Jug, Foliage Design, Cobalt, 4 Gallon, 14 1/4 In. 45.00
Jug, Gonner & Snedeker, Wheeling, W.Va., Cobalt Blue, 2 Gallon 55.00
Jug, Gray, Handled, Signed Warner, 1 Quart, 8 In. 45.00
Jug, Hamilton & Jones, Greensboro, Blue Design, 4 Gallon 250.00
Jug, Hamilton & Jones, Greensboro, Pa., Cobalt Blue, 2 Gallon 115.00
Jug, Harrington Lyons, Freehand Tulip, 2 Gallon 225.00
Jug, Haxton Ottman & Co., Fort Edward, Bird, Cobalt Blue, 1 Gallon 300.00
Jug, Impressed Albany Slip, Pouring Spout, 9 In. 20.00
Jug, Impressed S.Hart, Cobalt Blue, 1 Gallon 75.00
Jug, Impressed W.J.Seymour, Troy Factory, Flower & Leaf, 2 Gallon 145.00
Jug, Incised Swan, Gardinier Stoneware Co., C.1860, 1 Gallon 100.00
Jug, James Lowery, Syracuse, N.Y., 1 Gallon 42.00
Jug, Large Insect, Roberts, Binghamton, N.Y., 2 Gallon 250.00
Jug, M.Salzman Co., Purity Above All, Gray & Brown, 1/2 Gallon 45.00
Jug, Minnesota Stoneware Co., Redwing, Minn., Brown Glazed, 1 Gallon 65.00
Jug, Pink Roses, Green Ground, 1 Quart 10.00
Jug, Polka-Dot Bird, Stylized Foliage, 5 Gallon 475.00
Jug, Running Vine & Tulip, 1 Gallon 245.00
Jug, S.Hart & Son, Flower & Scroll, Blue Gray, 1 Gallon 95.00
Jug, S.T.Brewer, Havana, Flower, 1 Gallon 120.00
Jug, Scrolls & Roses, W.J.Seymour, 2 Gallon 185.00
Jug, Signed Pittman Bros. & Co., Ft.Edward, N.Y.Gray, 1 Gallon 26.00
Jug, Somerset Potters Works, Design, 2 Gallon 165.00
Jug, Stylized Bird, Whites Utica, Cobalt Blue, 11 1/2 In. 165.00
Jug, Stylized Florals, E. & L.P.Norton, Cobalt Blue, 4 Gallon 135.00
Jug, Thistle, Saugerties, N.Y., Dated 1892, Gray, 1 Gallon 265.00
Jug, Thompson & Tyler, Troy, N.Y., 1858, 2 Gallon 240.00
Jug, Tulip, Signed Cowden & Wilcox, Harrisburg, Pa., 1 Gallon 195.00
Jug, W.J.Seymour, Feathered Scroll, 1 Gallon 165.00
Jug, Whites Utica, Hen, Rooster, Wreath, C.1862, 2 Gallon 2800.00
Jug, Wisp Of Cobalt Blue, Grooved Handle, Gray Glaze, 11 1/2 In. 85.00
Jug, 5 Tooled Rings, Hartford, C.1815, Ovoid, 1 Quart 35.00
Mold, Cake, Brown, Large 42.00
Mold, Food, Bunch Of Grapes Design, 7 X 8 1/2 In. 48.00
Mug, Barrel, Blue & White .... 65.00 To 95.00
Mug, Beer, Double Cobalt Blue Rings, Gray, Set Of 6 .... 120.00
Mug, Blue & Gray, Fishscale & Rose 85.00
Mug, Buffalo, Blue & Gray 125.00
Mug, Buffalo, Utica, White 125.00
Mug, Cattails, Blue & White, Set Of 4 .... 380.00
Mug, Hawkeye Mustard, Vinegar & Pickle Works 45.00
Mug, Incised Bands 40.00
Mug, Root Beer, Buckeye, Figural Handle, 6 1/4 In. 52.00
Mug, Souvenir, Concord, N.H., C.1880, Beige & Red & Gold 8.00
Mug, Stenciled Rose, Blue & White 50.00
Pan, Milk, Spout, 2 Handles, 6 Blue Flowers, 1 1/2 Gallon 105.00
Pitcher & Bowl, Embossed Scrolls & Designs, Cream 150.00
Pitcher & Bowl, Rose Fishscale, Blue & White 225.00
Pitcher, Albany Slip, 10 In. 55.00
Pitcher, Apricot, Blue & White .... 65.00 To 100.00
Pitcher, Batter, Brown, Large 175.00
Pitcher, Beer, White & Co., Binghamton, Inside Strainer, 2 Quart 250.00
Pitcher, Bird On Twig, 2 Gallon 900.00
Pitcher, Brown & Tan, Commemorating Utah Into Union, 7 In. 185.00
Pitcher, Bumblebee, Blue, 2 Gallon 250.00
Pitcher, Butterfly, Blue & White .... 65.00 To 145.00
Pitcher, Buttermilk, Brown Glaze, 7 In. 45.00
Pitcher, Cattails, Advertising, Collinsville, Illinois, Large 165.00

Pitcher, Cobalt Blue Leafy Design, Signed Lyons, 1 Gallon 300.00
Pitcher, Cow, Blue & White .... 125.00 To 145.00
Pitcher, Cow, Brown .... 58.00 To 75.00
Pitcher, Cow, Yellow & Green, 6 In. 60.00
Pitcher, Cow, Yellow & Green, 8 In. .... 65.00 To 85.00
Pitcher, Cows, Green, Cream, 8 In. 50.00
Pitcher, Deer & Fawn, Blue & White, 8 In. 135.00
Pitcher, Dragonfly, Blue & Gray, 8 In. 185.00
Pitcher, Dutch Boy & Girl Kissing, Navy & Green, 6 In. 70.00
Pitcher, Dutch Boy & Girl, Blue & White, 8 In. 120.00
Pitcher, Dutch Scene, Blue & White, 8 In. 135.00
Pitcher, Eagle, Blue & White, 8 In. 400.00
Pitcher, Eagle, Brown, 8 In. 110.00
Pitcher, Edelweiss, Motto In German, 9 In. 150.00
Pitcher, Embossed Grapes, Blue & White, 8 1/2 In. 85.00
Pitcher, Figural, Cow, Blue, 7 In. 115.00
Pitcher, Figural, Cow, Ivory & Green, 8 In. 125.00
Pitcher, Floral Design, Lyons, 1 Gallon 275.00
Pitcher, Girl & Dog, Brown, 8 In. 90.00
Pitcher, Grape Pattern, Brown Glaze, 6 In. .... 22.00 To 45.00
Pitcher, Grape, Green, 8 In. 60.00
Pitcher, Gray & Blue Design, Impressed, 7 1/2 In. 65.00
Pitcher, Indian Boy & Girl, Blue & White, 8 In. 150.00
Pitcher, Iris, Brown, 7 In. 85.00
Pitcher, Lovebirds, Brown To Green, 8 In. 100.00
Pitcher, Marked Star, Grapes, Brown Glaze, 9 1/2 In. 50.00
Pitcher, Milk, Dutch Boy & Girl & Windmill, Blue & Gray 140.00
Pitcher, Milk, Raised Zinnias In Blue, Blue & White, 7 1/4 In. 78.00
Pitcher, Nichols & Afford, 1854, Hound Handle, 8 In. 150.00
Pitcher, Old Flemish Ware, Blue Gray, Hunting Scene, 9 In. 165.00
Pitcher, Pearl, Podmore Walker & Co., C.1834, 12 In. 150.00
Pitcher, Poinsettia, Blue & White, 9 In. .... 105.00 To 120.00
Pitcher, Rose & Fishscale, Blue & White, 9 In. .... 125.00 To 145.00
Pitcher, Rose & Trellis, Blue & Tan, 8 In. .... 55.00 To 65.00
Pitcher, Rose & Trellis, Blue & White, 8 In. 90.00
Pitcher, Rose Decal, Blue & White, 10 In. 135.00
Pitcher, Rose With Rose Band, Blue & White, 8 In. 125.00
Pitcher, Round Grape, Brown, 4 In. .... 30.00 To 65.00
Pitcher, Standing Deer With Fawn, Blue & White, 8 In. 150.00
Pitcher, Trees, Brown, 4 In. 30.00
Pitcher, Trees, White, 4 In. 55.00
Pitcher, Tulip, Blue & White, 8 In. .... 69.00 To 115.00
Pitcher, Washington Scene, C.1834, Podmore Walker & Co., 12 In. 140.00
Pitcher, Water, Fishscale & Roses, Blue & Gray, 9 3/4 In. 135.00
Pitcher, Water, Spirit Of 76, Ben Franklin, Blue, 9 In. 165.00
Pitcher, White, Green Band, 1 Gallon, 10 1/2 In. 110.00
Pitcher, Windmill & Bush, Blue & White, 6 1/2 In. .... 60.00 To 95.00
Plate, Pie, Impressed Scientific Electric, Blue & White 125.00
Plate, Pie, Yellow, Incised Derryshire Ironstone, 8 In. 65.00
Plate, Yellow Slip Glaze, 11 In. 200.00
Pot, Bean, Brown & Gray, Lettering, Covered, 3 Quart 40.00
Pot, Incised Fleur-De-Lis, Loop Handles, Ovoid, 11 3/4 In. 350.00
Rolling Pin, Blue & White 165.00
Rolling Pin, Blue Striped 95.00
Rolling Pin, Ft.Scott, Kansas 185.00
Rolling Pin, Wildflower .... 135.00 To 165.00
Salt, Apple Blossom, Wooden Lid 80.00
Salt, Apricot, Wooden Lid .... 60.00 To 135.00
Salt, Butterfly, Blue & White, Wood Lid 85.00
Salt, Butterfly, Wooden Lid 65.00
Salt, Butterfly, Wooden Lid, Blue & White 120.00
Salt, Daisy, Blue & White 195.00
Salt, Daisy, Blue & White, Wooden Lid .... 65.00 To 125.00

Salt, Eagle, Wooden Lid 215.00
Salt, Good Luck, Blue & White .... 50.00 To 75.00
Salt, Grape & Basket Weave, Blue & White 100.00
Salt, Hanging, Blue & White 145.00
Salt, Peacock, Blue & White 125.00
Salt, Raspberries, Wooden Lid, Blue & White 85.00
Salt, Rose, With Rose Band 125.00
Salt, Waffle Weave, Blue & White, Original Lid 110.00
Salt, Written In Gold, Blue & White 65.00
Soap, Beaded Rose 145.00
Soap, Bowtie, Bluebirds Decal, Covered 135.00
Spittoon, Blue & White 100.00
Spittoon, Leaf Design Circling Bowl, Blue & White 65.00
Spittoon, Lettered Elm Park Hotel 695.00
Spittoon, R.C.Remmey, Blue Design 205.00
Syrup, Log Cabin Shape 45.00
Tankard, Dutch Scene 115.00
Tankard, Kreussen, Enameled, Apostle Figures, 6 In. 200.00
Tankard, Wildflower, Bulbous, Blue & White 145.00
Teapot, Crabstock Handle, Spherical Shape, White, 3 7/8 In. 400.00
Tobacco Jar, Utica, Horsehead, White 90.00
Toothbrushes, Rose, Fishscale, Blue & White 80.00
Toothpick, Swan, Blue & White 50.00
Umbrella Stand, Tree Stump Shape, Signed, Norton, Worcester 225.00
Vase, Rainbow Striped, 8 1/2 In. 18.00
Wash Bowl, Bowtie, Blue & White 100.00
Wash Bowl, Wedding Rings, Blue & White 50.00
Wash Set, Bowtie, Rose Decals, 6 Piece 550.00
Water Set, Embossed Lady, Brown Glaze, 6 Mugs, Pitcher 65.00
Waterer, Chick, Blue Finial, Blue Stripe Over Joint, 1 Pint 135.00

STORE, see also Card; Coffee Grinder; Planters Peanut; Scale; Tool
STORE, Ashtray, Braille Alphabet, Dog In Center 10.00
Ashtray, Brand Prize Beer, Ceramic 35.00
Ashtray, Commonwealth Insurance, Copper 9.00
Ashtray, Coors 3.00
Ashtray, Dobbs Hat, Black Glass 14.00
Ashtray, Firestone Champion, Rubber Rim 15.00
Ashtray, Gibbons Beer, Red, White, & Black 3.50
Ashtray, Liberty Bank, Copper 6.00
Ashtray, Lord Calvert 3.25
Ashtray, Mack Bulldog 25.00
Ashtray, Marked Diamond Match 15.00
Ashtray, Old Hickory Bourbon 10.00
Ashtray, Rubber Tire, Kelly Springfield, Green 15.00
Ashtray, Yellow Cab Co. 10.00
Bank, Donkey, Listerine, Glazed Pottery, White 6.00
Barrel, Brill's Syn-O-Mon 130.00
Barrel, Ice Cream, Puritan Cone Co., Tin. 125.00
Beater, Rug, Shamrock 30.00
Beater, Rug, Wire 15.00
Bin & Sifter, Superior Flour, 3 1/2 Ft. 65.00
Bin & Sifter, Superior, Tin, 26 X 12 In.Diam. 98.00
Bin, Coffee, A. & P., Tin 350.00
Bin, Coffee, Dudleys Of Chicago, Lithograph On Tin 125.00
Bin, Coffee, Parkers Dry Roasted 125.00
Bin, Coffee, Roll Top, Tin, 22 1/2 X 20 1/2 X 12 1/2 In. 595.00
Bin, Draught Tea, Pictures Horses Pulling Wagon, 13 X 13 X 13 In. 295.00
Bin, Flour, Slant Front, Pine 125.00
Bin, Grain, Sloped Lid, Pine 350.00
Bin, Lion's Coffee 290.00
Bin, Ojibwa Tobacco, 11 In. 325.00

Bin, Race Match 275.00
Bin, Sugar, Lift-Top, Door For Scoop, Pine 500.00
Bin, Sure Shot Tobacco, Indian 325.00
Bin, Sweet Cuba Tobacco, 10 X 8 X 8 In. 135.00
Bin, Tea, Lady Pictured, 16 In.High 195.00
Bin, Tobacco, Polar Bear 145.00
Bin, Victor Matches, Tin, 21 X 15 X 10 In. 165.00
Bin, White Swan Coffee, Paper Label With Swan, 10 1/4 X 10 1/2 In. 135.00
     STORE, BOTTLE, see Bottle
     STORE, BOX, see Box
Bucket, Dr.Ridge's Lard, 2 1/2 In. 40.00
Bucket, Hellick's Peanut Butter, Tin, Wire Handle 10.00
Bucket, Naphey's Lard, 2 1/2 In. 40.00
Bucket, 50 Lbs. Of Home Rendered Lard, Pig On Side, Tin, 12 X 14 In. 48.00
Butcher Block, 6 Turned Legs, 5 Ft. 500.00
Button, Baltimore Orioles, Picture Of Bird Holding Bat, C.1960 .... 5.00
Button, Frank Howard, Washington Senators, C.1969 .... 5.00
Button, Green Bay Packers, Picture Of Bart Starr, 1964 .... 12.00
Button, New York Giants, C.1950 .... 10.00
Buttonhook, Wear-U-Well, Metal 8.00
Cabinet, Ampollina Dye, Slant Front, Cubbyholes, 24 X 15 1/2 In. 275.00
Cabinet, Angel Dainty Dye, Tin 60.00
Cabinet, Bronco Homoeopathic Remedies, 30 Sections, Oak, 15 X 19 In. 150.00
Cabinet, Diamond Dye, Court Jester 650.00
Cabinet, Diamond Dye, Evolution Of Woman 550.00
Cabinet, Diamond Dye, The Governess, Sliding Rear Door, Oak 425.00
Cabinet, Diamond Dyes, It's Easy To Dye .... *Illus* 300.00
Cabinet, Display, Collar Buttons, 1890s, Wooden, 11 X 7 In. 165.00
Cabinet, Display, Dr.Scholl's Remedies, 16 Products 85.00
Cabinet, Goff Embroidery Braid, 2-Drawer, Oak 100.00
Cabinet, Putnam Dye, Filled With Original Packages, Metal 110.00
Cabinet, Putnam Dye, Slant Tin Front, Wooden, 21 X 8 In. 75.00
Cabinet, Putnam Dye, Soldiers, Wooden, Tin Front, 21 X 10 X 8 1/2 In. 135.00
Cabinet, Putnam Fadeless Dye, Slant Front, Lithograph, Wooden 135.00
Cabinet, Shaving, 2 Shelves, Gray Enameled Finish, 6 X 7 3/8 In. 20.00
Cabinet, Slant Glass Front, Pipe 35.00
Cabinet, Sun Garter, Glass, Round 65.00
Cabinet, Sunset Soap Dye, Wooden, With Dyes 55.00
Caddy, Chase & Sanborn's Fancy Tea, Hinged Top, 8-Sided 35.00
Can Opener, Pabst, Counter Model 15.00

Store, Cabinet, Diamond Dyes, It's Easy To Dye

Can, Gas, Keen Kutter 15.00
Can, Penn Franklin Motor Oil, Tin 15.00
Canister, Arcadia Mixture, Tin 35.00
Canister, Buckingham Tobacco 22.00
Canister, Congress, Small Top 95.00
Canister, Dan Patch Tobacco, Cardboard 45.00
Canister, Dixie Queen, Tin 50.00
Canister, DuPont Powder 21.50
Canister, Dutch Masters 10.00
Canister, George Washington Cut Plug 20.00
Canister, Green River Tobacco, Cardboard 45.00
Canister, Just Suites, Small Top 90.00
Canister, Old Seneca Stogies 115.00
Canister, Pedro Tobacco, Cardboard 175.00
Canister, Real Thing, Tin 85.00
Canister, Red Indian Tobacco 130.00
Canister, Red, Rose Tea 75.00
Canister, Seal, North Carolina, Tin 115.00
Canister, Shedd's Peanut Butter, 5 Pound 10.00
Canister, Sir Walter Raleigh, Tin 30.00
Canister, Stag Tobacco, Tin, Small 25.00
Canister, Sterling 45.00
Canister, Sweet Burley Light Tobacco 105.00
Canister, Sweet Cuba, Green, Round, 2 X 8 In. 24.00
Canister, Sweet Mist, Cardboard 75.00
Canister, Tiger Tobacco, Cardboard 120.00
Canister, Tip Top Tobacco, Cardboard 45.00
Canister, Tobacco, Buckingham 18.00
Canister, Tobacco, Hunt Scene, German 15.00
Canister, Tobacco, Seal Of North Carolina, 5 1/2 In. 135.00
Canister, Union Leader, Uncle Sam, Pocket .... 20.00 To 22.00
Canister, Whip, Tin 275.00
Card, 3 Maids From School, Union Pacific Tea Co., 6 1/4 X 9 1/2 In. 7.50
Case, Barnum Cheese, 3 Glass Sides, Wooden, 22 X 21 X 19 In. 350.00
Case, Cheese, Rolltop Back, 3 Glass Sides, Wooden, 22 X 19 X 22 In. 395.00
Case, Counter, Slant Front, Pull-Out Drawers, 14 1/2 X 10 3/4 In. 55.00
Case, Fairbanks Soap, Fairy Christmas Box, 16 X 17 X 9 In. 150.00
Case, Lucky Strike Cut Plug Tobacco, Oak Bound, Dispenser 275.00
Case, Ribbon, 2 Glass Doors, 24 X 25 X 40 In. 625.00
Change Receiver, Cuticura, Glass 30.00
Cheese Safe, Advertising On Back, Mahogany, 22 X 18 In. 250.00
Coaster, Smith Brothers, Ale, Tin 7.00
Coffee Bean Roaster, Tin, Cylindrical, Long Handle 230.00
Container, James Lutted, Glass Log Cabin, C.1885 .... 475.00
Container, Kis-Me Gum, Glass, Lid 77.00
Counter, Victorian, General Store, Carved Front, Pine 550.00
Cover, Flue, Lady With 3 Little Girls, Large 20.00
Cover, Flue, Swiss Couple 14.00
Cover, Flue, Young Girl, Gold Border, Chain For Hanging 15.00
Creamer, Lipton Tea, Yellow 5.50
Crock, Apple Butter, Heinz, Label 120.00
Crock, Heinz Baked Beans 125.00
Crock, Heinz, Preserved Peaches, Label, Gallon 195.00
Cup, Ft.Bedford Peanut Butter, Tin 50.00
Cutter, Cigar, Art Nouveau Bell Shape, Pocket 48.00
Cutter, Cigar, Blowfish, White Brass, Pocket 85.00
Cutter, Cigar, Bowing Man, Head Turns, Cuts Cigar Inside Hat, 8 In. 685.00
Cutter, Cigar, Charles Denby, Countertop 175.00
Cutter, Cigar, Dexter, Wooden 28.00
Cutter, Cigar, Elks Emblem, 1915, Pocket 20.00
Cutter, Cigar, Figural, Spaniel, Bird In Mouth, Silver Plated, 5 3/8 In. 235.00
Cutter, Cigar, Indian Motorcycle, Pocket 9.50

Cutter, Cigar, Lop-Eared Spaniel, Hand Held, 5 3/4 In. 225.00
Cutter, Cigar, Mephistopheles, Brass, 3 X 1 3/4 In. 250.00
Cutter, Cigar, Muriel Cigars, Sterling Silver, Pocket 18.50
Cutter, Cigar, Scissors, Metal, Pocket 14.00
Cutter, Cigar, Shape Of Man, Bronze, Pocket 40.00
Cutter, Cigar, Silver Nails In Shoe, Squeeze Type, Scotch, Gold 225.00
Cutter, Tobacco, Brown's Mule, R.J.R. Tobacco Co. 50.00
Cutter, Tobacco, Champion 40.00
Cutter, Tobacco, Cupples Co., Marked Arrow 38.50
Cutter, Tobacco, Enterprise, 1871 .... 45.00
Cutter, Tobacco, No O-Yankee, On Pine Slab, Cast Iron, 6 X 13 In. 35.00
Cutter, Tobacco, Queen, Gilt Letters, Cast Iron, 17 1/2 In. 55.00
Cutter, Tobacco, Red Devil Thumbing Nose On Handle 30.00
Cutter, Tobacco, Spearhead, P.J.Sorgco, Old Red Paint, Cast Iron, 19 In. 90.00
Cutter, Tobacco, Yankee Slicer, 12 In. 42.00
Dish, Candy, Advertising Schraffts 600.00
Dish, Candy, Schepp's Cocoanut, Coconut Finial 250.00
Dish, Change, Napoleon Cigars, Cast Iron 23.00
Dish, Soap, Empire Cream Separator, Brass 32.00
Dispenser, Banquet Tea, Pea Pot Shape, Crockery 55.00
Dispenser, Base, Soda Fountain, Cordley's Stoneware 16.50
Dispenser, China, Hires, Hourglass 325.00
Dispenser, Cigarette, Elephant, Turntail, Cigarette Drops, Cast Iron 55.00
Dispenser, Delaware Punch, Milk Glass, Metal Base, C.1920 .... 165.00
Dispenser, Green River Syrup 325.00
Dispenser, Heinz Vinegar, Glass, 10 In. 90.00
Dispenser, Hires Hourglass, Complete 350.00
Dispenser, Hires Root Beer, Marble & Brass 500.00
Dispenser, Hires, Original Plunger, Porcelain 90.00
Dispenser, Mansfield Automatic Clark Gum Machine, C.1902 .... 500.00
Dispenser, Match, Kool Cigarette 15.00
Dispenser, Match, Kools, 1 Cent Pocket 25.00
Dispenser, Match, Stencils, Green Cabinet, 1 Cent, 4 X 10 In. 165.00
Dispenser, Matchbox, Countertop, Penny 150.00
Dispenser, Paper, 2-Sided, Multicolored, Wooden 250.00
Dispenser, Ribbon, Cast Iron 35.00
Dispenser, Richest 5 Cent Root Beer, Brass Legs, Marble Base 750.00
Dispenser, Smith Bros. Cough Drop, With 1 Box 95.00
Dispenser, Spearmint Gum, 1 Cent 135.00
Dispenser, String, Red Goose, Cast Iron 875.00
Dispenser, Syrup, Boweys Root Beer, With Pump 300.00
Dispenser, Syrup, Brass Spigot, C.1870, Copper, Square, 6 X 7 In. 90.00
Dispenser, Syrup, Cherry Smash, Maid Of Honor Pump 450.00
Dispenser, Syrup, Fan Taz, Pennant Winner, Baseball & Bat Shape 1050.00
Dispenser, Syrup, Magnus Root Beer 275.00
Dispenser, Syrup, Orange Crush, With Pump 400.00
Dispenser, Ward's Lemon Crust 345.00
Dispenser, Zeno Gum, Oak 450.00
Dispenser, 5 Root Beer, Brass Legs, Marble Base, Glass Bowl 750.00
Display Case, Boye Phonograph Needles, Tin, Packets 85.00
Display Case, Cutlery, Swing-Down Back, 10 Divisions, Glass Front 65.00
Display Case, Eveready Shaving Brush 40.00
Display Case, Kleencut Scissors 65.00
Display Case, Kola Gum, Glass Sides, Etched Lettering, 18 X 11 In. 650.00
Display Case, La Crosse Manicure Implements, 15 X 20 In. 100.00
Display Case, Mazda Auto Bulb, Tin 40.00
Display Case, Paris Garters 85.00
Display Case, Razor, Shelving, Oak, 2 Ft. X 2 Ft. X 3 In. 250.00
Display Case, Remington Knife, Wooden, 30 1/2 X 14 X 8 In. 75.00
Display Case, Ribbon, Oak, 3 Ft. 250.00
Display Case, Slidewell Collar, Contents, 49 1/2 X 7 X 6 1/2 In. 295.00
Display Case, Sunset Soap Dye, 26 Sections, 1915, 14 X 18 In. 135.00
Display Case, Tootsie Roll 75.00

Display Case, Winchester, Simmons Razor Blade 75.00
Display Vase, Claes & Lehnbeuter Of St.Louis, Cigar, Oak, 94 X 38 In. 2500.00
Display, Jacquins Cordials, Man, High Hat, Bulging Eyes, 2 Bottles 30.00
Display, Santa Claus, Mechanical, Rocks Forward, Arms Move, 6 Ft. ....
Door Pull, Dandy Bread 6.00
Door Push, Dr.Pepper, Good For Life, 4 X 8 In. 35.00
Door Push, Hires 22.50
Door Push, NuGrape, Porcelain 20.00
Egg Timer, Mueller's Macaroni, 1890s 22.00
Fan, Ceiling, Emerson, 4 Wooden Blades, 26 In.Diam. 315.00
Figurine, Baker's Chocolate, Lady With Tray, Crossed Sword, 14 1/2 In. 800.00
Figurine, Bulldog, Bulldog Lager Beer, Porcelain, 15 In. 235.00
Figurine, Delivery Man, Whitman's Sampler, 3-Dimensional, 26 In. 275.00
Figurine, Green River Whiskey, Black Man With Mule, 6 3/4 In. 325.00
Figurine, Hamden Ale, Accordion Player On Barrel, Plaster, 14 3/4 In. 250.00
Figurine, Pabst Blue Ribbon Fighter In Ring, Cast Iron, Lighted 90.00
Figurine, R.C.A.Dog, Plaster Of Paris, Large 900.00
Flashlight, Phillips 66, 1921 .... 12.50
Flyswatter, Clockwork, Original Paint & Blades, 1876, Cast Iron 475.00
Flyswatter, Leather .... 9.00 To 12.50
Holder, Letter, J. & B.Scotch 5.00
Holder, Napkin, Nar-O-Fold, Chicago, Milk Glass 20.00
Holder, Straw, Glass 40.00
Holder, String, Counter Model, Cast Iron, Claw Feet 35.00
Holder, String, Plantation Pharmical Co., Memphis, Glass Dome 145.00
Humidor, Havana Cigars, Embossed Top, Metal 45.00
Humidor, Prince Albert Tobacco, 1910, Glass 28.00
Humidor, Sunny Bank Tobacco, Ceramic 85.00
Jar, Adams Gum, Etched Lettering 85.00
Jar, Curtis Chico Peanut, Tin Lid & Base 145.00
Jar, Dad's Cookie Co., Glass 65.00
Jar, Imperial Cut Tobacco, Porcelain 45.00
Jar, Just Born, Brazils 5 For 5 Cents, Almonds 15 For 5 Cents, Lid 85.00
Jar, National Biscuit Co. 45.00
Jar, Prince Albert Tobacco, Dated 1910 .... 45.00
Jar, Ramon's Pills, Counter .... 45.00 To 70.00
Jar, Sharp & Dohne Lozenge, Weighted Lid, 12 In. 95.00
Jar, Squirrel Brand Salted Peanuts, Squirrel Embossing 40.00
Jar, The Nut, Embossed House, Glass, Round 60.00
Jar, Tobacco, Bagdad 55.00
Jar, Tobacco, Globe, Barrel Shape, Dated 1882, Amber 30.00
Jar, Tom's Toasted Peanuts, Red, Embossed Tom's On Knob, 5 Quart 12.00
Jug, I.W.Harper Whiskey, Kentucky 65.00
Jug, White Lily Rye 65.00
Label, Canadian Salmon, Indian Paddler, Housewife, Set Of 10 .... 7.50
Label, Fruit, Redman Pears 4.00
Label, Fruit, Skookum Apples, 1916 .... 4.50
Label, Grape, Owl .... .50
Label, Orange Crate, Homer Brand, Blackbird, 10 X 10 In. 10.00
Label, Sebastopol Queen Apples, Robed Queen, 9 1/2 X 11 In. 1.00
Lamp, Budweiser, Revolving Light, Model Horses & Wagon 425.00
Lifter, Milk Cap, Dewhirst Dairy 6.00
Lighter & Cigar Cutter, Spark, Double Brass Tanks, Wooden Case 250.00
Lighter, Cigar, Garcia Brand, Electric, Holds Cigar Box 43.00
Lighter, Cigarette, Royal Crown Cola, Bottle Shaped 6.00
Lighter, Cigarette, Shape Of Plane, Steel 35.00
Lock, Mail Pouch Shape, Tobacco, Brass & Cast Iron 65.00
Lunch Box, Bagleys Wild Fruit 65.00
Lunch Box, Blue & Scarlet 275.00
Lunch Box, Central Union Cut Plug, Wire Bail Handle 39.00
Lunch Box, Comet 35.00
Lunch Box, Dixie Kid, Black Boy 200.00
Lunch Box, Dixie Queen, Lady 70.00

Lunch Box, Fashion Tobacco .... 85.00 To 150.00
Lunch Box, Friend's 105.00
Lunch Box, George Washington Cut Plug, Blue & Red, 6 X 3 X 3 1/4 In. 45.00
Lunch Box, Green Turtle .... 115.00 To 135.00
Lunch Box, Joe Palooka, Tin 35.00
Lunch Box, Just Suits Cut Plug, Lithograph, 7 3/4 In. .... 40.00 To 60.00
Lunch Box, Kandies For Kiddies 85.00
Lunch Box, Lorillard 60.00
Lunch Box, Mayo .... 24.00 To 30.00
Lunch Box, North Pole 55.00
Lunch Box, Patterson Seal Tobacco 15.00
Lunch Box, Peanuts, 1973 .... 5.00
Lunch Box, Pedro Tobacco .... 50.00 To 125.00
Lunch Box, Peter Rabbit 45.00
Lunch Box, Round Trip, Handleless .... 65.00 To 110.00
Lunch Box, Sensation Tobacco, Christmas Design 65.00
Lunch Box, Sensible Tobacco .... 25.00 To 30.00
Lunch Box, Skookum's Tobacco, Apple Paper Label 225.00
Lunch Box, Tiger Chewing & Smoking Tobacco, 10 X 8 In. .... 30.00 To 80.00
Lunch Box, Tom Corbett 48.00
Lunch Box, U.S.Marine Tobacco 30.00
Lunch Box, Union Commander, Picture Of George Washington 50.00
Lunch Box, Union Leader Tobacco .... 12.00 To 45.00
Lunch Box, Victorian Child Walking With Mr.Beetle, German, Tin, Oval 85.00
Lunch Box, Wagon Train, Thermos 10.00
Lunch Box, Walton's Peanuts 7.00
Lunch Box, Warnick & Brown 35.00
Lunch Box, Wild Fruit 55.00
Lunch Box, Winner Tobacco, Racing Cars .... 100.00 To 125.00
Lunch Box, Winner, Trunk Shape 35.00
Lunch Box, Workers Tobacco, Alligator Grain 25.00
Lunch Pail, True Blue, Paper Label 45.00
Lunch Pail, Union Leader Cut Plug, Picture Of Eagle 22.50
Machine, Candy Cutting, Mill's, Iron & Brass 55.00
Machine, Climax No.10, Peanut Butter, Original Paint 750.00
Machine, Popcorn, Advance, 1920s 800.00
Machine, Popcorn, Holcomb & Hoke, Deluxe, Pair 2175.00
Mannequin, Baby, Wearing Hanes Underwear, C.1935 .... 185.00
Mannequin, Boy, Glass Eyes, C.1910 .... 165.00 To 175.00
Matchbox Holder, Dr.Pepper, Advertising, Wall 12.00
Measure, Grain, Advertising 30.00
Measure, Grain, Nesting Set Of 5, Oak, 1880 .... 295.00
Mirror, Pocket, Alaska Fur Mfg. Co. 25.00
Mirror, Pocket, Bell's Buffalo Soap 8.00
Mirror, Pocket, Blue Valley Butter, Oval 17.00
Mirror, Pocket, Buick 9.00
Mirror, Pocket, Cadillac 10.00
Mirror, Pocket, Calox Tooth Powder, Oval 15.00
Mirror, Pocket, Cascarets Did It, Round 20.00
Mirror, Pocket, Des Moines 8.00
Mirror, Pocket, Duffy's Malt Liquor 15.00
Mirror, Pocket, Edison Mimeograph 29.00
Mirror, Pocket, J. & P.Coats 12.50
Mirror, Pocket, Kauffmann's Dept. Store, Pittsburgh, C.1910, Celluloid 20.00
Mirror, Pocket, Kellogg Jeweler & Optician, Woodhull, Ill. 20.00
Mirror, Pocket, Old Reliable Coffee, Round 23.00
Mirror, Pocket, Overland Cars 10.00
Mirror, Pocket, Socony, Red, White, & Blue, 3 1/2 In. 22.00
Mirror, Pocket, State Life Insurance, Child's Face 8.00
Mirror, Pocket, Sterling Piano 25.00
Mirror, Pocket, White Cat Union Suits 30.00
Mirror, Pond's Extract For Inflamations & Hemorrhages, 14 X 17 In. 145.00
Mirror, Sullivan, 10 Cent Cigar, Woman, Oval, Pocket 28.50

Mirror, Wall, Marilyn Monroe	34.00
STORE, MOLD, see Pewter, Mold; Tin, Mold	
Money Changer, Motorman's, C.1910, Metal	24.00
Mug, A & W Root Beer, Small	5.00
Mug, Rochester Root Beer	30.00
Mug, Santa Fe Brand Coffee	6.50
North Pole Tobacco, Pocket	95.00
Opener, Cigar Box, Tampa-Cuba	18.00
Pail, Apples In Marmalade, Jensen & Co., Tin	25.00
Pail, Armour, Peanut Butter	55.00 To 85.00
Pail, Armour's, Peanut Butter, Mother Goose	150.00
Pail, Armour's, Shield, Pure Lard, Bail Handles, 4 Pound	10.00
Pail, Bell, Pure Lard, Pictures Bell, Swine, Lithograph, Metal	15.00
Pail, Blueberry, Bail Handle, Lithograph Label, Tin Plate, 6 In.	18.50
Pail, Buffalo Brand Peanut Butter, Handle, 1 Pound	47.50
Pail, Butternut Coffee	25.00
Pail, Candy, Lovell & Covell, 3 Ounce	95.00
Pail, Climax, Peanut Butter, Bail Handle, J.W.Beardsley's Sons, Tin	28.50
Pail, Credo, Peanut Butter	28.00
Pail, Dan Patch	25.00
Pail, Dixie Queen, Pictures	65.00
Pail, Dixie, Peanut Butter	20.00
Pail, E.G.Kemp Golden Glow Peanuts, Gold, Yellow, & Black, 10 In.	45.00
Pail, Frontenac, Peanut Butter, Lid & Handle, C.1928	22.00
Pail, Gold Flake, Peanut Butter	35.00
Pail, Harrison's Butter, Bail Handle	125.00
Pail, Hoof Stuffing Compound, Red, Woodenware	12.00
Pail, Joe Palooka	65.00
Pail, Lard, Armour Star, Green, White, Bail Handle	4.00
Pail, Larkin, Peanut Butter	35.00
Pail, Luzianne, Coffee, 3 Pound	25.00
Pail, Mammy's Favorite Brand Coffee, 4 Pound	95.00 To 125.00
Pail, Marine Tobacco, Green	10.00
Pail, McLaughlin, Coffee, 5 Pound	50.00
Pail, Nashe's Coffee	18.00
Pail, Nigger Hair, Picture Of African Native	105.00
Pail, Ojibwa Tobacco	45.00
Pail, Old King Cole, Peanut Butter	85.00
Pail, Ontario, Peanut Butter, 3 1/2 In.	9.00
Pail, Ox-Heart, Peanut Butter	26.00
Pail, Pal's, Peanut Butter, Bail Handle, 5 Pound	12.00
Pail, Peter Rabbit, Peanut Butter	85.00
Pail, Red Seal, Peanut Butter	85.00
Pail, Sap, 1891	10.00
Pail, Sears, Coffee, Wooden Handle, Green & Blue, 11 In.	125.00
Pail, Seven Up	250.00
Pail, Shamokin, Lard, Indian, 8 Pound	55.00
Pail, Shedd's, Peanut Butter, Bail Handle, 5 Pound	12.00 To 22.50
Pail, Squirrel Brand, Peanut Butter, 1 Pound	125.00
Pail, Staple Brand, Peanut Butter	35.00
Pail, Sultana, Peanut Butter, 2 Toddlers, Bail, 1 Pound	26.50 To 30.00
Pail, Sunny Boy, Peanut Butter, 1 Pound	75.00
Pail, Sweet Mist	75.00
Pail, Swift's Pure Lard, Bail Handle, 2 Pound	10.00
Pail, Teddie, Peanut Butter, Bail Handle, Label, 5 Pound	10.00
Pail, This Little Pig, Candy	25.00
Pail, Toyland, Peanut Butter	70.00 To 72.00
Pail, Upton's Peanut Butter, 1 Pound	80.00
Pail, Wizard Of Oz, Peanut Butter	165.00
Pennant, Ringling Bros., Felt	9.00
Periscope, Morton Salt, 1930	25.00
Pitcher, Orange Crush, Pink Glass, Red Writing	35.00
Pitcher, Pepsi Cola, 6 Tumblers	55.00

Pitcher, Water, Passport Scotch, Ceramic 4.25
Planter, Old Grand Dad Whiskey 4.00
Plate, Push, Ex-Lax, Porcelain 40.00
Plate, Union Pacific Tea Co., Bears On Edge, Tin, 1907 .... 40.00
Poster, Avalon Cigarettes, Bolero Gal, 1939, 11 X 16 In. 25.00
Poster, Avalon Cigarettes, Spanish Lady, 1937, 11 X 16 In. 30.00
Poster, Babbitt's Soap, Tom Sawyer Type Boy, Fishing, 1892, 27 X 14 In. 150.00
Poster, Bock Beer, Goat Wearing Clothes, Victorian Woman, 27 X 21 In. 165.00
Poster, Boston Rubber Shoe Co., Fairies Putting On Shoes, 18 X 24 In. 150.00
Poster, Buckshoe & Tiger Stripe Tobacco, Fishbowl, 1895, 28 X 14 In. 275.00
Poster, Burkhardt Beer, Pretty Girl, 1930s, 20 X 27 In. 30.00
Poster, Charles Denby Cigars, Black Boy With Box, Stand-Up, 13 In. 25.00
Poster, Cloth Of Gold Cigarettes, Victorian Blonde, 1895, 14 X 30 In. 295.00
Poster, Dam-I-Ana Invigorator, Nude People, 1900, 24 X 33 In. 575.00
Poster, Dilworth Bros.Cigars, Girl, Flowers, 1895, 2/ X 14 In. 170.00
Poster, Duke's Mixture, Spanish American Soldiers, 1899, 32 X 22 In. 395.00
Poster, Elgin Watch, Father Time With Watch, 1910, Framed, 16 X 22 In. 175.00
Poster, Epco 5 Cent Cigar, Giant Cigar, 1930s, 8 X 22 In. 5.00
Poster, Ferry Seed, Farmer Selling Tomatoes, Framed, 32 X 24 In. 165.00
Poster, Hammond Roach Powder, Tramp Panning For Gold, 1920s 145.00
Poster, Honest Scrap Tobacco, Cat & Dog Fighting, 1900, 30 X 23 In. 495.00
Poster, LaEsferia Cigars, Lady Holding Umbrella, 1895, 28 X 15 In. 275.00
Poster, Mother's Oats, Child In Tiger Skin, 1895, Framed, 28 X 22 In. 145.00
Poster, Orphan Boy Tobacco, 1930s, 13 1/4 X 20 1/4 In. 50.00
Poster, Raleigh Cigarettes, 1939, 11 X 16 In. 25.00
Poster, Red Cross Cotton, Negroes Picking Cotton, 1894, 33 X 24 In. 375.00
Poster, Red Man Tobacco, 1930s, 20 X 22 In. 65.00
Poster, San Felice Cigars, Woman Hugging Man, 1910, Framed, 18 X 24 In. 215.00
Poster, Satin Skin Powder, Stone Lighograph, Dated 1903, 42 X 26 In. 50.00
Poster, Silver Pine Healing Oil, Bleeding Horse, 1900, 28 X 21 In. 110.00
Poster, Target Cigarette, Roller & Pack, Dated 1931, 8 X 17 In. 10.00
Poster, Windish-Mulhauser Brewing Co., 1906, 16 X 22 In. 265.00
Pouch, Just Suits Cut Plug Tobacco 8.00
Pouch, Liggett & Myers Highgrade Chewing Tobacco, Leather 17.50
Pouch, Oceanic Tobacco, Cloth 6.00
Pouch, Red Eye Plug Tobacco 7.50
Pump, Beer, Hand-Operated, Wood & Brass Handle 25.00
Pumper, Balloon, Carnival, Cast Iron 75.00
Rack, Baker's, Pie, Open, 6-Shelf, Wooden 185.00
Rack, Display, Postcard, Cast Iron & Tin 55.00
Rack, Display, Winchester Flashlight, Holds 12, Red Paint 75.00
Roaster, Peanut, 4-Wheeled, Push, Clock Wind Mechanism Turns Nuts 3800.00
Ruler, Mutt & Jeff, Wooden, Souvenir Theatre House 5.00
Salt & Pepper, Penguin, Kool 15.00
Scoop, Airy Fairy Flour 9.00
Scoop, Flour, Eaco, Tin 10.00
Scoop, Ice Cream, Wooden Handle, Brass 25.00
Shaker, Horlick's Malted Milk, Lum & Abner .... 12.50 To 25.00
Sharpener, Pencil, Baker's Chocolate 10.00
Sharpener, Twinplex Razor 6.00
Sign, Ada Olive Oil, Girl, Olive Branches, Tin, 13 X 19 In. 135.00
Sign, Advertising Corsets, Clockwork 450.00
Sign, Aetna Insurance Co., 1920s, Porcelain, 12 X 18 In. 75.00
Sign, Agency, Shawnee Fire Ins.Co., Topeka, Ks., Porcelain, 12 X 18 In. 225.00
Sign, Akro Agate, Cardboard, Stand-Up, 15 1/2 X 13 In. 200.00
Sign, Alka Seltzer, 1920s, Cardboard, 20 X 12 In. 45.00
Sign, American Automobile Association, Porcelain, 22 X 5 3/4 In. 30.00
Sign, Anheuser Busch, Custer's Last Fight, Paperboard, 46 X 36 In. 350.00
Sign, Anheuser Busch, Dr.Stock, 1915, Tin, Self-Framed, 7 X 12 In. 40.00
Sign, Anheuser Busch, Woman, 4 Little Girls, Framed, 20 X 28 In. 1250.00
Sign, Antikamnia Tablets, 1912, Anita, 6 X 8 In. 65.00
Sign, Artificial Breeding, Embossed Tin, 1930s, 10 X 13 In. 20.00
Sign, Artificial Breeding, 1940s, Embossed Tin, 9 X 12 In. 20.00

Ivory, Figurine, Man Sitting On Bundle Of Sticks, C. 1880, 3¾ In.

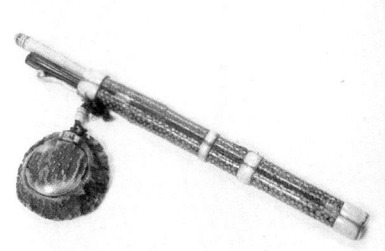

Scribe Set, Arrow Stand & Quiver, Edo Period, C. 1750

Painting, Reverse On Glass, Landscape, C. 1900, 13 X 19 In.

Furniture, Tambouret, Pyromania,
C. 1910

Furniture, Rocker, Wicker Caning
Over Wood Frame, C. 1880,
3 Ft. 1 In.

Furniture, Chair, Hall, Oak, 1905,
3 Ft. 10½ In.

Furniture, Easel, Victorian,
Renaissance Gothic

Furniture, Chairs, Side, Mahogany Stained, Upholstered Seat, 1840–50; Maple, Cane Seat, 1840–50

Furniture, Chairs, Side, Gothic Revival, Mahogany, 1835–50

Music, Phonograph, Victor, Upright,
Cabriole Legs, 4 Ft. 2¾ In.

Furniture, Chair, Victorian, Associated
With "Jeliffe"

Furniture, Chair, Arm, Hunzinger,
Colonial Revival, Walnut, 1890,
2 Ft. 10½ In.

Clock, Tall Case, Wm. Gilbert
Clock Co., Mission, Oak, 1910,
2 Ft. 5¼ In.

Furniture, Table, Occasional,
Ebonized Maple, Turned Legs,
1880, 1 Ft. 7 In. Diam.

Furniture, Chair, Papier-Mache, Lacquered, English, C. 1855;
Table, Tilt Top, Papier-Mache, Lacquered, English, C. 1855

Furniture, Desk, Wooton, Walnut, 1874–80

Doorknobs, Victorian

Furniture, Rocker, Colonial Revival, Walnut, Ebonized, Adapted From Spinning Wheel Parts, 1890

Doll, Mechanical, Boy Blowing
Bubbles, Bisque, French

Toy, Dog, Sandy, Stuffed,
1920s, 7 In.; Doll, Little Orphan
Annie, Composition, 1924

Toy, Furniture, Parlor, Gothic Revival, Germany, C. 1875; Doll, Woman, China Head,
Germany, C. 1875, 6½ In.; Doll, Man, Bisque Head, Germany, C. 1890, 6½ In.

Sign, Atkins Silver Steel Saws, Lithograph On Tin, 18 X 8 In. 160.00
Sign, Atlantic Coast Line, 1940s, Tin, 22 In.Diam. 75.00
Sign, Baldwin's Wind Pills, 1905, 26 X 20 In. 40.00
Sign, Bartholomay, Seminude Riding Wings, Paperboard, 26 X 36 In. 475.00
Sign, Bavarian Beer, Tin, 1930s, 6 X 9 In. 18.00
Sign, Beech Nut Tobacco, 1930's, 16 X 8 In. 20.00
Sign, Beef Wine & Iron, Great Restorative Tonic, C.1910, 26 X 40 In. 150.00
Sign, Bell Telephone Underground Cable, Porcelain, 2 1/2 X 7 In. 22.00
Sign, Bell Telephone, Porcelain, 11 X 11 In. 65.00
Sign, Benjamin Moore Paint, Reverse Painting On Glass, 35 1/2 X 8 In. 125.00
Sign, Berghoff Beer, Dogs, Snow March, Self-Framed, 13 X 21 In. 45.00
Sign, Better Made Ice Cream, On Mirror, 12 X 21 In. 30.00
Sign, Bird Roofing, Girl, 1920s, Porcelain, 14 X 20 In. 85.00
Sign, Blatz, 1913 Auto, Stretched Canvas, Frame, 35 X 26 In. 475.00
Sign, Blue Ribbon Bourbon, Lithograph On Canvas, 38 X 28 In. 395.00
Sign, Blue Star Coal, Blue Star, Tin, 22 X 14 In. 20.00
Sign, Boar's Head Tobacco, Porcelain, 7 X 24 In. 155.00
Sign, Bock Beer, Goat, Woman, Poster, 1893, 27 X 21 In. 165.00
Sign, Borden's Ice Cream, Reverse Painting On Glass, 21 X 12 1/2 In. 85.00
Sign, Brokhoff Ice Cream, Tin, 22 X 40 In. 29.00
Sign, Buckeye Beer, Embossed, Tin, 1930s, 3 X 18 In. 20.00
Sign, Buckeye Beer, Ship's Captain, Pub, Tin, 21 X 16 In. 125.00
Sign, Budweiser Girl, Red Dress, Paper, Wood, 1907, 36 X 21 In. 450.00
Sign, Buffalo Gasoline, Tin, 6 X 7 In. 15.00
Sign, Bull Durham, Paper, 1940s, 17 X 7 In. 35.00
Sign, Burger Beer, Man, Canoe, Beer, Tin, 21 X 16 In. 55.00
Sign, Burger Beer, Man, Canoe, Case Of Beer, Tin, 21 X 16 In. 55.00
Sign, Burger Brau, 1930s, Embossed, Tin, 9 X 13 In. 50.00
Sign, Burkhardt Beer, Lady Holding Glass, Cardboard, 20 X 27 In. 30.00
Sign, Busch Ginger Ale, 1920s, Porcelain, 11 X 21 In. 65.00
Sign, Buster Brown Shoes, Buster & Dog, Lithograph, 17 X 12 In. 95.00
Sign, Butcher's, Meat Saw, Bull On Top, Iron, 26 X 14 1/2 In. 475.00
Sign, C.H.Pendleton, Eye Doctor, Tin, 20 X 6 In. 30.00
Sign, California Fruit Chewing Gum, Child In Sailor Suit, 9 X 11 In. 90.00
Sign, Canada Dry, Bottles, Tin, 47 X 18 In. 25.00
Sign, Canada Dry, Shield Shape, Tin, 14 1/2 X 15 In. 15.00
Sign, Carter's Ink, Kittens Playing Baseball, Framed, 11 X 13 In. 35.00
Sign, Cetacolor, Prevents Fading, 1890s, Oilcloth, 36 X 25 In. 75.00
Sign, Champale, Champagne Glass Blinks, Electric, 12 X 5 In. 20.00
Sign, Chesterfield, Best For You, Shows 2 Packs, Tin, 34 X 12 In. 28.00
Sign, Chi-Namel Varnish, Chinaman, 1920, 2-Sided, 20 X 13 In. 195.00
Sign, Chief Paints, 1940s, Tin, 12 X 28 In. 25.00
Sign, Chippewa Salt, Paper Lithograph, 1918, 24 X 60 In. 65.00
Sign, Chrysler, Porcelain, 1930s, 24 X 36 In. 95.00
Sign, Citizen's Insurance Co., Reverse Painting On Glass, 22 X 16 In. 135.00
Sign, Clabber Girl Baking Powder, Tin, 1940s, 12 X 36 In. 25.00
Sign, Clark Thread, Advertising, 24 X 18 In. 65.00
Sign, Clicquot Club, Tin, 19 1/2 X 8 1/2 In. 35.00
Sign, Clover Leaf Soap, 1915, Embossed, Tin, 5 X 20 In. 35.00
Sign, Coca-Cola, Bottle Shape, Tin, 17 In. 25.00
Sign, Coca-Cola, Porcelain, 1923, 10 X 30 In. 150.00
Sign, Coca-Cola, 1940s, Self-Framed, Tin, 12 X 28 In. 95.00
Sign, Colonial Club, 2-Sided Steel, 1915, 8 X 18 In. 45.00
Sign, Columbian Beer, Embossed Bottle, Old Man, 14 X 10 In. 145.00
Sign, Columbian Rope, Sailor & Parrot, Oilcloth, 50 X 30 In. 450.00
Sign, Continental Brewing Co., Cardboard, 11 X 7 In. 14.00
Sign, Cook's Beer, Redhead In Long Dress, 1930s, Tin, 29 X 22 In. 175.00
Sign, Cook's Beer, 1940s, Tin, 16 X 24 In. 20.00
Sign, Cool Roasted Coffee, Orange & Black, 30 X 20 In. 20.00
Sign, Corby's Whiskey, Man, Newspaper, Tramp, Paper, 1910, 9 X 13 In. 250.00
Sign, Corby's Whiskey, Tramp With Drink, Paperboard, 1910, 31 X 23 In. 250.00
Sign, Cow Pass 300 Feet, Black & White, Cast Iron, 9 1/2 X 11 In. 130.00
Sign, Crisco, 1930s, Cardboard, 11 X 13 In. 15.00

Sign, Crown Teas, Tin, 1900, 14 X 20 In. 85.00
Sign, Dad's, Blue, Red, Yellow, Tin, 28 X 20 In. 59.00
Sign, Dari-Rich, 1930s, Tin, 10 X 24 In. 25.00
Sign, Davis Carriage Mfg. Co., Petersburg, Va., Tin, 7 X 20 In. 110.00
Sign, DeLaval Cream Separators, 5 Pictures, Tin, 41 X 30 In. 1250.00
Sign, DeLaval, Right Angle, Porcelain, Cream Separator, 18 X 27 In. 225.00
Sign, Denver Sandwich, 1940s, Tin, 12 X 28 In. 35.00
Sign, Der-Ma-Tine, 1930s, Cardboard, 7 X 12 In. 15.00
Sign, Devilish Good Cigar, 1910, Tin, 8 X 11 In. 95.00
Sign, Dewer's White Label, Distillery, Composition, 13 X 20 In. 8.50
Sign, Diamond Dyes, Page & Court Scene, Tin, 16 1/2 X 18 1/2 In. 135.00
Sign, Dill's Best, Cardboard, 24 X 29 In. 100.00
Sign, Dodge Bros., 1930s, Porcelain, 15 X 45 In. 95.00
Sign, Dolly Madison, 1910, Embossed, Tin, 5 X 20 In. 20.00
Sign, Dr Pepper, Good For Life 10-2-4, Scenes, Cardboard, 15 X 25 In. 18.00
Sign, Dr Pepper, Logo, Tin, 1920, 19 X 7 In. 25.00
Sign, Dr Pepper, Metal, 24 X 12 In. 75.00
Sign, Dr Pepper, Porcelain, 10 X 26 In. 115.00
Sign, Dr Pepper, Tin, 29 1/2 X 12 In. 22.00
Sign, Dr.Blumer's, Tin, 1915, 3 X 18 In. 25.00
Sign, Dr.Caldwells, Cardboard, 27 X 34 In. 300.00
Sign, Dr.Meyer's Foot Soap, Black & White Litho, Cardboard, 7 X 10 In. 10.00
Sign, Dr.Morse's Indian Root Pills, 3-Sided, Cardboard, 4 X 3 Ft. 67.50
Sign, Dr.Scholl's, Porcelain, 24 X 7 1/2 In. 60.00
Sign, Drink Braem's Bitter For Appetite, C.1906, Metal, 13 X 7 In. 27.00
Sign, Drink Hires, Bottle, Tin, 27 1/2 X 9 1/2 In. 12.50
Sign, Drink Nehi Orange, C.1940, Cardboard, 11 X 28 In. 15.00
Sign, Duluth Imperial Flour, Black Cook, Tin, 1910, 18 X 25 In. 750.00
Sign, Dupont, Cavalryman, Shooting Buffalo, Paper, 1895, 14 X 30 In. 295.00
Sign, Dutch Masters Cigar, Lithograph On Canvas, C.1910, 12 X 18 In. 125.00
Sign, Early Times Whiskey, Wooden Frame, Plaster, 23 X 29 In. 300.00
Sign, Ebbert Wagons, Self-Framed, Tin, 42 X 30 In. 1150.00
Sign, Ebling's Extra, Grand Old Beer, Cardboard, 9 X 14 In. 12.50
Sign, Edgar Bergen Coca-Cola, Paper, 1940s, 11 X 28 In. 80.00
Sign, Edison Mazda Lamps, Calendar 1930, Signed Parrish, 11 X 21 In. 250.00
Sign, Ehlermann, Founder's Face, Workers Picking Hops, Tin, 26 X 18 In. 650.00
Sign, El Bart Gin, Bulldog, Chained To Door, Tin, 1910, 9 X 13 In. 195.00
Sign, El Morris 5 Cent Cigar, 1930s, Cardboard, 10 X 13 In. 10.00
Sign, Enjoy Ice Cream, Chain Hanger, Glass, 10 X 10 In. 75.00
Sign, Everready Safety Razor, Metal & Glass, 18 X 40 In. 200.00
Sign, F.E.Draper Undertaker, Gold Leaf, Wooden, 16 X 26 In. 225.00
Sign, Fairbanks Morse, Porcelain, 9 X 50 In. 65.00
Sign, Fairbanks Morse, 1930s, Embossed, Tin, 10 X 28 In. 40.00
Sign, Fairy Soap For Toilet & Bath, Small Girl, Tin, 7 X 39 In. 225.00
Sign, Fairy Soap, 1920s, Cardboard, 11 X 21 In. 65.00
Sign, Falstaff Beer, Barbeque On The Range, Cardboard, 42 X 30 In. 45.00
Sign, Falstaff, The Peace Maker, 1910, Tin, Self-Framed, 31 X 23 In. 850.00
Sign, Favorite Straight Cut Cigarettes, Hunting Dog, Tin, 18 X 9 In. 125.00
Sign, Fire Escape, Enamel, 7 X 20 In. 15.00
Sign, Fisk Tires, Boy, Tire, New York Skyscrapers, Paper, 48 X 28 In. 60.00
Sign, Fleischmann's, 1910, Wood Framed, Tin, 15 X 40 In. 150.00
Sign, Ford Tractor, Masonite Board, C.1939, 11 X 22 In. 65.00
Sign, Fr.Blumer's Baking Powder, Tin, 1915, 3 X 18 In. 25.00
Sign, Ft.Worth Brewing Co., Bottle, Glass, People, Tin, 22 X 28 In. 500.00
Sign, Get Real Action, Thirst Your 7-Up Away, Tin, 41 X 31 In. 38.00
Sign, Golden Cola, 1940s, Embossed, Tin, 12 X 28 In. 30.00
Sign, Goldyrock Birch Beer, 1930s, Embossed, Tin, 11 X 22 In. 20.00
Sign, Good Will Soap, 1930s, Embossed Tin, 2 X 18 In. 25.00
Sign, Goodrich, 1930s, Two-Sided Porcelain, 18 X 23 In. 45.00
Sign, Grainbelt, Fish, Plastic, 13 X 7 In. 8.50
Sign, Grapenuts, Girl & St.Bernard, 1905, Self-Framed, Tin, 31 X 20 In. 650.00
Sign, Grapette, Glamour Girl With Bottle, Cardboard, 20 X 31 1/2 In. 18.00
Sign, Green River Whiskey, Black Man, Mule, 1899, Tin, 38 X 28 In. 650.00

Sign, Green River Whiskey, Man & Horse, Paper, Framed, 18 X 24 In. 125.00
Sign, Griffith & Boyd Co., Aluminum, 23 1/2 X 15 1/2 In. 20.00
Sign, Grocer's Straight 5 Cigars, Lithograph, Framed, 17 X 14 In. 60.00
Sign, Gulftane, Porcelain, 8 1/2 X 11 In. 12.50
Sign, Hair Grower, 1905, Cardboard, 9 X 12 In. 15.00
Sign, Hampden Ale, Waiter Holds Tray, Metal, 2-Sided, 27 X 17 In. 375.00
Sign, Hampden, Tin, 1930s, 11 X 9 In. 60.00
Sign, Harvard Rye, Drinking Graduate, Tin, Wooden Frame, 29 X 22 In. 450.00
Sign, Harvester Cigar, Oval Convex, Tin, 10 X 13 In. 75.00
Sign, Hazle Club, 1940s, Tin, 8 In.Diam. 9.00
Sign, Health Club, 1940s, Tin, 11 X 21 In. 50.00
Sign, Heinz Sweet Pickles, 20 X 15 In. 185.00
Sign, Helmar Cigarettes, Cardboard, 36 X 25 In. 295.00
Sign, Helmar Turkish Cigarettes, Soldier's Head, 26 X 25 1/2 In. 395.00
Sign, Hex Fine Chili, Reverse Painting On Glass, 6 X 9 In. 6.00
Sign, HGC For Colds, Man In Tuxedo, 1890s, Tin, 7 X 10 In. 95.00
Sign, Hi-Power Malt Tonic, 1920s, Tin, 8 X 10 In. 25.00
Sign, Hires In Bottles, Tin, 10 X 28 In. 20.00
Sign, Hires Root Beer, Girl, Cardboard, 12 In.Diam. 8.00
Sign, Hires Root Beer, Party Scene, Easel Back, Cardboard, 12 X 16 In. 8.00
Sign, Hires Root Beer, Tin, 30 X 12 In. 10.00
Sign, Hires, Embossed Tin, 1926, 11 X 28 In. 40.00
Sign, Hires, 2 Girls Sipping Drinks, Oval, 24 In. 850.00
Sign, Horses At A Walk, Motor Vehicles 10 MPH, Iron, 32 X 16 In. 265.00
Sign, Howe Scale Co., Rutland, Vt., Hand-Painted, Wooden, 13 X 36 In. 325.00
Sign, Howell's Root Beer, Tin, 27 X 8 In. 49.00
Sign, Hump Hairpins, Giant Hairpin & Camel, 1910, Tin, 16 X 14 In. 150.00
Sign, Ice, 1930s, Porcelain, 11 X 20 In. 75.00
Sign, Jax Beer, Blue, Orange, & White, Meal, 32 X 56 In. 125.00
Sign, Jed Clayton Whiskey, Framed Paper, Black Man, Jug, 20 X 30 In. 165.00
Sign, Jersey Ice Cream, Embossed, 1940s, Tin, 18 X 24 In. 30.00
Sign, Jetter Beer, Elk, Bottle, Landscape, Tin, 23 X 32 In. 650.00
Sign, Jewel Stoves & Ranges, Gold Crown, Self-Framed, Tin, 12 X 19 In. 225.00
Sign, Jeweler & Optician, Large Pocket Watch, Tin, 12 X 36 In. 90.00
Sign, Jeweler, Woman With Large Diamond Ring, Tin, 12 X 36 In. 95.00
Sign, Just Say J.A.Cigars, C.1920, Tin, 3 X 20 In. 15.00
Sign, Kato Beer, Convex Glass, Pictures Eagle, 16 In.Diam. 125.00
Sign, Kayo Chocolate, 1930s, Embossed, Tin, 28 X 14 In. 60.00
Sign, Kenyon Cards, Ira Vail Dirt Champion, Cardboard, 30 X 20 In. 110.00
Sign, Kerosene Electrolux Refrigerator, 1930s, Embossed, 13 X 19 In. 25.00
Sign, Kessler Brewery, Gunboat, War, Tin, 24 X 18 In. 245.00
Sign, Kessler Brewery, U.S.Gunboat Helena, Embossed Tin, 24 X 18 In. 395.00
Sign, Kingbury Beer, 14 X 8 In. 10.00
Sign, Knox Hosiery, 1920s Ladies, Die-Cut Cardboard, 16 X 16 In. 45.00
Sign, Korbel California Champagne, Tin, Girl, Grapes, 13 X 19 In. 175.00
Sign, La Fendrich Cigar, Tin, 10 X 30 In. 55.00
Sign, La Salle Wine, Redhead On Veranda, 1930s, Tin, 15 X 10 In. 110.00
Sign, Lacquerwax, 1930s, Embossed Tin, 13 X 20 In. 50.00
Sign, Ladies, Galvanized Bracket, Porcelain, 1930s, 4 X 15 In. 11.00
Sign, LaSalle Wine, Redhead, Red Dress, 1930s, Tin, 15 X 10 In. 110.00
Sign, Lash's Bitters, Victorian Lady, Lithograph On Wood, 14 X 21 In, ... 425.00
Sign, Lawrence Barrett Cigars, Curved, Porcelain, 21 X 31 In. 395.00
Sign, Lilac Rose Soap, 15 X 12 In. 75.00
Sign, Lime Cola, Tin, 28 X 10 In. 22.00
Sign, Lime Cola, 1940s, Embossed Tin, 3 X 18 In. 15.00
Sign, Lipton's Tea, Porcelain, Flange, 2-Sided, 11 X 16 In. 175.00
Sign, Lone Ranger, 1938, Paper, 12 X 8 In. 20.00
Sign, Lowenbrau, Raised Gold Lion, Plastic, 14 X 16 In. 15.00
Sign, Lowney's Cocoa, Pictures Lady, Paper, 8 X 10 In. 15.00
Sign, Magnolia Oil, 1930s, Porcelain, 30 In.Diam. 60.00
Sign, Mail Pouch, 1920s, Porcelain, 11 X 34 In. 60.00
Sign, Malt Nutrine, Tin, 8 X 12 In. 50.00
Sign, Marlow Coaster Brakes, Boys On Bikes, 1930s 95.00

Sign, Marvels, 1930s, Embossed Tin, 10 X 13 In. 60.00
Sign, Mazda Lamps, Tin, 19 X 5 1/2 In. 50.00
Sign, McCormick Dairy Equipment, Embossed, Tin, 1940s, 14 X 22 In. 25.00
Sign, McLean's, Liver-Kidney Balm, 1905, Cardboard, 5 X 20 In. 15.00
Sign, Memphis Electric, 1930s, Embossed, Tin, 9 X 20 In. 20.00
Sign, Meyercord Co., Chicago, Boy Holding Elgin Watch, Oak, 15 X 22 In. 175.00
Sign, Michelob, Chain, Anheuser Busch Logo, Electric, 20 X 5 In. 15.00
Sign, Mikado Pencils, Our Gang Stars At Desk, 1930s, Paper, 20 X 10 In. 75.00
Sign, Milk, Embossed, Tin, 1940s, 11 X 23 In. 30.00
Sign, Miller High Life, Champagne Of Bottle Beer, Plastic, 17 X 7 In. 5.00
Sign, Miller High Life, Girl On Moon, Tin, 24 In.Round 450.00
Sign, Min Lax, Embossed, Tin, 1930s, 16 X 20 In. 25.00
Sign, Model Smoking Tobacco, 1940s, Tin, 11 X 32 In. 35.00
Sign, Model Tobacco, Did You Say 10 Cents, Mustached Pipe, 10 X 34 In. 47.50
Sign, Monogram Tea, Blue & White, Porcelain, 12 X 36 In. 85.00
Sign, Moore's Ice Cream, Giant Cone, Poster, 1940, 15 X 21 In. 85.00
Sign, Moore's Ice Cream, 1940s, Embossed, Tin, 24 X 36 In. 25.00
Sign, Mother's Oats, Pictures Boy In Leopard Skin, 20 X 27 In. 165.00
Sign, Mountain Whiskey, Girl, Water, Still, 1910, Paper, 24 X 20 In. 150.00
Sign, Moxie, Cardboard, 14 X 11 In. 12.00
Sign, Moxie, Driverless Car Moving, 1933, Tin, 27 X 20 In. 495.00
Sign, Moxie, Horse In Car Passing Moxie Billboard, Tin, 19 X 27 In. 375.00
Sign, Moxie, People Entering Moxie Hall Of Fame, Tin, 54 X 19 In. 350.00
Sign, Moxie, Ted Williams, 1950s, Cardboard, 9 X 12 In. 85.00
Sign, Moxie, 1940s, 2-Sided Steel, 8 X 18 In. 50.00
Sign, Moxie, 1950s, Tin, 36 X 43 In. 35.00
Sign, Mt.Hood Brewing, Oregon, Incised Mountain, Brass, 18 X 24 In. 325.00
Sign, Munsingwear, Mother, Children In Union Suits, Framed, 33 X 21 In. 325.00
Sign, National Phonograph Co., Man, Woman, 1905, Paperboard, 31 X 24 In. 375.00
Sign, National Phonograph Co, Man, Phonograph, 1905, 32 X 24 In. 375.00
Sign, National Union Fire Ins., Reverse Painting, 31 1/2 X 19 1/2 In. 350.00
Sign, Navy Tobacco, Paper, 35 1/2 X 26 In. 290.00
Sign, Nebo Cigarettes, Tin, 1920s, 15 X 13 In. 125.00
Sign, Nehi Curb Service, 19 1/2 X 28 In. 35.00
Sign, Nehi Root Beer, 1940s, Embossed, Tin, 12 X 30 In. 30.00
Sign, No Parking, Metal, 12 X 18 In. 10.00
Sign, Nu Grape, Picture Of Bottle, Tin, 12 X 31 In. 28.00
Sign, O.F.C.Bourbon, Stags Drinking From Barrel, Tin, 26 X 42 In. 225.00
Sign, Occidental Flour, White Letters, Black Ground, Wooden, 46 X 6 In. 60.00
Sign, Oconto, Football Players, 3-D, Paperboard, 1930s, 22 X 29 In. 95.00
Sign, Old Continental Whiskey, Beveled Plate Glass, 16 X 16 In. 52.00
Sign, Old English Curve Cut Tobacco, C.1915, Cardboard, 14 X 22 In. 15.00
Sign, Old English, Men By Fireplace With Dog, 1900, Paper, 31 X 24 In. 225.00
Sign, Old Jed Clayton Whiskey, Hunters, Framed, Paper, 20 X 30 In. 220.00
Sign, Olympus Cigars, Cardboard, Framed, 12 X 15 In. 65.00
Sign, Optician, Large Eyeglasses, Tin, 12 X 36 In. 125.00
Sign, Orange Crush, Bottle Shape, Wood Frame, Tin, 16 X 4 In. 85.00
Sign, Owego Bridge Co., Boys Fishing, C.1905, Tin, 12 X 18 In. 185.00
Sign, P & G Soap, 1930s, Cardboard, 13 X 13 In. 15.00
Sign, Pabst Brewing, Factory, C.1910, Self-Framed, Tin, 36 X 48 In. 325.00
Sign, Pabst Brewing, Man, Bottle, Brewery, C.1900, Tin, 36 X 48 In. 450.00
Sign, Pabst, Hands, Bottle, Factory, Self-Framed, Tin, 36 X 48 In. 350.00
Sign, Packard Shoe Co., Self-Framed, Tin, 9 1/2 X 21 In. 125.00
Sign, Parking 30 Minutes, Metal, 13 X 18 In. 10.00
Sign, Pendleton, 1910, Embossed Tin, 5 X 20 In. 45.00
Sign, Penn Vacuum Cup Tires, Multicolored, Tin, 12 X 35 In. 125.00
Sign, Penn.Telephone, Blue & White Porcelain, 11 In. 75.00
Sign, Pennfield Motor Oil, Oil Well, 13 X 19 In. 30.00
Sign, Pepo Worm Syrup, 1920s, Embossed, Tin, 6 X 9 In. 30.00
Sign, Pfeiffer Beer, Another Winner, Self-Framed Tin, 15 X 18 In. 175.00
Sign, Phillip Morris, Johnny In Corner, Red Lettering, Tin, 10 X 27 In. 32.00
Sign, Piedmont Cigarettes, Washington, Mt.Vernon, Tin, 27 X 20 In. 225.00
Sign, Piedmont The Virginia Cigarette, Porcelain, 11 1/4 X 11 1/2 In. 45.00

Sign, Piedmont, Porcelain, 12 1/2 X 12 1/2 In. 60.00
Sign, Pilsner, Hoboken, N.J., Lady, Self-Framed, 20 1/2 X 17 In. 525.00
Sign, Polar Ice Cream, 1930s, Aluminum, 9 X 15 In. 15.00
Sign, Prince Albert, Cowboy, 1930s, Canvas, 3 X 6 Ft. 85.00
Sign, Products Of Johnson & Johnson, Framed, Wooden, 3 X 23 In. 55.00
Sign, Public Telephone, N.Y., 2-Sided Porcelain, 20 X 20 In. 125.00
Sign, R & G Corsets, Woman Wearing Corset, Mechanical, 24 X 36 In. 750.00
Sign, R.J.Campbell, Dentist, Double-Sided, Silver On Black, 36 X 14 In. 55.00
Sign, Railway Express, Porcelain, 7 X 7 In. 45.00
Sign, Rainbow Bread, Embossed, 1947, Tin, 3 X 18 In. 9.00
Sign, Rainer Beer, Monks Fanning Monk, C.1896, Cardboard, 18 X 22 In. 295.00
Sign, REA, Red, Green, Yellow, Metal, 12 X 70 In. 265.00
Sign, Red Cross Cotton, Blacks Picking Cotton, 1894, 33 X 24 In. 375.00
Sign, Red Cross Stove, Maltese Cross, Tin, 16 X 20 In. 125.00
Sign, Red Crown Gasoline, 1920s, Porcelain, 36 In.Diam. 115.00
Sign, Red Man, Paper Poster, 1930s, 20 X 22 In. 65.00
Sign, Red Man, 1940s, Tin, 5 X 14 In. 20.00
Sign, Red Rock Cola, 1940s, Cardboard, 11 X 14 In. 10.00
Sign, Reliable Coffee, Paperboard, 33 X 15 In. 80.00
Sign, Republic Tires, Eagle, Tire, 2-Sided, 1920, 36 X 24 In. 195.00
Sign, Rheingold Beer, Miss Rheingold On Yacht, Cardboard, 12 X 18 In. 15.00
Sign, Richmans Strait Cut, 1891, Celluloid, 20 X 30 In. 950.00
Sign, Robin Hood Flour, Embossed Tin, 1940s, 11 X 36 In. 25.00
Sign, Rochester Root Beer, Reverse On Glass, 9 X 11 In. 75.00
Sign, Rummy, 1930s, Embossed, Tin, 11 X 18 In. 45.00
Sign, Running Horse, Blacksmith Trade Sign, Sheet Iron, C.1860, 17 In. 350.00
Sign, San Felice Cigars, Red On Yellow, 23 X 11 In. 18.00
Sign, Schenley Pure Rye, C.1910, Lady & Gent, Tin, 19 X 25 In. 250.00
Sign, Schenley Pure Rye, Lady & Gent, C.1900, Framed, Tin, 23 X 19 In. 275.00
Sign, Schiltz, Logo In Stained Glass, Light-Up, 22 X 30 In. 65.00
Sign, Schlitz, Winged Nude Girl, Bottle, Stretched Canvas, 14 X 22 In. 275.00
Sign, Selz Shoes, Blue & White, Porcelain, 1910, 16 X 18 In. 135.00
Sign, Seven-Up, Bottle Shape, 48 In. 50.00
Sign, Sharples, Tin, 19 1/2 X 13 1/2 In. 75.00
Sign, Sharples, Woman Using Cream Separator, Cardboard, 28 X 9 1/2 In. 55.00
Sign, Shell Gasoline, Porcelain, 45 1/2 In.Diam 195.00
Sign, Shoe Repair, Boot Shape, Black & White, Sheet Iron, 31 X 23 In. 220.00
Sign, Silver Spring Brewery, 1915, Stone Lithograph, 20 X 20 In. 60.00
Sign, Ski Drink, 1950s, Tin, 11 X 32 In. 30.00
Sign, Smith Piano & Organ Co., Man Playing Piano, Paper, 31 X 23 In. 250.00
Sign, Smoke Beck's Hunting Tobacco, Yellow, Black, Tin, 5 X 13 In. 20.00
Sign, Spiffy Cola, 1940s, Embossed, Tin, 6 X 9 In. 25.00
Sign, Sprite, Boy, Tin, 14 X 36 In. 50.00
Sign, Squibb's, 1920s, Cardboard, 42 X 26 In. 95.00
Sign, St.Louis American Brewing Co., Celluloid, 9 X 6 1/2 In. 75.00
Sign, Standard Brewing Co., Wood, 24 X 18 In. 250.00
Sign, Star Tobacco, Blue, Yellow, Brown, Porcelain, C.1920, 12 X 24 In. 65.00
Sign, Sterling Beer, Clowns On Circus Horses, Tin, 21 X 28 In. 225.00
Sign, Stewart Hair Clipping Machine, Men, Horse, 1920s, Tin, 24 X 20 In. 250.00
Sign, Stonewall Jackson Cigars, Portrait, 1930s, Tin, 36 X 15 In. 175.00
Sign, Stroh's Beer, Gold, Crown, Raised Lion, Electric, 12 X 14 In. 15.00
Sign, Sultan Cigarettes, 18 1/2 X 23 1/2 In. 225.00
Sign, Sun Bleach White Goods, Beveled Reverse Glass, 12 X 18 In. 175.00
Sign, Sun Drop, Embossed Tin, 1940s, 48 X 18 In. 45.00
Sign, Suncrest, Porcelain, 10 X 16 In. 20.00
Sign, Sunny Brook Whisky, General Holding Bottle, Tin, 10 X 12 In. 80.00
Sign, Sunoco Motor Oil, 1920s, 2-Sided, Porcelain, 26 X 16 In. 110.00
Sign, Sunshine Special Chocolate Milk, 8 X 10 In. 15.00
Sign, Supreme Auto Oil, Manufactured By Gulf, Porcelain, 18 X 22 In. 75.00
Sign, Sweetheart Flour, Red Porcelain, White Letters, 5 In. 25.00
Sign, Sweetie Beverages, 1940s, Tin, 11 X 28 In. 25.00
Sign, Texaco Sky Chief, Feathers, T In Circle, Porcelain, 9 X 12 In. 35.00
Sign, Texaco Sky Chief, Porcelain, 18 X 12 In. 20.00

Sign, Texaco, 1930s, Porcelain, 36 X 36 In.	50.00
Sign, Texsun Citrus Assn., 1940s, Tin, 6 X 12 In.	15.00
Sign, The Temptation Of St.Anthony, Whiskey, Blacks, Tin, 19 X 13 In.	425.00
Sign, Tiger Tobacco, Picture Of Tiger, Framed, 30 X 36 In.	750.00
Sign, Tower Root Beer, 1940s, Embossed Tin, 18 X 9 In.	25.00
Sign, Trade, Ice Cream, Pictures Sundae, Wooden, 62 X 25 1/2 In.	150.00
Sign, Union Fire Insurance Co., Porcelain, 1920s, 12 X 18 In.	75.00
Sign, Union Stamps, 2-Sided, Tin, 13 X 9 In.	30.00
Sign, Usher's Whiskey, Reverse Painting On Glass, 26 X 15 1/2 In.	285.00
Sign, Utica Club, Embossed Tin, 1930s, 12 X 24 In.	35.00
Sign, Valvoline, Porcelain, Tin, 30 1/2 In.Diam.	32.50
Sign, Van Houten Cocoa, Lady Pouring, Cardboard, C.1910, 23 X 31 In.	350.00
Sign, Vica Oil, Porcelain, 1930s, 36 X 24 In.	80.00
Sign, Vigortone, Tin, 1940s, 18 X 14 In.	25.00
Sign, Virginia Dare Root Beer, Easel Back, Cardboard, 9 1/2 X 14 In.	8.00
Sign, W.Tasket, White Letters, Black, Wooden, 36 7/8 X 10 3/4 In.	65.00
Sign, Walkover Shoes, Cowgirl, Paper Under Glass, C.1911, 12 X 31 In.	175.00
Sign, Washington, Coffee, Metal, 10 1/2 X 17 1/2 In.	65.00
Sign, Welch's, Cutout Decal Of Grapes & Vine, 12 X 12 In.	20.00
Sign, Western Ammunition, Hunting Scene, Tin, C.1920, 13 X 21 In.	150.00
Sign, Western Ammunition, Signed A.Russell, Stand-Up Cardboard, 31 In.	285.00
Sign, Western Union, Porcelain, Blue & White, C.1905, 21 X 30 In.	265.00
Sign, Whitman's Chocolate, Green, White, C.1910, Porcelain, 13 X 40 In.	135.00
Sign, Wiedeman's Beer, Eagle, Shield, Keg, Light-Up, 15 In.Diam.	165.00
Sign, Wilson Whiskey, Carriage, People, Tin, 1902, 40 X 28 In.	550.00
Sign, Wilson Whiskey, Carriage, 1902, Tin, 40 X 28 In.	550.00
Sign, Winchester Punching Bags, Boxer, Shotguns, Cardboard, 7 X 12 In.	60.00
Sign, Winchester Tires, 1940s, Tin, 18 X 48 In.	35.00
Sign, Wine & Liquors For Medical Use, Cardboard, 1890s, 11 X 14 In.	16.00
Sign, Wings Cigarettes, Package With Red Letters, Paper, 12 X 18 In.	4.00
Sign, Wisconsin Dairy Barn Quarantine, Yellow & Black, 8 X 14 In.	35.00
Sign, Wiss Tinner Snips, Tin, 13 X 6 In.	55.00
Sign, Wolf Co., Flour Mill, Red Riding Hood, Paper, 20 X 14 In.	225.00
Sign, X Ray Headache Tablets, 1905, Cardboard, 5 X 14 In.	8.00
Sign, Yankee Girl, Tin, 20 X 6 1/2 In.	100.00
Sign, YB Cigars, Framed, 10 X 12 In.	45.00
Sign, Yellow Label Whiskey, Lady, Man In Chair, Tin, 13 1/2 X 10 In.	125.00
Sign, Zanzibar 50 Lb.Sausage, Tin	195.00
Sign, Ziegler's Beer, 1930s, Tin, 9 X 12 In.	25.00
Slate, School, Wooden Frame, Slate Pencil, 7 1/2 X 9 3/4 In.	15.00
Slicer, Meat & Cheese, Adjustable Thickness, Pre-1891, Iron & Wood	85.00
Spiffy Cola, 1940s, 2-Sided, Steel, 10 X 14 In.	30.00
Spool Cabinet, Belding Bros., 13 Drawer, 34 In.High	275.00
Spool Cabinet, Clark's, 2-Drawer, Ruby Glass	195.00
Spool Cabinet, Clark's, 3-Drawer, Ruby Glass	325.00
Spool Cabinet, J. & P.Coats, Thread, Oak, 20 3/4 X 16 1/2 X 22 1/2 In.	675.00
Spool Cabinet, J. & P.Coats, 4-Drawer	300.00
Spool Cabinet, J. & P.Coats, 4-Drawer, Leather Lift Top, Inkwell, Oak	395.00
Spool Cabinet, J. & P.Coats, 6-Drawer, Slanted Desk Top	600.00
Spool Cabinet, 5-Drawer, Walnut	550.00
Sprinkler, Dutch Cleanser, Red With Black Base, 5 1/2 In.	5.00
Stand, Display, Heinz, Glass	110.00
Stand, Teaberry Gum, Vaseline	22.00 To 35.00
Syrup, Karo, Metal	10.00
Target, Shooting Gallery, Fat Duck, Cast Iron, 4 X 6 X 1 1/2 In.	55.00
Target, Shooting Gallery, Hunter, Gun, Pack, Cast Iron, 7 X 4 1/2 In.	90.00
Teapot, Lipton, Yellow	12.00
Teapot, Salada, Cobalt Blue	12.00
Thermometer, Mailpouch Tobacco, 39 In.	29.50 To 42.00
Thermometer, Pepsi-Cola, 7 X 28 In.	14.00
Tieback, Aunt Jemima, 1940s, Hard Plastic, Set Of 6	24.00
Tin, Allspice, Round, Ann Page, Orange & Brown Paper, 2 1/2 In.	4.00
Tin, Angelus Marshmallow	20.00

Tin, Bagdad, Pocket	12.00
Tin, Bank Roll Cigars, 6 X 5 1/4 In.	35.00
Tin, Banquet Hall Cigars	35.00
Tin, Banquet Tea, Round, 10 In.	12.00
Tin, Bayuk Philadelphia Phillies Cigars	25.00
Tin, Bee Brand, Turmeric, McCormicks, Ivory, 3 1/2 In.	4.00
Tin, Besco Cigars	8.00
Tin, Big Ben Tobacco, Pocket	35.00
Tin, Biscuit, Art Nouveau, Crumksall & Cardiff, 10 In.	80.00
Tin, Biscuit, Book, Huntley Palmer	95.00
Tin, Biscuit, Figural, Organ Grinder, Crawford, English	325.00
Tin, Blanke's Mojav, Coffee, Lady, Riding Side Saddle, 2 Pound	75.00
Tin, Blue Boy Paper Inset, Biscuit	40.00
Tin, Bowl Of Roses, Short	65.00
Tin, Bright & Early Coffee, Picture Of Rooster, 8 In.	25.00
Tin, Buckingham Bright Cut Plug, 3 X 4 1/2 In.	20.00
Tin, Buckingham, Pocket	29.00
Tin, Buckingham, 1930, Pocket	5.00
Tin, Buffalo Brand Peanut Butter, 1 Pound	135.00
Tin, Buffalo Brand Salt Peanuts, 10 Pound	135.00
Tin, Bulldog, Pocket	70.00
Tin, Bunte, Marshmallow, Dated 1906	12.50
Tin, Calumet Baking Powder, Thank You Boy On Lid	70.00
Tin, Campbell Brand Coffee	45.00
Tin, Central Union, Pocket, 4 X 6 In.	25.00
Tin, Chase & Sanborn, Coffee, Paper Label	50.00
Tin, Chesterfield, Round	15.00
Tin, Cigarette, Bugler, Blue, 3 In.	4.00
Tin, Climax Plug Tobacco, Flat	9.00
Tin, Commodore Coffee	45.00 To 65.00
Tin, Continental Cubes, Tobacco, Pocket	148.00
Tin, Cream Dove, Peanut	90.00
Tin, Cuban Coffee Mills, 28 Pound	165.00
Tin, Cupid Bouquet Cigars	35.00
Tin, Dan Patch Cut Plug, Lithograph, 6 X 3 1/2 In.	22.50 To 28.00
Tin, Dill's Best Tobacco, Short Pocket	20.00
Tin, Dill's Best, 3 3/4 X 4 1/2 In.	10.00
Tin, Dixie Queen Tobacco	90.00
Tin, Dr.Johnson's Educator Crackers, Yellow & Black, 5 X 5 X 5 In.	35.00
Tin, Duco	20.00
Tin, Edgeworth Sliced Pipe Tobacco, Flat	7.50
Tin, Edgeworth Tobacco, Pocket	10.00
Tin, Elephant, Peanut	105.00
Tin, Eve, Pocket	42.00
Tin, Famous Cake Box Mixture, Gold Lettering, 5 X 6 In.	30.00
Tin, Fisher's Salted In Shell Peanuts, 10 Pound	85.00
Tin, Forest & Stream, Duck, Pocket	45.00 To 85.00
Tin, Forest & Stream, Pocket	100.00
Tin, Four Roses, Pocket	25.00
Tin, Fring's 3 Bros., Cigars	45.00
Tin, Full Dress, Pocket	85.00
Tin, George Washington	65.00
Tin, Great Pepper, Yellow & Red Label, C.1900, 4 In.	3.00
Tin, Half & Half Tobacco, Telescope	5.00
Tin, Hi Plane, Pocket	20.00
Tin, Holiday, Pocket	10.00
Tin, Honeymoon, Pocket	60.00 To 85.00
Tin, Horlick's Malted Milk, 25 Pound	185.00
Tin, Hoyt's But-A-Kiss Candy, 30 Pound	165.00
Tin, Huntley Palmer, Egyptian Casket	18.00
Tin, Jewel Tea, Cocoa, 1 Pound	10.00
Tin, Johnson & Johnson, Bandage, Round	10.00
Tin, Just Suits Tobacco, Pocket	75.00

Tin, Kipling Tobacco	40.00
Tin, La Lucrena Cigars	50.00
Tin, La Salle Wine, Redhead, Veranda, 1930, 15 X 10 In.	110.00
Tin, Log Cabin Syrup, 5 Lb.	30.00
Tin, Loose Wiles Fine Confections, 25 Pound	110.00
Tin, Lord Salisbury, 276 Cigarette Size	25.00
Tin, Lucky Strike Cigarettes, White, Pocket	245.00
Tin, Lucky Strike, Flat	9.00
Tin, Lucky Strike, Pocket, Flat	9.00 To 10.00
Tin, Luzianne Coffee, Cover, Red	38.00
Tin, Maltby's Cocoanut	35.00
Tin, Marple's Lotus Brand, Salt Peanuts, 10 Pound	125.00
Tin, Marshmallows, Campfire	50.00
Tin, Maryland Club	15.00
Tin, Mellow Smoke, Hasket & Marcuse, Green & Black, 6 X 3 1/2 In.	60.00
Tin, Millar's Mountain Brand Coffee, 7 In.	45.00
Tin, Model Tobacco	65.00
Tin, Monarch Tea, Picture Of Teapot	4.50
Tin, Monarch Tea, 1/2 Pound	12.50
Tin, Morrell's Snow Cap Lard, 8 Pound	25.00
Tin, Mothers B & B Peanuts, 5 Pound	45.00
Tin, Murad 100s, Flat	35.00
Tin, Oceanic Tobacco, Pocket, 4 X 6 In.	75.00
Tin, Old Colony, Pocket	55.00
Tin, Pipe Major, Pocket	70.00
Tin, Piper Champagne Chewing Tobacco	13.50
Tin, Porter Salve	3.50
Tin, Postmaster, Red	35.00
Tin, Prince Albert Tobacco, Pocket	3.00
Tin, Q-Broid, Oval	18.00
Tin, Red Jacket, Pocket	15.00 To 20.00
Tin, Rival Tobacco, 5 Pound	10.00
Tin, Rola Club Coffee, Pictures Polo Player	33.00
Tin, Roly Poly Storekeeper, Red Indian	425.00
Tin, Roly Poly, Dutchman	465.00
Tin, Roly Poly, Mammy	550.00
Tin, Roly Poly, Mammy, Mayo	450.00
Tin, Roly Poly, Satisfied Customer, Dixie Queen	350.00
Tin, Roly Poly, Satisfied Customer, Mayo	500.00
Tin, Roly Poly, Singing Waiter	395.00 To 500.00
Tin, Sargent Cigar Chest, Bridgeport, Conn., Pat.1908	25.00
Tin, Sir Walter Raleigh, Pocket, Flat	40.00
Tin, Snuff, Garretts, Sample	6.00
Tin, Sozodent Tooth Powder, Pictures Man	65.00
Tin, Stag, Pocket	24.00 To 40.00
Tin, Stag, Pocket, Upright	20.00
Tin, Superior, Peanut	75.00
Tin, Sweet Burley	85.00
Tin, Sweet Mist Tobacco	150.00
Tin, Talc, Cashmere Bouquet, Sample	12.00
Tin, Talc, Colgate's Baby, Picture Of Baby Holding Can, 6 X 2 1/4 In.	50.00
Tin, Talc, Joli Soir, Art Deco	15.00
Tin, Talc, Satin Skin, Lady On Front	20.00
Tin, Talc, Watkins, Art Nouveau	13.00
Tin, Tasty Food Limited, 4-Car Train, Pure Coffee, Brownwood, Texas	300.00
Tin, Tetley's Tea, Sunflowers	15.00
Tin, Tiger, Pocket, Cardboard	75.00
Tin, Tiger, Pocket, 4 X 6 In.	23.00
Tin, Tobacco, Bigger Hair, Round	140.00
Tin, Trout Line, Pocket	275.00
Tin, Tuxedo Cigarettes, Curved	8.00
Tin, Tuxedo, Pocket	5.00 To 18.00
Tin, Twin Oaks, Curved Top, Pocket	30.00

Tin, U.S.Marine Cut Plug 24.00
Tin, Union Leader Cut Plug, Eagle, Milk Can Shape, 9 1/2 In. 85.00
Tin, Union Leader, Eagle, Pocket .... 3.00 To 5.00
Tin, Union Leader, Pocket 4.00
Tin, Union Leader, Uncle Sam .... 20.00 To 25.00
Tin, Union Plug 35.00
Tin, Velvet Tobacco 7.00
Tin, Velvet, With Pipe, Pocket 4.50
Tin, Veteran Coffee 50.00
Tin, Weber's White Rose Lemon Oil, Man Polishing Car 22.00
Tin, Wernet's Powder, Sample 15.00
Tin, Yacht Club Tobacco, Flat 40.00
Tin, Ying Mee Tea, Paper Label 15.00
Tin, Yum Yum 50.00
Tray, A.Gettelman Beer 50.00
Tray, A.M.Smith Wine & Liquor, 3 Monks Eating & Drinking, 1900 .... 140.00
Tray, Anheuser Busch, Bevo, Non-Alcoholic, 1920s 100.00
Tray, Anheuser Busch, Cherubs 480.00
Tray, Anheuser Busch's Mal Nutrine, Beautiful Woman, 1905 .... 60.00
Tray, Bartels, Concave, Metal, 17 1/2 In. 130.00
Tray, Becks Beer, Buffalo's Best, Magnus Brewing Co., 14 In. 15.00
Tray, Berghoft Beer .... 30.00 To 40.00
Tray, Beverwyck Beer, Gold Flourishes, Green & White 20.00
Tray, Beverwyck Beer, Wood-Grain 25.00
Tray, Beverwyck Breweries, Billy Beaver Marching With Drums 35.00
Tray, Bolton Bros., Troy, N.Y., 4 Monks Sampling Brew, Oval 350.00
Tray, Budweiser Beer, Southern Scene 75.00
Tray, Budweiser, Man & Woman Mixing Beer In Fondue, 16 In.Diam. 275.00
Tray, Caffe Medaglia D'oro, Lady Drinking Coffee, Rectangular 32.00
Tray, Capitol Brewing Co., Jefferson City, Mo., Pre-Prohibition 100.00
Tray, Carstairs Whiskey, White Seal, Wood 26.00
Tray, Charles Daniels Brewing Co., Manistee, Michigan 285.00
Tray, Christian Feigenspan Breweries, Art Nouveau Lady, Dated 1910 ..... 125.00
Tray, Country Club Whiskey, Toothless Monk, Bottle, Barrel, 1900 .... 145.00
Tray, Croft Ale, Black Ground, Red Rim, White Letters, 12 In. 30.00
Tray, Cunningham Ice Cream, Factory, 1915, Oval, 18 In. 165.00
Tray, Dawes Brewery, With Horse, Enamel 200.00
Tray, Diamond Springs Ale, Yellow & Black, Red Edged, 12 In. 35.00
Tray, Diamond Wedding Rye, Woman In Red, Drinking, 1900 .... 195.00
Tray, Dicken's Ale, 2 Men, Hoisting Mugs, Red & White Ground, 12 In. 25.00
Tray, Dobler Brewing Company, Albany, N.Y., Pretty Lady, Red Ribbon 45.00
Tray, Douglas Ice Cream, Girl In Yellow, 1913 .... 125.00
Tray, Dow Old Stock Ale, Red Ground, White Letters, 12 In. 35.00
Tray, Dr Pepper, Girl With 2 Bottles 155.00
Tray, DuBois Brewing Co. 245.00
Tray, E Robinson's Sons Pilsener 55.00
Tray, Eagle Brewery, New Jersey, Pretty Girl, 1911, 10 X 13 In. 225.00
Tray, Edelweiss Girl, Pre-Prohibition 125.00
Tray, Ehrets Hell Gate, Beer, Oval 200.00
Tray, Enterprise Beer, Woman, San Francisco, 1905 .... 375.00
Tray, Escanaba Brewing Co., Michigan 250.00
Tray, F & S Beer & Ale, Bell Hop, Beer On Tray, Orange Ground, 12 In. 25.00
Tray, Falls City Beer 75.00
Tray, Falstaff Beer, Maiden Serving Sir Falstaff, 24 In. 35.00
Tray, Fehr's Beer, King Holding Goblet To Queen 125.00
Tray, Felsenbran, 17 Waiters Serving Beer, Brown Ground, 12 In. 20.00
Tray, Flenkenstein, Workers Eating & Drinking, 1910, 20 X 13 In. 275.00
Tray, Frank Jones Brewery, Portsmouth, Monk, 9 In. 175.00
Tray, Franklin Life Insurance 35.00
Tray, Fro-Toy, 1920s, Ice Cream 15.00
Tray, Genesee, 1, 000, 000 Barrels, Silver Plate, 12 In.Diam. 55.00
Tray, Gettelman Beer, Milwaukee 50.00
Tray, Gin Seng, Beverage Of Purity, Girl In Ricksaw .... 60.00 To 70.00

Tray, Green Rivers Whiskey, Black Man .... 110.00 To 135.00
Tray, Haberle Congress Brewing, Eagle 21.00
Tray, Haffenreffer, Pickwick Ale 75.00
Tray, Hampden Brewing Co., 13 In.Diam. 68.00
Tray, Hampden Mild Ale, Running Waiter, Tray Of Beer, Red Ground 25.00
Tray, Hanley's Beer, Bulldog, 12 In.Diam. 58.00
Tray, Harry & Bert Piels, Harry & Bert Comics, Multicolor, 13 In. 15.00
Tray, Heilman's Old Style Lager, Cream, Yellow, Red Ground, 13 In. 20.00
Tray, Hinckel's Beer, Elk 140.00
Tray, Hires Root Beer, Scene Of Boy, 16 1/2 X 13 3/4 In. 35.00
Tray, Hires, May 21, 1907, Oval 200.00
Tray, Holihan's Light Stock Ale, Coat Of Arms, Red Ground, 12 In. 35.00
Tray, Holland Custard & Ice Cream Co., 12 X 14 In. 48.00
Tray, Hot Diggity Dog, 1933, Cat & Dog Drinking Scene, Signed 55.00
Tray, Jani-Cola, Lady Hugging Horse, Oval 150.00
Tray, Jersey Creme 175.00
Tray, Koening Brau Premium 30.00
Tray, Kruger Beer 21.00
Tray, Labatt's, The Sign Of Good Cheer, Red Ground, 13 In. 25.00
Tray, Lager Beer, Wooden Shoe, Dutch Girls 85.00
Tray, Lakeside Grape Juice, 13 In.Diam. 65.00
Tray, Lawrence Welk With Lennon Sisters 20.00
Tray, Leisy Beer Co., Factory, Wagons, & Eagle, 1900s, Oval, 16 1/2 In. 425.00
Tray, Lemp Beer, 24 In.Diam. 250.00
Tray, Lemp, Falstaff Man, Pre-Prohibition, 16 In.Diam. 135.00
Tray, Miller Beer, Girl On Moon 18.00
Tray, Miller High Life, Girl On Quarter Moon, 13 In. 65.00
Tray, Moerlbach, 2-Headed Eagle, Dark Green, 4 1/4 In. 35.00
Tray, Monroe, King With Beer Mug, Multicolored, 12 In. 65.00
Tray, Myers & Company, Pure Fulton Whiskey, Nickel On Tin 65.00
Tray, Narragansett Beer 90.00
Tray, Neuweiler's Brew, Man Carrying Tankard, 13 In.Diam. 35.00
Tray, O'Keefe's, Vienna Beer, Cream, Edge In Gold, Blue, 13 In. 40.00
Tray, Old Dutch Beer, Catsaqua, Pennsylvania, 1950s 45.00
Tray, Old Pepper Whiskey, Soldiers Drinking, Flags, 1910, Oval 175.00
Tray, Old Ranger Premium Beer, Racoon Hat, Rifle, Multicolor, 12 In. 45.00
Tray, Olympia Beer, Cavalier Pouring Drink 155.00
Tray, Olympia Beer, Horseshoe & Waterfall, Pre-Prohibition 220.00
Tray, Oneida Brewing, Sparkling Cream Ale 45.00
Tray, Oneida Brewing, Utica, Dog 350.00
Tray, Orange Crush 35.00
Tray, Orange Julep, 1920s Bathing Beauty With Umbrella 155.00
Tray, Ortlieb's Beer 50.00
Tray, Pabst Beer, Old Man 40.00
Tray, Pabst Blue Ribbon, Portrait Of Woman 27.00
Tray, Pabst Breweries, Blue Leaves, White & Red Ground, 13 In. 20.00
Tray, Pacific Beer, C.1912, Wood Grain 115.00
Tray, Pepsi Hits The Spot 40.00
Tray, Pepsi-Cola, Girl At Bar, 1900 .... 500.00
Tray, Pepsi-Cola, Girl At Fountain 500.00
Tray, Pfeiffer's Beer, 3 Monks Eating, Drinking 195.00
Tray, Pickwick Ale, Bald-Headed Man Offering Toast, 12 In. 40.00
Tray, Pure Milk Co., Ice Cream, Milk Bottle By Plant, 1900 .... 110.00
Tray, Red Dot Cigar, Girl Under Glass 135.00
Tray, Red Raven Splits, Giant Bird With Bottle, 12 In.Diam. 225.00
Tray, Ringler Brewery, New York 250.00
Tray, Ruhstallers, Girl With Dove 100.00
Tray, Ruppert Beer & Ale, Cream, Maroon Ground, 13 In. 20.00
Tray, Sanitary Ice Cream, 1915 .... 110.00
Tray, Sanitol Tooth Powder 10.00
Tray, Santo's Supreme Ice Cream 30.00
Tray, Satin Cigarettes, 20 For 15 Cents, Lady 50.00
Tray, Scheidt's Valley Forge Beer 30.00

Tray, Schmidt's Pilgrim Beer	30.00
Tray, Schneider Brewing Co., Man & Woman	45.00
Tray, Sen Sen, Embossed	7.00
Tray, Simon Pure Ale, Winged Hop, Green Ground, 12 In.	22.00
Tray, Standard Tru-Age Beer	40.00
Tray, Star Brewing Co.	85.00
Tray, Star Fine Ale & Lager, Revolutionary Era, Blue Ground, 12 In.	25.00
Tray, Stegmaier's Gold Medal Beer, Double-Headed Eagle, Dated 1911	29.50
Tray, Stroh's Beer, Waiter, Striped Vest, Carries Tray	195.00
Tray, Tech Golden Pilsner, Black, Yellow Ground, 12 In.	15.00
Tray, Tip, Apollinaris Whiskey, Lady With Goblet	35.00
Tray, Tip, Baby Ruth Gum, Glass	150.00
Tray, Tip, Black Label Whiskey, Red & White, 6 1/2 X 4 In.	9.00
Tray, Tip, Black River & Western R.R., Ringoes, New Jersey	5.00
Tray, Tip, Caine Steel Co. On Reverse, 6 1/2 X 4 1/2 In.	5.00
Tray, Tip, Canadian R & R, Imported Whiskey, Hard Plastic, 6 1/2 In.	5.00
Tray, Tip, Canda Dry Sport Cola, Clock	20.00
Tray, Tip, Carnation Milk	32.50
Tray, Tip, Clark's Teaberry Gum, Glass, Amber	32.00
Tray, Tip, Columbus Brewing, Picture Of Columbus	65.00
Tray, Tip, Coors	25.00
Tray, Tip, Cottolene	40.00 To 85.00
Tray, Tip, Delaval Cream Separator, Lithograph, 4 3/8 In.	32.00 To 55.00
Tray, Tip, Dick's Beer, World's Fair	18.00
Tray, Tip, Diehl Brewery, Lady	40.00
Tray, Tip, Domestic Sewing Machine	45.00
Tray, Tip, Dr.A.C.Daniels Horse & Cattle Medicine	55.00
Tray, Tip, Evinrude Rowboat & Canoe Motors, Pictures Boat & Woman	52.50
Tray, Tip, Fairy Soap	30.00 To 80.00
Tray, Tip, Fiegenspan Brewery	40.00
Tray, Tip, First Lover 5 Cent Cigar	20.00
Tray, Tip, Franklin Life Insurance	20.00
Tray, Tip, Hebburn House Coal, Eagle	25.00
Tray, Tip, Household Credit Man	65.00
Tray, Tip, Hyroller Whiskey, 1910	15.00
Tray, Tip, Indianapolis Brewery, Bottle	50.00
Tray, Tip, King's Beer	30.00
Tray, Tip, Kings International Exposition	65.00
Tray, Tip, Kings Pure Malt, Waitress	25.00
Tray, Tip, Lily Beer, Rock Island, Illinois, 6 1/2 X 4 1/2 In.	45.00
Tray, Tip, Marilyn Monroe, Nude	20.00
Tray, Tip, Miller High Life, Ducks	9.00
Tray, Tip, Miller High Life, Red & White, 6 1/2 X 4 1/2 In.	8.00
Tray, Tip, Moxie, Blue Ground	125.00
Tray, Tip, Moxie, Girl Drinking	75.00
Tray, Tip, National Premium Beer	15.00
Tray, Tip, Oertel's Brewing, Lady, Dove	75.00 To 100.00
Tray, Tip, Old Angus Scotch Whiskey, Highlander & Baby Sheep	20.00
Tray, Tip, Opia Cigar	60.00
Tray, Tip, Premier Royal Range, Cook Stove Pictured	36.00
Tray, Tip, President Suspenders	35.00
Tray, Tip, Prudential Life Insurance	8.00 To 15.00
Tray, Tip, Quick Meal Ranges	40.00 To 60.00
Tray, Tip, Red Raven, Bird & Bottle	45.00
Tray, Tip, Resinol Soap	125.00
Tray, Tip, Reynaldo, Havana Cigar	23.00
Tray, Tip, Rockford Watches, Pretty Girl	65.00
Tray, Tip, Roy Rogers	15.00
Tray, Tip, Ruppert's Beer, Hans Flato, 1 Cent	50.00
Tray, Tip, Ruppert's Beer, Hans Flato, 3 Cent	50.00
Tray, Tip, S.S.Peirce, Wine & Spirit Merchants Since 1831	20.00
Tray, Tip, Savannah Brewing Co.	65.00
Tray, Tip, Simon Pure, Winged Hops	20.00

Stove, Faience, French, White & Yellow,
26 1/2 In. X 6 Ft. 6 In.

Tray, Tip, Standard Vitrified Conduit Co.	30.00
Tray, Tip, Stove Polish	8.00
Tray, Tip, Success Manure Spreader, Syracuse N.Y., Farmer & Spreader	85.00
Tray, Tip, White Rock, World's Best Table Waiter	50.00
Tray, Utica-Club, Talking Mugs, Red Ground, 13 In.	15.00
Tray, Vani Kola, Girl With Horse, Oval	165.00
Tray, Weatherly Ice Cream, Lady, Fur Hat & Stole, Holly, 1915	155.00
Tray, Wm.Hartwig Beer, Watertown, Wis., 3 Men On Lunch Break, 1905	290.00
Tray, Yuengling's Premium Beer, Bottle, Glass, Red Ground, 13 In.	25.00
Trunk, Cremo Cigar, Tin Over Wood, 28 1/2 X 18 1/2 X 19 1/2 In.	500.00
Tumbler, Bromo Seltzer, Cobalt Blue, Set Of 5	75.00
Tumbler, Old Crow Whiskey, Old Crow Front, Famous Smooth Mellow Back	5.00
Warmer, Hand, Gold Slide Cover, Pierced, Velvet Cover, C.1860, 3 X 5 In.	50.00
Washing Machine, Maytag, Salesman's Sample, Cast Iron	195.00
Whiskbroom, Pinocchio, 9 In.	22.50
Whistle, Poll Parrot, Tin	3.50
Whistle, Winchester	70.00

STOVE, Acorn Baseburner, 9 Tiles, Statue	2200.00
Birmingham Stove & Range Co., Madam Queen, Cast Iron, 18 1/2 X 20 In.	25.00
Brass & Copper, European Stove Shroud, 45 Tiles, 62 In.	1000.00
Coal, Art Deco, Chrome & Enameled, Ogee Feet, C.1930, 40 X 25 In.	300.00
Depot, Potbelly Magnum, 5 Ft.	350.00
Faience, French, White & Yellow, 26 1/2 In. X 6 Ft. 6 In. *Illus*	4500.00
Favorite Stoves & Ranges, Best In The World, Child's, Cast Iron	450.00
Galley, Railroad, Copper Water Tank, C.1920, Cast Iron	350.00
Globe, Warming Oven, Kettle, 3 Pans, Cast Iron, Salesman's Sample	450.00
Kitchen, Radiant Home, Top Ovens, 6 Burner, Oven Below, C.1880	3800.00
Parlor, Prizer Oak, Renickeled, 5 Ft.	1975.00
Parlor, Wood Burning, Round Oak Duplex, Cast Iron, Swinging Urn Top	800.00
Potbelly, Yale, 22 In.	82.00
Railroad Car, Iron, Marked	350.00
Reservoir, Warming Ovens, Copper Clad, Blue Porcelain	1800.00
Reservoir, Water, Lift Top, Copper With Blue Enamel	65.00
Saratoga Wood Burner, 1853, Warren, Sweetland & Little, Crescent, N.Y.	150.00
White Faience, German Rococo, Somerhuber, Iron Stand, 5 Ft. 7 In.	3000.00
Windsor No. 91-16, Lakeside Foundry, Chicago, Coal Or Wood, 5 1/2 Ft.	875.00
STRAWBERRY, see Soft Paste	

STRETCH GLASS, Bonbon, Footed, Covered, Green	35.00
Bowl, Berry, Red, 6 1/2 In.	60.00
Bowl, Celeste Blue, 5 In.	18.00
Bowl, Flat Bottom, Velva Blue, 10 In.	65.00

Bowl, Footed, Blue, 10 In.Diam.	28.00
Bowl, Opaque, 9 1/2 In.	45.00
Bowl, Red, 1 1/2 X 7 In.	90.00
Bowl, Rolled Edge, Blue, 7 1/2 In.	30.00
Bowl, 14-Panel, Amberina	240.00
Candlestick, Blue, Imperial Glass, 8 1/2 In., Pair	79.00
Candlestick, Clear, Green & White Trim, 9 In., Pair	70.00
Candlestick, Colonial, Olive, 5 1/2 In., Pair	60.00
Candlestick, Yellow, 8 3/4 In.	22.00
Compote, Footed, White, 7 In.	35.00
Compote, Imperial, Blue Gray, 8 1/4 In.	48.00
Compote, Imperial, Teal, 7 3/4 X 7 1/2 In.	50.00
Dish, Candy, Celeste Blue, Covered, 7 In.	38.00
Dish, Candy, Northwood, Covered, Topaz, 9 In.	45.00
Finger Bowl, Red, 5 In.Diam.	85.00
Hat	85.00
Jar, Candy, Covered, Celeste Blue	38.00
Jar, Candy, Northwood, Covered, Topaz	38.00
Plate, Imperial, Red, 8 In.	49.00
Plate, Pale Violet, 8 In.	10.00
Vase, Fan, Blue, 6 In.	25.00
Vase, Fluted, Pink, 5 In.	28.00
Vase, Vertical Cut, Blue, 10 In.	45.00 To 49.00

Sunbonnet Babies were first introduced in 1902 in the Sunbonnet Babies Primer. The stories were by Eulalie Osgood Grover, illustrated by Bertha Corbett. The children's faces were completely hidden by the sunbonnets, and had been pictured in black and white before this time. The color pictures in the book were immediately successful. The Royal Bayreuth China Company made a full line of children's dishes decorated with the Sunbonnet Babies.

SUNBONNET BABIES, Bonbon, Fishing, Spade-Shaped, 5 1/4 In.	190.00
Book Plate, Babe & Boy, Running, Signed, 6 X 8 1/2 In.	15.00
Book Plate, Riding On Sled, Signed Wall, 6 X 8 1/2 In.	15.00
Book, A.B.C., 15 Color Plates, By Eulalie Osgood Grover	55.00
Book, A.B.C., 1934	35.00
Bowl, Babies Cleaning, 3 1/4 In.	199.00
Bowl, Blue Mark, 6 In.	195.00
Bowl, Ironing, 5 In.	48.50
Box, Pine, Covered, Hinged, Burnt Wood, 4 X 4 In.	37.50
Cake Plate, Ironing Day, Handled, Blue Mark, 10 In.	220.00
Calendar, 1908, Cardboard	17.50
Candlestick, Blue Mark	395.00
Compote, Mending, Blue Mark, 2 3/4 X 5 3/4 In.Diam.	295.00
Compote, Washing, Blue Mark, 6 In.	375.00
Coverlet, Double Bed	125.00
Creamer, Cleaning	175.00
Creamer, Washing & Ironing, 3 1/2 In.	175.00 To 225.00
Cup & Saucer, Washing, Ironing, & Mending, Blue Mark	190.00
Cup, Loving, Ironing, 3-Handled, Miniature	285.00
Dish, Feeding, Children Darning	165.00
Dish, Fishing, Heart Shaped	145.00
Dish, Fishing, Spade Shaped, 5 1/4 In.	189.00
Dish, Relish, Washing, Blue Mark, 7 3/4 X 4 In.	225.00
Nappy, Mending, Blue Mark	240.00
Pitcher, Cleaning, Blue, Signed, 2 3/4 In.	160.00
Pitcher, Fishing, Blue Mark, 4 1/2 In.	175.00
Pitcher, Ironing, 6 1/2 In.	180.00
Plate, Babies Cleaning, 6 1/4 In.	110.00
Plate, Cleaning, Royal Bayreuth, 6 1/4 In.	110.00
Plate, Feeding Duck, Holding Doll, Green Dress, 6 In.	95.00
Plate, Feeding, Kiss & Make Up, 7 In.	89.50
Plate, Fishing, Blue Mark	165.00

Plate, Washing, 9 In.	185.00
Platter, Ice Cream, Twins In Center, 9 1/2 In.	85.00
Postcard, Monday	10.00
Postcard, Saturday	10.00
Print, Scrubbing Day, Signed Bertha Corbett, Framed	65.00
Print, September, Chromolitho, 1906, 6 X 8 In.	35.00
Print, Summer, Beach, Sailboat, Ullman, 1906, 6 X 8 3/4 In.	15.00
Quilt, 20 Appliqued Girls, 66 X 84 In.	90.00
Saucer, Sewing, Blue Mark, 5 1/2 In.Diam.	95.00
Tray, Mending, Diamond Shape, Signed, Small	135.00

Sunderland luster is a name given to a characteristic pink luster made by Leeds, Newcastle, and other English firms during the nineteenth century. The luster glaze is metallic and glossy and sometimes appears to have bubbles as a decoration.

SUNDERLAND, Plaque, Black Transfer Of Ship, 7 3/8 X 8 In.	75.00
Plaque, Black Transfer, Thou God, Angel, Wreath, 8 1/4 X 9 In.	40.00
Salt, Cloud Pattern, Luster	24.00
Shaker, 4 1/8 In.	85.00
Teapot, Cloud Design, Ribbed, Pink Iridescent, 7 X 11 In.	195.00

SUPERMAN, Bank, Rocket Ship	10.00
Box, Pencil	12.00
Button, Fan Club, 1966	18.00
Card, Gum, 1940	7.50
Figure, Wood, Jointed, Ideal, 1940, 13 In.	377.00
Game, Card	10.00
Juice, In Action, 1964	15.00
Lunch Box, Action Shot	35.00
Puppet, Hand, 1965, Ideal	20.00
Toy, Roll Over Tank	275.00
Valentine, 1940	18.00

SWORD, American Officer's, 1785-95, Silver Hilt, Eagle Head Pommel, 25 In.	2250.00
Artillary Officer's, 1821, Spread Eagle, Gold Wash, 31 In.	550.00
Bayonet, Arms Fit Inside Muzzle, C.1700, Blade 11 In.	125.00
Bayonet, Artillery, Scabbard, Spanish, C.1900, 6 3/4 In.	47.50
Bayonet, Brass Hilt, Marked 1873, Scabbard, 28 In.	30.00
Bayonet, Butcher, Simpson & Co., German, World War II	30.00
Bayonet, Mauser, German Marked Blade, Spanish	22.50
Bayonet, Needle, French, Matching Numbered Scabbard, Dated 1879	40.00
Bayonet, Remington, 1917	65.00
Bayonet, Saber, Brass Hilt, Leather Sheath, For U.S.Rifle	185.00
Bayonet, Sawtooth, Scabbard	40.00
Bayonet, Scabbard, Remington	65.00
Bayonet, Socket, C.1808, Marked, Blade 16 In.	39.50
Bayonet, Springfield, Brass & Leather Scabbard, 22 In.	25.00
Bayonet, U.S.Parade, Dated 1908, Metal Chrome Plated	22.50
Bayonet, U.S.Springfield, Civil War	30.00
British Life Guard, C.1910, Side Loop, Sharkskin Grip, 32 In.	110.00
Broad, English, Ornate Handle, 7 1/2 In.	13.00
Broad, Line Engraving, Leather Cover, Scottish, C.1700, 32 In.	650.00
Cavalry, Civil War, 1860	48.50
Cavalry, Russian, Dated 1905, Brass Handle	125.00
Cutlass & Bayonet, Scabbard, 1858 Enfield, Navy	185.00
Cutlass, American Naval, 1740-76, Oak Grips, 18 In.	325.00
Cutlass, British Navel, 1-Piece Cast-Iron Grip, C.1812, 29 In.	180.00
Cutlass, Naval, War Of 1812, Iron Guard, Marked, 27 1/2 In.	450.00
Cutlass, U.S.N., 1860, Brass Hilt Leather Grips, Marked Ames, Chicopee	275.00
Dagger, Armor Piercing, Applied Enamel Designs, Ivory Grip, Persian	140.00
Dagger, Cossack, Sheath, 1908	550.00
Dagger, Gambler's Push, Spear Point Blade, Wooden Handle, 6 1/2 In.	350.00

Dagger, Nazi Storm Trooper, Enameled Eagle & Swastika, Motto 135.00
Dagger, Pearl Tip On Handle, Civil War 35.00
Dagger, Pommel Pulls Out, Enclosed Tweezers, Greek, 8 1/2 In. 87.50
Dagger, Push, American, C.1820, T Cross Handle, Sawtoothed, 9 In. 84.50
Dagger, Stocking, British, Silver Mounted, Horn Grip, Sheath, 5 In. 115.00
Dagger, Walnut Handle, Bronze & Silver Case 40.00
Diplomat's, Italian, C.1850, Gilt Brass Hilt, Beaded Design 137.50
Dirk, Naval, Gilt On Brass Hilt, Eagle's Head Pommel, American, C.1810 .... 650.00
Dragoon Officer's, 18th Century, Crown Each Side, 27 In. 325.00
Dress, French Diplomat's, Etched Scenes, Toledo-1888, Leather Case 1295.00
Dress, Officer's, Bronze, C.1830, Lion Masks, 37 In. 143.00
English, C.1750, Brass Hilt, Etched Battle Trophies On Blade, 32 In. 225.00
Field, Bronze Handle, Civil War, Metal Sheath 250.00
Foot Artillery, Roman Pattern, Brass Hilt, Ames, Springfield, 1839 .... 225.00
Foot Officer's, Marked Horstmann, Phila., Leather Sheath 375.00
French Officer's, Double Fuller, Dated 1814, 44 3/4 In. 605.00
German, Dragoon Troopers, Bayonet, Brass Hilt, Dated 1868, 37 In. 80.00
German, Imperial Officer's, Bird's Head Pommel, Prussian Eagle, 32 In. 145.00
Hunting, C.1870, Brass Hilt, Clamshell Guard, German, 16 In. 145.00
Hunting, German, C.1800, Brass Hilt, Stag Handle, 17 In. 94.50
Infantry Officer's, Lion Head Pommel, Dated 1769, 25 In. 425.00
Infantry Officer's, 1850, Pierced Floral Design, 32 1/2 In. 325.00
Infantry, Recurved Guard, Prussian, 18 3/4 In. 85.00
Military, Presentation, American, Gilt Hand Guard, 36 In. 80.00
Naval Officer's, American Revolution, Carved Wooden Grips, 25 1/2 In. 375.00
Officer's, C.1790, Gilt Design, Geometric Panels, French, 33 In. 495.00
Pioneer's, Imperial Russian, Cyrillic Inscription, 14 1/2 In. 135.00
Pirate, Spanish, 17th Century, Horn Grips, Incised Carving, 26 In. 375.00
Police, C.1870, Brass Hilt, Issue Marks, Bavarian, 24 In. 110.00
Russian, Court, Mother-Of-Pearl Grip, Arms, Foliage, 37 In. 495.00
Saber Bayonet, French, 1877 Model, Scabbard 30.00
Saber, Calvary, Marked Roby, US 1865, Iron Sheath 185.00
Saber, Cavalry Officer's, Triangular Shaped Point, American 650.00
Saber, Cavalry, Stirrup Guard, Marked Wooley & Deakins 132.50
Saber, Confederate Cavalry, Brass Hilt, Leather Grips, 31 In. 325.00
Saber, Confederate, Brass Hilt, Leather Grips, Blade 35 In. 450.00
Saber, Double Fullers, Iron Hilt, British, Revolutionary War, 36 In. 265.00
Saber, German, 1826-89, Iron Hilt, Bird's Head Pommel, 30 In. 69.50
Saber, Horseman's, American Revolution, Brass Hilt, 34 In. 650.00
Saber, Horseman's, American Revolution, Flat Blade, 36 In. 795.00
Saber, Military Dress, Brass & Silver Hand Guard, 35 1/2 In. 55.00
Saber, Military, Civil War, Marked 1863, 41 In. 60.00
Saber, Officer's, War Of 1812, Brass Hilt, Scroll Bars, British, 30 In. 235.00
Saber, Revolutionary Horseman's, Double-Edged Blade, 35 In. 550.00
Saber, Scabbard, Cavalry, 1818, Iron Sheath, Marked 265.00
Saber, Souvenir New York City, C.1890, Metal, 6 In. 22.00
Scabbard, American Diplomat's, Minerva Pommel, 32 In. 695.00
Scabbard, Cavalry, Civil War, 35 In. 250.00
Scottish Basket, 18th Century, Sharkskin Grips, 32 In. 1450.00
Swordfish, Mounted With Brass Guard, Rosewood Handle, 35 1/4 In. 145.00
U.S.Military, C.1865, Crosby, W.Chelmsford, Mass. 225.00
Wilkinson, Short, Walnut Grip, Leather Scabbard, British, 16 In. 80.00
     TANKARD, see Stein
     TAPESTRY, PORCELAIN, see Rose Tapestry

TEA LEAF IRONSTONE, Bone Dish .... 55.00 To 75.00
Bowl, Apple, Scalloped, Footed 225.00
Bowl, Fruit, Square, Wilkinson, 10 In. 60.00
Bowl, Meakin, 3 7/8 In.Diam., 1 1/2 In.High 50.00
Bowl, Open Rectangular, Meakin, 6 3/4 X 9 1/2 In. 38.00
Bowl, Round, Meakin, 6 In.Diam. 72.00
Bowl, Soup, Grindley, 9 In. 28.00
Bowl, Vegetable, Burgess, 9 1/2 In.Diam. 64.00

Tea Leaf Ironstone, Creamer, 4 1/2 In.

Brush Holder, Meakin		160.00
Butter Chip, Arthur J. Wilkinson		8.50
Butter Chip, Mellor-Taylor		8.00
Butter Chip, Round, Unmarked, 3 In.Diam.		8.00
Butter Chip, Scalloped Edge, Square		15.00
Butter, Covered, Insert		95.00
Casserole, Lid, Vegetable, Shaw		100.00
Casserole, Lid, Vegetable, Wedgwood, 7 1/2 In.Long		90.00
Chamber Pot		150.00
Coffeepot		125.00
Compote, Footed, Wilkinson, 9 X 5 In.		85.00
Creamer & Sugar, Wedgwood		180.00
Creamer, Shaw		80.00
Creamer, 4 1/2 In.	*Illus*	38.00
Cup & Saucer, Burgess		55.00
Cup & Saucer, Coffee, Meakin		50.00 To 58.00
Cup & Saucer, Coffee, Mellor-Taylor		50.00
Cup & Saucer, Handleless, Shaw		85.00
Cup & Saucer, Handleless, Wedgwood		47.00
Cup & Saucer, Meakin		55.00 To 75.00
Cup Plate, Meakin, 3 1/2 In.Diam.		35.00
Cup, Egg, 2 1/2 In.Diam., 3 1/2 In.High		140.00
Cuspidor, Shaw, Men's Faces On Side		420.00
Dish, Bone, Mayer		70.00
Dish, Bone, Meakin		35.00 To 55.00
Dish, Meakin, 4 1/2 X 6 1/2 In.		24.00
Dish, Sauce, Meakin, Square, 4 1/2 In.		15.00
Dish, Soap, Insert, Covered, Luster		85.00
Dish, Soap, Lid & Drainer, Meakin		90.00
Dish, Vegetable, Meakin, Covered, 6 X 9 In.		90.00
Dish, Vegetable, Ribbed Sides, A.J.Wilkinson, Square		45.00
Dish, 4 3/4 In.		40.00
Gravy Boat, Meakin		45.00
Holder, Brush, Meakin		120.00
Ladle, Soup, 9 In.		30.00
Mug, Shaving, Shaw, Raised Berry		115.00
Mug, Shaw, 3 1/4 In.		92.00
Pitcher, Meakin, 9 1/2 In.		55.00
Pitcher, Milk, Meakin, 7 1/2 In.		135.00
Pitcher, Shaw, 6 In.		65.00
Plate, Clementson, 4 1/2 In.Diam.		17.00
Plate, Meakin, 6 1/2 In.		12.50
Plate, Meakin, 10 In.		16.00 To 20.00

Plate, Mellor-Taylor, 6 1/2 In.	12.00
Plate, Mellor-Taylor, 9 1/2 In.	12.00
Plate, Shaw, Lily-Of-The-Valley, 9 3/4 In.	55.00
Plate, Shaw, 7 3/4 In.	14.00
Plate, Shaw, 8 In.	12.50
Plate, Shaw, 9 3/4 In.	15.00
Plate, Square, Wilkinson, 8 1/2 In.	48.00
Plate, Wedgwood, 7 1/2 In.	12.00
Plate, Wedgwood, 8 3/4 In.	11.50
Plate, Wilkinson, 9 In.	12.00
Plate, 8 1/2 In.	5.50
Plate, 9 In.	12.00
Platter, Lily-Of-The-Valley, 14 3/4 X 10 1/2 In.	55.00
Platter, Meakin, 9 1/2 X 13 In.	20.00
Platter, Oval, Arthur J.Wilkinson, 10 1/4 X 14 3/4 In.	34.00
Platter, Oval, Mellor-Taylor, 8 3/4 X 11 3/4 In.	38.00
Platter, Rectangular, Alcock, 10 3/4 X 14 1/4 In.	24.00
Platter, Rectangular, Meakin, 8 3/4 X 12 In.	10.00
Platter, Rectangular, Meakin, 11 1/4 X 15 1/4 In.	24.00
Platter, Wedgwood, 11 X 15 3/4 In.	34.00
Platter, 11 X 14 1/2 In.	17.00
Platter, 14 In.	28.00
Platter, 16 In.	35.00
Potty, 12-Sided, Shaw	195.00
Relish, Handles, Wedgwood, Scalloped Edge, 7 In.	29.00
Sauce Tureen, Ladle, On Tray, Mellor-Taylor	200.00
Sauce, Rectangular, Covered, Meakin, 3 Piece	150.00
Sauce, Round, Mellor-Taylor, 4 3/4 In.Diam.	9.50
Sauce, Square, Wedgwood, Scalloped Edge, 4 1/4 In.	14.00
Saucer	6.00
Saucer, Round, Meakin, 5 In.Diam.	14.00
Sugar, Covered	47.00
Sugar, Meakin, Covered	30.00
Tea Set, Meakin, 5 Piece	200.00
Teapot, Mellor-Taylor	175.00
Vegetable, Open, Scalloped Edge, Wedgwood, 8 3/4 In.	45.00

Teco pottery is the art pottery line made by the Terra Cotta Tile Works of Terra Cotta, Illinois. The company was founded by William D.Gates in 1881. The Teco line was first made in 1902 and continued into the 1920s. It included over 500 designs, made in a variety of colors, shapes, and glazes.

TECO, Vase, Brown Matte, Price Tag & Factory Label, Signed, 11 In.	120.00
Vase, Brown, 5 1/2 In.	75.00
Vase, Matte Green, 9 1/2 In.	140.00
Vase, Molded Leaves & Flowers, Green, 9 In.	125.00
Vase, Oblate, Tricorn Top, Green, 4 1/2 In.	50.00
Vase, Ovoid, Green, 6 In.	60.00

TELEPHONE, American Bell Co., Wall, Gold Decal, Crank, 9 X 20 1/2 In.	225.00
Audio, Brass Bell	325.00
Booth, Wood	550.00
Candlestick, Black Finish Over Brass	125.00
Candlestick, Dated November, 1910, Converted For Use, Brass	215.00
Candlestick, Glass Mouthpiece, Long Receiver, Dated October, 1916	260.00
Candlestick, Kellogg, 1901	75.00
Crank, Bakelite, 1930	11.00
Crank, Oak	150.00
Danish, Wood Trim, Locking Door	85.00
Desk, 1912, Danish	55.00
Electric, Wall, Gold Decal, Crank, Writing Tablet, Oak, 20 1/2 In.	225.00

Fiddleback, Wall	250.00
Field, Army, Lineman's	20.00
Kellogg, Oak Bell Box	62.00
Police, Pole Mounted	79.50
Stromberg Carlson, Bell Box, Oak	35.00
Stromberg Carlson, Candlestick, Miniature	125.00
Switchboard, Table Top, Cherry	158.00
Wall, Dovetailed, Oak	85.00
Western Electric, Cradle Desk, Oak Bell Box, Cord & Batteries	60.00
Western Electric, Desk, Oak Bell Box, Brass Bells	55.00 To 75.00
Western Electric, Golden Oak Case	300.00
Western Electric, Pay Phone	53.00
Western Electric, Wall, Oak	225.00
3 Bar Magnetos, Brass Crank	15.00

Teplitz refers to art pottery manufactured by a number of companies in the Teplitz-Turn area of Bohemia during the late nineteenth and early twentieth centuries. The Amphora Porcelain Works and the Alexandra Works were two of these companies.

TEPLITZ, Basket, Woven Effect, Angles In Garlands, Amphora, 11 X 15 In.	595.00
Bowl, Enameled Poppies, Castle Mark, 10 X 9 In.	295.00
Bowl, Raised Enamel Poppies, Handled, Marked, Amphora, 4 X 3 1/2 In.	265.00
Bowl, Vase, Basket Of Grapes, 10 X 7 In.	225.00
Bust, Victorian Woman, Signed, Amphora, 12 X 16 In.	850.00
Compote, Black Berries & Leaves, Amphora	190.00
Dish, Enamel Design, Amphora, Oval, Flat, 8 X 4 In.	24.00
Dish, Nautilus Shape, Covered, Signed, Amphora, 8 X 2 X 5 In.	95.00
Dish, Sweet, Little Girl, Oblong	52.00
Ewer, Bulbous, Turquoise Handle, Gold Flower, Crown, 10 1/2 In.	120.00
Ewer, Enameled Purple, Gold-Trimmed Orchids, Blue Base, 13 1/4 In.	230.00
Ewer, Mosaic Panels, Mask Spout, Marked, 12 1/2 In. ....Illus	160.00
Ewer, Wine, Art Nouveau Maiden, Portrait Of Bacchus, Marked	1500.00
Figurine, Arab Merchant Leading Camel, Amphora, 18 X 18 In.	975.00
Figurine, Man, Standing Holding Book, Marked, 7 3/4 In.	155.00
Jug, Wine, Roman Figure, Blue Matte Ground, Amphora, High Glaze	115.00
Pitcher, Art Nouveau, Amphora, Imperial Mark, 14 1/2 In.	295.00
Pitcher, Boy & Goose, Open Handle, Brown, Large	95.00
Pitcher, Girl & Goose, Open Handle, Green, Large	98.00
Pitcher, Green, Girl & Goose, Open Handle	98.00
Pitcher, Green, Girl With Horn & Dog, Squatty	52.00 To 65.00
Pitcher, Yellow, Green, Red, Matte Finish, Signed, Amphora, 12 In.	195.00
Tray, Painted View Of Vienna, Impressed Wahliss ....Illus	700.00
Vase, Art Deco, Signed, Yellow, Green, & Pink, Amphora, 7 In.	125.00
Vase, Art Nouveau, Flower Form Neck, Amphora, 10 1/4 In.	265.00
Vase, Bird In Flight, Flowers, Amphora, 12 In.	145.00
Vase, Bird-Shaped Handles, Brown Finish, Amphora, 7 1/2 In.	145.00
Vase, Blown-Out Figure Of Lady In Colonial Dress, 9 1/2 In.	185.00
Vase, Bud, Rooster Head Medallion, Geometric Design, 5 1/2 In.	85.00
Vase, Children At Play, Signed, 10 1/2 In.	379.00
Vase, Embossed Gold Trees, Blue Base, Crown Mark, 8 In.	52.00
Vase, Female Head & Pansies, Crown Oakware, 12 1/2 In.	395.00
Vase, Figures Of Boy & Girl, Signed & Numbered, Amphora, 10 In.	359.00
Vase, Flower Form, Handle, Amphora, Green, Blue, & Pink, 10 1/4 In.	265.00
Vase, Flower Form, Leaves, Iridescent, Amphora, 10 In.	245.00
Vase, Glazed Ducks In Flight, Moon Design, Amphora, 8 3/4 In.	180.00
Vase, Gold Webbing, Jeweled, Amphora, Imperial Crown Mark, 7 In.	290.00
Vase, Gray To Green, With Enameled Florals, 13 In.	150.00
Vase, Green, Brown Ground, Yellow Roses, 6 In.	100.00
Vase, Hen & Chicks, Marked, Amphora, 5 1/2 In.	120.00
Vase, Leaves & Stems, Applied Lavender Poppies, Amphora, 12 In.	250.00
Vase, Lobster Throat, Silver Overlay, Amphora, 14 1/2 In.	745.00
Vase, Musician, Handles At Base, Gold Amphora Mark, 7 1/4 In.	85.00

Teplitz, Ewer, Mosaic Panels, Mask
Spout, Marked, 12 1/2 In.

Teplitz, Tray, Painted View Of Vienna, Impressed Wahliss

Vase, Pear Form, Bird, Abstract Design, Amphora, White, 13 In.	70.00
Vase, Portrait, Blue, Mauve, Green, Gilding, Amphora, 11 In.	1750.00
Vase, Portrait, Crowned Maiden, Amphora, Blue, Mauve, Green, 6 In.	1000.00
Vase, Portrait, Queenly Maiden, Forest, Marked, 6 1/4 In.	1000.00
Vase, Red & Pink Roses, Gold Stem & Bands, 10 1/2 In.	160.00
Vase, Stalking Lion On Base, Signed, Amphora, 11 In.	300.00
Vase, Swirling Poppy Leaves Form Handles, Amphora, Signed, 11 In.	250.00
Vase, Tapered, Jeweled, Gold Outlines, Handled, Amphora, 11 3/4 In.	210.00
Vase, Webbing With Center Band Of Birds, Amphora, 9 In.	295.00
Vase, Yellow Roses, Gold Trim, 4-Handled, Amphora, 7 In.	55.00
Vase, 2 Children Playing, Amphora, 13 In.	375.00
Vase, 4 Gold Handles, Yellow Rose, Amphora, Black Ground, 7 1/4 In.	90.00
TERRA-COTTA, Burial Piece, Female Figure, Nubian, 4 1/2 In.	300.00
Figurine, Nubile Maiden, C.1920, Marked, 19 In.	2400.00
Jardiniere, Oriental Design, 13 In.	45.00
Pitcher, Raised Dragon, Enameled, Handle, Japanese, 11 In.	360.00
Teapot, Animals On Lid, Spout, & Handle, Oriental Mark	65.00
Teapot, Applied Porcelain Leaves & Design, Signed	38.00

*Textile includes all types of table linens and household linens such as
coverlets, fabrics, etc.*

TEXTILE, Afghan, Red, Blue, Yellow, & Pink, Handmade, Wool, 5 1/2 X 3 1/2 Ft.	90.00
Bag, Marble, Chamois, Drawstring Top	5.00
Banner, Circus, World's Smallest Man, Canvas	395.00
Banner, Sideshow, Master Of Magic *Illus*	800.00
Bed Rug, Woven Rags, Light Colors, Shaker, 66 X 80 In.	65.00
Bedspread, Counterpane, Full Size	45.00
Bedspread, Crepe, Lace Inserts, Peach, 86 X 60 In.	40.00
Bedspread, Crib, Popcorn Stitch, Squirrels At Top, 36 X 43 In.	85.00
Bedspread, Crocheted, Diamonds, 96 X 66 In.	50.00
Bedspread, Crocheted, Stringed Edges, 120 X 120 In.	95.00
Bedspread, Crocheted, 78 X 90 In.	125.00
Bedspread, Hand-Painted Lovers, Damask, 96 X 84 In.	65.00
Bedspread, Lace Edges & Panels, Silk, 80 X 34 In.	135.00
Bedspread, Popcorn Stitch, Hand-Crocheted, C.1915, Double	225.00
Bedspread, Summer, Woven, Dark Blue & White Checks, 90 X 92 In.	225.00
Bedspread, Trapunto, 80 X 80 In.	400.00
Bedspread, World's Fair, 1893	350.00
Blanket, Homespun, Blue & White, Hand-Hemmed, 73 X 96 In.	145.00
Blanket, Homespun, Brown Stripes, Natural Ground, 70 X 90 In.	90.00
Blanket, Peruvian, Wool, Fringed, 72 X 98 In.	45.00

Textile, Banner, Sideshow, Master Of Magic
(See Page 683)

Blouse, Button Front, Black Lace	6.00
Blouse, Elbow Sleeves, Ruffles Down Front, Lace Trim, Chiffon	35.00
Blouse, High Neck, 40 Crystal Buttons, White	150.00
Bodice & Skirt, Pigeon Breasted, Bone Stays, Pink Silk	100.00
Bodice, Black Silk, 1870, Fiddleback, Bead Trim	45.00
Bodice, Leg O' Mutton Sleeves, Braid Trim, Satin, Waist 22 In.	25.00
Bonnet, Amish, C.1920, Black	30.00
Bonnet, Baby, Handmade, White Silk With Pink, Quilted, 19th Century	30.00
Bonnet, Baby's, Eyelet	10.00
Bonnet, Black Silk & Lace, C.1850, Ties Under Chin	65.00
Bonnet, Child's, Black, Original Box, C.1860	25.00
Bonnet, Child's, Quilted Black & White, Lined, Mennonite	50.00
Bonnet, Chocolate Brown Straw, C.1840, 7 X 9 1/2 In.	65.00
Bonnet, Doll, Chocolate Brown Straw, C.1840, 7 X 9 1/2 In.	65.00
Bonnet, Ruffled Edge, 1840s, Calico	55.00
Bridge Set, Bridge Hand-Embroidered Cloth, 4 Napkins	32.50
Caftan, Silver & Gold Embroidery, Moroccan, Velvet	450.00
Canopy, Crib, Crocheted	32.00
Cap, Lace, Dutch Type	35.00
Cape, Black Velvet	20.00
Cape, Doucet, 1870, Paris, Hip Length, Blue	150.00
Cape, Evening, Velvet Trim, Silk Fringe, Satin, Paris Label	125.00
Cape, Lady's, Black Silk, Victorian, Lace Trim	10.00
Cape, Ribbon & Jet Bead Trim, Short, Black	22.00
Cape, Velvet Binding, Floor Length, Wool	85.00
Cape, Vertically Striped Ribbon At Hem, Black Satin, 16 In.	35.00
Chemise, Embroidered	18.00
Coat, Collar Forms Scarf, Black Velvet	100.00
Coat, Evening, Fur Collar & Cuffs, Black Velour, 1920s	50.00
Coat, Flapper, Black Silk, Broadtail Fur Collar, Size 14	35.00
Coat, Hess Bros, Paris, Peter Pan Collar, Side Buttons, Fur Collar	125.00
Coat, Prince Edward	15.00
Coat, Puffed Sleeves, White Fur Collar, Black Velvet	50.00
Coat, Raccoon, Man's, Beaver Collar, Wool Lining, Large	200.00

Linen or wool coverlets were made during the nineteenth century. Most of the coverlets date from 1800 to 1850. Four types were made, the double woven, jacquard, summer and winter, and overshot.

Coverlet, Eagle, Tree Border, Dated 1845, Blue & White 395.00
Coverlet, Eagles, Blue & White, Signed Sarah E.Phillips, 1888 .... 750.00
Coverlet, Grapevine, Eagle, & Floral Center, Signed H.Stager, Mt.Joy 250.00
Coverlet, Hand-Woven, Navy, Gold, & Tan, Double Bed Size 275.00
Coverlet, Jacquard, Central Medallion, 76 X 76 In. 225.00
Coverlet, Jacquard, Floral Design, 1840, Wool, 82 X 92 In. 300.00
Coverlet, Jacquard, Red, White, & Blue, Flower Border, 80 X 84 In. 1320.00
Coverlet, Jacquard, Signed Susan Stone, 1844, 88 X 78 In. 375.00
Coverlet, Jacquard, Stylized Flowers, 1839, Wool, 78 X 84 In. 225.00
Coverlet, Overshot, American, Initialed Saw, 76 X 88 IN. 500.00
Coverlet, Overshot, Homespun, Geometric, Blue & White, 104 X 84 In. 175.00
Coverlet, Plaid, Embroidered Initials, 64 X 76 In. 65.00
Coverlet, Red Stitch Of Birds & Animals, 1906, 72 X 76 In. 125.00
Coverlet, Star Pattern, Cinnamon Red, 82 X 72 In. 350.00
Coverlet, Trapunto, Pink, Reverses To Green, 70 X 80 In. 35.00
Coverlet, Woven In Rust & Natural, Fringe, 82 X 90 In. 225.00
Curtain, Eggshell, Scranton Craftspun, Label, 2 1/2 Yards, 5 Pair 250.00
Curtain, Flower & Scroll Pattern, Rayon Lace, 6 Panels 80.00
Curtain, Lace, Floral & Scroll Border, 39 X 82 In., 6 Panels 100.00
Curtain, Tassels, Tan & Burnt Sienna, 100 X 48 In., Pair 65.00
Dress, Alexander Agatha, 1979, Lavender 275.00
Dress, Baby, Long Sleeves, 1920, White Cotton 10.00
Dress, Child's, Homespun, C.1860, Size 5 .... 25.00
Dress, Child's, White, Smocking, Tatting, 1930's 23.00
Dress, Child's, 1908, Cotton Batiste, Bib Ties 35.00
Dress, Christening, Hand-Embroidered 65.00
Dress, Christening, Tucked & Embroidered Yoke, 19th Century, 30 In. 28.00
Dress, Christening, Tucked, Openwork Yoke, Long Sleeves, 35 In. 40.00
Dress, Christening, Vertical Tuck & Lace Waist, Long Sleeves, 22 In. 25.00
Dress, Cocktail, Hand-Beaded, Signed Fanny's 110.00
Dress, Dinner, Handmade Point De Gaze Lace, C.1910, Waist 30 In. 650.00
Dress, Elbow Sleeves, Apron Panel, Sash Back, Brown Chiffon, 1900 .... 75.00
Dress, Evening, Bias Cut, Gold Metal Piping, 1920s, Brown Velvet 65.00
Dress, Evening, Fuchsia, 1940s, Padded Shoulders, Gold Beading 38.00
Dress, Evening, Lanvin, 1938-39, Black Taffeta ....*Illus* 300.00
Dress, Evening, 1920s, Black Net, Silk Underdress, Lace Accent 40.00
Dress, Flapper, Beaded, Silver Sequins, Ivory, Paris Label 85.00
Dress, Flapper, Beaded, 1920s, Sash, Beige 35.00
Dress, Flapper, Floral Design On Sheer Black, Beaded 65.00
Dress, Garden, Cream, Silk, 3 Rows Of Lace, Edwardian 90.00
Dress, Gold Silk, Liberty Of London & Paris, Some Embroidery, 1906 .... 125.00
Dress, High Neck, Lace & Voile, White 225.00
Dress, Lacy, C.1900, White 145.00
Dress, Party, 1920s, Bias Cut, Sheer, Flesh Color, Cap Sleeve 30.00
Dress, Puffy Sleeves, Padded Shoulders, Blue Velvet 27.50
Dress, Sequin Top, 1940s, Black Chiffon 20.00
Dress, Wedding, 1940s, Bouffant Style, Size 12 .... 50.00
Duster, Lady's, Cape Style, Medium Size 35.00
Duster, Riding 18.00
Embroidery, Japanese, Cranes, Foliage, Ivory, 4 Ft. 7 In. X 6 1/2 Ft. 1700.00
Flag, American, 46 Stars, 5 X 8 Ft. 120.00
Flag, Confederate, Star & Bars, 9 X 6 Ft. 165.00
Flag, Naval, Confederate, Stars & Bars, 3 Ft. X 5 Ft. 8 In. 1750.00
Flag, Rhode Island, 31 Star 150.00
Gown, Ball, C.1890, Short Train, Lace Over Ivory Satin 75.00
Gown, Ball, Fringed Bodice, 1860s, Gray Silk Taffeta, 2 Piece 75.00
Gown, Dressing, Chinchilla Band At Elbow & Cuff, Silk 165.00
Gown, Tea, Fortuny, Pleated Silk Satin, Sea Green ....*Illus* 3500.00
Gown, Tea, Printed Linen, Velvet Yoke 75.00
Handkerchief, Wedding, Balencienne & Anglaise Lace, 12 X 12 In., Pr. 115.00
Hat, Garden Party, Wide Brimmed, Brown & Beige, 1920s 30.00
Headband, 1920's, Black Velvet, Faux Diamonds & Feathers 8.00
Jacket, Dinner, Narrow Lapels, Padded Shoulders, 1900s 15.00

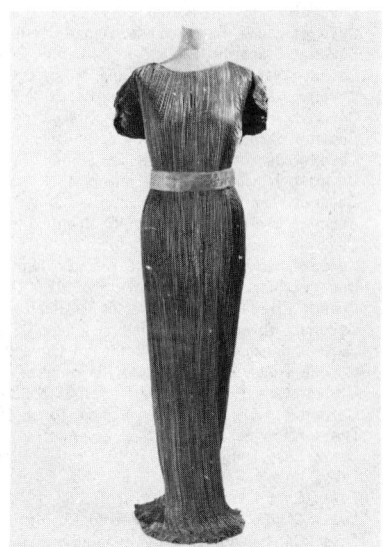

Textile, Dress, Evening, Lanvin, 1938-39,

Black Taffeta

(See Page 685)

Textile, Gown, Tea, Fortuny, Pleated

Silk Satin, Sea Green

Kimono, Encrusted With Gold Insects, Silk, Apricot 65.00
Kimono, Japanese, Silk, Chrysanthemum Clusters, White, Purple 150.00
Kimono, Rayon, Turquoise Ground, Floral Pattern, Red, Gold, Pink 20.00
Kimono, Wedding, Red Silk, Allover Floral & Bird Embroidery 250.00
Mantilla, Roses, Scalloped & Picot Edge, Black Lace, 42 In.Diam. 185.00
Mitts, White, C.1810, White 28.00
Needlework, Pheasant, Eliz.Forsett, Year 1786, Enfield, Framed, Pair 750.00
Nightcap, Lady's, Eggshell Crochet Over Blue Silk, 1800s 22.00
Overdress, Beige, Orange, Gray Floral Print, Sheer, 1920's 40.00
Panel, Needlework, 18th Century, Heraldic, 29 1/2 X 13 1/2 In. 275.00
Pantaloons 10.00
Pantsuit, Stewardess, Pan American, Periwinkle Blue, Size 4 .... 65.00
Petticoat, Boned & Fitted, Tucking & Lace, C.1860, Silk, 51 In. 110.00
Petticoat, Cotton, Lace Bottom, White 15.00
Petticoat, Embroidered, Long 35.00
Petticoat, Flannel Lined, Black Sateen 18.00
Picture, George Washington & Family, 1808, Silk, 20 X 24 1/2 In. 600.00
Picture, Memorial, Printed Silk Names 900.00
Picture, Mourning, Silk Ground, 16 X 16 In. 190.00
Picture, Needlepoint, Moses In Bulrushes, Framed, 30 X 38 In. 175.00
Picture, The Angelus, Woven Silk, 5 1/2 X 7 In. 95.00
Pillowcase, Crocheted Insert, Handmade, Pair 10.00
     TEXTILE, QUILT, see Quilt
Robe, Buggy, Racing Stripes, C.1900, Wool, 48 X 59 In. 45.00
Robe, Chenille, Peacock On Back 75.00
Robe, Lap, American Flag In Center 60.00
     TEXTILE, RUG, see Rug

Samplers were made in the United States during the early 1700s. The best examples were made from 1790 to 1840. Long narrow samplers are usually older than the square ones. Early samplers just had stitching or alphabets. The later examples had numerals, borders, and pictorial decorations. Those with mottoes are mid-Victorian.

Sampler, A.B.C., Sarah Lakeman, Dated 1825, Framed, 14 X 14 In. 395.00
Sampler, Alphabet & House, Signed Zawodsky Fesefa, 1853 .... 165.00
Sampler, Alphabets & Numbers Bands, Verse, E.Warren, 12 X 15 In. 150.00
Sampler, Alphabets, Numerals, & Verse, Dated 1852, 12 X 12 In. 140.00
Sampler, Ann Newell, 1838, Birds, Fruit Baskets, 18 1/2 X 17 In. 300.00
Sampler, Ann Shaw, June 3, 1801, Framed, 16 X 12 1/2 In. 200.00
Sampler, Apphia Gore Palmer, Aged 13 Years, 16 1/2 X 5 1/4 In. 165.00
Sampler, Mourning, Dated 110.00
Sampler, Pious Verse, Dated 1829, 15 X 17 In. 120.00
Sampler, Sarah Booth, Brandon School, 1761, Verse, 17 1/2 X 13 In. 275.00
Sampler, Signed Ann Higley, Tiverton, 1849, Linen, 10 1/2 X 10 In. 160.00
Sampler, Signed Ann Paine, Aged 6 Year, 1844, Linen, 12 X 12 1/2 In. 200.00
Sampler, Signed Catharina Lerch, 1832, Linen, 9 1/2 X 11 1/2 In. 70.00
Sampler, Signed Elizabeth Haller, 9 Years, 1867, 12 X 15 In. 180.00
Sampler, Signed Elizabeth Sharp, 9 Years, 1830, Linen, 7 1/2 X 11 In. 90.00
Sampler, Signed Hannah Askinson, 15 Year Old, Dated 1775 .... 525.00
Sampler, Signed Hannah Avery, 14 Years, 13 X 14 1/2 In. 170.00
Sampler, Signed Mary David, 19th Century, 21 X 26 In. 180.00
Sampler, Stitched Panels, Dated Ano 1871, Spanish, 27 X 34 In. 300.00
Sampler, Tapestry, European, Sheep Shearing Scene, 75 X 52 In. 225.00
Sampler, Worked By Sabina Wade, Halifax, 1822, 4 X 12 In. 150.00
Scarf, Piano, Silk & Cotton Damask, 56 In.Square 40.00
Scarf, Piano, Silk, Fringed, Peach 32.00
Shawl, Black Silk Embroidery, Fringe, Swedish, 34 In.Square 50.00
Shawl, Chantilly Lace, Black, Large 28.00
Shawl, Flowers, 3 Scalloped Sides, Spanish, Black Lace, 24 X 42 In. 135.00
Shawl, Fringe, Black Damask, 74 In.Square 25.00
Shawl, Paisley Border, Mulberry, Fringed, 64 In.Square 25.00
Shawl, Paisley, Floral Design, Wool, 71 X 70 In. 110.00
Shawl, Piano, Embroidered, Fringed, Silk 70.00
Shawl, Piano, Oriental, Rose Colored Silk, Clouds & Flowers 150.00
Shawl, Piano, Victorian, Coral Silk Crepe, 49 In.Square 78.00
Shawl, Silk Black Damask, Fringe, 71 In.Square 65.00
Shawl, Silk, Chinese, Floral, Peonies, Cherry Blossoms, 60 X 60 In. 300.00
Shawl, Thread Braid Trim, Black Taffeta 15.00
Shawl, Woven Paisley, 1860 .... 110.00
Shift, Homespun Linen, Cross-Stitch Initial, White 30.00
Skirt, 1800, Silk, Red Dots, Front Opens, Ruffle Edge 50.00
Slip, Child's, Crocheted 5.50
Stockings, Lace Pattern Below Knee, Gray Cotton 10.00
Suit, Fireman's, Child's, Cloth Over Fiber, 1800s, 3 Piece 22.50
Suit, Rhinestone Studded Lapels, Black Wool, Gloria Swanson, 2 Piece 45.00
Suit, Walking, Purple, Silk Damask, 1913, Cut-Glass Buttons 60.00
Swimsuit, 1930s, Man's 15.00
Tablecloth, Battenburg, Solid Center, Openwork, White, 28 In.Diam. 42.00
Tablecloth, Battenburg, 72 In.Diam. 100.00
Tablecloth, Carnations & Bowknots, Linen Damask, 72 X 106 In. 23.00
Tablecloth, Clover Design, Linen Damask, 160 X 86 In. 55.00
Tablecloth, Cluny Lace, Handmade, 65 In.Across 84.00
Tablecloth, Columbian Exposition, Washington & Columbus, Lace 165.00
Tablecloth, Crocheted Border, Lace Inserted Strips, 72 In.Diam. 150.00
Tablecloth, Crocheted Edge, 12 Napkins, Cross-Stitched, 92 X 78 In. 50.00
Tablecloth, Crocheted, Queen's Lace Pattern, Ecru, 66 X 80 In. 70.00
Tablecloth, Crocheted, 50 X 100 In. 50.00
Tablecloth, Damask, Fringe, Corner Monogram, 124 X 66 In. 45.00
Tablecloth, Embroidered, Linen, Oriental Design, 54 In. 65.00
Tablecloth, Embroidered, Linen, 34 In. 24.00
Tablecloth, Hand-Hemmed, Satin Damask, 8 Napkins, 66 X 82 In. 50.00
Tablecloth, Lace, Ecru, 76 X 108 In. 300.00
Tablecloth, Linen, Hemmed, 190 X 82 In. 50.00

Textile, Tapestry, Verdure, French, 7 Ft. 4 In. X 6 Ft. 3 In.

Tablecloth, Linen, White, C.1880, 5 X 6 Ft. 20.00
Tapestry, Arab Street Scene, Framed, 56 X 10 In. 55.00
Tapestry, Art Deco, Mideastern Warrior Scene, Belgium, 38 X 49 In. 55.00
Tapestry, Aubusson Style, Traveler In Courtyard, 46 X 38 In. 600.00
Tapestry, Aubusson, France, 1847, Signed, 5 Ft. 5 In. X 7 Ft. 2 In. 1300.00
Tapestry, Classical Ladies By Lake, Unframed, 33 X 24 In. 30.00
Tapestry, Flemish Verdure, Hunt Scene, 6 Ft. 5 In. X 7 1/2 Ft. 1000.00
Tapestry, Flemish, C.1600, Figures, 8 Ft. 5 In. X 14 Ft. 6 In. 3000.00
Tapestry, Flemish, Knight & Guards, 8 Ft. 9 In. X 3 Ft. 11 In. 2000.00
Tapestry, Flemish, Verdure, Dogs, Plants, 8 Ft. 1 In. X 6 Ft. 6 In. 1500.00
Tapestry, French, Genre, Maiden & Lord, 4 Ft. 8 In. X 3 Ft. 4 In. 1600.00
Tapestry, French, Verdure, 10 Ft. 11 In. X 4 Ft. 9 In., Pair 2600.00
Tapestry, Garden Scene, 4 Figures, Cream, Gray Ground, 6 1/2 X 8 Ft. 3200.00
Tapestry, Gros Point & Petit Point, French, 5 Ft. 11 In. X 4 Ft. 1300.00
Tapestry, Spanish Courtyard Scene, Belgium, 38 X 19 In. 26.00
Tapestry, Venetian Scene, Belgian, 20 X 37 In. 45.00
Tapestry, Verdure, French, 7 Ft. 4 In. X 6 Ft. 3 In. .... *Illus* 1500.00
Teddy, Lace Trimmed, Silk, Pink, Size 10 .... 22.00
Towel, Embroidered Roosters & Stars, Handwoven Linen, 16 X 43 In. 65.00
Towel, Irish Linen, 39 X 21 In., Pair 8.00
Towel, White Pattern, Fringed 7.50
Vest, Wedding, C.1850, Floral Velvet 45.00

THERMOMETER, Carter's Ink, Porcelain 85.00
Chesterfield Farm Supply, Wooden 25.00
Coburger Beer 350.00
Coca-Cola, Bottle Shape, 29 In. 55.00
Coca-Cola, 1954, 17 In. 25.00
Dad's Root Beer, Boxed 15.00
Dairy, Floating, Calibrated To Scalding, 8 1/4 In. 7.50
Distiller's, Copper, Large 18.50
Doan's Pills, Wooden, Shape Of Man With Backache 85.00
Dole Bananas, Tin 15.00
Edelweiss Light Beer, Round, 12 In. 50.00
Ex-Lax, Enamel, Tin, 8 X 36 In. 46.00
Ex-Lax, Porcelain, 36 In. 80.00

Fatima, Dated 1913, Porcelain	150.00
Figural, Black Boy, Dated 1949	20.00
Hires Root Beer, Bottle Shape, 28 In.	38.00 To 50.00
Hires, Bottle-Shaped	40.00
L. & M.Cigarettes, Raised Pack	25.00
La Fendrich 5 Cigar, Porcelain, 10 X 26 In.	95.00
Mail Pouch, Porcelain, 38 In.	40.00 To 68.00
Motorola, Tin, 38 In.	68.00
Moxie, Bottle & Man	135.00
Negro Boy, Dated 1949	15.00
Nevaleek Stoppers, Round	14.00
Old Buck Fuano, Richmond, White & Black Letters, 4 X 15 In.	25.00
Pepsi-Cola, Raised Bottle Cap, Yellow	25.00
Prestolite, 27 X 8 In.	18.00
Prestone, Winston	20.00
RC Cola, 25 X 10 In.	25.00
Winston Cigarettes, Multicolored, Round	12.80
Winston Cigarettes, 6 X 13 In.	10.00

TIFFANY BRONZE, Base, Lamp, Vinson Pattern, 3 Cylindrical Legs, Signed, 60 In.	3600.00
Box, Bronze Lattice Over Green Glass, Ball Feet, 5 1/2 In.	225.00
Box, Stamp, American Indian Pattern, 3-Section Tray	239.00
Desk Set, Bookmark Pattern, Inkwell, Letter Opener, Blotter	175.00

C. Tiffany Furnaces Inc. Favrile

Louis C. Tiffany

Tiffany glass was made by Louis Comfort Tiffany, the American glass designer who worked from about 1879 to 1933. His work included iridescent glass, Art Nouveau styles of design, and original contemporary styles. He was also noted for his stained glass windows, his unusual lamps, bronze work, pottery, and silver.

TIFFANY GLASS, Bottle, Cologne, Leaf & Vine Design, Gold, Signed, 6 In.	1750.00
Bottle, Perfume, Ribbed, Flattened Body, 8-Sided Stopper	550.00
Bowl, Blue & Violet Highlights, Ribbed, Signed, 2 1/4 X 4 In.	250.00
Bowl, Blue, Signed, 8 In.	575.00
Bowl, Diamond & Ribbed Interior, Pastel, Signed, 9 1/4 In.	575.00
Bowl, Dimpled Rim, Rainbow Highlights, Signed, 6 1/4 In.	495.00
Bowl, Fruit, Signed, Numbered, 6 1/2 In.	389.00
Bowl, Swirl Effect, Blue, Signed & Numbered, 7 In.	895.00
Bowl, Swirled, Paneled, Blue, 10 In.	725.00
Bowl, Underplate, Finger, Favrile, Yellow, Marked, 6 In.	500.00
Bowl, Vine & Leaf Pattern, Signed, 3 1/4 X 10 In.Diam.	595.00
Brandy Snifter, Threaded Lily Pad Design, Gold, 3 3/4 In.	350.00
Candlestick, Favrile, Yellow, Domed Foot, Signed, 11 3/4 In.	750.00
Candlestick, Stretch Glass Saucer, Gold Trim, Signed, 4 In.	195.00
Candlestick, Swirled Standard, Blue, Marked, 7 In., Pair	70.00
Candlestick, 3 Balls, Embossed Design, Blue, Signed, 12 In.	1325.00
Chandelier, Greek Key, Yellow Ground, 1907 Mark, 22 In.Diam.	5000.00
Chandelier, Leaded, 6 Lily Extended Shades, Jewels, 31 1/2 In.	9000.00
Compote, Favrile, Stretched, 1925, Signed, 7 5/8 X 2 1/4 In.	485.00
Compote, Intaglio Cut Vintage Pattern, Signed, 6 1/4 In.	650.00
Compote, Pedestal, Footed, Gold Aurene, Signed, 6 X 4 In.	600.00
Cordial, Dimpled Lower Body, 1 3/4 In., Signed	150.00
Cup, 2 Horizontal Green Bands, Gold Iridescent, 2 In.	250.00
Decanter, Free-Form, Engraved, Stopper, Signed, 11 1/2 In.	2500.00
Dish, Butter, Gold Iridescent, Scalloped, Signed, 3 In.Diam.	165.00
Dish, Candy, 8-Sided Conical Top, Iridescent Blue, 9 In.	130.00
Dish, Mint, Raised Edge, Gold Iridescent, Signed, 5 3/4 In.	110.00
Dish, Nut, Gold Iridescence, Silver-Blue Highlights, Signed	140.00
Dish, Nut, 4-Footed, Signed, Gold, 1 1/2 X 2 1/4 In.Diam.	150.00

Dish, Pink, 8 In.	300.00
Dish, Serving, Footed, Violet & Blue, Signed, 2 X 8 In.Diam.	425.00
Dish, Violet & Blue, Pedestal, Signed, 8 In.Diam.	425.00
Finger Bowl, Underplate, Signed & Numbered	389.00
Finger Bowl, Yellow Opalescent, Signed	150.00
Flower Bowl, Iridescent Gold, 5 Lily Pads, Signed, 11 1/2 In.	1250.00
Flower Frog, Opalene, Signed, 4 X 2 1/2 In.	225.00
Flower Frog, Verre-De-Soie, Signed, 3 In.	150.00
Globe, Paperweight, Gold Iridescent Ground, Signed, 8 X 5 In.	2500.00
Goblet, Hollow Venetian Stem, Yellow, Signed, 7 1/2 In.	385.00
Goblet, Yellow Green Venetian Stem, Pink, Signed, 7 3/4 In.	425.00
Letter Holder, Grapevine, 3 Section, Signed, 6 X 10 In.	289.00
Liquor Set, C.1892, Double Conical Base, Signed, Amber, 7 Piece	1100.00
Paperweight, Grapevine, 3 3/4 In.Diam.	125.00
Paperweight, Zodiac Pattern, Rectangular	150.00
Parfait, Rice Grain Design, Deep Blue, Signed, 6 1/2 In.	485.00
Pitcher, Water, Green Leaf Design, Gold Luster, Signed, 9 In.	3800.00
Plaque, Green Lobster, Peacock Blue Ground, 16 In.Square	1000.00
Plaque, Swirled Center, Scrollwork Rim, Signed, 12 3/4 In.	1500.00
Plate, Fuchsia Pastel, 11 In.	395.00
Plate, Stretched Edge, Marigold, Signed, 7 1/4 In.	160.00
Plate, Teardrop Pattern Center, Signed, Paper Label, 7 In.	225.00
Punch Glass, Spreading Hollow Stem, Signed, 3 1/2 In.	165.00
Salt, Aurene, Blue & Purple Highlights	175.00
Salt, Blue & Gold, Signed	250.00
Salt, Blue-Gold Thorn, Signed	225.00
Salt, Gold Aurene, Ruffled, Signed, 2 3/4 In.Diam.	140.00
Salt, Gold Favrile, Signed, 2 3/8 In.	125.00
Salt, Gold Highlights, Thorn Design, Signed	350.00
Salt, Gold Iridescence, Handled, Signed & Numbered, 2 1/4 In.	225.00
Salt, Gold Iridescent, Flared Rim, Ribbed, 2 1/4 In., Set Of 4	350.00
Salt, Gold Ruffled, Signed, 2 3/4 In.	135.00
Salt, Gold, 2 3/4 X 1 1/4 In.	125.00
Salt, Iridescent Sapphire Blue, Ruffled, Signed	235.00
Salt, Prunts, Footed, Green Iridescent	325.00
Salt, Pulled Handles, Gold, Signed & Numbered, 4 1/4 In.	210.00
Salt, Pulled Outsides, Gold Iridescent, Signed	150.00
Salt, Ribbed, Flared, Blue Iridescent, Numbered, Signed	250.00
Salt, Ruffled Edge, Flat Base, Master, Signed, 4 In.Top	325.00
Salt, Ruffled, Gold, 2 3/4 In.	180.00
Salt, Ruffled, Iridescent	120.00
Salt, Ruffled, Sapphire Blue, Signed	235.00
Salt, Scalloped, Blue, Signed, 3 In.Wide	275.00
Salt, Scalloped, Gold, Signed, 3 In.Wide	175.00
Salt, Turned-Out Rim, 2 Pull Handles, Signed, 2 1/4 In.Diam.	210.00
Sherbet, Pulled Prunts On Bowl & Pedestal, Signed, 3 1/2 In.	250.00
Shot Glass, Dimpled Sides, Gold Phantom Luster, Signed, 2 In.	130.00
Snifter, Gold, Miniature, 3 3/4 In.	350.00
Tile, Brown, Yellow, Red, & Green, Center Flower, 3 In.Square	60.00
Tile, Green, Red, Brown, & Yellow, Marbleized, 3 In.Square	55.00
Tile, Medallion Center, Dated 1881, Signed, 3 In.Square	75.00
Toothpick, Dimple On Each Side, Signed & Numbered, 1 3/4 In.	160.00
Toothpick, Favrile, Amber & Violet, 1 3/4 In.	175.00
Toothpick, Orange Iridescent, Dimpled, Signed, 2 In.	135.00
Toothpick, Pinch-Sided, Signed, 2 7/8 & 1 7/8 In., Pair	250.00
Tumbler, Threaded Midsection, Gold Iridescence, Signed, 4 In.	175.00
Urn, Egyptian, Gold Murano, Rainbow Iridescence, 9 1/2 In.	1800.00
Urn, Signed, Covered, Midnight Blue, 9 1/2 In.	1750.00
Vase, Apple Green, Pears & Apple, Ribbed Body, Signed, 7 In.	1150.00
Vase, Atomic Cloud, Gold Iridescent, Signed, 4 1/2 In.	375.00
Vase, Baluster Form, Blue Iridescent, Signed, 2 3/4 In.	350.00
Vase, Baluster Form, Blue Iridescent, Signed, 11 3/4 In.	975.00
Vase, Base Of Greens, Silver Over Gold Trim, Signed, 7 In.	2500.00

Vase, Blue Iridescent, Signed, 4 In. 375.00
Vase, Bronze Dore Holder, Iridescent Gold, 10 In. 485.00
Vase, Bud, Gold, Hexagon Shape, Knob Stem, Signed, 6 In. 375.00
Vase, Bud, Hexagon Shape, Ball Stem & Pedestal, Signed, 6 In. 395.00
Vase, Bud, Orange & Gold Design, Folds, Signed, 5 1/2 In. 2500.00
Vase, Bud, Pulled Green & Gold Feathers, White, Signed 1650.00
Vase, Bud, 2-Piece, Favrile, Peacock Blue, Signed, 15 1/2 In. 950.00
Vase, Butterfly Blue, Green, Gold, & Purple, Signed, 5 1/2 In. 1200.00
Vase, Calyx Flower Form, Green, White, Gold, Signed, 12 1/2 In. 1750.00
Vase, Cylindrical Form, Applied Blue Lily Pads, Signed, 7 In. 2400.00
Vase, Cypriote, Blue & Purple, Rough Texture, 5 1/2 In. 1100.00
Vase, Cypriote, Favrile, Ochre Overlay, Brown, Marked, 5 In. 8000.00
Vase, Cypriote, Gold Speckled, Black Overlay, Signed, 3 1/2 In. 2500.00
Vase, Cypriote, Rounded Bottom, Signed, 5 1/4 In. 1100.00
Vase, Cypriote, Textured, Purple, Iridescence, Signed, 5 1/4 In. 1100.00
Vase, Dark Green Over Light Green, Silver Trim, Signed, 7 In. 1200.00
Vase, Egyptian, Onion Shape, Green Veined, Signed, 10 In. 2000.00
Vase, Elephant Tails, Pink, Blue, Signed, 2 In. 165.00
Vase, Favrile, Gourd Shape, Yellow, Gold Design, Signed, 9 In. 500.00
Vase, Favrile, Ovoid, Blue Iridescence, Marked, 5 In. 475.00
Vase, Favrile, Peacock Eyes, Amber, Caramel, Signed, 15 1/2 In. 1550.00
Vase, Flared Edge, Gold Iridescent, Signed, 4 1/2 In. 300.00
Vase, Flared Top, Green & Cobalt Blue, Signed, 10 In. 700.00
Vase, Flared, Fluted, & Dimpled, Gold Iridescent, Signed, 6 In. 595.00
Vase, Flora Front & Side, Diana On Reverse, Handled, 11 In. 500.00
Vase, Flower Form, Blue Highlights, Gold, Signed, 9 7/8 In. 1200.00
Vase, Flower Form, Blue, Purple, & Pink, Signed, 11 In. 2500.00
Vase, Flower Form, Favrile, Green Leaves, Stems, Signed, 14 In. 2600.00
Vase, Flower Form, Gold Luster, Green Vine, Signed, 6 1/4 In. 1100.00
Vase, Flower Form, Gold, Blue Highlights, Signed, 9 7/8 In. 1200.00
Vase, Flower Form, Gold, Multicolored Inner Top, Signed, 11 In. 2250.00
Vase, Flower Form, Gold, Red, & Blue Iridescent, Signed, 11 In. 1095.00
Vase, Flower Form, Green Feather, White Ground, Signed, 11 In. 1650.00
Vase, Flower Form, Green Feathering, Signed, 15 In. 3500.00
Vase, Flower Form, Green, Gold Trim, Signed, 11 1/2 In. 1450.00
Vase, Flower Form, Green, Opalescent Rim, Signed, 15 In. 3150.00
Vase, Flower Form, Orange Gold Interior, Signed, 11 1/2 In. 2000.00
Vase, Flower Form, Pale Yellow, Signed L.C.T., 11 In. 1495.00
Vase, Flower Form, Yellow & Gold, Signed, 16 3/4 In. 1300.00
Vase, Free-Form, Pinched Shoulders, Gold, Signed, 3 1/2 In. 425.00
Vase, Gold Applied Threading, Black Ground, Signed, 5 1/2 In. 500.00
Vase, Gold Feather, Dore Bronze Holder, Signed, 15 1/2 In. 725.00
Vase, Gold Iridescence, Violet Highlights, Signed, 4 In. 575.00
Vase, Green Feather Design, Flared Opening, Signed, 6 In. 1500.00
Vase, Green Intaglio Leaves, 3 Curved Arms, Signed, 7 1/2 In. 2500.00
Vase, Intaglio Carved, Twisted Shape, Lay Down, Signed, 10 In. 2500.00
Vase, Intaglio Carved, Twisted Shape, Signed, 10 In. 2500.00
Vase, Iridescent Feather On Opalescent Body, Signed, 8 In. 550.00
Vase, Jack-In-The-Pulpit, Yellow & Gold, Signed, 13 1/4 In. 1300.00
Vase, Leaf Pattern On Lower Body, Ovoid, Blue-Green, 4 1/2 In. 600.00
Vase, Lemon Yellow Sides, Amber, C.1906, Signed, 11 1/2 In. 900.00
Vase, Lower Part Shaded Green, Silver Over Gold, Signed, 7 In. 2500.00
Vase, Millefiori, Peacock Blue, Marked, 8 In. 1500.00
Vase, Onion Shape, Green Leaf Design, Label, 12 In. 2400.00
Vase, Open Lattice, Gold, Blue Highlights, Purple, Signed, 4 In. 855.00
Vase, Oviform, Ribbed, Blue Purple, Signed, 6 1/2 In. 500.00
Vase, Oviform, Yellow, Green Leaves, Signed, 5 In. 900.00
Vase, Ovoid Body, Gold Iridescent, Signed, 4 3/4 In. 210.00
Vase, Ovoid, C.1916, Striated Feathers, Signed, 7 In. 650.00
Vase, Ovoid, Opaque Olive, Beige Band, Label, 12 1/2 In. 1400.00
Vase, Paperweight, Amber-Green, Red Berries, Signed, 8 In. 1425.00
Vase, Paperweight, Favrile, Purple Flowers, Signed, 8 In. 3000.00
Vase, Pinched-Open Lattice On Top, Purple, Signed, 4 In. 950.00

Vase, Pockmarked Yellow, Gold Globules, Lava, Signed, 5 In. 5500.00
Vase, Pulled Yellow Feather On Alabaster, 8 In. 550.00
Vase, Raised Design Of Circles & Ribs, Gold, Signed, 3 In. 425.00
Vase, Red, Favrile, Teardrop, Purple Overlay, Signed, 9 In. 5500.00
Vase, Rounded Bottom, Tapered Neck, Blue, Signed, 6 1/2 In. 750.00
Vase, Speckled Peacock Blue, Rounded Bottom, 6 1/2 In. 750.00
Vase, Spiral Handles, Blue-Silver Iridescence, Signed, 11 In. 1100.00
Vase, Stick, Conical, Gold Luster, Button Pontil, Signed, 14 In. 675.00
Vase, Swirled Feather, Green, Gold, & Violet, Signed, 3 1/2 In. 595.00
Vase, Thorn Pattern, Gold Iridescent, Signed, 5 In. 625.00
Vase, Trumpet Shape, White Bowl, Gold Foot, Signed, 1o 3/4 In. 2200.00
Vase, Urn Form, C.1919, Amber Foot, Signed, 10 1/4 In. 500.00
Vase, White Columns, Gold Scrolls, Yellow, Signed, 9 In. 920.00
Vase, 3-Tier Shape, Signed & Numbered, 2 In. 325.00
Vase, 4-Finger, Green, Gold, & Purple, Signed, 6 1/2 In.Diam. 1200.00
Wine, Flared Rim, Baluster Stem, Gold, 3 7/8 In., Pair 140.00
Wine, Intaglio Cut Grapes & Leaves, Gold, Signed, 5 1/2 In. 300.00
Wine, Rice Grain Design, Twisted Stem, Signed, 7 1/4 In. 425.00

TIFFANY GOLD, Earrings & Pendant, 18 K, Fitted Velvet Case 1500.00
Salt, Bowl Shape, 4-Footed, Signed, 2 1/4 X 1 1/2 In. 150.00

TIFFANY POTTERY, Vase, Old Ivory, 8 X 5 In. 285.00

TIFFANY SILVER, Ashtray, Porringer Form, Pierced Handle, 1 7/8 In., Set Of 4 .... 375.00
Basket, Pierced, Cobalt Blue Glass Liner, 5 X 3 1/2 In. 195.00
Bottle, Perfume, Sterling Connectors, Intaglio Cut, 7 In. 145.00
Bowl, Embossed Flowers, Handled, C.1875, Marked, 13 1/2 In. 1000.00
Bowl, Footed, New York, C.1854, 8 In. 320.00
Bowl, Old English B In Center, Pierced Band, 9 In.Diam. 475.00
Box, Etched Lift-Off Lid, Gold Wash Inside, Marked, 3 1/4 In. 225.00
Butter, Leaves, Floral, Covered, C.1890, 4 In. 440.00
Child's Set, Audubon Pattern, C.1871, Knife & Fork 95.00
Coffeepot, Japanese Style, C.1877 .... 1875.00
Compote, Footed, C.1865, 12 1/4 In. 950.00
Dish, Buds & Shells, C.1907, 11 1/4 In. 250.00
Dogtag, Beaded Chain, 14K Gold 300.00
Fork, Fish, Threaded Oval, 5 Prongs, Scrolls, Marked, 9 1/2 In. 145.00
Kettle On Stand, New York, 11 1/4 In. 550.00
Knife, Butter, Palm Pattern, Master 42.00
Ladle, Punch, New York, C.1880, 12 1/2 In. 700.00
Pencil, Pull-Out, Hang On Chain, Floral Repousse 120.00
Pitcher, C.1875, Covered, 9 In. .... *Illus* 750.00
Pitcher, Embossed Men & Women Among Putti, C.1915, 10 In. 950.00
Pitcher, Hot Water, Niello .... *Illus* 1200.00
Pitcher, Water, Spherical Form, C.1900, 7 In. 850.00
Plate, Butter, Engraved Design, Coin, 3 In.Diam. 45.00
Punch Bowl, Ladle, Chrysanthemum Pattern, Signed, 21 In.Diam. 6500.00
Salad Set, Vine Pattern 375.00
Server, Cake, Winthrop 225.00
Snuffer, Candle, Wood Handle, New York 70.00
Spoon, Parfait, English King, Set Of 8 .... 370.00
Spoon, Serving, Chrysanthemum, Kidney Shaped, Gold Wash Bowl 285.00
Spoon, Vine Pattern, Ruffled Edges 180.00
Strainer, Tea, 2 Openwork Handles 110.00
Sugar, Japanese Style, 2-Handled, C.1877 .... 2875.00
Tazza, Copper Trees, Foliage, C.1910, 8 In. 360.00
Tray, Card, Basket Shape, Pierced, Marked, 8 In.Diam. 90.00
Tray, Etched Dancers, Marked Christmas 1881, 13 In.Diam. 950.00
Tureen, Soup, Forked Handles, Flowerheads, 16 In. 2650.00
Vase, Pedestal, Horizontal Leaf Design, Marked, 7 3/4 In. 275.00
Vase, Reticulated, Cranberry Liner, C.1902, Signed, 8 In. 395.00
Vase, Trumpet Form, New York, C.1900, 20 In. 750.00

Tiffany Silver, Pitcher, C.1875, Covered, 9 In.   Tiffany Silver, Pitcher, Hot
Water, Niello

Vase, Trumpet Shape, Engraved Design, Footed, 12 In.	450.00
TIFFANY, Ash Stand, Favrile, Bronze, Hinged, Glass Liner, Signed, 26 In.	1300.00
Ashtray, Enamel Simulated Leather, Silvered Bronze, Signed, 5 In.	75.00
Ashtray, Gold Dore, Handled, Ribbed, Bronze, Signed, 4 In.Diam.	135.00
Ashtray, Gold Dore, Line Design, Round, Signed & Numbered, Set Of 4	375.00
Ashtray, Green Iridescent Insert, Signed	350.00
Ashtray, Jewels At Each Corner, Bronze, Signed, 5 3/4 X 3 1/2 In.	175.00
Ashtray, Nested, Bronze, Oval, Marked, Set Of 3	125.00
Ashtray, Zodiac, Center Symbol, Bronze, Signed, 4 X 3 In.	135.00
Blotter Corner, Pine Needle Pattern, Set Of 4	150.00
Bookends, American Indian, Mask, Scroll, Bronze, Signed, 4 1/2 X 6 In.	400.00
Bookends, Bronze & Abalone, Leaf Design, Signed, 5 1/2 X 5 1/2 In.	495.00
Bookends, Figure Of Woman Buddha, Bronze, Signed, 5 1/2 X 6 In.	350.00
Bookends, Geometric Enamel Pattern, Signed, Bronze & Enamel, 5 In.	300.00
Bookrack, Flower & Leaf Design, Signed, Bronze & Abalone, 19 In.	800.00
Bookrack, Ninth Century Pattern, Bronze & Jeweled, Signed, 19 In.	800.00
Bowl, Arabesque Border, Pedestal, Signed, 9 In.	125.00
Bowl, Centerpiece, Ribs All Around, Bronze, Signed, 2 X 8 In.Diam.	250.00
Bowl, Opalescent Stripes, Pink Pastel, Numbered, Signed, 6 3/4 In.	350.00
Bowl, Reticulated Border, Dated October 9, 1920, 6 1/2 In.	95.00
Box, Abalone Discs In Leaf Pattern, Bronze, Signed, 5 1/2 X 3 In.	525.00
Box, Abalone Grape Cluster, Silver Over Bronze, Signed	225.00
Box, Azalea Pattern, Bronze & Glass, Signed, 6 1/2 X 4 X 2 In.	395.00
Box, Bronze, Favrile, C.1890, Marked, 2 X 6 In.	70.00
Box, Cigarette, Venetian Pattern, Cedar Lined, Bronze, 5 1/2 In.	375.00
Box, Jewelry, Dore, Grapevine Design, Amber	395.00
Box, Leaf Pattern, Abalone Discs & Bronze, Signed, 5 1/2 X 3 1/2 In.	525.00
Box, Line Pattern Enameled In Blue, Footed, Bronze, Signed, 2 3/4 In.	300.00
Box, Puff, Gold Wash Interior, Engraved Lid, Marked, 3 3/4 In.	225.00
Box, Stamp, Chinese Pattern, Bronze	130.00
Box, Stamp, 3-Division Tray, Zodiac, Signed & Numbered	189.00
Brush, Pen, Graduate, Gold Finish, 2 1/2 X 2 In.	75.00
Butter, Deep Blue Iridescent, Scalloped Rim, Signed, 3 In.	225.00
Calendar Holder, Grapevine, Glass & Bronze, 8 1/4 X 6 3/4 In.	165.00
Candelabra, 6-Branch, Center Snuffer Holder, Bronze, Signed, 15 In.	2000.00
Candlestick, Bronze & Glass, Horseshoe Shape, Signed, 12 1/4 In.	750.00
Candlestick, Bronze & Glass, 4 Feet, Signed, 12 1/2 In.	750.00
Candlestick, Bronze, Signed Glass Hurricane Shade, 21 In.	1500.00
Candlestick, Bronze, Signed, 18 3/4 In.	375.00

Candlestick, Glass Shades, Signed, Pair 1300.00
Candlestick, Hurricane Shade, Signed, Bronze, 21 In. 1500.00
Candlestick, Ovoid Socket, Leaf Tipped Arms, Bronze, 10 In., Pair 625.00
Candlestick, Queen Anne's Lace, Signed, Bronze & Glass, 17 1/2 In. 750.00
Candlestick, Ribbed Glass Shade, Gold Trim, Bronze, Signed, 20 In. 2200.00
Candlestick, Ribbed Shade, Bronze Base, Signed, 12 In., Pair 1550.00
Candlestick, Twisted Stick Body, Signed, Bronze, 13 In. 300.00
Candlestick, 3-Prong Shade Holder, Bronze Base, Signed, 13 In. 1500.00
Chamberstick, Hammertone Design, Curved Arm, Bronze, Signed, 5 In. 275.00
Chamberstick, 2 Arms, Leaf Design, Bronze Snuffer, Signed 900.00
Chandelier, Moorish Turtlebacks, Glass & Bronze Balls, Signed 5000.00
Charger, Abalone Design, Bronze, Signed, 14 In. 200.00
Clip, Paper, Gold Dore Finish, Signed 95.00
Clock, Carriage, Double Pendulum, French Enamel Design, 12 In. 925.00
Clock, Desk, Zodiac Pattern, Marked, 5 1/2 In. 475.00
Clock, Ship's Wheel, Hygrometer, Barometer, & Compass, 7 In. 125.00
Clock, Swivel Cube, Hygrometer, Barometer, & Compass, Brass, 4 1/4 In. 225.00
Clock, Venetian Pattern, Chelsea Works, Bronze, 4 X 4 In. 650.00
Clock, 8 Day, Sterling Silver, 2 1/4 X 2 X 5/8 In. 395.00
Cocktail, Amber Faceted Stem, Gold, Signed, 5 1/4 In. 175.00
Compote, Green Pastel, Opalescent, Stem, Signed, 6 1/4 In. 650.00
Compote, Raised Leaf Pattern, Bronze & Glass, Signed, 6 1/4 In. 550.00
Compote, Seafoam Green To Clear, Grain Design, Signed, 6 In. 650.00
Desk Set, Bronze, Inkwell, Pen, Tray, Blotter, Letter Opener, Mirror 800.00
Desk Set, Bronze, Zodiac Pattern, Dore Finish, Signed, Set Of 9 .... 1575.00
Desk Set, Chinese Pattern, 4 Piece 995.00
Desk Set, Clock, Double Lamp Base, Bookends, 20 Piece 5400.00
Desk Set, Nautical Pattern, Bronze, Signed, 11 Piece 2000.00
Desk Set, Zodiac Pattern, Brown Patina, Bronze, Signed, 9 Piece 1295.00
Dish, Mint, Raised Edge, Gold Iridescent, Signed, 5 3/4 In. 110.00
Dish, Nut, Flared, Gold Iridescent, Signed, 1 1/4 X 3 In.Diam. 140.00
Dish, Nut, Gold, Blue Highlights, Signed, 4 1/2 X 2 1/2 In. 200.00
Dish, Stylized Floral Border, Dore Bronze, Signed, 6 In.Diam. 95.00
Finger Bowl, Underplate, Vintage, Gold Iridescent, Signed 325.00
Fixture, Hanging, Ribbed Globe, Bronze & Pastel, Signed, 11 In.Diam. 2500.00
Frame, Abalone Discs In Bronze Design, Signed, 8 1/4 X 5 3/4 In. 750.00
Frame, Bookmark Pattern, Perpetual Calendar, Signed, 6 1/4 X 5 In. 250.00
Frame, Bronze & Abalone, Leaf & Floral Design, Signed, 7 X 10 In. 750.00
Frame, Calendar, Easel Style, Bronze & Glass, Signed, 6 1/4 X 4 In. 225.00
Frame, Double, Azalea Pattern, Bronze & Glass, Signed, 10 1/4 X 7 In. 550.00
Frame, Grapevine, Oval Opening, Bronze & Glass, Signed, 6 X 8 In. 800.00
Frame, Oriental Pattern, Bronze, Signed, 6 1/4 X 9 In. 500.00
Glass, Ashtray, 2 Loop Handles, Signed, 4 In.Diam. 60.00
Globe, Hanging, Off-White, Bronze Collar, Signed, 12 X 9 In. 5500.00
Holder, Calendar, Venetian Pattern, Flip-Over, Bronze 230.00
Holder, Letter, Divider, Gilded Grapevine, Slag Glass & Bronze, 5 In. 120.00
Holder, Note Pad, Bronze & Jeweled Cover, Signed, 4 1/2 X 7 1/2 In. 300.00
Holder, Note Pad, Graduate, Gold Finish, 7 3/4 X 4 3/4 In. 95.00
Holder, Pen, Blotter, Adams, Bronze, Signed, Holder 9 1/2 In. 298.00
Holder, Pen, Double, Venetian Pattern, Bronze 550.00
Humidor, Brass Top, Copper Rim, Wave Design, C.1920, Signed, 7 1/2 In. 95.00
Inkstand, Bookmark Pattern, Bronze, 4 3/8 X 2 3/4 In. 330.00
Inkstand, Hexagon Shape, Hinged, Signed, 6 1/2 In. 295.00
Inkstand, Pedestal, Bronze 360.00
Inkstand, Venetian Pattern, Bronze, Marked, 5 1/4 In. 260.00
Inkwell & Pen Tray, Leaf Pattern, Signed, 12 In.Long 1000.00
Inkwell, Abalone Shell Discs On Body, Signed, 3 1/2 X 3 1/2 In. 300.00
Inkwell, Adams Pattern, Oval, Dore 190.00
Inkwell, American Indian Pattern, Bronze 245.00
Inkwell, American Indian Pattern, Bronze, Tapered 288.00
Inkwell, Art Nouveau, Curved Tray, Bronze, Signed, 8 In.Wide 1500.00
Inkwell, Bookmark Pattern, Bronze, Signed, Large 285.00
Inkwell, Double, Flute Player Center, Bronze, Signed, 9 X 12 1/2 In. 595.00

Inkwell, Graduate, Line Design, Glass Insert, Signed, 4 X 2 1/2 In. 225.00
Inkwell, Grapevine Design Over Green Marble Glass, Bulbous 300.00
Inkwell, Grapevine, Bronze Over Amber Slag Glass, Signed, 4 X 4 In. 325.00
Inkwell, Hinged Cover, Signed, Bronze & Abalone, 3 1/2 X 3 1/2 In. 300.00
Inkwell, Indian Pattern, Original Insert, Bronze, Signed 225.00
Inkwell, Nautical, Dolphin Feet, Bronze, Signed 575.00
Inkwell, Nautical, Sea Designs, Dolphin Feet, Bronze, Signed 575.00
Inkwell, Pen Tray, Art Nouveau Design, Bronze, Signed, 12 In.Long 1000.00
Inkwell, Pine Needle Pattern, Insert, Bronze 175.00
Inkwell, Pine Needle, Iridized Glass Insert, Bronze 290.00
Inkwell, Pyramid Shape, Blown Glass, Bronze Frames, Signed, 3 1/2 In. 1000.00
Inkwell, Pyramid Shape, Bronze Cover, Glass, Signed, 3 1/2 In. 1500.00
Inkwell, Spanish, Hinged Cover, Insert, Signed, 2 3/4 In.Square 450.00
Inkwell, Zodiac, Hexagon, Hinged Cover, Bronze, Signed, 6 1/2 In.Diam. 295.00
Jar, Enamel Over Brass Lid, 5 In. 550.00
Lamp, Acorn, Green Ground, Orange Acorns, Arms, Bronze, Signed, 10 In. 3250.00
Lamp, Adjustable Arm, Swirl Design Shade, Signed, Bronze, 19 1/2 In. 2800.00
Lamp, Base, C.1925, Dished Base, 4 Feet, Silvered Bronze, 25 1/2 In. 550.00
Lamp, Bell Shape, Gold Dore, Rib Design, Bronze, Signed, 15 In. 700.00
Lamp, Bell Shaped, Pink Striped Shade, Bronze, Signed, 15 In. 700.00
Lamp, Bellflower, Yellow, Ivory Ground, Bronze, Signed, 23 In. 9000.00
Lamp, Bridge, Curved Arms Around Shade, Lily Pad Feet, Signed, Bronze 1500.00
Lamp, Bridge, Turtleback Tile & Bronze, Signed, 22 In. 8500.00
Lamp, Bronze, Signed, Quezal Shade, Signed, 27 1/2 In. 2500.00
Lamp, Candle, Gold Luster Shade 345.00
Lamp, Candle, Lace Bronze Base, Gold Feather Shade, Signed, 24 In. 1800.00
Lamp, Candle, Matched Base & Shade, Silver Plated Fittings, 14 In. 775.00
Lamp, Candle, Ribbed, Gold Chimney, Damascene On Shade, Signed, 16 In. 1325.00
Lamp, Candlestick, Bamboo & 8 Trunk Base, Bronze, Signed, 15 1/2 In. 850.00
Lamp, Candlestick, Shade, Signed, Golden Amber, 11 1/4 In. 1550.00
Lamp, Candlestick, Turtleback Shades, Amber Glass, Signed, 19 In. 3000.00
Lamp, Dark Patina, Yellow & Green Shade, Signed, 17 In. 2450.00
Lamp, Desk, Abalone, 8-Paneled Shade, Bronze, Signed, 20 In. 4000.00
Lamp, Desk, Bell Shaped Shade, Feather Design, Bronze, Signed 1200.00
Lamp, Desk, Chinese Pattern, Octagon Shade, Bronze, Signed, 17 In. 3000.00
Lamp, Desk, Counterweight, Damascene Swirl Design, Signed, 13 In. 3500.00
Lamp, Desk, Flowers On Platform, 3 Arms Hold Shade, Bronze, Signed 2500.00
Lamp, Desk, Gold & Silver Swirl Shade, Signed, Bronze, 14 In. 1500.00
Lamp, Desk, Liberty Bell, Blue Glass, Bronze, Signed, 14 3/4 In. 4000.00
Lamp, Desk, Murano Design Shade, Bronze, Signed, 13 1/2 In. 3150.00
Lamp, Desk, Raised Petal Design, Bronze, Signed, Shade 10 In.Diam. 2500.00
Lamp, Desk, Wire Mesh & Bronze, Enamel Design, Signed, 17 1/2 In. 1100.00
Lamp, Desk, Zodiac, Oval Base, Bronze Shade, Adjustable, Signed, 10 In. 900.00
Lamp, Desk, 8-Paneled Fabrique Glass, Bronze, Signed, 20 In. 4000.00
Lamp, Desk, 18 Dichroic Panels, Bronze, Signed, 21 In. 3500.00
Lamp, Fabrique Shade, 10 Panels, Signed, Bronze, 21 In. 4000.00
Lamp, Favrile, Bronze Black-Eyed Susan, Flowerhead, Signed, 22 In. 6050.00
Lamp, Fleur-De-Lis, Orange Stem, Green Ground, Signed, 21 In. 6500.00
Lamp, Ivy Leaf, White & Blue, Bronze Cap, Signed, 22 In. 4500.00
Lamp, Kerosene, Green, Gold Damascus Shade, Gold Base, Signed, 17 In. 2300.00
Lamp, Lemon Leaf, Bronze Base, Signed, 25 In. 7500.00
Lamp, Lemon Leaf, Green To White, Stick Body, Signed, 22 In. 9500.00
Lamp, Lily, 3-Branch, Red Shades, Adjustable, Bronze, Signed 4500.00
Lamp, Lily, 7-Light, Amber Shades, Signed, Bronze, 20 In. 8000.00
Lamp, Lily, 10-Light, Gilt Bronze 7500.00
Lamp, Linenfold, Emerald Green, Gold Finish, Signed, 21 In. 3000.00
Lamp, Linenfold, Emerald Green, Signed Shade & Base, 19 In. 4600.00
Lamp, Mosque, Gold & Green Feather Pattern, Signed, 8 1/2 In. 1800.00
Lamp, Oil, Bronze, Turtleback Tiles, Signed 5000.00
Lamp, Ribbed, Scalloped Shade, Lily Pad Base, Bronze, Signed, 21 In. 7800.00
Lamp, Student, C.1900, Font, Adjustable Rod, Signed, Bronze, 24 1/2 In. 1500.00
Lamp, Student, Canister Holder, Adjustable Arms, Bronze, Signed 6000.00
Lamp, Student, Double, Pyramid Shaped Shades, Bronze, Signed 1800.00

Lamp, Student, Silver Finish, Openwork Design, 2-Light, Signed 6000.00
Lamp, Table, Bellflower, Wave Pattern, Bronze, Signed, 16 In. 9000.00
Lamp, Table, Chippendale, Allover Circular Design, Signed, 17 In. 2500.00
Lamp, Table, Favrile, Bronze, Green, Blue, Urn Form, Signed, 14 In. 990.00
Lamp, Table, Geometric Pattern, Green & White, Bronze, Signed, 22 In. 7500.00
Lamp, Table, Lemon Leaf, Striated & Mottled, Bronze, Signed, 25 In. 7500.00
Lamp, Table, Wire Mesh & Iridescent Glass, Bronze, Signed 1500.00
Lamp, Urn-Style Body, Damascene Shade, Signed, Bronze, 14 In. 2500.00
Lamp, 3 Arms On Foliate Base, Green Slag Shade, Bronze, 10 1/2 In. 200.00
Lamp, 3 Gold Iridescent Shades, Bronze, Signed, 22 In. 3250.00
Lamp, 3-Branch Lily, Red Shades, Bronze, Signed 4500.00
Lantern, 3 Blue-Green, 1 Red Turtleback, Rope Design, Signed, 9 In. 2200.00
Letter Opener, American Indian, Bronze 170.00
Letter Opener, Bookmark Pattern, Bronze 125.00
Letter Rack, American Indian, Closed Sides, Bronze 425.00
Letter Rack, Bookmark Pattern, 2 Section, Signed, 9 X 5 In. 300.00
Letter Rack, Indian Design, 2 Section, Signed, 11 X 5 In. 300.00
Letter Rack, Venetian Pattern, Closed Sides, Bronze 400.00
Letter Rack, 2 Compartment, Bronze & Abalone, Signed 325.00
Letter Rack, 2 Section, Pine Needle, Metal & Glass, Signed, 6 1/2 In. 350.00
Letter Rack, 9th Century, Bronze & Jeweled, Signed, 6 X 10 In. 550.00
Letter Seal, Form Of 3 Beetles, 1 3/4 In. 255.00
Magnifying Glass, Signed, Bronze & Abalone, 8 In. 350.00
Match Holder, Green Glass, Metal Stand 75.00
Medallion, Founding Of Cooper Union, N.Y., 1909, Bronze, 2 3/4 In. 65.00
Necklace, Gold, Pearl, & Opal, 12 Links, Signed, 14 In. 3500.00
Night-Light, Feather Design Shade, Bronze Base, Signed, 16 1/2 In. 700.00
Night-Light, Feather Pattern, Enameled Platform, Signed, 17 1/2 In. 1500.00
Ornament, Etched Metal & Glass, Bronze, Chain, 6 1/2 In.Long 350.00
Paperweight, Bulldog, Bronze, Signed & Numbered 325.00
Paperweight, Figural, Dog, Bronze, Signed, 2 1/2 X 1 1/2 In. 245.00
Paperweight, Lioness, Signed & Numbered, Bronze 395.00
Pendant, Dragonfly, Body, Silver, 6 In., Wingspan 10 In. 1250.00
Pitcher, Triangular Handle, Enamel On Copper, Signed, 14 In. 9500.00
Planter, Etched Bronze, Signed, Bottom 10 1/2 In.Diam. 425.00
Plate, Albacore Inserts On Border, 7 In.Diam. 75.00
Plate, Gold Engraved Bands, Marked, 10 In., Set Of 4 .... 250.00
Platter, Bronze, Deep Center Well, Signed, 9 In.Diam. 95.00
Platter, Bronze, Footed, Sunburst Design, Signed, 8 In.Diam. 200.00
Platter, Dore Bronze, Insert, Signed, 8 3/4 In.Diam. 200.00
Shade, Acorn, Mottled & Striated, 16 In.Diam. 2000.00
Shade, Candle Lamp, Gold, Signed, Fitter Rim, 2 5/8 In. 325.00
Shade, Frilled & Flaring Rim, Iridescent Gold, 7 In., Set Of 3 .... 350.00
Shade, Greek Key, Hanging, Green Mottled Ground, Orange, 22 In. 9000.00
Shade, Green Feather, Gold Broder, Signed 325.00
Shade, Iridescent Blue, Purple, Green, & Gold, Signed, 5 X 4 In. 300.00
Shade, Lily, Gold Feather, Mottled Body, Signed, 4 1/8 In. 275.00
Shade, Ribbed, Fluted Rim, Green Leaf Pattern, 7 1/4 In., Pair 120.00
Shade, Swirl Ribbed Body, Furled Rim, Gold, 5 In., Set Of 6 .... 250.00
Smoke Set, Geometric Design, Bronze & Enamel, Signed, 4 Piece 950.00
Tray, Card, Glass Center, Tab Handles In Enamel, Bronze, Signed 900.00
Tray, Gold Dore Over Bronze, Signed, 12 In. 200.00
Tray, Pen, Bronze With Green Glass Insert, Signed 160.00
Tray, Pen, Curved Line Design, Bronze & Mosaic, Signed, 7 3/4 In.Long 2200.00
Tray, Pen, Graduate, 4 Ball Feet, Gold Finish, Signed, 9 X 2 1/2 In. 95.00
Tray, Pen, Grapevine Pattern, Bronze Over Glass, Signed, 9 1/2 In. 150.00
Tray, Pen, Jewels Around Pattern, Bronze, Signed, 9 3/4 X 3 1/2 In. 225.00
Tray, Pen, Pine Needle Pattern, Bronze & Glass, 9 1/2 In.Long 150.00
Tray, Pen, 3 Compartments, Abalone Discs In Center, 8 1/2 In.Long 125.00
Tray, Raised Border, Geometric Design, Signed, Bronze, 14 In.Diam. 225.00
Tray, Serving, Floral Pattern, Abalone Discs & Bronze, Signed, 14 In. 300.00

Tiffin Glass Company of Tiffin, Ohio, was a subsidiary of the United States Glass Co. of Pittsburgh, Pennsylvania. Black satin glass, made by the company between 1923 and 1926, is very popular among collectors. Other types were also made.

TIFFIN, Bowl, Silver Overlay On Black Satin Glass, 8 In.	200.00
Candleholder, Satin, Black, 8 In.	20.00
Compote, Pedestal, Black Satin	30.00

TILE, see also listing by company name

TILE, Aztec Design, Claycraft, 6 X 8 In.	65.00
Calendar, 1902, Jones-McDuffie	50.00
Calendar, 1904, Jones-McDuffie	50.00
Calendar, 1905, Jones-McDuffie	50.00
Calendar, 1906, Jones-McDuffie	50.00
Calendar, 1907, Jones-McDuffie	50.00
Calendar, 1909, Jones-McDuffie	50.00
Calendar, 1915, Jones-McDuffie	50.00
Calendar, 1917, Jones-McDuffie	50.00
Calendar, 1922, Jones-McDuffie	50.00
Calendar, 1923, Jones-McDuffie	50.00
Calendar, 1926, Jones-McDuffie	50.00
Calendar, 1927, Jones-McDuffie	50.00
Calendar, 1929, Jones-McDuffie	55.00
Indian Woman, Wrapped In Robe, C.1840, Sepia, Staffordshire, 9 X 6 In.	325.00
Picture Of Harvard Medical School, Ceramic, 1908, 3 1/4 X 4 3/4 In.	78.00
Tray, Boy & Girl, Grass Handle, Copper Frame, Dutch, 14 X 8 In.	95.00
Zodiac, Moravian	45.00

TIN, see also Store; Tole

TIN, Biscuit, Bird Shape, McVitie & Price, Edinburgh & London	245.00
Box, Asphaltum, Compartments For Tobacco, Pipe, & Matches, 5 X 1 3/4 In.	78.00
Box, Candle, Cylinder, Black Paint, 10 1/2 In.	200.00
Box, Candle, Tabs For Hanging, Cylindrical	195.00
Box, Deed, Handle, 13 X 9 X 10 In.	35.00
Box, Deed, Stenciled, Farm Scene, Grazing Cow, Black Ground, 3 X 4 In.	550.00
Box, Deed, Tole, Green	65.00
Box, Document, Band Of Red Cherries, Wire Loop, White, 4 1/4 X 8 3/4 In.	275.00
Box, Document, Black, Vermilion Band, Shell Design, 8 X 4 X 4 In.	225.00
Box, Document, Polychrome Design, Brass Handle, 13 X 6 In.	275.00
Box, Hat, Brass Fittings, Oval, C.1830, Mustard Paint, 10 X 11 3/4 In.	125.00
Box, Hinged Lid, Painted Gentleman On Lid, Gold Border, 3 1/4 3/4 In.	145.00
Box, Knife, White Inside, Black Outside, C.1870, 9 X 13 1/2 In.	65.00
Box, Peter Rabbit, Oval	45.00
Box, Spice, Lift-Up Lid, Mexican Scene On Front, 11 X 8 In.	85.00
Box, Spice, Tole Type, Red Paint, Tin Bottle Insert, 4 X 2 X 2 In.	75.00
Box, Stenciled Pattern, Says Friendship, Covered, 6 3/8 X 3 1/4 In.	45.00
Bucket, Sugar, Finger Handle, Cover, Blue Paint, 11 X 10 In.	35.00
Cabinet, Spice, 8-Drawer, Painted White, 8 X 13 X 3 1/4 In.	135.00
Can, Kerosene, Cone Top, Strap Handle, Brass Collar, C.1870, 1 Gallon	25.00
Candle Sconce, Hanging, Crimped Edges, Peacock, Flowers, 9 3/4 In., Pair	175.00
Candleholder, Hog Scraper	24.00
Canister, Tea, Cylindrical, Embossed Oriental Design, 7 3/4 In.	15.00
Case, Comb, Hanging, Embossed, Pockets, Diamond Shaped Mirror, 7 In.	12.50
Case, Comb, Hanging, Pockets & Mirror, Embossed Pebble Design	20.00
Case, Document, Purse Shaped, Slide Catch, C.1860, 4 X 7 1/4 In.	27.50
Case, Map, Handmade, Lapped Seaming, C.1860, 3 X 30 In.	45.00
Case, Vest Pocket, 3 Cigars	12.00
Chamberstick, Dark Gray, Saucer, Push-Up, Embossed, C.1860, 4 In.	50.00
Coffee Set, Embossed Floral Medallion, C.1870	135.00

Coffeepot, Double Cone Shape, Pennsylvania, 19th Century 285.00
Cover, Flue, Corn & Pumpkin Harvest, Red Barn & Silo 8.00
Cup, Cyclist's, Embossed Couple On Tandem, Dated 1897, Folding 20.00
Cup, Trojan Powder Blasting 20.00
Feeder, Chicken, Royal Wire Handle, 7 1/2 X 7 1/2 In. 12.50
Flask, Body, Contoured, 7 1/2 X 11 1/2 In. 15.00
Foot Warmer, Pierced, Cherry Posts & Frame, Square 130.00
Frame, Victorian, C.1910, Oval, 14 X 24 In. 22.50
Hip Bath, Victorian, 19th Century, 39 In.Diam. 80.00
Hog Scraper, Candlestick, Iron Push-Up, 4 1/2 In. 50.00
Holder, Match, Hanging, Dark Gray, Twin Pockets, Shell Design, 5 In. 25.00
Horn, Fish, Cape Cod 35.00
Lantern, Darkroom, Front Hatch, Oil, Red Paint, 8 1/2 In. 35.00
Lantern, Dome Top, Floral Motifs, Glass Insets, 21 1/2 In., Pair 100.00
Lantern, Lighthouse Shape, Onion Waist, Star Vents, 17 In. 165.00
Lantern, Punched, Paul Revere Type, 13 In. 80.00
Match Holder, Striker Between 2 Pockets, C.1890, 4 1/2 X 4 3/4 In. 25.00
Match Safe, Crimped Top 26.00
Matchbox, Double, Striker, Mirror In Center, Gray, C.1880, 8 3/4 X 9 In. 30.00
Mold, Candle, American, 3 Holes, 10 X 16 X 12 In. 200.00
Mold, Candle, Cathedral, Drip Cup & Handle, Single, 17 3/4 In. 120.00
Mold, Candle, Double Handled, 12 Tube 110.00
Mold, Candle, Single, Crimped Base, 10 In. 52.00
Mold, Candle, 8 Tube 60.00
Mold, Candle, 12 Tube .... *Illus* 26.00
Mold, Candle, 12 Tube, Double Handle 110.00
Mold, Candle, 12 Tube, Handles At Each End 65.00
Mold, Candle, 48 Tube, 3 Rows, Folded Corners, 19 X 10 1/2 In. 210.00
Pail, Pink Inside, Blue Outside, Stripped, Bail, C.1860, 3 1/4 X 3 1/4 In. 25.00
Pitcher, Water, Dull Red, 2 7/8 In. 28.00
Plate, Embossed, Bust Of Washington, 13 Stars, 5 5/8 In. 65.00
Rattle & Whistle, Embossed For A Good Boy, C.1860, Tin, 6 1/2 In. 75.00
Rattle, Attached Whistle 15.00
Saltshaker, Cylinder Shape, Circular Foot, Handmade, 2 1/4 In. 27.00
Sconce, Candle, Crimped Pan & Top, Old Black Paint, 9 3/4 In. 85.00
Sconce, Punched, Hanging, 13 3/4 In. 250.00
Sugar Shaker, Handled, 4 In. 30.00
Tinderbox, Finger Handle, Striker, Flint & Wick, C.1830, 3 X 2 In. 130.00
Tinderbox, Snuffer Cover, Flint, Candle Top, Striker, Handled 235.00
Tray, Pin, Advertising, Republic Metalware Co., 2 X 2 1/2 In. 17.50
Tub, Bath, Baby, Painted 45.00
Washbasin 15.00

Tin, Mold, Candle, 12 Tube

Toby Jugs, Pearlware, Davenport; Pearlware, Yorkshire; Staffordshire

TOBACCO JAR, Figural, Black Boy, 5 1/2 In.	85.00
Figural, Black Girl, 5 1/2 In.	85.00
Figural, Jester	54.00
Figural, Man Smoking Cigar, Lid Is Feather In Hat, Marked	55.00
Figural, Mandarin, Papier-Mache	95.00 To 98.00
Figural, Sailor Comes Out Of Lid, Blue	115.00
Figural, Sea Captain	70.00
Girl, Golden Locks, Pink Turban	60.00
Marbleized Blues & Browns, Brass Frog, Porcelain, English, 4 In.	137.00
TOBACCO, TIN, see Store, Tin	

Toby jugs have been made since the seventeenth century.

TOBY JUG, see also Royal Doulton, Toby Jug

TOBY JUG, Colonial Man, Red Bowtie, Brown Hat, Occupied Japan	15.00
General MacArthur, Child's, Occupied Japan	35.00
Gold, Blue Blouse, White Hair, Occupied Japan, 2 1/4 In.	10.00
Indian, Occupied Japan, 3 In.	30.00
Pearlware, Davenport	*Illus* 250.00
Pearlware, Yorkshire	*Illus* 825.00
Seated Man, Willow Scenes, Staffordshire, 1825-35, 5 5/8 In.	325.00
Staffordshire	*Illus* 350.00
Tricorn, Smoking Pipe, Staffordshire, C.1780, 9 7/8 In.	355.00

Tole is painted tin. It is sometimes called japanned ware, pontypool, or toleware. Most 19th-century tole is painted with an orange-red or black blackground and multicolored decorations.

TOLE, see also Tin

TOLE, Bowl, Footed, Leaves, Flowers, Yellow, Black Ground, 3 In.	200.00
Box, Black Swag Design On Front & Sides, Yellow, 2 1/2 X 6 1/2 X 3 In.	165.00
Box, Document, American, 19th Century	*Illus* 260.00
Box, Document, Roses & Strawberries, 9 1/2 X 6 X 7 1/2 In.	585.00
Box, Hinged & Hasped Dome, Wire Loop, 1 7/8 X 2 7/8 X 1 3/4 In.	35.00
Box, Hinged, Multicolored Flowers, Green Leaves, 4 X 3 X 4 1/4 In.	18.00
Box, Shoeshine, Oval Handle, Iron Shoe Rest, Open Back For Brushes	50.00
Box, Wire Ring Handle, Rounded Hinged Cover, 6 1/4 X 3 X 3 In.	17.00
Bucket, Flowers On Black Ground, Tin, 9 3/8 X 6 In.	185.00
Caddy, Tea, White, Smoke Graining, Flowers, Blue, Red, Green, 5 3/4 In.	150.00
Candle Snuffer & Tray, Crosshatch Design, Gold Lines, Black	22.50
Canister, Cherries, Flowers, Red, Yellow, Green, Brown Ground, 8 In.	550.00
Canister, Tea, Flowers, Leaves, Red, Yellow, Black, Gold Ground, 5 In.	220.00

Tole, Sugar, American, 19th Century, Covered; Box, Document, American, 19th Century
(See Page 699)

Canister, Tea, Mirror Front, 19 1/4 In.	175.00
Chamberstick, Handle	10.00
Coffeepot, Urn Of Flowers, Strap Handle, Curved Spout, 10 In.	800.00
Container, Coffee, China Red, Coffee & Floral Design, 8 In.	30.00
Horn, Fish Peddler's, Original Japanning, C.1870, 13 3/4 In.	16.50
Jar, Hand-Painted Florals & Gold Panels, Cover, C.1870, 15 1/2 In.	175.00
Lamp, Kerosene, Original Shade	45.00
Lantern, Folding, Asphaltum, Mica Panes, Patent 1865, Folded 5 X 3 In.	130.00
Measure, Painted, Peck	15.00
Pitcher, Gold Panels, Florals, Folding Handle, Black, 13 1/2 In.	175.00
Snuffer, Candle, Tray, Dogwood Blossoms & Vining, Black Tin, 10 1/4 In.	85.00
Snuffer, Candle, Tray, Painted Design, Black Strippings, C.1840, 9 In.	50.00
Sugar, American, 19th Century, Covered .... *Illus*	300.00
Syrup, Painted Design	340.00
Teapot, Oval, Strap Handle, Fruit, Leaves, Red, Yellow, Green, 6 In.	950.00
Train, Child's, Engine, Passenger Cars, Red, Blue, C.1835, 12 1/2 In.	250.00
Tray, Bread, New England, 19th Century, Pierced, Hand Hold, 13 1/4 In.	200.00
Tray, Bread, Painted Designs, Japanned, 7 1/2 X 12 In.	55.00
Tray, Bread, Red, Yellow, Green, Black Ground, 12 In.	75.00
Tray, New England, Original Stenciling	650.00
Tray, Painted Design, Octagonal	125.00
Vase, Flowers & Scene, Hand-Painted, C.1800, French	50.00
TOM MIX, Badge, Decoder, 6 Gun, 1941	65.00
Badge, Star, With Tony	20.00
Bandana	57.00
Book, Scourge Of Paradise Valley, 1937	10.00
Card, Arcade, Set Of 5	20.00
Compass & Magnifier, Brass	20.00
Knife, Pocket, Ralston	32.00
Mirror, Pocket, Yankee Boy Play Clothes	35.00
Periscope	55.00
Pistol, Cap, Pluck	20.00
Ring, Ralston Straight Shooters	27.00
Ring, Slide Whistle	35.00
Spurs, Glow In The Dark	90.00
Telegraph Set, Red	95.00
Watch Fob, Gold Ore .... 25.00 To 38.00	
6-Shooter, Ralston Straight Shooter, Wooden	60.00

TOOL, see also Iron; Kitchen; Store; Tin; Wooden
TOOL, Adze, American Bowl, Short Handle, 3 1/2 In. 115.00
  Adze, American, Lipped 24.00
  Adze, Bowl, Impressed Heart On Curvature, Cutting Edge 3 1/2 In. 115.00
  Adze, Cooper's .... 17.00 To 20.00
  Adze, Handle Marked B & M R.R. 35.00
  Adze, Lipped, American, Spike 24.00
  Adze, Shipwright's, Lipped, Wooden Haft, Blade 5 In. 65.00
  Adze, Stirrup, Hand, Original Early Handle 95.00
  Anvil, Jeweler's, Brass, 3 In. 18.00
  Anvil, Jeweler's, 19th Century, Iron, 3 1/2 X 1 1/2 In. 20.00
  Anvil, Norn & Hardy, 14 Pound 60.00
  Anvil, Shoemaker's, Wooden 38.00
  Auger, Sugar Devil, Loosen Sugar In Barrels 125.00
  Ax Head, Winchester, Iron 45.00
  Ax, Double Bit Mortise, Pennsylvania, 19 1/2 In. 70.00
  Ax, Goosewing, Pennsylvania, D.Hofman 350.00
  Ax, Goosewing, Pennsylvania, D.Hofman, Lancaster, Pa., Blade 13 1/2 In. 375.00
  Ax, Goosewing, Signed Hibker, 4 Touchmarks, Blade 11 In. 275.00
  Ax, Ice, Straatsburg 30.00
  Ax, Ice, W.T.Wood & Co. 26.00
  Ax, Keen Kutter 15.00
  Ax, Marble's Arms 125.00
  Ax, Mortise, Double Bit, 19 1/2 In. 70.00
  Ax, Mortising, Double Bit, Wrought Iron, Original Handle, 12 In. 110.00
  Ax, Post Hole, H.Melling, Center Bit Mortising 60.00
  Ax, Post Hole, Signed I.Sener 72.00
  Ax, Tobacco, Cast Iron, Steel Blade, 18 1/2 In. 5.00
  Ax, Winchester, Goosewing 225.00
  Beader, Hand, Stanley, No. 66 .... 13.00
  Beader, Stanley, No. 66, 1 Cutter, 2 Fences 13.00
  Beam Brace, Blacksmith's, Iron, 18 In. 75.00
  Beam Brace, Blacksmith's, 21 In. 98.00
  Beater, Carpet, Wicker 20.00
  Bench, Cobbler's, Assortment Of Tools 295.00
  Bench, Cobbler's, High Back, 2 Drawers, Tools, 56 X 24 In. 875.00
  Bevel Square, Brass Lever To Secure Blade, Walnut, Stanley 9.00
  Bit, Auger, Russell & Jennings, 1855, No.100, Boxed 115.00
  Blowtorch, Brass 10.50
  Bolt Header, Blacksmith's, Hand-Forged Iron, 8 1/2 In. 10.00
  Bootjack, Wood Base, Cast-Iron Frame, Carpeted Top 35.00
  Box, Embossed The Superior, Cast Iron 30.00
  Brace & Bit, Keen Kutter .... 25.00 To 35.00
  Brace & Bit, Winchester 50.00
  Brace, Cage Head, Chamfered Iron Frame, Two Support, 15 1/2 In. 295.00
  Brace, Carpenter's, Wood & Brass 50.00
  Brace, Chairmaker's, Missing Ferrule 150.00
  Brace, Corner, Miller's Falls, Patent Feb. 18, 1890 .... 30.00
  Brace, F.W.Hens 12.00
  Brace, Fixed Quill Type Bit, Heavy Brass Ferrule 145.00
  Brace, Inlaid Ebony, Brass Frame 400.00
  Brace, Lignum Vitae Head, Sheffield, All Wood 135.00
  Brace, Octagonal Pewter Ferrule, Fixed Spoon Bit, Maple 250.00
  Brace, Ogee Styling On Top & Bottom, 4 Bit Pads, Maple 650.00
  Brace, Quill Bit, Sheffield, No. 119 .... 110.00
  Brace, Sheffield, Quill Bit, Lignum Head, No.119 .... 110.00
  Brace, Wagon Builder's, Pumpkin Head, Wrought-Iron Wing Nut 45.00
  Brace, Wood, Brass Ferrule, Fixed Quill, All Wood 145.00
  Brace, Wrought Iron, 4 In.Head, 34 In. 160.00
  Branding Iron, Bar, Hand-Forged Iron 21.00
  Brass Bit, Winchester, Wooden Handle, Cast-Iron Bits 65.00
  Broadax, American, C.1880, Old Blue Paint 95.00

Broadax, Barton, Rochester, N.Y., 1832, Original Paint	40.00
Broadax, Blade Marked, Simmons Cohoes, N.Y.	45.00
Broadax, Goosewing, Cooper's, Hand-Forged Iron, 34 In.	135.00
Broadax, Goosewing, Pennsylvania	325.00
Broadax, Keen Kutter	650.00
Broadax, Leather Whip, Braided Rawhide	35.00
Broadax, Wooden Handle, 6 X 10 1/4 In.	65.00
Broom, Splintered Birch, 19th Century, New York, 47 In.	110.00
Bruzz, Wheelwright's, W.Marples & Sons, Squares Axle Holes In Hubs	22.00
Cabinet, Watchmaker's, Oak, 5 X 16 1/2 In.	115.00
Calipers, Artist's, Glick's Masterstroke, Wooden, 14 In.	30.00
Calipers, Dancing Legs, Black Finish, 2 1/4 In.	45.00
Calipers, Dated 1880, Beech	110.00
Calipers, Straight Leg, Spring Loader, 9 1/2 In.	5.00
Carder, Wool, Tin Teeth, C.1890, Wooden, 11 In., Pair	12.50
Carpet Beater, Dated October 4, 1927, Batwing Shape, Wooden	13.50
Carpet Beater, Wicker	18.00
Chipper, Ice, Dated 1884, Turned Wood Handle	15.00
Chisel, Ice, Gifford	18.00
Chisel, Keen Kutter	3.00
Chisel, Splitting, Narrow	22.00
Chisel, Starting, Double Ended	27.00
Cigar Maker, Knife, Trimming Tool, Mold, Cast-Iron Press	75.00
Clamp, Austin & Eddy, 1860, Cabinet, Iron & Wood	67.50
Clamp, Marked R.Bliss Mfg. Co., Pawtucket, R.I., Jaws 6 In.	16.50
Clamp, W.J.Wood, Valley Forge, R.I., Jaws 7 In.	18.50
Compass, Cooper's, Brass Ferule, Closed, 16 In.	16.50
Compass, S.S.Wilson, Button	8.00
Cranberry Picker, 14 X 22 In.	145.00
Croze, Cooper's	35.00
Croze, Half Moon, Maple, 23 In.	75.00
Cutter, Buttonhole, Mechanical, Adjustable, Dated 1860, Iron & Brass	120.00
Cutter, Buttonhole, 18th Century, Hand-Forged Steel Blade, 3 In.	75.00
Cutter, Sole, Cobbler's, Cast Iron, 10 1/2 In.	15.00
Cutter, Washer, Leather	15.00
Cutting, Sliding Scale, Crawford Salerside, Pistol Grip	85.00
Dehorner, Cattle, Cast Iron	25.00
Dehorner, Keen Kutter, Cast Iron	25.00
Detector, Counterfeit Coin, Berrian Co., N.Y., , 1877	185.00
Die, Button, U.S.Navy Officer's, Eagle Over Anchor, 3/4 In.Diam.	74.50
Digger, Hole, Keen Kutter	25.00
Dividers, Hand-Forged, Railroad, 28 In.	125.00
Dividers, Sailmaker's, Brass Tightener Screw, C.1870, Pine	50.00
Draftsman's Set, Original Tools & Case, Dated 1899	35.00
Drawshave, Maple Handles, Brass Ferrules, 15 1/2 In.	15.00
Drill, Breast, Steel Pillar, Bronze Bevel Gears, Gear 5 3/4 In.Diam.	155.00
Drill, Gang, Grand Rapid Sash Pulley Co., To Mortise Sash Weight	65.00
Drill, Pump, Up-And-Down, Brass Flywheel, Adjustable Chuck	78.00
Ember Carrier, Iron Pan, Diamond Pattern, Wood Handle, Spring Pull Lift	350.00
Finger Stretcher, Pianist's, Mahogany & Brass	68.00
Finger, Spinning Wheel, Hand-Carved, Pine	10.00
Flattener, Cork, Wooden Base, Iron Handle & Teeth, 3 X 10 1/2 In.	12.00
Flax Hackle	20.00
Flax Wheel, 15 X 39 In.	175.00
Forge & Blower, Champion, Cast Iron, 14 X 19 In.	165.00
Forge, Blacksmith's, Blower, Anvil, Drill Press, & Vise, 1911	950.00
Frame, Quilting, Wooden, Round	55.00
Froe & Mallet, Basket Maker's	55.00
Froe, Handle, Cast Iron	12.00
Gauge, Double Sided, Calibrated Slide Bar, Maple	55.00
Gauge, Marking, Brass & Rosewood	24.00
Gauge, Mortise, Patent Sept. 5, '76, Solid Brass	185.00
Gauge, Sliding, Pair	20.00

Gauge, Spider, Coachman's, Oak Main Stem	10.00
Grater, Soup, Fels Naphtha Stamped On Handle, 9 In.	3.50
Grinder, Clamp Style, Cleveland Tool & Supply	12.50
Hacksaw, Iron, Wood Handle	40.00
Hammer-Hatchet, Pulling Claws	75.00
Hammer, Double Claw, Patent Date Nov. 4, 1902	185.00
Hammer, Log Marking, Diamond 6	145.00
Hammer, Slide, Nail Puller, Keen Kutter, Cast Iron	32.00
Hammer, Tinner's	16.00
Hammer, Winchester	70.00
Hatchet, Butchering, Farmer's, Small	10.00
Hatchet, Dated 1842	75.00
Hatchet, Ice	32.00
Hatchet, Produce, Kenn Kutter	30.00
Hatchet, Shingle	28.00
Hatchet, Tobacco, Cast-Iron Round Eye, Steel Blade, 18 1/2 In.	5.00
Hatchet, Winchester, Nail Puller, Single Bite	17.00
Hide Pounder, Wooden, 21 3/4 In.	35.00
Hoe, Cultivating, Wooden, 67 In.	50.00
Hoe, Winchester	40.00
Hydrometer, Dated 1910, Wooden Case	12.00
Ice Harvesting, Ringed 2-Prong Fork Bar	24.00
Inshave, Cooper's, 4 1/2 In. Radius Cutter, Iron & Wood, 20 In.	110.00
Iron, Branding, Initials CMs, HANDLE, 27 IN.	20.00
Iron, Branding, Letter R	20.00
Iron, Polishing, Pat.1848	75.00
Jack, Automobile, Model T Ford	27.50
Jack, Conestoga Wagon, Wood & Cast Iron	165.00
Jack, Wagon, 7-Stage Life, Cast Iron, 29 1/2 In.	25.00
Jagging Wheel, Hearts & Geometric Designs, Whale Ivory, 5 5/8 In.	800.00
Jointer, Razee, B.W.Smith, Mahogany, 3 X 17 In.	85.00
Key, Rope Bed, Wooden, Pair	42.00
Knife, Chamfer, Brass Stop, 19 In.	20.00
Knife, Draw, Cooper's	35.00
Knife, Draw, Folding Handle	27.50
Knife, Draw, Folding, Fulton	30.00
Knife, Draw, Mast, J.M.Sheffield, Stamford, Ct., 26 In.	28.00
Knocker, Snow, Hand-Forged Iron, Looped Handle, 7 3/4 In.	35.00
Knocker, Snow, Hand-Forged Iron, Wooden Shaft, 8 1/2 In.	30.00
Ladle, Plumber's, Cast Iron	7.00
Level, Baker McMillen Co., Akron, Ohio, Mahogany Block, 12 In.	15.00
Level, Brass Fittings, Top, Bottom, & Side Plates, Mahogany, 15 1/4 In.	75.00
Level, Carpenter's, Diston & Morse, 12 In.	15.00
Level, Carpenter's, Iron Handle	25.00
Level, Davis, 1883, Iron, 19 1/2 In.	65.00
Level, E.M.Chapen, 16 In.	20.00
Level, Jennings, Cast Iron, 24 In.	45.00
Level, Keen Kutter	25.00
Level, P.H.Vogel Mfg.Co., New Britain, Conn., Cast Aluminum, 24 In.	50.00
Level, Stanley, Brass Ends	8.00
Level, Stanley, Cast Iron, 24 In.	35.00
Level, Stanley, No.3, 24 In.	12.00
Level, Stanley, No.93, Brassbound Mahogany, 28 In.	45.00
Level, Stanley, Steel, 18 In.	40.00
Level, Stanley, 30 In.	25.00
Level, Stratton Bros., Brass Trim, Mahogany	75.00
Level, Stratton Bros., Eagle Trade Mark, Mahogany, 28 In.	25.00
Level, Surveyor's, Brass, D & E	75.00
Level, Surveyor's, Wooden Dovetailed Box	75.00
Level, Williamsburg, Steel, 12 In.	70.00
Level, Winchester	50.00
Log Marker, Marked P & M	45.00
Log Roller, Twisted Shaft, Ring Handle	90.00

Machine, Broom Making 350.00
Mallet, Cabinetmaker's, Burl, 12 X 4 In. 60.00
Mallet, Carpenter's, Lignum, Oak Handle 8.00
Mallet, Saddlemaker's, Round-Headed, Hang-Up Thong, 10 3/4 In. 40.00
Marking, Leather, Double Brass Wheeled, Wooden Handle, 4 1/4 In. 8.50
Marking, Letters A To Z, George Andes, Flat Box, 3 5/8 X 24 In. 48.00
Measuregraph, Measures Material 45.00
Measuring Gauge, Coachmaker's, Rosewood, Brass Slides, Thumb Screws 65.00
Miter Template, Sash, E.Preston & Sons, Brass, 6 In. 20.00
Multiplane, Stanley, No.45 .... 95.00
Multiplane, Stanley, No.55 .... 265.00
Nail Puller, Wrought Iron, 24 1/4 In. 12.00
Niddy-Noddy, Birch, 17 3/4 In. 55.00
Opener, Box, Simmons 8.00
Padlock, Keen Kutter, Brass 75.00
Picker, Huckleberry, 1 Piece 128.00
Pincer, Cobbler's 9.00
Pitchfork, Winchester 50.00
Plane, A.Kelly & Co., Center Bead 12.00
Plane, A.Kelly & Co., Center Bead, Ashfield, Mass., 3/16 In. 12.00
Plane, Andruss, Single, 2 In.Bead, Boxed 14.00
Plane, Bead, Andruss, Single Boxed, 1 In. 14.00
Plane, Bead, Boxwood Insert, Signed V.F.Scher, Maple 45.00
Plane, Bead, Sargent & Co., Double Boxed, 1/2 In. 10.00
Plane, Block, Moulson Bros., 24 In. 15.00
Plane, Cabinet Maker's, Sargent, Adjustable Front Sole Plate 32.00
Plane, Cabinet Maker's, Stanley, Block, Adjustable Throat 1050.00
Plane, Cabinet Maker's, Stanley, 3 3/4 X 1 1/2 In. 20.00
Plane, Conway Tool Co., Conway Mass., No.15, Hollow, 1850-51 .... 13.00
Plane, Cooper's, Sun, Barton, Rochester 85.00
Plane, Dado, Thos. L.Appleton, Boston, Brass Side-Mounted Stop 10.00
Plane, E.Safford, Albany, Round, 1 1/4 In., Iron 13.00
Plane, Fillaster, No.3061 .... 125.00
Plane, G.Ashley, Little Falls, No.18, Hollow 24.00
Plane, Gardner & Murdock, Boston, 1825-45 .... 40.00
Plane, Geo.Burnham, Jr., Amherst, Mass, 1849-53 .... 22.00
Plane, Grooving Match, Sandusky 10.00
Plane, Hand, Signed, Brass Frame, Ebony Center 230.00
Plane, Keen Kutter 25.00
Plane, L & I J White, Buffalo, No.16, Round 15.00
Plane, M.Copeland, Closed Handled, Tongue Match, C.1831, 11 3/8 In. 13.00
Plane, M.Copeland, Tongue Match, Closed Handle, 1831, 11 3/8 In. 13.00
Plane, Molding, Addison, Star & Sunburst Mark 18.00
Plane, Molding, Codified Core Type, S. & H.Hills, Amherst, Mass. 20.00
Plane, Molding, J.Kellogg & Co., Jack Handled, C.1849, 16 In. 65.00
Plane, Molding, J.MaCauly, Carved Blade, Wooden, 9 1/2 In. 16.00
Plane, Molding, P.B.Rider 32.00
Plane, Molding, Stanley, No.55, Original Cutters & Box 200.00
Plane, Molding, Wooden, Set Of 7 .... 70.00
Plane, Moulson Bros., Screw-Arm Plow, 8 Irons, Boxwood 325.00
Plane, P.B.Rider, Complex Molding, Single Boxing 32.00
Plane, Pill Box Maker's, For Windings To Form Box Sides 475.00
Plane, Plow, Boxwood Screw Arms, Marked Gladwin & Appleton, Boston 450.00
Plane, Plow, C.1820, Signed T.Tileston, Boston, Adjustable Arms 110.00
Plane, Plow, Depth Adjustment, Ohio Tool Co., Handled, Boxwood 235.00
Plane, Plow, Slide Arm, Wood, W.D.Wiley 65.00
Plane, Pump, Double Dowel Handles, Maple, 9 1/2 In. 30.00
Plane, Robert Wooding, London, Hollow, 7/8 In. 600.00
Plane, Round, L. & I.J.White, Buffalo, No.16 .... 15.00
Plane, Round, Safford, Albany, 1813-21, Plane 1 1/4 In. 13.00
Plane, Round, Worrall Patent Multiform Plane Co. 48.00
Plane, Rounding, Ram's Horn Wing Bolt, 18th Century, Pine, 15 1/2 In. 60.00
Plane, S & H Hills, Amherst Mass., Modified Core, 1829-30 .... 20.00

Plane, Sargent & Co., No.7, Hollow	9.00
Plane, Shipmaker's, Coffin Shape, Exotic Wood	58.00
Plane, Skewed Rabbet, Union Factory, H.Chapin, Chip Ejection Cut-Out	10.00
Plane, Slide Arm, Casey Kitchel & Co., Boxwood Wedges, 11 In. Arms	75.00
Plane, Slide Arm, W.D.Wiley, Captive Wedges	65.00
Plane, Spill, Blade Set At Hard Angle, Fruitwood, 1 3/4 X 2 1/4 X 6 In.	85.00
Plane, Splint, Wrought Hardware, Cherry, 3 1/2 X 7 In.	150.00
Plane, Stanley, No.2, Smooth	125.00
Plane, Stanley, No.5, 13 1/2 In.	40.00
Plane, Stanley, No.20, Circular	75.00
Plane, Stanley, No.20, Circular, Original Box	125.00
Plane, Stanley, No.28, Fore, Eagle Trademark	22.00
Plane, Stanley, No.40	25.00
Plane, Stanley, No.45, 8 Blades	55.00
Plane, Stanley, No.46, Combination, 10 Cutters, Wooden Box	100.00
Plane, Stanley, No.48	30.00
Plane, Stanley, No.51, Draw	12.00
Plane, Stanley, No.55, Combination, 4 Boxes Of Cutters	255.00
Plane, Stanley, No.64, Butcher Block	950.00
Plane, Stanley, No.78	37.50
Plane, Stanley, No.90, Rabbet, 4 In.Long	30.00
Plane, Stanley, No.130	20.00
Plane, Stanley, No.193, Fiberboard, Attachments & Cutters	115.00
Plane, Stanley, No.278, Rabbet & Fillister, With Fence, Japanned	160.00
Plane, Stanley, No.605, Bedrock	60.00
Plane, Stanley, 1886, 6 In.	16.00
Plane, Sun, Cooper's, Marked Mottram Cast Steel, Yellow Birch, 17 In.	95.00
Plane, Thomas Grant, New York, Panel Raising	325.00
Plane, Thumb, Coffin Shape, Pistol Grip, Beech, 1 X 1 3/8 In.	98.00
Plane, Worrall Patent, Multiform, No Handle	48.00
Planter, Corn, Original Green Paint, Patented 1870, Wood, Iron, & Tin	70.00
Planter, Potato, 1885, Wooden Handle, Cast Iron	15.00
Pliers, Fence, Keen Kutter	17.00 To 25.00
Pliers, Winchester	24.00
Plow Plane, Lamb & Brownell, New Bedford, Mass., 6 Irons	125.00
Plow, Bookbinder's, Oak Slides, Dark Beech, 24 In.	210.00
Plumb Bob, Cast Iron, 2 3/4 In.	3.00
Plumb Bob, Steel Point, Brass, 1 X 5 1/4 In.	22.00
Plumb Bob, Steel Tip, Brass, 6 In.	45.00
Plumb Bob, 8 Recess Circles, Cast Iron, 2 3/4 In.	3.00
Press, Cork, Hunting Dog, Cast Iron	52.00
Pricker & Stamp, Cracker, Oval Pattern, Handle, 1 1/2 X 2 1/2 In.	165.00
Printing Press, Hand, Galley Tray, Inking Stone, Rollers, C.1850	375.00
Pulley, Well	22.50
Pump Drill, Brass Flywheel, Signed W.D., 12 X 9 In.	95.00
Pump, Bicycle, Brass	6.00
Punch, For Cutwork, Wooden Tube, 2 1/2 In.	12.50
Punch, Leather, Adjustable, 6 Size, Marked Osborne	5.00
Rabbet, Stanley, No.79, Right & Left	20.00
Rake, Blueberry, Wood & Metal	25.00
Rake, Ole Olson Label, Wooden	45.00
Rake, Oyster, Vertical & Horizontal Bars, Hand-Forged Iron, 19 In.	85.00
Ratchet, Mechanic's, 10 1/2 In.	12.00
Rattle, Police & Fire, Oak	85.00
Router, Coachmaker's, Hand-Forged Iron, 9 1/2 In.	40.00
Router, Double Yoke	210.00
Router, Granny's Tooth, Signed R.F.Matthews, 1825, Beech, 6 In.Wide	49.00
Router, Quirk	34.00
Router, Stanley, No.71	18.00
Rule & Level, Stanley, Carpenter's, 1890, Cherry Wood	55.00
Rule, E.Smith, Illinois, Double Member Slide, Boxwood, 24 In.	85.00
Rule, Keen Kutter, Folding, Brass Ends, 24 In.	12.00
Rule, L.C. Stephens & Co., No.66, Lumberman's, Boxwood, 24 In.	60.00

Rule, Luftkin, No.781, Folding, 24 In. 35.00
Rule, Luftkin, 4-Fold, Brass Trim, Boxwood, 36 In. 12.00
Rule, Stanley, Folding, Boxwood, 24 In. 20.00
Rule, Stanley, Folding, No.78 1/2, 24 In. 55.00
Rule, Stanley, Folding, Wood & Brass, 24 In. 18.00
Rule, Stanley, No. 18, 2-Fold, Brass Trim, Boxwood, 24 In. 20.00
Rule, Stanley, No.36, Caliper, 2-Fold, Heart Trademark, Brass Trim 8.00
Rule, Stanley, No.63, Folding, Brass Trim, Boxwood 16.50
Rule, Starrett, Folding, Bronze, 3/4 X 24 In. 35.00
Rule, Starrett, Folding, Marked, 2 Feet 24.00
Rule, 2-Fold, Wood & Brass 15.00
Rule, 4-Fold, Brass Trim, Boxwood, Patd.12-3-18, 36 In. 12.00
Rule, 4-Fold, German Silver & Ivory Trim, 24 In. 295.00
Rule, 4-Fold, Ivory With German Silver, 24 In. 295.00
Saw, Carpenter's, Iron Handle 25.00
Saw, Dado, Adjustable, Maple, 7 3/4 X 2 3/4 In. 35.00
Saw, Fret, Sorrento Wood Carving Co., Boston, Mahogany, 22 In. 89.00
Saw, Hack, Wrought-Iron, Wooden Handle 40.00
Saw, Hand, Winchester, 18 In. 45.00
Saw, Ice 28.00
Saw, Jeweler's, Blades, Files, Pliers, Hammer 5.00
Saw, Jig, Clamp-On, Gilt Design, Trump Bros., Delaware 89.00
Saw, Keen Kutter 15.00
Saw, Keyhole, Brass Handle, 16 1/4 In. 35.00
Saw, Meat, Tension Blade, Wood Frame 25.00
Scissors, Horse Mane 8.00
Scissors, Keen Kutter, 12 In. 20.00
Scraper, Dough, Hand-Forged 39.00
Scraper, Stanley, No.12, Veneer, C.1886, Rosewood Handle 45.00
Scraper, Stanley, No.80, Cabinet 15.00
Scraper, Winchester, Cabinet 65.00
Screwdriver, Oak Handled, Brass Ferrule, 15 In. 8.00
Screwdriver, Winchester, Brass Ferule 18.00
Scribe, Ebony, Bushnell, Adjustable 65.00
Scribe, Encased In Brass, Ebony & Rosewood 85.00
Scribe, Rosewood, Panel 35.00
Scribe, Round Barrel End, Stemmed, Tiger Maple, 14 In. 35.00
Scribe, Thumb Crotch Grip, Black Walnut, 13 1/4 In. 60.00
Scribe, Wooden, Brass Slide, 9 In. 7.00
Seismograph, Revolving Drum, Stylus, Glass & Wood Case, 14 X 8 In. 50.00
Shave, Maple Handles, Brass, 2 In. Cutter 65.00
Shave, Mast, Rochester, N.Y., Tang Handles, 17 In. 12.00
Shave, Rabbet, Double Curved Walnut Handles, Brass Blade Cover 1125.00
Shave, Stanley, No.51, 10 In. 22.00
Shears, Brush Maker's, Bench Mounted, J.Brombacher, N.Y. 90.00
Shears, Mule 3.00
Shears, Sardine Can, Pair 8.00
Shears, Sheep, Keen Kutter 17.00
Shucker, Oyster, Beehive Shaped Burl Block, 5 1/2 In. 95.00
Shuttle, Net Mending, Set Of 8 .... 20.00
Shuttle, Tatting, Celluloid 10.00
Sickle, Barley, Hand-Forged Iron, 18th Century, Signed W.Fox 25.00
Slide Rule, Keuffel & Esser Co., Ivory, Leather Case 45.00
Slitting, Leather, Adjustments For Thickness & Angle, Mahogany & Brass 40.00
Smoother, Compass Bottom, Coffin Shape, Boxwood, 1 3/8 X 3 1/2 In. 95.00
Snip, Tin, Keen Kutter 20.00
Spade, Tile 22.00
Spirit Level, Engineer's, Brass, Polished, 5 In. 45.00
Splitter, Rein, Cast Iron 12.00
Spoke Shave, Stanley, No.51 .... 10.00 To 15.00
Spoke Shave, W-91 .... 95.00
Square, Carpenter's, Brass Inlay, Wood Handled 12.00
Square, Carpenter's, Eagle Square Mfg. Co., Iron, 24 X 17 In. 15.00

Square, Carpenter's, Hand, Brass Inserts In Handle	8.50
Staking Set, Jeweler's, 97 Punches, 18 Stumps, C.1900, Wooden Case	125.00
Stamp, Fabric, Lion Head, Tail Over Back, Wooden, 5 X 6 1/4 In.	48.00
Stocking Float, Gunsmith's, Shaping Stock, 5/8 In. Half Round	85.00
Straight Edge, Carpenter's, Rosewood, 15 In.	12.50
Stretcher, Bunion, Cast Iron	7.50
Stretcher, Carpet, Victor, 1889	80.00
Stretcher, Muskrat	8.00
Stretcher, Wire, Cast Iron	25.00
Sun Plane, Cooper's, Metal Throat Plate On Sole, D.R.Barton, N.Y., 1822	95.00
Sundial & Compass, A.Abraham Co., Liverpool, 19th Century .... Illus	800.00
Swift, Yarn, Table Clamp	55.00
Tape Loom, Cut-Out Crests, Reddish-Brown Stain, Poplar, 20 1/2 In.	310.00
Tape, Surveyor's, Winding, Leather Cased, England, 4 In.	25.00
Tongs, Blacksmith's, Gold Header	7.50
Tongs, Ember, Hand-Forged, Jointed Scissor Type	290.00
Tongs, Ice, Straatsburg	26.00
Torch, Jeweler's, Brass Wick Cap & Pick, Marked L.K., Copper, 8 In.	60.00
Traveler, Wheelwright's, Center Star Design, Wrought Iron	49.00
Trencher, Crushing Grain, Pine	85.00
Trencher, Pine, Tab Handles, 18th Century, 29 X 13 In.	165.00
Tripod, Warner & Swasey, 1898, Leather Case	200.00
Trowel, Edging, Brass	9.00
Universal Spoke Shave, Straight Bottom, Stanley, No. 67,	32.00
Vise, Harness Maker's, Stitching, In Slab Of Maple, Pine, 27 In.	30.00
Vise, Harness Maker's, Wooden, 34 In.	40.00
Wantage Rod, Cooper's, Brass, Gaskell & Chambers, 1/4 X 1/4 X 32 In.	72.00
Wash Stick, Carved Handle, Open Box End, Knob Top, 18 In.	85.00
Weaner & Poke, Calf, 18th Century, Cast-Iron Teeth, Wooden	70.00
Weaner, Calf, Daisy, Spikes, Cast Iron	9.50
Wheel, Jagging, Whalebone, Hearts, Circles, & Scrolls, 7 1/4 In.	750.00
Winder, String, Red Finish, Bentwood	50.00 To 55.00
Winder, Yarn, Table Model, Handmade	65.00
Witchet, Adjustable Rounder & Wood Screws, Marples & Sons, Boxwood	175.00
Witchet, Handmade, 18th Century, Oak & Brass	325.00
Wrench, Alligator, Pipe, Dated 1898, 15 1/4 In.	10.00
Wrench, Crescent, Crestoloy, 15 In.	15.00
Wrench, Crescent, Keen Kutter, Shapleigh's, 10 In.	15.00
Wrench, Double Open End S	37.50
Wrench, Ford Script, Cast Iron	3.50
Wrench, Hub, Automobile	6.00

Tool, Sundial & Compass, A.Abraham Co., Liverpool, 19th Century

Wrench, Keen Kutter, Adjustable	18.00
Wrench, Monkey, Ford	10.00
Wrench, Monkey, Wooden Facing On Handle, 10 In.	5.00
Wrench, Pipe, Keen Kutter, Cast Iron	25.00
Wrench, Tighten Rope Beds, Hand-Whittled Jaw, Pine, 15 X 14 1/4 In.	20.00
Wrench, Wagon, 2-Ended, Hand-Forged Iron, 18 In.	14.50
Yardstick, Rosewood & Ivory, Inlaid Dots, 19th Century	50.00
Yardstick, Sliding, Keen Kutter, 1948	6.50

Toothpick holders are sometimes called toothpicks by collectors. The variously shaped containers made to hold the small wooden toothpicks are of glass, china, or metal. Most of the toothpicks are Victorian.

TOOTHPICK, see also other categories such as Bisque; Slag; etc.

TOOTHPICK, Beveled Star, Clear	25.00
Birchbark, Irregular Shape, Silver Plated, W.Rogers, 2 1/2 In.	28.00
Blue Opalescent, Hobnail	40.00
Boot, Clear Glass, 6 1/4 In.	6.00
Brazilian, Clear	25.00
Columned Thumbprint, Clear With Gold	30.00
Cranberry, Vaseline Spatter, Frosted Leaf Mold	140.00
Figural, Cat & Top Hat, Glass	65.00
Figural, Dog Has Paw On Bone, By Basket	78.00
Figural, Frog, Bisque	12.00
Figural, Indian, Art Nouveau, Metal	28.00
Figural, Rabbit Carrying Basket, Glass, Blue	45.00
Gold Hexagon Star, Clear	26.00
Gold On Panels, Clear	35.00
Illinois, Clear With Gold	30.00
Leaf Mold, Cranberry & Vaseline	125.00
Manhattan, Clear With Gold	35.00
Ruffled Top, Gilding, Coralene Design, Jeweled	125.00
Stump, The Garden Of Gods, 1909	25.00
Take Your Pick, Silver Plate, 2-Handled	35.00
Top Hat Shape, Samurai Warrior Seated, Hand-Painted	95.00
Vermont, Green With Gold	45.00
White Enameled Figure, Footed, Oblong, Silver Plated	95.00

Tortoiseshell glass was made during the 1800s and after by the Sandwich Glass Works of Massachusetts and some firms in Germany. Tortoiseshell glass has been reproduced.

TORTOISESHELL GLASS, Tumbler, 3 3/4 In.	75.00

TORTOISESHELL, Box, Gold Shield Center, Mother-Of-Pearl Lines, 5 1/2 X 2 In.	295.00
Comb, Butterfly Wing Shape, Rhinestones & Flowers	12.00
Comb, Mantilla, Hand-Carved, Large	98.00
Comb, Mustache, Gold Filled Case, Hanging Loop, C.1920, 3 In.	65.00
Glass, Vase, Urn Shaped, Amber & Blue Handles, 7 1/2 In., Pair	570.00
Holder, Cigar	12.50
Plaque, Gold Design, 10 In.	250.00
Tea Caddy, George III, C.1790, Ivory Inlaid, 8 3/4 In.	990.00

TOY, Adding Machine, Add Up To 9999, Wolverine, Tin, 9 X 2 In.	20.00
Adding Machine, Wolverine	15.00
Adding Machine, Wolverine, Tin	6.50
Aeroswing, Windup, Chein	185.00
African Mailman, Ostrich Pulls Black Man, Yellow Cart, Lehmann, Tin	275.00
Airmail Hangar, Acrobatic Airplane & Dirigible, Marx, 19 In.	250.00
Airplane Set, Tootsietoy No.5698, Boxed	35.00
Airplane, Autogyro, Tootsietoy, Silver	25.00
Airplane, DV4, Metal, 17 1/2 In.Wide	30.00
Airplane, Girard, 1930	150.00
Airplane, Kingsbury, 1930	125.00
Airplane, Lindy, Hubley, Wing Span 10 In.	450.00

Toy, Army Tank, German, 20th
Century, Painted Tin

Toy, Beat-It The Komikal Kop, Clockwork,
Marx, Lithographed Tin

Airplane, Red, Iron, Miniature Anvil, 4 In.	20.00
Airplane, Spirit Of St.Louis Style, Tin, Huge Wheels	69.00
Airplane, 2 Motors, World War II, Red Wings, 15 1/2 In.	45.00
Alarm Clock, Bugs Bunny, Animated	165.00
Alps Old Time Car, Battery	95.00
Ambulance, Militaire Service De Sante, Peugeot, Tin, Windup	100.00
Amos N Andy, Open Air Taxi, Tin	325.00 To 450.00
Anti-Aircraft Armored Car, Battery, 13 In.Long	25.00
Army Cycle, Marx, Windup	38.00
Army Tank, German, 20th Century, Painted Tin .... *Illus*	175.00
Baby, Crawling, Celluloid, Key Wind	14.00
Badge, Junior Fire Chief, Tootsietoy	5.00
Badge, Shield G-Man, Club	20.00
Balky Mule, Marx, Windup	35.00
Band, Li'l Abner, Dogpatch	375.00
Band, Monkey, 6 Musicians, Leader, Stand, Marked Germany, 5 In., 8 Piece	160.00
Barbershop, Animal, Windup, Marx	40.00
Barnacle Bill, Windup	185.00
Barney Google & Sparkplug, Schoenhut, 1922, Boxed	975.00
Bartender, Charlie Weaver, Battery Operated, Boxed	45.00
Basset Hound, Blue Collar, Squeaker, Jointed Head, 1960s, 11 1/2 X 7 In.	75.00
Battleship, Slush Metal, Tootsietoy, 5 1/2 In.	15.00
Bazooka, Bob Burns	50.00
Beagle, Puppy, Jointed Head, Sitting, Red Collar, 4 1/2 In.	40.00
Bear, Alarm Rings, Bear Raises Up, Yawns, Windup	38.00
Bear, Balancing On Bicycle, Legs Peddle Bike, C.1800, Tin	75.00
Bear, Balloon Blowing, Battery	50.00
Bear, Beating Drum	25.00
Bear, Boxing, Battery Operated	135.00
Bear, Clockwork Windup, C.1915, 12 In.	265.00
Bear, Cryer, Steiff, 13 In.	95.00
Bear, Mechanical, Brown Fun, Key Wind, Head Moves Side To Side, 6 In.	15.00
Bear, On Wheels, 20 X 11 1/2 In.	250.00
Bear, Papa, Smoking, Battery	50.00
Bear, Roller Skating, Windup, Box	225.00
Bear, Smokes & Walks, Battery Operated	25.00
Bear, Twist & Turn, Papier-Mache, 6 X 4 In.	65.00
Beat-It The Komikal Kop, Clockwork, Marx, Lithographed Tin .... *Illus*	250.00
Bed, Doll, Brass, 24 In.	65.00
Bed, Doll, High Poster, Rope, Walnut, C.1820, 12 3/4 X 17 X 18 In.	175.00
Bed, Doll, Red, White Hand-Stitched Quilt, Mahogany, 11 1/2 X 7 1/2 In.	50.00
Bed, Doll, Spool, Ash, 24 X 15 X 13 In.	50.00
Bed, Doll, Springs, Brass, 13 In.	150.00

Bed, Doll, Tester, Beaded Top, Wooden, 20 X 16 X 18 In. 125.00
Bed, Doll, Victorian, Walnut .... 175.00 To 395.00
Bed, Doll, White, Wood, 15 1/2 X 9 In. 35.00
Bed, Doll, Wicker, Satin Lined, Pillows, C.1935, Germany, 10 1/2 X 16 In. 30.00
Bed, Doll, Wire Mesh Springs, Folding, 1890s, White, 9 X 20 In. 40.00
Beebop Jigger, Boxed, Marx 165.00
Beetle, Windup, Lehmann 80.00
Betty, Windup, Lindstrom, Tin 65.00
     TOY, BICYCLE, see Bicycle
Bird, Flying, Lehmann, Windup 475.00
Black Boy On Tricycle, Ives, Clockwork 825.00
Blocks, Puzzle, Lithographed Paper, Large, Set .... *Illus* 250.00
Blocks, Wood, Baseball Lithograph, Boxed 95.00
Blushing Willy, Battery Operated, Boxed 65.00
Boat, Candle Operated, Marx, Pt-10, 1941, 10 In. 50.00
Boat, Gun, Friction, White, Gold, Green, Red, Tin, 10 X 4 X 3 In. 125.00
Boat, Pontoon, Chein 20.00
Boat, Speed, Tin, Chein, Windup, 8 1/2 In. 10.00
Bomb, Cap, Yellow Kid 50.00
Bowler Andy Mill, 4-Story Tower, Glass Marbles, Tin, 4 X 6 1/2 In. 110.00
Boy On Trapeze, Windup, Signed Tik-Tak, 11 In. .... 69.00 To 125.00
Boy On Tricycle, Bell Ringer, Windup 265.00
Boy, Somersaults Over Bars, Windup, Celluloid, 6 In. 155.00
Bronco, Bucking, Lehmann 485.00
Buckboard, Yellow Striping, Green & Red Paint 495.00
Bucking Bronco, Windup, Tin, Lehmann 450.00
Buddy L, Truck, Ice Cream 50.00
Buggy, Cast Iron, 3 In. 25.00
Buggy, Doll, Metal Wheels, Seat & Back Cloth Covered, 12 X 6 X 12 In. 150.00
Buggy, Doll, Tin 85.00
Buggy, Doll, Wicker, Original Finish 85.00

Toy, Blocks, Puzzle, Lithographed Paper, Large, Set

Buggy, Dollhouse, Metal Top, Wooden, 4 X 4 1/2 In. 60.00
Buggy, Metal Wheels, Cloth Covered Seat, Metal, 12 X 6 X 12 In. 150.00
Bull, On Iron Wheels 225.00
Bulldog, Circus, Glass Eyes, Barks, Nods, Pull, 20 In. 675.00
Bulldozer, Caterpillar, 1956, Tootsietoy, Yellow 4.00
Bulldozer, Doetke Toys, 15 In. 50.00
Bumblebee, Windup, Flaps Wings & Crawls, Tin 45.00
Bureau, 2 Drawers, Brass Pulls, Bootjack Leg, 1890 .... 65.00
Bus, Arcade, 1930, Cast Iron 45.00
Bus, Double Decker, Cast Iron, 11 In. 14.75
Bus, Double Decker, Driver, Yellow Coach, Arcade, 1930, 13 In. 1250.00
Bus, Double Decker, Interstate, Strauss, Key Wind 265.00
Bus, Double Decker, Kenton, 1930, Iron, 6 1/2 In. 350.00
Bus, Double, Minic Tri-Anc Toys, London Transport, Tin, Windup 50.00
Bus, Fageot, Iron, Arcade, 8 In. 85.00
Bus, Greyhound Jumbo Torpedo, Tootsietoy, Silver 13.00
Bus, Greyhound, Buddy L 55.00
Bus, Greyhound, GMC 3751, 1948, Tootsietoy 2.00
Bus, Greyhound, 1936, Great Lakes Exposition, Cast Iron 150.00
Bus, London Double Decker, Red, Lone Star, London, 3 1/4 In. 20.00
Bus, Original Colors, Steel, 1920s, 23 In. 75.00
Bus, Royal, People, Driver, Luggage Rack, Trunk, Marx 125.00
Bus, Sightseeing, Germany, Windup 8.00
Bus, Sightseeing, Kenton 6500.00
Bus, White Rubber Tires, Kenton, Cast Iron, 9 In. 325.00
Busy Mike Monkey 12.00
Cab, Checker 300.00
Cab, Yellow, Friction 13.00
Cab, Yellow, Sedan, 1923, Tootsietoy, Gray 10.00
Cabinet, Hoosier, Porcelain Knobs & Top, Yellow, 22 X 15 X 39 In. 145.00
Camel, Felt Covered, Composition, Wood, Hair, Glass Eyes, 6 X 9 In. 365.00
Camel, Real Camel Hair, C.1900, 11 In. 50.00
Camel, Steiff, 11 In. 195.00
Camel, 1 Hump, Schoenhut 185.00
Canary, Singing, Germany, Windup 65.00
Cannon, Big Bang, Original Label, 24 In. 50.00
Cannon, Original Green Paint, Iron, 4 3/4 In. 20.00
Captain Video, Program, Pittsburgh Police Circus, 1954 .... 30.00
Car Coupe, Buddy L, Original Sticker, Cast Iron 850.00
Car, Arcade Yellow Taxi 295.00
Car, Brink's Armored, Battery Operated 28.00
Car, British, Tin, Mettoy, Windup 85.00
Car, Buick, Sedan, Arcade, Iron, 8 1/4 In. 1000.00
Car, Cadillac, Battery Operated, King Size 50.00
Car, Cadillac, Sedan, 1954, Tootsietoy, Yellow & Red 10.00
Car, Charlie McCarthy 225.00
Car, Chevrolet Coupe, Tootsietoy, Green 9.00
Car, Chevrolet, 1940, Forward & Reverse, Occupied Japan, Windup, Metal 48.00
Car, Chevy Coupe, Arcade, 1924, Cast Iron, 7 In. 375.00
Car, Chevy Utility Coupe, Cast Iron, 6 1/2 In. 355.00
Car, Chrysler, 1930s, Peddle 675.00
Car, CKO Volkswagen, Top Flips, Windup, Tin 100.00
Car, College Flivver, Whoopee Car, 2 Flappers 145.00
Car, Coupe, 1924, Tootsietoy, Green 12.00
Car, Coupe, 2 Side Windows, Arcade, C.1920, Cast Iron, 6 In. 65.00
Car, Cowboy Crazy Car, Whoopee Car, 1930s 175.00
Car, Crazy, Mortimer Snerd, 1950s, Windup 100.00
Car, El Camino, 1959, Tootsietoy 4.00
Car, Ford, Coupe, 1934, Cast Iron, 6 1/2 In. 165.00
Car, Ford, Customline Sedan, 1955, Tootsietoy, Red 10.00
Car, Ford, Model A, 1929, Nickel Plated Wheels, Cast Iron, 5 In. 130.00
Car, Ford, 1912, Gold Wheels & Steering Wheel, Tootsietoy 40.00
Car, G-Man, Boxed 45.00

Car, Hess Hessmobile, Chauffeur, Friction Crank Drive 485.00
Car, Highway Patrol, Battery 18.00
Car, Horseless Carriage, Lehmann, Pat.1903 .... 250.00
Car, Mercedes 250 Sedan, Friction 35.00
Car, Milton Berle, Windup, Marx, Boxed .... 125.00 To 185.00
Car, Model A Touring, Cast Iron 250.00
Car, Model A Tudor, Driver, Arcade, Cast Iron, 6 1/2 In. 350.00
Car, Model T Ford, 1914, Tootsietoy, Black 25.00
Car, Model T, Fliver Pickup, Buddy L, Cast Iron 575.00
Car, Mustang, F.B.I.Commander, Boxed, Friction 45.00
Car, Open, Penny Toy, Tin 50.00
Car, Pedal, Hudson, Original Paint, Lights, 1937 .... 550.00
Car, Pontiac Star Chief, 1959, Tootsietoy, Red 5.50
Car, Racer, Bobtail, Red, Wyandotte 55.00
Car, Racer, Cast Iron, Black, 5 In. 40.00
Car, Racer, Champion Hardware Co., Cast Iron, Red 110.00
Car, Racer, Driver, Iron, 9 In.Long 110.00
Car, Racer, Lupor Sparkling, Box 35.00
Car, Racer, Speed King 115.00
Car, Racer, Tin, Windup, Marx 20.00
Car, Racer, Tootsietoy 5.00
Car, Racer, Wooden Wheels, Lithograph, Windup, Tin 55.00
Car, Racer, Wooden, Made In Hungary 40.00
Car, Renault Caravelle, Friction, Boxed 25.00
Car, Roadster, Yellow, Red Top, Spare Tire On Trunk, 8 In. 85.00
Car, Sedan, Cast Iron, Blue, 4 In. 45.00
Car, Sedan, Green, Wyandotte, 15 In. 55.00
Car, Sedan, Silver Metal Tires, Cast Iron, Blue, 4 In. 50.00
Car, Sedan, Windup, Marx, Lithograph 15.00
Car, Sheriff Sam Whoopee, Original Box 45.00
Car, Speed King, Marx, Racer 165.00
Car, Station Wagon, Cadillac, Wyandotte, Tin 110.00
Car, Station Wagon, Pontiac Safari, Tootsietoy 10.00
Car, Station Wagon, Rambler, 1960, Tootsietoy, Blue 10.00
Car, Studebaker Convertible, 1925, Studebaker, Pedal 3200.00
Car, Studebaker, 1950, Windup, Gray, Metal, 8 In. 20.00
Car, Thunderbird, 1955, Tootsietoy, Black 2.00
Car, Touring, Old Red Paint, Iron, 1920s, 6 1/2 In.Long 185.00
Car, U-Drive-It No.501, Tin, Lithographed 19.50
Car, Uncle Wiggly 350.00
Car, Volkswagen 113 Bug, 1960 .... 10.00
Car, Whoopee, Cowboy 150.00
Car, Whoopee, Sheriff Sam, Boxed 45.00
Car, Wolverine Town & Country, Boxed 35.00
Car, 2-Tone Blue, Tipp, Windup, Tin, German 325.00
Carousel, Clockwork, Muller & Kadeder, 6 Bisque-Headed Dolls 8500.00
Carousel, Flag At Top, Velveteen Canopy, 3 Horses, 2 Boats, 1880s, Tin 1650.00
Carousel, Ride-A-Rocket, Windup, Chein, Kids In Rocket 125.00
Carpet Ball, Brown Sponge Pattern 110.00
Carpet Sweeper, Daisy 30.00
Carpet Sweeper, Daisy Duck, 1940 .... 32.50
Carpet Sweeper, Lithograph, C.1940, Tin 7.00
Carpet Sweeper, Merry Mousewife, Fisher Price 12.00
Carriage, Doll, Wyandotte, Painted, Tin, 9 In. 25.00
Carriage, Hand-Painted, Tin, German, Flowered Cloth Top, 6 In. 45.00
Carriage, Military, Open Field, World War I, 2 Horses, Cast Iron 125.00
Carriage, With Doll, Pennytoy 95.00
Cart, Butcher, Pulled By Pig, Windup, Dated 1905, German 330.00
Cart, Doll, Tin, Red & Mustard 165.00
Cart, Doll, 2 Wheels, Long Handle, Wicker 75.00
Cart, Fire Hose, Friction 375.00
Cart, Horse Drawn, Clown, Windup, Lehmann, 1903 .... 110.00
Cart, Push, Doll, Fenders & Handle 95.00

Cash Register, Chein, Tin	12.00
Cash Register, Little Tot, Tin	30.00
Cash Register, Michigan, Cast Iron	90.00
Cash Register, Tom Thumb, Tin	10.00
Cash Register, Uncle Sam, Tin	19.00
Cat, Felix, Schoenhut, 9 In.	250.00
Cat, In Basket, Glass Eyes, Windup	25.00
Cat, Knitting, Windup, Box	45.00
Cat, Papier-Mache	165.00
Cat, Trix, Gong Toy	245.00
Cat, With Ball, Windup, 1940s, Japan, Metal Base	100.00
Chair, Child's, Rocking, Pine	55.00
Chair, Twisted Wire, Rolled Top, Scrolls	75.00
Chariot, Driver, 3 Horse, Hubley, Cast Iron	300.00
Charlie Chaplin, Riding Bicycle	150.00
Chevy Coupe, Arcade, Cast Iron, 8 In.	365.00
Chicken & Hen, Hen Pushes Baby Carriage, Battery Operated, 10 In.	19.50
Chicken Pulling Cart, Tin, 8 In.	10.50
Circus Wagon, Overland, Kenton Hardware	250.00
Claw Digger, Remco, Original Prizes	37.00
Climbing Monkey, Lehmann, Boxed	165.00
Clock, Hickory Dickory, Musical, Mattel, 1952, Box	25.00
Clock, Nursery Rhyme Figures, Bisque, German, 10 1/4 In.	95.00
Clown Riding Pig, 1920, Windup	155.00
Clown, French Pierrot, Wooden Body, Composition Head, Windup, 10 In.	90.00
Clown, Hobo, Schoenhut, 8 In.	107.00
Clown, Mechanical, Tumbling, Windup, Celluloid & Tin	30.00
Clown, Mechanical, Turns Head, Rolls Eyes, Balances Ball On Foot, 16 In.	350.00
Clown, Musical, 1910, Fernand Martin	600.00
Clown, Skating, Lithograph, Rayon Pants, Windup	42.00
Clown, Spinning Chicken, Chein, Windup, Tin	35.00
Clown, Violin, Windup, Tin, Schuco, Boxed	95.00
Comic Construction Set, Blondie's, Whole Family, 1930s, 12 X 21 In.	65.00
Commando Joe, Windup, Tin, Boxed	40.00
Cop On Motorcycle, Iron, 5 In.Long	65.00
Cop On Motorcycle, Sidecar	40.00
Coronet, 8 Valves, C.1870, Tin	25.00
Costume, Zorro	38.00
Couch, Fainting, Doll, Wine Velvet Cover, 16 X 12 X 12 In.	150.00
Couch, Fainting, Upholstered, 21 In.Long	35.00
Cow, Borden's Elsie, Wooden, Push-Up	20.00
Cow, Hide-Covered, Nodding	165.00
Cow, On Wheeled Platform, Silver & Green, Tin, 4 1/2 X 3 1/2 In.	63.00
Cowboy On Horse, Battery, Cragston	150.00
Cowboy, Galloping, German, Windup, Tin	150.00
Cradle, Doll, Hand-Pegged, Spindle Spines, Pine, 12 X 23 In.	60.00
Cradle, Doll, Hand-Whittled, 1-Piece Poplar Log, Pegged Rockers	
Cradle, Doll, Jenny Lind, 4-Poster, 24 X 17 X 22 In.	325.00
Cradle, Doll, Spindle, Rocker Posts, Patchwork Quilt, 12 X 23 In.	45.00
Cradle, Folding, 1800s, Wire	22.00 To 30.00
Cradle, 4-Poster, Pine, Painted White, Rockers, 20 In.	45.00
Crane, Hubley, Orange Cab, Cast Iron	19.00
Crap Shooter, Cragston, Battery Operated, Boxed	45.00 To 65.00
Cupboard, Child's, Pine, 4 Doors & Drawers, 15 X 32 In.	225.00
Cupboard, Glass Doors, 27 In.	260.00
Cycle, Police, Auto, Battery, Boxed	60.00
Cyclist, Kiddy, Lithograph, Metal, Windup, 9 X 7 In.	100.00
Dagwood, In Airplane, Marx, Tin	525.00
Dancer, Ballet, Marx, Boxed	85.00
Dancing Couple, Celluloid, Windup, Occupied Japan	36.00
Deer, Shoebutton Eyes, Straw Stuffed, Princing Position, 8 In.	45.00
Deer, Steiff, 12 In.	65.00
Denny Dimwit, Comic Strip Toy, Boxed	225.00

Deputy Dawg, Windup, Tin 75.00
Desk, Rolltop, Price 1 Dollar, Oak, 18 X 14 3/4 In. 275.00
Dog, At Typewriter, Windup 15.00
Dog, Cast-Iron Face & Legs, Rabbit Fur Body, Pull, 10 X 10 X 5 In. 135.00
Dog, Chow, Felt Covered, White Rabbit Fur, Glass Eyes, 6 1/2 In. 60.00
Dog, Pull, Iron, Mini, Original Gold Paint, 3 1/2 X 2 1/4 In. 125.00
Dog, Rocking, Japan, Windup 48.00
Dog, Sandy, Tin 145.00
Dog, Scotty, Stuffed, Straw, Movable Head 35.00
Dog, Shakes Metal Shoe, Tin, Windup, Japan, 9 In. 95.00
Dog, Snappy, Marx 50.00
TOY, DOLL, see Doll
Dollhouse, Chest, 3 Drawer, Signed, 1878, 8 X 11 1/4 X 4 In. 85.00
Dollhouse, Coffee Grinder, Pewter, 2 In. 85.00
Dollhouse, Color Litho Paper Covered, Wooden, 9 X 6 X 12 3/4 In. 675.00
Dollhouse, Dutch Colonial, Wooden, White, Red Trim, 7 Rooms, 32 In. 175.00
Dollhouse, Dutch Colonial, Wooden, Yellow, Green, Red Roof, 20 In. 450.00
Dollhouse, Fence, Victorian, 19th Century, 3 7/8 In. .... *Illus* 275.00
Dollhouse, Gabled Roof, Red Shingles, American, 24 3/4 In. .... *Illus* 200.00
Dollhouse, German, Red Roof, Green Shutters, Yellow Sides, Papered Walls 900.00
Dollhouse, Lithographed Paper On Wood, German 2000.00
Dollhouse, Mansard Roof, Brick Front, 5 Room, 23 5/8 In. .... *Illus* 200.00
Dollhouse, Red Roof, Germany, 11 X 20 X 18 1/2 In. 485.00
Dollhouse, Wonderland, Cardboard 65.00
Dollhouse, Wooden, Gabled Roof, L-Shaped Cottage, Porch, 24 In. 200.00
Dollhouse, Wooden, Mansard Roof, Brick Front, Cream Rim, Red Door, 23 In. 200.00
Dollhouse, 2 Rooms, Schoenhut, With Furniture 175.00
Dollhouse, 2 Story, 4 Rooms, Furnished, 1930s, Wooden 450.00
Dollhouse, 21 Windows, Electrified, Handmade, C.1916, 4 1/6 X 2 1/6 Ft. 1500.00
Donkey Cart, Clockwork, German, Lithographed Tin .... *Illus* 150.00
Donkey Cart, Driver, Cast Iron 225.00
Donkey Pulling Clown, Lehmann, Windup 175.00
Donkey, Shoenhut, Brown, 8 In. 58.00
Donkey, Tin, Windup, Brown Felt, Glass Eyes 50.00
Donkey, Tremblin Toy, Windup, Celluloid 165.00
Drum, Lithograph On Tin, Sticks, Dated 1908 .... 45.00
Drum, Uncle Wiggly 75.00
Drummer, Mechanical, Chein 75.00
Duck, Friction, Original Yellow, Green, Red Paint, Tin, 8 X 5 In. 85.00
Duck, Walking, Windup, Tin, Chein, 3 3/4 In .... 20.00 To 28.00
Egg Laying Hen, Baldwin, Windup 23.00
Eggbeater, A. & J., Patent 1923, 5 1/2 In. 8.00

Toy, Stable, 2 Box Stalls, Feed Baskets, Horses, 23 X 19 3/8 In.

Toy, Dollhouse, Fence, Victorian, 19th Century, 3 7/8 In.

Toy, Dollhouse, Gabled Roof, Red Shingles, American, 24 3/4 In.

Toy, Dollhouse, Mansard Roof, Brick Front, 5 Room, 23 5/8 In.

Elephant, Bubble Blowing, Battery Operated	50.00
Elephant, Nodding, Composition, German, 20th Century, 8 X 5 In.	110.00
Elephant, On Wheels, Tin, 1900, 9 In.	190.00
Elephant, Painted Eyes, Schoenhut	90.00
Elephant, Pull, Nodding Head & Tail, German, 14 1/2 X 8 X 4 In.	140.00
Elephant, Steiff, 1930s, 21 In.	400.00

Elsie Cow, Borden's, Push-Up, Wood	20.00
Engine, Train, Key Wind, Cast Iron, 8 In.	250.00
Erector Set, Gilbert, Wooden Box	70.00
Erector Set, No.3 1/2, 1935	24.00
Erector Set, No.6 1/2, Tin Box	28.00
Erector Set, Oak Box	90.00
Erector Set, 1954	15.00
Felix The Cat, Swivel Head, Jointed Spool Arms, Wood	225.00 To 300.00
Felix The Cat, Wood Jointed, 1920s, 9 In.	195.00
Felix, Doll, Wood Jointed, 4 In.	50.00
Felix, On Scooter	175.00
Felix, Walking, Tin	195.00
Ferdinand The Bull, Tin, Windup	75.00
Ferris Wheel, Hercules, Chein, Windup	100.00
Ferris Wheel, Hercules, 6 Cars, Bell Rings, Chein, Windup, Tin, 16 1/2 In.	125.00
Ferris Wheel, Mickey Mouse, Key Wind	175.00
Fire Engine, Courtland, Tin, Windup, Red, Black, 8 3/4 In.	55.00
Fire Engine, Driver, White Wheels, Cast Iron, 5 In.	62.00
Fire Engine, Hill Climber, Friction, C.1905	95.00
Fire Engine, Live Steam, Weedon	2500.00
Fire Engine, Pumper, Cast Iron, 8 In.	13.75
Fire Engine, Pumper, Horse Drawn, Iron, 3 Horses, Red, Black, White	185.00
Fire Engine, Pumper, Smoker, Driver, 2 Horses, Iron, 21 In.	500.00
Fire Engine, 3 Horses, Man, Cast Iron, 11 1/2 X 4 1/2 In.	240.00
Fire Engine, 4 Ladder, Driver & Rider, Tin, Jeep, Citroen, 8 In.	100.00
Fire Truck, Hook & Ladder, Kingsbury, Metal	55.00
Fire Truck, Pumper, Red Paint, Cast Iron, 4 1/2 In.	22.50
Firehouse, Red, Mechanical Gates, Metal, 13 1/2 In.	125.00
Fireman, Climbing, Tin, Windup, Marx	60.00 To 155.00
Flintstone, Tank, Turnover	150.00
Flying Bird, Lehmann	350.00
Flying Bird, Lehmann, Windup	400.00 To 475.00
Flying Saucer, Battery	45.00
Fort, Tri-Ang Wood, England, Boxed	20.00
Fox Terrier, Bell Between 2 Large Wheels, Pull Toy, 11 In.	225.00
Fox Terrier, Felt Ears, 1950s, 4 In.	20.00
Fox Terrier, Homemade & Stuffed, Lithographed Cloth, 10 1/4 In.	35.00
Fox Terrier, Wirehaired, Mohair, Head Turns, Steiff, 17 In.	115.00
Fred Flintstone On Dino, Battery Operated	95.00 To 175.00
Froggie The Gremlin	75.00
Furniture, Bed, Doll, Victorian, Brass Post, Wooden Center, 14 In.	135.00
Furniture, Dollhouse, Armchair, Padded Seat, 1930s, Germany, 3 7/8 In.	12.50
Furniture, Dollhouse, Armchair, Tootsietoy	5.00
Furniture, Dollhouse, Bed, Oak, 32 X 16 In.	35.00
Furniture, Dollhouse, Bed, Painted, 1920s, Tin	6.50
Furniture, Dollhouse, Bellows, Moving Parts, Brass, England, 3 1/2 In.	12.00
Furniture, Dollhouse, Bench, Piano, 4 Legs, White, 2 7/8 X 1 5/8 In.	4.00
Furniture, Dollhouse, Birdcage, Candlestand, Cage 4 X 3 In. *Illus*	170.00
Furniture, Dollhouse, Buffet, Brown, Tootsietoy	8.00
Furniture, Dollhouse, Bureau, 3-Drawer, Walnut, 16 X 10 X 28 In.	325.00
Furniture, Dollhouse, Cabinet, Biedermeier	250.00
Furniture, Dollhouse, Cabinet, Kitchen, Iron, 11 In.	47.50

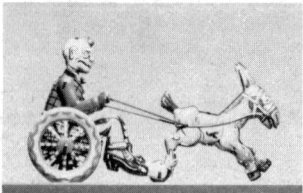

Toy, Donkey Cart, Clockwork, German,
Lithographed Tin   *(See Page 714)*

Furniture, Dollhouse, Candelabra, Fantasia 10.00
Furniture, Dollhouse, Candelabra, Royal 8.00
Furniture, Dollhouse, Candleabra, 2 Arm, 3 Cup, Brass, 1 In. 7.50
Furniture, Dollhouse, Candlestick, Brass, 1 5/8 In., Pair 15.00
Furniture, Dollhouse, Cedar Chest, Lift Top, Loop Handles, 4 X 1 1/2 In. 18.00
Furniture, Dollhouse, Chair, Cane Seat, Europe, Cast Lead .... *Illus* 310.00
Furniture, Dollhouse, Chair, Curved Legs, Pillow, C.1900, 3 3/8 In. 4.00
Furniture, Dollhouse, Chair, Dining, Guest, Petite Princess 12.00
Furniture, Dollhouse, Chair, Easy, Footstool, Beige, Suede 15.00
Furniture, Dollhouse, Chair, High Back, 3 3/8 In., Pair 6.00
Furniture, Dollhouse, Chair, Kitchen, Maroon, Set Of 3, Tootsietoy 10.00
Furniture, Dollhouse, Chair, Occasional, Ottoman, Blue, Petite Princess 12.00
Furniture, Dollhouse, Chair, Upholstered, 7 X 7 In. 5.00
Furniture, Dollhouse, Chair, Velvet Seat, Dark Finish, 4 1/2 In. 6.00
Furniture, Dollhouse, Chair, Windsor, Mahogany Stained 5.00
Furniture, Dollhouse, Chair, Wing, Brocade, Red 14.00
Furniture, Dollhouse, Chair, Wing, Red Brocade, Oriental Design 14.00
Furniture, Dollhouse, Chair, Wing, Red With Gold Print, Salon 10.00
Furniture, Dollhouse, Chaise Longue, Cylinder Pillow, Pink Satin 14.00
Furniture, Dollhouse, Chest, Attached Mirror 35.00
Furniture, Dollhouse, Chest, Palace, Petite Princess 10.00
Furniture, Dollhouse, Chest, 3 Drawers, 4 X 3 1/2 In. 12.50
Furniture, Dollhouse, Clock, Grandfather, Decorated Panels, Screen 25.00
Furniture, Dollhouse, Clock, Mantel, Tin, Germany, 1 3/4 X 2 1/2 In. 14.00
Furniture, Dollhouse, Closet, Mirror Door, Pewter Knobs, 2 7/8 X 3/4 In. 35.00
Furniture, Dollhouse, Commode, Tub, & Pail, Mirrored, Tin 85.00
Furniture, Dollhouse, Couch, Biedermeier 200.00
Furniture, Dollhouse, Couch, Chair, Rocker, Lamp, Radio, 6 Pieces 75.00
Furniture, Dollhouse, Cradle, Hooded, Rockers, 4 7/8 X 2 3/4 In. 20.00
Furniture, Dollhouse, Cupboard, Granny, Green, Tootsietoy 12.00
Furniture, Dollhouse, Cupboard, Kitchen, 2 Shelves, 2 Doors, Brass Knobs 35.00
Furniture, Dollhouse, Cupboard, Kitchen, 2-Drawer, 7 1/2 X 4 X 9 1/2 In. 75.00
Furniture, Dollhouse, Dining Set, Cabinet, Buffet, 4 Chairs 16.00
Furniture, Dollhouse, Dining Table, Brown, Tootsietoy 10.00
Furniture, Dollhouse, Dining Table, Gatelegs, 5 1/4 X 7 4/8 In. 12.50
Furniture, Dollhouse, Fireplace, Paper Brick Lined, 4 3/4 X 3 5/8 In. 15.00
Furniture, Dollhouse, Fireplace, Petite Princess 10.00
Furniture, Dollhouse, Hearthplace, Regency 18.00
Furniture, Dollhouse, Ice Cream Parlor Set, Wooden Seats, Metal, 5 Piece 200.00
Furniture, Dollhouse, Icebox, Green Paint, Galvanized Iron Over Wood 75.00

Toy, Furniture, Dollhouse, Birdcage,
Candlestand, Cage 4 X 3 In.

Toy, Furniture, Dollhouse, Chair,
Cane Seat, Europe, Cast Lead

Furniture, Dollhouse, Kitchen Set, Cabinet, 2 Chairs, Table & Stove	28.00
Furniture, Dollhouse, Kitchen, Tin	425.00
Furniture, Dollhouse, Lamp	150.00
Furniture, Dollhouse, Lamp, Table, Shade Unscrews, Brass, 1 1/2 In.	5.00
Furniture, Dollhouse, Lamp, With Shade, Wooden, 3 1/4 In.	2.50
Furniture, Dollhouse, Living Room, Victrola, Tootsietoy, 6 Piece	75.00
Furniture, Dollhouse, Mirror, Pier	175.00
Furniture, Dollhouse, Natural Wood, 8 1/2 In.	25.00
Furniture, Dollhouse, Piano, Upright, Paper Keys, Pine, 4 X 4 In.	12.50
Furniture, Dollhouse, Radiator, 8-Ribbed, Cast Iron, 2 X 1 1/2 In.	35.00
Furniture, Dollhouse, Red Velvet Upholstered, Walnut, 8 X 8 X 15 In.	150.00
Furniture, Dollhouse, Server, 2-Door, Crown Top, 3 7/8 X 3 3/4 In.	22.00
Furniture, Dollhouse, Settee, Curved Back & Arms, Cast Iron, 4 1/2 In.	25.00
Furniture, Dollhouse, Settee, Splint Seat, Handmade, 4 1/2 X 8 X 8 In.	45.00
Furniture, Dollhouse, Sideboard, Brown, Tootsietoy	7.00
Furniture, Dollhouse, Sink, Kitchen, Green, Tootsietoy	10.00
Furniture, Dollhouse, Sofa, Cretonne Covered, 2 Pillow, 4 X 3 In.	8.50
Furniture, Dollhouse, Sofa, Marked Arcade, Cast Iron, 7 X 3 3/4 In.	25.00
Furniture, Dollhouse, Stove, 2-Burner, Daisy, Cast Iron, 4 1/4 In.	20.00
Furniture, Dollhouse, Stove, 4-Burner, Double Oven, 3 1/2 In.	28.00
Furniture, Dollhouse, Table Set, Coffee, Salon	10.00
Furniture, Dollhouse, Table Set, Marble Top, Ashtray, Statue, Lighter	15.00
Furniture, Dollhouse, Table Set, Tier, Petite Princess	10.00
Furniture, Dollhouse, Table, Dressing, Royal, Pink, Petite Princess	20.00
Furniture, Dollhouse, Table, Occasional, Marble, Petite Princess	8.00
Furniture, Dollhouse, Table, Occasional, White With Lyre Design	6.00
Furniture, Dollhouse, Table, Pedestal, Stained Pine, 3 In.Diam.	6.50
Furniture, Dollhouse, Table, Scalloped Aprons, Cast Iron, Green, 5 In.	24.00
Furniture, Dollhouse, Table, Trestle, Pine, 2 1/2 X 2 1/4 In.	8.50
Furniture, Dollhouse, Tea Cart, Petite Princess	20.00
Furniture, Dollhouse, Tea Wagon, Wheels Turn, 4 1/2 X 2 3/4 In.	28.00
Furniture, Dollhouse, Toaster, C.1920	27.50
Furniture, Dollhouse, Toilet, Wood Cover, 2 1/4 In.	9.50
Furniture, Dollhouse, Tootsietoy, Metal, 38 Piece	195.00
Furniture, Dollhouse, Tray, Raised Edges, 1 5/8 X 2 1/4 In.	4.00
Furniture, Dollhouse, Trunk, 14 X 7 In.	10.00
Furniture, Dollhouse, Washboard	14.00
Furniture, Dollhouse, Washstand, 1-Drawer, Towel Bar, 13 X 6 X 16 In.	195.00
G.I.Joe Space Cap, Record, Suit, Official, Boxed	45.00
G-Man, Car, Windup, Tin	40.00
G-Man, Siren, Pocket, Tin, 1940	20.00
G-Man, Tommy Gun, Marx	24.00
Game Board, Double Face, Red & Mustard	185.00
Game Board, Parcheesi, Double Face, Red, Yellow, & Black	195.00
Garage, Automatic Door Opener, German, Tin, 11 In.	130.00
Gilbert Kaster Kit Moulds, Military Series, 1936, Boxed	75.00
Giraffe, Schoenhut	195.00 To 295.00
Giraffe, Steiff, 19 In.	65.00
Goat & Cart, Cast Iron	160.00
Goat, Pulling Cart, Late 19th Century, Cast Iron, 4 X 2 1/2 In.	125.00
Goose, Egg Laying, Pecking, Windup, Marx	60.00
Goose, Walks, Windup, 1910, German	49.00
Goose, Windup, Waddles & Lays Egg, Patented July, 1924, Tin	90.00
Gorilla, Windup	45.00
Grasshopper, Pull, Wooden	65.00
Grinder, Food, Cast Iron	45.00
Guitar, Gene Autry, Boxed	75.00
Gun, Atomic Disintegrator	45.00
Gun, Big Bang, 16f, Pershing Model Cannon, 16 In.Barrel, Boxed	125.00
Gun, Buck Rogers	40.00
Gun, Cap, American Bulldog	17.50 To 35.00
Gun, Cap, Animated, Iron, Figural, Locomotive Moves With Trigger, 5 In.	495.00
Gun, Cap, Animated, Lightning Express	100.00

Gun, Cap, Biff, Jr.	17.50
Gun, Cap, Big Chief, Octagon Barrel, Cast Iron	20.00
Gun, Cap, Bigger Bang	45.00
Gun, Cap, Border Patrol	15.00
Gun, Cap, Buffalo Bill	15.00 To 100.00
Gun, Cap, Cowboy	15.00
Gun, Cap, Double Barrel, Flintlock, Hubley	16.00
Gun, Cap, Eagle	30.00
Gun, Cap, Echo, Single Shot, Cast Iron	10.00
Gun, Cap, Fancy Filigree, Original Caps, Boxed	85.00
Gun, Cap, Flintlock Jr., Boxed	12.00
Gun, Cap, Gem	18.00
Gun, Cap, Hero	15.00
Gun, Cap, Hide-Away	8.00
Gun, Cap, Hubley Flintlock Jr.Dueling, Pair	7.50
Gun, Cap, Hubley Marshal 45, 250 Shot, Smoke Repeater, Original Card	20.00
Gun, Cap, Hubley No.210, On Card	10.00
Gun, Cap, Hubley, Large	20.00
Gun, Cap, Hubley, Tex	10.00
Gun, Cap, Invincible, New 50 Shot	12.50
Gun, Cap, Iron, Marked Cowboy, Leather Holster	15.00
Gun, Cap, Kilgore, Pal	12.00
Gun, Cap, Kit Carson	8.00
Gun, Cap, Lightning Express	200.00
Gun, Cap, Lion, Cast Iron	65.00
Gun, Cap, Magic	30.00
Gun, Cap, Marked Texas, Die Cast	4.00
Gun, Cap, Mick, Pat.Sept.11, 23	12.50
Gun, Cap, National No.380, Holster	50.00
Gun, Cap, Oh Boy	20.00
Gun, Cap, Pioneer, C.1940, Boxed	3.75
Gun, Cap, Pluck	12.50
Gun, Cap, Pluck, Miniature, Cast Iron	20.00 To 35.00
Gun, Cap, Punch & Judy	350.00
Gun, Cap, Sambo, Cast Iron	90.00
Gun, Cap, Scout, Stevens, 1890	35.00
Gun, Cap, Scout, Tin Body, Cast Iron Parts, 1918	17.50
Gun, Cap, Spitfire, Boxed	15.00
Gun, Cap, Spy	17.50
Gun, Cap, Sure Shot	20.00
Gun, Cap, Texan, Cast Iron, 1938	30.00
Gun, Cap, Texas, Metal	4.00
Gun, Cap, Trooper Safety	40.00
Gun, Cap, Trooper, Hubley, Cast Iron	10.00
Gun, Cap, Victor	70.00
Gun, Cap, Volunteer	60.00
Gun, Cap, Winner	20.00
Gun, Cap, Zip	17.50
Gun, Cowboy, Hubley	10.00
Gun, Dart, Daisy	25.00
Gun, Flash Gordon, Water, Boxed	100.00
Gun, Hubley Tex, Holsters & Belt, Pair	7.50
Gun, Ray, Captain Video	18.00
Gun, Red Ranger, Clicker, Tin	13.00
Gun, Rifle, Air, Red Ryder	25.00
Gun, Rubber Band	39.00
Gun, Space, Barnum & Bailey Circus	15.00
Gun, Space, Tom Corbett, Boxed	100.00
Gun, Sparker, Ronson	25.00
Gun, Submachine, Tom Corbett, Boxed	45.00
Gun, Tom Corbett, Sparking Space Cadet, Marx, Boxed	175.00
Gun, Wild Bill Hickok & Jingles, Holster, Boxed	68.00
Gun, Zap, Flintlock, Midget, Hubley, 5 3/4 In.	15.00

Gun, Zorro, Water, On Display Card 20.00
Ham & Sam, Minstrel Team, Strauss, Windup, 1921 .... 450.00
Hamper, Doll, Wicker, 12 In. 30.00
Hans Brinker, Skater, Metal, 2 1/2 In. 20.00
Happy Grandpa, Windup 40.00
Happy Hooligan, Jack-In-The-Box 75.00
Helicopter, S-58 Sikorsky, Tootsietoy 12.00
Hen, Lays Marble Eggs, Tin, Wyandotte 45.00
High Chair, Doll, Tray, Footrest, 9 X 9 X 29 In. 125.00
Hobbyhorse, Glass Eyes, Wooden 435.00
Hobbyhorse, Real Hair 350.00
Hobbyhorse, Trimmed In Horsehair, C.1850, All Original 975.00
Horse & Cart, Pull Toy, Marked Germany, 13 In. 800.00
Horse & Cart, Wood, American, Hand-Painted 165.00
Horse & Sulky, Moving Legs, White Rubber Wheels, Pedal 300.00
Horse, Appaloosa, Penny, Pulling Wagon 58.00
Horse, Circus, Schoenhut .... 85.00 To 125.00
Horse, Cloth Over Wood, 16 1/2 In. 20.00
Horse, Composition, Harnessed, Pull, Victorian 145.00
Horse, Composition, Pull, Small 75.00
Horse, Daja, Windup 28.00
Horse, Hide Covered, Pull, Victorian 210.00
Horse, On Wheels, Papier-Mache, 5 1/2 In. 35.00
Horse, Plush, On Wheels 105.00
Horse, Pull, Papier-Mache & Wood, White, Black, 11 X 10 In. 115.00
Horse, Red Leather Saddle, Red Bridle, 1950s, 5 1/2 X 5 In. 50.00
Horse, Running, Bell, Nickel Plated Cast Iron, 9 X 4 X 5 In. 170.00
Horse, Schoenhut, Dapple Gray 150.00
Howdy Doody, Jack-In-The-Box, Plastic, 5 In. 20.00
Hula-Hoop Girl, From India, Battery 85.00
Humphreymobile, Complete With Box 410.00
Hunter, Mechanical, German, C.1915, Painted Tin ....*Illus* 350.00
Ice Cream Parlor Set, Child's, Wooden Seats, Metal, 16 In., 5 Piece 350.00
Ice Skates, Men's, Clamp-On, Winslow Skate Co., Mass., 14 1/4 In. 16.50
Ice Skates, Racing, Brass Toes & Heels, Dated 1895 .... 28.00

Toy, Hunter, Mechanical, German,
C.1915, Painted Tin

Ice Skates, Winchester 35.00
Ice Skates, Wood, Iron Runners, Tie To Boots, Child's, 7 3/4 In. 70.00
Iron, Child's, Hollow Grip, Marked O, 3 In. 40.00
Ironing Board, Wood, Tin, & Iron 20.00
Ironing Board, Wooden .... 12.50 To 30.00
Jack Armstrong, Pedometer, Silver Border 20.00
Jack Armstrong, Secret Bombsight 25.00
Jalopy, Black, Red & Yellow, Marx, Tin, Windup, 7 In.Long 185.00
Jazzbo Jim, Banjo, Windup, Tin, Unique Art, Boxed 350.00
Jazzbo Jim, Black, Strauss, 1921 .... 245.00

Toy, Joe Penner, Clockwork, Marx, Lithographed Tin

Jeep, Desert Patrol, Battery Operated	60.00
Jeep, Jumping, Marx, Boxed	50.00 To 85.00
Jeep, Tootsietoy	5.00
Jigger, Black, Oriental Features, Tin, Windup	150.00
Jigger, Dapper Dan, Marx	260.00
Joe Penner, Clockwork, Marx, Lithographed Tin	*Illus* 190.00
Jolly Chimp, Battery, Musical, Boxed	45.00
Jolly Penguin, Windup	15.00
Kangaroo, Baby In Pouch, Ears & Pouch Beige Velvet, 16 In.	75.00
Kayo & Moon Mullins, Handcar, Boxed	470.00
Lamb, Pull, Man Pointing, 2-Sided, Tin	1500.00
Leopard, Glass Eyes, 1960s, 13 In.	150.00
Li'l Abner Dogpatch Band	350.00
Limping Lizzie, Black Auto, Marx, Tin, Windup, 7 1/4 In.	95.00
Lincoln Tunnel, 3 Cars, 2-Way Traffic, Windup, Tin, 24 In. Long	95.00
Lion, Reclining, Button-Glass Eyes, Steiff, 11 1/2 In.	50.00
Little Performer, Girl Playing Xylophone, Windup, 9 In.	20.00
Llama, Steiff, 11 In.	85.00
Loop Plane, Key Wind, Occupied Japan, Tin & Celluloid	25.00
Louie Armstrong, Rosko, Windup, Boxed	120.00
Lunar Loop	75.00
Magic Barn, Marx, Boxed	25.00
Mammy Sweeping, Linstrom, Boxed	165.00
Mammy Sweeping, Windup, Marx, Boxed	120.00
Mammy, Windup Walkers	145.00
Man In Tux, Shoots Pool, Penny	125.00
Man, Champion Weight Lifter, Battery Operated, Boxed	45.00
Marching Band, Lead, Brown Uniforms, Marked Cpyrt, 2 1/4 In., 5 Piece	135.00
Marionette, African, Tribal, Wood & Red Trade Cloth	275.00
Marionette, Bashful, Madame Alexander, 1930s	165.00
Marionette, Comic, Papier-Mache Head, Wood Torso, Arms, & Legs, 10 In.	125.00
Marionette, Dopey, Madame Alexander	125.00
Marionette, Mouseketeer, Jimmy, 13 In.	50.00
Marionette, Olive Oyl, King Features, Late 40s	45.00
Marionette, Pluto, Fisher Price, Wooden	65.00
Mary Had A Little Lamb, Jack-In-The-Box	65.00
Mask, Tom Mix, Full Face, Paper, Ralston Premium	25.00
Maxwell, The Coffee Drinking Bear, Battery	65.00
Mecki, Steiff	40.00
Merry-Go-Round, Blue, Red, Yellow, 5 Horses, Wolverine, 11 X 12 In.	125.00
Merrymakers Band, Marx	350.00 To 465.00
Microphone, Little Wonder, Stromberg-Carlson, Boxed	35.00
Mixer, Cement, Jaeger, Kenton	200.00
Monkey, Bombo, Windup, Swings From Tree, Unique Art, Boxed	35.00
Monkey, Bubble Blowing, Battery Operated, Boxed	45.00 To 75.00

Monkey, Clancy The Great, Battery Operated 100.00
Monkey, Climbing, Trixo, Strauss, Box 90.00
Monkey, Climbs Ladder, Penny 175.00
Monkey, Conductor, Windup 35.00
Monkey, Crap Shooting, Battery Operated .... 35.00 To 50.00
Monkey, Frankie, Roller Skating, Boxed 150.00
Monkey, Fur Covered, French, Windup 195.00
Monkey, Jocko, Fully Jointed, Early 1960s, 13 1/2 In. 125.00
Monkey, Mohair, Steiff, Jointed, 12 In. 30.00
Monkey, On Chair, Schoenhut 275.00
Monkey, On Tricycle, Steiff 150.00
Monkey, Playing Cymbals, Battery Operated .... 30.00 To 40.00
Monkey, Playing Guitar, Battery 65.00
Monkey, Riding A Wire Cart, Pull Toy, Steiff, Felt 225.00
Monkey, Swings Mouse, Tin, Windup, Schuco, Boxed 95.00
Monkey, Zippo, Tin, Climbs String, Marx, 10 In. 15.00
Monoplane, C.1928, Tin, 5 X 6 In. 85.00
Moon Rocket, Battery 35.00
Mother Goose, Unique Art 250.00
Motor Express, Hercules, Chein 125.00
Motorcycle, Cop, Tin Lithograph, Windup, Side Fins, 8 1/2 In. 125.00
Motorcycle, Delivery Attachment, Boy, Windup, Marx, Tin, 9 1/2 In. 115.00
Motorcycle, Mystic, Windup, Marx 50.00
Motorcycle, Policeman, Rubber Tires, Champion, Cast Iron, 7 1/4 In. 75.00
Motorcycle, Rider, Harley Davidson, Cast Iron 85.00
Motorcycle, Rider, Iron, 6 In. 35.00
Motorcycle, Sidecar, Smitty, Tootsietoy, Red & Yellow 90.00
Motorcycle, Sidecar, Windup, Tin, 7 In. 14.50
Motorcycle, Speedboy, Windup, Tin 28.00
Motorcycle, With Cop, Champion, Iron, 5 In. 32.00
Mountie, Royal Canadian, Lead, Hand-Painted, 2 1/4 In. 15.00
Moxie Mobile, Tin, Lithograph 475.00
Mule, Balky, With Cart, Marx 38.00
Mule, Ears Move Up & Down, Tail Spins, Windup, 1930s, 6 X 6 In. 40.00
Mule, Jenny Balky, Strauss 140.00
Mule, Jenny Balky, Windup 150.00
Mule, Kicking, Windup, Lehmann .... 110.00 To 150.00
Mutt & Jeff, Metal Ball Jointed, 8 In. 250.00
My Doll Nursing Set, 1930s, Japan, Boxed 15.00
Native On Turtle, Tin 55.00
Noah's Ark, Carved Animals, 15 In. 250.00
Noah's Ark, Hand-Carved Animals 350.00
Noah's Ark, Wooden People, 7 Animal Figures, Green, 8 X 4 In. 85.00
Ocean Liner, Wolverine Co., Windup, Tin, 15 In. 28.50
Old Man Drinker, Battery 45.00
Old Woman In Shoe, Filled With Small Dolls, Ives 3500.00
Ostrich Cart, Lehmann 375.00
Ostrich, On Roller Skates, Key Wind, Occupied Japan, Boxed 35.00
Paddy & Pig, Lehmann 325.00
Paddy On Pig, Tin, Windup, 4 1/4 In. 325.00
Pail & Shovel, Cowboys & Indians Lithograph, Chein 10.00
Pango Pango African Dancer, Tin, Windup, Boxed 65.00
Parrot, Dome Shape Cage, Papier-Mache Bird, Squeak, 19th Century, 5 In. 225.00
Parrot, Franzi, 1950s, Steiff 30.00
Parrot, Talking, Lights Up, Wings Flap, Perched On Tin Base, Marx, 18 In. 400.00
Parrot, Talking, Marx 525.00
Peacock, Hans Eberl 175.00
Penguin, Baby, Black Velvet Wings, Red Felt Feet, 4 1/2 In. 50.00
Penguin, Percy, Friction, Boxed 15.00
Penguin, Walking, Windup, Tin, Chein, 4 In. 28.00
Penguin, Walking, Yellow, Black & White, Wooden, 5 In. 22.00
Phonograph, Serenade, 1960, Record, Boxed 45.00
Phonograph, Victor Talking Machine Co., 1910, Bubble Records 175.00

Piano, Baby Grand, 12 Keys, Schoenhut, Engraved Name On Front 125.00
Piano, Bliss, 1911, 9 1/4 In. 35.00
Piano, Child's, Schoenhut, Lithographed Panel, Cupid, 21 X 13 In. 75.00
Piano, Schoenhut, Dated 1900 .... 87.50
Piano, Upright, Symphony, 10-Key, Pine, Picture Of Wood Nymphs, 11 In. 95.00
Piano, Upright, 15-Key, Wooden, Schoenhut, 20 X 17 In. 50.00
Piano, Upright, 17-Keyboard, International Pitch Symphony, 18 X 11 In. 60.00
Piano, Upright, 18 Keys, Schoenhut 150.00
Piano, 11 Keys, Schoenhut, Marked 80.00
Pif & Paf, 2 Tumbling Clowns, Windup, French, 21 In., 2 Trapezes 750.00
Pig, Cook, Flips Egg In Pan, Windup 39.00
Pikes Peak Mountain Climbing, Windup, Marx, 31 In.Long 110.00
Pipe, Bubble, Tin, Vermont, 7 In. 14.00
Pipsqueak, Ewe & Lamb, Polychrome Paint, 5 1/8 In. 155.00
Pipsqueak, Rooster, Polychrome Paint, 3 1/8 In. 95.00
Pistol, Bean Shooter, Ideal 22.50
Plane, Military, Tootsietoy 8.00
Plane, World War II, Metal, Hubley, Folding Wings, Retractable Wheels 65.00
Plane, Wyandotte 15.00
Play-A-Sax, 5 Paper Rolls 135.00
Polar Bear, Crawling, Battery Operated 55.00
Polar Bear, Key Wind 25.00
Policeman, Lead, English, Blue Uniform 10.00
Poodle, Jointed Legs, Mohair, Gray, 1950s, 6 In. 45.00
Poodle, Lambskin Covering, Canvas Body, Standing, 10 1/2 In. 75.00
Poodle, Schoenhut 140.00
Pool Players, Windup 130.00
Popeye Express, Parrot Pops Out 375.00
Popeye Paddlewagon, Boxed 40.00
Popeye The Pilot, Marx, Tin, Windup 375.00
Popeye, In Barrel 250.00
Popeye, Playing Basketball 525.00
Porky Pig, Windup, Marx, 1939, Large 550.00
Porky Pig, With Umbrella, Windup, Marx, 1939 .... 150.00
Prehistoric Animal, Linemar, Tin, Windup, Boxed 110.00
Projector, King, Electric, 7 Cartoons, 1930s 50.00
Pug Dog, Pull Toy, Molded Felt 210.00
Pump Organ, Cathedral Shape, Hand-Cranked Bellows, German, 6 3/4 In. 125.00
Pup, Peppy, Battery 35.00
Pup, Slurpy, Battery Operated 40.00
Puppet, Charlie McCarthy 125.00
Puppet, Court Jester, German 25.00
Puppet, Dream Baby, Paper Heart Label, 12 In. 300.00
Puppet, Hand-Painted, Wooden, 24 In. 160.00
Puppet, McAwful The Scott, With Record, 1948, Boxed 40.00
Puppet, Monkey Head, Hand, Composition 11.00
Puppet, Owl, Hand, Steiff 40.00
Puppet, Stick, Dancing Black Man 16.00
Rabbit, Eating A Carrot, Pull, Original Paint, 7 X 5 X 3 In. 40.00
Rabbit, Playing Drums, Windup 35.00
Rabbit, Pulling Cart 10.00
Rabbit, U.S.Zone Germany, Windup, Tin 35.00
Rabbit, Windup, Chein, Tin 28.00
Racing Horse & Man, 2-Wheel Holder, Cast Iron, Brown 99.00
Railroad, Silver Mountain 28.00
Railway, Street, Funny Andy, Lithographed, Tin, Pull, Trolley, 13 In. 125.00
Rattle, Wooden 8.00
Red Ranger, Wyandotte, Windup 48.00
Refrigerator, North Wind, Marx, Tin 18.00
Ride-A-Rocket, Carnival Ride, Mechanical, Tin, 18 In. 50.00
Rider, Tricycle, Bell Ringer, Windup, Cast Iron 215.00
Road Roller, Huber, 4 1/2 In. 50.00
Robot, Gigantor, Battery Operated, Box, 17 In. 100.00

Robot, Moon Explorer	50.00
Robot, Piston	55.00
Robot, Space Capsule	175.00
Robot, Space Warrior, Radio Controlled	45.00
Robot, Super Astronaut, Tin, Boxed	45.00
Robot, Super Giant, 17 In.	90.00
Robot, Video	48.00
Rocker, Child's, All Wooden, 12 X 14 X 18 In.	175.00
Rocker, Child's, Victorian, Wicker Back & Reel Spindles	30.00
Rocker, Splint Seat, Slat Back, 15 1/2 In.	35.00 To 40.00
Rocking Dog, Windup	48.00
Rocking Horse, Convertible, Pull, Cloth Covered, Victorian	420.00
Rocking Horse, Curved Legs, Shoofly Base, Original Paint	310.00
Rocking Horse, Dapple Gray, Wood	165.00
Rocking Horse, Hand-Carved, C.1880	525.00
Rocking Horse, Hide Covered, Glass Eyes	475.00
Rocking Horse, Original Black Paint Seat, 19th Century	475.00
Rocking Horse, Original Paint & Design, Converse Label	385.00
Rocking Horse, White, Red & Blue Bridle, Leather Saddle, 29 1/2 In.	425.00
Roller Coaster, Key Wind, Chein	35.00
Roller Coaster, 2 Cars, Windup, Tin, Chein, 20 X 10 In.	125.00
Roller Skates, Doll, Tin, 1 3/4 In., Pair	6.00
Roller Skates, Winchester	32.00 To 45.00
Rolmonica, 3 Rolls, Steel	85.00
Rooster, Marx	300.00
Rooster, Squeak	17.50
Rooster, Tags, Steiff, Multicolors, 8 In.	65.00
Rowboat, Black, Iron, 6 In.	10.00
Safe, Union, Combination, Cast Iron, Heavy Tin, 3 1/2 In.	40.00
Sailors, British, Lead, Hand-Painted, White Uniforms, 2 1/4 In., 12 Piece	120.00
Sand Pail, Snow White, 1932	15.00
Santa, Clock Works, Head Moves Side To Side, 1920, 13 X 21 In.	750.00
Santa, Drummer, Battery Operated	35.00
Santa, Riding Tricycle, Windup	15.00
Santa, Ringing Bell & Waving, Windup	20.00
Santa, Sleigh, Reindeer, Cast Iron, 17 In.	750.00
Santa, Windup Walkers	175.00
Saxophone, Spike Jones, Boxed	50.00
Scooter, Trike, 1920s	65.00
Seal With Ball, Friction, Tin, Lehmann, Germany, 3 X 4 In.	35.00
Seesaw, Gibbs, Hand-Painted	80.00
Service Station, Roadside Stop, 1930, Marx	165.00
Settee & Matching Armchair, Wicker, 9 In.Long	95.00
Sewing Machine, Betsy Ross, Electric, Carrying Case	45.00
Sewing Machine, British Zone, Germany	35.00
Sewing Machine, Child's, Vulcan, Working Model, Black, 5 X 9 X 6 In.	35.00
Sewing Machine, Junior Model By Gateway, Red, Metal	22.00
Sewing Machine, Little Miss, Lindstrom, Motor	45.00
Sewing Machine, Penny Toy	95.00
Sewing Machine, Singer, Child's, 1903	45.00
Sewing Machine, Stitch Mistress, Model No.49	25.00
Sheep, Pull Toy, Handmade, Oxidized Paint, Wooden	45.00
Sheep, Pull, Real Wool, Glass Eyes, Makes Noise, C.1880	275.00
Sheep, Woolly Coated, Papier-Mache Over Wood, 2 1/2 In.	22.00
Ship, Sky Rangers On Side, Red, Blue, Yellow, Tin, 9 In.	30.00
Shooter, Marble, Cast Iron	350.00
Shuttle, Coal, Child's, Orange Outside, Black Inside, Tin, Shovel	9.00
Skunk, Windup, Walks, Tail Wags, Tin & Cloth	65.00
Sled, Double Wicker Seats For Twins	175.00
Sled, Girl's, Paris, Bluejay Transfer, Red	195.00
Sled, Lightning Glider, Stenciling	40.00
Sled, Metal Runners, Floral Stenciling, Child's	185.00
Sled, Original Blue Paint	165.00

Sled, Red Steel Runner, Hand-Painted, Signed Kalamazoo, Mich., 1902 .... 190.00
Sled, Stenciled Snowflake Design, Blue Paint, South Paris, Maine 150.00
Sled, Wooden Side Grips, Cast-Iron Runners, Marked, C.1880, 45 1/2 In. 160.00
Sled, Wooden, Hungary, 10 In. 40.00
Sleigh, Child's, Iron, Blacksmith Made 65.00
Sleigh, Santa Claus, Strauss, Tin 485.00
Sleigh, Wicker 12.00
Sleigh, Wood & Metal 95.00
Snake, Green, Red & Yellow, Jointed, 14 In. 22.00
Snow Shoes, Wood, Pair 50.00
Snowman, Mechanical, 1930s, 28 In. 215.00
Soldiers, U.S.Cavalry Lead, Hand-Painted, 3 In., Set Of 5 .... 75.00
Soldiers, U.S.Cavalry, Mounted, Lead, Black Horse, C.1890, 3 In., Set Of 4 .... 60.00
Sparkler, Hand-Painted Santa Claus, Tin 125.00
Spelling Board, Wood, Pat'd 1886 .... 42.00
Squirrel, Nut In Paws, Steiff, 5 In. 45.00
Squirrel, Roly Poly, Celluloid 15.00
Stable, 2 Box Stalls, Feed Baskets, Horses, 23 X 19 3/8 In. .... *Illus* 250.00
Stable, 2 Horses, Bliss 295.00
Stagecoach, Iron, 5 1/2 In. 115.00
Stagecoach, Overland, Battery Operated, Action & Sound 65.00
Stagecoach, Wagon Master, Boxed 50.00
Station, Train, German, Bing Tin, 9 1/4 X 7 In. 50.00
Station, Train, Schoenhut 225.00
Steam Accessory, Bing, C.1915, Painted & Lithographed Tin .... *Illus* 150.00
Steam Engine, Burner, Wooden Base, 5 3/4 X 9 3/4 In. 55.00
Steam Engine, Iron & Brass, Weeden 90.00
Steam Roller, Fat Man At Controls, Battery Operated, Tin, Japan 48.50
Steam Roller, Huber, Heavy Metal, 8 X 5 1/2 In. 95.00
Steam Roller, Hubley, 9 1/2 In. 15.00
Steam Roller, Tipp & Co., German, Tin, 13 In. 375.00
Steam Shovel, Buddy L 145.00
Steam Shovel, Truck Hauler, Wyandotte, Windup 30.00
Store, Fold-Up, Cardboard Products, Tin 40.00
Stork, Straw Stuffed, 1930s, Stieff 95.00
Stove, Child's, Venus, 4 Burner, Embossed Sides, Iron, 6 X 5 In. 35.00
Stove, Eagle, Hubley, Gas, 3 1/2 X 8 1/2 X 6 3/4 In. 225.00
Stove, Gas, Royal, Cast Iron, 2 1/2 X 2 X 2 1/2 In. 22.50
Stove, Little Lady, Electric 40.00
Stove, Pet, Cast Iron, Pots, Shelf, Lids, Stack, 7 In. .... 65.00 To 70.00
Stove, Prize, Cast Iron 35.00
Stove, Roper, Gas, Tin 40.00

Toy, Steam Accessory, Bing, C.1915,
Painted & Lithographed Tin

Stove, Star On Door, Footed, Cast Iron, 6 3/4 X 9 In.	60.00
Stove, Stern, Metal, 5 Pans	95.00
Stove, 2 Burners, Cast Iron, 4 X 3 1/2 In.	35.00
Stroller, Green Wicker	75.00
Submarine, Blue & Red, Battery Operated, Tin	45.00
Submarine, Tin, Gold Paint, 53 In.	95.00
Submarine, Wolverine, Boxed	45.00
Sulky, Doll's, Wicker, 32 In.	125.00
Surrey, Fringed Top, Horse Drawn, C.1906, Cast Iron, 13 1/2 In.	175.00
Surrey, Stanley, Cast Iron	65.00
Swimmer, Celluloid, Wind-Up, Boxed	25.00
Table, Child's, Drop Leaf, Walnut, Trestle Legs, 8 X 16 In.	135.00
Table, Child's, Folding, ABC & Miss Muffet Pictured, 2 Chairs, Wooden	125.00
Table, Old Red Paint, Arcade, Cast Iron, 3 3/4 X 6 1/2 X 3 In.	9.00
Table, Sewing, Child's, Pine, Ruler, 9 3/4 In.Tall	45.00
Tank, Space, Tin, Boxed	85.00
Tank, Superman	140.00
Tank, U.S., No.4, Rubber, 5 1/4 In.	35.00
Tank, World War II, Marx, Windup	15.00 To 30.00
Target, Gorilla, Screams When Hit, Arms Fly Up, Battery	45.00
Taxi Meter, 1937, Clockwork	325.00
Taxi, Amos & Andy, Boxed	645.00 To 750.00
Taxi, Lincoln Zephyr, Cast Iron, 7 1/2 In.	285.00
Taxi, Tricky, Marx, Tin	17.00
Taxi, World's Fair, Cast Iron, 6 1/2 In.	295.00
Taxi, Yellow, Cast Iron	250.00
Tea Set, Marked Staffordshire, Blue & White, 23 Piece	300.00
Teakettle, Child's, Whistling, Red Handle, 4 X 3 In.	10.00
Teddy Bear, Black, Silver Tipped Mohair, Straw Stuffed, 11 1/2 In.	225.00
Teddy Bear, Button Ears, Brown, Tipped Beige, Overalls, Steiff, 10 3/4 In.	225.00
Teddy Bear, Fully Jointed, Straw Filled, Music Box, 16 In.	250.00
Teddy Bear, Glass Eyes, Jointed, Humped Back, Straw Filled, 19 1/2 In.	250.00
Teddy Bear, Handmade, Wool Canvas, Embroidered Face, Button Eyes, 10 In.	38.00
Teddy Bear, Jointed, Lamb's Wool, 12 In.	45.00
Teddy Bear, Jointed, Mohair, Steiff, Caramel, 10 In.	28.50
Teddy Bear, Jointed, Mohair, Steiff, Caramel, 20 In.	85.00
Teddy Bear, Mechanical, Jointed, Music Box, Teddy Bears' Picnic, 13 In.	135.00
Teddy Bear, Mortarboard Hat, Carries Cane, Glass Eyes	185.00
Teddy Bear, Movable Joints & Head, 16 In.	165.00
Teddy Bear, Musical, Glass Eyes, C.1920	150.00
Teddy Bear, On Iron Wheels, Dated 1910	350.00
Teddy Bear, On Wheels, Hermann, 5 1/2 X 5 In.	27.50
Teddy Bear, Pointed Face, Jointed, Steiff, 12 In.	225.00
Teddy Bear, Polar, On All Fours, White, Jointed Head, 6 In.	85.00
Teddy Bear, Shoe Button Eyes	375.00
Teddy Bear, Shoe Button Eyes, Fabric Nose, Beige, 11 In.	195.00
Teddy Bear, Shoe Button Eyes, 1920s, 10 1/2 In.	95.00
Teddy Bear, Steiff, 1920s, Gold, 9 In.	165.00
Teddy Bear, Straw Filled, Mohair Coat, Germany, 16 In.	175.00
Teddy Bear, Triangular Head, Shoebutton Eyes, Gold, 13 In.	185.00
Teddy Bear, Windup, German	90.00
Teddy Bear, 1950s, Steiff, Beige, 8 1/2 In.	155.00
Telephone, Hello-Hello, Chimes, Cast Iron	1750.00
Three Little Pigs, Schuco, Windup	240.00
Three Little Pigs, Washtub & Board, Lithograph, Tin	15.00
Tiger, Yellow With Brown Stripes, Wheels, Wooden, 4 1/4 In.	10.00
Tip Top Porter, Strauss, Boxed, Tin	200.00
Tool Chest, 12 Unused Tools, Paper Lithograph, 18 X 9 In.	85.00
Toonerville Trolley, Windup, Tin	450.00 To 600.00
Top, Spinning, Chien, 6 In.	7.50
Tractor, Allis Chalmers, Arcade, Cast Iron	37.50
Tractor, Allis Chalmers, Kaysun	150.00
Tractor, Allis Chalmers, Original Paint, Cast Iron, 7 In.	125.00

Tractor, Arcade	40.00
Tractor, Caterpillar, Tin	10.00
Tractor, Driver, Rubber Tires, Arcade, Cast Iron, Small	85.00
Tractor, Farm, Red Wheels, Man Driving, Tootsietoy, Gray & Red	35.00
Tractor, Fordson, Arcade, Steel Wheels, Cast Iron, 5 1/2 In.	110.00
Tractor, Hubley, Cast Iron	11.00
Tractor, International, Rubber Tires, Metal	10.00
Tractor, John Deere, Arcade Cast Iron	325.00
Tractor, John Deere, 1947	90.00
Tractor, With Cart, Arcade, Iron, 8 In.	50.00
Train Car, Pennsylvania R.R., Tootsietoy, 1938	35.00
Train, American Flyer, Iron, Tin Tender & Passenger Car	125.00
Train, American Flyer, No.1107	75.00
Train, Caboose, N.Y.C., Tootsietoy	1.00
Train, Caboose, Tootsietoy R.R.	2.00
Train, Car, Lionel, No.710	75.00
Train, Car, Old Dutch Cleanser	150.00
Train, Engine, Clockwork Wind, Cast Iron, 9 In.	250.00
Train, Engine, Pacific Overland, Engine No.M10003, Clockwork Mechanism	35.00
Train, Engine, Wood-Burning Type, Original Paint, Cast Iron, 7 In.	49.00
Train, Hill Climber, Large, Friction	129.00
Train, Honeymoon Express, Windup, Marx, Tin	35.00
Train, Lionel, Locomotive Set, C.1926	650.00
Train, Locomotive, Smokestack Wood Burner, Big 6, C.1888, 8 In.	350.00
Train, Locomotive, Steam, O Gauge, Bing, 7 1/2 In.	350.00
Train, Locomotive, With 1 Car, Pullman, Cor-Cor Toys, Sheet Metal, 18 In.	70.00
Train, Passenger Set, Union Pacific, O-Gauge, Lionel, 4 Piece *Illus*	750.00
Train, Santa Fe Diesel Switcher, Lionel 623, Boxed	125.00
Train, Set, O-Gauge, Karl Bub, 1920s, Clockwork, Tin, 4 Piece *Illus*	650.00
Train, Tippy, 2 Cars, Self-Winding, Tunnel, Bridge, 6 X 6 In.	95.00
Train, Track & Key, Schucco, Tin, 12 X 10 In.	350.00
Train, Wooden, Dark Green	110.00
Train, Wooden, 4 Piece	100.00
Trapeze Artist, Windup, Occupied Japan	125.00

Toy, Train, Passenger Set, Union Pacific, O-Gauge, Lionel, 4 Piece

Toy, Train, Set, O-Gauge, Karl Bub, 1920s, Clockwork, Tin, 4 Piece

Tricycle, Iron, 1920s	35.00
Tricycle, With Sidecar, Wicker, 10 In.	26.00
Trolley Car, Cast Iron, 4 1/2 In.	50.00
Trolley, Sunny Andy	55.00
Truck, Ace Am, Continental Express, Tin, Marx, 21 In.	15.00
Truck, Army Transport, Buddy L	40.00
Truck, Borden's Milk, Horse Drawn, Glass Milk Bottles	165.00
Truck, Chevy Stake, Cast Iron, 9 In.	650.00
Truck, City Fuel, 10 Wheels, Tootsietoy, Silver	40.00
Truck, Coca-Cola, 6 Cases & Bottles, Boxed	450.00
Truck, Cor Cor, Model A, 24 In.	125.00
Truck, Dairy, Toytown, Pulled By Horse	75.00
Truck, Daisymatic Cement Mixer, Battery	85.00
Truck, Dandy Digger, Buddy L, Boxed	55.00
Truck, Dump, Arcade, Cast Iron, 3 In.	25.00
Truck, Dump, Crank-Up, Steel, Large	150.00
Truck, Dump, Driver, Arcade, 1930, 10 1/2 In.	350.00
Truck, Dump, Friction	155.00
Truck, Dump, Hydraulic, Buddy L, Tin	35.00
Truck, Dump, Old Green & Yellow Paint, Tin, C.1915, 8 In.	85.00
Truck, Dump, Plastic Wheels, Tonka	10.00
Truck, Dump, Structo	80.00
Truck, Dump, Tin, Green & Yellow, C.1915, 8 In.	85.00
Truck, Dump, Tootsietoy, Red, 5 In.	10.00
Truck, Dump, Wyandotte, 15 In.	27.00
Truck, Ford Pickup, Tootsietoy, Red	18.00
Truck, Gasoline, Yellow, White Rubber Tires, 5 1/2 In.	35.00
Truck, Hydraulic Lift, Tonka, Red	8.00
Truck, Ice Cream, Buddy L, Cast Iron	50.00
Truck, Ice, Kenton, Cast Iron, 7 In.	165.00
Truck, International K5 Toy, Tootsietoy	5.00
Truck, LaFrance Fire, Tootsietoy	2.00
Truck, Lazy Day Farm	35.00
Truck, Log, Smith, Miller, Green	550.00
Truck, Mac Coal, 1925, Tootsietoy, Tan & Yellow	25.00
Truck, Mac Stake, 1925, Tootsietoy, Green & Tan	25.00
Truck, Mack B-Line Stake Trailer, 1955, Tootsietoy, Green	20.00
Truck, Mack Gasoline, Cast Iron, Tin Tank, 13 In.	695.00
Truck, Mack, Closed Sides, Yellow Wheels, Iron, Arcade, 5 1/4 In.	375.00
Truck, Mack, Hercules, Bulldog, Tin, Original Paint, 18 In.	40.00
Truck, Mack, Tootsietoy, Airmail Van	75.00
Truck, Milk, Hershey, Pot Metal, Silver, Rubber Wheels, 5 In.	150.00
Truck, N.B.C. T.V. Truck, Friction	65.00
Truck, National Biscuit, Horse, Tin Wagon	95.00
Truck, Oil Trailer, Domaco, Front Bumper, Tootsietoy, Orange & Cream	35.00
Truck, Oil, Seal Beam Headlights, Tootsietoy, Red	3.00
Truck, Panel, Buddy L, 24 In.	60.00
Truck, Panel, Service Routier, Peugeot, Tin, 6 1/2 In.	85.00
Truck, Pickup, Ford, Buddy L, 1921, Original Paint, Cast Iron, 12 In.	285.00
Truck, Pickup, Model A, Hubley, Boxed	20.00
Truck, R.C.A. T.V., Cast Iron	90.00
Truck, Sand Loader, Cast Iron	65.00
Truck, St.Louis Sand & Gravel, Metalcraft	95.00
Truck, Stake, Cast Iron, 1920s, 9 In.	125.00
Truck, Stake, Mack Bodied, Iron, Red Paint, 4 1/2 In.	65.00
Truck, Stake, Wyandotte, 15 In.	20.00
Truck, Sturditoy, Cast Iron	125.00
Truck, Sun Rubber Company	4.00
Truck, Telephone, Cast Iron, 7 In.	395.00
Truck, Texaco Tank, 1950s, Buddy L	55.00
Truck, Texaco, Buddy L	20.00
Truck, The Cannonball Express, Cow-Catcher Front, Bell	375.00
Truck, Tow, Arcade, Iron, No. 218	75.00

Toy, Turkey & Peacock, Squeak Base, Painted Plaster, 7 In., Pair

Truck, Tow, Buddy L, White, Cast Iron	45.00
Truck, Wrecker, Decal, World War II, Buddy L	35.00
Trunk, Doll, Wooden, Floral Design Inside, Hangers, 9 X 10 In.	100.00
Trunk, Tin	45.00
Turkey & Peacock, Squeak Base, Painted Plaster, 7 In., Pair .... *Illus*	475.00
Turkey, Pendulum Moves Head & Tail, C.1865, 8 1/2 In. .... *Illus*	1900.00

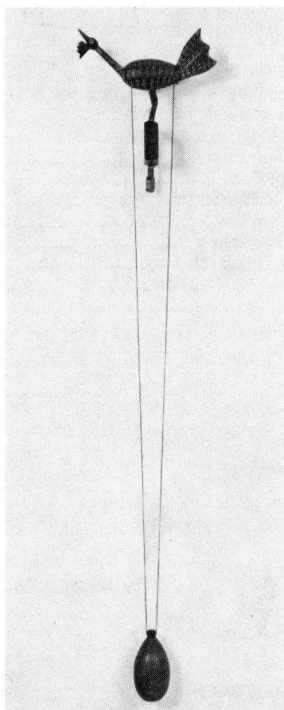

Toy, Turkey, Pendulum Moves
Head & Tail, C.1865, 8 1/2 In.

Turtle, Windup, Tin, American, 5 In.	8.00
Tut-Tut, Windup, Lehmann	500.00
Typewriter, Dial, Marx, Child's, Tin, Moving Carriage, 5 X 11 In.	35.00
Typewriter, Dial, Marx, No.2109	15.00
Typewriter, Simplex, Boxed	55.00
Typewriter, Tom Thumb, Carrying Case	10.00
Uncle Wiggly, In Car, Windup, German, Tin	3500.00
Village School, Master, 11 Boys & Girls, Lamb, Dunce Cap, 15 Pieces	500.00
Violin, Tin	17.50
Wagon, Beer, 8 Horses & Barrels, Iron, 35 In.	85.00
Wagon, Child's, Coaster	250.00
Wagon, Circus, 2 Horses, Driver, Iron, 8 1/2 In.	40.00
Wagon, Coaster, Paris, Hand Brake	325.00
Wagon, Dray, Team & Driver, Kenton	225.00
Wagon, Express, Pulled By Goat, Original Paint, Cast Iron	80.00
Wagon, Express, Wooden Wheels	175.00
Wagon, Hubley, 3 Horse, Ladder, C.1910, 28 In.	585.00
Wagon, Ice, Cast Iron, 12 In.	225.00
Wagon, Ice, One Horse, Red, Gold Wheels, Iron, 10 In.	70.00
Wagon, Milk, Borden's, Horse, Man, Wagon, & Bottles	200.00
Wagon, Milk, Bordens, Tin & Wood	75.00
Wagon, Milk, Windup, Marx	95.00
Wagon, Milk, 1 Horse, Althof Bergman, Tin	800.00
Wagon, The Overland, Dated 1906, Wooden Wheels, Oak Body	295.00
Wagon, Wood, Advertises Yeast Foam, 1906, 32 X 10 In.	70.00
Waiter, Celluloid, Black, Windup	45.00
Walker, Child's, Bentwood, Cherry, Round Seat	45.00
Washboard, Wooden Frame, Green Glass Insert, 4 3/4 X 9 1/2 In.	30.00
Washing Machine, Little Miss Housekeeping, C.1930	30.00
Washing Machine, Wringer, Tin & Glass Tub, Wood Rollers, 10 In.	50.00
Washtub, Tin	10.00
Whale, Moby Dick, Color Litho, Tin, Windup, 11 1/4 In.	50.00
Wheel Barrow, Child's, Wooden Wheels, Shovel, Rake & Hoe, 5 In.	8.00
Whistle, Bird, Blue & Yellow Paint, Tin, 4 1/2 In.	35.00
Whistle, Jack Webb, Offical Dragnet	5.00
Whistle, Pipe, Ed Wynn Fire Chief	55.00
Whistle, Sgt.Preston, On A Rope	5.00
Whistle, Slide, Hezzie & The Hoosier Hotshots, Boxed	50.00
Whoopee Car, Marx, Lithographed Tin _Illus_	175.00
Wild Mile Jack, Bell Ringer, 1900, Iron	475.00
Windmill, Sand-Powered, Marx, Lithograph, Tin	15.00
Wings, Airplane Pilot, Tootsietoy	15.00
Xylophone, Schoenhut, 22 In.	23.00
Xylophone, 1893	45.00
Zeppelin, 1920s, Germany, 6 In.	27.00
Zeppelin, 1930s, Marx, Boxed	170.00

Toy, Whoopee Car, Marx, Lithographed Tin

Tramp art is a form of folk art made since the Civil War. It is usually made from chip-carved cigar boxes.

TRAMP ART, Bowl, Church Scene Inside, Wooden	24.00
Box, Acorn Finial, Stars On Sides, Pine & Birchbark, 6 In.	80.00
Box, Bird Spears Cigarettes, Wood & Tin, 6 3/4 In. ....*Illus*	800.00
Box, Brass Nails, Leather Hinged Cover, Lined, 6 X 4 In.	55.00
Box, Carved Tiers, Hinged Top, Cherry, Maple, & Mahogany, 4 X 7 In.	65.00
Box, Cigarette, Bird On Hinge, Scallops, Hearts, 6 1/4 In.	880.00
Box, Mirror Sides	135.00
Box, Pyramidal Layers, Grooved Members, Lined, 6 1/2 X 9 X 4 In.	60.00
Box, Wooden, White & Stained Bown, Key, 3 In.Tall	10.00
Box, 2 Drawers, Scrolled Feet	120.00
Box, 3 Nested & Notched Pyramids, Diamond Overlay, 3 1/2 X 7 In.	45.00
Chest, Porcelain Knobs, Signed, Small	135.00
Chest, 14 X 11 X 10 In.	90.00
China Cupboard, Double Glass Doors, Central Drawer, 60 3/4 In.	575.00
Cupboard, Hanging, Seated Dog On Top	1175.00
Dresser, Doll's, Mirror	140.00
Dresser, 2 Drawer, Porcelain Knobs, Gray & White, 17 X 16 X 9 In.	115.00
Frame, Gold Paint, Heart & Leaf Design, 23 X 16 In.	70.00
Frame, Interlocking & Overlapping Crown Of Thorns, 34 X 19 In.	125.00
Tray, Cutlery	85.00
Wall Pocket, Hanging, Dark Green, Black, Yellow & Orange, 11 In.	105.00

Tramp Art, Box, Bird Spears Cigarettes, Wood & Tin, 6 3/4 In.

TRAP, Ant, Calpro Ant Extermination, 1925, Green Crockery	18.00
Bait, Creel Shape, C.1880, Tin, Gray, 3 1/4 X 3 1/4 X 2 1/2 In.	10.00
Bear, Double Spring, Hand-Forged	95.00
Bear, Kodiak, No.6	250.00
Bear, Newhouse, No.15	375.00
Bear, Single Spring, Hand-Forged	85.00
Bird, Spring Operated, 18th Century, For Banding, Wood & Iron, 8 In.	165.00
Eel, Basket, Wooden Plug, Delaware River Area, 21 In.	85.00
Eel, Hickory Splint, 24 In.	45.00
Fly, Clock Driven Cylinder, Chapel & Hubbard, 1872, 40 X 6 1/2 In.	130.00
Fly, Glass	65.00
Fly, Marked Patent Applied For J.J., Blown Glass, 7 In.	450.00
Mole	6.50
Mouse, Black Wire & Iron, C.1870	32.00
Mouse, McGill	4.50

Mouse, Victor 4-Way	4.00
Mouse, Wire Bail Handle, Wooden Floor, Spring Action, 6 X 6 X 11 In.	20.00
Newhouse No.3, Dated 1911, Double Spring	12.50
Rabbit, Wooden, 8 In. X 13 1/2 In.Long	22.50

Treen are small wooden objects such as mugs, spoons, and bowls. The term is early English but is used in the United States in many areas.

TREEN, Bowl, Eating, Oval, 5 1/4 X 5 1/2 In.	75.00
Bowl, Porridge, Old Cream Paint, Footed, C.1820, 5 1/4 X 5 1/2 In.	125.00
Box, Footed, 2 1/2 In.	11.00
Box, Pocket, Hinged, Contour Lip To Center, Burl, 2 7/8 X 3 3/8 In.	50.00
Box, Salt, Covered, 1 1/2 X 3 1/2 In.Diam.	60.00
Box, Spool, Ivory Grommets, 6 Thread Portholes, 4 1/4 X 2 1/2 In.	30.00
Candleholder, Black Tin Drip Cup, Picket Spike, Colonial, 10 1/4 In.	195.00
Candlestick, Butternut, 7 1/2 In., Pair	75.00
Dispenser, Medicine, Kit, H.Gilbertson & Sons, London, 4 Piece	125.00
Grinder, Spice	235.00
Holder, String, Keg Shaped	110.00
Inkwell, Pontiled Blown Glass Well, Quill Holders, Colonial	95.00
Jar, Lift Notches, Domed Cover, 5 1/4 X 4 In.	12.50
Mirror, Hand, Loop Handle, Beveled Glass Mirror, 4 3/4 In.Diam.	22.50
Mortar & Pestle, Concentric Lines To Top, C.1850, Pestle 8 In.	35.00
Mortar & Pestle, Herb	195.00
Mortar & Pestle, Mushroom Knob, Mortar 9 In.	85.00
Mug, La Pierre Mfg.Co., C.1901, Silver-Mounted, 8 1/2 In.	250.00
Pitcher, Cylindrical Form, Fitted Handle, 10 In.	165.00
Ponce Sander, Star Shape Sander, C.1820, Nutwood, 3 In.	50.00
Salt Maul	235.00
Salt Trencher, Irregular Contouring, Briar Burl, 4 X 5 In.	175.00
Sander	64.00
Shaker, Globe Powder, Bottom Screws On, C.1840, 6 1/2 In.	65.00
Sugar, Concentric Rings, Cover, 7 1/2 In.Diam.	95.00
Sugar, Footed, Covered	55.00
Trencher, Irregular Rim, Oval, Maple, 7 1/4 X 15 In.	160.00
Urn, George III, Covered, Lignum Vitae, 9 In.	245.00
Vessel, Drinking, Footed, Lemony Color, 1 Piece Maple, 4 In.	12.50
Wine, Free-Carved Ring, Pedestal, 4 3/4 In.	22.50

Trivets are now used to hold hot dishes. Most of the late nineteenth- and early twentieth-century trivets were made to hold hot irons. Iron or brass reproductions are being made of many of the old styles.

TRIVET, Brass, Doodles Dream, 8 In.	13.00
Brass, English, Circular, Scrolling Base, 10 In.	60.00
Child's, Sensible, Iron, 4 1/2 In.	30.00
Enterprise Mfg., Cast Iron	15.00
Flatiron Shape, B. & D. In Lacy Center, Iron	8.50
Fleur-De-Lis, Cast Iron	15.00
Floral Pattern, Marked W.B.R., Handled, Footed, Cast Iron	85.00
Fruit Center, Brass, Rectangular, 5 1/4 X 12 In.	85.00
Hand With Heart Inside, 3 Interlocking Circles Handle, Brass	65.00
Heart Shaped, Peacock Feathered Interior, Iron	25.00
Heart, Iron, 3-Footed, 4 1/2 In.	60.00
Heart, Knob-End Legs, 18th Century, Brass, 5 3/4 X 4 In.	85.00
Heart, Wrought Iron, 3 1/2 X 6 In.	80.00
Horseshoe Shaped, Brass, 7 In.	10.00
Horseshoe Shaped, Good Luck To All Who Use This, Brass	50.00
Kettle, Open Heart Center, Rays, Cast Iron, 8 In.	75.00
Maltese Cross, Cast Iron	18.00
Odd Fellows, Brass	55.00
Order Of Cincinnati, Brass, Heart Handle, 5 X 9 In.	95.00
Our Ain Fire Side, Brass	45.00
Pineapple & Heart, Footed, Iron	22.00

Scalloped & Holed, Iron, 6 1/8 In.Diam. 25.00
Serpentine, Form, 3 Drawn Legs, 18th Century, Wrought Iron, 7 In. 150.00
Square, Baluster Shaped, Circular Base, Brass, English, 10 In. 25.00
Star & Sunburst 18.00
Turtle Feet, Lacy Center, Iron 8.00
Urn Design, Openwork, 3-Footed, Cast Iron 30.00
Victorina, Crown Shape, Twisted Wireware, 6 1/4 In.Diam. 25.00
Wire, Diamond Design, Round 12.50
3 Initails, Refer To W.B.Pineby, 19th Century, Cast Iron, 12 3/8 In. 85.00
3 Legs Extend Into Center, Wrought Iron, 6 X 8 In.Diam. 65.00

TRUNK, Brassed Tin Locks, Tin, Wood Interior, 10 X 6 X 6 In. 40.00
Camel Top, C.1760, Finger-Painted Interior, Blue Paint 850.00
Chest, Seaman's, Cape Cod, C.1820, Pyramid Shaped 325.00
Dated 1867, Lock & Key, Norwegian, Interior Salmon Paint, 45 In.Wide 850.00
Doll, Humpback 65.00
Dome Top, Embossed Metal Designs, Wood Slats 100.00
Dower, Rosemaled, Norwegian, Dated 1880 .... 895.00
Front Design Of Leaves & Vines, Flat Topped, Brown, Pine, 31 X 14 In. 235.00
Immigrant, Dated 1775, Norwegian, 48 In.Wide 950.00
Immigrant, Norwegian, Dated 176i & 1829, Lock & Key 1400.00
Ironbound, Leatherized Covering, Dome Top, Handled, 30 In. 40.00
Oriental, Red Leather, Foo Lion, Brass Bail, 21 In. 100.00
Rosemaled, 1852, Norwegian 550.00
Stagecoach, Cylindrical, Leather Cover, Iron Lock, C.1840, 23 1/2 In. 175.00
Stagecoach, Tooled Design, Brass Buttons, Dated 1868, Leather 225.00
Wallpaper Lined, Whalen Harness & Trunkmaker, 26 X 17 3/4 In. 50.00

TURQUOISE, Vase, Carved Flowering Plant, Ovoid, 2 7/8 In. ....*Illus* 500.00

TUTHILL, Bowl, Cut Rose Pattern, 8 In. 300.00
Bowl, Intaglio Cut Rose Pattern, Signed, 8 In.Diam. 295.00
Bowl, Vintage Pattern, Rolled Rim, Pedestal, Signed, 12 In.Diam. 1075.00
Celery, Primrose Pattern, Signed, 13 X 5 In. 425.00
Sherbet & Underplate, Copper Well Engraving, Signed, Plate 6 In. 100.00
Sugar & Creamer, Phlox Pattern 450.00
Tumbler, Wild Rose, Signed 60.00
Vase, Allover Geometric Cut, Corset Shape, Signed, 10 In. 175.00
Vase, Bud, Floral, Wheel Cut, Signed, 12 In. 275.00
Water Set, Geometric Design, Signed, 7 Piece 495.00

Turquoise, Vase, Carved Flowering Plant,
Ovoid, 2 7/8 In.

TYPEWRITER, Bennett, Portable, Case, Patent Date 1908, 10 3/4 X 4 3/4 In. 35.00
  Harris Visible No.4 .... 12.50
  Lambart 250.00
  Multiplex 150.00
  Oliver, 1909 .... 75.00
  Schmidt Premier, 1892 .... 95.00

UMBRELLA, Handle, Art Nouveau, Sterling Silver 45.00
  Handle, Sterling Silver Overlay, Scrolling, On Abalone, 7 1/8 In. 48.00
  Parasol, Bamboo, Ivory Tip, Material, Victorian 20.00
  Parasol, C.1890, 8 Gold Tips For Frame, C.1890, French, Gold Mounted 400.00
  Parasol, Child's, Ivory Handle, Brass Fitting, Ivory End Knob 25.00
  Parasol, Child's, Pink Paper & Bamboo 20.00
  Parasol, Japanese, Lacquered, Black 25.00
  Parasol, Oriental 35.00
  Parasol, Oriental, Painted Paper & Wood, Marked Chicago 1933 .... 5.00
  Wedding, White 85.00

UNION PORCELAIN WORKS GREENPOINT N.Y.

Union Porcelain Works was established at Greenpoint, New York, in 1848 by Charles Cartlidge. The company went through a series of ownership changes and finally closed in the early 1900s.

UNION PORCELAIN WORKS, Oyster Plate, Dated 1879, 9 1/2 In. .... 65.00 To 95.00
  Pitcher, Uncle Sam & Chinaman 875.00

UNIVERSITY CITY, Vase, Bottle-Form, C.1915, Olive Glaze, Maroon Flecks, 8 In. 385.00
  Vase, White Glaze & Crystals, Outlined, Marked, 3 1/2 In. 100.00

Val St Lambert

Val St.Lambert Cristalleries of Belgium was founded by Messieurs Kemlin and Lelievre in 1825. The company is still in operation.

VAL ST.LAMBERT, Base, Bronze Overlay, Cobalt Blue Lining, C.1910, 12 In. 565.00
  Bowl, Birds & Butterflies, Cobalt Blue, Signed, 8 1/4 In. 650.00
  Bowl, Canoe Shape, Copper Over Cobalt Blue, Signed, 8 1/4 In. 650.00
  Bowl, Flower, Signed 75.00
  Candlestick, Virgin Mary, 3 Cherubs, Frosted, Marked, 12 In. 120.00
  Decanter, Cameo, Violets, Frosted Ground, Signed, 9 1/2 In. 670.00
  Ice Bucket, Enameled Violets, Plated Rim, Marked, 9 In. 300.00
  Paperweight, Flowers, Blue Ground, Marked, 2 3/8 In. 375.00
  Paperweight, Frosted Mushroom, 3 1/4 In. 15.00
  Paperweight, Frosted Squirrel, 3 1/4 In. 15.00
  Plate, Rubens & Rembrandt, Dated, Signed, 8 In., Pair 60.00
  Vase, Cameo, C.1920 ....*Illus* 2250.00
  Vase, Fluorogravure, C.1905, Purple Overlay, Signed, 9 1/4 In. 450.00
  Vase, Tree Design, Signed, Green, 10 In. 150.00
    VALENTINE, see Card, Valentine

Vallerysthal

Vallerysthal Glassworks was founded in 1836 in Lorraine, France. In 1854 the firm became Klenglin et Cie. It made table and decorative glass, opaline, cameo, and art glass. The firm is still working.

VALLERYSTHAL, Dish, Covered, Squirrel Finial, 6 X 5 In., Pair 175.00
  Dish, Setter Dog Cover, Blue, Signed, Milk Glass 150.00
  Dish, Shell Cover, Shell Finial, Milk Glass 95.00
  Dish, Snail Cover 80.00
  Dish, Squirrel On Acorn, White Opalescent 75.00
  Plate, Thistle Pattern, Signed, Green, 8 In. 70.00

Val St.Lambert, Vase, Cameo, C.1920

Van Briggle Pottery was made by Artus Van Briggle in Colorado Springs, Colorado, after 1901. Mr.Van Briggle had been a decorator at the Rookwood Pottery of Cincinnati, Ohio, and he died in 1904. His wares were original and had modeled relief decorations with a soft dull glaze. It is still being made.

VAN BRIGGLE, Ashtray, Hopi Maiden, Turquoise, Marked, 5 1/2 In.	75.00
Ashtray, Indian Woman Grinding Corn, White, Signed	145.00
Bookends, Figural, Owl, Turquoise	100.00
Bookends, Peacocks, Dark Rose	80.00 To 100.00
Bookends, Squirrel, Marked, Persian Rose, 6 1/2 In.	115.00
Bowl, Console, Caped Seated Woman, Signed Walker	245.00
Bowl, Console, Siren Of The Sea, Flower Frog	325.00
Bowl, Half-Moon Shape, Blue	17.50
Bowl, Molded Flowers, 1905, Marked, Green Glaze, 7 1/2 In.Diam.	385.00
Bowl, Pinecone, Anniversary, Signed, Dated 1974, 9 X 5 In.	125.00
Bowl, Yellow-Green Glaze, Dated 1906, 4 X 7 In.	950.00
Conch, Persian Rose, Numbered, 3 X 9 In.	65.00
Conch, Persian Rose, 12 1/2 In.	35.00
Dish, Heart Shaped, Turquoise, 6 In.Diam.	15.00
Figurine, Donkey, Turquoise	45.00
Figurine, Elephant, Turquoise, 13 X 8 1/2 In.	28.00 To 45.00
Figurine, Girl With Corn, Turquoise	55.00
Figurine, Owl, On Stump, Brown Glaze, 9 3/4 In.	300.00
Figurine, Rabbit, Signed	12.00
Flower Frog, AA Mark, Blue	10.00
Flower Frog, Brown, Dated 1916, 3 Frog	55.00
Flower Frog, Seated Girl, Skirt & Cape, Blue Green, 8 1/2 In.	140.00
Flower Frog, Tri-Cornucopia Shaped, 4 3/4 X 5 In., Pair	45.00
Lamp, Damsel From Damascus, Original Shade	265.00
Lamp, Indian, 3 Face, Blue Finish, 11 1/2 In.	140.00
Lamp, Persian Rose, 16 In.	65.00
Lamp, Pressed Flower Shade, Blue, 12 In.	150.00
Mug, Dark Green Lava Over Lighter Green Body, 4 3/4 In.	150.00
Owl On Stump, Browns, High Glazed, Signed	295.00
Paperweight, Figural, Rabbit, Green To Brown, 6 1/2 X 2 3/4 In.	58.00
Pencil Holder, Blue Flower, Dated 1934	25.00
Pitcher, Black Glaze, Set Of 8 Tumblers	95.00
Planter, Conch Shell, 17 In.	42.50
Planter, Raised Tulips, Turquoise, Blue, 9 X 6 In.	30.00
Plate, Triangular Shape, Handle, Shaded Blue & Speckled, Small	25.00

Pot, Turquoise, Butterfly Design, Signed	22.50
Rose Bowl, Butterfly Design, Red & Blue Glaze, 3 1/2 In.	65.00
Tobacco Jar, Brown With Green, Signed Nunn, 1920	115.00
Vase, Art Deco, Dated 1905, Green & Eggplant Glaze	300.00
Vase, Art Deco, Handled, Turquoise, 7 1/2 In.	40.00
Vase, Blue Glaze, Floral Design, 2-Handled, 4 1/2 In.	195.00
Vase, Blue-Green, Swirl, 4 1/2 In.	25.00
Vase, Brown & Green, Incised Design, 6 1/4 In.	35.00
Vase, Bud, Brown & Green Glaze, 7 In.	25.00
Vase, Bud, Triple, Signed, Beige Drip, Brown, 7 In.	35.00
Vase, Bulbous, Art Nouveau, 4 1/2 In.	35.00
Vase, Craig Brown & Rose, 8 In.	50.00
Vase, Dark Persian Rose, Blackish-Blue Highlights, 6 In.	80.00
Vase, Dated 1916, Violet Plum Glaze, 6 In.	350.00
Vase, Deco Shape, Turquoise Matte, Signed, 9 In.	25.00
Vase, Green Matte, Leaf At Top, Signed & Dated, 2 In.	145.00
Vase, Green, Blue-Green, Dated 1916, 10 1/2 In.	500.00
Vase, Handled, Blue & Green, 5 In.	22.00
Vase, Indian, Ouray & Chipita, Turquoise, Pair	225.00
Vase, Lavender, Spiderwort Design, 5 In.	90.00
Vase, Lorelei, Turquoise	75.00
Vase, Lotus, Blue, 4 In.	18.00
Vase, Persian Rose Dragonflies, 9 3/4 In.	75.00
Vase, Persian Rose, 1917, 3 3/4 X 4 1/2 In.	40.00
Vase, Persian Swirl, Blue Highlights, 7 In.	95.00
Vase, Persian, 1928, 10 In.	50.00
Vase, Tones Of Purple, 7 1/2 In.	75.00
Vase, Turquoise & Blue, Raised Tulip, 9 In.	30.00
Vase, Turquoise Glaze Over Leaves, 1906, Marked, 9 1/2 In.	220.00
Vase, Turquoise, 3 Bats, Outstretched Wings, Marked, 11 In.	175.00
Vase, Turquoise, 7 In.	25.00
Vase, Urn Shape, 2 Curled Handles, Turquoise Glaze, 5 In.	12.00
Vase, 3-Handled, 1914, Matte Green, 6 1/2 In.	50.00

Vasa Murrhina is the name of a glassware made by the Vasa Murrhina Art Glass Company of Sandwich, Massachusetts, about 1884. The glassware was transparent and was embedded with small pieces of colored glass and metallic flakes. Some of the pieces were cased. The same type of glass was made in England. Collectors often confuse Vasa Murrhina glass with aventurine, spatter, or spangle glass. There is much confusion about what actually was made by the Vasa Murrhina factory.

VASA MURRHINA, see also Spangle Glass

VASA MURRHINA, Basket, Crimped & Ruffled Rim, Thorn Handle	65.00
Ewer, Mica Flaking, White Lining, Ruffled, Blue, 8 1/2 In.	135.00
Pitcher, Cobalt Blue, Gold Flecks, Amber Handle, 4 3/4 In.	235.00
Rose Bowl, Blue To Clear, Silver Flecks, Crimped, 3 3/4 In.	120.00
Rose Bowl, Egg Shape, Gold Spangled, Yellow, 4 In.	85.00
Rose Bowl, Gold Spangled, Yellow, Egg Shape, 4 In.	95.00
Rose Bowl, White Lining, Mica Flaking, Peach, 3 1/2 In.	110.00
Rose Bowl, 8-Crimp, Silver Spangled, Coral Pattern, 3 3/4 In.	95.00
Vase, Amber, Oval, 11 X 7 In.	110.00
Vase, Crimped, Swirled Mica Flakes, White Lining, 6 1/2 In.	65.00
Vase, Fan Shape, Fluted, Green Spatter & Mica, 11 1/2 In., Pair	650.00
Vase, Ruffled Top, Crystal Trim Down Sides, 9 3/8 In., Pair	195.00
Vase, Ruffled, White Lining, Mica, Pink & Maroon, 9 1/8 In.	195.00

Vasart is the signature used on a late type of art glass made by the Streathearn Glass Company of Scotland.

VASART, Vase, Hat Shape, Mottled White, Pink Brim, Signed, 2 In.	45.00
Vase, Signed, 7 In.	60.00

Vaseline glass is a greenish yellow glassware resembling petroleum jelly. Some vaseline glass is still being made in old and new styles. Pressed glass of the 1870s was often made of vaseline-colored glass. The old glass was made with uranium, but the reproductions are being colored in a different way. See Pressed Glass for more information about patterns that were also made of vaseline-colored glass.

VASELINE GLASS, Basket, Drape Design, Pink Opalescent Band, Crimped Top, 7 In	245.00
Berry Set, Flora, Opalescent, 7 Piece	285.00
Bottle, Perfume, Crystal, Matching Stopper, 3 1/2 X 6 In.	75.00
Bottle, Perfume, Daisy & Button, Ground Stopper, 4 1/2 In.	55.00
Bowl, Garlands Of Roses, Frosted, 10 In.	95.00
Bowl, Scalloped, 11 In.	40.00
Box, Gold Design, Enameled, Partially Opaque, 4 In.Diam.	110.00
Butter Pat, Tree Of Life, 3 In.	28.00
Butter, Dewey, Covered	75.00
Butter, Iris Meander, Opalescent, Covered	185.00
Candlestick, Knobbed Cup, Baluster Stem, 7 In., Pair	175.00
Candlestick, Knobbed Cup, Hexagonal Base, 7 1/2 In., Pair	125.00
Candlestick, 6 Knobs On Cup, Loop Pattern Base, 7 In., Pair	150.00
Castor, Pickle, Daisy & Button, Silver Plate Framed & Tongs	145.00
Celery, Arch Pattern, Cascade Base, 11 1/2 In.	385.00
Celery, Wild Flower	55.00
Compote, Diamond Pattern, Pedestal, 7 1/2 X 6 3/4 In.	47.50
Compote, Jelly, Stemmed, Iris Meander, Opalescent	60.00
Compote, Rose In Snow, Covered, 10 In.	110.00
Creamer, Dewey, Large	65.00
Creamer, Leaf Mold, Cranberry Spatter	75.00
Creamer, Oaken Bucket	45.00
Creamer, Three Panel	38.00
Cruet, Diamond Point	65.00
Cruet, Hobnail, Clear Stopper, 6 In.	22.50 To 35.00
Dish, Candy, Argonaut & Shell, Pedestal	38.00
Dish, Sauce, Square, Footed, Finecut & Panel	9.00
Feeder, Invalid, Pink & Gold Floral Design	75.00
Goblet, Daisy & Button With Thumbprint	25.00
Goblet, Diamond-Quilted With Star	25.00
Goblet, Fine Cut	45.00
Hat, Daisy & Button	35.00
Inkwell, 6-Sided Diamond Shape, Hinged, 2 5/8 X 2 7/8 In.	110.00
Lemonade Set, Basket Weave, 5 Goblets & Tray, 7 Piece	235.00
Lighter, Cigarette, 7 In.	37.00
Mug, Dewey	60.00
Mug, Thousand Eye	32.00
Mug, Three Panel	40.00
Perfume Set, Pin Dish, Bottle, 3 Piece	125.00
Pitcher, Water, Bagware	85.00
Pitcher, Water, Divided Block With Sunburst	28.00
Pitcher, Water, Ransom	80.00
Plate, ABC, ABC's Around Rim, Marked	85.00
Rose Bowl, Beaded Panels, Opalescent Rim, Pedestal, 5 1/2 In.	40.00
Salt, Diamond Pattern	8.00
Shoe, Bow	20.00
Shoe, Daisy Pattern, Lion At Top Front, 5 1/4 In.	20.00
Spooner, Alternating Daisy & Button, Pedestal, Clear	35.00
Spooner, Inverted Thumbprint	25.00
Spooner, Scroll, Acanthus, Opalescent	45.00
Spooner, Three Panel	35.00
Spooner, Two Panel	30.00
Sugar & Creamer, Palm Beach	135.00
Sugar, Dewey, Covered	65.00
Sugar, Diamond Spearhead, Opalescent, Covered	90.00
Sugar, Medallion, Covered	55.00

Syrup, Inverted Thumbprint, Pinched Base	50.00
Syrup, Rope & Thumbprint	55.00
Syrup, Rope & Thumbprint, Pedestal, Pewter Lid, Dated '84	75.00
Table Set, Fluted, Scroll, Opalescent, 4 Piece	445.00
Toothpick, Daisy & Button, Master's Hat Shape	48.00
Toothpick, Daisy, Kettle Shape	26.00
Toothpick, Thousand Eye	28.00
Tray, Serpentine, Large	45.00
Tray, Water, 2 Panel	44.00
Tumbler, Block & Star	20.00
Tumbler, Daisy & Button, On Bottom Half	22.00
Tumbler, Mitered Diamond	25.00
Tumbler, Pressed Diamond	25.00
Tumbler, Thumbprint, 3 3/4 In., Pair	15.00
Vase, Blown, Opalescent Top, 6 In.	45.00
Vase, Car, Impressed Florals, Pair	35.00
Vase, Flared Top, Ribbed, Smoked, Silver Plated, 3 1/2 In.	130.00
Wine, Austrian	120.00

Venetian glass has been made near Venice, Italy, from the thirteenth to the twentieth century. Thin colored glass with applied decorations is favored, although many other types have been made.

VENETIAN GLASS, Candlestick, Honey Color, 1700s, 12 In., Pair	325.00
Candlestick, Lady Holding 2 Candles, Light Blue, 10 1/2 In.	110.00
Juice, Multicolored Canes, Filigree, Goldstone, Set Of 4	50.00
Rose Bowl, Ruffled, Gold Mica Design, Footed	95.00
Vase, Pink Applied Leaves, Yellow, 11 In.	45.00

Verlys glass was made in France after 1931. Verlys was also made in the United States. The glass is either blown or molded. The American glass is signed with a diamond-point-scratched name, but the French pieces are marked with a molded signature.

VERLYS, Ashtray, Swallows, Signed, Blue	125.00
Bowl, Birds & Honeybees, Opalescent, 11 1/2 In.Diam.	250.00
Bowl, Electric Blue, Frosted, Marked, 11 3/4 In.	165.00
Bowl, Roses, 5 In.	25.00
Bowl, Thistle, Frosted, Script, Clear, 8 3/4 In.	55.00 To 65.00
Bowl, Thistle, Signed, 11 3/4 In.	110.00
Bowl, Water Lily, Frosted, Signed, 13 3/4 In.	185.00 To 235.00
Bowl, Water Lily, Signed, 13 3/4 In.	235.00
Centerpiece, Blown-Out Large Angelfish, Signed, 12 3/7 In.	250.00
Charger, Royal Blue, Blown-Out Fish & Birds, Signed	350.00
Planter, Applied Opalescent Berries, Frosted Ground, 7 X 6 2/8 In.	150.00
Plate, Bird Motif, Signed, 11 3/4 In.	165.00
Plate, Opalescent Gulls, 10 1/2 In.	165.00
Vase, Berries & Rose Pattern, Clear, Frosted Body, Signed, 4 In.	110.00
Vase, Birds, Frosted, Tint Of Brown, Signed, 12 1/2 In.	450.00
Vase, Half-Moon, Lovebirds, Frosted, Signed, 6 1/4 X 4 1/2 In.	90.00
Vase, Lance, Signed, Frosted	150.00
Vase, Lovebirds, Fan Shape, 6 1/2 In.	40.00
Vase, Lovebirds, Frosted To Clear, 4 1/2 In.	30.00
Vase, Mandarin In Garden, Frosted, Signed, 9 1/8 In.	80.00
Vase, Opalescent, High Relief, Signed, 6 X 6 1/2 In.	175.00
Vase, Roses, Frosted, Molded, Signed, 5 1/2 In.	35.00
Vase, Seasons, Spring, Autumn, Artist Signed, 8 1/4 In.	275.00
Vase, Summer & Winter Scene, Signed, 8 In.	250.00
Vase, Thistle Pattern, Deep Blue, Frosted, Signed, 10 In.	215.00
Vase, Thistle, Opalescent & Clear, 9 1/2 In.	195.00

Verre de soie glass was first made by Frederick Carder at the Steuben Glass Works from about 1905 to 1930. It is an iridescent glass of soft white or very, very pale green. The name means glass of silk, and it does resemble silk. Other factories have made verre de soie, and some of the English examples were made of different colors. Verre de soie is an art glass and is not related to the iridescent pressed white carnival glass mistakenly called by its name.

VERRE DE SOIE, see also Steuben

VERRE DE SOIE, Basket, Raspberry Prunts On Handle, Monogrammed, 4 1/2 In.	85.00
Bottle, Perfume, Jade Flame Stopper, 4 1/2 In.	135.00
Bowl, Melon Ribbed, Applied Rosaline, 19 In.Diam.	265.00
Bride's Basket, Enameled Floral, Silver Plated Holder	275.00
Compote, Stylized Floral, Hawkes, 5 X 7 In.Diam.	225.00
Salt, Copper Wheel, Sterling Silver Pedestal, Steuben	55.00
Salt, Engraved, Sterling Silver Pedestal, 1 3/4 In.	55.00
Shade, Optic Rib, Gold Machine-Threaded	100.00
Sherbet, Underplate, Monogrammed	65.00
Vase, Baluster Form, Etched Floral Swag, 11 3/4 In.	100.00
Vase, Diamond Optic, Green Reeding, 6 1/2 In.	150.00
Vase, Pedestal, 3 1/4 X 5 1/4 In.	30.00
Vase, Rosaline Threading, 6 In.	175.00
Vase, 3 Applied Green Lily Pads, 6 Dimples, 5 1/2 In.	125.00
VESSIERE, Vase, Pink Flowers, 11 French Words, Cameo, Signed, 12 In.	785.00

Vienna Art plates were round metal serving trays produced around the turn of the century. The designs, copied from Royal Vienna porcelain plates, usually featured a portrait of a lady encircled by a wide, ornate border. Many were used as advertising or promotional items and were produced in Coshocton, Ohio, by J.F. Meek's Tuscarora Advertising Co. and H.D. Beach's Standard Advertising Co.

VIENNA ART, see also Coca-Cola

VIENNA ART, Plate, Brunette, Low-Cut Dress, Schoeny Grocers, 1905	65.00
Plate, Calendar, 1907, Harvard Brewing Co., Pretty Lady	225.00
Plate, Jamestown, 1607-1907, Smith, Pocahontas, 10 In.	75.00 To 95.00
Plate, W.W.Lawrence & Co., Paints, Dated 1905, Lady, 10 In.	40.00

VIENNA, see Beehive; Royal Vienna

Villeroy & Boch Pottery of Mettlach, Germany, was founded in 1841. The firm made many types of pottery, including the famous Mettlach steins.

VILLEROY & BOCH, see also Mettlach

VILLEROY & BOCH, Box, Hand-Painted, Mercury Mark, 3 1/2 X 4 X 3 1/2 In.	55.00
Dish, Vegetable, Blue Underglaze, Oval, Covered, 10 In.	75.00
Gravy, Attached Platter, White, Blue Flowers, 9 In.	55.00
Mug, Applied Green Leaves & Branches, Twig Handle, 3 In.	38.00
Pitcher, Blue Flowers, Cobalt Blue & Gold Handle, 7 In.	40.00
Pitcher, Family Scene, Gray, 10 1/2 In. ....*Illus*	210.00
Plaque, Boat Scene, Blue & White, 10 1/4 In.	90.00
Plaque, World War I Battleship Scene, 12 In.	200.00
Plate, Elves, Green & Turquoise, 7 3/4 In.	18.00
Plate, Hanging, Delft Type, Pronghorn Sheep, 12 In.	75.00
Platter, Dresden Pattern, Open Handles, 9 X 11 3/4 In.	40.00
Punch Bowl, Underplatter, Raised Red & Green Leaves	65.00
Sauceboat, Onion Pattern, Attached Tray	25.00
Tureen & Underplate, Blue & White Castle, Lake Scene	200.00
Tureen, Soup, Portraits Of Kaiser & Empress, Marked, 15 In.	975.00
Vase, Applied Leaves & Vines, Silver Luster, Seal, 8 In.	75.00

Villeroy & Boch, Pitcher, Family Scene,
Gray, 10 1/2 In. *(See Page 739)*

VOLKMAR
Corona N.Y. *Volkmar pottery was made by Charles Volkmar of New York, from 1879 to about 1911. He was part of several firms including the Volkmar Ceramic Company, Volkmar and Cory, and Charles Volkmar and Son.*

VOLKMAR, Etching, Ducks At A Pond, Initialed, Framed, 7 1/2 X 11 In. 220.00
    Lamp, Oil, Mottled Green & Yellow, 12 X 7 1/2 In. 200.00
    Pitcher, Matte Green 100.00
    Plaque, Under The Elms, Blue Spatter, Marked, 11 1/4 In. 175.00
    Plaque, Washington's Headquarters, Blue Spatter, Marked, 11 1/4 In. 175.00

Volkstadt was a soft paste porcelain manufactory started in 1760 by Georg Heinrich Macheleid at Volkstadt, Thuringia. Volkstadt-Rudolstadt was a porcelain factory started at Volkstadt-Rudolstadt by Beyer and Bock in 1890.

VOLKSTADT, Figurine, Mouse, Sitting Astride Walnut Shell, Marked, 3 In. 125.00
    Tureen, Tulip, 18th Century, Iron Red Streaked, Marked, 7 1/2 In. 800.00
           WALLACE NUTTING, see Print, Nutting
           WALT DISNEY, see Disneyana
           WALTER, see A. Walter

WANNOPEE, Pitcher, Marked, High-Glaze Green, 4 1/2 In. 50.00

Warwick china was made in Wheeling, West Virginia, in a pottery factory founded in 1887.

WARWICK, Ale Set, Dog Portraits, 6 Mugs 350.00
    Biscuit Jar, Melon Shape, Hand-Painted Flowers, Semiporcelain 95.00
    Bowl, Gold Trim, 9 In. 50.00
    Bowl, Horn Of Plenty, Floral, Cobalt, 11 In. 250.00
    Butter Pat, Pink Roses, Blue Ribbons 8.50
    Butter, Plantation, Covered 65.00
    Chocolate Pot, White, Cherry Design, 8 In. 85.00
    Ewer, Rose Design, IOGA, 7 In. 65.00
    Goblet, Plantation 25.00
    Jar, Tobacco, Indian Head 100.00
    Mug, Beer, Brown Glaze, Cardinal In Red, IOGA 45.00
    Mug, Brown, Gent, Top Hat, Playing Guitar, 5 In. 47.00
    Mug, Elk, B.P.O.E., Brown Ground 50.00
    Mug, Shaving, Portrait Of Indian 120.00
    Pitcher, Cider, Monk, IOGA, Red 140.00

Pitcher, Lemonade, Portrait Of Gypsy Girl, IOGA	75.00
Pitcher, Monk, Brown, 7 1/2 In.	95.00
Pitcher, Pink Roses, Gold Speckled, Old Mark, 7 In.	35.00
Pitcher, Water, Floral & Strawberries, Red Helmet Mark	115.00
Planter, Dutch Scene, Windmills, 3 1/4 In.	98.00
Plate, Elk, 10 1/2 In.	75.00
Plate, Indian Chief, 9 1/2 In.	140.00
Tankard, Brown Tones, Indian Chief, 11 In.	375.00
Vase, Brown, Floral Design, Bulbous, 7 In.	50.00
Vase, Brown, Poinsettia, Twig Handles, Marked, 10 In.	85.00
Vase, Flower Design, Handled, IOGA, 10 In.	60.00
Vase, Gibson Girl Portrait, Holding Flowers, 12 In.	100.00
Vase, Gypsy Lady, Twig Handles, Signed IOGA, 10 1/2 In.	145.00
Vase, Orange Flowers On Vine, Twig Handle, IOGA, 12 In.	85.00
Vase, Portrait, Duchess, Gray Ground, IOGA Mark, 8 In.	125.00
Vase, Portrait, Nude, 10 In.	38.50
Vase, Portrait, Young Girl, 8 In.	100.00
Vase, Senator, Brown Floral, 11 1/4 In.	90.00
Vase, Stick, Orange Poppies, 12 In.	75.00
Vase, Trumpet, Brown, Floral Design, 15 In.	110.00
Vase, Yellow & Brown, Floral Design, IOGA, 9 In.	85.00

Watch fobs were worn on watch chains. They were popular during Victorian times and after.

WATCH FOB, Abraham Fur Co., Brass	65.00 To 90.00
Adams Road Grader	10.00
Amber Glass, Profile Of Classical Goddess	8.00
American Legion, Des Moines	12.50
American Legion, Milwaukee, 1941	18.50
American Rubber Bowling League, 1919-20, Brass	22.50
Anniversary Of Rock Island R.R., 1850-1922, President Lincoln	50.00
Atlas Life Insurance	10.00
Avery Bulldog, Brass	55.00 To 85.00
Avery Kerosene Tractor, Brass	75.00
Beck Sweet Feed, Donkey, Memphis, Tenn., Red Celluloid	45.00
Black & Gold Beads	15.00
Buffalo Bill, Pawnee Bill, Gold Plated	45.00
Buick Motor Cars, Valve In Head	80.00
Bulldog, Avery	90.00
Case Plow Works	65.00
Case, Centennial, 1837-1937	55.00
Case, Eagle	50.00
Century Of Progress, 1934	30.00
Chalmers Motor Co., Porcelain	60.00
Chero-Cola	20.00
Chicago World's Fair, 1933	20.00
Columbia Tool & Steel Co., Enameled Shield & Stripes	20.00
Covered Wagon, Oxen, K.C., Mo., 1913, Santa Fe Trail	27.50
Cyrus McCormick, Reverse, 2 Men, Horse, & Reaper, 1831-1931	50.00
Daisy Williams, Sterling Silver	60.00
DC21	25.00
DeLaval Separators	65.00
DeLaval, Porcelain	95.00
Diamond Edge, Bone & Sterling Silver	50.00
Diamond T Trucks	17.50
Dr Pepper, Billiken	65.00
Dr Pepper, Louisiana Purchase Exposition	65.00
Dry Cell Batteries, Celluloid	65.00
Egyptian Scenes & Symbols, Signed	50.00
Egyptian, 4 Linked Sections, H.Carter Portrait, Signed	95.00
Erie, Foundry Machinery	11.50
Euclid Caterpillar, Brass	17.50
F.O.E., Eagle In Flight, Brass	27.50

Fisher Body	35.00
Fordson Tractor	75.00 To 100.00
Gold Shield, English Sterling Silver	35.00
H.Miller Mfg. Co., Gate Valve, Brass	90.00
Hand-Tooling In Crest Design, English, 9K Gold	95.00
Harley Davidson	65.00
Heinz 57	22.50
Heinz, Girl In White Cap	26.50
Hoffman Barber Supplies	25.00
Hub Furniture, Wagon Wheel Hub, Porcelain	75.00
I.O.O.F., 1910, Brass	19.50
Inidan Motorcycles, Figural Arrowhead	55.00
International Harvester, Bucking Bronco	35.00
International Harvester, 2 Worlds	60.00
Iowa State Capitol Building, Enameled	15.00
Iowa State Traveling Men's Assoc.	17.00
J.D.Adams Co., Man On Grader & Man Pushing Wheelbarrow	55.00
John Deere Emblem, Pearl Shield	10.00
John Deere, Mother-Of-Pearl Shield, Silver Deer	100.00
John Deere, 4-Legged Deer, Oval, Blue Porcelain	125.00
K.C., Mo., 1913, Sante Fe Trail, Embossed Covered Wagon	40.00
Kelly Springfield Tires, Women & Tires, Brass	95.00
Keystone Lumber, Pittsburgh, Pa., Elephant	15.00
King Oscar 5 Cent Cigars, Embossed Picture	47.50
Knights Of Pythias, Brass	17.50
Labor Day, Des Moines, September 1, 1913	32.00
Lady's Head, Art Nouveau	35.00
Lion Brand Fertilizer, Embossed Lion	45.00
Locomotive Works, Davenport, Iowa, Brass	15.00
Lone Star Cement, Porcelain	25.00
Magobar	50.00
Maltese Cross Shape, Horseshoe Center, 1 1/2 In.	22.00
Meadow Gold Butter, Celluloid Insert	40.00
Merchant's Life Casualty, Minneapolis, Celluloid Center, Brass	22.00
Mesh, Figural, Hand Saw, E.Atkins Co., Silver Steel Saws	65.00
Milwaukee, Wisconsin	15.00
Monarch Ranges	65.00
Northern Rock Island Plow, Brass	85.00
Ohio Gas & Oilman's Assoc., White Metal	17.50
Oliver Cleartrac	40.00
Oliver O C 9 Crawler	55.00
Orange Rifle Powder & Laflin Powder Co., Embossed Cannon	37.50
Order Of Railroad Telegraphers, Ribbon Type	47.50
Order Of Railway Conductors, Embossed Passengers, Conductor	75.00
Our Choice, Bryon Kern, Brass	20.00
P. & O.Canton Plow	85.00
Page Dragline	18.00
Patterson & Stevenson Co., Minneapolis, Beaver Hats, Brass	35.00
Pepsi-Cola Co., New Bern, N.C., Delicious Pepsi-Cola, Healthful	125.00
Pepsi-Cola, Embossed Eagle & 2 Bottles, New Bern, N.C.	225.00
Polar Bear Flour, Figural Bear	35.00
Polarine Motor Oils, Embossed Bear	35.00
Poll Parrot Shoes, Celluloid Inset, Brass	60.00 To 75.00
Red Diamond Overalls & Shirt, Brass	30.00
Remington, National Letter Writing Contest, 1913	125.00
Remington, 100th Anniversary, 1916, Brass	125.00
Reo	40.00
Rock Island Plow Co., Blue Porcelain	75.00
Roosevelt, Fairbanks	27.00
Rumely, Brass	115.00
Salvation Army Blue, Brass	12.00
Satisfaction Coffee, Brass	50.00
Sealed Stark Trees Bear Fruit, Stark Bros, Missouri, Tin	25.00

Watch, European Watch & Clock Co.,	Watch, Cartier, C.1920, Diamond,
Diamond & Platinum, 1925	Platinum, & Gold

St.Louis Livestock Exchange Calf Show, Embossed Calf's Head	27.50
St.Louis World's Fair	12.00
Standard Varnish Works	22.50
Starrett Tools	25.00
State Of Texas, Bronze	25.00
State Seal Of Iowa	35.00
Statue Of Liberty, White Metal	10.00
Steer's Head, Kansas Pacific Railway, 1874	28.50
Swift & Co., Bakelite Heart On Ribbon, Steer Other Side	70.00
Talon Clutching Gold Ball, Victorian, 14K Rose Gold	125.00
Texas Centennial	27.50
Tractomotive Machinery	20.00
Trojan ♣ Wheeler	12.00
Ultman Taylor, Chicken, Bronze	75.00
Union Tool	10.00
University Of Iowa, 1915	52.00
University Of Wisconsin, 1910	15.00
Washburn Crosby Flour, Brass	25.00
Whaling Scene, New Bedford Semicentennial, 1847, Silver Plated	20.00
William Taft	35.00
Woodman Accident Assoc., 4-Color, Brass	26.00
Woodsmen Of The World, Gold, Braided Human Hair Chain	75.00
Yosemite National Park, Bear, Brass	20.00
1917 Gypsy Tour	65.00

WATCH, Albert Bale & Co., Pocket, Key Wind, Swing-Out, Silver, English	250.00
Auger & Gueret, Pocket, Benjamin Morgan Palmer, 15K Gold	1400.00
Babe Ruth, Wristwatch	325.00
Bristol, Pocket, Key Wind, Coin Silver	125.00
Cartier, C.1920, Diamond, Platinum, & Gold	Illus 2200.00
Cartier, Lever Movement, Silver Dial, Art Deco, Gold Strap, 18K Gold	1650.00
Chevalier & Cochet, Musical, 1790-1805, 18K Gold	8500.00
Cinderella, Pink Hands & Numerals, Wristwatch, Metal Band	24.00
Dudley, Pocket, Masonic, Display Type Case	1950.00
Elgin, Father Time, 24 Jewel, Base Metal Case	145.00
Elgin, Military, 5 Positon Adjustable Time, Second Hand	225.00
English, Open Face, 15K Gold, Grotesque Mask, Gold Chain, Hallmarked	1210.00
European Watch & Clock Co., Diamond & Platinum, 1925	Illus 3250.00
Frederick Richard, Hallmarked London, 1763, Silver & Tortoiseshell	412.00
Fusee, Mother-Of-Pearl, Musical, Leather Lined, 2 X 1 1/2 In.	8500.00
Gruen, Pocket, 14K Gold, Thin	350.00
H.R.Ekegren, Pocket, Repeating, C.1880, 18K Gold, Enamel Dial	4675.00
Hamilton, Pocket, 21 Jewel, Open Gold Filled Case	285.00
Hamilton, Pocket, 21 Jewel, Silver Case	250.00
Hamilton, Porcelain Dial, Red Second Track, Double Roller, 17 Jewel	100.00

Hamilton, Railroad, Montgomery Dial, 21 Jewel	95.00
Hamilton, Railway, 17 Jewel	175.00
Hampden, Molly Stark, Pocket, Hunting Case, 14K Gold	275.00
Hampden, Pocket, 14K Gold Hunting Case, Railway, C.1889	650.00
Home Watch Co., Pendant, Gold & Enamel, 18K, C.1920	2100.00
Howard, Chronometer, Swing-Out Case, Yellow Gold Filled	325.00
Howard, Hunter, N	350.00
Howard, Pocket, Gold Filled, 17 Jewel	125.00
Howard, Pocket, 17 Jewel, Open Face, Yellow Gold Filled	90.00
Howard, Swing-Out Case, Second Track, 17 Jewel	150.00
Illinois Sangamo Special, Pocket, 23 Jewel	400.00
Illinois, Bunn Special	350.00
Illinois, Bunn Special, Railroad, Pocket, 21 Jewel, Yellow Gold Filled	150.00
Illinois, Pocket, Open Face, Gold Filled, Chain, J.H.Monogram	125.00
Ingersoll, Pocket, Three Pigs & Big Bad Wolf, Animated Eyes, Signed	325.00
Jos. Catherwood & Son, Key Wind, C.1799, 2 Silver Cases	500.00
Krumhuber, C.1795, Enamel Dial, Silver & Horn	375.00
Lapel, Marcasite, Sterling, Tobias Movement	145.00
London, Pocket, Verge Fussee, Silver, Hallmarked, Sansom Of London	300.00
Longines, Blued Steel Hands, C.1930, Wristwatch, Leather Strap	475.00
Lord Elgin, Pocket, Open Face, 15K Gold	295.00
Lord Elgin, Pocket, 1952 World Champions, New York Yankees	575.00
Matthew Jeantet, C.1870, Train Jump Quarter Seconds, Silver	357.00
Minute, Repeating, Chronograph, 18K Gold Hunting Case, C.1890	3000.00
Mori, Remembrance Of Death, Carved Ivory Skeleton Case	*Illus* 4500.00
P.S.Bartlett, Hunting Case, C.1898, 3-Color 14K Gold, 17 Jewel	1320.00
Patek Philippe & Co., Self-Winding, 37 Jewel, Gold, 34 Mm.Diam.	880.00
Patek Philippe, Pocket, 18 Jewel, 18K Gold, Matching Numbers	950.00
Pedometer, C.1850, Steel Movement, Enamel Dial, Skeletonized Center	195.00
Pendant, Lady's, Engraved Back, 15K Gold	300.00
Pocket, Concealed Erotic Automaton, 15K Gold, Repeater	2090.00
Pocket, Open Face, Key Wind, Tricolor, Gold	*Illus* 475.00
Pocket, White Dial, Black Numerals, Gold Hunting Case	*Illus* 450.00
Quarter, Repeating, Chronograph, 14K Gold Hunting Case, C.1900	1000.00
Repeating, Micrometer Regulator, Arabic Numerals, Wristwatch, Gold	4950.00
Reverside Maximus, 0-19	195.00
Rolex, Oyster, Perpetual Date, 18K Gold Band, Wristwatch, 14K Case	2200.00
Santa Fe Special, 16-21	185.00
Seth Thomas, Hunting Case, 1887, Gold Plated, Chain	105.00
Snow White, Pink Hands & Numerals, Wristwatch, Original Strap	28.00
Spiro Agnew Character, Wristwatch, Boxed	115.00
Tiffany & Co., Open Face, Man's, Stem Wind, 18K Gold	875.00
Trans-Pacific Railroad, 21 Jewel	45.00

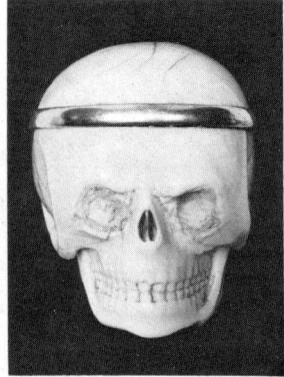  

Watches, Pocket, White Dial, Black Numerals, Gold
Hunting Case; Open Face, Key Wind, Tricolor Gold

Watch, Mori, Remembrance Of Death,
Carved Ivory Skeleton Case

Watch, Waltham, Pocket, Hunting
Case, Rose & Green Gold

Watch, Wm.Ellery, Hunting Case,
C.1882, 14K Gold

Vacheron & LeCoultre, Up & Down Power Dial, Gold 195.00
Vanguard, 16S, 21J, Double Minute Chapter 315.00
Waltham, Box Hinge Hunting Case, C.1888, Enamel Dial, Engraved Flowers 1210.00
Waltham, Hunting Case, C.1883, Enamel Dial, Arabic Numerals 385.00
Waltham, Hunting Case, Design, 14K Gold 150.00
Waltham, Hunting Case, Gold & Enamel Box Hinge, C.1879, Enamel Foliage 880.00
Waltham, Lady's, Hunting Case, C.1903, 14K Gold, Arabic Numerals 195.00
Waltham, Model 1883, Santa Fe Route On Dial, Walnut Case 500.00
Waltham, Pocket, Christopher Columbus In Solid Gold On Back 175.00
Waltham, Pocket, Gold Hunting Case, 14K, Box Hinged, C.1882 .... 750.00
Waltham, Pocket, Hunting Case, Rose & Green Gold ....*Illus* 300.00
Waltham, Pocket, Ligne Maximus, Open Face, Yellow Gold 125.00
Waltham, Pocket, Vanguard, 23 Jewel, Gold Filled Case 350.00
Waltham, Pocket, Vanguard, 23 Jewel, Open Face, Lever Set 400.00
Waltham, Pocket, 14K Gold Hunting Case, Feather Scrolls, C.1895 .... 1100.00
Waltham, Pocket, 15K Gold, 7 Jewel 250.00
Waltham, Up-Down, 16-23 .... 365.00
Wm.Ellery, Hunting Case, C.1882, 14K Gold ....*Illus* 750.00

> *Waterford type glass resembles the famous glass made in the Waterford*
> *Glass Works in Ireland. It is a clear glass that was often cut for*
> *decoration. Modern glass is still being made in Waterford, Ireland.*

WATERFORD, Bowl, Scalloped, Pedestal, Cobalt Blue, 11 In. 20.00
Compote, Diamond Cut Body, Paneled Baluster, C.1920, 5 In., Pair 60.00
Cordial, Alana 20.00
Decanter, Wine, Lismore Pattern 100.00
Goblet, Alana 27.50
Pitcher, Milk, 5 3/4 In. 85.00
Urn, Pedestal, Oval Flutes, Bull's-Eye Below, 14 In. 275.00
Wine, Alana 27.50

> *Wave Crest glass is a white glassware manufactured by the Pairpoint*
> *Manufacturing Company of New Bedford, Massachusetts, and some French*
> *factories. It was then decorated by the C.F.Monroe Company of*
> *Meriden, Connecticut. The glass was painted in pastel colors and decorated*
> *with flowers. The name Wave Crest was used after 1898.*

WAVE CREST, Atomizer, Perfume, Egg, Roses, 5 1/2 In. 295.00
Biscuit Barrel, Pewter Top, Brown & Yellow Roses, 8 In. 195.00
Biscuit Jar, Bulbous, Florals, Hallmarked Sterling Silver Band 295.00
Biscuit Jar, Egg Crate Pattern 375.00
Biscuit Jar, Egg Crate Pattern, Square, Flowers 385.00
Biscuit Jar, Egg Crate Pattern, 8 In. 295.00
Biscuit Jar, Egg Crate, Yellow & Pink Roses 150.00

Biscuit Jar, Flowers, Cream Ground, Bail Handle	175.00
Biscuit Jar, Flowers, Ivory Ground, Silver Plate Rim & Cover	150.00
Biscuit Jar, Flowers, Sterling Silver Cover, Numbered, Square	375.00
Biscuit Jar, Pansies, Paneled	375.00
Biscuit Jar, Pink Clovers, Oyster White Ground, Puffy	475.00
Biscuit Jar, Signed CFM, Square	355.00
Box, Baroque Shell, Hinged, Red Banner Mark, 7 1/4 In.Diam.	325.00
Box, Baroque Shell, Hinged, Signed, 4 1/2 In.Diam.	350.00
Box, Blown-Out Zinnia Lid, Turquoise Base, Signed, 4 1/2 In.	595.00
Box, Bulbous Cover, Stylized Palmetto Leaves, C.1900, 3 1/4 In.	60.00
Box, Christmas Trees & Cupids, Embossed, 4 In.	450.00
Box, Collar, Red Banner Mark, 8 X 7 1/2 In.	750.00
Box, Egg Crate, Tobacco Front, Floral Top, Signed, 5 X 5 In.	450.00
Box, Enameled Floral, Green, Lined, Signed, 9 1/2 X 4 X 4 1/4 In.	875.00
Box, Enameled Swirled Blossoms, Lined, Red Banner Mark, 3 1/2 In.	255.00
Box, Floral Decorated, Erie Twist, Covered, 4 1/2 In.	180.00
Box, Hand-Painted Flowers, Lined, Embossed Lid, 7 3/4 In.Diam.	885.00
Box, Helmschmied Swirl, Enameled Flowers, 5 1/2 X 3 1/2 In.	435.00
Box, Helmschmied Swirl, Round, Covered, Jewel, 6 In.Diam.	275.00
Box, Hinged Lid, Red Crown Mark In Red Wreath, 6 In.Diam.	130.00
Box, Hinged, Original Lining, Signed, 5 1/2 In.	290.00
Box, Hinged, Pink Base, Crown Top, 4 1/2 In.Diam.	345.00
Box, Jewel, Floral On White, Silver Plated Rim, Covered, 6 In.	275.00
Box, Jewel, 2 Cherubs Gardening, Green, Signed, 5 1/2 X 3 1/4 In.	525.00
Box, Jewelry, 5 X 3 1/4 In.	325.00
Box, Molded Swirl Lid, Red & Blue Flowers, 8 X 6 3/4 In.	775.00
Box, Old Woman, Child, Chicken, Field, Signed, 3 1/2 In.	200.00
Box, Ormolu Feet, Brass Collar & Lid, 5 In.	250.00
Box, Overall Design Of Pink & Blue Flowers, 4 X 7 In.Diam.	450.00
Box, Pin, Blown-Out Design, Pink Floral, Marked, 10 X 1 1/2 In.	75.00
Box, Pin, Blown-Out Flower, Ormolu Rim, Marked, 14 X 2 In.	125.00
Box, Pink Forget-Me-Nots, Signed, 5 1/2 In.	275.00
Box, Pink Zinnia Lid, Turquoise Base, 4 1/2 In.	690.00
Box, Powder, Floral, Enameled	200.00
Box, Powder, Orange, Yellow Roses, Blue Ground, 7 In.	550.00
Box, Red & Blue Flowers, White Center, Ormolu Base, Legs, 8 In.	775.00
Box, Scenic Cover, Woman, Child, & Chicken, Signed, 3 1/2 In.Diam.	200.00
Box, Shell Lid With Daisies, Blue, Blue Mark, 4 In.	275.00
Box, Shell On Lid, Top Lined, Signed, 4 X 2 3/4 In.	355.00
Box, Swirl, Applied Flowers, 4 X 7 1/2 In.Diam.	475.00
Box, Swirl, Blue Enameled Dots On Cover, Signed, 4 1/2 In.	225.00
Box, Swirl, Hinged Cover, Lined, Signed, Pink & Blue, 7 X 4 In.	450.00
Box, Swirl, Pink To Green Enameled Flowers, 6 3/4 X 3 3/4 In.	650.00
Box, White & Gold, Signed, Hinged, 5 X 2 1/2 In.	225.00
Box, Yellow Middle, Floral Sprays, Red Banner Mark, 7 X 5 1/2 In.	775.00
Creamer, Mauve Violets, Green Leaves, Silver Plated Top	175.00
Creamer, Sterling Silver Top	90.00
Creamer, Swirled, Roses, 3 1/2 In.	95.00
Dish, Blown-Out Enameled Floral Trim, Signed, 3 1/2 In.Diam.	95.00
Dish, Floral On Beige, Open, Signed, 3 In.	90.00
Dish, Pin, Sunflower Shape, Ormolu Handles, 3 1/2 In.Diam.	95.00
Fernery, Brass Liner, Hinged, Signed, 7 In.	350.00
Holder, Card, Brass Rim, Enameled Flowers, 4 X 2 1/2 In.	279.00
Holder, Letter, Hand-Painted, Dore Bronze Fittings, 5 3/4 In.	345.00
Holder, String, Scene Of Girl & Boy, Peach Ground	35.00
Humidor, Cigar, Shell Lid, Red Banner Mark	350.00
Inkwell, Enameled, C.1890, Marked, 3 1/8 In.	120.00
Jar, Cigarette, Red Banner Mark, 4 In.	195.00
Jar, Dresser, Signed, 5 1/2 In.Diam.	400.00
Jar, Powder, Red Banner Mark	240.00
Jardiniere, Raised Dots, 8 Cupids At Top, Signed, 8 X 9 In.Diam.	595.00
Napkin Ring, Blue, Forget-Me-Nots, White Ground, Marked	125.00
Planter, Blue Flowers, Original Insert, Signed, 5 1/2 In.	190.00
Salt & Pepper, Blue Forget-Me-Nots, Yellow	125.00

Salt & Pepper, Floral Design 75.00
Salt & Pepper, Forget-Me-Nots 65.00
Salt & Pepper, Puffy Floral 95.00
Salt & Pepper, Scenic 195.00
Salt, Dog, Daisy Shape 85.00
Sugar & Creamer, Helmschmied Swirl, Blue To Ivory Satin, Florals 425.00
Sugar & Creamer, Mushroom Patch, Blossoms, Silver Plated Rim 295.00
Tray, Bonbon, Handled, Hand-Painted Lavender & Blue Florals 115.00
Tray, Pin, Flowers, Blue & Pink, Signed, 4 1/2 In. 145.00
Tray, Pin, Handled 125.00
Tray, Pin, Ormolu Handles, Signed 115.00
Tray, Pin, Purple & Blue Flowers, Handled, Black Mark, 4 In. 85.00
Tray, Pin, Rosebuds, Blue, Double Shell, 3 In. 150.00
Tray, Pin, 1 Handle, Blue Mark 72.00
Tray, Trinket, Ormolu Footed, Signed, 7 In. 450.00
Vase, Brown & Pink Florals, Cream Ground, Signed, 5 1/2 In. 185.00
Vase, Enameled, Pair, Signed 295.00

WEAPON, Ax, Boarding, Civil War, Cast Steel, Oak Handle 450.00
Ax, Boarding, French, Japanned Finish, Wood Handle, 21 1/2 In. 375.00
      WEAPON, BAYONET, see Sword, Bayonet
Chakram, India, Steel Quoit, Gold Inlaid, 19th Century 225.00
Derringer, Double Barrel, Remington, Type II, 41 Caliber, 5 In. 160.00
Grenade, Revolutionary War, Hollow Iron Ball, 3 1/2 In.Diam. 225.00
Halberd-Tomahawk, American, C.1700, Forged 1 Piece Iron, 12 In. 550.00
Halberd, American, C.1700, Leaf-Shaped Top Blade, Polearm, 17 In. 750.00
Halberd, Ax Blade, Curved Back Spike, C.1560, German, 56 In. 375.00
Halberd, Colonial, C.1750, Full Maple Shaft, 6 Ft. 2750.00
Halberd, English, C.1740, Tapered Spike, Hickory Shaft, 6 Ft. 5 In. 850.00
Jambiya, 1-Piece Horn Grip, Brass Studs, Arab, 8 1/4 In. 62.50
Lance, India Cavalry, Bamboo Haft, British, 7 Ft. 6 In. 80.00
Machete, Zulu Wars Period, British, 20 In. 80.00
Pesh-Kabz, Pierced Iron Hilt, Balls In Hollow Chamber, Persian 275.00
Pike, U.S.Constitution, 1797, Wood Shaft, 37 In. 1750.00
Spear, C.1800, Brass Socket, Engraved Base, Siamese 85.00
Spear, Trench, American Revolution, Hand-Forged, Iron Straps 135.00
Spontoon, American, C.1750, Pierced Blade, Maple Shaft, 5 Ft. 8 In. 1095.00
Spontoon, German, Engraved St.Jacobus On Blade, Dated 1771 .... 450.00
Stiletto, 19th Century, Whalebone & Metal, 17 In. 100.00
Tomahawk, Spike, American, C.1750, Curved Spiked Back, 8 1/2 In. 295.00

WEATHER VANE, Arrow, Copper & Iron 210.00
Arrow Form, Iron Post, 8 Ft. 8 In. 375.00
Black Hawk Horse 575.00
Butterfly, Feeler Weighted, Yellow, Sheet Metal, 19 In. 1100.00
Cow, Arrow, Tin & Cast Iron, 15 X 9 X 28 In. 175.00
Cow, Figural, Copper .... 3200.00 To 4500.00
Cow, Full-Bodied, 6 1/4 X 9 In. 200.00
Cow, Lightning Rod, Tin 190.00
Cow, Mounted On Tin Piece, Copper Lightning Rod 155.00
Cow, With Letters, Copper 500.00
Cow, 19th Century, Rod & Directional, Copper, 5 Ft. 10 In. 250.00
Dog, Setter, Full-Bodied, Copper 3200.00
Eagle On Ball, Wings Spread, Directional Arrow, 6 Ft. 1800.00
Eagle, Copper, Full-Bodied, Outstretched Wings, 79 In. 750.00
Eagle, Copper, Spread Wings, On Ball, Arrow, 42 In. 550.00
Eagle, Glass Eyes, Mounted On Oak Base, Wingspread 6 Ft. 3200.00
Eagle, Pennsylvania Post Office, Cast Iron 395.00
Eagle, Spread Wings, Ball & Arrow, Copper, 28 In. 200.00
Filigree On Arrow & Twisted Stems, Copper, C.1850 .... 350.00
Firehouse, Made From Fireman's Hat & Horn, Zinc 900.00
Fish, Wooden, Gray, Tapering Chamfered Spire, 67 In. 175.00
Horse & Jockey, Carved Wood 2050.00
Horse & Jockey, Sulky, 19th Century 3000.00

Weather Vane, Horse, Full-Bodied, American, Copper

Horse, Copper Body, Zinc Head, Directionals, 16 3/4 In.	425.00
Horse, Dempster, Cast Iron	195.00
Horse, Figural, Traces Of Mustard Paint, Copper	725.00
Horse, Full-Bodied, American, Copper	*Illus* 1800.00
Horse, Molded Copper & Zinc, 19th Century	2750.00
Horse, Profile, Wooden, Walking Stance, White Body, 21 In.	575.00
Horse, Rearing, Tin	70.00
Horse, Riveted Tin	275.00
Horse, Running, Circus, Tin & Iron, 10 X 8 In.	135.00
Horse, Running, Full-Bodied, Copper, 32 In.	375.00
Horse, Running, Full-Bodied, Flowing Mane, 29 In.	200.00
Horse, Running, Pressed Copper, 28 In.	325.00
Horse, Running, Sheet Iron, Black & White, 43 X 20 In.	235.00
Horse, Running, Sheet Metal, Yellow Paint, 38 X 19 In.	275.00
Horse, Running, Silhouette, 19th Century, Metal, 24 1/2 In.	500.00
Horse, Tin	85.00
Horse, Trotting, Full-Bodied, 7 1/2 X 9 3/4 In.	200.00
Horse, With Letters, Copper	500.00
Horse, Wooden, Black Spots, Cream Ground, 20 1/2 In.	2750.00
James Rooster, Stand & Red Lightning Ball	250.00
Large Eagle, Some Original Gold Leaf Showing	985.00
Man In Sulky, Trotting Horse, Copper & Brass, C.1860	550.00
Milking Cow, Curved Horns, Molded Copper, 32 In.	250.00
Peafowl, Iron, Applied Feathers, Rotating, 20 In.	700.00
Pig, Arrow Length, 20 In.	950.00
Pig, Full-Bodied, Copper	175.00
Pig, Lightning Rod, Cast Iron Directional, Zinc Pig 15 X 8 In.	200.00
Pig, Lightning Rod, Tin	125.00
Pig, Lightning Rod, Tin & Cast Iron, 9 X 5 In.	130.00
Pig, Zinc & Iron, Lightning Rod, 22 X 5 X 1/2 In.	145.00
Rooster, American, 19th Century, Full-Bodied, Copper, 28 In.	1600.00
Rooster, Copper, 24 X 26 In.	275.00
Rooster, Old Gold Leaf & Paint, Sheet Tin, 23 X 17 In.	265.00
Rooster, Stand & Red Lightning Ball	250.00

Sea Horse, Full-Bodied, Scrolling Tail, Gray, 22 In. 5500.00
Sea Serpent, Wood, Yellow & Red Polychrome, Iron Strips 4750.00
Stallion, Running, Copper, Flowing Mane, 28 In. 325.00
Sulky & Driver, Directionals & Shaft, 43 In. 7500.00
Sunflower, C.1880, Copper 550.00
3 Men Riding In Donkey Cart, French, Flat Sheet Metal, 22 In. 400.00
3 Owls, Different Sized, Copper, Mounted On Iron Bar, 35 In. 200.00

Webb glass was made by Thomas Webb & Sons of Stourbridge, England.
Many types of art and cameo glass were made by them during the Victorian
era. The factory is still producing glass.

WEBB BURMESE, Bowl, 2 1/2 X 3 1/2 In. 248.00
Lamp, Fairy, Acid Finish, Marked Clarke Base, 4 In. 175.00
Lamp, Fairy, Florals, Pink To Yellow, Mirror Base, Marked, 5 In. 450.00
Lamp, Fairy, Marked Clarke Base, 3 X 4 In. 175.00
Lamp, Fairy, On Mirror Plateau, Clarke Base, Triple Shades 2250.00
Lamp, Fairy, Ruffled Base, Clarke Insert, Signed, 5 5/8 In. 675.00
Rose Bowl, Egg Shape, Yellow Ruffled Foot, 2 1/2 In. 275.00
Rose Bowl, 2 1/4 In. 235.00
Sconce, Wall, Leaf & Berry, Beveled Mirror, 4 X 2 1/2 In. 325.00
Vase, Ball Shape, Green Leaves, Brown Branches, Pink, 3 5/8 In. 365.00
Vase, Berry Prunt, Brass Tripod Holder, 3 3/4 In. 525.00
Vase, Bottle Shape, Encircling Ivy, Pink To Lemon, Signed, 7 In. 650.00
Vase, Columbine Design, 3 1/2 In. 485.00
Vase, Egg Shape, Footed, Acid Finish, 3 1/2 X 2 1/2 In. 265.00
Vase, Floral Spray, High Glaze, Ruffled Top, 2 X 2 1/4 In. 70.00
Vase, Fluted & Crimped, Columbine, 3 1/2 In. 485.00
Vase, Fluted, Pedestal Foot, Pink To Yellow, 6 In. 395.00
Vase, Mums Design, Signed, 12 In. 1550.00
Vase, Pedestal, Signed, 4 1/2 In. 295.00
Vase, Red Berries, Leaves, Star Shaped Top, Footed, Signed, 4 In. 395.00
Vase, 5-Petal Flower Design, Yellow Handles, Signed, 5 In. 795.00
Vase, 5-Petal Flowers, Petal Top, Pedestal, Signed, 5 3/4 In. 650.00

WEBB PEACHBLOW, Bottle, Oriental Design, Gold Butterfly, Silver Lid, 6 In. 795.00
Bottle, Scent, Gold Prunus & Butterfly Design, 4 3/4 In. 495.00
Jar, Sweetmeat, Gold Prunus & Branches, 4 1/2 In. 450.00
Pitcher, Cream Lining, Rose Shaded To Pink, 3 5/8 In. 295.00
Punch Cup 250.00
Rose Bowl, Matsu-Noke Design, Pinch-Pleat Top, Cream Lining 1150.00
Vase, Bird In Flight, Off-White Lining, 4 X 8 In. 295.00
Vase, Bottle, Flower Design, Gold Bee, Red To Pink, 8 In. 375.00
Vase, Butterfly & Blossoms, Handled, Propeller Mark, 5 In. 500.00
Vase, Egg Shaped, Dimpled, White To Pink, 8 1/2 In. 325.00
Vase, Flowers & Leaves, Dragonflies, Handles, 7 1/2 In. 395.00
Vase, Foliage & Flowers, Gold Bee, Propeller Mark, 5 1/4 In. 250.00
Vase, Gold Daisies & Leaves, Dragonfly, 6 7/8 In. 695.00
Vase, Gold Floral Design, Double Gourd Shape, 8 In. 825.00
Vase, Gold Leaves & Flowers, Bird, 8 In. 295.00
Vase, Red To Pink Lining, Gold Flower & Butterfly, 3 1/4 In. 375.00
Vase, Ruffled Top, Rose To Cream, Cranberry Handle, 11 In. 475.00
Vase, Ruffled, Gold Trim, Enameled Flowers, 11 In. 475.00
Vase, Satin, Gold Daisies, Dragonfly, Rose To Cream, 6 7/8 In. 695.00

WEBB, Base, Bronze, Glass, Flared Top, 5 X 10 In. 650.00
Bonbon, Footed, Rainbow, Polka Dot, 6 3/4 In. 80.00
Bottle, Perfume, Embossed Sterling Silver Border, Citron, Signed 2250.00
Bowl, Diamond-Quilted, Mother-Of-Pearl, 6 Crimp, Apple Green, 4 1/4 In. 695.00
Bowl, Diamond-Quilted, Yellow Threaded Feet, Signed, 3 1/4 In. 100.00
Bowl, Pink Liner, Enamel Flower Design, 3 Amber Feet, 7 1/2 In.Diam. 350.00
Bowl, Prunus Blossoms, Gold Butterfly, Brown Satin, Footed, 5 3/4 In. 650.00
Bowl, Salad, Gold Prunus & Butterfly, Sterling Silver Spoon & Fork 850.00
Bowl, Satin, Prunus, Butterfly, Cream Lining, 8-Crimp Top, 2 1/4 In. 395.00

Webb, Bride's Bowl, Wilcox Silver Base, Signed

Bride's Basket, Enameled Design, Silver Plated Holder	300.00
Bride's Bowl, Pink & White Outside, 8 Ruffles, 10 3/8 In.Diam.	375.00
Bride's Bowl, Wilcox Silver Base, Signed	*Illus* 2800.00
Candleholder, Paperweight Style, Striker Bottom, Signed, Pair	135.00
Chalice, Cameo Flowers, Diaper Pattern Around Collar, 2 1/4 In.	635.00
Chalice, English Cameo, Brown Ground, Floral Design, 2 1/4 In.	395.00
Compote, Blown-Out Cherries, Signed, 6 1/2 In.	275.00
Cruet, Blue Ground, Clear Amber Base, Signed, 10 1/2 In.	325.00
Cruet, Blue, Clear Amber Base, Twisted Handle, 10 1/2 In.	325.00
Cup, Loving, Bronze Glass, Pedestal, 5 1/2 In.	75.00
Flask, Head Of Duck, Yellow Bill, Signed T.W. & Son, 8 3/4 In.	1950.00
Jar, Amberina, Honeycomb, Covered, British Touchmarks	425.00
Lamp Base, Kerosene, Lemon With Blue, Signed	295.00
Perfume, Brown, Hinged Lid, Zeus Head, Lay Down, 5 In.	235.00
Pitcher, Flowers, Butterfly, White Interior & Handle, Signed, 5 1/2 In.	565.00
Rose Bowl, Alexandrite Honeycomb, 2 1/2 In.	725.00
Rose Bowl, Cameo, Pink & White Frosted, 2 3/4 In.	1850.00
Rose Bowl, Gold Prunus Blossoms, Box-Pleated Top, 2 1/2 X 3 3/4 In.	375.00
Rose Bowl, Satin Glass, Buue, Gold Prunus Blossoms, Cream Lining	375.00
Tumbler, Diamond-Quilted, Mother-Of-Pearl, White Lining	145.00
Tumbler, Diamond-Quilted, Pink To Raspberry, Signed	145.00
Vase, Alexandrite Dainty Petal Top, 6 In.	750.00
Vase, Blue Body, White Cameo Carved Flower, Bud Leaves, 3 1/2 In.	850.00
Vase, Butterfly, Citron Color, 4 3/4 In.	1200.00
Vase, Cameo, Lime & White, 4 1/2 In.	600.00
Vase, Cameo, Vines & Flowers, C.1900, 4 In.	175.00
Vase, Cerise, White Cased Inside, Lace Design, Signed, 7 In.	320.00
Vase, Coinspot Mother-Of-Pearl, Enameled Flowers, Marked, 11 In.	650.00
Vase, Cut Flowers, Vine, & Leaves, Butterfly On Back, Citron, 7 1/4 In.	1640.00
Vase, Dark Pink To Off-White Pink, White Acorns, Leaves, 8 In.	285.00
Vase, Diamond-Quilted, Metal-Footed Base, Blue, 5 7/8 In.	200.00
Vase, Enameled Flowers & Butterfly, 6 1/2 X 12 In.	295.00
Vase, English Cameo, Roses, White, Royal Blue, Signed, 9 In.	3500.00
Vase, Floral, White Collar Top, Carved Flowers & Leaves, Blue, 10 In.	2450.00
Vase, Gold Leaves, Stems, & Blossoms, Butterfly, Yellow Ground, 7 1/2 In.	350.00
Vase, Gold Prunus, Yellow Satin, Cream Lining, 4 1/4 In.	265.00
Vase, Morning Glory & Butterfly, Red Body, Double Band, 6 In.	2350.00
Vase, Mother-Of-Pearl, Butterfly & Flowers, Gold & White, Marked, 12 In.	498.00
Vase, Raindrop Design, Pink & White Morning Glories, 10 In.	475.00
Vase, Satin Glass, Blue Plums, Gold Branches & Leaves, Rose Pink, 7 In.	375.00
Vase, Shaded Rose To Blue Plums, Gold Branches & Leaves, 7 In.	375.00
Vase, Stick, Blue Satin, Gold Enameled, 8 In.	395.00
Vase, Stick, Bronze Glass, 3 X 3 1/2 In.Diam., Pair	75.00
Vase, Stick, 3-Color, Day Lily Cameos, 13 In.	3900.00
Water Set, Dogwood & Fern, Gold On Clear, 5 Tumblers	135.00

WEDGWOOD *Wedgwood pottery has been made at the famous Wedgwood factory in England since 1759. A large variety of wares has been made, including the well-known jasperware, basalt, creamware, and even a limited amount of porcelain.*

WEDGWOOD, see also Gibson Girl

WEDGWOOD, Barrel, Biscuit, Blue & White, Classical Figures	265.00
Barrel, Biscuit, Lilac & White	525.00
Barrel, Bisquit, Blue & White, Jasper, Classical Figures, Marked	90.00
Basket, With Underplate, Creamware, Twig, Brown Trim	425.00
Biscuit Jar, Acorn & Leaf Design, Acorn Knop, C.1925, 8 1/2 In.	350.00
Biscuit Jar, Blue & White, Jasperware, Silver Mounts, 6 In.	225.00
Biscuit Jar, Blue & White, Ladies, Cupids, Lion's Head, 6 In.	145.00
Biscuit Jar, Blue & White, Raised White Figures, Marked	145.00
Biscuit Jar, Classical Figures, Sterling Silver Lid, Blue	265.00
Biscuit Jar, Jasperware, Blue, White, Marked, 5 3/4 In.	145.00
Biscuit Jar, Jasperware, Front Design, Blue & White	135.00
Biscuit Jar, Jasperware, Gold, Black, & White, Marked, 6 1/2 In.	750.00
Biscuit Jar, Jasperware, Portrait Medallions, Marked, Covered, 7 In.	325.00
Biscuit Jar, Lavender, 7 In.	390.00
Biscuit Jar, Sterling Silver Collar & Handle, Blue & White	225.00
Biscuit Jar, White Figures, Green, 5 1/2 In.	125.00
Bottle, England, Black Jasper Dip, 5 In.	125.00
Bottle, Green, Blue, Lilac & White, C.1850	2800.00
Bowl, Basalt, Covered, Draped Figure Design, 4 1/4 In.	50.00
Bowl, Basalt, Lady Templetown Design, C.1790, 7 1/4 In.	1275.00
Bowl, Black Basalt, C.1900, 16 1/4 In.Diam.	80.00
Bowl, Butterflies, Fairyland Luster, 3 7/8 In.	250.00
Bowl, Butterfly Luster, Blue & Gold Interior, 3 X 6 1/2 In.Diam.	349.00
Bowl, Candy, Jasperware, Blue & White, Covered, Marked, 7 In.	170.00
Bowl, Centerpiece, Queensware, Grape Leaves & Grapes, 10 In.Diam.	25.00
Bowl, Classical Figures In White, Dark Blue, 4 X 2 1/2 In.	70.00
Bowl, Dark Blue, Classical Figures, White Ground, 4 X 2 1/2 In.	70.00
Bowl, Daventry Luster, Orange & Blue Interior, Signed, 9 1/4 In.	1350.00
Bowl, Dragon Luster, 4 1/4 In.	90.00
Bowl, Dragon Luster, 6 1/2 In.	395.00
Bowl, Dragon Luster, 8 1/8 In.Diam.	600.00
Bowl, Fairyland Luster, Chinese Garden, Marked & Numbered, 11 In.	2600.00
Bowl, Fairyland Luster, Hummingbirds, Orange Luster, 4 1/2 In.	275.00
Bowl, Fairyland Luster, Octagonal,Fiddler In Tree, 8 In.	1600.00
Bowl, Fairyland Luster, Orange, Butterflies, 4 X 2 1/2 In.	300.00
Bowl, Fairyland Luster, 8-Sided, Dragons Center, 3 X 5 In.Diam.	375.00
Bowl, Fairyland, Orange, Butterflies, Gold Greek Key, 4 In.	300.00
Bowl, Fruit, Fairyland Luster, Garden Of Paradise, 11 In.	1850.00
Bowl, Hummingbird, Luster, 9 1/2 In.	595.00
Bowl, Jasperware, Applied White Figures, Salmon Ground, 3 X 2 In.	55.00
Bowl, Jasperware, Blue & White, Silver Cover, Marked, 6 In.	250.00
Bowl, Jasperware, Cupid With Bow, White Sides, 10 3/4 In.Diam.	395.00
Bowl, Luster, 5 Hummingbirds, Bird & Orange Luster Inside, 4 In.	185.00
Bowl, Mother-Of-Pearl Luster Inside, Crane Outside, 3 X 4 3/4 In.	325.00
Bowl, Octagonal, Chinese Red With Blue & White, 12 In.Diam.	450.00
Bowl, Oriental Design, Luster, Octagonal Shape, 4 3/4 X 3 In.	350.00
Bowl, Sugar, Basalt, Covered, Red & Cream Swag, 2 5/8 In.	50.00
Bowl, Waste, C.1925, Olive Green, 4 1/2 X 2 1/4 In.	150.00
Box, Butterfly, Lilac, Covered, 2 1/2 X 3/4 In.	45.00
Box, Crimson & White Design, Women & Cupid On Cover, 3 In.	325.00
Box, Dragon Luster, Widow's Finial, Covered, Blue, 6 In.Diam.	650.00
Box, Green, White Design, 2 X 3 In.	45.00
Box, Heart Shape, C.1925, Olive Green, Covered, 3 1/2 X 4 1/4 In.	250.00
Box, Heart Shape, Jasperware, Black, Covered	39.00
Box, Hummingbird, Widow's Finial, Blue Luster Exterior, 5 5/8 In.	695.00
Box, Jasperware, Green Classical Motif, Covered, 5 In.	60.00
Box, Jasperware, Heart-Shaped, Covered, 5 X 3 1/2 In.	550.00

Box, Jasperware, White Figures, Lidded, Round, 1 1/2 X 2 1/2 In.	125.00
Box, Powder, Blue & White, Jasper, Marked, 5 In.	40.00
Bracelet, Cameo & Medallion, Bell-Shaped	95.00
Bust, Burns, Black Basalt, 14 1/2 In.	675.00 To 850.00
Bust, Homer, Basalt, 11 1/2 In.	950.00
Bust, Milton, Parian, E.W.Wyon, 8 1/4 X 14 1/4 In.	850.00
Bust, Washington, Basalt, C.1820, 14 In.	1250.00
Butter Tub, Jasperware, Lidded, Blue & White, Signed	90.00
Candlestick, Black Basalt, Grecian Figures, 6 3/4 In., Pair	185.00
Candlestick, Dark Blue, 10 In., Pair	325.00
Candlestick, Jasperware, Blue, 8 In.	60.00
Candlestick, Lady With Lyre, Dark Blue, 6 In.	95.00
Candlestick, Terra-Cotta, Enamel Flowers, Marked, 7 In., Pair	225.00
Chamber Pot, Blue Willow	65.00
Cheese Dish, Jasperware, Covered, Adams, Green	260.00
Cheese Keeper, Light Blue, 1890s, 8 X 10 In.	400.00
Clock, Mantel, Blue & White, Jasperware, Ivory Dial, Marked, 8 In.	375.00
Coffeepot, Black Basalt, Capri Enameled, Marked, 6 In.	250.00
Coffeepot, Caneware, Glazed, 9 In.	225.00
Compote, Flying Cranes, Temple Dogs, Blue-Green Ground, 3 In.	485.00
Condiment Set, Bamboo Lattice, Tricolor, Silver Plated Holder	425.00
Cookie Jar, Jasperware, Blue	148.00
Cookie Jar, Jasperware, Green	165.00
Cookie Jar, Jasperware, Lilac	265.00
Cracker Jar, Blue, White Design	175.00
Cracker Jar, Classical Figures, Blue Ground, Marked	125.00
Cracker Jar, Cupids, Myth, Blue	145.00
Cracker Jar, Jasperware, Black	445.00
Creamer, Black, Bulbous, 5 In.	85.00
Creamer, Blue Jasper, White Figures, Marked England	50.00
Creamer, Glazed Interior, C.1925, Olive Green, 3 3/4 X 3 1/2 In.	135.00
Creamer, Jasperware, Cherub Playing Flute, Green, 3 1/2 In.	55.00
Creamer, Jasperware, 1867, Blue	120.00
Cup & Saucer, Caneware, Yellow	275.00
Cup & Saucer, Flowers, Royal Ironstone, White	8.00
Cup & Saucer, Fruit In Basket Pattern, Blue Trim	15.00
Cup & Saucer, Jasperware, Blue & White, Birds	395.00
Cup & Saucer, Jasperware, Classical Appliques, 6 Sets	255.00
Cup & Saucer, Landscape & House On Both Pieces, Dark Green	225.00
Cup & Saucer, Lusterware, Silver Rim, Demitasse	395.00
Cup & Saucer, Queensware, Grape Leaves & Grapes	18.00
Cup & Saucer, White Figures, Dark Blue, Jasperware	125.00
Cup, Lusterware, Bird In Middle, Handleless, Small	195.00
Cup, Peach Melba, Fairyland Luster, Leapfrogging Elves, 4 1/4 In.	795.00
Cup, Tea, Black Basalt, Enamel Flowers, Marked	75.00
Dish, Game, Caneware, Insert, 10 In.	425.00
Dish, Lilac, Oval, 5 X 3 1/2 In.	30.00
Dish, Peach Melba, Hummingbird Luster, Flame Inside, 3 1/4 In.	275.00
Dish, Serving, Green, Embossed Leaf, 8 3/4 X 11 3/4 In.	40.00
Eggcup, Gold Trim, Drab Glazed	125.00
Ewer, Basalt, Gilded, C.1860, 15 In.	1850.00
Ewer, Jasperware, Impressed Flowers, Cameo Of Woman, Pink, 6 In.	250.00
Ewer, Water, Gilded Basalt, 15 In.	225.00
Figurine, Bear, Black Basalt, Striding, Marked, 4 5/8 In.	250.00
Figurine, Blackbird, Glass Eyes, C.1916, Marked, 4 3/4 X 4 3/4 In.	575.00
Figurine, Bulldog, Black Basalt, Standing, Marked, 4 1/2 In.	200.00
Figurine, Cupid & Psyche, Basalt, Pair	1900.00
Figurine, Polar Bear, Creamware, C.1927, Marked & Signed, 7 X 10 In.	450.00
Figurine, Squirrel, Sitting On Hindquarters, Glass, 6 In.	95.00
Figurine, The Birth Of Venus, White, Biscuitware, 7 In.	2500.00
Figurine, Winston Churchill, Black Basalt, Marked, 7 In.	40.00
Gravy Boat, Lion's Head On Each Side, C.1915, 9 In.	25.00
Heel, Shoe, Lady's, Green, Pair	295.00

Heel, Shoe, Lady's, Jasperware, Blue, 1950s, Pair 200.00
Holder, Plant, Blue & Cream, Figural, 15 In. 450.00
Humidor, Cylinder Shape, Blue & White 275.00
Inkstand, C.1820, Black 950.00
Jar, Condiment, Light Blue, Dark Blue, White, 3 1/2 In. 345.00
Jar, Ginger, Fairyland Luster, Rainbow, 8 In. 2200.00
Jardiniere, Basalt, Lion Heads, Swags Of Grapes, 5 1/4 X 5 1/2 In. 175.00
Jardiniere, Blue & White, 6 1/4 In. 220.00
Jardiniere, C.1925, Olive Green, Flared, 8 1/4 X 7 1/2 In. 550.00
Jardiniere, Jasperware, Figures, Lion Heads, Marked, 2 3/4 In. 88.00
Jardiniere, Jasperware, Mythological Scene, 4 1/2 X 5 1/4 In., Pair 440.00
Jardiniere, Tricolor, Black Grecian Figures, Yellow Ground, 7 In. 440.00
Jug, Ale, C.1870, 8 In. 110.00
Jug, Eglinton Tournament Series, Knight In Armor, Flow Blue, 6 In. 150.00
Jug, Hot Water, Queensware, Grape Leaves & Grapes 75.00
Jug, Jasperware, Raised Ladies Around Sides, White Bands, 7 In. 125.00
Jug, Milk, Hinged Pewter Lid, Raised Grape Border, Blue, 8 In. 260.00
Jug, Milk, Rope Handle, Silver Plated Cover, C.1860, 7 In. 165.00
Jug, Molasses, Figures, Spade Shaped Metal Lid, Rope Handle, 7 In. 250.00
Lamp, Jasperware, Brass Footed, Blue, 26 In. 210.00
Loving Cup, Animal Luster, 3-Handled, Signed & Numbered, 2 In. 225.00
Marker, Wine Cask, Parian 85.00
Paperweight, Liberty Bell, Black Basalt, Impressed Mark 25.00
Pitcher, Clasical Figures, Deep Blue, 8 In. 195.00
Pitcher, Classical Figures, Green, 8 In. 495.00
Pitcher, Classical Figurines, Dutch Green, 4 In. 210.00
Pitcher, Drabware, Blue Raised Figures, 4 1/2 In. 300.00
Pitcher, Franklin & Washington Medallions, Rope Handle, 8 1/2 In. 500.00
Pitcher, Grecian Ladies, Cobalt, 4 In. 125.00
Pitcher, Greek Key & Classical Figures, Blue, 5 1/2 In. 95.00
Pitcher, Hunting Scene, Blue & White, 9 1/4 In. 150.00
Pitcher, Hunting Scene, Hound Dog Handle, 7 In. 110.00
Pitcher, Hunting Scene, Silver Luster, Marked, 6 3/4 In. .... *Illus*   95.00
Pitcher, Jasperware, Acorns, Leaves & Figures, Marked, 4 1/8 In. 110.00
Pitcher, Jasperware, Blue & White, 5 In. 85.00
Pitcher, Jasperware, Classical Figures, Blue, 8 In. 115.00
Pitcher, Jasperware, Rope Handle, Green, 8 In. 110.00
Pitcher, Knob Finial, Barrel Shaped, Covered, 1875-90, 6 1/2 In. 120.00
Pitcher, Transfer, Garfield, Born 1831, President 1881 .... 650.00
Pitcher, Water, Jasperware, Blue & White, Pewter Cover, 8 In. 125.00

Wedgwood, Pitcher, Hunting Scene, Silver Luster, Marked, 6 3/4 In.

Pitcher, White Figures, Grapevine Border, Dark Blue, 5 In.	100.00
Planter, Olive Green, 6 1/2 In.	290.00
Plaque, Elizabeth II & Philip Coronation, Blue, Framed, Pair	250.00
Plaque, James II, Oval, C.1840, 2 1/4 In.	80.00
Plaque, Jasperware, Blue & White, Psyche, Marked, 8 1/4 In.	190.00
Plaque, Jasperware, Gilt Frame, 4 X 8 In.	175.00
Plaque, Jasperware, Rococo, Lady, Cupids, 7 In.	25.00
Plaque, Jasperware, White Figure, Flowers, Green, Signed, 9 In.	120.00
Plaque, Napoleon, Light Blue & White, C.1820, 8 1/2 In.	590.00
Plaque, Sage Green, White, Jasperware, Wood Frame, 19 X 7 In.	875.00
Plaque, White Figure, Yellow Green, 7 1/2 In.Diam.	250.00
Plate, Black & Red, 10 In.	30.00
Plate, Black & White, Jasperware, Trophy Ware, C.1900, Chariot, 8 In.	325.00
Plate, Botanical Series, Enameled Flowers, 10 1/4 In.	25.00
Plate, C.1820, Floral & Prunus Blossoms, Marked, 8 1/8 In., Set Of 8	150.00
Plate, Christmas, 1970, Trafalgar Square, Light Blue	30.00
Plate, Commonwealth Ave., Boston, Brown & Cream, 8 In.	55.00
Plate, Creamware, Hand-Painted, Fortune & The Infant, 9 3/8 In.	135.00
Plate, Creamware, Nude Lady, Child, Gold Scalloped, Marked, 9 3/8 In.	135.00
Plate, Dragon Luster, Gold & Blue Border, Marked, 9 1/8 In.	350.00
Plate, Game, Creamware, Dog Standing, Gun, Game, 9 In.	140.00
Plate, Gunston Hall, 10 In.	15.00
Plate, Ivanhoe, Brown, White, Pastel-Colored Border	300.00
Plate, Ivanhoe, Rebecca Repelling The Templar, Blue & White, 10 In.	55.00
Plate, Jasperware, Black, 10 In.	45.00
Plate, Jasperware, Queen Elizabeth Bust	14.00
Plate, Library Of Congress, 9 In.	28.00
Plate, Little Red Riding Hood, 10 1/2 In.	125.00
Plate, Louise, Bird, Berries, Flowers, Red, Yellow, Marked, 9 In.	39.00
Plate, Majolica, Reticulated Edge, 9 In.	45.00
Plate, Mandarin, C.1905, 10 In.	18.00
Plate, Massachusetts Institute Of Technology, 1930	30.00
Plate, Mayflower, Plymouth Harbor, 9 In.	28.00
Plate, Mt.Vernon, 9 In.	28.00
Plate, Old London View, Sepia Design, Cream Ground, 1941, 10 1/2 In.	35.00
Plate, Patrician Pattern, 10 1/2 In.	10.00
Plate, Queensware, Grape Leaves & Grapes, 8 1/2 In.	12.50
Plate, Return Of The Mayflower, Blue & White, 10 In.	35.00
Plate, Return Of The Mayflower, 9 In.	48.00
Plate, Serving, Creamware, C.1800, 8 In.	110.00
Plate, Spirit Of '76, Blue & White, 10 In.	35.00
Plate, The Capitol, 9 In.	25.00
Plate, University Of Maine, 1931, Blue & White, 10 In.	38.00
Plate, White House, 9 In.	25.00
Platter, Cows, Blue Ground, 17 In.	95.00
Platter, Devon Sprays, 13 1/2 In.	30.00
Platter, Edme Pattern, C.1920, White, 19 1/2 X 15 1/2 In.	82.50
Platter, Raised Leaf & Strawberry, Ironstone, 1856, 16 X 18 In.	125.00
Pot, Posy, Deep Lilac, Green Leaves, C.1810, 3 5/8 In.	600.00
Pot, Wine, Creamware, 18th Century, Signed	450.00
Salt & Pepper, Jasperware, Figures, Cupids, Blue, White, Marked, 4 In.	110.00
Sherbet, Fairyland Luster, Flying Cranes & Temple Dog, 3 X 4 In.	525.00
Sucrier, Caneware, 6 In.Diam.	245.00
Sugar & Creamer, Classical Figures, Dark Blue, White	150.00
Sugar & Creamer, Jasperware, Cobalt	125.00
Sugar & Creamer, Jasperware, Dark Green	140.00
Sugar & Creamer, Mottled Majolica, Silver Plate Mounted, 4 1/2 In.	400.00
Sugar & Creamer, Patrician, Cover	35.00
Sugar & Creamer, Queensware, Grape Leaves & Grapes	90.00
Sugar, Black Basalt, Globular, Covered, Marked, 4 1/2 In.	110.00
Sugar, Queensware, Coronation Of Edward VII, Relief Busts, Cover	30.00
Tea Set, Black Basalt Ware, Classical Figures, Marked, 4 Piece	275.00
Tea Set, Fluted Bodies, Brown & Gold Prunus Trees, 5 Piece	160.00

Tea Set, Jasperware, Dark Blue, 3 Piece 295.00
Tea Set, Silver Coated, 3 Piece 1000.00
Teapot, Blue & White, Jasperware, Classical Figures, Marked 175.00
Teapot, C.1925, Olive Green, 5 1/4 In. 225.00
Teapot, Capriware, Black, C.1840 .... 385.00
Teapot, Devon Sprays 35.00
Teapot, Drabware, C.1820, 3 1/2 In. 310.00
Teapot, Drabware, Lavender, 19th Century, Crested Front, 9 1/4 In. 250.00
Teapot, Dragon Handle & Spout, Empressed 1864 Code 225.00
Teapot, Jasperware, Classical Figures, Dark Blue 145.00
Teapot, Jasperware, Conical Top, White On Blue Ground, 5 In. 50.00
Teapot, Jasperware, 4 X 6 1/2 In. 95.00
Teapot, Queensware, Coronation Of Edward VII, Relief Busts 75.00
Teapot, Queensware, Grape Leaves & Grapes, Large 95.00
Teapot, Redware, Lotus Blossoms, Bamboo Handle, Marked 150.00
Teapot, Rosso Antico, C.1820, 3 1/2 In. 310.00
Teapot, Salt Glaze, C.1820, 5 1/2 In. 350.00
Teapot, Stand, White, Stoneware, Flower, Leaf, C.1835, Marked 200.00
Teapot, Two Doves, Dark Blue, 6 In. 250.00
Tile, Calendar, 1903 .... 55.00
Tile, Calendar, 1910 .... 55.00
Tile, Calendar, 1912 .... 55.00
Tile, Calendar, 1922 .... 55.00
Tile, Calendar, 1929 .... 40.00
Tile, Little Red Riding Hood, C.1850, 6 In. Square 42.00
Tobacco Jar, Scroll & Trellis Pattern, White, Lilac, Green, Marked 230.00
Tobacco Jar, Terra-Cotta, Covered, Classical Figures, Marked 170.00
Toothpick, Dark Blue, 3 Scenes 28.00
Toothpick, Jasperware, Black 38.00
Toothpick, White Figures, Signed 95.00
Tray, Dresser, Jasperware, Blue 45.00
Tray, Pin, C.1925, Olive Green, 2 1/8 X 5 7/8 In. 135.00
Tray, Serving, Divided, Playing Cards, People, Verses, 1910 .... 150.00
Tureen, Saucer, Queensware, Covered, Floral Knob, Marked, 8 In. 80.00
Urn, Basalt, Satyr, Wedgwood & Bentley, C.1775, Miniature, 5 In. 1675.00
Urn, Black Jasperware, White Ladies, Covered, Marked, 10 In. 695.00
Urn, Brown Mottled, Creamware, C.1782, 11 In. 2800.00
Urn, Dancing Hours, 19th Century, Blue & White, 9 In., Pair 1350.00
Urn, Mottled Design, Creamware, Basalt Plinth, Signed, 13 In. 3500.00
Urn, Polychromed & Glazed, Covered, Marked, 9 3/4 In. 70.00
Vase, Birds In Flight, Mottled Blue, 8 1/2 In. 450.00
Vase, Black & White, Grecian Scene, 5 In. 270.00
Vase, Blue & White, Jasperware, Pear Form, Classical Figures, 7 In. 180.00
Vase, Blue Jasperware, White Ladies, Foliage, Marked, 14 1/2 In. 895.00
Vase, Blue Luster, Gold Dragon Design, 12 In. 485.00
Vase, Bottle, Deep Blue, White, Classical Ladies, 7 In. 135.00
Vase, Bud, Blue & White, Jasperware, Pear Form, Cherub, Marked, 5 In. 90.00
Vase, Bud, Hummingbird Luster, Blue, 5 1/4 In. 195.00
Vase, Bud, Mustard Yellow, Black, Marked, 7 In. 625.00
Vase, Bud, Yellow & Black, Jasperware, Teardrop Form, Marked, 7 In. 275.00
Vase, Creamware, Marked, 6 1/2 In. 50.00
Vase, Creamware, Posey, 8 In. 85.00
Vase, Crimson, White Jasperware, Baluster, Marked, 6 1/8 In. 750.00
Vase, Cylinder, Classical Scene, Black & White, 6 In. 140.00
Vase, Dragon Luster, Covered, Blue, 12 In. 485.00
Vase, Dragon Luster, Mother-Of-Pearl Inside, Marked, 8 3/4 In. 495.00
Vase, Fairyland Luster, Gold Dragon On Blue, 8 In. 299.00
Vase, Fairyland Luster, Ship & Bridge, 8 In. 1600.00
Vase, Ferrara, Deep Blue, Marked, 9 In. 75.00
Vase, Flat, Blue, White Enamel, 12 X 6 In. 95.00
Vase, Handled, Jasperware, Figures, Black & White, 10 1/8 In. 475.00
Vase, Hummingbird Luster, Blue, Gold, Flame Interior, Signed, 8 In. 395.00
Vase, Jasperware, Blue & White Scenes, 5 1/4 In. 60.00

Vase, Jasperware, Classical Figures, 3 3/4 In. 38.00
Vase, Jasperware, Figures, Black & White, 10 1/8 In. 475.00
Vase, Jasperware, Portland, Black & White, 5 In. 195.00
Vase, Jasperware, Portland, Blue & White, 5 1/4 X 7 In. 375.00
Vase, Jasperware, Tricolor, Oval Medallions, Marked, 5 X 4 In.Diam. 750.00
Vase, Jasperware, White Figures, Deep Blue & White, 10 1/4 In. 625.00
Vase, Jasperware, White Relief, Blue Ground, Marked, 7 In. 125.00
Vase, Light Blue & White, C.1850, 4 In. 110.00
Vase, Luster, Dragon & Oriental Design, Powder Blue, 4 1/2 In. 240.00
Vase, Portland, Black & White, Jasper, Classical Figures, 8 In. 325.00
Vase, Portland, Dark Blue, 7 In. 235.00
Vase, Spill, Caneware, Crescent Shape, Floral, 3 1/4 In. 750.00
Vase, Spill, Caneware, Palmette, Bellflowers, Marked, 3 1/2 In. 100.00
Weight, Pearlware, Signed & Regulatory Marks, Set Of 4 .... 650.00

LOUWELSA
WELLER

Weller pottery was first made in 1873 in Fultonham, Ohio. The firm moved to Zanesville, Ohio, in 1882. Art wares were first made in 1893. Hundreds of lines of pottery were made including Louwelsa, Eocean, Dickens, and Sicardo before the pottery closed in 1948.

WELLER, Ashtray, Fox, Marked 20.00
Base, Bonito, 2-Handled, Signed, 6 In. 40.00
Base, Marvo, Brown, 10 In. 45.00
Basket, Burntwood, Hanging, Geometrics, 9 X 5 In. 27.00
Basket, Forest, Hanging 125.00
Basket, Lustre, Purple, 6 1/2 X 5 In. 30.00
Basket, Malvern, Marked, Green, Tan & Purple, 6 X 8 In. 28.00
Basket, Souevo, Hanging, Stylized Wave Crest, Brown, 6 1/2 In. 60.00
Bottle, Water, Ollas, 2-Color, Marked, 12 In. 35.00
Bowl, Barcelona, 9 In. 38.00
Bowl, Bonito, Flower Frog, Artist Signed, 10 1/2 In. 90.00
Bowl, Breton, Green, 4 In. 60.00
Bowl, Claywood, Swimming Duck, 2 3/4 In. .... 30.00 To 35.00
Bowl, Console, Evergreen, 12 In. 15.00
Bowl, Console, Gloria, Brown 40.00
Bowl, Console, Roma, Shell Feet, Roses, 6 X 10 In. 75.00
Bowl, Coppertone, 10 1/2 X 2 In. 165.00
Bowl, Coppertone, 13 1/2 In. 75.00
Bowl, Fairfield, 4 X 7 In. 75.00
Bowl, Nut, Figural Squirrel 55.00
Bowl, Souevo, 5 3/4 X 5 3/4 In. 85.00
Bowl, Turkis, 3 In. 12.00
Bowl, Woodcraft, Squirrels, 3 1/2 In. 95.00
Bowl, Woodcraft, Squirrels, 6 In. .... 68.00 To 125.00
Bowl, Woodcraft, 13 In. 85.00
Candleholder, Clarmont, 12 In. 25.00
Console Set, Lavonia, Flower Frog & Candleholders, Bowl, 3 X 15 In. 60.00
Console Set, Rozane, Candlesticks, Turquoise, Bowl 12 In. 100.00
Console Set, Rozane, Candlesticks, 1940s, Brown, Bowl 14 In. 90.00
Console Set, Silvertone, 12 In., 4 Piece 250.00
Console, Coppertone, 10 1/2 X 2 In. 160.00
Cornucopia, Cameo, Blue, 7 In. 12.00
Cornucopia, Rozane, Turquoise 90.00
Cornucopia, Wild Rose, Pink 25.00
Doorstop, Roma 175.00
Ewer, Cameo, Blue, 10 In. 40.00
Ewer, Cameo, Green, 10 In. 20.00
Ewer, Gloria, Brown, 9 In. 55.00
Ewer, Gloria, Green, 9 In. 20.00
Ewer, Oak Leaf, Pedestal, Shaded Green Ground, 6 1/2 In. 24.00
Ewer, Roba, Orange 55.00
Fernery, Warwick Design, Round, 6 In. 90.00

Figurine, Girl, Blue, 11 In.	80.00
Flower Frog, Coppertone, 4 In.	70.00
Flower Frog, Malvern, White Flakes, Brown, 5 X 2 1/4 In.	12.00
Flower Frog, Silvertone	45.00
Flower Frog, Woodcraft, 6 Raised Openings, Center Hole, 6 X 3 1/2 In.	20.00
Flower Holder, Muskota, Frog On Lily	70.00
Flowerpot, Flemish, 7 In.	55.00
Jar, Ginger, Panella, Script Mark, Gray To Aqua, 6 1/2 In.	30.00
Jardiniere, Blue Ware, Pedestal, 28 1/2 In.	750.00
Jardiniere, Bonito, Ink Stamped, 10 X 9 In.	60.00
Jardiniere, Burntwood, 9 X 11 In.	150.00
Jardiniere, Cameo Jewell, 8 In.	185.00
Jardiniere, Etna, Frog Peeping Over Edge, Water Lilies, 9 X 9 1/2 In.	250.00
Jardiniere, Evergreen, 13 1/2 X 10 1/2 In.	60.00
Jardiniere, Flemish, Green, Pink Floral, 8 1/2 In.	75.00
Jardiniere, Flemish, Paneled Grapes & Apples, Footed, 10 In.	105.00
Jardiniere, Forest, 4 1/2 X 5 1/2 In.	45.00
Jardiniere, Forest, 8 In. .... 58.00 To 85.00	
Jardiniere, Indian Swastika Design, Signed, 6 X 8 In.	175.00
Jardiniere, Ivory, Classic Florals, Brown Ground, 6 3/4 In.	28.00
Jardiniere, Ivory, Pedestal, 31 1/2 In. .... 20.00 To 325.00	
Jardiniere, Ivory, 4 1/2 In.	45.00
Jardiniere, Ivory, 8 1/2 In.	70.00
Jardiniere, Knifewood, 8 1/2 X 10 In.	130.00
Jardiniere, Louwelsa, Art Nouveau .... *Illus* 400.00	
Jardiniere, Louwelsa, Leaf Design, 10 1/2 In.	110.00
Jardiniere, Louwelsa, Shaded Golden Flowers, Brown, 10 X 8 1/2 In.	350.00
Jardiniere, Marvo, Brown, 8 In.	22.00
Jardiniere, Narona, Pedestal, Ivory	400.00
Jardiniere, Pearl, 8 X 10 In.	55.00
Jardiniere, Roma, Raised Roses, Open Handles, 8 In. .... 40.00 To 65.00	
Jardiniere, Roma, Rose Garlands, Cream Ground, 3 1/4 X 6 1/4 In.	20.00
Jardiniere, Roma, 4-Paneled, Foxes & Chickens, 9 In.	125.00
Jardiniere, Woodcraft, Overlapping Leaf Design, 9 1/2 In.	75.00
Jug, Louwelsa, Cherries, Handled, 6 In.	95.00
Lamp, Base, Coppertone	150.00
Mug, Burntwood, Flower Design, 5 In.	35.00
Mug, Creamware, Hand-Designed, 5 In.	65.00
Mug, Dickens Ware, Chief Bald Eagle, Full Headdress, J.Butterworth 1200.00	

Weller, Jardiniere, Louwelsa, Art Nouveau

Mug, Dickens Ware, Thistles, 7 In. 275.00
Mug, Etna, Flowers, Pink, 5 1/2 In. 125.00
Mug, Louwelsa, Cherries, 6 1/2 In. 125.00
Pitcher, Cream, Marbleized 20.00
Pitcher, Forest, Glossy, 6 In. 100.00
Pitcher, Forest, 6 In. 50.00
Pitcher, Louwelsa, Brown, 5 1/2 X 3 In. 155.00
Pitcher, Louwelsa, Orange Flower, Green Leaves, Handled, Signed, 3 In. 110.00
Pitcher, Louwelsa, Pansies 125.00
Pitcher, Louwelsa, Pansy Design, Signed Madge Hurst, 3-Footed, 5 In. 200.00
Pitcher, Marvo, Carmel, 8 In. 150.00
Pitcher, Marvo, Green, 6 In. 45.00
Pitcher, Naked Black Boy Handle, 3 1/2 In. 20.00
Pitcher, Pierre, Ivory, 7 1/2 In. 25.00
Pitcher, Zona, Cameo Forest On Reverse, 8 In. 275.00
Pitcher, Zona, Duck, Dark Blue 75.00
Pitcher, Zona, Kingfisher, Green 80.00
Planter, Blue Drapery, 4 1/4 X 5 1/2 In. 32.50
Planter, Cactus, Coppertone, Frog On Pad Holding Open Lily 60.00
Planter, Cameo, Creamware, 4 In. 35.00
Planter, Creamware, Pierced, With Liner 36.00
Planter, Marvo, Orange, 13 X 6 In. 50.00
Planter, Roma, Clay Liner, 3 X 6 1/4 In. 50.00
Planter, Roma, Lion Corners, Insert 35.00
Plaque, Lincoln, 1904 St.Louis Fair .... 45.00 To 85.00
Spittoon, Claywood 75.00
Tankard, Aurelian, Fruit Design, 10 1/2 In. 160.00
Tankard, Dickens Ware, Chief Hollow Horn Bear, E.L.Pickens, 12 In. 1395.00
Tankard, Louwelsa, Berries & Ivy, 6 Mugs, Brown To Green 175.00
Tankard, Louwelsa, Dog Portrait, Blake, 11 In. 425.00
Tankard, Louwelsa, Indian Portrait, Signed, 12 In. 1000.00
Tea Set, Zona, 6 Cups 300.00
Teapot, Tearose 59.00
Teapot, Zona 45.00
Tile, Fleur-De-Lis On White, California Faience 55.00
Tobacco Jar, Dickens Ware, Incised Monk 250.00
Tobacco Jar, Dickens Ware, Irishman 530.00
Tobacco Jar, Dickens Ware, The Turk 550.00
Tub, Flemish, 5 1/2 X 10 1/4 In. 45.00
Tumbler, Drink Hager's Cider, Etched 14.00
Umbrella Stand, Cameo Jewell 375.00
Urn, Souevo, 5 X 8 In. 50.00
Vase, Alvin, 7 In. 16.00
Vase, Aurelian, Brown To Yellow, Holly Design, 3-Handled 155.00
Vase, Baldin, Marked, Green Top, 4 X 7 In. 24.00
Vase, Besline, Orange, 9 In. 300.00
Vase, Blossom, Green, 9 In. 32.00
Vase, Blue Drapery, 6 In. 45.00
Vase, Blue Drapery, 6 1/2 In. 37.50
Vase, Blue Ware, Lady Picking Grapes, Cylinder, 10 In. .... 80.00 To 90.00
Vase, Bonito, 4 In. .... 40.00 To 42.00
Vase, Bonito, 5 In. 25.00
Vase, Bonito, 7 1/2 In. 55.00
Vase, Bonito, 9 In. 90.00
Vase, Breton, Burnt Orange, 9 In. 25.00
Vase, Bronze Ware, 12 In. 145.00
Vase, Bud, Alvin, Marked, Satin Matte Glaze, 8 1/2 In. 25.00
Vase, Bud, Burntwood, Flowers & Vines, Flared Base, Hexagonal, 5 In. 20.00
Vase, Bud, Coppertone, Frog Climbing Reeds, 9 In. 125.00
Vase, Bud, Roma, Triple, 7 In. 12.50
Vase, Bud, Warwick, Marked, 7 1/2 In. 30.50
Vase, Burntwood, Birds, Flowers, 8 3/4 In. 150.00
Vase, Burntwood, Dogwood Blossoms, Wide Band, 5 X 4 1/2 In. 65.00

Vase, Burntwood, Fish Design, 16 1/2 In.	75.00
Vase, Burntwood, Underwater Scene, Fish, 6 In.	65.00
Vase, Burntwood, 5 X 5 In.	20.00
Vase, Burntwood, 5 1/8 In.	10.00
Vase, Burntwood, 9 3/4 In.	85.00
Vase, Cameo, Blue, 13 1/2 In.	25.00
Vase, Claywood, 3 1/2 In.	30.00
Vase, Claywood, 4 In.	30.00
Vase, Cloudburst, Orange Luster, 10 In.	55.00
Vase, Coppertone, 4 Frogs Emerging From Base, 12 In.	110.00
Vase, Darsie, Blue Matte, 6 In.	12.00
Vase, Darsie, Turquoise, 5 1/2 In.	10.00
Vase, Dickens Ware, Boy Golfer, 9 1/2 In.	450.00
Vase, Dupont, 7 1/4 In.	55.00
Vase, Eclair, Black, Red Roses	45.00
Vase, Elberta, Green Shading To Cream, 4 1/4 In.	20.00
Vase, Elberta, 4 1/2 In.	30.00
Vase, Eocean, Pink Floral, Dark Blue To Gray, Signed, 9 In.	175.00
Vase, Etna, Carnations, 10 In.	145.00
Vase, Etna, Floral, Dark Smoke Blue, Cream, Lavender, 11 In.	130.00
Vase, Etna, Grape Cluster, 15 In.	450.00
Vase, Etna, Handled, 4 In.	40.00
Vase, Etna, Pope Pius X, Rosary Design, 10 1/4 In.	385.00
Vase, Etna, Rose Colored Blossoms, Pink, White, & Gray, 8 1/2 In.	85.00
Vase, Etna, Rose, 10 In.	125.00
Vase, Etna, Signed	170.00
Vase, Etna, 5 In.	60.00 To 70.00
Vase, Flemish, Floral, 9 In.	45.00
Vase, Flemish, 14 In.	150.00
Vase, Floral, Hand-Thrown By S.R.McLaughlin, 10 1/2 In.	300.00
Vase, Floral, Long Thin Neck, 6 1/8 In.	170.00
Vase, Florenzo, Fan-Shaped, Vines & Blueberries, Marked, 5 1/4 In.	26.00
Vase, Forest, Fan-Shaped, Marked, 9 X 7 In.	70.00
Vase, Forest, Pedestal, 7 3/4 In.	250.00
Vase, Forest, 6 X 11 3/4 In.	110.00
Vase, Forest, 8 In.	79.00
Vase, Forest, 9 In.	45.00
Vase, Forest, 12 In.	135.00
Vase, Forest, 13 In.	200.00
Vase, Glendale, Yellow Birds & Flowers, 9 In.	185.00
Vase, Greora, Fan-Shaped, Marked, 7 X 7 In.	40.00
Vase, Greora, 4 1/2 In.	35.00
Vase, Greora, 5 In.	22.00
Vase, Greora, 9 1/4 In.	55.00
Vase, Handled, Cameo Green, Bulbous, Script In Mold, 8 1/2 In.	35.00
Vase, Hudson, Apple Blossoms, Pink To Blue, Signed, 7 In.	185.00
Vase, Hudson, Crocus Design, Pink Vellum Ground, Signed, 6 1/2 In.	275.00
Vase, Hudson, Floral, Artist Signed, 8 In.	375.00
Vase, Hudson, Flowers & Leaves, Mauve, 7 1/2 In.	185.00
Vase, Hudson, Gourd-Shaped, White Ground, 10 In.	100.00
Vase, Hudson, Iris, 12 In.	550.00
Vase, Hudson, Spray Of Hibiscus In White, Gray Ground, 8 In.	225.00
Vase, Hunter, Horse, Dog, & Tree, Blue & White, 9 In.	160.00
Vase, Indian Portrait, 9 In.	1500.00
Vase, Jewell, Shaded Pinks & Greens, Signed, 9 1/2 In.	150.00
Vase, Kenova, 9 In.	60.00
Vase, Knifewood, Daisies & Butterflies, 7 In.	120.00
Vase, Knifewood, Horned Owls, 8 1/4 In.	140.00
Vase, Knifewood, 7 1/2 In.	85.00
Vase, LaSa, Iridescent, 5 1/4 In.	175.00
Vase, LaSa, Scenic, 12 In., Pair	600.00
Vase, LaSa, Signed, 5 1/2 In.	175.00

Vase, LaSa, 15 1/2 In.	1200.00
Vase, Lorbeek, 12 In.	75.00
Vase, Louwelsa, Blue, 11 In.	700.00
Vase, Louwelsa, C.1900, Flowers & Foliage, Brown Ground, Marked, 36 In.	1050.00
Vase, Louwelsa, Chrysanthemums, 17 X 10 In.	290.00
Vase, Louwelsa, Cylindrical, Poppies, 10 In.	145.00
Vase, Louwelsa, Daffodils, 7 In.	115.00
Vase, Louwelsa, Floral Design, Signed, 12 In.	275.00
Vase, Louwelsa, Gray, 10 In.	30.00
Vase, Louwelsa, Mums, Artist Signed, 4 X 5 In.	350.00
Vase, Louwelsa, Pedestal, Wild Roses, 5 1/2 In.	155.00
Vase, Louwelsa, Trumpet Neck, Floral, 10 In.	140.00
Vase, Luxor, Incised Flowers & Vines, Bark Ground, 11 In.	40.00
Vase, Malvern, Molded Leaves & Branches, Twig Handles, 7 In.	44.00
Vase, Marvo, Brown, 10 In.	45.00
Vase, Marvo, Green, 9 In.	30.00
Vase, Neisha, Handled, Mottled Yellow, 7 3/4 In.	25.00
Vase, Oak Leaf, Green, 6 In.	22.50
Vase, Patra, Green Rim & Handles, Orange Skin Finish, 5 In.	25.00
Vase, Patra, 8 In.	50.00
Vase, Patra, 10 In.	48.00
Vase, Patricia, White, 8 1/2 In.	48.00
Vase, Pearl, Rose, Olive, & Gold, Black Accents, Ivory Ground	175.00
Vase, Portrait, Monk, 12 In.	1100.00
Vase, Roba, Green	53.00
Vase, Roba, Yellow, 6 1/2 In.	30.00
Vase, Roma, Cameo, 4 In.Square	50.00
Vase, Roma, 9 In.	18.00
Vase, Rosemont, Browns & Yellows, Label, 4 3/4 In.	22.00
Vase, Scandia, 7 In.	30.00
Vase, Scandia, 7 1/2 In.	35.00
Vase, Selma, 7 1/2 In.	110.00
Vase, Sicardo, C.1905, Iridescent Glaze, Signed, 4 3/4 In.	110.00
Vase, Sicardo, Wine, 6 In.	190.00
Vase, Sicardo, 3 3/4 X 7 1/4 In.	325.00
Vase, Sicardo, 10 In.	360.00
Vase, Sicardo, 16 In.	500.00
Vase, Silvertone, Butterflies, 12 In.	170.00
Vase, Silvertone, Butterfly & Flowers, 11 3/4 In.	175.00
Vase, Silvertone, Lilies & Daisies, Trumpet Shape, 10 1/2 In.	55.00
Vase, Silvertone, Peony, Rainbow Background, Signed, 9 1/4 In.	100.00
Vase, Silvertone, Purple Grapes, 6 1/2 In.	60.00
Vase, Silvertone, Twisted Handle, 11 In.	175.00
Vase, Silvertone, 2-Handled, 8 1/2 In.	95.00
Vase, Silvertone, 6 In.	65.00
Vase, Softone, Pink, 11 In.	11.00
Vase, Souevo, 5 X 5 In.	42.00
Vase, Sydonia, Green Base, Mottled Green Top, Signed, 9 1/2 In.	50.00
Vase, Tupelo, Pink & Green, 9 In.	60.00
Vase, Turkis, 1 Handle Top, 1 Handle Bottom, Plum Drip Glaze, 7 In.	55.00
Vase, Velva, Brown, 11 In.	50.00
Vase, Velva, Light Brown, 6 In.	30.00
Vase, Wall, Woodcraft, Squirrel	100.00
Vase, Wild Rose, Green, 2-Handled, 9 In.	22.00
Vase, Woodcraft, 9 In.	15.00
Wall Pocket, Blue, Drapery	30.00
Wall Pocket, Euclid, Roses	50.00
Wall Pocket, Fairfield, 10 In.	70.00
Wall Pocket, Flemish, 9 1/2 In.	125.00
Wall Pocket, Oakleaf, Rust, Signed	30.00
Wall Pocket, Roma, 8 In.	40.00
Wall Pocket, Woodcraft, Owl	85.00 To 125.00

Willets, Tankard, Hand-Painted Grapes, Artist Signed, 14 In.

Wall Pocket, Woodcraft, Squirrel .... 85.00 To 105.00
WHEATLEY, Vase, Applied Leaves & Flowers, C.1880, Marked, 9 In. 175.00

BELLEEK

WILLETS

Willets Manufacturing Company of Trenton, New Jersey, worked from 1879. The company made Belleek in the late 1880s and 1890s in shapes similar to those used by the Irish Belleek factory.

WILLETS, Bowl, Black Rim, Blackberries, Gold Lizard Handles, 4 1/2 In. 195.00
Bowl, Wildflower Pattern, Ruffled Rim, Small 75.00
Butter Tub, Ivory 28.00
Chalice, Portrait Of Monk Drinking, Green, Leafy Ground, 11 In. 325.00
Cider Set, 6 Tumblers, Pitcher 425.00
Compote, Stemmed, Hand-Painted Grape & Leaf Design, Signed, 11 In. 150.00
Cup, Gold Paste Florals, Cream Ground 45.00
Eggcup, Lily, Pink Shading, Red Serpent Mark 74.00
Mug, Bulldog, 4 In. 125.00
Mug, Hand-Painted Blackberries, Shaded Blue Ground 72.00
Pitcher, Blue & Green, Gold & Blue Handle, Signed, 7 In. 149.00
Pitcher, Claret, Gold Paste Design, Mask Spout, Dragon Handle 360.00
Pitcher, Floral & Gold, 6 In. 150.00
Pitcher, Pastel Roses On Both Sides, Twig Handle, Jewels, 5 In. 185.00
Pitcher, White, Raised Gold Leaves, Gold Sponge Work, 3 3/4 In. 450.00
Salt, Pearlized Interior, Green Leaves, 3-Footed 19.00
Sherbet, Flowered Silver Overlay, Pink 125.00
Tankard, Hand-Painted Grapes, Artist Signed, 14 In. .... *Illus* 160.00
Tankard, Hand-Painted Raspberries & Flowers, 14 In. 375.00
Tea Set, Cane, Gold Sponge & Brush Work, Red Serpent Mark, 3 Piece 350.00
Teapot, Pink Roses, Turquoise Forget-Me-Nots, Gold Design 585.00
Vase, Apple Blossoms, Rose & Blue Ground, Marked, 8 In. 175.00
Vase, Floral Design, Belleek, Hand-Painted, 1909, 11 1/2 In. 229.00
Vase, Hand-Painted Roses, 15 1/2 In. 95.00
Vase, Peacocks, Lavender Luster, 17 In. 295.00
Vase, Red Roses, Lavender Ground, 14 In. 250.00
Vase, Roses, Serpent Mark, 12 In. 375.00
Vase, Violet Design, 9 In. 225.00
    WILLOW, see Blue Willow

WINDOW, Schlitz Beer, Chicago Saloon, 38 X 69 In. 2900.00
Stained Glass, Illinois Jewelry Store, Sandrock 155.00
Stained Glass, Religious, 1 3/4 X 32 X 61 In. 725.00

Wood Carving, Bird, 19th Century, Wire Legs,
Painted, 6 3/4 In.

Wood, Carving, Angel, Polychrome,
Italian, 14 1/4 In., Pair

WOOD CARVING, Angel, Polychrome, Italian, 14 1/4 In. .... *Illus* 1100.00
  Ashtray, Black Bellhop, Green Coat, Spats, 37 In. 1320.00
  Bird, Glass Eyes, Bristle Comb, Signed Schifferl 630.00
  Bird, 19th Century, Wire Legs, Painted, 6 3/4 In. .... *Illus* 400.00
  Board, Mangling, German Verses, 17th Century, 32 1/2 In. 700.00
  Box, Carved Nautical Design, Sailor Art 85.00
  Cake Board, Signed J.Conger, C.1800, Reverse Relief, 11 1/4 In. 300.00
  Cane, Carved American Flag, Snake, Red, White, Blue & Black 140.00
  Cane, Carved Clenched Fist On End 100.00
  Cane, Man's Head On End, Diamond-Shaped Carvings, Signed WB 165.00
  Eagle, American, Raised Wings, Speckled Feathers, 10 In. 2750.00
  Eagle, American, W.Schimmel, Penna., 19th Century, 6 1/4 In. 4750.00
  Eagle, New England, Painted, 10 1/4 In. .... *Illus* 2500.00
  Eagle, The Sentinel, Basswood, 2 X 16 X 16 In. 130.00
  Figurine, Apostles, Gilt, 3/4 Relief, 9 In. 425.00
  Figurine, Bear With Fish In Mouth, 13 In. 50.00
  Figurine, Crouching Lioness, Oak, 13 In. 50.00
  Figurine, Ecclesiast, Gilt, Full Relief, Glass Eyes, 12 In. 225.00
  Figurine, Elf, Horn Feet, German 170.00

Wood Carving, Eagle, New England, Painted, 10 1/4 In.

Wood Carving, Figurine, Water Buffalo, Oriental, 19th Century

Wood Carving, Pheasant, New England, Painted, 9 1/4 In., Pair

Figurine, Hen, Painted	185.00
Figurine, Horned Owl, Cypress, 1 1/4 X 4 In.	65.00
Figurine, Lady With Fan, In Horseshoe, 7 3/4 In.	170.00
Figurine, Owl, 1920s, Green Eyes, 15 X 6 1/2 X 6 In.	235.00
Figurine, Poodle, Black Eyes & Nose, Red Mouth	375.00
Figurine, Rooster, Painted	265.00
Figurine, Saint, C.1790	200.00
Figurine, St.John, Holding The Infant Jesus, Full Relief, 7 In.	100.00
Figurine, St.Michael, Gilt, Full Relief, Pedestal Base, 21 In.	475.00
Figurine, Swan, Extended Wings, C.1740, Pine, 31 X 21 1/2 In. 3300.00
Figurine, The Lamenting Virgin, Full Relief, Glass Eyes, 21 In.	625.00
Figurine, Water Buffalo, Oriental, 19th Century .... *Illus* 950.00
Mask, Grotesque, Devil & Dragon, 34 In.	165.00
Ornament, Coiled Snake, Dragonlike Head, Metal Teeth	650.00
Ornament, Pineapple, Sign Of Hospitality, Basswood, 8 X 18 In.	45.00
Pheasant, New England, Painted, 9 1/4 In., Pair .... *Illus* 3500.00
Rifle, Pine, 19th Century, 39 In.	55.00
Uncle Sam, Holding Flag, Painted, Art Deco, 27 In.	65.00
Whirligig, Soldier, Swing Arms, Original Paint, 13 In.	65.00
Whirligig, Uncle Sam, Full-Bodied, Traditional, 26 In. 3850.00

WOODEN, see also Kitchen; Store; Tool
WOODEN, Barrel, Apple Cider, Bentwood Rings, 14 X 19 3/4 In. 75.00

Barrel, Fig, Wooden Plug, Iron Rings, C.1900, 5 1/2 X 6 1/4 In. 25.00
Barrel, Impressed Our Centennial Best, 1777-1876, Swing Handle 60.00
Billy Club, Policeman's 4.50
Bootjack, Pine, Hole For Hanging, 4 1/2 X 20 In. 14.50
Bootjack, Wall Hanging, 29 1/2 In. 20.00
Bowl, American, Burl Walnut, 4 3/4 X 18 In.Diam. 185.00
Bowl, Burl, Dated 1822, 22 In.Long 1400.00
Bowl, Burl, Mid-19th Century, American, Chestnut, 5 X 15 In. 300.00
Bowl, Burl, Turned Line Design, American, 18th Century, 9 1/8 In. 325.00
Bowl, Burl, 2 1/2 X 7 In.Diam. 325.00
Bowl, Burl, 12 In.Diam. 60.00
Bowl, Burl, 19th Century, 3 1/2 X 10 In.Diam. 125.00
Bowl, Chopping, Rectangular Form, Flat Bottom, Red Paint, 2 In. 300.00
Bowl, Dough, Late 1800s, 3 1/2 Ft.Long 130.00
Bowl, Dough, Oblong, 22 In. 35.00
Bowl, Gold, Red & Black, Russian, 6 3/4 X 3 1/2 In. 35.00
Bowl, Lathe-Turned Ornamental Rings, Burl, 10 1/4 In.Diam. 485.00
Bowl, Original Red Paint, 16 X 29 In.Diam. 350.00
Bowl, Speckled American Ash, 3 X 13 In.Diam. 475.00
Bowl, Tiger Maple, 10 In. 30.00
Bowl, 13 In.Diam. 30.00
Box, American, 19th Century, Appliques, Painted, 9 In. 750.00
Box, Bentwood, Circular Form, Fruits, Berries, Vines, 8 3/4 In. 715.00
Box, Candle, Carved, Sliding Lid, Cream Ground, Smoke Design, 10 In. 385.00
Box, Candle, Hanging, 2 Drawers, 18th Century, Buttermilk Red, Pine 385.00
Box, Candle, Pine, Old Red Paint, Table Model, Slide Cover, 6 X 7 In. 95.00
Box, Candle, Pine, Sliding Lid, Dovetailed, 5 1/2 X 6 X 10 In. 80.00
Box, Candle, Sliding Lid, Flowering Tulip, Red Ground, 9 In. 1100.00
Box, Cheese, 2 Pounds 4.00
Box, Cheese, 5 Pounds 6.00
Box, Chopping, Natural Finish, 8 3/8 In.Square 20.00
Box, Glove, Hand-Carved, Lid 25.00
Box, Herb, Bentwood, Circular, Red, Yellow Ground, 3 1/4 In. 412.00
Box, Inlaid Top, Secret Lock, 5 1/4 X 9 3/4 X 4 1/2 In. 25.00
Box, Knife, Mahogany, Scalloped Ends, Divider, 16 X 10 In. 275.00
Box, Magic Yeast, 3 1/4 X 5 1/4 X 8 1/2 In. 4.00
Box, Ming Tea, Hand-Painted Floral Picture, 5 X 4 1/2 X 6 In. 4.00
Box, Pill, Round, 2 Fingers, Wooden Pegs, 2 In.Diam. 40.00
Box, Recipe, Oak 8.00
Box, Winchester Ammunition, 9 X 9 X 14 In. 10.00
Bucket, Molasses, Iron Bands, Bail Handle 65.00
Bucket, Old Green Paint 22.00
Bucket, Sap, Metal Bands, Original Red Paint 30.00
Bucket, Stave-Sided, Old Hunter Green Paint, Handled, C.1809, 9 In. 75.00
Bucket, Sugar, Copper Nails, Signed B.R.Jenkins, Salmon Paint 125.00
Bucket, Sugar, Wire Bail, White Over Blue, 6 1/2 X 11 In.Diam. 37.50
Bucket, Sugar, Wooden Hoops, Wood Handle, Covered, 12 X 12 In. 35.00
Bucket, Wire Bail, 13 1/4 X 13 In. 35.00
Bucket, 2 Iron Bands, Old Red Paint, Stave Handle, 7 X 5 1/2 In. 225.00
Carrier, Cheese, Iron Folding Handle, Bentwood, For 50-Pound Wheel 60.00
Carving, Bearded Man, C.1850 .... 650.00
Carving, Naked Lady, Wood, Gold Paint, 9 1/4 In. 175.00
Carving, Whale, Wooden, Metal Button Eye, Salem, Mass., 28 In. 90.00
Case, Heinies Beer 9.50
Chest, Spice, Dovetailed, 8-Drawer 95.00
Crate, Old Dobbin Ale, Erie Brewing Co., Erie, Penna., 16 X 11 X 8 In. 12.50
Drainer, Cheese, C.1830, Maple, 8 5/8 In.Diam. 175.00
Egg, Hand-Painted, Striations Of Black, Pullet Size 3.50
Horse, Harness Maker's, Dapple Gray, Full Size 1600.00
Ink Sander, 2 1/2 In. 55.00
Jardiniere, C.1800, Gilt Metal Mounted, Satinwood, 12 1/2 In. 1100.00
Kaleidoscope, Brass, Leather, 14 In. 715.00
Keg, Oyster, Staved, Lock-Lapped Hoops, 6 X 10 In. 95.00

Keg, Rum, Hand-Forged Iron Hoops, C.1770, 5 X 3 In.Diam.	200.00
Mallet, Judge's	12.50
Measure, Chamfered Side Lapping, Bentwood, 6 1/4 X 11 1/2 In.Diam.	35.00
Mold, Cigar, Dated 1875, American	40.00
Mold, Cigar, 2 Parts	22.00
Mortar & Pestle, Spice	25.00
Mortar, Grinding Corn, Hollowed Maple Tree, 21 In.	165.00
Paddle, Butter, Edge Of Bowl Hook, 10 In.	250.00
Plaque, American Eagle, New England, C.1860	8000.00
Rack, Candle Dipping, Removable Sticks	145.00
Rack, Towel, Pegged Together, J.Turiks Impressed, Old Green, 3 Arms	115.00
Salt, Old Green Paint Over Original Red Paint, 2 1/4 In.Diam.	20.00
Stand, Wash Boiler, Fold-Up	7.00
Tray, Center Marquetry, Sterling Silver Gallery, Handles, 2 X 14 In.	100.00
Trencher, Hand-Scooped, Tab Handles, C.1870, 11 1/4 X 21 3/4 In.	160.00
Wash Stick, Corrugated, Hand-Hewn, 18th Century, 28 In.	150.00
Wash Stick, Hand-Carved, Maple, 2 1/2 In.	25.00
Whistle, Original Black & Red Paint, 6 In.	35.00
Winnower, Blueberry, 13 Rollers, Filter, C.1900, Pine, 14 1/2 X 24 In.	45.00

Worcester porcelains were made in Worcester, England, from 1751. The firm went through many name changes and eventually, in 1862, became the Royal Porcelain Company. Collectors often refer to Dr. Wall, Barr, Flight, and other names that indicate time periods and artists at the factory.

WORCESTER, see also Royal Worcester

WORCESTER, Bowl, Reticulated Cover, Tans & Greens, 6 In.Diam.	385.00
Creamer, Floral Design, Bamboo Handle, Gilded, Ivorene, 4 In.	135.00
Cup & Saucer, Flight & Barr	85.00
Mustard, Three Flowers Pattern, C.1775, Floral Knop, 3 7/8 In.	440.00
Pitcher, Exotic Birds, Dr.Wall, 10 In.	400.00
Pitcher, Exotic Birds, Dr.Wall, 1760, 8 In.	650.00
Teapot, Bouquets & Sprigs Of Flowers, C.1780, Covered, 6 In.	385.00
Tureen, Sauce, 1813, Impaling Of Williamson, F.B.& B., 7 In.	220.00
Vase, Hand-Painted Blackberries & Foliage, 3 3/4 In.	225.00
Vase, Highland Cattle Scenes, Signed, 16 In., Pair	4750.00

WORLD WAR I, Buckle, Anson Mills, U.S. Balloon Forces, 1916-19	15.00
Helmet, Spiked, Prussian, Dated 1915	80.00
Helmet, Trench, Austrian, Leather Liner	97.50
Pick & Shovel, Folding, U.S.	11.00
Stretcher, 1917, Navy, Oak & Canvas	95.00
Uniform, Doughboy	32.00

WORLD WAR II, Bayonet, Nazi Dress	22.50
Cap, Officer's, Nazi	95.00
Coat, Stormtrooper's, Leather, German	100.00
Dagger & Scabbard, Nazi, Fireman's	62.00
Helmet, German, Blue Painted Steel	22.50
Helmet, Italian, Liner	7.50
Helmet, Nazi Police, Black Finish, Aluminum	165.00
Jacket, Ike, Army	6.50
Lantern, Signal, Battleship, Pair	400.00
Light, Signal Blinker, Battleship, Pair	350.00
Mask, Gas, German	35.00
Medal, Mother's, Nazi	25.00
Micrometer, Navy, Oak Box, Set	330.00
Pin, Lapel, Ruptured Duck	10.00
Pouch, Ammo, 3 Section, German	10.00

WORLD'S FAIR, Ashtray, Firestone Tire, Rubber Rim, Glass Insert, Logo, 1939	15.00
Ashtray, 1939, New York, Hemisphere On Top, Metal	15.00
Banner, 1940, Trylon & Perisphere, Satin, 21 X 21 1/2 In.	23.00
Bottle, Hemisphere, 1939, Milk Glass	15.00

Bottle, Perfume, Century Of Progress, 1933, Screw Top 24.00
Box, Cigarette, 1939, New York, Celluloid, Russian, 4 In. 22.00
Cane, 1934 .... 20.00
Card, Playing, 1933 .... 12.00
Creamer, St.Louis, 1904, Administration Building Picture 15.00
Goblet, Stemmed, Ruby Flashed, 1893 .... 50.00
Handkerchief, 1893 .... 10.00
Hatchet, Head Of Washington, World's Fair 1893 On Head, Blue 38.00
Knife, St.Louis 40.00
Locket, 1904, Aluminum, Heart Shape 8.00
Match Holder, St.Louis, 1904, Metal 15.00
Medal, 1939, New York, Bronze, Symbol On Front, Poster On Back 20.00
Mug, Chicago, 1933, Red, 4 1/2 In. 15.00
Mug, Lithophane Machinery Hall Base, St.Louis 150.00
Napkin Ring, St.Louis, Brass 10.00
Salt & Pepper, Chicago, 1933, Glass 10.00
Salt & Pepper, 1939 .... 10.00
Salt, 1893, Cased Over Pink, Melon Ribbed, Gold Washed Rim 125.00
Scarf, Golden Gate International Exposition 12.00
Scarf, 1939 .... 9.00
Tie Holder, Chicago, 1933 .... 6.00
Tray, Chicago, 1933,.Oval 6.00
Tray, Crumb, 1933, Boxed 11.00
Tray, St.Louis Exposition, Picture Of Jefferson, Brass 25.00
Tumbler, St.Louis Exposition 20.00
Tumbler, 1893, Ruby Flashed Glass 45.00
Tumbler, 1939 .... 7.00
Vase, St.Louis World's Fair 1909, Cranberry, 7 3/4 In. 58.00
1933, Whiskbroom Holder, Chicago, Signed 8.50

YELLOWWARE, Bedpan 15.00
Bedpan, Male Urinal 22.50
Bowl, Advertising, 8 In. 12.00
Bowl, Banded, White, 10 1/2 In. 25.00
Bowl, Bands Of White & Cobalt Blue, Marked, 11 3/4 In. 30.00
Bowl, Blue Sponge Spatter, 4 In. 40.00
Bowl, Blue Sponge Spatter, 8 3/4 X 2 1/2 In. 150.00
Bowl, Braiding On Edge, Impressed Shield, 12 3/4 In.Diam. 48.00
Bowl, Brown Striping, 14 In.Diam. 29.00
Bowl, Country, Thick Rim, C.1850, Stamp On Base, 8 In. 85.00
Bowl, Dripped Mocha Banding, White, 8 In. 25.00
Bowl, Embossed, 14 X 6 1/2 In. 40.00
Bowl, Marked R.Boston Pottery, 19th Century, 11 1/2 In. 110.00
Bowl, Pouring Spout, Embossed, 9 In. 12.00
Bowl, Pouring Spout, 8 In. 35.00
Bowl, White Bands, 7 In. 9.00
Bowl, White Bands, 9 In. 13.00
Bowl, 2 Cream Bands, 2 Brown Bands, 8 In. 35.00
Bowl, 6 In.Diam. 15.00
Butter Crock, Cover & Insert 68.00
Cup, Custard, Flat Rim, C.1850, 3 3/4 X 2 1/4 In., Pair 75.00
Cup, Custard, 12 Paneled Sides, 4 X 1 3/4 In., Pair 18.50
Cuspidor, 8-Sided, Embossed, Molded Scroll Design 45.00
Mold, Bundt 60.00
Mold, Corn Design 28.00
Mold, Pudding, Grape Design 45.00
Pan, Milk, Graduated Set, 11 1/2 In., 10 1/4 In., 9 1/2 In. 110.00
Pitcher, Blue Bands, 6 1/4 In. 40.00
Pitcher, Rose, Basket Weave, 7 In. 60.00
Plate, Pie, 10 In.Diam. 50.00
Pot, Chamber, White Stripes, 2 3/4 In. 25.00
Rolling Pin .... 100.00 To 110.00
Rolling Pin, 8 In. 110.00

Spittoon, Embossed Scrolls, Victorian Gothic 45.00
Tenderizer, Dated 1877 .... 50.00 To 51.00

ZANE WARE

*Zane pottery was founded in 1921 by Adam Reed and Harry McClelland
in South Zanesville, Ohio. It was sold in 1941.*

ZANE, see also Peters & Reed

ZANE, Wall Pocket, Moss Aztec, Roses, Vine, & Leaves, 5 X 8 In. 25.00

LA MORO

*Zanesville Art Pottery was founded in 1900 by David Schmidt in
Zanesville, Ohio. The firm made faience, umbrella stands, jardinieres, and
pedestals. It worked until 1962.*

ZANESVILLE, Vase, Pansies, La Moro, Signed, 4 1/2 In. 195.00

ZS BAVARIA, Pitcher, Apostle, Cream Colored 125.00
Vase, Madame La Brun, Brown Ground, 9 3/4 In. 125.00

*Zsolnay pottery was made in Hungary after 1862, and was characterized by
Persian, Art Nouveau, or Hungarian motifs. A series of new Zsolnay
figurines with green-gold luster finish is available in many shops today.*

ZSOLNAY, Boat, Gravy, Wild Flowers 50.00
Bowl, Cream Ground, Polychrome Flowers, Melon Shape, Signed, 5 In. 140.00
Bowl, Floral Enamels, Melon Shape, Cream Ground, Signed, 5 In. 140.00
Bowl, Heart-Shaped Panels, Foliage Inset, Ivory Ground, 10 1/2 In. 200.00
Bowl, Yellow Poppies, Lavender Florals, Marked, 12 In. 150.00
Compote, Scalloped, Foldover, Reticulated, Steeple Mark, 6 X 8 In. 375.00
Cup & Saucer, Orange, Portrait 30.00
Ewer, Multiflorals, Griffin Handle, C.1900, Olive Green, 9 1/2 In. 350.00
Figurine, Bird, Green, Signed, 6 In. 85.00
Figurine, Boy In Tree, Scotty Dog Near, 10 1/2 In. 175.00
Figurine, Doe, 2 1/2 In. 20.00
Figurine, Fox, 4 In. 30.00
Figurine, Nude Lady, 1930s, Green Iridescent, 9 1/2 In. 135.00
Pitcher, Molded Maidens, Green & Gold Luster, 6 1/2 In. 85.00
Pitcher, Persian Design, Cabochon Prunts In Relief, 8 1/4 In. 400.00
Pitcher, Standing & Stooping Women, 6 In. 185.00
Planter, Gold, Blue, Red, Green, Floral Design 125.00
Tumbler, Nudes Holding Cups, Vineyard, Gold And Green, 6 1/2 In. 85.00
Vase, Allover Reticulation, Steeple Mark, 6 1/2 In. 420.00
Vase, Blue, Iridescent Luster, Scalloped Top, Old Flame Mark, 8 In. 95.00
Vase, Bud, Enamel Design, 3 1/4 In. 60.00
Vase, Cobalt, Gold, Reticulated, 6 1/2 In. 375.00
Vase, Cobalt, Gold, White Decoration, Double Walled, 6 1/2 In. 389.00
Vase, Deco Nude Girl Bending, 10 In. 185.00
Vase, Double Gourd, Marked, 5 1/4 In. 125.00
Vase, Filigree Handles, Figures Traced In Gold, Signed, 13 In. 295.00
Vase, Persian Temple Jar Shape, Jeweled Handles, Signed, 8 1/2 In. 245.00

INDEX

769

pot, Bennington, 29; pot, Nanking, 397; and sugar tray, Duncan & Miller, 199; whipper, 338
Cream jug: Belleek, 27; mocha, 383; silver, 624
Cream pitcher: Jackfield, 323; Limoges, 356; milk glass, 380; Weller, 758
Creamer. See specific makers and materials
CREAMWARE, 126
Credenza, 245
Creel basket, 23
CREIL, 126
Creme de menthe, Heisey, 294
Crib, 245; canopy, 684
Cribbage board: Coca-Cola, 112; game, 275; scrimshaw, 604
Cribbage box, ivory, 320
Cricket: cage, ivory, 321; jar, Nippon, 405, 406
Crimper, onion, 420
Crock, 330; Bennington, 29; Red Wing, 531; redware, 532; salt glaze, 597; stoneware, 653; store, 659. See also specific makers, materials, and types of crock
Crockett, Davy. See Davy Crockett
Crocus pot, porcelain, 457
Chronometer, nautical, 398
Croquet game, 275
Cross: gold, 324. See also Crucifix
Crossword game, 275
CROWN DERBY, 126
CROWN DUCAL, 127
CROWN MILANO, 127
Crown Tuscan. See Cambridge
Croze, 702
Crucifix: Belleek, 27; cut glass, 135; silver, 630. See also Cross
CRUET, 127. See also specific makers and materials
Crumb set, Roycroft, 576
Crumb tray: Chicago World's Fair (1933), 766; copper, 120; and scraper, aluminum, 4
CT GERMANY, 127
Cuckoo clock, 105
Cucumber server, silver, 631
Cuff links: box, Royal Bayreuth, 553; gold, 324; Mickey Mouse, 176
Cup. See specific makers, materials, and types
CUP PLATE, 128; Dedham, 146; ironstone, 319; Leeds, 349; Pairpoint, 431; Staffordshire, 641; tea leaf ironstone, 680
Cupboard, 245–46; tramp art, 731
Curd breaker, 330
Curio: cabinet, 232; table, 263
CURRIER, 130–31
CURRIER & IVES, 129–30
Curry dish, Canton, 71
Curtain, 685; pull ring and coaster, North Dakota School of Mines, 415; tieback, see Tieback
Cuspidor. See specific makers and materials
Custard cup: Autumn Leaf, 12; Depression glass, 163; Heisey, 294; Rockingham, 534; spongeware, 639; stoneware, 653; yellowware, 766
CUSTARD GLASS, 131–33
CUT GLASS, 133–39
Cuticle knife, silver, 631
Cutlass, 678
Cutlery: box, Shaker, 608; display case, 660; tray, tramp art, 731
Cutter. See specific types
Cutting board, 329; Shaker, 608

Dagger, 678–79; silver, 620, 631; World War II, 765
Daguerreotype, 447–48; case, 447
Dance: apron, Indian, 310; shield, Indian, 313
D'ARGENTAL, 139
Darkroom: lamp, 448; lantern, tin, 698
Darner, 606; Aurene, 10; onion, 420; peachblow, 437; Sandwich glass, 598; Shaker, 609; spatter glass, 637
Dart(s): board, Hopalong Cassidy, 301; Coca-Cola, 112; gun, 719; pistol, 452
DAUM NANCY, 139–42
D'AURYS, 139
DAVENPORT, 142. See also Flow blue
DAVY CROCKETT, 142
Daybed, 227, 246
DE MORGAN, 142
DE PANTIN, 142
DE VEAU, 142
DE VEZ, 142–43

Deanna Durbin doll, 181, 184, 189
Decanter. See specific makers and materials
Decanter stand, 246
Decoder: Captain Midnight, 72; Orphan Annie, 427
Decoy, 143–45; Indian, 312
DEDHAM, 145
Deed box: tin, 697; wooden, 42
DeGrazia collector plate, 117
Dehorner, 702
DELATTE, 146
Deldare. See Buffalo Pottery Deldare
DELFT, 146–47
Demitasse cup and saucer. See specific makers and materials
Demitasse set: Limoges, 354; Rosenthal, 543; RS Germany, 577; Satsuma, 601
Demitasse spoon: plique a jour, 453; silver, 629
Democratic party: donkey mug, 223. See also Political
Dental, 147; bellows, 372; box, 372; chair, 372; tool, 373
DEPRESSION GLASS, 147–74; Adam, 147–48; Adam & Sierra, 147; American sweetheart, 148–50; Aunt Polly, 150; avocado, 150; beaded block, 150; block optic, 150–51; boopie, 151; bowknot, 151; bubble, 151; cameo, 151–52; Cape Cod, 152; cherry blossom, 152–53; chinex classic, 153; circle, 153; cloverleaf, 153–54; colonial, 154; coronation, 154; cubist, 154; diamond quilted, 154; Diana, 156; dogwood, 156; Doric, 156; English hobnail, 156; Fairfax, 156; fine rib, 156; floragold, 156; floral and diamond band, 156; floral, 156–57; Florentine No. 1, 157; Florentine No. 2, 157–58; forest green, 158; fortune, 158; Georgian, 158; grape, 158; hobnail, 158; holiday, 158–59; homespun, 159; Indiana custard, 159; iris, 159; lace edge, 159, 161; laurel, 161; Lincoln Inn, 161; Madrid, 161–62; Manhattan, 162; Mayfair federal, 162; Mayfair open rose, 162–63; Miss America, 163; moderntone, 163; moondrops, 163–64; moonstone, 164; Mt. Pleasant, 164; new century, 164; Newport, 164–65; No. 610, 165; No. 612, 165; No. 615, 165; No. 616, 165; No. 618, 165; No. 620, 165–66; Normandie, 166; old cafe, 166; oyster and pearl, 166; patrician, 166; peacock and wild rose, 167; petalware, 167; primo, 167; princess, 167–68; Queen Mary, 168; radience, 168; raindrops, 168; ribbon, 168; rose cameo, 168; rosemary, 168; roulette, 168; round robin, 168; roxana, 168; royal lace, 168–69; royal ruby, 169; S pattern, 170; sandwich hocking, 170; Sharon, 170–72; sierra, 172; spiral, 172; strawberry, 172; sunflower, 172; swirl, 172; sylvan, 172–73; tea room, 173; thistle, 173; victory, 173; Waterford, 173; Windsor, 174; X design, 174;
DERBY, 174
Derringer, 747
Dessicator jar, Cambridge, 63
Desk, 246–49; basket, Shaker, 608; railroad, 527; Roycroft, 576; weight, bronze, 52
Desk set, 438; bronze, 49; copper, 120; Royal Bayreuth, 555; Tiffany, 694
Dessert: dish, cut glass, 136; fork, silver, 615; plate, Belleek, 28; plate, Fiesta ware, 208; service, silver, 614, 627; spoon, silver, 614, 616, 628
Dessert set: KPM, 339; Royal Crown Derby, 560; RS Prussia, 583
DEVILBISS, 174
Diaper Dan thermometer, 33
Dice, coin-operated, 115
DICK TRACY, 174–75; Christmas tree light bulb, 97; game, 275
Dickensware. See Royal Doulton; Weller
Dictionary stand, 249
DiMaggio, Joe: baseball card, 72
Dinah's Shack matchbook, 33
Dining: chair, 236; table, 263
Dinner: bell, Aunt Jemima, 32; bucket, graniteware, 280; fork, silver, 615; gong, iron, 317; pail, graniteware, 281; plate, see specific makers and materials; set, Cauldon, 93
DIONNE QUINTUPLETS, 175; calendar, 58; dolls, 181, 189; paper dolls, 432
Dipper, 331; blue willow, 34; graniteware, 280; onion, 420; Shaker, 609
Dish. See specific makers, materials, and types

Microscope, 372
Milk: bottle, 40; bottle, Hopalong Cassidy, 301; bowl, salt glaze, 597; can, graniteware, 280; cap lifter, 651; mug, Leeds, 349; pail, 335; pail, graniteware, 281; sign, 668
MILK GLASS, 378–82. See also specific makers and articles
Milk jug: Adams, 2; Belleek, 27; Crown Derby, 126; Judaica, 326; Noritake, 414; silver, 615; Wedgwood, 753
Milk pan, 335; redware, 533; Rockingham, 534; stoneware, 655; yellowware, 766
Milk pitcher: amberina, 5; Autumn Leaf, 13; carnival glass, 78, 87, 89, 91; Copeland, 119; copper, 120; flow blue, 214; Gaudy Welsh, 277; Haviland, 289; ironstone, 319; McCoy, 371; mulberry, 390; Niloak, 402; Nippon, 407; opalescent, 423; Pickard, 449; Rose Tapestry, 542; Royal Bayreuth, 557; RS Prussia, 584; ruby glass, 591; Shawnee, 610; Staffordshire, 643; stoneware, 656; tea leaf ironstone, 680; Waterford, 745
MILLEFIORI, 382
Miner's lamp, 346, 347
Minnie Mouse, 175–78; Christmas tree light bulb, 98; cookie jar, McCoy, 370
Mint dish: Belleek, 27; Cambridge, 62; Tiffany, 694
MINTON, 382–83
Mirror, 252–53; advertising, 662; Belleek, 28; bronze, 52; Buster Brown, 56; celluloid, 93, 94; Coca-Cola, 113; Disneyana, 176; dresser, guttapercha, 284; dresser with, 249; Elvis Presley, 201; gutta-percha, 284; Hopalong Cassidy, 302; Howdy Doody, 302; Masonic, 368; Planters Peanuts, 452; political, 454; Shaker, 609; silver, 631; silver plate, 612; Tom Mix, 700; treen, 732
Miter template, 704
Mitts, 686
Mix, Tom. See Tom Mix
Mixing bowl, 329; Autumn Leaf, 12; Depression glass, 159; graniteware, 280; McCoy, 370; mocha, 383; spatterware, 637; spongeware, 638
Mixing spoon, onion, 421
Moccasins, Indian, 313
MOCHA, 383–84
Model ship, 399
Molasses: bucket, wooden, 764; jug, Wedgwood, 753
MOLD. See specific types
Mole trap, 731
Money: changer, 663; clip, 324–25
Money order & general delivery window, post office, 8
Monkey wrench, 708
MONMOUTH, 384
Monroe, Marilyn: calendar, 58; mirror, 663; paper doll, 443; tip tray, 675
Mont Joye. See Mt. Joye
Moonshine still, copper, 120
MOORCROFT, 384–85
Mop, 334
MORGAN, MATT, 369
MORIAGE, 385–86
Mortar: bronze, 52; wooden, 765
Mortar & pestle: Akro agate, 3; brass, 47; bronze, 52; iron, 318; onion, 420; porcelain, 458; treen, 732; wooden, 334, 765
Mortician's table, 373
Mortise gauge, 702
MOSAIC TILE CO., 386
MOSER, 386–87
MOSS ROSE, 387
Motorcycle, toy, 722
MOTHER-OF-PEARL, 387
Mouse trap, 731–32
Movie: handbill, 434; poster, 460; projector, Mickey Mouse, 176, 177; projector, Moxie, 448
Moxie: fan, 203; mobile, 722; projector, 448; sheet music, 395; sign, 668; thermometer, 688; tip tray, 675
Mr. Peanut: bank, 20; clock, 103; coloring book, 433; doll, 181, 191; letter opener, 352; marble, 365; nodder, 412; pencil, 439; Valentine card, 73. See also Planters Peanuts
MT. JOYE, 388
MT. WASHINGTON, 389. See also Burmese; Crown Milano
MUD FIGURE, 390
Muffin: dish, silver, 615; mold, 334; pan, 281; 334, 335; tin, 334, 338; warmer, silver, 628

Muffineer: cranberry glass, 124; Crown Milano, 127; cut glass, 137; Locke Art, 358; Longwy, 360; Mt. Washington, 389; Smith Brothers, 633
Mug. See specific makers, materials, and types
MULBERRY, 390
MULLER FRERES, 390
Multiplane, 704
MUSIC, 390–95; box, 42, 391–92; box, Mickey Mouse, 176; rack, 254; stand, 253. See also Sheet music; and specific instruments and music-making devices
Musical: Christmas tree stand, 100; clock, 105, 106
Musket, 283
Muskrat stretcher, 707
Mustache: comb, silver, 630; comb, tortoiseshell, 708; curler, silver, 630; iron, silver, 631
MUSTACHE CUP, 396; moriage, 386; & saucer, 396
Mustard: Autumn Leaf, 13; Capo-Di-Monte, 72; cut glass, 137; Fenton, 205; Fiesta ware, 207; Heisey, 297; keg, Red Wing, 532; ladle, silver, 615; milk glass, 380; New Martinsville, 401; Nippon, 407; Noritake, 414; Old Ivory, 420; onion, 420; Royal Bayreuth, 556; Roycroft, 576; RS Germany, 578; RS Prussia, 584; satin glass, 600; silver, 627; spoon, silver, 616; Staffordshire, 642; tin, Buster Brown, 56; Worcester, 765
Mustard jar: Crown Milano, 127; custard glass, 132; Depression glass, 167; Heisey, 296; Pratt, 462
Mustard pot: graniteware, 281; mocha, 384; Nippon, 407
Mustard set: Fostoria, 220; Hall, 285; Nippon, 407
Mutoscope, 116
MZ AUSTRIA, 396

Nail buffer set, RS Germany, 578
NAILSEA, 396
NAKARA, 396
Name clip, political, 454
NANKING, 397
Nantucket basket, 23
Napkin holder, 661
NAPKIN RING, 397–98; cut glass, 137; ivory, 322; Kate Greenaway, 327; Kewpie, 328; milk glass, 380; Nippon, 407; Noritake, 414; Shaker, 609; St. Louis World's Fair (1904), 766
Nappy: carnival glass, 75, 80, 83, 85, 86, 89, 91; chocolate glass, 97; cranberry glass, 124; custard glass, 132; cut glass, 137; Depression glass, 168; Fenton, 205; Fiesta ware, 207; goofus glass, 279; Greentown, 282; Harlequin ware, 288; Hawkes, 290; Heisey, 297; Limoges, 354; Nippon, 407; Noritake, 414; Royal Bayreuth, 556; Sunbonnet Babies, 667
NASH, 398
NATZLER, 398
NAUTICAL, 398–99; blunderbuss, 283; clock, 105, 106, 108; cutlass, 678; desk, 248; knife, U.S. Navy, 339; lantern, 348; micrometer, World War II, 765; pistol, 283; pump, brass, 47; whistle, 619, 631
Necklace, 325; Indian, 313; ivory, 322
Necktie, political, 454
Needle: basket, Indian, 311; book, 607; box, 43; case, 606; holder, 606, 607; threader, 608
Needlework, 686; panel, 686
Negro. See Black
Net mending shuttle, 706
NETSUKE, 399–400
NEW MARTINSVILLE, 400. See also Peachblow
New Year's card, 72
New York World's Fair (1939–1940): ashtray, 765; banner, 765; bottle, 765; cigarette box, 766; medal, 766; poster, 460; salt & pepper, 766; scarf, 766; tumbler, 766
NEWCOMB, 401
NEWHALL, 401
Nez Perce bag, Indian, 310
Nickelodeon, 393
Niddy-noddy, 704
Night-light: Belleek, 28; bisque, 31; Galle, 272; Howdy Doody, 302; Popeye, 457; Tiffany, 696
Night table, 267. See also Bedside table
Nightcap, 686
NILOAK, 402
NIPPON, 402–12
NODDER, 412–13; Donald Duck, 176; papier-mache, 435; Roy Rogers, 552